26.95

# Contemporary North American
# Film Directors

# A Wallflower Critical Guide

wallflower

LONDON and NEW YORK

First published 2000, reprinted 2001
This edition published 2002 by
Wallflower Press
5 Pond Street, London NW3 2PN
www.wallflowerpress.co.uk

ISBN 1-903364-52-3



Book Design by Rob Bowden Design

Printed in Great Britain by Antony Rowe, Chippenham, Wiltshire

# Contemporary North American Film Directors

# A Wallflower Critical Guide

wallflower

LONDON and NEW YORK

# Contents

# Praise for the First Edition

'MUST BUY. Threatens to become indispensable. An invaluable reference tool and thoroughly enjoyable read ... the prose is clear and accessible'
*Empire Magazine*

'The first comprehensive dictionary of American cinema in quite some time ... A worthy successor to Andrew Sarris's *The American Cinema: Directors and Directions 1929 – 1968* ... it is not too much to say that this volume reconfigures and transforms the landscape of contemporary cinema criticism. Stunningly comprehensive ... a book that should be welcomed by academics and laypersons alike'
Wheeler Winston Dixon, *Film Quarterly*

'The entries are concise, pithy and on the nose ... there is no quarrelling with the inclusiveness and intelligence that the book has to offer. Put it on you shelf – you'll be reaching for it very often'
Barry Forshaw, *Starlog*

'An excellent launch for the series and a real bargain for the quality ... the judgements are informative, perceptive, and on the mark. Highly recommended for all film studies collections'
*Library Journal*

'A valuable tool for film students or enthusiasts'
*Variety*

'This volume is comprehensive and up-to-date ... a handy reference guide'
*Film Review*

'Truly fantastic'
Peter Curran, *The Big Picture*, BBC London Live

# Editors' Preface

The *Critical Guides to Contemporary Film Directors* are a series of multi-volume reference guides that focus on hundreds of well-established and newly-emerging directors. Each volume in the series is made up of entries that include brief biographical material and a comprehensive feature filmography, and engage with the film-makers' main body of work, highlighting their prominent themes, concerns and styles. The entries have been specially commissioned from a wide-ranging mix of film critics and journalists, industry practitioners, and established academics and postgraduate students of film.

*Contemporary North American Film Directors: A Wallflower Critical Guide* is an enlarged and updated second edition of the first volume. The second in the series was published in 2001 and focuses on British and Irish directors. *Critical Guides* on Continental European directors and World Cinema directors are in production.

In compiling the *Critical Guide*, certain inclusion criteria have had to be employed. We have tried to cover most, if not all, film-makers who have had fiction feature films released for theatrical exhibition in the last decade or so. In some cases, film-makers who have had animation films or documentaries released have been included, but we have not been able to extend the present *Critical Guide* to cover all film-makers of non-feature-length or non-fiction films. This is not to give artistic or industrial priority to the fiction feature film but is purely a reflection of organisational constraints – we hope to cover animation, documentary and shorts in subsequent editions.

Furthermore, certain issues exist with regard to the inclusion of film-makers not native to North America. Our understanding of a 'North American director' is someone making feature films within the American and Canadian film industries, mainstream and independent. Thus directors such as John Woo, Paul Verhoeven, Wim Wenders, Peter Weir, Lasse Hallström, Milos Forman and Christopher Nolan are all included here although they are not American or Canadian by birth. Indeed some directors will appear in more than one volume because a substantial body of their work has been produced in different countries.

Each volume of the *Critical Guide* will continue to be periodically revised and updated to incorporate each director's latest works and also to include new entries on emerging film-makers. Every edition will thus provide a unique ongoing resource and critique of contemporary film-making.

Every effort has been made to ensure the accuracy of information, yet details on works that are stated as currently in production may be subject to change. Should there be any factual inaccuracies present in the book, do feel free to let us know. Also, we welcome contributions on new directors and so please send all comments, suggestions and queries to info@wallflowerpress.co.uk.

Finally, the Editors would like to very warmly thank all the contributors for their original entries and their assistance in updating them, and everyone involved in the commissioning, research, editing and production of this unique reference resource, especially Laura Bushell, Alexander Hadziioannou, Chris Kasrils and Ian Haydn Smith. A special mention should also go to Howard Seal for conceiving the original idea.

We hope you continue to find this collection helpful and stimulating.

Yoram Allon
Del Cullen
Hannah Patterson

3 October 2002

# List of Contributors

| | | | |
|---|---|---|---|
| MA | Michele Aaron | AL | André Loiselle |
| RA | Richard Armstrong | WL | William Luhr |
| JA | Jonathan Aronoff | JMa | John Manuel |
| PB | Paul Bamford | BM | Ben McCann |
| WB | William Beard | SM | Scott McGee |
| OB | Oliver Berry | JM | Jay Morong |
| MB | Mark Bould | JO | Joseph Oakley |
| LB | Laura Bushell | HO | Harvey O'Brien |
| RC | Robert Cagle | CP | Charlie Palmer |
| EC | Elayne Chaplin | HP | Hannah Patterson |
| SCh | Stephen Charbonneau | JPa | Jason Paul |
| RCh | Robert Chilcott | MBP | Monica B. Pearl |
| JC | James Clarke | BP | Barbara Pederzini |
| IC | Ian Cooper | JP | Jim Penn |
| WWD | Wheeler Winston Dixon | HPe | Hugh Perry |
| JD | Jacqueline Downs | HR | Hannah Ransley |
| REH | Robert Edgar-Hunt | JR | Jonathan Rayner |
| MF | Martin Flanagan | PR | Pauline Reay |
| IG | Ian Garwood | SRe | Sean Redmond |
| FG | Frankie Good | MR | Matthew Reynolds |
| AG | Alexander Graf | SR | Sandy Robertson |
| LH | Leigh Hallisey | MRo | Michael Rowley |
| SH | Stuart Hanson | HS | Howard Seal |
| THa | Todd Harbour | SSc | Sheldon Schiffer |
| KH | Kevin Harley | SJS | Steven Jay Schneider |
| DH | Douglas Hildebrand | ES | Emily Shaw |
| PH | Peter Homden | JS | Jason Silverman |
| TH | Tanya Horeck | SS | Sunil Singhvi |
| CH | Christopher Howard | CS | Christopher Smets |
| DHo | Dawn Howat | RHS | Richard Harland Smith |
| RH | Reynold Humphries | IHS | Ian Haydn Smith |
| NI | Natalie Ivemy | MS | Martha Snowdon |
| NJ | Neil Jackson | CSo | Chris Sodring |
| DJ | Deborah Jermyn | CSt | Christina Stojanova |
| EJK | Eyun Jennifer Kim | AS | Andrew Syder |
| AK | Anton Kozlovic | TT | Tony Todd |
| SK | Sabrina Krinsky | PWa | Paul Watson |
| TK | Tanya Krzywinska | BW | Barnaby Welch |
| SL | Samantha Lay | PW | Paul Wells |
| PL | Peter Lehman | JW | Jerry White |
| JL | Jacqueline Levetin | LW | Lysandra Woods |

# Contributors' Profiles

Michele Aaron is Lecturer in Film Studies at Brunel University, with a special interest in cinematic representations of gender, sexuality and Jewishness.

Richard Armstrong is an Associate Tutor affiliated to the British Film Institute. He has written extensively on director Billy Wilder and is currently researching the subject of realism in film.

Jonathan Aronoff is a doctoral student at the University of Chicago, with a special interest in the theory and history of montage, historical representations in film and science fiction.

Paul Bamford is a freelance film critic with a special interest in contemporary Hollywood cinema. He lives in Chesterfield, UK.

William Beard is Associate Professor in the Film and Media Studies Program at the University of Alberta, with a special interest in contemporary Canadian cinema.

Oliver Berry is a freelance writer and film critic with special interests in Alfred Hitchcock, 1960s and 1970s cinema, and comedy in film. He lives in Cornwall and London, UK.

Mark Bould is Senior Lecturer in Film and Media Studies at Buckinghamshire Chilterns University College, with special interests in Marxism, science fiction and American film. He is currently working on a book on John Sayles for the Wallflower Press *Directors' Cuts* series.

Laura Bushell is a freelance film journalist working in London.

Robert Cagle is a freelance writer on film and popular culture, with special interests in Canadian cinema and underground film.

Elayne Chaplin is Lecturer in Film Studies at the University of Northumbria at Newcastle, with special interests in fantasy film and television, animation and post-classical Hollywood.

Stephen Charbonneau is a graduate of the Film School at New York University/Tisch School of the Arts. He is presently a postgraduate student at the University of Warwick with special interests in globalisation and contemporary Hollywood.

Robert Chilcott studied Film at the London College of Printing. He is a freelance writer and film-maker living in London, UK.

James Clarke is a film-maker and playwrite based in Herefordshire. He has a BA in Film and Literature from the University of Warwick and a Postgraduate Diploma in Film and TV Production from the University of Bristol.

Ian Cooper is a film-maker and Lecturer of contemporary cinema and media at Birkbeck College, University of London, with special interests in the horror film and American independent cinema.

Wheeler Winston Dixon is the James Ryan Endowed Professor of Film Studies, Professor of English at the University of Nebraska, Lincoln, Series Editor for the State University of New York Press Cultural Studies in Cinema/Video, and the Editor-in-Chief of the *Quarterly Review of Film and Video*. He has written many books on the subject of cinema.

Jacqueline Downs is the Curriculum Team Leader for Film and Media at South Thames College. Her special interests include the melodrama, American independent cinema, particularly Jim Jarmusch and John Cassavetes, the films of Ozu, Kurosawa and Kaurismaki, and the British cinema of the 1960s.

Robert Edgar-Hunt is Lecturer in Film and Television at The College of Ripon and York, with a special interest in contemporary cinema.

Martin Flanagan is lecturer in Film Studies at Bolton Institute. He is currently researching generic and cultural aspects of Hollywood action cinema, as well as the salience of Mikhail Bakhtin's theories of spectatorship.

Ian Garwood is Tutor in Film and Television at Glasgow University, with special interests in music and characterisation in narrative film, and road movies.

Frankie Good is a freelance writer with a special interest in women film directors in Australasian and US cinema. She lives in London, UK.

Alexander Graf graduated with a PhD in Film Studies at Edinburgh University. He has recently published a monograph on Wim Wenders within the Wallflower Press *Directors' Cuts* series. He currently works as a translator in Berlin.

Leigh Hallisey is Lecturer in Film and Television at Boston University, with special interests in genre theory and representations of race and gender.

Stuart Hanson is Lecturer in Media and Film Studies at the University of Birmingham, with special interests in the development of multiplexes and post-war British cinema.

Todd Harbour is founder and moderater of *Mobius Home Video Forum*, and a freelance film and DVD critic with interests in genre, independent and world cinema. He lives in Austin, Texas.

Kevin Harley is a freelance film and music journalist. He has written extensively on cinema and popular culture for various publications, and lives in London, UK.

Douglas Hildebrand recently completed his MA in Film Studies at Concordia University, Montreal. His film interests include genre, authorship and reception.

Peter Homden is a doctoral student and tutor at Brunel University, specialising in gender and early silent cinema.

Tanya Horeck recently completed a doctorate at the University of Sussex. Her thesis centred on representations of rape in contemporary literature and cinema.

Christopher Howard recently graduated with an MA in Film and Television Studies from the University of Warwick and is currently researching East Asian and Japanese cinema.

Dawn Howat is a writer and freelancer in film production. She lives in Toronto, Canada.

Reynold Humphries is Professor of Film Studies at the University of Lille, with special interests in the horror film, film noir, contemporary Hollywood and film theory.

Natalie Ivemy is a journalist with a degree in Media and Sports Science and an interest in British social realist film. She lives in London, UK.

Neil Jackson is a doctoral student at the University of Westminster, with research interests in screen violence, contemporary Hollywood cinema and film genres.

Deborah Jermyn is Lecturer in Film Studies at Southampton Institute, with special interests in feminism and film, Hollywood cinema and melodrama. She has recently published a co-edited collection on Kathryn Bigelow for the Wallflower Press *Directors' Cuts* series.

Eyun Jennifer Kim is a doctoral student at the CUNY Graduate Center in New York City. She received her BA from Pomona College in Claremont, CA.

Anton Kozlovic is a doctoral student at The Flinders University of South Australia, with special interests in representations of religion in film and the biblical epics of Cecil B. DeMille.

Sabrina Krinsky is a freelance film critic with special interests in women directors and contemporary French cinema. She lives and works in Paris, France.

Tanya Krzywinska is Senior Lecturer in Film Studies at Brunel University, with special interests in science fiction, occult fictions and cinematic sex. She has recently published a co-edited collection on the interfaces of videogames and the cinema for Wallflower Press.

Samantha Lay is Senior Lecturer in Media Theory at Trinity and All Saints College, University of Leeds. She has recently published a volume on British Social Realism for the Wallflower Press *Short Cuts* series.

Peter Lehman is Professor in the Interdisciplinary Humanities Program and the Hispanic Research Center at Arizona State University.

André Loiselle received his PhD from the University of British Columbia in 1995 and teaches Film Studies at Carleton University in Ottowa. Having written on Canadian directors and cinema, he is currently researching the films of Michel Brault.

William Luhr is Professor of English at Saint Peter's College and Co-Chair of the Columbia University Seminar on Cinema and Interdisciplinary Interpretation.

John Manuel is Lecturer in Film Studies at Staffordshire University, with special interests in scriptwriting, authorship theories, and British and Hollywood cinemas.

Ben McCann is currently completing a PhD in 1930s French cinema. His other interests include Jack Lemmon, Japanese films and *Singin' in the Rain*.

Scott McGee holds an MA in Film Studies from Emory University. He works as a staff member with the Turner Classic Movies cable network in Atlanta, Georgia.

Jay Morong is a freelance writer and graduate student at Boston University, with special interests in 1970s American film and cinema's relationship to theatre and television.

Joseph Oakley is a freelance film critic with a special interest in the work of Peter Weir. He lives in London, UK.

Harvey O'Brien is a Government of Ireland Research Council for Humanities and Social Sciences Post-doctoral Research Fellow working out of University College Dublin.

Charlie Palmer is a postgraduate student at the University of Warwick, with a particular interest in contemporary Hollywood cinema and postmodern film.

Hannah Patterson is Series Editor of the *Critical Guides to Contemporary Film Directors* and Assistant Editor at Wallflower Press. She is also a freelance film writer and is currently working on an edited collection on Terrence Malick for the Wallflower Press *Directors' Cuts* series.

Jason Paul is a graduate student at Emory University, with special interests in cinema and ethics, Andrei Tarkovsky and Gilles Deleuze.

Monica B. Pearl is Lecturer in American Studies at Keele University, with special interests in cinematic and literary representations of illness.

Barbara Pederzini is a graduate from the University of Warwick, with a special interest in studies of spectatorship and new media. She lives in Italy.

Jim Penn holds an MA in Film Studies from the University of Warwick. He has taught at Cheltenham and Gloucester College and is currently working in the television industry.

Hugh Perry is a journalist based in London, with interests in popular culture, particularly contemporary American cinema.

Hannah Ransley is a writer with special interests in British cinema and the avant-garde. She lives in London, UK.

Jonathan Rayner is Lecturer in English Literature and Film at the University of Sheffield, with research interests in Australian and New Zealand cinema.

Jacqueline Levitin is a film-maker and teaches Film and Women's Studies at Simon Fraser University in Vancouver.

Pauline Reay is Lecturer in Film and Media Studies at West Herts College, with a special interest in American independent cinema.

Sean Redmond is Senior Lecturer in Film Studies at Southampton Institute, with research interests in the cultural representations of whiteness and cinematic transgressions. He is co-editor, with Deborah Jermyn, of a collection on Kathryn Bigelow within the Wallflower Press *Directors' Cuts* series.

Matthew Reynolds is a graduate student at the University of Rochester currently undertaking a critical evaluation of the Hollywood Redevelopment Project.

Sandy Robertson is an experienced music and film journalist, with a special interest in old horror movies, 'lost' film, cuts and censorship. He lives in London, UK.

Michael Rowley is studying for a degree in Film Studies. He is a freelance film reviewer with a special interest in American cinema.

Howard Seal is Technical Director of Wallflower Press.

Sheldon Schiffer is an independent film-maker and Assistant Professor of Communication at Georgia State University in Atlanta. He teaches acting and directing for film and television.

Steven Jay Schneider is a doctoral student in Philosophy at Harvard University and in Cinema Studies at New York University, with a special interest in the history and theory of the horror genre. He has recently published a co-edited collection on cult and underground American film for Wallflower Press, and is currently working on a monograph on Wes Craven for the Wallflower Press *Directors' Cuts* series.

Emily Shaw holds an MA in Film and Television from the University of Warwick. Having provided educational opportunities for disadvantaged film-makers, she is now training to be a barrister specialising in media law.

Jason Silverman is the artistic director of the Taos Talking Picture Festival and a curatorial assistant for the Telluride Film Festival.

Sunil Singhvi is a graduate of the University of Southampton and is currently programme-making for the BBC's new Black music station 1Xtra.

Christopher Smets is a screenwriter and playwright with a keen interest in digital film-making, the French New Wave and any movie that features a multitude of ravenous, flesh-eating zombies. He lives in Toronto and New York.

Richard Harland Smith is a playwright, screenwriter and film critic living in New York City.

Ian Haydn Smith is a freelance film critic and postgraduate student at the University of Westminster, with a special interest in East Asian cinema. He is currently working on a monograph on Ang Lee for the Wallflower Press *Directors' Cuts* series.

Martha Snowdon is a postgraduate student of film at the University of Southampton, with special interests in structures of audience identification and European film.

Chris Sodring is a postgraduate student in film and literature at Bristol University, with a special interest in cinematic representation of the works of Shakespeare.

Christina Stojanova is a film critic and a post-doctoral fellow at York University in Toronto, with special interests in ethnic and historical representation in Central and Eastern European cinema, inter-war German cinema and Québecois cinema.

Andrew Syder is a doctoral student at the University of Southern California in Los Angeles, with special interests in psychotronic cinema, phenomenology and the relationship between film and society.

Tony Todd is Lecturer in Visual and Cultural Theory at The London Institute's College of Printing. He is currently completing his doctorate on David Lynch at Southampton University.

Paul Watson is Programme Leader of Media Studies at the University of Teesside, with special interests in film theory and animation.

Barnaby Welch is a freelance writer and is the Editor of highangle.co.uk, a film review website, and has particular interests in the films of David Lynch and surrealist cinema.

Paul Wells is an award-winning radio and television programme-maker and Professor of Media and Cultural Studies at the University of Teesside. He is the author of two volumes within the Wallflower Press *Short Cuts* series, on the horror genre and animation.

Jerry White is Assistant Professor of Film Studies at the University of Alberta, and President of the Canadian Association for Irish Studies. He has also undertaken programmatic and educational work for the Philadelphia, Edmonton, Taos and Telluride film festivals. He is the editor of a collection on Canadian cinema within the Wallflower Press *24 Frames* series.

Lysandra Woods is taking her Master's Degree at Concordia University. In her spare time, she cannot stop watching old Hollywood melodramas.

# Foreword to the Second Edition

## Absolute Beginnings: sage advice about film-making from a complete novice
by Neil LaBute

When the good people at Wallflower Press asked me to write a foreword to their Critical Guide to Contemporary North American Film Directors, I replied with an emphatic "Yes!" I leapt at the chance. Now, after some five months of stalling and basic procrastination, here it is. I think the reason that it took me a little while to get going on this is because of that simple yet primal fear of having nothing to say. Don't get me wrong, I can ramble on forever, blathering on endlessly about practically nothing at all. No problem. But actually having something informative and useful to impart is another matter entirely. What could I possibly have to say about film-making or film-makers? True, I make films and have met a few directors over brunch, but that's about the extent of my expertise. I realise now, however, that that in itself is a kind of expertise. I know as much as the next guy about this weirdly fascinating world we call movies. I've made five of them and I still consider myself a complete novice. Take it from me, I know as much and as little as anybody else on the subject.

So, if you're looking for answers, keep reading. And no, I don't mean this foreword, I mean 'elsewhere'. To bastardise a quote by Brigham Young and use it for my own means, "This is surely not the place." Don't get me wrong, I'm going to do my best here, to say something about the process of film-making and my involvement in that process, but the actual usable answers will, no doubt, be few and far between. I'll do my best to be creative and honest and helpful, but that's about as good as it'll get. Answers, like most things in life, are hard to come by.

Maybe that's a good place to start, actually. The concept of 'answers'. I used to ask a lot of questions about my profession before I was a working member of that profession. I would pour over magazines, books, articles ... anything I could find on the subject. My first love was the theatre, but I was a constant moviegoer in my youth and had a pretty healthy interest in the subject. I could tell you who won what Academy Award in a given year, but precious little about how they did it. Actually, in much of that reading, the guiding force for me was usually a fairly simple set of concerns: "How did they do it? How did they get started? How can I do what they do? What were they doing when they were my age?" The answers, happily, were all over the proverbial map. I say 'happily' because what that meant was that there was no one way to fail or succeed. There were as many possibilities and variations as I could dream up.

The greatest piece of information that I've learned in this ongoing process called 'my career' is that there is no direct, obvious or singular path to follow. Unfortunately, that's also the bad news. I have never been able to find a universal way in which things would work out, if only I would utilise the simple, easy-to-use set of directions. I came into the world of film-making through the backest of doors, stumbling in blindly and with little thought or care of it becoming my profession. I simply made a film because I was sick of waiting for other people to make it. I should explain: I was approached by a film company – a good one out of New York – to adapt a play of mine into a screenplay. At the time, this simply meant that I should type "Fade in" at the beginning of the play and that was about it. However, the company liked what I did well enough to try and raise money to make the thing. This process, the 'financing' portion of independent film-making, turned out to be a nightmare of high expectations, dashed hopes and interminable waiting. I did not have the temperament for it. After the initial option period for the screenplay ran out, I refused to hand over another, opting instead to try and make a film on my own. A silly idea, really, for someone with no formal (or informal, for that matter) training, limited resources and no cash. The result was *In the Company of Me*, shot in eleven days and filmed for the tidy sum of $25,000. No matter what one thinks of the results (and the critical reaction ran the gamut from 'classic' to 'snuff film'), the end product was a film. True, I was older than Orson Welles when he made his first film (one of my earliest 'how did he do it?' heroes) and I hadn't followed any of the rules that I'd been searching for along the way, but I did have a motion picture under my belt for the effort. I don't advocate that anyone pursue the quirky, serpentine route that I followed to make that movie, but it does help prove two of my pet theories about films: 1) No one knows anything, and 2) You must make your own way on this journey.

My calling card to the world of film-making was also my first foray behind the camera. No film school. No short film paid for with the money set aside for my braces. Just a wordy, static think piece that went against most of the established conventions of American film. It garnered a few awards and got me over to the Cannes Film Festival, which was about five thousand miles further than I had ever allowed myself to dream. So it goes. One success story in a million. And I have no idea how I did it. Each day I just went out with a small group of talented, committed people and worked away at it, setting up each shot as we went and finally, days later, a film existed. True, it was a pile of rushes that had to be waded through, but it was in there somewhere. And so far, some four films later, that's the way it always seems to go. You go to work, you listen to everybody, you make decisions and, eventually, you start shooting. It doesn't matter what the budget is (I've worked with everything from $25,000 to $25 million), you always need a little more money and a lot more time. You always spend up to your means, and then a bit more. It never seems to get easier (or much harder, for that matter) and the pressure always seems to be about the same: steady, constant, noticeable.

The process of film-making still feels new to me and so I remain something of a zealot. I love what I do and am thrilled that I have the opportunity to do it on a semi-regular basis. The controlled chaos that is a film set has become addictive to me and I long for it when I am away from it. I still haven't found a useful set of rules to follow, to get to that next step in my 'career'. Actually, I'm not much of a planner. The idea of a 'five-year plan' is almost laughable to me. I can barely plan the next five minutes. But I do know that I'm going to keep at it. If I can't follow in the direct footsteps of Elia Kazan or Eric Rohmer or Federico Fellini or Sidney Lumet, then I'll have to make my own way. I've been doing it a few years now and it seems to be working. And that's the best advice I can give, I suppose. Keep going, believe that it's not a matter of 'if' but 'when'. Don't take 'no' for an answer. 'No' simply means ask again or ask somebody else.

This is the best I can do. To tell you that if I can do this, God knows anyone can. Your greatest weapon and virtue is yourself because there is no one quite like you. Before I begin to sound like Oprah I'm going to shut up, but I will tell you that this is it. There are no rehearsals, no do-overs. The world has never been more open to different ways of making films, different formats of presentation, different voices calling out with new ideas about technique and content. Whether it's Dogma 95 or your grandmother's Super 8, the world is poised and ready to have its collective breath taken away. People like Harmony Korine, Paul Thomas Anderson, Todd Solondz, Lisa Cholodenko and Vincent Gallo are out there pushing the envelope. Folks like Steven Soderbergh, The Coen Brothers, Todd Haynes and Atom Egoyan have already pushed through and are on their way to the next envelope. Are all these people just genius-freaks, dripping with talent and so completely different from you and me? Well, yes, they are talented, no doubt. But most of them are also just hard working dreamers who refuse to give in, give up or give way. They start from scratch each time out, fitting the format and film stock to the needs of the dream. The dream is all.

As this collection shows, contemporary American and Canadian film-making is rich and varied. Many of the directors included here no doubt started by taking polaroids, playing with images and ideas, and worked hard to bring their visions to the screen. So begin to dream... tomorrow may be too late.

# Introduction to the First Edition

## Back to the Brats
by Nick James, Editor of *Sight and Sound*

When asked to write an introduction to this, the first volume of the Critical Guides to Contemporary Directors, I began thinking about the world of the North American director today and kept coming back to a rumour I heard recently (circa July 2000). Apparently Harvey Weinstein, the notoriously uncompromising co-head of Miramax, the influential Disney-owned production and distribution company, had flown to the Cinecitta studios in Rome where Martin Scorsese was shooting *The Gangs of New York*, a nineteenth-century crime drama starring Leonardo DiCaprio. Weinstein had gone to stop the budget from ballooning out of control beyond its reported $90 million. He is said to have walked onto the 1860s New York set barking, "worker, stop working!" at bemused, possibly mono-lingual, Italian set builders.

Unremarkable, you might think, but what is irresistible about this story is that in one snapshot you have a director from the 'movie brat' generation (Scorsese, who made *Mean Streets*, *Taxi Driver*, *Raging Bull*, *GoodFellas* and *Casino*), given a budget way beyond anything he has had before in twenty-five years of film-making (a near-blockbuster $90 million), working for the most influential movie company of recent years (Miramax), on a film shot far away from Hollywood (Cinecitta), but where English remains the language of money. If we expand a little on each of these elements, one by one, something of the reality of contemporary North American film-making emerges.

Scorsese is, of course, one of the 'movie brats', the cinephiles who came out of film school and formed a second wave of maverick film-makers, joining the older film-makers in bringing the independent rock 'n' roll spirit of the 1960s and 1970s to a hidebound Hollywood or – if you subscribe to Peter Biskind's alternative view in his book *Easy Riders, Raging Bulls* – hoping to indulge their monstrous egos with sex and drugs excess. Of the first maverick wave, mostly men born in the 1930s who are now in their late 60s or 70s, only the affable likes of Warren Beatty, Woody Allen and Robert Altman still work regularly, and only Beatty is a force in the industry – unless you count the high-profile acting kudos that comes with being cast by Allen.

Another of them, William Friedkin – married to Paramount chair Sherry Lansing – has attempted comebacks with *Jade* (1995) and *Rules of Engagement* (2000), with-out ever looking convincingly like the director who made *The Exorcist* (1973). Otherwise, putting aside deceased greats and near greats such as Stanley Kubrick, John Cassa-vetes, Alan Pakula and Biskind's hero Hal Ashby, it is a tale of brief glory followed by prematurely arrested careers. Francis Coppola (*The Godfather, Apocalypse Now*) mostly executive produces, significantly for his daughter Sofia, whose recent directorial debut *The Virgin Suicides* is a big prestige movie success. Others, such as Peter Bogdanovich, Dennis Hopper or Arthur Penn, are increasingly invisible or retired.

Of the movie brats who came after them in this great experiment and who might be expected still to dominate the industry, Scorsese, Steven Spielberg, Paul Schrader and Brian De Palma have kept working, the latter two only in fits and starts. George Lucas stepped down from directing after completing the Star Wars trilogy and only recently returned with the prequel *Star Wars: Episode 1 - The Phantom Menace*. Terrence Malick did not make a film for twenty years between *Days of Heaven* (1978) and his triumphant comeback *The Thin Red Line* (1998). As Biskind tells it, the careers of most of these mavericks crashed in the 1980s with the coming of corporate Hollywood: the new world of pitch meetings, plot paradigms and executive narcissism so deftly etched in acid by Altman's comeback movie *The Player* (1992).

It is necessary to sketch some history here because it was in the 1980s that the movie business reconstituted itself out of the ashes of the old studio system. And it was two movie brat directors who were responsible indirectly for conjuring the world of *The Player*. Where many 1970s innovators sought to merge a European sensibility with Hol-lywood-level success, coming up with such prestige masterpieces as *The Godfather, The*

*Last Picture Show* and *Chinatown*, Spielberg and Lucas took a very different approach. With just two movies, *Jaws* (1975) and *Star Wars* (1977), they changed the way the industry works forever. So successful were their attempts to make big versions of 1950s-style B-movies for teenagers that the newly corporatised studios were encouraged to formularise the production and distribution processes to better exploit these kinds of movies, specifically targeting that teen boy demographic. Event movies, as they would come to be called, soon became the benchmark for studio success. What ensued is well known: the rise of multiplex cinema chains, the re-expansion of the moviegoing audience and a return to the idea of the movie as pure spectacle on a scale not seen since the days of D.W. Griffith and Cecil B. DeMille.

The Event movie was refined and taken to another level of sensation by a new generation of film-makers hired from other countries and other related industries. British director Ridley Scott is typical: his two films *Alien* (1979) and *Blade Runner* (1982) had nearly as much cultural impact as *Jaws* and the *Star Wars* trilogy. Event movies had to be 'high concept', meaning that their essential idea could be put across grippingly in two or three sentences. Requiring larger-than-life, machine-like stars such as Arnold Schwarzenegger and Sylvester Stallone, and plenty of special effects, these films were fantastically expensive. The need to put together a package of talent sufficiently impressive to justify gambling huge sums with confidence led to a substantial increase in power for both agents and actors in Hollywood.

Perhaps the key arbiters of the new approach were producers Don Simpson and Jerry Bruckheimer (and one should not forget their mirror image Joel Silver). Simpson (*An Officer and a Gentleman*, *Flashdance*, *Top Gun*, *Beverley Hills Cop*, *Days of Thunder* and *Bad Boys*) in particular was a vulgarian with an instinct for what sells movies to the archetypal teenage boy in Des Moines – more gorgeous scantily clad women, more explosions and more smartass one-liners – and Bruckheimer was the cut control freak, using directors for hire in the old Hollywood manner and kicking them out of the cutting room. Simpson was a crucial influence in shifting script development in Hollywood away from funky auteurism. Using ideas developed by writers steeped in the structure of folk tales, such as Joseph Campbell, Simpson demanded scripts built around an accepted paradigm, a rigid structure of three acts with a chain of action beats arcing upwards towards a big climax and featuring mythical archetypes from typical quest narratives. Campbell's ideas were easily grasped, as were those of screenwriting gurus such as Robert McKee and Syd Field. Smart studio executives soon gained the confidence to do more than question the quality of screenplays. Now they could also dictate their own changes.

One by-product of the movie brat era that survived this bigger-is-better onslaught was a bastardised version of the European concept of the auteur director. It suited the talent-packaging approach of executive Players that there should be an A-list of 'hot' directors – people who could enforce their vision even on a huge, unwieldy blockbuster machine. (Some say that directing such movies involves so many daily logistical decisions that they are often, in effect, 'directed' by the cinematographer – hence the promotion from lighting camera to director of Jan De Bont, who made *Speed* and *Twister*). It is a process that happens almost invisibly for those being assessed. This A- and B-listing meshes well with a similar director-as-star mentality in the music and advertising industries. Another hot corporate concept of the 1980s evidenced by the growth of movie merchandising and encouraged by the burgeoning growth of multi-media conglomerates was 'synergy'. The mutual marketing interests of music and film ensured an increasing supply of new directors who had cut their teeth in the fast-cutting, dutch-tilting, luridly colourful promo video world.

Of the directors who came to prominence through blockbuster Event movies few are US-born. James Cameron (*Terminator 2*, *Titanic*) is Canadian, Paul Verhoeven (*Total Recall*, *Basic Instinct*) and Jan De Bont (*Speed*) Dutch, Ridley and Tony Scott (*Blade Runner*, *Top Gun*) British, Roland Emmerich (*Independence Day*) German, Renny Harlin (*Die Hard 2*) Finnish, and John Woo (*Face/Off*, *Mission: Impossible II*) Hong-Kong Chinese. All of these directors you will find in this volume, although some may feature in companion volumes too; the very fact that the decision cannot be cut and dried points to the increasing globalisation of the movie industry itself. Questions are regularly asked as to whether, if a movie as seemingly North American in subject matter as *The Patriot* (2000), has two Australian lead actors (Mel Gibson and Heath Ledger) and a German director (Roland Emmerich), there is any point in trying to identify anything about it that is specifically national. Or does funding alone denote the national ownership of contemporary films?

The Event movie has taken US cinema across the globe in an unprecedented fashion, both in its Big Loud Action incarnation (*Mission: Impossible II*) and its more recent Natural Disaster sister form (*The Perfect Storm*) but no Event movie has yet made any claims on social realism, on reflecting North American life as it is lived. For that we usually turn elsewhere. If there is an authentic North American cinema today we expect to find it in the much-praised US indie sector. At present there is a strong whiff of misanthropy about non-mainstream movie tastes. Directors such as Todd Solondz (*Welcome to the Dolls House, Happiness*) and Neil LaBute (*Your Friends and Neighbours, Nurse Betty*) seem to want to vilify ordinary people for their gormless behaviour and they find a weird echo in the mainstream 'idiot' comedy of directors like the Farrelly brothers (*There's Something About Mary*). In contrast, hot young directors such as Paul Thomas Anderson and Kevin Smith offer a more forgiving view of humanity. And perhaps most heartening is the level of formal experimentation we have seen in Anderson's *Magnolia*, Kimberly Peirce's *Boys Don't Cry*, Harmony Korine's *julien donkey-boy*, Spike Jonze's *Being John Malkovich* and Mike Figgis' *Timecode*. It is almost as if the aesthetics of the movie brat era were being reborn.

The 1960s and 1970s was a uniquely cinephile era during which it was felt to be essential for a young person of intelligence to have an in-depth knowledge of cinema. During the boom post-*Easy Rider* years, a complex supportive structure of repertory cinemas and specialist cinemas built up across the USA and Canada, that was happy to play gay films, classic films, subtitled films and even avant-garde films. The early independent film-makers of the 1980s relied on that circuit to reach the public's attention. Film-makers such as John Sayles and Jim Jarmusch plotted very careful financial routes to survival outside of the mainstream, taking care to earn enough with one film to make another, and ensuring where possible that they would retain ownership of the print.

The typical mode of the 1980s US indie film might be loosely characterised as disjointed, instinctual or magic realist narrative structures married to a cool, downbeat visual style. It was (and is still) a rich field. While Jarmusch (*Stranger Than Paradise, Mystery Train*) explored the farce of miscommunication in a milieu of leftover landscapes and hip sainthood, Sayles (*Eight Men Out, City of Hope*) made serious issue-based dramas. David Lynch (*Blue Velvet, Wild at Heart*) became the prince of surreal weirdness, the Coen brothers (*Blood Simple, Miller's Crossing*) were cinephile black comedians, Hal Hartley (*The Unbelievable Truth, Trust*) got student angst around lust and literature down pat and Spike Lee (*She's Gotta Have It, Do the Right Thing*) used every aesthetic strategy he could to bring an African-American perspective to bear on race issues. These are somewhat sketchy summaries of the often subtle and complex approaches of these indie directors, but they give a flavour of the 1980s scene, an alternative that built its own institutions, only to see them absorbed by the greater industry.

Take the Sundance Film Festival. Ever since Steven Soderbergh won the Cannes Palme d'Or in 1989 with his low-budget indie film *sex, lies and videotape*, a Sundance audience hit which went on to make a lot of money, the festival has changed its character from a place where independent cinema is celebrated for its own sake to a kind of auction block for Hollywood. So many directors have now been plucked from obscurity into mainstream action after just one success there that the films submitted to Sundance are nearly all of a 'calling card' nature. And just as Hollywood has taken a step streetside to talent hunt, so has the independent sector transformed itself into a marketing- and multiplex-friendly operation.

Two names best epitomise this process: Quentin Tarantino and Miramax. Tarantino's success with the complex jewelry-store heist movie *Reservoir Dogs* was a transitional moment in independent film. Most of the directors already mentioned under the indie rubric were middle aged and well established and a new generation of filmgoers were impatient to discard the auteur icons of their parents and older siblings. With its glee for violence, its chopped-up structure borrowed from Kubrick and its brilliant pop-culture referencing, *Reservoir Dogs* somehow made Tarantino into an instant household name. Tarantino's success was cemented by his second film *Pulp Fiction* and by two others made from his scripts, Tony Scott's *True Romance* and Oliver Stone's *Natural Born Kill-*

*ers*. These quartet of films seemed to redefine the possibilities of independent cinema in a way that also suited the plans of Bob and Harvey Weinstein at Miramax.

The Weinstein brothers learnt much of their trade initially from Steve Woolley and Nik Powell of the British company Palace Pictures. Woolley and Powell had gone a long way by buying and distributing undervalued video titles such as *Diva* and *The Evil Dead* from a range of genres. What the Weinsteins did was to hone the process of marketing niche films while upping their production values so that they could play in the multiplexes. This meant that films that once would have only played independent circuits, such as costume dramas and noir thrillers, could now viably play in multi-screen cinemas. (The Miramax approach also tended to be one in which films would be recut to the Weinstein's own conception.) This has tended to create a greater marketing divide between such typical 'Miramax movies' as, say *Pulp Fiction* or *The English Patient*, and low-budget independents. It has also put Miramax-sponsored directors like Tarantino up into the same mid-budget bracket as Michael Mann, Oliver Stone and Kathryn Bigelow – auteurs whose epic scale always forced them to work with the mainstream. It is little wonder then that US independent directors who want to retain control now look for funding outside of the USA.

These then are the parameters of contemporary North America cinema. There are now really only two layers of commercially plausible releases in the USA and (to a perhaps lesser extent) Canada, and they are stratified pretty much by their budget. Or, to put it more simply, nearly everything that is not a blockbuster, a teen comedy, a kid's animation or a women's picture is a Miramax type movie. And the modern North American film-maker doesn't even have to plow one furrow or the other. It would have seemed impossible a few years ago for an up-and-coming duo like the Wachowski brothers to make the sharp, dark and sexy B-movie style thriller *Bound* one year, and the big-budget special-effects movie *The Matrix* the next. You could not imagine John Dahl (*The Last Seduction*), for instance, making that leap. But then who would have thought that Gus Van Sant would be capable of such a quintessential 'Miramax movie' as *Good Will Hunting*?

The hot young directors of the future, though, will not be able to rely even on these verities. Today, you can still take your first movie to Sundance and be sure that someone at the studios will have caught it and, if enough people are excited, offers beyond your wildest calculation may beckon. But what about tomorrow? Never has William Goldman's industry maxim "nobody knows anything" been truer. The movies, more than any other culture industry, now labour under the Chinese curse of interesting times. US and Canadian cinema is one of the most creatively fertile cinemas in the world but there is no clear picture yet of how a digital future in which moving image piracy may be rampant, and in which the internet provides the calling card shop window for all future directors, will work. What is significant is that although there are hundreds of directors working in North America today, they stem from, and work within, a still limited number of modes and models. It is thus a timely opportunity to consider the shifting parameters of the contemporary North American film industry, and illuminate the variety of currently-working film-makers, as brought together in this eclectic collection of auteurs, movie brats, studio hacks and independent artists. It may very well be that, as cheaper movie-making technology enables more people to be included in directories such as this, the cinema will become richer and stranger. I hope so, but I also believe that something like the collective movie experience as we know it will remain.

When I think of the determined struggle that the supreme cinephile director Martin Scorsese has put up to keep on working with the full resources of Orson Welles' "best train set a boy could ever have" at the highest level of quality, I have nothing but admiration. I hope *The Gangs of New York* matches *Taxi Driver, Raging Bull* and *GoodFellas* as an unimpeachable chunk of North American cinema at its best. There is something well rounded in the possibility of an original movie brat perhaps reaching the summit of artistic and commercial success at the very moment when a new generation of directors is beginning to make formal experiments in narrative, structure and shots not unlike those made by Scorsese's peers back in the 1970s. The past year has brought us *American Beauty, Boys Don't Cry, Being John Malkovich, Magnolia, The Insider, The Wonder Boys* and *Nurse Betty*, all of whose directors need not be ashamed in that company.

# Jim ABRAHAMS

Jim Abrahams is a director of wacky comedies that often plumb the depths of vulgarity but can also be ruthlessly satirical. A former private investigator, born in Milwaukee in 1944, Abrahams' life changed drastically when he went into partnership with old friends David and Jerry Zucker to found the Kentucky Fried Theater in Wisconsin, operating as a centre for live improvisation and filmic comedy. The trio went on to write and direct the hugely successful *Airplane!* (1980) and *Top Secret!* (1984), both of which were distinguished by an unending stream of puns and coarse visual gags.

Their next film, *Ruthless People* (1986), was marginally more restrained, posing the question: what happens when you kidnap someone that nobody wants back? Bette Midler is the termagant spouse whom Danny DeVito was going to murder anyway, and who intimidates her amateur kidnappers more than they do her. Crudely drawn caricatures are employed to accent the callousness of late twentieth-century society, where fidelity has no meaning and money is the new god.

This is a motif echoed by the first of Abrahams' lone projects, *Big Business* (1988). Made in the same year as Ivan Reitman's *Twins*, *Big Business* uses trick photography to present two sets of Bette Midlers and Lily Tomlins who become mixed up at birth. One pair are rural, the other urban industrialists, pitted against each other over the sale of a subsidiary firm in Jupiter Hollow, where they were all born. Complications arise when they come together, but this idea is not new. Indeed, Laurel and Hardy were using it before the director himself was born in *Our Relations* (1936).

Winona Ryder's performance is really the only commendable thing about *Welcome Home, Roxy Carmichael* (1990). Reprising the role of kooky misfit from *Beetlejuice* (1988), the gifted young actress commands much of the attention and provides essential comic relief in this otherwise stilted small-town story.

However, *Hot Shots!* (1991) heralds a return to the potent days of *Airplane!*, with the fighter pilot film *Top Gun* (1986) acting as a prime target for Abraham's wit. Charlie Sheen ensures he will never again be taken seriously (just like Leslie Nielsen) after being seen frying eggs on Valeria Golino's stomach. But the rapid-fire raillery, albeit occasionally hit-and-miss, married with a succession of movie references (*9½ Weeks*

(1986), *Dances With Wolves* (1990) and *Gone with the Wind* (1939) to name but three), helps to occupy the mind. The sequel – *Hot Shots! Part Deux* (1993) – delivered more of the same, using *Rambo* war films as a framework.

Abrahams' next film of merit was made for television. *...First Do No Harm* (1997) is a well respected 'lapse' into sombre family medical drama. Filmed in Canada, this is the true story of the Reimullers and their son's battle with epilepsy. Puissant performances by Meryl Streep (nominated for an Emmy and Golden Globe) and Fred Ward pragmatically convey the frustration and distress of the parents, but young Seth Adkins eclipses them both as the ailing child. This film is a prime example of the medium being used to functionally instruct and pronounce sentence on social matters.

This is in marked contrast to *Jane Austen's Mafia* (aka *Mafia*) (1999), which is a belated spoof of the *Godfather* (1972, 1974, 1990) series. Like the earlier *Spy Hard* (1996) or *Dracula: Dead and Loving It* (1995), this film merely affirms that the genre is desperately repeating itself. The jokes are more incongruous than comical (using a donkey's hind quarters as a hiding place or riddling the late Lloyd Bridges' Don with bullets as the macarena plays) and at certain points even nugatory (Jay Mohr's bewildering melée with a hose). This is a merciless reminder that the glory days have long since passed. **PB**

# Andrew ADAMSON

*Shrek* (2001) Before lensing *Shrek* (2001), DreamWorks' animated hit of 2001, Andrew Adamson and Vicky Jenson never previously directed a film. Notable for bringing the fairytale genre up to date, and for its use of irreverent humour, *Shrek* has crossed many boundaries in film animation: it appeals to all ages, was accepted for Cannes and won the first ever Academy Award for an animated film in 2002.

Adamson's background was in computer animation on commercials and station IDs in his native New Zealand. In the 1980s, he was recruited by PDI in America, where he progressed eventually to work on Barry Levinson's *Toys* (1982). He subsequently worked on *Double Dragon* (1993) and *Angels in the Outfield* (1994) and as a visual effects supervisor for *Batman Forever* (1995) and *Batman and Robin* (1997), both of which were finalists for an Academy Award nomination for Best Visual Effects. Vicky Jenson started as a background artist at Hanna-Barbera in 1977, became a storyboard artist for Warner Bros., Marvel and Disney Television, and variously worked as a production designer, art director and co-producer. In the mid-1980s she worked on the team responsible for the development of the visual style for 'Mighty Mouse' and 'Ren & Stimpy', and was art director for *Ferngully* in 1992. Jenson first worked for DreamWorks as a production designer and story artist on the 2000 animated feature *The Road to El Dorado*.

With producer and DreamWorks partner Jeffrey Katzenberg and the animators at PDI/DreamWorks (responsible for *Antz* (1998)), Adamson and Jenson built on the success of their previous visual accomplishments to create a funny, post-modern fairytale. Based on a children's book by William Steig, the film plays with the genre's conventions whilst maintaining the fairy story spirit, taking a few pot shots at arch-rival (and Katzenberg's former employer) Disney on the way. Featuring the voices of Mike Myers, Eddie Murphy, Cameron Diaz and John Lithgow, *Shrek* tells the story of a gloomy green giant who 'wants to be alone' but is tricked into setting out on a quest to rescue a princess in distress. Assisted by a talking donkey, skilfully voiced by Murphy, they rescue the unconventional damsel by way of several tongue-in-cheek nods to a movie-literate audience, young and old, satirising amongst others 'Beauty and the Beast' and *The Matrix* (1999). Around 275 team members at PDI/DreamWorks spent three years developing *Shrek*. Katzenberg had a lot of input in the film, but the visual effects and humour that the directors brought to the film are much in evidence. Adamson has commented that he 'grew up watching MTV, *Fawlty Towers* and *Monty Python* ... so we ended up with a fairly broad spectrum of comedy in the movie'. Jenson believes that her animation experience honed her comic timing. Though stylised, the use of cinematography and camera operation, using perspective and techniques to intentionally create 'faults' to simulate live action, gives the film an edge over CGI films to date.

DreamWorks, who are continuing to rival Disney with their animation output, are already at work on the sequel, with Adamson tipped to direct solo. First, though, he is rumoured to be writing with Joe Stillman, a co-author of *Shrek,* and directing *Truckers*, a DreamWorks movie that will mix live action and animation, based on the novel by science fiction writer Terry Pratchett. Vicky Jenson is slated to direct an upcoming DreamWorks CG project that has yet to be announced.                                    **FG**

# Alan ALDA

Best known for his role as Hawkeye Pierce on the television series 'M*A*S*H', Alan Alda has put together an extensive resume that spans over four decades. With his light-hearted charm and devotion to humanity Alda has consistently created work that has enlightened as well as entertained.

*The Four Seasons* (1981)
*Sweet Liberty* (1986)
*A New Life* (1988)
*Betsy's Wedding* (1990)

Born in New York City in 1936, Alda followed in his father's acting footsteps and began his career working in stock theatre companies in the eastern United States. While attending Fordham University, he travelled to Europe and continued to act in various stage and television shows. After returning, Alda continued to act on Broadway and broke into films with his role in *Gone are the Days* (1963). Since then he has acted steadily in films, television, and on the stage.

With 'M*A*S*H' Alda was given the opportunity to direct and write many of the episodes. This opportunity helped Alda to define the show's themes and showcase his talents beyond acting. He received five Emmy awards for his work on 'M*A*S*H' and is the only person to win an Emmy award for acting, writing, and direction. This led to several other television directorial efforts such as '6 Rms. Riv Vu' with Carol Burnett, and work on a Marlo Thomas special 'Free to Be – You and Me'. He also wrote and produced several other specials and shows, most memorably 'We'll Get By'.

As his writing and directorial talent was being well-cultivated on television, Alda was finally given the opportunity to direct the feature film *The Four Seasons* (1981). The film, which Alda also wrote and starred in, co-starred Carol Burnett, Jack Weston, and Bess Armstrong. It chronicles the lives of three middle-class couples as they vacation during different seasons of the year. Alda deftly handled the serious nature of the film and showed his unique ability to present different sides of people's lives. Warm and funny, the film did well and was later made into a short-lived television series that Alda co-produced.

After spending years of directing 'M*A*S*H' episodes on television Alda got one last chance to direct the 4077, as he directed the final episode, *M*A*S*H: Goodbye, Farewell, & Amen* (1983). This special two-hour episode was a smash and continues to be the highest-rated network television show ever. Again Alda used comedy and compassion to present our last glimpses of the familiar television icons.

1986 saw Alda working on the big screen again, directing *Sweet Liberty*. The director again also wrote and starred in this charming look at film-making, small-town values, and human wants and desires. The film was wonderfully sarcastic, but also touching in its portrayal of what people will go through to make movies. Michael Caine and Bob Hoskins co-starred.

Alda again tackled couples and divorce in *A New Life* (1988). He completed the trifecta (directing, writing, and acting) again as he showed a married couple facing their lives alone in the big city. *Betsy's Wedding* (1990) also dealt with family relations as Alda presented the plans and preparations for a wedding. The film centred particularly on Alda's character as he tries to give his daughter the perfect lavish celebration. This is arguably Alda's best outing as a director; a wonderful social comedy that is filled with truthful observations about family life. For the last ten years Alda has taken a break from directing. He has been hosting 'Scientific American Frontiers' on PBS and making several television, movie and stage appearances, most notably on 'ER' and in the Broadway production of 'ART'.                                    **JM**

# Woody ALLEN

Woody Allen (Allan Stewart Konigsberg) is probably American cinema's most consistent and prolific film-maker, having written and directed an average of a film a year for the past thirty years. He also acts in many of these films, and they are frequently interpreted as autobiographical exercises about his own neuroses. But does his art really imitate his life? Are his films really examples of *cinema-à-clef*, or is it simply a case of mistaken

*What's Up Tiger Lily?* (1966)
*Take the Money and Run* (1969)
*Bananas* (1971)
*Everything You Always Wanted*

identity? And, moreover, why are we so interested? The last of these questions can in part be answered by reference to the scandals surrounding his private life in recent years. Fans and critics have, however, been attempting to locate the 'private' Woody in his work for decades – a game seemingly encouraged by the films themselves, despite Allen's claims to the contrary. Note, for example, how often psychoanalysis pops up in his films, and how often his protagonists are writers or directors.

Born in Brooklyn in 1935, Allen began his career as a highly regarded stand-up comic and gag writer. He first branched into film in the mid-1960s, penning the script for, and acting in, *What's New Pussycat?* (1965), then dubbing new dialogue over the soundtrack of a Japanese James Bond clone in the hilarious *What's Up Tiger Lily?* (1966). His first original films as a director – which have since been labelled his 'early, funny ones' – were a brilliant set of out-and-out comedies in which the gag ruled over every other consideration. The basic, recurring formula of these films was to take Allen's schlemiel character and put him in ever more ridiculous situations. In *Take the Money and Run* (1969) he plays a hapless career criminal who even has difficulty stealing from a gumball machine; in *Bananas* (1971) his efforts to impress a girl lead him to accidentally take part in a fictional Latin American country's revolution, eventually becoming its dictator; *Everything You Always Wanted to Know About Sex, But Were Afraid to Ask* (1972) sees him play, amongst other memorable characters, a reluctant sperm; *Sleeper* (1973) places him in a science fiction narrative in which he is frozen and wakes up two hundred years into the future; and *Love and Death* (1975) finds him inserted into a spoof of nineteenth-century Russian literature.

While these films focus primarily on slapstick and verbal comedy, a vein of intellectualism can be detected running just beneath the surface: a metaphysical as well as a physical comedy. Who else would combine banana skin gags with jokes about Pushkin and Antonioni? This intellectualism found its footing in the 'nervous romance' *Annie Hall* (1977), a comic examination of a failed relationship. This is the psychoanalysis movie par excellence: it starts with a joke by Freud, ends with one about a psychiatrist, and the moments between are filled with enough concealments, displacements and fragments of memory to keep a shrink busy for months. Allen must have struck a chord with therapy-obsessed Hollywood, as the film was honoured with Academy Awards for Best Picture, Director, Actress (Diane Keaton) and Original Screenplay. It also introduced a philosophy of Allen's that has resurfaced in many of his later works: be happy you're only miserable.

He followed the success of *Annie Hall* with *Interiors* (1978), a bleak and sombre family drama in which neither Allen nor his one-liners appeared. The film was the first of a number of kammerspiel dramas to reveal his admiration for the work of Ingmar Bergman, later seen in works that include *September* (1987) and *Another Woman* (1988). The standard critical account of Allen continues to paint him as desperately attempting to emulate Bergman. While there may be some truth in this description, it is a somewhat misleading view in that it tries to characterise the split between Allen's comedies and his dramas within a Romantic framework of the suffering artist: that he aspires towards serious and profound art, but cannot shrug off his jester's bells. This seems fallacious, not only because Allen has always been able to make the films he wants to make, but also because it misleadingly stereotypes Bergman as a purveyor of doom and gloom, when he too made a number of comedies. Indeed, Allen's light and magical *A Midsummer Night's Sex Comedy* (1982) was influenced by Bergman's *Smiles of a Summer Night* (1955), and perfectly evokes the enchantment of a fairytale.

Certain auteurs tend to be associated with a particular city, and Woody Allen is no exception. Nowhere is this more clear than in *Manhattan* (1979), his valentine to New York City. Filmed in lush black-and-white CinemaScope – Allen is one of the few film-makers to still shoot frequently in black-and-white – *Manhattan* marks the highpoint of his collaboration with cinematographer Gordon Willis, who shot all of Allen's films between 1977 and 1985. (Future collaborations would see Allen further augment his interest in European cinema by teaming up with both Bergman's cinematographer, Sven Nykvist, and Antonioni's, Carlo Di Palma.)

In a scene in *Annie Hall*, Allen is pressured for his autograph by two thuggish men who have seen him on television, showing a side to celebrity that is expanded in the darkly comic *Stardust Memories* (1980). A variant on Preston Sturges' *Sullivan's Travels* (1941) and Federico Fellini's *8½* (1963), in which Allen plays a film-maker struggling to make a serious film whilst attending a retrospective of his comedies, *Stardust Memories* comes across as a long, heartfelt cry of despair. Yet it is not without humour, and Allen spoofs critical opinion of his own films with particular venom. For example, he opens the movie with what appears to be a painfully pretentious Bergman homage, but is really a film-within-a-film, while in another scene he meets a group of space aliens who profess a preference for his early, funny films.

*Zelig* (1983), *Broadway Danny Rose* (1984), *The Purple Rose of Cairo* (1985), and *Radio Days* (1987) are all small gems about small lives, exploring how different characters respond to mundane existences. *Zelig* is a brilliant pseudo-documentary about a human chameleon who assumes the appearances of others as a method of seeking acceptance. It has been interpreted as an allegory for the Jewish experience, but could be a metaphor for any form of insecurity or 'passing' in which one suppresses one's own identity in order to gain social approval. In *Broadway Danny Rose*, Allen gives arguably his best performance as a legendary small-time talent agent who finds himself on the run from the Mob in a case of mistaken identity. The film finds its heart in rooting for the underdog, with Danny Rose remaining absolutely devoted to his low-rent, variety act clients, even when he realises that his own chances at the big-time have all but evaded him. *The Purple Rose of Cairo* is a bittersweet, Depression-era fantasy in which Jeff Daniels plays a movie character who steps down off the silver screen to romance a lonely, lovelorn Mia Farrow. Blurring the line between reality and fiction, it expertly shows how cinematic escapism helps to lift us up at our lowest moments but remains ultimately incompatible with actual existence. *Radio Days* is similarly nostalgic. A virtually freeform collection of memories of 1940s New York, the film interlaces stories of a family's life with tall tales about famous radio personalities.

*Hannah and Her Sisters* (1986) and *Crimes and Misdemeanors* (1989) proved to be his biggest critical successes of the decade, both earning Allen Best Director nominations. The former is a serio-comic look at a group of characters suffering mid-life crises and searching for some kind of meaning or direction in their lives. It finds Allen at his most metaphysical and, like much of his later work, weaves a multi-narrative tapestry with an A-list ensemble cast – winning Academy Awards for Dianne Wiest and Michael Caine, as well as another screenwriting award for Allen. *Crimes and Misdemeanors* is one of Allen's most ambitious films, intercutting between two stories of strikingly different tone: a very sombre drama in which Martin Landau plays a wealthy doctor who arranges to have his mistress murdered, and a comic tale in which Allen plays a lowly documentary film-maker involved in a marital indiscretion with a colleague. What interests Allen are moral and spiritual crimes (rather than the legal variety) and the question of God's existence. Landau is never caught for his crime, but he is left with the fear that God may have been watching and, perhaps worse, that his conscience will prevent him from ever being able to continue a normal family life.

'Oedipus Wrecks' is the acknowledged high point of *New York Stories* (1989), a largely uninspired compendium of short tales about the city by Allen, Martin Scorsese and Francis Ford Coppola, and it remains the ultimate Jewish mother film. *Alice* (1990) is a disappointing fantasy in which Mia Farrow takes magical herbs that make her invisible. *Shadows and Fog* (1992) is a witty, Kafkaesque tale shot in remarkable, expressionistic black-and-white – although anyone familiar with Allen's play *Death*, upon which it was based, is likely to feel the film did not quite realise the potential of its source material.

The question of where the real Woody Allen ends and the *reel* Woody Allen begins has been nowhere more hotly debated than with *Husbands and Wives* (1992), a film about a marriage break-up that has become inseparable from Allen's own very public split from Mia Farrow. The film, however, remains among his most dynamic and penetrating works – perhaps all the more powerful for it – with Allen astutely anticipating the speculations of the ensuing media circus in his one-liner that life doesn't imitate art, it imitates bad television.

His first film after the scandal, *Manhattan Murder Mystery* (1993), surprised everyone with its sprightliness. Allen in fact seems to be poking fun at critics who confuse the person and the persona by staging the film's dénouement at a cinema playing *The Lady From Shanghai* (1948). Not only does his shootout mimic Welles' hall-of-mirrors finale, he also quips, 'I'll never say art doesn't imitate life again!' *Manhattan Murder Mystery* also sees him attempting a thriller for the first time, in a Bob Hope-meets-Hitchcock vein. While *Husbands and Wives* had employed handheld cameras to heighten the rawness and emotional immediacy, here they are used to keep the audience on the edge of their seats with suspense, perfectly translating the nervousness of his comedy into an adrenaline rush of jumpy thrills.

A theatrical farce, *Bullets Over Broadway* (1994) again posed questions about the role of the artist, with John Cusack playing a pretentious 1920s playwright who enters into a Faustian pact with a local gangster in order to get his play produced. Here, Allen gives a new twist to the old dilemma about whether one would choose to save from a burning building the last known copies of Shakespeare's plays or an anonymous person. Cusack's playwright aspires to humanist ideals but is never more than second rate, whereas one of the gangster's henchmen, Cheech (Chazz Palminteri), is a literary genius who thinks nothing of bumping off a bad actress to save the play.

A disappointing adaptation of Allen's play about American tourists stranded behind the Iron Curtain, *Don't Drink the Water* (1994) was shot for television and might more aptly be titled *Don't Tread the Water*. *Mighty Aphrodite* (1995), his next film, is undeniably witty and features the clever gimmick of a Greek chorus, but offers little that Allen hasn't done better elsewhere. *Everyone Says I Love You* (1996), however, proved to be a thoroughly charming attempt at recreating an old-style Hollywood musical – albeit one in which the actors don't need to be able to sing or dance well. The fun the cast are evidently having is infectious, but the sight of Allen pairing himself up romantically with Julia Roberts is almost as creepy as his singing voice.

More recently, Allen has often returned to the frameworks of his earlier career. *Deconstructing Harry* (1997) and *Celebrity* (1998) are both very distressing films about authorship and stardom, and similar to *Stardust Memories*. In the former, Allen blurs the boundaries between reality and fiction as he plays a *roman-à-clef* writer who must deal with the repercussions of having written about the lives of the people around him. It is a dark and complex film that once again sees Allen reworking Bergman, this time *Wild Strawberries* (1957). It also features some of his most inventive gags, such as keeping Robin Williams deliberately out-of-focus and casting Billy Crystal as the devil. *Celebrity* on the other hand is felled by an irritating Woody impersonation from Kenneth Branagh and remains as shallow as its subject matter – which might of course be the point.

*Sweet and Lowdown* (1999) returns to the fictional biopic format of *Zelig*, detailing the footloose and pompous life of Emmett Ray, the *second* greatest jazz guitarist of the 1930s. It is a funny and light film about Allen's passion for jazz, and all the more potent for seeming so effortless. *Small Time Crooks* (2000) marked the beginning of an alliance with DreamWorks, as well as a return to the tone of his early, funny films. It feels a little like two separate films clumsily stuck together, but it is crammed with many great one-liners and proved to be his biggest opener in twenty years. *The Curse of the Jade Scorpion* (2001) spoofs the hardboiled detective genre, but falls somewhat flat. Too many jokes miss their target and the script contains little suspense or mystery, mainly because the audience is always three or four steps ahead of Allen's detective. In his most recent offering, *Hollywood Ending* (2002), he plays a director fallen on hard times who has the chance to direct another big film; temporarily blind, he attempts to keep his condition from the producer in order to complete the shoot. Its reception has been decidedly lukewarm.

Ultimately, Allen remains as enigmatic as Zelig and as blurry as Robin Williams – no doubt just as he intended. Like the perfect Freudian paradox, by seeming to reveal everything about himself he ends up revealing nothing at all. Perhaps the best way to look at his films is to remember the advice of that friendly little alien from *Stardust Memories*: 'You want to do mankind a real service? Tell funnier jokes.' As for searching for the 'real' Woody Allen? Don't waste your time, because there isn't one. Only Allan Stewart Konigsberg. **AS**

# Roger ALLERS

*The Lion King* (1994)  After a lengthy association with the Disney corporation (which included pre-production work on the visually innovative, live-action feature *Tron* (1982) and story credits for the films which re-established the company's animated division, *The Little Mermaid* (1989) *Beauty And The Beast* (1991) and *Aladdin* (1992)), Roger Allers' directorial debut was made (in collaboration with Rob Minkoff) on the enormously successful *The Lion King* (1994).

Consolidating the Disneyfication of the globe, the film presents an African jungle landscape replete with Western conservative family values and familiar fantasy archetypes, from mighty patriarchal beasts to wisecracking wildlife. That the cute lion cub Simba (voiced in adulthood by Matthew Broderick) should undergo a gradual rites of passage in order to fulfil the law of his regal father, Mufasa (James Earl Jones), underlines the conservative view familiar from all Disney animation. Banished into exile upon the death of his father, Simba briefly subscribes to a 'problem free philosophy' but returns to restore order to his rightful kingdom when he reaches maturity. As in many contemporary action films, the treacherous villain, Scar (Jeremy Irons), is given a European voice – indeed, in order to maintain the purity of Simba, the final confrontation displaces his revenge (Scar was responsible for Mufasa's death) onto the disgruntled hyenas, themselves defined as cowardly, disloyal and destructive. However, the film is consistently entertaining, despite the curiously forgettable songs (by Tim Rice and Elton John). Combining state of the art computer animation techniques with traditional methods, the film proved popular enough to spawn a direct-to-video sequel and Broadway show.                                                **NJ**

# Michael ALMEREYDA

Michael Almereyda, born in 1960, and a product of the American Midwest, turned to feature film directing after completing his first short, *A Hero of our Time* (1985), and providing a screenplay for Steve DeJarnatt's science fiction comedy *Cherry 2000* (1987). *Twister* (1988), a $3 million adaptation of Mary Robison's 'Oh!', is an amusing chronicle of the meltdown of an atypical nuclear family. Filmed in Kansas, the film boasts a quietly knowing performance by Harry Dean Stanton as the paterfamilias to children Suzi Amis and Crispin Glover. Almereyda's above-average support cast includes Dylan McDermott, Jenny Wright, Lois Chiles and Beat author William Burroughs in a wry cameo. When *Twister*'s financier, Vestron, went bankrupt, the film (from which only three prints had been struck) was given a few urban art-house playdates before being sold off to home video. Little seen at the time of its limited theatrical run, Almereyda's 'cursed cult film' was driven further underground by the 1996 release of Jan de Bont's effects-laden blockbuster of the same name.

*Twister* (1988)
*Another Girl, Another Planet* (1992)
*Nadja* (1994)
*At Sundance* (1995)
*The Rocking Horse Winner* (1997)
*Trance* (1998)
*Hamlet* (2000)
*Happy Here and Now* (2001)

At just over an hour, Almereyda's follow-up, *Another Girl, Another Planet* (1992), received greater attention, more because it was filmed with a discontinued toy camera – the high-speed Fisher-Price PXL 2000 – than for its merits as a work of art. Almereyda's 'pixie camera' afforded this black-and-white love letter to New York's East Village the fragmented, cottony aspect of an opium dream. Shot with a six-person crew ('not counting the elephant trainer'), the short film received sufficient word of mouth and critical acclaim to urge Almereyda towards his second feature film, the contemporary vampire opus *Nadja* (1994), which reunited him with the star of *Another Girl, Another Planet*, Elina Löwensohn.

Executive produced by David Lynch (who financed the film with his own money when the original funding fell through) and Mary Sweeney, *Nadja* was influenced by discussions of Carl Theodor Dreyer's *Vampyr* (1932) and Lambert Hillyer's *Dracula's Daughter* (1936) by William K. Everson, author of 'Classics of the Horror Film'. *Nadja* inverts the latter film by marginalising its heterosexual male hero (Hal Hartley regular Martin Donovan) in favour of a seduction/romance between Löwensohn's lesbian bloodsucker and Galaxie Craze's disenchanted wife. Almereyda bucks vampire chic by refusing to make his undead protagonist a counter-culture role model in the vein of Anne Rice's brooding revenants. In drawing a parallel between Euro trash and vampires, *Nadja* honours the narrative intention of 'Dracula' author Bram Stoker more faithfully than that novel's countless adaptations, and is a rare American attempt to deal with vampirism within the context of family. Almereyda again used Pixelvision to communicate the other-worldliness of New York's nightlife (underscoring the bizarre happenings with a lush, multi-tiered soundtrack by British composer Simon Fisher-Turner). The medium's coarse, third-generation aspect said as much about *Nadja*'s doomed genealogy as did Almereyda's elliptical script. He tied for the Best Director award at the 1995 Catalonian International Film Festival.

Following two more short features, the documentary *At Sundance* (1995), and his award-winning adaptation of a D. H. Lawrence story, *The Rocking Horse Winner*

(1997), Almereyda returned to the theme of tortured families with *Trance* (1998). Even less accessible than *Nadja*, *Trance* – described by one critic as 'a Val Lewton film run amok' – follows the dreamlike voyage of a dysfunctional Manhattan family to their boggy ancestral home on the coast of Ireland. Suffering premonitions of death, and crossing paths with the IRA, husband and wife must also endure the unnerving presence of Christopher Walken as a half-blind uncle who keeps a two-thousand-year-old mummified druid stashed in the basement. *Trance* is Almereyda's only film to date made with a major studio – indie financier Trimark, who denied its writer-director a final cut and dumped the film onto the video market under the alternative title *The Eternal*.

Almereyda received considerably more press for his updating of *Hamlet* (2000), which lays the melancholy Dane's identity crisis within the context of New York's corporate jungle. Ethan Hawke, who helped develop the project, plays his brooding prince as video-obsessed, shooting his own tortured soliloquies and playing back the 'dailies' to make sense of his existence. Patterned after Kurt Cobain, this tragic hero is not insane, but decidedly depressed. Shot by British cinematographer John de Borman on Super 16, the film employs surveillance techniques to evoke a post-modern take on court intrigue. Almereyda's support plays include such theatrical heavyweights as Diane Venora and Sam Shepard, as well as Bill Murray.

Any success Almereyda may have enjoyed with *Hamlet*, however, has not helped his most recent film, the New Orleans-set *Happy Here and Now* (2001). The story follows a teenage girl to the Big Easy, on a search for her missing sister, and aided by a retired private detective; she is drawn further into the mystery by online messages from an anonymous computer geek who goes by the alias 'Eddie Mars' – a reference to Raymond Chandler's 'The Big Sleep'. Eschewing the Mardi Gras aspect of most films set in New Orleans, Almereyda utilises the intangible aspect of cyberspace in the same way that dream imagery functioned in his earlier films. Shot in 2000, the film has yet to find a distributor, and Almereyda has since helmed a documentary about the Los Angeles staging of Sam Shepard's play 'The Late Henry Moss'.                      **RHS**

# Robert ALTMAN

Robert Altman is American cinema's greatest iconoclast. Prolific, experimental, visionary and ambitious, he is a director whose career spans over five decades and includes over thirty feature films. Known as a maverick director (a label he denies), Altman eschews the market-oriented climate of Hollywood, refusing to bow to studio demands and insisting on total control over his material. The result is an eclectic body of work that moves across several genres, each picture effectively dismantling the generic conventions on which it draws. The critique of social institutions and the portrayal of social outsiders are Altman's central preoccupations; his oeuvre can be read as an attempt to revise American history by subverting some of its most trenchant myths. Motivated by what interests him, Altman has admitted to going broke in order to shoot a picture he believes in. It is this kind of fervent dedication to his craft that has earned him a reputation as one of America's most independent and innovative film-makers. Happy with a cast of hundreds, Altman loves to direct groups of people, painting a broad picture of their complex interactments and entanglements. Yet while he may be most famed for his large-scale pictures, his interest in exploring the inner life of his characters should not go ignored. His stylistic hallmarks are readily recognisable: the inventive use of overlapping sound and dialogue, mock documentary realism and improvisation – one of the most interesting features of Altman's work is his use of cinema to explore the ever-shifting boundary between reality and fantasy.

Born in Kansas City in 1925, Altman had already lived a few lives before becoming a film-maker: he was a B-54 bomber pilot, an engineering student, and the inventor of a machine for tattooing identification marks on dogs. He learned the tricks of the film trade when he started working on industrial pictures (documentaries, employee training films, and advertisements) in his native Kansas City. Rarely seen, *The Delinquents* (1957), is Altman's admittedly mediocre directorial debut. The poor man's version of *Rebel Without a Cause* (1955), Altman produced, directed and wrote the film for $63,000. His next film, *The James Dean Story* (1957), is another unremarkable directorial effort, though Alfred Hitchcock is said to have divined Altman's future genius after seeing it, contracting the young director to shoot two episodes of 'Alfred Hitchcock Presents'. By the time he started doing work for television, Altman was more than conversant with the technical intricacies of film-making: camera, sound and editing. His ability to work fast made him an ideal director for television and during the late 1950s and the early 1960s he directed a number of television episodes, including 'Bonanza' and 'Hawaiian Eye'. Altman credits his early experience as a television director with the improvisational method that later became one of his trademarks.

Countdown (1968), a fictionalised account of the first moon landing, is Altman's first feature film after working in television, but he considers That Cold Day in the Park (1969), a psychodrama starring Sandy Dennis, to be his most important early work. His first big commercial success was M*A*S*H (1970), a black comedy centred on doctors at a Korean mobile army surgical hospital. Starring Donald Sutherland, Alan Alda and Elliott Gould (an actor who would go on to appear in several Altman films), M*A*S*H is a pivotal movie for Altman, introducing several of his directing techniques – the use of a large cast, the mobile camera and a prominent score. Especially notable is Altman's self-reflexive use of the loudspeaker system, which serves as a link between scenes and provides a pointed commentary on the on-screen action. The callous, politically incorrect treatment of the Sally Kellerman (Hotlips) and Robert Duvall (Frank Burn) characters led to accusations of misogyny and homophobia. Against these charges Altman insists that his film is not indicative of his own opinions of women and homosexuals, but, rather, is a truthful documentation of the reality of how minority groups are treated. Yet the cruelty of these images reappear in some of Altman's later films. Buoyed by the success of M*A*S*H, the director took creative license with his next film, Brewster McCloud (1970), an eccentric picture about a boy who wants to fly in the Houston Astrodome. Although some critics found the film hilarious, it is no match for the exquisitely crafted McCabe and Mrs Miller (1971). With wonderful cinematography from Vilmos Zsigmond (whose partnership with Altman resulted in some of the director's best work), this revisionist western, full of dark grey skies and wet snowfalls, is a haunting, incredibly atmospheric film. First-rate performances from Warren Beatty, as the small-time hustler McCabe, and Julie Christie, as the madam Mrs Miller, along with a brooding Leonard Cohen soundtrack, make for a deeply moving film.

Images (1972), a film inspired by Ingmar Bergman's Persona (1966), stars Susannah York as the mentally unhinged heroine. The film is a striking example of Altman's facility for probing examinations of the psyche. Shot in Ireland (with cinematography from Zsigmond), it is a clever mix of fantasy and reality that continually manages to keep the spectator uncertain as to which 'realm' we are in. The Long Goodbye (1973), his ironic take on Raymond Chandler and the 1940s hard-boiled detective novel, has a screenplay written by Leigh Brackett, the same writer who co-scripted the 1946 Bogart-Bacall version of Chandler's 'The Big Sleep'. Transporting detective Philip Marlowe (Elliott Gould) into the debauched world of 1970s Los Angeles, Altman's version is a clever condemnation of the American dream.

Altman's father was an inveterate gambler and Altman himself is known to gamble. California Split (1974) is a rambling, non-judgmental exploration of the world of gambling. The film features great improvisational acting from its two leads, Elliott Gould and George Segal. Deft characterisation and acting is also present in Thieves Like Us (1974), a film that deserves more recognition than it usually receives. Scripted by Joan Tewkesbury (an Altman regular), it is a brilliantly unconventional period piece of 1930s Americana.

Nashville (1975), Altman's subsequent film, is a classic two-and-a-half-hour epic study of ambition, greed, talent and politics in American culture, with the country and western music business serving as a microcosm of American society. The best of Altman's films from the 1970s, it is also, arguably, one of the best American movies ever made. Following the intertwined lives of 24 protagonists during a long weekend in Nashville, Tennessee, the film is shot in quasi-documentary style and features smart performances from its cast (which includes cameos from Julie Christie and Elliott Gould playing themselves). The recipient of five Academy Award Nominations, including Best Director and Best Picture, the film is a showcase for Altman's directorial skill and flair. His penchant for overlapping dialogue, ensemble acting and self-reflexive use of a number of communication devices (including songs, telephones, televisions, radios and loudspeaker systems) are all perfected here. Several of the actors wrote their own country music songs and Keith Carradine won the Academy Award for Best Song for his performance of 'I'm Easy'.

*Buffalo Bill and the Indians, or Sitting Bull's History Lesson* (1976), based on Arthur Kopit's far more interesting play 'The Indians', is Altman's most tedious attempt to revise American history. However, his next film, the hypnotic *3 Women* (1977), found him back on the terrain he explored in *Images*. He has said that the idea for the film came to him in a dream, and the sensitive rendering of Millie (played by Shelley Duvall in a profoundly moving performance) and Pinkie (Sissy Spacek) rank among the most fascinating portrayals of female characters in contemporary cinema. Described by Altman as a film about 'personality theft', it explores questions of identification and identity assault, but works most effectively when it is simply observing Millie's attempt to interact with the social world that excludes her. *A Wedding* (1978) sees Altman moving outwards again, with another huge ensemble cast. Lacking the warmth and compassion of *3 Women*, the cruelty of *M\*A\*S\*H* resurfaces here, with an especially pointless and troubling undercurrent of misogyny and homophobia. Altman concluded the decade with the pretentious science fiction picture *Quintet* (1979), and the mildly amusing comedies *H.E.A.L.T.H.* (1979) and *A Perfect Couple* (1979).

The 1980s are generally recognised as a difficult decade for Altman. *Popeye* (1980), featuring Robin Williams in his first starring role, is a dreadful film version of the comic strip. On better form in *Come Back to the Five and Dime, Jimmy Dean, Jimmy Dean* (1982), he incisively directs a wonderful cast, including Sandy Dennis, Cher and Karen Black. With *Streamers* (1983), the story of four young recruits about to be sent to Vietnam, Altman raises provocative questions about masculinity, homosexuality and race relations. It is one of the darkest films of this period of his career. *Secret Honor* (1984), shot on a shoestring budget as a class project during his stint at the University of Michigan, is an eccentric but suggestive journey into the mind of Richard Nixon. The film consists of a powerfully delivered 85-minute monologue from Philip Baker Hall (who played the role on stage). *O.C. & Stiggs* (1985), one of the more underrated teen flicks of the 1980s, sat on the shelf for several years; a reference-laden, quirky tale of two teens' summer adventure, it is full of energy. *Fool for Love* (1985) is Altman's fourth film from the 1980s to be adapted from a stage play. Written by Sam Shepard, who also stars alongside an electric Kim Basinger, the film is full of inventive direction. Set in a desert motel, the visuals are fantastic, and the flashbacks deserve special mention. *Beyond Therapy* (1987), also based on a play, is a misdirected comedy filmed in Paris but set in New York. Altman's unexceptional interpretation of Rameau's 'Les boreades' appears in *Aria* (1987), a film in which ten different directors interpret their favourite operatic aria.

One of Altman's best films of the 1990s, the masterly *Vincent and Theo* (1990), is curiously unlike any of the director's other work. The story of Vincent Van Gogh (Tim Roth) and his relationship with his brother Theo (Paul Rhys), it probes the themes of artistic obsession, creativity and madness. Always an outsider in Hollywood, *The Player* (1992) is Altman's most explicit critique of the business in which he holds such an uneasy position. Sharply scripted by Michael Tolkin (who adapted his novel of the same name), much of the delight of this satirical, self-referential film comes from star-spotting the over fifty celebrities who appear as themselves, including Whoopi Goldberg, Cher and Anjelica Huston. From the complex, opening tracking shot, the directing is virtuoso.

Heralded as Altman's comeback, *Short Cuts* (1993) is arguably the most fully realised of his works. From start to finish the film bears the imprint of his unique directorial style, and is a veritable tour de force of acting, direction and editing. Perhaps even more effectively than its predecessor, *Nashville*, the film successfully weaves together several different interlocking tales, based on the short stories of Raymond Carver. The eagerly anticipated *Prêt-a-Porter* (1994), following on the heels of *Short Cuts*, was a major disappointment. Intended as a biting critique of the vagaries of the fashion industry, the film is a shambles, failing precisely where *Short Cuts* succeeds.

Altman has described *Kansas City* (1996) as a 'jazz memory'. Born and raised in Kansas City, Altman lovingly recreates the atmosphere in and around jazz clubs, where the various interactions among the actors are likened to jazz riffs. Although the film fails as a crime thriller, it does manage to elicit an unexpectedly powerful performance from Harry Belafonte. His next, *The Gingerbread Man* (1998), is the most interesting film adaptation of a John Grisham novel to date. Inventive directorial tricks and attention to detail lift this above a run-of-the-mill crime thriller. *Cookie's Fortune*

(1999), released a year later, stages a return to the ensemble acting so characteristic of an Altman film, albeit not as convincingly as his best work. A slow-paced, and at times tedious picture, the film offers a whimsical portrayal of small-town folk in the Deep South. Irony is strangely absent from the film and stereotypes of 'cute' Southern folk prevail.

Now in his mid-seventies, Altman continues to attract big name actors to his quirky and ambitious projects. *Dr T. and the Women* (2000), another film scripted by his close collaborator Anne Rapp, is set in the socialite world of Dallas, Texas, and focuses on relations between the sexes, a pet Altman theme. The gynaecologist's waiting room, filled to the brim with chattering female patients jostling to get an appointment, is a central paradigm for the film's exploration of the women (wife, lover, daughters, sister-in-law, patients) who surround the popular doctor, played by Richard Gere. The film includes all the Altman hallmarks of an ensemble cast and overlapping stories, but it plays more like a soft-focus romantic comedy than the biting satire on class and gender it is intended to be. There are some incredibly mawkish and awkward scenes between Gere and Farrah Fawcett (who plays the doctor's mad wife) that play like a television movie of the week. Despite some amusing moments, the film eventually unravels; one is left feeling uncertain about its attitude regarding male-female relations. For some critics, it is simple: the film is a misogynist rant, in which women are nothing more than reflections of pathetic male fears and fantasies – the sexually independent jock, the lesbian, the sexually frustrated spinster. It is worth noting that no matter which role they inhabit, all the women characters are played by identikit pert blonde actresses, including Fawcett, Tara Reid, Kate Hudson, Laura Dern, Shelley Long and Helen Hunt. For Altman's proponents, however, the film reveals the director's deep affection and love for the women who have always played such a central role in both in his personal life and his film-making career. While the charge of misogyny may be a tad harsh, there is something uncomfortable and irritating about the portrayal of the women in the gynecologist's waiting room as a hysterical, neurotic, needy throng, desperate to get in to see Dr T., the doctor who has a way with a speculum.

Altman is in better form, and on safer ground, with his latest movie, *Gosford Park* (2001), his most critically acclaimed and commercially successful film of recent years. A classic English country house murder mystery, which features a stellar British cast, including Maggie Smith, Helen Mirren, Kristin Scott Thomas, Michael Gambon and Jeremy Northam, *Gosford Park* is elegant and amusing, if a little thin on narrative and plot. Its 'upstairs, downstairs' storyline and critique of English class relations is also peppered with gentle jibes at Americans, who are represented by the characters of a Hollywood film director and a young male actor. During his stay in Britain, where *Gosford Park* was filmed, Altman outraged certain extreme right-wing groups in America by reportedly criticising American patriotism and George W. Bush. As Altman's defenders point out, the charges that he is a 'traitor' to his country are nothing short of outrageous: in addition to having devoted his entire career to making affectionate and artful films about American people and culture, Altman also boasts a prestigious military record, having served in Vietnam.

He is currently working on a comedy starring Joaquin Phoenix titled *Voltage*, based on the Robert Grossbach novel 'A Shortage of Engineers'.                    **TH**

# Jon AMIEL

At first sight Jon Amiel's oeuvre seems an unlikely and distinctly disparate collection. Moving from the gentle satire of *Tune in Tomorrow/Aunt Julia and the Scriptwriter* (1990), his debut Hollywood feature, to the spectacle and big action thrills of *Entrapment* (1999), in the first decade of his film-making career he has shifted between romance, comedy, action and period drama with unusual ease, demonstrating a versatility that can be better understood in the light of his diverse pedigree.

Born in London in 1948 and educated at Cambridge, Amiel started out in theatre, eventually becoming a director at the Royal Shakespeare Company, before moving to the BBC as a story editor. Whilst there he directed Dennis Potter's 'The Singing Detective' (1986), a phenomenal success which won an array of international awards. This background in television and theatre has no doubt contributed to Amiel's reputation as a collaborative director who enjoys close working relationships with both actors and writers. A spell in advertising in the late 1980s, including two mini-dramas for the British government's controversial AIDS-awareness campaign, and his directorial film debut, *Queen of Hearts* (1989), followed before Hollywood beckoned.

Although shifting between genres, Amiel's early work maintained a recurrent interest in the unusual and provocative, lending these films an element of risk or inclination towards the unexpected, which distinguishes them from many Hollywood productions. *Tune in Tomorrow*, based on a Mario Vargas Llosa novel, explored the social constraints of 1950s America, specifically centring on the relationship of a younger man and older woman, also weaving a surreal and satirical relationship between the lives of these characters and the fictional ones of the radio soap opera that develops within it. The period drama *Sommersby* (1993), with its broody post-Civil War setting and dénouement, had many of the trappings of a conventional romance, yet Amiel defied generic and institutional expectations in the film's ending, where the hero sacrifices himself, for capitalism as much as love. Widely seen as a remake of *The Return of Martin Guerre* (1982), the film has an air of myth about it that reflects Amiel's interest in the line between truth and fiction, as both characters and audience ponder who and what to believe.

Amiel next moved from love story to dark thriller to make *Copycat* (1995), a disturbing but original take on the serial killer movie. Holly Hunter and Sigourney Weaver were cast as the two investigative leads, complicating criticisms that the film took misogynist pleasure in the pursuit of its post-modern murderer, a killer who is replicating the crimes of the twentieth century's 'greatest' serial killers. This premise allowed Amiel to open up a reflective look at the genre, making the process of watching familiar territory a critical and uncomfortable process. The sequence where Hunter and Weaver examine scene-of-crime photos of the murdered girls is something of a generic convention, but Amiel's use of ponderous panning and classical choral music here leave the audience feeling distinctly troubled by it.

A return to comedy followed with *The Man Who Knew Too Little* (1997), where a case of mistaken identity propels Bill Murray into an assassination plot. However, Amiel's highest-profile work to date came next with his big-budget extravaganza about a pair of ingenious thieves, *Entrapment* (1999). He proved here that he could also turn his hand to frivolous but spectacular action, and the scene where Catherine Zeta Jones bends and weaves her way through a web of laser lights to reach her prize is one of the most compelling and dazzling moments the genre has produced for some years. Amiel's career seems likely to continue to surprise and, with a recent producer credit on *Simply Irresistible* (1999), to develop along new paths. Indeed his next directing credit will add yet another genre to his oeuvre. *The Core*, due for release in 2002, will be his first foray into sci-fi, as NASA send a team of scientists and 'terranauts' to the earth's core to adjust its temperature and save the planet following revelations that the Earth is about to stop spinning. **DJ**

# Allison **ANDERS**

Border Radio (1987)
Gas, Food, Lodging (1992)
Mi Vida Loca (1993)
Grace of My Heart (1996)
Sugar Town (1999)

The near-tragic, routinely violent and picaresque early life of Allison Anders, born in Kentucky, USA, in 1954, forestalled her career as a film-maker until her mid-thirties. A correspondence with Wim Wenders led to a job for the UCLA film school graduate as a production assistant on the German director's 1984 film *Paris, Texas*. Anders then co-wrote and co-directed the road movie *Border Radio* (1987) with former classmates Kurt Voss and cinematographer Dean Lent.

A black-and-white homage to LA rock and punk, co-starring non-actors Chris D (of the Flesh Eaters), Dave Alvin (of the rockabilly group The Blasters) and John Doe (of X), *Border Radio* has a suitably bedraggled vibe; bleak and semi-improvised, it had limited commercial appeal and remains something of a cult item.

Anders worked with Lent again on her 1992 solo directorial debut, the well-received *Gas, Food, Lodging* (1992). –The heartfelt drama of two young sisters living in the desert with their divorced mother was both a critical and commercial success, giving Anders enough of the industry clout necessary to finance another non-commercial and unflinching character study, *Mi Vida Loca* (1993), the story of the violent and hopeless existence of Chicano gang girls in east Los Angeles. The relationship between the biological sisters Trudi and Shade in *Gas, Food, Lodging* sees its extension in the friendship of 'blood' sisters Mousie and Sad Girl, who are turned against one another by the sexual interference of a man.

Anders was subsequently invited by fellow independent film-makers Quentin Tarantino and Robert Rodriquez (who had recently had respective successes with the crime comedies *Pulp Fiction* (1994) and *El Mariachi* (1992)) to contribute to the omnibus film *Four Rooms* (1995). Anders' vignette, 'The Missing Ingredient', paired the writer-director with pop icon Madonna in a darkly comic tale of contemporary urban witches attempting to resurrect their goddess. Although reviews of the film were uniformly scathing and receipts slim, Anders was propelled towards her most expensive and commercial film to date, *Grace of My Heart* (1996), a tribute to 1960s-era pop composers and thinly-veiled biopic of singer/songwriter Carole King, executive produced by Martin Scorsese. It harks back to *Border Radio* in its bid to connect music to a specific place, time and set of circumstances.

Having acted as an executive producer on Lisa Addario's *Lover Girl* (1997), Anders re-teamed with Kurt Voss for *Sugar Town* (1999), an updated take on the LA rock scene. A tale of comers, players and industry hopefuls, she employed such 1970s and 1980s music icons as Michael des Barres, John Taylor (of Duran Duran) and Martin Kemp (of Spandau Ballet). Anders and Voss have since co-written *Things Behind the Sun*, a deeply-felt drama shot on video and inspired by the director's past. The story focuses on a rock journalist forced to come to terms with his own dark past when interviewing an up-and-coming Florida rocker (Kim Dickens) who was raped as a young girl. Featuring a characteristically eclectic cast (whose number includes Rosanna Arquette, Don Cheadle and Eric Stoltz) and a soundtrack that includes musicians such as Nick Drake, Sonic Youth and Manfred Mann, the film received very positive reactions from audiences at the Sundance Film Festival. Rather than opt for a limited theatrical distribution, Anders chose instead to have a cable viewing, thus ensuring a much greater initial audience.

Celebrated more for her strong female characters than the films they inhabit, Allison Anders is nonetheless an intensely personal film-maker whose lesser work remains heads above most Hollywood product. **RHS**

# Jay Todd ANDERSON

Jay Todd Anderson worked for years as a storyboard artist on an array of films, including, most significantly, those of the Coen brothers, such as *The Big Lebowski* (1998) and *Fargo* (1995). Anderson's directorial debut, *The Naked Man* (1998), was written with the assistance of mentor Ethan Coen. It is clear that his directorial style has been affected by theirs: the film features very similar narrative devices and tropes, in particular the use of wide-angle lenses to alienate the audience from the subjects of the film. The effect both confuses the audience and leads them to new perspectives of the story. The film is a bizarre comedy surrounding a chiropractor turned wrestler, filled with surreal sequences that beg the question 'what is dream and what is reality?' The action sequences are split neatly between those on screen and those that we are left viewing only the aftermath. Despite careful mimicking of the Coen brothers, it is an average film, a fact that only serves to highlight their clear superiority in directing.

More recently, Anderson has returned to the storyboard to collaborate with the Coen Brother's on *O Brother, Where Art Thou?* (2000) and *The Man Who Wasn't There* (2001). **SS**

*The Naked Man* (1998)

# Paul ANDERSON

Newcastle-born Paul Anderson graduated from Warwick University with a degree in film studies and an MBA. Early work as writer and director includes *The Spiral Cage*, a documentary about cartoonist Al Davidson, and the short drama *Speed*; he was also principal writer on the television crime series 'El CID'.

His feature-length directorial debut, which he also wrote, was *Shopping* (1994), an attractive-looking (if very dark) tale of thrill-seeking car thieves, joy riders and ram-raiders set in what is presumably intended to be a near-future London, although some of the cultural references suggest that it is an alternative version of the present. This would-be *Clockwork Orange* for the 1990s is ultimately little more than a moody melodrama of sullen teenage rebellion and marginal criminal existence in a rubble-strewn post-

*Shopping* (1994)
*Mortal Kombat* (1995)
*Event Horizon* (1997)
*Soldier* (1998)
*Resident Evil* (2002)

industrial wasteland, interspersed with some well-staged car chases and scenes of violent destruction. The US version – some 18 minutes shorter – removed much of its pretentiousness along with some of the complexity of the characters and relationships.

Of the several movies adapted from computer games, *Mortal Kombat* (1995) best captures the kineticism and loopy disregard of conventional plot typical of the medium. A supernatural fantasy featuring a set-up appropriated from *Enter the Dragon* (1973), the film employs endless fight sequences, charmless protagonists, humour so broad as to not be funny, tacked-on platitudes about teamwork and proper motives, and acting so listless and rudimentary that Cary-Hiroyuki Tagawa's performance – more an embodiment of Oriental Evil than a character – seems well-rounded. The fights are unimaginatively choreographed but increasingly well-served by the camera, and the attractive production design and cinematography help Anderson's stylish fragments to cohere.

*Event Horizon* (1997) is a magnificently silly blend of science fiction and horror in which it is easy to spot elements appropriated from twenty or thirty other movies by directors as varied as Clive Barker, John Carpenter, Stanley Kubrick, Nicolas Roeg, Joel Schumacher, Andrei Tarkovsky, Fred M. Wilcox, and Robert Wise. This restless bricolage is anchored by solid performances and, once again, impressive production design and cinematography.

Anderson's next movie, *Soldier* (1998), is something of a backward step. Rumoured before its release to be set within the *Blade Runner* universe (but not a direct sequel), the two movies are connected by a single passing reference to Tannhauser Gate, but screenwriter David Webb Peoples reworks the central character and situation of his *Blade Runner* and *Unforgiven* scripts one more time. Kurt Russell, uttering various grunts and growls and less than eighty words, plays a soldier trained from birth who is made redundant by a new, genetically engineered breed of warrior. Left for dead on a garbage planet, he awkwardly integrates into an improbable community of shipwrecked colonists, kills the new warriors, and saves his old comrades. Dubious CGI effects, inept montage sequences, and an excessive use of slowmotion to convey the significance of things, all detract from some attractive visuals. Russell's eloquent silence includes a couple of minor twitches which communicate an appropriate degree of despair.

Anderson's most recent film, *Resident Evil* (2002), is another computer game adaptation, a horror film starring Milla Jovovich. Initial reactions have been mixed. **MB**

# Paul Thomas ANDERSON

Born in California in 1970, Paul Thomas Anderson emerged as one of the most exciting young directors in Hollywood, with two epics as vast and sprawling as the San Fernando Valley in which they are set – *Boogie Nights* (1997) and *Magnolia* (1999). His films already show the hallmarks of a distinctive vision and are marked by a surprising maturity, delving deep into themes of family, loneliness and the ghosts of the past.

His debut feature, *Hard Eight* (1996), is a steady drama set in and around the casinos of Reno, in which a young and naïve John (played by John C. Reilly) is taken under the wing of veteran gambler Sydney (Phillip Baker Hall). Anderson focuses not on the glitz of the casinos, but rather the murkier depths of character. Only towards the end of the film do we learn of the dark secret that motivates Sydney's kindliness. Indeed, the theme of the repression and concealment of one's past lies at the heart of this cool and controlled film, and is neatly conveyed through the final shot of Sydney carefully hiding a blood-stained cuff under the sleeve of his coat.

Conversely, his breakthrough, *Boogie Nights*, is a big, bold and giddy film: a celebrated portrait of a 'family' of pornographers in the 1970s and 1980s, which is refreshingly free of moralising and won Anderson an Academy Award nomination for his screenplay. Inspired by the life of John C. Holmes – many of the films-within-the-film are exact replicas of Holmes movies – *Boogie Nights* is also structured like a backstage musical, charting the rise and fall in the adult entertainment industry of well-endowed newcomer Dirk Diggler. Its detractors have argued that it presents an overly utopian view of the 1970s, but the strength of the film is the way it reveals a profound sadness underlying the hedonism, evident in the way the funky, upbeat disco songs are underpinned by Michael Penn's melancholic, broken-down merry-go-round score.

Some critics have noted imitations of the works of Martin Scorsese, Robert Altman and Jonathan Demme, but Anderson's *mise-en-scène* is never simply faddish or plagiaristic. For example, he often borrows from Scorsese's use of lengthy steadicam shots in *GoodFellas* (1990), yet Anderson seems to have more purpose for them. In particular, his camera is wonderfully promiscuous, drifting between different characters and storylines: not only conveying the promiscuity of the times and pastiching the use of long-takes in porn films, but also commenting on the connections between people. This is most notable during the bravura steadicam shots at the beginning and end of the film, which take in virtually all of the major characters to document the changes in their lives.

Similar themes of interconnectedness also permeate the mystical *Magnolia*, a three hour cine-poem which reunited much of the cast of *Boogie Nights* and features Tom Cruise in an award-winning turn as an foul-mouthed self-help guru who instructs men to 'seduce and destroy'. In particular, the film employs its interweaving multi-narrative format to comment on the connections people make (and break) with one another, especially those between several sets of parents and their alienated children. Moreover, Anderson uses the ensemble structure to fashion a tale about chance and fate, opening with three unrelated tales of extreme coincidence which seem to point towards something beyond mere happenstance. As several characters pronounce that although we may be through with the past, the past is not through with us, we are given the sense of a greater order of the universe – strikingly represented in a concluding storm of biblical proportions, foreshadowed by several oblique references to Exodus 8:2.

Anderson's most recent feature, *Punch-Drunk Love* (2002), features Adam Sandler as the bullied brother of horrible sisters, who manages to find romance with a mysterious girl played by Emily Watson. Not as lauded as *Magnolia*, on the whole it was well-received in Cannes; while some writers have criticised Sandler's over-the-top acting persona, others have found it a worthy, if not ground-breaking, addition to the director's body of work. **AS**

# Steve ANDERSON

Steve Anderson began his career in television, working as co-producer on 'To The Moon Alice', a 1990s rags-to-riches show about a homeless immigrant family that finds shelter on a movie set, duly becoming Hollywood stars in their own right. That obscure and terribly old-fashioned one-off bodes little for a career, and the two feature projects the director has completed, some five years apart, suggest Anderson has never really made it out of the starting blocks.

*South Central* (1992)
*Dead Men Can't Dance* (1997)

His debut feature, 1992's *South Central*, which he also wrote and co-produced, is part of a whole string of features that attempted to cash in on the success of John Singleton's *Boyz N the Hood* (1991). *South Central*, with its tale of an ex-con struggling to stay straight in a tough ghetto world, is predictable in its plotting, and hangs too much on the aspect of *Boyz N the Hood* that Singleton only just managed to pull off: grand, moral speeches about the hard-knock life. You need a definite writing ability to generate such tension and drama, something Anderson just does not have, and the film climaxes with the unfortunate platitude, 'Prison sure turned you stoopid', which is the kind of line no actor should ever have to say. Made on a low budget, with some obviously worthy intentions, *South Central* now looks like just a vague hope that someone in the video store may pick it up by mistake when they should be watching the far superior *Boyz*.

The video store is the only place you could hope to find Anderson's second film, *Dead Men Can't Dance* (1997). Starring Michael Biehn, the actor who found charisma only when under Industrial Light and Magic's incredible morphing effects in *Terminator 2: Judgement Day*, it is hi-octane nonsense about a crack weapons team cut off from safety in North Korea. Where the geographic location of the film is tastelessly redolent of old Cold War anxieties, the film is strictly functional video fare. As the last of Anderson's projects to come to the screen, it is a step down from *South Central* which, although unsuccessful, at least had virtue in its conception where *Dead Men Can't Dance* has, simply, nothing. **CSo**

# Wes ANDERSON

Born in Texas in 1969, Wes Anderson co-wrote the three films he has directed to date with Owen Wilson, whom he met whilst studying philosophy at the University of Austin.

*Bottle Rocket* (1996)
*Rushmore* (1998)

Their first collaboration, *Bottle Rocket* (1996), originated from a $100, 13-minute short that came to the attention of the Svengali-like producer James L. Brooks. However, after spending $5 million on re-shooting as a feature, the film was never released nationally; Columbia TriStar finding the film's asinine, pithy comedy too frivolous to risk backing a nationwide release. Yet the film did create a buzz of approval amongst the Hollywood community, so much so that Anderson's next project, *Rushmore* (1998), had no trouble in finding a backer, ultimately proving to be a hit with both industry and critics alike.

    *Rushmore* is an intelligent, crisp reworking of the high-school romantic comedy. Set in a prestigious private school, Rushmore Academy, Jason Schwartzman plays Max Fischer, the bespectacled, braced, blazered, and bereted high-school geek. However, Max, like the film itself, defies expectations. Beating beneath the stereotypical nerdish, loner's exterior is the heart and drive of an obsessive, self-absorbed sociopath. Max is obsessed with all things extracurricular at Rushmore, from the debating team to the wrestling squad, yet his over-devotion to these trivial pursuits ultimately renders him an under-achiever in the classroom. Because of his failing grades Max is threatened with expulsion and, to add to his troubles, he falls hopelessly in love with an older, unattainable woman, teacher Rosemary Cross (Olivia Williams). In danger of losing all the objects of his desire, Max sets out on a deterministic course of self-destruction as he lies, cheats and manipulates friends, contemporaries, and authority figures in order to achieve his ends.

    Shot through with equal doses of melancholia and madness, *Rushmore* drops the usual trend of sophomoric humour that normally proliferates in the misfit-finding-love teen comedy. Instead the film is a quirky examination of fixation, delusion and dejection that defies categorisation. As Anderson himself says, 'because there is no genre, there is nothing to fall back on'. Particular high points of the film are Bill Murray's portrayal of the washed-out, tycoon alcoholic Herman Blume, Max's sometime nemesis, confidant, and love rival, and the plethora of surreal, inventive details Anderson drops into the plot (such as the dramatised stage version of *Serpico* (1973) that Max stages for the school).

    Whimsical comedy, forgiveness and melancholic misfits struggling for acceptance continue to be the key theme in Anderson's and Wilson's next collaboration, *The Royal Tenenbaums* (2001). The narrative focuses on the attempts at reconciliation and acceptance between various members of the eponymous Tenenbaum family after 'two decades of failure, betrayal and disaster'. The family comprises of the long-separated Royal Tenenbaum, an untrustworthy and unkempt lawyer played with shifty aplomb by Gene Hackman, his flamboyant wife Etheline (Anjelica Huston) and their three oddball prodigies, Margot, a gifted yet reclusive playwright, Richie, a former tennis ace, and Chas, a paranoid business entrepreneur who breeds Dalmatian mice. Essentially a family melodrama that deals with Sirkian concerns such as sibling rivalry, suicide, drug addiction, incest and lies, the film presents the American family as a concept riddled with tragedy, capricious deceit and misunderstanding, although Anderson's family, as a collective comprising of alienated genius eccentrics, are more Munsters than Magnificent Amberson's. As with *Rushmore*, plot and narrative are never subordinated to the comedy, and without ever allowing us to feel truly sympathetic towards any character the film keeps the audience guessing and never spirals into predictability. This unpredictability and uniqueness of script ultimately resulted in the film being nominated for an Academy Award for Best Screenplay.

    With a distinctive visual style that steers clear of the gross plagiarism of many post-Tarantino thirtysomething directors, Anderson sets himself apart from most of his contemporaries. His work is as refreshing and visually inspiring as any Coen brothers' film, and restores faith in the idea that Hollywood can still produce an idiosyncratic black comedy once in a while. **PH**

# David ANSPAUGH

David Anspaugh's films share the theme of the second chance: the opportunity to reflect on past mistakes and move on to fulfilling a dream that once seemed unattainable.

    Born in Decatur, Indiana in 1946, his feature debut came with *Hoosiers* (1986), the story of former university basketball coach Norman Dale (Gene Hackman), who seeks to regain a measure of self-respect by coaching a small-town high-school team in

Indiana. Although facing opposition from obstinate townspeople, he eventually takes the team to the state championship. Despite its vast popular appeal, *Hoosiers* is an insipidly sentimental film, with strictly pedestrian direction and scripting (by Angelo Pizzo). The Jerry Goldsmith score is similarly cloying and intrusive – meant, far too obviously, to inspire and rouse the audience. Anspaugh uses an extremely heavy hand and never moves beyond the most obvious, clichéd techniques, relying on musical montages and slow motion to move the story. Supporting characters are seemingly put in place merely to act as barriers to the coach's goal.

*Fresh Horses* (1988), based on the play by Larry Ketron, is the story of a wealthy Ohio college student who breaks off his engagement to his 'proper' fiancée (Chiara Peacock) when he falls for a poor stranger (Molly Ringwald), who he meets in a seedy house party in Kentucky. As her sordid past and present are gradually revealed to him, he must decide if he is willing to accept her as she is. Although the film is able to break free of its theatrical roots, Anspaugh's direction is still at a strictly pedestrian level. The scripting seems to make little sense at many points in the film, and the performances are uniformly dull, although McCarthy plays his part earnestly. With two stars, McCarthy and Ringwald, at the heights of their 1980s fame for teen-appeal movies, *Fresh Horses* is somewhat unconventional. However, any individuality it has comes more from incomprehensibility than originality.

*Rudy* (1993) follows closely in the saccharine footsteps of *Hoosiers*. It is the story of Rudy Ruettiger (Sean Astin), a young Illinois man in the early 1970s, who is a life-long Notre Dame football fan, and who dreams of playing for the team. He fails to get the grades necessary to attend the university, but when his close friend (predictably) dies in a work accident, he is inspired to chase the dream as far as it can go. He attends a junior college, makes the grades, makes the team, and – of course – sees himself play for the team in the last minutes of the last game of his last season. *Rudy* comes from another Angelo Pizzo script and Jerry Goldsmith once again composes the score. Although veteran actors Ned Beatty and Charles S. Dutton are forceful in their supporting roles, Astin's Rudy is dull. It is difficult to sympathise with someone who is such a loser, and the sentimentalism reaches absurd, almost parodic, heights by the film's conclusion.

Anspaugh's best film to date is *Moonlight and Valentino* (1995), about a group of women who rally behind repressed young widow Rebecca Lott (Elizabeth Perkins), who is learning to deal with the recent accidental death of her husband. Dispatching with the hackneyed, formulaic fables of his past, Anspaugh's camera becomes closely intimate with Rebecca, her best friend Sylvie (Whoopi Goldberg), younger sister Lucy (Gwyneth Paltrow), and ex-stepmother Alberta (Kathleen Turner). Written by Ellen Simon, and based on her play, the film is heavy with dialogue but manages to be genuine and moving through the strength of its performances. The occasional touches of melodrama are woven into the film effectively so as to never be overbearing.

Anspaugh's largely unremarkable body of work indicates that he is more comfortable with the smaller scale of television, where he got his start directing and producing the television series 'Hill Street Blues', for which he received two Emmy Awards. He has also directed episodes of 'St. Elsewhere' and 'Miami Vice' as well as the television movies *Deadly Care* (1987), *In the Company of Darkness* (1993) and *Swing Vote* (1999). His most recent film is the Mariah Carey vehicle, *Wisegirls* (2002), the story of three waitresses working in a restaurant run by the Mafia. **DH**

# Gregg ARAKI

Once considered to be the leading agitator of 'New Queer Cinema', Gregg Araki can just as profitably be seen in the wider context of the early 1990s 'rise of the indies'. Certainly he focuses on a generation's pursuit of the old goals – love, lust, a life – under the burden of 1990s self-consciousness. His characters talk like they know they are in a film, and his mode of cine-literate pastiche mimics Hollywood genres with Godardian playfulness. It could be argued, too, that their apparent superficiality is a consequence of Araki's grasp of cinema as surface, a relocation of encoded depth to surface juxtaposition, and postmodern pushing of genre and soundbite culture aesthetics to a logical extreme. But his films often feel forced in their plot lurches and doe-eyed doldrums; for all their energy and mildly satirical empathy for youth, they tend to leave critical and emotional engagement behind.

Born in 1959 in California, Araki went on to graduate in Cinema from the University of Southern California School of Cinema-Television, and taught a course, Independent-Guerilla-Underground-American New Wave-Neo-realist Cinema, at UC Santa Barbara. His first few films capitalised nicely on their 'guerilla' aesthetics. The aptly titled *Three Bewildered People in the Night* (1987) and *Long Weekend* (*O'Despair*) (1989) capture their characters' angst and anomie in their rough black-and-white and claustrophobic settings.

Araki describes the latter as his response to the smug 'yuppie' schtick of *The Big Chill* (1983), and certainly both – as much in form as content – reveal a determination to get inside Hollywood conventions and mess with their workings. Nonetheless, the shallow ennui of both films dominates so much that they verge on being unwatchable, a problem Araki emphatically solved with *The Living End* (1992). He dubbed it 'An Irresponsible Movie By Gregg Araki', which was prescient, given the sniffy response this irreverent tale of two HIV-positive gay lovers on the road received from many gay critics. Still, there is an irresistibly confrontational energy to its hot-wired mix of combustible screwball comedy and self-consciously Godardian flourishes. If there was any doubt that Araki's films are about cinema as much as anything else, it is evident in his casting of a key character (Jon) as a jaded movie critic, and another (Luke) as a cross between Jean Paul Belmondo and Marlon Brando. That Luke shoots a couple of gay bashers wearing *Drugstore Cowboy* and *sex, lies and videotape* T-shirts both situates the film in the context of the 'rise of the indies' and highlights his antagonistic relationship to it.

Nonetheless, Araki's next film, the first instalment in his 'teen apocalypse trilogy', betrays a kinship with Richard Linklater's debut feature, *Slacker* (1991). Araki dubbed *Totally F\*\*\*ed Up* (1993) 'A Movie In Fifteen Random Celluloid Fragments', drawing attention to similarities with the '15 Precise Facts' of Godard's *Masculin Féminin* (1966). Yet its combination of straight-to-camera confessions and ensemble traipsing through teenage group dynamics views like Linklater's film re-played in a 'queer soap opera' style. Like *Slacker*, it is a deliberately unformed film about a generation feeling its way towards formation, with a sobering edge granted by its starting point: a newspaper clipping detailing rising rates of suicide among teenage gays. If this suggests a more sensitive approach than *The Living End*, Araki's script cannot rise to the challenge, resulting in an alterna-rock spin on *The Breakfast Club* (1984) that is darker – but not much deeper – than what it wants to subvert.

Still, it earned Araki his first proper budget, $1 million, which he used to fine effect in the dazzling dayglo pop expressionism of *The Doom Generation* (1995). Set in the clubs, storefronts, motels and parking areas of a dystopian America, Araki's fifth feature is a road movie with its foot firmly on the pedal, played out in a series of interiors. Like most road movies, it is about America's frontiers, with appropriately-named slacker lovebirds Jordan White and Amy Blue picking up the lascivious Xavier Red and hitting the road in search of safe pockets of sexual utopia, armed only with their goofball repartee. Araki dubbed it 'A Heterosexual Movie', although it purposefully pushes homoerotic coding in heterosexual movies to breaking point with its spunk-munching and threeways. At once erotic and exhilarating, it is also bold enough to end on a truly chastening note, as both Araki's American dreamers and the very surface of his film are lacerated by a quite horrifying vision of American conservatism.

For all its strengths, however, it is tough to swallow Araki's apparent conviction that naïve romanticism is any kind of answer to the entropy he depicts. Dubbed 'The Gregg Araki Movie', as if it were his ultimate statement, *Nowhere* (1997) grafts the rapacious omnisexuality and eye-candy aesthetic of its predecessor onto a film that is about twice as gauche. His sales pitch for this one was 'Beverly Hills 90210 on a bad trip'. That fits his high-school teenagers' subjection to rape, suicide, alien abduction and pop-art death-by-soup-can perfectly, with entropy and waste vividly displayed in scenes of gorging and vomiting. It is fair to say, however, that Araki's aesthetic is equally bulimic, as *Nowhere* greedily gorges on John Waters-style aesthetics and regurgitates them messily. That may make it the ultimate youth movie, or the ultimate Araki movie, but when 'Dear Diary, what a day' is as probing as the dialogue gets, you've got problems. That said, it is preferable to the soap suds and sloppy screwball of *Splendor* (1999), a spin on Noel Coward's *Design for Living* (1933), via Lubitsch, with shreds of *His Girl Friday* (1939), *The Philadelphia Story* (1940) and *The Graduate* (1967) to garnish. Kathleen Robertson is fine as Veronica, a twentysomething self-consciously jaded by dating, who finds herself dating two men at once, but all the film's goofball fun is crammed into the early scenes, where the bickering threesome shack up together. As soon as Araki introduces elements of responsibility via Veronica's pregnancy, *Splendor* falls through the holes in his characteristically lightweight script. Plots have never been Araki's poison, but here he seems to have lost his bite too, with the film's borderline, insipid faux-charms summed up by its couldn't-care-less directorial credit. Seen in the context of the rest of his career, 'A Gregg Araki movie' seems to translate as something almost as wilfully entropic as the America he has been exploring.

It's perhaps not surprising that Araki was last spotted directing a film for MTV, namely *This Is How the World Ends* (2000), and indicative of how retrogressive his career has been of late; while *Splendor* was not distributed in the UK, he was having trouble getting MTV to show his latest film. **KH**

# Denys ARCAND

After the stunning success of *The Decline of the American Empire* (1986) (nine Genies, Canada's highest film award, Film Critic's Prize at Cannes and an Academy Award nomination), followed in 1989 by the no less successful *Jésus of Montréal* (twelve Genies, the Jury Prize at Cannes and another Academy Award nomination), Denys Arcand emerged as one of the few 'star' directors in Canada, on a par with Atom Egoyan and David Cronenberg. Before his breakthrough, however, Arcand was labelled as an unbankable trouble-maker, the kind of film-maker who made politically explosive documentaries and equally controversial, socially conscious and overly critical fictions.

Born in 1941 and raised in a small riverside village not far from Montreal, Arcand is what they call 'Québecois pur lin de souche' – dyed-in-the-wool, old stock Québecer. He attended Jesuit school in Montreal, studied history at the francophone Université de Montréal, where he spent some time in theatre groups and co-directed his first documentary in 1962 about the life of a first-year student, *Seul ou avec d'autres*. Later he went to join the National Film Board of Canada and made his first three short documentaries – a sort of trilogy focused on the discovery of the North American continent and its colonisation. But it is *Cotton Mill/On est au coton* (1970), a biting socio-political critique of the textile industry in Montreal, that won him the reputation of the enfant terrible of Québec cinema. The NFB management declared the film biased and banned it for six years. *Cotton Mill*, along with his two subsequent feature documentaries – *Québec: Duplessis and After.../Québec: Duplessis et après...* (1972) and *Comfort and Indifference/Le confort et l'indifference* (1981), and his first three fiction films form a coherent period in Arcand's artistic evolution as an auteur (he has scripted all but three of his films, edited four and shot one of them), a merciless critic of the political establishment, and a keen observer of a society in transition.

Arcand's debut feature fiction, *Dirty Money* (1971), is shot in the bleak industrial Montreal East and the hostile Québec countryside. Strongly influenced by nineteenth-century Naturalism, it is a dark fatalist tale about an impoverished working-class couple who rob and kill an uncle for his life-savings. Arcand subverts the crime genre with long takes and shots, and slow-paced editing, thus diverting the attention from the action towards the socio-psychological depths of the story.

If *Dirty Money* takes its aesthetic cues from *Cotton Mill*, then *Réjeanne Padovani* (1973) continues the examination of political corruption in Montreal, initiated with *Québec: Duplessis and After....* Inspired by a real event (the much-opposed construction of a Montreal highway), it tells the story of construction boss Vincent Padovani's assassination of his estranged wife during the celebration over Padovani's new highway contract which she has been fighting, along with her Jewish boyfriend and a group of environmentalists. Contained within the walls of Padovani's suburban Montreal mansion, the *mise-en-scène* makes good use of the social symbolism implicated in the design of the celebration: Padovani's powerful supporters are entertained in the living room, while the employees are confined to the basement. The influence of Luis Buñuel's claustrophobic settings and dark ironies – that inform Arcand's entire body of work – is strongly felt throughout the film.

*Gina* (1975) is structured as a parody of the western genre and features the reconstruction of events from the shooting of the ill-fated *Cotton Mill*. Arcand takes the action to a small town lost somewhere in the usually romanticised Québec countryside where Gina is a stripper in a dingy hotel. She befriends the documentary film crew, staying at the same hotel, but soon after is gang-raped by a group of unemployed men. A ridiculous succession of parallel events is set off with each sub-plot following the logic of its genre (the western or the documentary) and providing the other with a satirical comment. Gina's agent arrives at the scene to seek bloody revenge while the film is stopped by the NFB under pressure from the textile company; Gina leaves for Mexico while the film director goes off to shoot a commercial. Arcand's brilliant blending of fiction and documentary accounts for the rich social, moral and political subtext of the film, and for its sharp critique of Québec society.

Before *The Decline of the American Empire*, Arcand made three episodes for the CBC mini-series 'Empire Inc.' (1983) and scripted and directed his first big-budget film, *Murder in the Family/Le crime d'Ovide Plouffe* (1984), an accurate but impersonal and dispassionate adaptation of Roger Lemelin's novel of the same title.

*The Decline of the American Empire* focuses on eight francophone intellectuals, four men and four women, who have gathered to spend the weekend together. While the women relax at a beauty parlour the men cook a gourmet dinner. The editing juxtaposes rather graphic – even titillating – conversations about sex on both sides of the gender divide. The evening, however, does not evolve into a carnal orgy as one might have expected. Once around the table the characters engage in a futile – albeit heated – mouthing of sophisticated insights into contemporary culture, the human condition, or the state of the world. Here, like in *Gina*, the misplaced or alienated sexuality stands for artistic compromise and creative impotence, and vice versa. The only drive that gets immediate satisfaction in this almost convivial picture is the urge for betrayal – yet another of Arcand's favourite ethical leitmotifs. He suggests that these cynical, over-educated, over-sexed, middle-class baby-boomers cannot come to terms with the world they live in for they have lost somewhere along the way a basic human skill – genuine affection and compassion.

Many critics rightfully link the social scepticism and intellectual nihilism of *The Decline of the American Empire* with Arcand's pessimistic documentary *Comfort and Indifference*, based on Machiavelli's 'The Prince' and reflecting on Québec's anxieties in the wake of the failed 1980 independence referendum.

In his subsequent film, *Jésus of Montréal*, deservingly qualified as his masterpiece, Arcand brilliantly brings together stylistic, thematic and philosophical tendencies discernible in his previous works. While remaining concerned with the state of things in his native province, he expands his frame of reference to incorporate ideas from a higher metaphysical plane, such as the existence of an ultimate moral order and the possibility for redemptive love. Like *Gina*, the film blurs reality and fiction and makes plausible the alternations between the two planes of its meta-narrative (play-within-a-film). The principal fabula event – staging an open-air version of the 'Passion Play' on Mount Royal by a Montreal theatre group – allows Arcand to use well-known biblical archetypes as a vehicle for his assiduously sarcastic observations on the present-day social and spiritual malaise, articulated so well in *The Decline of the American Empire*. The examination of the hedonistic-voyeurist culture acquires baroque dimensions here: television programmes, commercials and shooting of porno films intertwine with scenes (both dramatic and/or hilarious) from the staging of the play and from the life of lay and clerical personages involved. Like corrupt politics and big business in *Réjeanne Padovani*, contemporary religion and entertainment industry merge in Jésus of Montréal. Their unholy alliance to provide the insatiable consumerist culture with mythical rituals and cult figures is mirrored by the ill-fated love affair between a Catholic priest and an actress.

While *The Decline of the American Empire* could be compared to a baroque Concerto Grosso where the males and the females form two orchestral groups and each participant has the right to a solo within the contrapuntal structure, *Jésus of Montréal* resembles a classical Concerto, where the solo of the actor portraying Christ and the orchestration of the numerous plot lines are of equal importance for the development of the basic leitmotifs of betrayal and compassion. Thus the transformation of this failure of an actor into a Christ-like figure unravels Arcand's deepest transcendental concerns with the causality of human actions in life as well as in art.

Arcand's first English-language film, *Love and Human Remains* (1993), grafts his favourite themes into the English-Canadian social environment. This time, unemployment forces the personages out of the 'unbearable lightness' of their middle-class being; sexual frustrations leave the intellectual domain and turn into violent criminal drives; the narrative abandons its playful ambiguity and the multifaceted huis clos ethical discourse is reduced to a straightforward sermonising. Whether because this is the first film scripted not by the director himself but by the famous Anglo-Canadian gay writer Brad Fraser (based on his cult theatre piece 'Unidentified Human Remains and the True Nature of Love'), because he is out of his element shooting in English, or because the group of characters under scrutiny is a generation younger, *Love and Human Remains* lags far behind *The Decline of the American Empire*, its artistic and thematic prototype.

Arcand's two other films from the 1990s could be compared to variations, or rather light potpourri, on themes from his earlier works. *Seen from Afar* – his instalment in the 1991 avant-garde six-part travelogue *Montreal Sextet* (helmed by five other star directors: Léa Pool, Michel Brault, Atom Egoyan, Jacques Leduc and Patricia Rozema) is scripted by Paule Baillargeon and represents a parody of a diplomatic cocktail party. It contains original character sketches and hilariously funny observations on the rich and the powerful, trademarked by Arcand's familiar mixture of styles, but without the sarcastic edge of his vintage social satire. The same holds true for *Poverty and Other Delights* (1996). A scriptwriting debut for Claire Richard, it is an anecdote-laced journey into Montreal's lower depths, where the two main characters are seen as happy-go-lucky fellows who have consciously chosen the freedom of panhandling over the constraints of the regimented life (captured perfectly) on the other side of the economic divide.

*Stardom* (2002), Arcand's latest film, is a big-budget star-studded production shot in English. Scripted by the director, it is a story of a beautiful young girl (Jessica Paré, Arcand's discovery) who is plucked from the obscurity of Québec hinterlands and thrust into the spotlight of the glamorous world of supermodels – the perfect milieu for Arcand to globalise his dexterity for grasping the social, political and cultural idiosyncrasies of our times.

The film opened at the Toronto IFF in 2000 amidst mixed reviews and even more mixed audience reactions. Arcand's success has always been precariously contingent on the masterful balance of original artistic style with palpable ideological theses. To use the musical analogy again, the principal character's imposing leading theme pushes that balance in favour of the didactic thesis, at the expense of the somewhat erratic orchestration of satirised, one-dimensional characters. The rise of Tina Menzhal from a provincial athletic beauty to a supermodel is used to deconstruct the trajectory of the popular rags-to-riches Hollywood fairytales. The appearance of the famous Québec director Robert Lepage in the role of the documentary film-maker whose cinema-vérité camera follows Tina obsessively, emphasises the self-reflexive nature of the narrative. Tina is a girl with character and, thanks to the intricate antics of Arcand's and Jacob Potashnik's script, moves like a loose cannon through scandalous love affairs, two marriages and an uneven catwalk career, ripping through the lustre and exposing the predictably repulsive underbelly of the world of haute couture. And although she never manages to express herself verbally – her agent, her boyfriend or an arrogant television host finish her sentences – she knows what she wants. Or rather – what she does not. Arcand makes good use of Paré's powerful, albeit fairly inert, presence and endows her character with the mythic powers of *l'élan vital*. Like the 'Passion Play' actor from *Jésus of Montréal*, Tina becomes a litmus test for moral resilience. Unlike *Jésus of Montréal*'s self-sacrificial, Agnus Dei pathos, however, *Stardom*'s heroine is presented as a veritable instrument of the Wrath of God – of Denys Arcand, the auteur and uncontested demiurge of his cinematic world, that is. *Stardom* is the closest Arcand has ever come to making a film programmed to be commercially successful. And although it does not share the psychological and philosophical depths of *The Decline of the American Empire* and *Jésus of Montréal*, *Stardom* is informed by Arcand's commanding authorial presence, unmistakably discernible in his propensity for biting social criticism, moralising and ironic commentary on the never-ending human comedy.                                  **CSt**

# George ARMITAGE

Although most famous for the box-office hit *Grosse Pointe Blank* (1997), the less-than-prolific George Armitage began as an associate producer in television with 'Peyton Place'

*Private Duty Nurses* (1971)
*Hit Man* (1972)

before entering the film business as a scriptwriter for Roger Corman's *Gas-s-s!* (1970). Like so many of his contemporaries, particularly Jonathan Demme, Armitage was given his directorial break through Corman's New World Pictures, with the exploitation film *Private Duty Nurses* (1971). This was followed by *Hit Man* (1972), a reworking of Mike Hodges' *Get Carter* (1971), written by Armitage. Its emphasis on a seedy and down-at-heel milieu revealed a directorial style that blended attention to detail and visual flair with a keen sense of pace.

Armitage's 1976 feature *Vigilante Force* was his first for a major studio and his first with a recognised lead (Kris Kristofferson). The film's apocalyptic plot – a group of Vietnam vets are hired to restore order in a oil-producing town in the midst of a nation-wide energy crisis and then take over the town for themselves – and highly stylised violence was a not-too-subtle satire on the American way. Disliked by the studio, the film was a commercial failure and Armitage was cast, or cast himself (the story varies), into the wilderness for thirteen years, punctuated only by a television film called *Hot Rod* in 1979. Salvation came in the shape of Demme, who passed Armitage a novel by Charles Willeford centring on a policeman called Hoke Moseley, and which Armitage adapted and filmed in 1990 as *Miami Blues*. Redolent of *Hit Man* in its downbeat visual style, dark humour, and emphasis on violence, *Miami Blues* features career-best performances by Alec Baldwin, Jennifer Jason Leigh and Fred Ward.

The dark humour and amorality at the heart of *Miami Blues* is also carried over into Armitage's last and most successful film to date, *Grosse Pointe Blank*. The film is a satire about hitman Martin Blank (John Cusack), who goes to his ten-year high-school reunion, pursued by a bevy of fellow hitmen, orchestrated by Mr Grocer (Dan Aykroyd), angry at his refusal to join their hitmen's union. Armitage's contribution is more than that of director-for-hire – although he had no part in the script – since his wry approach to the subject matter of the hitman wrestling with the moral issues of killing for money rests on both an appreciation of the inherent absurdity of the plot and the dark humour necessary to overcome it. Both *Miami Blues* and *Grosse Pointe Blank* suggest a director at ease with the complexities of humour and violence, camera and characterisation, although who knows how long we will have to wait for his next film?

Armitage has recently been linked with *Larceny for Lovers*, a romantic comedy starring Pierce Brosnan about two con artists that fall in love while travelling through Europe. **SH**

# Darren ARONOFSKY

Born in Brooklyn, USA, in 1969, Darren Aronofsky graduated from Harvard Film School with his short film *Supermarket Sweep* and went on to make one of the most original and unsettling films of 1998, *π* (Pi). Inspired by Shinya Tsukamoto's *Tetsuo – The Iron Man* (1988) and the comic books of Frank Miller (The 'Sin City' series in particular), *π* tells the story of reclusive mathematician Max Cohen, and his search for numerical order within the seeming randomness of the New York Stock Exchange. Referred to as a 'Digital Faust Story' by its star Sean Gullette, the film charts the rapid descent into madness by a man who is attempting to control the uncontrollable. The Greek letter Π (3.1416 ... ad infinitum) serves as a metaphor for this futile search. Max's belief that 'mathematics is the language of nature' and 'everything around us can be represented through numbers' suggests not only the novels of William Gibson, but also Baudrillard's idea of the simulacrum – in this case, an endless string of zeros and ones that signal the absence of a basic reality. By placing us within the fragile mind of his self-destructive genius, Aronofsky nihilistically suggests that humankind cannot exist productively in such an environment.

He followed *π* with a film based on Hubert Selby Jr.'s 'Requiem For A Dream' – a frantic and bleak portrayal of addiction and shattered dreams that confirms the director's precocious and unusual talent. Made within the confines of the American mainstream, *Requiem for a Dream* (2000) is just as powerful, unconventional and startling as his first feature. Yet it lacks the novelty element, which was, arguably, a central part of *π*'s success. It is also let down by a patchy, unconvincing script (co-written by Aronofsky and Selby JR.) and has an unfortunate moralistic attitude toward drug use that plays at odds with its liberated camerawork and *mise-en-scène*. However, it does confirm Aronofsky's commitment to pushing the boundaries of the visual image. Shot in colour by Matthew Libatique, *Requiem for a Dream* utilises the hyper-real, comic book intensity of *π* to explore the downward spiral of drug dependency.

Aronofsky is currently in pre-production with *Batman: Year One*, his long awaited collaboration with cartoonist Frank Miller. A self-confessed comic book addict, he could well be the perfect director for this project; it will be interesting to see how his distinctive visual style sits alongside previous imaginings of Gotham City's hero. Aronofsky is also at work as a producer of *Below*, a film based on his script 'Proteus' and is in discussions to make *Last Man* a 'metaphysical post-*The Matrix* sci-fi film', starring Brad Pitt and Cate Blanchett.                                                                                            **BW**

# Miguel ARTETA

A graduate of the film programme at Wesleyan University and the American Film Institute's directing programme, Puerto Rican director Miguel Arteta has been involved in film in various capacities for many years, including crew work on Sidney Lumet's *Q&A* (1990) and Jonathan Demme's *Cousin Bobby* (1992).

*Star Maps* (1997)
*Chuck & Buck* (2000)
*The Good Girl* (2002)

Arteta's ambitious first feature as a director, *Star Maps* (1997), was a hit at the Sundance Film Festival. It follows the story of a young Mexican-American named Carlos (Douglas Spain), an aspiring actor living in Los Angeles, who goes to work for his pimp father Pepe (Efrain Figueroa) as a street hustler under the guise of a salesman of maps of celebrity homes. One of Carlos' customers is beautiful soap opera actress Jennifer (Kandeyce Jorden), who promises him a small part on her show in exchange for his regular services. This enrages Pepe, who wants to maintain control over his son. Meanwhile, Carlos' sister Maria (Lysa Flores) is left to take care of their delusional mother (Martha Velez).

Arteta wrote and directed the film with the aid of veteran Mexican cinematographer Chuy Chavez, who gives the film an astounding vividness, despite a meagre budget. Arteta has been criticised for making his white characters one-dimensional, but the film is concerned with Los Angeles Latinos and the Hollywood stereotypes they deal with on a daily basis. Arteta's camera is intimate to the point of intrusion, following Carlos even into his own delusions and passive sexual encounters. However, the film is somewhat unfocused, with dramatic lines at odds with one another.

Arteta's second film, *Chuck & Buck* (2000), was another popular success at Sundance. It is the story of an obsessive man named Buck (Mike White, who also scripted), a young adult stuck in childhood stasis. Buck continually relives the best years of his life, when he was close friends with Chuck (Chris Weitz), who has since moved to Los Angeles and is engaged to be married. Buck moves there as well after he and Chuck meet again at the funeral for Buck's mother. Buck bitterly resents Chuck's fiancée (Beth Colt) and stages a play that closely resembles their current conflict. By the end, Chuck forces himself to make a difficult decision regarding how he will proceed with the increasingly strange Buck. The film received almost unanimous critical praise, largely thanks again to Chavez, who shot the film on digital video, allowing the film-makers angles truly unique to mainstream American cinema. White's screenplay has also been the subject of much praise.

*The Good Girl* (2002), Arteta's most recent film, stars 'Friends' star Jennifer Aniston as a married woman who has an affair with an eccentric young man (Jake Gyllenhaal). Also written by White, the film premiered, yet again, to a very strong reception at Sundance. Arteta has worked extensively in television, directing episodes of the series 'Homicide: Life on the Streets', 'Snoops' and 'Freaks and Geeks'. He has also directed the short films *Everyday is a Beautiful Day* (1990), which premiered at Berlin Film Festival, and *Lucky Peach* (1995), his Masters thesis at the American Film Institute.                                                                                      **DH**

# ASH

With a supposedly raw, 'guerrilla' aesthetic, Ash (Ashley Baron Cohen) has been touted as one of America's more controversial independent film-makers. Not only are his films highly intelligent, but they also prove to be very skilfully crafted, evoking a real complexity and subtlety of feeling between their more visceral moments. Perhaps also

*Bang* (1995)
*Pups* (1999)

telling is that in his critique of both institutional corruption and America's amoral culture of violence, Ash's 'heroes' appear more as easy-going outsiders rather than as refractory dissidents.

Born in London in 1964, Ash was originally a student of experimental psychology, but was subsequently expelled from a course at the Pasadena Art Centre. Thereafter he managed to make a handful of well-received short films before directing his first feature, *Bang* (1995). The film tells the story of a young Japanese-American woman (Darling Narita), who, after being sexually harassed by a police officer, steals his uniform and masquerades as a cop herself. Wonderfully attentive to the different pleasures and pains the unnamed woman takes from her new identity, the engaging, free-flowing feel of the film belies the way its episodic structure is meticulously organised. In her role as an anonymous representative of authority, the film subtly charts the woman's gradual ascent from awkwardness to confidence, only then to witness her overwhelmed by the darker side of modern urban life.

With an interesting slant on identity politics, the woman refuses to put aside her cultural identity and congenial personality. However, in the end, not only does an ill-feigned attempt to 'save' a reluctant Asian-American prostitute persuade her to relinquish her police persona, but it also convinces her of the lack of solidarity in the world at large. Yet the film ends on a more optimistic note, with a transitory but amicable exchange with the prophetic Adam (Peter Greene), the spaced-out eccentric she earlier met that day.

Ash's second film, *Pups* (1999), treads the familiar territory of the failed bank-job-cum-hostage crisis. With no interest in glamorising its adolescent criminals, the film instead concentrates on their destructive amorality, which here appears to be a direct result of over-exposure to the simplified, ersatz violence of television and film. Like *Bang* the film has a 'colourful' array of supporting characters, and Ash even managed to procure the services of Burt Reynolds as the cop responsible for hostage negotiation. Whilst attempting to reveal the frightening reality of actual violence, the film also makes ironic, self-reflexive gestures that force the audience to recognise they are still watching a film, and indeed are in many respects deriving pleasure from viewing violence.

Ash manages to cultivate real tension throughout the film and also delivers a spectacular finale. However, the intellectual intentions result in a rather dry film that lacks the enjoyable looseness of *Bang* as well as any nuanced sense of characterisation. Both films, however, suggest that Ash could go on to become a significant film-maker should he find a more suitable and consistent tone.                                        **CH**

# Michael AUSTIN

*Killing Dad* (1989)
*Princess Caraboo* (1994)

Michael Austin's directorial debut, *Killing Dad* (1989), makes an ineffectual attempt to be darkly satirical. Adapted from Ann Quinn's novel 'Berg' it is a hapless ramble into the tribulations of lower-class family life. With a promising premise, set in an out-of-season seaside town with a cast of top British comedy actors (including Anna Massey and Julie Walters), the film could have been an effective black comedy. However, Austin aspires to, but does not achieve, the wit and accuracy of Mike Leigh. The first film funded by Scottish Television, it is a desperate story of Ali, a hair tonic salesman (Richard E. Grant) whose dad (Denholm Elliott) is attempting to return to the family nest after deserting Ali as a baby. Still nurturing a deep grudge, Ali feels threatened and decides to kill his dad. Missing the opportunity to be tasteful, amusing and compassionate, Austin's first film is patronising and bland.

Five years later, Austin returned to direct *Princess Caraboo* (1994), from a script which he co-wrote. A palatable fable, successful as a family-friendly light comedy, the film is based on a true story of an esoteric girl (played by Phoebe Cates) who appears mysteriously in the West Country. Her identity is in question: is she a real Princess, or is she an over-imaginative servant girl who has invented this identity to parody the class that exploits her own? A newspaper reporter, Gutch (Stephen Rea), suitably falls in love with the alleged Princess whilst investigating; however, few sparks fly in this unbelievable romance. Set in the nineteenth century, an era when begging was punished by flogging, the film's superlative moments arise from its satire of class consciousness. With a darker perception and a more authentic portrayal of the era, Austin's second film could have been more provoking and memorable.                                        **NI**

# Stefan AVALOS

Born in 1968, Stefan Avalos was trained as a classical violinist, winning competitions and playing with the Philadelphia Orchestra at an early age. He made several shorts while still at high school, and went on to study film-making at college. He produced and directed commercials before securing television work with 'Rescue 911', 'Frontline', and MTV. After the concert movie *Vine in Concert* (1992), he directed and edited his feature debut, the low-budget (US $200,000) *The Game* (1994), and made a further concert movie, *Cut It Up* (1996).

The Game (1994)
The Last Broadcast (1998)

*The Last Broadcast* (1998), co-written, co-directed, and co-produced with Lance Weiler (Avalos also edited the movie, composed the score, and appears as Steven Akvast) saw him dubbed by *Wired* magazine as one of the 25 people helping to reinvent entertainment. This low-budget horror movie, made for just US $900, raises important questions about the implications of data collection and manipulation in the digital age.

After some festival success, Avalos and Weiler formed Wavelength Releasing to facilitate *The Last Broadcast*'s theatrical release. On 23 October 1998, using borrowed equipment, the movie was digitally encoded, beamed via satellite to theatres in Minneapolis, Orlando, Philadelphia, Portland, and Providence, routed through Windows servers and then digitally projected. Subsequent distribution has been via the internet and cable modems, as well as more conventional media. **MB**

# Roger AVARY

Born in Flin Flon, Canada, in 1965, Roger Avary is a gonzo pioneer of the 1990s video store generation of film education; a semantic, creative style bred by the obsessive absorption of thousands of films through repeated viewings on home video. Referential without being derivative, Avary's style is the distilled cinematic essence of French New Wave, Hong Kong action cinema, 1970s American action and German expressionism, with a deep infusion of modern pop culture from a decidedly male perspective.

Killing Zoe (1994)
The Rules of Attraction (2002)

Avary attended film school at the Art Center College of Design in Pasadena, California, a well respected training ground for the advertising industry. His early creative output is closely tied to writer/director Quentin Tarantino, a former cohort and co-worker at Video Archives, a video store in Manhattan Beach, California. Avary and Tarantino collaborated on many cinematic ideas, chewing through countless screenplay drafts and revisions that eventually became the seminal foundation for *True Romance* (1993) and *Pulp Fiction* (1994). Avary shared the Academy Award for Best Screenplay in 1995 for *Pulp Fiction* with Tarantino.

Avary's directorial debut, *Killing Zoe* (1994), is a blood-spattered, drug-fuelled crime thriller filmed with panache and a European sensibility. Beneath its noisy and viscerally violent Bastille Day bank-heist-gone-wrong exterior, the film is a dark, Herzogian descent into madness and hysteria marked with yin/yang character relationships and an ambiguous ending evocative of 1970s American cinema.

His next project, *The Rules of Attraction* (2002), is based on Bret Easton Ellis' book of the same title. **THa**

# John G. AVILDSEN

A professed Frank Capra fan, it is tempting to see John G. Avildsen's film projects as the playing out of all the themes Capra held dear – stories with definite heroes, the underdog overcoming tremendous odds, the surrogate father – and his career as a conscious and deliberate attempt, however unsuccessful, to translate the template of 1930s and 1940s narratives onto a cynical and increasingly individualistic 1970s and 1980s. The paucity of his work in the last decade hints at a director out of tune with modern cinema's sensibilities – since Tarantino and *Die Hard* (1988), audiences are used to foul-mouthed and visceral anti-heroes rather than those that overcome all the odds. It is tempting to see his films as an antidote to the growing despondency and world-weariness of the 1970s – Watergate, Vietnam and assassinations. Avildsen's films airbrush these out of history and concentrate on the integrity of the individual against the machinery of the corrupt 'state' (whether in the boxing ring, the dojo or apartheid South Africa). His style is gritty and no-nonsense, and was first

Turn on to Love (1969)
Joe (1970)
Guess What We Learned
in School Today? (1970)
Okay Bill (1971)
Cry Uncle! (1971)
Save the Tiger (1973)
The Stoolie (1974)
W.W. and the
Dixie Dancekings (1975)
Fore Play (1975)
Rocky (1976)
Slow Dancing in the

articulated in his early experiences working on industrial films and commercials for IBM and Shell.

Born in Oak Park, Illinois, in 1935, he worked in the armed services before entering the world of cinema, seesawing between advertising work and film production experience. Known as a director of 'crowd-pleasers', it is ironic that his breakthrough came with *Joe* (1970), a film about a despicable racist's blackmail of a killer. Starring Peter Boyle, the film became a template for numerous future projects, including Michael Winner's *Death Wish* (1974) and Gus Van Sant's *Drugstore Cowboy* (1989). Avildsen's direction makes audience identification almost impossible but at the same time asks the kind of questions that mainstream film would not ask for several more years about the treatment of racists, junkies and gritty urban living.

*Save the Tiger* (1973) won Jack Lemmon his first Academy Award in this intelligent exploitation film of the garment business, but Avildsen really came to the mass audience's attention in 1976 with his Academy Award-winning direction for *Rocky*. Sylvester Stallone's title character is a near loser, a Philadelphia no-hoper given one shot at winning a title fight. He loses of course, but at the same time certifies the American dream for mass consumption. The film spawned four more money-spinning sequels and created a cultural icon that came to typify US spirit and indominability in the late 1970s and early 1980s. Appropriated as a Reaganite symbol of achievement through hard graft, the film is a glowing pæan to America's favourite sport while equally a mythopoeic examination of fragile masculinity in a post-Vietnam world. Avildsen revisited this territory 14 years later in *Rocky V* (1990), by which time the sequels had plumbed the depths of clunking exposition and ham-fisted direction; he at least managed to steer the film back to its original setting of underdog versus establishment. This time Rocky turns trainer to his son – cue Bill Conti's score, slow motion training and shameless flag-waving.

*Slow Dancing in the City* (1978) shamed audiences with its final-reel bathos. This is a charge that is constantly levelled at the director; he sacrifices narrative plausibility and downbeat closure for over-the-top climaxes that often scupper the rest of the film's tone. As *Variety* aptly wrote, the film has so much heart 'Avildsen's aorta is showing'. It is the balance between feelgood and realism that categorises Avildsen's most successful ventures and but this only happens one film in every half-dozen. After the promising start of *Slow Dance in the City*, the film was cut by executives. This is a constant problem for Avildsen: nearly all his non-commercial ventures have been tinkered with and retouched, denying him the chance to articulate his offbeat ideas.

*The Formula* (1980) was a wasted opportunity for Avildsen to flex his directing muscles and he begged MGM executives to take his name off the picture. Watchable as George C. Scott and Marlon Brando are, Avildsen's direction of a pedestrian tale of a cop who falls in with a mysterious group of scientists and oil tycoons is uninspired.

Its failure was followed by a run of pallid and artless films. *Neighbors* (1981) was John Belushi's last film, and his epitaph deserved more than this unfunny 'comedy' about neighbours from hell in small-town suburbia. A run of unambitious duds came to an end with *The Karate Kid* (1984). Shamelessly cannibalising his own work, Avildsen simply remade *Rocky*, but tapped into the mid-1980s zeitgeist and forged a film full of warmth and affirmation. *The Karate Kid* trilogy (1984, 1986, 1989) proved the rule of diminishing returns, but not before refashioning the *Rocky* treatment for the baby-boomer generation. The real pleasure in Avildsen's direction of the three films is the lilting partnership between the boy and wise owl teacher. The surrogate father-son relationship never jars, and the endlessly quotable dialogue and thrilling, if telegraphed finale, is a worthy panacea to the artifice and hollowness of 1980s cinema.

Despite its production difficulties, *Happy New Year* (1987) is an enjoyable caper in which Peter Falk and Charles Durning pose as elderly gents casing a jewellery store in preparation for a heist. *For Keeps* (1988) was another worthy attempt to highlight a child's response to adult responsibilities (this time a pregnant Molly Ringwald). A standout in recent times was *The Power of One* (1992), a film full of depth, dimension and excellent casting. Bringing together a cast as eclectic as Morgan Freeman, Stephen Dorff and John Gielgud payed off for Avildsen, allowing him free rein to mount a captivating tale of a young boy's awakening in colonial South Africa and meld it to a boxing drama. Much of the film's impact stems from Avildsen's intelligent editing (he edits most of his films) and the lush Zimbabwe photography by Dean Semler.

In recent years, Avildsen's output has been of a mediocre quality; however off-beat the rodeo drama *8 Seconds* (1994) purports to be, it still smacks of a rehash of *Rocky* but without the charisma and clout of its predecessor. Moreover, a film about a sport full of cuts, bruises and dirt needs to be reflected in the filming; instead, this is rose-coloured and wholly schematic. *Coyote Moon* (1999), an action film starring Jean-Claude Van Damme as a veteran soldier, is equally lacking in originality of style or thought.                     **BM**

# Jon AVNET

A prolific producer-director comfortably and successfully working within Hollywood cinema, John Avnet has repeatedly proven his facility for creating engaging, star-driven dramas.

Born in Brooklyn in 1949, Avnet broke through as a director with *Fried Green Tomatoes at the Whistle Stop Café* (1991), which might arguably be seen to have announced the revival, to some small degree, of the woman's picture which had once been a very real and significant Hollywood genre. *Fried Green Tomatoes* starred Kathy Bates as Evelyn Couch and Jessica Tandy as Ninny Threadgoode. With this film Avnet announced his real skills as an actor's director rather than possessing a distinctive and individual sense of *mise-en-scène*. Adapted from the novel by Fannie Flagg, *Fried Green Tomatoes* tells of the friendship between Evelyn and Ninny, with the film built around a flashback-driven narrative taking the audience back to the 1930s and the character of Idgie Threadgoode, a proto-feminist. As Evelyn learns more about Idgie, she becomes inspired to adopt her sense of liberty and individuality. Evelyn effectively starts her life afresh, taking more control of it in the process. *Fried Green Tomatoes* shows Avnet revelling successfully in melodrama. The film also marked the start of his ongoing collaboration with composer Thomas Newman, who has scored all of Avnet's films to date.

He followed *Fried Green Tomatoes* with *The War* (1994), which told the story of a father, Stephen, back in America from Vietnam and struggling to find work in an impoverished southern community. The 'War' of the title refers to battles fought on several fronts – obviously Vietnam, as referenced by the film's refreshingly low-key flashbacks; the war of living from day to day – with all its attendant financial difficulties, frustrations, and lack of opportunity; the war with oneself for dignity and a sense of purpose; and the war between Stephen's children and friends with a rival gang over the ownership of an incredible tree-house. The film evokes memories of *Stand by Me* (1986) but is more melancholy and melodramatic. It also provides Kevin Costner, as Stephen, with one of his strongest roles to date as the anxious, inarticulate, gentle father who always tries to do the right thing. Witness the scene where he sits on the bench outside the diner talking with his son, or the scene where Stephen tearfully embraces his son in the woods. In *The War*, Avnet conjures a nostalgic and sentimental story, enhanced by strong performances from both his adult and child leads, especially Elijah Wood.

Avnet followed *The War* with a romantic comedy-drama, *Up Close and Personal* (1996), starring Michelle Pfeiffer and Robert Redford. The romantic drama follows a young woman, Sally Atwater, who achieves her ambition of breaking into broadcast news journalism and who falls in love with the man, Warren Justice (Redford), who hired her. Not as sentimental as *Fried Green Tomatoes* or *The War*, *Up Close and Personal* thrives most on its lead performances, again demonstrating that Avnet's best contribution comes in his handling of actors.

The thriller *Red Corner* (1997) stars Richard Gere as Jack More, a lawyer framed for murder in present-day China. More must negotiate the labyrinthine Chinese legal system in an attempt to prove his innocence. Again Avnet elicits a charismatic and appropriately sympathetic performance from his star, but the film as a whole fails to truly engross, and it relies perhaps a little too much on the familiar narrative devices of legal thrillers.

Avnet has emerged as an efficient director of mainstream film, utterly confident in crafting a story and characters, in the classic style, with whom the audience can empathise, yet never really igniting the screen with images that surprise or remain burned into our movie-going memories. As a producer, Avnet has been highly prolific and successful, his films including *Risky Business* (1983), *Tango and Cash* (1989), *The Mighty Ducks* (1992), and *George of the Jungle* (1997). He has recently written and directed *Uprising* (2001) for television, narrating the story of the Jewish fighting organisation in Nazi-occupied Warsaw.                     **JC**

*Fried Green Tomatoes at the Whistle Stop Café* (1991)
*The War* (1994)
*Up Close and Personal* (1996)
*Red Corner* (1997)

# B

## Beth B

Trained at Chicago's Art Institute and the New York School of Visual Arts, Beth B exploited the rise of New York's underground cinema in the late 1970s and early 1980s. Like contemporaries Eric Mitchell and Amos Poe, she utilised a punk/new wave aesthetic to make a series of experimental 8mm shorts. Seeing film-making as a logical extension of her other artistic endeavours, she directed films with husband Scott, or collaborated on photography, script and music in his films. Early 8mm works were characterised by evocations of violent worlds of cruelty and dehumanisation, authority and organisation, expressed in non-traditional forms, and known as a kind of cinema of transgression.

*Black Box* (with Scott B, 1978) is a film about degradation and torture, whilst *G-Man* (with Scott B, 1978) combines documentary, narrative and experimental techniques. It uses self-reflexivity, such as the long pan across downtown Manhattan that has been compared to the continuous zoom in Michael Snow's *Wavelength* (1967).

B, however, professes to dislike experimental styles 'if it's nothing but a formalist or conceptual idea'. Thus her films have stories to tell. *Letters to Dad* (with Scott B, 1979) uses a variety of performers, artists and musicians, to recite extracts from letters written to the Reverend Jim Jones before the mass suicide of his Jonestown followers. Her 1980 short *Trap Door* discusses the ways society rigidifies people, reflected in a more stable camera and peripheral framing.

Her first 16mm feature, *Vortex* (with Scott B, 1983), utilised a crew out of necessity and thus altered the Bs' working practice, restricting freedoms from improvised dialogue and camera moves. It is a film of dark interiors and an atmosphere of isolation. Like *G-Man* and Scott B's *Offenders* (on which she was co-screenwriter and cinematographer), there is a crime narrative involved in the story of a female private detective investigating a Howard Hughes-like billionaire. Frequent B collaborator and performance artist Lydia Lunch heads the cast.

After venturing into rock videos Beth B wrote, produced, and directed her first solo feature, *Salvation! Have You Said Your Prayers Today?* (1987), a satirical look at television evangelists, using performers from B's sub-cultural environment, including alternative rock singer Exene Cervanka, Viggo Mortensen and Rockets Redglare. The

*Vortex* (1983)
*Salvation! Have You Said Your Prayers Today?* (1987)
*Two Small Bodies* (1993)
*Visiting Desire* (1996)
*Voices Unheard* (1998)
*Breathe In, Breathe Out* (2000)

subject was timely – the title refers to the reverend's pre-coital catchphrase – and uses fantasy sequences, high-angle camera work which twists into close-ups, and tight editing to clarify the difference between the reverend's (Stephen McHattie) land of luxurious promise and the housewife Rhonda's own reduced circumstances.

After contributing to a Franco-American collection of short works by video artists (*Trans-Voices*, 1992) B adapted her next feature from Neal Bell's play about a detective investigating the disappearance of a single mother's children. The film uses more mainstream actors (Fred Ward and Suzy Amis) but remains typical of B's work in mood and atmosphere. The themes of violence, perversity and sexuality which pervade her work are here, too, with issues of child abuse and female identity to the fore. Unsettling and claustrophobic, the film is ambiguous about the nature of the couple's relationship, not allowing the audience to place them in expected and comfortable roles as a seemingly official visit becomes a violent physical confrontation.

A move further into the documentary form followed, with docu-drama *Visiting Desire* (1996), wherein strangers were locked up together and encouraged to express their fantasies. Interviews with professional therapists and ordinary people about their definitions of desire were cut with the group confessing and exploring their own definitions.

*Voices Unheard* (1998) documents sexual offenders' treatment centres and *Breathe In, Breathe Out* (2000) shows B, three Vietnam veterans and their grown-up children revisiting Vietnam to try to reconcile past and present lives. The latter film marks a visual difference in B's work, although themes of guilt, cruelty, and violence remain, as does her refusal to allow the audience to become comfortable with the viewing experience.

JD

# John BADHAM

John Badham has sustained an enduring Hollywood career spanning nearly 25 years. Widely considered as a seasoned craftsman rather than an auteur, he has directed a number of critically respectable and commercially successful movies across a range of genres, although more recently he has established himself rigidly within the action and comedy thriller cycle.

Born in the UK in 1939 and having emigrated to the US at the age of two, Badham attended Yale School of Drama where he was awarded his BA and MA in drama. Despite his educational achievements, Badham followed the more traditional career path by starting as a mailroom assistant at Universal before rising through the ranks to associate television producer. Following a brief spell directing movies for television, he moved into film directing in the mid-1970s. His first feature, *The Bingo Long Travelling All-Stars and Motor Kings* (1976), was an engaging but slight period comedy depicting the adventures of a 1930s amateur black basketball team shooting for the big time. Although the film received reasonable critical notices, it was more a measure of the low commercial expectations of *Saturday Night Fever* (1977) that the relatively inexperienced Badham got to direct what turned into one of the biggest grossing films of the year.

*Saturday Night Fever* was based on an article written by New York journalist Nick Cohn entitled 'The Tribal Rights of the New Saturday Night', which chronicled the rituals of the then little-known disco sub-culture. The film, which narratively amounts to little more than a clichéd tale of a working-class youth seeking to escape his grim life through dance, is most interesting in the manner in which it represented a shift towards a greater realism in the musical through its unsentimental North Brooklyn locations and the script's glut of profanities. In its original manifestation, however, disco had been a glamour-heavy reaction to rock music by such subordinate groups as African Americans, Hispanics and gays, which had taken form in obscure New York nightclubs. Subsequently, and most obviously, through the casting of an Italian American lead in the shape of John Travolta (who went on to become an international superstar) and through the white-Australian Bee Gees soundtrack that became a multi-million selling aural staple of that year, the film has been seen in certain circles as being instrumental in bringing about a white, middle-class colonisation of disco.

Badham's next picture marked a move to more mythical territory. *Dracula* (1979) was a big-budget, highly stylised affair with an enthused Frank Langella in the lead role. While the film, shot in England, drew praise for its atmosphere and design, many purists objected to a matinee idol romanticism that aligns the Count more with

Casanova than vampirism. Changing direction again, Badham's next feature was *Whose Life is it Anyway?* (1981), a screen adaptation of Brian Clark's static stageplay, in which Richard Dreyfuss plays a wisecracking, bed-ridden sculptor paralysed in a car crash. While the subject matter clearly imposes formal constraints, the overly vigorous oral performance of Dreyfuss and a certain emotional depth turned the film into a surprise commercial success. Badham's next two films saw him engaging with the effects of military technology. The first, *War Games* (1983), proved the marginally more interesting of the two. The film only threatens to exploit an interesting conceit in which an adolescent (Matthew Broderick) unwittingly triggers a full-scale East/West nuclear alert by tapping into the Pentagon Defence Department's computer. The film generates a degree of suspense, but this is ultimately undermined through a narrative that careers into the path of teen romance and humanitarian cliché. *Blue Thunder* (1983) constitutes the hackneyed tale of a vigilante-type LA police officer (Roy Scheider) haunted by his experience of service in Vietnam, and who becomes the pilot of the very latest high-tech helicopter. For all its narrative shortcomings, however, Badham proved himself adept at directing accomplished action sequences that would stand him in good stead.

With *American Flyers* (1985) Badham addressed themes of sibling rivalry through a punishing long-distance bicycle race set against a burning Colorado landscape. The film, which cast Kevin Costner in an early lead, is a modestly engaging tale (if sentimental and unsurprising) that visually exploits the transcendental tradition of American landscape photography. By way of complete contrast, Badham followed with the successful family movie *Short Circuit* (1986). The film tells the tale of a small military robot which is struck by lightening and develops human intelligence. Thus ensues a briskly paced chase caper (replete with nutty scientist, Steve Guttenberg) in which the robot takes refuge with a pet lover (Ally Sheedy). While such fare is hardly the mark of a traditional auteur, Badham again proved adroit at fashioning solid formulaic entertainment.

If his oeuvre to date had defied any consistency of theme, Badham's next four films established something of a loose pattern for him within the comedy-adventure genre. The first of this short cycle, *Stakeout* (1987), brought Badham considerable box-office success. The film depicts a love/hate cop relationship that develops between Richard Dreyfuss and Emilio Estevez during a sustained period of house surveillance in downtown Seattle. Much to the comic chagrin of his colleague, Dreyfuss falls for the partner (Madeleine Stowe) of the escaped murderer whose apartment he is staking out, which gives rise to the anticipated chase/action sequences. The success of *Stakeout* eventually precipitated a sequel, *Another Stakeout* (1993), in which Badham failed to repeat the success of the original. In the sequel, the Dreyfuss/Estevez relationship is comically confused with the introduction of a female officer (Rosie O'Donnell) as the threesome pose as a family on vacation while they stakeout a couple suspected of harbouring a fugitive. Commenting on the latter, but equally applicable to the former, Trevor Johnston observed, 'Comedy and suspense sensibly packaged; but very old hat'. Sandwiched between the *Stakeout* movies were two other comedy-adventures. The first, *Bird on a Wire* (1990), functions as a chase comedy and star vehicle for Goldie Hawn and Mel Gibson. The picture, which, despite its star pairing, did not go down well at the box office or with critics, sets up Hawn (a lawyer) and Gibson (in hiding under a witness protection scheme) as reunited ex-lovers on the run from rancorous murderers. Again Badham displayed a good sense of pace and an eye for the impressive set piece, but there remains a perfunctory ambience to the proceedings with a feeling of the same action scenarios being re-enacted only in different locations.

If not commercially, then easily the most critically successful of the four was *The Hard Way* (1991) for which Badham returned to the urban badlands of New York. Where its immediate predecessors were polished but prescribed, *The Hard Way* is refreshingly inventive, with an improbably successful comic interplay between the film's two stars, James Woods and Michael J. Fox. Fox plays a smug but cloistered film star who joins up with Woods' hardened and antagonistic homicide cop to gain 'real-life experience' for an upcoming role. Unwilling to make any concessions to his unwelcome companion's fragile sensibilities, Woods ceaselessly pursues a homicidal criminal, leading Fox into a series of life-threatening scrapes. As with its predecessors, *The Hard Way* is punctuated with impressive action sequences, and the film also makes concession to the usual Hollywood structuring, with the antagonistic couple coming to 'respect' each another.

Yet the proceedings are delivered here with a nice feeling for self-irony, hitherto absent in Badham's work.

Badham turned to more earnest fare with *The Assassin* (aka *Point of No Return*) (1993), a slavish but doomed remake of Luc Besson's cult favourite *Nikita*. Bridget Fonda plays a drug addict who, having killed a cop, is offered a choice between the electric chair and working as an undercover government agent. Understandably opting for the latter, Fonda is fetishistically re-groomed and trained as an assassin. Amidst the typically accomplished action sequences, this preposterous espionage hokum is imbued with the requisite love interest, with Gabriel Byrne and Dermot Mulroney contesting Fonda's affection. Despite this film's mediocre box office and critical showing, Badham had by now firmly established a niche for himself as a consummate director of mechanical action adventures.

This position was further secured with his next film, *Drop Zone* (1994). All the Badham traits re-emerge in a sky-diving adventure escapade. The movie's contrived plot, which has Wesley Snipes' US Marshal pitched against Gary Busey's typically unhinged, bad guy sky-diving expert, is primed solely to facilitate the bracing sky-diving sequences. More conceptually interesting, but ultimately flawed, was Badham's next feature, *Nick of Time* (1995), ostensibly a Hitchcockian thriller with the (relatively) fresh pretext of being shot in real time. On arrival at LA's Union Station, Johnny Depp (peculiarly out of type) has his young daughter kidnapped and is given a gun, a photograph and instructions to carry out an immediate hit if he wishes to see his daughter alive again. Although Christopher Walken puts in his expected entertaining turn as the chief bad-guy, the film's broad conspiracy theme doesn't suit the ninety-minute time frame.

The box-office nonentity, *Incognito* (1997), was critically slated. Once more working within the contrivances of the formula thriller, the film, with Jason Patric in the lead, is set in Europe and centres on the world of art forgery. Nor is there anything in Badham's subsequent two projects – *Floating Away* (1998), a comedy road movie casting together Rosanna Arquette, Paul Hogan and Judge Reinhold, and *The Jack Bull* (1999), a revenge western starring John Cusack and John Goodman – to suggest any radical change of direction for a respected director whose reputation is likely to remain one based on solid craftsmanship rather than the pursuit of any personal vision. His most recent works, the political drama, *The Last Debate* (2000) and the thriller *Brother's Keeper* (2002), were both made for television. **TT**

# Steven BAIGELMAN

*Feeling Minnesota* (1996) Born in Toronto, Steven Baigelman moved to New York after a year of college in order to study acting at the Neighbourhood Playhouse under the tuition of Sanford Meisner, later studying painting at City College. While working as a production assistant, he exhibited in New York and Europe before turning to screenwriting. His as yet still unproduced adaptation of Rick DeMarinis' 'Year of the Zinc Penny' brought him to the attention of Danny DeVito's Jersey Films. Following his attendance at the Sundance Institute's Director's Lab, they produced *Feeling Minnesota* (1996) which, at the age of 35, he directed from his own screenplay.

Although the powerful opening sequence suggests a rather different story will follow, Baigelman's literate script plunges Cameron Diaz and Keanu Reeves – in one of his best performances – into the kind of situation one expects to find only in Jim Thompson novels or Coen brothers' movies. A twisted tale of family ties, greed, dishonesty, manipulation, and stupidity, *Feeling Minnesota* blends family melodrama with black comedy, at times rather uneasily. Some slippery plot logic and a rather unbelievable twist are more than made up for by strong casting, which includes well-played minor roles for Tuesday Weld, Delroy Lindo and Courtney Love, and a terrific performance from Vincent D'Onofrio. A humorous soundtrack, well-observed scenes of desultory filial competition and conflict, and handsome cinematography round out a rather sly critique of the American dream. **MB**

# John BAILEY

*The Search for Signs of* With a distinguished and eclectic career as cinematographer already well established *Intelligent Life in the* thanks to his work on some of the most accomplished films of recent years, John Bailey

has ample reason to rest on his laurels. He has also developed an intriguing career as *Universe* (1991)
a director in his own right, however. With experience in a variety of genres, including *China Moon* (1994)
horror, noir, western, documentary, comedy and even filmed stage plays, Bailey's films *Via Dolorosa* (2000)
are marked by an ability to underpin thematic concerns and performances with an
astonishingly broad array of styles and an expansive cinematic imagination. His own
directorial concerns have been more low-key, mainly focusing on detailed acting and a
fascination with the film-making process.

Born in Missouri in 1942, Bailey graduated from the USC Film School and initially
gained experience on low budget films in the seventies and as a camera operator on
Terrence Malick's doomed *Days of Heaven* (1978). His talents emerged on critically
acclaimed *Boulevard Nights* (1979), and then *American Gigolo* (1980), his first
collaboration with Paul Schrader, in which Bailey's evocative lighting and camerawork
conjure the film's sleazy, erotic mood. Other collaborations with Schrader displayed a
similar command of imagistic language. *Cat People* (1982) is heavily reliant on Bailey's
lavish lighting and ability to contrast the intimacy of erotic thriller and the showy gore of
psychological horror; *Mishima* (1985), a virtuoso display of cinematography ranging from
technicolour, lavish fantasy to spare black-and-white childhood flashback. Bailey's career
elsewhere has been similarly disparate, with the ability to photograph action, comedy
and drama with equal success, thanks to his broad command of a multitude of cinematic
techniques and the capacity to weave style and narrative into a seamless whole.

Bailey's own directorial career began with a film version of a solo theatrical
performance piece, an idea precedented by his photography of the one-man show
*Swimming to Cambodia* (1987). *The Search for Signs of Intelligent Life in the Universe*
(1991) was an acclaimed Broadway hit for its star Lily Tomlin, in which she plays a
variety of characters in a meditation on the absurdities of human life. The remarkable
thing about this debut is its lack of ego; Bailey entirely subsumes his obvious command
of film-making to Tomlin's performance, delivering a stripped-down, straight recreation of
theatrical experience. This lack of overt style on Bailey's part is itself stylistic, illustrating
his understanding of the need to marry cinematic treatment with the demands of
material, here becoming near-invisible to lay emphasis on the central performance.

*China Moon* (1994) is, on the other hand, consciously stylised. It is a 1990s noir
update that deliberately employs genre hallmarks – perpetual rain, under-lighting, liberal
shadows, narrative twists – in order to draw attention to its themes of murder, passion,
betrayal and double-crossing. Highly erotic, with tense thrills and good performances,
it is principally a film about film-making; the way in which our own preconceptions and
filmic associations can be employed and subverted by invocation and manipulation of
genre conventions. Bailey's command of style makes him eminently capable of this kind
of postmodern film-making. *Via Dolorosa* (2000), his most recent effort, is a filmed
version of David Hare's monologue 'On a Westerner's Journey to Israel'.          **OB**

# Stuart BAIRD

Stuart Baird graduated from University College London with degrees in economics and *Executive Decision* (1996)
international relations. After working as Lindsay Anderson's assistant on *If...* (1968), *US Marshals* (1998)
he began a decade-long association with Ken Russell, working as assistant editor on
*The Devils* (1968), sound editor on *Savage Messiah* (1972), as editor on *Lisztomania*
(1975), *Tommy* (1975), and *Valentino* (1977), and as associate producer on *Altered
States* (1980). During the 1970s and 1980s, he edited *The Omen* (1976), *Superman
II* (1980), *Outland* (1981), *Five Days One Summer* (1982), *Beyond the Limit* (aka *The
Honorary Consul* (1983)), *Revolution* (1985), *Ladyhawke* (1985), on which he was also
second unit director, *Lethal Weapon* (1987), and *Lethal Weapon 2* (1989). He received
Academy Award nominations for the editing of *Superman* (1978) and *Gorillas in the
Mist* (1988). Working as full-time staff editor at Warner Bros. during the early 1990s,
he supervised the editing of *Tango and Cash* (1989), *Die Hard 2* (1990), *New Jack City*
(1991), and *Robin Hood: Prince of Thieves* (1991), among others. More recently, he
edited *The Last Boy Scout* (1991), *Radio Flyer* (1992), *Demolition Man* (1993), and
*Maverick* (1994).

If editing Russell's extravaganzas did not prepare Baird for directing contemporary
Hollywood spectacle, then editing Donner's humorous, hyperbolic, and typically
efficient action movies would have. His directorial debut (which he also co-edited) was

the cannily-cast *Executive Decision* (1996), starring Kurt Russell and Steven Seagal. Despite an ending too many, it is one of the best airborne *Die Hard* (1988) imitators, playing out its genre twists and tropes with admirable gusto. It is, however, marred by the anti-Muslim sentiments which have become increasingly common in contemporary US action cinema.

Baird's next project was to revive Sam Gerard for a sequel to *The Fugitive* (1993) called *US Marshals* (1998). John Pogue's screenplay opts to set an innocent, but eminently proficient, man on the run, and then makes Gerard's team, expanded to include an African-American woman, the main focus of a hackneyed conspiracy narrative. Although the movie is centred around Gerard, his dogged and intelligent character is rewritten as one who is merely determined and indestructible. There are some exciting sequences, but the action seems mostly laboured, reducing the pretensions of *The Fugitive* to mere plodding. It is perhaps significant that Baird did not edit the movie.

As an editor, he has more recently worked on two high-profile action films, *Mission Impossible II* (2000) and *Lara Croft: Tomb Raider* (2001), and is currently in production as a director on the latest in the Star Trek series, *Star Trek: Nemesis*.          **MB**

# Ralph BAKSHI

To understand Ralph Bakshi's work one must understand the state of American animation prior to the early 1970s. Before Japanese *anime* made the portrayal of extreme violence and sexuality marketable to audiences around the world, animation in the United States was viewed almost exclusively as a medium for families and children. Bakshi sought to re-invent animation, directing feature-length films for adults that would address serious themes and important social issues. As Bakshi himself has said of his own work: 'I had this dream that animation could be the medium of the people ... if Disney worked for the middle class, I was gonna work for the kids in the street.'

Born in 1938 and raised in Brooklyn, New York, Bakshi began his career as an animator for the Terrytoons studio producing off-beat cartoon heroes such as 'Diaperman' and 'Ropeman' for CBS television. Bakshi's first feature was the cult classic *Fritz the Cat* (1972), which immediately established his reputation. The film was a raunchy, X-rated adaptation of R. Crumb's infamous comic-strip about a horny feline on the prowl in an urban fantasy world of sex, drugs and violence.

His next feature, *Heavy Traffic* (1973), was supposed to have been an adaptation of Hubert Selby's novel 'Last Exit to Brooklyn'. However, a falling out with the writer forced Bakshi to develop a more autobiographical project. *Heavy Traffic* told the story of a young animator whose drawing board visions and fantasies come to vivid life. It remains a unique and brilliant film, combining a realistic portrayal of street life with the fantasy world of Bakshi's imagination; a world which sought to represent both the perils and pleasures of Brooklyn in the 1970s as well as to escape that same world through artistic inspiration. *Heavy Traffic* also introduced Bakshi's aesthetic trademark, the technique of 'rotoscoping' in which human forms are filmed first through a camera and then projected onto a matte where the animator can then manipulate the image and background. Such a technique produces an uncanny effect in Bakshi's films: his figures are brought to life through animation yet retain the density and form of the human figure.

The director's next film was the controversial *Coonskin* (aka *Streetfight* (1974)), about a rabbit who journeys to Harlem from the South, only to become trapped by the conditions of the ghetto and forced into a life of drugs and violence. African-American groups boycotted the movie and it was pulled from theatres after only a week of release. Reeling from the controversies and accusations of racism, Bakshi retreated to the world of fantasy and nostalgia. *Wizards* (1977) was a compelling and well-executed film set in a post-apocalyptic world of magic where two twins struggle against each other with the aid of sorcery on one side and the technologies of mass destruction on the other. Bakshi followed this with an adaptation of Tolkien's masterpiece. Taken on its own terms, *The Lord of the Rings* (1978) is a fine realisation which inevitably suffers from its attempts to condense the detailed books into two hours.

Bakshi returned to the streets for the animated epic *American Pop* (1981), the story of four generations of Jewish musicians and their journey from the pogroms of Russia to the drug-infested streets of New York. The film's title refers both to the importance of music to the formation of an American character as well as to the patriarchal lineage of talent and genius.

His next two films returned to the idea of rivalry and warfare, but were both set in drastically different periods. *Hey Good Lookin'* (1982) was the story of opposing gangs battling for turf in New York, while *Fire and Ice* (1983) was a return to the fantasy worlds of *Wizards* and *The Lord of the Rings* and told the story of two kingdoms trying to conquer each other. While *Fire and Ice* received decent reviews it was never able to find a large audience, and Bakshi would not make another feature for nearly a decade. Instead, he worked as an art director and animator on smaller projects and videos, including the Rolling Stones' 'Harlem Shuffle'.

The runaway success of the combined live-action-animation hit *Who Framed Roger Rabbit* (1988) allowed him to make *Cool World* (1992), his latest feature-length project. The film was characteristic of Bakshi's oeuvre, combining elements of fantasy and realism with his vision of a gritty urban world of drugs, sex and vice. Like *Who Framed Roger Rabbit*, *Cool World* mixed live action with animation. Yet despite the presence of budding superstar Brad Pitt and the voice of Kim Basinger, who played the animated Holli Would, the film was unsuccessful with audiences and critics.

Following *Cool World*, Bakshi returned to television with several series and a made-for-television movie, but controversy followed him there as well. His Saturday morning cartoon series 'The New Adventures of Mighty Mouse' was pulled from the airwaves after parents' groups protested about a scene in which the superhero appears to snort a white powder. As a film-maker and animator unafraid to take thematic or stylistic risks, Bakshi's career has been marked by such controversies. In addition, the director has been unable to shake the criticism that his films consistently employ, rather than undermine, racial and ethnic stereotypes. Bakshi insists he is trying to do the latter and to use animation to represent a certain kind of social realism. Whatever the case, Bakshi's career marks a turning point in the history of American animation.    **MR**

# Carroll BALLARD

In an age where the term 'family film' is frequently synonymous with bland, banal story-telling, Carroll Ballard's contributions to the genre are exceptions that prove the rule. His three most enduring films are not only confidently told, potent pieces of drama but also attest to the opportunities that exist for film-makers to evoke the natural world as an expressive aspect of a story – it can be more than just a picture postcard backdrop.

*The Black Stallion* (1979)
*Never Cry Wolf* (1983)
*Nutcracker: The Motion Picture* (1986)
*Wind* (1992)
*Fly Away Home* (1996)

Born in Los Angeles in 1937, Ballard was originally a cinematographer who became part of Francis Coppola and George Lucas' brave new world at American Zoetrope in late 1960s San Francisco. He benefited from the association a decade later when he contributed second unit work to *Star Wars: A New Hope* (1977) (shooting the Tusken Raider attack on Luke Skywalker). He made his directorial debut with *The Black Stallion* (1979), from a screenplay by Melissa Mathison and William Witliff, adapted from the novel by Walter Farley. Mathison went on to pen *E.T. The Extra-Terrestrial* (1982).

*The Black Stallion* is a simple and boldly poetic film that tells the story of a boy named Alec (Kelly Reno) who befriends a black stallion after they both wash up on a Mediterranean island, having survived the sinking of their ship. Ballard's film explores the bond that develops between the boy and his horse. They are finally rescued and returned to America, where Alec falls under the wing of a horse trainer, Henry Dailey (Mickey Rooney). The film concludes with Alec riding the stallion to victory in a thrillingly edited race. *The Black Stallion* abounds with poetic images – such as the hooves of the horse beneath the sea as it treads through the water. For much of its running time the film operates as a silent piece, and there is an affecting, unsentimental melancholy running through the narrative as it charts the orphaned boy's need to make new attachments to father figures, whether human or animal. The film possesses a near-fairytale quality as it follows his emotional growth.

*Never Cry Wolf* (1983) followed. Produced by Walt Disney Pictures, the film is another adaptation of a literary piece – by Farley Mowat – telling the story of a man's solitary, empowering, and illuminating experience studying wolves in Canada. Tyler, the protagonist, goes unprepared for the savage winter. Barely surviving, he is rescued by an Eskimo. Spring comes and Tyler finds himself in an idyllic wilderness where he develops a mutually trustful and engaging relationship with the wolves. This harmonious existence is threatened by the intrusion of caribou hunters. As in all his films, Ballard elicits a fine lead performance, on this occasion from Charles Martin Smith as Tyler.

Ballard followed *Never Cry Wolf* with *The Nutcracker: The Motion Picture* (1986) and then with *Wind* (1992), made under the auspices of Francis Coppola and set in the world of yacht racing and the Americas Cup – again, an opportunity for Ballard to capture the motion of the sea and place the audience vividly in the environment, despite the film's somewhat inert drama. Again, the crucible for the human drama is the natural world.

Ballard's most recent film was *Fly Away Home* (1996), from a screenplay by Robert Rodat – who went on to write *Saving Private Ryan* (1998). The film tells the story of a girl whose mother has died in a car accident. The girl is reawakened and restored when she discovers and nurtures, with the help of her father, a flock of orphaned goslings until they are ready to make the flight to the Southern states. As with *The Black Stallion* and *Never Cry Wolf*, Ballard dovetails the symbols available in nature with the drama to create an expressive whole in which a vigorous, sincere engagement with nature encourages a process of healing and illumination in the human characters.

Ballard is rumoured to be working on an IMAX version of 'Young Black Stallion' for Disney.                                                                                    **JC**

# Charles BAND

*Last Foxtrot in Burbank* (1973)
*Crash!* (1977)
*Parasite* (1982)
*Metalstorm: The Destruction of Jared-Syn* (1983)
*The Alchemist* (1984)
*Trancers* (1985)
*The Dungeonmaster* (1985)
*Meridian* (1990)
*Crash and Burn* (1990)
*Trancers II* (1991)
*Doctor Mordrid* (1992)
*Prehysteria* (1993)
*Dollman vs. Demonic Toys* (1993)
*Hideous!* (1997)
*The Creeps* (1997)
*Blooddolls* (1999)

Charles Band is the son of exploitation film-maker Albert Band, and brother of film composer Richard. Born in Los Angeles in 1951 but raised in Rome during the 1960s, he made a number of Warhol-esque shorts, but his feature debut came with *Last Foxtrot in Burbank* (1973). In 1977 he produced the soft-porn movie *Cinderella*, but more significantly he established Meda Home Entertainment (now Media Home Entertainment), produced Michael Pataki's horror movie *Mansion of the Doomed* (1977), John Hayes' science fiction movie *End of the World* (1977), and his own occult car-chase feature *Crash!* (1977), accomplishments indicating much of what was to come.

Two 3-D science fiction movies followed. *Parasite* (1982) – one of Demi Moore's earliest films – blends *Shivers* (1975), *Alien* (1979), and *Mad Max* (1979): the creator of the eponymous creature flees government forces into a desert occupied by the kind of punkish mutants indigenous to the post-apocalypse. *Metalstorm: The Destruction of Jared-Syn* (1983) is an even less distinguished effort, in which a power-crystal-wielding megalomaniac and desert settings provide a pretext for some naff astral plane symbolism and dreary western antics on wheels. Inexplicably, Jared-Syn (Mike Preston) survives. With the profits from these, Band established Empire International, a company responsible for a slew of lively low-budget science fiction, fantasy, and horror movies. Sometimes inventive, they typically featured ragged plotting, barely adequate performances, and truncated special effects sequences of variable quality. Based in Italy, Empire flourished from 1984–88, and it seemed for a while that Band might actually achieve his declared (if not entirely serious) intention of 'a thousand films by the year 2000'.

*The Alchemist* (1984), pointlessly set in the 1950s, is a minor horror movie featuring a far better score (from Richard Band) than it requires or deserves, and demonstrating ambition far in excess of Band's budget and then ability. Band directed one-and-a-bit movies for Empire. Basically a showreel anthology, *The Dungeonmaster* (1985) sees Paul (Jeffrey Byron) transported to the realm of Mestema (Richard Moll) where, aided only by his computer wristwatch thing, he must face seven challenges in order to rescue his girlfriend. Each segment was written and directed by a different director, except Steve Ford's 'Slasher', which was written by Byron. In addition to the linking material, Band directed the segment 'Heavy Metal', appropriately casting WASP as demons. Of Band's co-directors, all but Ford and Turko immediately went on to helm Empire projects. 1985 was also the year of Band's masterpiece, *Trancers*, a cross between *Blade Runner* (1982) and *The Terminator* (1984), with nods to Cronenberg and Romero, and a plot conveniently borrowed from television's 'The Invaders'. Jack Deth (Tim Thomerson) must travel three hundred years back in time, take over the body of an ancestor, and prevent Whistler (Michael Stefani) and his evil Trancers from killing the ancestors of Earth's ruling council. He also falls in love with Leena (Helen Hunt).

The witty script, by Danny Bilson and Paul DeMeo, benefits from tight, if opportunistic, plotting. Exposition is delivered with bravura economy, and self-conscious humour affectionately mocks genre expectations (a cop wearing a noirish mac in 1985 Los Angeles and a threat from Whistler found in a fortune cookie). The movie, which unusually provides diegetic sources for its predominantly red and blue lighting, retains the vigorous look of a good comic book, although the costumes and special effects have aged badly. A model of low-budget science fiction inventiveness, it exemplifies the best of Band's output, as both director and producer. Many of his shortcomings – lackadaisical plotting, humourless dialogue, unimaginative visuals – are on display in *Trancers II* (1991), which demonstrates a strong grasp of the possibilities of time-travel narratives but fails to deliver.

Band sold Empire to producer Irwin Yablans after the collapse of the lira led to financial difficulties. Band's subsequent company, Full Moon International, has grown to significant proportions. The names of its subdivisions – including Action Xtreme, Alien Arsenal, Alchemy, Cult Video, Filmonsters, Monster Island, Pulp Fantasy, Pulsepounders, Surrender Cinema – suggest the nature of its product, as do Band's own pictures. *Meridian* (1990), *Crash and Burn* (1990), *Doctor Mordrid* (1992), and *Prehysteria* (1993) feature, respectively, a family curse, some nudity, a synthoid killing machine, rival sorcerers from another dimension, and tiny dinosaurs. Band's taste for miniature monsters is further indulged in *Dollman vs. Demonic Toys* (1993) – in which Judith Grey (Tracy Scoggins) is rematched against the Demonic Toys, this time assisted by Brick Bardo (Tim Thomerson), the 13-inch tall alien cop from *Dollman* (1991) – and *The Creeps* (1997) – in which Dracula, the Werewolf, the Mummy, and Frankenstein's monster are brought to life, only three feet tall. Regaining their former stature is doomed in every sense except the physical.

Band has producer or executive producer credits on over seventy movies, with screenwriting credits on three of them and story credit on another nine. Apart from *Last Foxtrot in Burbank* (1973) and *Blooddolls* (1999), he has produced all of the movies he has directed. He is currently working on *Pulse Pounders*, a trilogy of horror shorts comprising a full-length film. **MB**

# Clive BARKER

Clive Barker is a celebrated name in the literary world, specifically in the areas of horror and the *grand fantastique*. Yet his impact on the cinematic scene has been less impressive since his commercial debut as a director in 1987. However, this may have more to do with the constraints imposed on him by both the film studios and the medium rather than any lack of enthusiasm or ability on his own part.

*Hellraiser* (1987)
*Nightbreed* (1990)
*Lord of Illusions* (1995)

Born in the UK in 1952, Barker entered the world of film indirectly via theatre and fiction. Film was perhaps a natural progression for him, as yet another way of communicating his far-reaching ideas. His little-seen avant-garde shorts *Salomé* (1973) and *The Forbidden* (1978) reveal many of Barker's preoccupations – such as sexuality, violence and religion – as well as reflecting his love of puzzles (which would resurface in his maiden feature). The black and white images occasionally recall the expressionist films of Lang and Wiene – by way of Jean Cocteau's experimental work – but are nevertheless pure Barker, unencumbered by the restrictions of classical storytelling.

Much later the scripts he wrote for *Underworld* (aka *Transmutations*) (1985) and *Rawhead Rex* (1986), a short story from his challenging 'Books of Blood', were ravaged by director George Pavlou, and this motivated Barker to make the next adaptation himself. *Hellraiser* (1987) is the consequence, based on his own novella 'The Hellbound Heart'. Remarkably, Barker's first film is also his most accomplished. It is one of the finest horror films of all time, belying its apparent sado-masochistic and video-nasty trappings. Its story is a variation on the Faustian pact, but the movie also contains direct and indirect references to such diverse sources as ancient Greek legends (specifically Pandora's box), Frankenstein, Hamlet and Snow White. A dissection of the nuclear family from the 1980s with incestuous overtones, *Hellraiser* is very visceral in its content ('Chekhov with gore' was how one reviewer described it). However, all the skinless bodies and blood never detract from the truly dark atmosphere, which is supplemented whenever the sadistic Cenobite demons are present. It is to Barker's credit that these are his most memorable characters despite the fact that they are only allowed minimal screen time – the leader 'Pinhead' is now a pop horror icon alongside Jason and Freddy. *Hellraiser*'s ascendancy ensured that sequels would follow, which gradually American-ised the mythos. Barker was involved in these in a purely advisory capacity.

*Nightbreed* (1990), again from one of his books – 'Cabal' – is a creditable endea-vour, examining the condition of celluloid monsters from an original perspective. Like *Alien Nation* (1988) before it, this film confronts racism and bigotry by substituting the exotic – in this instance the undead – for the real victims of prejudice (it is surely no coin-cidence that the Nightbreed are located in redneck territory). There is no question as to who the real monsters are, but the heavy-handed battle near the end overstresses this doctrine. In addition, the fragmented narrative and weak performances (particularly from erstwhile director David Cronenberg and lead actor Craig Sheffer), combined with studio interference, bridle Barker's good intentions. Following this catastrophe he emigrated to California seeking greater control over his work.

Barker executive produced, rather than directed, his other most successful film, *Candyman* (1992), based on his short story about a hook-handed killer who appears when you look in a mirror and say his name five times. The film raises salient questions about the nature of urban folklore: if enough people believe in something, does that make it real? But by shifting the setting from Liverpool to Chicago, director Bernard Rose also embraces issues of culture and class, the latter most notably through the institu-tions of academia. Tony Todd gives a strong performance as Barker's tragic villain and Virginia Madsen is perfect as his reincarnated love. Some mention should also be made of Philip Glass' superlative score.

With *Lord of Illusions* (1995), Barker returned to the director's chair. A gratifying, if somewhat laboured, chiller, this attempts to marry the noir and horror genres with little success. 'Quantum Leap' star Scott Bakula is Barker's archetypal detective hero Harry D'Amour, and Bond vixen Famke Janssen is his love interest, exploring the origins of real magic against a backdrop of depthless stage shows. But not even the pre-release altera-tions, made after test screenings, could weed out the blemishes.

In recent years, Barker has concentrated mostly on the written word in books like 'Everville', 'Sacrament' and 'Galilee'. He has written the story for a successful computer game, 'Undying', produced a horror film based on his own comic book series, and assisted with the writing of another *Hellraiser* sequel, *Hellraiser VI: Hellseeker*, which has yet to be released. Another of his stories, 'Tortured Souls', is also slated for adaptation.   **PB**

# Matthew BARNEY

*Cremaster 4* (1994)
*Cremaster 1* (1995–96)
*Cremaster 5* (1997)
*Cremaster 2* (1999)
*Cremaster 3* (2002)

Born in New York in 1967, Matthew Barney studied medicine before moving into art, which may explain some of the iconography behind his work on film. Obsessed with the body as architecture, physical locality, and transgressive or non-existent sexual states, Barney's *Cremaster* series treads a fine line between film, sculpture and art installation.

The *Cremaster* series have not been made in sequence and disregard narrative form in favour of baroque, visual excess and visual contradiction. Named after the muscle that retracts the testicles due to cold or fear, the films are concerned with sexual differentiation, imprisonment and escape, physical transformation and the formulation of identity. Barney, however, only alludes to these themes in his films, producing work that is difficult to read or place within the greater art and film world.

*Cremaster 4* (1994) has Barney dressed as a red-haired satyr and contains sequences of underwater tap-dancing off the coast of the Isle Of Man. *Cremaster 1* (1995–96) parodies a Busby Berkley dance routine. *Cremaster 5* (1997) stars Ursula Andress and contains allusions to Harry Houdini, Hungarian Opera, and water nymphs. *Cremaster 2* (1999) is based on Norman Mailer's novel 'The Executioner's Song', and explores the link between mass-murderer Gary Gilmore and Houdini, to whom he was related.

For Barney, each film explores a different physical arena but is concerned with sexual transfiguration and the ironic status of the male in today's society. In many of his pieces, the male body is disguised (*Cremaster 5*), transformed (*Cremaster 1*), or destroyed (*Cremaster 2*). Sexual identity in his films is confused and inverted – in *Cremaster 5*, male water nymphs are played by female body builders, and Barney's genitals are disguised by prosthetics.

Barney rarely gets involved in discussions about his work, adding to its mysterious appeal. His complex system of codes and references can only be guessed at and the work exists both as dense, beautiful landscape and complex intellectual and cultural comment.

The final installment, *Cremaster 3*, was completed in early 2002; the work as a whole will be exhibited at various venues, including the Guggenheim Museum in New York. **BW**

# Paul BARTEL

Paul Bartel's work as a director straddles a fine line between witty social satire and bawdy farce. His thematic interests consist almost entirely of the stuff of exploitation cinema: sex and violence. Yet he has consistently attempted to rebel against such a label by developing a style more attuned to the literary than the lurid iconography of exploitation. As a former playwright, his films use clever wordplay rather than elaborate camera style, cluttered *mise-en-scène*, or complicated montage. His best work – *Death Race 2000* (1975) and *Eating Raoul* (1982) – combine black comedy with a keen eye for cultural critique in a way that implicates the viewer, yet also allows audiences to laugh at themselves and the absurdities of their predicaments. *Death Race 2000* centres on a post-apocalyptic road race whose object is not so much reaching the finish line as it is the mutilation of as much humanity as possible along the way. The film basks in its own violence and gore yet still manages to be a biting indictment of the growing importance of media spectacle to an increasingly jaundiced viewing public. *Eating Raoul*, while not as explicit or fantastic as *Death Race 2000*, uses a humorous take on the subject of cannibalism as a way of addressing a number of social issues; from our fascination with sex and food, to illegal immigration, racism, and conservative morality.

Born in Brooklyn in 1938, Bartel began working in movies at an early age as an assistant animator for UPA (United Production of America). Later, he studied film at UCLA, worked as an animator on student projects and began writing plays. After graduating, he won a prestigious Fullbright scholarship, which he used to continue his education in animation at Rome's Centro Sperimental di Cinematografica. He got his first jobs making military films until he caught the eye of exploitation mogul Roger Corman. Corman produced Bartel's first short film project as a director, *The Secret Cinema* (aka *Paul Bartel's The Secret Cinema* (1969)). Combining the style of *cinéma vérité* with exploitation film's lurid subject matter, *The Secret Cinema* tells the story of a young secretary whose daily life begins to fall apart for no apparent reason. She slowly begins to realise that she is the subject of a documentary film whose director is encouraging her bad luck in order to make a more compelling movie. His first feature-length project, *Private Parts* (1972), was a well-received but financially unsuccessful black comedy about a young runaway who finds shelter at a hotel populated by murderers, oddballs and perverts.

Bartel's next project was the cult favourite *Death Race 2000*. A low-budget re-telling of the 1975 film *Rollerball*, *Death Race 2000* is a much more effective send-up of public obsessions with sport and violence. Bartel followed his success with another low-budget, cross-country race flick for Corman, the forgettable *Cannonball* (1976).

Bartel spent the next six years subsidising his writing through a number of acting roles and attempting to find funding for various film projects. He earned good reviews for 1982's *Eating Raoul*. The film tells the story of the Blands, a moralistic married couple disgusted by the sexual perversions of modern society. Taking matters into their own hands, Mary Bland masquerades as a prostitute while husband Paul kills the prospective johns and sells their bodies to the local dog-food plant. When their Hispanic delivery boy, Rauol, catches on, the couple hatch a plan to kill, cook, and eat him.

*Not for Publication* (1984) was a modernisation of the classic screwball comedies of the 1930s and 1940s, but updated with Bartel's unique stylisations. The film featured an assortment of strange sexual practices and human oddities, telling the story of a tabloid reporter who works her way into the good graces of a sleazy mayor and uncovers political corruption.

*Lust in the Dust* (1985) found Bartel mocking the western genre with the story of Rosie Velez, played by Divine, the king (queen?) of drag performers, in search of lost treasure in the town of Chili Verde. The plot hinges on the discovery of a map to the treasure which is tattooed on the rear-ends of Rosie and her nemesis, Marguerita. The set-up makes for a great deal of scatological humour which offended as many viewers as it pleased. The film's intentionally campy reworking of films like *Duel in the Sun* (1946) again divided audiences who either embraced or loathed the raunchy humour and B-movie aesthetic, with little consensus falling somewhere in between.

Over the next ten years, Bartel would only manage to make three films: *The Longshot* (1986), *Scenes from the Class Struggle in Beverly Hills* (1989), and *Shelf Life* (1993), all of which served as continuations of his attack on mainstream America and the hypocrisy and absurdity of everyday life. Of the three, *Scenes From the Class Struggle in Beverly Hills* was the most critically and commercially successful, due to the presence of Jacqueline Bisset as an ageing sit-com queen whose servants and relatives manage to sabotage her chance at reviving her dormant career. The film's strengths lie in its conflation of the American dream with the sexual goals and perversions of its characters: the plot hinges on the male servants bet concerning which one of them will be able to bed the other's boss. However, the frequently acute observations somehow manage to get lost in the film's slow pace and stagy direction.

Perhaps best known as a recognisable character actor who has appeared in nearly seventy films, Bartel has nevertheless managed to carve out a very unique and individualised niche as a director. His combination of satire and sex, humour and horror, violence and comedy attests to his desire to take cinematic forms to different places and to tweak the expectations of audiences well-conditioned by mainstream Hollywood cinema. While the results have been mixed at best, Bartel's work nevertheless situates the director as a maverick personality unafraid of risk amongst an industry driven through its attempts to appeal to as many as possible. Paul Bartel died in May 2000.    **MR**

# Michael BAY

*Bad Boys* (1995)
*The Rock* (1996)
*Armageddon* (1998)
*Pearl Harbour* (2001)

Born in 1965 in Los Angeles, Michael Bay's aesthetic credo might be 'bigger, better, faster, with more filters'. For all his undoubted visual acuity and ability to orchestrate broad action, his films frequently lack emotional and narrative complexity, and his pedigree is that of Tony Scott rather than James Cameron (the director that one feels Bay would like to emulate). Like Scott, Bay has repeatedly worked with action producer Jerry Bruckheimer.

Akin to the incremental progression of a series of action set pieces, Bay's four films to date have trumped each other in expense and grandiosity, but seem to be losing the sense of fun that redeems debut feature *Bad Boys* (1995). Coming to this vehicle for black comic stars Will Smith and Martin Lawrence from a background in adverts and music videos, Bay instils proceedings with the required gloss and concentrates on making Smith (in particular) look good for the camera. Lovingly photographed against reddening LA skies using Bay's soon-to-be-trademark 360° circling shot, Smith emerges as a star. Lawrence is the comedy foil, and the banter between the two is amusing. On the downside, Bay seems unable to make Tea Leoni's supporting role count, or indeed register femininity at all except in terms of an endless parade of scantily-clad neighbours, victimised escorts and half-dressed gangster's molls. The story discreetly sexualises the close bond between Smith and Lawrence: they are forced to swap lifestyles to keep Leoni's witness in the dark about their identities, with lothario figure Smith threatening to disrupt Lawrence's perfect family life. Lawrence's macho insecurities and Smith's loneliness are played for laughs, while simultaneously underscoring Smith's heterosexual appeal.

Bay's next protagonist, Stanley Goodspeed (Nicolas Cage), in the film *The Rock* (1996), develops a more ambiguous model of masculinity; an early scene depicts the Beatles-loving biochemical expert sitting naked playing guitar, while his girlfriend returns home from work and announces their pregnancy. Cage is the perfect contemporary star to render a looser sense of masculinity, and the movie cleverly defines Cage's 'new man' persona against the ex-SAS mercenary played by Sean Connery, a star who embodies a more traditional model of the action hero. Connery is on good form, and *The Rock* is an enjoyable and muscular action film, with darker tones emerging through a (rather underwritten) role for Ed Harris as a disenchanted Gulf War commander who holds the government to ransom.

The impressive returns achieved by Bay's first two films led to Disney's greenlight for the largest initial budget ever approved by a studio ($140 million). The resultant action epic, *Armageddon* (1998), revisits the familiar terrain of masculine relationships tried in adversity. Recalling the star dynamic of *The Rock*, Bruce Willis' experienced driller Harry Stamper has a junior partner (Ben Affleck) of whom he disapproves but must learn to trust for the sake of their mission (to destroy a meteorite headed for Earth). The film also retains other elements of its predecessor such as an awkward and inexpressive father-daughter relationship that suddenly blossoms (Bruce Willis and Liv Tyler supplanting Connery and Claire Forlani). *Armageddon* deliberately foregrounds the mixing of gender-identified genres; the schizophrenic switch of focus between the Affleck/Tyler romance plot and the impending disaster (rendered in glorious CGI) destabilises the film's macho posturings, and judging by promotional materials, was clearly conceived to echo the cross-gender appeal of Cameron's cash cow *Titanic* (1997). In the end, the story of Affleck and reluctant father figure Willis seems to interest Bay more, and generates authentic audience engagement.

The spectre of *Titanic* seemed to spur Bay on to his most bombastic, most lazily offensive and least ironic film yet, *Pearl Harbor* (2001). Whereas the earlier films played with macho archetypes, *Pearl Harbor* sets up a straight love triangle involving two airmen (Affleck and Josh Hartnett) and Kate Beckinsale's nurse. In hospital scenes, Bay adopts a more edgily intimate style to attempt to reflect the bewilderment of surprise attack, but the emphasis of the film is on the twin spectacles of the lovers' reunion and the CGI mounting of the attack itself. Bay can certainly effect a stylish battle, but one can't help but feel that the development of CGI technology can and should deliver more than a point-of-view shot from the perspective of a falling Japanese bomb. The conflicted perspective of the Japanese military is hinted at, but such scenes feel like concessions to political correctness rather than expressions of cultural awareness. The end result is at once utterly unsurprising and completely overwrought. *Pearl Harbor* was only a moderate success, considering cost, and Bay can do much better. He is currently in production with *Bad Boys 2*.                                                                 **MF**

# Henry BEAN

Henry Bean's directorial debut, *The Believer* (2001), develops the thematic concerns of his writing on *Internal Affairs* (1990) and *Deep Cover* (1992), primarily his exploration of character duality. The story of a Jew, Danny Balint, who becomes a member of a Neo-Nazi organisation, the film focuses on an individual who rails against the belief system he has grown up with and chooses its antithesis as a way of life; having felt constant conflict between the strict teachings of orthodox Judaism and doubts that at first left him guilt-ridden, he explodes into anger and rebellion. The film charts this decline, from flashbacks of Danny's dissension at school, through his induction into the fascist group and rise through its ranks, to his exposure as a Jew and final demise.

A challenging and unsettling film, Bean steers clear of the excessive violence and simplistic moralising of *American History X* (1998), preferring to delve instead into the roots of his character's fears and prejudices. He is aided by a remarkable performance from Ryan Gosling, who conveys the confusion and desperation of a man who is capable of beating an orthodox Jew for what they represent, yet at the same time treats the sacrosanct relics of Jewish religion with respect. Any lack of overall style is more than made up for by an intelligent and articulate narrative; unafraid to leave audiences with the task of formulating their own ideas, the ending is ambiguous.                    **IHS**

*The Believer* (2001)

# Warren BEATTY

Warren Beatty is an actor-director who only picks up the camera himself when he feels sufficiently inspired or impelled to do so. Naturally this means that the films he has made are especially personal to him, or in some way evince his own particular preoccupations. Born in 1937 in Vancouver, Beatty started out in the business as a child actor, starring with sister Shirley MacLaine in amateur theatre productions organised by their mother. Parts on television and Broadway led to a film career, with his portrayal of gangster Clyde Barrow in Arthur Penn's *Bonnie and Clyde* (1967) a pivotal moment in his acting career.

*Heaven Can Wait* (1978) was Beatty's first directorial assignment, a duty he shared with Buck Henry, as well as taking the lead role as a sportsman who dies before his

*Heaven Can Wait* (1978)
*Reds* (1981)
*Dick Tracy* (1990)
*Bulworth* (1998)

time. A retelling of *Here Comes Mr Jordan* (1941) – which itself was based on a Harry Segall play – this gentle comedy of spiritual errors is waggishly enjoyable. Exploiting perceptions of the afterlife, and the yearning for reincarnation, the film nevertheless deals with the topic in a capable, if theologically tepid, way. The love story is tempered with just the right amount of verbal and visual humour, and although he treads the fine line between farce and fantasy, Beatty always restrains the piece before it goes too far.

However, *Reds* (1981) is terribly self-indulgent. The first of Beatty's pictures to dwell on his love of politics, this is a weighty epic set in the 1915–21 period. Once again Beatty stars and directs, easing into the role of headstrong US journalist John Reed, and the film focuses on his turbulent romance with writer Louise Bryant (Diane Keaton), initially in New York, then later in Petrograd. This provides the ideal opportunity to reflect on Marxist doctrines through those they meet. Yet the continual flitting between affairs of the state and those of the heart eventually takes its toll, and although Beatty's enthusiasm for the project is apparent (ultimately earning him an Academy Award for direction), it fails to excite the audience in quite the same way – possibly because of its lengthy three-hour running time.

This is a criticism that could never be levelled at *Dick Tracy* (1990). The production designs, cinematography (by *Apocalypse Now*'s (1979) Vitorrio Storraro) and costumes alone are a feast for the eyes. Sumptuous cartoon colours – yellows, reds, blues, and greens – help bring Chester Gould's acclaimed 1930s comic strip detective to life. Also the wealth of songs (by Madonna and Mandy Patinkin) lend the production a certain Hollywood musical glamour. A shame, then, that the story lets the film down, with Tracy (Beatty) stumbling from one stylised gun battle to the next, facing prosthetic rogues like Big Boy Caprice (an unrecognisable Al Pacino) and Dustin Hoffman's Mumbles. The flat characterisations do little to endear those involved to the viewer.

In *Bulworth* (1998), Beatty turned the lens on politics again, but tarried much closer to home this time. The pitch of the film (and its contemporaries – *Wag the Dog* (1997), *Primary Colours* (1998)) epitomises political problems in the US over recent years. *Bulworth* presents us with a statesman who must move with the times to avoid professional oblivion, frankly speaking his mind about every subject. As a satire on modern civic affairs, the movie does sterling work, although the sight of Bulworth (Beatty) rapping down in South Central to reinvent himself is embarrassing in the extreme. **PB**

# JEAN BEAUDIN

Born in 1939, after studying at the Zurich School for design, Jean Beaudin joined the animation unit of the National Film Board of Canada (NFB) in 1964 and soon started directing films of a pedagogical nature. He made his first short fiction piece, *Vertige*, in 1969, which was followed by two mediocre commercial features, *Stop* (1971) and *Le diable est parmi nous* (1972). Beaudin eventually came into his own as a film-maker in the mid-1970s with *J.A. Martin Photographer/J.A. Martin photographe* (1976). Set at the beginning of the twentieth century, the film follows a photographer and his wife as they tour villages in rural Québec. Slow-paced, beautifully photographed by Pierre Mignot (a regular collaborator of Robert Altman's), and focusing on the relationship between the two main characters and their difference to the people they encounter on their journey, *J.A. Martin photographe* comprises the elements of style and narrative that recur through most of Beaudin's oeuvre. Many of his films encompass the narrative of a complicated but loving relationship set against, and contrasted with, an environment that is styled to highlight the difference between the central characters and their surroundings. Sometimes appearing as a mere decorative backdrop as in *Le Matou* (1985), or as a slick visual mosaic as in *Being at Home with Claude* (1992), this environment is always at odds with the couple at the films' core.

This structure is evident in the first of his many literary adaptations, *Cordélia* (1979), which is based on Pauline Cadieux's novel *Une lampe à la fenêtre*, about a lively, free-spirited woman and her lover who are stigmatised and wrongfully accused of murdering her husband by members of the conservative nineteenth-century culture, whose codes of behaviour the lovers disregarded. Similarly, in Beaudin's most recent film *The Collector/Le Collectioneur* (2002), this time based on Chrystine Brouillet's novel of the same name, the tender relationship between a female police officer and two troubled teenage boys is set against her investigation of a series of brutal murders. In *Mario* (1984), an adaptation of Claude Jasmin's novel, the imaginary world of an autistic child and his teenage brother contrasts with the realism of the island where they live (Îles-de-la-Madeleine). In *Memories Unlocked/Souvenirs Intimes* (1998), which is based on a book by Monique Proulx entitled *L'Homme invisible à la fenêtre*, the affection between a compassionate paraplegic painter and his close circle of friends clashes with the extreme violence of his past, as revealed through a web of flashbacks, when a woman he raped returns to confront him.

It is in *Being at Home with Claude*, however, that the dialectic between a loving relationship and the horrific world in which it exists is most strikingly articulated. Adapted from René-Daniel Dubois' play and probably Beaudin's best film since *J.A. Martin photographe*, it is the story of a male prostitute who has killed his lover and surrendered to the police but refuses to divulge his motive. The film opens with a startling nine-minute preface shot in black and white, in which fast-edited images and a feverishly mobile camera trace the events that precede the play proper. From the very first shot the film-maker establishes a clear dichotomy. There are two opposite yet complementary realities: the city riotously vibrating under the intoxicating sounds and sights of a jazz festival, and the intimate intercourse of two men, the prostitute, Yves (Roy Dupuis), and his lover, Claude (Jean-François Pichette). As the two lovers reach orgasm, Yves grabs a knife and slashes Claude's throat. Claude's blood gushing on the walls, furniture and appliances, are the first colour images in the film. The drama proper focuses on the police interrogation as an Inspector (Jacques Godin) seeks to understand why Yves killed his lover.

Through this initial arrangement of sounds and images, Beaudin manages to summarise the main contention at the core of the subsequent dramatic discourse, a dialectical opposition between a threatening open space peopled with brutal or, at best, indifferent, individuals and a closed, comfortable realm where lovers can enjoy intimacy. It is only at the end of the film that the prologue is explained, when Yves finally reveals the impetus behind the slaying of Claude. He slit his throat to preserve the instant of pure ecstasy from the corruption of the outside world; it is doubtlessly the most vivid illustration of the film-maker's preoccupation with the clash between intimacy and the world 'out there'.

Beaudin has also directed an extremely popular television series, *Emily/Les Filles de Caleb* (1990–91), based on Arlette Cousture's novel) about a teacher in rural Québec. **AL**

# Harold BECKER

New Yorker Harold Becker's strength, as the director of a number of dependable mainstream thrillers, has been in his precise and seemingly authentic depiction of various public bodies. Whilst there is nothing original in the premise that his protagonists will scrap with the institutions which they come across or belong to, Becker's films generally take a deal of care setting up the particular rules of engagement which each body imposes, whether it be the police (*The Onion Field* (1979), *Sea of Love* (1989)), the mayor's office (*City Hall* (1996)) or the medical establishment (*Malice* (1993)). His attention to detail with regard to the more mechanical components of his narratives, such as plausible plotting, has been less scrupulous, and he has yet to convince in his depiction of the private circumstances endured by his troubled male protagonists.

Considering his subsequent involvement in the quintessentially Hollywood genres of the tough cop drama and the conspiracy thriller, Becker's first film, *The Ragman's Daughter* (1972), was an anomaly. Indeed, nothing in his career to that point, as an art school graduate, a photographer, a designer, and commercials director, suggested he was an appropriate choice to direct British playwright Alan Sillitoe's kitchen sink drama. Becker struggled with both time – eschewing period detail in the film's many flashback sequences – and place – representing Nottingham through a series of clichéd signifiers of either working-class life or, in the flashback scenes, wistfully remembered romance. By placing its analysis of various social relationships and institutional pressures within the unfolding of a love story, the film laid bare an expressive awkwardness in Becker's portrayal of romantic situations that has been evident throughout his career.

Becker has shown himself to be far more comfortable with material that observed men amongst men, as evidenced in his first Hollywood feature, *The Onion Field*, an

*The Ragman's Daughter* (1972)
*The Onion Field* (1979)
*The Black Marble* (1980)
*Taps* (1981)
*Crazy for You* (1985)
*The Boost* (1988)
*Sea of Love* (1989)
*Malice* (1993)
*City Hall* (1996)
*Mercury Rising* (1998)
*Domestic Disturbance* (2001)

authentic dramatisation of a real-life cop-killing case, penned by Joseph Wambaugh. Becker provided a suitably low-key directorial presence in bringing the script to the screen, after Wambaugh insisted that there should be no repeat of the cinematic liberties taken with his source material by Robert Aldrich in *The Choirboys* (1977). As such, there was a novelistic attention to detail in the initial characterisations of the small-time psychotic (James Woods), his easily manipulated partner (Franklyn Seales), and the cops they kidnap (Ted Danson and Jon Savage). There was also a meticulous, if occasionally openly parodic, reconstruction of the labyrinthine courtroom procedures that followed the shooting of one of the cops, as the accused pursues every avenue available to him to escape punishment. Whilst some of Becker's thrillers have stalled due to an unnecessary commitment to genre procedures, *The Onion Field* benefited by taking the swamping of its characters' lives in legal procedure as a central theme.

After another collaboration with Joseph Wambaugh on the more light-hearted *The Black Marble* (1980) – a hybrid of the screwball comedy and police buddy movie – Becker's next film turned its attention to a different law-enforcing institution: the US military. *Taps* (1981) detailed a siege situation in a cadet training academy and obviated the need for an explanation of the protagonists' domestic circumstances, thus eschewing the type of narrative detours that had proved, and would continue to prove, unconvincing in Becker's work as a whole. This repression of the outside world did focus attention onto the struggle between the old-school military values represented in the training school and the faceless functionaries of modern combat sent in to repress their revolt. However, it did little to suggest where the film's sympathies lie in respect to the adversaries' opposing ideologies, fetishising the military hardware used by both sides in a manner consistent with the macho Reaganite entertainments in vogue at the time.

*Crazy for You* (1985), a teen movie set in the world of high-school wrestling, provided a less hyperbolic variation on the theme of young men developing their own code of honour as they battle against institutional pressures. *The Boost* (1988) worked as a melodramatic companion piece to *Taps* in its mapping out of the monetary, rather than militaristic, values associated with America in the 1980s. As a down-on-his-luck advertising executive, James Woods performed at the hysterical pitch evident in his portrayal of the cop killer in *The Onion Field*. Viewing his breakdown through the prism of the personal (in his deteriorating relationship with his wife (Sean Young)), rather than the professional, the film exposed Becker's perennial inability to find a convincing dramatic mode with which to depict intimate relationships.

There was a more satisfying integration of the professional and the personal in *Sea of Love*, Becker's biggest commercial success. Indeed, the film took as its theme the compromising of public duty with private obsession, as a troubled detective (Al Pacino) embarks upon a stormy romance with the prime suspect (Ellen Barkin) to a murder case he is working on. Whilst the twists and turns of the investigation were sometimes clumsily sign-posted, Pacino was highly convincing essaying his character's mood swings between the paranoid and predatory. There was also a satisfying deferral of violent action until the dénouement, which both complemented and allowed room for the simmering tension and unresolved suspicions evident in the central relationship.

*Malice* featured some astute observations on the deep-rooted power relations existing between two old school friends (Bill Pullman and Alec Baldwin) when they resume contact years later. As usual Becker's attention to institutional detail was telling in his depiction of the two work environments to which the male leads belonged (one a university lecturer, the other a renowned surgeon). However, the film failed to follow up on its more intriguing premises, focusing instead on a wholly unconvincing, needlessly complicated, conspiracy plot, masterminded by Nicole Kidman's cartoonish femme fatale.

*City Hall*'s chief failing, by contrast, consisted of a lack of complexity in its conspiracy narrative. The initial set-up – the accidental killing of a young black child on the streets of New York in a shoot-out between a drug dealer and an apparently corrupt cop – promised more than the perfunctory revelation of a chain of responsibility that led, inevitably, all the way up to the mayor (Al Pacino). The route by which political corruption was exposed – an unlikely collaboration between the mayor's young, idealistic assistant (John Cusack) and a lawyer (Bridget Fonda) out to expose the cover-up in his offices – was drawn with an equally sketchy hand. However, there were impressive setpieces that matched the film's evident heavyweight ambitions, chiefly Pacino's cynically manipulative oration to the mourners at the young child's funeral.

The espionage thriller *Mercury Rising* (1998) gave Bruce Willis the chance to audition for his role in *The Sixth Sense* (1999), as he struck up another on-screen friendship with an unusually gifted child, this time equipped with the ability to crack the most complex government codes. Willis' character, a haunted ex-secret service agent, also added to Becker's gallery of tortured but sentimental macho male leads. Unfortunately, the director's predilection for unlikely plotting provided the narrative with a less welcome authorial signature whilst, unusually, there was little compensation to be had in his detailing of the film's chosen milieu: the peculiarly under-staffed sub-section of the CIA attempting to silence Willis' charge, lacking the sense of authenticity Becker has brought to his depiction of more commonplace working environments.

Becker's most recent film, *Domestic Disturbance* (2001), stars John Travolta in the role of Frank Morrison, who discovers that the new husband of his ex-wife is involved in a murder.                                                                                    **IG**

# Richard BENJAMIN

If there ever was a director who could be considered an heir to the throne of the studio era's workhorse director, Richard Benjamin might just fit the bill. Born in New York in 1938, he began his career in the early 1960s as a struggling stage actor, finally achieving a considerable measure of fame on Broadway, and later in Hollywood. Benjamin became an important featured actor in a number of films, including *Goodbye, Columbus* (1969), *Catch-22* (1970), *Westworld* (1973), *The Sunshine Boys* (1975), and *Love at First Bite* (1979), before earning the chance to direct his first feature film in 1982.

*My Favorite Year* was a critical success, even though the box office did not exactly suggest a new superstar behind the camera. Inspired by behind-the-scenes stories of early live television, quite possibly those of Mel Brooks, whose company produced the film, *My Favorite Year* is a madcap nostalgia trip that is powered by an Academy Award-nominated performance by Peter O'Toole. Benjamin's rookie effort suggests a film-maker with a strong sense of sentiment, a conventional eye and a talent for working within genre parameters. From the Preston Sturges-like comedy of *My Favorite Year,* Benjamin embarked upon *City Heat* (1984). Starring two of the biggest box-office draws of the late 1970s and early 1980s, Burt Reynolds and Clint Eastwood, it came on the heels of the creation of a new genre, the buddy action picture, as exemplified by Walter Hill's *48 Hrs.* (1982). Set in 1930s Kansas City, the story revolved around the relationship between Reynolds and Eastwood. The film's period setting brings a definitive nostalgic appeal that contrasts unfavourably with the chaotic, slapstick tone that Benjamin injects into it, a tone that is reminiscent of Eastwood's *Every Which Way But Loose* (1978). The film suffers from a lack of tonal consistency, oscillating between broad comedy and violent action and Benjamin relies too much on the rapport between the two lead superstars, which did not translate that well onto the screen. *City Heat* turned out to be a critical and box office disappointment, particularly given the power that both lead stars wielded at the box office.

Benjamin rebounded with his next film, a coming of age tale called *Racing With the Moon* (1984). Starring a new generation of actors – Sean Penn, Nicholas Cage, Elizabeth McGovern – Benjamin's choice of material made commercial sense, given the popularity of the genre and the success of *Breaking Away* (1979), *Diner* (1982), *The Outsiders* (1983), and John Hughes' *Sixteen Candles* (1984) and *The Breakfast Club* (1985). Benjamin's handling of the material is deft, sensitive and confident enough to have not relied on overwrought nostalgia in place of real emotion. His direction of the appealing lead actors and the evocative period detail won kudos from virtually all critics, even though he received a few demerits for a slow pace.

After a two-year hiatus, Benjamin was unable to capitalise on the success of *Racing With the Moon*. Indeed, he instead chose to stay with conventional genre films that featured top-name stars. *The Money Pit* (1986) is a suburban nightmare satire that is hybrid of a 'Three Stooges' short and *Mr. Blandings Builds His Dream House* (1948), starring Tom Hanks and Shelley Long. Unfortunately, the comedy suffered too much Stooges-type comedy and not enough witty insight into the suburban existence that is evident in *Mr. Blandings*. Benjamin followed *The Money Pit* misfire with an indisputable mistake, an attempt at broad comedy called *My Stepmother Is an Alien* (1988). Suffering from a miscasting of Kim Basinger with Dan Aykroyd, the film never escapes the impression that it is nothing more than a one joke movie that relies too heavily on special effects and sophomoric humour.

Benjamin wisely followed up with a change of pace and *Little Nikita* (1988), an intriguing Cold War spy thriller that posits River Phoenix as the son of parents who are actually 'sleeper' agents for the USSR, and Sidney Poitier as an FBI agent out to intercept them. Despite the fact that Poitier had returned to the screen after semi-retirement from acting for *Little Nikita* and *Shoot to Kill* (1988), his performance seems to be the only spark of interest in the film. In 1989 he returned to comedy with *Downtown* (1990), a sly, urban and more successful 'buddy' movie starring Anthony Green and Forrest Whitaker.

Benjamin's next four films characterise the same genres and themes that he returns to again and again. *Mermaids* (1990) is a coming of age tale told from the perspective of a teenage Winona Ryder growing up with a free-spirited mother (Cher). *Made in America* (1993) makes a fair attempt at racial humour with the semi-romantic matching of Ted Danson and Whoopi Goldberg. *Milk Money* (1994) is a sweet natured comedy about a single father (Ed Harris) whose children try to match him up with a kind-hearted prostitute (Melanie Griffith). *Mrs Winterbourne* (1996) is a prince and the pauper story of poor, single mother Rickie Lake assuming the identity a dead woman whom she meets just before the woman is killed in a train wreck. All four of these comedies are rather bland and, with the exception of *Made in America*, not even approaching the unconventional. Despite his lack of refined comedic pace and the failure to rise above the ordinary, Benjamin's direction of actors is solid.

Taking a break from directing feature films to concentrate on acting, he appeared in Woody Allen's *Deconstructing Harry* (1998). Aside from directing television movies – *Tourist Trap* (1998), *The Pentagon Wars* (1998), *Laughter on the 23rd Floor* (2000), and *The Sports Page* (2001), he helmed the straight-to-video *The Shrink is In* (2000), starring the off-screen couple Davd Arquette and Courteney Cox. He is currently in production with *Marcia X*, a comedy starring Lisa Kudrow, who plays a young Jewish woman who suddenly finds herself in charge of a hardcore rap label.          **SM**

# Anna BENSON GYLES

*Swann* (1996)   Anna Benson Gyles began her career as an editor for the BBC before producing and directing a variety of biographical films on literary/cultural figures as varied as Virginia Woolf, Ernest Hemingway, John Malkovich and Vincent Van Gogh. This interest in artistic figures reveals itself in *Swann* (1996), her sole feature film to date. Concerned with the wider meanings generated by artists from the past, the film shows how the poetry of Mary Swann (axed to death by her farmer husband) effects the lives of Rose (Brenda Fricker), the guardian of Mary's work and Sarah (Miranda Richardson), a feminist writer intent on writing a book on the poet. The pain of Mary's life, revealed in snatches of her verse, is contrasted to the various motivations of those who have posthumously championed her work. Furthermore, the precious scraps of paper on which the poetry is preserved (although this in itself takes on great significance) reveal a life of domestic oppression, a detail ironically contrasted to the revelation of the profits to be made from the recycling of forgotten literature. The truth about the surviving scraps of work measures the value of art as antiquated museum display or genuine emotional experience. Strikingly photographed in Ontario, the film unfolds at a measured pace, balancing the layers of experience and realisation inspired by a gifted but downtrodden woman.          **NJ**

# Robert BENTON

*Bad Company* (1972)
*The Late Show* (1977)
*Kramer vs Kramer* (1979)
*Still of the Night* (1982)
*Places in the Heart* (1984)
*Nadine* (1987)
*Billy Bathgate* (1991)
*Nobody's Fool* (1994)

Robert Benton, born in Texas in 1932, has not enjoyed as high a profile as some of the film-makers who rose so quickly through the ranks with him in the late 1960s, but he has achieved a career longevity that has eluded many of his peers. He was aligned with the French New Wave from the beginning, when both Truffaut and Godard buzzed around his and David Newman's script for *Bonnie and Clyde* (1967) (before Arthur Penn eventually took up the directorial reins). A commitment to New Wave mentor André Bazin's advocacy of a pose of watching and listening, rather than overtly judging, on the part of the director, has been evident in Benton's subsequent work. This commitment to self-effacing observation has been combined, occasionally uncomfortably, with a *Twilight* (1998) willingness to populate his films with Hollywood's biggest stars, and to operate within classic generic scenarios, such as film noir and family melodrama.

*Bad Company* (1972), Benton's first film as writer/director, revisited the central theme of Bonnie and Clyde, re-contextualising its young heroes' attempts to create themselves as myths within the Old West rather than Depression America. The film's wry commentary on the tension between the protagonists' youthful idealism and their more pragmatic struggle to survive was exemplified by the ironic deployment of a piously moral voiceover culled from the journals of the Methodist-turned-outlaw lead (Barry Brown).

There was a shift of focus to a different generation for his next directorial effort, *The Late Show* (1977), which anticipated *Twilight* (1998) in its study of a private eye (Art Carney) coming to terms with both a classically contrived noirish conspiracy and his failing professional abilities. The film also marked a closer collaboration with his actors, inspired by discussions with producer Robert Altman.

*Kramer vs Kramer* (1979) consolidated Benton's attachment to the French New Wave, with the addition of Truffaut's cinematographer Nestor Almendros to his film-making team. Almendros' most significant contribution was his extensive use of the *plan séquence*, a method of filming a scene without resorting to cuts, which integrated, rather than foregrounded, the actor's performance within its realistically rendered setting. Whilst this might seem to attribute a neutrality to the camera's judgment over a highly emotive scenario – the struggle between two divorcees for the custody of their son – the script undoubtedly favoured the claims of the father (Dustin Hoffman) over the mother (Meryl Streep). The chamber music that accompanied scene changes enhanced the sense of the morality play over the pseudo-documentary, while the film could not resist climaxing with grandstanding courtroom testimonies from both stars, revealing its tendency towards melodrama rather than realism. Nevertheless, there was much fruitful interplay between the two modes, with the tension between moments of emotional outburst and low-key stillness reflecting the father's search for an even pitch at which to pace his life.

The film noir, *Still of the Night* (1982), like *The Late Show* before it and *Billy Bathgate* (1991) after, was too in thrall to genre conventions to breathe properly, and was not helped by a blank, rather than alluringly enigmatic, performance from Meryl Streep as the femme fatale. Its origins as a mooted remake of Hitchcock's silent classic *The Lodger* (1926) demonstrated the cinephilia that provided another link to the sensibility of the French New Wave, even in his more impersonal projects (a proposed collaboration with Truffaut on a remake of *Mildred Pierce* (1945) never came to fruition).

The Depression-set agrarian drama *Places in the Heart* (1984) was a more intimate enterprise. Set in his home state of Texas, it plunders his own family's history and, like *Kramer vs Kramer*, courting accusations of sentimentality in its melodramatic stacking of the odds against an indomitable hero (played by Sally Field, who, like Hoffman before her, exploited the opportunity for a crowd-pleasing turn to Academy Award-winning effect). Benton moved forward twenty years but stayed in Texas for his next film, *Nadine* (1987), which offered a return to the caper comedy of *The Late Show*, but gained emotional gravitas from the nervous groping towards marital reconciliation of its central partnership. The re-use of Jeff Bridges, co-star of *Bad Company*, signalled actors' willingness to re-submit themselves to Benton's direction, as was proved when Dustin Hoffman, Bruce Willis, and Paul Newman all extended their work with Benton over various projects.

*Billy Bathgate* saw Benton directing someone else's script for the first time, with disappointing results. By Benton's own admission, Tom Stoppard's adaptation of E. L. Doctorow's novel never got to grips with the task of translating the book's first-person narration into cinematic terms. The legacy of Coppola's *The Godfather* (1972) also cast a shadow over Benton's gangster pic, which wavered uneasily between genre revisionism and more straightforward homage, an uncertainty of tone that had also manifested itself in *The Late Show*. This uneasiness of style invaded both Almendros' uncharacteristically theatrical cinematography and Dustin Hoffman's mannered performance as mob leader Dutch Schultz.

Benton's most assured work to date came with *Nobody's Fool* (1994), a 'snow movie' that charted a crabby construction worker's long overdue acceptance of his familial responsibilities, just as he reaches pensionable age. The script's expert sense of place was enhanced by Paul Newman's finely-judged portrayal of the stubborn loner Sully, for whom the small-town community in which he lives represents a wintry husk which both shelters and entraps him. The integration of setting and theme extended to the film's deliberate pacing, which ensured that the reconciliation between Sully and his son was as much of a struggle as the father's daily trudge, inhibited by a crippled knee, through the town's snow-bound streets.

*Twilight* (1998), reuniting Benton with Newman, opened with the image of a young, naked woman that had originally been envisaged (in the shape of Faye Dunaway) in the original script for *Bonnie and Clyde* (Arthur Penn eventually opted for the iconic close-up of Dunaway's lips instead). However, as in *Nobody's Fool*, the film's focus was on the more weathered and lined features of its older protagonists (with Newman supported by Gene Hackman, Susan Sarandon, and James Garner). Compared to the subtle observation of a gradual thawing of relationships between Sully and his son, *Twilight*'s scenario appeared excessively contrived: a *menage à trois* conducted between a retired private eye (Newman) and his moneyed and married housemates (Hackman and Sarandon), set against a complicated murder inquiry that reunited the aging detective with an old colleague (James Garner). The combined star quality of the cast burdened their characters with inappropriate levels of charisma, the lengthy two-shots that showcased their interactions introducing a valedictory note to their representation which interfered with a mapping out of the dramatic situation. However, as with *The Late Show* and *Nobody's Fool*, *Twilight* did demonstrate Benton's admirably unfashionable interest in characters who, after long, not quite full, lives, were forced to confront the truth voiced by Hackman's terminally ill actor: 'there's nothing that concentrates the mind like the prospect of death'.

Benton is currently working on an adaptation of the Philip Roth novel 'The Human Stain', starring Anthony Hopkins and Nicole Kidman.                    **IG**

## Peter BERG

*Very Bad Things* (1998)  Peter Berg is one of the many American actors who recently attempted a shift of career towards directing. Born in New York in 1964 and having studied theatre at the Macalaster College in St Paul, Minnesota, Berg gave particularly interesting performances in John Dahl's *The Last Seduction* (1994) and in the television series 'Chicago Hope'. In the 1990s he turned to directing and scriptwriting. His debut feature was *Very Bad Things* (1998), a black comedy starring Cameron Diaz in an extreme performance similar to the ones she gave the same year in *There's Something About Mary*, and in *Being John Malkovich* (1999).

Apparently following Tarantino's lesson on the aesthetics of violence for its own sake, Berg's first film is characterised by ultra-violence and comic exaggeration. In fact, far from underplaying the violent actions in the film, the humorous narrative style and their irrationality make them even more gratuitous and unsettling. Exaggeration also marks the performances in the film, with all the actors indulging in over-excited acting, further underlined by the fast-paced and nervous camera movements. Consistent with this atmosphere, the film displays an interesting metafictional typecasting in Christian Slater's villain, which seems to reflect much of the actor's real-life experience with crime.

After *Very Bad Things*, Berg has completely abandoned acting and has been writing and directing his own medical drama, ABC's 'Wonderland'. Once more the style of his direction is extremely fast-paced, yet Berg seems to have found here a greater balance in the semi-documentary mode.                    **BP**

## Andrew BERGMAN

*So Fine* (1981)
*The Freshman* (1990)
*Honeymoon in Vegas* (1992)
*It Could Happen To You* (1994)
*Striptease* (1996)

Born in New York in 1945, Andrew Bergman published the well-regarded academic textbook 'We're in the Money: Depression America and Its Films' before embarking upon his screenwriting and directing career. As such it is not surprising that so many of his comedies have been marked by the style of the screwball classics of that era and infused with a generosity of spirit, commonly attributed to Frank Capra, particularly in their everyman protagonists.

In keeping with the spirit of the Depression, the movies Bergman has written and directed all chart their heroes' attempts to rescue themselves from debt, often accrued to caricatured mobsters who act as if they are auditioning for a Warner Bros. gangster film. This is the point where his films diverge from their templates, however. Bergman's romantic comedies are often classically styled, but can be as capricious as they are Capraesque: their protagonists' progress towards homely wisdoms often interrupted by the upstaging antics of a garishly rendered supporting cast. Whereas Capra's heroes stand at the centre of communities who look to them for inspiration and invigoration, the peripheral figures of Bergman's camply drawn comic worlds remain resistant to such moral instruction.

Bergman's first screenplay, 'Tex Mex', was broad enough to attract the attention of Mel Brooks and Richard Pryor, who reworked it into the hit western spoof *Blazing Saddles* (1974). The *In-Laws* (1979), Bergman's second writing assignment established his fondness for convoluted plotting. Both these elements were in place for his directorial debut, *So Fine* (1981), which saw Ryan O'Neal's unworldly academic press-ganged into taking over his father's ailing clothing business by a cartoonishly thuggish loan shark. A climax featuring the protagonists hijacking a production of Verdi's 'Othello' to act out their various animosities signalled Bergman's propensity to interweave his own narratives with other cultural reference points – in this case the climax to the Marx Brothers' film *A Night at the Opera* (1935).

This intertextual referencing was doubled in *The Freshman* (1990) by the casting of Marlon Brando in the Corleonesque role of mobster Carmine Sabatini. The presence of Matthew Broderick's ingenue film student, currently working on *The Godfather* (1972) in class, ensured that the task of deconstructing Coppola's classic movie was evenly spread amongst on screen characters, Brando's self-reflexive playing of his role and the knowledgeable viewer in the audience.

Bergman's *Honeymoon in Vegas* (1992) was his most fully achieved combination of comic and kitsch to date. Once again, the narrative involved its lead (Nicolas Cage) attempting to escape debt, this time by hiring out his fiancée, on the eve of their wedding, to a mobster (James Caan) who has fleeced him in a poker game. Both Cage and Caan are motivated by obsessive attachments: Cage to the advice of his mother, who commanded him never to get married on her death bed; Caan to his dead wife, who uncannily resembles Cage's girlfriend. This mirroring between hero and villain left little room for Sarah Jessica Parker's fiancée to make her mark but meshed effectively with the display of masculine obsession that provides the film's gaudy backdrop – the parade of Elvis impersonators who swarm around the Las Vegas hotel in which the couple intend to spend their honeymoon.

*It Could Happen To You* (1994), also starring Cage, was Bergman's straightest pastiche of Capra to date, as its original title, 'Cop Gives Waitress $2 Million Tip', suggests. The use of spinning newspaper headlines to signal plot progressions is evidence of both an old-fashioned storytelling mode and, unusually for Bergman, an attempt to demonstrate the galvanising effect of the leads' morally exemplary behaviour on their fellow citizens. The presence of classic pop songs on the soundtrack and the significant deferral of the leading couple's eventual coupling also placed the film in the 1990s genre of chaste romances alongside *Sleepless in Seattle* (1993). However, the revelation that Angel, the film's wise vagrant narrator, was actually an undercover newspaper photographer, indicated a sardonic tone that leavened the film's more saccharine elements.

*Honeymoon in Vegas* in particular owed its success to the ability of Nicolas Cage to provide a performance broad enough not to disappear against the vivid contributions of the supporting cast. The ill-received *Striptease* (1996) demonstrated what could happen when the star (Demi Moore) failed to pitch her performance appropriately. The film's squeamishness about its chief selling point – Moore playing a stripper – resulted in an unconvincing compromise whereby her routines were cast as indexes to her psychological state at any given moment. Her credentials as a good mother were bolstered at every opportunity. This worthy posturing fitted uneasily with Bergman's otherwise characteristically brash interpretation of Carl Hiassen's novel, which included silicone-enhanced strippers being strangled by their stage snakes and Burt Reynolds in a leather thong, his body glistening with Vaseline. Bergman's latest film, *Isn't She Great* (2000), has also been criticised for its unconvincing mixture of camp and coyness, sidestepping the question of the sexuality of its subject, Jacqueline Susann, cult author of 'Valley of the Dolls'. **IG**

# Kathryn BIGELOW

Born in California in 1952, Kathryn Bigelow is one of the few women directors working successfully in Hollywood today. She is certainly exceptional in that much of her work has been made within the traditionally male-dominated arena of big-budget action movies, a choice of field that has earned her a reputation as quite a maverick. However, Bigelow's films often reflect a different approach to these genres because she consistently explores themes of violence, voyeurism and sexual politics; ultimately, she seems to be concerned with questioning the very nature of the boundaries between particular genres. Her visual style echoes this thematic complexity, often introducing elements of an art-house aesthetic.

The framing of Bigelow as a visual stylist is perhaps unsurprising, given that she emerged from the New York art scene of the 1970s, having won a Whitney scholarship to study painting. She later transferred to the Columbia University film programme where she made *The Set-Up*, an experimental short film, which counterposed graphic images of two men fighting, with a soundtrack of philosophical musings and reactions to the images. An early example of her concern with violence, it also demonstrates Bigelow's tendency to merge pure spectacle and adrenaline with a more thoughtful analysis. Such amalgamation often sits uneasily. Critics such as Yvonne Tasker have commented on and identified this unease and awkwardness as a unique quality of Bigelow's film-making: 'Her contradictory position reflects what is so distinctive about her movies; an artful immersion in generic popular culture that is simultaneously stylish, seemingly ironic, but also so deeply romantic we're left unsure how to take it.'

Bigelow's subsequent career has been marked by her control and involvement with her productions, often developing the idea and script behind her films. Her first feature, *The Loveless* (1983), is typical of this approach. Recognisably art-house in style, the film has a thinly-developed narrative thread and focuses heavily on visual style. It examines the impact of a small group of bikers has on the inhabitants of a small town. The iconography of the 'biker movie', made recognisable by *The Wild One* (1953) and Kenneth Anger's *Scorpio Rising* (1964), is undercut by the ending, which focuses on the feminine and leaves Willem Dafoe's Vance powerless to prevent the destruction that entails.

Bigelow's subsequent film, *Near Dark* (1987), is a more typical generic exploration that fuses the vampire movie with the western. The vampire family are coded as outlaws – there is even the obligatory shoot-out scene – and ultimately Adrian Pasda's cowboy rides to the rescue on his horse. This updating and combining of two genres is partially successful, the element of romance which Tasker has described providing the only false note as Pasda's vampire love interest is restored to humanity by a blood transfusion. *Near Dark* is most significant in that it is the first introduction to a visual landscape that can be seen time and again in Bigelow's films. Shot mainly at night, the film is filled with tones of blue and black and glistening reflections. Aware of the quality of light, Bigelow colours the film to add depth to her visuals. In one scene where the vampires' hideout is shot out, the bullet holes in the walls let in shafts of light, taking on an almost three-dimensional quality. This use of light is echoed in *Blue Steel* (1990), but can be seen throughout her films. It adds an almost sculpted quality of texture to the look of her films and an overt stylisation that has become a hallmark.

*Blue Steel* again clearly disturbs generic expectations, but this time – for added measure – distorts the audience's conceptions of gender. Bigelow has stated that 'it all began with the idea of doing a woman action film. Not only has no woman ever done an action thriller, no woman has ever been at the centre of one as the central character'. Throughout the film, Bigelow plays with the notion of Jamie Lee Curtis' Megan as woman, highlighting the place of both the actress and the character in a traditionally male role. The opening shots show Curtis putting on her police uniform; the frilly lace of her bra at odds with the crisp lines of the uniform, 'masculine' and 'feminine' attire are starkly juxtaposed. Curtis' character becomes decidedly androgynous. The figure of the androgynous female who is capable of violence is a recurrent one throughout Bigelow's films, the association of the two often combining to give an erotic charge. This is made explicit in *Blue Steel*: the killer Eugene's fixation on Megan is linked to her possession of, and ability to use, her gun (leaving the film wide open to psychoanalytical and feminist readings).

The 1991 film *Point Break* is Bigelow's biggest commercial success to date, perhaps because it most successfully conforms to its action genre. The film focuses on the relationship between Keanu Reeves' Johnny Utah, an FBI agent, and his chief suspect in a series of bank robberies, Patrick Swayze as surfing guru Bodhi. Its examination of masculine relations and the lines between right and wrong is complimented by adrenaline-pumping action sequences. Bigelow's familiar group of outsiders living by different rules are presented here as whole-heartedly cool.

*Strange Days* (1995) is a neo-noir set against the backdrop of the eve of the new millennium and a dystopic Los Angeles, which is on the verge of erupting into race war. The film was a critical if not commercial success, building upon recognisable Bigelow motifs. It is a rich tapestry of narrative threads, stunning visuals and soundtrack, all of which compete for attention. Perhaps this dense layering of material fighting for audience attention ultimately explains the film's lacklustre reception. *Strange Days*, in line with Bigelow's other films, also switches traditional roles. Here the hero Lenny (Ralph Fiennes) is largely ineffective, with the action role filled by Angela Bassett, who plays Mace, a kick-boxing security specialist. Interestingly, in a storyline reminiscent of Michael Powell's *Peeping Tom* (1960), the film deals in part with a murderer who films his kills and, through S.Q.U.I.D. technology, relays the images and emotions back to his victims. The bathroom scene featuring rape and murder caused controversy on release, and in the same manner as *Peeping Tom* (1960), raises questions of voyeurism, relating it to the wider context of the cinema audience.

Her subsequent film, *The Weight of Water* (2000), is a thriller based on Anita Shreve's critically acclaimed novel and stars Catherine McCormack, Sean Penn and Sarah Polley. It juxtaposes two stories and draws thematic comparisons between each. The first, which is set in 1873 and told in flashback, focuses on a murder and trial in New England. The second takes place over 100 years later and revolves around a journalist who is writing a story about the case. Replete with issues of jealousy, desire and repression, the story of intrigue is further enhanced by Bigelow's visual acuity.

On the surface, her latest work, *K-19: The Widowmaker*, seems to mark a return to the action genre. It is based around the true story of Russia's first nuclear ballistic submarine and its captain (Harrison Ford) who, after a malfunction on-board, has to race to stop the sub's nuclear reactor from exploding. The casting of Ford, signalling mainstream Hollywood adventure, the tightly enclosed male world of the submarine, and the exploration of the relationship between Captain Vostrikov and his Executive Officer Mikhail Polenin, all hark back to *Point Break*. It is a precept ripe for Bigelow's trademark subversion – it is not often, after all, that a Hollywood film set at the time of the Cold War casts the Russians in the role of heroes. Bigelow has stated, 'The story of *K-19* will examine the heroism, courage and prowess of Russia's submarine force in ways we've never seen before'. However, as the film's title points out, courage and heroism don't exist in isolation, but in relation to the consequence of action; Bigelow's research involved her meeting and interviewing Captain Zateyev's widow, survivors and family members. With *K-19*, her significance continues, not only as a rare successful female director working within Hollywood, but as a director who manages to combine thematic complexity, technological experimentation and a sophisticated visual style with a populist approach.                                                                                    **HR**

# Charles BINAMÉ

Television has always been a solid training ground for emerging Canadian and Québec film-makers, and Charles Binamé has learned a great deal from the form. His feature films bear the mark of his television work; they are lucid, visually straightforward, although never static, and always have great emotional impact. He has slowly evolved into a solid, always-interesting film-maker with a good sense of how to work with actors.

*Eldorado* (1995)
*Le coeur au poing* (1998)
*La beauté de pandore* (2000)

His first feature film, *Eldorado* (1995), visualised Montreal as a complex, unstable place where people are very infrequently what they appear to be. Although it had a large ensemble cast and a totally de-centred narrative (similar to Robert Altman's films), the film's star is Pascale Bussières, a young woman who is the most famous, prolific Québecois actress of her generation. Bussières' fame is well deserved, and seeing her play a displaced, deceptive homeless woman supplies ample proof of this. Binamé makes the most of Bussières here: encouraging her to both emote and internalise to dramatic effect. The rest of the actors are dealt with equally well and throughout the film Binamé rides a fine line between a style that is loose and unstable and one that is tightly controlled, always pointing towards a biting critique of what it means to be young in contemporary Québec. It is a dualistic, complex film, one that fits well alongside such recent Québec cinema as Robert Lepage's Le polygraphe (1996) and Denis Villeneuve's Un août 32 sur terre (1998).

Binamé continues to work in television, and has recently made the features Le coeur au poing (1999) and La beauté de pandore (2000). These have not played widely in Canada or the United States, and have received a lukewarm response in Québec.   **JW**

## Brad BIRD

*The Iron Giant* (1999)  In the world of contemporary animation, Brad Bird is both a radical and a traditionalist. Born in Corvallis, Oregon, in 1963, he was mentored in his early teens by legendary Disney animator Milt Kahl (one of the company's fabled Nine Old Men). He went on to hone his craft at the California Institute of the Arts, where he studied alongside future mavericks Tim Burton and Pixar's John Lasseter. Bird first gained attention directing the Burton-designed short *Family Dog*, which aired as a segment of Steven Spielberg's late-1980s anthology programme, 'Amazing Stories'. He later acted as executive consultant on the prime-time series 'The Simpsons' and 'The Critic', where he was credited with helping to bring a cinematic sweep to the once static form of television animation.

*The Iron Giant* (1999), Bird's first full-length feature, is a witty Cold War fable that seamlessly combines state-of-the-art computer techniques with eccentrically rendered characters, naturalistic voice direction and glorious background work. A colourful rebuke to the established Disney formula of recent years, *The Iron Giant* contains no musical numbers, no goofball sidekicks, and no movie star vocal turns. Indeed, it may be the first major non-Disney release since *The Secret of NIMH* (1982) to attempt to do so. Loosely based on the book by poet Ted Hughes, *The Iron Giant* tells the story of Hogarth, a small-town boy who befriends the giant of the title, a peaceful visitor from outer space whose appearance arouses the distrust and ultimate aggression of the US government. While charming and sentimental on its surface, Bird deftly weaves in satiric references to Sputnik, 'duck and cover'-style educational films, and nuclear age monster movies, sharply evoking the Red Scare paranoia of the McCarthy era and creating a decidedly adult vision of a world gripped by the threat of nuclear war. In Bird's subtly revisionist version of the Norman Rockwell 1950s, salvation is to be found in the left-wing counterculture, represented here through the heroic beatnik character voiced by Harry Connick Jr. *The Iron Giant* is also one of the rare animated films to be grandly composed for anamorphic widescreen, lending the film an epic scope even while it playfully (and rightfully) pays homage to the preferred aspect ratio of the late 1950s setting.

Bird's next feature, *The Incredibles*, revolves around a dysfunctional family of superheroes.                                                                    **CS**

## Jamie BLANKS

*Urban Legend* (1998)  Born in Australia in 1971, Jamie Blanks made several horror shorts at film school in
*Valentine* (2001)  Victoria, including *Silent Number* (1993). Subsequently, he worked as a commercial director and editor, and as a camera operator and composer on *The Huntsman* (1993). His directorial debut, aged 26, was *Urban Legend* (1998) – variously known as *Mixed Culture* and *Urban Legends* – a post-*Scream* slasher movie which successfully integrates most of its hip self-referentiality. The inevitability of the twist in the opening sequence for example, foreshadowed by a Bonnie Tyler sing-along, makes it work. Handling familiar material with some skill, the film pursues an endearingly loopy plot: on the twenty-fifth anniversary of a campus massacre, a young woman, deranged by her boyfriend's death, sets about killing the two women she holds responsible, plus their friends and random

others, usually, but not always, in the manner of urban legends, thus securing her soon-to-be new boyfriend's journalistic career while wreaking her revenge. Attractive young television stars, variously brutal and inventive deaths, sinister and publicity-shy faculty, a security guard who idolises Pam Grier, astute cameos (Brad Dourif, Robert Englund, John Neville, Julian Richings), a plucky heroine (a well-cast Alicia Witt whose cynical TV persona overcomes some of the improbabilities), and sundry loose ends are all in the mix. Well-edited, with occasional stylish compositions, it is a reasonably effective addition to a subgenre renowned for its limited permutations. Energetic direction, especially during the set-pieces and running around, suggest that action movies might prove more amenable genre for Blanks.

However, his follow-up picture, *Valentine* (2001), is another slasher, loosely based on the novel by Tom Savage. In reworking the standard template with a bigger budget, the movie attempts to transform its familiar tropes by allowing the school-friend victims to be successful twentysomethings before the killer seeks revenge. This attempt to render the genre a little more mature is a disastrous failure. It is impossible to care for the soon-to-be victims, and thus we are forced to endure their company for much too long between the fairly uninventive murders. The pacing is badly off and the narrative collapses into incoherence. Loose ends abound, suggesting that the movie was trimmed from a greater length or that too many (or perhaps too few) writers were involved. Blanks succeeds in establishing some very rudimentary tension in the set-pieces, and again he demonstrates his eye for attractive compositions, but that is insufficient reward for even the most tolerant of viewer. Of the cast, only David Boreanaz emerges unscathed, largely through playing his role as an unvampiric Angel.  **MB**

# Don BLUTH

In a much publicised 'walk-out' from the Disney studios in 1979, Don Bluth effectively made a prescient statement about the decline of Disney's production values and outlook. Bluth and his colleagues, Gary Goldman and John Pomeroy, along with eleven others, left in dismay at the poor work which had characterised the studio's output since *Robin Hood* (1973). Having long abandoned the scale of investment and quality assurance championed in 'the golden era', Disney only re-addressed these issues much later, when the Michael Eisner and Jeffrey Katzenberg era recognised that the classical animation tradition had all but disappeared and Disney's fate as a company was intrinsically bound up in its resurrection and success.

Born in 1937, Bluth moved to Santa Monica with his family in 1954 and attended Brigham Young University. He sent his portfolio of artwork to the Disney studios, and was hired immediately as an assistant animator on *Sleeping Beauty* (1959). Bluth's initial period at Disney was a brief one, however, leaving in 1957 to pursue spiritual interests for three years with the Mormon Church in Argentina, and then, working with his brother Fred, producing musical theatre in Culver City, California. Returning to the Disney studio, Bluth was an omnipresent part of the Disney animation unit during the 1970s, and directed the scene-stealing animation sequences in *Pete's Dragon* (1977), a live-action feature, and *The Rescuers* (1977), as well as writing songs. He also directed *The Small One* (1978), the story of the little donkey who takes Mary to Bethlehem, while simultaneously working on his own short film, *Banjo, the Woodpile Cat* (1978). When Disney passed on its release, the film effectively became a showreel which won him a $6.5 million offer to direct his own feature. Having left Disney, he established an animation team at Studio City, before re-locating to Ireland to form the Sullivan Bluth Studio, with Morris Sullivan in the early 1980s.

The Disney 'tradition' was in effect first resurrected in the studio's initial film, based on Robert C. O'Brien's book, 'Mrs Frisby and the Rats of NIMH', *The Secret of NIMH* (1982), and later in the Stephen Spielberg/Amblin-funded *An American Tail* (1986). The latter suffers, however, from Spielberg's influence as a 'cartoonal' cinephile, in allying Warneresque speed to Disney-style sentiment, rather than embracing the more hyper-realist, character-driven, tragi-comedy of the authentic Disney formula, more fully played out in Bluth's next feature, *The Land Before Time* (1988). Bluth's commitment to quality animation in character movement and storytelling as an emotional journey completely reflects the Disney ethos, so crassly lost, for example, in the poorly designed, adult-oriented *Oliver and Company* (1988), the Disney film directly competing with *The*

*Land Before Time* that year. A re-working of *Bambi* (1941), the film tells the story of the fatherless Littlefoot, a baby dinosaur who endures the barren plains, the loss of his mother, massive earthquakes and the 'sharp-tooth' T-Rex, before arriving at the lush Great Valley, having reconciled the differences between species among his friends, and finding his grandparents. An epic and optimistic, rather than sentimentalised story, the film also reflected the resurgence of interest in dinosaurs by children, thus also astutely finding its market.

Recognising that the studio would also have to establish itself with adult audiences, Bluth made an altogether darker piece in *All Dogs Go to Heaven* (1990), an uneven hybrid of the musical adventure, gangster film and 'second-chance-on-Earth' fantasy. Charlie, a canine convict, voiced by Burt Reynolds, breaks out of jail and seeks to resume his illegal gambling and rat-racing business venture with former partner, Carface, voiced by Vic Tayback. Carface, however, kills Charlie, who ascends to heaven, only to be given an opportunity of coming back to earth, to redeem his mortal sins. He exposes Carface's rat-race fixing scam; protects those abused by him; endures nightmares of a descent into hell (a tour-de-force of design); and finally, fights Carface in a brutal climax. American critics allied the directness and spirit of the film with the work of Ralph Bakshi, praising the ways in which mature themes were handled; British critics, however, felt that Charlie's path to redemption was still characterised by the worst kinds of Disneyesque cuteness and sentimentality.

*Rock-a-Doodle* (1992), a rollicking musical, followed, but only consolidated the view that Bluth was a brilliant technician, but a creative figure unable to fully emerge as an auteur in the medium. Ironically, having arguably provoked Disney's necessary improvement, Bluth's work became a victim in comparison to it. *A Troll in Central Park* (1994), about a non-conformist troll named Stanley, was a pleasant but ultimately unsatisfying diversion; while *Thumbelina* (1994), his adaptation of the Hans Christian Anderson story, pales by comparison to the intrinsic modernity of *Aladdin* (1992) by not fully exploiting the potential of CGI or embracing Warneresque knowingness in its narrative style. The retreat to the 'cute and cuddly', and the lack of investment in the 'emotional journey' model renders the work dated, and uncertain of how to embrace the more theatrical model working so well for Disney. *The Pebble and the Penguin* (1996), like *Thumbelina*, using songs by Barry Manilow, also suffers from the same kind of anonimity, part-manic Warner, but more often the same unimaginative and clichéd Disney of the 1970s that Bluth had been so critical of.

Bluth's *Anastasia* (1998) is a partial return to form in the sense that his work finally has the courage to compete with Disney at the level of telling an adult story, animating adult characters and fully embracing CGI. Inevitably, its historical context, the Russian Revolution, provoked here by the sorcerer, Rasputin, rather than by the rise of the disempowered masses, is rendered bland in preference to the 'rags to riches' destiny narrative of the foundling, Anastasia, who ultimately attains her royal ascendence to the Romanov dynasty after years of amnesia and absence. She also ultimately finds her fullest contentment in the pursuit of romance, with the ever loyal (if contradictory and manipulative) Dimitri. This is a timely reminder of the singularity of purpose, not merely in Bluth's work, but in American Disneyesque feature animation overall, to preserve a highly sentimentalised account of human endeavour even in despite of the often horrific and contradictory aspects of its narrative sources. The assassination of Tsar Nicholas and his family in 1918, which included a multiple stabbing of Anastasia, and was concluded by 'burial' in a mineshaft where sulphuric acid was poured over the faces of the family to prevent identification, self-evidently has no place in this schemata; it provides further evidence for the consistent insensitivity on the part of the leading American production houses in regard to other cultures and histories. 'History' in effect does not matter. The aesthetic highpoint of the film – Paris depicted through picturesque reference of its most renowned artists – merely reinforces the absence of ideological and political engagement. The film also spawned a sequel for one of its cute comic sidekicks, Bartok the bat, in *Bartok the Magnificent* (1999).

*Titan AE* (2000) fully combines computer generated spacecraft and atmospheric exteriors with cel-animated characters, and seeks to update the 'community in crisis' theme following planetary destruction. Bluth's longevity and achievements should not be undervalued. His stand against the decline of Disney was one of the crucial moments, not merely in the recovery of the Disney Studio, but given Disney's place as the industry leader, in the field of feature animation in general. His approach also ensured that Stephen Spielberg's emergent Ambimation Studio was characterised by work of quality and authority, and his continuing presence in the field, now with a distribution deal facilitated by Twentieth Century Fox, means that alongside DreamWorks SKG and Warner Bros. Animation, Bluth is still challenging the Disney brand by insisting on quality in the art and craft of the animated form. He is slated to co-direct *Dragon's Lair*, an animated feature based on the legendary laserdisk videogame. **PW**

# Peter BOGDANOVICH

Peter Bogdanovich's career trajectory is exemplary of a certain strain of film-literate, highly skilled, but self-destructively egotistical directors that emerged in the late 1960s to shake up a staid Hollywood (William Friedkin and Bob Rafelson are other notable members of this group). The formula seems to be: find early success with some great movies, become insufferable, turn in a string of duds, then disappear. Bogdanovich followed the blueprint to the letter.

However, one thing that could never be said about Bogdanovich was that he did not know about, and passionately care for, Hollywood movies. Born in New York in 1939, he entered the industry as a film programmer for a New York cinema. He first became known for a series of critical monographs on the pantheon craftsmen of the classical era: John Ford, Howard Hawks and Alfred Hitchcock. Fitting in perfectly with the turn towards auteurism that criticism was taking in the 1960s, under the guidance of *Cahiers du cinéma*-influenced commentators like Andrew Sarris, Bogdanovich's position as movie writer for *Esquire* magazine enabled him to get close to his idols. It even provided the opportunity to observe Ford on set directing *Cheyenne Autumn* (1964), an experience that Bogdanovich not unreasonably said was better than attending film school as a way of learning the director's craft (Bogdanovich subsequently paid further homage when he released the documentary *Directed by John Ford* in 1971). When he hit his directing stride in the early 1970s, Bogdanovich's films would be drenched with the influence of such old masters. His first opportunity, however, was handed to him by a man whose name would seem slightly incongruous in such classical company. Legendary exploitation producer/director Roger Corman took the cinephile writer on as second unit director on Peter Fonda's breakthrough movie *The Wild Angels* (1966) before giving him autonomy on the sniper thriller *Targets* in 1968. Typically for the resourceful Corman, the only conditions on Bogdanovich's appointment as director were that the budget stay below $125,000, and that a part be found for ageing horror icon Boris Karloff, who owed Corman two days shooting time. The film flopped (given its subject matter, it was felt by the director to have suffered from a release date insensitively close to the assassination of Martin Luther King), but established Bogdanovich within New York critical circles as a director to watch.

Bogdanovich's next three pictures would set a high standard of critical and commercial success that he would find impossible to maintain, propelling him to the fore of the new breed of Hollywood directors when he perhaps had more in common with the previous generation. Adapted from Larry McMurtry's novel, *The Last Picture Show* (1971), a desolate Fordian meditation on growing up in a small town and the various betrayals of adolescent relationships, earned eight Academy Award nominations. Revolving around the closure of the local cinema, a metaphor for the disintegration of an innocent and unspoilt way of life, Bogdanovich underlined his style of nostalgic classicism by casting Ford regular Ben Johnson in the role of town patriarch Sam the Lion. The movie also launched the careers of Jeff Bridges and Cybill Shepherd (for whom Bogdanovich would leave his wife and collaborator Polly Platt, often credited with playing a significant role in his early successes).

Bogdanovich's next move was similarly informed by Hollywood's past; an attempt to revive the moribund genre of the screwball comedy so strongly associated with his hero Howard Hawks. After the monochrome gravitas of *The Last Picture Show*, Bogdanovich showed an admirable, and perhaps unexpected, lightness of touch in steering stars Barbra Streisand and Ryan O' Neal to huge box-office and critical success in *What's Up, Doc?* (1972). In spirit a remake of Hawks' *Bringing Up Baby* (1938), right from the self-consciously Hawksian 'page-turning' opening credits, the film is notable for Streisand's engaging performance as disaster-prone kook Judy Maxwell and O'Neal's skilful send-up of his leading man image as hen-pecked, strait-laced musicologist Howard Bannister. Genuinely romantic and blistering withscattershot, tongue-twisting dialogue, the movie is perhaps the director's finest moment. Its visual gags and physical comedy are executed perfectly. The wistful (and for the irreverent early 1970s, rather unfashionable) nostalgia for the heyday of the studios was still in place, and Bogdanovich clearly saw himself as heir to the legacy of his auteurist heroes. To the *New York Times* he revealed that he measured himself not against his contemporaries but against the likes of Hawks, Lubitsch, Welles, Ford,

Renoir and Hitchcock. It was a mixture of this arrogance and a craving for the autonomy of the true auteur that led to Bogdanovich's co-founding, in 1973, of the ill-fated 'Directors Company' alongside fellow 'young turks' Francis Ford Coppola and William Friedkin. Bankrolled by Paramount's eccentric owner Charlie Bludhorn, the alliance would yield two flops in its three-picture existence (Bogdanovich's *Daisy Miller* (1974) and Coppola's *The Conversation* (1974)) and ultimately combust in a not entirely unpredictable display of ego, as each director aimed to score points off the other and financial squabbles over the profits from the single hit film tore them apart.

That film was Bogdanovich's *Doc* follow-up, *Paper Moon* (1973). The director was coerced into making the film by Paramount executive Peter Bart after his plan to film a Larry McMurtry-scripted western with John Wayne, James Stewart and Henry Fonda collapsed (Bogdanovich felt Wayne's involvement was discouraged by John Ford; the script would eventually become the hit television mini-series 'Lonesome Dove'). *Paper Moon* is another exercise in nostalgia, although an accomplished and affecting one, a beautifully filmed Depression-era tale centring on Ryan O'Neal's conman and the nine-year-old companion who may or may not be his daughter (Tatum O'Neal). The film was a solid commercial success, Bogdanovich's third in a row.

The self-enchanted director was, the Hollywood community secretly felt, overdue for a fall. That fall came with his second picture for the Directors Company, the Cybill Shepherd-starring Henry James adaptation *Daisy Miller*. When Bogdanovich followed this misfire with the expensive musical disaster *At Long Last Love* (1975), also starring his muse, Shepherd, the writing was on the wall for the self-proclaimed auteur. Undeniably talented, a craftsman able to emulate the classical feel of the studio era and to conjure minor masterpieces out of *What's Up, Doc?* and *The Last Picture Show*, Bogdanovich perhaps lacked the natural spark, the talent for re-invention and pure cinematic imagination that allowed his peers Coppola, Scorsese and Altman to repeatedly bounce back from disasters *like One From the Heart* (1982), *New York, New York* (1977) and *Popeye* (1980). Suffering a personal tragedy in 1980 with the murder of his lover, ex-Playboy model Dorothy Stratten (recounted in Bob Fosse's 1983 movie *Star 80*), Bogdanovich's reputation would diminish with each successive film: the charmless homage to silent film, *Nickelodeon* (1976); the botched Paul Theroux adaptation, *Saint Jack* (1979); the flat romantic comedy, *They All Laughed* (1981), leaving him high and dry by the mid-1980s. The human interest drama *Mask* (1985), directed with competence and warmth, marked something of a return to form, but this was not an auteur picture, the statement of a genius fit to stand alongside Hawks and Hitchcock, and his early promise seemed to have been squandered. Presumably this sense of premature irrelevance prompted Bogdanovich to return to the scene of his greatest triumph for *Texasville* (1990), the tardy sequel to *The Last Picture Show*, centring once again on Bridges and Shepherd. The film was another flop and, although not without moments of humour and genuine emotion (especially those featuring Timothy Bottoms' quietly insane, ghostly Sonny, marooned in the 1950s time frame of the original film), it largely failed to recapture the subtle majesty and pathos of the original.

Bogdanovich will probably never again be considered a major director, although he is hardly the only film-maker from the 1970s to fail to grow in talent as well as in ambition and vanity. Many of his directorial works in the 1990s were for television, notable exceptions being the stage farce adaptation *Noises Off* (1992) and *The Thing Called Love* (1993), the final film of River Phoenix. However, as an emblematic figure of the bold, highly romanticised 'movie brat' era, the well-connected Bogdanovich has been able to re-establish a foothold in film culture as a quotable source for writers and documentarians researching the heyday of the studio system. Several of his books remain in print, including the well-regarded 'This Is Orson Welles'. The resurgence in interest in the directors of the 'New Hollywood' era (fuelled by writers such as Peter Biskind) has presaged Bogdanovich's return to a bigger cinematic platform; in 2002 he will release *The Cat's Meow* (2002), an account of an incident in the relationship between William Randolph Hearst and Marion Davies. The subject matter establishes a link between Bogdanovich and his mentor Orson Welles (who treated similar material, in thinly-disguised form, in his masterpiece *Citizen Kane* (1941)). The film stars Kirsten Dunst as Davies and Edward Herrmann as Hearst. That the classically inclined Bogdanovich should focus on the 1920s Hollywood milieu of Hearst, Davies, Charlie Chaplin and legendary gossip columnist Louella Parsons is no surprise. Less predictably, Bogdanovich has recently made several acting appearances on American television, contributing a self-deprecating cameo to ex-wife Shepherd's sitcom 'Cybill', and filling a more substantial role as a psychotherapist in David Chase's acclaimed HBO drama 'The Sopranos'.

Ultimately too mannered a director to transcend the influences of his classical forebears and define his own style, Bogdanovich nevertheless epitomises an important stage in the history of Hollywood, his early 1970s work reflecting the transition from old to new that enabled the regeneration of the beleaguered American cinema.     **MF**

# Lizzie BORDEN

Blending art and activism, film-maker Lizzie Borden was a key figure in American independent cinema of the 1980s. While she has done important work in the 1990s – *Erotique* (1994) and *Love Crimes* (1991) – Borden is best known for her feminist classics, *Born in Flames* (1983) and *Working Girls* (1986). These films set the stage for a body of work that consistently explores the root causes of gender inequality within the context of the workplace, the family and relationships.

Born in 1955, Borden was raised in Detroit, Michigan and went on to receive degrees in the fine arts at Wellesley College and Queens College of the City University of New York. Her initial foray into film production took place when she directed the experimental *Regroupings* in 1976 but it was *Born in Flames* that really put her on the map. The film constructs an imaginary future in which a socialist revolution as been enacted in the United States. Despite the revolutionary fervour, many familiar social ills persist prompting women to organise and take power away from the men in charge. Her overt address of gender issues and their intersection with class and race made this film a 'big bang' on the independent film scene. It highlighted an intelligent feminist sensibility just as the Reaganite 1980s were getting started.

She followed up this explosive debut with *Working Girls*. While no less powerful, *Working Girls* is a much more refined and accomplished film. Distressed by the victimisation of prostitutes in mainstream movies, Borden conducted months of research in preparation for a film that would highlight the world of middle-class prostitution. *Working Girls* takes as its setting a brothel in which men politely come and go, often acting as friendly or as casually as they might at a barber shop. But the vantage point of the film is strictly held within the subjectivity of a female protagonist. From this point of view the film not only highlights the perspective of the prostitute but it also traces for us the metaphorical nature of the brothel as representative of the workplace in general. The interaction between the women workers and the male clients underscores more commonplace female roles such as the hostess, secretary, or girlfriend. Traditional sexual roles are critiqued via a non-traditional look at prostitution.

After the success of *Working Girls*, Borden directed an episode of the TV series 'Monsters' which she then followed up with her next feature, *Love Crimes* (1991). The film follows investigations of a District Attorney (Sean Young) into a man (Patrick Bergin) who, posing as a famous photographer, manipulates women both sexually and economically. Next, Borden directed a film called *Inside Out* (1992) and a segment of *Erotique* (1994). The latter project was produced in Germany with the intention of having three women film-makers explore the topic of sexuality. Borden's segment, 'Let's Talk About Sex', features an aspiring actress who works a daytime job as a phone-sex operator. Things change, however, when she finds herself drawn to a caller who is willing to listen to her desires. Like her previous films, this short work concerns the ways in which economics and sex intertwine with one another in an endless patriarchal power play.     **SCh**

# Rob BOWMAN

Rob Bowman began his career in television, as a second unit director for Stephen Cannell Productions in 1982. He was first given the opportunity to direct (an episode of Cannell's short-lived action series, 'Stingray') in 1985. Since then, Bowman has been a prolific television director (particularly of science fiction and genre television), most notably featuring as a regular contributor to 'Star Trek: The Next Generation' and 'The X–Files'.

Bowman's first feature film, *Airborne* (1993), is a modest coming-of-age movie, concerning laid-back Californian surfer Mitchell Goosen (Shane McDermott), who goes to live in snow-bound Cincinnati with his aunt, uncle, and eccentric cousin, Wiley (Seth Green). The initial structural opposition between Mitchell's sunny, middle-class optimism and the cold, blue-collar aggression of the Cincinnati schoolroom is (predictably) complicated when Mitchell embarks upon a romance with the sister of the school's gang-leader. *Airborne* uses sport (in this case, roller-blade racing) to resolve Mitchell's problems and the climactic, dangerous race through city streets serves as a rite-of-passage for the teenage boys.

Whilst the directorial style displayed in *Airborne* is generally economical, Bowman's 'signature' is apparent in his use of exaggerated colours and strong lighting contrasts within the *mise-en-scène*. Consider, for example, the saturated orange of a Californian sunset in the early sequences, and later, the expansive, grey skies of Cincinnati and the shadowy school corridors, where silhouetted figures move through small pools of light.

Bowman's second feature film, *The X–Files: Fight the Future* (1998), is an altogether different movie. Unusually, this film is directly related to an ongoing television series (forming a bridge between seasons five and six), unlike the 'Star Trek' films, for example, that followed the television franchise of each series. Consequently, the film-makers had the difficult task of maintaining the narrative arc established on television, while simultaneously offering audiences a different (i.e. more cinematic) experience. As Bowman had been one of the most frequently employed directors on 'The X–Files', the task of reinforcing a 'brand identity' was perhaps the easiest to achieve. Indeed, Bowman remains faithful to the formal and narrative parameters delineated by the series creator, Chris Carter.

Once again, however, Bowman's visual style is most clearly marked by his use of lighting. There are recurring shots of human silhouettes against wide, bright landscapes (the polar ice of the opening and closing sequences and the bleached heat of the flat, sandy terrain of the Southern states, where the investigation commences). In contrast, there are moments of darkness, where moving shadows are barely discernible within the frame. Such images reinforce the sense of social alienation and mistrust that lies at the heart of 'The X–Files'.

Whether Rob Bowman will go on to develop a clear authorial signature in cinema is still in question. His most recent work, *Reign of Fire* (2002), is something of a change in direction, though still a fantasy. Set in a post-apocalyptic England, it has been described as a cross between *Dragonslayer* (1981) and *Mad Max* (1979), and involves a brood of fire-breathing dragons that awake from their slumber seeking to dominate the planet. **EC**

# Michel BRAULT

Michel Brault belongs to the first generation of French-Canadian film-makers associated not only with Québec's cultural and political awakening or the 'quiet revolution' from the 1960s but also with the emergence and establishment of the Québec cinema that has occurred since that time. Born in Montreal, in 1928, he has enjoyed a successful career since 1958 and his name as either director of photography and/or director appears in the titles of some of the most important films produced in Québec. He joined the National Film Board in 1956 where he collaborated in the production of the short documentary film series *Candid Eye* and was instrumental in the establishment of a French-only unit. The short film he made with Gilles Groulx, *Les raquetteurs/The Snowshoers* (1958) became a manifesto of the French film-makers and later provoked the changes in the structure and practices of the NFB. It also set the aesthetic and political tone for numerous short and long documentaries Brault made with Groulx, Claude Jutra and others over the next few years.

In 1959, he was invited to present *Les raquetteurs* in California where he met Jean Rouch who later offered him work in France, sharing his passion for direct cinema. Brault shot Rouch's classics, *Chronique d'un été* (1961) and *La punition* (1963) and continued to work on topical, socially engaged documentaries and fictions with French film-makers Mario Ruspoli, William Klein and Annie Tresgot. He established his reputation as a master of direct cinema but also as a firm believer in its ethics as means for moral awakening. The result of this quest was *Pour la suite du monde (For Those Who Will Follow)*, made in 1963, where a simple story about an island fishing community acquires almost mythic dimensions. The film was unanimously recognised as the Best Canadian Film of the year.

*The Last Period/La Derniere Shabat Shalom!* (1992) *Mon amie Max* (1994) *The Long Winter/Quand je serai parti ... vous vivrez encore* (1999)

In the 1960s, Brault tried his hand in fiction film both as director of photography (for Claude Jutra's *A tout prendre/Take It All* (1964)) and as director (the short *Le temps perdu*, 1964). Certainly, *Entre la mer et l'eau douce* (1967) stands out as the most original example of his masterful merging of fiction and direct cinema that is so typical of the Québec cinema in the 1980s. The film is loosely based on the life of its principal actor, popular singer Claude Gauthier, who shares the lead with the most famous Québec actress, Geneviéve Bujold, to tell the story of a Québec country boy who makes it big on the Montreal pop-scene.

In the 1970s, Brault lent his brilliant cinematographer's talent to other well-known Québec directors and shot a series of nationalist-minded documentaries, most notably *Un pays sans bon sens!/Wake-up, mes bons amis!* (1970). He also produced a vast number of episodes for the television series 'Le son des Français d'Amérique' and 'La belle ouvrage' reflecting on various customs and traditions prompted by fear of the disappearance of the French population in North America. The centre-piece of this period in Brault's career is his 'documented fiction' *Les Ordres/Orders* from 1974, a sombre account of the random arrest of five people, their moral torture and eventual release without explanation or apology in the wake of the War Measures Act, introduced by the Federal government in October 1970. The excellent acting of the five young stars of the films and its imagery brought him the Prize for *Mise-en-scène* at Cannes and the Canadian Best Director Award.

When Brault was not making his own films, he was helping others create their masterpieces. In the 1970s he shot such landmark Québecois films as *Mon oncle Antoine/My Uncle Antoine* (1971), proclaimed the best Canadian film of all times, *Kamouraska* (1973), and *Les bons débarras/Good Riddance* (1980). In the 1980s he continued to work as director of photography on a number of documentaries and was showered with awards: the Canadian Film Award for *My Uncle Antoine*; Genie for *Good Riddance*, amongst may others. In 1986, the Québec government awarded him with the Albert-Tessier prize.

It was not before 1989, however, that he repeated the success of *Orders* with *Les noces de papier/The Paper Wedding*, which one again starred Bujold. Made for television, the film told the simple story of a Montreal intellectual who agrees to a bogus marriage with a Latin American former revolutionary in order to save him from deportation but then falls in love with him. *A Paper Wedding* made quite a splash at the Berlin Film Festival mainly because of the subtle and dark charisma of its images. It marked the beginning of Brault's original experiments with shooting on different formats (16mm, video) and then transferring the image to 35mm.

*The Last Period/La Dernière Partie* is Brault's instalment in the 1991 avant-garde six-part travelogue *Montreal Sextet* (helmed by five other star directors, Léa Pool, Denys Arcand, Atom Egoyan, Jaques Leduc and Patricia Rozema). This tragic love story, shot during a hockey game at the Montreal Forum, intercuts slapshots, goals and fights with a couple's own divorce game.

*Shabat Shalom!* (1992), another film made for television, juxtaposes a closely knit Hassidic-Jewish family with the dysfunctional family of the City Mayor. The controversy linked to the building of a new synagogue constitutes the basic conflict in the film and parallels that between the Mayor and his alienated son. Both conflicts find their melodramatic resolution when the son falls in love with a Jewish girl.

Thanks to the enigmatic presence of Bujold, *Mon amie Max* (1994) succeeded in overcoming the melodramatic sentimentality of the story about a woman looking for her son, abandoned at birth 25 years earlier; it prepared the ground for Brault's first period film, *Quand je serai parti ... vous vivrez encore/The Long Winter* (1999). Once again the 72-year-old director proved his versatile originality and youthful daring in tackling yet another sensitive historical subject, the French-Canadian insurgencies against the British colonial armies in the early 1800s.                                                            **CSt**

# Martin BREST

*Hot Tomorrows* (1977)
*Going in Style* (1979)
*Beverly Hills Cop* (1984)
*Midnight Run* (1988)
*Scent of a Woman* (1992)
*Meet Joe Black* (1998)

Born in 1951 in the Bronx, Martin Brest directed the laudatory student project *Hot Dogs for Gaugin* (1972), starring a then unknown Danny DeVito and his future wife Rhea Perlman, while attending New York University. He went on to write, direct, produce and edit *Hot Tomorrows* (1977) for the American Film Institute for $33,000. In this black and white film, Ken Lerner plays a young New York writer who has moved to LA and who spends his days writing about his elderly aunt, when he is not busy exploring his obsession with death. Though highly praised by critics, few people since have been able to see it.

Brest's early efforts garnered attention from Warner Bros. and the studio eventually hired him to direct the legendary George Burns, Art Carney and Lee Strasberg in the comedy drama *Going in Style* (1979). The seasoned direction of the film did not betray Brest's very young age and it looked as if Hollywood had another film school *wunderkind* on its roster. Brest developed the teenage-oriented suspense film *Wargames* (1983), but he was fired from the production of the eventual blockbuster after an on-set confrontation with the producers. For nearly two years, Brest was virtually blacklisted, surfacing only for an acting assignment in *Fast Times at Ridgemont High* (1982). The director made a successful comeback with the enormous hit *Beverly Hills Cop* (1984), a Jerry Bruckheimer and Don Simpson-produced high-adrenaline blockbuster that further cemented the popularity of star Eddie Murphy. The story was originally developed as a vehicle for Sylvester Stallone, and given Murphy's invaluable contribution to the anarchic screenplay, it might appear doubtful that Brest would have delivered as popular a film at the box office. Brest's next film proved how good a director he actually is when it comes to fast-paced, action comedies for *Midnight Run* was a bright spot at the box office in 1988. The convoluted plot centred around a cynical bounty hunter (Robert De Niro) trying to deliver and protect an FBI informant and convicted embezzler (Charles Grodin) from the cops, the Mob, and other rogue bounty hunters. Sharp, funny, exciting, and violent, *Midnight Run* proved that Brest's ability to turn in an action comedy that makes sense was a talent, not a fluke. The film is aided immeasurably by the chemistry between Grodin and De Niro. Their love/hate interaction earns real emotion – by the end of the picture we have a relationship that is sincere and not contrived like so many other action comedies.

Brest took another four-year break before he tackled *Scent of a Woman* (1992), starring a bombastic Al Pacino. It portrays an embittered, hard-drinking, cantankerous, blind ex-soldier who hires a student companion (Chris O'Donnell) for the weekend. While the schmaltzy sentiment of the film becomes overbearing at times, not to mention Pacino's performance, the film does succeed on its own terms as being a grittier, more hard-edged *Dead Poets Society* (1989). Brest could perhaps be criticised for not reigning in Pacino, but other directors have fared no better in controlling Pacino's scenery-chewing acting. Brest scored a personal victory by earning an Academy Award nomination for Best Director but lost to Clint Eastwood for his direction of *Unforgiven* (1992). Pacino won the Best Actor statuette.

Brest did not capitalise on his Academy Award nomination but chose instead to take yet another four-year break in between projects. A remake of *Death Takes a Holiday*, the 1934 Fredric March vehicle, the fiasco of *Meet Joe Black* (1998) has done much regrettable harm to Brest's reputation as a director. Spanning an inexcusable three-hour length, the film was apparently conceived and directed as a potential Academy Award contender, given the sumptuous production design, the awkward combination of metaphysical ruminations and the innocent naïveté of the Forrest Gump-like lead character, played by Brad Pitt. The length of the picture created a new chapter in the ongoing debate regarding the ever-increasing length of feature films. But in the case of *Meet Joe Black*, no one was particularly willing to defend its length, as they did for *Saving Private Ryan*, released that same year. One reason may be because they sensed the material did not warrant such a lengthy screen time.

He is currently in production with *Gigli*, a comedy with Ben Affleck and Jennifer Lopez.   **SM**

# Manon BRIAND

The 1996 anthology film *Cosmos*, which had six young film-makers directing short episodes about a taxi driver in Montreal, was meant to announce a new generation of Québec film-makers; the results, so far, have been mixed. Some of the participants have done nothing since (Jennifer Alleyn, Marie-Julie Dallaire), one has made a very good feature that was much more ambitious than his entry (Denis Villeneuve, who made 1998's *Un août 32 sur terre*), and Manon Briand has made one feature that did not live up to the promise of the *Cosmos* work.

His episode of *Cosmos*, titled 'Boost', was a simple story about two friends driving around a snowy Montreal, as one of them tries to put off going to get the results of his AIDS test. Briand showed a real restraint with the actors – much of the dialogue feels improvised – and did not let the melodrama of this simple storyline overwhelm its execution. The camera, while restrained, made use of Montreal's gorgeous urban landscape, hinting at a promising start for a film-maker who had up to that point only made a few shorts.

Briand's big break came in 1998, with the feature film *Deux secondes*, which played at the Sundance Film Festival and enjoyed a modest North American theatrical release. This was a major step backwards, a cliché-filled, visually showy and self-consciously hip narrative about a bike messenger in Montreal. The lead actors, Charlotte Laurier and Dino Tavarone (who plays a grumpy bike-shop owner that finds happiness by coaching Laurier for a big bike race), are competent at dealing with unoriginal material. Marie-Claude Loiselle wrote that 'for all this vain agitation, all this vain demonstration of know how, there is only the impression of pure expenditure. Is this what one expects today from a *jeune cinéma*?'

Following *Deux secondes*, he shot the documentary, Heart: The Marilyn Bell Story, about a Canadian Teenager who won a swimming race across Lake Ontario in 1954. He recently completed *La turbulence des fluides*, starring Genevieve Bujold.          **JW**

*Deux secondes* (1998)

# Matthew BRIGHT

Matthew Bright was raised as a military child at Fort Leonard Wood, Missouri, where he became a fan of the visceral films of Sam Peckinpah, Sam Fuller and Russ Meyer at the movie house on base. After paying his dues as a veteran screenwriter of genre and cult films such as Richard Elfman's *Forbidden Zone* (1980) and *Modern Vampires* (released later in 1998) and Tamra Davis' *Guncrazy* (1992), Bright scored his first directorial opportunity when friend Richard Rutowski passed along Bright's script for *Freeway* (1996) to future executive producer Oliver Stone. Bright had vowed to start directing his own scripts after director Tamra Davis softened the hard edge of his *Guncrazy* script.

*Freeway* is a sassy, urban white-trash take on the Little Red Riding Hood fairytale. Containing an explosive performance by Reese Witherspoon as feisty teen hellcat Vanessa Lutz, Bright subversively skewers politically correct sensibilities through Vanessa's devilishly innocent eyes en route of this hilariously foulmouthed, blood-spattered California road trip. Bright's skillful balance of naïvety and worldly-wise sophistication absolves Vanessa of victim status and brings a comfortable irony to her battles against sexual predators, the welfare culture and the judicial system. Strong, young female characters are a staple in Bright's stories – Stone describes him as 'like Lewis Carroll, but nothing perverted'.

*Freeway II: Confessions of a Trickbaby* (1999) is a similarly themed film that fashions the story of bulimic, criminal, teenaged, lesbian runaways around the framework of the Hansel & Gretel fairy tale. Filmed on half the budget of *Freeway* with Natasha Lyonne in the lead role, it matches the earlier film's explicit excesses without quite matching its strong performances and sharply written screenplay.

Bright is currently in production with *Tiptoes*, starring Kate Beckinsale and Gary Oldman, with the latter playing a dwarf that becomes romantically involved with his brother's pregnant wife.          **THa**

*Freeway* (1996)
*Freeway II: Confessions of a Trickbaby* (1999)

# Albert BROOKS

Born Albert Einstein in Los Angeles in 1947, Albert Brooks is the son of the radio comedian, Harry Einstein. As a comedian, actor, writer and director, he has created a strong

*Real Life* (1979)
*Modern Romance* (1981)

comic persona in the five films he has directed. As an actor, he is known for major roles in *Taxi Driver* (1976) and *Broadcast News* (1987), and smaller but memorable roles in *Twilight Zone: The Movie* (1983) and *Out of Sight* (1998).

In the 1970s he joined the cast of the US television show 'Saturday Night Live' and began directing short comic films for the show. Fittingly, television was the subject of his directorial debut, *Real Life* (1979). In this pointed satire about 'fly-on-the-wall' shows, Brooks is a director making the definitive documentary about a 'real' American family, the Yeagers from Phoenix, Arizona (played by Charles Grodin and Frances Lee McCain). The (fictional) director invades the privacy of his subjects in a succession of bizarre and annoying ways, from attempting to film Mrs Yeager at the gynaecologist to an attempt at lifting them out of a depression which involves dressing as a clown. The film accurately exposes the pretensions of *vérité* film-makers with Brooks' character declaring his aim to 'depict a day-to-day living in contemporary America and at the same time hold a motion picture audience spellbound'. Although the film is well written and often very funny, Brooks' performance often exposes his roots in stand-up. This is a quibble, however, and the question of the star-writer-director and his ego can be seen to inform and even complicate our responses to Brooks' character. How much is Brooks lampooning artistic styles while indulging in his own?

*Modern Romance* (1981) doesn't stray too far from the milieu of films and filming, as Brooks plays a film editor who falls in and out of love with Kathryn Harrold. There are some amusing observations about Hollywood but this feels insubstantial. The mean wit that informs his debut is largely absent here but the neurotic persona on show is one that recurs in Brooks' work. A kind of West Coast Woody Allen, Brooks also owes something to other Jewish comic writers/performers who deal in neuroses – Neil Simon, Mel Brooks and Gene Wilder.

*Lost in America* (1985) is Brooks' best film, both extremely funny and a cutting comment on the yuppie materialism of the period. Brooks plays an LA advertising executive who, disappointed at being passed over for promotion, walks out of his job. Successfully imploring his wife (Julie Hagerty) to quit her job, the two of them set out, inspired by *Easy Rider* (1969), to travel across America in a luxury mobile home to 'find themselves'. Brooks is concerned with the vacuity of the yuppie existence, the differences between the 1960s and the 1980s, and the pretensions of the middle classes who hope to 'drop out' in comfort. Predictably, the characters lose everything and *Lost in America*, although hiding its withering observations under some hilarious material, can be seen as a variant on the 'yuppie nightmare' cycle of this decade – Martin Scorsese's *After Hours* (1985) and Jonathan Demme's *Something Wild* (1986).

*Defending Your Life* (1991) is something of a let-down after the peak of *Lost in America*. Brooks is killed in a car crash and 'relocates' to Judgement City where the fate of his soul is to be decided in a courtroom. Despite strong support from Rip Torn as Brooks' Defence Attorney and Meryl Streep as the love interest, the afterlife isn't open to Brooks' withering sarcasm as much as television documentaries or yuppie pretensions. The film ends up delivering some New Age platitudes about living ones life to the full and seizing every opportunity. One thing that does work to amusing effect is the Judgement City setting, which is like contemporary California, sterile and hi-tech, populated by cheerful folk greeting everyone with a 'Have a nice day'.

*Mother* (1997) is considerably less aggressive than one might be led to expect. Brooks plays a writer who moves back in with his mother (Debbie Reynolds) after a bitter divorce. There are some nice observations about strained family ties as the son has to come to terms with his mother's sexuality and his hatred and envy of his younger, more successful brother (Rob Morrow). Although Hollywood cinema frequently concerns itself with family as a subject, it is often aspirational and saccharine. While Brooks doesn't exactly provide the earthy alternative to this sweetness, he does bring a sober, largely unsentimental eye to mother-son relations.

Despite an intriguing premise, *The Muse* (1999), Brooks' most recent film, was not a success. Brooks is a screenwriter with writer's block who is put in touch with Sharon Stone, a muse and descendant of Zeus, who is responsible for Hollywood's 'inspiration'. There is an unsatisfying sting in the tale and Brooks does little with the comic possibilities. There are good cameos from James Cameron and Martin Scorsese, and the notion that the Muse offers not innovative artistic works but generic Hollywood blockbuster material is a good one. Still, this is minor Brooks.

Despite a hit-and-miss filmography, Brooks is a talented writer and director who, at his best, offers very funny comedy with a sharp edge.                                                **IC**

# James L. BROOKS

Dubbed 'the master of the sophisticated big-screen soap opera' by one critic and clearly influenced by his extensive experience as a producer of television sitcoms, James L. Brooks has achieved popularity directing films with an appealing blend of quick humour and heartfelt emotion. Born in New Jersey in 1940 and educated at New York University, he began his career as a copyboy with CBS News in New York and worked his way up to the position of TV newswriter. After moving to Los Angeles and into documentaries he conceived the idea for 'Room 222', the first of his many successful and long-running television series. Aside from acting in *Real Life* (1979) and *Modern Romance* (1981) he has also co-created 'The Mary Tyler Moore Show' (for which he won an Emmy as executive producer), 'Taxi', 'Lou Grant', 'Rhoda' and 'The Simpsons'.

Brooks' initial move from television into film was as a screenwriter on Alan J. Pakula's Burt Reynolds vehicle *Starting Over* (1979). In 1983 he directed his own first feature, *Terms of Endearment*, which was adapted from a novel by Larry McMurty and focused on the development of a turbulent mother-daughter relationship. Despite receiving criticism for its mawkish and manipulative treatment of cancer it won five Academy Awards, including Best Script, Best Director and Best Picture, and secured Brooks' reputation as a first-class artist able to effectively handle big stars (Jack Nicholson, Shirley MacLaine and Debra Winger) and potentially uncommercial material.

Having formed his own production company – Gracie Films – at Twentieth Century Fox, Brooks drew upon previous experiences at CBS for his next feature, *Broadcast News* (1987). A tale of love, ambition and greed set against the hectic backdrop of television news, it is a witty and well-observed comedy featuring a range of quirky, insightful performances from Holly Hunter, Albert Brooks and William Hurt.

*I'll Do Anything* (1994) was a less successful project both in its production and reception. Originally a musical about Hollywood with songs written by Prince, it suffered from poor test screenings and had to be recut several times as well as having the songs removed. The narrative is remarkably coherent despite the last-minute changes but even the energetic Nick Nolte, as the desperate, out of work actor, fails to give the film the spark it needs to adequately compare to Brooks' other work.

His subsequent and most recent film, *As Good as it Gets* (1997), put him firmly back on the popular track and into Academy favour once again. Featuring the familiar and involving soap opera close-ups and medium shots, it is a glossy comedy-drama that centres on the lonely life of an obsessive-compulsive writer. Enormously popular and successful, it received a Best Actor Academy Award for Jack Nicholson and Best Actress for Helen Hunt.

Aside from his own work, Brooks has produced a variety of successful films ranging from the more mainstream – *Big* (1988) and *Jerry Maguire* (1996) – to smaller independents such as *Bottle Rocket* (1996).                                **HP**

# Mel BROOKS

Mel Brooks' (born Melvin Kaminsky) name is synonymous not just with humour but also with a particular form of parody. Born in Brooklyn in 1926, like many comics of his generation, Brooks began professional life as a stand-up comedian in the Catskills, honing a particular comic sensibility and also a particular style. It is possible to believe the anecdote that one of Brooks' favourite activities is to leap from his car whilst waiting for traffic lights to change, run to the cars behind and hammer on the windows shouting 'Look it's me, Mel Brooks'. True or not, this oft-quoted tale epitomises Brooks' approach to his subject matter and also to his audience. If anything sums up a 'Brooksian' style it is brashness, vulgarity, and a forthright quality that others seem reluctant to use or often overplay to disastrous effect.

He further honed his skills writing with such greats as Neil Simon, Woody Allen, and Carl Reiner for Sid Caesar. Later, working with Carl Reiner he created the 'classic' 2,000-Year-Old Man. With Buck Henry he created the spy spoof 'Get Smart', which ran throughout the late 1960s and has been repeated ad nauseam ever since. The series utilised a device which Brooks has employed throughout the rest of his career: the spoof. This early television series shows a subtlety and wit that seems to be increasingly removed from his comedic work in recent years.

'Get Smart' identifies not only an embryonic movie style but also a subject for his talents. Brooks tends to focus on movie genres themselves rather than on broader philosophical or personal concerns. He has never attempted to become 'serious' with his own directorial work, perhaps an impossible task when the main point of parody is something which is itself often frivolous. Perhaps the most significant exception in the Brooks canon is *The Producers* (1968), which first used the talents of Gene Wilder to full effect. Whilst commenting on the trials and tribulations of the Broadway show (something Brooks had been involved in), it was concerned with two overtly Jewish characters who are (in the best tradition of Jewish narratives) doomed to failure. Whilst there may be a distinctly Jewish-American sensibility about Brooks' work, it is a facet that he has chosen to leave out from this point on. This is apart from a notable Yiddish-speaking Native American chief in *Blazing Saddles* (1974), comments in the non-Brooks-scripted *To Be or Not To Be* (1983), and the 'trailer' for the never-to-exist *History of the World Part II*, featuring 'Jews in Space'. *The Producers*, whilst firmly establishing Brooks as an important comic talent, was an impossible act to follow, and the director has never surpassed this film. Brooks himself stands outside the majority of Jewish comics and film-makers in his lack of self-derision and in the success of his main characters, but he retains a cynicism about the world that is evident in the majority of his works.

Brooks' next outing came with *The Twelve Chairs* (1970), which was received badly by both audience and industry alike, and whilst dissimilar from the remainder of his catalogue, it is certainly very different to *The Producers*. It is the story of a Russian family who discover that their family jewels have been hidden in a set of twelve chairs and their subsequent quest to find the furniture. Once again, Brooks directed and co-wrote, but this time he chose to star in the film. It seems that the less Brooks takes on board, the more successful his films are.

After several years of isolation, he struck back with a characteristically tasteless western sheriff. Directed, co-written, and co-starring Brooks (albeit in two very small roles), *Blazing Saddles* was one of the year's success stories. At this point the director began to formulate something of a troupe who would appear in his later films – the existing Gene Wilder, Harvey Korman and Madeline Kahn, to be joined later by Cloris Leachman and Dom Deluise. *Blazing Saddles* is the first cinematic example of Brooks' return to his genre spoofs, but it is unique in the canon of his work in being a biting social satire about racism as much as a comment on portrayals of the west. For an audience then, it is a piece which works on many levels, a feat that Brooks never seemed to be able to repeat to the same degree.

What seems evident from a viewing of the director's recent work is that a great deal depends on the ability of the performers to add another dimension to the 'raw' and 'harsh' quality of the scripts. An audience will go to a Brooks film with a clear notion of what to expect and the performance is no exception.

Brooks then went on to create a string of comedy films. *Young Frankenstein* (1974) was his next attempt and this parody of the Frankenstein movies was a hit equal to *Blazing Saddles*. Whilst the film boasts superb comic portrayals it is the attention to detail that really grabs the audience. In the greatest tradition of the satirist it is 90 per cent pastiche with only 10 per cent parody. This was a pattern he emulated with his next successes, *Silent Movie* (1976) and *High Anxiety* (1977), both of which he directed, co-wrote and starred in. It is noteworthy that while most of his later work is a gentle attack on the industry in which he works, *High Anxiety* is more of a homage to Alfred Hitchcock, in which Brooks places himself (as actor) in the role of an object of derision. It has been suggested by many critics of Brooks' work that it is his desire to control all, even down to singing the theme tune to *High Anxiety*, that has displaced an objective view of what will work. These latter two films, whilst certainly of comic value, never managed to reach the comic potential of *Young Frankenstein*, either in performance or in production values.

*History of the World Part I* (1981) presented a humorous look at various events in history – including the Roman Empire, the Spanish Inquisition, and the French

Revolution – and takes a broader perspective than his other works. However, it still retains its playfulness with filmic convention, including the historical epic and the Cecil B. DeMille dance routine. It is with this that Brooks returns to a clear and joyous use of bad taste as a vehicle for his humour, such as the Spanish Inquisition as a musical.

*Life Stinks* (1991), in which Brooks served in his usual four positions, was a huge disappointment to fans and critics alike. This is another example of self-indulgence on Brooks' part and suffers from a narrative which is plagued by a wholly uncharacteristic sentimentality. Although sentiment may be present there is always a pun to follow. *Life Stinks* also lacks the greatest of Brooks' comic devices, vulgarity. Whilst much of his later work has met with fierce attack from critics it consistently appeals to audiences, using a joyous vulgarity as a 'common denominator'.

*Life Stinks* seems to have been something of an aberration, sandwiched as it is between *Spaceballs* (1987) and *Robin Hood: Men in Tights* (1993). These two films, along with the most recent, *Dracula: Dead and Loving It* (1995), seem to show a new formula for Brooks which possibly suggests the old master of parody has run out of steam. Where other works have taken sweeps at genres, these films focus on very specific films as their point of reference – *Star Wars* (1977), *Robin Hood: Prince of Thieves* (1991), and *Bram Stoker's Dracula* (1992). While the comic value of these films is debatable, there is no doubt that they are narrow in focus. They are also a prime example of parodying something that was trivial in origin and partially parodic anyway.

Criticism of his most recent work aside, Brooks has not just taken the lead in creating some of the screen's best-known and loved parodies, he has diversified into 'serious production'. However, rather than use his own readily associable name and face, he created his own production company, Brooksfilms. The company has produced many acclaimed films, including *The Elephant Man* (1980), *The Fly* (1986), *Frances* (1982), *My Favorite Year* (1982), and *84 Charing Cross Road* (1986), which was also produced by Brooks. With this effective move into production Brooks has allowed himself to plough two furrows equally well. He continues to appear on television; recent outings include 'Mad About You', 'The Simpsons', 'Frasier', and 'The Tracey Ullman Show'.

Despite many negative comments from critics Brooks still maintains an audience and a world-wide fan base. Humour may be Brooks' own defence mechanism against the world, but it is a defence that has served him well and has provided him with a place in the history of movie comedy.                                                                 **REH**

# Hilary BROUGHER

Born in New York in 1959, Hilary Brougher started making Super 8 shorts at the age of 14. She was accepted into the New York School Of Visual Arts and graduated in 1980. Her first feature, *The Sticky Fingers of Time* (1997), is a complex rumination on creative awakening and time travel. Made on a budget of $250,000, the film effectively portrays the perils of time travel without the use of special effects. Instead, it concentrates on the logistics of being able to live your life in any order that you choose, without living the same moment twice.

*The Sticky Fingers of Time (1997)*

Part Hal Hartley, part 'The Twilight Zone', the film is, for the first act, incomprehensible. Brougher chooses to leave the exposition and explanation of events up to the audience, maintaining an uneasy atmosphere that mirrors the confusion of her time-travelling hero Drew (Nicole Zaray). The lesbian sub-plot is hinted at, but never exposed completely – Brougher's belief that a character cannot be defined by sexuality alone is a welcome counterpoint to most queer cinema. Although the film's plot is difficult to comprehend, the film is always engaging and manages to avoid most of the stereotypes commonly associated with science fiction.

Unlike most low-budget film-makers, Brougher is more interested in making horror and science fiction than human drama, forcing her to stretch her resources to the limit and reinvent generic constructs to suit her budget – something that has been achieved successfully in this film.                                                                 **BW**

# Amnon BUCHBINDER

Born in Kansas City, Missouri, in 1958, Amnon Buchbinder gained acclaim in the 1980s as a director of short films – such as the award-winning student work *Criminal*

*The Fishing Trip (1998)*

*Language* (1982), as well as the later *Oroboros* (1983) and *Seed* (1988). Raised in St. Louis and Toronto, this graduate of the California Institute of the Arts – and current Toronto screenwriting professor – has been a prominent figure in many Canadian and international film festivals. He made his feature film debut directing and producing *The Fishing Trip* (1998), based on a screenplay by his student M. A. Lovretta.

*The Fishing Trip* is the story of two sisters, Kirsti and Jessie (Jhene Erwin and Melissa Hood), both past victims of sexual abuse at the hands of their step-father Harold (Jim Kinney). When Kirsti comes home from university to confront Harold, she learns he has taken her little brother Jacob (T. J. Grist) to the same fishing cabin in which she was victimised, so she recruits Jessie and her friend Murdoch (Anna Henry) to hit the road to save the boy and deal with Harold. Although the film's extremely low budget meant sacrificing many flourishes, Buchbinder maintains the camera's focus on the characters, for whom he clearly has an affection. Although some of the dialogue feels somewhat stilted, the performances of Erwin, Hood, and Henry are refreshingly honest, and their collective inner pain is palpable. Indeed, *The Fishing Trip*'s bleakness is intrinsically related to its authenticity.

Buchbinder proves he has a deep psychological understanding of – or at least sympathy with – his central characters, and it is perhaps for this reason that Kinney's Harold comes across as less than fully rounded. Nonetheless, the film feels genuine in its handling of a painful subject matter.                                                              **DH**

# Chris BUCK

*Tarzan* (1999)  Chris Buck has worked on a number of projects for Disney, where he worked as an animator on films such as *The Fox and the Hound* (1981). Alongside Kevin Lima, he directed the full-length animated feature *Tarzan* (1999). Rigidly adhering to the structure of the Disney blockbusters, the film is a retelling of a classic story, which involves the central protagonist's battle to find his place in society.

*Tarzan* displays all the gloss and technical precision that has become associated with the new wave of Disney movies following the release of *The Little Mermaid* (1989). An interesting development is the reduced scale of the music in the film compared to earlier Disney (although it should be noted that Phil Collins did win an Academy Award for the score); it is now a sideline rather than the central narrative tool it once was. Positing the central character as a surfer, the action moves at a startling speed and the jungle itself seems constantly alive. Although *Tarzan* is a competent piece of film-making, much of its child-like charm (which is such an excellent part of the film's predecessors) is reduced, perhaps because of the advanced computer usage.                                                     **SS**

# Edward BURNS

*The Brothers*  Born in New York in 1968, Edward Burns writes, directs, produces, and stars in each
*McMullen* (1995)  of his own films, exerting considerable artistic influence over almost every aspect of
*She's the One* (1996)  the creative process. Originally an independent film-maker, his first film, *The Brothers*
*No Looking Back* (1998)  *McMullen* (1995), was made for $25,000 and won the Grand Jury Prize at the
*Sidewalks of New York* (2001)  Sundance Film Festival. His work was quickly recognised and appropriated by Hollywood for its mainstream sensibility and commercial appeal and he was given a budget of $3 million to develop his next, starrier project, *She's the One* (1996). Writing people-based, dialogue-led comedy dramas, he has occasionally been labelled as 'bland' and 'middle-of-the-road' and received criticism for failing to explore the more experimental, avant-garde potential of cinema. He has countered these allegations, declaring that his central aim as a film-maker is to write honestly and simply about what he knows best. His love for New York settings and his fondness for analysing familial and romantic relationships have also brought comparisons with Woody Allen, a director and writer whom Burns himself has cited as the main source of his inspiration.

*The Brothers McMullen* focuses on the inter-connected lives of three Irish-American brothers at a moment of crisis, examining the effects of a Catholic upbringing and tackling issues of guilt, love, lust and commitment. At times humorous, at others unexpectedly poignant and insightful, it is a film that improves on viewing, as one becomes acquainted with the characters and the specifics of their soul-searching angst. Told from a predominantly male perspective, its treatment of female characters is disappointingly inclined toward the stereotypical. This is a problem that is manifest in all of his work to date. Men are usually portrayed as the more complex creatures, suffering moments of anxiety and doubt as they attempt to make their life choices, while women tend toward the two-dimensional, acting as emotional sounding-boards rather than fully-rounded individuals. Stylistically, Burns favours a static camera and an understated, naturalistic approach, emphasising the unfolding drama over and above production values or cinematic excess.

On the surface, *She's the One* (1996) is a much glossier, high-profile film, featuring performances from well-known actors Jennifer Anniston, Cameron Diaz and John Mahoney. It is still surprisingly low-key both in its atmosphere and style, narratively echoing *The Brothers McMullen* through its narrow focus on two brothers and their tumultuous relationship with their father and loved ones. An engaging if not wholly satisfying piece of film-making, it consolidated Burns' reputation as a director able to work within the Hollywood mainstream, managing more experienced actors and a larger budget.

His third film, *No Looking Back* (1998), is the story of a thirtysomething man (Jon Bon Jovi) who returns to his childhood home in Queens and the friends and girlfriend he left behind years earlier. It received mixed reviews on its release, failing to generate any major publicity or commercial success. With a delayed release due to the events of 11 September, *Sidewalks of New York* (2001) has since opened to a warmer reception. Recognisably Allenesque in both tone and subject matter, it focuses on the inter-connected, complicated love lives of three couples living in the city. Scenes during which they individually talk to camera, answering questions about traditional and modern mating rituals, intersperse the action. This plays well to an audience already versed in 'Sex and the City' mores but packs less punch than the television series; its humour is wry rather than biting. The situations, on occasion, feel too contrived, but Stanley Tucci is reliably watchable as the oleaginous, morally dubious, selfish husband who, unable to resist the lure of an extra-marital affair, eventually ends up alone. Heather Graham plays his relentlessly chirpy and dissatisfied wife with a bright energy and it is her transformation that most helps to drive the film's narrative.

Burns has managed to achieve a great deal of success in front of the camera, playing central roles in Steven Spielberg's *Saving Private Ryan* (1998) and, more recently, John Herzfeld's *15 Minutes* (2001). He is determined, however, to continue writing and directing his own work, returning to explore the subjects and environments with which he is most familiar, New York and Irish Catholicism. He has his own production company, Irish Twins, which he owns with his brother Brian, and is currently in production with *Ash Wednesday*, the story of two brothers trying to come to terms with their past, starring Oliver Platt and Elijah Wood.                                                  **HP**

# Tim BURTON

Tim Burton is one of the most successful post-classical Hollywood film-makers working within the mainstream today. Often autobiographical, his fantasy film work is part self-conscious parody and part homage to pulp media – including kids' comic fantasy, gothic horror and television monster movies from the 1950s. Visually compelling and spectacle-driven, it soars to the kitschly-decorated heavens.

Born in California in 1958, Burton was considered a prestigious talent from the beginning. He studied animation at The California Institute of Arts after being awarded a fellowship from Disney, for whom he went onto work. While at Disney he animated on such family entertainment films as *The Fox and the Hound* (1981), but was also given creative and production time to work upon two personal projects: *Vincent* (1982) and *Frankenweenie* (1984).

*Vincent*, six minutes in duration, is both biography and homage, charting as it does the story of a boy who wants to grow up to be just like Vincent Price (Burton's childhood idol). Based on a Burton poem, and a fine example of claymation, the film introduced the audience to what would become consistent Burton themes and styles: the wildly inventive cinescapes of fantasy and gothic horror; a macabre sense of humour; the power to shock mid-sentence; the use of the crane to create operatic cinematography, often accompanied by an operatic, classical film score; and the characterisation of an awkward, sometimes tormented outsider (a Burton persona) as the central narrative agent.

*Pee-wee's Big Adventure* (1985)
*Beetlejuice* (1988)
*Batman* (1989)
*Edward Scissorhands* (1990)
*Batman Returns* (1992)
*Ed Wood* (1994)
*Mars Attacks!* (1996)
*Sleepy Hollow* (1999)
*Planet of the Apes* (2001)

*Frankenweenie*, his first short, live-action film, was considered so unsuitable for children, by Disney, that it was never released. In a clear sense this crystallises what the audience later take as Burton traits: his deliciously subversive take on cinefantastic and his single-mindedness when working on a project. *Pee-wee's Big Adventure* (1985), Burton's first full-length feature, owes much to the central star performance of Paul Reubens, or Pee-wee Herman, who also part-scripted the film. The gender-bending Pee-wee Herman goes on a road-movie search for his stolen fantasy bike. Although the film does work as a star-franchise vehicle for Reubens, Burton clearly authors the film through the insanely juvenile *mise-en-scène* – Pee-wee's front garden is kept watered by a rotating, brightly coloured garden Octopus – and the constant blurring of fact and fiction within the narrative. Pee-wee, a richly camp, queer transgressor of male identity, also locates the film as Burtonian. *Pee-wee's Big Adventure* was an enormous box-office hit, ensuring in a sense that Burton would continue to work within the Hollywood mainstream.

*Beetlejuice* (1988), his subsequent film, is pure Burton with its excessive (mock gothic) visual spectacle, its undercutting of fantasy codes, and the macabre, surreal manner in which the story unfolds. Michael Keaton gives an excellent, hysterical performance, and went on to work with the director again on his next venture, *Batman* (1989), one of the most successful films and movie franchises of all time. It is also one of the great pulp comic adaptations, breathing cinematic life into the Batman character who becomes, under Burton's direction, a tortured, alienated hero. *Batman* is pure bricolage, blending gothic horror interiors and exteriors with science fiction spectacle, noir and cartoon-like capers. The set-piece 'blow everything up' ending shifts texture, tone and mood as the film takes the viewer from the insane chaos of Gotham City, with its skeleton-clad hitmen motorcyclists, to the impossibly supreme Batman soaring towards The Joker in his phallic flying car. However, *Batman* is also a film that explores male/sexual dysfunction under the cloak of its fantasy landscape and, with an in-built racist ideology, operates problematically. The scarred and criminally murderous Joker walks, raps and jives like a blackman-in-whiteface, often to the funk beats of the Prince soundtrack. Finally, *Batman* also represents the more general move by multi-media, transnational corporations to have products related through synergy. See *Batman* the film, listen to *Batman* the soundtrack and invest in a wide range of high-quality *Batman* merchandise.

*Edward Scissorhands* (1990), his next film, is one of Burton's most beguiling. Coded as a fairytale, it beautifully captures the naïveté and awkwardness of the scissors-handed frankenstein prince (Johnny Depp) as he is embraced by a dream-like small-town girl, played by Winona Ryder. However, the film undercuts the surface beauty, through its parody of the identikit middle-class suburb where much of the film takes place, and the townspeople's rejection and expulsion of the ill-fitting prince (imagined very like the director himself). It is in the towering gothic castle outside and above the town, the audience are told, where life truly takes place, not in the death-like routine of the primary-coloured town below. The end of the film, where Winona Ryder dances in the falling snow, in slow motion, is pure heavenly, excessive display.

Tim Burton returned to the *Batman* franchise with his next film, *Batman Returns* (1992), having secured total control of the entire production process, a testimony to his then auteur, sure-fire hit status in Hollywood. *Batman Returns* is a much darker film in tone, intent and journey. The grotesque and excessively dangerous Penguin (Danny DeVito) emerges as a mutated orphan from the sewers to castrate and pollute his way through the film. Batman, now dressed in a metallic-like body armour, is re-presented in a hyper-masculine form, while Catwoman (Michelle Pfeiffer), a literal femme fatale, is hyper-feminine/feminised. Death litters the film, yet the architecture, the cinematic spaces that the audience are taken to, remain as incredible and spectacular as ever.

If there is one film in Burton's oeuvre that is personal to him it is *Ed Wood* (1994), and although the film was a box-office failure it received some of the best critical reviews that the director has ever had. A fictionalised/factionalised account of the life and times of the worst American film-maker ever is more readily seen as another Burton homage and adoption of the 'other' (Depp again plays Wood as if he is playing Burton). The homage is not just to Ed Wood, but to kitsch culture in general, and to the media spaces between the mainstream and the high art. Burton reconstructs a canon, a criteria of value, in sharp contrast to, say, Andrew Sarris, or cultural elitists. Comics, Hammer horror, B-movie sci-fi, and bubblegum playing cards are the most highly valued texts in this particular cultural canon. In *Ed Wood*, Burton lovingly reconstructs some of the worst moments from Wood's movies, interconnecting these dual texts together.

*Mars Attacks!* (1996) is a Burton film that is authentically connected to such low-art sources, based as it is upon a series of 55 bubblegum 'Mars Attacks!' trading cards from 35 years ago. Ferociously tongue-in-cheek and excessively bloody, it once again did badly at the box office but received strong critical reviews. The film works as a critique of both Spielbergian science fiction and of gung-ho militaristic encounters with the 'other'. The green, boggle-eyed Martians laser everything human in their path, thus wiping most of the star cast out way before the film's narrative closure. The caustic parody of the military, science, the media and the American government is wonderfully delivered; like all of Burton's movies, it is a visual treat, reconstructing, for example, the neon kitsch of LA and its commodity centre with garish, knowing vulgarity. It also has a nostalgic yearning for the past, however, and is thus a retreat from, or a rejection of, the present.

*Sleepy Hollow* (1999) saw Burton return to (pay homage to) the gothic horror film and also to narrative slippage: it is both an investigative and supernatural thriller. Adapted from Washington Irving's short story 'The Legend of Sleepy Hollow', the narrative focuses on Ichabod Crane (Johnny Depp), a methodical, scientific policeman who is sent to *Sleepy Hollow* to investigate a series of decapitations. The film flows with, and through, gothic horror reference points – pounding horse hooves, screeching carriages, the shrill sound of the wind – and sets Ichabod's rationalism in opposition with unexplainable supernatural forces (an opposition between day-world and night-world, faith and disbelief). Burton sets up a whole web of inter-textual reference points, from James Whale's *Frankenstein* (1931) to Terence Fisher's *Dracula* (1958), within the diegesis of the film. The film thus becomes culturally layered, particularly post-modern, as pastiche fuses with parody and with authenticity in a circuit of reference points.

Burton's 2001 re-imagining of Pierre Boulle's 'Planet of the Apes' is his most disappointing film to date, although it did extremely well at the box office. It seems to be both a homage to, and a parody of, the original 1967 film and consequently seems confused and dislocated. Visually, it is stilted, lacking imagination, and even the science fiction feels flat and uninspiring. If industry rumours are correct this could be the result of studio interference – rather than a 'Burton' film, then, it becomes a studio 'event' movie. Nonetheless, it does deal with Burton's pet issues of difference and belonging.     **SRe**

# Steve BUSCEMI

Steve Buscemi was born in New York in 1957, and upon graduating from high school studied to be an actor with John Strasberg, also in New York. Renowned for his eccentric and often violent supporting roles, Buscemi's angular features have made him a staple inclusion in the catalogue of actors employed by independent directors in Hollywood, such as the Coen brothers, Quentin Tarantino, Jim Jarmusch, and Alexandre Rockwell. He made his directorial debut in 1996 with *Trees Lounge*.

*Trees Lounge* (1996)
*The Animal Factory* (2000)

Partly autobiographical, the film – set in a bar on Long Island – has been praised as a debut that is equally fresh, funny and unique. Written by, and starring, Buscemi, *Trees Lounge* is virtually plotless. Tommy Basilio is a man with an unhealthy longing for his past, who faces an unavoidable future of alcoholism and premature death. The director's vision is both nihilistic and sombre, and he never allows the viewer to feel sympathy towards the downbeat characters by opting for comedy over melodrama. Shot in a deadpan visual style, the film offers a Cassavetian approach to film-making, particularly with Buscemi's incorporation of a series of comic vignettes and cameos from the likes of Samuel L. Jackson and Mimi Rogers. Yet the real dynamism and power of the film lies with the inspired writing and delivery by the two leads, Buscemi and Chloe Sevigny as Debbie, a Lolita-like figure that Tommy falls for.

Buscemi's recent feature, *The Animal Factory* (2000), is a prison drama adapted by Edward Bunker from his own novel, starring Willem Dafoe, Seymour Cassel and Buscemi himself. Shot in a downbeat, low-key style, it perfectly combines sentiment with reality in its investigation of prison life, the relationships which are deformed in institutions and the effects of the justice system. It sees his reputation sealed as an accomplished director as well as a respected actor.     **PH**

# C

## James CAMERON

As a key figure in the contemporary cinema of spectacle, James Cameron has emerged as an important technical innovator with a shrewd sense of commercial judgment. Effectively fusing the science fiction and action genres, the bulk of his work displays an apparent mistrust of technological advancement which is curiously at odds with his extensive deployment of state-of-the-art cinematic technology. Moreover, the widely discussed use of female action heroes in several of his films sits alongside his repeated collaboration with the ultimate body-conscious male superstar (Arnold Schwarzenegger) and an almost fetishistic concentration on scientific and military hardware. Both as a writer (*Rambo: First Blood, Part Two* (1985), *Strange Days* (1995)) and director, Cameron's post-Vietnam and post-feminist action narratives have proved highly influential, with the repeated gender and class themes manifesting themselves regardless of the historical, contemporary or futuristic settings.

Born in Canada in 1954, an early career as both an effects technician and set designer for Roger Corman's New World Pictures led to Cameron's first directorial assignment on *Piranha 2: Flying Killers* (1981). The film is notable chiefly for its pre-figuring of Cameron's later theme of scientific and corporate intrusion upon the natural world (and beyond). His breakthrough came with *The Terminator* (1984), a science fiction/action thriller that drew upon both technological and nuclear anxiety in the midst of Ronald Reagan's resurgent Cold War politics. The eponymous figure (Schwarzenegger, in a role he was seemingly born to play) emerges as one of the great cinematic monsters, embodying the fear of technology run rampant and accentuating it through his sheer physical presence. This threat is countered by the emergence of Sarah Connor (Linda Hamilton) as the first of Cameron's action heroines, her eventual vanquishing of the murderous Terminator merely a prelude to her role as mother of humankind's future messiah figure. Also touching upon both time travel and the Frankenstein myth, the film is nevertheless extremely taut and avoids pretension through its relentless narrative drive. It has been much imitated but never bettered.

In *Aliens* (1986), Cameron wisely avoided replicating its often brilliant predecessor (*Alien* (1979)) and devised instead another science fiction/action scenario. Reducing

*Piranha 2: Flying Killers* (1981)
*The Terminator* (1984)
*Aliens* (1986)
*The Abyss* (1989)
*Terminator 2: Judgment Day* (1991)
*True Lies* (1994)
*Titanic* (1997)

the emphasis on the almost sexualised characteristics embodied by the title creature in Ridley Scott's original, the aliens are this time presented as a threat to both military might and Ripley's (Sigourney Weaver) maternal instincts. Stripped of her professional status and discredited by the sinister 'company', Ripley is set against not only her alien foes but also oppressive corporate and military hierarchies. Her rescue and protection of a young girl foregrounds her role as both mother figure (Ripley's own daughter has died during her unusually long hyper-sleep) and resourceful heroine and it is she, not the military 'grunts', who is left to stand alone in the final reel. Cameron's concentration on the tensions between the space marines and their superiors highlights the inadequacies of military firepower against an elusive, invisible enemy (shades of Vietnam), while the 'grunts' themselves emerge as tools rather than instigators of aggression. Characterised visually by cold, metallic hues, the film's take on the title creatures lacks the sinister quality achieved in the original (they are often so much cannon fodder). However, their design and execution (by Stan Winston from original designs by H. R. Giger) generate a genuine frisson, particularly in Ripley's final showdown with an alien 'queen' enraged at her nemesis' arbitrary destruction of her unborn offspring.

Cameron's next film, *The Abyss* (1989), which was based on a short, displays an admirable ambition which is ultimately beyond its reach. The 'abyss' of the title takes on multiple significance as a global nuclear crisis, a crumbling marriage, a deep sea mission, and alien contact grapple for narrative space but are never satisfactorily unified into a thematic whole. Again, Cameron foregrounds the tensions resulting from the imposition of military authority, this time upon an oil rig crew, as they attempt to salvage a nuclear submarine. The film places great emphasis on the ultimate reconciliation and sacrifice of the estranged husband and wife (Ed Harris, Mary Elizabeth Mastrantonio). In the face of both personal and global catastrophe, this is taken as a symbol of humanity's essential capacity for positive change by a race of mighty yet benign sub-aquatic aliens. The themes of personal and political communication run solidly through the film but are never adequately explored to overcome the somewhat pat conclusion. However, the film compensates with a series of brilliantly orchestrated action set-pieces, notably Harris' final journey into the deep to meet his non-terrestrial benefactors. This climax, while lacking the sense of the infinite achieved by its obvious model *2001: A Space Odyssey* (1968), crystallises the film's emotional core. Unfortunately, this is marred by a descent into sentimentality which threatens to de-stabilise the film in its final stages.

*Terminator 2: Judgment Day* (1991) continues Cameron's concern with late Cold War contexts, consolidating themes hinted at in his original film and developing the nuclear issues expressed in *The Abyss*. This time, Schwarzenegger's Terminator character is presented as the protector of humanity's future saviour (initialled J. C.) and the introduction of the paternal man-machine effectively balances the maternal theme carried over from *Aliens*. As Sarah Connor overcomes her incarceration and oppression to combat the corporate figures responsible for the imminent Armageddon, she becomes a mother figure not only to her own son but to generations of children to follow (a point driven home by a dream sequence in which she witnesses a playground disintegrating in a nuclear fire). Emphasising 'the value of human life' in its final voice-over, the film softens Schwarzenegger's screen persona (under solemn oath not to kill anyone, he merely maims his enemies), allowing the film to channel its sadistic impulses through the truly astounding, liquid metal Terminator, a shape-shifting cyborg sent to eliminate humankind's potential saviour. Implicating computer technology for its central role in the apocalypse, the film nevertheless utilises the very same to create some of its innovative and hugely influential visuals. Sarah guides the young secular messiah (nurtured ironically by the very technological being created by humanity's destroyers) into an uncertain future, prepared for a global catastrophe which may no longer be imminent.

Given the fears expressed previously over the machinations of the military-industrial complex, *True Lies* (1994) is a curious enterprise. Transferring the fear of nuclear annihilation onto deranged Arab terrorist forces, the film shifts uneasily between domestic comedy and straightforward action adventure. As a consequence, those concerns often expressed earnestly in previous films become trite and superficial. While the film is based loosely on the French film *La Totale* (1991), Cameron accentuates the best elements of the James Bond model while magnifying its more objectionable aspects. Especially notable is Jamie Lee Curtis' role as Schwarzenegger's bored wife, totally unaware of his secret life as a secret agent. Probably the most thankless role

Cameron has written for a woman, her two key sequences involve her psychological torture and absolute sexual objectification. While Schwarzenegger is allowed to further develop the family image he keenly developed throughout the 1990s, he is most effective in the numerous action sequences. In keeping with Cameron's previous villains (be they human, alien or cyborg), the terrorists are appropriately sadistic and dehumanised.

Cameron's instinct for expensive yet commercially viable entertainments found its ultimate expression in *Titanic* (1997). Utilising elements of the disaster movie, costume drama and soap opera, this fictionalised account of the ill-fated ocean liner became the most financially successful film of all time and won eleven Academy Awards. Returning to the class and gender themes which marked Cameron's work before *True Lies*, the film defines the vessel as a simple metaphor for old world (read 'modern') social structures, while its romantic leads (Leonardo DiCaprio and Kate Winslet) attempt to bridge the two stratas. Once more suggesting that corporate folly and vanity is responsible for catastrophe, the film locates its historical tale within a contemporary framework in which a group of deep sea explorers come to realise their own greed in pursuit of an elusive diamond thought lost in a safe aboard the ship. While somewhat simplistic and clichéd in its series of character and narrative oppositions – DiCaprio's Jack is sensitive, artistic and courageous while his love rival (Billy Zane) is oppressive, spoiled and cowardly – the sheer sweep of the film is admirable and Cameron's handling of the Titanic's slow descent into the Atlantic is an impressive technical feat. Furthermore, Winslet's active, rebellious Rose emerges as the historical forebear of Ripley and Sarah Connor. Yet the film seems divided by its utilisation of such a terrible event and its presentation as state-of-the-art spectacle. Given both the sheer volume of character stereotypes and the use of actual footage from the bottom of the Atlantic, it is hard to avoid the sense of calculation in the film's attempt to manipulate the emotions. Beyond the spectacular surface effects, the film is ultimately hollow, a feeling reinforced by the often synthetic sheen of the computer-generated visuals.

Having worked in television on the series 'Dark Angel' as a director, writer and producer, Cameron is currently in the running to direct the sequel to *True Lies*, once again starring Schwarzenneger and Curtis.                                        **NJ**

# Danny CANNON

Born in London in 1968, Danny Cannon began making films when he was 16. By 18 he had written, produced and directed over a dozen short films and videos, including a forty-minute short for television which won the BBC's Film-maker of the Year award in 1987.

*Young Americans* (1993)
*Judge Dredd* (1995)
*I Still Know What You Did Last Summer* (1998)

He went on to study at the National Film and Television School, where he made two short films to some acclaim. The second, *Play Dead* (1991), was bought for television transmission by Britain's Channel 4.

His first feature, which he also wrote, was slightly reminiscent of *Play Dead*, dealing again with a gangster lifestyle. *Young Americans* (1993), a British movie with an Anglo-American cast including Harvey Keitel, was clearly designed to call loudly to Hollywood. The film's production style was slickly American, as was its story about a street-wise American policeman sent to London to investigate a drugs ring. A gangster-style thriller set in London's Soho clubland, the movie utilised MTV-style editing and the steel blues and greys favoured by the makers of glossy Hollywood fare. Its fast pace and youthful energy certainly appealed to Hollywood – Cannon was summoned to direct the $80 million *Judge Dredd* (1995), starring Sylvester Stallone. The studio and star's action movie sensibilities clashed with Cannon's attempts to produce a film of heightened reality with a symbolic *mise-en-scène*. It is visually incoherent, a combination of influences from superior films like *Metropolis* (1929), *Ben Hur* (1959), *El Cid* (1961), and *Blade Runner* (1982) with none of the visual style and clarity of those films.

Like Rachel Talalay's *Tank Girl* (1995) and the Hollywood *Batman* franchise, the film's budget works against it and its director. A cult comic transferred to film cannot count on a mainstream cinema audience, and cult audiences cannot begin to recoup such vast budgets, a factor not unnoticed by Hollywood. With *Dredd* a critical and commercial failure, Cannon was forced to back off from Hollywood for a while, and he returned to Britain where he executive produced Paul Hill's *Boston Kickout* (1995), an affectionate look at working-class youth. He then directed *Phoenix* (1998) – a drama about the problems of four detectives operating in Phoenix, Arizona – for Sky Television.

Cannon returned to directing for Hollywood with a sequel to one of the latest, seemingly endless, horror franchises (of which Wes Craven's *Scream* franchise is the most successful) with *I Still Know What You Did Last Summer* (1998). Capitalising on the youth market dollar and using new stars like Freddie Prinze Jr, Jennifer Love Hewitt, and Brandy, the film must serve as something of an embarrassment to Cannon: he was offered and rejected the original, and here he seems duly chastised. The film is a series of slow-turning doorknobs, shadows, 'behind you' mentality, and the narrative relies on the 'it's only a dream' excuse too often for its audience to accept the film's events as frightening. Cannon has said that in creating the look and atmosphere of this film he wanted to evoke the terror and intrigue of *The Shining*'s (1980) Overlook Hotel. In this, he shows himself to be almost as deluded as the inhabitant of that terrifying place.

At this stage in his career Cannon still appears to be attempting to discover his own voice in Hollywood. In terms of future directing projects, his name has been linked to *Wicker Park*, a remake of the 1996 French thriller *L'Appartement*.                    **JD**

# Joe CARNAHAN

*Blood, Guts, Bullets and Octane* (1998)
*Narc* (2002)

Joe Carnahan's solitary feature to date recalls the early DIY cinema exploits of Robert Rodriguez. Shot for just over $7,000, on 16mm film stock, *Blood, Guts, Bullets and Octane* (1998) is an energetic work that suffers only from repetition and over allusiveness. Indeed, the shadows of Sam Peckinpah and Sergio Leone, via Quentin Tarantino and Oliver Stone (particularly *Natural Born Killers* (1994)) loom so large here that they threaten to overwhelm any spark of originality the film displays. However, the kinetic editing, temporal distortion and pop culture savvy enhance the tale of two used car salesmen (one played by Carnahan himself) hotly pursued by both the FBI and a gang of criminals. The budgetary constraints obviously dictated the film's chaotic aesthetic, encapsulated succinctly in the title.

His most recent feature, *Narc* (2002), stars Ray Liotta as an ex-policeman who is brought back on to the force to investigate the death of a colleague. It has screened favourably at festivals.                    **NJ**

# Glen Gordon CARON

*Clean and Sober* (1988)
*Wilder Napalm* (1993)
*Love Affair* (1994)
*Picture Perfect* (1997)

Born in Oceanside, New York in 1954, Glenn Gordon Caron, like his early mentor James L. Brooks, is an occasional film director who has made his name in television, writing for such series as 'Remington Steele' and 'Taxi'. He then went on to create the groundbreaking 'Moonlighting' and, more recently, the science fiction drama 'Now and Again'. Caron's are character-driven pictures that operate with varying degrees of success, but he appears most comfortable when his material dictates an edgy coalition of comedy and drama.

This sensibility is best displayed by his first film, the blackly comic recovery tale, *Clean and Sober* (1988). Anchored by funnyman Michael Keaton in a performance of great truth and desperation, Caron finds just the right tone of monochromatic starkness from which to unfold this story of a drug-and-alcohol-addicted salesman who enrols in a 21-day recovery program to hide out from the cops. Caron locks down his camera in each scene, observing Keaton's gradual journey to sobriety as if waiting for his main character to arrive at the same sense of stillness. There is nothing cold about Caron's approach, however. In crafting a docudrama about people who descend into addiction so they don't have to feel, he manages to find the small moments of human interaction and painful longing that occur when those smothered emotions break through.

In stark contrast to the grungy realism of his first film, Caron's sophomore effort, the long-delayed *Wilder Napalm* (1993), is a misguided, nearly unbearable exercise in brightly coloured whimsy. Too cute and contrived by half, this muddled screwball comedy – about pyrokinetic brothers in love with the same woman – is the kind of picture that finds its ending with a chorus of singing firemen. If it is an attempt to recapture the romantic flights of fancy that made 'Moonlighting' such a beloved fixture, this overstuffed turkey crashes and burns before leaving the tarmac.

Caron's next undertaking was the Warren Beatty/Annette Bening vehicle *Love Affair* (1994). Already filmed twice by George Cukor (the second time as *An Affair to Remember* (1957)), it is a gorgeously mounted but ultimately hollow exercise, empty of all charm and spontaneity. Little of the blame can ultimately be foisted upon Caron, who does what he can, but reportedly bounced back and forth between the whims of Beatty and veteran cinematographer Conrad Hall like a skinned tennis ball. The film is the wax museum of romantic weepers.

*Picture Perfect* (1997), for at least its first three-quarters, is a smashing return to form. Brisk and engaging, the film stars Jennifer Aniston as a driven single woman who 'hires' wedding photographer Jay Mohr to act as her fiancé in order to angle a promotion at her conservative advertising firm. Caron lets his tale of romantic longing and professional ambition unfold with a heartbreaking bitterness (especially in a sustained dinner scene between the *faux* couple and Aniston's bosses, in which their web of lies breaks and is re-spun over and over again), echoing Billy Wilder's similarly themed *The Apartment* (1960), before his well-crafted narrative suddenly crumbles and gives way to a forced happy ending that appears to have been dictated by a particularly unkind test audience.　　**CS**

# John CARPENTER

Born in New York in 1948, John Carpenter made his mark with a succession of horrors and thrillers that, while often breaking new ground, never stray far from schlock-value, camp and perhaps teenage boy wish-fulfilment. In a career that swings between thrillers and light-hearted comedies, his magnum opus is *Halloween* (1978), a stalker movie that set the blueprint for countless horror films in its wake, and has also spun off into a number of sequels.

Carpenter exercises as much control over his films as possible. As a pointer to this, many have the suffix 'John Carpenter's' in the title (such as *John Carpenter's The Thing*). He also composes the score, writes and produces most of his films, and still finds the time to fit in the occasional cameo acting role.

*Dark Star* (1973) is variously hailed as a classic of the science fiction genre and as comic low-budget camp. With an increasingly bizarre and surreal plot, the film is set on board a spaceship where a cryogenically suspended commander and a bomb with a personality problem complicate the mission of four astronauts. A fun, ensemble feeling is retained and the film moves rapidly on. Following this was *Assault on Precinct 13* (1976), a violent and breathless shoot-em-up and a good example of the director's pacing ability and his occasional punchy effectiveness. The body count is high, as are the low-budget explosive thrills set among urban warfare.

The cornerstone of Carpenter's career, *Halloween*, is a classic horror film, which set out the stall for the stalker/slasher genre. So many elements in the film now seem overwrought and obvious, but Carpenter was among the first to introduce many crucial features to the genre: the underlying scariness and alienation of small-town America; the last girl standing; the masked psychopath; the terrorised baby-sitter. Actress Jamie Lee Curtis is genre-defining as the heroine who fights off Michael Myers, stalker *par excellence*, with the aid of Dr Loomis (Donald Pleasance). It is perhaps telling that Carpenter is at his scariest when dealing with human terror, rather than any supernatural or alien threat. *Halloween* has, at the last count, spawned five sequels, including the most recent entry, *Halloween H20: Twenty Years Later* (1998), which brought Curtis back into the fold.

A television movie made in 1979 began Carpenter's association with Kurt Russell. In *Elvis*, a biopic of the first true rock star, Russell is surprisingly effective in the title role, and has enough on-screen charisma to carry the part. Carpenter impresses with a film that – while its ambitions and budget are those of a TV movie – remains a strong example of its art. His next feature, *The Fog* (1980), is a sporadically effective horror movie, which now looks very much of its time. Phantoms move through the fog in a coastal town, wreaking terror on its inhabitants, and for the most part, Carpenter has fun with the plot. Although it occasionally slips from the grasp and fails to consistently ring true in the way the *Halloween* did so successfully, it is nevertheless underscored by a feeling of unease and foreboding that carries it through.

*Escape from New York* (1981) is rated by Carpenter die-hards as a classic. Hard-bitten war veteran Snake Plissken (Kurt Russell) is shanghaied by the US government into going into New York City – which has become the toughest-of-tough penal colonies – to rescue the President. Enlivened by its cast, such as Ernest Borgnine as the taxi driver, and by some interesting ideas, the film is ultimately hampered by a lack of clarity, and what seem now to be unoriginal views on a dystopian future. Perhaps a fault that Carpenter is guilty of elsewhere, the film has periods of dead air where it could have benefited from better pacing.

A genuinely chilly film, *The Thing* (1982) continued Carpenter's working relationship with Russell. Set in a research station in Antarctica, a shape-shifting creature first kills, then takes over, the forms of humans, wreaking havoc and causing increasing paranoia and panic. The film resonates of Ridley Scott's *Alien* (1979), and to excellent effect. With inspired use of special effects, the tension is built in an enterprising and highly effective way – where is there to hide when you are stranded in a frozen outpost?

One in a procession of Stephen King novels turned into films, *Christine* (1983) nonetheless stands out as one of the more successful adaptations. High-school kid Arnie becomes obsessed with a 1958 red Plymouth Fury, but the car, in true King fashion, turns malevolent, possesses Arnie, and starts killing people. The car is imbued with a real sense of personality, and Carpenter maintains the tension and thrills. This was followed by *Starman* (1984) which sets out to charm the viewer, and for a while this story of friendly extra-terrestrial contact succeeds. Ultimately, however, despite a typically strong and measured Jeff Bridges in the lead role as the gentle alien, it is a touch whimsical and smacks too much of Hollywood naïveté.

*Big Trouble in Little China* (1986) is a quirky film, which spans a number of genres. Melding Eastern mysticism with Western action-comedy, Carpenter came up with a tipsy and odd film. His contribution to the chop-socky canon is enjoyable and bizarre in equal measure. Soon to follow was *Prince of Darkness* (1987), a low point in Carpenter's film-making. Flimsy plotting, weak acting and implausible special effects make this one of the worst horror movies ever made, and it seems uncharacteristic of Carpenter's touch with the genre. Even a cameo from goth-rock star Alice Cooper as a zombie can't disguise the dearth of ideas. One for Carpenter die-hards only.

Entertaining and engaging, the high-concept *They Live* (1988) has a construction worker, Nada, who discovers a pair of sunglasses that strip away the facade of the world. He sees that some people are in fact aliens, and that subliminal messages are being transmitted through the television to keep people subdued. Nada – the name not too subtly euphemistic for 'nothing' – ultimately begins a struggle against the alien oppressors; among its shots at the Reagan era, *They Live* gives plenty of grist to the mill for conspiracy theorists, and for those paranoid about the new world order.

One of many films derived from H. G. Wells' novel 'The Invisible Man', *Memoirs of an Invisible Man* (1992) opts for the comic spin on the tragic tale. Chevy Chase is lively enough as the man who becomes invisible after a freak accident, mugging in all the right places, and the pace rolls along easily enough. Carpenter seems quite at home with the lightweight spoof elements of the film and these succeed better than may be expected.

*In the Mouth of Madness* (1995) is standard horror fare about a horror writer whose creations break free from his pages. The film's release was followed in the same year by a modern adaptation of John Wyndham's novel 'The Midwich Cuckoos', *Village of the Damned* (1995), which has alien children posing as humans and terrorising a small town. Christopher Reeve and Kirstie Alley are out of their depth in the lead roles. Then Snake Plissken made an inauspicious return in *Escape from LA* (1996), a tired sequel to *Escape from New York*. Plissken is sent to the Los Angeles penal colony to rescue the President's daughter, coming up against resistance from the freedom fighter residents. Russell seems rather detached in the reprisal of his earlier role, and he is let down by a wandering and loose script, which occasionally seems riddled with clichés. The special effects fail to paper over the cracks, and the frequent and extreme violence is stagy, camp and cartoon-like.

His subsequent film, *Vampires* (1998), is curiously uninvolving and meandering, despite staking its claim for the viewer's attention by being a veritable gorefest, it underplays its assets, which include actor James Woods, and seems to have little sense of where to take itself. *Ghosts of Mars* (2001) is equally aimless, a sci-fi/horror hybrid set in a future colony on Mars. **HPe**

# Willard CARROLL

The career of Willard Carroll, a USC Cinema-Television School graduate, has been largely that of producer and writer of animated children's television programs. His two major films, however, have been a B-grade supernatural thriller/horror film, *The Runestone* (1990), and a dramedy ensemble piece, *Playing by Heart* (1998). Each seems as far away from Carroll-produced shows such as 'Brave Little Toaster Goes to Mars' and 'Christmas in Oz' as they do from each other; one might think he was working in two or three separate businesses. Despite a third feature, the children's fable *Tom's Midnight Garden* (1999), which debuted at the 1999 Seattle Film Festival but has not yet gained wide release, Carroll's work seems more akin to the family-friendly product of his primary career. All, however, deal in some way with the power of imagination.

*The Runestone* (1990)
*Playing by Heart* (1998)
*Tom's Midnight Garden* (1999)

*The Runestone* is the story of a Norse monster that has been let loose in New York when an ancient rock is accidentally unearthed and an archeologist's romantic jealousy makes him susceptible to its powerful influence. A grizzled police detective in the Columbo tradition examines the mysterious random murders in the city while a teenager discovers his calling in life and a vaguely Scandinavian clockmaker realises evil is extant. While much of the film is extremely underwritten, *The Runestone* may actually be a sharp, if inadvertent, parody of this type of film, which was so prevalent in the 1980s. To its merit as well, it is anchored by an affecting David Newman score, and in at least one scene, Carroll proves he has seen F. W. Murnau's famous vampire film *Nosferatu* (1922) with an explicit visual homage.

Carroll's next feature-length film, coming eight years later, is an entirely different work that reveals a more serious intention toward cinema. *Playing by Heart* is a vast ensemble piece that encompasses six separate but intertwining narratives in Los Angeles. It is perhaps notable for its wide range of well-known actors including Sean Connery, Gena Rolands, Ellen Burstyn, Angelina Jolie, Gillian Anderson and Madeleine Stowe, amongst others. Carroll directs this eclectic mix very effectively, particularly the iconic Connery, who is playfully serene, and whose remembrance of a 25-year-old near-affair threatens his marriage on the eve of its fortieth anniversary celebration. For all its smart interconnectedness, however, the film lacks the needed epiphany at its conclusion to make it particularly memorable. Instead, Carroll opts for a rather contrived and obvious revelation about the characters in question. Nonetheless, with *Playing by Heart*, Carroll proves undoubtedly that he is able to move beyond the juvenile adventures of the characters from his children's programming, as well as those of *The Runestone*, to a more thoughtful, adult environment.

Narratively, *Tom's Midnight Garden*, adapted from the Philippa Pierce novel, seems more akin to Carroll's children's programmes – a live-action piece that deals with a young boy's night-time imaginings. However, much like the rest of Carroll's work, thematically – and on this point he bears comparison to Stanley Kubrick and *Eyes Wide Shut* (1999) – it shows how simple imagination can be the catalyst to greater things. **DH**

# Nick CASSAVETES

The son of independent film actor-director John Cassavetes and actress Gena Rowlands, Nick Cassavetes has continued the family profession to pursue both acting and directing. Born in New York in 1959, he studied at the American Academy of Dramatic Arts in Pasadena and appeared in some of his father's early films. He has subsequently acted alongside his mother on stage in 'The Third Day Comes' and in a variety of television series and films including 'LA Law', *The Wraith* (1986), *Mrs Parker and the Vicious Circle* (1994) and, more recently, John Woo's *Face/Off* (1997) and *The Astronaut's Wife* (1999).

*Unhook the Stars/Décroches les étoiles* (1996)
*She's So Lovely* (1997)
*John Q.* (2002)

Having written the screenplay for his debut feature, *Unhook the Stars* (1996), he was unable to find American financing and turned for help to Gérard Depardieu. A devotee and distributor of John Cassavetes' work in his own country, Depardieu arranged for French production funding; he also took on the small but important role of the Québecois truckdriver. Starring Rowlands as a middle-class suburban mother who befriends and looks after a neighbour's six-year-old son, *Unhook the Stars* is a sensitive and mature piece of film-making that takes time to ruminate upon the problematic nature of family dynamics and generational differences. Although it shares thematic similarities with the films of John Cassavetes, stylistically it is significantly more controlled, gentle and wistful in tone rather than hard-hitting or cynical. The acting is uniformly excellent – Rowlands is particularly moving – and it remains the most fully formed and satisfying of Nick Cassavetes' films.

Based on a script written by his father, Cassavetes' next movie, *She's So Lovely* (1997), is charged with a more raw intensity. Originally a vehicle for Sean Penn to direct, the actor ended up starring opposite his wife Robin Wright and winning the Best Actor prize at Cannes. The story centres on a freewheeling couple, forced to split up after the husband accidentally shoots a police officer and is admitted to a mental asylum for ten years; he later returns to claim her from her new husband (John Travolta) and her middle-class, suburban existence. With a much better first half than second, *She's So Lovely* nevertheless provides unusual viewing, proving that Cassavetes is capable of producing first-class and varied independent films.

By contrast, his most recent release, *John Q.* (2002), bears all the hallmarks of a studio movie. Denzel Washington plays a blue collar worker whose son has a heart condition and is in urgent need of a transplant. Lacking the necessary insurance cover to pay the hospital costs, because his employers have changed their policy, John Q takes matters into his own hands, holding the inhabitants of an emergency room hostage until his son is placed on the recipient list. The police and the press gather outside and the customary double-crossing and histrionics ensue. When the emphasis shifts away from the schmaltzy family drama, the dialogue between the hostages hints at a more interesting film, one that seeks to investigate the very real impact on American citizens who cannot afford decent medical insurance coverage. Overly schematic, however, the characters tend towards the one-dimensional. James Woods is given the chance to shine as a fat cat surgeon who eventually succumbs to the common cause but a great supporting cast, including Robert Duvall and Ray Liotta, are generally underused.   **HP**

# Jeremiah CHECHIK

Born in Montreal, Jeremiah Chechik went to Toronto early in his career and trained as a photographer and a painter. In the late 1970s he became *Vogue* magazine's leading fashion photographer in Milan before making commercials for Nike and Diet Coke. His first feature was the Chevy Chase vehicle *National Lampoon's Christmas Vacation* (1989), in which Chase decides to give his family an old-fashioned Christmas at home. Coming from the John Hughes stable of late 1980s film-making, the film is full of saccharine comment on the American family unit and the deification of traditional apple-pie homilies. Chechik's direction is lazy and unfocused, concentrating on facile humour and the decidedly unwinning charm of his leading actor.

His follow up, *Benny & Joon* (1993), displayed a level of originality and wit that temporarily earmarked Chechik as the director of more off-beat features. The film concerns the three-pronged relationship between a mentally disturbed woman, her over-protective brother and her new beau (played by Johnny Depp). The latter expresses himself in a series of silent Keaton and Chaplin mimes, and the film, often merely a collection of glib pleasantries, possesses a kooky charm all of its own that lifts it out of the increasingly clichéd romantic comedy. While *Tall Tale: The Unbelievable Adventures of Pecos Bill* (1995) is an endearing, and not unsuccessful, attempt to mix the kids movie and the western, the rest of Chechik's *oeuvre* is categorised by mind-numbing modernisations of previous cult television shows and French art-house classics.

*Diabolique* (1996) is a remake of the Henri-Georges Clouzot classic *Les Diaboliques* (1954) that supposedly prompted Hitchcock to up the ante on *Grand Guignol* horror and come up with *Psycho* (1960). Unlike Gus van Sant's 1998 shot-for-shot remake of *Psycho* (1998), which at least added a new, if not totally interesting, slant on the original in its use of colour, novelty value and Bates' 'visions', Chechik's remake fails on all basic narrative and aesthetic levels, leading the audience into a ponderous web of clichés, rickety lines and mugging. The costumes look sumptuous and Isabelle Adjani excels in the early scenes, but the heavy-handedness of her relationship with Sharon Stone's character, and the typecasting of surly Chazz Palminteri, divests the film of a campness that could have lightened proceedings. The film was roundly panned and added further credence to the myth that Hollywood continues to dull art-house gems.

*The Avengers* (1998) became a rather bad punchline in Hollywood after its wretched critical and commercial success. Promoted as one of those blockbusters that boasts a first-rate cast (Academy darlings Ralph Fiennes, Uma Thurman and Sean Connery), state-of-the-art special effects and a heavy dose of tongue-in-cheek humour, the film failed on every conceivable level. Cut by frightened studio bosses on the eve of its release, narrative continuity is negligible, with basic time and space rules flagrantly violated, and the prerequisite charm of Steed and Peel is muted by a script that allows for very little chemistry between the leads. The film hopes to remain true to the 1960s spirit of the television series and to that end, Chechik has designed the film as if the 1960s never ended – cars and clothes hint at a twee, ersatz Englishness which is epitomised by the film's opening scene in which Fiennes fends off attack from a milkman. Connery is employed as a counterpoint to 007 (one scene is a clever rehash of *Goldfinger* (1964)) but for the remainder of the film he struts and frets in a kilt. Chechik has airbrushed all of the original's TV-style theatricality and campness and replaced it with bland euphemisms and nonsensical plot twists; indeed, an apt metaphor for a director who has made a career out of trashing high-concept projects.           **BM**

# Peter CHELSOM

Born in Blackpool, UK, in 1956, as a former stage and television actor turned writer-director, Peter Chelsom's film career can perhaps best be epitomised as a kind of rag-bag of competing genres that never fully fuse into a satisfying narrative whole. While admirers of his genre-bending and convention-defiance highlight his ability to coax quirky performances from established stars (Sharon Stone, Warren Beatty, Goldie Hawn) and harness cult actors to his projects (Oliver Reed, Ned Beatty, Harry Dean Stanton), it is a shame that much of his work is characterised by a no-substance gloss that frequently falls under the weight of its own expectations.

*Hear My Song* (1991) – which Chelsom also co-scripted with actor Adrian Dunbar – is perhaps the most successful of his films, due in part to its modest aspirations and its narrative orthodoxy. Dunbar runs a nightclub catering for Liverpool's Irish community and aims to fight off his creditors by bringing renowned Irish tenor Josef Locke out of retirement for one last gig. Based on a real incident in which Locke did indeed flee Britain due to tax difficulties, it allows Chelsom – who remembers Locke from his own Blackpool childhood – to fuse a story of redemption and small-town values that is greatly aided by Ned Beatty's performance as Locke. Expertly photographed by Sue Gibson, the images are inflected with a nostalgia and sensitivity that underpins the rest of the story.

With his new kudos, Chelsom remained in the north of England for his next film, *Funny Bones* (1995). Described by *Variety* as a 'postmodern tragicomedy that couldn't find an audience', this film typifies Chelsom's film-making; a scatter-gun approach that attempts to fuse a variety of genres into some kind of statement on the nature of comedy. Is it a drama about smuggling, an acerbic riff on the desperation of performance, or a father-son melodrama? Chelsom packs the film with an Altman-esque array of oddballs and losers (Leslie Caron, Oliver Reed, Jerry Lewis, Oliver Platt) and makes interesting visual comparisons between Las Vegas and Blackpool. At just over a couple of hours, *Funny Bones* benefits hugely from the energy of Lee Evans – his part in the vertiginous climax is exhilarating.

*The Mighty* (1998) charts the tentative friendship of two Cincinnati children, one whose father is in prison, the other who suffers from a bone disease. At times too sentimental, with metaphors sign-posted, Chelsom coaxes powerful performances from his two young leads – Kieran Culkin and especially Elden Hensen – as well as Sharon Stone and Gena Rowlands as the recurring mother figures. Kevin's love of Arthurian legend is given a neat twist with the sight of knights crossing a bridge (only just staying the right side of Python-esque parody) and his capturing of small-town Americana befits that of an English director fascinated by the iconography of the unfamiliar. All this is perfectly complemented by Harry Dean Stanton's trademark hang-dog expression.

*Town and Country* (2001) has most recently highlighted Chelsom's thematic contradictions rather than cohesiveness. The shoot has already been canonised as one of the most troubled in Hollywood history (re-writes, re-shoots, a two-year delay in release, fights between producer and director). The comedy about marital infidelity is criminally unfunny; writer Buck Henry's forced one-liners and slapstick shtick are laboriously performed, while the glittering array of acting talent (Beatty, Keaton, Hawn, Jenna Elfman, Josh Hartnett) is profligate at best. Chelsom tries to inject some of his trademark quirkiness and physical humour into the mix, but the emotional trials and tribulations fails to find any resonance. The reported clashes between Beatty and Chelsom may in part explain the unevenness of tone. One is left with the sense that Chelsom was merely a director-for-hire, reined-in and unable to bring any level of shape or personal slant to this tired and uninvolving attempt at satire.

*Serendipity* (2001) marked a return to form for Chelsom, allowing him to atone for his previous bloated effort and instead fashion a gooey melodrama that keyed in to the post-11 September desire for escapism and well-told tales. Teaming together John Cusack and Kate Beckinsale as the New York couple who are reunited ten years after an eventful Christmas meeting is a canny move – the actors generate the requisite rom-com chemistry, while Marc Klein's witty (if somewhat manipulative) script allows the sparks to fly. *Serendipity* trawls fairly familiar territory – Chelsom mixes Woody Allen-esque one-liners with Nora Ephron schmaltz, Manhattan is filmed in dewy technicolour, and Ronan Keating and Annie Lennox warble romantically. After the *Town and Country* farrago, Chelsom is obviously playing it safe here, guaranteeing Miramax a moderate box-office success rather than experimenting with his peculiar brand of physical humour and twisted satire. What is encouraging, however, is Chelsom's continuing ability to coax subtle performances from eclectic actors, his 'stranger-in-a-strange-land' look at New York and his playful exploration of well-worn genres.                              **BM**

# Joan CHEN

*Tian yu* (1998)
*Autumn in New York* (2000)
Having begun her acting career in China, where she was born in 1961, in Shanghai, Joan Chen is best known for her roles in David Lynch's 'Twin Peaks' television series, Oliver Stone's *Heaven and Earth* (1993), Danny Cannon's blockbusting *Judge Dredd* (1995), and Donald Cammell's final movie *Wild Side* (1995), which she also co-produced. She returned to her native country to make her directing debut, the self-written and produced *Tian yu* (1998) (known to Western audiences as *Xiu-Xiu: The Sent-Down Girl)*. Based on the book by Geling Yan, who also co-wrote the screenplay with Chen, the film is a moving, beautifully told and filmed account of a period of Chinese history – the 1970s – when Chinese lives were seriously affected by the Cultural Revolution. The story concerns Xiu-Xiu, who is sent to a remote part of China to be 're-educated' into rural ways, at the expense of her urban upbringing. Through the relationship between Xiu-Xiu and the Tibetan herder she is forced to live with, the film examines the conflicts in Chinese society, eschewing Hollywood-style morality for complex and subtle representations. Although not overtly political, the film, and Chen, fell out of favour with the Chinese government; like Chen Kaige's 1993 film *Farewell my Concubine* and *The Blue Kite* (Tian Zhuangzhuang, 1993), it has never been officially released in its country of origin.

Chen's second feature, made for Hollywood, has none of the subtlety of her debut and has been less well received. Written by Allison Burnett, *Autumn in New York* (2000) pairs the ageing Richard Gere with the ever-youthful Winona Ryder (the match producing criticism) in a terminal illness melodrama set against the red tones of an autumn in the city. A throwback to the 1950s melodrama so favoured by studio bosses and the female audiences that attended in droves, this lacks the subversive elements of its earlier counterparts, which were afforded a depth beyond their melodramatic surfaces. Glossy and romantic, it is ultimately contrived and empty, offering none of the visual promise suggested by Chen's debut.                              **JD**

# Lisa CHOLODENKO

*High Art* (1998)
*Laurel Canyon* (2002)
Lisa Cholodenko's one feature, *High Art* (1998), was commercially astute, appealing to a niche lesbian audience and simultaneously pleasing the art-house crowd. Detailing the relationship between two women in physical and emotional close-up, bathing their story in overripe pastels, and playing it against the backdrop of New York's loft bohemia, *High Art* moved out of the New Queer Cinema ghetto and became an unexpected hit.

Cholodenko was born in California in 1964 and after working for the American Film Institute became an assistant editor on such features as *Boyz N the Hood* (1991) and *To Die For* (1994). She then signed up for the film programme at Columbia University where *High Art* was developed.

Charting the attempt at the big-time of photography journal assistant Syd, via the resurrection of legend Lucy Berliner, *High Art* transparently resonates with Cholodenko's own bid for recognition through her casting of 1980s Brat Pack star Ally Sheedy as Lucy. Pencil-thin and garbed in chic black hipsters, Sheedy's reinvention is both a calling card and Cholodenko's gift to American art cinema. Influenced by 1980s photographers Nan Goldin and Jack Pierson in its sultry mood, and the films of John Cassavetes in its framing and emotional acuity, Cholodenko's debut throbs in time with Syd and Lucy's longing. The voyeurism abounds as cinematographer Tami Reiker probes every shadow in rooms and on faces, lending washes to the image which render psychological moods into tangible atmosphere.

Cholodenko's film won her the Waldo Salt Award for Best Screenplay at the Sundance festival in 1998. Her forthcoming film, *Laurel Canyon* (2002), is the story of a relationship between a Los Angeles record producer and her newly-engaged conservative son, and stars Kate Beckinsale and Christian Bale.                **RA**

# Roger CHRISTIAN

Rather like his films, Roger Christian's career has shown pockets of brilliance in a frustratingly incomplete whole. Born in London in 1944, Christian initially displayed prodigious talent in art direction, graduating to direction in the early 1980s, yet the potential promised by his visual ability has never been fulfilled. Mostly action thrillers, his films employ strong psychological threads to explore the nature of heroism and its conflict with oppression, tyranny and terrorism. However, high-concept ideas, moments of cinematic vision, and his panache for sophisticated action direction have too often been betrayed by dreadful scripts and lack of narrative depth, hinting at a director whose enthusiasm for the medium has regularly outstripped his sense of what is cinematically viable.

*The Sender* (1982)
*Lorca and the Outlaws* (1985)
*Nostradamus* (1994)
*The Final Cut* (1995)
*Underworld* (1997)
*Masterminds* (1997)
*Battlefield Earth* (2000)

Christian's first break came as art director on Peter Hall's experimental *Akenfield* (1974), a semi-documentary of Suffolk village life contrasted with fantasy reconstruction of its Edwardian heritage. His command of powerful image was further proved as set decorator on *Star Wars* (1977), transforming earthly locations into otherworldly evocations of Lucas' concept of 'used space' where 'the future is already old'. This experience of mixing futuristic machinery and organic mutation proved vital for his Academy Award-winning, and hugely influential, art direction of *Alien* (1979), which contrasted gloomy futuristic interiors with the Freudian drama of the H. R. Giger-designed Alien. His eye for cinematic setting and landscape as image gave Monty Python's *Life of Brian* (1979) a similarly lavish, period-specific look. Christian's greatest strength is his ability to supplement narrative themes with evocative art direction; as director, however, he was to learn that films cannot survive on looks alone.

Following *The Dollar Bottom* (1980), an intelligent short about a schoolboy protection racket, Christian made his first feature, *The Sender* (1982), a psychological horror involving a madman who telepathically transmits his deranged visions. The film prefaces Christian's later directorial career – an intriguing concept, an impressive look, striking hallucinatory images, let down by below-par acting and periods of derivative, schlocky direction. Christian's interest in psychodrama and the battle with supernatural forces is a recurrent theme in his work, as is his impressive use of visual effects. *Lorca and the Outlaws* (1985) repeats the pattern. A space adventure pitting tyrannous androids against oppressed humans, Christian commands the action and setting with aplomb but the film is too superficial to make any impact. Both films fared badly and Christian's directorial career already appeared to be in terminal decline.

After a gap of several years during which he gravitated inexorably towards Hollywood, came *Nostradamus* (1994), part biopic, part reconstruction of the famous prophet's life. The psychological trauma of Nostradamus' gift, particularly its estranging effect on his personal relationships, is explored with a bravura range of cinematic tricks – hallucinations, flashbacks, cross-cuts, flash-forwards, slow-motion – and is powerfully evoked by a contrast of styles ranging from documentary to violent fantasy. As an unwilling 'hero' locked in internal conflict, Nostradamus is also a textbook subject for Christian.

The idea recurs in Christian's next three films. In *The Final Cut* (1995) a retired bomb defusal expert is forced to battle a mad terrorist. In *Underworld* (1997) an ex-con plays cat-and-mouse mind games in order to discover his father's killer and in *Masterminds* (1997) a young hacker must outwit a computer wizard holding his friends hostage. Christian identifies the opposed sides as symbiotic döppelgangers, with contrary goals but a necessarily shared mindset in the best serial killer/detective tradition. The psychological battle is as much with internal demons as with real adversaries. As is so often the case, however, the intelligent premises are not fulfilled cinematically; Christian's command of correlating theme and visual image, so prevalent in his early work, never surfaces, perhaps due to the new pressures of a Hollywood budget. Instead, competent action sequences, visual thrills and exhaustive editing replace technical innovation and cinematic imagination, turning potentially involving psychological thrillers into pedestrian, forgettable no-brainers.

Christian is highly capable of delivering stunning, visceral film-making, though, as displayed in the action sequences he produced as Second Unit Director on *Star Wars: Episode 1 – The Phantom Menace* (1999). His most recent film, *Battlefield Earth* (2000), displays the same talent for broad set-pieces, epic sweep and bone-jarring editing. The flair for apocalyptic future landscapes, the variety of camerawork ranging from noir to war film, and the well-worn theme of the triumph of the human spirit, all demonstrate Christian's enthusiasm for the genre and for the art. Sadly, his eagerness to overcompensate for another dire script simply result in confused, unintelligible film. Christian's films work like production sketches: though full of ideas, there is the inescapable sense that many of them should never have got past the drawing board. **OB**

# Jerry CICCORITTI

Born in Toronto in 1955, Jerry Ciccoritti has proven himself to be one of Canada's most versatile talents, with a string of successes as writer, producer and director of several film and television projects that stretch back nearly twenty years. His works cover a wide spectrum of styles and illustrate the director's continued growth and development as an artist.

Ciccoritti first became interested in the world of movies while growing up in Toronto. After graduating from high school he briefly attended York University before deciding to direct the funds set aside for his education toward film-making costs. In 1978, he co-founded Toronto's famous Buddies in Bad Times Theatre Company where, in 1980 he directed his own translation of Genet's 'The Maids'.

In 1985 Ciccoritti wrote, produced and directed his first feature, *Psycho Girls*, a send-up of the slasher genre that has, over the years, developed a cult following on the home video market. The next year he wrote and directed the stylish *Graveyard Shift* (1987), the story of a vampire who takes a job as a night-shift cab driver to connect with potential victims. *Graveyard Shift* proved to be financially successful enough to spawn a sequel, *The Understudy: Graveyard Shift II* (1988), which Ciccoritti also directed. More self-reflexive than its precursor, *The Understudy* details the further misadventures of the cabbie-vampire, now moonlighting as an actor assigned to play a vampire in a low-budget movie.

That same year saw the production of *Skull: A Night of Terror,* a film about a police officer who is forced to take on a group of terrorists who are holding his family hostage, co-written by Ciccoritti with director Robert Bergman. Ciccoritti tackled more controversial material with his next feature, *Paris, France* (1993). The film, adapted by Tom Walmsley from his novel, is a story of desire, compulsion and exploitation in which a young poet (Peter Outerbridge) finds himself the object of three people's obsession. The film played at several international festivals and in addition to becoming a scandalous success for its frank depiction of sexual situations, established its director as one of Toronto's hottest talents.

In 1994 Ciccoritti began working in television and over the next five years won five Gemini Awards for his direction of episodes of 'Catwalk', 'Due South' and 'Straight Up', and the television film *Net Worth* (1997). He also directed episodes of 'Poltergeist: The Legacy', 'Lonesome Dove', 'The Hitchhiker', 'Top Cops', 'E.N.G.', 'Forever Knight', and 'Sweating Bullets'.

*Boy Meets Girl,* Ciccoritti's 1998 feature film, represents yet another shift in this gifted director's stylistic oeuvre. A light romantic comedy that pays homage to such classic movies as *Artists and Models* (1955), *Breakfast at Tiffany's* (1961), and *The Umbrellas of Cherbourg* (1964), *Boy Meets Girl* stands out as distinctly more optimistic than Ciccoritti's earlier works. The film's lush, Technicolor-inspired palette and nostalgic *mise-en-scène* call to mind the Cinemascope musicals popular in the 1950s and 1960s. Sean Astin, Kate Nelligan, Joe Mantegna and Kevin McDonald star in this cinematic Valentine about life and love in Toronto's Little Italy district. Despite less than stellar reviews and limited theatrical distribution, the film became a hit on home video and has sold briskly on the US market. It also introduced Ciccoritti discovery Emily Hampshire in the role of Angelina, the shy Italian waitress who is the emotional centre of the film. As Angelina, Hampshire shines with a star presence that is reminiscent of a young Natalie Wood or Connie Francis.

Hampshire appears again in Ciccoritti's 1999 feature, *The Life Before This*. An eloquent meditation on the vicissitudes of fate, the film details the lives of several characters whose paths cross one night at a Toronto coffee shop where, without warning, a violent robbery takes place. Many critics were quick to point out the similarities between the events of the film and a similar tragedy that had taken place not long before at a well-known Toronto cafe. Rather than dwelling on the violent crime, however, Ciccoritti's film spends time with each of its characters and illustrates how even seemingly insignificant choices may have profound consequences. The film features an ensemble cast of Canadian and international talents including Catherine O'Hara, Stephen Rea, Joe Pantoliano, Sarah Polley, Joel S. Keller, Bernard Behrens and Callum Keith Rennie.

Ciccoritti's latest completed project is *Chasing Cain* (2000) a Salter Street Films Production for the Canadian Broadcasting Corporation. Cain is the first of a series of two-hour telefilms that follow a pair of Toronto detectives through the culturally and ethnically diverse neighbourhoods of the city. The film stars Peter Outerbridge and Alberta Watson. Ciccoritti is also at work on a new feature film about Toronto's punk music scene of the 1970s and 1980s. **RC**

# Michael CIMINO

Michael Cimino's career would appear to represent a cautionary tale for all aspiring Hollywood auteurs. Born in New York in 1943, and educated at Yale University in painting, his best films marry a distinct aesthetic and formal grandeur with a complex, often incoherent interrogation of the social structures of the United States.

In many ways he is the modern heir to both John Ford and Sam Peckinpah through his critical examination of the tensions inherent in the mythic foundations of the nation. Unfortunately, the dominant perception of him is that of the megalomaniac *wunderkind* whose fall from grace single-handedly toppled a studio with the financial excesses of one film. Consequently, and in the grand tradition of Welles and Peckinpah, some of his films have been severely mutilated by studio chiefs. This is a great pity, since Cimino's most distinguished work is amongst the richest and most provocative that contemporary American cinema has to offer.

Early success as a co-screenwriter on *Silent Running* (1971) and *Magnum Force* (1973) led to his first directorial assignment on *Thunderbolt and Lightfoot* (1974). This variation on the buddy/road movie demonstrated Cimino's interest in the dynamics of masculine interaction and their homoerotic underpinnings. It also provided Clint Eastwood with a welcome variation on his thus far rigidly defined screen persona. Quirkily ambitious, yet modest in its execution, it remains – due largely to Jeff Bridges' performance – Cimino's most personable film.

*The Deer Hunter* (1978), on the other hand, is the work of a film-maker entranced by the mythic grandeur of his material. Charting the effect of the Vietnam war on a Pennsylvania steel town, the film considers the individual ethos of its title character (Robert De Niro) amid the crumbling ideals of community and nation. The fascist inflections of the De Niro figure, while never satisfactorily resolved, are countered by the mediating presence of Christopher Walken's character. Indeed, the film has been accused (wrongfully) of pandering to right-wing instincts. Alluding to literary and historical antecedents (the novels of James Fenimore Cooper, the American log cabin ideal), the film's immense richness is beset by ideological confusion and ambiguity. Yet its intricate weaving of spectacle and intimacy consolidates a formal audacity rarely seen in the Hollywood cinema. A grand wedding celebration, a game of Russian roulette and a picturesque hunt in the mountains form part of a loose yet elaborate structure in which ritual and ceremony define and shape key themes and motifs. Even the war itself is conceived as a grotesque metaphor wherein the gun is both forcefully and consensually turned to one's own head. Featuring a brilliant cast (including Walken, Meryl Streep and, in his final role, John Cazale) the film also considers the socio-sexual tensions and ruptures which define the character relationships in the domestic sequences. Particularly memorable is Cazale's homophobic rant at De Niro amidst the Pennsylvania mountains and a homoerotically tinged game of pool in which the men raucously dance and sing along to 'I Love You Baby' in a bar. Despite controversy surrounding the alleged misrepresentation of the Vietcong, the film received Academy Awards for Best Film, Supporting Actor (Walken), Editing and Direction, and such institutional endorsement elevated Cimino to major recognition.

Cimino followed his Academy Award success with the notorious *Heaven's Gate* (1980), a film discussed chiefly for its tumultuous production, extreme cost and catastrophic box-office performance (for a full, yet crucially one-sided history, read Stephen Bach's fascinating book, 'Final Cut'). Hindsight and retrospect reveal the film as one of the best of its time. Expanding upon its predecessor's formal audaciousness, the film infuses the western with layers of political and social detail, enriching its admittedly thin tale of Wyoming settlers. Indeed, the sacrifice of a clearly defined narrative line seems the major objection to the film and Cimino opts instead to enhance the elliptical nature of *The Deer Hunter* in order to convey the sweep of a little-known slice of nineteenth-century American immigrant history. However, this is partly the essence of the film's achievement. In its conception of the nation's infancy as a class and race struggle, *Heaven's Gate* injects its mythic aspirations with startling visual detail – one executive commented upon viewing early footage, 'It's like David Lean decided to make a western' – but its interest goes far beyond that. The Harvard graduation, a communal skating event and the final bloody, dust-strewn battle confirm Cimino's fascination with the ceremonial and ritualised aspects of his story, in which symbolic and enigmatic detail assume meaning equal to any classical notions of character or narrative exposition. Magnificently photographed (by Vilmos Zsigmond) and often beautifully played (by, among many others, Kris Kristofferson, Isabelle Huppert and John Hurt), this is, in terms of its historical, industrial and generic status, a seminal American film. (Note: The above comments refer to the full 219-minute version. The final US release version of 149 minutes is best avoided.)

After a five-year hiatus, Cimino returned to directing with *Year of the Dragon* (1985). Scripted by Oliver Stone, this is a typically audacious yet deeply troubling film in which the protagonist, a racist New York police captain (Mickey Rourke, too young for the role despite his best efforts) battles Chinatown mobsters. The film seems unable to formulate a coherent attitude to the Rourke figure and consequently it oscillates between condemnation and sympathy with his racially defined crusade. His Vietnam veteran status is reiterated constantly as a justification for his hatred of Orientals yet he embarks on an extra-marital affair with a Chinese-American news reporter (Ariane). Nevertheless, the film contains some stunning sequences and is particularly fascinating in its take on the socio-historical permutations of Chinese gangsters and their relationship to the established Mafia structures of the USA.

Cimino's subsequent career has been patchy to say the least. *The Sicilian* (1987) charts the complex interrelationship of organised crime, religion and nationalist politics in post-war Italy. Cut by around thirty minutes in the US by the studio, the film is only partially engaging even in its full version. Both *The Desperate Hours* (1990) and *The Sunchaser* (1996) are deeply disappointing, the former a remake of William Wyler's 1955 suspense thriller, the latter revisiting the road movie motifs of *Thunderbolt and Lightfoot* and marrying them with New Age mysticism. Against the flamboyance of the earlier work, these two films demonstrate a marked loss of confidence.    **NJ**

# Richard CIUPKA

Relatively little-known Canadian director Richard Ciupka has headed a total of five features to date, two of which were made for television. However, for a decade spanning from 1975, he established himself as a cinematographer on 14 features – as well as working as a camera operator in 1977 – before turning to direction in the early 1980s.

Curtains (1983) was Ciupka's debut feature, and one for which he took the pseudonym Jonathan Stryker after the murderous film director at the centre of this adequate slasher flick. Six actresses at an audition in an isolated house find themselves the victims of a knife-wielding masked lunatic, a routine premise for this genre of horror. Detractors have argued for the script's inconsistencies and the bad quality of the characterisation, although opinions differ with regard to the effectiveness of the work as an example of the horror genre. His next, Coyote (1992), is a comic drama based upon a teenage love affair. Set against the backdrop of Québec and Ontario, this film is also an example of Ciupka's co-writing, yet remains decidedly tricky to trace.

In the interlude between cinema features came two television series, the first of which was '10-07: L'affaire Zeus' (1995), a French-Canadian police drama. This was followed in 1998 by 'Emily of New Moon', the story of Emily Starr, an aspiring writer who, upon being orphaned, is sent to live with her eccentric aunts. Set at the turn of the century on Prince Edward Island it was based upon the classic Canadian novels by L. M. Montgomery.

Ciupka's French-Canadian film Le Dernier Souffle (1999, follows a Montreal police officer as he travels to Arkansas to solve the mystery surrounding the murder of his brother. Opening on an underwater shot of a body being fished out of a river, the film starts out promisingly, yet the tension and suspense soon disintegrate. It is clear from this film that Ciupka is trying to escape from his television background, taking on larger issues and the big-screen format, unfortunately at the expense of character insight.

His most recent film, La mysterieuse mademoiselle (2001), a comedy about an elementary school teacher, has invited comparisons with the 2001 French hit, Amelie.                                                                                   **LB**

*La mysterieuse mademoiselle (2001)*

# Bob CLARK

This often underrated director started promisingly as a maker of effective low-budget horror films. Born in New Orleans in 1941, his first film, *Children Shouldn't Play with Dead Things* (1972), credited to Benjamin Clark, was made for $50,000. Starring and co-written by Alan Ormsby (who would go on to write Paul Schrader's glossy *Cat People* (1982), the film owes a great deal to George Romero's *Night of the Living Dead* (1968). This story of a group of hippy film-makers making a horror movie on a deserted island mixes its horror with slapstick comedy, anticipating the two strands of Clark's later work. The gruesome final scenes are played straight, however, and demonstrate the director's ability to scare an audience. Clark and Ormsby followed this with *Dead of Night* (1972), a reworking of the W. W. Jacob's short story 'The Monkey's Paw' with a soldier returning from Vietnam as a blood-drinking zombie. The film works as a gory horror flick and as political allegory, the war leaving the protagonist with a literal taste for blood. It also anticipates the crazed veterans of *Taxi Driver* (1976), *The Deer Hunter* (1978), and Ted Kotcheff's *First Blood* (1982).

After serving as an (uncredited) producer on Ormsby's excellent black comedy *Deranged* (1974), Clark wrote and directed *Black Christmas* (1974). This is a seminal slasher movie about a psycho loose in a university sorority house over Christmas. The film anticipates a number of plot twists and visual motifs that would become commonplace in the slasher sub-genre after *Halloween* (1978). These include the use of a subjective camera to represent the killer's point of view and scary phone-calls that originate from inside the victim's house. The stylish murders, including suffocation by plastic sheeting and stabbing with a crystal ornament, would seem to owe something to the baroque Italian horror of Mario Bava and Dario Argento. The film also has a terrific cult cast including Keir Dullea, Margot Kidder and John Saxon, and Clark gets considerable mileage out of the Yuletide setting. If *Black Christmas* looks disappointing to contemporary viewers that may well be due to its shocks being diluted through repeated imitation. The Clark and Ormsby films are good examples of low-budget horror from this period, being violent, blackly comic and visibly, almost defiantly, low-budget.

Clark's next film was *Breaking Point* (1976), his first outside the horror genre and considerably less successful. Bo Svenson is a judo teacher turned avenger battling the Mob in a convoluted addition to the 1970s vigilante cycle that included *Death Wish*

*Children Shouldn't Play with Dead Things (1972)*
*Dead of Night (1972)*
*Black Christmas (1974)*
*Breaking Point (1976)*
*Murder by Decree (1979)*
*Tribute (1980)*
*Porky's (1981)*
*Porky's II: The Next Day (1983)*
*A Christmas Story (1983)*
*Rhinestone (1984)*
*Turk 182! (1985)*
*From the Hip (1987)*
*Loose Cannons (1990)*
*It Runs in My Family (1994)*
*Baby Geniuses (1999)*
*I'll Remember April (2000)*

(1974) and Phil Karlson's *Walking Tall* (1974). Although the film has a couple of effective action scenes it is largely unremarkable, ending on a ridiculous note as Svenson uses a bulldozer as a weapon against the mobsters.

*Murder by Decree* (1979) saw Clark back on familiar ground, melding Conan Doyle's Sherlock Holmes with the Jack the Ripper murders. A remarkable cast includes Christopher Plummer and James Mason as Holmes and Watson plus support from John Gielgud, Donald Sutherland, Genevieve Bujold and Frank Finlay. The film sets up a conspiracy that implicates the Royal Family but loses the courage of its convictions and the film's ending is a bit of a letdown. But Clark creates an atmospheric London, foggy and noirish, and the film uses a strikingly gothic *mise-en-scène*.

*Tribute* (1980) showed Clark once more distancing himself from the horror genre. The film tells of a carefree joker (Jack Lemmon) who falls ill and the way this impacts on his troubled relationship with his son. It is basically a stage show opened out for the screen and there is little for Clark to do with what boils down to a showcase for Lemmon.

Clark followed this with what is still, to date, his biggest commercial hit, *Porky's* (1981). A sex comedy about horny students at a Florida college in the 1950s, the film owes much to the gentler *American Graffiti* (1973) and the funnier *National Lampoon's Animal House* (1978) but despite a critical mauling, it is often funny. From the opening shot of an erection pushing up bed sheets through to naked shower scenes and a hoax phone-call for 'Mike Hunt' (leading to an attractive barmaid calling 'Has anyone seen Mike Hunt?' to a leering crowd), the humour is broad and coarse. There is an attempt to inject a sub-plot about anti-Semitism but this is lost amongst the bare breasts and pranks. The simplicity of *Porky's*, with an unknown cast and Clark's directing with few of the directorial flourishes of his earlier work, led to the film being one of the big sleeper hits of 1981. This success spawned two sequels, the first, *Porky's II: The Next Day* (1983), directed by Clark, and numerous imitators, including the recent *American Pie* (1999).

Clark's films since have failed to achieve the quality of his horror films or the box office of *Porky's*. The small-scale but affecting *A Christmas Story* (1983) based on stories by Jean Shepard and co-written and narrated by the author, garnered good reviews, unlike the country and western turkey, *Rhinestone* (1984) with Sylvester Stallone and Dolly Parton. *Turk 182!* (1985) was a low-key attempt to make a Frank Capraesque comedy-drama hampered with a terrible title. Timothy Hutton wages a graffiti war against the city to avenge his disabled fireman brother, played by Robert Urich. Like a number of his later films, there is an almost deliberate anonymity about the direction. *From the Hip* (1987) is an uneasy mix of courtroom comedy and thriller, co-written by David E. Kelley, later creator of 'Ally McBeal' and pits a dull Judd Nelson against an excellent performance by John Hurt as a wife murderer. The inane comedy *Loose Cannons* (1990) was something of a career nadir for Clark, with Gene Hackman and Dan Aykroyd as cops dodging Nazis and Israeli agents hunting for a porno movie starring Adolf Hitler.

Despite some prestigious work for television, such as an adaptation of Arthur Miller's 'American Clock', Clark's work in the 1990s has been disappointing. A sequel to *A Christmas Story*, *It Runs in My Family* (1994) was average, and the strange children's film *Baby Geniuses* (1999) was poor. Clark's latest is a British/US co-production. *I'll Remember April* (2000) is a drama about Japanese-American relations in the period preceding Pearl Harbour. As Japanese-Americans are placed in internment camps, a young boy befriends a Japanese sailor who is in hiding after a submarine accident off the California coast. The cast includes Mark Harmon, Pam Dawber (of 'Mork and Mindy'), Pat Morita and Haley Joel Osment. *Unleashed* and *Now and Forever* are awaiting distribution.                                                                                         **IC**

# Larry CLARK

*Kids* (1995)
*Another Day in Paradise* (1998)
*Bully* (2001)

Born in 1943 and one of the most outspoken chroniclers of contemporary American society, Larry Clark has been attacked for, what some people consider to be, his amoral body of work. A Vietnam veteran and celebrated photographer, he first attracted controversy with his 1971 book 'Tulsa', which documented the lives of drug-addled youths living in his home town in Oklahoma. Following two further photo journals of

America's dispossessed, 'Teenage Lust' (1982) and 'Perfect Childhood' (1992), Clark ventured into film-making.

With a script penned by Harmony Korine, *Kids* (1995) aroused a storm of protest and criticism from both ends of the political spectrum, which resulted in calls for a ban. An account of the lives of teenagers growing up in New York, the film follows Telly, who will only have sex with virgins in an attempt to avoid contracting AIDS. Unaware that he is HIV Positive, he is pursued across the city by Jennie, a girl he has infected, who attempts to stop him before he spreads the disease any further. Drowning her pain in a cocktail of drink and drugs, she catches up with him too late, after he has seduced another unsuspecting virgin and been raped by his friend. Telly and his friends enact what they believe to be an adult lifestyle, but without the responsibilities associated with adulthood. Parents or guardians, other than older teenagers who imbue in them their own moral code, are almost entirely absent – Telly's mother makes a cursory appearance in one scene, but shows no interest in her son – and they live without control or guidance. Sex is neither emotional nor important to Telly and his friends. It is merely an act that alleviates the boredom of their pointless existence.

Frank in its detail of underage sexual activity and substance abuse, *Kids* was shot in an urgent, *vérité* style. With convincing performances from a cast of non-professionals – although both Chloe Sevigny and Leo Fitzpatrick have since become regulars on the American independent cinema scene – Clark's film is occasionally exploitative, but never less than honest in its attempt to offer a convincing and frightening portrait of America's urban youth.

His second feature, *Another Day in Paradise* (1998), proved to be something of a disappointment. Featuring James Woods, Melanie Griffith, Natasha Gregson Warner and Vincent Kartheiser as couples on the run from the law, it lacked the immediacy of his debut. With a pedestrian script, and solid but uninspired direction, the film is memorable only for the impressive performances of the leads.

With *Bully* (2001), Clark has returned to more familiar territory. A faithful adaptation of journalist Jim Schutze's book 'Bully: A True Story of High School Revenge', the film traces the incidents that led a group of Florida students to kill one of their classmates. Shot in just 21 days and on a minuscule budget, *Bully* is a raw, graphic, and profoundly disturbing film. In focusing on a group in their late teens, Clark presents a more explicit document of American youth, and the result blurs the line between exploration and exploitation. The teenagers' bodies are treated fetishistically, and certain shots are undeniably gratuitous; an accusation even Clark himself has gone on record to admit. In his review, director Bruce LaBruce saw the representation of the teenagers sexuality as honest yet problematic, referring to the film as 'Vogue Bambini meets the Dead End Kids'. Alongside Nan Goldin and, more recently, Harmony Korine, Clark offers a chilling portrait of the underbelly of America's youth culture.

Clark is currently working on a companion piece to *Kids*: *Ken Park* (2002), written by Harmony Korine, will look at the lives of the parents absent in his debut.     **IHS**

# Ron CLEMENTS & John MUSKER

Ron Clements and John Musker have become the most distinctive and successful working partnership in the new era of Disney animation. Their work has been prominent in raising the quality of the animation at the Disney Studios, after an acknowledged lull. They are arguably responsible for re-inventing the Disney ethos for modern audiences. In prioritising 'adult' stories over animal adventures, Iowa-born Clements, and Musker, born in Illinois, have prompted extensive criticism from advocacy groups and cultural critics, fiercely opposed to what they argue are the unacceptably sexist, racist, religious, and nationalist stereotypes in these films.

*Basil, The Great Mouse Detective* (1986)
*The Little Mermaid* (1989)
*Aladdin* (1992)
*Hercules* (1997)

Ron Clements immersed himself in cinema from an early age, making a short animated film called *Shades of Sherlock Holmes* as a child, a story which he would re-visit later in his work on *Basil, The Great Mouse Detective* (1986). John Musker attended the Loyola Academy in Wilmette, Illinois, where he was a cartoonist for the Academy newspaper, honing his skills in caricature and demonstrating the significant influence of the artists at *Mad* magazine. He won a partial scholarship to the California Institute of the Arts, studying alongside Henry Selick and John Lasseter. In 1977, he joined Disney on the same Animation Training Development Programme as Clements.

Clements and Musker seek in all their films to establish an overall design strategy which properly embraces the underpinning thematic and narrative clarity of the text, its approach to comic events – significantly different, for example, in *Basil* and *Aladdin* (1992) – and in the sense of performance. *The Little Mermaid* (1989) provoked one critic to suggest that the message of the film was 'it's alright to be a bitch if you're cute and privileged', a long way from the intention of the directors to tell a story about the necessity for parents to love and protect their children, but to let their children go, and let them make their own mistakes. *Aladdin* provoked extensive criticism from the Muslim community, objecting to the representation of the Arab world, and the Disney studio were forced to change the lyrics of the opening song, 'Arabian Nights', and actively defend their film in the light of the potential loss of a major market.

Clements and Musker argue that their chief interests were in creating a story that resisted the 'greed is good' ethos, promoting instead a return to inner values, independent thought (especially embodied in the character of Jasmine), and the symbolic quest for personal fulfilment in the face of the cultural entrapments that could inhibit such growth. With *Hercules* (1997), Clements and Musker prioritise a coherent design strategy, but move away from the reinforcement of the Disney tradition of 'cute' by adopting the freer, harsher and more fluid styling of English satirist and caricaturist, Gerald Scarfe. Further, they enhance the more ironic and self-reflexive elements of the text to comment upon the representational and commercial agendas, so often the currency of Disney criticism, within the narrative itself. Hercules is simultaneously 'masculinity in crisis' and a marketable 'action figure'. The Greek myths are hollowed out to make way for simple narratives, but are maintained as archetypes of human challenge and moral myth-making. Clements and Musker have significantly progressed Disney from 'product' back to 'classic', raising and engaging with all the key questions that need to be addressed about the power and effect of the Disney text in the contemporary era, and the art of feature film animation in general.

Their next project will be an animated adaptation of Robert Louis Stevenson's 'Treasure Island', entitled *Treasure Planet*.                                                    **PW**

# Graeme CLIFFORD

*Frances* (1982)
*Burke and Wills* (1985)
*Gleaming the Cube* (1989)
*Ruby Cairo* (1993)

With a diverse and often challenging body of work, Graeme Clifford has proven his ability in all areas of film-making, though he has never achieved the success as director he deserves. Initially an innovative and progressive film editor, Clifford began directing in the early 1980s. Often tragic in tone, Clifford's films deal with themes of concealment, freedom and personal quest, but are most concerned with the power of the visual image to suggest as well as explicate, and how its use in cinematic narrative can inspire and manipulate emotion.

Clifford developed his command of filmic language collaborating as editor with leading counter-cultural directors of the 1970s. Following assistant work for Robert Altman, he edited *Images* (1972), Altman's exploration of madness and hallucination through the juxtaposition of images as memories. Clifford's work with Nic Roeg on *Don't Look Now* (1973) and *The Man Who Fell To Earth* (1976) continued the use of editing to evoke mood, theme and time and subvert the constrictions of linear narrative, while *The Rocky Horror Picture Show* (1975) demonstrated his ability to deliver flamboyant spectacle. His later work, though more conventional, continues to use fluent editing to oppose and contrast conflicting outlooks, philosophies, and emotional states, creating dramatic conflict and character depth, as in the social melodrama *F.I.S.T.* (1978).

*Frances* (1982) was Clifford's feature debut, the story of Frances Farmer, the doomed 1930s Hollywood starlet who was lobotomised as a result of emotional instability and rebellious non-conformity. Principally a detailed character study, the film is filled with oppositional forces; Farmer's free spirit and the oppressive forces of studio, media and family; the schism between her glitzy public persona and tortured inner self; the pressures of fame and the desire for normality. Clifford uses visual contrast – compare the bright glamour of Farmer's Hollywood life in the first half with the dark, surreal quality of the asylums in the second – and skilful editing to support these themes of emotional and social division. The delight in making image work as spectacle, suggestion and narrative tool is one of the key elements of Clifford's work.

His concurrent fascination with ideological pioneers reacting against restrictive systems is further treated in *Burke and Wills* (1985), an epic recounting the fateful journey of the eponymous Australian pioneers. Lavish cinematography and a newly displayed competence for action combine with Clifford's skill in using setting, music and image to form emotional tableaux, as in the final scene where the last survivor tells his tale. The story itself, however, with its tendency toward melodrama, marks Clifford's move towards a more conventional period of work.

*Gleaming the Cube* (1989) sets a skateboarder against a corrupt Vietnamese crime ring responsible for his brother's murder. Clifford's delight in the visual potential of the sport, demonstrated by some stunning action sequences, is the real strength of the film, which otherwise is disappointingly conventional in dealing with its themes of freedom and hidden truths. The same is true of *Ruby Cairo* (1993), a film in which a wife discovers that her late husband has secreted a fortune around the globe. Again, it involves the need to re-evaluate the past and discover the truth behind visual facades and mysterious 'symbols' like the baseball cards that act as the 'treasure map'.

Clifford's later work, though beautifully shot, sacrifices his original use of cinematic, image-driven narrative for over-explicative direction, a disappointment for a director so capable of suggestive, elusive film-making and perhaps driven by a need for commercial return. Clifford has found more freedom in television; directing episodes of 'Twin Peaks', the Lynch-driven surreal melodrama whose love of symbol and visual suggestion seems tailor-made for Clifford, as well as straighter drama such as 'The Last Don'.          **OB**

# Stacy COCHRAN

Stacy Cochran is a difficult director to categorise. Her first feature, *My New Gun* (1992), made shortly after her graduation from Columbia Film School, indicates the emergence of a wryly feminist sensibility, but *Boys* (1996), her second, concentrates on the yearnings and tribulations of an adolescent male. What the two films share, and what can be considered Cochran's trademark, is an investment in detail, an ability to render the quotidian as a drama of its own, rife with tension, humour and petty, yet daunting, obstacles. All of these factors, under Cochran's direction, achieve a quiet force. In both films, an outside element is introduced into the confines of a self-enclosed world: the gun into the respectable existence of a New Jersey housewife, and an older, mysterious woman into the all-male academy. While these elements harbour an aroma of the clandestine, and possibly the criminal, Cochran's focus remains fixed instead on their catalytic effects.

*My New Gun* (1992)
*Boys* (1996)
*Drop Back Ten* (1999)

Cochran's view that oppressive environments stifle individuality, freedom and fun is hardly groundbreaking, nor especially insightful, but by paring down her scenarios to the bare essentials, she argues that daily oppression has reached the point of banality, and banality is too often confused with security. That the banal can be so radically interrupted marks the specious nature of security, and Cochran takes a certain glee in watching the insulation crumble.

Released the year after *Thelma and Louise* (1991), *My New Gun* is a subdued take on the themes of the former. Instead of hitting the highway with a girlfriend, Cochran's Thelma-like protagonist stays at home with her lunkhead husband. Copying his friend, he presents his wife with a gun, 'just in case'. It is an idea that seems practically ludicrous to her – what could possibly happen in their generic environs? There is much of course, for the gun's presence wakes her from marital stupor, setting of a chain of absurdity that points up the shortcomings of her relationship, whilst allowing her a fresh self-perspective. Failing commercially, the film garnered much critical attention for its masterfully understated structure; as one critic wrote, 'the world [Cochran] creates is full of tiny eccentricities and delights. It's a doll's-house world, tiny but whole.'

*My New Gun* was received by some as an update of Ibsen's 'The Dollhouse'. By contrast, her second feature, *Boys*, was viewed as a recasting of 'Snow White'. Only now, Snow White is a booze-addled woman, and the dwarves are boys. Like *My New Gun*, *Boys* gains momentum by translating the mundane into the ominous. John Baker's (Lukas Haas) attempt to hide a female fugitive from a sea of raging hormones is a delicate task. The stoners down the hall, who are dumb, albeit comforting allies, take on a menacing quality when they discover his secret. However, *Boys'* strongest feature, the perfectly parleyed rhythms and power plays of male adolescence, also proves its greatest limitation. The juvenile sensibility of its protagonist becomes the film's own, and, ultimately, it too easily bypasses the dilemmas it has so painstakingly raised.

Following *Boys*, Cochran made a short documentary, *Richard Lester!* (1998), before returning to fiction with *Drop Back Ten* (1999). This film, nominated for the Grand Jury prize at Sundance, investigates the most modern of ailments: the power of media hype. However, Cochran remains low-key about her own buzz; commenting on her absence from the film's premiere due to the birth of her first child, she simply stated: 'I'm not thinking about that. I never win anything.'                                                                     **LW**

# Joel COEN

Joel Coen, born in Minneapolis in 1954, is credited as director on each of the Coen brothers' films, but he and brother Ethan share the roles of director, producer and editor. Their quirky and idiosyncratic films have defied many of the aesthetic and commercial rules of Hollywood, earning them critical respect and a loyal following of cinephiles for their ability to make devilishly ingenious parodies of classical and post-classical Hollywood genre clichés. The brothers have also found the respect of big-name actors and crew for their unassuming manner on the set and intense pre-production planning. Their films are difficult to categorise. Calling up the ghosts of genres past, they ask the viewer to spot film references and be alert to incongruities and departures from convention. Expect no action-hero supermen in a Coen brothers' film; instead their characters are far more likely to find themselves in a situation spiralling out of control.

After film school in New York, Joel Coen worked as an assistant editor on Sam Raimi's *The Evil Dead* (1982). Innovative mobile camera work used on the film, particularly the low-tracking 'stalker' shot, migrated into many subsequent Coen brothers' films. Joel and Ethan went on to co-write the manic screwball-noir *Crimewave* (1985) and *The Hudsucker Proxy* (1994) with Raimi.

The brothers' first feature was the acclaimed *Blood Simple* (1984), which dwells on Hitchcock's famous comment that killing a man is not an easy task. It is also indebted to the crime and passion novels of James M. Cain, a writer with a rich pedigree in 1940s film noir. *Blood Simple* has all the sparseness of a Cain novel: events are pared down to a primal level, to the lurid domain of adultery, sex and murder. Hired by an embittered husband to follow and then kill his wife and her lover, *Blood Simple*'s detective (M. Emmett Walsh) is perhaps one of the most abject and loathsome sleazeball villains in cinema. The detective here is a universe away from the figure of identification provided by the laconic Sam Spade. There is no noirish glamour, no gleam of satin or stockings or smoky-voiced narrator. Instead the film de-mystifies the spectacle of murder by making it banal, brutally messy, and senseless. The raw nature of the film extends beyond the sphere of action into surface textures, such as the exposed brickwork in the wife's (Frances McDormand) apartment, the cold earth that covers the face and body of the not-quite-dead husband, and the pipes that are the detective's last earthly view. Echoes of expressionism are evident in the neo-noir lighting and through the pervading trope of the return of the repressed. This is a cold-blooded film with little sympathy for its characters. As Georg Seeslen has said in its praise, it is a nasty and very un-American film.

*Raising Arizona* (1987) and *The Hudsucker Proxy* are both indebted to Hollywood screwball comedy. *Raising Arizona* focuses on a couple's (Holly Hunter and Nicolas Cage) desire for a child. It draws on Hawks' *Bringing Up Baby* (1938) but the leopard 'baby' is replaced by the capture of a real one, snatched from a family with quintiplets. The couple's efforts to make themselves into perfect parents are hindered by, amongst others, two escaped prisoners and a demonic biker figure borrowed from *Mad Max* (1979). The latter seems to be an extension of H.I.'s (Nicolas Cage) repressed 'wild' side, and emerges directly from his dreams. The film's main preoccupation is with the problems of masculinity, particularly the tension between fatherhood and individualism, reflected perhaps in the mix of genres used (road/biker movie, prison/crime movie, and romantic/screwball comedy). *The Hudsucker Proxy* is more closely aligned to classical screwball than *Raising Arizona*. The film charts the rise and literal fall of a 'dumb' employee (Tim Robbins) of Hudsucker Industries, chosen to replace the company's recently deceased chairman. His honesty and naïveté is contrasted with a manipulative and tough newspaper woman (Jennifer Jason Leigh), making for an odd-couple-style romance. She is a facsimile of Rosalind Russell's character in *His Girl Friday* (1940), which Leigh embellishes with a convincing rendition of Katharine Hepburn's voice. The film is stylistically characterised by big-city art deco buildings with steely grey interiors, within which the 'human' warmth of romantic comedy is intentionally made ill at ease. Both films deploy a supernatural presence to achieve their happy endings that can be construed as an ironic comment on Hollywood's tendency to favour narrative resolution.

*Miller's Crossing* (1990) is perhaps the most enigmatic film made by the Coen brothers. Like *Blood Simple* it does not include a comic dimension to relieve the darker aspects of the human psyche evoked. Like their other films, this too plays with audience expectations, and as Ulrich Kriest has said, the viewer's contract with the films is constantly shifting and under negotiation. *Miller's Crossing* appears to be a typical gangster film. Set during the 1920s during the prohibition period, it is the story of rival mobs. The Coens bring a multicultural angle through the tension between the Irish and Italian groups to this convoluted tale of double-dealing. This provides the context within which Tom (Gabriel Byrne) falls for the boss's girlfriend, Verna (Marcia Gay Harden), but it is a love affair with no happy ending. In existential no-man's-land, Tom is constantly unsure of his own motives and allegiances. Barry Sonnenfeld's pristine cinematography and muted colour palette contributes to the visual appeal of the film. It could be described as the least hysterical of the brothers' films, yet it nevertheless focuses on a character whose identity is an enigma to himself.

*Barton Fink* (1991) also refers back to classical Hollywood, not simply through reference to genre but by direct reference to the industry. Barton Fink (John Turturro) is a scriptwriter newly arrived in Hollywood after the success of a play in New York. Written when the Coen brothers became stuck with writing the script for *Miller's Crossing*, the film centres on Fink's inability to churn out a script for a wrestling movie. His idealistic vision of writing for the common man jars against the hack, formulaic writing demanded by the industry. Looking for a story, he is blind to so many that arrive in his purview, but only when his apparently nice-guy neighbour turns out to be a serial-killing Nazi can he get on with writing the script. Fink's writer's block and the use of wide-angle low tracking shots through the ill-lit corridors of the hotel he stays in echo aspects of *The Shining* (1980). This hotel from hell is both literal and mythic. It has sodden peeling wallpaper as well as demonic inhabitants and the image of fiery hell is evoked as the hotel burns at the end of the film. The vision of horror contrasts with sunny California of idealised Hollywood and marks the use of incongruity as the main source of the film's ironic comedy. The lesson seems to be that people are not always what they seem. Well received by the critics, it was awarded the Palme d'Or at Cannes in 1991 for Best Film, Director and Actor.

Like many other Coen brothers films, *Fargo* (1996) hinges around a kidnapping. Lacking power within his own family, due mainly to a bullish and successful businessman father-in-law, Jerry Lundegaard (William H. Macy) is a pathetic and naïve character desperately in search of some self-esteem. He hires a couple of oddball hoods to kidnap his wife with the aim of earning some money to bail himself out of financial difficulties. His actions, born of stupidity and near-sightedness, just get him in deeper and lead to the deaths of his wife and father-in-law, plus a series of other people who just happened to get in the way of the kidnappers. Wryly re-working the 'macho' cop genre movie, the detective figure here is a heavily pregnant woman. Margie Gunderson (Frances McDormand) has a homespun approach to her police-work and has none of the fetishistic glamour of other Hollywood girl-cops. Faced with the killer in the process of wood-chipping his sidekick, she remains calm and matter-of-fact, before single-handedly bringing him in. With its striking white snowfields, oddball characters and Scandanavian speech patterns of the people of Brainerd, the film delights in well-observed local idiosyncrasies, for which the Academy Award for Best Screenplay was well deserved.

Following this came *The Big Lebowski* (1998), the Coen brothers' most commercially successful film to date. Aided by its comparatively gentle comedy and sympathetic portrayal of The Dude (Jeff Bridges) and Walter (John Goodman), the off-Hollywood feel of the film gives it an appealing quality. The film's premise seems to be built on the question: what if a hippy accidentally blundered into *The Big Sleep*? Once again generic incongruity provides the impetus for the film (Cheech and Chong meets Humphrey Bogart). The Dude is a freewheelin' individualist, suffering from dope-induced inertia, his life revolving around the bowling alley and his unattached male buddies. He echoes Bogart's laconic individualism in *The Big Sleep* (1946) and is similarly used as a key figure in a frame-up. The Dude's sense of self-esteem evolves around a tendency to self-mythologise (hence his name and the fact that he talks about himself in the third person). The bowling alley provides both the film and his life with a certain punctuating structure. It features strongly in The Dude's imagination and appears in his dreams as a Busby Berkeley extravaganza. Like many of the other Coen films, *The Big Lebowski* is a male fairytale, juxtaposing the banality of everyday life with something more magical and imaginary.

The typical Coen brothers cross-genre strategy is also present in *O Brother, Where Art Thou?* (2000). Aspects of the classical Hollywood crime caper are mixed with the musical, comedy, and Homer's classical adventure tale 'The Odyssey', which the brothers say they have never read. Set in the Depression era, three prison escapees set out to find a hidden horde of cash. The central protagonist then struggles against the odds to return to his wife who is about to be remarried. The film was nominated for a Palme d'Or at Cannes in 2000.

Their most recent film, *The Man Who Wasn't There* (2001) takes its generic cue from existential noirs. Pulp fiction dialogue, striking angles, and chiaroscuro lighting make for rich cinematic pleasures, working effectively with a tale of solitude and disillusionment. Infidelity and blackmail are dovetailed with a Lolita-style romance in this downbeat treatment. Typically for the Coen brothers, the central character is caught up in events beyond his control, but his reactions are the laconic opposite of screwball hysteria exhibited by characters in their other films. The tag-line 'the more you look the less you really know' adds to the atmosphere of noir-tragedy. Unlike *Fargo*, *The Big Lebowski* and *O Brother, Where are Thou?*, the film was aimed at an art cinema audience. It has had mixed reviews from Coen fans and critics, but tied for Best Director at Cannes in 2001. The central character has none of the warm, endearing qualities of The Dude, which, for some, precludes an all-important audience sympathy for his plight. There are quirky and darkly funny moments, yet melancholy and dry disenchantment are key signatures.

The Coen brothers' films might lack the high artistic or philosophical intent of Lynch or Cronenberg, but they do have an auteurist sense of absurd incongruity, in addition to an ear for the peculiarities of colloquial speech. Laced in strangely surreal black comedy, intertextual references and mischievous re-workings of genre conventions, their films draw on the collective archetypes of Hollywood. From the bleak noir negativism of *Blood Simple* to the endearing comedy of *The Big Lebowski*, their films delight in self-reflexive play, leading some critics to claim them for a postmodern aesthetic. Others praise their films as a rare mix of intelligence, parody and entertainment.

Joel Coen is rumoured to be working on *Intolerable Cruelty*, a comedy starring George Clooney and Catherine Zeta-Jones as a lawyer and client. **TK**

# Larry COHEN

Larry Cohen is perhaps best known for his darkly comic, horror B-movies. With its raw energy and bizarre monsters – like the killer yoghurt of *The Stuff* (1985), the murderous mutant babies of *It's Alive!* (1974) and *It Lives Again* (1978), and the hermaphroditic messiah of *God Told Me To* (1977) – Cohen's work has attracted a loyal cult following. Cohen's visual style is economical (rather than flamboyant) yet his films are notable for their rich textual detail, their strong central performances, and their radical critiques of American patriarchal capitalism.

Born in New York in 1938, Cohen attended the City College Film Institute in New York after which he worked mainly in television, where he created such series as 'Branded' and 'The Invaders' whilst regularly contributing to 'Kraft Television Theater' and 'Columbo' amongst others. Cohen formed his own production company (Larco) in 1965, in order to develop projects for the big screen. Since then, he has been a prolific independent film-maker, producing and directing from his own original screenplays, while continuing to write and produce for other directors.

Cohen's first film as director, *Bone* (1972), is his most experimental work. Influenced by contemporary political radicalism (anti-Vietnam War protests, feminism, and black power movements), Cohen removes the veneer of white, middle-class respectability to expose the pernicious effects of cultural stereotypes. Thus, when a menacing black criminal, Bone (Yaphet Koto), mysteriously appears at the home of a white, middle-class couple, audience preconceptions are systematically overturned. Bone is revealed to be a sensitive and vulnerable man, brutalised by a life of racist oppression, while his 'victims' are a child molester and murderer. Here (as in subsequent Cohen films) there is no reassuring separation of good and evil, victim and monster.

*Wicked Stepmother* (1989)
*The Ambulance* (1990)
*Original Gangstas* (1996)

Cohen continued to focus upon race in his next two films, *Black Caesar* (1973) and a hastily produced sequel, *Hell Up in Harlem* (1973). Capitalising on the box-office success of blaxploitation movies like *Shaft* (1971) and *Superfly* (1972), whilst also referring to the gangster movies of Classical Hollywood (particularly *Little Caesar* (1930)), these two films chart the rise and fall (and rise) of Tommy Gibbs (Fred Williamson), from shoe-shine boy to black 'godfather'. Where legitimate avenues of social affirmation are denied to Cohen's anti-hero, a life of crime accords him both wealth and respect. Like Bone in Cohen's earlier film, Gibbs' propensity for violence is explicitly presented as an internalisation of racist brutality (the savage beating he receives from a vindictive white police captain is edited into subsequent scenes of Gibbs' violent actions). Black pride is celebrated in the montage sequences of colourfully dressed gang members striding through city streets to the accompaniment of a raging James Brown soundtrack, yet Gibbs' victories are achieved at the expense of his humanity.

*It's Alive!* is arguably Cohen's most popular and critically acclaimed film. Produced during a resurgence of American horror cinema during the 1970s (as seen in the early films of George Romero, Tobe Hooper and Wes Craven), Cohen's film makes literal the movement's dominant tendency of presenting monstrousness as something endemic to the American family (rather than as a foreign/alien invader). The film begins with the birth of an animalistic, mutant baby to an otherwise unremarkable middle-class family. The father of the child, Frank Davis (John P. Ryan), is torn between his paternal emotions and his desire to maintain a position of social respectability. In Ryan's wonderful portrayal, Davis is a parody of masculine stoicism, tight-jawed, unyielding and monstrously large within the frame. A moment of catharsis finally occurs when (in a scene that echoes the climax of John Ford's classic western *The Searchers* (1956)), Davis chooses to embrace rather than destroy his son.

References to Frankenstein run throughout the movie (the title is drawn from James Whale's 1931 film), as Frank repeatedly tries to separate his identity from that of his monstrous 'creation', but here there is no mad scientist to blame for the monster rather the film obliquely refers to the excesses of anonymous corporate capitalism (pollution and inadequate drug testing) when trying to find a cause for the mutation.

There have been two sequels to *It's Alive! It Lives Again* follows the same narrative trajectory as the earlier film. Here, Frederic Forrest plays the father who finally overcomes his hostility toward a mutant son, with the help of Frank Davis (now a surrogate father to two other mutant babies, Adam and Eve).

In *Island of the Alive* (1987), Stephen Jarvis (Michael Moriarty) is the father of an adult mutant son. Mutants have been living peacefully on a remote island, until an illness attacks their community. Embittered and socially ostracised during the early scenes of the movie, Jarvis experiences an emotional rebirth when he agrees to take responsibility for a mutant grandson. In the film's happy ending, Jarvis drives out of the frame, with his ex-wife (Karen Black) and their grandson, toward an outlaw existence.

*God Told Me To* is a fascinating, perplexing film that critically examines the patriarchal traditions of Judeo-Christianity. New York is the setting for a series of random multiple-murders that have apparently been willed by God. The police detective investigating the killings, Peter Nicholas (Tony Lo Bianco), is a devout catholic and profoundly unhappy man. Indeed, throughout the film, religion is an oppressive, destructive force that offers pain, rather than redemption. The scene in which a man describes the way in which he murdered his wife and young children because 'God told him to' is particularly chilling. Nicholas' enquiries lead to a secretive religious sect (dominated by middle-class white businessmen) and a genderless, telepathic messiah (who happens to be his half-brother). After a climactic confrontation with the god, Nicholas abandons his faith, career and personal relationships. Like so many of Cohen's heroes, he finds no possibility for emotional fulfilment within social conformity.

*The Private Files of J. Edgar Hoover* (1977) is a biopic that rapidly charts the fifty-year career of the legendary FBI chief who was 'America's top cop' and 'number one blackmailer'. The film posits a link between Hoover's closeted homosexuality (particularly in his long-running relationship with his deputy, Clyde Tolson (Dan Dailey)), and his obsessive search for the dark secrets of public figures. However, Hoover is not presented as an aberrant figure on the political landscape of the United States, but rather as a symptom of a corrupt system. All of the politicians portrayed here are shown to be as hypocritical and vindictive as Hoover.

Following the teen-werewolf comedy, *Full Moon High* (1981), Cohen embarked upon an adaptation of the Mickey Spillane novel 'I, The Jury' for the studio American Cinema. When creative differences led to him being fired mid-way through the shoot, Cohen immediately began work on his next (independent) production, the contemporary monster-movie, *Q – the Winged Serpent* (1982). Here, a police detective (David Carradine) leads the hunt for a predatory flying reptile that is terrorising New York. He spends much of the film trying to determine whether the creature is the manifestation of an Aztec god (Quetzelcoatl), or simply a monster that can be destroyed. This is something of a red herring, however, in that in Cohen's world-view there is little difference between the two. However, the film is dominated by the presence of Michael Moriarty as a cowardly, small-time crook who, in structural opposition to the monster, is unable to intimidate (even when carrying a loaded gun).

Moriarty has (so far) appeared in four Cohen-directed movies, bringing an endearing sense of playfulness, spontaneity and vulnerability to his characterisations. In *The Stuff*, he plays an industrial saboteur investigating a highly addictive, yoghurt-style dessert that is actually a parasitic life-form, feeding upon those who consume it. The film's thematic concern with the greed of corporate capitalism and the myth of consumer sovereignty is enriched by the dessert's connotative association with 'Americanness' (it is white, 'natural', and bubbles like crude oil from American soil). A small band of eccentrics (including a hilariously caricatured right-wing survivalist (Paul Sorvino)) try to warn a gullible public, but at the close of the movie, the product has been renamed and is back on sale.

*A Return to Salem's Lot* (1989) is a (loosely drawn) sequel to Tobe Hooper's television movie of Stephen King's vampire novel 'Salem's Lot'. Here, Moriarty portrays an anthropologist who moves to Salem's Lot with his teenage son, only to discover that the conservative New England town, replete with rolling lawns and white picket fences, is actually a community of vampires, who have been thriving, undetected for three hundred years. The teenager decides to become a vampire in order to gain immortality (and avoid growing up). Subsequently, the film explores the ways in which the norms of adult masculinity can be seen as restrictive and repressive. When a vampire hunter (played by movie director Samuel Fuller) arrives in Salem's Lot, the narrative moves toward a gleeful destruction of the community and all it represents.

Whereas *Wicked Stepmother* (1989) is an unsatisfactory supernatural farce (primarily known for being the last film of Bette Davis who quit, amid some acrimony, during the shoot), *Original Gangstas* (1996) marks a return to form for Cohen. Here, the stars of 1970s blaxploitation movies (including Fred Williamson, Jim Brown, Richard Rowntree, Pam Grier and Ron O'Neal) are former gang-members who join forces to avenge the (gang-related) death of Grier's son. Against a backdrop of urban decay and ghetto poverty, the film contrasts the experiences of contemporary black youth with those of the 'original gangstas', whilst implicitly reflecting upon the ideology of 1970s black action cinema.

In a film industry that too often values expensive special effects over conceptual originality, Cohen's films display a maverick perceptiveness in their combination of radicalism, suspense and sentimentality. Larry Cohen is, simply, one of American cinema's most undervalued independent auteurs.                                    **EC**

# Peter M. COHEN

*Whipped* (2000)  As writer, producer and director of *Whipped* (2000), it would be difficult for Peter M. Cohen to apportion the blame for one of the singularly most offensive American films in recent memory. While the Farrelly Brothers may be pretty inexcusable, bar one or two humorous moments, and the recent work of Tom Green something of a nadir, Cohen mistakenly believes himself to be taking a pseudo-feminist, quasi-provocative approach.

The story focuses on three male buddies who think of females as potential notches on the bedpost. Alarmed when they find themselves trying to win over the same attractive woman – the perennially underwhelming Amanda Peet – their worlds are turned upside down. At best competently directed, it is a wholly unedifying, juvenile, and frankly boorish affair that makes the insights into relationships expounded by the characters in 'Sex and the City' seem like Nietzsche. Even more distressing, Cohen also has the chutzpah to give himself a small cameo role – fine for Ed Burns but not a good sign for this kind of director. In the final analysis, with its faux enlightenment and table-turning attitudes to the predatory nature of male and female sexuality, *Whipped* is nothing short of dismal. **JWo**

# Rob COHEN

Born in New York, USA, in 1949, Rob Cohen began his career in film during his sophomore year at Harvard when he assisted director Daniel Petrie. After graduating, he moved to Los Angeles and became Director of Television Movies at Fox TV. His television directorial credits included an Emmy-nominated episode of 'Miami Vice' as well as episodes of 'thirtysomething', 'Hooperman', 'A Year in the Life', and 'Private Eye'. He is also a renowned producer, setting up the Motown Corporation and then establishing the Badham-Cohen Group with fellow director John Badham. His notable productions include *The Witches of Eastwick* (1987) and *The Hard Way* (1991).

His feature debut, *A Small Circle of Friends* (1980), is the kind of eclectic and intertextual film that went on to characterise Cohen's career and concerns the trials and tribulations of Harvard men at the end of the 1960s. Written by Ezra Sacks, Cohen presumably had much affiliation with the film given its autobiographical content and setting, and it is an uneven yet ambitious cocktail of sex, comedy, politics and melodrama. The humour is extremely knowing, relying too much on an audience's prior knowledge of a specific time and place.

*Scandalous* (1984) is certainly bizarre. British-financed, Robert Hays plays a television reporter who gets a taste of his own medicine when his wife is kidnapped by Pamela Stephenson and a leather-clad John Gielgud. The film flaunts its small-screen origins as well as its inherent smut and soft-core image – it is notable only for wasting the talents of all concerned (including Dave Grusin's music and Jack Cardiff's cinematography). *Dragon: The Bruce Lee Story* (1993) is a lively if somewhat watered-down biopic that introduced the world to Jason Scott Lee (no relation) and tried to decipher the myth that adorns every student's bedroom wall. Cohen's film succeeds largely due to its excellent recreations of exiting Bruce Lee films (especially *Enter The Dragon* (1973)); as a hagiographic study, its style is both haunting and unsettling.

*Dragonheart* (1996), his next film, was one of the first to successfully meld fantasy, CGI graphics and a distinctly 1990s cast in its portrayal of medieval knights and a splendidly-voiced dragon (Sean Connery). Cohen modelled the dragon's voice modulations and facial tics on the actor, and the result is never less than miraculous. Dennis Quaid tries manfully to incorporate everything into a coherent whole, but it is left to the typical British villain (not Alan Rickman or Jeremy Irons this time, but David Thewlis) to bring a certain swaggering campery and amiability to the role of the evil king. Julie Christie and John Gielgud also make an appearance, and the whole event smacks of childish enthusiasm and a love of a long-stagnant genre.

Cohen burnt his bridges somewhat with the over-indulgent Sylvester Stallone vehicle *Daylight* (1996), combining state-of-the-art SFX with cardboard cut-out characters. The disaster movie enjoyed something of a renaissance during 1996 (the year that *Twister* was also released) and Cohen must have been hoping that the audience would not become too disgruntled by the lack of plot on show here: a group of Americans are trapped in a tunnel; the audience are invited to guess who will be the first to die; and it is up to Stallone, like Gene Hackman in *The Poseidon Adventure* (1972), to lead them to safety.

Cohen followed with *The Skulls* (2000), the story of an impoverished student (Joshua Jackson) who enters the secret Skull society at an Ivy League university but soon falls into trouble when he discovers that his room-mate has been murdered. Cohen and screenwriter John Pogue unfortunately bungle this fascinating idea, for the film is hopelessly in thrall to a lifestyle it purports to condemn. It is hard to feel any sympathy for the murdered student (earnest student journalist Hill Harper) when his death falls against the backdrop of fast cars and easy money. The Skulls society is presumably based on the Skull and Bones club at Yale University (with contained both Bush presidents as members), but instead of exploring complex issues such as Faustian pacts, class systems and education, Cohen opts for simple conspiracy thriller generics, complete with shadowy eminence grise, a Fatboy Slim soundtrack and 'Dawson's Creek'-style acting. Although not 'the execrable frat flick' that some reviews labelled it, the film feels routinely lightweight, lacking the kind of gravitas that Donna Tartt's best-selling novel 'A Secret History' (which tackles the same themes) had in abundance.

Cohen's return to form, and entry into the blockbuster pantheon, was assured by *The Fast and the Furious* (2001). Paul Walker is an undercover officer who infiltrates a gang of LA racers (led by Vin Diesel) to trap a hijacking ring. Where the film succeeds is in its intensity (rarely have drag races seemed so exciting), its smouldering performances (Diesel's basso profundo tones sit well with his granite physique) and Cohen's clever direction, whose fast and furious style finds its niche. An eclectic hip-hop and thrash metal soundtrack adds to the kineticism. Unlike Dominic Sena's earnestly prosaic *Gone in Sixty Seconds* (2000), *The Fast and the Furious* recognises its own script limitations and focuses instead on non-stop action, testosterone-fuelled banter and the kind of ending Hollywood baddies should get more often.

Cohen's most recent feature, *XXX* (2002), is a James Bond-style adventure in which Vin Diesel is recruited by a government agency to infiltrate a Russian crime ring. Samuel L. Jackson also stars. **BM**

# Chris COLUMBUS

Chris Columbus is a director and screenwriter of phenomenally successful – if elementary – comedies, who has in the last few years also explored the genres of melodrama and science fiction. His no-nonsense style is both his anchor and Achilles' heel, providing straightforward plots that often fail to satisfy the more mature observer.

Born in 1959 in Pennsylvania, a graduate of New York University, Columbus had sold his first screenplay, *Jocks*, before leaving. In time he went on to write scripts for a number of Spielberg-produced films, most prominently *Gremlins* (1984) and *The Goonies* (1985).

In the tradition of prescription romps like *Risky Business* (1983) and *After Hours* (1985), *Adventures in Babysitting* (1987) begins with Elisabeth Shue looking after two children, and proceeds as a naïve, imbecilic hash in which she heads across night-time Chicago to help a friend – with her charges in tow. The presence of Shue almost justifies this doltish jaunt, as she exposes flashes of brilliance that would re-surface in *Leaving Las Vegas* (1995). But as a rule this offering is half-baked trumpery that refuses to enthral. However mediocre his debut may be, however, it never stoops as low as *Heartbreak Hotel* (1988), possibly the greatest insult to the memory of Elvis Presley since his demise. Kidnapped post-concert by Charlie Schlatter in 1972, Elvis (David Keith) is taken to meet and greet the lad's mother (Tuesday Weld). In a bizarre turn of events the singer finds himself nestling in the bosom of their small hometown, offering counsel and disentangling the family's problems. The saccharine ending is truly excruciating, as is the German Accordion Band's tribute to the king – a shameless and shameful abuse of the star's reputation.

Luckily Columbus' next film would establish him in Hollywood for life. The coup that was *Home Alone* (1990) proved just as much of a mystery to executives at Fox as it did a hit with punters the world over. Prolific writer-producer John Hughes' implausible plot strands eight-year-old cherub Macaulay Culkin in the house alone for the Christmas vacation, then pits him against infelicitous burglars Joe Pesci and Daniel Stern. Alternating radically between repellent simpering and virtually sadistic Three Stooges slapstick – triggered by Culkin's makeshift defences (Pesci attacked with a blowtorch, Stern's encounter with a six-inch nail) – in all the commotion it is easy to forget that the whole scenario rests upon a serious case of child neglect.

Another Hughes favourite, John Candy, takes the lead in *Only the Lonely* (1991), a romantic comedy with too few ingredients from either genre to triumph. Candy plays a bashful Chicago cop in love with a mortician's daughter, Ally Sheedy. The obstacle in their way: his bigoted, browbeating, dictatorial mother – a choice role for Maureen

O'Hara, returning to films after twenty years away. Mildly diverting and at times uncannily familiar, *Only the Lonely* does provide a spruce overview of the difficult search for love in a big city.

*Home Alone 2: Lost in New York* (1992), however, holds few revelations, being nothing more than a replay of the original, trading the suburban family home for a metropolitan hotel. Once more, Culkin is chastised by his parents and accidentally mislaid; he boards a plane for New York while they head for Florida. Coincidentally, he clashes with the same two thieves from *Home Alone*. If anything, the violence is more acute, but that said, it still numbered amongst the biggest box-office draws of the year.

As indeed did *Mrs Doubtfire* (1993), with takings totalling $200 million in the US alone. An obvious *Tootsie* (1982) clone, this time comedian Robin Williams dons the dress, camouflaging himself in order to see his children and estranged wife (Sally Field). The quality moments are the most salient ones, where Williams indulges in manly pursuits dressed in drag or performs exhaustingly quick changes to be in two places at the same time. The film also balks at suggesting any magical Hollywood solutions to the family's plight – actually providing evidence that concerns about Williams' lack of responsibility were well-founded.

Apart from a handful of droll scenes, *Nine Months* (1995), Columbus' graceless attempt to turn Hugh Grant into a latter-day Cary Grant, is a trifling rumination on pregnancy in the professional age. An upwardly mobile couple inadvertently conceive, thus initialising a series of dubious comedic set-pieces interspersed with navel-gazing and stock-in-trade screwball mix-ups. The circular narrative barely penetrates the outer layer of the subject, Tom Arnold and Joan Cusack are held up as arguments both for and against parenthood, and Robin Williams' encore as a foreign obstetrician is too preposterous for words in this mismanaged remake of Patrick Braoudé's *Neuf Mois* (1994).

In *Stepmom* (1998), however, actresses Julia Roberts and Susan Sarandon compete for Academy Award attention – the former as a vivacious fashion designer, the latter as a mother having to come to terms with Roberts as 'stepmom' to her kids. This results in highly charged emotional interplay, swiftly exacerbated by the onset of Sarandon's cancer. A quintessential 'tear-jerker' with only Ed Harris' insensitive father poorly-served by the script. Another melodrama superseded this, albeit one unconvincingly masquerading as science fiction. In *Bicentennial Man* (1999) Robin Williams makes his third appearance in a Columbus movie, here as a robotic tin man who craves the frailties of humanity. Based on Isaac Asimov's short, it spans two centuries and applies the latest in special effects technology to construct one of the most credible visions of the future ever filmed. Unfortunately, James Horner's obtrusive score, ham-fistedly signalling the more touching scenes, and Columbus' gauche moralising about the nature of our race enervate its admirable intentions.

After creative differences between first-choice director Steven Spielberg and creator J. K. Rowling, Columbus won the privileged job of bringing that most famous of schoolboy wizards to life in *Harry Potter and the Sorcerer's Stone* (2001). The quintessential British ambience is retained from the book, and actors like Robbie Coltrane and Dame Maggie Smith even outshine the prerequisite magical effects and striking sets. Total unknown Daniel Radcliffe is also inspirationally cast as Harry, and Columbus' previous experience with the children's market is a significant advantage. All these factors coalesced to make this one of the most successful films of all time, and Columbus is directing the two sequels: *Chamber of Secrets* and *The Prisoner of Azkaban* (scheduled for 2002 and 2004 respectively). **PB**

# Bill CONDON

Bill Condon has established himself as an important contributor to the horror/thriller genre over the last decade. Inspired by the films of Alfred Hitchcock and James Whale, he has produced a body of work whose most common thread, beyond mere association with the horror genre, is a thematic insistence on dealing with one's past. From *Sister, Sister* (1987) to the seminal *Gods and Monsters* (1998), the passage of time is a central dilemma facing Condon's protagonists.

Born in New York in 1957, Condon attended Columbia University and majored in philosophy. An interest in films eventually led him to California, where he began writing

*Sister, Sister* (1987)
*Candyman II: Farewell to the Flesh* (1995)
*Gods and Monsters* (1998)

for several film journals, 'American Film' being the most prominent. His writing caught the attention of a producer who subsequently invited Condon to write scripts for him.

His first two scripts to be produced were for horror films, *Dead Kids* (1981) and *Strange Invaders* (1983). Michael Laughlin directed both and Condon had the opportunity to observe the production process at work. Confident about his own directing potential, Condon wrote and directed the gothic thriller *Sister, Sister*, starring Jennifer Jason Leigh and Eric Stoltz. Following this debut came a string of films for television: *Murder 101* (1991), *White Lie* (1991), *Dead in the Water* (1991), and *Deadly Relations* (1993). For *Murder 101*, which starred Pierce Brosnan, Condon won the Edgar Award from the Mystery Writers of America.

In 1995, he directed *Candyman II: Farewell to the Flesh*. The film afforded the director the opportunity to return to the silver screen and intertwine his nuanced approached to horror films with the sensationalism of the slasher genre. He returned to television to direct *The Man who Wouldn't Die* (1995), a thriller starring Roger Moore and Malcolm McDowell. However, it was *Gods and Monsters* (1998) which raised Condon's implicit thematic concerns (time and memory) to a whole new level.

An adaptation of Christopher Bram's novel, *Gods and Monsters* is a biographical look at acclaimed film-maker James Whale in the final weeks of his life. Deploying cinematic devices from Whale's own films, Condon paints a complicated portrait of a man who, at the twilight of his life, is unable to appreciate his own achievements. At the heart of the film is the relationship between the openly gay Whale (played by Ian McKellan) and his gardener, ex-marine Clayton Boone (Brendan Fraser). While the relationship is largely fictionalised, the Boone character is framed and characterised as a sort of loveable 'monster'. Flashbacks highlighting details of Whale's past are cleverly interwoven throughout the film, blurring the distinctions between past/present and fantasy/reality. **SCh**

# Theresa CONNELLY

*Polish Wedding* (1998)
Theresa Connelly is typical of a new breed of American directors that eschew mainstream, spectacle-based entertainment for a more European, character-driven, personal experience. Having grown up in a Polish Community outside Detroit, Connelly utilises her unusual background in her first screenplay, *Polish Wedding* (1998). Accepted to the Sundance Screenwriters and Directors Lab in 1994, she managed to secure backing for this – her first and only film – in 1998.

*Polish Wedding* tells the story of the Pzoniak family who inhabit a Polish suburb outside of Detroit. Halle (Clare Danes) is the strong willed and rebellious daughter who, by getting pregnant by the local policeman, disrupts not only her links with her family, but also falls into what she was attempting to avoid – repeating the mistakes of her mother. Gabriel Byrne as the cuckolded father is overbearing and unsympathetic whilst Lena Olin, as the matriarchal head of the family, produces a brash and stereotypical performance that seems to have no basis in reality.

Connelly has stated that she was so inspired by the inner strength of the people in her life that she felt compelled to make this film. Although she clearly has a feel for dialogue and comedic situations, her first attempt is not fully realised and is under-developed.

Connelly still continues to direct for the stage. **BW**

# Martha COOLIDGE

*David: Off and On* (1972)
*Old-Fashioned Woman* (1974)
*More than a School* (1974)
*Not a Pretty Picture* (1975)
*Valley Girl* (1983)
*The Joy of Sex* (1984)
*City Girl* (1984)
*Real Genius* (1985)
*Plain Clothes* (1988)
*Rambling Rose* (1991)

Born in Newhaven, Connecticut, in 1946, celebrated as an icon for women in the film industry, and one of the most prolific film-makers working, Martha Coolidge started making independent documentary films at the age of 26. *David: Off and On* (1972) is about Coolidge's brother's drug addiction and reveals a distinctive style of direction which characterised much of her early work. Although concerning a subject intimately related to herself, Coolidge maintains a distanced relationship between her brother and her camera, not allowing her own bias or attitude to perceptively intrude at all. She sits back and watches him, making acute filmic observations of the traits of his addictive persona: his nervous chain-smoking, an action which she feels stands on its own as a signifier of David, becomes a feature of her patient, languid gaze.

In 1974 Coolidge made *More than a School* and was also involved in a collaboration of work called *Roots*, which comprised four shorts from different directors (including *Italianamerican* from Martin Scorsese) about their heritage. Her film, called *Old-Fashioned Woman* (1974), is about her grandmother's life, and is a montage of old photographs, tied together by Mabel Tilton Coolidge's bold opinions on family, family-planning and society. It too reveals an objective style which distances Coolidge's own politics from those of her grandmother, while at the same time painting a generous and loving portrait of her.

Continuing this exploration of autobiographical history, Coolidge's most personal film, *Not a Pretty Picture* (1975), which deals with her rape as a teenager, is also her most political. The role of the rapist as a retrospective adult seeks to emphasise man's injustice to women, and there is little nostalgia in this film set mostly in 1962. It is in some ways an anti-period piece, letting contemporary thought and action represent the time instead of a fastidious recreation of the fashions they wore. But the exact reconstruction of her story seems to be a therapeutic externalisation of her own trauma, rather than something which successfully implicates the social attitudes which may have allowed it.

Coolidge's major breakthrough came in 1983, after further writing credits and some television work, with a film called *Valley Girl*. About shopping mall culture in 1980s California, Coolidge quietly satirises the highly fashion-conscious girls as they pressure each other in some sort of co-dependency to remain the same, but again pushes very little judgment forward. She explores the minor dilemmas the girls put themselves through with a persistent but benign curiosity, which simultaneously exposes their emptiness and renders them worthy of our attention. The film earned Coolidge critical and financial success and she followed it up with a project which had begun before *Valley Girl*, but which had floundered financially. After the arrival of Peter Bogdanovich as executive producer, *City Girl* was made and released in 1984. With her characteristically detached perspective, Coolidge explores the professional and romantic afflictions of a young female photographer in Toronto, her film refusing to be an apologist for the self-centred protagonist. It is unromantic and tough, and though a little melodramatic at the end, many felt it was one of the most realistic portrayals of the modern woman, and helped establish her reputation as a progressive-thinking feminist. It also effectively brings Coolidge's filmography up to date with her age: after the lessons she learnt from her foremother and revisits to various stages of girlhood, *City Girl* was the film whose central concern most resembled her own.

Unfortunately, the success of her last two films earned her the attention of Hollywood, and in an unwise move Coolidge started making films for the big studios. First came *The Joy of Sex* (1984), a very joyless high-school coming-of-age comedy which lacks any of her formerly displayed sensitivity. In 1985 came *Real Genius*, written by *Police Academy* writers Neal Israel and Pat Proft, and starring Val Kilmer as a gifted science student. Coolidge seems out of her depth with the technicalities demanded by the subject, and she does little to challenge this very predictable genre. *Plain Clothes* (1988) is yet another high-school picture, this time using the old trope of disguising an adult as a student and watching what happens. It is satisfactorily tongue-in-cheek, but still disappointing from the director who brought such originality to *Valley Girl*.

In one glimpse of former brilliance, Coolidge made *Rambling Rose* (1991), starring the mother and daughter team of Cheryl Ladd and Laura Dern. Set in 1971 with an ageing man reminiscing about his first love back in 1935, the film deals confidently with the sexual double standards that oppressed women in that society. Visually, though, the film is gentle and quaint, evoking the pre-war innocence of the American South, but this sentimentality also invades upon the potent subject of female oppression. By confining the matter to the past, an active political objective is submerged, and the evident nostalgia for the period really blunts the edge of Coolidge's potential blade. The film was well received, however, and benefited from strong acting performances.

Coolidge's detached approach to film-making, and her reputation as an 'actor's director', earned comments that she imposes no particular style on her films. This criticism could be endorsed by several of her recent films, including *Neil Simon's Lost in Yonkers* (1993), a bland film adapted from the Pulitzer Prize-winning play about teenagers living with their grandparents in the wartime summer of 1942. In 1994 she directed *Angie*, the strengths of which are in the recognition of the complexities of a modern woman's (and mother's) life, but the film amounts to little more than a showcase for Geena Davis' post-*Thelma and Louise* (1991) talents. However, an unexpected ability to produce hilarity is exhibited in the birthing scene, when the mother-to-be is advised to sing as she pushes. *Three Wishes* (1995) is described by *Variety* magazine as 'a pallid re-working of *It's a Wonderful Life*', which, despite some emotive moments and pleasing special effects, suffers from a clumsy script and a twee Little League obsession. *Out to Sea* (1997) pairs the dependable Jack Lemmon and Walter Matthau in a cruise ship adventure, but with a partnership which guarantees humour and sparkling on-screen antagonism, the film did not really demand anything of the director.

Her subsequent film, *Introducing Dorothy Dandridge* (1999), was a biography of the black actress, starring Halle Berry. Not really comparable to the powerful Tina Turner story *What's Love Got to Do With It* (1993), it is generally unremarkable, and it seems Coolidge has lost her conviction. Where once her subtle approach allowed incisive observations to become evident, as she moved further and further into melodrama and sentimentality, her own stylistic personality became overridden. Her next feature, *Aurora Island*, will star Kim Basinger and Joaquin Phoenix.                                    **MS**

# Francis Ford COPPOLA

*Tonight for Sure* (1961)
*Dementia 13* (1963)
*You're a Big Boy Now* (1966)
*Finian's Rainbow* (1968)
*The Rain People* (1969)
*The Godfather* (1972)
*The Godfather Part II* (1974)
*The Conversation* (1974)
*Apocalypse Now* (1979)
*One From the Heart* (1982)
*The Outsiders* (1983)
*Rumble Fish* (1983)
*The Cotton Club* (1984)
*Peggy Sue Got Married* (1986)
*Gardens of Stone* (1987)
*Tucker: The Man and His Dream* (1988)
*The Godfather Part III* (1990)
*Bram Stoker's Dracula* (1992)
*Jack* (1996)
*The Rainmaker* (1997)

Francis Ford Coppola, with the likes of Martin Scorsese, George Lucas, Robert Altman, and Brian De Palma, was one of the so-called 'movie brats' who, from the late 1960s through the 1970s, were responsible for creating what is widely considered as an artistic apex in Hollywood history. Like most of his peers, Coppola came to film-making through degree and Masters programmes and was awarded his Master of Cinema from UCLA in 1968 for *You're a Big Boy Now* (1966). Most general accounts of Coppola's work have identified recurrent familial themes, while visually he has come to be understood as something of a guru of the extravagant. However, neither of these positions is entirely sustainable across an oeuvre that on closer inspection discloses considerable formal and thematic scope.

Born in Detroit, 1939, Coppola's commercial directorial career began at UCLA in less than auspicious style with the soft-core 'girlie' picture *Tonight for Sure* (1961). Things improved in the following year when Coppola won a Samuel Goldwyn Award for his unproduced screenplay *Pilma Pilma*, which in turn led to a contract with Roger Corman at American International Pictures. After a period of production work in various capacities, Coppola directed the low-budget horror *Dementia 13 (The Haunted and the Hunted)* (1963), a gruesome tale of the axe murders of an aristocratic Irish family. Coppola would not direct again for another four years, but in the meantime he continued to work within the industry, predominantly in a writing capacity.

*You're a Big Boy Now* reflected some of Coppola's more scholarly influences. He incorporated self-reflexive formal strategies originally conceived in the European New Waves into a film that was effectively an Oedipal screwball comedy. The film was well received by public and critics alike and its female star, Geraldine Page, received an Academy nomination for her performance. It was also the first evidence of Coppola's reputation for eliciting outstanding performances from his stars. In the following year, he moved into new generic territory with the musical *Finian's Rainbow* (1968). The film had a very tight budget – for a musical – and Coppola was obliged to shoot on a Warner's back lot rather than on location, as he wanted. The director was unconvinced of the project's merit from the outset but took it on because, as he put it, 'Musical comedy was something that I had been raised with in my family, and I thought, frankly, that my father would be impressed.' The film, which attempted socio-economic allegory through the story of a leprechaun seeking the retrieval of gold taken to America, was a disaster at the box office and not well-received critically.

*The Rain People* (1969) saw Coppola on happier turf. It is the first of his films to deal thematically with the family and was based upon an incident in Coppola's own childhood during which his mother temporarily left home. The film, a road movie shot entirely on location, depicts a travelling pregnant woman in the midst of an identity crisis. Although *The Rain People* never achieved the lofty box-office heights of its contemporary, *Easy Rider* (1969), it was a more contemplative, resonant film that implicitly questioned the long-term wisdom of the 'drop-out' counter-culture philosophy.

Within his peer circle, *The Rain People* held a wider significance for Coppola's growing reputation as an auteur. Firstly, it was during the production of the film that he, with his friend and colleague George Lucas, conceived of the idea of an independent production company set up to nurture artistic talent in rebellion of Hollywood. Established at a converted warehouse in San Francisco, the company came to fruition in 1969 as American Zoetrope (with Lucas as its Vice President). Secondly, in what was seen as an unprecedented act of creative self-assurance, Coppola backed *The Rain People* with $20,000 of his own money (such courage of conviction would later prove the downfall of Zoetrope). Coppola's reputation continued in ascendance the following year when he received an Academy Award for co-writing credits on *Patton* (1970). Even given his growing reputation, the most optimistic insider could not have envisioned the astonishing commercial and critical success of his next picture, *The Godfather* (1972). Taken together, *The Godfather, The Godfather Part II* (1974), and *The Godfather Part III* (1990), form a nine-hour familial triptych spanning three generations of Italian-American Mafia life. Despite the relative critical and commercial success of *Part III*, it is, however, the first two films that are extolled in Hollywood myth.

Initially reluctant to work on a picture that was someone else's material, but heavily pressed to repay debts accrued through Zoetrope, Coppola agreed to direct the screen version of Mario Puzo's populist novel. But whereas in his previous films Coppola had sought to experiment with formal strategies learned from the likes of Godard and Fellini, the narrative codes employed in *The Godfather* (and its successors) were conceived with the visual composition of primitive cinema and Victorian family portraiture very much to the fore. Organised fundamentally as a set of tableaux, the film, with its now famous autumnal hue, plays with analogous contrasts of light and dark in a manner unprecedented in a mainstream Hollywood cinema then characterised by high-key lighting. The film is also widely acclaimed for the performances of its ensemble cast. Indeed, Coppola fought hard with Paramount executives over the casting of Pacino (an unknown in the lead role) and the almost inaudible Brando (by now notoriously recalcitrant) as Don Corleone. In terms of narrative the films deal with the amorality of American capitalism, yet all three instalments eschew the wider social repercussions of organised crime, focusing instead on the mechanisms of a family of murderous racketeers. For this reason, some critics saw the film/s as ethically irresponsible, but by and large *The Godfather* was viewed by critics and paying public alike as something of a masterpiece, with Pauline Kael describing it as 'the greatest gangster picture ever made'.

Despite being one of the highest-grossing films in history, and laden with Academy Awards for Brando, Best Picture and Screenplay, there had been considerable bad blood between Coppola (who felt he had been exploited) and Paramount studio executives, and he was initially less than happy with the idea of a sequel. By Peter Biskind's account, Coppola only agreed to script and direct a sequel for the sum of $1 million (he had been paid $60,000 for directing the first film) and on a commitment from Paramount to finance Coppola's pet project *The Conversation* (1974). This period was to prove the pinnacle of Coppola's career. Both preceding and proceeding the events of the first picture, and spanning a total of around 75 years, *The Godfather Part II* surpassed the narrative ambition of its predecessor and although the film's convoluted structuring proved too perplexing for some, was generally acknowledged as significantly superior to its predecessor.

*The Conversation* is a much more intimate work (and Coppola's favourite). With Gene Hackman taking the lead as an alienated surveillance expert, this brilliant paranoid thriller focused upon the world of aural electronic surveillance and has thus often been read as microcosmic of the Watergate era. Formally, the film returns to the spirit of European art cinema, but it was Coppola's experimentation with sound that is most ingenious, with the lonely Hackman punctiliously adjusting recorded abstract sounds until they gradually form audible conversations. Coppola found himself in the enviable position of being the first film-maker to be in competition with himself for Best Picture Academy Awards. In total, *The Godfather Part II* received eleven nominations and *The Conversation* three, with the former winning six awards including Best Picture and Best Director.

Lurching from one crisis to the next, the cataclysmic events surrounding the production and post-production of Coppola's next film, the Vietnam epic *Apocalypse*

*Now* (1979), are ingrained in the annals of cinematic folklore (and nicely chronicled in Bahr and Hickenlooper's 1991 documentary film *Hearts of Darkness: A Filmmaker's Apocalypse*). Overblown in every respect, Coppola's interpretation of Conrad's 'Heart of Darkness' has Martin Sheen heading up-river into Cambodia to assassinate a renegade American colonel played by a T. S. Eliot-quoting Marlon Brando. One would be pushed to challenge the view held by J. Hoberman that narratively the film 'can't help but go down in flaming futile pretension and intellectual disarray'. As a spectacle, however, the film is mesmeric – a wide-angle flaming jungle replete with neon, surfing GIs and a troupe of Playboy bunny girls. Defying all logic for a film that is said to have tripled its original budget, *Apocalypse Now* did enough business to leave Coppola with a very healthy personal profit. Additionally, the film received five Academy nominations and shared the prestigious Palme d'Or at the 1979 Cannes Festival.

If Coppola had thought (understandably enough) that his career was blessed, his next venture, the musical *One from the Heart* (1982), was to bring about a very hasty and categorical fall from grace. Initially conceived as a modest antidote to the excesses of *Apocalypse Now*, the film ballooned into an experiment (using the very latest video technology) of gargantuan, tragic proportions. Although the film's sumptuous Vegas design and slight romantic narrative has been subject to fond critical re-evaluation, at the time of its release the film was slated and bombed at the box office. *One from the Heart* bankrupted Coppola and subsequently marked an immediate shift in his career to more modest projects.

In 1983 Coppola made back-to-back movies adapted from S. E. Hinton novels that have retrospectively acquired something of a cult status. *The Outsiders* (1983) amounts to little more than an distracting rites-of-passage teen picture but one notable for its ensemble 'brat pack' cast including Tom Cruise, Emilio Estevez and Matt Dillon in early roles. Like its predecessor, *Rumble Fish* (1983), the film focuses upon Tulsa gang culture, with Matt Dillon playing the idolising brother of Mickey Rourke, who is colour-blind and deaf following endless and pointless 'rumbles'. Peculiarly shot (given the subject matter) in rapturously expressionistic monochrome (with colour fish), the film amounts to little more than a grand exercise in style over substance. Coppola followed with the ill-conceived *The Cotton Club* (1984). Although the film featured some inspired choreography, its depiction of prohibition-era gangster life convergent upon the famous Harlem club was almost unanimously seen as a miserable attempt to exploit the glories of past formulas. Much more successful was *Peggy Sue Got Married* (1986) in which Kathleen Turner (never better) faints at her school reunion and wakes up twenty years earlier. Despite some syrupy closure, the film, about second chances (should Turner marry her dim-witted childhood sweetheart, Nicolas Cage?), is an unassumingly thoughtful counter to the sentimental nostalgia and pyrotechnics of *Back to the Future* (1985). Coppola's next film, *Gardens of Stone* (1987), a story of a soldier training troops for a (Vietnam) war he doesn't believe in, was well received critically but was blighted by personal tragedy when Coppola's son, Gian Carlo, died in a boating accident during production. His next film, *Tucker: The Man and His Dream* (1988), is a visually inventive biopic of the single-minded postwar American car-maker who failed gallantly to challenge corporate monopoly. The narrative has often been read as analogous of Coppola's own career, although the film is too affectionately reminiscent to denote any bitterness on Coppola's part.

Following on from the calamitous sentimentality of 'Life Without Zoë' – his contribution to the three shorts that made up *New York Stories* (1989) – and *The Godfather Part III*, Coppola directed a faithful adaptation of *Bram Stoker's Dracula* (1992). Although Coppola stated that he initially envisioned *Dracula* as minimalist fare, the film turned out as a predictably gothic and immoderate pleasure that is narratively organised around all manner of stylistic devices and which features an appropriately grandiloquent performance by Gary Oldman as the Count. Coppola respectfully directed two more films in the 1990s, the Robin Williams vehicle *Jack* (1996), and an adaptation of John Grisham's novel, *The Rainmaker* (1997), but it is *Bram Stoker's Dracula* that stands as his last recognisably 'Coppolian' flourish.

Whether or not Coppola, as a writer-director, has a great picture left in him remains to be seen – his new film, *Megalopolis*, is certainly eagerly awaited – but his ambition, integrity and oeuvre secure him canonical status within the history of American cinema. **TT**

# Roman COPPOLA

Born in 1966, Roman Coppola is the son of Francis Ford Coppola, one of the major CQ (2001) figures in American film. His family connections also include actor cousins Nic Cage and Jason Schwartzman, actor aunt Talia Shire and sister Sofia Coppola, who made her disastrous career-start performing in *The Godfather Part III* (1990), before redeeming herself with a striking directorial debut, *The Virgin Suicides* (1999).

Like Sofia, who worked on her father's films within various capacities, from costume designer to screenwriter, Roman began his career working for Coppola senior. He appeared in *The Godfather Part II* (1974) at the age of eight, and *Apocalypse Now* (1979) – although he was unseen until the 2001 release of *Apocalypse Now Redux*. He also worked on the impressive *Rumble Fish* (1983), the neglected *Bram Stoker's Dracula* (1992) and the wonderful *Jack* (1996). Away from the family fold, he made his name working as a video promo director, making videos for Green Day, Wyclef Jean and Moby.

His sole directorial feature to date is the offbeat drama, *CQ* (2001), which features a fantastic cast including Jeremy Davies, Elodie Bouchez, John Phillip Law, Jason Schwartzman and Gérard Depardieu. The film deals with a sci-fi fantasy movie being made in 1969, set in the year 2000, that runs into trouble when the director (Depardieu) becomes fixated on his leading lady. Davies plays an angsty American brought in to finish the film only to become obsessed himself with the actress and her character, the sexy Barbarella-ish Dragonfly. The resulting movie is pleasingly weird, with Billy Zane doing Castro, Cubans on the moon and some of the grooviest sets since Joseph Losey's offbeat *Modesty Blaise* (1966). Not only does the movie seem destined for cult status, it also suggests Coppola is a talent to watch. *CQ* is, as yet, unreleased in the UK. **IC**

# Sofia COPPOLA

Born in New York during the filming of *The Godfather* in 1971, Sofia Coppola might The Virgin Suicides (1999) well have laid to rest her rather inauspicious introduction to the film business with the release of *The Virgin Suicides* (1999). Following co-writing credits for 'Life Without Zoë', her father Francis Ford's critically mauled contribution to *New York Stories* (1989), Coppola was injudiciously cast (she is an untrained actor) by her father in the central role of Mary Corleone in *The Godfather Part III* (1990). While the film received warm notices, Coppola's performance was broadly viewed as the film's Achilles' heel and her father stood accused of nepotism. Given such ignominious beginnings, it is perhaps not surprising that Coppola chose to pursue careers in photography and fashion design over the following decade.

In 1999 (the year in which she married actor/director Spike Jonze) Coppola resumed her career in the family business, this time as the screenwriter/director of *The Virgin Suicides*, an adaptation of Jeffrey Eugenides' cult novel. Produced through her father's production company American Zoetrope, the film, which boasts an impressive cast including James Woods and Kathleen Turner, chronicles the tragi-comic events surrounding the apparently motiveless suicides of five adolescent sisters from Michigan, as told twenty-five years on from the perspective of a young man who had been a boyhood neighbour of the girls. Combining dreamlike slow motion sequences with hazy close-ups, the film drew enthusiastic praise at both the Cannes and Sundance Film Festivals. **TT**

# Frank CORACI

Born in New York in 1966, Frank Coraci graduated from the Tisch School of Arts New Murdered Innocence (1995) York University. After several shorts, travel documentaries and music videos, he made his The Wedding Singer (1998) directorial debut with the thriller *Murdered Innocence* (1995), which he also co-wrote. The Waterboy (1998)

In his freshman year at college Coraci met Adam Sandler, Jack Giarraputo and Tim Herlihy. This led to work as the creator and director of visuals for Sandler's 1997 comedy/rock tour, his HBO concert movie *What the Hell Happened to Me?*, and his 'Steve Polychronopolous' music video. Coraci also wrote for and performed on Sandler's comedy CDs 'What the Hell Happened to Me?' and 'What's Your Name?'. In turn, this led to Coraci directing two vehicles for Sandler's gentle, self-effacing brand of screen-humour, both written by Herlihy and produced by Giarraputo

The nice but dim protagonist of *The Wedding Singer* (1998) is devastated when he is ditched at the altar. A co-worker (played by Drew Barrymore) persuades him to help her to prepare for her own wedding to a yuppie who thinks he is Don Johnson circa 'Miami Vice'. Sandler and Barrymore fall in love, and various complications ensue before a happy ending. Typically, such a vehicle would depend entirely upon the appeal of its star, but *The Wedding Singer* gives almost equal weight to its leading lady. Much of the humour is still quite broad, but the charm of Barrymore and Sandler (here doing a Dustin Hoffman impersonation) in these roles make this a quietly effective comedy-drama. Revelling in the appalling fashions of its 1985 setting (although Barrymore's costumes are largely exempt) and a spot-on soundtrack of successful but dreadful 1980s pop music, the movie depends heavily upon retro humour. This is to its advantage; when the *mise-en-scène* makes the audience laugh the narrative does not have to be gag-driven. Coraci's direction is generally unobtrusive, but betrays a lack of confidence in the screenplay's rather perfunctory plot-reversals. Jon Lovitz and Steve Buscemi, in particular, make much of their wonderful cameos.

*The Waterboy* (1998) reverts to a more typical episodic, gag-driven vehicle. Fired from his job as the Cougars waterboy, Sandler – playing Forrest Gump as a cross between Jerry Lewis and Andy Kaufman – joins the no-hope American football team, the Mud Dogs. Against his mother's wishes, he enrols at college, falls for a local sexpot and becomes a star linebacker, taking his team to a Louisana Bourbon Bowl confrontation with the Cougars. The movie seems uncertain as to whether it is following or mocking a formulaic template; given that such conventions have become so familiar that they are funnier when played straight, this is problematic. Coraci's direction is competent, but seems rather less suited to this kind of movie.　　　　　**MB**

# Roger CORMAN

One of the most innovative and influential directors of the second half of the twentieth century, Roger William Corman was born in 1926 in Detroit, USA. When he was a teenager his parents moved to Beverly Hills, California, where Corman attended Beverly Hills High School, and immediately fell in love with film. After graduation he attended Stanford University, where he majored in engineering, obtaining his BA, and then enlisted in the Navy for three years. By this time, however, Corman knew that he was no longer interested in engineering and, with his family's blessing, obtained employment as a runner at 20th Century Fox, eventually graduating to script reader.

After a brief trip to England, where he studied English literature for one semester as a graduate student at Oxford, Corman returned to Los Angeles and hammered out a low-budget script that he eventually sold to Allied Artists. Ever the shrewd negotiator, Corman insisted on associate producer credit on the project, which was released under the title *Highway Dragnet* (1954). Artistically disappointed with the film, and believing that he could a better job as a producer, he pooled all his money and produced *Monster from the Ocean Floor* (1954) on a budget of $12,000, letting Wyott Ordung handle the director's reins. After selling the film to Lippert Pictures outright for a profit of $100,000, Corman scripted and produced *The Fast and The Furious* (1954), which was directed by the film's star, John Ireland. Shot in ten days, the film was a big step up for Corman; he passed on distribution offers from Columbia and Republic to join up with Jim Nicholson and Samuel Z. Arkoff, who were forming a small company called American Releasing Corporation. Corman gave ARC *The Fast and The Furious* for their first release on the condition that ARC would provide immediate financing for a second film. Nicholson and Arkoff agreed, and ARC, later renamed American International Pictures, was launched, with Corman as its house director.

Corman immediately began cranking out films at an incredible pace, taking over the director's chair with his next film, *Five Guns West* (1955), a ten-day western. This was followed in rapid succession by *Swamp Women* (1955), *Apache Woman* (1955) and *The Oklahoma Woman* (1956), all low-budget films that demonstrated Corman's early feminist leanings: he assigned the major action roles to a series of self-sufficient female protagonists rather than the typically generic leading man. In 1956 and 1957, Corman turned to science fiction, horror and teen exploitation films, directing *It Conquered the World*, *The Day the World Ended* (both 1956), along with *Not of This Earth*, *Attack of the Crab Monsters*, *Teenage Doll*, *The Undead*, *Sorority Girl*, *Rock All Night*, *Naked*

Paradise, and *Carnival Rock* (all 1957). All of these films, shot on budgets hovering around the $100,000 range, were substantial hits for AIP and Woolner, a New Orleans distributor who also bankrolled some of Corman's early projects. With lurid posters and aggressive advertising campaigns, Corman's films soon found acceptance with AIP's target audience, teenagers, and Corman's directorial style displayed a verve and vigour that many other low-budget films lacked. Corman kept creating films at a frantic pace, directing *War of the Satellites*, *Teenage Cave Man* (with a young Robert Vaughn), *She Gods of Shark Reef*, *The Saga of the Viking Women and Their Voyage to the Waters of the Great Sea Serpent*, *Machine Gun Kelly* (with Charles Bronson in an early leading role) and *I, Mobster*, all in 1958.

In 1959 Corman turned his hand to black comedy with the classic satire *A Bucket of Blood*, in which talentless artist Walter Paisley (Dick Miller) finds instant acclaim when he accidentally kills his cat, and then covers the body with plaster, displaying the end result as a 'lifelike' sculpture at a local coffee house. Soon, demand for new sculptures forces Walter to randomly kill various acquaintances to create new works, displaying the plaster-covered remains in a triumphant one-man show. With a superb script by Corman's long-time collaborator Charles B. Griffith, *A Bucket of Blood* was a significant departure from the straightforward melodramas Corman had previously been directing. He followed it with one of his most famous works, *The Little Shop of Horrors* (1960), which he shot in two days on leftover sets, with one night of exterior shooting to flesh out the project. The film, documenting the misadventures of flower-shop employee Seymour Krelboined (Jonathan Haze) and his pet man-eating plant, remains one of Corman's most original and idiosyncratic films, and was subsequently revamped as a Broadway musical, and then a big-budget Hollywood remake.

It was also during this period that Corman produced his most personal film, *The Intruder* (1961), featuring a very young William Shatner as a virulent racist determined to stir up trouble in a small Southern town. Shot in gritty black and white for a budget of $90,000, using local actors and no permits, the film received superb reviews, but failed at the box office. Corman, who had mortgaged his house to partially bankroll the project, was deeply upset. While no studio, even AIP, would touch the project, Corman had still intensely believed in the message of the film. Yet, in the wake of the film's commercial failure, Corman began to back away from films with an overt message, and concentrate on genre works that contained coded social commentary within a highly commercial genre framework. This was a strategy that he would pursue for the rest of his career as a director and film-maker; after the financial disaster of *The Intruder*, Corman never again forgot the importance of the bottom-line.

Yet times were changing. The short-schedule, black and white films that were Corman's trademark were beginning to lose their market, and so Corman convinced AIP to let him direct a larger-budgeted 'A' picture, *The Fall of the House of Usher*, in 1960. Starring Vincent Prince, and shot in CinemaScope, the film was a huge commercial hit, and started Corman on a series of Edgar Allan Poe adaptations, including *The Pit and the Pendulum* (1961), *Tales of Terror* (1962), *The Premature Burial* (1962), *The Raven* (1963), *The Haunted Palace* (1963), *The Masque of the Red Death* (1964) and *The Tomb of Ligeia* (1965). Ever cost-conscious, Corman finished many of these films ahead of schedule and budget, and on one occasion created an entirely new film, *The Terror* (1963), on left over sets from *The Raven*, using Boris Karloff, Dick Miller and Jack Nicholson to complete the bulk of the film in another two-day shooting session. All of these Corman color films were extremely stylish in their set design, photography, and their use of fluid, moving camera shots to accentuate an atmosphere of mounting dread.

With each new film, Corman increased his budget and his shooting schedules, working with such established talent as Vincent Price, Basil Rathbone and Ray Milland, and up and coming cineastes Francis Ford Coppola, Peter Bogdanovich and Monte Hellman. In 1966 Corman's film *The Wild Angels* scandalised the American public with its documentary-style depiction of the Hell's Angels motorcycle gang, and in 1967 he directed *The Trip*, the first major studio film to deal with the effects of LSD. Corman, however, was beginning to clash with Nicholson and Arkoff over artistic matters, particularly editorial interference on *The Trip* (AIP wanted to push the film as an anti-drug tract, while he, typically, remained noncommittal). Incensed, he went over to 20th Century Fox to direct one of the most brutally effective gangster films of the 1960s, *The St. Valentine's Day Massacre* (1967). But Corman was frustrated working for a big studio; with little

*The Last Woman on Earth* (1960)
*The Fall of the House of Usher* (1960)
*Atlas* (1960)
*The Pit and the Pendulum* (1961)
*The Intruder* (1961)
*Creature from the Haunted Sea* (1961)
*Tales of Terror* (1962)
*Tower of London* (1962)
*The Premature Burial* (1962)
*The Young Racers* (1963)
*X: The Man with the X-Ray Eyes* (1963)
*The Terror* (1963)
*The Raven* (1963)
*The Haunted Palace* (1963)
*The Secret Invasion* (1964)
*The Masque of the Red Death* (1964)
*The Tomb of Ligeia* (1965)
*The Wild Angels* (1966)
*The St. Valentine's Day Massacre* (1967)
*The Trip* (1967)
*Target: Harry* (1969)
*Bloody Mama* (1970)
*Gas-s-s-s, Or It Became Necessary to Destroy the World in Order to Save It* (1970)
*Von Richthofen and Brown* (1971)
*Frankenstein Unbound* (1990)

control over the production process, he felt that both time and money were being wasted. Furthermore, he was feeling burned out; by the time he directed *Von Richtofen and Brown* (aka *The Red Baron*) (shot in 1970, released in 1971) for United Artists, Corman decided that the time had come to take a break from the rigours of directing, and concentrate on producing his films for his own company.

Thus, in 1970, he formed New World Pictures, and released a pick-up picture, *Angels Die Hard*, as their first effort. This was followed by *Student Nurses* (1970), a soft-core sexploitation comedy, the first film that New World actually produced, shot at a studio that Corman converted from a lumber yard in Venice, California. Both were enormous hits. Corman began a policy of aggressively booking his films not only in regular theatres, but also in drive-ins that were then fading from the American scene and desperate for product. In the years that followed, Corman produced a stream of low-budget exploitation films, including *Women in Cages* (1971), *Boxcar Bertha* (1972), *Caged Heat* (1974), *Eat My Dust!* (1976), *Grand Theft Auto* (1977) and *Rock and Roll High School* (1979), offering employment opportunities for an entire new wave of directors, including Jonathan Demme, Martin Scorsese, Ron Howard, Joe Dante, Paul Bartel and James Cameron. Simultaneously (and somewhat paradoxically), he served as the American distributor for Ingmar Bergman's *Cries and Whispers* (1972), Federico Fellini's *Amarcord* (1974), François Truffaut's *Small Change* (1976), Volker Schlöndorff's *The Tin Drum* (1979), Bruce Beresford's *Breaker Morant* (1980), and other European 'art' films that were being shut out of the lucrative US market. Corman marketed these films in the same manner as his homegrown efforts, with aggressive ad campaigns and saturation bookings, garnering impressive box-office results from films the major studios found impossible to sell.

However, with the collapse of the drive-in market and the rise of cable, videocassettes and DVDs, Corman recognised that New World's days as a producer/distributor were numbered. Accordingly, he sold New World in January 1983 and almost immediately formed a new, more competitive company, Concorde-New Horizons. Aimed strictly at the home video and direct-to-cable market, Corman's Concorde films included such titles as *Suburbia* (1984), *Stripped to Kill* (1987), *Slumber Party Massacre II* (1987), *Big Bad Mama II* (1987), *Dune Warriors* (1990), *Carnosaur* (1993), and numerous other action and science fiction thrillers. These later films are extremely problematic for most viewers. In the first place, they are all but invisible to the public, being released solely through US cable networks, or on straight-to-home-video deals. Secondly, in the age of digital special effects, Corman's newer films suffer because of their low-budget look. Finally, the excessive amounts of sex and violence in the Concorde films makes many viewers uncomfortable; from the relatively tame sexploitation of *Student Nurses*, more recent Corman productions such as *Don't Sleep Alone* (1997), *Detonator* (1998) and *Hard as Nails* (2001) seem devoid of any artistic impulse whatsoever, designed solely to make money. While Corman's pace of production hasn't flagged, his films have become more and more marginal.

In the mid-1990s Corman struck a deal with Showtime for a series of made-for-cable films, often based on older titles in his library, and as the straight-to-video market evaporated, he moved ahead with a television series for the Sci-Fi Channel, an American cable network, entitled *The Black Scorpion*, which began production in 1998. In early 2000 Corman sold the Venice studio, and began to relocate his production activities to Ireland, where he had purchased a film production facility. Presently in his seventies, Corman's production schedule has come to a halt as he concentrates on wringing the last dollar out of existing product.

While Roger Corman has been instrumental in furthering the career of numerous young talents within the industry, it may be that his influence in this area is coming to an end. While numerous Corman alumni now hold major studio positions, a younger generation of directors are finding work within the majors to be the fastest route to promotion, partly as a consequence of the hyper-conglomerisation of Hollywood which has all but killed off independent production. Corman's films as a director, and the success of his numerous proteges, are his real legacy; in his films for AIP, one can sense the hand of a genuine and caring artist at work. Honoured at numerous retrospectives of his work throughout the world, Corman has become something of an elder statesman in Hollywood, despite the fact that he hasn't directed a film since *Frankenstein Unbound* in 1990. He has recently forged something of a new career for himself as an actor in major

Hollywood films such as *Philadelphia* (1993) and *Apollo 13* (1995), often playing a smooth-talking heavy. With more than three hundred films to his credit as a producer, and more than fifty as a director, Roger Corman has had an undeniable impact upon the industry both as a business and an art form.                              **WWD**

# Michael CORRENTE

Born in Rhode Island in 1960, Michael Corrente began his career writing and directing for the theatre, and his feature films possess a character-centred intimacy and sincerity reminiscent of theatrical productions, while employing distinctly cinematic imagery and themes. Yet the biggest distinction of Corrente's films lies in their depiction of a working-class, New England milieu and its people. His three releases, *Federal Hill* (1995), *American Buffalo* (1996), and *Outside Providence* (1999), were all filmed and set in various parts of the director's native state, Rhode Island, and while Corrente's love of the region is obvious, the films reflect the struggle and tension that the characters face as they try to break out of their limited and often bleak lives.

*American Buffalo* (1996)
*Outside Providence* (1999)
*A Shot at Glory* (2002)

*Federal Hill* (1995)

*Federal Hill*, his debut feature, was originally conceived as an off-Broadway play. The gritty, black and white film, set in the Italian-American section of Providence called Federal Hill, has drawn comparisons to Martin Scorsese's *Mean Streets* (1973) in its portrayal of the friendship between two young men, as one falls in love with a wealthy college student, while the other becomes increasingly entrenched in a life of crime. At its heart, the film depicts the lives of people whose youthful promise and hopes have quietly passed them by without their notice.

Corrente continued with the subject of crime and foiled ambition with *American Buffalo*, an adaptation of a David Mamet play. The three-player film has the look and feel of a stage piece and has the lengthy and rapid-fire dialogue characteristic of a Mamet play. Most notably, it features admirable performances from its three stars: Dustin Hoffman as an ageing small-time con-man hoping for a big-time score, Dennis Franz as a non-committal pawn shop owner, and Sean Nelson as his eager young apprentice.

*Outside Providence*, partly set in Corrente's hometown of Pawtucket, and based on a novel by fellow Rhode Island film-maker Peter Farrelly, is a coming-of-age comedy about a young slacker's pivotal year at a Connecticut prep school in the mid-1970s. This film marked the most mainstream commercial effort by the director, and the success of the Farrelly brothers' *There's Something About Mary* (1998) made for a deceptive publicity campaign comparing the two films, whose only similarity was in their jokes aimed at the physically handicapped. Unlike the director's first two films, *Outside Providence* presents a more cheerful and hopeful future for its protagonist, Tim Dunphy, engagingly played by Shawn Hatosy, and paints an idyllic picture of the New England countryside, in stark contrast to the decrepit and empty town that offers no opportunities for its inhabitants. Yet the message of the film centres on the importance of family and staying loyal to the past as Tim returns to Rhode Island upon graduating, on better terms with his beleaguered and brusque father played by Alec Baldwin, affecting an authentic local accent. With the exception of Tim's love interest, most of the prep school students prove to be a group of ne'er-do-wells who succeed by privilege or money, and Tim stands as a moral centre. In spite of yearning to escape, Tim finds that the best place is home. Corrente's most recent feature, *A Shot at Glory* (2002), is about a lower-league Scottish soccer team and stars Michael Keaton.                              **EK**

# George P. COSMATOS

George P. Cosmatos (sometimes credited as George Pan Cosmatos or Yorgo Pan Cosmatos) was born in Italy in 1941. He worked unaccredited as assistant director on the Greek-British co-production *Otan ta psaria vgikan sti steria* (*The Day the Fish Came Out*) (1967) before directing *The Beloved* (1970) from his own screenplay. This was followed in 1973 by the French-Italian co-production *Rappresaglia* (aka *Massacre in Rome*), an adaptation of Robert Katz's 'Death in Rome', co-scripted by Cosmatos. Based on a true story, the movie focuses on the relationship between an Italian priest (Marcello Mastroianni) and a German colonel (Richard Burton), who has been ordered to execute ten Italians for each one of 33 German soldiers killed in an explosion. Rousing Vatican ire for its portrayal of their complicity in the events depicted, *Rappresaglia* lacks

*The Beloved* (1970)
*Rappresaglia* (1973)
*The Cassandra Crossing* (1976)
*Escape to Athena* (1979)
*Of Unknown Origin* (1983)
*Rambo: First Blood Part II* (1985)
*Cobra* (1986)
*Leviathan* (1989)

subtlety and fluctuates wildly between the pretentious and the banal. Listing the names of those who were murdered adds insult to the injury the movie does their memory. Cosmatos' next movie, for which he also received story and screenplay credits, was *The Cassandra Crossing* (1976), a thriller about a train whose passengers are infected with plague. A doctor on board finds a cure, but the authorities would prefer to see the train and its passengers destroyed. Energetic camerawork keeps the ludicrous plot going, but ultimately the movie cannot rise above the indifferent performances of its impressive cast as they struggle with weakly-delineated characters and weaker dialogue. This was followed, in 1979, by the bloated caper movie *Escape to Athena*, in which POWs, the Greek resistance, local prostitutes, and a nice German join forces to variously escape, destroy a submarine base and a rocket launch site, and steal the treasure from a nearby monastery. Cosmatos' camerawork is restless, and there are a couple of effective action sequences, but again a good cast struggling with weak material becomes torpid.

The era of the internationally-cast European picture came to an end, and Cosmatos' next project was the Canadian giant-rat-on-the-loose picture *Of Unknown Origin* (1983). Coming a year after *The Rats* (1982), which was adapted from James Herbert's best-seller, *Of Unknown Origin* is oddly proleptic of Cosmatos' subsequent career, in which his movies have either ridden on the coat-tails of more popular pictures or been part of a mini-cycle.

In 1985 he directed *Rambo: First Blood Part II*, a sequel with a more substantial budget ($25 million) than its predecessor. Co-scripted by Sylvester Stallone and James Cameron, it rewrites John Rambo as an unstoppable force, but remains slightly more complex in its negotiation of post-Vietnam politics and American national identity than the popular perception would allow. Its depiction of the Vietnamese and Chinese is, however, repellent. Cosmatos' competent direction saw him reunited with Stallone for the vigilante-cop movie *Cobra* (1986), an intensely reactionary manifestation of the Reaganite retrenchment of 1960s and 1970s liberal gains, scripted by Stallone from Paula Gosling's 'Fair Game' (aka 'Running Duck'). Some of the action sequences are exciting.

*Leviathan* (1989) was one of four movies that year in which the crew of an undersea base encounter aliens. More accomplished than either *DeepStar Six* (1988) or *Lords of the Deep* (1989), it comes a poor second to *The Abyss* (1989). An unimaginative rehash of elements from countless earlier movies, its weak script – in which mismatched characters are drawn too broadly to be sufficiently convincing – is poorly served by weak performances. Cosmatos' direction is remarkable only in its ability to leach any residual suspense from the scenario.

*Tombstone* (1993) – attractively shot by William A. Fraker, and featuring another laughable character role for Val Kilmer – reached the screen before *Wyatt Earp* (1994), but the two movies seem almost to belong to different genres. Whereas Kasdan's elegy is stately, sometimes ponderous, Cosmatos' hyperbolic western lacks only a cattle train, marauding Indians, and a cavalry charge to complete its attempted encapsulation and recapitulation of the entire genre. Familiar faces recur as the movie strings incident after incident, but it has none of the revisionist drive of, say, *Posse* (1993), *Bad Girls* (1994), or Sam Raimi's sublime spaghetti homage *The Quick and the Dead* (1995). A commercial success, it is probably Cosmatos' best work to date, but as he increasingly – and without clear rhyme or reason – cannibalises and appropriates from other movies, both better and worse than his own, he has come to seem more and more anonymous as a director.

His plundering and growing invisibility continued with *Shadow Conspiracy*, the slightest of 1997's slight Whitehouse thrillers. **MB**

# Kevin COSTNER

Kevin Costner was born in California in 1955. So far his directorial career has proved interesting for the ways in which he has used the films to expand upon his star persona in features such as *The Untouchables* (1987), *Field Of Dreams* (1989), and *JFK* (1991). The concentration upon mythic images of America has been especially striking, as has the focus on the frontier ethos of the lone hero, both in a romanticised past and an imagined future.

*Dances With Wolves* (1990) places its white hero, Lt. John Dunbar (played by Costner) amidst the initially hostile but eventually accommodating Sioux tribespeople.

Introduced during the American Civil War, Dunbar emerges initially as an ironic Christ figure, 'resurrected' after miraculously surviving a suicidal charge on confederate troops. His desire to see the frontier 'before it closes' is conveyed through his gradual rejection of nominally 'civilised' America and his embracing of the environment and its indigenous people. The Native Americans themselves are represented by a split between the Sioux and the more overtly aggressive Pawnee, a characterisation which some see as an undermining of the film's attempts to revise traditional western representations and humanise the Native American. Indeed, Dunbar's intervention in the tribal feuding is epitomised by his presentation of firearms to the Sioux, a troubling inversion of the film's overarching liberal impulse to preserve Native American culture. However, as seen through this white hero's eyes, the Sioux emerge as a rounded, dignified community (especially in the extended 230-minute version) and the film's conservative undercurrents and its obvious emotional cues do not dissipate its good intentions and genuine sweep. Avoiding the vilest racial atrocities of the US Army (see *Little Big Man* (1970) and *Soldier Blue* (1970)), the ultimate elegiac tone allows for a small victory as Dunbar is rescued from his white captors. The film is enhanced by its range of performances (notably Graham Greene and Mary McDonnell), and as a first-time director, Costner proves more than adept in both the film's intimate and epic moments. A risky project from the outset, it was rewarded by both widespread popular appeal and a brace of Academy Awards.

*The Postman* (1997), on the other hand, was met with both critical derision and public rejection. This time the western hero (again played by Costner) is reconfigured in a post-apocalyptic future. As if to underline the film's relationship to the genre, Costner includes a brief moment wherein images of Ford's *She Wore a Yellow Ribbon* (1949) digitally morphs into the narrative. Like *Dances With Wolves*, this is a film centered on mythic notions of America, but the futuristic setting gives rise to all manner of fresh tensions and ruptures. The rejection of military demagoguery is explicit, but the film seems only able to find an alternative in the leadership proffered by the patriarchal (if gently ironic) title character.

This yearning for such alternative father figures sullies the call for communication amongst the masses (who are often characterised as passive and helpless) and echoes Costner's closing monologue in *JFK*. His sexual virility is crudely contrasted with the impotence of the quasi-fascist Bethlehem (Will Patton) but the film doesn't expand upon the rich possibilities of such psycho-sexual oppositions. The film's allegorical aspirations give rise to all manner of confusion – the references to ethnic cleansing once more echo Costner's first feature, but this time he seems content to conveniently resolve such ideological impulses once the pantomime villain has been eliminated. Yet, for all its faults, this is an unusually ambitious Hollywood blockbuster and did not deserve the drubbing it received from those critics who judged it as much on Costner's celebrity as its individual merits. Yearning for a lost notion of Americanism, *The Postman*'s need to believe infuses it with a fresh spin on the western myth, highlighting, as well as succumbing to, the tensions inherent in the form. His next film, *Open Range*, is a western due for release in 2003. **NJ**

# Alex COX

Although a director in his own right, Alex Cox is probably best known to British readers as the host of BBC2's long-running film series 'Moviedrome' (1987–94). The series focused on movies that were cultish, obscure, marginal or simply bizarre, and the same adjectives are equally applicable to Cox's own career. Not unlike Orson Welles, Cox has not been afraid to antagonise the Hollywood studios and has similarly 'started at the top and worked his way down'.

Born in the UK in 1954, Cox studied law at Oxford followed by film at Bristol University, and subsequently won a Fulbright Scholarship to study film at UCLA, where he made a well-received short film, *Sleep is for Sissies* (1980). His debut feature, the cult classic *Repo Man* (1984), is still perhaps his most famous and admired film. Inspired by countless Hollywood B-movies (notably Robert Aldrich's 1955 noir, *Kiss Me Deadly*), the film follows a group of car repossessors, sinister government agents, street punks, religious nuts and ufologists, as they chase after a Chevy Malibu with dead aliens in the trunk being driven around Los Angeles by a lobotomised nuclear scientist who may have created the neutron bomb. Besides launching the career of Emilio Estevez (for which Cox later apologised), *Repo Man* has a cast filled with many great character actors (Harry Dean Stanton, Tracey Miller, Sy Richardson) and a soundtrack featuring some of the top west coast punk bands of the period (Black Flag, The Plugz, The Circle Jerks). *Repo Man* is also an important example of Cox's political leanings and his penchant for zany conspiracy theories. The film is fiercely anti-nuclear and anti-Reaganite (all the characters really care about is money), and works as a fine satire of LA's car culture.

Cox's attachment to the punk scene is even clearer from his next project, *Sid and Nancy* (1986), an account of the last days of Sid Vicious and Nancy Spungen, played with total conviction by Gary Oldman and Chloe Webb. More a pure love story than a simple biopic (Cox's original title was *Love Kills*), the film deftly laces documentary-style realism with more abstract, dreamlike imagery. *Sid and Nancy*, however, would mark the beginning of the end of Cox's studio career, which seems to prove how difficult it is to make explicitly political films in Hollywood, and which is marked by equal parts stubbornness, foolishness and integrity.

His next film, *Straight to Hell* (1987), was perhaps the most spectacular and interesting failure of his *oeuvre*. Following a fund-raising concert for the Sandinista National Liberation Front, Cox was involved in persuading a number of musicians – including Joe Strummer, The Pogues, Elvis Costello – to tour Nicaragua in August 1986. However, they were unable to raise money for the tour, so instead enlisted the musicians to appear in a movie, the result of which is the modern day spaghetti western *Straight to Hell*. The final film however is a shambles, and was the first nail in Cox's coffin.

This was followed by the unjustly maligned *Walker* (1987), starring Ed Harris. In 1855 William Walker, an American, invaded Nicaragua and ruled the country as a dictator for two years. Cox retells these events as an indictment of Reagan's intervention in Central America, even using historical anachronisms (such as helicopters, limousines, Zippo lighters and Walker appearing in contemporary journals) to imply that not much has changed since 1855. *Walker* remains an interesting study of how history is represented and features a haunting score by Joe Strummer. Although it ended Cox's relationship with Hollywood, one must also admire his intentions: *Walker* was conceived as a means of spending as many US dollars in Nicaragua as possible, in order to help boost the economy. It remains today the second highest grossing movie ever in Nicaragua, behind *The Sound of Music* (1965).

Since *Walker*, Cox's output has been patchy at best, with little or no distribution. After a five-year hiatus, he returned to directing with *El Patrullero* (aka *Highway Patrolman*) (1992), a Spanish-language film made in Mexico. Dramatising the tenet that no good deed goes unpunished, the film follows the struggles of a young policeman to resist corruption, and was shot by Cox using an impressive grasp of the possibilities of the long take. *El Patrullero* garnered his best reviews since *Sid and Nancy*, but was the last of Cox's films to acquire a significant release. Cox continued his love affair with Latin America in 1996, with an adaptation of Jorge Luis Borges' 'The Death and the Compass', in which Cox himself played Borges. Stylish and provocative, it was expanded from a 50-minute short film that he had made for the BBC four years earlier. Also in 1996, he made the Las Vegas drama *The Winner*, but subsequently disowned it after the producers recut it and replaced the score with what could best be described as porno music.

Shortly thereafter, Cox was removed from his adaptation of *Fear and Loathing in Las Vegas*, to be replaced by Terry Gilliam – although he fought for (and won) a screenwriting credit with his collaborator Tod Davies. However, in 1997 he formed 'Exterminating Angel Productions' with Davies, and his career would appear to be on the turnaround. The first film from this production company was the Cox-directed *Three Businessmen* (1998), a typically bizarre and existential comedy in which he also stars as one of two businessmen (the third is otherwise engaged) who meet at Liverpool's Adelphi Hotel and spend the evening talking and being mysteriously transported to different cities around the world, including Amsterdam, Tokyo and Hong Kong. Cox has since completed the documentary *Kurosawa: The Last Emperor* and a futuristic update of 'Revenger's Tragedy'.          **AS**

# Wes CRAVEN

*Last House on the Left* (1972)   Wes Craven first entered the film scene as part of a new wave of horror directors in the
*The Hills Have Eyes* (1978)   early 1970s. While the careers of many of his contemporaries (such as George Romero

and Tobe Hooper) stalled in the 1980s, he has managed to sustain his position at the forefront of horror for three decades. Despite an uneven career, he regularly manages to produce a hit film at just the crucial moment.

Before entering the movie business Craven, born in Cleveland, Ohio, in 1939, was a humanities professor; the presence of a brain behind the blood and guts that fill his films has been a key to his success. Indeed, a number of film scholars (most notably Robin Wood) have identified the modern American horror film as one of the most progressive genres for radical social and political critique – with the monster representing the return of that which society represses. Craven's films are no exception: he positions the bourgeois family as a locus of violence and horror and examines such topics as child abuse, racial exploitation and the postmodern condition.

Having been tempted out of academia by producer Sean S. Cunningham, Craven made his feature debut with the infamous and gruelling *Last House on the Left* (1972). A reworking of Ingmar Bergman's *The Virgin Spring* (1962), the film depicts the brutal, backwoods murder of two teenage girls by a gang of psychopathic killers and the subsequent retribution suffered by the gang at the hands of one of the victim's parents. The film presents a challenge to the American family by forming a dual structure of ostensibly 'good' and 'bad' families, then blurring the two to reveal the latent violence behind respectable middle-class veneers. After committing their horrendous murders, the killer family are forced to assume the appearance of model houseguests; conversely, the victim's bourgeois family unleash the dormant violence within themselves. Craven has spoken about how the film tapped into his feelings about the Vietnam War and it remains a potent metaphor of the ideological attempts made by conservative America to repress its own immorality.

The same dual family structure is also evident in Craven's next film, *The Hills Have Eyes* (1977). One of his finest achievements, the film tells of a middle-class, 'whitebread' family who break down in the desert and are forced into battle with a family of ravenous cannibals who attack their motor home. *Last House on the Left* is disturbing because of its blunt artlessness: rejecting many horror techniques such as chiaroscuro lighting and nail-biting suspense, all of its atrocities occur in broad daylight and are shot in a plain, documentary style to heighten the sense of naturalism. However, with *The Hills Have Eyes* Craven crafted a stylised, suspense classic in which the knife-edge tension never lets up. He returned with a sequel in 1985, but it was a lacklustre affair in which much of the running time is padded with 'flashback' footage lifted from the first film (including one from the point of view of a dog).

Based on Lois Duncan's novel of the same name, *Summer of Fear* (1978) marked the first of Craven's frequent forays into television. It is a chilling tale of witchcraft, but Craven's skill with explicitly violent material is clearly stunted by the limitations of network television. This is a problem that dogs many of his small screen outings, forcing him to focus more on atmospheric frights than messy gore. *Chiller* (1985) was a popular thriller about a corporate executive who is revived from being cryogenically frozen, but returns without his soul. *Night Visions* (1990) is a serial killer movie with a psychic twist. He also directed several episodes of 'The Twilight Zone'. *Invitation to Hell* (1984), however, remains perhaps his most satisfying television work. A family moves to a nice, clean, suburban neighbourhood in California and are encouraged to join a local health spa to which the entire community belongs. Only the father is suspicious that evil may lurk within. While offering little not already found in *The Stepford Wives* (1975), Craven finds a perfect pitch of clinical sterility to produce an unnerving experience.

*Deadly Blessing* (1981) and *Swamp Thing* (1982) were two unremarkable theatrical features that did little to advance his career. The former is another rural thriller, dealing with a repressive sect of Hittites (who we are told 'make the Amish look like swingers'), and features an early performance by Sharon Stone. Aimed more at a family audience, *Swamp Thing* is a fairly sweet-natured, DC Comics monster-movie and was followed by a sequel and a television spin-off, but ranks among Craven's least memorable endeavours.

Just when he seemed to have lost the spark of his 1970s work, Craven's next film hit a surprise home run and gave us a new horror supervillain: the dream monster, Freddy Krueger. *A Nightmare on Elm Street* (1984) again examined corruption in the family structure, touching on themes of child abuse, alcoholism and parental neglect. Freddy may terrorise the children, but they are the innocents paying for the sins of their parents.

The film also began a shift from rural to (sub)urban settings in Craven's work – allowing his sociological critiques to be even more specific.

To date there have been six more Elm Street films. Craven co-wrote the third, but only directed the final one, *Wes Craven's New Nightmare* (1994). Miraculously breathing life into the moribund franchise, Craven injected postmodernism into the horror film. Taking the series' blurring of reality and nightmares to a new extreme, Freddy crosses over to attack the film's makers in the 'real' world. Playing himself, Craven argues it is the job of storytellers to capture the essence of 'evil' (of which Freddy is a manifestation) and hold it prisoner in their tales. In a witty spin on the series, we learn that Freddy escaped and is on the loose because the Elm Street franchise became so watered down and commercialised – the only solution is to make another film and make him scary again.

*Deadly Friend* (1986) tells the story of a teenage whiz kid that uses a microchip implant to resurrect the recently deceased girl next door. It remains campily entertaining, but sees Craven less successfully reworking elements from *A Nightmare on Elm Street* – suburbia, nightmare sequences and child abuse. However, he does deserve kudos for the tremendous beheading-by-basketball scene.

*The Serpent and the Rainbow* (1988) is an atmospheric and intelligent chiller starring Bill Pullman as a chemist investigating a 'zombie' drug in Haiti during the revolution. Craven deftly combines contemporary social chaos and ancient superstitions to produce a surrealistic nightmare for both Pullman and the audience. In contrast, *Shocker* (1989) was a rather blatant (and failed) attempt to create another franchise-spawning supervillain: executed mass-murderer Horace Pinker, a poor man's Freddy Krueger. Craven again employs the technique of blurring reality and nightmares, but in such a casual way that he makes absolutely no effort to provide a logical explanation for it. However, the climatic battle 'inside' a television system – with the hero and villain inserted into sitcoms, newsreels and tele-evangelist shows – is great fun and shows signs of Craven's developing interest in postmodernism.

*The People Under the Stairs* (1992) tells of an evil brother and sister team of landowners trying to squeeze black families out of their homes for profit. When a small ghetto kid named Fool breaks into their house in search of gold, he finds himself trapped alongside a community of near-zombies the couple have imprisoned in their cellar. Turning his sights to the plight of exploited minorities in the inner city, Craven successfully grafts these concerns onto a self-conscious fairy tale structure in what is perhaps his most underrated film. The Eddie Murphy vehicle *Vampire in Brooklyn* (1995) focuses on similar themes of urban racial exploitation. In particular, Murphy's steadily decaying manservant, who maintains a misplaced sense of loyalty despite his own demise, serves as a powerful metaphor for crack and the exploitation of one set of African-Americans by another.

Having experimented with postmodernism in *Shocker* and *Wes Craven's New Nightmare*, Craven upped the laughs and found a winning formula with another decade-defining smash hit: *Scream* (1996). Not only did the film kick-start Craven's career again, it resuscitated the entire horror genre and spawned countless imitations. Its concept was simple: the suburban teens in a slasher movie themselves watch slasher movies and are aware of all the clichés and conventions. Conceived as a trilogy, Craven also directed the two sequels to *Scream*. Both films were just as successful at the box office, but neither is as satisfying as the original. The imaginatively titled *Scream 2* (1997) apes the conventions of slasher movie sequels but is also itself a victim of those conventions (such as sequels never being as good or original as the first film). Set in Hollywood, *Scream 3* (2000) was shockingly conventional and pedestrian, proving how quickly the formula had become stale. The series arguably has little new to offer beyond generic deconstruction and both sequels seem to mistake in-joke tomfoolery and smug self-reflexivity for the subtle plays on convention in the first *Scream*. The original works because it is really one great double bluff: by exposing the conventions of the genre the audience expect something else to happen, but the film then plays by those very same conventions.

The success of *Scream* allowed Craven the opportunity to direct *Music of the Heart* (1999), a pet project and his first major departure from the fantasy/horror genre. A heartfelt true story of a violin teacher (Meryl Streep) in the inner-city projects, it was perceived by his fans as something of an anomaly. However, despite its generic difference, it revisits many of the same urban and racial concerns of *The People Under the Stairs* and *Vampire in Brooklyn*. Other horror directors who have ventured out of the genre with pet projects have usually returned, swiftly, to it. It will be interesting to see whether Craven attempts to pursue this new direction further in the future or attempts to mine new gold in postmodern horror. Like Freddy Krueger, he is likely to pop back up and surprise us with yet another hit franchise just when we thought he was dead; it could be with *Alice*, his next film, which sees an older Alice retuning to Wonderland to find it darker and changed.                                               **AS**

# Jeanne CRÉPEAU

Born in Montreal in 1961, Jeanne Crépeau's career is typical for a Québecois indie *Revoir Julie* (1998)
director. With her background rooted in history and anthropology, she entered the busy Montreal film scene thanks to a 1985 professional programme for young film-makers offered by the National Film Board of Canada. Her subsequent pursuits include various trainee jobs, specialisation at the Canadian Centre for Higher Cinema Studies (Toronto), as well as eight low-budget short and medium-length films, and two video installations.

The medium-length *Justine's Film* (1989), about a woman in the throes of an unrequited love, and the subsequent short *Claire and the Darkness* (1992), an adaptation of a choreographic spectacle inspired by an actual assassination of a female dancer, brought Crépeau awards and recognition. They consolidated her visual style by proving that the video could be every bit as artistically versatile as the film and established her feminist stance. Her latest animation, *The Solitude of Mr Turgeon* (2000), reconfirmed her taste for elegant bitter-sweet humour and experimentation.

Jeanne Crépeau produced, directed and wrote her first feature film, *Revoir Julie* (1998). Acted and shot in a refreshingly natural manner, it revisits the themes she has explored so far: solitude, love and lesbianism. The autobiographical touches account for the seductive mixture of mild irony and poeticism that drive the story of Juliet and Julie, who rediscover each other after 15 years of silence amidst the beautiful farming landscapes not far from Montreal.                                               **CSt**

# Michael CRICHTON

Michael Crichton (born John Michael Crichton in Chicago, 1942) graduated with an MD *Pursuit* (1972)
from Harvard Medical School, having worked in the Emergency Room of Massachusetts *Westworld* (1973)
General Hospital. His first and main success is as a thriller writer, winning the 1968 *Coma* (1978)
Mystery Writers of America Edgar Allan Poe Award for Best Mystery Novel with 'A *The First Great Train*
Case of Need'. Although he denies writing science fiction, his many best-sellers utilise *Robbery* (1979)
old-fashioned science fiction tropes (the lost world, rampaging robots, aliens, and ESP) *Looker* (1981)
and draw on his medical background to focus on techno-scientific matters. Movies *Runaway* (1984)
based on his novels include *The Andromeda Strain* (1971), *Dealing: Or the Berkeley- Physical Evidence* (1989)
to-Boston Forty-Brick Lost-Bag Blues* (1972), *The Carey Treatment* (aka *Emergency Ward* (1972)), *Pursuit* (1972), *The Terminal Man* (1974), *The First Great Train Robbery* (1979), *Jurassic Park* (1993), *Rising Sun* (1993), *Disclosure* (1994), *Congo* (1995), *The Lost World: Jurassic Park* (1997), *Sphere* (1998), and *The 13th Warrior* (aka *The Thirteenth Warrior* (1999)). Most, if not all, of his other novels have been optioned.

Crichton's screenwriting credits include *Westworld* (1973), *Extreme Close-Up* (aka *Sex Through a Window* (1973)), *Coma* (1978), *Looker* (1981), *Runaway* (1984), *Rising Sun* (1993), and *Twister* (1996). He also has credits as executive producer of *Disclosure*, producer of *Twister, Sphere, The 13th Warrior*, and *Jurassic Park 3* (2001), and creator and executive producer of NBC's 'ER', which was developed from a screenplay he wrote in 1974.

With its central theme of autonomy and control, its paranoid fascination with, and distrust of, an increasingly mechanised and simulacral society, and the contradictory relationship between its technophilia and grandstanding technophobia, *Westworld* is the movie most representative of Crichton's work. At its most effective in the sequences set in impersonal technological spaces, the direction of *Westworld* is fairly unremarkable, despite some nice compositions. Paradoxically, this is one of the movie's greatest strengths: that it all looks so familiar, that the supposed recreation of the authentic west looks like a western television show. Yul Brynner, playing the menacing android cowboy, adds depth to its concern with simulation. In keeping with its theme, *Westworld* established Crichton's intention to exercise control over adaptations of his work; *The Terminal Man*, the best effort at generating ambiguity from a technophobia which even Spielberg's simple-minded moralising was hard-pushed to reduce any further, is the major exception.

*Coma*, adapted from Robin Cook's best-selling debut novel, provided Crichton with his greatest critical and commercial success as a director. The stylistic mish-mash characteristic of his work is here at its most effective, moving from the chilling formalism of operating theatres and naturalistic domestic scenes, which make excellent use of off-screen space, imbalanced compositions, doorways and other vertical lines, to suspenseful action sequences and formulaic technophobic gothicism. Despite portraying a fairly strong and independent heroine, the movie is ultimately as reactionary as any of Crichton's work. The awkward gender politics revealed in the coincidence of male domination and the rather less frightening, less plausible, spare-parts surgery conspiracy are forgotten in a conclusion in which the conspiracy is exposed and patriarchal status quo is reinstated.

The underrated *The First Great Train Robbery*, based on a true story, is Crichton's least typical movie and arguably represents his best work as a director. Beautifully shot, it is meticulous in its 1880s period design, and great fun. His next movie, *Looker*, was a virtual remake of *Coma* without any of its merits; it has, however, received some critical attention for its concern with the simulation and commodification of the androgynous female body. *Runaway* casts Tom Selleck as a future cop specialising in disabling household robots which have gone haywire. *Physical Evidence* (1989) is a dull thriller about a tough cop accused of murder, and the public defender who comes to his aid. Crichton's only directorial work since then has been the extensive, uncredited, re-shoots on the over-budget, over-schedule *The 13th Warrior*, described by *Interzone* as 'Hollywood's first-ever Original Novelist's Cut of a film version written and directed by other people'. **MB**

# Michael CRISTOFER

Michael Cristofer is a Pulitzer Prize-winning playwright and screenwriter turned director of often sexy and lurid films. Born in New Jersey in 1945, he worked as an actor in television from the mid-1970s and his play 'The Shadow Box' was adapted as a television movie in 1980 with Paul Newman directing. This led to screenwriting jobs on a number of high-profile films, including the curiously old-fashioned reworking of David Lean's *Brief Encounter* (1945), *Falling In Love* (1984), starring Robert De Niro and Meryl Streep, and *The Witches of Eastwick* (1987), a scrappy and disappointing version of the John Updike novel. He also wrote Mike Figgis' *Mr. Jones* (1993), a Richard Gere vehicle which re-teamed the actor with the British director after the excellent *Internal Affairs* (1990). This second collaboration was badly botched, however, in no small part through studio interference.

Cristofer's directorial debut was shot for television and won six Emmies. *Gia* (1998) was a 'rags to riches to death' biopic of the supermodel Gia Carangi, who died of AIDS in 1986 at the age of 26. Cristofer cast the then unknown daughter of Jon Voight, Angelina Jolie, and although *Gia* is well done, it is notable mainly for Jolie's performance. The lifestyle of the bisexual, drug-addicted model may well have helped draw Cristofer to the project; his work since has often returned to sensationalised sexual subject matter.

*Body Shots* (1999) is an example of such treatment. Despite the self-important tag-line – this is a movie that helps 'define a decade' – it offers a superficial and flashy treatment of teenage sexual mores, including the hot topic of date rape. Employing a technique best described as a kind of MTV *Rashomon*, David McKenna – whose previous script for *American History X* (1998) was another example of an empty exploration of serious themes – seems to think the alcohol-fuelled sex games in his screenplay have hugely symbolic significance. The title, which refers to tequila, sex and violence sums this up. Despite these pretensions to seriousness, the film offers similar pleasures to the far superior *Cruel Intentions* (1999) and *Wild Things* (1998), namely the chance to see gorgeous young people behaving badly. There is a good movie to be made around the issue of date rape and the way the boundaries between rough sex and sexual assault can blur and often dissolve, but *Body Shots* is not it.

Cristofer's most recent film, *Original Sin* (2001), has seen him re-team with the now A-list Jolie in a risible erotic thriller. Adapted from the novel by the cult writer, Cornell Woolrich, this is another slice of sub-Hitchcock-soft-porn-noir (like the superior *Body Heat* (1981), *Basic Instinct* (1992), *Jade* (1995) and numerous direct-to-video outings), with only the period setting to distinguish it. In nineteenth-century Cuba, Antonio Banderas gets a mail-order bride (Jolie) who, after some badly lit, choreographed writhing, runs off with his money. The settings look cheap, Banderas never seems comfortable acting in English and even the usually sparky Jolie is dull (and, surprisingly, unsexy). This is glossy rubbish, not even bad enough to be fun.     **IC**

# David CRONENBERG

Between the aphrodisiacal slugs of *Shivers* (1975) and the bio-ports of *eXistenZ* (1999), David Cronenberg has devoted himself to the cause of transformation by fusion with immensely fertile results. Just as his films fold science fiction into horror, or intellectual rigour into emotional and physical intensity, so they have consistently mapped out a mind/body tension. Little wonder that Gavin Smith has dubbed him 'cinema's patron saint of symbiosis', or that, given his singular consistency, many consider him a definitive auteur. For feminist and queer critics, however, this singularity is the rope Cronenberg hangs himself by, its result a self-indulgent body of work packed with monstrous and/or passive women, or, in adapted work, conspicuously toned-down 'queer' themes. Not surprisingly, this remains a dichotomy Cronenberg cannot seem to fuse; and yet, on the whole, his films are more complex and often more ambiguous than his critics allow for.

Born in Toronto in 1943, the product of a 'cosy' (his word) bourgeois upbringing, Cronenberg did not take any formal film education. If this partially accounts for his unique vision, so his studies in Science and English Language and Literature hint at sources for his quasi-scientific themes and richly figurative visual language. The influence of the New York underground on Cronenberg was more practical than aesthetic. Their methods prompted him to form the Toronto Film Co-op with Ivan Reitman in the 1960s, in typically quiet Canadian rebellion against Hollywood. A comparative glance at Reitman's subsequent career – from *Ghostbusters* (1984) through *Twins* (1988) and *Kindergarten Cop* (1990) to *Dave* (1993)– reveals how assiduously Cronenberg has stuck to his word.

If Cronenberg is a neo-conservative film-maker, he didn't show it in his prototypical debut feature, *Shivers*. He had already mapped out his territory in a series of shorts: *Transfer* (1966) introduced themes of addiction and psychoanalysis, while *Stereo* (1969) and *Crimes of the Future* (1970) laid some foundations with their minimal settings, lean pacing and bizarre institutions. For its part,

*Shivers* plays host to one of Cronenberg's first purposeful diseases, in the shape of a parasitical cross between a slug, a turd and a penis. Ostensibly designed to cure over-rationality, it effectively cures the occupants of a sterile Montreal residential tower block, Starliner Towers, of bourgeois repression by turning them into orgiastic zombies.

The result marked Cronenberg's entrance into a pantheon of 1970s horror film-makers (also including Wes Craven, John Carpenter and George A. Romero), but it's no mere generic workout. If Romero's *Night of the Living Dead (*1968) thematised a civil rights context, so *Shivers* looks like a post-sexual revolution movie, with an air of catch-all sexual liberation to belie numerous accusations of sexual disgust. Sexual panic is a theme, but it is not the film's end point. The same can be said of its companion piece, *Rabid* (1977), a quasi-vampire movie in which Cronenberg infects most of Montreal after a woman's skin tissue implant mutates into a blood-sucking 'cock thing' (Cronenberg's words). Montreal's sexual panic is captured with keen ambiguity, and porn star Marilyn Chambers' engaging lead performance amounts to more than mere monstrous sexual predatory, a charge levelled by feminists at *Rabid*. Played by Samantha Eggar, the monstrous female character at the heart of *The Brood* (1979) did not endear Cronenberg to feminists either. Nonetheless, despite an unforgiving intensity, arguably generated by Cronenberg's marital breakdown prior to making the film, *The Brood* signals a shift from concept to plot in his career. There is some of the former in its theme of an addictive doctor-patient relationship hinged on the idea of psycho-plasmics – therapy based on physically transformative expressions of emotion – but the real meat of this smarting bruise of guilt, hatred and homicidal jump-suited dwarves is Cronenberg's deliberate inversion of the 'family values' movie. Famously, he dubbed it his *Kramer vs Kramer* (1979), and the result boasts an artful ferocity elevated by Howard Shore's almost knowing score: think Bernard Herrmann, lacerated.

*Scanners* (1981) emphasised Cronenberg's flair for weaving concept into plot. The much-admired exploding head sequence is an extraordinary feat of conceptual imagery, and the film's key conceit of the political conspiracies surrounding a group of atomised, telepathic warriors – scanners – offers plenty to chew on. These themes of conspiracy, coupled with the censorious critics Cronenberg's films had started attracting, segue into *Videodrome* (1983). Many consider this to be Cronenberg's finest, and James Woods' shabby Max Renn was the director's strongest character at that point. Yet it is a messy film. All semblance of plot disintegrates as Renn succumbs to physically transformative hallucinations after tumour-inducing exposure to a private snuff television show, 'Videodrome'. The point is to dissolve Cronenberg's *Videodrome* into the 'Videodrome' within the film, but the result leaves you with little more than a mish-mash of generic conservatism and fragmentation, with any points about censorship lost to a noirish detective story-cum-Philip K. Dick-style conspiracy tale steeped in sado-masochistic imagery. Cronenberg did not quite manage to integrate concept on the level of plot here.

When Cronenberg announced that he was to adapt Stephen King's 'The Dead Zone', it sounded like he was either taking time out after *Videodrome*'s intensity or dumbing down for the mainstream. As it happened, *The Dead Zone* (1983) proved to be a richly satisfying interior transformation tale, ably carried by Christopher Walken's tortured portrayal of a schoolteacher who wakes from a coma to find himself the unhappy bearer of psychic abilities. Consequently, Cronenberg's next film, *The Fly* (1986), turned out to be a stunning fusion of emotional and physical viscera. 'You could come back to my lab' is the line that leads Veronica Quaife (Geena Davis) to Seth Brundle's (Jeff Goldblum) place to check out his telepods. What follows is a classic doomed love story, a red-raw 'Beauty and the Beast' that shifts the partial transformation from the 1958 film version of *The Fly* to a fusion between Brundle and housefly at molecular level. The first stages of this transformation signal the clearest initial impact of existentialism in Cronenberg's work, with Brundle showing tendencies to 'wax messianic' and crack the shell of the archetypically impotent Canadian hero: from car-sick nerd to barroom brawler. Still, his near-Hollywood self-made man shtick stalls as he decomposes and reassembles as a six-foot fly, to Veronica's distress. The film's coupling of intimacy and genuine tenderness – it isn't *The Brood* – with a vivid expression of self/other fusion made for a happy, if brief, marriage between Cronenberg and the mainstream.

Instead of capitalising on it, Cronenberg went on to make the uncompromising *Dead Ringers* (1988), a project he had been stewing on since *The Dead Zone*. There is precious little viscera to contend with, but it proved to be even more affecting than *The Fly*. Partly adapted from the book 'Twins', the tale of symbiotic twin gynaecologists (the Mantle twins in the film, the Marcus twins in real life) found dead in their flat, it is a sombre, sonorous, character piece that spreads Cronenberg's fascination with the mind/body schism across Jeremy Irons' stunning performance as both twins. Genevieve Bujold makes a strong showing as the richly characterised actress who Beverly Mantle falls for, and the result shows how thoroughly Cronenberg had overhauled the horror genre in his own name by this point.

True to form, however, he chose to reject suggestions of the Marcus brothers' homosexuality, much to the consternation of queer critics. Similar concerns overshadowed his decision to adapt William S. Burroughs' 'Naked Lunch' in 1991: how could this relentlessly heterosexual director adapt the hero of sexual transgression's key work? Cronenberg argued that Burroughs was more ambiguous about his sexuality at that point than is presupposed, and the film fuses the sensibilities of director and writer in a witty, ingeniously antic discourse on drugs, creativity, censorship and sexuality. It's something of a droll libidinous riot, and for Christine Ramsay's criticism that Cronenberg's films are 'littered with dead queers', it is worth noting that this is the first of his films not to end in a ritual death. Peter Weller's Bill Lee writes his way out of that fate.

It's hard to see why *M. Butterfly* (1993), Cronenberg's adaptation of David Henry Hwang's stageplay, received such a poor reception. Perhaps it was because it emerged close to Neil Jordan's *The Crying Game* (1992), a similarly-themed film, although Cronenberg's tale of an affair between a European diplomat and a cross-dressing Chinese opera singer is the more subtle and complex of the two. He maps a study in colonialism onto themes of sexuality as a mutually constructed fantasy with great acuity, and the revelation of John Lone's opera singer's penis is mercifully free of the shrill hysteria that accompanied a similar scene (on and off-screen) in Jordan's film.

Still, nothing could anticipate the onslaught that greeted *Crash* (1996). Cannes gave this adaptation of J. G. Ballard's counter-cultural novel an award for 'audacity', but it proved too audacious for some. In Britain, the *Daily Mail* and *Evening Standard*'s attacks resulted in it being banned in Westminster. Ted Turner, the boss at Fine Line, its US distributor, delayed its release in the States until March 1997. The film itself, a cool, ingeniously metaphorical study in chrome and copulation, detailing how a couple's numbed sex life is ambiguously revived by a Dr Vaughan's (Elias Koteas) fixation on car crashes, almost disappeared in the thick of the controversy.

Ironically, despite the bleatings of neo-conservative critics and the film's hypnotic pull, other critics found the film deeply conservative. Certainly its explorations of sexuality betray the ambivalence that Cronenberg has been accused of. Vaughan introduces sexual transformation into the lives of Catherine and James Ballard only to be killed off once he's had sex with the latter and, implicitly, tried to penetrate him

Cronenberg pointed out that Vaughan and James share the film's first face-to-face kiss, and yet there remains a whiff of Hollywood cliché to Vaughan's death and James' penetration anxiety. That the other character to emphatically die in the film is a man dressed as a woman makes Ramsay's comment about 'dead queers' seem doubly pertinent. It's disappointing, especially coming after the wittily charged initial meeting between Vaughan and a badly injured James, the doctor cruising his patient's every crack.

He subsequently went on to deliver his cheekiest film yet. In part, *eXistenZ* (1999) is a meditation on censorious resistances to image-as-metaphor, coloured by Cronenberg's meeting with Salman Rushdie and, arguably, the *Crash* debacle. If Cronenberg's first film from an original script since *Videodrome* recalls that film by ingeniously collapsing its plot into the plot of the bio-technological game-within-the-film, eXistenZ, that is not to say he is stuck in a rut. He has clearly moved on from *The Fly*, where computers needed to be taught about the flesh. The cross-over between biology and flesh is complete here, as the game is played via inserts into spinal 'bio-ports' that feed off its players' nervous systems.

Considerably experienced in engaging his own audience's nervous systems, Cronenberg weaves meditations on cinema per se into his film, allowing existential themes of life-as-performance to emerge organically from the material. These conceptual layers are more rigorously worked out than in *Videodrome*, and yet more lightly. Despite the odds stacked against him circa *Crash*, Cronenberg was at the top of his game with this fresh, funny and intellectually frisky film: having fun with his material and playing it like a pro – not least at the expense of his male hero's fear of being penetrated.

A brief flirtation with Hollywood followed, which, characteristically for Cronenberg, never came off. Perhaps that's for the best – it's hard to imagine the director's singular style fusing with Sharon Stone and a second *Basic Instinct* film. Instead, Cronenberg decamped to London to make *Spider* (2002), an adaptation of Patrick McGrath's neo-gothic, first-person (and he's a profoundly unreliable narrator) novel centred on one Dennis Cleg, aka Spider, a man haunted by the traumatising death/murder of his mother. Set in the east end of London in the 1950s, the novel is a transformation narrative of sorts, focused on Spider's decidedly problematic relationship with his body.

On the subject of body works, there are rumours that Cronenberg has a script in the pipeline called *Painkillers*, about the French 'carnal artist' Orlan. To date, Orlan has had no less than nine plastic-surgery operations, through which she models herself on various figures from myth and history: Europa, Diana, Psyche, the Mona Lisa, and so on. At the time of writing, Cronenberg had offered no confirmation of the project. However, given Orlan's multiple transformations and talk of 'life as an aesthetically recuperable phenomenon', it is easy to see the director being drawn to the subject matter. **KH**

# Cameron CROWE

Born in Palm Springs in 1957, writer-director Cameron Crowe is a student of classic studio comedy, a throwback to Golden Age Hollywood. Like Frank Capra, Preston Sturges and Ernst Lubitsch, Crowe has demonstrated a rare ability to invest characters with depth and dignity while still making audiences laugh. During an era in which coarse and easy humour has dominated Hollywood comedy-making, Crowe's early works have served as a refreshing alternative, offering intelligent, funny, and often moving investigations of contemporary American life.

Crowe was notably precocious. At 14 he became the rock critic for San Diego's daily newspaper and, a few years later, Rolling Stone's youngest editor, having shocked the staff there by turning in a profile of Led Zeppelin, a band who had previously refused contact with the magazine. Before he was 21, Crowe had interviewed Bob Dylan, David Bowie, Neil Young and Eric Clapton, and at 22 he returned to high school under an alias, collecting material for what became the best-selling book 'Fast Times at Ridgemont High: A True Story'. Universal Pictures optioned the book while still in galley form, releasing Fast Times at Ridgemont High (1982) a year later. The film, directed by Amy Heckerling from Crowe's screenplay (nominated for a Writers Guild of America award), received some criticism for being exploitative. However, Fast Times is anything but typical teen soft porn; it offers a frank, realistic portrayal of suburban teen life.

After nearly seven years of frustration, Crowe saw the release of his directorial debut, the mature and charming teen romance Say Anything (1989). The story traces the evolving relationship between a valedictorian and a determined young suitor. Sweet but not saccharine, hopeful but not naïve, Say Anything is a minor classic. Although conventional in structure, the film is radical in its treatment of its characters, investing them with a humanity too rarely seen in contemporary Hollywood film-making.

Crowe's next work, Singles (1992), explores the romantic trysts among a group of friends living in a Seattle apartment building. The director struggled with Warner Bros. executives over the tone and content of the film throughout the production and post-production stages. Perhaps as a result of the disagreements, or maybe because of its ensemble cast, Singles is something of a mishmash, lacking the clarity and carefully developed characters that define Crowe's other works. His subsequent project, Jerry Maguire (1996), became one of the most successful films of the 1990s. The plot is Capra-esque: a brilliant young sports agent (Tom Cruise) attempts to insert some humanity into a world dominated by greed and cynicism. Nominated for six Academy Awards (Cuba Gooding Jr. won Best Supporting Actor), Jerry Maguire is a triumph, demonstrating Crowe's remarkable talent as a director of actors and his ability to invest his storybook tales with contemporary realism and a sense of social conscience.

After publishing 'Conversations with Wilder', an acclaimed and highly personal collection of interviews with director Billy Wilder, Crowe recently returned to work behind the camera. In Almost Famous (2000), a semi-autobiographical story about the 1970s rock'n'roll scene, he creates an entertaining, if uneven, account of a teenager's early experiences as a music critic. Almost Famous features the kind of energetic performances that Crowe's films have become known for: Kate Hudson playing a groupie and Frances McDormand as a nervously permissive mother were both nominated for Academy Awards; Philip Seymour Hoffman is also excellent as a cynical critic. It remains engaging even when it loses focus. Satisfying both as a rites-of-passage film and a rockers-on-the-road chronicle, it won Crowe his first Academy Award (for original screenplay) and has attracted something of a cult following, particularly after the release of a DVD director's cut.

Having spent his first decade as film-maker creating films that are smart, funny, sensitive and familiar, and which celebrate the power of humour and idealism in a corrupt world, after Almost Famous it would have been easy to pigeon-hole Crowe. Existing in a kind of cinematic netherworld, he is too old-fashioned to be associated with the generation of hip, ironic American independent auteurs, yet has a far deeper concern for his characters than the typical Hollywood director.

With the release of Vanilla Sky (2001), however, his profile changed considerably. This Tom Cruise vehicle, updated from Alejandro Amenábar's Abre Los Ojos/Open Your Eyes (1997), is an Escher-like box-inside-a-box thriller that features Cruise as a millionaire playboy disfigured in a harrowing car crash. The film, a strange choice for Crowe (whose finest work rests, solidly, in the familiar), works better as a metaphysical exercise than as a piece of convincing storytelling. Some critics were intrigued by its alienating qualities – its cool, polished veneer, its red herrings, its indecipherable layers of flashback – while others attacked it as a muddled vanity project for Cruise, who also produced. **JS**

# Alan CUMMING

Both actors, Alan Cumming and Jennifer Jason Leigh met while performing in 'Cabaret' *The Anniversary Party* (2001) on Broadway and, sharing similar sensibilities, decided to write, produce and direct their debut feature film, *The Anniversary Party* (2001), together. Born in California in 1962, Leigh had previously established a career specialising in intense, often challenging, roles in a range of edgy and off-beat films, such as *Last Exit to Brooklyn* (1989), *Rush* (1991), *Short Cuts* (1993), *The Hudsucker Proxy* (1994) and *Mrs Parker and the Vicious Circle* (1994). Born in Perthshire, Scotland, in 1965, Cumming began acting in British theatre and television, and more recently forged an American career after roles in *GoldenEye* (1995), *Circle of Friends* (1995) and *Emma* (1996) brought him to Hollywood's attention, where he has since starred in *Flintstones in Viva Rock Vegas* (2000) and *Spy Kids* (2001). Before conceiving *The Anniversary Party,* Cumming had directed a short film, *Burn Your Phone*, about a telecom operator who receives malicious calls, in 1996, and Leigh had produced Ulu Grosbard's *Georgia* in 1995.

Calling on an array of friends, including Gwyneth Paltrow as a spoilt ingénue and Kevin Kline as an over-the-hill leading man, Leigh and Cumming used improvisation to develop the script for this movie about a writer turned director and his insecure actress wife who celebrate their renewed marriage by throwing a sixth anniversary party. Potentially self-indulgent, the film is actually witty and subtle for the most part, eliciting strong performances from an interesting cast (Phoebe Cates, Jennifer Beals and John C. Reilly also lend credible support), and producing an intimate portrait of a rocky relationship. Shades of Edward Albee's play 'Who's Afraid of Virginia Woolf?', which was filmed by Mike Nichols, are evident in the couple's searing arguments and the manner in which they draw friends and colleagues into their marital misery.

Shot fast and cheap on digital camera, by cinematographer John Bailey, it has a spontaneous visual style. However, despite Bailey's best efforts, the movie cannot help but evoke the cheapness of digital film. Still, the mode of filming serves the raw emotional subject matter effectively; it is this type of small, fiery movie that the technology is perfectly suited to. It is only when the characters take the Ecstasy brought to the party by Paltrow's character that the film's does stray towards self-indulgence. On the whole, though, it is vividly acted and accurately observed – a positive start for the pair, whose edgy styles and reputations promise much for future projects. **JD**

# Vondie CURTIS-HALL

Born in Detroit in 1956, Vondie Curtis-Hall first found success as an actor, appearing in *Gridlock'd* (1997) over thirty movies to date, as well as playing series regular Dr Dennis Hancock in CBS' *Glitter* (2001) 'Chicago Hope'.

His directorial debut, which he also scripted, was *Gridlock'd* (1997), a comedy starring Tim Roth and Tupac Shakur as two junkies who, following a friend's near-fatal overdose, pick the wrong day to try to kick the habit. As they attempt to get emergency medical insurance so they can get into a rehab programme on the same day, they run foul of a drug dealer (D-Reper, played by Curtis-Hall) who has murdered their own dealer, with supposedly hilarious consequences. There is, however, nothing Kafkaesque about their situation. As they are sent from pillar to post, their poorly-paced tour – interrupted by flashbacks which do not succeed in adding depth to their relationship – reveals a collapsing healthcare system and the helplessness and occasional intolerance of those working within it. Too full of second-hand stylishness to tell its story well or to generate any sympathy for its characters, the movie lacks the ironic distance or satiric bite to compensate, and undercuts its anti-drugs message by failing to depict the junkie's existence as being any worse than that of someone who is merely a cog in the city's bureaucratic machine or just plain poor. Even Roth's trademark low-key quirkiness and a cameo from John Sayles cannot redeem this tasteless exercise in shallowness.

Curtis Hall's last film, *Glitter* (2001), was an indifferently received Mariah Carey vehicle. **MB**

# D

## John DAHL

John Dahl has stylistically tapped into the dark side of America with his fresh brand of melodramatic potboilers. His best storytelling, full of beautiful, double-crossing femmes fatales and desperate, working-class protagonists, is a respectful throwback to the film noir of the late 1940s and early 1950s, evoking films such as *Out of the Past* (1947) and *A Place in the Sun* (1951). Born in Montana in 1956, Dahl is the reverse of his jaded and conflicted characters, having experienced a pleasant and uneventful upbringing as the son of an insurance salesman. He attended the University of Montana to study art, and later completed a degree in film production at Montana State. He continued his education in the director fellowship program at the prestigious American Film Institute and graduated to work as a storyboard artist on such films as *Robocop* (1987) and the Jonathan Demme projects *Something Wild* (1986) and *Married to the Mob* (1988). He honed his directing skills by filming a handful of music videos for such artists as Joe Satriani, Kool & The Gang and Nia Peeples.

Dahl's first foray into feature directing was *Kill Me Again* (1989), a straight-up noir thriller. Starring the husband and wife team of Val Kilmer and Joanne Whalley-Kilmer, the film is an assured but derivative tale of a private detective played for a fool by a sexy, double-crossing siren on the run from a troubled past. There is a lot to like about *Kill Me Again* – especially the breezy but dangerous sexuality of Whalley-Kilmer, and the fast-paced, twisting narrative – but most importantly the film serves as a fascinating trial run for characters and themes that Dahl revisits more successfully in his next two films.

*Red Rock West* (1992) and *The Last Seduction* (1994), two low-budget projects that had difficulty finding theatrical distribution because of shortsighted financial backers, are the crown jewels of Dahl's career. Deliciously wry, provocative and clever, both films are benchmark examples of how to translate classic film noir themes to contemporary period pieces. *Red Rock West* follows Nicolas Cage as a sympathetic, downtrodden protagonist who becomes victimised by a number of inescapable circumstances that twist back on him like a relentless nightmare, including such noir chestnuts as a questionable play for quick money, and a hot, sexually charged affair with a dangerous, manipulative, backstabbing femme fatale. John and Rick Dahl's script is

*Kill Me Again* (1989)
*Red Rock West* (1992)
*The Last Seduction* (1994)
*Unforgettable* (1996)
*Rounders* (1998)
*Joy Ride* (2001)

crisp, efficient and unpredictable, gleefully piling on surprise after surprise to great effect. *The Last Seduction* is Dahl's mesmerising update to the femme fatale myth in the form of a scheming, cold-hearted, white collar professional brought to life in a career-best performance by Linda Fiorentino. She is a gorgeous, man-shredding vixen who aspires to a more privileged life of luxury and power at any cost, including ruthless betrayal, manipulative violence and ferocious sex with unwitting, small-town boy toys. Her excesses are restrained just enough by Dahl to avoid camp, keeping the film grounded in unpredictable intrigue with a splash of black humour.

*Unforgettable* (1996), a Dino De Laurentis production, began a shift for Dahl towards work on larger budgeted projects with less creative control. Although scattered with familiar elements, *Unforgettable* is a departure from Dahl's established (and more successful) neo-noir formula to the fantastic realm of science fiction-based melodrama. If its ludicrous leaps in logic and confessing killer dénouement can be forgiven, *Unforgettable* is a solid thriller made better by skilful camerawork and several visually creative set pieces. Much of the film is told in dialogue-free flashbacks, giving Dahl an opportunity to showcase his directorial muscle. While Ray Liotta gives a convincingly conflicted performance as a police medical examiner obsessively haunted by his wife's homicide, co-star Linda Fiorentino is sadly wasted as his one-dimensional expositor sidekick.

In *Rounders* (1998) Dahl applies a standard 'sympathetic lead character who loses everything and fights to regain it back by the film's end' premise to the underground poker community in New York City. The film is saved from mediocrity by its colourful, lingo-heavy dialogue and on-target supporting performances. Dahl is the right director for the material, bringing a stylish gloss and suspense to the gambling sequences without getting bogged down in tedious gaming strategies. The film loses its edge, however, when it turns away from its absorbing characters and falls back on servicing its underlying plot engine.

More recently, Dahl has edged a few steps back towards his suspense roots for *Joy Ride* (2001), a horror thriller about a cross-country road trip gone awry that had the ill-fated timing of making its US debut mere weeks after the 11 September terrorist attacks. Although brimming with the kind of hard edged black humour that works so well in *The Last Seduction*, the collective nerve of American filmgoers was still raw and unprepared for suspenseful escapism – and violence of any form – so this very effective, expertly directed genre film never found its audience. *Joy Ride*'s barren Americana isolationism blisters with tension and dread, and exploits the device of the never-seen, open road stalker with style and precision. Feeling more like a heady update of *Breakdown* (1997) than *Duel* (1971), *Joy Ride* is perhaps a quart low in narrative originality, but it is still superb, well-oiled popcorn entertainment. **THa**

# Joe DANTE

Born in New Jersey in 1946, Joe Dante indulged his early fascination with film in an on-going project called *The Movie Orgy*, conducted between 1967 and 1975, in which he compiled and edited sequences from forgotten B-movies, early television kinescopes, and Schlitz beer commercials. The film was shown year by year in college campuses, repertory theatres and drive-in parks. Dante's skills in editing earned him work cutting trailers at Roger Corman's New World Studio, and the opportunity to co-direct (with Alan Arkush) *Hollywood Boulevard* (1976), before gaining prominence through the John Sayles-scripted *Piranha* (1978), acknowledged by Steven Spielberg as the most persuasive *Jaws* (1975) parody he had seen. *The Howling* (1980) maintained Dante's profile, foregrounding state-of-the-art transformation effects, and demonstrating his penchant for ironic revisionism, and the subversive critique of genre staples.

Although much has been made of Dante's background with Corman, his appreciation of exploitation and trash aesthetics, and his witty engagement with the horror genre, the pivotal moment in his career was arguably his segment in the Spielberg-produced *Twilight Zone – The Movie* (1983). 'It's a Good Life' highlighted Dante's recognition of the absurdist ambivalence of the cartoon sensibility and his gift for choreographing the surreal brutalities of cartoon violence. An implied critique of 'Uncle Walt' and the sentimentality of the Disney canon, this prefigures Dante's work in *Gremlins* (1984) and *Gremlins 2: The New Batch* (1990), which turns Disneyesque 'sweetness' and WASP suburban security into a nightmare of technological failure, while also satirising media complicity and consumerist complacency.

This combination of the sensibility of a cartoonist and social satirist reaches its zenith in Dante's work in the part-animated *Small Soldiers* (1998), an anti-*Toy Story* vehicle which shows the brutality of gung-ho action figures as they take on their sworn enemies, the essentially peace-loving and fun-seeking Gorgonites, trashing the middle-American liberal ethos as outmoded and naïve. Dante plays out an ambivalence in the appeal of the far-right agenda through the figures of Chip Hazard (voiced by Tommy Lee Jones) and his Commando Elite (voiced by the surviving actors from *The Dirty Dozen*). Dante condemns the violence of the US military as self-evidently 'wrong' and lampoons the heroic glorification of soldiering in war movies, but the wit, ingenuity and selfless commitment of the soldiers remains exciting and persuasive. Dante's witty parodies of *Patten* (1970) and *Apocalypse Now* (1979) merely enhance the credentials of the 'right' in the face of the ineptitudes and nostalgia of the 'centre'. Although Dante critiques Globotech's corporate abuse of merchandising opportunities and communications technologies, this ultimately only highlights generational anxiety in the light of late capitalism. The Baby Boomer generation are both disempowered at the socio-economic level, and more importantly, out of touch with the context in which their children live – a context informed by a vast ideological and ethical vacuum which the less scrupulous are eager to exploit. Although the small soldiers are ultimately defeated by the enterprising youngster Alan, his girlfriend Christie, and a combination of geeks and suburban bumblers, Globotech, the makers of the Commando Elite toys, merely pay off the inconvenienced at the end of the film, and still perceive a use for the toys in rebel guerrilla warfare elsewhere. Although the surviving Gorgonites sail off in pursuit of their mythical home, Dante does not let sentiment interfere with reality.

Dante's preoccupation with exposing the dark underbelly of small-town America is also evident in *The 'burbs* (1989) – a farcical take on xenophobia and petty voyeurism – and in his gothic twist on the youth-orientated sitcom-cum-soap crossover, 'Eerie Indiana'. Directing the first five episodes, Dante set the tone for a series that has drafted the supernatural and the paranormal into everyday scenarios, collapsing the distinction between imagined and experienced 'horror'. This has tragi-comic consequences in many instances, and highlights Dante's playfulness in consistently recognising that black humour is a significant way of addressing and dealing with increasingly arbitrary and ambiguous codes of lived experience. This approach also figures in his other television work, most notably, his episodes of 'Police Squad' (1982) and 'Amazing Stories' (1985).

While possessing an often insightful and subversive social sensibility, Dante has never lost sight of his second generation 'movie brat' credentials, and continually references his movie influences as a resistance to what he believes is Hollywood's preoccupation with the centrality of spectacle, and the lack of respect for other models of world cinema, and the 'art' of cinema in general. *Gremlins 2*, for example, has particular disdain for a television channel showing *Casablanca* (1945) in a colour version with a happier ending. All of his films have visual references to a variety of media forms and aspects of popular culture. *Matinee* (1993) is Dante's own respectful tribute both to the film culture of the mid-1950s and to the B-movies which have often become the unacknowledged source for big-budget blockbusters in the contemporary era. John Goodman plays Lawrence Woolsey, a character based on B-movie director William Castle. The film within a film, 'Mant' (Half-Man! Half-Ant! All Terror!) brilliantly parodies movies as various as *Them!* (1954), *Tarantula* (1955), and *The Incredible Shrinking Man* (1957). *Explorers* (1985) also features aliens who have learned all they know from television culture, while *Innerspace* (1987) is Dante's re-working of the Raquel Welch vehicle, *The Fantastic Voyage* (1956).

Dante's achievement is considerable. His films constitute a canon of work which has continually undermined and subverted American mythologies, pointing up the particular complicity of the arts and media in the United States in perpetuating unsustainable ideological and socio-cultural agendas. His playful yet black comic sensibility, allied to his encyclopaedic knowledge of popular culture, has enabled him to critique the conservatism of American political and social experience, and lament the triumph of late capitalism over distinctive and imaginative cultural identities. Inexplicably, Dante has been overlooked while film-makers like Tim Burton and David Lynch, engaging with much the same terrain, have been critically lauded. Acclaim for the consistency and creativity in Dante's oeuvre is long overdue.

Forthcoming projects include *Blood Relative*, in which a genetics student discovers disturbing secrets from his family past.                                           **PB**

# Frank DARABONT

Born in 1959, Frank Darabont paid his Hollywood dues as a set dresser and production assistant on movies like *Hell Night* (1981) and Ken Russell's *Crimes of Passion* (1984), before graduating to screenwriting, where he carved a niche for himself in the horror genre with credits including *The Fly II* (1989), *The Blob* (1988), and *Mary Shelley's Frankenstein* (1994).

His directorial debut, the Stephen King adaptation *The Shawshank Redemption* (1994), established the hallmarks of his storytelling style: deliberately slow pacing, attention to narrative detail, respect for the intelligence of the audience, astute casting (Tim Robbins and Morgan Freeman took the lead roles), and the panache to carry off the occasional set-piece (Robbins' prison escape and triumphant emergence into the rain). The film fared poorly at the US box office, but its slightly anachronistic ring of 'quality' earned it several Academy Award nominations, which helped it to find a huge audience on video and television. By the end of the 1990s, the movie was regularly placed in Best Film polls.

In 1999, Darabont released *The Green Mile*, to initial critical reservations about the wisdom of tackling two Stephen King prison-bound dramas in a row. As expected, many of the elements that had earned *Shawshank* its reputation were in place: epic length, a sympathetic racial pairing (Tom Hanks as Death Row warder Paul Edgecomb and Michael Clarke Duncan as the mysterious gentle giant, John Coffey), and a certain nostalgia for a more innocent cinematic era (where *Shawshank* employed icons such as Rita Hayworth, *The Green Mile* featured *Top Hat* (1935) as a motif of pure, uncomplicated happiness). Both films share themes concerning wrongfully accused men whose innate decency is eventually recognised, and Darabont has spoken of his artistic debt to Frank Capra. His latest release, *The Majestic* (2001), is also Capraesque. Set in 1951, it stars Jim Carrey as a blacklisted writer who loses his memory after a car accident and ends up in a small town where he is confused for a local war hero who has been missing.

In demand as a writer (with uncredited rewrites on *Eraser* (1996) and *Saving Private Ryan* (1998)), Darabont's reputation as a director seems to rest less on visual style than on subtlety, characterisation, and an unfussy, detailed approach to narrative craft. His next film will be a new take on Ray Bradbury's 'Fahrenheit 451'.                **MF**

# Julie DASH

Despite the funding problems that have plagued her films, Julie Dash has become one of America's most respected independent film-makers and a particularly crucial figure for black feminist critics.

Born in New York in 1952 and later graduating from City College there, Dash elected to move to the West Coast where she enrolled on the film production programme at the American Film Institute. During this period she no doubt became acquainted with the highly political, Afrocentrist ideals of 'third cinema'. Of equal importance to Dash's development was the work of black feminist novelists such as Toni Morrison and Alice Walker. Dash's AFI graduation film *Illusions* (1982) is a dazzling piece of cinema and went on to be voted best film of the decade by the Black Filmmakers Foundation.

With her interest in narrating the 'forgotten history' of black women, the film is set in a Hollywood studio during World War Two and concerns the relationship between Mignon (Lornette McKee), whose light skin colour allows her to pass as a white executive, and the darker-skinned Ester (Roseanne Katon), a singer who is used to dub white musicals. Despite their differences, the film depicts the increasing sensitivity of Mignon towards Ester's exploitation, and her recognition of the need for solidarity between black women.

One of the most astonishing features of Dash's work is the amount of historical research she does for her projects, and the film is meticulous in the detail of the clothes, hair and make-up of each woman, revealing the positive way in which the women care for themselves. But what particularly adds to the emotional depth of the film is the visual texture: the exquisite lighting and tonality of the black and white cinematography, and haunting images such as that of the dispossessed Ester somehow dubbing a love song out of sync with her own voice.

Dash has always stressed the need for artistic control over her projects. However, such a determination has meant that she has struggled to find funding for her, work and the long battle to produce her first feature *Daughters of the Dust* (1991) has been well documented. Dash does, however, hold the accolade of making the first film by a black woman to get national distribution.

The film is perhaps the closest cinematic equivalent to the literary work of Morrison and Walker, with Steven Spielberg's adaptation of *The Color Purple* (1985) roundly condemned by black feminist critics for being adapted to suit a white, liberal audience. *Daughters of the Dust* is set on the Sea Islands off South Carolina at the beginning of the twentieth century and recounts the final meeting of a black family just as they are about to migrate to the American mainland. Central to the work is the tension between Nana (Cora Lee Day), who wants the family to stick to their roots on the island, and the other members who look to the future. The film, however, uses the interesting device of narrating the story both from Nana's perspective and that of an unborn child, whose retrospective commentary suggests that the family history will continue to be told into the family's diasporic existence.

The film thus not only puts black female characters at the centre of narrative events, but through stressing the importance of the African traditions of oral storytelling also marks the women as the guardians of ancestral history. Despite the attention given to the nuances of individual characters, there is always an emphasis on the shifting relations within the family group as a whole. Not only does Dash organise the dramatic space to constantly highlight group interaction, but she also sets this against the rich natural landscape to give the film a deep, spiritual feeling.

Together with *Illusions*, *Daughters of the Dust* was originally intended as part of a series of films dealing with the experiences of black women across the last century, but again Dash has unfortunately suffered funding difficulties. Recently, however, she has made several movies for television; *Incognito* (1999), *Funny Valentines* (1999), *Also Love Song* (2000), and *The Rosa Parks Story* (2002). Whilst lacking the visual brilliance of the earlier films, *Funny Valentines*, the story of a woman travelling back to visit her family in the deep South, is again able to reprise these themes of memory and history in a profound and moving way. Given the brilliance of her earlier films one can only hope that this might lead to greater opportunities for Dash in the future.          **CH**

# Andrew DAVIS

In clambering for a critical toehold in the mirror-polished surfaces of Andrew Davis' brand of visceral cinema, it is tempting to turn to the long-forgotten term *metteur en scène*, introduced into film criticism by the *Cahiers du cinéma* critics to distinguish the artisan from the artist. Accordingly, the few reviewers and critics who have attempted to deal with Davis' films tend to revert, with uncanny predictability, to a handful of pithy terms such as set-piece virtuosity, machine-tooled efficiency, visual sensation, and kinetic energy. Indeed, it is difficult to find a review of a Davis film which doesn't contain one version or another of the platitude: 'Davis handles the action sequences well.' Starting from the presupposition that he must be a mere director, as opposed to an auteur, his work is then reduced to 'empty' concept-driven formalism or pure spectacle, variously praised by 'thrill-cognisants' for its neat stereotypes and rhapsody of physical exhilaration at the expense of psychological nuance, or chided by critics hung-up on forms of content such as character and thematics.

Accepting this crude form/content opposition, the more pallid critical statements figure Davis as an exponent of what Larry Gross terms 'the big loud action movie', and what other critics more vituperatively refer to as the 'dumb action movie', or the 'by-the-numbers-blockbuster', that is, precisely the sort of corporate entertainment which traditional models of criticism are either unable or unwilling to cope with. Latterly, however, more productive criticism has concentrated the action film's kinship with the 'pure' cinematic logics of both the pre-1914 'cinema of attractions' and the European formalism of Bresson and Tarkovsky thus clearing the ground for the reappraisal of this

*Stony Island* (1978)
*The Final Terror* (1981)
*Code of Silence* (1985)
*Above the Law* (1988)
*The Package* (1989)
*Under Siege* (1992)
*The Fugitive* (1993)
*Steal Big, Steal Little* (1995)
*Chain Reaction* (1996)
*A Perfect Murder* (1998)
*Collateral Damage* (2002)

putative genre fodder in artistic and aesthetic terms. And it is to this extent that the pre-emptive titular exultation of action of many of Davis' films – *Under Siege* (1992), *Chain Reaction* (1996) – stand as *leitmotif* for the paradigm of film-making which has, since the early 1980s, rapidly reconfigured the economic strategy and creative alignment of post-classical Hollywood production. As such, like Jan De Bont, Paul Verhoeven, James Cameron, John McTiernan and the other contemporary high priests of high-concept movies, Davis belongs to a new breed of auteur who aesthetically kow-tow to the corporate form to the extent that that form becomes the mark of their artistry. So while Davis lacks the postmodern irony of Verhoeven and the mega-buck capital investment of Spielberg or Lucas, and cannot be described as a neo-epic director like Ridley Scott, what explicitly separates Davis' best films from the generic chaff, making him more than an incidental figure, is the distinctive gestalt of his degree-zero style. It is somewhat of a paradox, therefore, that the relative success of Davis' films is more or less proportional to the effacement of his authorial presence. It is in this sense that one of the more perceptive critics imagines his directorial intervention less in terms of afflatus than of a 'consummate *apparatchik*, endlessly checking the logistics of each stunt and story-boarding every shot to within an inch of its life'.

Born in Chicago in 1942, Davis grew up in the creative milieu of repertory theatre. Behoved by his parents' relationship to director and cinematographer Haskell Wexler, Davis' film career began as his assistant cameraman on *Medium Cool* (1969). Indeed, together with his journalistic education, Davis frequently cites Wexler's ultra-realist, Bazainian approach to film-making as paradigmatic of his own directorial credo. It is perhaps no accident, therefore, that while working in the crew on 15 studio and independent features, Davis cut his professional teeth working as a director of photography in the more clinical forms of the television commercial and documentary special.

Underscored by an unlikely inspirational brew of Fellini, Bertolucci, and the youthful work of Kubrick and Friedkin, Davis' early work is a *via media* of vicarious generic fodder and personal stylistic refinement. His semi-autobiographical directorial debut, *Stony Island* (1978), is a little-known yet modestly acclaimed independent musical which he co-wrote and produced. Despite its neat reflexive surfaces, *The Final Terror* (1981) is perhaps more notable for its inauguration of Daryl Hannah and Rachel Ward, while the subsequent rigid Chuck Norris vehicle, *Code of Silence* (1985) not only marked Davis' full-time commitment to directing, but is also the most clear presage of his longstanding kinship with the action genre.

While on the one hand the historical accounts of CIA involvement in narcotic racketeering and the military experiences of co-writer and star Steven Segal invest *Above the Law* (1988) with a patina of authenticity, on the other hand it is precisely the abnegation of psychological complexity and historical specificity to the primacy of kinaesthetic sensation that stakes out this reduced generic but volumetric aesthetic territory as Davis'. Indeed, the acutely didactic yet turbid script, as well as the crude distillation of plot into self-contained set-pieces, is curiously offset by the kinetic élan of the action's balletic choreography, theatrically staged amidst the urban scenography of Chicago. And, with the exception of *Steal Big, Steal Little* (1995) – a timid and ultimately hackneyed rehash of the good twin/bad twin *deceptio visus* scenario – and *A Perfect Murder* (1998) – a hueless remake of Hitchcock's thriller *Dial M for Murder* rescued only by the camp laconism of Michael Douglas' performance – Davis' work has consistently revisited and refined this empty formalism.

The hazardous thrills of *The Package* (1989) and the feckless orgy of destruction delivered by *Under Siege* (1992) graduated Davis to the A-list of Hollywood action directors. Structured around an inexorable logic of concatenation, these films not so much abandon narrative to spectacle, but rather represent the narrativisation of spectacular pleasure, a *modus operandi* summed up by Philip Strick, who noted what the latter film has in mind 'is action, not polemic'. However, despite the *alieni generis* of its improvised shooting process, and somewhat in spite of the philanthropic performances by Harrison Ford and Tommy Lee Jones, it is *The Fugitive* (1993) which not only stands as paradigmatic of fin-de-siècle post-classical film-making, but which best captures the gestalt of Davis' auteurist engineering. The relentless hero-in-jeopardy narrative logic fuses with the phantasmagoria of the image and the dynamic hyper-fidelity soundtrack to produce a styleless style of cinema which hardwires itself into the audience's sensorium. Seen from this angle, the breathtaking velocity and explosive splendour of the film's train crash sequence which sets the narrative's domino-toppling structure in motion, stands as an exemplar of post-classical plot advancement through set-piece spectacle, a process which returns us to cinemas pre-classical history. Moreover, in disavowing psychological and historical complexity and atavistically relocating narrative motivation in the graphic potential of the frame, *The Fugitive*, and its logical but not so gratifying precipitation, *Chain Reaction* (1996), in fact skilfully collapse the shop-worn form/content narratology into high-concept visceral aesthetics. And it is precisely to this extent that Davis' films have been as responsible as any for codifying the trope of the chase as the *lingua franca* of the contemporary action movie. Indeed, critics nostalgic for the psychological pleasures of classicism are perhaps right when they suggest that there's little more to Davis' cinema than meets the eye.

His most recent feature, *Collateral Damage* (2002), suffered long release delays after the events of 11 September. Starring Arnold Schwarzenegger as a man out for revenge after his wife and childcare killed in a terrorist bombing, its subject matter was considered too delicate.                                                                            **PWa**

# Tamra DAVIS

Tamra Davis is one of a few female directors steadily employed in the commercial film industry. A graduate of the Los Angeles City College's cinema programme, she followed the path of such feature film directors as David Fincher, Felix Gary Gray and Spike Jonze by starting a career directing music videos for artists like Sonic Youth, NWA, Tone Loc and New Kids on the Block, among others. It was through her close connection with the music scene that she met her husband, Michael Diamond (aka Mike D.) of the Beastie Boys. Primarily, Davis is a director-for-hire on teen-oriented comedy projects, and she brings a youthful attitude and street credibility to her work. Indeed, her career path is remarkably similar to that of Penelope Spheeris, another female director with strong roots in punk and heavy metal music but with a filmography marked by blockbuster 'Saturday Night Live' alum-comedies like *Wayne's World* (1992).

Davis' first break into feature films was her most personal and interesting project, *Guncrazy* (1992), a loose but spunky update of Joseph Lewis' classic cult film noir *Gun Crazy* (1950). Honouring the well-mined 'young doomed lovers awry of the law' genre represented by such classics as *You Only Live Once* (1937), *They Live By Night* (1949), and *Bonnie and Clyde* (1967), Davis successfully moves the genre forward to the early 1990s with a pair of angst-ridden, trailer-trash lovers struggling for self worth and affection against a desolate backdrop of abusiveness and violent gunplay. *Guncrazy* is strikingly filmed with a clever, unexaggerated tone that respects the sometimes over-the-top satire and sharp pacing of Matthew Bright's script. Lead actors Drew Barrymore and James LeGros bring an attractive innocence to their non-traditional relationship, and cult actor Joe Dallesandro is a welcome sight as Barrymore's mother's bloated, sleazy ex-boyfriend. Davis graduated from her intriguing debut to helm mainly lowbrow comedy features (interspersed with music video projects during her downtime) over the next nine years.

*CB4* (1993) is rap music's disappointing answer to the groundbreaking parody of the rock music industry, *This Is Spinal Tap* (1984). Although competently directed, the film fails to be insightful, clever, or even mildly funny. *Billy Madison* (1995) is a lame juvenile vehicle for comedian and 'Saturday Night Live' refugee Adam Sandler, rehashing the standard story of the incompetent son who bumbles through a seemingly impossible rite-of-passage at the behest of his successful father. Unlike *Back to School* (1986), which tweaked genre conventions to great effect, *Billy Madison* remains tiresomely shackled to predictability. Sandler does exhibit a few brief moments of amusing comic idiocy, but not enough to sustain the picture's feature-length running time.

*Best Men* (1997), billed as an 'action comedy', is a convoluted mess, unabashedly recycling action sequences from *True Lies* (1994) and *Butch Cassidy and the Sundance Kid* (1969), and sporting Tarantino-esque dialogue riffs without ever finding a comfortable comedic tone. Although not a complete success, *Half Baked* (1998) has its bong-filled, politically incorrect highlights, with sporadic but solid belly laughs and a few scene-stealing celebrity cameos that appeal to viewers on both sides of the recreational drug lifestyle fence. *Skipped Parts* (2001) is a low-budget adaptation of Tim Sandlin's

1991 coming-of-age novel of the same name, a book Davis fell in love with while editing *Guncrazy*. Evocative of characters in 'Catcher in the Rye' and 'The Last Picture Show', and feeling occasionally like *Rumble Fish* (1983), the film is a faithful but uneven translation of the book. Although Davis gets the most out of her Saskatchewan location and $2 million budget, its tone is awkward at best, and the sexually explicit humour flat, bordering on painful. *Crossroads* (2002), notable as the feature film debut of pop princess Britney Spears, is an unremarkable, derivative road trip movie aimed at young girls that is creatively strangled by its extreme overprotection of Spears' pure-as-the-driven-snow public image. One can only hope that this dreadful poppycock banishes Britney back to pitching Pepsi-Cola, and motivates Davis to reclaim her credibility by finding a project with a decent script. **THa**

# William DEAR

A writer-producer-director, William Dear has carved out a career as a purveyor of popular comedy and drama, often with generic overtones, in both film and television. Dear's movies have, for the most part, told tall stories with enough authenticity to make them sufficiently engaging, ranging from spectral baseball players to teen agents to a bigfoot moving into suburbia.

Dear's career began with a fruitful collaboration with Michael Nesmith, an ex-Monkee with whom Dear created the first ever 'video album', 'Elephant Parts' (1981), which went on to win a Grammy. With Nesmith bankrolling him, Dear then directed a feature entitled *Timerider: The Adventures of Lyle Swann* (1982).

In 1985 Dear's major breakthrough came when he directed a very well received episode of the short lived series 'Amazing Stories' (created and executive produced by Steven Spielberg). Entitled 'Mummy Daddy' (from a screen story by Spielberg), the half-hour horror comedy had some of the most generous reviews that the 'Amazing Stories' could muster. It also set the template for many of the features that Dear would go on to direct – the story of an average guy whose life is touched by elements of the fantastic. The piece told of an actor playing a mummy in a horror film who is chased across country en route to the birth of his child.

The successful reception of this episode paved the way for Dear's first major motion picture from his own script, *Harry and the Hendersons* (1987), which was made for Spielberg's Amblin Entertainment. In the spirit of other Amblin-produced films in the 1980s the feature explored the drama inherent in the fantastic colliding with the mundane and everyday. *Harry and the Hendersons* followed the experiences of a bigfoot when knocked over by a holidaying middle-American family who decide to take him back to suburbia. In a pattern established by *E.T. The Extra-Terrestrial* (1982), Harry's suburban idyll is disrupted – in this case by the encroaching force of a game hunter. A fantasy comedy – typical of many Hollywood fantasy movies at the time – *Harry and the Hendersons* was successful enough to lead to a sitcom spin-off.

Over the years Dear has contributed several times to the fantasy genre. He directed *Teen Agent* (1991) about a teen James Bond style character who goes on a high-school trip from America to France and becomes swept up in international espionage. Proving Dear's facility with the tall story, the teenager is kitted out like a real life James Bond as he strives to defeat the power-hungry villain. In the same year Disney released one of the best, most underrated and charming 1990s fantasy movies, the charming *The Rocketeer* (1991), based on the seminal comic strip by Dave Stevens. William Dear co-wrote the screen story.

All of Dear's films are marked by a sense of whimsy and wish fulfilment but none more so than his family fantasy for Disney – *Angels in the Outfield* (1994), starring Christopher Lloyd, Danny Glover and Tony Danza. The film, a remake of the 1951 film of the same name, was an undemanding, sentimental and lightweight fantasy comedy in which a boy in a foster home hopes for miracle that will reunite him with his widowed father. Sure enough real angels arrive and only the boy can see them. Soon enough the angels are helping out in other ways too.

Dear followed *Angels in the Outfield* with a feature based on real events. *Wild America* (1997), again made for Disney, tells the story of the three Stouffer brothers growing up in the 1960s who dream of being naturalists. The film charts their adventurous journey across America, recording it as they go on film. Whilst not breaking any new ground, the film belongs to a long-established Disney tradition of well-crafted, engaging wilderness-based films for young viewers. His latest film was a made-for-TV comedy, *Santa Who?* (2000), starring Leslie Nielsen. **JC**

# Jan DE BONT

Working chiefly in the action/spectacle genres, Jan de Bont's films in this area have thus far oscillated between the definitive and the execrable. His one foray into the horror film proved ill-advised.

De Bont was born in the Netherlands in 1943. After a long and distinguished career as a cinematographer in both Europe and Hollywood, de Bont made his directorial debut with *Speed* (1994). Stripping the action genre to its narrative core, the film draws equally from the disaster cycle, and is structured upon three extended set-pieces in which a falling elevator, a speeding bus, and a rushing train fulfil the sensory pleasures suggested in the title. Appropriately, its machine gun editing, relentless pace and restless, swirling, swooping camera define speed as the film's aesthetic, with all other elements becoming subsidiary to this primary ethos. While briefly suggesting a link between crazy hero (Keanu Reeves) and psycho villain (Dennis Hopper), the film wilfully drains any social significance from its antagonist's terror campaign, and the moral positions of the adversaries are clearly distinguished. The limitations of Reeves and Sandra Bullock (as the unfortunate civilian forced to drive a bus rigged to explode) as actors is more than compensated by their subservience to the overall design, and the former exudes a likeable, cocky bravado. Any sub-textual elements (Hopper's class resentments, the media infiltration of disaster) are barely expanded upon and the film is content to reject them as secondary to the admittedly spectacular surface effects. Essentially, this is the Hollywood action film *par excellence*.

Working from a Michael Crichton script, *Twister* (1996) gave de Bont the opportunity to survey the spectacular potential of natural disaster. Pitting humans against the elements, the film foregrounds the crumbling marriage of its leads (played by Bill Paxton and Helen Hunt) against their research into the destructive force of tornadoes, a crude device which predictably serves to accommodate their ultimate reconciliation. Hunt's childhood trauma and personal obsession is coupled with Paxton's fearless instincts and, indeed, the film's take on scientific inquiry transforms it into the realms of extreme sports. Unlike *Speed*, the film injects a variety of themes (instinct vs. technology, innovation vs. corporate infiltration) which are barely developed anyway. However, de Bont excels again in the sheer spectacle of the tornado attacks (they function almost as *Godzilla*-style environmental monsters) and the CGI effects are among the most impressive ever deployed, retaining a sense of the natural as opposed to the synthetic quality so often produced by this increasingly predominant technique.

*Speed 2: Cruise Control* (1997) is a disaster movie in every sense. Seemingly intent on rejecting all of the elements which made the original work, the film introduces ill-advised attempts at humour, 'fleshed-out' characters (one senses star input in this regard), and flaccid, static action sequences which only serve to stop the film dead. Reversing the speed ethos of its predecessor, its chief achievement is to make a crashing ocean liner appear uninteresting. Appropriately, Jason Patric makes for one of the dullest action heroes in memory.

*The Haunting* (1999) operates on the basic premise that a contemporary horror film has to create its scares via an oppressive array of computer generated images. Appearing barely weeks after *The Blair Witch Project* (1999), their relative impact appears to prove the contrary. Indeed, whereas Robert Wise's (frankly overrated) original adaptation of Shirley Jackson's novel 'The Haunting of Hill House' relied on subtly designed scares, de Bont's version is crass and superficial despite its impressive production design. The film culminates in a vision of the afterlife so saccharine and overblown that it almost negates Lili Taylor's sometimes effective central performance. **NJ**

# Guillermo DEL TORO

Born in 1964 in Guadalajara, Mexico, Guillermo Del Toro's part in the current renaissance in contemporary Mexican cinema as evidenced by such recent successes

*Speed* (1994)
*Twister* (1996)
*Speed 2: Cruise Control* (1997)
*The Haunting* (1999)

*Cronos* (1993)
*Mimic* (1997)

as *Amores Perros* (2000) has been pivotal. Beginning his career in film as an executive producer on homegrown Mexican titles such as *Doña Herlinda y su hijo* (1985), Del Toro's career as a director began with three episodes of the popular Mexican television series 'Hora Marcada'. A stint followed as a special effects make-up artist on several features – including the internationally well-received family drama *Bandidos* – before his career-changing feature debut, *Cronos*, emerged in 1993.

The film, which relates the tale of an elderly antiques dealer (Federico Luppi) who discovers an alchemist's trinket containing the gift for eternal life, still stands as one of the most remarkable contemporary horror fables in recent memory. Del Toro injects fresh blood into the vampire genre, mixing dry wit and sombre pacing into a narrative that eschews special effects and bland trickery to explore the rapidly deteriorating Luppi's desire to maintain a bond with his wife and young granddaughter. Apart from the spattering of fine performances, particularly those of veteran Luppi and the underused Ron Perlman, and Guillermo Navarro's sumptuous photography, it is the director's confident hand and sheer imagination that really elevates the film.

An instant cult favourite across the world, *Cronos* also caught the eye of Bob Weinstein and the writer-director was lured across the border for the 1997 film *Mimic*. Remaining within the broad confines of the horror genre, Del Toro and co-writer Matthew Robins (Steven Soderbergh also contributed a draft) fashioned a deeply impressive allegory about the horrors of genetic manipulation in an allegorical tale about huge people-eating cockroaches in the subways of New York. Working on a more expensive canvas – the special effects featuring human-sized roaches send a distinct shiver down the spine – Del Toro never for one moment substitutes style for substance. Displaying a sensibility that errs toward the subversive, he establishes a personal, visual style in which dark, gothic and often subterranean interiors are shot with precision and a highly attuned sense of colour and composition.

Committed to indigenous cinema, Del Toro returned to his homeland for *The Devil's Backbone/El Espinazo del Diablo* (2001). Produced by Pedro Almodovar's company, the film re-teamed Del Toro with Navarro, who has also returned to Mexico having worked as a director of photography on films such as *Jackie Brown* (1997). The take is a deliciously dark ghost story about a remote Spanish orphanage during the final days of the Spanish civil war whose young inhabitants are terrorised by Santi, a decomposing spirit who stalks the building's dark decaying hallways seeking vengeance for his murder. Once again, it is a gently political, highly allegorical piece about greed, corruption and the scarring of innocence (Del Toro often features children in his work). A visceral and thrilling film – with a truly explosive finale – it often feels like a more action-packed companion piece to Victor Erice's *The Spirit Of The Beehive* (1973). Del Toro ably demonstrates his eye for the disturbing and the macabre, creating cavernous interiors in which ungodly forces linger, and a simmering atmosphere.

Del Toro's most recent film is the sequel to *Blade*, Stephen Norrington's 1998 working of the popular black vampire comic-book hero. Starring a returning Wesley Snipes alongside Kris Kristofferson and Ron Perlman, *Blade 2* (2002) has performed extremely well, further proof that he is one of the smartest and most imaginative directors currently working. His next project is *Hellboy*, an account of a black magic demon conjured by the Nazis to help their ailing cause at the end of World War Two.     **JWo**

# Jonathan DEMME

In an era of pat sentiment and cynically calculated optimism, few film-makers have infused their films with as much authentic joy and generosity as Jonathan Demme. He seems fascinated with humanity and his films overflow with its celebration, resulting in a body of work as rich, diverse and vibrant as that of any other contemporary director. He shows a rare understanding of the relationship between cinema and music, he embraces the collaborative nature of film-making, and he has worked across a range of formats, from feature film to documentary. Of these different modes of production, Demme has said, 'When you're doing a fictional film, the whole aspiration most of the time is to try and make it as real as possible; but when you're making a documentary – I've discovered – you try and make reality as entertaining as possible. I like the difference'. Indeed, the fact that he has become one of the most interesting documentarians currently working is often overlooked.

Demme was born in Long Island in 1944. Like many other prominent directors of his generation – including Martin Scorsese, Francis Ford Coppola, Peter Bogdanovich and Ron Howard – his first films were produced under the auspices of exploitation king Roger Corman: *Caged Heat* (1974), *Crazy Mama* (1975), and *Fighting Mad* (1976). The first two of these are especially interesting as films that laid the groundwork for much of his later work. Both films take the bare bones of the exploitation film (employing the quick-and-cheap style and the regular bursts of nudity or violence central to the form) to present feminist themes about the position of women at the edges of American society. *Caged Heat* uses the women-in-prison formula to explore the relationships between a group of women fighting against the system as they attempt to escape from an inhumane prison and its sadistic warden – although one might argue that such feminist sentiments are compromised somewhat by the frequent shower scenes and cat-fights. Similarly, *Crazy Mama* transcends its status as one of Corman's cycle of *Bonnie and Clyde* rip-offs, emerging as a fertile and joyful period film about three generations of women who take to the road for an absurdist crime spree across America.

*The Silence of the Lambs* (1991)
*Cousin Bobby* (1992)
*Philadelphia* (1993)
*The Complex Sessions* (1994)
*Beloved* (1998)
*Storefront Hitchcock* (1998)
*The Truth About Charlie* (2002)

Following the revenge thriller *Fighting Mad*, in which a peaceable Peter Fonda is driven to violence by a ruthless landowner, Demme helmed *Citizens Band* (1977), a light-hearted ensemble comedy in which a series of characters and vignettes are interconnected by way of the crowded airwaves of the CB radio craze. The film's sprawling cast and freewheeling structure have been often likened to the work of Robert Altman – especially *Nashville* (1975) – but this is perhaps a rather superficial comparison. In particular, he rarely seems to view humanity with the cynicism or pessimism found in most Altman films. Throughout his oeuvre, Demme never looks down on his working-class characters, displaying instead a compassion and empathy that shines through in *Citizens Band*.

After directing an episode of 'Columbo' in 1977, Demme shot the tense thriller *Last Embrace* (1979), in which Roy Scheider's CIA agent believes somebody is out to kill him after his wife is assassinated and he receives a cryptic Jewish death threat. Clearly inspired by Hitchcock – particularly the climax at Niagara Falls – *Last Embrace* demonstrates the aptitude for taut suspense that Demme would successfully return to years later in *The Silence of the Lambs* (1991).

*Melvin and Howard* (1980) was his first significant critical success, winning a Best Director award from the New York Film Critics Circle and two Academy Awards (Original Screenplay and Supporting Actress for Mary Steenburgen). The film was based on the true story of Melvin Dummar, a milkman who produced a copy of Howard Hughes' will in which he was named as a beneficiary of $156 million. Despite counter-claims that Dummar was a fraud, it seems emblematic of Demme's approach that he never doubts the veracity of the story as he chronicles the socio-economic struggles of Dummar's blue collar life, from his act of generosity to an injured Hughes in the desert at the start of the film to the cruel dismissal of his claim at the end. Indeed, the film is a paean to mundanity that provides a poignant meditation on the disparity between human aspirations and the myths of the American dream, revealing how luck and opportunity are rarely the privilege of the lower classes.

*Who am I This Time?* (1981) was an adaptation of the Kurt Vonnegut story for television, while *Swing Shift* (1984) was released to the worst notices of his career. For many years Demme refused to talk about the film because his original cut – a feminist parable about women sticking together during wartime factory work – was re-edited by Warner Bros. into a bland romantic comedy intended to capitalise on the off-screen coupling of its two stars, Goldie Hawn and Kurt Russell.

While struggling over *Swing Shift* in the day, Demme used his nights to create one of his finest achievements: *Stop Making Sense* (1984), a film record of Talking Heads in concert. This was the first of a number of documentary and 'performance' films that Demme has continued to make alongside his fiction films, including *Haiti Dreams of Democracy* (1988), a film born out of Demme's long interest in that country, and *Cousin Bobby* (1992), a powerful documentary about Demme's relationship with his cousin, Father Robert Castle, a minister working in Harlem. *Stop Making Sense*, like his subsequent performance films *Swimming to Cambodia* (1987) and *Storefront Hitchcock* (1998), demonstrates Demme's sensitivity to the process of adapting live theatre and performance to film, carefully harmonising the stage act with the demands of cinematic representation. It was revolutionary for eschewing the many clichés of concert films – rock razzmatazz, back-stage interviews, screaming fans – favouring instead a classical, almost minimalist *mise-en-scène* that seeks to provide the audience with 'the best seats in the house'. The film also demonstrates Demme's ear (and eye) for music: treating each song as a separate visual drama, and favouring uninterrupted long takes of the performers rather than faddish, MTV-style fast cutting.

This subtlety is equally evident in *Swimming to Cambodia*, a film of Spalding Gray's one-man-show monologue. Aided by Laurie Anderson's sound design, Demme creates a riveting and hypnotic atmosphere to draw us into the monologue, but his direction is also a model of restraint that never lets the focus stray from the liveness of the performance. This becomes even clearer if one compares the film to later Gray monologues directed by Nick Broomfield (*Monster in a Box*, 1991) and Steven Soderbergh (*Gray's Anatomy*, 1996), the *mise-en-scène* of which are increasingly stylised and intrusive. Similar traits also run through *Storefront Hitchcock*, Demme's film of musician Robyn Hitchcock which pays homage to The Squat Theatre, a Dutch theatrical company who perform in storefront spaces, using the shop window to reveal and mobilise the street space outside.

Of Demme's subsequent fiction films, *Something Wild* (1986) and *Married to the Mob* (1988) are perhaps his two most vivacious and colourful. The former is a whirlwind, screwball comedy that remains for many the quintessential Demme film. Shot through with the spirit of The Troggs' anthem 'Wild Thing', it follows the liberation of Jeff Daniels' straight-laced businessman when he is abducted for a joyride by a sexy and unrestrained Melanie Griffith. However, some might find the rather conservative resolution of Griffith's narrative at odds with Demme's fondness for wild women elsewhere. *Married to the Mob* has been seen as a lighter and more frivolous film, but its story of Michelle Pfeiffer's pampered Mafia wife opting for a more honest, working-class life continues Demme's interest in the joys and hardships of women struggling to make it on their own in society. Similarly, his kindness to his characters is neatly summarised by Leonard Maltin's remark that only Demme could make a mob movie with likeable characters in it.

The multi-Academy Award winning *The Silence of the Lambs* was a phenomenon that needs little introduction and remains Demme's biggest hit. As many critics have pointed out, it is something of a problem film within his oeuvre, although in Jodie Foster's Clarice Starling we are again presented with a strong independent woman at the film's centre. It also benefits greatly from not talking down to its audience and is at times a gratifyingly mischievous film that harks back to Demme's exploitation days – and even features Roger Corman in a cameo as the head of the FBI.

Much of his subsequent work has been less satisfying, and increasingly less frequent. The AIDS drama *Philadelphia* (1993) and his adaptation of Toni Morrison's *Beloved* (1998) were disappointing treatments of important issues: homophobia and racism, respectively. Whereas his previous films seem to have been about the embracing of life, these two films are preoccupied with death and dying – and worse still, seem to have had all the life drained out of them. Working as a writer-director for the first time since *Fighting Mad*, Demme returned to more lighthearted material with *The Truth About Charlie* (2002). A remake of Stanley Donen's chic comedy-thriller *Charade* (1963), the film sees Mark Wahlberg and Thandie Newton filling the shoes of original stars Cary Grant and Audrey Hepburn.                                                                **AS**

# Ted DEMME

Born in New York, USA, in 1964, Ted Demme completed six feature films before his death in 2002, working on both big-budget studio films and also smaller budget independents. Before moving into features, he worked on music videos, and co-created and produced 'Yo!MTV Raps', the daily glimpse at hip-hop culture. He also directed music videos for artists such as Salt 'n' Pepa and Dave Stewart, and co-directed the video for Bruce Springsteen's 'Streets of Philadelphia' with his uncle, director Jonathan Demme. Demme's production company, Spanky Pictures, produced Demme's own *Monument Ave.* (1998), as well as *Rounders* (1998) and *Tumbleweeds* (1999).

Whilst at MTV, Demme directed some of comedian Denis Leary's promotional spots and comedy specials which led to his first feature, *Who's The Man?* (1993), an MTV tribute starring Leary, as well as Dr Dre, Ice-T and a variety of rap artists in cameo roles. The film is a comedy about two bungling barbers who are reluctantly turned into cops and surprisingly clean up the streets of Harlem, becoming heroes. Demme's next feature, *The Ref* (1994), was his first for a major studio, Touchstone. The film again stars Leary, this time as Gus, a robber on the run, who accidentally kidnaps a yuppie couple played by Judy Davis and Kevin Spacey. Gus becomes trapped between the bickering couple and their dysfunctional family in this black comedy set on Christmas Eve. The film was a success with the critics but not at the box office.

For *Beautiful Girls* (1996), Demme worked with US indie Miramax. Influenced by *The Deer Hunter* (1978), Demme wanted to make a 'buddy picture', but the film bears more of a resemblance to *The Big Chill* (1983). Scott Rosenberg wrote the screenplay and the ensemble cast includes Timothy Hutton, Matt Dillon, Mira Sorvino and Uma Thurman. A character piece set in an East Coast American town; *Beautiful Girls* is a drama about male camaraderie and boy-girl relationships, aimed at the 'post-MTV audience'. It is the story of Willie Conway (Timothy Hutton), a city boy who returns to his small hometown for a ten-year high-school reunion and also to ponder his future – should he marry his girlfriend or hold out for someone he likes better? While waiting, he observes his friends as they mistreat and harass the women they love.

*Beautiful Girls* was acclaimed critically and Demme followed with *Monument Ave.*, the story of an extended Boston-based Irish-American family, again starring Denis Leary. The actor plays the role of a car thief whose loyalty is put to the test when his boss kills one of his friends. For *Life* (1999), Demme worked with Universal and a budget of $75 million, his biggest so far. The movie stars Eddie Murphy and Martin Lawrence as two criminals who discover the value of life after being sentenced to life imprisonment. Aiming to be a comedy with serious overtones, above all it is a celebration of friendship and the human spirit. Despite a patchy reception with the critics, the film was a box-office success.

Demme's most recent project, *Blow* (2001), became his final and best-known film. Produced by New Line, with a screenplay by Nick Cassavetes, *Blow* is a biopic of George Jung, a cocaine smuggler who was responsible for 85 per cent of the cocaine that entered the USA in the late 1970s and early 1980s. Starring Johnny Depp as Jung and Penelope Cruz as his demanding wife Mirtha, the drug-smuggling drama is filmed on an epic scale spanning three-decades. There is effective use of voiceover and a number of montage sequences to show the passing of time as Jung moves from a go-getting youth to a drug-frazzled and desperate middle age. An accomplished work that depicts Jung's rise-and-fall pursuit of the American dream and his betrayal by those closest to him, it features an outstanding performance from Depp, who manages to make the drug pusher's character attractive.

When Ted Demme died he left behind a compact career during which he demonstrated his talent as a director of character-driven films with strong dialogue and a knack for comedy. **PR**

# Brian DE PALMA

Brian De Palma represents a dying breed in Hollywood. Self-consciously baroque and formal and often criticised for favouring stylistic flamboyance over substance, he is one of the few contemporary American film-makers exploring the unique visual possibilities of cinema. Although championed by the critic Pauline Kael in the 1970s and 1980s, many were alienated by his alleged misogyny and transformation of violence into elaborate spectacle. Moreover, the accusation that his work is slavishly imitative of Alfred Hitchcock's has negated De Palma's re-interpretation of Hitchcockian motifs. This, however, is lazy criticism which stops at the dazzling, allusive surfaces, ignoring the complex engagement of his best films with a dense sexual/political undercurrent, concepts of cinematic illusion and an often subtly deceptive and reflexive construction.

Born in New Jersey in 1940, De Palma was introduced to film-making at Sarah Lawrence College after a spell at Columbia University studying physics. His self-confessed, unsettled adolescence (due to his mother's inattentiveness and his father's infidelity, an event which inspired De Palma to photograph his adulterous activities) seems to have inspired the troubled sexual politics of his psycho-thrillers. Like Hitchcock, De Palma's exploration of voyeurism and perversion lends itself easily to psychoanalytic perspectives. Robin Wood sees a pronounced castration anxiety through many of the films, a view underlined by their monstrous females and weak, ineffectual male figures.

*Greetings* (1968)
*Murder à la Mod* (1968)
*The Wedding Party* (1969)
*Dionysus in '69* (1970)
*Hi, Mom!* (1970)
*Get To Know Your Rabbit* (1972)
*Sisters* (1973)
*Phantom of the Paradise* (1974)
*Obsession* (1976)
*Carrie* (1976)
*The Fury* (1978)
*Home Movies* (1979)
*Dressed To Kill* (1980)
*Blow Out* (1981)
*Scarface* (1983)
*Body Double* (1984)

Early work was inspired by both the radical campus politics of the late 1960s and the politicised films of Jean-Luc Godard. *Greetings* (1968) and *Hi, Mom!* (1970) were inexpensive but inventive products of the counter-culture, featuring early performances by Robert De Niro. *Hi, Mom!* prefigures De Palma's voyeuristic explorations as De Niro films his sexual encounter with a neighbour from an adjacent apartment block. After the frustrations of *Get To Know Your Rabbit* (re-cut by the studio before its 1972 release), came De Palma's first obvious Hitchcock homage, *Sisters* (1973). The film utilises the voyeur and double themes which figure prominently in De Palma's later thrillers, equating the oppression of its title characters (played by Margot Kidder) with patriarchal domination, be it personal or institutional in origin.

The playful rock updating of *The Phantom of the Opera* (1925), *Phantom of the Paradise* (1974), and *Obsession* (1976) (a homage to *Vertigo* (1958)), were followed by De Palma's first mainstream success, *Carrie* (1976), an adaptation of Stephen King's original novel. The film defines its tormented, telekinetic protagonist as the victim (and ultimate avenger) of both social oppression and religious mania. The central blood metaphor (beginning with Carrie's first period in the communal school shower and climaxing with her dousing with pigs blood at the school prom) has encouraged the film to be read as an expression of teenage menstrual fury, yet the presentation of Carrie's final humiliation and revenge as an elaborate visual spectacle seems cruel. The final bluff is a shock sequence much imitated ever since. *The Fury* (1978) re-visited elements of *Carrie*, but was less accomplished in its fusion of horror and conspiracy thriller. An outrageous pay-off, in which John Cassavetes' villain is exploded telekinetically, anticipated David Cronenberg's *Scanners* (1981).

The experimental *Home Movies* (1979) utilised a crew of De Palma's film students, recalling the late 1960s work, but it was *Dressed To Kill* (1980) which consolidated his reputation as master of suspense narratives. Provoking a campaign by British feminist protesters amidst the Yorkshire Ripper murders, the film elaborates upon *Psycho* (1960), featuring a murderous transsexual awaiting final transformation. The film is replete with visual allusions to the doppelgänger theme amidst its socio-sexual ambiguities. The film's murder victim, Kate (beautifully played by Angie Dickinson), is punished ostensibly for her casual adultery, but her death is linked more forcefully to the collective indifference and condescension afforded her by the male characters – her husband, her psychiatrist (Michael Caine), and the police officer in charge of her murder investigation (Denis Franz). Similarly, the prostitute and murder witness, Liz (Nancy Allen), is defined constantly through her exploitation by her clients or the police. While the film's female characters seek sexual assertion, the males are presented as either sexually inadequate (Kate's husband), murderously repressed (Dr Elliott), venereally afflicted (Kate's lover), or curiously asexual (Kate's son). Featuring several brilliantly orchestrated sequences, notably a silent courtship and pursuit in an art gallery, the film frames its flamboyant set-pieces in a surreal, nightmarish ambience, imbuing the urban locale with an elegantly sinister sheen.

*Blow Out* (1981) is arguably the best-realised work to date, a paranoid conspiracy thriller reflecting the social anxiety provoked by political assassination and cover up in the US. Drawing themes from Antonioni's *Blow Up* (1966), the film is buoyed by a deceptively engaging performance by John Travolta as a film sound effects technician convinced he has recorded a political assassination. Making full use of the visual possibilities afforded by the material, the film fuses its protagonist's paranoia with the nature of the cinematic experience itself, using both the Panavision frame and sound design to accentuate thematic and symbolic resonances. Travolta's recording and unravelling of the title event and the final, desperate chase through Philadelphia during the Liberty Day celebrations are superbly choreographed and culminate in an extraordinarily cynical pay-off. The film represents a fading counterforce to the onslaught of high-concept, feel-good films which would dominate the ensuing decade.

Ironically, in light of the last comment, *Scarface* (1983) represented to many the worst extremes of both the decade and the director himself. Featuring perhaps cinema's most venal portrait of a gangster's moral corruption, Al Pacino's title performance begs little sympathy from the audience in a film replete with reprehensible characters. Written by Oliver Stone, the focus on Cuban gangsters in 1980s Miami lends the film an exotic backdrop to its procession of excess. Yet amidst the rivers of blood and mountains of cocaine emerges a consistent interrogation of the murderous extremes of capitalism.

So overwhelming is the film's take on the seductive quality of the criminal capitalist structure that its incestuous sub-plot feels tacked on and underdeveloped.

Body Double (1984) returned to the allusive territory of the Hitchcockian thriller. Partly inspired by De Palma's use of a stand-in for Angie Dickinson in Dressed To Kill, it is his most self-reflexive film. Evoking both Rear Window (1954) and Vertigo, the film uses the narrative device of a witnessed murder to emphasise limits of perception and the nature of cinematic illusion, repeatedly drawing attention to its own artifice and construction. Projected backdrops, film within film, a music video interlude, and a camera crew revealed in a mirror all consolidate the film's exploration of cinema's illusionistic codes. Delicately balancing the implications of its male protagonist's claustrophobia and voyeurism, it is less successful in the consideration of its beautiful female object figure and her gory death by power drill, invoking the phallus forcefully and problematically as a means to murderous assertion. This seems particularly disturbing in light of De Palma's original wish to shoot the film as a hard-core feature using porn actors.

The gangster comedy Wise Guys (1986) was a critical and commercial failure but huge success came the following year with The Untouchables (1987), a dazzling play on the gangster genre's surfaces and moral polarities. Each character, from Kevin Costner's Elliot Ness to Robert De Niro's Al Capone, is a broad, knowing caricature. Written by David Mamet, and evoking both the western and Eisenstein's Battleship Potemkin in its action set-pieces, the film is De Palma's most consistently entertaining, earning Sean Connery an Academy Award.

Casualties of War (1989) is sporadically successful In recounting an actual incident during the Vietnam War. Transplanting De Palma's familiar theme of misogyny onto a different canvas, the film does not adequately negotiate its complex moral implications. However, it does attempt to personalise its doomed Vietnamese victim, albeit via a disturbing rape metaphor. Dissatisfaction with the film is irrelevant compared to that of Bonfire of the Vanities (1990), a frankly disastrous interpretation of Tom Wolfe's seminal 1980s novel. Ill-conceived and executed, from its ludicrous casting to its empty, elaborate form, the film is a profoundly depressing experience.

Solace was sought in the self-parodic suspense thriller (Deranged! Demented! De Palma! screamed the publicity) Raising Cain (1992), and a confident return to the gangster film, Carlito's Way (1993). Teaming again with Al Pacino, the 1970s-set film is more romantic than Scarface in its view of the gangster figure's tragic dimensions. Featuring an outstanding performance by Sean Penn, the film culminates in another brilliantly executed chase across Grand Central Station. Yet the film's romanticism is conspicuous amidst the postmodern inversions of the gangster film proffered by Quentin Tarantino and his progeny.

Mission Impossible (1996) featured a series of impressive action/suspense set-pieces yet any deeper engagement with the film is overcome by the strict adherence to spectacle. At least the film gave De Palma a new commercial foothold. Snake Eyes (1998) marked a return to the conspiracy thriller and is boldly experimental in its examination of the limits of human (and by extension, cinematic) point of view. Featuring a charismatic performance by Nicolas Cage and an audacious opening shot, the film draws heavily on modern surveillance culture, making it a companion piece to Blow Out in its linking of the political and personal responsibilities of voyeurism. Thematically at least, it is the most characteristically 'De Palma' film since the early 1980s and as such it represents a refreshing antidote to the dominantly conservative Hollywood climate.

Mission to Mars (2000), a universally panned science fiction film, is one of De Palma's most silly and insubstantial works yet. Visually diverting and narratively uninspiring, it wastes the talents of its actors (particularly Tim Robbins) and does little for the director's reputation. His most recent release, Femme Fatale (2002), is a thriller starring Antonia Banderas as a photographer trying to uncover a woman's mysterious past. **NJ**

# Johnny DEPP

Born in Kentucky in 1963, Johnny Depp is known primarily for his work in front of the camera, but took the opportunity to call the shots with his 1997 offering The Brave.

The Brave (1997)

Based on a novel by Gregory McDonald, the screenplay, by Depp, brother Danny and Paul McCudden, tells the story of a poverty-stricken Native American who agrees to die on camera to give his family a better life. Previewed in competition at Cannes, the film received much criticism, as highlighted by John Hurt's comments regarding its inclusion in the festival, stating that it was simply not good enough and had only been considered in order to attract some big-name stars. In fact, the film was the subject of great derision at the initial press screening. The criticism thrown at the film has been mainly concerned with two key faults. Firstly, rather than placing others under the spotlight – as Oldman did with *Nil By Mouth* (1997) (also in competition that year) – Depp decided on the narcissistic approach, seemingly content to look at as much footage of his bandanna'd head and shirtless body as possible. The second area of criticism centred on the film's pacing, which, whilst intending to evoke desert languor, ended up being just plain leaden. However, despite all this, the film does remain oddly haunting, if only for its sheer eccentricity, maintaining Depp's association with the weirder, independent side of cinema. For now, however, he will remain solely in front of the camera. **CP**

# Howard DEUTCH

Having cut his teeth on music videos and film trailers, director Howard Deutch moved into the movie director's chair in the mid-1980s thanks to the patronage of teen titan John Hughes, for whom Deutch would make eventually turn out three features. Despite the considerable pleasures of his early work, Deutch has ultimately distinguished himself as a middlebrow hack, crafting films without the benefit of style, rhythm or personality.

If John Hughes' *Sixteen Candles* (1984) is the *Rio Bravo* (1959) of the 1980s teen flick cycle, then Deutch's first two films are, respectively, its *El Dorado* (1966) and *Rio Lobo* (1970). Like Howard Hawks' trio of similarly-plotted John Wayne westerns, *Pretty in Pink* (1986) and *Some Kind of Wonderful* (1987) form the second and third parts of a trilogy of Hughes-penned movies that share a high-school love triangle, a rumpled but understanding father figure, and a bouncy modern rock soundtrack. The two men's individual stylistic approaches to the same material, however, are markedly different. In his prime, Hughes was the teen picture's pop maestro, a stylist fond of oblique camera positions, deadpan master shots, absurdist jump-cuts and oddball music cues – part Sergio Leone, part Jean-Luc Godard. Deutch, on the other hand, directs both *Pink* and *Wonderful* to be both gently observed and warmly naturalistic; his only nod to Hughes' postmodern sensibility is the actor Jon Cryer's incredulous glance at the audience during *Pretty in Pink*'s prom finale. He also displays a gift for working with actors, particularly new, untested talents, many of whom (Gina Gershon, James Spader, Elias Koteas) got early breaks under Deutch's tutelage.

Unfortunately, just as Hughes left making teen pictures behind to concentrate on writing and producing such broad high-profile kid comedies as *Home Alone* (1990) and *Dennis the Menace* (1993), Deutch soon floundered once he began dealing with main characters who were actually old enough to have graduated. His final movie for Hughes, the John Candy/Dan Aykroyd vehicle *The Great Outdoors* (1988) suffers from its overbearing quest for laughs, broadening his style and loosening the directorial reins until every actor turns in an unpleasant, obvious caricature of a performance. Deutch tried a more adult approach with his next project, the comic veteran's hospital saga *Article 99* (1992), but his attempt to deliver a black, rebellious satire of the order of *Catch-22* or *M\*A\*S\*H* (both 1970) fell far short of his ambitions. Shackled by a shallow script and muddied politics, and directed at an antic, unfocused pace, the film was an artistic and financial disaster.

After *Article 99*'s failure, Deutch seemed to resolve to make only straight, inoffensive comedies, hooking up with fellow Hughes alumnus Macaulay Culkin for the weak family-oriented crime caper *Getting Even With Dad* (1994). The story of an ex-con (Ted Danson) whose plot to heist a rare coin collection is jeopardised by the appearance of his estranged son, *Dad* features pale variations on *Home Alone*'s anarchic crook-foiling gags coupled with a cloying, insincere sweetness. Deutch then took it down a notch with 1995's halfway-decent *Grumpier Old Men*. A likable, if somewhat sitcom-level, sequel to the 1993 Jack Lemmon/Walter Matthau pairing *Grumpy Old Men* (directed by Donald Petrie), *Grumpier* proved to be something of a no-brainer. Deutch may have elicited his best performances since the early Hughes-scripted films, but with such veterans as Lemmon, Matthau, Burgess Meredith, Ann-Margret and (in a rare Stateside appearance) Sophia Loren at his disposal, all he needed to remember was which end of the camera to look through. Tragically, Lemmon and Matthau were of little help in saving Deutch's next picture, the long-delayed sequel to Neil Simon's *The Odd Couple* (1968). *The Odd Couple II* (1998) falls far short of both its predecessor and Deutch's previous collaboration with the two old-timers, thanks to a half-baked screenplay delivered by Simon himself. Deutch tries his best, but as always, his lack of inspiration is responsible for never elevating the material far above the level of mediocrity. Deutch's last theatrical release, *The Replacements* (2000), is a comedy starring Keanu Reeves and Gene hackman about the 1987 professional football player's strike.          **CS**

# Danny DeVITO

Since founding his production company, Jersey Films, in 1992, Danny DeVito has steadily acceded to prominence as a major Hollywood mandarin. As a producer, he has, for the most part, picked his projects astutely, standing behind films such as *Pulp Fiction* (1994), *Get Shorty* (1995), *Man on the Moon* (1999), and *Erin Brockovich* (2000). His impish physique belies not only his considerable talent as an errant character actor, but also a saturnine comic eye as a director. Indeed, if anything links his performance persona to his directorial corpus it is, with the notable exception of *Hoffa* (1992), the same disproportionate cartoonal aesthetic that distinguishes his physicality.

*The Ratings Game* (1984)
*Throw Momma From the Train* (1987)
*The War of the Roses* (1989)
*Hoffa* (1992)
*Matilda* (1996)
*Death to Smoochy* (2002)

Born in 1944 in New Jersey, DeVito abandoned his job as a hairdresser in his sister's salon to attend the American Academy of Dramatic Arts. Cast by Michael Douglas in an off-Broadway production of Ken Kesey's 'One Flew Over the Cuckoo's Nest', DeVito, after a string of bit-parts, made a lasting impression by reprising his performance as the psychotic Martini in Milos Forman's 1975 cinematic version of Kesey's novel. He turned down the television spin-off to play miserable Louie De Palma in the sitcom 'Taxi', and it was this show that afforded DeVito the chance to direct.

Following a string of acclaimed comic performances and some noteworthy television directorial credits, DeVito made his cinematic debut as director with *Throw Momma From the Train* (1987). The film, which proceeds from a neat parody of the murder scenario in Hitchcock's *Strangers on a Train* (1951), derives much of its bleak comic perturbation from the performative rasp between the neurotic tirades of Larry (Billy Crystal) and the absurd quasi-psychosis of Owen (DeVito). Indeed, in its best moments, *Throw Momma From the Train* achieves a degree of formal abstraction which enables DeVito to invest the narrative with an ambiguity between comic and tragic modes more usually associated with the distilled comic tropes of the cartoon.

The sadistic hysteria of *The War of the Roses* (1989) represents a significant refinement to this pared-down logic insofar as plot is almost entirely superseded by form. The film self-consciously renews the *amantes sunt amentes* friction between Michael Douglas and Kathleen Turner, established most notably in *Romancing the Stone* (1984) and *The Jewel of the Nile* (1985), only to reduce characterisation to hyperbolic caricature. As such, framed by a pseudo-fairytale ruse, *War of the Roses* plays out a series of formal comic exercises structured around the Roses' increasingly obsessive attempts to inflict on one another ever more humiliating cruelty. In this way, the cynical and ultimately nihilistic comedy of DeVito's film approaches the emptied-out formalism of Chuck Jones' work.

It is ironic, given the success of *War of the Roses*, that it is precisely the same inattention to plot and narrative which vitiates the otherwise impressive *Hoffa* (1992). Written by David Mamet, Hoffa attempts to thresh the chaff from the seed of the life of notorious American labour organiser, union demagogue and vicarious Mobster, Jimmy Hoffa. Indeed, while critics and reviewers were quick to wire the film into the circuit of contemporaneous biopics, its stench of political conspiracy, particularly around the ambiguities and uncertainties of Hoffa's putative murder, locate the film closer to the political paranoia and assassination narratives of Oliver Stone's *JFK* (1991) and Spike Lee's *Malcolm X* (1992).

However, as one critic quite appositely pointed out at the time, although 'scene to scene, Hoffa feels like a near-masterpiece', and notwithstanding the force of Jack Nicholson's performance as the titular protagonist, the film's stubborn attempt to squeeze the entirety of Hoffa's seesaw career into 140 minutes not only leads to some glaring contextual confusions, but sacrifices narrative unity to hyper-individualised historical minutiae.

*Matilda* (1996), while not as nihilistic as *War of the Roses*, certainly revisits DeVito's predilection for macabre humour. Indeed, risking distortion by analogy, the cruel comic excess of Roald Dahl's quasi-moral narratives and the grotesque disproportionality of Quentin Blake's illustrations provide not only the material of the film's cartoonal physical comedy, but can be read as the literary equivalent to DeVito's comic directorial corpus. Indeed, notwithstanding the film's wonderfully nasty caricatures and computer-generated visual comedy, the strength of the film is that DeVito resists offering any firm desiderata for determining whether the warm-hearted moral in tow is genuine or, in the spirit of Dahl's books, yet another wicked joke at our expense.

He has recently returned to directing with the film *Death to Smoochy* (2002), a comedy about the fierce feud between two children's television stars, featuring Edward Norton and Robin Williams. His following project, *Duplex*, will star Ben Stiller and Drew Barrymore. **PWa**

# Tom DiCILLO

*Johnny Suede* (1991)
*Living in Oblivion* (1995)
*Box of Moon Light* (1996)
*The Real Blonde* (1997)
*Double Whammy* (2001)

Born in Florida in 1954, Tom DiCillo graduated from Harvard Film School with a Masters in film-making in 1976. He started off as a cinematographer on numerous films, including Jim Jarmusch's *Permanent Vacation* (1982) and *Stranger Than Paradise* (1984). His first film, *Johnny Suede* (1991) starred a then-unknown Brad Pitt and introduced a number of themes that recur in DiCillo's work: the crisis of masculine identity; the impossibility of maintaining artistic principles in a world that has none; the seductive power of the image; and the fluidity of reality and fantasy that allows his characters to survive in a meaningless environment. The heroes of all DiCillo's films are on a metaphysical search, desperate to find meaning and resonance within an otherwise purposeless existence. Although the influence of working with Jarmusch is evident in most of his films, DiCillo rarely manages to attain the same level of poignancy or complexity as Jarmusch does in *Down By Law* (1986) or *Mystery Train* (1989).

*Living in Oblivion* (1995) is the highpoint of his career so far. DiCillo's predilection for advancing narrative through fantasy sequences is utilised extensively and successfully to blur the distinctions between art and life, reality and fantasy. Audience expectation is constantly questioned and subverted as the lines between what is real and what is fantasy deteriorate. The film's 'Noises Off' quality and complex interweaving of relationships add to its farcical nature. The scene where Nicole's (Catherine Keener) performance is slowly dissolved through a number of takes focuses the entire film and could act as a metaphor for the entire process of film-making.

DiCillo's third film, *Box of Moon Light* (1996), is a slight and unconvincing parable of mid-life crisis and the desperate need to regain an identity that has been lost to structure and routine. Al Fountain (John Turturro) – a character who lives by the clock and worships rules and regulations – attempts to relive his childhood after the harsh realisation that his life has no meaning; again, it is through fantasy sequences that this is made explicit. When he meets The Kid (Sam Rockwell), Al comes to the slow realisation that he has not led an authentic life and eventually finds meaning beneath the surface of his previously automaton existence. Utilising an aesthetic heavily reminiscent of the photographer William Eggleston, DiCillo also attempts his first portrait of provincial America. It is obvious, however, that he feels more at home within the confused confines of the city.

*The Real Blonde* (1997) is a thematically complex but ultimately confused film that redeems itself in DiCillo's understanding of his characters and the world they inhabit. The use of a speech from Arthur Miller's 'Death of a Salesman' sets the ideological tone for the film, but the power of the reference is never utilised due to the film's refusal to expose the harsh reality that it attempts to criticise. The references to the vapid and empty world of television and modelling are self-conscious and obvious (Empty-V and a designer perfume called Depression). This, coupled with a second-rate performance by Maxwell Caulfield as Bob, gets in the way of any serious investigation of the issues DiCillo is attempting to bring to the fore. The attempt to reinvent the themes so successful in *Living in Oblivion* therefore fails dramatically. In addition, his peripheral understanding of sexual politics and the crisis of masculinity are never explored successfully, merely superficially placed in order to advance the plot. DiCillo never seems to show allegiance to Bob's secure but shallow existence, thereby producing an unfocused work devoid of any solid critical basis.

His next film, *Double Whammy* (2001), has not been theatrically released in the UK and performed modestly at the American box office. A quasi-existential story of a New York cop (Denis Leary) attempting to regain his reputation, *Double Whammy* suggests that DiCillo is finally out of ideas. Derivative and clichéd, it has little of the quirkiness or understanding of character shown in his previous films and is thick with self-parody. DiCillo seems stuck in the comfortable world of late 1980s/early 1990s US independents. Where other directors have shifted and changed with the times – Jarmusch's *Ghost Dog: The Way of the Samurai* (1999) being a case in point – DiCillo has remained static and seems weary of exploring new situations or styles that would breathe new life into his tired and ethnographically specific work.          **BW**

# Erin DIGNAM

Born in California in 1955, former professional tennis player Erin Dignam is a strong and original voice in US independent cinema. Careful to avoid the clichés that dominate the terrain her films focus on, Dignam's take on the family drama has attracted an impressive roster of actors.

In *Loon* (1991), Robin Wright Penn plays Sarah, a housekeeper whose memories of an intense relationship are rekindled when she encounters an old friend. By using extended static and long-shots to accentuate the loneliness and pain endured by Sarah, Dignam's rigid, almost clinical directorial style results in a film that is too dour to convince. However, her formal approach to filming domestic drama and the close working relationship she enjoyed with Penn paid dividends in her second film.

*Loved* (1997) is similar to its predecessor in displaying Dignam's refusal to simplify the complexities of her subject matter. Avoiding a sensationalist approach to domestic violence and its impact upon both the victim and their family, Dignam crafts an intelligent and emotionally charged study of a woman whose life is haunted by the memories of an abusive relationship. Using a sparse *mise-en-scène* and cutting between long-shots, close-ups and hand-held camera, Dignam contrasts Hedda's inner state of mind with the world around her. The austerity of both the courtroom and Hedda's parents' home is contrasted with the tranquillity of a local swimming pool and the house of her attorney, the only places she appears to feel at ease. Similarly, Dignam's script is also used to separate Hedda from her surroundings. When testifying against her former lover, she employs a different language to the one used by lawyers, re-humanising events which the law had made cold and unemotional. As a result, Hedda is a more convincing character than *Loon*'s Sarah, giving *Loved* more depth and warmth than Dignam's first film.

At the film's beginning, Sean Penn, playing one of LA's dispossessed, tells William Hurt's attorney of the boundaries people build to prevent themselves being hurt, but which also stop them loving and being loved. An overview of the film's themes, the speech not only displays Dignam's ability to work well with actors, but also highlights her intelligence as a writer and director.          **IHS**

*Loon* (1991)
*Loved* (1997)

# Roger DONALDSON

As a journeyman director who has been doing the rounds in Hollywood for two decades, Roger Donaldson can lay claim to introducing the cinema-going public to some of film's rising stars. Mel Gibson, Kevin Costner, and Robin Williams all worked with him early in their careers, and he has been repaid in kind by being offered some of Hollywood's more cherished projects.

Born in Australia in 1945, he moved to New Zealand and became one of New Zealand's only feature film-makers (the formulaic action-thriller *Sleeping Dogs* (1977); the overtly symbolic family drama *Smash Palace* (1981)) before his breakthrough with *The Bounty* (1984). Assembling a cast as eclectic as Olivier, Hopkins and Day-Lewis proved the coup, but the end product was a stolid rehash of the MGM classic, with Donaldson displaying none of the verve and vigour of Frank Lloyd's 1935 original. *No Way Out* (1987) heralded Donaldson's arrival in Hollywood, as well as Costner's. The film is a gripping remake of *The Big Clock* (1947) in which Costner is the Pentagon

*Sleeping Dogs* (1977)
*Nutcase* (1980)
*Smash Palace* (1981)
*The Bounty* (1984)
*Marie* (1985)
*No Way Out* (1987)
*Cadillac Man* (1990)
*White Sands* (1992)
*The Getaway* (1994)
*Species* (1995)
*Dante's Peak* (1997)
*Thirteen Days* (2000)

official convinced his boss (Gene Hackman) is guilty of murder, despite all the evidence pointing to himself. Donaldson injects proceedings with tension, double-crosses and shock surprises, while the final-reel twist anticipates *The Crying Game* (1992) and *The Usual Suspects* (1995). From *Cadillac Man* (1990), in which the early promise of a Robin Williams/Tim Robbins collaboration is spoiled by clunking farce and lachrymose sentimentality, Donaldson begins to lose his way, producing the kind of painting-by-numbers film-making that categorises him as at best a hired hack. This is exemplified in *White Sands* (1992) in which the assembled cast (Sarandon, Dafoe, Mastrantonio) fail to assert themselves above the endless twists and turns of the narrative. Set in New Mexico, the deputy Sheriff (Dafoe) gets mixed up with the CIA, the FBI and arms dealers whilst investigating a murder. Again Donaldson seems capable of hiring big name stars but then doesn't seem to know what to do with them. All look far from comfortable, despite the director's attempts at sultry chemistry and murky intrigue.

The Getaway (1994) is remarkable only for the lack of on-screen chemistry between real-life couple Kim Basinger and Alec Baldwin. A remake (again) of the 1972 Peckinpah classic, Donaldson creates the requisite hot and sweaty Mexican milieu, but the increasing reliance on shoot-'em-ups and scenery-chewing from Michael Madsen and James Woods means that the film never rises above the generic straightjacket that it tries so hard to escape from. The same is true of *Species* (1995), one of the first batch of B-movie rehashes that have become standard seasonal fare in Hollywood. A hybrid created from alien and human DNA escapes and runs amok in downtown LA. Part science fiction and part high-school fantasy (the alien is supermodel Natasha Henstridge), the direction and writing are efficient but lack the necessary humour that a Joe Dante, or the satire that a John Carpenter, would have brought proceedings. Containing the immortal line 'Something bad happened here', this is an apposite imprimatur of Donaldson's oeuvre.

His next project was the long-cherished *Dante's Peak* (1997) which was that year's first of two volcano films (along with Mick Jackson's *Volcano* (1997)). Starring erstwhile 007 Pierce Brosnan, the film follows the traditional *Jaws*-style disaster movie logistic (lone voice crying out against backdrop of community complacency and ignorance) before the full-scale pyrotechnics and CGI effects override the narrative. The characters are badly sketched, the dialogue sophomoric and the reliance on a dog for emotional weight is an apt metaphor for the film's and the director's intentions. What could have been an exercise in tension and community reaction in the face of danger is quickly eschewed, and Donaldson relies too heavily on the volcanic eruption for effect.

His most recent release, *Thirteen Days* (2000), is set during the 1962 Cuban Missile Crisis and centres on how President Kennedy (Bruce Greenwood), Attorney General Robert Kennedy (Robert Culp) and others handled the explosive situation. He is currently in production with *The Farm*, the story of an instructor (played by Al Pacino) at the CIA training facilities who is suspected of being a double agent. **BM**

# Richard DONNER

Richard Donner is a director who has dallied in virtually every known genre during his lengthy career, from horror to comedy, westerns to action, and even children's movies. Although he has delivered modest and intimate films, he is probably more widely recognised as an advocate of the Hollywood blockbuster, most notably through his alliance with the producer Joel Silver.

Born in 1930 in New York, the son of a wood carver, Donner was the first of his immediate family to go into show business, initially as an off-Broadway actor. He soon discovered he was better at giving direction than taking it, and after being guided by director Martin Ritt he moved to California in 1958. In the next decade-and-a-half he established a name for himself in the television world, but he also sporadically directed feature films.

*X-15* (1961) tells the story of a record-breaking aircraft and its crew, but is impeded by a muddled plot and over-reliance on technical explanations and military jargon. As one critic commented at the time, it is more like a training film than a piece of entertainment. A rare opportunity to study the emotional and domestic challenges of such pilots is wasted, with only Charles Bronson and James Gregory eliciting any bona fide audience sympathy. Certain key scenes are capably handled by Donner, betraying his TV roots, but on the whole *X-15* is a disjointed and now terribly dated piece of Army Air Corps propaganda. British production *Salt and Pepper* (1968) is infinitely more rewarding, if only because it does not have aspirations above its station. A slapstick comedy in the traditional sense, its dizzying pace, carefree attitude and visual panache also capture the spirit of the 1960s perfectly. In a deft piece of casting, singer Sammy Davis Jr, displaying the same comedic flair he would later draw on for the 'Cannonball' series, is paired up with Peter Lawford as the Soho night-spot managers of the title, always in trouble with the authorities.

England is also the setting for the opening portion of *Twinky* (1969, aka *Lola*), and heralded Charles Bronson's return to serious acting. Exploiting the sexual freedom of its era, the film centres on a naïve young nymphet's relationship with an older man. Unlike many similar scenarios, the imprudent marriage of the two and consequent problems that ensue hold the interest without depressing the viewer, and Susan George's vigorous portrayal of the lead is a revelation. Unfortunately, the sudden shift from Britain to New York can be interpreted as more of a practical necessity than an artistic decision, and effectively cuts short the promising interchanges between Twinky and her family (including Honor Blackman as the mother and Michael Craig as her stifling dad).

*The Omen* (1976) provided Donner with the hit he needed to free him from television obscurity. His mandate, to 'eliminate the obvious' horror film accoutrements, sets the motion picture apart from the majority of its peers. Concentrating on the figure of the Antichrist as a child (Harvey Stephens), Donner is able to further destabilise the family unit and incapacitate American values to reflect the mood of the time. Using reputable actors like Gregory Peck and Lee Remick as Damien's parents, and religious texts such as The Book of Revelation for its authorisation, *The Omen* manages to achieve what few films past or present have done, giving Satanism a mainstream, mass-market appeal.

'You'll believe a man can fly' promised the pre-publicity for *Superman* (1978), and unusually for a comic strip adaptation, verisimilitude is a primary concern. The garish campness of Adam West's Batman is rejected in favour of an earnest presentation of the myth, still spell-binding in its execution. Christopher Reeve takes the part of the alien messiah in a position to offer hope to mankind, and although supposedly a world figure, Superman is the perfect righteous American – thanks to his upbringing in the wheat fields of the west, a fact the movie never lets us forget. However, we also witness his human frailties, proving that even those with power occasionally make mistakes: something equally true of world leaders and superheroes alike.

In contrast to the lavish fantasy excesses of *Superman, Inside Moves: The Guys from Max's Bar* (1980) has more in common with an independent picture. An exploration of everyday life from a disabled point of view, it is more interested in the personalities than their individual afflictions. Based loosely on Todd Walton's novel, it introduces us to a group of remarkable individuals, surprisingly at ease with their predicaments, counterbalancing with recently-crippled John Savage, who has to gradually regain his self-respect. *Inside Moves* is a legitimate and sensitively-handled 'word-of-mouth' movie that neither offends nor insults.

With *The Toy* (1982), however, Donner attempts to take another delicate subject and use it as the grounds for a disgracefully irreverent comedy caper. Richard Pryor is the unemployed black journalist 'bought' by bigoted millionaire Jackie Gleason as a play thing for his spoilt son. The nauseating scene where Pryor is tied up with a pink ribbon and given to the child sets the precedent for innumerable indignities ahead. The fact that Pryor cannot secure a job because of racist hiring policies, and the obvious parallels to slavery, ensure that *The Toy* can only work on the most rudimentary of levels. And the final reel, wherein everything miraculously resolves itself – father and son become closer, Pryor gets back to journalism – is simply another example of Hollywood wish fulfilment, ignoring the highly questionable ideological foundations on which the film is constructed.

Donner worked with producer Steven Spielberg next for *The Goonies* (1985) and the influence is manifest. A post-Indiana Jones children's adventure, it recounts the escapades of a gang of young misfits in a small coastal town. In short it is the effectuation of every wayward pre-pubescent's wild imaginings: chasing pirate treasure, investigating crime, outwitting villains and earning the admiration of their elders.

Donner's other film of 1985, *Ladyhawke*, is a fantasy in every sense of the word, part of the 'Sword and Sorcery' revival of the 1980s which also embraced the *Conan* (1982/

1984) saga, *Red Sonja* (1985), and *Legend* (1985). As with *Superman*, the world of this fairytale is totally compelling, absorbing and self-contained, owing mainly to the beautiful Italian surroundings. The story, sadly, is hackneyed and customary, detailing Rutger Hauer and Michelle Pfeiffer's struggle to break a wizard's spell – he transforms into a wolf at night, while she becomes his winged companion during the day.

*Lethal Weapon* (1987), is a modification of the 'good cop/bad cop' formula, capitalising on Mel Gibson's *Mad Max* image – here as another widower policeman with a death wish. His chemistry with older partner Danny Glover, who functions as his straight man, makes the package cogent. And thanks to an interminable stream of action set-pieces one never really notices the illogical nature or vulnerability of Shane Black's screenplay.

*Scrooged* (1988) is an extremely aware updating of Dickens' 'A Christmas Carol', substituting a television executive for the more familiar money-counter. Cynical and satirical in-jokes, such as 'Dynasty''s John Forsythe as an undead Marley figure, and more fashionable ghosts (the highlight being Carol Kane's malicious fairy) instil the proceedings with a whimsy of their own. That said, Bill Murray's caricature is less than convincing, and *Scrooged* is forever on the verge of lapsing into a bilious philanthropic sermon, particularly during the comic's final cringe-making address.

In the *Lethal Weapon* sequels (1989 and 1992), Glover and Gibson develop their double act, offering yet more banter and mayhem. The tenability and credulity are stretched to ridiculous lengths, and not even the introduction of foul-mouthed Joe Pesci and ex-model Rene Russo can divert the attention away from those same old explosions and car chases. Which probably explains why Donner returned to a smaller canvas with *Radio Flyer* (1992), a deeply personal film about two boys' dreams of building a flying machine so they can escape their stepfather's cruel behaviour. Emotive, fantastic, and inspirational to varying degrees, only the irksome script and ham-fisted narration (by Tom Hanks) conspire against it.

*Maverick* (1994), as well as being an exaggerated western comedy, was part of a rash of nostalgic television remakes in the 1990s (*The Addams Family* (1991), *The Flintstones* (1994), *The Avengers* (1998) and so on). Mel Gibson is excellent as the scoundrel gambler in this unpretentious and candidly amusing yarn, which has a wonderful time sending up the limitations of the genre – in particular screenwriter William Goldman's liberal references to his own *Butch Cassidy and the Sundance Kid* (1969). James Garner (the original Maverick) is present, too, as is Jodie Foster, playing against type as a quick-witted temptress.

Both *Assassins* (1995) and *Conspiracy Theory* (1997) take risks, but they back-fire spectacularly. The former's convoluted plot follows the antics of angst-ridden killer-for-hire Sylvester Stallone, stepping down as number one and trying to avoid being Antonio Banderas' next mark. However, in contrast with Luc Besson's immeasurably superior *Leon* (1994), there is little attempt to endear these shallow hitmen to the general public, nor is there sufficient justification for their actions. Similarly, Mel Gibson's chronically paranoid character in *Conspiracy Theory* is almost impossible to empathise with, even when he uncovers a secret government cabal. A retrograde pursuit thriller in the *Three Days of the Condor* (1975) mould, it feeds all too readily off society's 'Big Brother' concerns in a pre-millennial age.

Donner's last film, *Lethal Weapon 4* (1998), is, however, possibly his worst. The third *Lethal Weapon* follow-up is frankly one too many. Now that Gibson has found a new love (the pregnant Russo), Glover is his best friend, and they have both been promoted, the original impetus has faded away. Despite their protestations to the contrary, the seemingly indestructible duo are getting way too old for all this juvenile nonsense, and it shows.

Donner's next project, *Timeline*, is the story of a history professor from the near future trapped in fourteenth-century France, based on Michael Crichton's novel of the same time.                                                                                    **PB**

# Anthony DRAZAN

Born in Detroit in 1955, Anthony Drazan has directed three films – *Zebrahead* (1992), *Imaginary Crimes* (1994), and *Hurlyburly* (1998) – that are all perfect examples of the character-based screenplay, in which development of character is the primary narrative drive. His films feature few visual flourishes – he directs in an economical, low-key fashion, allowing the actions of his characters and the subtle curves of the script to lead the way. This can alternately be touching or tedious, depending on the film in question.

The Oliver Stone-produced *Zebrahead*, a Sundance award-winner, is set in a Detroit high school, where a white teen, Zack (Michael Rappaport), falls for Nikki (N'Bushe Wright), the cousin of his black best friend Dee (DeShonn Castle). As Zack is particularly enamoured with Black-American culture, some are suspicious of his intentions with Nikki, but only when another teen, black gang-banger Nut, becomes interested in her, do petty prejudices erupt into violence. As an exploration of human relationships, the apparently autobiographical film is particularly adept at getting beneath the obvious manifestations of racism, attempting, refreshingly, to see each character as an individual, rather than a part of a collective group-mentality.

The little-seen *Imaginary Crimes*, based on Sheila Ballantynes' autobiography, continues in the path set by its predecessor, albeit in an entirely different fashion. A quaint coming-of-age tale set in early 1960s Portland, the film tells the story of Sonya Weiler (Fairuza Balk), the daughter of Ray (Harvey Keitel), a perennial loser/inventor/con-man. Sonya, a burgeoning writer, uses her father's exploits as the focus of her stories, and it is the reading of these stories which serves as the film's narration. Although the Oregon mountains of *Imaginary Crimes* would appear to be a major leap from the urban jungle of *Zebrahead*, the film feels strikingly similar with Drazan's connection to his characters. Like Zack in *Zebrahead*, Sonya has been forced to grow up without her mother, and this continues to have reverberations throughout her young life, including a household dominated by an eccentric father. Again, Drazan refuses to boil his characters down to mere concepts, choosing instead to see each one as a fully-formed, though flawed, human being.

*Hurlyburly*, based on David Rabes' popular play about a group of cocaine-fuelled men who work in various aspects of the movie business, is perhaps Drazan's least successful film, despite the many years he spent trying to make it. Eddie (Sean Penn) and Mickey (Kevin Spacey) are roommates in a large Hollywood Hills home, where they spend their days doing drugs and having sex, while Eddie tries to make some sense of his life. The film is further populated by an assorted, eccentric group of characters. Drazan still closely examines his characters in *Hurlyburly*, but the whole is mired by the unpleasantness of their personalities, and the film still feels very theatrical as it rarely moves out of Eddie's living room. However, in exploring the alternate side to the existence of *Zebrahead* – that of the urban rich – Drazan shows that it is still the relationships people form that define the satisfaction they feel in their lives.    **DH**

# Dennis DUGAN

The filmography of Dennis Dugan, born in Illinois in 1946, indicates a predisposition towards, and fetishisation of, bodily functions and other assorted obscenities – to the point that one might be led to believe the director is in fact a kindergarten student. However, Dugan has been in Hollywood as an actor since the 1970s. In the mid-1980s he began directing episodes of popular television series such as 'Hunter', 'Moonlighting', and 'L.A. Law'.

Dugan made his inauspicious feature film debut with the critically despised *Problem Child* (1990), a comedy about a man (John Ritter) who adopts a child (Michael Oliver) with severe behavioural problems. The film performed well commercially and spawned two sequels, but it remains that *Problem Child* is the type of film that replaces humour with crudity, expecting the latter to generate the same reaction as the former. *Brain Donors* (1992), Dugan's second film, faired just as poorly with critics as it did with audiences. An unauthorised remake of the classic Marx Brothers film *A Night at the Opera* (1935), the film does have a popular following, but those who are familiar with the earlier film find the remake's additional vulgarity difficult to accept.

Dugan revitalised his film career through his work with 'Saturday Night Live' comedian Adam Sandler in *Happy Gilmore* (1996), the story of a failed hockey player (Sandler) who takes up golf to in order to save his beloved grandmother's (Frances Bay) house from government repossession. His violent behaviour shocks the sedate golf world and leads him into conflict with a cocky professional (Christopher McDonald). Although the film is no less crude than Dugan's previous work, Sandler's charisma is strong enough to sustain the film for at least its first half. The actor seems altogether incapable of sincerity, so when the film's tone turns somewhat serious, it drags to a slow, implausible finale. There are, however, moments of true hilarity and the film has gained a wide, enthusiastic audience since its release on video.

*Happy Gilmore*'s follow-up, *Beverly Hills Ninja* (1997), stars the late Chris Farley, also of 'Saturday Night Live', as a clumsy white ninja who travels from his Japan home to California to stop a counterfeiting ring. Farley depends solely on his great girth and pratfalls for humour and, because he lacks Sandler's personality, *Beverly Hills Ninja* is unable to surpass the limited potential of its minimal plot or transcend its director's lack of cinematic imagination.

Dugan has expressed a fondness for working with Sandler, and *Big Daddy* (1999) is another Sandler vehicle. After his girlfriend dumps him, failed law student Sonny Koufax (Sandler) takes custody of his roommate's (Jon Stewart) young son to prove he is a responsible adult. He teaches the child all his own bad habits, but connects with him on a more emotional level when Social Services threatens to take the boy away. Although reviled by most critics, the film was a massive commercial success. Sandler had been gaining in popularity since *Happy Gilmore*, and *Big Daddy* cemented this fame. His personality carries the film and once again it only begins to slow when its tone turns serious. The sentimentality simply does not gel with Sandler's abrasive style.

Dugan's films have neither a personal signature nor any intellectual edge, marking them as a by-product of the Hollywood machine – that which appeals to the basest of cultural tastes. Since becoming a director he has also maintained a steady acting career, appearing as periphery characters in many of his own films as well as others, including *Can't Buy Me Love* (1987), *She's Having a Baby* (1988), and *Parenthood* (1989). He has continued to work in television, directing episodes of 'NYPD Blue', 'Chicago Hope', and 'Ally McBeal', as well as the television movies *Columbo: Butterfly in Shades of Grey* (1994) and *The Shaggy Dog* (1994).

Dugan's most recent release, *Saving Silverman* (2001), is a comedy about two young men (Jack Black and Steve Zahn) who try to prevent their friend's impending marriage. His next project, *National Security*, is an action comedy starring Martin Lawrence, slated for a 2003 release.                                                    **DH**

# Christian DUGUAY

With a career that has moved between cinema and television features as well as television series, Christian Duguay's directorial output encompasses a variety of genres including science fiction, crime and real-life dramas.

'The Hitchhiker' was a television series of mystery-thrillers that ran from 1983 to 1989, for which Duguay was one of a plethora of directors. The episodes took on a new narrative each week based around a supernatural theme, introduced and concluded in a Hitchcockian style, by the narrator in person.

For his first feature Duguay continued where Cronenberg left off with the sequel *Scanners II: The New Order* (1991) and followed a year later with *Scanners III: The Takeover* (1992). Taking up the narrative of the telepathic fighters warding off the forces of evil, the immediate successor sees a scanner's latent power being exploited by sinister forces in an indolent, messy plot. Described by critics as superfluous and visually clichéd, it is fair to say that taking on a Cronenberg sequel was a little over-ambitious for a first feature. The next instalment is another 'good versus evil' plot in which all but one of the Scanners is drugged and turned evil. Poorly scripted, with a bad cast, it went straight to video. Where the first of the two films gained some attention for its inventive special effects, this feature is little more than a slur on Cronenberg's original idea. 1992 also saw the release of *Live Wire,* another thriller/horror that debuted on cable television and featured Pierce Brosnan as a bomb disposal expert investigating a case of a new invisible explosive that detonates once ingested into the human body.

Duguay's next four features were made for television. The first, *Adrift* (1993), for which he additionally worked as steadicam operator, was the tale of a shipwrecked couple taken aboard another boat only to discover something more sinister behind the crew's hospitality. *Snowbound: The Jim and Jennifer Stalpa Story* (1994) operates along a similar narrative thread with a couple being caught in a snow-drift. *Model by Day*, which followed in the same year, is an implausible story of a model who turns to crime fighting at night aided by her karate master. *Million Dollar Babies*, based on a true story set in 1930s Canada, follows the plight of quintuplets born into a poor Ontario family who find themselves turned into a freak show and was nominated for both ASC and Gemini awards.

It was in 1995 that Duguay moved away from real-life drama made for television back towards the sci-fi/horror with the feature *Screamers*. Based on a Philip K. Dick novel, it follows the alliance soldiers on a quest for peace in a 2078 wasteland planet and their battle against the eponymous screamers, the self-replicating flying blades. With a limited budget, it favours spectacle over intelligence, ultimately at the expense of its characters.

*The Assignment* (1997) opens on a Steadicam shot operated by Duguay as he returns once again to the technical side of film-making which he had developed in his earlier years. Starring Aiden Quinn as both a terrorist and the family man whose uncanny likeness leads to his to impersonation of the killer, the film combines documentary stylistics with a fiction narrative. More than any of his other work this film shows Duguay's ability to create suspense and develop strong characters.

Unfortunately, despite an interesting premise, *Jeanne d'Arc* (1999) fails to follow through into a successful feature, though it is more successful at portraying Jeanne as a human being rather than idolising her, as other productions have. Duguay's most recent film, *The Art of War* (2000), stars Wesley Snipes as a UN Agent caught up in a political murder plot.                                                                                                    **LB**

# Griffin DUNNE

Better known as a gifted actor in films such as *An American Werewolf in London* (1981) and *After Hours* (1985), Griffin Dunne, born in New York in 1955, began producing movies in 1979 and has continued, with his New York-based production company and partner Amy Robinson, to produce a variety of socially conscious or unconventional stories. *Running on Empty* (1988) – about a couple continually on the run from the FBI since their part in bombing a university defence installation in 1971 – and *White Palace* (1990) – about a bereaved young middle-class man who embarks on a relationship with an older working-class waitress – typify his output as producer.

*Addicted to Love* (1997)
*Practical Magic* (1998)
*Famous* (2000)

As a director Dunne utilised his darkly comic abilities in *Addicted to Love* (1997), a black comedy about obsessive love and revenge, seemingly at odds with the cheery, clean-cut promise of its stars Meg Ryan and Matthew Broderick. When astronomer Sam's (Broderick) long-term girlfriend leaves him and their small town for a job in New York, he follows her and sets up surveillance in the apartment opposite. He is surprised and upset to discover that not only does his ex have a new man, but that the new lover's ex (Ryan) has already set up her own spying facilities and is fastidiously keeping watch and plotting revenge. The film is a refreshingly brutal tale, with sado-masochistic undertones, disguised as a romantic comedy. Dunne spares his leads no embarrassment as the camera obscura rigged up by Sam reflects the new couple's rampant sex life right into their cockroach-infested lair. This reinforces Sam, whom we first see spying on Linda through a telescope in their hometown, as an unsavoury peeping Tom usually to be found in thrillers. Although dark and cynical, there is a moment of lightness when Sam realises he loves Maggie, and the film ends with two happy couples. However, Dunne's film seems to undermine this in the context of what has gone before – we have to question whether the couples can recover from the orgy of voyeuristic sadism that has befallen them, especially because the film eschews the idealism of young love for bitterness and hatred.

Dunne's next film, *Practical Magic* (1998), stars Nicole Kidman and Sandra Bullock in a comedy drama about two sisters who take up the witchcraft previously practised in their family and taught to them by their two aunts. The dualities of the sisters and their aunts are explored through this ghostly love story, dealing with the light and dark aspects in our lives and relationships in a similar way to *Addicted to Love*. Not as pleasingly vicious or coherent, the film again shows Dunne as someone interested in the nature of female power and dark romantic forces. He may reduce the potential for exploring this power in favour of emphasising a sugary romance but, like his previous film, this shows that Dunne is capable of handling shifts of mood between fun and romantic escapism and the darker forces unleashed by our desire to love and be loved.

*Famous* (2000) represents a thematic departure for Dunne. A parody of *cinéma vérité*, it is about a documentary film-maker following a struggling New York actress on the verge of fame. When a sexy advertising campaign buys her some unexpected notoriety, the film-maker hopes he can ride his subject's coat-tails to stardom. Despite a string of cameos from the likes of Sandra Bullock, Buck Henry, Linda Blair, and Spike Lee, the film has thus far been seen as a self-indulgent take on a predictable subject, showing little of the darkness and flair for comic timing of Dunne's previous work, and told in too conventional a format.

Dunne's next project, *Nailed Right In*, is a crime drama starring Johnny Depp.  **JD**

## Evan DUNSKY

*The Alarmist* (1998)  Evan Dunsky worked on the fringes of Hollywood for many years, first as an assistant director on the second-rate comedy-horrors *Magic Sticks* (1987) and *My Demon Lover* (1987). He also co-wrote the horror film *Voodoo Dawn* (1990) and acted in Todd Haynes' *Poison* (1991).

Dunsky's directorial debut, *The Alarmist* (1998), was based on the 1990 Keith Reddin play 'Life After Wartime', the title by which the film was originally known at its Toronto Film Festival premiere. The mainstream release of the film was delayed for over a year; even then it was only shown in very few theatres. It suffered from a lack of publicity, and could find a niche in neither art-house nor megaplex programming.

The consistently negative critics of *The Alarmist*, which certainly did not help its already limited commercial potential, were largely correct in their reading of the film, which suffers from a severe lack of focus and weak acting from David Arquette, whose Tommy Hudler is the story's protagonist. Tommy has just accepted a sales position at a security systems company run by Heinrich Grigoris (Stanley Tucci). Tommy falls in love with his first customer, Gale (Kate Capshaw), and begins to question his career choice when he sees Heinrich committing crimes to encourage sales of more systems. When Gale is murdered in her home, Tommy believes Heinrich is responsible and sets out for revenge.

Arquette's confused performance – nervous and twitchy at all times – is indicative of the direction of the whole film, which seems to waver between light comedy, dark comedy, romantic drama, and postmodern revenge fantasy. There are also some interesting quick shot-counter-shots, but these further the confusion by giving it a documentary feel. Only Tucci's undeviating sharpness keeps the film on an even plane.  **DH**

## Robert DUVALL

*We're Not the Jet Set* (1975)  The work of playwright and sometime film-maker Horton Foote makes an ideal entry-
*Angelo My Love* (1983)  point to the film work of Robert Duvall. Like Foote, Duvall makes small, modest works
*The Apostle* (1997)  that sink deep into your consciousness, resting there quietly as their meanings slowly grow, speaking to you in ever more complex ways. Born in San Diego in 1931 and one of the most passionate and thoughtful actors of his generation, Duvall has been in a few Foote plays and acknowledged this link. 'My career at one point was like a railroad track,' he told *Film Comment*. 'After I did *The Godfather* (1972), pretty many things happened, and the other railroad track I had was Horton Foote's work. If I had had nothing but that, it would have been a nice little career.' As with Foote's work, the three films that Duvall has directed – *We're Not the Jet Set* (1975), *Angelo My Love* (1983), and *The Apostle* (1997) – are relatively little-known.

His first film, the documentary *We're Not the Jet Set*, portrayed a Nebraska farm family that he had met while filming Coppola's *The Rain People* (1969). *Angelo My Love* was a fictional narrative about a Romany family in New York that used only non-actors playing themselves. It has been praised for its sympathetic but utterly unromantic look at their lives. Foote's impact is visible in Duvall's most widely seen feature film, *The Apostle*. With its gentle but realistic humanity, its close attention to the actor's craft and its occasional flashes of self-conscious artistic technique, this appears the work of a director working within certain industrial constraints. Unable to imagine making work any other way, by second nature he makes everything he does organic with apparently modest resources. Duvall will also star in his next feature, *Assasination Tango*, where a hired killer is sent to Argentina to kill a General and becomes romantically involved with a local tango dancer.  **JW**

# Clint EASTWOOD

Clint Eastwood is such an icon of the cinema that it is easy to forget that he has also had a rich and productive career as a director over the past thirty years. Indeed, he exerts such a control over his films (through his Malpaso production company) that it is often difficult to distinguish between those films he directed and those in which he only starred. Born in San Francisco in 1930, he is famed for his performances as rugged male anti-heroes – most notably 'Dirty' Harry Callahan and the lone gunslinger from Sergio Leone's *Dollars* (1964/65/66) trilogy – rather than as an auteur. However, he has used that control over his films to fashion one of the longest and most fascinating examinations of masculinity in American cinema, especially with respect to themes of individuality, violence, and more recently, ageing. Furthermore, this masculinity has been inseparable from the national culture in which it is conceived, with Eastwood's films consistently exploring his country's myths and legends through such emblematically American genres as the western, the road movie and the action film.

Already established as a top box-office draw, Eastwood made his directorial debut with *Play Misty for Me* (1971), a precursor to *Fatal Attraction* (1987), in which Eastwood plays a DJ who is terrorised by a female fan after their one night stand. It is an expert psychological thriller which, like Don Siegel's *The Beguiled* (1970), infuses the masculinity of Eastwood's hero with vulnerability and more than a hint of crisis: punishing his philandering by revealing to him that he does not have the control over women that he believes he possesses.

While *Play Misty for Me* was clearly influenced by the films Eastwood made with Siegel, whom he cast as Murphy the Bartender, the gothic *High Plains Drifter* (1972) took his 'Man With No Name' character from the Leone films to a new extreme. One of a cycle of 'apocalyptic westerns' made during the Vietnam era, the film offers a demonic variant of the *High Noon* narrative, with Eastwood playing a mysterious angel of vengeance who drifts into a small community that was complicit in the murder of its Sheriff. Westerns have traditionally examined the township as a birthplace of civilisation, but *High Plains Drifter* marks the most dystopic end of the spectrum. The community is almost entirely aligned with imagery of death and corruption and the ghostly stranger literally sends the town to hell for its sins. In 1985, he returned to play a similar, though more benevolent apparition in *Pale Rider*, which sees him defending a community of miners rather than seeking revenge. Closer to *Shane* (1953), the film seems to offer another reading of male heroism by arguing that while Eastwood's stranger is skilled in violence in a manner valued by traditional tropes of masculinity, it is precisely those skills which prevent his assimilation into the family and community.

A folksy romance, *Breezy* (1973), marked a striking departure for Eastwood – both in terms of subject matter and by the fact that he chose not to act in it himself – but with hindsight it remains a defining film for him as a director. In particular, through the inter-generational love affair between William Holden's middle-aged Frank Harmon and a free-spirited hippy chick called Breezy, the film demonstrates Eastwood's interest in character-driven narratives, as well as his compelling use of a no-nonsense film style that exudes a romantic attachment to realism.

*The Eiger Sanction* (1975) is a disappointing Cold War thriller which degenerates into a battle of machismos, as Eastwood and other climbers take on the north face of the Eiger mountain. However, *The Outlaw Josey Wales* (1976) is a rich western which many count among his finest achievements. Once again, the film details the Eastwood character's estrangement from family life, with his wife and child being murdered in the opening moments. However, this time the narrative focuses on Eastwood forming an extended surrogate family from the people he picks up or rescues on his journey of revenge – which, as Edward Gallafent has noted, makes a specific case for reconstruction that addressed feelings about the Vietnam war.

*The Gauntlet* (1977) is the mayhem movie *par excellence*: an effective, pared-down action movie in which Eastwood's cop is charged with escorting Sondra Locke's prostitute from Las Vegas to Phoenix. Worthy of a cult following, the film is essentially a fun satire of the police: most notably during three set-pieces that were inspired by the saturation gunfire the police had used against the SLA, in which a car, a bus and an entire house are demolished in a riddle of bullets.

The Capra-esque *Bronco Billy* (1980) took on the theme of Americans as dreamers, and demonstrated that Eastwood was capable of more than just the violent loner figure. Following his naïve New Jersey shoe clerk as he sets up a travelling Wild West show, it touches on themes of friendship, loyalty, and individuality; celebrating the courage to realise a dream and say, 'I am who I want to be'. Though not without optimism, *Honkytonk Man* (1982) has Eastwood playing a dying country musician in a film about the American hero being destroyed by his culture – and alongside *The Beguiled* (1970) is one of only two films in which his character dies.

*Firefox* (1982) proved to be another disappointing Cold War thriller, in which Eastwood steals a new Russian jetfighter, and is of note only for its aerial action sequences. *Sudden Impact* (1983) was the fourth of the Harry Callahan films and the only one directed by Eastwood himself. It is arguably the creepiest entry in the series – with Harry falling for Sondra Locke's homicidal rape victim – but it is also the silliest, featuring a farting dog called Meathead. Meanwhile, *Heartbreak Ridge* (1986) explores the question of what happens to men when they become obsolete. Eastwood plays a warrior without a war; an ageing, alcoholic sergeant on the verge of retirement, who has sacrificed his life and family for the army and sets out to end his career on a high note by training a group of disgruntled new recruits.

*Bird* (1988), on the other hand, is about a man whose candle burned short but bright, presenting a collage of passages from the life of saxophonist Charlie Parker. Not only did the film allow Eastwood to indulge his passion for jazz, it also marked a turning point in his critical reputation, winning him the Golden Globe for Best Director. *White Hunter, Black Heart* (1990), a film based on John Huston's experiences during the shoot of *The African Queen* (1951), continued this critical favour, but failed to set box-office tills rolling. Like *Bird*, it also presents a portrait of the creative artist as a contradictory and mythologised figure, focusing on themes of obsession and egotism as the Huston character attempts to indulge his vanity and masculinity by shooting an African elephant. However, as if to prove his own inconsistency as an artist, Eastwood made *The Rookie* the same year: a cartoonish, virtually incoherent riff on the Callahan films, in which stuntmen outnumbered actors by more than two to one.

However, the majestic *Unforgiven* (1992) finally brought Eastwood success at the Academy Awards. Moreover, it seems to have forced critics to re-evaluate his earlier work. Eastwood was now at last an auteur. The film was acclaimed for its revisionist view of the myths of the western genre, but along with *White Hunter, Black Heart* it also marks the beginning of Eastwood's move away from violent mayhem movies towards a more reflective stance on the damaging effects of violence. It also shows Eastwood continuing to examine the implications of ageing within his star persona.

*A Perfect World* (1993) found Eastwood at his most existential yet: a haunting and melancholic road movie starring Kevin Costner as an escaped convict who kidnaps (and bonds with) a seven-year-old boy. It is a naturalistic and deliberately paced film that is all the more effective for flying in the face of current conventions – as does *The Bridges of Madison County* (1995), a touching Midwestern, middle-aged romance adapted from Robert James Waller's bestseller. *Midnight in the Garden of Good and Evil* (1997), though, is a lacklustre adaptation of John Berendt's novel about murder in Savannah high society.

*Absolute Power* (1997) and *True Crime* (1999) are both pleasingly old-fashioned thrillers in which Eastwood plays ageing professionals (cat-burglar and journalist, respectively) trying to maintain relationships with their children while struggling to get to the bottom of crimes of great political importance. Both films add further textures to his older, wiser persona – as does *Space Cowboys* (2000), Eastwood's first foray into science fiction, which chronicles a group of old-timers being sent into orbit on an important and dangerous mission. His forthcoming film, *Blood Work*, is about a retired FBI director who has a heart transplant and is then hired to investigate the death of his donor.                                                                                                                **AS**

# Blake EDWARDS

Born in Oklahoma in 1922, Blake Edwards is the last major Hollywood director currently working who began his career during the studio era. He has successfully adapted to extensive changes in the film industry and has also worked in a variety of other performance media, including radio, television and theatre. His career is marked not only by its diversity but also by his desire for creative control over his work in highly collaborative media. He considers himself primarily a writer but, to maintain creative control, has assumed the roles of director and producer on many of his projects.

His greatest visibility is as a director of comedy and two of his films – *A Shot in the Dark* (1964) and *Victor/Victoria* (1982) – are on the American Film Institute's list of the 100 Best American Film Comedies. His comedies themselves display great diversity, from 'sophisticated' ones like *Breakfast at Tiffany's* (1961) to the physical comedy of the Pink Panther films to movies like *Victor/Victoria* which blend both. He is certainly the most distinguished contemporary director to draw upon the slapstick traditions of the silent era. Many of his most accomplished films, such as *Days of Wine and Roses* (1962) or *Wild Rovers* (1971), however, are not comedies at all.

His work has been internationally respected for decades. Its quality was praised by writers like Jean-Luc Godard at *Cahiers du cinéma* in France in the late 1950s and is still honoured at international film festivals. He has received countless awards, including the prestigious Preston Sturges Award (given jointly by the Directors' and Writers' Guilds of America) and the French Legion of Honour.

Although creative control is important to Edwards, he is also known for his remarkably long-lived creative collaborations. His 35-year television and film relationship with Henry Mancini may be the most extensive and successful major director/composer partnership in film history. Both Peter Sellers and Julie Andrews have appeared in numerous Edwards films and are widely associated with his work.

Although Edwards is associated with Hollywood 'entertainment' film-making, a serious examination of his work reveals not only great formal skill, but also a profound cultural critique. He is particularly incisive in depicting the desperation of the heterosexual white male during the post-World War Two era in which his traditional cultural dominance was eroded by large-scale social changes. Much of this desperation plays itself out in the realm of sexuality, reflecting Edwards' long-standing interest in psychoanalysis.

Edwards' adoptive father worked in the film industry and was himself the son of silent film director, J. Gordon Edwards (famous for directing many Theda Bara films). Edwards thus considers himself a third generation film-maker and he spent much of his

*Bring Your Smile Along* (1955)
*He Laughed Last* (1956)
*Mister Cory* (1957)
*This Happy Feeling* (1958)
*The Perfect Furlough* (1958)
*Operation Petticoat* (1959)
*High Time* (1960)
*Breakfast at Tiffany's* (1961)
*Experiment in Terror* (1962)
*Days of Wine and Roses* (1962)
*The Pink Panther* (1963)
*A Shot in the Dark* (1964)
*The Great Race* (1965)
*What Did You Do in the War, Daddy?* (1966)
*Gunn* (1967)
*The Party* (1968)
*Darling Lili* (1970)
*Wild Rovers* (1971)
*The Carey Treatment* (1972)
*The Tamarind Seed* (1974)
*Return of the Pink Panther* (1974)
*The Pink Panther Strikes Again* (1976)
*Revenge of the Pink Panther* (1978)
*10* (1979)
*S.O.B.* (1981)
*Victor/Victoria* (1982)
*Trail of the Pink Panther* (1982)
*Curse of the Pink Panther* (1983)

youth around film sets. His active involvement in the film industry began as an actor in the early 1940s. Feeling that he could do better than many film-makers of the era, he co-authored and co-produced (with John Champion) two independent films – *Panhandle* (1948) and *Stampede* (1949) – in the late 1940s. He also began working in network radio in 1949 with his creation of the popular 'Richard Diamond: Private Detective' series. He wrote many of the episodes for this and other radio shows, such as 'Yours Truly', 'Johnny Dollar', and 'The Lineup', throughout the 1950s. In 1954 he began his television career with 'Four Star Playhouse'. In the late 1950s he created the popular and innovative 'Peter Gunn' and 'Mr. Lucky' television series, on which he also served as writer, producer and director.

During the 1950s he also entered the Hollywood studio system as a writer and director for Columbia and, later, Universal studios. He directed 'B' films in the mid-1950s and moved up to 'A' films, involving higher budgets and stars of the status of Cary Grant, with *Operation Petticoat* in 1959. In the early 1960s he directed a number of films of astonishing diversity. With *Breakfast at Tiffany's* he earned a reputation as director of stylish, sophisticated comedy; *Days of Wine and Roses* demonstrated his skill at a dark drama on alcoholism; *Experiment in Terror* (1962) showed his talent in making a grim thriller. *The Pink Panther* (1963) revealed his flair for slapstick and introduced the character of Inspector Clouseau, played by Peter Sellers. *A Shot in the Dark*, also featuring Clouseau, followed and one of the most successful series in film history was born.

This burst of creative energy combined with popular and critical acclaim was followed by a period of ambitious films that failed to find such success. *The Great Race* (1965) and *What Did You Do in the War, Daddy?* (1966) were comedies on a grand scale; the first a homage to silent era film-making, the second a World War Two satire. Both, however, did poorly at the box office and with critics. *Gunn* (1967) and *The Party* (1968), the only non-Clouseau film Sellers made with Edwards and his personal favourite, went largely unnoticed. *Darling Lili* (1970) marked Edwards' first film with Julie Andrews, who also became his wife. Its purported financial excesses, combined with battles with studio executives on *Wild Rovers* and *The Carey Treatment* (1972), gave Edwards a reputation for being difficult to work with. He found the pressures of this period so distressing that he left Hollywood for a time, making *The Tamarind Seed* (1974) in England.

In the mid-1970s, with both Edwards' and Sellers' careers at low points, they revived Clouseau with spectacular success in *Return of the Pink Panther* (1974). They quickly capitalised upon this with *The Pink Panther Strikes Again* (1976) and *Revenge of the Pink Panther* (1978).

The Clouseau films reveal preoccupations that come up again and again in Edwards' work. Clouseau is very much a hysterical white male and much of the films' comedy comes from the ludicrous gap between his presumptions of cultural superiority and his idiotic behaviour. He feels free to treat his Asian manservant, Cato, brutally, and proclaims his mastery over women, yet he is spectacularly inept at nearly everything he attempts and is constantly humiliated. Clouseau's humiliations are particularly evident in a subtext of the films involving his sexual embarrassment and failure. In the first film he constantly fails to seduce his own wife, while she, at the same time, is sleeping with his arch-enemy. At the film's end he goes to prison for his enemy's crimes. The endings of these films are revealing. As the next three films conclude, he is about to engage in romantic activity with a woman, but is attacked by Cato. They close with him frustrated and in chaos.

*Revenge of the Pink Panther*, however, signals a shift indicating a planned end to the series. Uncharacteristically, the film ends peacefully: Clouseau and his romantic soulmate quietly walk off together. Earlier films would have had Cato attacking them at this moment and ruining everything, but here all remains peaceful.

After the phenomenal success of the revived Pink Panther series, Edwards made three critically acclaimed films that marked a significant departure in his career: *10* (1979), *S.O.B.* (1981), and *Victor/Victoria*. *10* and *Victor/Victoria*, both successful with the public as well as critics, dealt overtly with sexual themes that had previously been subtextual. A central theme of *S.O.B.*, a film about Hollywood, was the very process of dealing explicitly with sexual themes. *10* and *S.O.B.* also point to the increasingly autobiographical nature of Edwards' films: the former dealing with a musician's mid-life crisis, the latter with a film-maker's battles for artistic control of his work. *S.O.B.* and *Victor/Victoria* point to the growing importance of remakes in Edwards' career: *Victor/Victoria* remade the 1932 German film *Viktor und Viktoria*. In *S.O.B.* a producer remakes his own G-rated film into an X-rated one.

Edwards' next two films, *Trail of the Pink Panther* (1982) and *Curse of the Pink Panther* (1983), attempted to revive the Pink Panther series after the death of Peter Sellers. The former featured outtakes of scenes with Sellers from the previous films and the latter introduced Ted Wass as a bumbling detective figure who replaces Clouseau. Both films failed with the public and critics alike and the remainder of the 1980s were difficult for Edwards both in terms of box office and critical reputation.

Edwards' overt exploration of sexual themes surfaced again in his remake of François Truffaut's *The Man Who Loved Women* (1983), a film about a compulsive womaniser. Stylistically, it marks a shift in Edwards' comic style: whereas many of his previously films had been all-out comedies going for maximum laughs, increasingly in the 1980s he made sombre, reflective films with just one or two wildly comic scenes. *The Man Who Loved Women* has a morose tone and ends with the death of its central character. A sequence with its star Burt Reynolds hiding in a lover's closet when her husband unexpectedly returns, however, is hilarious and ends with Reynolds escaping after accidentally getting a dog stuck to his hand with Crazy Glue. Similarly, *Skin Deep* (1989) deals grimly with an alcoholic womaniser but also includes brief scenes of hilarity. In one, star John Ritter attempts to walk after receiving electrical shock treatments and, in another, viewers see little more than two glow-in-the-dark condoms when Ritter gets caught making love to a woman after her lover unexpectedly enters the dark room. Perhaps most extreme is *That's Life!* (1986), an autobiographical film centred around the central character's sixtieth birthday: he is having a late mid-life crisis; his wife is secretly awaiting the results of a possible cancer biopsy; and their adult children are experiencing various family tensions. In the midst of this, a wildly comic scene occurs when Jack Lemmon stands to speak during a church service. Seized with an outbreak of itching, he twists and contorts his body in a desperate effort to carry on.

In contrast to these dramas punctuated by brief bursts of comedy, Edwards made several 1980s films at the opposite end of the spectrum: *A Fine Mess* (1986) and *Blind Date* (1987) virtually banish serious narrative, character and thematic development, replacing them with elaborately developed sight-gags. *A Fine Mess* began as a remake of Laurel and Hardy's *The Music Box* (1932) but Edwards cut the central scene of stars Ted Danson and Howie Mandel moving a piano up a huge flight of stairs only to discover it to be the wrong address. He also cut the planned dedication to Laurel and Hardy, although the film's title recalls Hardy's oft-repeated remark to Laurel, 'This is another fine mess you've gotten us into'. Both *Blind Date* and *A Fine Mess* grow out of Edwards' profound respect for the silent slapstick tradition wherein the process of structuring physical comedy takes precedence over dialogue, theme, plot and character development. In fact, the structure of the comedy becomes all of those things. These films have deceptively simple stories. Much as *The Party* (1968) can be summarised as little more than an evening wherein a party is disrupted and a house destroyed, *Blind Date* can be summarised as little more than a disastrous evening wherein a dinner party is disrupted and a car destroyed. Critics have always been particularly hard on Edwards' fondness for working in this tradition, something about which he has expressed dismay.

Edwards' most recent films and related projects have once again focused upon remakes and sexuality. *Switch* (1991) is a companion piece to *Victor/Victoria*. In the latter Julie Andrews plays a woman who pretends to be a man pretending to be a woman; in the former a man dies and returns as a woman (Ellen Barkin).

With *Son of the Pink Panther* (1993) Edwards once again failed to revive the series without Peter Sellers. Although *Switch* enjoyed some success in Europe, as *Son of the Pink Panther* did in Italy, neither film did well in the US. Since their release, Edwards has taken a hiatus from film-making and focused on theatre, most notably with his high profile Broadway production of 'Victor/Victoria' in 1995. Edwards served as writer and director as well as one of the producers. The play is a theatrical remake of his film, which was itself a remake of an already existing film. He also wrote and directed another musical comedy, 'Big Rosemary', that was staged at the Helen Hayes Theater in Nyack, New York in 1999. Another gender-bender, 'Big Rosemary' is also a theatrical remake, this time an unacknowledged one of an early Edwards film, *He Laughed Last* (1956), in which a woman becomes the head of the Mob in Depression-era Chicago. The theatre productions, along with Edwards' life-long commitment to painting and sculpture (that culminated with a one-man show in Los Angeles in 1988), reveal a career of dazzling variety. Edwards is currently planning to direct a film of his original screenplay, *It Never Rains*. Like *That's Life!*, the autobiographical script deals with a family crisis. Edwards has remained an active presence in the industry since World War Two, making him one of the most prominent film-makers of his generation.                    **PL & WL**

# Atom EGOYAN

Atom Egoyan hinges his metatextual cinema on themes of emotional and psychological displacement. While biographical readings are often suspect, it is easy – given how candid Egoyan is with personal details in interview – to see how his own background of displacement influences his films. Although born in Cairo in 1960, he was brought up in Victoria, British Columbia, from the age of three. The move separated his family from any sense of community, and the search for some kind of 'real' community in a world populated by shattered, isolated individuals who project their inner, emotional lives onto images is central to his films.

It could be argued that he straddles two traditions of Canadian cinema. His success can be traced back to the early 1980s and the emergence of a group of Canadian film-makers dubbed the 'Ontario New Wave' by Carole Desbarats. Both the Ontario Film Development Corporation and the 1984 Toronto Festival of Festivals – where Egoyan's first feature, *Next of Kin* (1984), debuted – were central to their emergence. These developments increased in pace in 1987 with the likes of Egoyan's *Family Viewing* and Patricia Rozema's *I've Heard the Mermaids Singing*. Egoyan's fame increased when *Wim Wenders*, impressed by *Family Viewing*, gave the newcomer the $5,000 award he had received for *Wings of Desire* (1987) at Montreal's Festival of New Cinema and Video.

However, as Geoff Pevere has commented, Egoyan also sits comfortably with an older tradition of Canadian cinema in which characters are distinguished by their profound inertia and paralysing immersion in structures bigger than themselves. If any one director has drawn a line of demarcation between Hollywood's victorious individuals and Canada's decentred half-heroes, Egoyan has, with characters who exist in states of extreme emotional self-detachment.

*Family Viewing* and then *Speaking Parts* (1989) established Egoyan's reputation as a bleakly witty cine-poet of technological alienation. In these films, his characters fetishise their feelings and desires surrounding ambiguous familial relationships via audio-visual technology. In *Family Viewing*, a father binges on video porn while his son replays video footage of his hospitalised grandmother. In *Speaking Parts*, a scriptwriter obsessed with a video of her dead brother masturbates via a video-conference link over a hunky actor who resembles him. It comes as no surprise to learn that Egoyan wished he had coined the title *sex, lies and videotape* before Steven Soderbergh.

Despite the omnipresence of video in many of his films, Egoyan doesn't demonise the medium. He is more interested in plotting the processes by which his characters become metaphors of their experience and their subsequent quest for some sort of 'real' experience. These initially opaque plots only gradually fall into revelatory place, partly because Egoyan wants to implicate his audience on every level. He layers theme, form, plot and language in a way that forces us to follow the same path as his characters.

By saying that he treats his camera like a character in a film, or by mixing video and film footage, he betrays a fascination with why and how we watch images. How do we know what we know? How do we create knowledge from the information we are given? This audience scrutiny received a witty treatment in his early short, *Peep Show* (1991), with a young man visiting a technological pornography emporium only to have the erotic machines offer him images of himself.

Video technology takes a back seat to vocation and photography in *The Adjuster* (1991), Egoyan's most fully realised film up to then. Its characters are still at one remove, still ritualising their troubles, still at odds with self-knowledge. The film centres on an insurance loss adjuster, Noah Render (Elias Koteas), who treats having sex with his clients as part of his job and obsesses over photographs of their belongings while his wife works as a classifier of sex acts in pornography films. Language plays an increasingly evident role in the traps Egoyan's characters struggle with here, with Noah's fraught expression telling a wholly different story to his empty corporate speak.

Egoyan has been criticised for not trading in 'real' characters with 'real' inner lives. On the one hand, this misses the point: his films interrogate the concept of character by setting his characters at odds with themselves. On the other hand, his films are coloured by their empathy and compassion. *Calendar* (1993) certainly did not lack emotional conviction. Describing it as his take on Armenian consciousness, Egoyan cast himself as a Canadian photographer of Armenian ancestry who visits Armenia with his wife (Arsinée Khanjian, Egoyan's wife) to take photographs for a calendar. Back home, the photographer reflects on how his wife left him for an Armenian guide, ignores her answer machine messages and suffers several excruciating dinner dates. Alongside Egoyan's deft juggling of time, place and video with 16mm film, what rings clear here is the desperate poignancy of a relationship breaking up.

Egoyan's breakthrough film was the lush, moody *Exotica* (1994). This haunting and emotionally shattering tale of a taxman's obsession with a table dancer almost ignores video entirely. Instead, Egoyan puts the image of the table dancer who dresses as a schoolgirl at the core of the film's highly charged circuit of trauma. Although meticulously plotted, this tale of people's emotional baggage shaping how they relate to self and others unfolds with an uncannily organic and unwavering precision, suggesting that we cannot know someone without first unpacking the baggage – figurative and literal – that they carry. Egoyan described its steadily unravelling structure as a striptease, but there is nothing prurient about this wrenching, deeply empathic film. It deservedly earned him the International Critics Prize at Cannes and a string of other international awards.

His two subsequent films were relatively frustrating. Egoyan seemed to be displacing himself anew by turning to adaptations of other people's work, although the way that both films tease out *Exotica*'s peripheral themes suggests that he was working in that film's shadow. *Exotica* closes with the suggestion that Mia Kirshner's table dancer dresses as a schoolgirl because she is trapped in a legacy of being abused as a child. Although mainly concerned with the tale of a town devastated by the deaths of its children in a school bus accident, *The Sweet Hereafter* (1997), an adaptation of Russell Banks' novel, hones in – awkwardly – on the father/daughter incest theme. Likewise, while *Exotica*'s plot coils around the murder of a child, Egoyan's mostly faithful but haphazard adaptation of William Trevor's novel, *Felicia's Journey* (1999), centres on the relationship between a teenage girl and a serial killer of young girls.

Fittingly for a director whose work is metacinematic, both films use 'stranger in a strange town' plots. The former stars Ian Holm as a lawyer exorcising his estranged relations with his daughter by urging the mourning town to push for a lawsuit. In the latter, Felicia (Elaine Cassidy) leaves her home in Ireland to find the father of her child in Birmingham. Where he previously worked from his own screenplays, in both these films Egoyan is a stranger himself as adapter. Likewise, it is surely no coincidence that both films centre on children and corrupted innocence. Egoyan's own child was born following an appearance – via a pregnant Khanjian – in *Exotica*.

For all their flaws, both see Egoyan exploring and broadening the emotional scope of his work. He is also wrestling with mediums; having once described his films as 'almost operatic', 1998 saw him direct an English National Opera production of Gavin Bryar's 'Dr Ox's Experiment' in London and a production of 'Salome' in Toronto. More recently, 2002 saw him exploring themes of formative memories and the means by which they're stored in 'Steenbeckett', an installation based on his film of Beckett's play, 'Krapp's Last Tape'. In addition, his most recent film, *Ararat*, about the Armenian holocaust of 1915, is a hugely ambitious film. Instead of taking the *Schindler's List* route of recreating, as if unproblematically, images of the holocaust, Egoyan's film-within-a-film centres on a director making a historical epic about the period.                    **KH**

# Harry ELFONT

Constant collaborators, Harry Elfont and Deborah Kaplan have written films such as *Very Brady Sequel* (1996) and *The Flintstones: Viva Rock Vegas* (2000), and a host of other films for which they are un-credited.

*Can't Hardly Wait* (1998)
*Josie and the Pussycats* (2001)

Their feature directorial debut, *Can't Hardly Wait* (1998), is a teen-oriented comedy that takes place the evening after high-school graduation at a house party for the entire graduating class and follows several characters in their romantic exploits. It focuses on Preston (Ethan Embry), who longs to express a long-held crush on recently-singled prom queen Amanda (Jennifer Love Hewitt). It is an unpretentious film, well-paced and humorous, that unfortunately cannot shake off its resemblance to so many teen films of the past. Appealing to teens with short memories for pop-culture, it is blatantly derivative and feels calculated to please, with a host of stock characters. Nonetheless, Kaplan and Elfont show tremendous affection for thee characters and an excellent ability to maintain focus on their individual plights despite frequent narrative jumps. The film's uniqueness lies in its taking place in a single night in, mainly, a single setting; accordingly, it never lingers long on any one narrative line.

Kaplan and Elfont continue to work exclusively together. Their most recent feature, *Josie and the Pussycats* (2001), is a live-action adaptation of the 1970s comic strip about a crime-solving rock group. They have written the upcoming romantic comedy *Surviving Christmas*. **DH**

# Roland EMMERICH

Roland Emmerich is a director who works almost exclusively within the science fiction genre, sometimes infusing his pieces with action and horror staples. Since his partnership with actor-turned-producer Dean Devlin, he has gone on to sire some of the biggest hits of the 1990s, reintroducing mainstream audiences to the delights of the 'what if...' science fiction extravaganza.

Born in Stuttgart in 1955, Emmerich began his career in his native Germany, studying production design while at film school in Munich. After gravitating towards direction, he made a diploma movie that opened the 1984 Berlin Film Festival and was sold to over twenty countries around the world.

*Das Arche Noah Prinzip/The Noah's Ark Principle* (1984) is evocative of science fiction serials from Hollywood's golden age, as well as role model George Lucas' own student film, *THX 1138* (1970). A prophetic and uncanny parable about weather experimentation emboldens this amateur endeavour, as does Emmerich's handling of widescreen and stereo sound, plus Bavaria Studio's startling budget effects. Its greatest problem remains a lamentable dearth of excitement and dialogue, which causes the 100-minute running time to drag.

The following year's *Joey* (1985) is another German film, this time with an English-speaking cast, headed by Joshua Morrell as the perspicacious 11-year-old of the title. This Spielbergian tale, which also looks to movies such as *Magic* (1978), *Carrie* (1976) and *Neverending Story* (1984) for stimuli, is little more than the sum of its parts and suffers badly from the same scripting shortfalls as its predecessor. The same can also be said of Emmerich's confusing *Ghost Chase* (1988), which is reliant on the science fiction and horror cinema archives for charisma. What should have been a quirky comedy about two dilettante film-makers encountering phantoms is sabotaged by homages to films like *Gremlins* (1984) and *E.T. The Extra-Terrestrial* (1982), a fitful plot and self-indulgent constitution.

Happily, in *Moon 44* (1990) Emmerich exhibits some of the style that would make his name in Hollywood, uniting two very contrary sub-genres under the science fiction umbrella: the fighter-pilot film and prison drama. Like Peter Hyam's *Outland* (1981) this is set on a corrupt outer space mining colony and contains a wry sideswipe at 1980s big business psychology. Granted there are untold clichés, like the weakling technofreak (played by Dean Devlin) who befriends the hero, futuristic slang, and incessant macho posturing. Its exemplary overall appearance, however, gives the impression of a much more extravagant and discerning piece.

For his principal US movie Emmerich chose *Universal Soldier* (1992), which Devlin rewrote for him. In its own sphere this Jean-Claude Van Damme vehicle is certainly among his finest. Standardised, loud and baneful, *Universal Soldier* does have the benefit of a very provocative core idea – that deceased soldiers from the Vietnam War might be brought back to life, then exploited again today – and the film at least touches on the question of how their loved ones would react if they found out. Add to this roles that bring out the best in stars Van Damme and Dolph Lundgren, namely high-kicking Herculean zombies, and the result is an above average late night enterprise.

The subsequent *StarGate* (1994), co-produced and co-written by Devlin, marked Emmerich's watershed Hollywood film. Epic in scale and aspiration, the visuals are reminiscent of the literary tradition of Edgar Rice Burroughs, Jules Verne and H. Rider Haggard, but also the cinematic feats of D. W. Griffith and Cecil B. DeMille. This is not to say that *StarGate* is perfect, but James Spader and Kurt Russell are agreeable enough as protagonists, and Jaye Davidson's androgynous – but thoroughly evil – Ra is so far removed from any previous genre villain he enhances the movie's status ten-fold.

Emmerich and Devlin's next project, *Independence Day* (1996), proved to be their most triumphant, becoming one of the largest grossing films of all time. Unquestionably and unashamedly a compound of many different invasion flicks, *Independence Day* also makes use of 1970s disaster movie and nuclear war film conventions: the destruction of entire cities and national monuments, incredible coincidences, a multitude of characters – all stereotypes. Without a doubt the abhorrent flag-waving, which reaches a crescendo during the president's speech, is merely an advertisement for the US government and their military aptitude. At the heart of the film though is a global message about putting aside differences for the common good (in the spirit of a British World War Two film).

It is a pity that the pair should follow *Independence Day* with *Godzilla* (1998), an exercise in crass commercialism and high-concept film-making. This time the Japanese Gojira monster movies, *King Kong* (1976) and Spielberg's dinosaur outings are the source, but the veneration is not as tolerable as before. None of the elements work – not the characterisation of Matthew Broderick, Jean Reno and Maria Pitillo, the dismal rain-soaked computerised effects, not the bland action sequences, and especially not the new look of the creature on which the entire vacuous production depends. To make matters worse, however, Emmerich even stoops to cannibalising his own back-catalogue (the helicopter battles from *Moon 44*, character names from *StarGate*, the exploding buildings of *Independence Day*). 'Size Does Matter' the tag line says, but so too does storyline, plausibility and distinctiveness.

Dubbed '*Braveheart* in America', the duo's summer 2000 blockbuster, *The Patriot*, took them in another direction altogether. Working from Robert Rodat's screenplay Emmerich has constructed an ambitious – though not entirely credible – historical action composition, starring Mel Gibson as Benjamin Martin, reluctantly battling against the British in the War of Independence. Complimented by an exhilarating John Williams score and authentic production design, this film demonstrates that Emmerich can approach serious topics with just as much vigour.          **PB**

# Nora **EPHRON**

Nora Ephron is one of the most prolific and profitable female directors in Hollywood today. Born in New York in 1941, to screenwriter parents Phoebe and Henry Ephron, she began her career as a journalist and novelist before making a successful transition to screenplay writing with credits such as *Silkwood* (1983) and *When Harry Met Sally* (1989). The films she has directed are sentimental contemporary fables reminiscent of the romantic comedies of the 1940s. Although they might appear conservative and simply constructed, they have been praised by critics for their acerbic wit and emotional vitality.

Ephron made her directorial debut in 1992 with the poorly received *This is My Life*. Adapted from Meg Wolitzer's novel, this is a comedic familial melodrama that follows the fortunes of Dottie Ingels (Julie Kavner) as she struggles to juggle family, love, and her desire to become a stand-up comedienne. Partially autobiographical, the film sets the tone for her future directorial work, with its thematic emphasis on the vicissitudes of human emotion and love.

Her second feature, *Sleepless in Seattle* (1993), is a hopelessly romantic film with repeated allusions to Leo McCareys' *An Affair To Remember* (1957). The film has the essential ingredients required to make a classic weepy, including two perfectly cast leads (Tom Hanks and Meg Ryan), who bring an intelligent warmth to the would-be lovers whose romantic destiny is guided by Hank's eight-year-old on-screen son. The film took $17 million in its opening weekend in the US, earning Ephron her third Academy Award nomination and ensuring her status as a commercially dependable director.

*Mixed Nuts* (1994), Ephron's next project, failed to capitalise on the commercial success of *Sleepless in Seattle*. A somewhat confused farce starring Steve Martin, the film generated little critical acclaim. However, her next film, *Michael* (1996), found the director returning to form with the story of an archangel (John Travolta) playing cupid on earth to a series of misfits, pessimists and unethical grotesques. Reaching number one at the US box office, the film employs the typical Ephron mix of sentimentality, cynicism and saccharine-sweet, unabashed charm.

*You've Got Mail* (1998) saw Ephron teaming up again with the winning combination of Tom Hanks and Meg Ryan in a loose reworking of *The Shop Around the Corner* (1940). The film is unashamedly schematic in its simplistic rendering of innocent love blossoming between two business rivals. Critics have decreed *You've Got Mail* to be 'contrived, ephemeral and bland', yet the chemistry that Ephron extracts from her two leads proved irresistible at the box office. It is a feat that Ephron attempted to emulate with her next release, *Lucky Numbers* (2000), which saw her again directing John Travolta in the lead role this time opposite 'Friends' star Lisa Kudrow. Unfortunately Ephron's decision to make the characters asinine and self-centred rather than saccharine and soft-centred in this rather black comedy, based loosely on the Harrisburg lottery scam, proved anathema to both critics and public alike.

Overall, Ephron's work to date can be read as a series of sentimental homages to a romantic cinema of the past. The subject matter she deals in – sensitive women, conservative men, and the formalised hetero-relationship, leading to an idyllic, utopian union – has led some critics to criticise her as a storyteller that deals in the conceit that all women really want is a good man; while they are hardly revolutionary or subversive, their enduring popularity is testament to their appeal. **PH**

# Emilio ESTEVEZ

After a couple of years acting in small movies and television shows, Emilio Estevez, born in New York in 1962, was launched into movies proper with a sizeable part in Francis Ford Coppola's *The Outsiders* (1983) and a leading role in Alex Cox's consumerist satire *Repo Man* (1984). One of the 1980s Hollywood 'Brat Pack', he made his name in the tabloids and in movies like John Hughes' *The Breakfast Club* (1984) and Joel Schumacher's *St Elmo's Fire* (1985).

His screenwriting debut, *That Was Then, This Is Now* (1985), in which he also starred, saw him consolidate his role as one of the sharpest of the Brat Packers, able to see that they could not ride the wave of group youth movies forever, and realising that he had to add other strings to his bow.

The following year he made his directorial debut, with *Wisdom* (1986), a modern-day Robin Hood story about lonely and disenfranchised John Wisdom, who robs banks and destroys mortgage records to help the people he feels are taken advantage of by the financial institutions. The film is passionate in its evocation of youthful angst and revolutionary tendencies (perhaps learned from his actor father Martin Sheen) but is also naïve and conventional, a self-pitying tale blandly told and heavy on the symbolism: the film opens and closes with Estevez lying in a bath watching the water drain down the plug hole in a clumsy metaphor for his wasted life and opportunities.

Meanwhile he continued acting, and wrote and directed his second film (co-starring his brother Charlie Sheen) in 1990. *Men at Work*, a so-called black comedy about two refuse collectors who find a political candidate's body in a bin and become embroiled in a toxic waste plot, the film tries to have good intentions but is inept in its reliance on nursery school jokes and scatalogical humour. Estevez shows himself unable to hold onto a coherent narrative, with the film including random and ignored plot devices.

However, his next directorial effort proved something of a departure. Set in Texas in 1972, *The War at Home* (which he also produced) starred Estevez as a man unable to readjust to life after Vietnam. Including performances from Martin Sheen and sister Renée Estevez, the movie deals with a dysfunctional family's attempts to keep up appearances. Described as 'The Brady Bunch' meets *Ordinary People* (1980), the film uses flashbacks to predictably counter the past and present, and despite this structure the film demonstrates a lack of any real social, political, or historical context. As a result it is reduced to a conventional depiction of the troubled father/son relationship, lacking insight into the theories of violence and war, and rendering the characters as ciphers. Obviously adapted from James Duff's stage play 'Homefront', it is talky but well-performed, involving (in the manner of soap opera), and has some dramatic punches.

At times moving, and usually competently directed, the film offers nothing new to any debate about the legacy of the Vietnam war.

His latest movie, *X Rated*, is a biopic about porn film producers Jim and Artie Mitchell, who made their fame and fortune on the back (so to speak) of their star actress, the infamous Marilyn Chambers. The perils of fame (excessive bouts of sex, drugs, drink, and the spending of their fortune) are predictably handled with none of the style of Paul Thomas Anderson's acclaimed *Boogie Nights* (1997). Comparisons might be odious but they are also inevitable when another film touches on a subject such as the porn industry. These comparisons can also be seen to exist on another, more tongue-in-cheek level, in the casting of Charlie Sheen, himself having fallen very publicly to the kinds of excesses described in the film. **JD**

# Pierre FALARDEAU

Born in 1946, Pierre Falardeau started using video as a means to study various aspects of Québec culture and society after completing his studies in anthropology at the Université de Montréal. His first, *Continuons le combat* (1971), revisits the theme of professional wrestling already observed in a classic direct-cinema documentary of the National Film Board of Canada (NFB), *Wrestling/La Lutte* (1961), directed by Michel Brault, Marcel Carrière, Claude Fournier and Claude Jutra. But whereas Brault *et al.* offer a whimsical look at one of the favorite pastimes of French Canadians, Falardeau denounces the practice outright. Denunciation became Falardeau's *modus operandi*. From his short video *Le magra* (1975), which exposes institutionalised despotism at the Police Academy of Nicolet (Québec), to his most recent feature film, *15 février 1839* (2000), a harsh criticism of the British Imperial regime and its treatment of the French-speaking rebels who led an insurrection in Lower-Canada (now Québec) in 1838, Falardeau's oeuvre points an accusatory finger at those who oppress the powerless and disenfranchised. His first feature fiction film, *Le Party* (1990), revolves around a burlesque show organised in a jail and performed before both inmates and prison officials. In the course of the show, a few prisoners are given a venue to express their anger at the penal system – one song in particular, performed by folk singer Richard Desjardins in the role of an inmate, voices the rage that the film as a whole expresses – while guest performers get to know the prisoners and realise the oppression of which they are victims. Parallel to the activities surrounding the burlesque show, one prisoner carries out his escape while another one commits suicide.

While Falardeau's films attack all those whom he perceives as oppressors, his main target is the English-speaking establishment of Canada. A staunch supporter of Québec's national independence, Falardeau has made a number of short films, such as *Speak White* (1980) and *Le Temps des bouffons* (1985), which condemn Anglophone capitalist federalism. His most accomplished work dealing with the issue of Québec's nationalism is his feature *Octobre* (1994), which looks at the events of October 1970, when members of the Front de Libération du Québec kidnapped a British diplomat, James Cross, and a Québec politician, Pierre Laporte. Falardeau focuses on the handful

*Elvis Gratton – le film* (1985)
*Le Party* (1990)
*Le Steak* (1992)
*Octobre* (1994)
*Miracle á Memphis* (1999)
*15 février 1839* (2000)

of FLQ members who held hostage and eventually killed Laporte. While sympathetic to the cause of the FLQ, Falardeau manages to draw a complex picture of the kidnappers, where political ambitions are mixed with personal rivalries and self-doubt. Purposefully agonising, the long closing segment of the film, following Laporte's failed attempt to escape during which he was badly hurt, shows two FLQ members debating whether to bring Laporte to a hospital and turn themselves in or to simply put the man out of his misery by strangling him. Although other films have provided serious examinations of the October crisis, in particular Michel Brault's masterpiece, *Les Ordres* (1974), *Octobre* is the only production that succeeded in giving a human face to a group of young radicals who have generally been demonised by history. A difficult film to watch, *Octobre* remains Falardeau's best feature.

In addition to being Québec cinema's most radically politicised film-maker, Falardeau is also one of its most irreverent jesters. Interviews with him generally include a mixture of harsh political commentary and wickedly funny insults (usually against the powers-that-be but sometimes even against the interviewers themselves). Some of his films exhibit this peculiar blend of vicious political attacks and rude but amusing sarcasm. *Le Temps des bouffons,* for instance, is so vulgar in its tirade of insults against members of the prestigious 'Beaver Club', that it becomes more amusingly absurd than politically engaging. Falardeau's bizarre sense of humour is most obvious in *Elvis Gratton – Le film* (1985) and *Miracle à Memphis* (1999), both starring Bob Gratton, an Elvis Presley impersonator who embodies for Falardeau all that is wrong with a segment of the French Canadian population that blindly adopts American ideology and culture. The fat, tacky, rude, ignorant Gratton, played by Julien Poulin who also co-directed the films, first appeared in three shorts, *Elvis Gratton* (1981), *Les Vacances d'Elvis Gratton* (1983), and *Pas encore Elvis Gratton!* (1985), that were compiled into the feature-length *Elvis Gratton – Le film*, which has enjoyed tremendous success on video. *Miracle à Memphis* also enjoyed a very successful theatrical release. The popularity of the two Elvis Gratton movies speaks volumes about Falardeau and Poulin's ability to hold up an ironic mirror to the people of Québec, throwing their follies back at them in the distorted form of an idiot in an Elvis outfit. While sometimes genuinely hilarious (although often moronic and juvenile), these comedies are as denunciative of American capitalism and Canadian federalism as the humourless *Octobre* and *15 février 1839.*          **AL**

# Jim FALL

*Trick* (1999)    Born in New York in 1962 and thus growing up in the 1970s, Jim Fall was dismayed with much gay representation which, from his perspective, usually followed one of two routes: self-loathing or psychosis. At a young age Fall decided that he wanted to make 'gay movies' and, after dropping out of New York University film school, and a stint in television production, this is what he did, making his first feature film, *Trick*, in 1999. Foregoing self-loathing and psychosis, the protagonist of *Trick* is more concerned that he does not fit into the gay lifestyle 'culturally': he worries he is not 'cool' enough to meet a man or sustain a relationship.

The film brings a freshness to the typical quandaries of the romantic comedy, most notably by incorporating elements of the musical. Initially, the numbers play out in a stilted manner, and the film's *leitmotif* song 'Enter You' sounds unwieldy and amateurish. However, such stiff beginnings work thematically. As the film progresses, the protagonist becomes more comfortable with both his romantic life and his own body and, appropriately, the numbers themselves become more vital. Remaining chaste, *Trick* falls well within the musical tradition, having its characters channel their sexual energy into a tune or a turn on the dance floor.

Part homage, part reinterpretation of the musical genre, *Trick* garnered accolades at the 1999 Berlin Film Festival, where it received the Siegressaule Award, and a nomination for the Grand Jury Prize at the 1999 Sundance Film Festival.          **LW**

# Rick FAMUYIWA

*Blacktop Lingo* (1996)    A graduate of the University of Southern California, born in Los Angeles in 1973, Rick
*The Wood* (1999)    Famuyiwa's first film, *Blacktop Lingo* (1996), is already lost to obscurity but it cemented a writing partnership with Tod Boyd that continued to his second feature, *The Wood*

(1999). Self-consciously distancing itself from the ghetto in its Inglewood, California setting, *The Wood* details the efforts of three friends to make it to a wedding, before diving into flashbacks of their teenage years. It demonstrates real potential, managing to portray the lives of young black men whilst avoiding the lashings of gangsterism that can so easily be piled onto the subject matter. The sequences from their youth work best and Famuyiwa has received critical praise for his sensitive direction of actors – it is certainly far superior to that seen in more high-profile releases of 1999 (*American Pie* being the most notorious example). However, *The Wood* is MTV-produced and the barrage of music is irritating, occasionally disrupting the rhythms of the film.

Famuyiwa's forthcoming production, *Brown Sugar*, is a romantic comedy in the mould of *When Harry Met Sally* (1989). **CSo**

# Peter & Bob FARRELLY

Rhode Island brothers Peter and Bob Farrelly, born in 1957 and 1958 respectively, have developed a reputation as the contemporary masters of 'low culture' comedy. Accused by critics on both sides of the Atlantic as being 'the boys who dumbed down America', the brothers' unique brand of tasteless schoolboy humour can be seen to be symptomatic of an anti-establishment comic tradition in cinema. From the anarchic slapstick of the Mack Sennett silents through to John Walters' world of the gross caricature, comedy in cinema has always been a source of transgressive pleasures and in today's politically correct world nothing offers a more socially aberrant experience than a Farrelly brothers film.

*Dumb & Dumber* (1994)
*Kingpin* (1996)
*There's Something About Mary* (1998)
*Me, Myself & Irene* (2000)
*Osmosis Jones* (2001)
*Shallow Hal* (2001)

The often-debauched comic themes that distinguish their work can be seen in *Dumb & Dumber* (1994), directed by Peter and co-produced by the pair. Jim Carrey and Jeff Daniels play two hapless losers, Harry and Lloyd, who embark on an event-filled journey to return a suitcase full of money to its rightful owner, played by Mary Swanson. With the film's emphasis on bodily functions – there are jokes about diarrhoea, flatulence, urination and vomiting – social status is abandoned in favour of a more fluid concept of identity. In the Farrelly brothers' grotesquely comic world the two incongruous fools, in classic carnivalesque tradition, fart and rise above their servile positions in society to become kings for a day.

*Kingpin* (1996), their second feature – co-directed by both – continues in this same vulgar vein, with an added dimension of surrealism. Woody Harrelson plays Roy Munsun, an ex-ten-pin-bowling champ hampered by a prosthetic rubber hand and a drug-smuggling Amish bowling partner played by Randy Quaid. Again the focus is on taboo subjects such as physical deformity and bestiality. However, the absurd, Beckett-like, surreal nature of the characters and settings allows for these normally sensitive subjects to be openly confronted and laughed at.

*There's Something About Mary* (1998) has been the brothers' biggest success to date. A series of set comic pieces – involving a grossly swollen penis, a dead dog and, most infamously, semen mistaken as hair gel – ensure that the infantile comedy comes thick and fast. The humour is rude, obtrusive and liberating in both its celebration of immaturity and its affront to authority and middle-class taste. Candidly straightforward in its quest for laughs, the comedy is strictly aimed at the gleeful humiliation of all the male characters in the film (Ben Stiller, Matt Dillon *et al.*) as they blindly pursue Mary (Cameron Diaz).

The larger-than-life Jim Carrey has a tendency to dominate, *Me, Myself & Irene* (2000). On the run with Renée Zellweger, who is escaping from her gangster lover, he plays a schizophrenic alternating between his nice-guy cop Charlie and his angry alter-ego Hank. Less inventive and hilarious then *There's Something About Mary*, it still features all the familiar visual gags, challenges every aspect of political correctness, and brims with energy.

Their next directorial effort saw a distinct shift for the brothers in both style and content. *Osmosis Jones* (2001) is a part live-action, part animated story of a sluggish and typically gross Farrellyesque zoo worker, Frank (Bill Murray), who contracts a deadly virus after consuming an egg contaminated by monkey spit. Partly set inside the ailing body of Frank (animated with restrained flair by Tom Sito and Piet Kroon), the film quite literally offers a unique chance for the Farrelly's to take the gross-out inside. However, the film is far more restrained and subtle than one would expect. This is partly due to the nature of the experiment – which is more ingenious than odious – and partly due to the PG audience at which the film is aimed.

*Shallow Hal* (2001) sees the brothers return to more familiar territory. Superficial deadbeat Hal (Jack Black) has his perceptions of feminine beauty altered by self-help guru Tony Robbins (played by Tony Robbins), which results in him falling in love with a grossly obese woman (Gwyneth Paltrow). The film itself is oddly paradoxical in that it deals with the subject of obesity, a prime subject for the Farrelly's normally merciless brand of humour, yet it is far more empathetic than any of their previous films. The humour in *Shallow Hal* is subtle rather than palpable and conveys a sense of maturity that is unexpected and at times philosophically refreshing.

Despite this newfound maturity, the Farrelly brothers can be seen as comic voyeurs who are carrying on the tradition of *Animal House* (1978) using low humour as a means of taking the human body, rather than gender difference, as a source of comedy.     **PH**

## Jon FAVREAU

*Made* (2001)   The writer and star of the hit film *Swingers* (1996), Jon Favreau has fared less well with his directorial debut, *Made* (2001). A comedy about two would-be hoodlums, Favreau plays Bobby, a boxer and bodyguard, who is forced to carry out a courier job for Peter Falk's Mob boss after he beats up a prospective client. Enlisting the help of Ricky, his loud-mouthed friend, they set off for New York, where Ricky's inability to follow orders results in confusion, betrayal and their near execution at the hands of a rival gang.

Whereas *Swingers* offered a refreshingly funny take on a group of twentysomething men enjoying life without love in LA, *Made* is an all-too-familiar journey into an over-parodied genre, populated by a collection of tired stereotypes. Missing the directorial flair that Doug Liman brought to the earlier film, *Made* soon descends into broad farce, only occasionally hitting its target. It is left to Vince Vaughan to inject some energy into the film. Playing Ricky as an imbecilic show-off, his performance veers between the offensive and embarrassing, and he is certainly deserving of better material. Although Sean Coombs offers a fine cameo as the duo's New York contact, neither his nor Vaughan's performances are capable of rescuing such a mediocre film.     **IHS**

## John FAWCETT

*The Boys Club* (1997)   Born in Canada in 1968, John Fawcett enjoyed a career directing episodes for high-
*Ginger Snaps* (2000)   profile sword and sorcery and action adventure television shows such as 'Xena: Warrior Princess' and 'La Femme Nikita', before directing his debut feature, a coming-of-age saga, *The Boys Club* (1997). Though little seen, the film fared well in Canada, earning the first-time director a prestigious Genie award nomination.

The tale opens on three feuding friends who stumble across a mysterious man in their secret shack in the wood. Both wounded and armed, they decide to help him rather than make a report to the authorities; the film goes on to follow the moral and ethical crisis that escalates from their collective error in judgment. Dominic Zamprogna, Stuart Stone and rising star Devon Sawa are well equipped to play the increasingly fractious chums and Chris Penn as the stranger oozes intrigue and charm. Ultimately, however, the film is elevated above generic counterparts such as *Stand By Me* (1986) and *River's Edge* (1986) by the quality of Peter Wellington's script and Fawcett's confident and relaxed direction.

After a brief return to television, Fawcett achieved critical success and attention with his feature *Ginger Snaps* (2000). A horror movie aficionado, he took the conventions of the werewolf genre and smartly turned them on their head, imbuing the film with such disparate themes as small-town ennui, outsiderism, familial dysfunction and the onset of female puberty. The result is a strangely beguiling and highly effective hybrid, part *Carrie* (1976), part *American Werewolf in London* (1981) via Todd Solondz. Once again, Fawcett gathered a talented cast – newcomers Emily Perkins and Katharine Isabelle are perfect as pubescent siblings Brigitte and Ginger, and Mimi Rogers delivers a neat cameo as their mother. Fawcett's strong-minded co-writer, Karen Walton, lends the proceedings the requisite feminine (and feminist) authenticity.

Despite a disappointing dénouement that revealed the limitations of the budget, *Ginger Snaps* is genuinely original fare, and it is to be hoped that Fawcett, a perceptive director able to inject fresh blood into flagging genres, will more permanently make the move from small screen to large. **JWo**

# Guy FERLAND

Guy Ferland understands the holy trinity of modern American moviemaking: sex, violence and rock 'n' roll. Directors from Scorsese to Tarantino have built some of the most imaginative cinema of recent years on these basic blocks; what matters is the style in which you treat them. Style is something Ferland has shown in abundance, dealing with various genres and narrative modes with intelligence and a flair for visual storytelling. However, his easily packaged plots and lack of real commercial punch have resulted in few international releases for his films, and most of them having been unjustly relegated to the straight-to-video market.

*The Babysitter* (1995) opens in a straight, naturalistic vein – a couple hire a babysitter, who invites her boyfriend over for company. Real events then become subsumed beneath layers of erotic, voyeuristic and even violent male fantasy towards the babysitter; events occur and repeat only to be distorted, ending differently according to the outlook of each fantasist, who include her boyfriend, her employer, and even the young boy she is babysitting. Principally a meditation on male objectification of women, the film is intriguing in its admission of complicity; it is as much about the way movies, necessarily including Ferland's own, have distorted male views of women. Though difficult to follow and somewhat overwrought, this is nevertheless an intriguing example of stylised, non-linear film-making.

*Telling Lies in America* (1997) is more conventional, thanks largely to an over-earnest script from Joe Eszterhas. A rites-of-passage drama set in 1960s Cleveland, the film is the story of Karchy, a young Hungarian immigrant seduced by the promises of the American dream, symbolised by outrageous DJ Billy Magic. Ferland's themes of illusion and fantasy fulfilment resurface here: the brash, ersatz and sexy rock 'n' roll image of Magic inevitably gives way to a cynical and corrupt heart, and Karchy's American dream emerges as self-delusional fantasy, as does his idealised image of love-interest Diney. Again, Ferland's style underpins his themes, with his own seductive camerawork and art direction of the Magic world becoming increasingly fake as the story progresses – an interesting slant, given the part cinema may have played in attracting immigrants to an unrealistic image of America.

Ferland's more recent work – not theatrically released – has continued his interest in experimenting with the conventions and styles of traditional genre stories. *Delivered* (1998) is essentially a straight psychological thriller in which a pizza delivery boy unwittingly glimpses a murder and becomes embroiled in a deadly pursuit. The story betrays Ferland's fascination with exploitation and manipulation, and his imaginative realisation of the chase – facilitated by a tape-recorded diary and one-by-one killing of Will's friends – is aided by some tense direction and sly homages to celebrated thrillers and directors of the past. *After the Storm* (2001) is based on a Hemingway short story in which a luxury yacht goes down in bad weather, and examines the breakdown of relationships and morals in the race to acquire the yacht's lucrative salvage. Another example of Ferland's ability to marry impressive cinematography and atmospheric action, with his interest in duplicity and betrayal, this is slick if unremarkable film-making, heavy on style but rather lacking in substance. This may be a recurrent motif of his films to date, but to hit truly consistent form or box-office success, he deserves more than the straight-to-video bin has to offer. **OB**

*The Babysitter* (1995)
*Telling Lies in America* (1997)

# Abel FERRARA

Born in the Bronx in 1952, Abel Ferrara started making amateur films on Super 8 in his late teens before making his official debut with violent low-budget productions such as *Driller Killer* (1979) and *Ms. 45* (1981). Referred to by one critic as the 'seediest low-down renegade in American cinema', Ferrara continues to produce films marked by visceral extremity and existential confusion. However, his films can also be read as moral parables. He continually dwells on issues surrounding religion, salvation, and self-destruction, and although the plethora of unsavoury characters that live within his pessimistic, bleak cityscapes always have the slim chance of redemption, few seem

*Driller Killer* (1979)
*Ms. 45* (1981)
*Fear City* (1984)
*China Girl* (1987)
*Cat Chaser* (1989)
*King of New York* (1990)
*Bad Lieutenant* (1992)
*Body Snatchers* (1993)

able, or willing, to take it. Equally erratic and prolific, Ferrara sets out to exploit, shock, and outrage his audience with his increasingly introspective views of the morally corrupt human condition.

His first feature, *Driller Killer*, sets the tone for his later films. Upon its release in the UK, the film found itself caught up in the folk-devil frenzy surrounding 'video nasties'. Consequently the film remained banned until 1999. It would, however, be a mistake to think that the film is a simplistic exercise in gore-terrorism. The story of the frustrated artist (played by Ferrara), driven by his irksome noisy neighbours to drill everyone to death, is more in the tradition of 'high art' exploitation films, such as Polanski's *Repulsion* (1965), rather than being a careless exploitation flick. Nihilistic and sickly humorous, the film manages to capture a hopeless vision of urban and moral decay, and has the savage intelligence that characterises Ferrara's later work. Basking in his reputation as a 'shock' director, Ferrara enhanced his infamous standing with his next offerings. The critically well-received *Ms. 45* came first, a violent role-reversal film exploring the vengeful mind of a rape victim, followed by the hypercharged and excessively brutal *Fear City* (1984). After working in television for the next two years on shows such as 'Miami Vice' and 'Crime Story', Ferrara returned to the big screen in 1987 with his modern adaptation of the 'Romeo and Juliet' story. *China Girl* is a tale of star-crossed lovers from rival youth gangs in New York City and marks a departure from explorations of the darker side of city life. His next project, the straight-to-video *Cat Chaser* (1989), was a confusing and essentially dull adaptation of an Elmore Leonard novel.

It was not until the release of his next film, *King of New York* (1990), that Ferrara would cement his reputation as a film maverick. Christopher Walken plays the maniacal Mafia boss who pathologically instils fear in all he meets and extracts a terrible vengeance on all who dare to cross him. As a parable on malignancy, the film offers Walken one his most memorable roles to date and paves the way for Ferrara's bleakest film yet, the visceral and immensely powerful *Bad Lieutenant* (1992). Here Ferrara elicits a truly nightmarish performance from Harvey Kietel as a corrupt New York detective hell-bent on a course towards self-destruction. Although at times difficult to watch, this is quintessential Ferrara, bathed in Catholic guilt, remonstration and redemption. *Bad Lieutenant* has endlessly courted controversy since its release, but its combination of exhibitionism, drugs, and blasphemy is considered by many to be the director's masterpiece – Martin Scorsese went as far as saying it was the film he wanted his *Last Temptation of Christ* (1988) to be. The film also marked the beginning of a period of frenetic intensity for Ferrara.

Over the next six years he would release eight films, including *Body Snatchers* (1993), an eerie re-working of the Don Siegel classic, *Dangerous Game* (1993), a relentlessly grim film within a film, and *The Addiction* (1995), an allegorical vampire movie shot in black and white. *The Addiction* serves to perfectly illustrate Ferrara's obsession with the collapse of moral order as Lili Taylor, the philosophy student-turned-reluctant vampire, finds herself in moral turmoil as she is torn between self-denial and her insatiable desires.

In 1996 Ferrara revisited the gangster genre with *The Funeral*, a period piece with an existential vision of familial violence. Christopher Walken again provides Ferrara with a deadpan canvas on which to paint his vision of a man tormented by inner demons. It is essentially a film about mood and emotion, and is, in some respects, an answer to the hyper-reality and oblique posturing of other Mafia movies of the period. *The Blackout*, Ferrara's 1997 tribute to Hitchcock, switches location from his favoured seedy New York backdrop to the opulent vogue of Miami. Like *Dangerous Game* this is a film within a film, with Matthew Modine playing a movie star with a dreadful secret. The protagonist wallows in an all-consuming self-obsession, and his eventual confrontation with his inner demons results in confession and violent retribution. *New Rose Hotel* (1998) sees Ferrara taking a sojourn into the cyber-punk genre. Based on William Gibson's short story, the film captures the bleakness and despair of a man, Willem Dafoe, trapped within a nightmarish world of his own making. The film was panned by critics in the US, confusing audiences with its bleak vision and unconventional use of narrative flashbacks. Subsequently the film has failed to achieve a UK release.

Ferrara continues to split the critical vote with his work. His films are seen as either passionate near-masterpieces or aberrations of visceral extravagance. Love him or loathe him, it is patently clear that his continuing fixation with the shocking, sometimes subversive, nature of his protagonists – the gangsters, murderers, maniacs, corrupt cops, and philosophising vampires – renders him an auteur in his own right. Yet beyond the brutality and pessimism of his films Ferrara continually, and perhaps surprisingly, offers salvation as a possibility. As he says: 'Redemption is a moment-to-moment reality … it's a struggle between heaven and hell.' His recent *R' Xmas* has yet to be widely released.                                                                                   **PH**

# Todd FIELD

Born in California in 1964, Todd Field is an experienced actor, most famously playing the *In the Bedroom* (2001) mysterious pianist Nick Nightingale in Stanley Kubrick's *Eyes Wide Shut* (1999). Having made a variety of shorts – *Nonnie & Alex* and *When I Was A Boy*, amongst others – he directed his debut feature, one of the most successful and well-reviewed family dramas in recent years, *In the Bedroom* (2001). A slow-burner and sleeper hit, it unexpectedly caught the public imagination, further buoyed by Sissy Spacek winning a Golden Globe and an Academy Award nomination for Best Actress; the acting is uniformly excellent.

Set in a coastal town in Maine, the opening shots invoke an idyllic atmosphere – Natalie (Marisa Tomei) is having a relationship with Frank (Nick Stahl) and the two are in love. But gradually, a more problematic situation emerges: she is the mother of two young boys with an estranged and angry husband, and he is about to go to college to study; their disparity in age is a cause of concern, particularly to his mother Ruth (Spacek). Frank's father, Matt (Tom Wilkinson), is less interfering. When tragedy occurs, however, and Frank is killed, Ruth and Matt are forced not only to face and come to terms with their loss, but also to crucially deal with the drift of their own relationship.

An adult drama, the material is intelligently and sensitively handled. The dialogue is entirely plausible as are the character choices and reactions. With the family unit rendered apart, the parents slowly realise how their past choices have come to affect their current lives: Matt works as a doctor rather than on the sea catching lobsters as he would like to; Ruth has never had another child and it is now too late. They vent their frustrations on one another. While the film's events are by their nature dramatic, they are never sensationalised and for this type of Hollywood genre piece, the ending is unusual and challenging. Writer David Lodge has suggested that the reason *In the Bedroom* was so unexpectedly popular at a specific time in America is due to the events of 11 September: people could relate to the fact that the mother and father wanted to create their own justice system and exact revenge or retribution – feeling empathetic, they were less inclined to moralise.                                                                   **HP**

# Mike FIGGIS

Born in Carlisle, UK, in 1948, Mike Figgis was raised in Nairobi, and relocated with his *Stormy Monday* (1988) family to Newcastle when he was eight. He is an adept writer, composer and musician, *Internal Affairs* (1990) as well as one of the most innovative and independently minded directors working today. *Liebestraum* (1991) He is critical of Hollywood and sees it as an environment where creativity and vision are *Mr Jones* (1993) stifled in order to maximise profits and maintain its hierarchical structure. During his *The Browning Version* (1994) teenage years Figgis' first love was music; he was in a band, Gas Board, with future Roxy *Leaving Las Vegas* (1995) Music frontman Bryan Ferry. After moving to London to study music he joined avant- *One Night Stand* (1997) garde theatre troupe The People Show as a musician and performer and toured around *The Loss of Sexual Innocence* the world. After leaving The People Show in 1980, he formed his own theatre company, (1999) The Mike Figgis Group. It was at this point that he began his work in film, producing *Miss Julie* (1999) multi-media productions. Some of his early experimental works caught the attention of *Time Code* (2000) Channel 4 and they funded his first film, a television feature, *The House* (1984). *Hotel* (2001)

He wrote, scored and directed his breakthrough feature, *Stormy Monday* (1988). Set in Newcastle's jazz scene, the loving attention to detail and the construction of its edgy, smoky milieu illustrates Figgis' familiarity with, and sympathy for, the environment. It also works as a homage to Hollywood film noir, featuring an impressive cast including Sting, Tommy Lee Jones and Melanie Griffith, as well as some beautiful and highly stylised cinematography. The plot, however, moves along at an uneven pace that stifles the momentum. A moderate success, it brought Figgis to the attention of Hollywood.

His first American feature, *Internal Affairs* (1990), was a hard-hitting tale of police corruption, and here Figgis further perfected the sharp and stylish. The film boasts superb performances from Richard Gere as the creepy crooked cop, and Andy Garcia, his nemesis, resurrecting the former's career and making a star out of the latter. A box-office success, it also cemented Figgis' reputation as a bankable director.

His next feature, *Liebestraum* (1991), did not fare so well. Critics complained that its plot was convoluted, bordering on the nonsensical. The saving grace of this story of dark family secrets and corruption is the modish, economical way Figgis draws out the psychological agonies of his complicated characters. His next feature, *Mr Jones* (1993), did not mark a return to form. Trying his hand at romance, he produced an uneven work centring on the romance between Richard Gere, as a charming manic-depressive, who falls in love with his psychiatrist, played by Lena Olin. The film was a commercial flop and critics failed to warm to Gere's unstable charms.

Another commercial failure followed with *The Browning Version* (1994), a remake of the 1951 classic starring Michael Redgrave, which was adapted from Terrence Rattigan's 1948 play. In Figgis' film, Redgrave's character, Andrew Crocker Harris, is played by Albert Finney. This is no *Goodbye Mr Chips* (1939); the schoolmaster has no faith in the future, himself, his wife, or his profession. His despair is encapsulated in his poignant rhetorical question, 'How can we mould civilised beings if we no longer believe in civilisation?' Despite sterling performances from Finney, Greta Scacchi, and Michael Gambon, Figgis' *Browning Version* does not match up to the original. After a period of successive failures, the director finally found the project that would bring him international success. *Leaving Las Vegas* (1995) earned four Academy Award nominations, and won Nicolas Cage the Best Actor award. The film centres on Ben Sanderson, an alcoholic screenwriter hell-bent on drinking himself to death in Las Vegas. He forms an unlikely and uncomfortable bond with prostitute Sera, played by Elisabeth Shue. Unable to comprehend why he is so dedicated to his own destruction, he refuses to make her understand. They accept each other as flawed individuals, however; Sera does not save him and we do not know if she can even save herself. The relationship goes beyond the usual romantic love and beyond the Hollywood happy endings. This is a deeply human story of redemption – who receives it, who shuns it, and who deserves it. For Ben, if there were redemption available he would refuse it. Sera's redemption is Ben, or at least the care she shows him, and the dignity with which she does it. *Leaving Las Vegas* achieved enormous critical and box-office success, particularly for an independent film shot on Super 16mm.

*Leaving Las Vegas* was a difficult film to follow and Figgis' next project, *One Night Stand* (1997), did not live up to expectation. It is a weak drama starring Nastassja Kinski, Robert Downey Jr and Wesley Snipes, and was a box-office and critical failure. The film follows Max (Snipes), a successful LA-based professional who arrives in town to spend some time with his friend Charlie (Downey) who has been diagnosed with HIV. Whilst in New York he has an encounter with Karen (Kinski), a married woman – the 'one night stand' of the title. This is a disappointingly weak tale that seems to lead nowhere.

The *Loss of Sexual Innocence* (1999) marks his first foray into experimental cinema since his days with The Mike Figgis Group in the 1980s. It is an autobiographical, intensely personal portrayal of sexual awakening, longing and experiment, told through the re-working of the Adam and Eve story. Figgis' film caused controversy for casting a black Adam and a white Eve. He had attempted to make the film some years before, but the financial backers were unhappy with the script. He lays the blame at the door of the distributors, saying: 'The distributors basically said, "I don't like the idea of a black man fucking a white woman"'; when they asked him to reverse the roles Figgis, quite rightly, refused.

His stylish direction and experimental concerns are highly evident in *Miss Julie* (1999), his adaptation of August Strindberg's play. The film is thematically concerned with the chasms dividing class and gender, played out against the backdrop of a Swedish Count's estate. Miss Julie, the Count's daughter, seeks love and affirmation after being jilted by her fiancé. Jean is her 'below stairs' lover, an avowed social climber. Each of the characters crave what they perceive the other has to offer; theirs is a pragmatic, selfish kind of love. Figgis used some highly innovative techniques to construct the dense and claustrophobic *mise-en-scène*. He had a 360-degree one-room stage constructed for the entire film. The action was shot using two hand-held Super 16mm cameras, one in the hands of the cinematographer and one operated by Figgis himself. The action was filmed in sequence, in long, 15-minute takes. A tight space is created around characters, forcing the audience to focus on their expressions, their mannerisms and movements, while the lighting works in expressionistic contrasts of light and shade. *Miss Julie* was not made to achieve commercial success, but rather to continue the director's passion for cinema in all its forms. Some critics disapproved of the film, arguing it was more like theatre than film. Figgis agrees, arguing, 'Theatre is gorgeous and film is theatre – unfortunately most films are bad theatre'.

His most audacious and experimental film to date, *Time Code* (2000), splits the screen into four sections to show four separate but intertwining stories played out in one continuous take using digital cameras, in real time. In the top left-hand corner is Salma Hayek's grasping wannabe starlet. Next to her in the top right-hand corner runs the tale of a down-trodden and lonely wife, played by Saffron Burrows. She is married to a film producer, played by Stellan Skarsgård, who is featured in the bottom left-hand screen at a movie production meeting, and bottom right, escaping the meeting to cheat on his wife with Hayek's character. *Time Code* received mixed reviews: some critics were stimulated by his experimentalism and others saw the split screen as nothing but a gimmick.

Two of Figgis' recent projects have seen him return to his experimental roots after too long in Hollywood. *Hotel* (2001), a project set in Venice that is similar to *Time Code*, involves over thirty actors, including Salma Hayek and David Schwimmer, who worked without a script. In a period of change generated by digital technology Figgis is excited by new possibilities and also interested in exploring ways of using digital projection to turn any space with seating into a digital cinema. A film based on the battle between strikers and the police in 1984 during the mining strikes, titled *The Battle of Orgreave*, may well be screened late 2002/early 2003.                                                  **SL**

# David FINCHER

Born in Colorado in 1963, one of the more accomplished directors to have emerged from the field of music video (several of which he made for Madonna), David Fincher has thus far demonstrated a striking consistency of vision. Notable for their focus on dystopian despair, societal decay and moral breakdown, his films are equally distinctive through their thoroughly postmodern cynicism. This is complemented by a recurring commitment to striking formal and stylistic design which frame the films' thematic resonances in an often stunning visual schemata.

*Alien³* (1992)
*Se7en* (1995)
*The Game* (1997)
*Fight Club* (1999)
*Panic Room* (2002)

Given the reports of director/studio antagonism during its production, it is intriguing in retrospect how much *Alien³* (1992) prefigures Fincher's later work. Expanding the parameters of the *Alien* series, the film rejects the action heroics and Reaganite, militaristic inflections of *Aliens* (1986) and instead develops Ripley's (Sigourney Weaver) status as woman and mother figure in an all-male prison environment populated almost exclusively by murderers and rapists. This is compounded by the repeated references to contamination and disease, an apt metaphor for the fear the monster figure embodies in the AIDS era. The sexual threat embodied by the alien in Ridley Scott's original film is partly supplanted here by that represented by the convicts. The film also contrasts the nurturing instincts of the monster with those of Ripley as, devastated by the loss of her adoptive child from the previous film, she discovers the presence of an alien foetus in her body. Aware of the far greater threat her condition poses (the foetus is an egg-laying queen), Ripley becomes the sacrificial Christ figure, especially ironic given the prison community's supposed new-found religious convictions. Fincher accentuates the claustrophobia of this prison planet through constant low angled shots and a copper-toned colour scheme which is at once oppressive and mournful. Suffering from both murky characterisation (Weaver's role excepted) and misguided adherence to generic convention (the regular dispatch of minor characters, repetitive subjective alien-eye shots), the film nevertheless utilises the series' mythology in order to form its own distinct identity. Ripley's final self sacrifice, at once strangling and embracing her alien infant as she plunges into a fiery furnace, echoes the similar plunges into space taken by her foes in the climaxes to the previous films in the series. By taking the fall herself, Ripley foils the powers intent on using the creature for militaristic ends and seemingly ensures that the devastating, polymorphous power of the alien perishes, clasped to her bosom.

While Fincher's first film located its futuristic vision of decay in the far reaches of space, *Se7en* (1995) depicts a thoroughly contemporary, postmodern nightmare. Its presentation of an evil figure counteracting sin in an oppressive urban milieu is played against the notion of secular and spiritual faith as it resides in both of the protagonists, Detectives Mills (Brad Pitt) and Somerset (Morgan Freeman). The film balances Somerset's despair at the ongoing apathy of modern living with its relentless presentation of a city defined by its adherence to sin. Through repeated literary and religious allusion, the concept of sin is transformed from its theological basis into a tangible trait of the population of the film's unnamed city. The central symbol of Mills and his wife's (Gwyneth Paltrow) home vibrating to the rumble of passing trains underlines the tenuous nature of perceived traditional values in this environment. The ultimate revelation of the avenging, demonic killer as a literal 'John Doe' (for that is the only name he is given) is chilling for the way in which it connects his own recognition of his surface banality with the extremity of his often ingenious acts. Striking in both its visual and sound design, the film is one of the key works of Hollywood in the 1990s, distinguished not only by its despairing tone but also by its thoughtful screenplay (written by Andrew Kevin Walker) which reconfigures themes and motifs from the detective and serial killer sub-genres. It also boasts one of the most striking title sequences ever. Its bleakness of tone is not alleviated in any way and this alienated several commentators. Indeed, the film might be accused of the very 'apathy' that Somerset himself berates – the 'shock' climax and subsequent spiritual defeat of its protagonists defies convention and has a powerful thematic force but offers no viable alternative to the dystopia it presents.

*The Game* (1997) is a relative disappointment, a reworking of the paranoid conspiracy thriller in which a millionaire investment banker (played by Michael Douglas) partakes in the bizarre and elaborate 'game' of the title. The film suggests that wealth and power begets stasis and complacency and that stimulation is therefore only possible through the systematic stripping of personal and financial assets. The sinister corporation which orchestrates this scenario therefore lays bare the illusory nature of power. Lacking the political dimension which distinguishes many of the conspiracy thrillers of the 1960s and 1970s, the film ultimately plays as an elaborate hoax, reflecting its treatment of an age in which even fear and paranoia are manufactured and consumed. In the wake of *Se7en*, the final redemption of the film's protagonist seems trite, as if Fincher had listened to the voices which objected to his previous film's unforgiving dénouement. Submitting to the same suicidal fate of the father whose lasting influence he has long resisted, Douglas survives to discover the true nature of the game and its controlling figures, thus negating the narrative symmetry that the film has seemingly worked towards. While never less than intriguing on a narrative level, the film is ultimately as hollow as its central figure.

*Fight Club* (1999) represents a thematic and stylistic summation of Fincher's work to date. Encompassing the disenfranchised male community of *Alien³*, the urban despair of *Se7en*, and the narrative conundrums of *The Game*, its dazzling surfaces provide an apt canvas for its enactment of masculinist assertion in a sterile world. Starting literally in its protagonist's (Ed Norton) brain, the film plays as a quasi-Freudian conflict between his ego and id (as represented by Brad Pitt's Tyler Durden). The 'fight club' of the title (in which men pummel each other to a pulp in pursuit of a vaguely sado-erotic fulfilment) proves merely the starting point for a wider terrorist movement which seeks to dismantle the corporate structures of the USA. In contrast to *The Game*, the struggle against powerful corporate forces is depicted from the lower end of the social scale with Norton's character actively (or, given the film's ultimate narrative twist, unconsciously) choosing to shed his middle-class trappings. Through this linking of masculinist and anarchic drives, the film deviates from Fincher's previous work through giving full expression to its central characters' frustrations. The oppressive urban landscape is quite literally dismantled by the film's conclusion and in turn the underlying economic forces are thrown into disarray. Criticised by many for its fascistic (or, at least, Nietzschean) undertones, the ultimate sense is that of chaos rather than control. Once again Fincher is left with a world of moral and spiritual confusion with seemingly nowhere better to go.

Dividing critical opinion, *Panic Room* (2002) can be seen as either an above-average thriller or David Fincher on autopilot. His weakest film after *Alien³*, it stars Jodie Foster and Kristen Stewart as a mother and daughter held captive by a group of thieves, trapped in the panic room of their new home, with the object that the thieves want. What follows is a battle of nerves between the criminals and Foster's resourceful mother, and though lacking the originality of both *Se7en* and *Fight Club*, and less playful than *The Game*, *Panic Room* remains an engrossing thriller. From the opening credits, with its echoes of Saul Bass' graphic work for *North by Northwest* (1959), Fincher's film is both homage to Hitchcock and a showpiece for his technical virtuosity. In the most impressive scene, Fincher shoots the break-in, à la *Rope* (1948), as though it were one continuous shot, during which his camera passes through a banister, a room partition and the aperture of a coffee jug. Later, as Foster runs across one level, the camera pans down to reveal the thieves crossing the floor below. A reference to *The Lodger* (1926), it both impresses and draws attention away from the holes in David Koepp's script. Foster and Forrest Whittaker are well cast in their roles of captive and captor, though they hardly break new ground. Fincher, meanwhile, appears to have fun working on a smaller scale. Oddly, although the film's action takes place in only a few rooms, it is his least claustrophobic work.

Fincher has recently signed up to direct Tom Cruise in *Mission Impossible 3* (scheduled for 2004). **NJ & IHS**

# Thom FITZGERALD

One hopes that Thom Fitzgerald is not a one-hit wonder. One of many gay film-makers to emerge from North America in the mid-1990s, his films explore the complexities of memory through attention to surface, form and structure, balanced with a ripe sensuality, bawdy good humour and emotional ballast (not surprisingly, Fitzgerald admires Terence Davies' films). Still, his debut feature, *The Hanging Garden* (1997), showed a keener grip than its follow-up, a top-heavy film about the muscle magazines of the 1950s called *Beefcake* (1999).

*The Hanging Garden* (1997)
*Beefcake* (1999)

Fitzgerald was born in New York in 1968 and, after graduating from the Nova Scotia School of Art and Design, moved to Halifax and struggled to develop his debut feature for over three years. Ironically, when *The Hanging Garden* emerged it turned out to be a film about the persistence of family roots. When Sweet William, a twentysomething gay man, returns to his fraught family in rural Nova Scotia, he finds the past lingering. Most potently, in an astutely handled surreal twist, William's overweight and suicidal ten-year-old self still hangs from a tree in his father's lush garden. Fitzgerald almost swamps the film with densely poetic symbolism (the religious implications of the father's garden paradise, characters named after flowers, an elaborate colour scheme) but smartly grounds any formal fancies in emotionally complex writing and excellent casting. The result won the Toronto City Award for best Canadian feature at the 1997 Toronto International Film Festival.

From 'trouble in paradise' motifs to explorations of the body and memory, *Beefcake* carries many themes over from its predecessor. A queer reclamation of the muscle magazines of the 1950s, it gleefully shows how Bob Mizer's 'Athletic Model Guild' and 'Physique Pictorial' offered well-oiled images of self-improvement to McCarthy's American youth that appear, in retrospect, plainly homoerotic. Sadly, despite its geniality, Fitzgerald's conspicuously formal offering juggles undigested gobbets of documentary footage, variable personal recollections, arid courtroom drama and cheesy B-movie recreation to diffuse effect. Indeed, he almost swamps his film's key tension: witness the fun he has with these clandestine 'stroke mags' and the contention that Mizer exploited youths fresh off the bus in LA for both sex and 'body fascist' imagery. Still, if *Beefcake*'s potential to do for the muscle magazines what *Boogie Nights* (1997) did for the 1970s porn industry goes to waste, its ambition, scope and thematic richness are still to be admired.

Fitzgerald has been out of the limelight since then, although he hasn't stopped working. In *Wolf Girl* (2001), directed for television, he folded a teen-angst tale into classic lycanthropy mythology. For *The Wild Dogs*, the tale of a Canadian pornographer who becomes involved in Romanian street life which is currently in production, he has adopted a docu-drama style. He is also working on *The Event*, which boasts an excellent indie cast – Parker Posey, Don McKellar, Brent Carver and Sarah Polley. **KH**

# Gary FLEDER

A director whose initial fame derived from his debut's loose thematic and structural association to the films of Quentin Tarantino, Gary Fleder has proven himself to be

*Things to Do in Denver When You're Dead* (1995)

a solid director. Over two features he has progressed from a flippant spin on the conventional gangster film to a big-budget thriller, honing his talent to the demands of mainstream Hollywood.

Purporting to be more hip and knowing than it actually is, *Things to Do in Denver When You're Dead* (1995) profits from an impressive ensemble of actors and fine dialogue from Scott Rosenberg. Andy Garcia plays Jimmie 'The Saint' Tosnia, an ex-gangster required to complete one last job for a crippled mobster, Christopher Walken's 'The Man With The Plan'. When the job goes wrong and the mobster puts a contract out on Jimmie's crew, the film attempts to become elegiac in tone, as Jimmie and his friends reminisce about their times together and share their regrets of a life tainted by crime.

Fleder's fluid direction belies the overly schematic plot and occasional nastiness that undermines *Things to Do in Denver When You're Dead*. He also manages to move the action forward at a fair speed and draws a number of fine performances from an eclectic cast. Most impressive are the scenes involving Christopher Lloyd's 'Pieces'. A man who has spent most of his life suffering and who waits for his death as a welcome alternative to the years of pain and misery, Fleder and Lloyd work well together to emphasise the pathos of Rosenberg's tragic character. Fleder also proves himself adept at changing pace and mood with relative ease. Jimmie's relationship with the women in his life offer lighter moments against the backdrop of the impending tragedy, before both strands merge, for an interesting, if pat, resolution. However, although intermittently entertaining, Fleder's feature debut could have benefited from a less mechanical plot and more character depth.

*Kiss the Girls* (1997) is based on the first of James Patterson's phenomenally successful Alex Cross novels. Drawing obvious comparisons with *The Silence of the Lambs* (1991), Fleder's film is a taut thriller that once again profits from two excellent central performances. Morgan Freeman plays criminal psychologist Cross, who becomes involved in an investigation to hunt down a serial killer when his niece is kidnapped. With the help of the one woman who escaped from her abductor, Cross tracks down the killer whose pleasure lies not in killing his victims, but imprisoning them.

A disturbing thriller, *Kiss the Girls* works most effectively in its opening hour, when Ashley Judd's Kate McTiernan is abducted. Fleder effectively conveys both Kate's disorientation in her new environment and the fear of the other abductees. Her escape from the labyrinthine corridors of the underground prison is handled with considerable verve. Shot mostly in close-up, the chase is made terrifying through its economic use of space, never revealing the distance between victim and captor. Although the later stages of the film lack both the tension and paranoia of the earlier scenes, *Kiss the Girls* is an improvement on *Things to Do in Denver When Your Dead* and reinforces Fleder's position as a capable director.

*Don't Say a Word* (2001) is something of a disappointment. A run-of-the-mill thriller, it features Michael Douglas as a psychologist coerced by a gang of criminals into discovering a secret, that will reveal the whereabouts of a priceless gem, concealed within the damaged psyche of Brittany Murphy's patient. With a visual style somewhere between a pop promo and a car advert, it is at best an entertaining diversion. Fleder's direction lacks subtlety, undermining any of the thrills of Anthony Peckham's script. With Douglas acting on autopilot, and Sean Bean – having now overtaken Steven Berkoff as the resident bad Brit in Hollywood – hammy as the chief villain, only Murphy and homicide officer Jennifer Esposito inject any emotion or intelligence into the film.

Originally conceived as a short feature for television, *Imposter* (2002) is an effective adaptation of a Philip K. Dick short story. Set in a distant future, when the Earth is under attack from an alien power, Gary Sinise plays a scientist involved in the construction of a super-bomb that will annihilate the enemy. While awaiting the arrival of a dignitary, he is apprehended by Vincent D'Onofrio's investigator, who believes he has in fact been replaced by a replicant whose body conceals an explosive device, set to trigger within close proximity of the super bomb.

The anti-war message present in Dick's original story is entirely absent in Fleder's film. What remains is a collage of images culled from dystopian science fiction films of the last twenty years, accompanied by an exhausting chase through the urban sprawl of an all-too-familiar metropolis in a state of severe decay. Sinise, D'Onofrio and Madeleine Stowe, as the doctor's wife, compensate for the lack of originality in Scott Rosenberg's lazy script. Fleder also does his best to engage the audience. However, the film betrays its origins and remains little more than a diversion in the career of a director who quite obviously has much more to offer than his recent record has shown. **IHS**

# Richard FLEISCHER

Born in New York in 1916, son of animation pioneer Max Fleischer and brother of minor actress Ruth, Richard Flesicher began his mainly distinguished film-making career after training in the drama department at Yale University. In 1942, he joined RKO's New York studios to work on the RKO-Pathé newsreel operations where he wrote and directed the 'This is America' series and 1944's *Memo for Joe*, a short documentary about the US Community Chest Wartime Charity Program. The success of his work allowed him to move to RKO's Hollywood feature film studio.

He began his fictional film-making career with some socially conscious dramatic works such as *Child of Divorce* (1946), in which he offered one of the first serious treatments of the subject, focusing on its impact on the divorcees' child. The Hays Production Code, very much in evidence during this period, disallowed the notion of any 'immorality' to be attached to divorce and demanded Fleischer's thoughtful, tactful approach. He followed with another drama, *Banjo* (1947), a family movie about a girl sent to live in Boston after a lifetime growing up on her family's farm. Her faithful dog, the eponymous Banjo, follows her, and, in true 'Lassie' style, the film follows their misadventures. Another misadventure theme was worked into Fleischer's next film, *So This is New York* (1948), the story of a rural man who is dragged to New York City by his upwardly mobile wife and sister – the usual fish-out-of-water tale.

Fleischer's subsequent feature is notable now for its relationship to the great American independent auteur Robert Altman: 1948's *Bodyguard* was based on a story by Altman and filmed as a pretty routine thriller bolstered by a strong performance from Lawrence Tierney. The visual style evokes film noir, something that would become evident in several of Fleischer's subsequent films. *Follow Me Quietly* (1949), *Trapped* (1949), and *The Clay Pigeon* (1949) all mark a very productive period of noir-style crime thrillers, dealing as they do with variations on counterfeiting and including darker hints of violence, conveyed with a compact and effective directorial touch. During this time, Fleischer put his name to an uncharacteristically lighter movie – the oddly titled *Make Mine Laughs* (1949) – a compilation of RKO comedy material fashioned in the vaudeville vein.

*Armored Car Robbery* (1950) and *His Kind of Woman* (1951, on which John Farrow is credited as director) mark a return to darkness and crime. The former is a tautly constructed and executed thriller about a well-planned robbery which goes horribly wrong, resulting in the deaths of both the police and the robbers. Robert Mitchum stars in the latter as a gangster planning to return to the US via a Mexican resort. Notable for his performance and its murky tone, the film is a satisfying and occasionally gripping crime noir.

In *The Narrow Margin* (1952), Fleischer appeared to have consolidated the subject and style he had been flirting with, to produce a deft thriller with an evocative visual style. The story of a woman testifying against the mob, and under protection as she takes a train journey from Chicago to Los Angeles, the film utilises the naturally claustrophobic setting of the train and its corridors to convey the dark themes and the sense of threat.

Fleischer made a brief return to comedy with *Happy Time* (1952), a domestic misadventure story about a family in French Canada during the 1920s. He followed this with the 3D flop *Arena* (1953), a rodeo-set story with Gig Young and Polly Bergen, about a rodeo-rider whose marriage is in danger because of his love of the sport. Although the rodeo scenes are captured with a degree of excitement and authenticity, the film itself is on the melodramatic side, like a watered down, less sexually political version of Nicolas Ray's *The Lusty Men* (1952), with which it shares certain thematic similarities.

With *20,000 Leagues Under the Sea* (1954), Fleischer got his first big commercial break. This family movie, a perennial holiday season favourite, has an all-star cast including Kirk Douglas, James Mason and Peter Lorre. This adventure/science-fiction movie about a ship sent to investigate mysterious sinkings and encountering an advanced submarine commanded by the infamous Captain Nemo, proved to be spectacular – both in style and box-office returns. A gloriously old-fashioned family yarn, its models and special effects still hold up today.

Fleischer returned to crime with *Violent Saturday* (1955) in which a gang of hooligans, including Lee Marvin, make plans to rob a small-town local bank. Their story is interwoven with stories from other inhabitants of the small town, including a gentle female librarian, fallen on hard times, and (in a brilliantly ironic stroke which proves that American liberalism goes only so far) an Amish farmer (played by Fleischer regular Ernest Borgnine) who lays down his pacifism and picks up a rifle as protection. Episodic in structure, the film offers a 'slice-of-life' heist movie, reminiscent of the socially conscious drama arising from parts of American film and television, and concurrently being produced in the British film industry.

Fleischer's next few films provided a mix of subjects and styles: the turn-of-the-century crime drama *The Girl in the Red Velvet Swing* (1955), is based on the real murder of famous architect Stanford White; *Between Heaven and Hell* (1956) is a vaguely anti-war action thriller about a spoiled wealthy southerner whose experiences in a mixed-race platoon in the Pacific during World War Two force him to question his values. *Bandido* (1956), an enjoyable western-action adventure movie about an arms dealer and a mercenary who cross swords, once again stars Robert Mitchum and a Mexican setting.

Veering more towards the action and adventure with which he was becoming familiar, Fleischer's following film, *The Vikings* (1958), starred Tony Curtis and Kirk Douglas as Eric the former slave and Einar the great warrior. Unaware that they are half-brothers, the two compete for the throne of Northumbria in tenth-century Britain. One of the highest grossing films of the 1950s, the film combines extraordinary set-pieces featuring battles on the high seas and the coasts of Britain in a fast-moving adventure yarn, crisply and beautifully photographed by Jack Cardiff.

*These Thousand Hills* (1959), a western about a Montana cattle-man's journey of self-discovery, is notable mainly for developing Fleischer's skills in shooting action sequences. It was followed by his take on the Leopold-Loeb crime, *Compulsion* (1959). Filmed by Alfred Hitchcock as *Rope* (1948) and more recently by Tom Kalin as *Swoon* (1992), the story of these bored, privileged kids whose psychosis goes too far when they murder a teenager for kicks, has proved an enduring one. Orson Welles plays it straight as the lawyer whose performance is based on Clarence Darrow's real address to the court, lending the film a documentary air which is, on occasion, somewhat stifling. The rather slow *Crack in the Mirror* (1960) stars Welles again in another courtroom drama, this time setting a young lawyer and his ageing mentor against one another in a murder case. The comedy-action-adventure *The Big Gamble* was released in the following year; following a small group of men who re-locate to a remote African town to set up a new business, it unsuccessfully attempted to combine too many disparate moods.

Fleischer's religious epic *Barabbas* – about the man chosen to live at the expense of Jesus Christ – was released in 1962, part of a trend of Hollywood movies that were clearly feeling the competition from television. The equally epic *Fantastic Voyage* (1966) is one of his best fantasy-adventure movies, the story of a submarine and its crew, shrunk to microscopic size and injected into the bloodstream of an endangered diplomat. The plot, though thrilling and action-oriented, is full of holes; disbelief can be willingly suspended, however, thanks to Fleischer's visual and narrative imagination, some gripping set pieces and wonderfully old-fashioned sets. Another family picture, *Dr Dolittle* (1967) followed, featuring Rex Harrison as the eponymous vet who can talk to the animals.

*The Boston Strangler* (1968) reunited Fleischer with Tony Curtis in a career-best role as the infamous serial killer, who was considered at that time to be Albert de Salvo. It is a chilling and murky account of the serial killer and his crimes, which effectively uses split-screen cinematography to afford the audience a simultaneous view of the murders, the dead bodies and the futile attempts of the police and passers-by to prevent or discover the crimes. This heralded Fleischer's move into darker, more stylised crime movies, the kind of less-mainstream Hollywood fare that could be made within the studio system at the time.

Next, Fleischer made two conflict-themed movies. *Che!* (1969) offers a typical American ideological approach to Guevara and Castro in this fictionalised biography starring Omar Sharif in the title role and the distinctly non-Cuban looking Jack Palance as Castro. *Tora! Tora! Tora!* (1970), named for a Japanese battle cry, details the events leading up to the attack on Pearl Harbour. Surprisingly ambiguous and complex in its approach, Fleischer directed the American section, and Kinji Fukasaku and Tashio Masuda were responsible for the Japanese sections; Akira Kurosawa dropped out due to pressure from the American producers to impose restrictions on his vision.

Fleischer moved to Britain to make his next film, *10 Rillington Place* (1971), which, like *The Boston Strangler,* deals with a real-life murderer. Demonstrating his ability to render such material with an appropriately dark tone, Fleischer perfectly evokes the seedy milieu in which actors Richard Attenborough and John Hurt are able to flourish, committing to the screen a commendable portrait of Britain at the time of the crimes. He remained in Britain for *See No Evil* (1971), a creepy, atmospheric thriller, reminiscent of Terence Young's 1967 chiller *Wait Until Dark*, starring Mia Farrow as the blind woman who is unaware that her murdered family and their killers are in the same house.

A return to the US saw Fleischer revisiting old ground with a well-made if unexceptional crime drama, *The Last Run* (1971), about a former getaway driver retired to a Portuguese fishing village and asked to do one more job. The double crosses and plot twists, particularly the well-executed chases, are reminiscent of Fleischer's earlier films. 1972's *The New Centurions* stars George C. Scott and Stacy Keach as the retiring cop and the rookie respectively in what could easily have been a staid, clichéd account of the infamous 'cop's last day on the job' scenario. The Hollywood 'downer ending' of the 1970s is also evident in his follow-up the 1973 *Soylent Green,* a science fiction thriller set in 2022. Here a haunting score is synthesised perfectly with the sepia-toned images to provide a chilling visualisation of the film's themes. The cast, which includes Edward G. Robinson and Joseph Cotten, and Charlton Heston in the hero role, is excellent. Famed for its narrative pay-off (doesn't everyone know what Soylent Green *is*?), the movie is an assured piece of paranoia film-making.

Fleischer's take on the gangster movie and the western, with *The Don is Dead* (1973) and *The Spikes Gang* (1974), saw him reunited with stars Anthony Quinn and Lee Marvin. The former is an over-violent and under-developed attempt to reap the box-office benefits of Francis Ford Coppola's *The Godfather* (1972), whilst the latter pitches Marvin as an outlaw who takes a trio of teens (amongst them Ron Howard) and teaches them how to rob banks. Both films mark Fleischer's move with the times to deal with more overtly violent work, in keeping with much studio output of the period, and interspersing such ventures with a lighter comic touch.

Elmore Leonard wrote Fleischer's next film, *Mr Majestyk* (1974), about the Vietnam war. Charles Bronson stars as the titular melon farmer and Vietnam veteran fighting for his livelihood against the corrupt men whose aim is to run his business down and buy up his land cheaply. An odd combination of action and melodrama, like a significant degree of Fleischer's work, the film offers little in the way of Vietnam exploration, instead giving Bronson the chance to hone his *Death Wish* persona.

One the one hand controversial and ill-received, though reclaimed as a subversive masterpiece, *Mandingo* (1975) is concerned with a slave owner who, during the mid-nineteenth century, trains his slaves as bare-knuckle fighters, and discovers his prize fighter has been intimately involved with the female members of the family. Over-ripe performances from Susan George and James Mason, and a camera that leers over the naked, sweating flesh of Richard Ward's Agamemnon, the film is melodramatic – slave-porn for mainstream America.

At this point in his career, Fleischer descended into an undistinguished and at times bewildering array of directorial choices. *The Incredible Sarah* (1976) sees him revisiting the biopic with a bland portrait of actress Sarah Bernhardt's early career; *Crossed Swords* (1978) (better known in the UK as *the Prince and the Pauper)* is a family swashbuckler starring Oliver Reed and Mark Lester, about the young Edward VI changing places with a beggar in order to reveal some courtly betrayal, notable mainly for Jack Cardiff's photography; *Ashanti* (1979) is a faintly ludicrous but brutal tale of a diplomat's wife kidnapped by slave traders.

Next, followed a series of utterly pointless remakes and sequels. *The Jazz Singer* (1980) was designed – preposterously – as a Neil Diamond vehicle, and co-starred a hammy Laurence Olivier. *Amityville 3-D* (1983) exploits 3D effects built around dubious plot devices. *Tough Enough* (1983), the story of a country singer finding new success as a boxer, includes some sparky fight scenes.

*Conan the Destroyer* (1984) and *Red Sonja* (1985) demonstrate sword-and-sorcery theatrics in overblown set pieces. The former is more of the material that John Milius offered in his 1981 *Conan the Barbarian*; the latter attempts to out-do them all in its ill-advised setting and storyline. Hulking brutes, evil queens and laughable dialogue make both a waste of Fleischer's and the viewers' time. Although Fleischer directed a short action-adventure-sci-fi film, co- written by British comic writer and actor Chris Langham, *Call From Space*, in 1989, his most recent feature, 1987's *The Million Dollar Mystery*, is a lame comedy about a dying man who tells four strangers that he has hidden $4 million in separate hiding places. Lacking in the style and pace that made a group of his films stand out throughout his career, it seems that antipathy, lack of material, and Hollywood's insistence on ignoring the talents of its loyal directors, has affected Fleischer in much the same way it has countless classic film-makers before him.          **JD**

# Andrew FLEMING

*Bad Dreams* (1988)
*Threesome* (1994)
*The Craft* (1996)
*Dick* (1999)

Andrew Fleming has tapped into the American teenage consciousness with three of his four films to date. These three films all feature packed soundtracks and stories that appeal to the teen market while perhaps alienating older audiences. Likewise, the films themselves come as a full package that caters to a particular trend, targeting the changing waves of popular fashion and attitudes. Yet Fleming's films deliver good, satirical, and knowing fun, featuring casts of fresh-faced and fully game actors who appeal to young audiences.

Fleming studied film-making at New York University's Tisch School of the Arts. Although his first film, *Bad Dreams* (1988), received little notice, his second, *Threesome* (1994), was significant for its titillating and risqué subject matter. A sort of sexual coming-of-age film in a college setting, it featured Josh Charles as a sexually confused young man slowly coming to terms with his homosexuality. The complication of the story ensues when the college mistakenly assigns a woman to the triple-size dorm room, and the three roommates struggle with their attractions for one another. The culminating 'threesome' sex scene seems to champion a kind of omni-sexuality, yet the film panders to gender and sexual stereotypes in the depiction of the sensitive, literate gay character; the boorish, frat-boy jock straight male; and the straight woman who really wants the gay guy because he's so sensitive but has to settle for the straight one.

Fleming's next feature, *The Craft* (1996), was a more cinematically entertaining film that drew upon the contemporary interest in the occult and examined themes of teenage insecurities. This film had more appeal to teen audiences than Fleming's earlier films and featured a cast of strong young women, notably Fairuza Balk and Robin Tunney, in addition to Neve Campbell, who would go on to star in the more successful series of *Scream* films (1996, 1997, 2000). Like those teen slasher films which were remarkable for their tongue-in-cheek appreciation and imitation of the teen horror film genre, *The Craft* drew heavily from earlier works that examined the same subjects of teen alienation and witchcraft, *Carrie* (1976) in particular. Like the protagonist of Brian De Palma's film, the four aspiring witches of *The Craft* are outcasts from their school's various social cliques. When they discover they can use magic to change their insecurities or flaws and gain whatever they desire, the film becomes an enactment of the revenge fantasy of every teenager who has suffered humiliation. The girls' transformations from timid and shunned wallflowers to post-punk Southern California riot grrrl vixens also pandered to contemporary fashion trends and the grunge sensibilities of the mid-1990s pop culture. The use of special effects makes a minimal impression in the film – the girls change hair colour, move objects, levitate – instead, the real enjoyment and entertainment comes from Fairuza Balk's hilarious and increasingly hysterical portrayal as an out-of-control witch.

*Dick* (1999) re-examined the 1970s and offered a mocking, clueless teen's-eye-view of the Watergate scandal that toppled the Nixon administration. The film imagines that the mysterious informant called 'Deep Throat' who provided journalists Carl Bernstein and Bob Woodward with incriminating evidence that caused the scandal and resulted in Richard Nixon's resignation was in fact a pair of dim-witted teenage girls who had accidentally stumbled onto the Watergate break-in and later became pals with the President as White House dog-walkers. Featuring a motley cast of comedians in intentionally parodic portrayals of key Watergate figures, *Dick* brings a 'Saturday Night Live' take on the one of the most sombre and complex events in US history. From the music to the wardrobe and the innocence of the teenagers, Fleming's film maintains that the 1970s were a nutty time.          **EK**

# Rodman FLENDER

Although Rodman Flender has to date only directed a quartet of low-budget genre pictures – most recently the teen gorefest, *Idle Hands* (1999) – he has already enjoyed a prolific and varied professional career. A native New Yorker who grew up watching late-night monster movies on television, Flender did his undergraduate work at Harvard University, where he occasionally teamed with future 'Late Night' host Conan O'Brien, writing for the Harvard Lampoon comedy magazine. He also spent his time making idiosyncratic student films such as *Bloody Mutilators*, an animated production featuring supermodel-eating rats, which a local paper commended as 'savagely satiric'. This indelicate blending of comedy and horror, obviously inspired by such established gross-out auteurs as Sam Raimi and Peter Jackson, has remained a staple of Flender's work.

After graduating from Harvard in 1984, Flender moved to Los Angeles in the hopes of securing a job in the movie business. Having sent infamous indie schlockmeister Roger Corman (whose sex 'n' monster pictures had enthralled him as a child) a tape of one of his films, Flender took a position at the iconoclastic mogul's newest production house, Concorde-New Horizons, where he worked his way up to Vice President of world-wide marketing and distribution, and eventually, to film-maker and Vice President of production. In only three years, Flender produced a remarkable 23 independent pictures, low-budget fare mostly, with such transparent titles as *Demon of Paradise* (1987), *The Terror Within* (1988), and *Body Chemistry* (1990).

Eager to showcase his creative talents, Flender began offering his services as a writer, editor, and short-order director. His feature debut came in 1991 with *The Unborn*, a science fiction thriller starring Brooke Adams as a young wife whose doctor inseminates her with mutated sperm. The result is something straight out of *It's Alive!* (1974): a monstrous foetus so tough it manages to survive its attempted abortion. A year later, Flender wrote and directed another Corman project, *In the Heat of Passion* (1992). This soft-core neo-noir has Sally Kirkland playing the part of a rich, bored housewife whose lover accidentally murders her husband. As with *The Unborn*, *In the Heat of Passion* managed to transcend – if only just – its exploitative subject matter and shabby production values due to strength of acting and directorial competence.

In 1993 Flender received a break when Trimark Pictures recruited him to helm *Leprechaun 2*, a horror-fantasy hybrid featuring a sadistic and super-powerful leprechaun on the prowl for an Irish bride. Owing a great deal to such 'mad trickster' horror films as *A Nightmare on Elm Street* (1984) and *Child's Play* (1988), this derivative affair has little to recommend it. Fortunately for him, Flender managed to bridge into television around this time, directing well-received episodes for such popular shows as 'Party of Five', 'Dawson's Creek', 'Tales From the Crypt', 'Chicago Hope', and 'Millennium'.

Despite being panned by reviewers, ignored by the public, and heavily criticised for having a release date not long (enough) after the Columbine High School massacre in Littleton, Colorado, Flender's next feature film, *Idle Hands*, deserves credit for its clever take on the old 'possessed limb' sub-genre. Littered with references to everything from *Mad Love* (1935) to *An American Werewolf in London* (1981), this ultra-black comedy/horror stars Devon Sawa as Anton, an adolescent pot-head whose right hand is suddenly possessed by an evil spirit, committing bloody acts of murder against its owner's will. Taking the self-reflexive horror humour of *Scream* (1996) to absurd lengths, the movie failed to bring in its teenage target audience, though it may gain new life on the cult video circuit. Flender has subsequently returned to television. **SJS**

# John FLYNN

John Flynn is a 'tough guy director' whose pulpy thrillers are in the tradition of Don Siegel, Robert Aldrich and Sam Fuller. Although his work by-and-large falls short of these film-makers, he has made a couple of unfairly neglected movies. His first credit was as an assistant director on the comedy *John Goldfarb, Please Come Home* (1965). Nothing special, it is a bit of a curio, having been written by the screenwriter of *The Exorcist* (1973), William Peter Blatty, and directed by another (largely unsung) 'tough guy' director J. Lee Thompson.

Flynn's directorial debut was *The Sergeant* (1968). Owing much to John Huston's impressively insane *Reflections in a Golden Eye* (1967), this is the story of an eponymous soldier (Rod Steiger) who, fearful of his desire for a handsome recruit (John

Phillip Law), tortures himself (and Law). Although the film looks pretty dated today – and would make a fine double bill with Robert Aldrich's equally overwrought lesbian drama, *The Killing of Sister George* (1968) – it is still powerful. Steiger eschews his habitual hamminess in a raw and highly watchable performance. Flynn followed with the dull thriller *The Jerusalem File* (1972), which is notable only for a strong cast: Bruce Davison, Nicol Williamson, Donald Pleasence, and Ian Hendry.

His next film remains his best. *The Outfit* (1974) is an adaptation of a novel by Donald Westlake and although it doesn't quite match up to John Boorman's Westlake movie, *Point Blank* (1967), it is still good, hardboiled fare. Robert Duvall is a con fresh from prison; out to avenge his brother's death, he comes up against the Mob in the process. Like an American reworking of Mike Hodges' similar *Get Carter* (1971), or an updated revenge western, *The Outfit* is a tense action piece, and far removed from the steroid-crazed, sub-James Bond blockbusters that have passed for action movies since the 1980s. Duvall is no Stallone or Seagal: his Macklin is a career criminal out of his depth. Like Peckinpah's *The Getaway* (1972) and Siegel's *Charley Varrick* (1973), this is a thriller that actually thrills: it is depressing that in later Flynn films the stars would be the likes of Seagal and Stallone, worlds away from Duvall's cool loner. The film also features an excellent supporting cast, from Karen Black, Timothy Carey and Elisha Cook Jr. to the hard men Joe Don Baker, Robert Ryan and Richard Jaeckel.

Flynn's subsequent film, *Rolling Thunder* (1977), was another good action thriller, the story of a Vietnam veteran (William Devane) who, after losing his wife, child and hand to a band of thugs, goes on the revenge trail. Lean and exciting, it provided an early role for Tommy Lee Jones and fashions some well-staged fight scenes. Often overlooked, Quentin Tarantino is a great champion of the film. After a dull television movie about Marilyn Monroe, and the corny Jan-Michael Vincent vehicle, *Defiance* (1980), Flynn made the rather dull soapy romance, *Touched* (1983) and then returned to familiar hardboiled territory with *Best Seller* (1987). A slick and violent thriller, the ever-reliable duo of Brian Dennehy and James Woods play well in the a story of a cop-turned-writer and his relationship with a psychotic criminal.

Flynn's films since have been disappointing and include the average Stallone prison picture, *Lock Up* (1989), the dreadful Seagal movie, *Out for Justice* (1991), and the recent, 'just about watchable' Mob movie, *Protection* (1999), starring Steven Baldwin. The release of *Final Guardian* is imminent. **IC**

# James FOLEY

A student of medicine and psychology at the University of Buffalo, New Yorker James Foley entered film school with the ambition only to earn extra credits. Eventually graduating from the University of Southern California's film and television programme, Foley eked out a tour of duty as a script writer and production assistant before his directorial debut, *Reckless* (1984), an occasionally risible but competently lensed and acted amalgam of themes cobbled from such classic troubled youth films as *The Wild One* (1954) and *Rebel Without a Cause* (1955). Future director Chris Columbus' script concerned a heated steel town high-school war between the haves and have-nots. While the film was sold on the attractiveness of its young stars (Aidan Quinn and Daryl Hannah, both clearly postgraduate), the best performances were turned in by old-timers Kenneth McMillan (as Quinn's alcoholic father) and Lois Smith (who had acted opposite James Dean in *East of Eden* (1955)).

Also set on the wrong side of the tracks, Foley's sophomore effort was considerably darker, an exercise in what might be called Pennsylvania Dutch Noir. A violent tale of blue-collar criminality (Nicholas Kazan's script was based on true events), *At Close Range* (1986) told of the uneasy partnership between career felon Christopher Walken and his worshipful but conscience-addled heir (a characteristically sensitive performance by Sean Penn). Penn's brother Chris contributed a memorable turn as a victim of Walken's increasing paranoia, and Foley's supporting cast benefited greatly from the presence of Crispin Glover, David Straithairn and Mary Stuart Masterson.

Casting Sean Penn's then-wife Madonna (who had provided *At Close Range* with a pop hit theme song) as a sassy ex-con who makes life miserable for uptight social climber Griffin Dunne, Foley's comedic follow-up, *Who's That Girl* (1987) was a miserable, grating misfire. The director enjoyed a return to form with *After Dark, My*

*Sweet* (1990), an adaptation of the deeply cynical novel by Jim Thompson. Jason Patric starred as punch-drunk ex-pug 'Collie' Collins, who is lured into a doomed kidnapping caper by lowlifes Rachel Ward and Bruce Dern. Varying only slightly from Thompson's source novel, *After Dark, My Sweet* found Foley on firmer ground, and he would remain within the realm of crime-based dramas for his second decade behind the camera.

After helming an episode of David Lynch's surreal television series 'Twin Peaks' (1990–91), Foley returned to the big screen with an acclaimed adaptation of David Mamet's searing Pulitzer Prize-winning Broadway play, *Glengarry Glen Ross* (1992), a chronicle of intrigue and betrayal among the employees of a New York real estate office. If Foley and Mamet (who adapted his own script) were not entirely successful in freeing the text from its theatrical origins, the piece was uplifted by an appropriately apoplectic performance by Al Pacino and an abrasively hilarious cameo by Alec Baldwin.

Pacino and Foley would reunite for 1995's *Two Bits* (aka *A Day to Remember*), a benign coming-of-age drama penned by producer Joe Stefano (author of the screenplay for Alfred Hitchcock's *Psycho* (1960)). Primarily a vehicle for Pacino (in a performance informed more than slightly by Marlon Brando's elderly Don Corleone), the Depression-era character study was further enlivened through the efforts of Mary Elizabeth Mastrantonio (Pacino's sister in *Scarface* (1983)) and child actor Jerry Barrone. The theme of a grandfather's hold on an impressionable youth was continued in *The Chamber* (1996) (Foley's adaptation of the novel by lawyer-novelist John Grisham). Chris O'Donnell stars as an idealistic young defence lawyer attempting to save grandfather Gene Hackman from Death Row despite his contempt for the man's racist beliefs.

Foley's eighth feature film, *Fear* (1996), was an upscale psycho-thriller, with former white rapper Mark Wahlberg as a hunky sociopath whose designs on nubile Reese Witherspoon urge father William Peterson to defensive measures. Despite Foley's competently taut direction, the end result erred on the side of predictability and excess. Wahlberg and Foley would re-team for Foley's next film, the violent Chinatown thriller *The Corruptor* (1999), which co-starred Hong Kong action star Chow Yun Fat in his second American outing. Again, the finished film did not seem to live up to expectations as either a high-octane Hong Kong crime variant or the sort of relationship drama for which Foley is best known. Depending on the source, Foley's best work remains either long past or yet to come. 'It gets more and more difficult,' the director expressed in an interview with the *Toronto Sun* in 1999. 'If I make many more movies, I'll explode.' The accuracy of this prediction will be tested with his forthcoming feature, *Confidence*, a thriller starring Dustin Hoffman and Andy Garcia.                **RHS**

# Milos FORMAN

Milos Forman is one of few European *émigré* directors to have achieved critical and commercial success in America. In a career showered with accolades, he has won the Academy Award for Best Director twice (for *One Flew Over the Cuckoo's Nest* (1975) and *Amadeus* (1984)). Although his detractors suggest that his body of work is not inventive or daring enough to warrant such a critically distinguished career, Forman is a self-confessed popular film-maker. Known as a champion of the common man, his films explore questions of personal freedom, social conformity, and the oppression of the individual. Deeply informed by his experience of living under a Communist regime, much of Forman's American work can be read as a paean to his adopted country.

Born in Czechoslovakia in 1932, his parents were killed in Auschwitz and Buchenwald by the Nazis. A student of direction at the Prague Film School, Forman went on to become a leading director of the Czech New Wave in the 1960s. Friends and colleagues with several leading Czech figures (writer Milan Kundera was his teacher), Forman cites two of the geniuses of early Czech cinema – the comedy director Martin Fric and the avant-garde Alfred Radok – as major influences. When Russian troops invaded Prague in 1968 Forman left Europe for the United States, becoming an American citizen in 1975. In the late 1970s he taught at Columbia University and eventually became co-director of its film programme.

After directing two short films, *Audition* (1963) and *If It Weren't For Music* (1963), Forman embarked on his feature film career with *Black Peter* (1963), *The Loves of a Blonde* (1965), and *The Fireman's Ball* (1967) (the last two were both nominated for

*Black Peter* (1963)
*The Loves of a Blonde* (1965)
*The Fireman's Ball* (1967)
*Taking Off* (1971)
*One Flew Over the Cuckoo's Nest* (1975)
*Hair* (1979)
*Ragtime* (1981)
*Amadeus* (1984)
*Valmont* (1989)
*The People vs. Larry Flynt* (1996)
*Man on the Moon* (1999)

the Academy Award for Best Foreign Film). Classics of the Czech New Wave, these films are recognised for their ironic humour and biting social satire. While the first two films were made in a time of relative openness, *The Fireman's Ball* was banned in Czechoslovakia for what the censors viewed as its unforgivable attack against the government. Censorship is an issue close to Forman's heart and he has worked tirelessly to protect the rights of film-makers. He has long served on the Director Guild of America's National Board, winning the 1997 John Huston Award for Artist Rights.

*Taking Off* (1971), a comedy about the generation gap between parents and children, is Forman's first American film. Although the film was not a box-office success, it received quiet acclaim for its funny depiction of American lifestyles. Two years later Forman directed an unmemorable segment, 'The Decathlon', in *Visions of Eight* (1973), a film in which eight different directors give different views of the 1972 Olympics (among the other directors are John Schlesinger and Mai Zetterling). *One Flew Over the Cuckoo's Nest*, Forman's third American film, is recognised as one of his best. It is the second of three movies – *It Happened One Night* (1934) and *Silence of the Lambs* (1991) are the others – to win the top five Academy Awards: Best (Adapted) Screenplay (Laurence Hauben and Bo Goldman), Best Actress (Louise Fletcher), Best Actor (Jack Nicholson), Best Picture and Best Director. Based on the novel by Ken Kesey, the film is an allegorical tale about the conflict between the individual and the social forces of conformity. Featuring one of the best screen villainesses in cinema history (Fletcher as the cool and calculating Nurse Ratched), the film also boasts an excellent supporting cast, including Brad Dourif and Danny DeVito. Forman's final picture of the decade, *Hair* (1979), the screen adaptation of the cult Broadway musical of the 1960s, is a daring if silly piece of Americana. Its anti-war, pro-peace statement fits in with Forman's overall thematic concerns.

*Ragtime* (1981) is a disjointed representation of E. L. Doctorow's great American novel but is worth watching simply to catch James Cagney's last film appearance. The ambitious *Amadeus* is a lavish production, set in the salons, opera houses and palaces of Vienna in the late eighteenth century. A story about musical talent, God, genius and jealousy, the film won nine Academy Awards, including Best Picture, Best Director, Best Screenplay, Best Actor (F. Murray Abraham), Best Costumes, Art Design, Make Up, Art Direction and Sound. *Valmont* (1989), based on Choderlos de Laclos' eighteenth-century novel 'Les Liasons Dangereuses', suffered from its comparison to Stephen Frears' highly successful *Dangerous Liasons*, released one year earlier. While it may not match the dark intensity of Frears' version, the film is nevertheless a light and entertaining romp.

Forman only released two films in the 1990s, both biopics of eccentric, controversial American men. *The People vs. Larry Flynt* (1996) is Forman's biography of the legendary *Hustler* editor and his First Amendment struggles. The film sparked outrage from Gloria Steinem, among other feminists, for its supposed glorification of the outrageous pornographer and his sexist and racist sensibilities. In fact, as many reviewers remarked, the real difficulty with *The People vs. Larry Flynt* is its sanitisation of the more dangerous and problematic aspects of Flynt and the pornography he champions. Forman has professed his disgust at *Hustler*, a magazine he claims never to have glanced at until the making of the film; this admission is reflected in his failure to engage his subject matter more explicitly. The result, as one critic memorably noted, is a movie that 'champions the uncensored while blurring its own crotch shots'. Despite its rather predictable direction, the film's fascinating subject matter, along with a bright performance from Courtney Love as Flynt's girlfriend, makes it compelling viewing.

*Man on the Moon* (1999), the story of American comic Andy Kaufmann, is written by Scott Alexander and Larry Karaszewski, the same writers who scripted *The People vs. Larry Flynt*. The film wins points for not attempting to explain Kaufmann's outrageous behaviour or the motivating force beneath his comic genius. It contains a clever opening scene in which Kaufmann (played by Jim Carrey) directly addresses the cinema audience. However, the rest of the film does not quite match this opening. The main problem is that the film never pauses to question what it means to tell the story of one of America's most maverick and unconventional comics in such a conventional, generic way. Just as *The People vs. Larry Flynt* told the story of a pornographer's life without considering pornography, so some critics complained that *Man on the Moon* told the story of comedian Kaufmann's life without considering how his innovative use of comedy challenges classic dramatic structure.

Forman is currently invloved in two projects, an adaptation of Donald E. Westlake's novel 'Bad News' and another biographical film based on the life of Goya.   **TH**

# John FORTENBERRY

Although John Fortenberry may be responsible for directing arguably two of the worst films of the 1990s, he has managed a consistent career in television, working on some of the most highly regarded comedy series of the decade, including 'Everybody Loves Raymond', 'Spin City', and the short-lived but critically acclaimed 'Action'. However, Mississippi-born Fortenberry's big-screen, feature-length outings have lacked anything resembling coherence or humour. At running times of only 85 and 82 minutes respectively, *Jury Duty* (1995) and *A Night at the Roxbury* (1998) still suffer from being too long. They are essentially elongated television sketches. The director unsuccessfully tries to use sketch comedy techniques for his films, failing to understand that what is mildly funny for three minutes can barely be sustained for even the shortest of feature-length running times.

*Jury Duty*, a vehicle for MTV 'personality' Pauly Shore, tells the story of a pathetic layabout who learns he has been called for jury duty. He aims to be put on the longest-running trial he can find so he will be sequestered in a hotel, and concocts a series of antics to ensure he will remain there. In *A Night at the Roxbury*, two brothers, Doug (Chris Kattan) and Steve Butabi (Will Ferrell), whose sole interest is clubbing, set out to own an exclusive night-club with the help of actor Richard Grieco (himself) and a jovial businessman (Chazz Palminteri). The two face the wrath of their conservative father (Dan Hedaya) and a domineering neighbour (Molly Shannon) who has her eye on Steve, but all resolves itself by the conclusion.

The films are both exercises in stylistic and narrative cliché, with no apparent thought put into either – in fact they seem to be a celebration of stupidity. While this is a common trend in American films, there is little charm in any of Fortenberry's characters, and the hackneyed plotting, lack of humour, and lazy direction make it all the more apparent. He has since worked in television.   **DH**

*Jury Duty* (1995)
*A Night at the Roxbury* (1998)

# Jodie FOSTER

Jodie Foster is something of an anomaly in Hollywood: an independent female director who exercises creative control over her own material. Born in Los Angeles in 1962 and in show business since the age of two, Foster grew up on Hollywood film sets, becoming one of the few performers to make the successful transition from child star to adult actress. Foster's intelligent, strong-willed performances make her the first actress in cinema history to win two Best Actress Academy Awards (for *The Accused* (1988) and *Silence of the Lambs* (1991)) before the age of thirty. But it is as a director that Foster says she most wants to be remembered.

Her warmly received directorial debut, *Little Man Tate* (1991), tells the story of the relationship between a child prodigy and his single working mother (played by Foster). A thoughtful movie about the difficulties of a brilliant child, many critics read the film as a thinly-veiled documentation of Foster's own childhood experiences (a suggestion she vehemently denies). In 1992, Foster's production company, Egg Pictures, entered into a three-year production agreement with Polygram Filmed Entertainment. The deal grants Foster funding to develop and produce projects under her creative directorship.

*Home for the Holidays* (1995), produced by Egg Pictures, is Foster's second directorial effort. Billed as a comedy, the film explores the dynamics of family life through the eyes of Claudia (Holly Hunter), a single mother visiting her childhood home for Thanksgiving. Through its affectionate depiction of the close relationship between Claudia and her gay brother Tommy (Robert Downey Jr in a show-stopping performance), the film offers a sharp critique of the traditional nuclear family as represented by ultra-conservative sister Joanne, her dull husband and two obnoxious children. Although the film at times appears to rely on the sentimental clichés of family drama it wants to critique, it is in the sensitive portrayal of marginalised individuals that Foster's strength as a director lies.

Foster's next planned project is *Flora Plum*, the story of a poor girl who joins the circus.   **TH**

*Little Man Tate* (1991)
*Home for the Holidays* (1995)

# Marc FORSTER

Born in Germany in 1969, Marc Forster grew up in Switzerland before moving to America in 1990 to study film at New York University. His short *Loungers* won the Audience Award at the 1996 Slamdance Film Festival and was praised for its arresting visual style. His debut feature, *Everything Put Together* (1999), is an articulate and moving account of one woman's journey through the process of grieving; it also works as a satire on the emotional vacuum of modern-day suburbia. Radha Mitchell plays Angie, whose life falls apart after her newborn child becomes a victim of Sudden Infant Death Syndrome. Consumed with grief, she finds herself alone when her friends, most of whom are either mothers or expecting their first child, exclude her from their social group. To them, Angie represents their worst fear; that their children could die at any time. She also threatens the happy veneer of their existence in a world seemingly free from trouble. *Everything Put Together* closely resembles Todd Hayne's *Safe* (1995) – with a nod to Polanski's *Repulsion* (1965) and *Rosemary's Baby* (1968) – and contemporary suburban America is portrayed as being so normal that it threatens the health and sanity of those who exist in it. Angie's psychosis may initially be the result of her grieving, but it is her treatment at the hands of her friends that pushes her over the edge.

Shot on DV, *Everything Put Together* is an unnerving film that fully conveys Angie's trauma and the feelings of solitude she experiences; stylistically, Forster's follow-up could hardly be more different. *Monster's Ball* (2002) is a slow-burning drama set in the Deep South that once again explores the nature and effects of grief. Halle Berry plays Leticia Musgrove, whose husband is executed on death row. Shortly after, she begins an affair with Hank who, unbeknown to her, was one of the prison guards present at her husband's execution. Equally stricken, Hank's relationship with Leticia initially offers some comfort but interference from his racist father and his past threaten their chances of happiness. *Monster's Ball* profits from excellent performances by Berry, Billy Bob Thornton and Peter Boyle. Occasionally the script is overly schematic, but Forster's unfussy direction allows the drama to unfold at an unusually measured pace, eschewing histrionics in favour of more restrained emotions. As with his debut, Forster successfully captures the debilitating effect of grief and the pressure of having to carry on living.

Forster's forthcoming film *Neverland* stars Johnny Depp, Kate Winslett, Radha Mitchell, Julie Christie and Dustin Hoffman. Based on J. M. Barrie's encounter with four fatherless children, which inspired him to write 'Peter Pan', Forster once again explores the process of grieving, only this time looking at the fantasy games children play in order to cope with their suffering. **IHS**

# Jonathan FRAKES

Born in Pennsylvania in 1952, Jonathan Frakes is a director better known as William T. Riker from 'Star Trek: The Next Generation'; it thus comes as no surprise that his film-making experience is almost entirely 'Trek'-related. As an actor he appeared in television shows from the late 1970s onwards, including 'The Doctors' and 'North and South', before making the role of Riker his own in 1987. The first cast member to also step behind the camera, he cut his teeth on segments of his own show, 'Deep Space Nine' and 'Voyager'. So, when Paramount sought someone to direct an eighth *Star Trek* picture, Frakes was the natural choice.

*Star Trek: First Contact* (1996) thrives where most of the others faltered: it entices a broad non-fan-based audience by selecting an all-action approach and spotlighting bio-mechanical enemies called the Borg. In addition, Patrick Stewart's Captain Picard makes an authentic hero, while Brent Spiner's android Data continues his Pinocchio-like quest to be human. More emotional than brooding, *Star Trek: Insurrection* (1998) resuscitates the hoary 'lost fountain of youth' myth, but flavours this with a timely Kosovo ethnic cleansing rebuke. Other cast members, such as Michael Dorn and Marina Sirtis, are used to much greater effect than before, but in the end the film's mustiness wins out.

Of late, Frakes has been involved in another sci-fi television programme, as executive producer and director on 'Roswell High', although he did find time to direct *Clockstoppers* (2002) – a terrible teen sci-fi film in the *Back to the Future* (1995) and *Bill & Ted's Excellent Adventure* (1989) mold. From the loud MTV-style opening to the inexcusable bastardisation of scientific theories and glaring narrative inconsistencies, it screams disaster. Ironically a similar premise was used to much greater effect in an episode of Fraker's own 'Star Trek' television series. **PB**

# John FRANKENHEIMER

John Frankenheimer stands today as one of the last remaining auteurs in an era of blockbusters and conglomerates. His body of work is notable for both its immensity (having directed thirty feature films, four films for cable, and over fifty plays for television) and its influence. What is most remarkable about this director, however, is his pioneering of the modern-day political thriller; Frankenheimer began his career at the peak of Cold War politics in the 1950s and subsequently carved a niche in Hollywood.

During the radical 1960s, he developed a tremendous propensity for exploring the political situations which ensnare his characters, often blurring the line between good and bad (*The Manchurian Candidate* (1962)), but along with this strong sense of environment came an obsession with the psychological dilemmas of his male protagonists (*Seconds* (1966)). Considering the problematics behind brute masculinity is a fundamental Frankenheimer theme and is evident from his earliest work (Warren Beatty's troubled Berry-Berry in *All Fall Down* (1962)) to his latest (Gary Sinise as George Wallace in *George Wallace* (1997)). While critics either consider him a fading auteur or a Hollywood hack for hire, Frankenheimer's ability to both explore complex social situations and psychological ordeals has made him one of the most important film-makers of the last forty years.

Frankenheimer was born in 1930 and grew up in New York City. His father was a stockbroker, a partner in a stock exchange firm and, while he was Jewish, his mother was Irish Catholic. As a result, Frankenhiemer was raised Catholic until he was 17 years old, when he decided that he 'couldn't do it anymore'. He was always interested in movies and could recall as a child going to the Lone Ranger serials every Saturday. At Williams College, in Williamstown, Mass., he studied English and graduated in 1951 with an eye towards acting as a career. But, in his own words, 'it wasn't until I got into the Air Force that I really started to think seriously about directing'.

Once in the Air Force, Frankenheimer joined a film squadron based in Burbank, California. It was this experience that initially gave him the directing bug. The first film he ever shot was made during this experience, a documentary about the production of asphalt. He would take cameras home with him at the weekends and 'shoot all manner of stuff'. At this point Frankenheimer also began reading classic film theory like Sergei Eisenstein as well as a handful of how-to books on film-making.

In 1953, his tenure was finished and he moved to New York, where he was eventually hired at CBS as an assistant director. This initial television work turned out to be an invaluable learning experience for the blooming director. He worked as an assistant under the likes of Sidney Lumet and eventually graduated to direct teleplays himself. His work during this time included *The American*, starring Lee Marvin, and a series of adaptations including F. Scott Fitzgerald's 'Winter Dreams' and 'The Last Tycoon', William Faulkner's 'Old Man', and Ernest Hemingway's 'Fifth Column', 'The Snows Of Kilimanjaro', and 'For Whom the Bell Tolls'.

Frankenheimer's emergence as a film-maker in the 1960s coincided with a crisis in the Hollywood studio structure. Faced with staggering competition related to the proliferation of television as well as other leisure activities during the 1950s, Hollywood began to lose its rigorous hierarchical character as the old studio oligarchs jumped ship. This opened up the industry for experimentation and made way for directors like Frankenheimer, whose critical eye had been shaped by television and the rumblings of European art cinema.

All of Frankenheimer's films during the 1960s – he made eleven of them – were critical and commercial successes, with the exception of *Seconds*. After directing *The Young Stranger* in 1956, he began the decade with *The Young Savages* (1961). The film starred Burt Lancaster, who would go on to star in four more Frankenheimer films before the decade was over. Concerning the death of a Puerto Rican boy at the hands of three Italian youths, the film follows Hank Bell (Lancaster), assistant to the District Attorney, on his investigation. Highlighting Frankenheimer's attentiveness to the complexity of social situations, Bell's initial belief that this case will be a relatively simple one turns out to be illusory. By underscoring the politics of poverty and blind ambition, *The Young Savages* established Frankenheimer as a unique social realist.

1962 marked a watershed year for Frankenheimer. He directed three films in the span of one year: *Birdman of Alcatraz*, *All Fall Down*, and *The Manchurian Candidate*. *Birdman of Alcatraz* also starred Burt Lancaster and depicted the true story of Robert Stroud, a prisoner in America at the beginning of the twentieth century who develops an internationally renowned expertise on birds and their illnesses. Again illustrating Frankenheimer's talent for representing complex social situations with ease, the film helped to establish Lancaster as one of the premiere American actors. *All Fall Down* explored the dynamics of a family whose idealistic faith in their eldest son, Berry-Berry (Warren Beatty), betrayed a tendency to disregard his destructive qualities and inevitably leads to a violent encounter between brothers.

Next came Frankenheimer's classic, *The Manchurian Candidate*. Starring Frank Sinatra, Angela Lansbury, and Janet Leigh, this film functioned as a damning critique of McCarthyite scapegoating, associating it with much irony to the subversion of American democracy. The plot revolves around a Korean War veteran, Raymond Shaw, who has been programmed by the Communists – using hypnosis – to serve as an assassin. Major Marco (Frank Sinatra), who was also hypnotised, soon realises what is going on and attempts to save Shaw. However, it is revealed that Shaw's mother is an operative for the Communists and is also controlling her husband, a blowhard senator clearly mimicking the exploits of Joseph McCarthy. At the orders of his mother, Shaw kills her husband's leading political rival, an outspoken liberal senator. Marco finally frees Shaw's mind but fails to stop him before he kills his mother, stepfather, and himself.

The controversy that swirled around this film's release can be attributed to the fact that it was still taboo in the early 1960s to paint a satiric anti-McCarthyite picture. Yet the film was too good to be brought down by political sensitivities. Propelled forward by the support of critics and Sinatra's star persona, *The Manchurian Candidate* became a huge success and is still today Hollywood's canonical political thriller. It paved the way for Stanley Kubrick's *Dr Strangelove* (1963) and skilfully interwove psychological dilemmas with a scathing political critique.

Frankenheimer followed the success of *The Manchurian Candidate* with two films in 1964, *Seven Days in May* and *The Train*. *Seven Days* follows the same lines as its predecessor by depicting a political world where there are plots within plots. Kirk Douglas stars as an upstanding colonel who uncovers a plan to overthrow the president by some of his military colleagues, upset over an arms treaty signed with the Soviet Union. The narrative in *The Train* turns this around so that audiences identify with the plotters. This film is set during the eve of Paris' liberation from the Nazis and concerns the resistance efforts of patriotic French railworkers.

In 1966 Frankenheimer made what was to be his darkest film yet, *Seconds*. A brilliantly told tale of middle-aged Arthur Hamilton (John Randolph) who, while wealthy, is extremely dissatisfied with his life. Soon, through a message from a friend that he had thought dead, Hamilton is led to the headquarters of a corporation whose primary aim is to provide wealthy clients with new lives, befitting their lost ambitions. Key to this transformation is the physical reconstruction of the body. Hamilton emerges from the surgery as a painter named Tony Wilson, played by Rock Hudson. When Wilson discovers that this new life is as meaningless as the previous, he returns to the corporation to ask for a third chance. They reply that this is possible, but only on the condition that he recommends a new client for their exploits. When he refuses, they decide to use his corpse for the next customer.

*Seconds* was unique in that it prioritised delving into the psychological dimensions of alienation over the socio-political conditions of Frankenheimer's previous thrillers. The film is extremely subjective, situated as we are in Hamilton/Wilson's point of view throughout. This enabled Frankenheimer to deploy surrealistic imagery in a manner he had not before (note the fish-eye lens). Similarly, the film was a tremendous deconstruction of a star persona, namely Rock Hudson. Casting Hudson in the role of the 'ideal' painter persona, Tony Wilson, constituted a rich critique of the emptiness of stardom. When the film premiered at the 1966 Cannes Film Festival, it was so panned that Paramount lost all confidence in the film and it went on to be a commercial failure.

*Grand Prix* (1966) was next, a grand visual spectacle about race cars shot in 70 mm. This was followed by *The Fixer* (1968), a historical drama set in Tzarist Russia; *The*

*Extraordinary Seaman* (1969), a comedic spoof on war; and *The Gypsy Moths* (1969), the story of sky-divers who flirt with death. Frankenheimer then pushed full-steam ahead into the 1970s with a series of strong films: *I Walk the Line* (1970), *The Horseman* (1971), *Impossible Object* (1973), *The Iceman Cometh* (1973), *99 and 44/100% Dead* (1974), *The French Connection II* (1975), and *Black Sunday* (1977). These films continue Frankenheimer's previous concerns with psychological dilemmas and social realism. Most notable is *Black Sunday*, a film about the efforts of Middle Eastern terrorists to murder a whole stadium crowd on Super Bowl Sunday which could have descended into empty clichés in the hands of a lesser film-maker. But Frankenheimer, in typical fashion, transcends standard good/bad characterisations by underlying the fact that both sides have blood on their hands.

In the next thirteen years (1977–90) Frankenheimer made only six films: *Prophecy* (1979), *The Challenge* (1982), *The Holcroft Covenant* (1985), *52 Pick-Up* (1986), *Dead Bang* (1989), and *The Fourth War* (1989). It is important to note that by the late 1970s the studio system was reasserting its authority over content and the blockbuster mentality was sinking in. This changing climate meant that film-makers did not have the artistic freedom they enjoyed in the 1960s and early 1970s. Like nearly every other director, Frankenheimer's career was impacted by this new reality of the industry. Most notable of these films is *The Fourth War*, a political thriller that focuses on an American military officer (Roy Scheider) trying to find his way in a post-Cold War world.

The 1990s marked Frankenheimer's return to television, albeit cable. After directing *The Year of the Gun* (1991), he made *Against The Wall* (1994) and *The Burning Season* (1994) for HBO, followed by *Andersonville* (1996) for TNT. All three films won Frankenheimer an Emmy for Best Director and affirmed his status as a true auteur. Given the restraints of the film industry, cable television – being a relatively new development – granted Frankenheimer an artistic license that, in many ways, recalled his early years in television. He ventured back into Hollywood when trying to pick up the pieces of a failing production entitled *The Island of Dr Moreau* (1996). Wrought with production problems from the outset, the film was a disaster waiting to happen, a critical and commercial failure when released.

After the experience of *Dr Moreau*, Frankenheimer understandably went back to cable, where he made *George Wallace* for TNT. The film starred Gary Sinise and provided Frankenheimer with the opportunity to return to form. The subject matter was perfect for him: a biographical study of controversial Alabama Governor George Wallace. In this story, the protagonist is faced with changing social conditions that are forcing him to face up to his own prejudices.

Most recently, Frankenheimer has directed two films: *Ronin* (1997) and *Reindeer Games* (2000), both of which leave much to be desired for fans of the director's work. *Ronin* is a post-Cold War political thriller and *Reindeer Games* is a run-of-the-mill action piece lacking in the social realism that Frankenheimer traditionally brings to such films.

In spite of these last examples, Frankenheimer has proven to be one of the most important artistic voices in film-making today. His knack for capturing the complicating nature of social situations while still delving into the psychology of his characters is a rare and unique skill. As a testimony to his influence, in 1996 the Museum of Modern Art and the Museum of Radio and Television in New York, working jointly for the first time ever, launched a retrospective of Frankenheimer's body of work. Such an event is the perfect homage to an indisputable cinematic talent. John Frankheimer died in July 2002. **SCh**

# Carl FRANKLIN

Born in California in 1949, Carl Franklin began his career working as an actor in television and film. However, as an African-American, a lack of quality roles and stereotyped casting led him to enrol as a graduate student at the American Film Institute, where he studied direction. His early films – *Nowhere to Run* (1989), *Eye of the Eagle 2: Inside the Enemy* (1989), and *Full Fathom Five* (1990) – were all generic pot-boilers made for Roger Corman's production company, which allowed Franklin learn the craft of film-making while subsidising the director's academic education.

It wasn't until the 1991 movie *One False Move* that he established himself as an important, groundbreaking film-maker. *One False Move* is the story of two thieves, one black and one white, who begin to distrust each other's motivations while hiding out with the help of the girlfriend of one of the men. Compounding the situation is the fact that the local white sheriff, awaiting his chance to make a name for himself by capturing the fugitives, appears to have a connection to the young black woman hoping to aid their escape. Under Franklin's controlled direction the film never uses the issue of race as a platform for sermonising. Instead, he utilises the racially-charged setting of the film to increase the tension between his characters as well as to emphasise their humanity. He followed it up with a made-for-television movie, *Laurel Avenue* (1993), about a young black family whose lives are disrupted by random violence.

His next film was *Devil in a Blue Dress* (1995), adapted from Walter Mosley's novel of the same name. It starred Denzel Washington as 'Easy' Rawlins, an unemployed African-American factory worker living in the racially segregated Los Angeles of the 1950s. When he is offered $100 to investigate the disappearance of the mayor's girlfriend, a white woman known to frequent black bars and juke-joints, he becomes embroiled in political corruption and murder. It is an exemplary film which draws comparisons to Polanski's *Chinatown* (1974) (also set in Los Angeles), but differs in its attempt to re-draw the map of film noir from the inside-out. *Devil in a Blue Dress* is set within the urban spaces which induce fear, paranoia, and dread in the typical noir protagonist. In Franklin's film it is the corrupted white world which becomes the true source of dread and fear, not the world of the street, the black neighbourhoods which are so often coded as the shadow worlds which define film noir. Both *One False Move* and *Devil in a Blue Dress* were meticulously crafted thrillers with complex visual styles that revealed in Franklin's work a concern and interest with context. *One False Move* takes place in the racially charged environment of rural Arkansas. By contrast, *Devil in a Blue Dress* is set in the re-created urban spaces of a racially segregated black Los Angeles. While both films deal with issues of race, they are more concerned with the manner in which setting influences character and action.

Franklin took a slightly different direction in *One True Thing* (1998), the story of an up-and-coming young reporter who is called home to care for her mother who has just been diagnosed with cancer. The film struck many critics as an odd choice in that it deals with the concerns of an upper-middle-class white family and is entirely devoid of the racial overtones which have informed his best work. A fairly straightforward melodrama, *One True Thing* nevertheless maintains Franklin's concern for social and class constraints and showcases the director's talent, illustrating the manner in which setting and place determine the fates of his characters.

Franklin's latest film, *High Crimes* (2002), a thriller starring Morgan Freeman and Ashley Judd, finds the latter playing a successful lawyer who is caught in a web of intrigue when her husband is arrested and tried for the murder of South American villagers during his service in the marines. Another thriller, *Out of Time*, starring Denzel Washington, is planned. **MR**

# Stephen FREARS

*Gumshoe* (1972)
*The Hit* (1984)
*My Beautiful Laundrette* (1985)
*Prick Up Your Ears* (1987)
*Sammy and Rosie Get Laid* (1987)
*Dangerous Liaisons* (1988)
*The Grifters* (1990)
*Accidental Hero* (1992)
*The Snapper* (1993)
*Mary Reilly* (1996)
*The Van* (1996)
*The Hi-Lo Country* (1998)
*High Fidelity* (2000)
*Liam* (2000)

A significant figure in British cinema, within the last decade or so Stephen Frears has directed such landmark American films as *The Grifters* (1990) and *The Hi-Lo Country* (1998). His range is remarkable, taking in 1980s social realism, biography, comedy, and historical drama within the mediums of film, television and theatre. Frears is often described as a 'writer's director' and has enjoyed long and fruitful working partnerships with a range of quality writers.

Frears was well positioned to helm the series dedicated to British cinema, 'Typically British'. Not many movements and moments have passed this director by – Frears worked with the angry young men in the 1960s, turned to television in the 1970s and 1980s, and in the 1980s worked with the new 'alternative comedians' on the 'Comic Strip Presents...' series for Channel 4.

Born in Leicester, UK, in 1941, after studying Law at Cambridge, Frears became interested in theatre and joined London's Royal Court. His first work in film was as assistant director to Karel Reisz on *Morgan* (1966). A year later he made his first film, a short entitled *The Burning*, which foregrounded some of his later concerns about race and ethnicity. He continued working as an assistant director for Reisz, Lindsay Anderson and Albert Finney before directing his first feature, *Gumshoe* (1972), starring Finney as a day-dreaming Liverpudlian bingo caller who advertises his services as a private investigator. *Gumshoe* satirises American detective films; having received mixed critical reactions at the time of its release, it has enjoyed something of a renaissance in recent years.

Frears worked mainly in television throughout the 1970s and early 1980s, working with writers like Alan Bennett and Tom Stoppard on plays and films for British television. He has been quoted as saying that 'television gives an accurate account of what it's like to live in Britain – about men and women who lead somewhat desperate lives'. He was to find that he could do this just as accurately and effectively on film.

His next feature, *The Hit* (1984), is a taut, suspenseful, compact crime-thriller which, like *Gumshoe*, has an interesting take on the genre. Terence Stamp plays an informer located by two assassins, John Hurt and Tim Roth, who take him back to Paris to pay for his 'treachery'. It has been argued that for all its style and panache, the film has a disappointingly weak resolution. Whilst this criticism is justified, *The Hit* is about the journey to Paris and, ultimately, the journey to death. The film received some favourable reviews but was not a box-office success. However, as with his earlier *Gumshoe*, *The Hit* is now regarded as a minor British classic.

Through the exploration of relationships which cross boundaries of gender, sexuality, class and ethnicity, Frears' next three features critique Thatcherism. *My Beautiful Laundrette* (1985) was shot in 16mm for £700,000. According to Frears himself, the film was his and screenwriter Hanif Kureishi's swipe at the new entrepreneurial spirit of Thatcherism. Some critics argue that *My Beautiful Laundrette* is the definitive critique of Thatcher's Britain. Others see the film as a direct descendant of the social realist films of the 1950s and 1960s, prompting one critic to describe it as 'a story which empties the contents of three kitchen sinks into one washing machine'. The film is set in South London where a thriving Pakistani community lives alongside the hopeless underclass of 'native' England. This tension clearly articulates Frears and Kureishi's concerns in reflecting both sides of Thatcher's economic miracle. The film also critiques the air of sexual repression in Britain in the 1980s via explorations of relationships that call into question family values and the marginalisation of gay men.

Gay relationships and class distinctions are also central to Frears' next feature, *Prick Up Your Ears* (1987), adapted from John Lahr's biography of playwright Joe Orton. Gary Oldman plays Orton, with Alfred Molina as Orton's lover and subsequent murderer, Kenneth Halliwell. Eschewing a faithful biographic approach, Frears focuses on the relationship between Orton and Halliwell rather than mapping the standard chronology. The film begins with Orton's murder, allowing the audience to concentrate on the character dynamics that lead to his death. While not explicitly concerned with class difference and sexual and social inequalities, the Orton-Halliwell relationship articulates the problems of love across class boundaries and against society's norms. The film takes Orton and Halliwell, pitting them first against the system, and finally against each other.

During the 1980s Frears made several feature films for television (*Bloody Kids* (1979), *Loving Walter* (1986), *Saigon: Year of the Cat* (1983), and two films for the 'Comic Strip Presents...' series, *The Bullshitters* (1984), and the superior *Mr Jolly Lives Next Door* (1988).

His next feature, *Sammy and Rosie Get Laid* (1987), saw him reunited with writer Kureishi. It is a multi-layered look at the social relations of a liberal, mixed-race couple, Sammy (Ayub Khan Din) and Rosie (Frances Barber), and contains similar themes to *My Beautiful Laundrette*. Sexual, ethnic, and class politics are dramatised against a carefully crafted backdrop of a decaying, changing England. The action is again based in South London and provides a critique of the repressive morality of Thatcher's Britain. At the time of its release, Frears stated that the film was intended to bring the government down. Of course it did not achieve this, marking the end of his vociferous attacks on the government of the day. The director conceded that he 'did not have anything else to say about England right now'; his films of the 1980s remain among the most caustic cinematic attacks on Thatcherism. In 1988, Frears made his Hollywood debut with *Dangerous Liaisons*, a sumptuous adaptation of a Christopher Hampton play (itself based on Choderlos de Laclos' eighteenth-century novel). Some critics felt it to be too lavish, too highly stylised, and lacking in the cinematic sincerity Frears had become associated with in his British films. However, these criticisms fail to take into account the way the sets, costumes and the stylisation work within the narrative to amplify the superficiality of the characters and their motives.

Frears describes his next Hollywood feature, *The Grifters* (1990), as a cross between Shakespeare and a B-movie. *The Grifters* marries a highly stylised vision of a timeless Southern California with the grittiness that had informed his British films of the 1980s. This curious timeless quality comes in part from the fact that the film is adapted from the novel by Jim Thompson, which is set in the 1950s, while the film is set in the 1980s. The three central characters, Roy Dillon (John Cusack), Lily Dillon (Anjelica Huston), and Myra Langtry (Annette Bening) are compelling. Cusack provides a sympathetic centre for the film, whilst Anjelica Huston's portrayal of Lily, Roy's mother, is perhaps her finest performance to date. *The Grifters* was a success at the box office and was highly acclaimed by critics; it is regarded as a classic of contemporary Hollywood cinema.

His next Hollywood feature is possibly Frears' least successful film to date. *Accidental Hero* (1992) seems to have everything: capable director, major Hollywood-star cast (Dustin Hoffman, Geena Davis, Andy Garcia, Chevy Chase) and an intriguing plot. It should, in theory, work; in practice, it does not. *Accidental Hero* is a comic parable about the nature of heroism, and society's need for the right kind of hero. It focuses on a gruff, shallow petty criminal, Bernie Laplante (Hoffman), who reluctantly saves passengers from the wreckage of a crashed jet plane, only to disappear before taking the credit. Andy Garcia's serene down-and-out, John Bubber, then steps into the frame claiming to be the Angel of Flight 104. A number of factors prevent an interesting script from gaining the momentum it needs: Hoffman's characterisation of Laplante is too much of a caricature rather than a character – somewhere between Ratso Rizzo and Columbo's evil twin. The plane crash sequence is wholly unconvincing, too clean and too bloodless, and the editing is too slow to create the sense of urgency such a scene requires. Frears himself explained that part of the problem with *Accidental Hero* was that he had no conception of how to shoot a plane crash. The film was a commercial failure and failed to ignite the imaginations of the critics, despite fine performances from Davis and Garcia.

Frears' next project, *The Snapper* (1993), was the screen adaptation of Roddy Doyle's book. A minor controversy was caused at the BBC's reluctance to allow the film cinematic exhibition, choosing to air it on television first – all the more galling since the film enjoyed theatrical release in Europe. On the whole, American critics saw *The Snapper* as a warm-hearted Irish comedy and it was generally well received. In Britain, critics tended to compare the film either with the novel or with Alan Parker's *The Commitments* (1991), the first episode of Doyle's Barrytown Trilogy. From this perspective, the film fared less well critically in Britain. *The Snapper* focuses on Sharon Curley, a young working-class woman who hides the fact she is pregnant until it becomes too obvious to hide. Speculation and rumours fly within her local community as to who the father is, but Sharon refuses to identify him. This is a film about family, love and acceptance, and while the Curleys' are far from the 'ideal family' (they brawl, they gossip, they drink), Sharon's pregnancy serves to bind them closer together. Some critics saw *The Snapper* as a return to Frears' low-budget, social-realist roots, yet the film is too warm, and too uncritical of social and sexual prejudice, the family or community to provide anything other than surface realism. It lacks the biting critique of *Sammy and Rosie Get Laid* or *My Beautiful Laundrette*.

*Mary Reilly* (1996), starring Julia Roberts, was a box-office failure and was virtually ignored by the critics. The film is based on Valerie Martin's novel, which was itself based on Robert Louis Stevenson's classic 'The Strange Case of Dr Jekyll and Mr Hyde'. The eponymous heroine, Mary Reilly, played by Julia Roberts, is the maid who falls in love with Dr Jekyll (John Malkovich). The victim of childhood abuse at the hands of her drunken father, Mary is confused but not surprised by the duality of her employer since she is used to loving and fearing men at the same time. In line with the demands of the story, both Roberts and Malkovich deliver unusually restrained performances. 'Dr Jekyll and Mr Hyde' is, after all, widely interpreted as an allegorical comment on Victorian sexual, emotional and psychological repression, as well as playing out cultural fears about science and progress. The studio wanted a more upbeat ending but Frears held out. Jekyll must be punished and there can be no romantic coupling. *Mary Reilly* was Frears' second collaboration with writer Christopher Hampton, and despite a solid script and Frears' restrained direction, the film received poor reviews.

There are two problems with the film. First, it is difficult to believe that Roberts' character does not recognise her boss to be the evil Mr Hyde. As one critic said: 'That a hairstyle keeps Mary from linking Hyde with Jekyll is as believable as Lois Lane not recognising Superman because he's wearing glasses.' Second, critics clearly struggled to place the film within a generic context: was it Gothic horror, psychological thriller or historical melodrama? With no handy labels available, the critics chose to ignore it altogether, and consequently audiences stayed away. This does the director a disservice as *Mary Reilly* is at least stylish.

His next feature, *The Van* (1996), based on the third instalment of the Barrytown Trilogy, fared little better with critics and audiences. Frears again examines unemployment and its effects on family life. It follows the fortunes of two Dubliners, Bimbo (Donal O'Kelly) and Larry (Colm Meaney), who decide to escape unemployment by investing in a fish and chip van. The van is a big success but this success puts a strain on the pair's friendship. From here the film degenerates into a series of noisy arguments and fights between the two leads and little else. Watching *The Van* it is necessary to remind oneself that it is directed by the same angry voice of the 1980s. Social conscience has been traded in for surface realism and Doyle's sharp, human and insightful humour replaced by cheap gags and pointless screaming matches. *The Van* performed poorly at the box office and critics expressed disappointment.

Frears returned to form with *The Hi-Lo Country*, described by one British critic as 'the finest Sam Peckinpah western the man himself never made'. Set in the 1940s, it centres on the relationship between Big Boy Matson (Woody Harrelson) and Pete Calder (Billy Crudup). It is an atmospheric film that delivers a powerful sense of a decaying old west gradually giving in to a new era, not so much through *mise-en-scène*, but through characterisation. Despite its 1940s setting, the central plot is classic western material: the hero's hometown is at the mercy of ruthless cattle baron Steve Shaw (Lane Smith). Pete and Big Boy go to work for Shaw's rival, Hoover, played by James Gammon, who represents the town the boys left behind after they received their call-ups. Critics welcomed *The Hi-Lo Country* as a genuine attempt to get 'back to basics', after years of science-fiction cross-overs (*WestWorld* (1973), *Back to the Future III* (1990), *Wild Wild West* (1999)), post-feminist chick-flicks (*Bad Girls* (1994), *The Quick and the Dead* (1995)), and stylistically overblown epics (*Young Guns* (1988), *Dances with Wolves* (1990), *Tombstone* (1993), *Legends of the Fall* (1994)).

*High Fidelity* (2000) was adapted from Nick Hornby's bestseller of the same name. The film drew much criticism from some areas of the British press because of the relocation of the action – Chicago, rather than the North London setting of the novel. Frears himself had reservations about this but later argued that the film 'kept the spirit of the book but universalised the story'. He handles the comedy of Hornby's modern classic with relish. John Cusack plays the list-obsessed Rob Gordon who compiles his top five break-ups. *High Fidelity* has it all: crackling wit, polished performances and crisp direction.

Frears' next project was an impressive television film, *Fail Safe* (2000), which caused quite a stir in the States where it was screened by NBC. A Cold War thriller, it asks the audience to imagine a nuclear bomb has been launched by accident on Moscow. It was filmed as if it were 'happening now' in black and white to suggest a 1950s American broadcast.

The director's most recent project, *Liam* (2000), is a drama set in Liverpool during the Depression. Once again, Frears is concerned with the effects of poverty on family life; here, it is in an historical setting. The story follows the fortunes of Liam (Anthony Borrows) and his family and much of the film's action is filtered through Liam's eyes, as his father loses his job as a docker and they descend further into poverty. Liam's father (Ian Hart) becomes increasingly bitter and turns to a far-right group in order to vent his anger. Scripted by Jimmy McGovern, this film is hard-hitting in places and sincere in its intent to convey a humanist message. Frears' eye for detail is evident in the way he constructs a believable milieu for his characters to inhabit on screen. There are also some genuinely comic moments, mostly concerning young Liam's Catholic education. The film received some modest reviews, but generally critical opinion seems to be that an association between Frears and McGovern should have yielded greater results. He is currently in production with *Dirty Pretty Things*, a crime thriller with a London setting. **SL**

# Bart FREUNDLICH

Born in 1970, writer-director Bart Freundlich's first feature, *The Myth of Fingerprints* (1997), established him as a loose, natural storyteller whose film-making style is evocative in its very restraint. Set in and around a rambling country house, the film delicately traces the course of a Thanksgiving weekend among an extended family of New England WASPs, weaving a tone of quiet oddness and autumnal yearning that is closer to Chekhov (one character makes an explicit reference to 'The Seagull') than the catalogues of wild dysfunction found in the similarly-geared *Home for the Holidays* (1995) and *The Ice Storm* (1997). It is a film of grace notes, structured around keen, funny observations of behaviour and speech rather than plot points. Freundlich takes a less-is-more approach, never letting a scene last longer than it should, and conveying information with the lean economy of a short story writer.

A theme of lost connections and forgotten memories runs through what amounts to an ensemble piece, but the emotional centre of the story rests with Noah Wylie, effective as the long-absent son who attempts to resolve issues with his distant father, played – in a performance of wry contempt – by Roy Scheider. Freundlich is spare in suggesting just how haunted these two men are by the past. A pair of flashbacks conjoin like puzzle pieces to reveal the cause of the rift between Wylie and his father, while a scene late in the film, played silent as Scheider sadly watches old home movies by himself (Freundlich simply holds on the actor's weathered face) hints at deeper levels of loss and regret.

*World Traveller* (2002), a drama starring Billy Crudup and Julianne Moore about a man running away from his family only to realise its value during his travels, has received a lukewarm critical reception. **CS**

# William FRIEDKIN

Instrumental in the commercial transformation of Hollywood in the early 1970s, the films of William Friedkin often display a cold cynicism that belies the popular appeal of his short-lived commercial success. Friedkin was born in Chicago in 1939 and unlike many of his 'New Hollywood' contemporaries, he served his apprenticeship in the world of television (a medium to which he has often returned) before progressing to full-length documentaries (notably, *The People vs. Paul Crump*) and features by the end of the 1960s. Renowned for a volatile, dictatorial approach on set, his biography is replete with tales of confrontation and arrogance which arguably infuse his best films with their bitter edge.

*Good Times* (1967), an inauspicious vehicle for then-married singing duo Sonny and Cher, led to an adaptation of Harold Pinter's 'The Birthday Party' in 1968, the light comedy *The Night They Raided Minsky's* (1968), and, most impressively, *The Boys in the Band* (1970). This adaptation of Mart Crowley's play anticipates Friedkin's later film *Cruising* (1980) in its theme of the denial of homosexuality and uses its single set to good effect. However, none of these films anticipate Friedkin's commercial and critical breakthrough, *The French Connection* (1971). Based on a real-life police case, the film draws stylistically on its director's documentary background, utilising hand-held cameras, de-saturated colour and bleak, urban locations to evoke the painstaking investigation into an international narcotics operation. The fascistic undertones of Gene Hackman's 'Popeye' Doyle police character (a role he reportedly despised) echo those of Clint Eastwood in Don Siegel's *Dirty Harry* (1971), a cop driven as much by frustration and vendetta as any investigative drive. Yet the film remains ambivalent toward its protagonist, a figure boosted considerably by the charisma of Hackman himself. Despite this, the film is undeniably exciting and contains a brilliantly edited car chase which, for its raw encapsulation of the central pursuit theme, remains a benchmark in action cinema. The film received five Academy Awards, including one for Friedkin himself, thus thrusting him into the pantheon of young Hollywood auteurs.

Friedkin fully consolidated his newfound control with *The Exorcist* (1973), a tale of faith and the demonic possession of a 12-year-old girl, which became one of the highest grossing films of all time. Buoyed by an excellent cast (including Max Von Sydow, Lee J. Cobb, Jason Miller and Ellen Burstyn), the film is often crude in the rendition of its thematic core, but also direct and economical in its narrative drive. *The Exorcist*'s early, effective deployment of sinister stillness and silence is jarringly punctuated by heightened sound and montage (notably the use of almost subliminal flash cuts), bringing these elements together in the final exorcism sequence. It also seems reluctant to actually state its position on the science/faith dichotomy, a result of the creative tensions inherent in Friedkin's interpretation of writer/producer (and avowedly Catholic) William Peter Blatty's source novel and screenplay. While this often results in rich ambiguities, the theological themes struggle incessantly to be heard amidst the sheer emotional and sensory effects which are the film's chief assets. *The Exorcist* remains one of the seminal horror films.

Many feel that Friedkin's next film, *Sorcerer* (1977), a remake of Henri-Georges Clouzot's *The Wages of Fear* (1953), symbolises the egomania and ill judgment rampant amongst Hollywood wunderkinds of the period. The story of four men transporting nitro-glycerine across an alien, hostile Latin American landscape, the film strips its existential themes to the core and, driven by a series of striking images, ultimately goes one step further than Clouzot by suggesting that humankind is subject not only to the vagaries of fate and nature but to its own vengeful, venal essence. Despite this bleak outlook, the film contains an effective score by Tangerine Dream and some extraordinary action sequences, notably the hazardous crossing of a fragile bridge during a rain storm. Unlike Clouzot's film, Friedkin does not allow for easy identification with any of the central figures and despite Roy Scheider's impressively physical central performance it remains emotionally aloof. The film was a significant box-office failure and Friedkin would never regain his commercial instincts.

After the heist comedy *The Brink's Job* (1978), Friedkin embarked on *Cruising* (1980), an adaptation of Gerald Walker's novel. Plagued on-set by gay protesters concerned at its perceived homophobic content, the film is one of the most troubling interrogations of brutalising masculinity Hollywood has ever produced. A young police officer (played uncomfortably by Al Pacino) is hired to work undercover to bait a killer stalking New York's sado-masochistic homosexual sub-culture. The film suggests, but never explicitly states, that the cop himself is a repressed homosexual and that his inability to come to terms with this unleashes his own murderous instincts. Friedkin, through a highly elliptical narrative, transforms ambiguity into confusion and incoherence, seemingly less interested in the identity of the killer than the contaminating nature of male violence in general. The oppressive sadism of the investigating police officers finds its reflection in the parodic, carnivalesque but no less sinister ambience of the cavernous night-clubs haunted by Pacino in his investigation. This Jungian shadow motif is crystallised in an extraordinary, grotesque sequence in which an innocent suspect is intimidated and slapped by a giant black man clad only in boots, jock strap and a stetson during a police interrogation. Universally vilified upon release, the film has been reclaimed by some critics, both gay and mainstream. It remains the director's most challenging film and the revelation in a recent interview with Mark Kermode that he originally prepared a much longer version remains a tantalising prospect for admirers of this sorely neglected work.

The satire on arms dealing, *Deal of the Century* (1983), did little to restore Friedkin's commercial foothold. *To Live and Die In L.A.* (1985), on the other hand, proved that he could still construct an exciting action narrative while retaining a cold ambivalence toward his central characters. Showcasing another brilliantly orchestrated car chase, the film also systematically deconstructs the themes and character conventions of the crime thriller (and its attendant homo-erotic underpinnings), blurring the distinctions between pursuer and pursued and subjecting the masculinist tendencies of the genre to a thorough interrogation. Unlike *Cruising*, it is crystalline in its cynical detachment from its protagonist (William L. Petersen) while repeatedly emphasising the seductive elegance of his vicious quarry (Willem Dafoe). Aided immeasurably by cinematographer Robby Muller's imaginative visualisation of the Los Angeles landscape, the film forms an effective trilogy with *The French Connection* and *Cruising* in its interpretation of the police procedural thriller. Where it differs (and arguably benefits over those films) is in its control, clarity and consistency of vision. In this sense, it is arguably Friedkin's best work.

Clarity and coherence are the last qualities one could bestow upon *Rampage* (1988) given that it exists in two, significantly different and ideologically contradictory versions, both prepared by the director himself. Concerned with the legal and moral intricacies of the death penalty in the case of a ritual serial murderer, the film was poorly distributed, reflecting Friedkin's own commercial downfall during the decade. This is a shame as, despite its occasional recourse to TV movie stylistics, the film is sporadically effective, particularly in its early sequences.

Friedkin's subsequent career has been only fleetingly interesting. *The Guardian* (1990) is a supernatural horror film which ransacked many of the clichés the director overcame with his avowedly realist approach in *The Exorcist*. *Blue Chips* (1994) is an equally disappointing effort, never totally transcending sports film conventions in the tale of a college basketball coach (Nick Nolte) coming to terms with corruption. Friedkin's best film of recent years is *Jade* (1995), a much-maligned variation on the 'erotic thriller' cycle initiated by *Basic Instinct* (1991). Like that film, it uses a Joe Eszterhas script but, unlike many examples of the sub-genre, critiques the essential ugliness beneath the sleek, glossy exteriors of the figures involved. While much of the film is dictated by convention, Friedkin's signature, cynical outlook breaks through periodically, not least in a final sequence, which echoes that of *To Live And Die In L.A.*

*Rules of Engagement* (2000) proved to be Friedkin's most commercially successful project since the 1970s, a military courtroom drama set amidst the increasingly incendiary US involvement in middle-eastern politics. During the evacuation of the American Embassy in Yemen (a brilliantly orchestrated but disturbing action sequence), Col. Childers (Samuel L. Jackson) orders his men to open fire on a hostile crowd, resulting in the deaths of 83 people. Insistent that the order was necessary to save the lives of American marines, Childers is tried for murder and defended by his long-time friend and fellow combat veteran, Col. Hodges (Tommy Lee Jones). Addressing themes of loyalty, morality, responsibility and honour in warfare, the film drew widespread criticism for its seemingly jingoistic stance. What the film actually attempts is to draw clear lines of demarcation between the combat soldier and military/political bureaucracy. In doing this, Childers' misguided and catastrophic actions are somehow perceived as a lesser evil against the corruption of National Security Advisor Sokal (Bruce Greenwood). Friedkin manages to inject a degree of ambiguity into the film's pivotal massacre, fully demonstrating the dire consequences but suggesting (in an almost subliminal flash) that a young girl rendered legless by the event actually fired upon the marines. Ultimately, however, the film is more concerned with upholding the integrity of Childers while never actually wholly endorsing his acts. Furthermore, despite Friedkin's provocative approach to topical material, the film also plunders shamelessly from the time-worn cliches of courtroom drama – a burnt-out lawyer takes on one last case, defending his client against a hot-shot prosecutor (Guy Pierce) and overcoming seemingly insurmountable odds. The coda (in which a former Vietcong officer salutes Childers) is one of the most bizarre climaxes to any recent Hollywood film. Friedkin has called the ending his attempt to 'bring some sort of closure to the Vietnam war' – this may be so, but it seems a rather crass statement given the film's inability to credibly resolve many of the issues arising from its more immediate frame of reference.

Friedkin is currently at work on *The Hunted*, yet another re-working of *The Most Dangerous Game* (1932), which reunites him with Tommy Lee Jones.  **NJ**

# Antoine FUQUA

*The Replacement Killers* (1998)
*Bait* (2000)
*Training Day* (2001)

Born in Pittsburgh in 1966, Antoine Fuqua began his career directing music videos for artists as diverse as Arrested Development, Prince, and Stevie Wonder. He won a Music Video Production Award for his work on Coolio's 'Gangsta Paradise' as well as the Sinclair Tenebaum Olesiuk and Emanuel Award for the trailer to the 1995 film *Dangerous Minds*. After making the transition to features, he has since made three films which combine his trademark showy camera work with a judicious use of hip-hop and gangsta rap.

*The Replacement Killers* (1998) has much to recommend it, not least in its eclectic casting. By pairing Academy Award-winning character actress Mira Sorvino alongside Chow Yun-Fat in his English-language debut, Fuqua establishes a complex relationship that lends weight to the film. At a brisk 87 minutes, the plot is a virtual reprisal of Yun-Fat's most iconic role in *The Killer* (1989). He plays a hitman whose debt to the Mob will be written off if he carries out one more job on a corrupt cop's son. Where the film excels is in Fuqua's fluid direction – his sinewy camera fetishises gadgets and guns with obvious delight, and he impressively edits gunfights to the hip-hop beats that run throughout, skilfully utilising his music video experiences. The real masterstroke is the way Ken Sanzel's script pares down the dialogue to a bare minimum – Yun-Fat utters few words, while the action set-pieces are frequently conducted in silent slow motion. With John Woo as Executive Producer, Fuqua's stylistic techniques are necessarily cannibalistic, though never lifeless or impersonal. Especially interesting is Yun-Fat's almost Zen-like aura of invincibility and the kind of easy charm and hip chic that recalls Alain Delon in *Le Samourai* (1967).

Fuqua's second feature, *Bait* (2000), has yet to be released in the UK, perhaps due to its poor critical and commercial reception in America. Straying into the action-comedy genre, the film stars Jamie Foxx as an ex-con used by police to lure a criminal out of hiding. Where Fuqua's kinetic camera moves suited the theme and style of his debut film, the constant use of crashing zooms and skewed close-ups quickly begin to grate here, as he tries to inject some energy into a flaccid storyline. As a Malkovich-like villain, David Morse is always interesting to watch, but the rest of the supporting cast (including David Paymer and *Sopranos*-regular Robert Pastorelli) are left unused and underdeveloped. Foxx is no Eddie Murphy (the plot is a virtual rehash of *48 Hours* (1982)), and the absence of fast-mouth action or black comedy highlights the lack of originality in script and direction.

*Training Day* (2001) was heralded as one of the year's most impressive films, not only marking a return to form of Fuqua but elevating him to A-list status. Again Fuqua sources another work, this time *Internal Affairs* (1990), to fashion a film that contains a stunning performance from Denzel Washington as a corrupt cop, Alonzo Harris, who is guiding raw recruit (Ethan Hawke) through a LAPD 'training day'. Although clearly an 'actor's film', Fuqua provides solid direction, again showcasing his flashy camera moves and voyeuristic delight in all things technological and ballistic. Most impressive is his use of music to underscore mood, the assembling of a strong support cast (Scott Glenn, Tom Berenger, Dr. Dre) and a key scene in which Hawke is left to play cards with an assortment of killers and rapists. The tension in this scene is unbearable, and Fuqua's nervy camera and non-moralistic stance shows signs of maturity and panache. Yet the real star is Washington, who finally puts years of noble performances behind him. With his winning smile, hip-hop swagger and shallow morality, he excels in a role that justly rewarded him with an Academy Award. Hawke received a nomination, and the interplay between the two actors is facilitated by a mix of Fuqua's impressive direction and slick editing.

His next film, *Hostile Rescue*, which is due for release in 2003, stars Bruce Willis. **BM**

# Sidney J. FURIE

Born in Toronto in 1933 and educated at the Carnegie Institute of Theater, Sidney J. Furie showed early promise, writing plays for television performance. His feature film career began here with a film for which he raised the funds himself, *A Dangerous Age* (1958), about a teenage elopement. Concentrating on character and emotion, with a careful if conventional construction, the film gave an early indication of Furie's later British social conscience youth movies. This was sustained in his second film, *A Cool Sound From Hell* (1959), which took rebellious youth, jazz, and beat poetry, rendering them with harsh and evocative photography and the sensitivity to atmosphere evident in his debut.

Furie moved to England in 1960, where he made a range of films establishing a penchant for showy camera work. He wrote, produced, and directed several films a year. *Doctor Blood's Coffin* (1961) and *The Snake Woman* (1961), both hoary Hammer-style films, were separated by three movies all released in the same year. *During One Night* deals sincerely with the sexual inexperience of an American soldier in wartime England, suffering the trauma of his friend's suicide; *Three on a Spree* provides a lively new version of the play (and later film) 'Brewster's Millions'; *The Young Ones* marked the first of two films with Cliff Richard, the second being *Wonderful Life* in 1964. Both are characterised by their star's toothy zest, jaunty choreography and implausibly naïve plotting.

Furie's move into more socially conscious work came with *The Boys* in 1962, a courtroom drama about four East End youths accused of the brutal murder of an elderly garage worker. Opened out by flashback detailing the events of the night and the lives of the boys, the film utilises grainy photography, location shooting and naturalistic lighting, and eschews a manipulative score and traditional happy ending to evoke an austere social commentary.

1963's *The Leather Boys* provokes careful debate about homosexuality within the boundaries of mainstream cinema, following on the heels of Basil Dearden's *Victim* (1961). Initially concerned with the story of a young newlywed couple, the film goes on to introduce issues surrounding male relationships as a young man enters the couple's lives. Shot in close-ups to reinforce the intimacy of the story, the ending is necessarily compromised considering the time and the legal status of homosexuality, but overall Furie manages observant, careful direction of a difficult subject.

Furie's reputation was cemented with what remains the highlight of his long career. *The Ipcress File* (1965) (adapted from Len Deighton's spy thriller) launched Michael Caine's Harry Palmer upon a world used to the suave sophistication of James Bond. Shown in thick spectacles, proudly brandishing his East London accent, into cookery and supermarket shopping, Caine's Palmer is an anti-authoritarian counterculture hero asserting his individuality and investigating the typical establishment spy facade. Furie's visual style became more significant in this film, as he utilises canted camera angles and demonstrates a penchant for shooting through parking meters, rear-view mirrors and clashing cymbals to provide a distorted and distinctive view.

Typically, Hollywood sat up and took notice of this surprise success, and Furie moved to the US in 1966. His first studio film (for Universal) was *The Appaloosa* (1966), a western weighed down by Marlon Brando's desire to develop his passion for the plight of the Native American Indians at the expense of the film. Furie's distinctive style edges over into parody with a disruptive variety of oddly angled shots attempting to invest the tiniest of actions with significance.

After directing duties on the J. Lee Thompson-credited *The Eye of the Devil* (1966), Furie made *The Naked Runner* (1967), with Frank Sinatra as an ex-spy travelling with his son while Peter Vaughan's dubious boss coaxes him into one last murder. An attempt to mimic the success and style of *The Ipcress File*, this film revitalises the genre in many ways but suffers from Furie's now intrusive style.

*The Lawyer* (1970), which he also wrote from an earlier discarded script, went on to form the basis for the television lawyer series 'Petrocelli', starring the film's star Barry Newman in the title role. A fictionalised account of the trial of Dr Sam Sheppard (a case which also inspired 'The Fugitive'), the film briefly returns to Furie's more socially concerned period, dealing implicitly with racism and small-town hypocrisy. Here, with a successfully researched legal script, Furie rejects his idiosyncratic style for a keen sense of environment and character detail to some success.

*Little Fauss and Big Halsy* (1970) marked the beginning of Furie's career re-working popular films at studios' behest. An unoriginal but competently achieved biker movie following two minor league racers on their journey across America, the film borrows from a variety of popular counter-culture sources, including Arthur Penn's *Bonnie and Clyde* (1967) and *Easy Rider* (1969) with no sense of Furie's own concerns stamped over them. A range of disparate elements (the William Burroughs-reading hippy girl; the tortoise and hare fable) are unified self-consciously with a return to Furie's trademark shooting: close-ups of flies on food; races filmed from beneath wheels; shooting the white trash family through their home's screen door.

Furie's next feature, a biopic of jazz singer Billie Holiday, *Lady Sings the Blues* (1972), an old-fashioned telling of Holiday's eventful life and career, was a box-office hit. Like Furie's *Gable and Lombard* (1976), about the scandal surrounding these Hollywood stars, the movie endorses inaccuracies and composites, using cliché and stereotypes, preferring gloss to grit in a sentimental and unquestioning account of Holiday's life. 1973's *Hit!*, about a Federal agent taking action against the drug gang who killed his daughter, demonstrates Furie's intermittent desire to reinvigorate genre, in this case the thriller, to varying success. *Sheila Levine is Dead and Living in New York* (1975) – an oddity which was buried at the box office, was followed, after *Gable and Lombard*, by an attempt to replicate Robert Altman's war movie *M\*A\*S\*H* (1970). *The Boys in Company C* (1978) is reminiscent of Furie's early British work in its emphasis on male bonding and social context but avoids any serious debate by placing emphasis on old-fashioned team spirits, and showing how rebellion can be easily re-modelled as patriotism. Even the peace-loving hippy fires up with the rest of them, and 'bad' soldiers were always so, rather than corrupted by a war. Despite its ellipses and overlaps, à la Altman, the film is more confusing than groundbreaking and is ultimately tearfully sentimental.

*The Entity* (1981), a schlock-horror cashing in on recent cinematic hits, was based on an allegedly true story of a woman terrorised by a supernatural force, and demonstrates how easy it is for a director of erstwhile note to become a hack. *Purple Hearts* (1984) followed, a simple love story set against a Vietnam hospital, and Furie's involvement with three of the *Iron Eagle* films (the first, second and fourth, made in 1986, 1988 and 1995 respectively, with the sequels capitalising on the success of Tony Scott's airborne adventure *Top Gun* (1986)). Endorsing right-wing Rambo-style politics through the unidentified but obviously Middle-Eastern villains, the films are glossy and ridiculous, and a studio-imposed soundtrack (a legacy of *Top Gun*) reduces the airborne combat to the level of pop video. In between, Furie directed *Superman IV* (1987), completing the franchise's box-office decline with a poorly structured visually disconnected movie. *The Taking of Beverly Hills* (1991) and *Ladybugs* (1992) have completed his devolution into jobbing studio hack.

The 1990s saw Furie embark on two film projects which were then partly abandoned: *On The Run*, due to start filming in Ireland in 1995, and *In Her Defense*, which went into production in 1998 and appears only to have secured Canadian release at present. *Top of the World* (1997), *Hollow Point* (1995), and *The Rage* (1997) achieved limited theatrical release. *Tripwire*, *The Collectors* (a traditional crime thriller) and *Cord* (released in 2000) were all completed in 1999, a remarkably industrious year for Furie. He has also busied himself with television films including *Married to a Stranger* (1997), and *The Rage* (1999), an FBI-set action thriller.

Furie is still hard at work: *My 5 Wives* (2000), a comedy written by and starring Rodney Dangerfield as a real estate agent, received a limited theatrical release. *A Friday Night Date* (2000) is narratively reminiscent of Steven Spielberg's *Duel* (1971), taking as its main story Casper Van Dien's nice-guy hero, fresh from saving a pretty college student from a domestic situation, becoming involved in a chase with a crazy truck driver as he drives the student home. Elements of tension in this attempt-at-thriller fail to compete with Spielberg's spare, fresh rendition of the story.

Furie has consistently worked, mainly in Canada, with his films, covering a variety of genres. *Going Back* (2001) is the story of Marines returning to Vietnam as part of a television show; *Global Heresy* (2001) oddly casts British theatricals Joan Plowright and Peter O'Toole in a tale about a rising rock band whose lead singer disappears on the eve of a European tour; *Donzi: The Legend* (2001) is the action-adventure 'life and times' of legendary boat designer and off-shore racing champion Don Aronow. Whilst he seems to have given up the idea of investing his work with personal style and concerns, and takes on projects that are destined for limited release, Furie still demonstrates that he is as productive as ever.                                                   **JD**

# G

## Vincent GALLO

*Buffalo 66* (1998)

Vincent Gallo, a successful model, painter, musician and actor whose screen credits include *Arizona Dream* (1993), *The Funeral* (1996), *Palookaville* (1996), and *Truth or Consequences* (1997), was born in Buffalo, New York in 1956. He made his critically acclaimed directorial debut in 1998 with *Buffalo 66*.

Gallo's film is as idiosyncratic and gaunt as the ex-Calvin Klein model himself. It is, as noted by reviewers, self-obsessed, intelligent, satirical, and expressive. The film itself is a loosely-connected group of set-pieces following the cathartic quest of a sociopathic hero, Billy Brown, played by Gallo, who returns to the place of his birth upon his release from prison to rid himself of the memory of his abusive childhood. During the course of his journey he abducts a white-trash tap-dancing teenager (Christina Ricci) who is forced to pose as his wife during a visit to the home of Billy's maniacal parents (played by Angelica Huston and Ben Gazzara). Billy's redemptive journey is a character-based study that, like other performer-turned-director cinematic efforts, foregrounds performance style over narrative and spectacle. However, Gallo's spirited use of the camera ensures that simple empathy with the central protagonist is never fully guaranteed. By employing techniques such as shooting on reverse stock, using often drawn-out and vainglorious stretches of dialogue, and utilising innovative methods of editing – particularly in the flashback sequences – the audience is constantly alienated from the world that Gallo creates; a world of bleak tableaux settings inhabited by misfits, suburban louts, bullies and Billy's own self-obsessive paranoia.

Gallo presents us with a contemporary fable in which he explores the dysfunction of blue-collar suburbia, with a special emphasis on the turgid and often heartless drama of American family life. **PH**

## Mick GARRIS

*Critters 2: The Main Course* (1988)
*Sleepwalkers* (1992)

Successfully ensconced in genre film and television as a writer-director-producer, Mick Garris has proven himself adept at combining horror and fantasy without recourse to too much postmodern irony. Alongside directors John Carpenter, Rob Reiner and Frank

Darabont, Garris is the other key interpreter of Stephen King's fiction for the screen. Garris, though, has worked primarily within the framework of television and the mini series with King's work. He has directed mini-series adaptations of *The Stand* (1994) and *The Shining* (1997), and has recently directed three episodes of the television supernatural drama, 'The Others', executive produced by Steven Spielberg. Garris' career to date has been consistent, demonstrating a sincere commitment to the horror genre. As a writer he has been responsible for numerous television pieces and also supplied the story for the Stan Winston-directed Michael Jackson promo, 'Ghosts'. Garris has also provided the stories for the films *Hocus Pocus* (1994), *The Fly 2* (1988) and *batteries not included* (1987).

A self-confessed genre fan all his life, Garris began as a freelance, supplying articles to such legendary fan boy bibles as *Cinefantastique*, *Fangoria* and *Starlog*. From there he began producing behind the scenes promos for film distributor Avco, documenting the making of films such as *The Fog* (1980), *The Howling* (1980), and *Escape from New York* (1981). In 1982 Garris, now at Universal, handled publicity on *E.T. The Extra-Terrestrial* (1982) and three years later was a major player in the production of Steven Spielberg's anthology series, 'Amazing Stories'.

Garris made his theatrical feature debut with *Critters 2* (1988), the sequel to the 1986 horror comedy about alien furballs who maraud and munch their way through America. After another spell in television, he returned to the theatrical format with an adaptation of another Stephen King novel, *Sleepwalkers* (1992), essentially a vampire story about a monstrous mother and son who feed off a local virgin. To date, Garris' most confident and successful contribution to horror adaptation has been his epic and involving adaptation of 'The Stand' – a mini-series project which took its time in building character. His small screen version of 'The Shining' was scripted by King himself and as one might appreciate, is markedly different to Kubrick's take on the tale. Garris has planned to direct an adaptation of Stephen King's novel 'Desperation'.                    **JC**

# Mel GIBSON

*Man Without a Face* (1993)
*Braveheart* (1995)
Born in New York in 1956, Mel Gibson shot to public prominence as the avenger cop, Max Rockatansky, in the post-apocalyptic *Mad Max* trilogy (1979, 1981, 1985). Gibson then switched continents and reinvented himself, as LAPD detective Martin Riggs, in the *Lethal Weapon* films (1987, 1989, 1992, 1998). These macho cop sagas showcased Gibson's penchant for physical comedy and personal eccentricity, while firmly establishing his international reputation as a bankable action star. These two iconic characters were peppered among a string of respectable performances in a variety of genres.

Gibson's debut feature as director, *Man Without a Face* (1993), is a coming-of-age drama set in 1968 Maine, and is a competent, diligent, and credible directorial effort. The story revolves around the relationship between Justin McCleod (Gibson), a gruff, internally scarred misanthrope, and twelve-year-old Chuck Norstadt (Nick Stahl), who wishes to escape his dysfunctional family by getting into a private military academy. During this allegory on alienation, intimate bonds are formed, innocence is lost, regained, and lost again, as fear grows into friendship. Although cynically referred to as a 'Mel-o-drama', it frequently avoids cheap sentimentalism. Gibson's directorial eye was intelligent, daring, technically strong, and yet understated.

*Braveheart* (1995) won Gibson Academy Awards for Best Director and Best Picture, plus the Golden Globe Award for Best Director. Exquisitely realised in a grimy medieval atmosphere, the film is full of sex, treachery, battle, and passion. Gibson stars as a charismatic Scot, William Wallace, another internally scarred soul. Revelling in its raw energy, the film graphically depicts disfigurement on a grand scale with sickeningly savage realism.

Gibson cinematically cogitates upon the values of freedom and human dignity, particularly amongst the Machiavellian machinations of small-minded Scottish noblemen and powerful English kings. Directed with a sure hand and less experimentation than before, Gibson re-tapped the hero cycle and went one better by making Wallace messianic, complete with a suspended crucifixion pose on a cross. *Braveheart* graphically explores issues of honour, nobility, love, loss, life and death; the quintessential elements of human existence, and the director's neophyte preoccupations.

Gibson's cinematic legacy is irrevocably assured. However, since his Academy Award-winning directorial triumph he has not attempted to direct again, preferring to relegate himself to acting and producing via his development company Icon Productions.    **AK**

# Jim GILLESPIE

Before working on his second feature *D-Tox* (2002), a formulaic Sylvester Stallone vehicle, Jim Gillespie entered into the film-making profession with *I Know What You Did Last Summer* (1997), little being known about his previous offering *Joyride* (1995). Whilst the opening scenes work to establish the somewhat complex relationships between the teen protagonists and those around them, the film soon loses steam and ends up looking poor in comparison to the likes of *Scream* (1996), released in the previous year. Perhaps the main problem for Gillespie was having to make something of Kevin Williamson's relatively lame screenplay, one that returns to more straightforward horror conventions and with considerably weaker dialogue than we have come to expect. As a result, the film lacks any major thrills, although Gillespie manages to make up for this with the relentless promise of such delights, working – occasionally to great effect – with the audience's generic literacy. Furthermore, Gillespie's playful shot of a victim's body being carried on the killer's hook is truly comical, going some way to make up for the distinct lack of ironic humour and self-awareness elsewhere. The film also looks good (for its genre), and the director clearly understands how to generate the required amount of tension. Unfortunately, *I Know* looks tired and formulaic on repeated viewing, although it would be wrong to blame Gillespie for this generic fault. Furthermore, whilst the film may be weak in comparison to some of its contemporaries, one need only look at Danny Cannon's sequel to see how bad things can get. Of course, the sequel may never have existed were it not for Gillespie's delightful 'the-killer-lives' ending, one that leaves the audience feeling ultimately satisfied.

His next project (which he will also co-write) is *Julian*, a horror film about a girl whose imaginary friend starts murdering people around her.    **CP**

# Terry GILLIAM

Terry Gilliam is best known for films that inventively combine the gothic and romantic. His trademark soaring flights of fantasy are often set to attack dogged rationality and grey-minded bureaucracy.

Gilliam was born in Minneapolis in 1940 and after university his ability to draw and anarchic brand of humour led him to work for *Help!* magazine (1962–65) in New York. Here he rubbed shoulders with cult artists such as Robert Crumb, and met John Cleese after seeing him in a pre-Python comedy show, 'Cambridge Circus'. Entranced by the presence of real castles and disillusioned with America, Gilliam travelled to Europe, ending up in London in the late 1960s. His first break came as a resident artist on a television show, followed by some animation commissioned for 'Do Not Adjust Your Set' (1967–69), a British children's television show featuring several subsequent Pythons. On joining the 'Monty Python's Flying Circus' team, Gilliam's main task was to create the animated segments that bridged the sketches. Combining cut-outs, often taken from medieval and renaissance paintings, with airbrushed caricatures, Gilliam's animation lent a certain surreal richness to the show, as well as adding an extra-textual dimension. Working to flout expectations and often using grotesque imagery, Gilliam's animations are one of the stylistic hallmarks of Python humour.

Python provided Gilliam with the chance to realise his ambition to direct live action. After dissatisfaction with the treatment of the first Python film, the Pythons sought to maintain control over their next film by keeping the direction within the team. Sharing the role, Gilliam and Terry Jones took rather different approaches to the task of directing *Monty Python and the Holy Grail* (1975). Gilliam's focus was on creating a film full of visual interest, whereas Jones and other members of the crew treated the production process in much the same way as a television show. Despite the problems experienced by the two neophyte directors the film was a box-office success and continues to have cult status. Although largely ignored by critics of British cinema, the satirical technique of deglamourising the Arthurian legend has been read as bringing politics and history back into the myth. Since *Holy Grail*'s active rejection of the gleaming and super-clean

Hollywood presentation of the Arthurian myth, no Arthurian romance – straight or comic – has ever looked the same again. Gilliam's fascination with the filthy and fetid aspect of the medieval world recurs in his later films. *Holy Grail* fuelled Gilliam's desire to direct, and shortly after he went on to make another medieval comedy based on a nonsense poem by Lewis Carroll.

Co-written by Gilliam, *Jabberwocky* (1977) was carefully storyboarded and he claims that the directorial experience was far easier on this picture because of the presence of actors. The film is an atmospheric, gruesome fairytale set in the middle ages, yet has Pythonesque humour – perhaps because of the pressure to build on the success of *Holy Grail*. For viewers expecting pure Python the film was a disappointment and it is the only film Gilliam has made that does not enjoy a current video release. It is, however, full of innovative eccentricity as well as featuring a slew of British comedy actors, including Max Wall. Some critics seemed to find the film far-fetched and simply not funny enough. However, for others, its visual invention and unorthodox approach are its strengths. It also seems to have influenced John Boorman, who allegedly studied the film's style before he set out to shoot *Excalibur* (1981). Gilliam did not direct the next Python film, *Life of Brian* (1979), but worked mainly as the film's designer, as well as contributing to the acting, screenwriting and some animation.

Funded by George Harrison's Handmade Films, *Time Bandits* (1981) was written by Gilliam and Michael Palin. The film bends the laws of the physical universe, often using eccentric camera angles, wide-angle lenses and disparate scale, to create a combination of science fiction, fantasy and slapstick that revolves around a small boy named Kevin (Craig Warnock). His adventures begin when a band of dwarves accidentally arrive in his bedroom after having stolen a map of time gateways from God. The film's lesson is that heroes are less than what they seem, lending the film a wistful sense of the impossibility of the ideal. In many of Gilliam's films fantasy is figured as creative and imaginative escape from reality, but it also carries with it an air of loss. This often evokes a violent and abrupt response, as is the case with the presence of the descending gigantic squashing foot that appears in the animated Python credits. At the end of *Time Bandits* it is tempting to read the unexpected explosion of Kevin's middle-class gadget-obsessed parents as an expression of anger at the loss of the fantasy world and it potential heroic father figure, King Agamemnon (Sean Connery). This anger, alongside an anarchic pleasure in overturning expectation, prevents Gilliam's films from becoming overly sentimental.

Two of Gilliam's recurring themes, the power of the imagination and the fight against corporate or bureaucratic culture, are taken up in the section he directed in the last Python film, *The Meaning of Life* (1983). Entitled 'The Crimson Permanent Assurance' it is a tale of swashbuckling on the high accountant sea. After having made the management walk the plank, the anchor is pulled on the City of London building and the rebellious and rather elderly Dickensian crew set sail, with accompanying heroic music, towards the New York corporate accountants to launch a take-over. The mixture of live action and cut-out animation allows the building to become a ship and office furniture transform into weapons. The sequence provides a pseudo B-movie to the main feature and intrudes on the other film at one point. It is a remarkable sequence borrowing from 'Boy's Own' tales of high romance to stage an attack on and poke anarchic fun at the captains of corporate culture.

Co-written with Charles McKweon and Tom Stoppard, *Brazil* (1985) is perhaps Gilliam's best known film to date and is stylistically stunning. Bringing a 1940s veneer to modern day technology, Gilliam produces a technocratic nightmare by revealing the innards of machines, as with the intestinal ducting in all the buildings in the film. Sam Lowry (Jonathan Pryce) escapes the banality, and later horror, of Orwellian bureaucracy and totalitarian control through fantasies of free-soaring flight and heroic deeds. As in many of Gilliam's films this is double-edged. Lowry's fantasy life acts as a buffer, preventing him from doing anything about the status quo. During the post production of the film Gilliam staged his own battle against the Hollywood studio with a stake in the project. Universal's newly hired boss would not take delivery of the film for US distribution until it was given a new 'romantic' ending and significantly cut, leaving Gilliam little option as to his course of action. Quality prevailed, however, and after the so-called 'director's cut' won awards and a general campaign, spearheaded by Gilliam, took hold of the American media the film was eventually released in the US, but with little publicity from the studio. It nevertheless gained two Academy Award nominations.

Gilliam's next film, *The Adventures of Baron von Munchausen* (1988), is a wild vision that breaks all the rules of time and scale. Charting the heroic tall-tales of the Baron (John Neville) the film, like *Brazil* and *Time Bandits*, is concerned with the power of fantasy, and the villain is a dogged pragmatist. Set during the eighteenth-century Enlightenment, the film plays with philosophical ideas such as the mind-body split, and juxtaposes earth-bound science with a balloon flight to visit the King of the Moon. There are some outstanding cameo performances in the film, including Robin Williams' hysterical King of the Moon and Oliver Reed's explosive, cuckolded Vulcan. In some ways less bleak than *Brazil*, it still carries a certain sense of nostalgia and loss. Partly funded by Columbia Pictures, the film ran into financial difficulties, halting production and forcing changes to Gilliam's plans, mainly due to poor production management. The grandeur of the sets and the film's rather rambling structure has a capricious charm. Despite its failure to recoup its cost at the box office, it nevertheless stands as testimony to Gilliam's visionary imagination.

*The Fisher King* (1991) began a cycle of films made in the US that were directed, but not written, by Gilliam. After the ordeal of *Munchausen*, Gilliam launched into an American studio picture based on a screenplay by Richard LaGravenese which focused on characters rather than stunning special effects. Its appeal for Gilliam lay in its status as a modern grail story, the combination of the themes of redemption and love, and its critique of 1980s self-serving values. Robin Williams plays a crazy down and out, named Parry, whose personal tragedy and naïve romanticism facilitates the redemption of an ex-yuppie DJ (Jeff Bridges). In this world, events are connected and actions have consequences, making it a type of medieval morality tale shifted onto the streets of New York. The city is transformed into a fairytale landscape, including a castle that houses the grail that Jack must retrieve to revive Parry from coma. Gilliam adds individual touches to the screenplay, such as the Central Station commuters breaking into a waltz. The film benefits from ad-libbed dialogue and largely avoids a mawkish approach, while retaining a sense of human failings and frailties. Bob MacCabe claims that this was the film that 'melded Gilliam's inner vision to the outside world'.

*12 Monkeys* (1995) has Gilliam's trademark textural density and brings his signature gothic technology to the film's vision of the future. Past, present, and future are connectively layered into a story that unites love with madness, action chases and desperation. The central character, Cole (Bruce Willis), is a time traveller looking to pinpoint the moment in the past when a deadly germ was released. Confused by the shock of time travel and conflicting messages, Cole begins to believe that he is psychotic, partly as a way of staying with the woman he has fallen in love with. Following clues left by the '12 monkeys' graffiti, Cole and his girlfriend realise that they have been following a false trail, and that history has mis-read the signs as forewarning the release of the germ. In the closing scenes Cole, as a child, watches himself being shot in pursuit of the germ carrier. It becomes clear that he cannot save five billion people from dying, but, unknown to him, his actions mean that the germ can be analysed by future scientists, with the aim of decontaminating the surface of the earth. The film confronts the paradox of time travel and comes out with an innovative and complex approach to pre-determination.

Gilliam's most recent film, *Fear and Loathing in Las Vegas* (1998), is in many ways as close as a Hollywood film can get to stream-of-consciousness form, and this is its strength. Based on Hunter S. Thompson's novella, the film revels in recreating the various drug-induced psychoses experienced by Raoul Duke (Johnny Depp) and Dr Gonzo (Benecio Del Torro). But this is not simply an 'out of it' movie; Gilliam brings a certain ironic distance to the mindless excess that is meant to be the nemesis of the American dream. Depp's performance is finely tuned, particularly through the inarticulate hand gestures that speak his character's subjective hyper-turmoil. The wide-angle lenses and extreme tilts, which recur in most of Gilliam's films, find a fitting context here, and the hallucinatory sequences are convincingly rendered. While the film might be assigned to the realms of cultdom, it is, nevertheless, full of surreal intelligence and interest.

From medieval dragons to Las Vegas lounge lizards, Gilliam's films collectively resemble a postmodern bestiary. Offbeat heroes do battle with mind-numbing institutions, grey bureaucracies, and psychoses and no one gets off such encounters lightly. Setting his mettle against the Hollywood leviathan, Gilliam's skewed visions, coupled with his independent and often uncompromising approach, establish his status as contemporary auteur. *Good Omens*, a comedic fantasy based on the novel by Neil Gaiman and Terry Pratchett, is his next planned project. **TK**

# François GIRARD

François Girard has, on the basis of a relatively small filmography over the course of the last six years, received much acclaim and recognition for his work. Born in St-Felicien, Québec, in 1963, he studied communications in Québec City and Montreal, going on to develop a career in video art and music videos (including a Peter Gabriel concert film), before taking the step in film directing.

At the head of his oeuvre is his quasi-documentary *Thirty Two Short Films About Glenn Gould* (1993). Charting the life of the extraordinary Canadian pianist, Girard eschews the traditional narrative approach of the biopic, and opts for a more interesting examination of the multi-faceted, and often contradictory, nature of one of the major musical figures of the century. Taking the structure of his film from Bach's 'Goldberg Variations' (one of Gould's signature pieces), Girard offers perhaps more insight than a conventionally linear narrative might allow. With some sections dedicated to 'fictionalised re-enactments' of moments from Gould's life (featuring a remarkable performance from Colm Feore as Gould), and others featuring 'documentary' interviews with people who knew him (family, friends, colleagues, and so on), the film seems to get to the heart of Gould as artist and individual. Girard also adopts an occasional 'abstract' section, one of which – the importing into his own film of an abstract animation tribute to Gould by fellow Canadian Norman McLaren – makes explicit the links Girard would seek to adopt with established canons of Canadian culture. Aesthetically, the film is marked by an absolute economy of means; very simple camerawork and editing.

For his second feature, *Le Violon Rouge* (*The Red Violin*) (1998), Girard takes on a more straightforward narrative, though still not fully linear. Once again, he pursues a musically-oriented narrative, this time with a violin as the protagonist. The film charts the history of a single violin from its creation, through its various owners over the course of three hundred years, and the power the instrument exerts on them. As a portmanteau film, *Le Violon Rouge* follows its predecessor in adopting a musical form, this time the fugue, as the basis for the narrative structure. Girard exhibits his ability to handle a more expansive and emotional narrative form and aesthetic (underpinned by John Corigliano's Academy Award-winning score), even if the ultimate secret about the violin's origins becomes readily apparent fairly early on. Where the film really impresses, however, is in the connecting device of a present-day auction; the scene is replayed throughout the film, revealing more information and characters' differing interpretations of it (a contemporary take on Kurosawa's *Rashomon* (1951) principle), and is handled with real verve and originality.

Neatly bridging the two feature films is a television documentary, *The Sound of the Carceri* (1997), made as part of the series 'Yo-Yo Ma: Inspired By Bach', in which cellist Ma collaborated with a range of film-makers to produce a series of six films around his performances of Bach's six suites for solo cello. In his film, Girard utilises advanced computer special effects techniques to recreate the Carceri d'Invenzione etchings of the eighteenth-century Italian architect Giovanni Battista Piranesi. The film attempts to seek the link between the purely visual elements in architecture (the artist's plans) and music (the composer's notes), and how these are to be realised by their interpreters. The film explores how a musical performance is built, and how it can be represented visually. Coming as it does between the two musically-oriented feature films of the director, *The Sound of the Carceri* seems to stand as a very clear representation of Girard's project to date.

Forthcoming work includes *Stompanato*, a film based on the true story of the affair between mobster Johnny Stompanto and actress Lana Tana (starring Antonio Banderas and Sharon Stone) and *The Magician's Wife*, adapted from the novel by Brian Moore about a French official in Algieria. **JP**

# Paul Michael GLASER

Born in Cambridge, Massachusetts, in 1943, this actor-turned-director became a household name in the 1970s playing Detective Dave Starsky in the successful cop show 'Starsky and Hutch'. He also achieved an unenviable fame through family tragedy as his wife and two children contracted HIV, which led to her death and later the death of Glaser's daughter from AIDS in the 1980s.

The Cutting Edge (1992)
Air Up There (1996)
Kazaam (1996)

Leonard Maltin has described his work as a director as 'affably minor'. The judgment is not unfair. His directing debut was the silly television movie *Amazons* (1985), in which the descendants of female warriors plot subversion in contemporary Washington. The film is notable only for the presence of former blaxploitation star Tamara Dobson, and a pre-stardom Madeleine Stowe. Glaser followed this with his first theatrical feature, *Band of the Hand* (1986). The story of a Vietnam veteran who trains Miami street kids in the Florida everglades so they can combat drug dealers, the film plays like a poor 1970s vigilante movie produced a decade too late. Despite the involvement of Michael Mann, the creator of 'Miami Vice' who emerged as a major American director in the 1990s with *Heat* (1995) and *The Insider* (1999), the film is shoddy and derivative. Like Mann's 1980s television work, *Band of the Hand* contains some ugly stylistic excesses – such as loud rock music accompanying any action scenes – that led to the film looking dated almost as soon as it was released. There are a number of talented performers in the cast, including Laurence Fishburne, Lauren Holly and a magnificently slimy James Remar, but they are wasted in a film that seems to offer violence against coke dealers as a kind of bonding exercise.

The violent content of the film may well be what landed Glaser his next project, *The Running Man* (1987), his most prestigious film to date. Featuring Arnold Schwarzenegger, it was based on a book by Richard Bachmann (a pseudonymous Stephen King). In this reworking of Ernest B. Schoedsack's *The Most Dangerous Game* (1932), Schwarzenegger is a contestant on a gladiatorial game show in a futuristic dystopian America. The film offers the familiar, dubious pleasures of an 1980s Schwarzenegger vehicle, with lots of violence and accompanying one-liners. Glaser is no James Cameron or Paul Verhoeven, however, and *The Running Man* never achieves the gloss of either *The Terminator* (1984) or *Total Recall* (1989). It looks cheap and despite reliable support from Yaphet Kotto, the end result is boring.

After a five-year gap, Glaser made *The Cutting Edge* (1992), a restrained affair about an ice-hockey star who becomes an ice-dancer and his romance with his skating partner. Glaser seems more comfortable with the sweet-natured relationship here than with the brutal fisticuffs of his previous picture. D. B. Sweeney and Moira Kelly make a fairly convincing couple in this formula but absorbing love story. Particularly effective is the way footage of the leads is skilfully and seamlessly matched with doubles in the ice-dancing sequences.

*Air Up There* (1996) was something of an oddity – a kind of African tribal sports satire with Kevin Bacon. He plays a slimy basketball agent scouting for stars in Africa who gets involved in tribal warfare. Despite expecting its audience to swallow the notion that ancient conflicts can be solved by a basketball game, it is amiable and well-intentioned. There is some awareness of the cynicism at the heart of US sports but it is mild compared to William Friedkin's hard-hitting *Blue Chips* (1994) and Steve James' *Hoop Dreams* (1996). The cast includes members of African tribes, who served as the models for the films' fictional adversaries, and also two African-born American college Basketball stars. There are considerable attempts made to ensure the film avoids the traditional patronising Hollywood stereotypes and this attempt at careful handling of racial/cultural issues adds something to the viewers' enjoyment. Despite Glaser's economical direction, the film performed disappointingly at the box office. It remains, however, the director's best work. The super-hero fantasy *Kazaam* (1996) followed. Primarily a vehicle for the 'acting' talents of the athlete Shaquille O'Neal, this children's movie about a genie was a backward step after *Air Up There*. Cheap special effects and television movie production values make this a weak addition to the director's oeuvre.

Glaser is currently in production with *Untitled Peppermint Lounge*, which stars Chazz Palminteri and Bruno Kirby. He has worked hard to distance himself from his TV cop persona, directing some well-intentioned if lightweight movies. As yet his directing has not yet eclipsed his acting, and with the regular re-runs of 'Starsky and Hutch' and the thirst for 1970s nostalgia, there is little sign this will change in the future.                                                                                  **IC**

# Arne GLIMCHER

After starting his adult career as an art dealer and establishing an excellent reputation for his New York Pace Gallery, Arne Glimcher broke into cinema with a small acting role as an auction bidder in 1984's *Still of the Night*. He earned some respectable producing credits for *Legal Eagles* (1986), *Gorillas in the Mist* (1988), and *The Good Mother* (1988), gleaning the information and skills required to create a film, and patiently waited until the opportunity arose to direct himself. Born in 1938, Glimcher was 54 when *The Mambo Kings* opened in 1992, and was rewarded for his bold career move so late in life with a warm reception to his adaptation of the Pulitzer Prize-winning novel by Oscar Hijuelos.

Swathed in nostalgia, it is the story of two Cuban brothers immigrating to New York in 1952, amid the heat of mambo music's popularity. The American dream they seek with their band, the eponymous Mambo Kings, inevitably effects a strain on the Castillo brothers' relationship in a film about familial ties that bind but also strangle. The casting is excellent, with Antonio Banderas in his first English-speaking feature. He is strong as the younger, more introspective brother Nestor, who finds the expression of his soul in music. Armand Assante gleams as the older and feistier brother, Cesar, the driving force behind the pair's musical act. Glimcher lets himself down, however, with his handling of the disintegration of their personal relationship, which is threatened by a romantic interest in the same woman; the gradual resentment and tension comes across as tired and formulaic. Indeed, the only thing saving the film from the routines of melodrama is Glimcher's privileging of music as the central feature. The camera moves with the rhythm and tempo of mambo; exciting the audience, making them dance. This is enhanced by the sharp editing, which often cuts against the beat, keeping the visual-musical dynamic lively and driven.

The commercial success of *The Mambo Kings* (Warner Bros. reimbursed Glimcher his personal investment of $1 million after it exceeded box-office expectations) meant that Glimcher was guaranteed a bigger and better production for his next film. He chose to make another adaptation and filmed *Just Cause* (1995), from John Katzenbach's successful legal thriller. From the premise alone, this project seems bound to impress, with a high-profile cast including Sean Connery and Laurence Fishburne, a chilling Florida Everglades location, a market-tested narrative and an audience already primed for dark thrillers in the wake of *Cape Fear* (1991) and *Silence of the Lambs* (1991). All the film delivers though is a limp plagiarism of the terrifying psychological intricacies visited by those films: the performances are derivative (particularly Ed Harris' shamelessly overacted Hannibal Lector homage), there is no coherency and sense to the plot, and eventually the uneven pace brings us to a bewildering climax. As if in one last effort to make a feature of the lush location, Glimcher's camera returns insistently to the crocodiles that live in the swampland. Instead of adding to the tension, they detract from the narrative issues, and then suddenly and unnecessarily, one of the criminals gets eaten.

Glimcher's most recent work *The White River Kid* (1999), a film about teenage angst, largely escaped critical notice due to its modest production and low-profile cast.     **MS**

# Eric GOLDBERG

Eric Goldberg is one of the latest collaborators of the Disney animation crew. In tune with the recent resort to computer generated imagery, his direction and animation are particularly reliant on a fast pace and highly accomplished visuals, which, combined, have produced such amazing achievements as Pocahontas' hair, or the yo-yoing flamingo in *Fantasia 2000* (1999).

Born in 1955, his first task as director was a partnership with Mike Gabriel on *Pocahontas* (1995). This Disney cartoon feature is the first to display a clearly unhappy ending and has a partially serious, and politically committed, tone. The writers (Carl Binder, Andrew Chapman, Susannah Grant, and Philip La Zebnik) drew on the real (albeit highly mythologised) story of British coloniser John Smith and his love for Native American Pocahontas. In the contemporary American climate of compulsive political correctness, they made every possible step to ensure that the representation of Pocahontas and her tribe was as neutral and idealised as possible. The usual caricatural characterisation inherent in the Disney features is applied only to the animal side-kicks and to the colonisers, thus creating a striking opposition of style and representation between the protagonists and the more marginal characters. However unbalanced this delineation is, the film is firmly kept together by the remarkable use of blue airy colours and by the incredible fluidity of the animation, which seems to move along to the rhythm of the Academy Award-winning music and original song.

Goldberg then worked as supervising animator of Philoctetes on *Hercules* (1997). It was only in 1999 that he had another chance to direct, in the ensemble feature *Fantasia 2000*. Conceived as a completion for the original *Fantasia* (1940), according to Disney's original concept of a constantly updated project, this collection of pieces seems to lack the sensory unity achieved by the previous instalment yet has its most accomplished pieces in Goldberg's two episodes. Goldberg takes complete control over the projects (writing as well as directing) to achieve sequences where the use of colour and animation are just a continuation of the music. *Rhapsody in Blue* is particularly successful, drawing on the style of caricaturist Al Hirschfeld to create the perfect frantic protagonists for Gershwin's New York, whereas *Carnival of Animals* is slightly over-reliant on the impressively fast and accomplished animation.

Goldber's next project is an animated feature, *Where the Wild Things Are*, which is based on Maurice Sendak's picture book about a little boy that retreats into his imaginary world. **BP**

# Allan A. GOLDSTEIN

In a career that has spanned 17 years, Allan A. Goldstein has directed no fewer than 18 films, some of which he has also written, produced and starred in. He debuted in 1983 with the feature *True West*, which starred John Malkovich and Gary Sinese in the leading roles as rival siblings. Malkovich plays the drifter brother to Sinese's screenwriter, whose life he turns upside-down when he makes an unscheduled arrival, causing a psychological battle of wits. Originally aired on television, *True West* is a filmic rendition of the Steppenwolf Theatre Company's production of the original Sam Shepard play.

Taking key issues of ethnic, cultural and self-identity, *The Outside Chance of Maximilian Glick* (1998) marks a successful move back into cinematic features after Goldstein's 1984 television movie *The Dining Room* and *Some Men Need Help* (1985).

A tale of a young Jewish boy from an overbearing orthodox family, set against 1950s Canada, *The Outside Chance* (1989) received four Genie nominations of and won Best Motion Picture. It also won Best Film at both the Vancouver International Film Festival and the Toronto Festival of Festivals, although it was not released in the USA until two years after its Canadian release. *Cold Front* (1989) followed, after another television movie, *The Phone Call*, in the same year. Martin Sheen takes the lead as an American cop in what has to be one of the most disappointing performances of his career and also Goldstein's. After the critical acclaim of his previous feature, Goldstein imbues *Cold Front* with too many clichés to make it a success.

Nonetheless, Goldstein was back on the Genie wish list with a Best Motion Picture nomination for his next film, *Chaindance* (1990). The film works on the premise that the best way to reform a troublesome prisoner is to chain him to the wheelchair of a surly, rebellious man with cerebral palsy. This forced proximity, it is assumed, will placate both of them and clearly allows Goldstein a reason to re-examine issues of identity and perceptions that permeated his previous work.

It seemed at this point that Goldstein was setting a career pattern, following each critically credible film with a career nose-dive, this time in the shape of *Death Wish V: The Face of Death* (1994). With his sensitivity to explorations of identity, it is incomprehensible why Goldstein chose the fifth instalment of a Charles Bronson vehicle as his seventh feature. It seems even more dated in style and tone than the original, which was made twenty years before.

The visibly low-budget film *Spill* (1996) uses an ecological theme to try to gain credibility, following an ex-bodyguard who saves the day (and Yellowstone Park) when a mass of deadly chemicals goes awry. With critics arguing that Goldstein's main concern here was to create enough explosions and fights to make an interesting trailer, it is no surprise that this went straight to video.

Goldstein's next venture was *Memory Run* (1996), a futuristic thriller in which a man's brain is transplanted into his dead girlfriend's body by the virtually omnipotent Life Corporation. Raising questions about genetics, transplantation, power and exploitation, it would seem like common territory for Goldstein but the film has slipped into obscurity. *Jungle Boy* of the same year, the story of a boy raised by animals in the jungle, also remains obscure. However, his fourth feature of 1996, *Black Out*, is widely considered to be an entertaining work although it remains of B-movie status. It centres on an amnesiac banker, John Gray, whose flashbacks do not fit his current life. After an attempt on his life and the murder of his wife, Gray moves to LA to solve the mystery.

In 1998 Goldstein released *Home Team*, with Steve Guttenberg, and *When Justice Fails*, both of which remain little-known, as does *2001: A Space Travesty* (2000), co-written by and starring Leslie Nielsen. It seems a shame that with such a promising start and the ability to consistently complete pictures, Goldstein has not produced more interesting work. Up next is *One Way Out*, a thriller starring James Belushi about a detective whose gambling addiction leaves him with a great debt that can only be paid off through his collaboration in a murder plot.                               **LB**

# Tony GOLDWYN

A Walk on the Moon (1999)
Someone Like You (2001)

Grandson of Sam Goldwyn, Tony Goldwyn, born in Los Angeles in 1960, is perhaps best known as an actor in films such as *Ghost* (1990), *The Pelican Brief* (1993), and *Nixon* (1995). More recently, he supplied the voice for the title character in Disney's animated *Tarzan* (1999).

As a director, his first and most widely seen effort is *A Walk on the Moon* (1999), a family comedy-drama set in a Catskills resort against the so-called 'Summer of Love' in 1969. Frustrated in her marriage to a television repair-man (Liev Schrieber), Pearl (Diane Lane) embarks on an affair with a hippy salesman Walker (Viggo Mortensen) while the married couple's daughter, Alison (Anna Paquin) meets her own first boyfriend. The film contrasts the rebellion and self-discovery of Alison with the adultery of Pearl, as their respective love affairs inevitably impinge upon each other's personal realisations. Demonstrating the shifting values of marriage in the 'free love' era, the film recreates the famous Woodstock festival for a key narrative turning point. It also weighs the roles of personal responsibility against sexual liberation. Intercutting the first moon landing with Pearl and Walker making love, the film demonstrates the significance of its themes in relation to the grander social and political events of the time. Slipping into romantic cliché on occasion, the film is nevertheless affectionately made and avoids the crude stereotyping of its period so familiar from other nostalgic renditions of the 1960s.

Goldwyn's second feature, *Imaging Nathan* (1999), is without distribution at the time of writing. *Someone Like You* (2001) successfully paired Ashley Judd and Hugh Jackman, in a romantic comedy about a television producer who is dumped by her boyfriend and begins to research men's sexual behaviour.                               **NJ**

# Jenniphr GOODMAN

The Tao of Steve (2000)

Jenniphr Goodman graduated with honours from New York University Film School in 1994, where she had won a series of awards for her short films. *The Tao of Steve* (2000), set in her native Santa Fe, is a romantic comedy that earned standing ovations in competition at Sundance. Unusually for the genre, it manages to appeal equally to men and women; its male lead is fat, unethical and cynical, but has lots of success tricking women into bed then dumping them. Although the misogynist has appeared in films from *Alfie* (1966) to Neil LaBute's *In the Company of Men* (1997), rarely have we seen him challenged by a woman, particularly in an otherwise traditional rom-com. *Tao* was co-written by Goodman, her actor sister Greer and Duncan North, upon whom the character is based. North was a college buddy of Goodman's husband with whom they stayed after her graduation. She became fascinated by his ideas on life and religion and amazed at his success as a serial seducer of women. Greer insisted they should write a film script. Third sister Dana also has a small role, and friends signed up to crew with enthusiasm reflected in the end result.

Dex (Donal Logue) is a hefty slacker who believes that 'doing stuff is overrated' and uses cod psycho-philosophy from Heidegger through Steve McQueen (hence the title) to

Lao-Tsu to attract women, for example 'We pursue that which retreats from us, and if the man retreats, the woman will pursue him'. This works until he re-encounters Syd (Greer Goodman), a former college friend acquainted with his methods and who forces him to re-examine his approach and its underlying causes. Logue's unsentimental performance elicits sympathy as the character so obviously lacks self-esteem; in answer to what he looks for in a woman, he replies 'low standards'. The comfort of genre allows the audience to enjoy his antics with the knowledge that his redemption is surely nigh, but the film is still enjoyable. The direction is a little self-consciously quirky, and a glut of pop culture references achieve varying results, but the dialogue and soundtrack are good, and the Santa Fe landscapes are stunning.

It is rumoured that Jenniphr and her sister are planning another collaboration; a family drama about a man with a football obsession and his three daughters that Goodman originally wrote in film school. **FG**

# Keith GORDON

Born in New York in 1961, the son of New York actors, Keith Gordon followed his parents' lead and as an actor logged numerous roles in television, theatre and film. He is best know as teen loner Arnie Cunningham in John Carpenter's *Christine* (1983) and Ernie Blick in the underground hit *Static* (1985), which he also wrote. Between these oddball roles Gordon garnered himself a certain cult status among the young, male, geek circuit, a crowd he did not disappoint when he turned his hand to directing. His films tend to focus on the plight of outsiders – outside being the only space of integrity – as they attempt to navigate their ostracism, only to discover that any radical action will, finally, be co-opted.

*The Chocolate War* (1988)
*A Midnight Clear* (1991)
*Mother Night* (1996)
*Waking the Dead* (2000)

Gordon's first feature *The Chocolate War* (1988), based on Roger Cormier's novel, is set in a Catholic boys' school (Gordon's films usually reside in the masculine sphere). Newcomer to the school Jerry Renault refuses to pitch in for the annual chocolate sale, a move of indifference that is read as, and soon becomes, an act of defiance. Worried about the effects of Renault's attitude on school morale, the headmaster joins forces with a dominant boys' club to force Renault's acquiescence. Shot in an austere, controlled manner, the film is hardly typical teen fare, as Renault's holdout results not in victory but in the realisation that avoiding incorporation is an impossibility. Ultimately, his stance proves easy fodder for yet another school project, as he must fight his nemesis – the rich boy – in front of a paying, bloodthirsty audience: Renault's personal act of resistance effortlessly translated into crude public spectacle.

Gordon's second feature, *A Midnight Clear* (1991), graced many Top Ten lists for 1991. Its story of a US intelligence unit – the members of which become increasingly unnerved by the fact that the German unit in their vicinity simply refuses to fight – continues Gordon's thematic interest in power and resistance as they are played out in the masculine world. Noteworthy for its sympathetic portrayal of Nazi soldiers – who, like the Americans, are tired of war, do not want to die, and long for home – the film recasts the war as one between the military elite and the foot soldiers. It targets the egotistical, wilfully ignorant authority figures, playing with their men like a handful of toy soldiers, as the true horror. Like *The Chocolate War*, asserting humanity in an inhumane world has ephemeral success but fails in the long run to effect concrete change.

*Mother Night* (1996), based on the Kurt Vonnegut novel, is the next logical step in what can be regarded as an ongoing examination of the – perhaps misguided – faith in the transcendence of the personal. The film never makes clear if its protagonist, Howard W. Campbell Jr, is an American agent or solely working for the Nazis, and in a sense it does not matter, for the results are the same. Allegorically, the film can be read as America's complicity with fascism, as Campbell meditates on the possibility that, unwittingly or not, he is guilty of war crimes.

Gordon's films are set at one remove from reality; the school in *The Chocolate War*, the abandoned house in *A Midnight Clear*, and the prison in *Mother Night*, are all infused with a hazy, murky light, as if the landscape is always already a psychic projection. The characters battle with themselves as much as with the brutish, stifling power structures. The revolution is a process rather than an act: the individual act will fail, but it must be made, if only to gauge the size of the opponent. Stuck between the radical and the reactionary, Gordon continues the honed American tradition of championing the individualist, yet he treats the individual as an impotent force. If his protagonists triumph, they do so for the very side against which they were struggling. Moments of personal resistance, despite grand plans, prove unable to vanquish the overarching oppression.

Gordon continues to mine the collision of the personal and the public in his fourth feature, *Waking the Dead* (2000), in which a congressional candidate experiences a breakdown of sorts after an encounter with his former, and presumed dead, lover. His next film, *The Singing Detective*, is based on the BBC mini-series and will star Mel Gibson and Robert Downey Jr.                                          **LW**

# Stuart GORDON

Born in Chicago in 1947, Stuart Gordon is a veteran director of over-the-top bloodthirsty horror and science fiction films, and the man responsible for popularising classic writer H. P. Lovecraft's unnerving tales in the mid-1980s. He was partly to blame for Disney's 'big' family movie *Honey, I Shrunk the Kids* in 1989, having co-written the original story with Brian Yuzna and Ed Naha.

Gordon's background is in theatre. He directed a university production of 'Peter Pan' which was hit by obscenity charges (Never-Never Land in this instance being a drug-induced hallucination), co-founded Chicago's notorious Organic Theater in 1969 and spent 15 years there as its artistic director, working on productions such as David Mamet's 1974 'Sexual Perversity in Chicago'.

Gordon's approach to *Re-Animator* (1985), his low-budget feature debut, was equally theatrical. Loosely interpreting Lovecraft's short, Gordon fashioned a grisly, often darkly amusing, frightener. Jeffrey Combs plays the stereotypical mad scientist, Herbert West, who can bring the dead back to life with a fluorescent green serum but fails to consider the true consequences of his experiments. There is some effort to grapple with the morality of West's actions and Combs' rendering of a man obsessed with his work is worrisomely believable, although, as a rule it is the outré set pieces and effects that have the greatest impact, due primarily to the way they are composed by Gordon and shot by Mac Ahlberg; the basement scramble after a resurrected cat and the fracas in the morgue are such examples. Many will undoubtedly be dissuaded by the excessive gore on display, or by the exploitation of heroine Barbara Crampton as an object of sexual gratification (by the living and the deceased).

Sex is very much at the heart of *From Beyond* (1986), though not in the sense one might imagine. A machine called 'The Resonator' allows creatures from another dimension to tap into characters' sexual desires via their frontal lobes, freeing them from repression but also hideously altering them. A zealous and intrepid production, this also stars Combs and Crampton but reverses the roles this time. Unfortunately poor distribution and a more serious tone meant that the picture was shunned by all but the most ardent Gordon proponents.

*Dolls* (1986) was Gordon's homage to James Whale's 1932 film *The Old Dark House* and the more astute viewer will spot references to the original (particularly given the change of title), despite the fact that it follows a similar plot route – several travellers forced to spend the night in a mysterious and sinister old house because of a raging storm. Here they are assessed by owners Guy Rolfe and Hilary Mason, accompanied by an army of malicious dolls, and judged good or bad by whether they are innocent in their hearts. Much-maligned at the time, *Dolls* is hardly the failure it was reported to be, providing the requisite volume of suspense and shocks, encouraged by reasonable special effects. The addition of a less than heroic 'hero', Stephen Lee, also makes for a pleasant change.

The vampire telefilm *Daughter of Darkness* (1990) did nothing to revive Gordon's career, even after an uncut theatrical release in Europe, but it did introduce him to horror icon Anthony Perkins, an artist he had admired for so long – tragically, Perkins passed away before they could collaborate on a worthier project. During this time financial problems plagued Gordon's first science fiction film, *Robot Jox* (1990), which were made all the more infuriating by the sudden collapse of Empire Pictures. Set 50 years or so in the future, it envisions an era when superpowers will settle their grievances not by wars, but with manned 120-ft robots fighting like gladiators to the death – which is underlined by the main operator's classical name, Achilles. A relevant proposition when conceived three years earlier, by the time the movie came out the Cold War was virtually over, dating the 'Russian as villain' dogma terribly. *Robot Jox* was also shamefully supported by some atrocious miniature effects work shot in the Mojave desert, which betrayed its meagre $6.5 million budget.

*The Pit and the Pendulum* (1990), is a remake of the Roger Corman film and also an expansion of Edgar Allan Poe's famous torture tale. In Gordon's version, he delves into the history of the Spanish Inquisition, focusing on its figurehead Torquemada (an august performance by Lance Henriksen). The story is a commendable one, stressing not only how easy it is to be swept up by mass hysteria and paranoia (an allegory of both Nazism and McCarthyism), but also how ordinary people can inadvertently contribute to heinous acts of cruelty. Realism is communicated through the costume design and location shooting in producer Charles Band's own Italian castle. Oliver Reed appears briefly, exacerbating unavoidable comparisons with Ken Russell's *The Devils* (1971) – a film that was frequently discussed by actor and director on set.

Gordon switched back to sci-fi in 1993 for *Fortress*, but learnt well from his previous mistakes. The film is a grim Orwellian nightmare intertwined with pulp action, forewarning what might happen if the world's population continues to grow exponentially. Christopher Lambert and Loryn Locklin are the couple imprisoned in the Fortress – a hi-tech underground jail with automated guards – for exceeding society's one-infant limit. The mind-set trades on the same cynical distrust of large corporations evidenced in films such as *Alien* (1979) and falls victim to accustomed incarceration clichés. That said, it has more than enough intrigue, gimmicks and brisk movement to compensate.

After penning Abel Ferrara's modern take on the 'body snatchers' myth, Gordon made *Castle Freak* (1995), which effortlessly matches the standard of his earlier work. Members of the director's stock company reunite again, including Combs and Crampton, for this disquieting tale of a recovering alcoholic (who accidentally killed his son and blinded his daughter in a car accident) trying to begin again in an inherited castle abroad – oblivious to the nasty creature lurking in its cellar. Dennis Paoli's psychologically-driven script enhances the overall feel of the piece, making it a better-than-average monster flick and deserving of a warmer reception than it received.

Though relatively bigger in terms of production values and distribution, *Space Truckers* (aka *Star Truckers* (1997)) has much less of a coherent identity, and finds no comfortable place in Gordon's canon. Unsuccessfully combining iconoclastic comedy with a 1950s science fiction mentality, it regards itself more as a desultory video game in the *Super Mario Bros.* (1993) mold. There are some acceptable touches, such as the traffic lights in space and the square livestock genetically engineered to fit in the cargo hold, but the plot is meandering, the characters inconsistent and the special effects cartoon-like. Also to abuse talented actors such as Dennis Hopper and Charles Dance (playing a trucker and lunatic cyborg respectively) in this manner is almost a cinematic crime in itself.

As disparate again is *The Wonderful Ice Cream Suit* (1998), a PG-certificated 'feelgood' comedy fantasy scripted by science fiction guru Ray Bradbury. It chronicles Joe Mantegna's attempts to purchase a brilliant white suit he has seen in a local store, pooling together resources from a guitar player (Esai Morales), an orator (Gregory Sierra), a young lad (Clifton Collins Jr.), and a tramp (Edward James Olmos), who are all the same size. Regardless of its fairytale proclivity – the suit has the power to make dreams come true – this movie is *au fond* about the developing kinship of the consortium. As Collins Jr. puts it: 'This morning I had no friends, but tonight I have many friends!' thus verbalising the true magic of the outfit.

Gordon has not turned his back on horror. He provided the story for Brian Yuzna's alien insemination film *The Progeny* (1999), and his most recent venture is yet another Lovecraftian movie, *Dagon* (2001), which incorporates ideas from the author's story of the same name and also his 'The Shadow Over Innsmouth' fable. Based on a script written 15 years ago to tentatively follow *Re-animator*, it tells the tale of shipwreck survivors in Spain who encounter monsters from the sea, rendered by a blend of computer graphics and more traditional methods. Gordon develops the mythos of the 'Deep Ones' well, but this is really just another creature feature to add to the already burgeoning list in the horror genre.          **PB**

# Raja GOSNELL

Raja Gosnell began his career working as a driver for Robert Altman in Los Angeles, before becoming apprentice editor on four of his features and graduating to assistant director on his musical-comedy Popeye (1980). Having completed his first project as solo editor on the short The Silence (1982), he went on to edit over 15 major films, including Pretty Woman (1990), Mrs Doubtfire (1993), Nine Months (1995), and Miracle on 34th Street (1994). It was John Hughes who gave him the opportunity to direct his debut feature, Home Alone 3 (1997), after he had worked with the writer/producer on previous successes Home Alone (1990) and Home Alone 2: Lost in New York (1992).

Although a solid and adequately directed film, Home Alone 3, the third in an already tired film franchise, is in no way remarkable. This time without Macaulay Culkin but still childishly slapstick in a similar vein to its predecessors, it sees the young hero getting himself into impossible scrapes with a group of terrorists before predictably saving the day. Despite making it admirably less sentimental than the first two, with his next effort, Never Been Kissed (1999) Gosnell opted for the all-out feelgood factor. Starring Drew Barrymore as a 25-year-old copy editor who gets the chance to revisit high school as an undercover reporter pretending to be 17, the film embraces the whole range of teen stereotypes. Predictably, the heroine is placed in humiliating situations, reminiscent of her earlier childhood experiences but, very publically and unbelievably, ends up winning the love of her English teacher. The film is again adequate but still in no way remarkable.

Big Momma's House (2000) stars Martin Lawrence as an undercover cop who poses as a southern grandmother to lure a criminal. Mildly amusing but on the whole disappointingly slight, it treads old Eddie Murphy ground and the cases of mistaken identity soon begin to pall. If Gosnell is ever to make his mark as an interesting director, instead of remaining a jobbing studio hack, he really needs to seek out some original material, and Scooby Doo (2002), his most recent film, is not it. A hybrid live-action and CGI feature based on the popular animated series, it stars Freddie Prinze Jr., Sarah Michelle Gellar and Matthew Lillard.                                    **HP**

# Felix Gary GRAY

Felix Gary Gray has managed to produce three very different features in his short body of work. Born in 1970, he began his career producing music videos for artists such as Babyface, TLC and Coolio.

His inaugural film work was the Ice Cube and Chris Tucker vehicle Friday (1995), in which he helped create a cartoon image of the ghetto lifestyle, attributing the inherent disorder more to boredom than inner city turmoil. The film works as a comedy piece, with Chris Tucker exuberant as the drug-smoking joker, but hides a strong anti-gun message created by the dislocated voices and memories endured by Ice Cube's character as he battles with the local hoodlum.

The female-dominated piece Set It Off (1996) is a world away from Friday. The story focuses on a group of black women so betrayed by the world around them they turn to bank robbery to escape. Yet the dynamics become altered as the group become increasingly masculinised with the introduction of guns, cars and drugs. This blurring of the gender divide is best portrayed by the frighteningly aggressive Queen Latifah (for whom Gray had previously produced a music video). The culmination of the plot meets with a delight for overblown scale that Gray uses more in his later piece, resembling a reworking of the infamous O.J. Simpson chase as the LAPD chase the girls across the city.

The Negotiator (1998), like Gray's other works, relies perhaps too heavily on the acting talents of the central characters. Kevin Spacey and Samuel L. Jackson put in admirable performances but cannot escape the stumbling plot. The piece is best viewed for Gray's over-the-top illustration of the scale of police presence, which resembles an army far more than the local authorities.

Gray is planning a remake of the 1969 classic The Italian Job and an action film starring flavour of the month action star Vin Diesel.                            **SS**

# James GRAY

Having directed just two films, James Gray has swiftly become recognised as a distinctive and confident young voice in American film. Born in 1969, while growing up in Queens he immersed himself in film, often skipping class to go to the movies, subsequently enrolling at the University of Southern California School of Cinema-Television. When producer Paul Webster saw his student film, *Cowboys and Angels*, he encouraged Gray to write his first full-length script, which then became *Little Odessa* (1994); on its release, the film received critical acclaim and won the Venice Film Festival's prestigious Silver Lion Award. Despite Gray's young age, *Little Odessa* is a remarkably assured and mature film that distinguishes itself from the Tarantino-primed independent landscape of the 1990s. On the surface it appears to share similar concerns – hitmen, mobsters and lowlifes occupy the screen – but the comparisons remain superficial. Gray's style has little in common with such postmodern, self-conscious excess. Naturalistic, considered and austere, his film-making has more in common with that of 1970s 'New Hollywood'; it is no surprise he referred to *Apocalypse Now* (1979) and *Raging Bull* (1980) as 'the last gasp of American cinema'.

Although *Little Odessa* is a crime movie, Gray's main concern is the oppressive intensity and torment of familial relationships. Music, sound, and bleached colour blend to paint a convincing portrait of communal and familial dysfunction, and emotional deprivation. The story focuses on a detached hitman (Tim Roth) who has to return to his Russian-Jewish neighbourhood in Brooklyn in order to carry out an assassination. Although difficulties in his past make it dangerous to return, the real impediment is his father, played with intensity by veteran Maximilian Schell. Gray forges a complex picture, which strives to investigate an array of issues such as the threat of assimilation and the undermining of traditional values within urban modernity. Above all, he manages to elucidate its powerful themes of love and redemption.

Emotionally and physically, Gray's subsequent feature, *The Yards* (2000), shares much with *Little Odessa*. Once again, he locates his film in an unforgiving environment – shadowy business deals and corruption in New York railway yards – but familial ties and loyalties are really at stake. Here it is Leo (Mark Wahlberg) who has returned to the old neighbourhood, having been released from prison and taking the fall for his friends; attempting to get his life back in order, he hits a downward spiral. Howard Shore's unremittingly oppressive score increases the sense of looming tragedy and while the script doesn't quite hold up to this boldly operatic style, the sharp verbal exchanges work better than the declarative monologues interspersed throughout. Individual characterisations are scrupulously detailed; James Caan, in particular, is excellent, subtly conveying the guilt and exhaustion of a lifetime of cumulative compromise. Avoiding obvious gangster clichés, the film brings some genuinely original flourishes to the genre – the cavernous subway yards are wonderfully evoked as a metaphor for tortured, confused ambition – yet on occasion, Gray seems overwhelmed by his own ambition and the film's narrative power sometimes falters.                                                        **HS**

# John GRAY

Mainly forging a successful career as a director of American television movies and series, John Gray has nevertheless made sporadic forays into the feature film industry with very disparate material: social melodrama, children's film, and big-budget action. Fluent in the language of popular Hollywood cinema – solid three-act structures, firmly delineated characters, the climactic payoff – Gray's work has consistently delivered competent entertainment that is never groundbreaking but shows technical assurance and visual imagination.

Initially Gray worked outside the Hollywood system, gaining experience on small, low-budget productions. His first film, *Footlights and Flatfeet* (1984), never received an extensive cinema release but paved the way for a second independent production, *Billy Galvin* (1986), a father-son drama set in working-class Boston. Focusing on the pressures of blue-collar life and the desire for escape and betterment, the film is reminiscent of old-fashioned social drama. Gray's intimate camerawork, juxtaposing work and family life and father-son opposition, makes for an unshowy style which allows the strong central performances to shine. The facility for well-crafted emotional drama led to a lengthy period of directing television movies, often focusing on topical issues and true stories. *The Marla Hanson Story* (1991), *An American Story* (1992), and *A Place for Annie* (1994) dealt with the assault and disfigurement of a model, American soldiers, and the adoption of an HIV positive child, respectively.

*Footlights and Flatfeet* (1984)
*Billy Galvin* (1986)
*Born to Be Wild* (1995)
*The Glimmer Man* (1996)

*Born to Be Wild* (1995) marked Gray's move into bigger-budget Hollywood production and the constrictions of rigid genres and studio demands. The story of a troubled teenage boy who befriends a captive gorilla, the film details a child-animal relationship whose venerable genre reaches from the days of 'Lassie' in the 1950s to *Free Willy* (1993) in the 1990s. Identifying the isolation and mistreatment of the gorilla with the disenfranchised loneliness of teenagedom, the film follows a uniform structure – befriending followed by separation, escape into peril, final struggle for freedom – while Gray's opposition of the manipulative adult world with the endangered friends mixes the requisite comic moments and thrills. The film shows Gray's ability to work to the conventions of genre while creating smaller, individual moments of originality like the comic escapades of the escape – entertaining if predictable film-making targeted at a specific audience.

*The Glimmer Man* (1996) follows the same trend. It is a vehicle movie for its star Steven Seagal that follows a martial arts expert and wisecracking cop in pursuit of a serial killer who crucifies his victims. Gray again fulfils all the demands of the specific genre – terrific explosions, elaborate chases, bone-crunching falls and fights – while toying with the directorial styles of Bond movies, psychological thrillers, and the martial arts flick. Gray's ability to both use and individualise conventions of the genre, together with his unerring sense of his audience, make for a film that delights its intended fans but depresses those who are not. This is a very Hollywood method of film-making – targeted, well-executed, proficient, but ultimately soulless – that seems at odds with Gray's early heartfelt social drama and more in keeping with the formulas of television direction, the medium for which all of his subsequent work has been made.     **OB**

# David Gordon GREEN

*George Washington* (2000) Born in 1975 in Texas, David Gordon Green studied film-making at the North Carolina School of the Arts (NCSA) and worked in the film industry in New York and Los Angeles, both for independent and studio companies. He has written and directed short fiction and documentary films, among them *Pleasant Grove* (1996), *Artificial Insemination* (1996), *A Biography of Barrels* (1997), and *Physical Pinball* (1998). *George Washington* (2000), his first feature-length film, is one of the more memorable of recent years. An astonishingly assured, meticulous and involving film, the story intelligently privileges the perspective of children and involves a group of young friends who live in a rural town in Northern Carolina and play together amongst derelict houses, playgrounds and ghost trains, befriending adults or avoiding them as necessary. Nasia, a twelve-year-old, narrates some of the events, and the opening scene when she and her boyfriend Buddy earnestly discuss their relationship and its demise is a measure of the film's subtle mix of maturity and wry humour. But it's George, the boy she thinks she is in love with, that is really the centre of the piece, a kid who wants to become President and dresses as a superhero to do good deeds.

As many critics have pointed out, and Green himself has demurred, he wears the influence of another director from the Deep South on his sleeve, Terrence Malick, and not only through the use of voice-over. The visual image is fetishised, saturated with colour and plays at odds with the downtrodden indigence of the characters' lives (Tim Orr is the director of photography). The deliberate pace intensifies both the suggestion of heat-filled days and the growing sense of unease that something out of the ordinary is about to happen. Deservedly lauded by critics, Green in currently working on his next project, *All the Real Girls*, which is also set in small-town America.     **HP**

# Maggie GREENWALD

*Home Remedy* (1988) The films of Maggie Greenwald can be said to address the social roles and expectations
*The Kill-Off* (1989) which, as a result of gender, serve more often to confine than liberate.
*The Ballad of Little Jo* (1993)     Born in 1955, Greenwald began her career as an actor and dancer and went to film
*Songcatcher* (1999) school at the age of twenty. She worked as an editor, and then later as a sound editor, and began searching for a way to finance her own projects. *Home Remedy* (1988), her first feature, was about a young New Jersey businessman who quits his job to live the life of a hermit in his comfortable suburban home. However, his peace is interrupted by his intrusive neighbours. In this film, Greenwald reverses the gender stereotypes, positioning

the main male protagonist as a passive victim to his beautiful but sexually aggressive female neighbour. *Home Remedy* made the rounds at a number of film festivals and allowed the director to finance her next project, *The Kill-Off* (1989).

In *The Kill-Off*, Greenwald adapted pulp novelist Jim Thompson's novel about a vicious matron of a small town who uses gossip as a way of controlling the inhabitants and bending her neighbours to her own will. The movie's washed-out, grim visual qualities, combined with its realism, struck a chord with fans of Thompson's novels and fitted in nicely with a series of 'neo-noirs' produced at around the same time. It earned Greenwald excellent reviews and a strong overseas following.

She followed *The Kill-Off* with *The Ballad of Little Jo* (1993), a revisionist western which tells the story of a young society woman whose family forces her to give up her only child after she gives birth out of wedlock. Now an outcast, Josephine Monaghan changes her name to 'Little Jo', moves out West, and lives the rest of her life as a man. Film theorist and historian Tania Modleski noted that the film should be understood as a 'landmark in the history of women's cinema and a major artistic achievement by almost any standard'.

*Songcatcher* (1999) – shown only at Sundance at the time of this writing – follows the life of a turn-of-the-century musicologist who gives up her career in academia after being continually passed over for promotion at her job. She moves to a rural Appalachian community where she finds a new life studying and recording the folk music of the surrounding regions.

While all four films differ in tone, style, and realisation, Greenwald's concerns as a film-maker can be viewed through the narratives she constructs (Greenwald has written the screenplays for all four of her films). She consistently writes strong female characters, forced into taking on different roles as a result of their situations, but who nevertheless adapt and thrive once they have left tradition behind. Because of the subject matter of her work she has frequently been labelled a 'feminist' director. However, such a label at once acknowledges the concerns and issues which inform her work while it has simultaneously (and unfortunately) marginalised her work and limited her audience. **MR**

# Robert GREENWALD

Trained as a theatre director, Robert Greenwald's career began with a series of television movies with sensational titles: *Sharon: Portrait of a Mistress* (1977), *Katie: Portrait of a Centerfold* (1978), and *Flatbed Annie & Sweetiepie: Lady Truckers* (1979). However, during the past fifteen years Greenwald has increasingly become known for his ambitious made-for-television films, which often explore controversial issues. He also has developed a strong reputation with actors, as evidenced by the stars his projects attract.

Greenwald has directed 14 films and, through his production company, produced more than two dozen more, a body of work which has earned him 23 Emmy nominations. Greenwald's first feature was *Xanadu* (1980). This bizarre, if colourful, update of *Down to Earth* (1948) was created as a vehicle for the singer Olivia Newton-John. Early critical success came with the made-for-television film *The Burning Bed* (1984), an Emmy-winning and explosive exploration of domestic violence starring Farrah Fawcett. Subsequent serious-minded works include *Shattered Spirits* (1986), starring Martin Sheen as an alcoholic, and *A Woman of Independent Means* (1995), which follows Sally Field's character through seven decades of love and loss.

*Sweet Hearts Dance* (1988) uses a strong ensemble cast (Jeff Daniels, Don Johnson, Susan Sarandon, and Elizabeth Perkins) to explore love and romance in a New England town. Despite some breathtaking cinematography and realistic dialogue, it succumbs too much to sentimentality to be a truly searing exposé of adult relationships. *Hear No Evil* (1993), an embarrassingly overblown thriller, features Marlee Matlin as prey for a stalker and Martin Sheen. Greenwald's most accomplished feature is *Breaking Up* (1997), with Russell Crowe and Salma Hayek as two lovers who dissect the dissolution of their relationship. Although flawed, lacking a greater social awareness, the film is intriguing and well-played by the two leads. His latest project, *Steal This Movie!* (2000), a lively, thorough, and ambitious biopic following the strange life of 1960s civil rights activist Abbie Hoffman, has received a limited theatrical release. it is rumoured that next Greenwald will direct an adaptation of James Ellroy's 'My Dark Places'.          **JS**

# John GREYSON

John Greyson's films are political, but, engaging with postmodern critical theories, deride the seriousness of politics and the artificiality of any medium seeking to propound an ultimate truth. One of Toronto's most creditable video and film-makers in the independent documentary tradition, his primary interest is in challenging how the 'factual' can represent and define. Although he finds documentary frustrating he continually returns to it. 'The experience of being represented is always difficult for your subject,' he says, and hates being represented himself, even by the most empathetic. 'There's always going to be a disjunction.' Refusing to be pigeonholed, he has set out to explore homosexuality in many forms of expression, from diverse approaches and within different genres, from performance to low-budget video to feature film. He uses strategies such as Brechtian distanciation and juxtaposition to shock people out of their accepted norms. His films are consciously 'queer', satirising diversely but remaining thematically consistent. Critical, but not heavy-handed, he uses absurdist humour, biting satire and a plethora of cultural references to examine power structures and break down accustomed cultural beliefs.

Greyson lives in Toronto but grew up in London, Ontario. Born in 1960, he has described his childhood as 'lonely ... Catholic ... fed by that sort of dark romanticism of despair'. He has been involved in gay activism for *Body Politic*, a famous gay/lesbian liberation magazine in Toronto, and AIDS-Action-Now. In 1982 he joined the Jumper Video Collective and collaborated in a series of leftist videos: *Disrupting Diplomacy*, a documentary short on civil disobedience at the UN; *Manzana Por Manzana*, a multi-media look at the Sandinistas; and *Changing the Current* on students' reactions to racism. In 1985 he depicted the predicament of Ontario's farm workers in *To Pick is Not to Choose*. This period also saw him reflecting on the limitations of representation by traditional narrative structure. In *Moscow Does Not Believe in Queers* he used Rock Hudson in *Ice Station Zebra* (1968) to underline his thoughts on his visit to the 1985 Moscow Youth Festival. A year later he made *You Taste American*, examining 'bathroom raids' in Ontario through fictional lovers Tennessee Williams and Michel Foucault, unravelling in 100 rolls of toilet paper. *The Kipling Trilogy* exposed imperialist Britian's peculiar relationship with homosexuality, using *If* and *The Jungle Book*, amongst other films. In 1987, a piece intended for exhibition in a shopping mall exposed the reality in the life and death struggles endemic within words and representations. Called *The ADS Epidemic*, it lampooned regressive attitudes to AIDS using *Death In Venice* (1971) and a song called *ADS: Acquired Dread of Sex*. It explores the dichotomy between 'good' monogamous gays and 'bad' promiscuous gays, finding the notion culturally contrived and retrograde, a theme that runs through much of Greyson's work.

His first feature-length film, *Urinal* (1988), part documentary, part cultural critique, expounds on similar themes. Greyson explores police raids on public toilets, an issue which remains politically divisive even amongst the gay community. *Urinal* posits that 'bathroom sex' is only a crime when so created by the police. Next came *Zero Patience* (1993), an AIDS fantasy musical with a double meaning: the zero patience that people with AIDS experience every day, and Patient Zero, ascribed as the first person to bring the syndrome to North America. This idea was proposed by Randy Shilts' best-selling book 'And The Band Played On'. Although a general indictment of government indifference to the epidemic, Greyson had a problem with its basic premise, already disproved at the time of publication and, he believes, included only as a cynical marketing ploy. In Greyson's film, Patient Zero returns as a ghost to speak to a Victorian sexologist, now alive and working on an AIDS installation for The Toronto museum. He videotapes interviews with Zero's friends and family, but, edited out of context, they often state the opposite to the interviewees' intentions. With musical production numbers, styled a la Busby Berkley/Esther Williams and featuring singing anuses, he underlines the ludicrousness of the culture of blame. The piece is fatuous, but too poignant not to be taken seriously. Greyson states, 'I think there is a real perversity in taking such a fluffy empty, discredited genre like the musical and filling it with AIDS activist content'. The film critiques the HIV-hypothesis as the sole cause of AIDS, and asks why the mainstream media uphold the scapegoat theory. Greyson subverts history as the truth and evinces it as both authentic and illusory.

His following film, and perhaps his most popular is *Lillies* (1996), a period drama from an original play by Michel Marc Bouchard. *Lillies* confronts the arguments on positive gay representation as a sole position. It finds a use for 'negative' representation and underlines the pretence within this stance. *Uncut* (1997), his next feature, was largely dismissed in the US as avant-garde nonsense. Greyson, however, claims to react against the modernist avant-garde who alienate audiences, but also roundly condemns those who patronise by explaining every detail. He admits that he brings some strange ideas to the table, but asserts that 'dialogue is more interesting ... than pronouncements'. *Uncut* is about the penis, circumcision and censorship, with Greyson finding penile euphemisms everywhere and an unlikely homoeroticism in former Canadian Premier Pierre Trudeau.

His most recent feature, *The Law of Enclosures* (2001), is based on a novel by Dale Peck. It is set in 1991 in a provincial town in Ontario during The Gulf War, which underpins the destructive relationships of two younger and two more mature lovers. The fires rage ceaselessly in Kuwait as does the rancour between the couples. The style is direct and unromanticised but with an off-kilter palette. The film's structure is palindromic and audiences either loved or hated it, largely depending on their ability to let go of their preconceived notions of narrative. Along with all Greyson's work it remains largely ignored or misunderstood in the US.                                              **FG**

# Ulu GROSBARD

Ulu Grosbard, born in Belgium in 1929 and best known as a director of Broadway dramas, began in film as an assistant director for Elia Kazan (*Splendor in the Grass* (1961)), Robert Wise (*West Side Story* (1961)), Robert Rossen (*The Hustler* (1961)), and Sidney Lumet (*The Pawnbroker* (1965)) before making his own directorial debut with 1968's *The Subject Was Roses*. This adaptation of Frank D. Gilroy's Pulitzer Prize-winning Broadway play about a war veteran's emotional homecoming launched the film career of Martin Sheen, netted Jack Albertson an Academy Award for Best Supporting Actor, and marked actress Patricia Neal's return to cinema following a debilitating stroke. The kitchen sink realism of Grosbard's first film is characteristic of the attention to minute detail evident in this former diamond cutter's subsequent film work.

Grosbard's sophomore effort, the black comedy (co-written with playwright Herb Gardner) *Who Is Harry Kellerman and Why Is He Saying Those Terrible Things About Me?* (1971), was a critical and box-office failure despite the casting of Dustin Hoffman (as a neurotic composer of popular songs plagued by unhappy relationships with his parents and a string of girlfriends) relatively fresh from his success in Mike Nichols' *The Graduate* (1967), and remains Grosbard's most elusive title (and is to date still unavailable on video). Grosbard would replace Hoffman as the director of the gritty prison drama *Straight Time* (1978), an adaptation of Edward Bunker's 'No Beast So Fierce'. Hoffman's intense portrayal of an ex-con attempting to adapt to a 'straight' life was ably supported by Harry Dean Stanton, Gary Busey and M. Emmet Walsh, as Hoffman's bullying parole officer.

Grosbard returned to the crime genre in 1981 with *True Confessions*, an adaptation of John Gregory Dunne's speculative novel about the still-unsolved 1947 'Black Dahlia' murder case. Robert Duvall and Robert De Niro co-starred as estranged brothers, one a homicide cop, the other a highly-placed Catholic priest, whose respective ethical and moral blind sides are exposed in the wake of the grotesque murder of a Hollywood hanger-on. Despite a literate but gritty script, stunning vintage detail (captured by *Straight Time* cinematographer Owen Roisman) and a strong supporting cast (Charles Durning, Kenneth McMillan, Burgess Meredith, Cyril Cusack and Rose Gregorio), audiences seemed indifferent to the desensationalised resolution and the against-type casting of De Niro as the benign (but conflicted) Father Des Spellacy. Furthering Grosbard's passion for troubled families, *True Confessions* ends with a bittersweet coda in which Duvall promises his dying brother that he will sing an Irish song at the wake.

De Niro and Grosbard teamed up again for 1984's *Falling in Love*, which attends the love affair between city-working suburbanites (De Niro and Meryl Streep), whose collision in a New York bookstore jammed with holiday shoppers causes them to mix up their gifts to their respective spouses (Jane Kaczmarek and David Clennon). Despite the nuanced performances of De Niro and Streep (both heartbreaking and hilarious as she tries on outfits for her first stab at infidelity), as well as those of a stellar cast of New York film and theatre actors (Harvey Keitel, George Martin, Dianne Wiest, and Victor

Argo), the film is ultimately bland and rarely mentioned in the *curriculum vitae* of its principal players.

A full decade would pass before Grosbard again got behind the camera for *Georgia* (1995), which returned to the theme of the tenuous ties between siblings – in this case, the obligation of successful country singer Mare Winningham for her dissolute and untalented sister (Jennifer Jason Leigh). Grosbard again assembled a splendid supporting cast (with Ted Levine, Max Perlich, and musician John Doe particularly noteworthy), but the film was praised predominantly for the performances of the female leads and quickly forgotten. Grosbard's last film to date, *The Deep End of the Ocean* (1999), starring Michelle Pfeiffer – about the return of a woman's missing son after a nine-year absence – continues the director's recurring theme of the difficulty of maintaining strong family bonds.                                                                          **RHS**

# Christopher GUEST

Best known for his role as Nigel Tufnel, lead guitarist in Rob Reiner's famous 'mock-rockumentary' *This Is Spinal Tap* (1984), which he also co-wrote, Christopher Guest has been working in film since the early 1970s. Born in New York in 1948, he became better known in the mid-1980s for roles in *Little Shop of Horrors* (1986), *The Princess Bride* (1987), and 'Saturday Night Live'. Guest has made many friends working in film and television, and this is apparent in the many star cameos and recurrent faces in his films.

Guest's first film as director was *The Big Picture* (1989), which he co-wrote with Michael Varhol and *Spinal Tap* partner Michael McKean. It is the story of an award-winning film school graduate who is wooed into the Hollywood studio system only to see his arty feature idea transformed into a sordid comedy. When the project is finally scrapped, he is forced to begin anew. *The Big Picture* is an unassuming comedy with strong performances by Kevin Bacon, Martin Short and J. T. Walsh. Guest's plotting moves slowly at times and there are several clumsy delusion scenes, but it is an otherwise confident first film with cameos by many Hollywood insiders.

Guest worked on several other projects before directing his second film, *Waiting For Guffman* (1996), a 'mockumentary' in the *This Is Spinal Tap* vein, about the production of a Broadway-style show being put on by an amateur theatre company in a small Missouri town for its sesquicentennial (150th anniversary). Lead by the ambitious Corky St. Clair (Guest), the show's cast includes many of the town's denizens, including its dentist (Eugene Levy), travel agents (Fred Willard and Catherine O'Hara) and Dairy Queen cashier (Parker Posey). The film examines the idiosyncrasies of small-town America, but never with viciousness or condescension. Guest shows a reverence for his characters and their Hollywood pretensions. The characters are the true focus of the film, and their absurdities make them sympathetic without being sentimental. Guest, who co-wrote the film with Levy, also composed its score with *Spinal Tap* bandmates McKean and Harry Shearer.

*Almost Heroes* (1998), Guest's subsequent film, is a comedy set in the early nineteenth century about an explorer duo (Chris Farley and Matthew Perry) trying to reach the Pacific before the legendary Lewis and Clark. Farley plays a brash, hard-drinking woodsman named Hunt, and Perry an effete glory-seeker named Edwards; together, they lead a group of misfits played by many Guest regulars. *Almost Heroes* traverses the line between crude comedy and modern satire, and ends as a rather mediocre, though inoffensive, compromise between both. Generally unpopular with critics, it lacks the sharpness of Guest's previous films.

*Best in Show* (2000), Guest's most recent film, is yet another mockumentary, this time focusing on the world of dog shows. Featuring a host of characters played by familiar faces (himself, Levy, McKean, O'Hara, Posey, Willard and others), the film follows them on their respective journeys to the annual Mayflower Kennel Club Dog Show in Philadelphia. It is the characters' eccentricities that are truly on display, however, with competitors attributing all manner of personality traits to their dogs. The highpoint comes in the final third at the dog show; Willard is hilarious as the television commentator for the show, better used to football banter than dog talk. *Best in Show* is on par with *Waiting for Guffman* as truly one of the best comedies of its era, and while it may seem a little too easy to pick on such an absurd group of people, one cannot help but go along with Guest's ribbing.

Alongside his directing, Guest has continued acting in a number of film and television productions, including Rob Reiner's *A Few Good Men* (1992). He also directed and produced the short-lived television series 'Morton & Hayes' in 1991 along with McKean, and directed the television movies *Attack of the 50ft. Woman* (1993) and *D.O.A.* (1999), which was co-written by Levy. **DH**

# Davis GUGGENHEIM

Born in 1964, a relative newcomer to the world of feature film directing, Davis *Gossip* (2000)
Guggenheim is no stranger to moviemaking. With a promising film career ahead, he has carved out an impressive resumé and continues to challenge audiences with his gritty style and approach to film-making.

Much of Guggenheim's early career was spent working on various documentary film crews with his father Charles Guggenheim. Acting, producing, and other crew jobs led to his directorial debut, the short film, *Breaking and Entering* (1992). Turning his eye to television, he found himself directing several episodes of the hit ABC police drama 'NYPD Blue'. During that time Guggenheim showed his ability to handle seasoned actors and dramatic content with relative ease. His work on 'NYPD Blue' garnered high praise and provided further opportunity. After directing several episodes of the series, he branched out to other television series such as 'Party of Five', 'ER', and 'The Visitor'. Each one of these series furthered his craft and showcased his skill at creating realistic and compelling characters on screen.

With *Gossip* (2000), Guggenheim was finally given the opportunity to direct a major studio picture. The film centres on a college campus and what happens when words take on a life of their own. Working with an ensemble cast that included Edward James Olmos and Joshua Jackson, Guggenheim not only showed his ability to produce fine results from actors, but also his tendency to tackle issues in a highly stylised manner. The film, although not well received by critics, can be viewed as a successful experiment because of Guggenheim's deftly handled execution of subject matter and themes.

While filming *Gossip*, Guggenheim turned his attention to a subject that he felt very deeply about, education. Through the Teachers Documentary Project, Guggenheim teamed up PBS and producer Julia Schachter to tell the story of five new schoolteachers working in the Los Angeles school system, titled *Teach*. Guggenheim, using digital technology and documentary technique pick-up from his many years working with his father, has created a heartfelt moving depiction of life in the education system. The film earned Guggenheim a certficate of merit from the San Francisco Film Festival. He also helped to produce the box-office success *Training Day* (2001), starring Denzel Washington and Ethan Hawke.

Guggenheim is currently working on several projects with the Teachers Documentary Project as well as directing more television – his most recent effort is the critically successful Fox drama '24'. **JM**

# Sturla GUNNARSSON

After working extensively within Canadian television and making several politically *Such a Long Journey* (1998)
conscious documentaries for the National Film Board of Canada, Sturla Gunnarsson *Rare Birds* (2001)
emerged onto the international scene in 1998 with the narrative feature *Such a Long Journey*, an adaptation of the Rohinton Mistry novel.

This came at a time when Canadian film-makers seemed particularly interested in questions surrounding the India/Pakistan conflict – Deepa Mehta's *Earth* (1998), also about the partition, was released the same year – and although it was an adaptation, it avoided any literary pretence in favour of visual inventiveness. Indeed Gunnarsson, like Mehta, seemed to be answering the Merchant-Ivory portrayal of the place, filling his frames not only with melodrama, teeming masses, and the sense of 'something important', but also with arguing neighbours, faith healers and the small tribulations of the third-world middle class. Set in 1971 (just as India and Pakistan were about to go to war), the history of colonialism hangs heavy over the film, but there are no pompous British liberals wrestling with what post-colonialism means to them. Instead, Gunnarsson visualises the sub-continent in an insular way. There is clearly a world outside of India and Pakistan, but Gunnarsson does not acknowledge it; for him western

Asia is too complex. His 1997 documentary *Gerrie and Louise* was a portrait of another post-colonial country in transition, examining the state of post-apartheid South Africa.

His latest film, *Rare Birds* (2001), stars William Hurt as a restaurant owner living in small-town Newfoundland who concocts a plan to attract tourists by claiming that a near-extinct bird has now re-appeared; Molly Parker co-stars. The film has been (favourably) compared to *The Shipping News* (2001), which was released at the same time and is also set in Newfoundland. Also adapted from a novel, *Rare Birds* is based on the book by Edward Riche.                                                                **JW**

# Lawrence GUTERMAN

*Cats and Dogs* (2001) Raised in Montreal and Toronto, Lawrence Guterman made his first short films when he was a teenager. He studied physics at Harvard, where he edited and illustrated the satirical magazine 'The Harvard Lampoon' and during summer breaks returned to Canada to study animation at the Sheridan College of Art in Toronto. Following graduation, he studied at the USC School of Cinema, paying his way by teaching undergraduate physics. He found work for Joel Silver, reading scripts and working on computer graphics, and in production development at Columbia Pictures. By 1996 he had sold two feature scripts and co-written one of the 'Tales From the Crypt' series. He also made short films for the Web, earning critical acclaim for pieces such as *Headless,* a short about a 'dumb and dumber' couple who have a twisted idea of how to make money. Guterman's first outing as director was a video game based on the 'Goosebumps' series and he went on to direct several sequences for the computer-animated film *Antz* (1998). His first major release, *Cats and Dogs* (2001), is a state-of-the-art computer generated/live-action movie.

The story is fairly standard. Professor Brody (Jeff Goldblum) is a scientist searching for a cure for canine allergies. His son's dog is part of the research programme but it disappears, kidnapped by feline villain, Mr Tickles (modelled on Blofeld's moggy). Mrs Brody replaces the dog with a puppy who is quickly recruited by the secret dog service then finds himself under attack from evil moggies. Dog and child bond, and the cats fail. Initially conceived as an animated feature, Guterman decided instead to use real animals, thus capitalising on their individual quirks. The film is live-action Disney meets *Babe* (1995), at its best when it focuses on the animals. The script is weak and predictable but there are creative moments.                                                          **FG**

# Philip HAAS

Philip Haas' career began in London, as an assistant director with the Royal Shakespeare Company, and as a documentary film-maker who, in films including Money Man (1992) and the four-part television series 'Magicians of the Earth', investigated oddities of the art world. Although his roots are in theatre and non-fiction film-making, Haas has created a cinematic, highly stylised and notably ambitious series of feature films.

As a fiction film-maker, Haas has worked in close collaboration with his wife Belinda Haas, who has co-written and edited each of the films. Their first film was the streamlined and effective adaptation of Paul Auster's novel 'The Music of Chance'. A study of two gamblers who find themselves cornered on the estate of two eccentric millionaires, The Music of Chance (1993) stays true to the heightened reality of Auster's novel. In the film, Haas explored several themes central to his later work, including the power of material objects and the arbitrary nature of the rules governing human society.

Both themes were further unpacked in Angels and Insects (1995), adapted from A. S. Byatt's novella 'Morpho Eugenia'. A splendid response to the standard chamber drama, Angels and Insects follows a naturalist whose study of insects leads him to consider the ways in which humans interact. Haas digs gleefully beneath the artifice of Victorian culture to reveal some anarchic, shriekingly coloured, and troubling truths. The film was nominated for an Academy Award for costume design.

Haas' next film, The Blood Oranges (1997), was adapted from John Hawkes' novel and explores a series of infidelities between two couples in a remote Mexican village. At once brilliantly colourful and emotionally austere, The Blood Oranges is a striking, ambitious, and inconclusive experiment. Haas' most recent film, Up at the Villa (2000), was adapted from W. Somerset Maugham's novella. Lacking the depth and consequence of the director's previous films, it nevertheless retains a strong sense of style. However, the melodramatic period piece, set in Italy, was poorly received by critics. **JS**

# Taylor HACKFORD

Taylor Hackford is the sort of director that early film academics would have called a *metteur-en-scène*, an almost anonymous figure behind the camera, one who doesn't instil his personality onto the film. He is probably best known as the husband of actress Helen Mirren, yet he is a film-maker of genuine ability.

Hackford was born in Santa Barbara in 1945 and studied political science before becoming an investigative reporter, making documentaries for public television in Los Angeles (for which he won two Emmy Awards). A foray into fiction (the short film *Teenage Father* (1978)) was rewarded with an Academy Award, and sealed his move to the big screen on a permanent basis. His first feature, *The Idolmaker* (1980), is an uninventive, formulaic story about 1950s rock 'n' roll, in which an audacious young man becomes the manager of a new singer, manipulatively exploiting both the singer and the adolescent audience along the way. Although not a remarkable movie, it is marked by a fine eye for period detail, and indicates Hackford's seemingly natural ability for storytelling and pacing, and his skill at handling actors.

1982 saw the release of the director's second feature, *An Officer and a Gentleman*. The story of a misfit (Richard Gere) trying to seek acceptance by becoming a fighter pilot, the film is a not wholly successful hybrid of high melodrama and a masculine rites-of-passage narrative. The characters are two-dimensional, with little depth or development, but somehow it doesn't seem to matter. Hackford's control of narrative pace is strong, and the dénouement of the movie, a much-parodied scene where the newly qualified pilot Gere swoops into his estranged lover's workplace to literally sweep her off her feet, is one of the great iconic moments of 1980s cinema. The film also features an Academy Award-winning performance from Lou Gossett Jr as Gere's drill-sergeant; a tyrannical military man, naturally, but a feelgood tyrant, who we realise early on will be the catalyst for Gere's redemption, and for whom Gere (and the audience) will develop a begrudging respect by the story's conclusion.

*Against All Odds* (1984), Hackford's subsequent film, is another two-dimensional melodrama, in which a has-been football star, Jeff Bridges, is hired by a former colleague (James Woods) to act as a private detective and track down his lover (Rachel Ward), who has run off to Mexico. A loose remake of Jacques Tourneur's *Out Of The Past* (1947), the movie, whilst well paced, moves along to an inevitable conclusion with limited tension. Hackford again gets strong performances from his cast, particularly Woods and Bridges.

A year later came the release of *White Nights* (1985), a Cold War political thriller in which Russian defector Mikhail Baryshnikov is involved in a plane crash behind the Iron Curtain, and convinces a Western defector (Gregory Hines) to assist him in returning to the West. Neither particularly political nor genuinely thrilling, the film is most effective in the dance sequences, where Hines' tap and Baryshnikov's ballet collide (the only time there is a genuine sense of the opposition of American and Soviet cultures). This film, along with the two previous features, is the cinematic equivalent of a blockbuster novel; proficient, slick and fast-paced, but superficial, uninventive and uninspiring. *White Nights* was followed by a brief foray back into documentary work, *Chuck Berry, Hail, Hail, Rock'n'Roll* (1987). The film is partly a profile of the legendary performer, and partly a concert film featuring Berry and the likes of Eric Clapton, Little Richard, and Jerry Lee Lewis.

His next feature, *Everybody's All American* (1988), is altogether more interesting. The story of a collegiate football hero and his prom queen girlfriend, the narrative covers thirty years of American history, as it happens around the hero (Dennis Quaid). Retaining some stylistic features of Hackford's work (the control of pace, the innate narrative handling and the ability with actors), the film is also much deeper in terms of character, and has a more intelligent narrative. Moving from a youthful naiveté, Quaid's football star goes through life from the mid-1950s to the 1980s, against the backdrop of political change (notably the development of racial politics), yet it is only at the film's conclusion that Quaid realises his world has moved on, leaving him behind, unwanted. As with *The Idolmaker*, there is a strong attention to period detail, with the eras nicely differentiated, and there are strong performances from Quaid and Jessica Lange. The principal problem is in Hackford's choice of episodic narrative structure, where unsignalled narrative jumps forward in time happen at the expense of genuine character development.

This problem also mars Hackford's next film, *Blood In, Blood Out* (1993), a three-hour film examining life for three Hispanic cousins in Los Angeles from their adolescence, through gang battles, and their individual developments and separate paths into adulthood (where they end up as a drug-addicted artist, a narcotics policeman, and a violent prison-gang godfather). The ambitious narrative is well handled, and Hackford avoids many of the potential problematic clichés of the Hispanic settings, but the narrative necessity to focus on one character at a time for large sections, as well as narrative leaps, leads to little in the way of character development, and ultimately they are unconvincing. The audience is left with little dramatic involvement.

*Dolores Claiborne* (1995) is a successful adaptation of a Stephen King non-horror novel, in which the central character, played by Kathy Bates, is a woman whom the population of a town are convinced killed her husband many years ago. The case was unproven, but a subsequent death with Dolores' involvement again looks like murder, and it is down to her daughter (Jennifer Jason Leigh) to deal with the repercussions. For the first time, Hackford focuses on central feminine characters, which introduces a new dynamic to his narrative handling. His pacing is very tight, and the decision to film the flashback elements of the narrative in pristine colours and the present settings in grey, grainy, filtered tones is successful. The performances from Bates, Leigh, and Christopher Plummer (as the jaded policeman desperate to secure a conviction where he failed years earlier) are very effective.

1997 saw the release of *Devil's Advocate*, a legal thriller with Faustian elements. Keanu Reeves plays the arrogant hotshot lawyer tempted to join the firm led by Al Pacino, a devil played to the hilt of camp ham-acting (Pacino clearly relishing the part). Hackford manages to instil the movie with genuine suspense and an air of palpable eeriness. The film's climactic scene, a 15-minute sequence in which the conflicts between Reeves and Pacino are revealed and resolved, is a remarkable achievement (it has the electricity of live theatre), and is clear proof of Hackford's ability as an actors' director. On the whole, the film is absolute hokum, but it is hokum of the highest and most entertaining kind.

Hackford's most recent release came in 2000 with *Proof of Life*, in which Russell Crowe plays Terry Thorne, a hostage negotiator assigned to secure the release of kidnap victims in the world's political troublespots. Thorne is sent in to negotiate the release of engineer Peter Bowman (played by David Morse), whose company's proposed oil pipeline strays into a Latin American military junta's financially supportive drug production region. Thorne's work also involves him in the emotional re-assurance of Bowman's wife Alice (played by Meg Ryan), and inevitable sexual tension between the two only serves to complicate Thorne's involvement in the case. Critically, the movie was overshadowed by the off-screen romance between the film's stars, and in retrospect it is a far better film than it was initially given credit for. Hackford's narrative pace, in combination with an intelligent script from Tony Gilroy (who had worked with Hackford on *Devil's Advocate*), allows for a sustained increase in tension across the whole movie, and an almost *Fitzcarraldo*-esque insistence on filming in the Ecuador mountains lends a real sense of precariousness to the movie. In fact, the admirable avoidance of CGI effects in the action sequences helps the movie retain a semblance of realism, and the sheer physicality of the infiltration and rescue climax enhances the excitement of a bravura, if rather gung-ho, piece of film-making. Where the film really suffers, though, is in the romantic subplot between Thorne and Alice; given the off-screen reality of the situation, Crowe and Ryan bring negligible chemistry to the screen, in a narrative strand that adds little, if anything, to the story as a whole. Ryan in particular seems unconvincing in this aspect, and the film comes across, for her, as an unsuccessful attempt to throw off the baggage of her romantic-comedy screen persona.

Hackford is current developing a new project, *Julia Pastrana*, the true story of a mid-nineteenth-century circus freak, and the relationship between her and the freak-show owner who discovers her. Some twenty years on from the success of *An Officer and a Gentleman*, it should see Hackford re-united with Richard Gere. **JP**

# Randa HAINES

Born in Los Angeles in 1945, Randa Haines is a graduate of the AFI Directing Workshop for Women. Her student film, *August/September* (1976) gained her the attention of television executives and landed her scriptwriting work on the popular 1970s television

*Children of a Lesser God* (1986)

*The Doctor* (1991)

series 'Family'. Haines forged a successful career in television, directing several episodes of 'Hill Street Blues' and 'Knot's Landing'. Her award-winning television drama about incest, *Something About Amelia* (1984), led to her first feature, *Children of a Lesser God* (1986), although she continued to work in television throughout the early years of her film-making career ('Tales from the Crypt' and 'Alfred Hitchcock Presents').

*Children of a Lesser God* is based on Mark Medoff's Tony Award-winning drama. The film centres on a speech instructor (William Hurt) and the stubborn deaf woman (Marlee Matlin) with whom he falls in love. This is a tender film directed with sensitivity and integrity, but it was not without its critics, who saw the film as somewhat cynical, prompting one to argue, 'making a sound movie about the deaf is a little like making a silent movie about the blind. It may be well made, but doesn't it evade the point?' Despite the criticisms, *Children of a Lesser God* was an auspicious start to Haines' career and was nominated for five Academy Awards, including Best Picture.

*The Doctor* (1991) saw the director again teamed with William Hurt, who plays an arrogant and cold-hearted surgeon who goes through a humbling and humanising process as he is diagnosed and treated for throat cancer. Particularly notable is Hurt's performance (and Haines' remarkable sensitivity to it) as we see this intractable and arrogant man come to terms with his mortality and the mortality of others.

The director's next feature, *Wrestling Ernest Hemingway* (1993), is a charming, challenging and thought-provoking film, largely due to the two charismatic leads (Robert Duvall and Richard Harris). The plot is simple enough: two elderly men with seemingly nothing in common meet in retirement in Florida. Gradually their characters unfold as they discuss life, news, films, their passions, and we observe their routines. This is a near-flawless study of the fears of old age: declining virility, lost dreams, loneliness. The film's core is the close observation of manly behaviour, and as in some of Hemingway's stories, we get a tremendous sense that the real action is simmering away under the small-talk, indicating to the audience that larger, murkier issues are lurking beneath the men's surface humour and bravado.

Haines' most recent feature, *Dance With Me* (1998), is a romantic drama set in the world of dance. The film's central character, Rafael (Chayanne), comes to America from Cuba after his mother's funeral, in search of his real father. His father (Kris Kristofferson) runs a highly successful dance studio and Rafael joins up in time for the World Dance Championship, failing to tell Kristofferson that he is in fact his son. A weak plot but some energising set dance pieces, and a fine performance from a strong cast, including Vanessa Williams, Joan Plowright and Harry Groener, *Dance With Me* is an enjoyable feelgood flick, but disappointing in the light of Haines' masterful direction in her first two features. Indeed, in comparison to *Children of a Lesser God* and *Wrestling Ernest Hemingway*, *Dance With Me* has been described as the film equivalent of fast food.

Haines is a director with enormous potential, as yet only half fulfilled. She is gifted in the way she can weave two central characters close together, and when working with craftsmen such as Hurt and Duvall, she produces a magical, personal, and intense cinema that is a rarity in mainstream Hollywood films.                    **SL**

# Lasse HALLSTRÖM

Lasse Hallström is one of the few contemporary European directors who has been successful in producing distinctive films within the studio system of Hollywood. Born in Stockholm in 1946, he made seven films in his native country between 1973 and 1983 including *Father to Be* (1979) and *The Rooster* (1981). Concentrating mainly on the issues of marriage, divorce and childhood, these films indicated an interest in themes that Hallström would explore and expand on later in his career. It was not until 1985 that the world started to take notice of this quiet and subtle film-maker – with the release of *My Life as a Dog*, Hollywood rapidly courted Hallström.

*My Life as a Dog* is an affectionate, episodic portrait of childhood and a child's ability to withdraw and ultimately triumph over adversity. Telling the story of Ingemar (Anton Glanzelius) and his journey into the Swedish countryside to live with relatives after the death of his mother, the film is emotionally generous and heart-warming without being sentimental. It is also the blueprint for most of Hallström's following films. His fascination with the forced maturation of children due to stressful or pressured external forces shows itself bravely in the character of Ingemar, who retreats from his traumatic existence into a rational world of 'life stories'. It is a child's ability to withdraw in this way that captures Hallström's imagination. Whilst adults tend to get stuck in problems, children seem to have a remarkable talent for moving on and erasing those problems from memory. Comparisons with Bergman are inevitable, but although both directors understand and exploit the cathartic power of film, Hallström has said that the process of making films has unlocked hidden childhood traumas of which he was previously unaware.

Hallström made two further films in Sweden: *The Children of Noisy Village* (1986) and *More About the Children of Noisy Village* (1987), based on the memoirs of author Astrid Lindgren. After being fired from the set of *Mermaids* (1990), Hallström debuted in Hollywood with the coolly received *Once Around* (1991). Starring Richard Dreyfuss and Holly Hunter, the film revives Hallström's popular themes of family dysfunction and thwarted love. His next effort, however, is probably his strongest American work.

*What's Eating Gilbert Grape?* (1993) is a methodical and slightly surreal vision of small-town America. Proving that he is more at home dealing with children and young adults, Hallström paints an affecting portrait of Gilbert and his family, who are struggling to maintain some level of normality in their lives when the odds are firmly against them. Gilbert (Johnny Depp) is a young man responsible not only for his brother (Leonardo DiCaprio), who has a severe learning disability, but also for his 500-pound mother, who cannot leave the confines of her house. Gilbert is forced to adopt the role of parent and provider, leading to an internal conflict and, more importantly, a contempt for his restrictive surroundings. Described as a 'sentimental film that eschews sentimentality', Hallstrom's humanist vision shines through his love of, and identification with, his characters.

After contributing to *Lumière and Company* (1995), in which 150 directors were challenged to make a film on the original Lumière camera – each segment consisted of 52 seconds and a single shot – Hallström went on to make the instantly forgettable *Something to Talk About* (1995), with Julia Roberts and Dennis Quaid.

*The Cider House Rules* (1999), produced by Miramax and based on the John Irving book of the same name, tells the story of the aptly named Homer Wells (Tobey Maguire) and his odyssey from a deserted New England orphanage, where he was born and grew up, into the wide world and back again. Although on first glance the screenplay seems to be a continuation of Hallström's work, he never quite lays his distinctive vision onto Irving's script. *The Cider House Rules* features excellent performances from both Maguire as the naïve Homer and Michael Caine as Dr Larch, the ether-addicted head of the orphanage, but the film is remarkably flat and old-fashioned. None of the pertinent issues raised (abortion, race, and incest) are investigated to any satisfying degree; as a result, Homer's journey seems a clichéd and unsatisfactory variation of the metaphysical Hollywood road movie. Irving's naïve morality seems at odds with Hallström's intense character study and the film is unable to find its centre. From his first view of the ocean to his first perfunctory sexual experience, Homer drifts impassively from the safe haven of the orphanage to the safe haven of the Cider House, seemingly detached from the war that is raging in the rest of the world. Hallström seems to have increasingly abandoned the peripheral characters that made his earlier works so distinctive: Fransson, the roof repair man in *My Life as a Dog*, and Betty Carver, the sex-starved housewife in *What's Eating Gilbert Grape?*, were characters that extended their scope and added to their unstable and surreal atmospheres. *The Cider House Rules*, however, is a strangely conservative morality tale that signals Hallström's complete acceptance by the mainstream.

*Chocolat* (2000), Hallström's subsequent film for Miramax, is another conservative piece which is packaged as somehow 'different'. Based on the best-selling novel by Joanne Harris, it tells the story of Vianne Rocher (Juliette Binoche), a chocolate maker who opens a chocolatier in Lansquenet, a small village outside of Toulouse during Lent. Seen as a corruptive influence on the God-fearing population, Vianne is ostracised by most of the villagers. Slowly, however, her chocolate shop takes the place of the church as a centre of confession and solace, and she is accepted as part of the community. The film seems made-to-order by Miramax, and Hallström goes through the motions he knows so well, portraying an isolated community ravaged by mistrust and over-dependence on religion. Although his distinctive character-studies are present in Josephine Muscat (Lena Olin), the battered wife and borderline neurotic, and Armande Voizin (Judi Dench), the cantankerous old lady with a heart, they are shadowed by the over-powering radiance and cloying sweetness of his leading lady.

The Shipping News (2001) does nothing to dispel Hallström's reputation as the king of the soft-core literary adaptation. Based on E. Annie Proulx's novel, the story once again takes place in an isolated community (this time Newfoundland) and its goal is to find closure and redemption for the long-suffering Quoyle (Kevin Spacey). Although central performances are strong, and the film is beautifully shot by Oliver Stapleton, it misses many of the subtle nuances of character that are present in its source material and is, ultimately, a rather dull repeat of themes that have been better explored in Hallström's previous films. He seems constantly drawn to this type of material and explores it with utter conviction. Yet his belief in the redemptive power of the human spirit, and the insistence with which he plays into the hands of a guaranteed and approving audience, is rapidly diminishing his interest and importance as a director.

His next film is rumoured to be another adaptation, this time of David Liss' book 'Conspiracy of Paper'. **BW**

# Tom HANKS

*That Thing You Do!* (1996) By the mid-1990s, actor Tom Hanks – born in California in 1956 – had revived what many perceived as his rapidly faltering career. With his creative and commercial power assured, Hanks followed in the well-established tradition of Hollywood's (predominantly) male stars and turned to writing and directing feature films. His debut feature, *That Thing You Do!* (1996), was a bright, upbeat and peppy nostalgic drama set in the mid-1960s in which a pop band – The One-Ders – form in the American heartland and for a short time burn brightly. The film charts their aspirations and frustrations as dreams and reality collide under the watchful gaze of their manager, played by Hanks. Like Hanks' familiar 1980s screen persona, the film is energetic and charged with good humour whilst also effectively venturing into more sombre drama. With its catchy theme tune written by Chris Cunningham of the American band, Fountains of Wayne, the film marked a breakthrough for several of its leads, notably Liv Tyler, Giovanni Ribisi (Phoebe's brother Frank in 'Friends'), and Steve Zahn.

Although the film was received with lukewarm enthusiasm, it is refreshing for its unassumingly modest ambition – unlike some actors' directorial debuts it is not self-important. If Hanks' style resembles any director with whom he has worked it would be Ron Howard. His approach is unfussy and straightforward. It is likely that audiences and critics expected something more showy, though it would be hard to deny Hank's skill in making the audience share the band's excitement when they first hear their song, 'That Thing You Do', air on the radio. It is the film's standout moment – crafted with real Hollywood savvy and panache.

Hanks has since moved into producing, notably the television series about the American space program, 'From Earth to the Moon', for which he directed the pilot episode. He is recently co-produced, with Steven Spielberg, the television series 'Band of Brothers', based on the experiences of American soldiers in World War Two. **JC**

# Curtis HANSON

*Sweet Kill* (1972)  A former photographer and entertainment journalist, and erstwhile editor of the industry
*The Little Dragons* (1980)  magazine *Cinema*, Curtis Hanson came late to cinematic success. Born in Nevada in
*Losin' It* (1983)  1945, having forged a solid if unspectacular career directing studio thrillers, it was only
*The Bedroom Window* (1987)  with his assured adaptation of James Ellroy's epic novel *LA Confidential* in 1997 that he
*Bad Influence* (1990)  found widespread critical and commercial success. A keen film historian and chairman
*The Hand That Rocks*  of the UCLA Film Archive, his films often pay homage to past greats, particularly the
*the Cradle* (1992)  films of Alfred Hitchcock and the classics of noir.
*The River Wild* (1994)  Like many of his contemporaries, Hanson cut his cinematic teeth on the low-budget
*LA Confidential* (1997)  thrillers and suspense films of the late 1970s and early 1980s, initially as a contract
*Wonder Boys* (2000)  screenwriter. After co-writing *The Dunwich Horror* (1970), a schlock-horror from the
*8-Mile* (2002)  Roger Corman stable, his first film was *Sweet Kill* (1972), a serial-killer thriller which made little impression but much use of moody lighting and the fetishes of its main character. Six years on, his screenplay for *Silent Partner* (1978), a crime caper revolving around an insider bank job and a cross-dressing Christopher Plummer, demonstrated an emerging interest in noirish themes and convoluted plotlines. Having briefly experimented with kids' movies in *Little Dragons* (1980), Hanson co-wrote the controversial

(and widely-banned) race parable *White Dog* (1982) with maverick director Sam Fuller, in which the 'white' dog of the title, trained to attack black people, is used as a metaphor for social conditioning and racial hatred. Much maligned and widely misunderstood, the film nevertheless demonstrated Hanson's desire to confront difficult themes in his work.

Following the teen sex comedy *Losin' It* (1983), in which a young Tom Cruise and gang of cohorts set out to lose their innocence and inhibitions in 1960s Mexico, Hanson found more consistent success with a run of tightly-directed psychological thrillers, strong on suspense and atmosphere and loaded with narrative twists, ulterior motives, and character reversals. *Bedroom Window* (1987), a sub-Hitchcock thriller in which a businessman witnesses a murder *in flagrante* with his boss' wife, showed brief glimpses of Hanson's developing skill with the mechanics of suspense, but rarely strayed from conventional lines and failed to turn Steve Guttenberg into a convincing leading-man. *Bad Influence* (1990), scripted by David Koepp, offered more original thrills, the *Strangers on a Train* (1951) tale of a frustrated corporate executive, played in typical sleazeball style by James Spader, who is seduced by the rakish lifestyle of man-about-town Rob Lowe only to discover his new buddy is also a closet psychopath. *The Hand That Rocks the Cradle* (1992) follows a similar vein and scored Hanson his first box-office hit. Annabella Sciorra plays a woman who is molested by her gynaecologist. Following the doctor's suicide during the ensuing investigation, his bitter wife (Rebecca de Mornay) poses as Sciorra's nanny and takes sadistic revenge on her family from within. Hanson subtly explores parental paranoia with some finely crafted suspense, atmospheric camerawork and a chilling central performance from de Mornay, though the film is strongest when building the air of menace surrounding her rather than during the inevitable overblown conclusion. Overtones of Hitchcock and his domestic psycho story *Shadow of a Doubt* (1943) again hint at Hanson's awareness of his thriller heritage, and the two powerful female leads make a welcome change. Hanson's next film, the big-budget studio picture *The River Wild* (1994), swapped moody interiors for the great outdoors, and follows a fractured all-American family on a rafting expedition who become entangled with a motley collection of escaping criminals. The various characters – jealous husband (David Strathairn), plucky kid, roguish villain (Kevin Bacon), and feisty matriarch (Meryl Streep) – are off-the-shelf, and too much generic action and too few real thrills mean Hanson rarely manages to elevate this above the ordinary.

*LA Confidential* (1997) is anything but ordinary; a complex, engrossing and impeccably made *film policier* mixing up the spirits of hardboiled crime fiction, modern cop thrillers, and good old-fashioned noir. The film follows three different detectives through the underbelly of 1950s Los Angeles: political straight-lace Ed Exley (Guy Pearce), fresh out of officer school; loose-cannon tough guy Bud White (Russell Crowe), oddly the most idealistic of the three; and the cynical Jack Vincennes (Kevin Spacey), adviser to a Hollywood cop show and off-duty informant to the tabloid rags. Brilliantly adapted from one of James Ellroy's most complicated novels, the script blends gangland murders, tabloid journalism, sex scandals, porn rings, racism, police brutality and official corruption, but never loses sight of its characters, each struggling with their own internal conflict between duty, justice and integrity. Filmed with meticulous attention to period detail and packed with every trick in the noir repertoire – moody camerawork, suggestive locations, narrative twists, and double-crosses – it is one of the most carefully crafted films to come out of Hollywood in years, the 1990s heir to classics of the genre like *The Big Sleep* (1946), *The French Connection* (1971), and *Chinatown* (1974). It also continued to explore one of Hanson's favoured themes: the conflict between reality and illusion, here set appropriately in the consummate city of make-believe. The film won huge critical and public acclaim, but was swamped at the Academy Awards by James Cameron's juggernaut *Titanic* (1997); Hanson and co-writer Brian Helgeland won only the award for Best Adapted screenplay, though Kim Basinger also won Best Supporting Actress as the Veronica Lake lookalike prostitute Lynn Bracken.

The success of *LA Confidential* has allowed Hanson to move out of the director-for-hire bracket he inhabited for much of the 1990s and develop more personal projects. His most recent film, *Wonder Boys* (2000), was another convoluted story adapted from a successful novel, focusing on Grady Tripp, a depressed, dope-addled creative writing professor, played by Michael Douglas. Battling with second book syndrome, Tripp becomes embroiled in a comedy of errors involving his bisexual editor, his ex-wife, a mysterious writing student, a dead dog, and Marilyn Monroe's jacket. Hanson mixes up screwball comedy and sentimental drama in an engaging if contrived tale about losing one's way in life, in which the oddball cast of characters are all searching for something – friendship, happiness, fulfilment and meaning. Though many of the ideas it throws up are better suited to the book than the cinema screen, Hanson's film is witty and full of heart, and continues to show him as a director unusually concerned with old-fashioned values of care and craft. Nevertheless, *Wonder Boys* fared badly at the box office after a mismanaged marketing campaign, and little better during a re-release in time for the 2000 Academy Awards.

His forthcoming film *8-Mile* is a hip-hop drama starring Eminem in his first film role. **OB**

# Renny HARLIN

Born in 1959 in Finland, Renny Harlin decided in his youth that he wanted to be a film director. He is now associated with the archetypal big-budget, blockbuster Hollywood action movie. The red-baiting *Born American* (1986) – set in Finland but American in its subject matter – established the style and tone for all of Harlin's subsequent films: emotional distance from characters, rapid cutting and a fast-moving narrative. Its macho sensibilities also signalled an appeal to young male audiences.

His next feature, *Prison* (1988), was a horror flick, effective in its use of shock and drawing good performances from its B-list cast, though like much of Harlin's work it displays a gloating attitude to violence. *A Nightmare on Elm Street 4: The Dream Master* (1988) was already part of a tired franchise when Harlin was given the job of directing, and added nothing to the original premise. For Harlin the film served to increase his credentials as a director at ease with the multi-genre conventions of the action/horror film. It led to him being offered the job of directing infamous stand-up comic Andrew Dice Clay in *The Adventures of Ford Fairlane* (1990). Eschewing Clay's racist, homophobic and misogynist reputation, Harlin fashioned a film that failed to capitalise upon Clay's off-screen persona or add anything to the private-eye genre. Nevertheless, Harlin's growing reputation with producers led to *Die Hard 2: Die Harder* (1990), a big-budget sequel to the surprise box-office hit *Die Hard* (1988). Trapped between the need to retain the key narrative elements and characterisation of the first film, *Die Hard 2* simply rehashed them on a grander scale but with less tension. However, it did confirm Harlin's ability to master large-scale film production, including huge sets, special effects and location shooting in extreme conditions.

*Cliffhanger* (1993), starring Sylvester Stallone – about a pair of mountain rescue guides forced to help a group of robbers find some suitcases full of money – is perhaps Harlin's most well-realised and straightforwardly entertaining film. It avoids the bombast of *Die Hard 2* and a reliance on a series of disjointed action scenes. Though the stunt work is impressive, particularly in the electrifying opening scenes of the mountain-top rescue and the mid-air heist, the film also attempts to link the action together into a coherent narrative. Ultimately, Harlin cannot resist the imperative of action over character, and the film also relies on some rather lazy stereotypes.

Harlin came crashing down to earth, or to be exact into the sea, with the $60 million turkey *CutThroat Island* (1995). In many ways the film's main elements are no different to Harlin's previous films – plenty of action, impressive stunt work, huge sets pieces – however, the film simply does not work on any level. The action is repetitive, the lead actors (Geena Davis and Matthew Modine) are uncharismatic, and the supporting characters are inconsequential. Fatally, the film seems out of time, in that it neither convinces as a historical drama or as an action film able to appeal to contemporary audiences.

Nevertheless, Harlin was still able to secure finance for his next film, *The Long Kiss Goodnight* (1996), the story of a former CIA assassin called Charly (Geena Davis) who, as a result of amnesia, becomes a primary school teacher. With the help of Samuel L. Jackson's private eye, she slowly begins to regain her memory. Whilst the rather hackneyed plot acts as a vehicle for a series of violent set-pieces, the film rivals *Cliffhanger* in the Harlin catalogue for enjoyable thrills. Unlike *Cutthroat Island*, the lead characters are both charismatic and enjoy a visible on-screen chemistry, whilst the action never overwhelms them. The film is also notable in its use of a female central protagonist, though its accent on family values is cloying. Its polish, like that of all Harlin's films, lies in its steadfast desire to be nothing other than a piece of genre entertainment.

*Deep Blue Sea* (1999), the story of a group of scientists trapped in a marine laboratory complex, pursued by genetically enhanced, 'intelligent' sharks, is an efficient reworking of a variety of film plots. It is essentially '*Jaws* meets *Alien'*. The characters resemble cardboard cut-outs and half the fun of the film is in trying to guess who will be eaten next. This does not detract from the film's merits as a piece of efficient if cold entertainment, however.

In Harlin's most recent film, *Driven* (2001), he teams up once more with Sylvester Stallone in a story of an aging racing driver brought out of retirement to help guide a younger driver to glory. As if to demonstrate the difficulty of making motor car racing interesting cinematic fare, Stallone's script and Harlin's uninspired direction pile on the crashes and spills but leave very little space amidst the noise and cacophony for characterisation. In some ways this is a blessing for the audience since Stallone's 'Rocky in a racing helmet' character is unconvincing (he is too old for this sort of thing now), whilst his mumbled delivery obscures what little of the dialogue we can hear. This kind of action vehicle is a long way from the vertiginous heights of *Cliffhanger*. Harlin's current project, *Mindhunters*, stars Val Kilmer.                    **SH**

# Ed HARRIS

Born in Englewood, New Jersey, in 1950, Ed Harris had long since established himself     *Pollock* (2000)
as a notable, charismatic leading man of integrity and repute in films such as *The Right Stuff* (1982), *Walker* (1987), and *Glengarry Glen Ross* (1992) when, after a long gestation period, he made his directorial debut, *Pollock* (2000).

An absorbing portrayal of Jackson Pollock, one of the twentieth century's greatest painters, the film features a typically committed performance by Harris himself, who also produced. Physically, the actor is extremely close to his subject; but his performance goes beyond the physical to capture something of the essence of the depressive, alcoholic, and frequently volatile artist. Equally good is the often-underused Marcia Gay Harden as the artist's wife and muse, Lee Krasner – her performance earned her a Best Supporting Actress Academy Award. Supporting roles are filled with the dependable likes of Bud Cort and John Heard. A deeply impressive debut, Harris proves himself as capable and assured behind the camera as in front of it. Beginning in post-war Greenwich Village, it is an evocative and highly authentic work, for the most part shot on Pollock's former Long Island Estate, that not only acts as an engrossing biopic but which also seriously attempts to consider its subject's contribution to contemporary art, a feat that many other similarly themed works singularly fail to achieve.                **JWo**

# James B. HARRIS

James B. Harris, born in New York in 1928, originally wanted to be a jazz drummer and     *The Bedford Incident* (1965)
studied music at the Julliard School. In 1947 he joined a film exporting company, and     *Some Call It Loving* (1973)
the following year became a distributor with Realart Pictures. In 1949 he co-founded     *Fast-Walking* (1982)
Flamingo Films which distributed movies to television, and during the Korean War he     *Cop* (1987)
served as a cameraman in the US Army Signal Corps. He formed Harris-Kubrick Pictures     *Boiling Point* (1993)
in 1954, and produced Kubrick's *The Killing* (1956), *Paths of Glory* (1957), and *Lolita* (1962). The partnership with Kubrick ended during the preparation of *Dr Strangelove: or, How I Learned to Stop Worrying and Love the Bomb* (1964) when the opportunity arose for Harris to direct *The Bedford Incident* (1965). Later, he produced Don Siegel's *Telefon* (1977).

Adapted by James Poe from Mark Rascovich's novel, *The Bedford Incident* is a gripping thriller about the pursuit of a Soviet submarine which has violated Greenland's territorial waters. It is the only movie directed by Harris which he did not also write. With strong performances by Eric Portman, Martin Balsam, and especially Richard Widmark as the 'effortlessly mean bastard' in command of the US vessel in pursuit, it also offered Sidney Poitier his first role in which race was not an issue, although the script still requires him to be the bearer of white liberal conscience. Bridging between the Cold War paranoia of 1950s cinema, and the countercultural paranoia of the late 1960s and early 1970s, *The Bedford Incident* depicts conflicts of personality and world-view, painted a little too broadly, as they inexorably develop against a backdrop of the tense and realistic procedurals of the pursuit. If the grim comedy of the preceding year's *Dr Strangelove* makes it seem a little too much in earnest, it is not the failed seriousness of *Fail Safe* (1964), with its impossibly noble and self-sacrificing characters; and *The Bedford Incident*'s accidental triggering of a nuclear exchange is funnier and scarier than anything in Kubrick's movie.

*Some Call It Loving* (1973), based on John Collier's 'Sleeping Beauty', is Harris' most personal film and his first extended meditation on his key themes of innocence and corruption, fantasy and reality: a jazz musician buys a woman who has slept for eight years, but when he wakes her his female companions initiate her into their ménage, and the only way to 'save' her is to return her to sleep. It is all much too straight-faced to have aged well.

*Fast-Walking* (1982) stars James Woods as a guard who schemes to earn himself two fat fees by pretending to assassinate an imprisoned black activist and by helping him escape. Attractively shot in Montana, it develops Harris' themes into an exploration of ideals and human frailty within systems which tend to render individuals powerless. Although it is often taken for a quintessential reactionary violent-cop movie, *Cop* (1987), adapted from James Ellroy's 'Blood on the Moon', is a grim investigation of the possibility of maintaining liberal principles in a world in which everyone, from serial killers to state institutions, is utterly opposed to them. The fairytale motif recurs and is made more pungent as the protagonist (again played by Woods) uses the form to tell his young daughter about his encounters with criminals, to prepare her for the world and to protect her from it. The best of Harris' crime trilogy, its weakness lies in its troubling gender politics, which leave the protagonist's conviction that all women subscribe to impossibly naïve and therefore dangerous beliefs unchallenged.

*Boiling Point* (1993), adapted from Gerald Petievich's novel, attempts to rise above the cop-thriller formula by reconstructing it as a character-driven narrative. A rather ponderous failure, it is an object lesson on the need for interesting characters to drive such narratives. Devoid of tension, it labours the parallels between the romantic and professional entanglements of a treasury agent and the criminals he is pursuing, and depends on some implausible interconnections between their lives. It is the only movie Harris has directed which he did not also produce. **MB**

# Trent HARRIS

Call it underground, avant-garde or cult film-making, there can be few more original, uncompromising and downright odd directors in American cinema than Trent Harris. A documentor and explorer of the stranger sides of American life, in particular his home state of Utah (as detailed in one of his books, 'Mondo Utah'), Harris' films simply defy categorisation. Sometimes documentary, sometimes fantasy, sometimes tragic realism, genres clash together in quite unthinkable ways. Practically impossible to find – often only available directly from the film-maker himself – and rarely receiving a theatrical release, Harris' films celebrate not only the wilful oddity of backwater America, but also the art of low-budget film-making. They are poised somewhere between the lowbrow high camp of Troma and John Waters, European art-house, and guerrilla independents. A sometime lecturer at Utah University, Harris has directed a number of experimental documentaries, including *The Greatest Love Story Ever Told* (the story of a beauty queen who ravishes a Mormon missionary) and *The Burning Man* (a film about the crazed yearly festival that occurs in the Nevada desert).

*The Orkly Kid* (1985) is perhaps his most widely known short, a hilarious fantasy in which a small Idaho town is shocked by a young man's burning desire to impersonate Olivia Newton-John in drag. The film features Crispin Glover, another oddball of American cinema who was to become a regular in Harris' work.

*Rubin and Ed* (1992) is Harris' biggest-budget studio venture; an odd couple story in which a real estate agent and a reclusive Seventies throwback embark on a quest through the Utah desert to find the perfect burial spot for a frozen cat. The perfect example of Harris' distinctive tone, mixing satire and affection in equal measures, the film is packed with comic imagination and detail – a range of targets including squeaky toys, self-help real estate companies and water-skiing cats – ridiculous, incomprehensible and very funny. Harris' films are never all joke, however; with excellent desert cinematography and some subtle musings on loss and alienation, *Rubin and Ed* is more than a self-consciously wacky oddity. The joke, of course, went way over the studio's head. *Plan 10 from Outer Space* (1994) is no more mainstream; a woman finds a bronze plate in Utah, which transpires to be linked both to Mormon doctrine and an invasion of earth by sex-crazed aliens. Again peopled by a cast of bizarre characters, the film is part sci-fi spoof (hence the title, the next plan on from Ed Wood's *Plan 9* (1965), part theological exploration. Filmed on a minuscule budget, it is now only available to Utah locals or direct from Harris.

*Beaver Trilogy* (2001), a three-parter, promises to be Harris' most interesting work yet: combining a multi-format mix of documentary footage of the inspiration for the *Orkly Kid* (the eponymous Beaver Kid), a fictionalised version starring a young Sean Penn, and the third version, the *Orkly Kid* short, with Crispin Glover. Imaginative, individual and incomprehensible, there is no doubt Harris has a vision; as an audience, the challenge is just to try and keep up.                                                                  **OB**

# Matthew HARRISON

Born in New York in 1959, Matthew Harrison is an art-house sensation in embryo. With three features and numerous shorts to his name, he has yet to make that hit which places him in the company of other innovative film-makers such as Hal Hartley, Spike Lee and Richard Linklater. Chronicling lives which have fallen through the ventilation grates of inner urban milieux, Harrison's work simultaneously dramatises his protagonists' trajectories whilst drawing on the experiences of his own life.

Born of British parents, Harrison studied experimental film-making at New York's Cooper Union School of Art under postwar underground luminary Robert Breer. Regularly citing Stan Brakhage as an influence, he has said: 'Everything I do is about form.' He took up the camera around 1971 and remembers directing infant actors. These lessons in improvisation lend recent works a feeling for character and a looseness reminiscent of early Godard. Driven by the need to make films cheaply, Harrison and eleven producers and directors established the Film Crash organisation. Key to the ethos is to stay active: 'We call them "prune films" because they keep us regular'.

The demonic *Spare Me* (1992) revolved around a bowling genius on the skids who falls for a beautiful siren whose psychotic brother comes in pursuit. Overripe – 'When you hear thunder, God is bowling' – it also displayed Harrison's knack for uncovering microscopic worlds, foreseeing *Rhythm Thief* (1994). Scarcely reviewed, the film went straight to video.

*Rhythm Thief* explodes onto the screen as its enigmatic hero addresses the camera: 'Watch me!' Fighting shy of a gallery of grizzled street types as he plies bootleg music tapes on the Lower East Side, Simon is auteur of his own life. Returning to the 'downwardly-mobile white guy themes' of the shorts, Harrison's film was shot in the old neighbourhood by Howard Krupa on high-contrast monochrome stock, and jump-cut to a pounding indie soundtrack. Unabashedly stylish, *Rhythm Thief* tells of individuals seeking identities. His actors' piquant turns are desperate bids for recognition. Simon (Jason Andrews) and sister remember their mother in a club as projected imagery plays across their bodies. The plight of characters as *mise-en-scène* is difficult to miss. *Rhythm Thief* won Harrison the Jury Prize for direction at the 1995 Sundance Film Festival.

Then came a $3 million budget, Hollywood action movie, *Code 99* (1996) which never found a British distributor, and the independent feature *Kicked in the Head* (1997). It revolves around a character – played by Kevin Corrigan, the lovesick nerd who obsessed over hard-nosed beauty Cyd in *Rhythm Thief* – who falls for an air hostess (Linda Fiorentino) whilst attempting to overcome his adolescence. The little guy chasing the big-time is symptomatic of Harrison's own trajectory as a resolutely independent director. However, whilst *Rhythm Thief* resounded at festivals from Montreal to Cambridge to Berlin, October Films didn't know whether to push *Kicked in the Head* as comedy or drama, and so it found few reviews and fewer screenings.

Aside from recent forays into mainstream television making, on programmes such as 'Sex and the City', Matthew Harrison remains a dark horse of the festival circuit, his career so far seeming to epitomise the tangled fortunes of the independent leftfield.                                                                  **RA**

# Mary HARRON

Canadian-born Mary Harron, a graduate of Oxford University, helped found 'Punk', the first punk magazine. Author of the first Sex Pistols interview to appear in an American publication, she has written music, theatre, and television criticism for the British broadsheet and music press. As a researcher on LWT's 'The South Bank Show' she contributed to programmes on The Velvet Underground, Warhol, Pollock, and Chandler. She has also directed segments of BBC's 'The Late Show', several short films and documentaries for Channel 4 and BBC/PBS, and episodes of 'Homicide: Life on the Street' and 'Oz'.

Her feature-film debut, which she also wrote, was *I Shot Andy Warhol* (1996), a biopic of Valerie Solanas, founder of the Society for Cutting Up Men (SCUM) and would-be killer of Warhol (in whose movie, *I, A Man* (1967), she appeared). Stylistically-varied and richly textured, especially in the opening stages, this biographical and intellectual collage, whose prismatic approach echoes that of co-producer Tom Kalin's *Swoon* (1992) is torn between presenting Solanas-as-text and producing conventional biopic dramatics. Its cool gaze remains external to the characters, offering a detached view of Solanas and her bemused isolation from the hollow men and women of Warhol's entourage. Initially the marginal framing and involvement shared by Solanas and Warhol suggests they are kindred spirits, but Warhol is soon shown to be cowardly and ineffectual. Despite hailing The SCUM Manifesto as a feminist classic, the decision to finally depict Solanas as a delusional psychotic undermines its importance.

For her next project, *American Psycho* (2000), from which she was briefly removed during pre-production, Harron and Guinevere Turner somehow produced a screenplay from Bret Easton Ellis' badly-structured novel about a yuppie serial killer. From the title sequence's witty use of nouvelle cuisine, it is clear that this is a work of distinction. Handsomely shot, with well-balanced compositions utilising the width of the frame, it is precise in its period detail, from the Robert Longo prints to its hilarious retro soundtrack. The conversion of the novel's interpolated dissections of such 1980s pop luminaries as Huey Lewis, Phil Collins, and Whitney Houston, into stone-faced monologues is inspired, illustrating how Harron's distance from her characters is here integrated into her investigation of surface and superfice. Unfortunately, the ambiguity about the reality of the depicted events seems to be resolved in the wrong direction: surely the movie's own ironies demand that they did, in all their hideous and incredible detail, happen. **MB**

# Hal HARTLEY

A distinctive voice in contemporary American cinema, Hal Hartley has garnered a reputation for off-beat drama that deals, primarily, with an assortment of bohemians – 'Young. White. Middle-class. College educated. Unskilled. Broke'. Educated at the State University of New York at Purchase, Hartley's films draw on a wide array of literary and filmic influences, achieving a predominantly cult following, and presenting, what critic John Fried has referred to as, 'a genre of comic cynicism in the relentless pursuit of youth'. Drawing on his background amidst the blue-collar suburbs of Long Island, where he was born in 1959, his debut feature, *The Unbelievable Truth* (1989), blossoming relationship between an angst-ridden teenager (Adrienne Shelly) and a mass-murdering car mechanic (Robert Burke). Hartley's painterly eye for composition, and, in particular, his unique direction of actors and their deadpan speech patterns (resulting in a bizarre kind of 'anti-performance'), has attracted comparisons with both David Mamet and Harold Pinter – drawing attention to the failure of language in communicating the irrationality of human emotions. Hartley, remaining within the limits and framework of his stylised naturalness, delights in the use of epigrammatic statements and precocious, bewildering aphorisms, offering an otherworldly examination of small-town life populated by weird and wonderful creatures.

*Trust* (1990) is a darker companion piece to Hartley's first feature. Once again featuring Shelly as the rebellious daughter, it introduces Hartley regular Martin Donovan as an apathetic but brilliant television engineer, who carries a grenade with him at all times, 'just in case'. Like its predecessor, characters talk across each other, displaying a preference for proclamations over conversation, and in a world of dreary, depressing colour, Hartley's film offers both pathos and humour. In his portrait of domestic life – people caught amidst the web of ambivalence and mistrust generated by the arrival of an enigmatic stranger – Hartley presents his emergent idiosyncratic view of small-town USA. Taking a brief hiatus from feature films, Hartley directed three short films for television. *Theory of Achievement* (1991) and *Ambition* (1991) are littered with allusions to the French New Wave, offering a wittier, more frivolous Hartley than is evident in his features. *Surviving Desire* (1991) also wears its *nouvelle vague* influences on its hip, one scene having Donovan's Dostoyevsky-obsessed lecturer breaking into a glorious impromptu dance sequence (a recurring motif that litters much of Hartley's later work) after the promise of romance from Mary Ward's thrill-starved student. A tragi-comedy of love and speech, trouble and desire, the film is one of Hartley's most impulsively resonant and fully realised works, offering a beautiful, tightly controlled study of deception and miscommunication.

A significant progression from *Trust*, Hartley's third feature, *Simple Men* (1992), further explores his fascination with the clashing of class and culture. It traces the journey of two brothers, one an overconfident bank robber, the other a shy philosophy student, as they search for their father, himself in hiding, caught in a transitional state between crime and the possibility of self-fulfilment. On the surface the film appears to critique male relationships, but it digs deeper to examine men's perception of women and how they define their existence in terms of their dependence on them. Shot in unspecified locations in Texas, with fractured dialogue and long silences, *Simple Men* shows clear signs of a transformation in Hartley's work, an increase in scope, character and narrative arcs, and ambition – a deliberate move away from his roots and his yearning for a more urban, cosmopolitan setting.

Before torturing his former colleague, a character in *Amateur* (1994) reflects 'I was younger then. I didn't know any better. I've moved up. I'm more realistic now'. Ironically, Hartley avoids realism at all costs, rarely allowing his actors to emote, even smile, and whilst this stylistic departure includes familiar ingredients of the archetypal thriller – chases, country hideaways, murderous hitmen – this is no conventional genre piece. Distinctly European in form (not least due to the presence of Isabelle Huppert), the café scenes, the bobbed hairstyles of the two female leads, and the prostitutional vocations of their characters, recall Anna Karina in *Vivre Sa Vie* (1962). Pitched somewhere between Godardian absurdism and Bressonian necessity, Hartley strips his trademark dialogue patter to the bare essential, discarding the bookish intellectuals and frustrated idealists of his native Long Island features. Wiping his canvas clear and shifting the action to New York, the film opens with an image that closed *Surviving Desire* – Martin Donovan waking up in the gutter – and discards any preconceptions, literally, by making him an amnesiac. As the title suggests, like Hartley, all the characters are exploring uncharted territories, and colliding in transition. Virginal Isabelle (Huppert) forsakes the church to write for dirty magazines, whilst porn star Sophia (Elina Löwensohn) quits X-rated videos to become 'a mover and a shaker' (though ends up in the convent). Donovan's Thomas, unable to remember his existence as a sadistic, exploitative pornographer, becomes more humane, whilst Edward's (Damian Young) initially sympathetic accountant ends up a brainwashed, gun-toting thug. Hartley is acutely aware of the direction he is heading, as Donovan wearily laments 'Whatever else I was, this is me now. What else can I do?'

The first segment of *Flirt* (1995) was shot several months before *Amateur*, using older screenplays, with dialogue so familiar it verges on the parodic. The same script was filmed again for a further two shorts, using different actors and slight text variations, in Berlin and Tokyo. Passers-by offer brief, pragmatic therapy to the perplexed trio of flirts. Hartley suggests progression through repetition and deviation, gradually paring down, once again, to the necessary, building meaning through action – the silent choreographed dance rehearsals of the Japanese section substituting the mannered speech patterns of the former New York milieu.

Following this, *Henry Fool* (1997) posits a self-reflective return to the suburbia of his early works. The mysterious ex-con stranger of *The Unbelievable Truth* re-emerges, this time as a would-be rapist, and as a newcomer to Hartley's repertory, *Thomas Jay Ryan* – bearing a floppy-haired resemblance to Donovan's angry and shambolic *Trust* character, some seven years on. Dysfunctional families, another *Trust* theme, is also emphasised, and Hartley enriches his palette by touching on new subjects such as creativity, child abuse, and the internet. Indeed, just as Ryan seems to be imitating a warped apparition of Donovan, James Urbaniak, as the mild-mannered Simon Grim, appears to be playing an early version of Hartley himself – the quiet, emerging artistic suburbanite. As with *Amateur*, the clashing and ultimate transference of personalities are manifested in Simon's intellectual awakening – guided, encouraged and liberated by Henry, whom he gradually begins to usurp.

*The Book of Life* (1998) expands Hartley's fascination with computers; one scene even fetishes the Apple Mac logo and its start-up icons. After a four-year absence Martin Donovan returns, in the befitting role of Jesus, sent down to New York City on the eve of the millennium with girlfriend Magdalena (PJ Harvey). Hartley portrays Christ as a confused wanderer in a sharp suit, troubled by the expectations of him from his demanding Father, and ambivalent about his role as administrator of the apocalypse. Ryan reprises his Henry Fool character, appropriately, as the Devil, given to hanging out in dimly-lit dive bars, quoting passages from the Book of Revelation and dealing trade-offs on people's souls. Shot on strobing DV as part of the '2000, Seen By' series for French television, consistently playful – the prophets are scheming lawyers, the Seven Seals are stored on a laptop, manufactured in Egypt 'and the warrantee has expired' – yet no less significant for it, the few, mostly festival, audiences, regard it as Hartley's finest hour, a precise compression the themes and concerns of one of the decades most important film-makers.

As with Godard and other 1960s European cineaste directors, Hartley views film as a continuous process, each successive work both an extension and a departure. Yet, like many of his early 1990s US indie contemporaries, Hartley seems to have fallen out of fashion of late. Following *Amateur*, his art-house talking point status was eclipsed by the emergence of Takeshi Kitano, Wong Kar-Wai, and a host of new Asian film-makers. Quirky New York coffee shop dialogue gave way to luscious romanticism and sombre, taciturn reflection from the Far East. The disappointing performances of both *Flirt* and *Henry Fool* meant that *The Book of Life* failed to secure UK distribution. This descent of his reputation as purveyor of all things hip may free him up to achieve his best work, and leave behind the burden of his early image as folk-hero to disenchanted students everywhere. His films offer the possibility of disaster and the possibility of perfection, his characters all equally helpless, all perfectly lost, yet all deserving of forgiveness.

All the more tragic then, that the much anticipated *No Such Thing* (aka *Monster*, 2001), failed to live up to these expectations. Ostensibly a reworking of 'Beauty and the Beast', it tells the tale of a murderous, foul-mouthed monster disgusted with society and evolution, who massacres a television crew, but is eventually befriended by a pretty and wide-eyed young journalist (Sarah Polley). Hartley, under Francis Ford Coppola's Zoetrope production company and working with his largest budget to date, seems ill at ease with CGI special effects, prosthetic creature make-up and starry supporting players. Helen Mirren is embarrassingly miscast as the office bitch in lame scenes of media satire, while Julie Christie is underused as a foreign doctor. The film opens well with a typically Hartley-esque monologue from its disaffected, misanthropic anti-hero (played by Robert Burke) – 'I've changed. I'm not the monster I used to be.' – and Polley's plucky ingenue recalls Adrienne Shelly from *The Unbelievable Truth* and *Trust*. Though the two leads are on familiar Hartley territory – the tale of the girl-next-door seduced by the mysterious stranger – here it is taken to its logical extreme, and in doing so, fails to progress its themes or satisfy its set-up. The narrative takes several clumsy turns: Polley is involved in a plane crash en route, then patched up in an Icelandic hospital, which pointlessly delays her inevitable and all-too-brief meeting with Burke; the action then returns to New York, where the monster becomes lionised by the press. With scenes so dull, one cares little for the film's feeble dénouement.                                    **RCh & IHS**

# Todd HAYNES

*Poison* (1991)
*Safe* (1995)
*Velvet Goldmine* (1998)
*Far From Heaven* (2002)

Todd Haynes makes provocative, complex and experimental films; he is a rarity in that sense alone. Perhaps unsurprisingly, these historically acute, formally daring, cinematic excavations of popular culture forms and genres engender strong responses for the models of identity they imply. The religious right have balked and he remains one of few American directors to have a film banned. On the other hand, he has moved from being an avatar of what was called New Queer Cinema – though he makes more emotionally resonant films than such New Queer contemporaries as Tom Kalin and Gregg Araki – to being one of the most critically respected directors working in any genre today.

Born in 1961 in Los Angeles, Haynes rejected mainstream approaches early on. He wrote and co-produced a film in high school called *The Suicide*, later commenting that disgust at its Hollywood-style trimmings – limousines, hierarchies, script girls – prompted him to pursue an experimental route. As a student of Art and Semiotics at Brown University, he made a quasi-punk Super 8 film called *Assassins: A Film Concerning Rimbaud* (1985). After graduating in 1985, he moved to New York and formed an independent production company with Barry Ellsworth and producer Christine Vachon called Apparatus.

Haynes' next film established him as a keen commentator on body politics and identification in popular culture with a knack for encoding theme in form. *Superstar: The Karen Carpenter Story* (1987) pinpoints a period in the early 1970s – post-Vietnam, pre-Watergate – when US popular culture seemed to be glossing over its country's ailments. Haynes' masterstroke was to use Barbie and Ken dolls to play Richard and Karen Carpenter as semi-Stepford types without ignoring Karen's suffering from anorexia. It takes real empathy to get an audience to feel for a Barbie doll and Haynes did it. Not that this affected Richard Carpenter and A&M Records, who promptly had the film banned.

Haynes turned down subsequent offers from the likes of Disney and United Artists to make his first feature for £200,000. An opaque triptych inspired by Jean Genet, *Poison* (1991) established him as New Queer Cinema's brightest hope. Its implicit, bracing rejection of 'positive image'-oriented gay cinema for a formally deviant take on the societal construction of deviancy prompted, in part, by the American right's dismissal of the AIDS crisis, still looks radical. This is largely because Haynes doesn't tell us why three stories – 'Hero', a suburban mockumentary; 'Homo', a prison drama; 'Horror', a pustulating B-movie pastiche – and several styles occupy one film. Instead, he invites us to trace the connections through the trail of spit and spunk that links each story. Eschewing the close reading this demands, Reverend Donald Wildmon and his American Family Association condemned *Poison* as porn in a campaign against the National Endowment for the Arts, from whom Haynes received a minor completion grant. Fittingly, for a film partly concerned with accepting the terms by which minority groups are oppressed only so as to turn them against the oppressor, Wildmon effectively boosted *Poison*'s box office.

Haynes' next film, a short made for PBS Television called *Dottie Gets Spanked* (1993), was another daring exploration of identification in popular culture, this time centred on the tension between a seven-year-old boy's fixation on a 1960s 'I Love Lucy'-style sitcom and his own sexual development. *Safe* (1995) followed. If we lived in the America Wildmon would like to see, it might look like the bleached-out San Fernando Valley home of *Safe*'s Carol White (Julianne Moore as a dead ringer for Superstar's Barbie doll). Something like *The Boy in the Plastic Bubble* (1976) via the stylistic sensibilities of Stanley Kubrick's *2001: A Space Odyssey* (1968) and Chantal Akerman, *Safe* is extraordinarily moving despite its apparently icy detachment. Alex Nepomniaschy's wide-angle shots and Moore's selfless performance create an atmosphere as 'hyper-sensitive' as Carol; the film's very form mirrors her pain and uncertainty as she develops allergies to her environment and turns to the 'new age' Wrenwood Centre for help. The Wrenwood section of *Safe* slyly critiques the 'self-love' philosophies – philosophies based on myths of centred selfhood – sold to gay men with AIDS by writers such as Louise L. Hay. Slyly, because Haynes doesn't state this directly; he implies, but with great acuity, again demanding that we read closely.

After Carol's whisper and Wrenwood's philosophy of 'moderation in dress' and silent mealtimes, the 'maximum volume' and exquisitely immoderate dress of *Velvet Goldmine* (1998) comes as a blast. If *Superstar* and *Safe* represented early 1970s and late 1980s America respectively as noxious and suffocating, *Velvet Goldmine* looks to the other side of the Atlantic, finding in early 1970s British glam rock a stack-heeled riposte to myths of unified selfhood. Not that Haynes sees glam through rose-tinted glasses. The film achieves a bittersweet tang from its retrospective, *Citizen Kane*-style narrative and the operatic melancholy of the soundtrack's early Roxy Music songs, charting a rock star's rise and fall as a parable for a generation's lost idealism.

Haynes managed a skin-tight grip on the tensions between history, popular culture and identity, and knew exactly how to convey them cinematically. Matching glam's gloriously Wildean vision of decentred identities and sexuality as performance, he mixed styles, eras, genres, real individuals and fictional characters into a kaleidoscopic fantasy that – despite a dizzying plot – coheres by sheer force of concept and directorial will. No wonder he took a breather after what looks like a majestic summation of his career to date. Like the rest of his work, it is quite an act to follow.

Haynes has recently completed shooting on his fourth feature which is due for release at the end of 2002. *Far from Heaven* (2002) reunites the director with Julianne Moore and producer Christine Vachon for a Douglas Sirk-styled, 1950s suburbia-set melodrama – the title recalls Sirk's *All that Heaven Allows* (1955) – made with Haynes' biggest budget to date, $14 million. When Moore's character catches her husband (Dennis Quaid) having sex with a man, she turns to their African-American gardener (Dennis Haysbert) for solace. Clearly, all kinds of complications follow in a drama that Haynes describes as hinging on 'the claustrophobia of domestic life and social systems'. **KH**

# Amy HECKERLING

Declaring Amy Heckerling the 'female John Hughes' makes for a good soundbite, but there is really no need to equate her with anyone else; she stands on her own as having a unique read on the culture of the American teenager and, to a greater degree, the dysfunctional families from which they spring.

Born in the Bronx in 1954, Heckerling studied Film and Television at New York University and received a Master's Degree in Film from the American Film Institute. Her first film, *Fast Times at Ridgemont High* (1982), chronicled the adventures of a group of high-schoolers in Southern California, and was based on the real-life escapades of a group of teenagers, as chronicled by the film's writer, Cameron Crowe.

*Fast Times* is filled with the usual teen angst over love, relationships, and just how stoned is too stoned to go to class, but it is a darker and more realistic look than most films in the teen genre. Parents are virtually non-existent in this film, and the kids are growing up fast. All of them hold thankless jobs in the hub of teen life, the mall. Whereas many teen films, like *Porky's* (1981) and *American Pie* (1999), focus on the sexual escapades of boys, Heckerling creates some strong female characters that explore their sexuality. Linda, played by Phoebe Cates, is already jaded and cynical about men and relationships. Stacy, played by Jennifer Jason Leigh, loses her virginity to an older man in the bleachers at a stadium, to just 'get it over with', and the look of boredom and pain on her face is almost too difficult to watch. She then has to face an unwanted pregnancy and an abortion, a subject that nearly twenty years later is still considered taboo in both film and teen television dramas. *Fast Times* was a springboard for many actors, including Sean Penn and Judge Reinhold.

*Johnny Dangerously* (1984), a comedy starring Michael Keaton, Marilu Henner and Joe Piscopo, and set in the 1930s, is a parody of old-school gangster movies. The film showcases Heckerling's humour, which is often steeped in her awareness of the conventions and stereotypes of the genre. *European Vacation* (1985), the follow up to National Lampoon's successful *Vacation*, brings back the Griswold family in all of its glorious dysfunction and follows their wacky antics across Europe. It is interesting to note that John Hughes co-wrote *European Vacation*, as the humour in the film, aside from Chevy Chase's usual brand of mugging and slapstick, is grounded in the film's point of view, which is sympathetic towards the kids, Audrey and Rusty, who are at that awkward adolescent stage where every moment with their parents (played by Chase and Beverly D'Angelo) brings sheer horror and embarrassment. Despite, and perhaps in Heckerling's view because of, their youth, they seem to have more common sense and worldliness than their parents.

Heckerling's adult female protagonists are still struggling with the burdens of men and relationships, as seen in *Look Who's Talking* (1989) and *Look Who's Talking Too* (1990), both light-hearted romantic-family comedies. In the first film, Mollie (Kirstie Ally) becomes pregnant while having an affair with a married man. He dupes her into believing that he will leave his wife and help her raise the baby together, but abandons her after the baby is born. Mollie spends the rest of the film searching for a father for Mikey (Bruce Willis narrates Mikey's inner monologue), who turns out to be right under her nose (James, played by John Travolta). The film is very much a product of the 1980s in its depiction of a 'superwoman' trying to have it all, balancing a career and single motherhood, as well as its concern with class issues. In one scene, Molly tries to picture herself married to James, a cab driver, and sees them living with ten kids in complete squalor, her barefoot and pregnant and him with an enormous beer gut, teaching the kids to belch. *Look Who's Talking Too* is essentially *Look Who's Talking* after the charm of a talking baby has outworn its welcome. Mollie's family expands with the addition of a new baby girl (as voiced by the nails on a chalk-board stylings of Roseanne Barr), but once again love and family triumph over chaos.

*Clueless* (1995) marked the triumphant return of Heckerling to the teen movie genre, and arguably the rebirth of the genre itself. A modern version of Jane Austen's novel 'Emma', *Clueless*, written and directed by Heckerling, is the story of Cher (named after the singer and played by Alicia Silverstone), her best friend Dionne, and the burden of being rich, beautiful, popular teenagers in Beverly Hills. As with *Fast Times*, *Clueless* is immersed in the music, clothing, language and icons of teenhood. Like teens themselves, *Clueless* is anything but when it comes to having its finger on the pulse of pop culture, with an endless stream of references to television, film, books and trends. On the surface, Heckerling's teens appear to be one-dimensional, blatant stereotypes in terms of class and gender (asked by her hypertensive lawyer father what she did in school, Cher replies 'I broke in my new purple clogs'), but usually this is a function of the film's awareness of the stereotypes. When compared to the all-white teen films that came before it, Heckerling's depiction of a group of white, black, and gay friends adds much needed depth and diversity to the genre. Sure, they fight, drink, have sex, smoke pot, and engage in stereotypical rites-of-passage that are depicted in countless teen movies, but Heckerling's teens are smart, strong, self-reliant, sympathetic and kind.

Since the success of *Clueless*, there has been a virtual 1980s renaissance with a slew of teen movies (*10 Things I Hate About You* (1999), *Cruel Intentions* (1999), *She's All That* (1999), *Idle Hands* (1999) – to name but a few) as well as television shows ('Dawson's Creek', 'Buffy the Vampire Slayer', 'Roswell High', 'Popular' and so on). Heckerling's latest instalment in her teen oeuvre, *Loser* (2000), received a lukewarm reception from critics and at the box office. The film is a fish-out-of water story starring Jason Biggs as Paul, an earflap-adorned kid from the sticks that goes to college on a scholarship in New York and gets a crash course in city living and the depths of human nastiness from his rich, party-boy roommates. His roommates scheme to get him kicked out of the suite because his studious ways are cramping their style, and Paul is assigned a room in an animal hospital. Ultimately, the message of the film is that nice guys do finish first, for in the end Paul does get Dora, the girl of his dreams (played by *American Beauty*'s Mena Suvari), and in a refreshing approach to the teen genre, doesn't have to change the quirky person he is to do so.

It is easy to see how *Loser* could get lost in the recent groundswell of gross-out teen comedies like *American Pie* (1999) (also starring Biggs), perhaps because its humorous, yet often painful portrayal of youthful awkwardness hits a bit too close to home for an audience who would rather lose itself in pie-fornicating fantasies. **LH**

# Brian HELGELAND

A graduate of Loyola Marymount University in Los Angeles, born in Providence, Rhode Island in 1961, Brian Helgeland at first seemed set to follow in the footsteps of H. P. Lovecraft, one of his hometown's most famous former residents, providing the story and screenplay for *Nightmare on Elm Street 4: The Dream Master* (1988), writing the screenplays for *976-EVIL* (1988) and *Highway to Hell* (1992), and making his television directorial debut in 1989 with HBO's 'Tales from the Crypt'. However, he abandoned the genre to write the screenplay for *Assassins* (1995), an everyday tale of rival hitmen; its Peckinpah-ian aspirations are merely ponderous. Helgeland's next effort, *L.A. Confidential* (1997), based on James Ellroy's book, and co-written with director Curtis Hanson, won the Academy Award for Best Adapted Screenplay, and was a critical and commercial success. His screenplay for *Conspiracy Theory* (1997) reunited him with Richard Donner, and was rather more successful than their previous collaboration, but his adaptation of David Brin's post-apocalyptic novel resulted in the long and boring box-office disaster *The Postman* (1997).

Helgeland made his feature film debut directing *Payback* (1999), an adaptation of 'The Hunter', the first of Donald Westlake's Parker thrillers (written under the pseudonym

*Payback* (1999)

*A Knight's Tale* (2001)

Richard Stark). As with John Flynn's *The Outfit* (1974), the movie suffered from the lazy comparisons made by reviewers and critics to John Boorman's *Point Blank* (1967), many of whom considered *Payback* to be an impertinent remake of an unapproachable classic. Helgeland, however, very clearly returned to the source novel for his screenplay, to which it remains quite faithful, even utilising some of its dialogue. And if Mel Gibson's gruff bear persona, further moderated by an intrusive voice over, is just not unpleasant enough to do justice to Westlake's existentialist protagonist, neither was Lee Marvin's performance. Unjustly maligned, Helgeland's blackly and brutally humorous romp is an efficient genre picture bloated by the presence of its star but, unlike *Point Blank*, lacking in portentousness. The movie offers good minor roles for William Devane, James Coburn and Kris Kristofferson, and its washed out cinematography is never unattractive.

*A Knight's Tale* (2001) is basically a one-joke movie. The story of a common-born man, William Thatcher (Heath Ledger) who pretends to be a knight so that he can compete in jousting tournaments, it derives considerable light humour from its self-conscious anachronisms, such as having the crowd sing along to Queen's 'We Will Rock You'. Written, produced and directed by Helgeland, it is handsomely shot, with well-staged action sequence, but it is too long for such slight material, and lacks sufficient conflict (depending on the contradictory and idiotic characterisation of Lady Jocelyn (Shannyn Sossamon) to provide complication). The likeable cast includes Paul Bettany as Geoffrey Chaucer, Rufus Sewell as an admirably villainous Count Adhemar, James Purefoy as the Black Prince and the woefully underused Laura Fraser as William's blacksmith, Kate. The sum is considerably less than the parts.

Helgeland has since co-written the script for *Daredevil* (2003) and is currently working on *The Sin Eater*, due for release in 2003 and again starring Ledger.     **MB**

# Monte HELLMAN

Monte Hellman, born in 1932, stands out as something of an anomaly in the Roger Corman stable of film-makers. Corman's success and longevity in the exploitation field was largely a result of his shrewd commercial sense: keeping his budgets low and peppering the films with liberal sprinklings of sex, violence and teen appeal. The early work of such Cormanites as Jonathan Demme, Martin Scorsese and Francis Ford Coppola are testaments to such a philosophy. Hellman's work, however, steadfastly ignores these commercial instincts. His budgets were equally low, but his are perhaps the most cryptic and esoteric films to have been produced by Corman, sitting more comfortably with the European art cinema tradition.

Many of Hellman's films have tended towards terminal self-destruction. His career has been no different. Over the last twenty years, his output has been sporadic and rarely seen. However, at the beginning of his career, Hellman's first few films were of the more traditional Corman ilk. His debut feature, *The Beast From Haunted Cave* (1959), boasted the tag-line: 'Screaming young girls sucked into a labyrinth of horror by a blood-starved ghoul from Hell'. With a zippy script by Charles B. Griffith, the film fused the heist film with the creature-feature, as a group of gold thieves who have fled to the wintry wildernesses of South Dakota find themselves up against a mysterious, spider-like monster.

Following uncredited work on *Ski Troop Attack* (1960) and *The Terror* (1963), the latter alongside fellow newcomer Francis Ford Coppola, Hellman went to the Philippines for the back-to-back shooting of two low-budget action films: *Back Door to Hell* (1964) and *Flight to Fury* (1966). For many people, they remain mostly of interest because of Hellman's collaborator, a young, little known actor and screenwriter called Jack Nicholson. *Back Door to Hell* is a World War Two thriller about a group of Americans (including Nicholson) who team up with Filipino freedom-fighters to win back a town from the Japanese. It was picked up for distribution by Twentieth Century Fox. *Flight to Fury* follows a group of adventurers whose plane crash lands in the jungle, resulting in them fighting against one another (and bandits) over a stash of stolen diamonds. The incident-packed script was written by Nicholson, who gave himself a peach of a role as a psychotic smuggler.

Following Corman's reasoning that if you are going out on location to shoot one movie you might as well shoot two, Hellman subsequently made another set of back-to-back movies with Nicholson. The results were two of the most extraordinary westerns of the decade: *Ride in the Whirlwind* (1965) and *The Shooting* (1967). In the former, Nicholson and Cameron Mitchell star as cowboys who are mistaken for outlaws and hunted down by a vigilante posse. Written by Nicholson, using dialogue adapted from diaries of the period for authenticity, the film is a poignant and melancholic rumination on violent fate and helplessness. A tangible sense of futility hangs over the picture, most eloquently conveyed in a sequence in which the protagonists hide out at a family's ranch: self-consciously reversing *Shane* (1953), in which the gunfighter hero helps to unearth a stubborn tree trunk, *Ride in the Whirlwind* depicts the farmer slugging away endlessly at the stump with no hope of ever defeating it.

The existential tone of *Ride in the Whirlwind* is even more pronounced in *The Shooting*. Warren Oates (in the first of several Hellman films) plays an ex-bounty hunter who is hired by a mysterious woman to lead her through the barren and lifeless Utah desert. Before long, as the sun beats down on the cast, which also includes Nicholson as a psychotic, phantasmic hired gun, Oates begins to realise he has been enlisted in a deadly manhunt, the motives for which remain oblique and unresolved. It should come as no surprise to anyone who has seen the film that when Hellman first arrived in Hollywood he staged a version of 'Waiting for Godot' as a western: based on a script by Adrien Joyce/Carole Eastman (*Five Easy Pieces* (1970)), *The Shooting* is equal parts Anthony Mann, Franz Kafka and Jean-Paul Sartre (especially 'No Exit''s vision of a group of characters trapped in their own hell).

Although successful in Europe on the festival circuit, both westerns had difficulty securing distribution and were not released until several years after their completion. Hellman served as editor on Corman's extremely successful *The Wild Angels* (1966), which initiated a swarm of biker films, but he did not direct again until *Two-Lane Blacktop* (1971), for Universal. Centred around a cross-country road race between a middle-aged driver named GTO (Warren Oates) and two young drag car racers, known only as The Driver (James Taylor) and The Mechanic (Dennis Wilson), *The Cannonball Run* (1980) it is not. As the film progresses, the race assumes less and less importance and is eventually all but forgotten, as though Hellman has sought deliberately to excise all the potential for narrative tension suggested by the premise. The dialogue is sparse, the road is long and desolate, and the final shot says it all: as The Driver returns to the racing circuit, the film begins to 'jam' in the projector, before burning away to nothingness.

However, *Cockfighter* (1974) is perhaps even more bleak and extreme. Oates again stars, playing a man who has taken a vow of silence after losing a cockfight. Like Sam Peckinpah's *Bring Me the Head of Alfredo Garcia*, which was made the same year and also stars Oates, it is a film that explores the connections between male violence and sexual impotence. Complex and uncompromising, it is a true American art film which has unfortunately become very difficult to locate – no doubt due in large part to the nature of its subject matter. It was based on a novel by Charles Willeford, produced by Corman and exquisitely shot by Nestor Almendros.

Hellman went on to edit Peckinpah's *The Killer Elite* (1975) and worked on the cult television show 'Baretta' the same year, before directing the spaghetti western *China 9, Liberty 37* (1978). Less successful than his earlier westerns and showing signs of production difficulties, it once again features Oates, playing a landowner whose young wife (Jenny Agutter) takes off with a hired gunman (Fabio Testi). It also introduces Peckinpah as an actor, in a small (but telling) role as a journalist looking to turn the protagonists' story into a piece of Old West mythology: 'I just want to buy a little legend, the lies we all need.'

Hellman finished *Avalanche Express* (1979) after the death of its credited director, Mark Robson, but he has barely been heard from since. *Iguana* (1988) was the violent tale of a nineteenth-century sailor who declares war on mankind. It was shot in the Canary Islands with Swiss money, but received little or no distribution. *Silent Night, Deadly Night III: Better Watch Out!* (1989) is, ironically, one of his most readily available yet least interesting films. Although an improvement on most slasher films, one can only assume that Hellman churned it out to pay some bills.

His career looked like it might be revived in the early 1990s, following a fortuitous relationship with Quentin Tarantino: Hellman executive-produced *Reservoir Dogs* (1992), having had an eye to directing it himself at one point. Further projects, including an adaptation of Elmore Leonard's 'Freaky Deaky', have been rumoured, but nothing has come to fruition. If only Tarantino and Nicholson could throw together a few dollars for a new Hellman film, contemporary cinema might be a happier (though existentially tormented) place. **AS**

# Stephen HEREK

Born in San Antonio in 1958, in the early 1980s Stephen Herek graduated from The University of Texas in Austin, where he studied under the legendary director Edward Dmytryk, then moved to Los Angeles to work for Roger Corman. He subsequently wrote and directed the low-budget genre movie *Critters* (1986), which was successful enough to generate two sequels. Amusing and well-made, featuring dazzling effects and some anarchic humour, it is often seen as a mere *Gremlins* (1984) rip-off but is actually more inventive; Herek maintains that *Critters* was conceived before Joe Dante's better-known film.

He captured the zeitgeist with his next feature, *Bill & Ted's Excellent Adventure* (1989), a film that had failed to flourish in either Frank Oz's or Rick Rosenthal's hands. Largely due to word of mouth from initial screenings, it was a massive hit. Keanu Reeves and Alex Winter play two engaging but lame-brained boys who brush up their history knowledge by time travelling, collecting famous people from history who must then negotiate the shopping malls of modern America. For many audiences, it has become Reeves' defining role, despite his attempts to achieve a more serious status within cinema. The film's self-aware imbecility, amusing dude-speak and exhilarating energy and originality make it the best of a series of films including *Wayne's World* (1992) and *Dude, Where's My Car?* (2000), which feature apathetic duos.

More hits followed, first the parody *Don't Tell Mom the Babysitter's Dead* (1991), which uses the 'Home Alone' premise to entertaining effect, and then *The Mighty Ducks* for Disney in 1992, a low-budget film that lacked the inventiveness of his past movies and surprised everyone by becoming a hit and sparking a professional hockey team. Creatively, however, the move to Disney seems to have limited Herek. *The Three Musketeers* (1993) was successful, a lavish swashbuckler with Charlie Sheen, Chris O'Donnell and Kiefer Sutherland, but then the classic adventure story rarely fails. Next Herek bewilderingly attempted a dramatic change and tackled the story of a dissatisfied music teacher (Richard Dreyfuss) who comes to learn the joy of mediocre success within his family and community. This quiet, sentimental movie appealed to older audiences and received some critical success, although many argue that it was vastly overrated, particularly by undermining its own message with an over-the-top feelgood ending. In 1996 Herek returned to his younger audience, with a live-action remake of the Disney animated classic, *101 Dalmatians* (1961), starring Glenn Close as Cruella De Vil. A box office success with excellent set and costume design, the characterisation is poor.

Having had such commercial successes, Herek directed and produced *Holy Man* (1998), starring Eddie Murphy as a home-shopping channel new-age guru who captures a vast audience by dispensing advice alongside consumer goods. Despite its vast potential for satire, the film was a commercial disaster. Using flashy camera work, Herek failed to take advantage of Murphy's talent for improvisation.

*Rock Star* (2001) is loosely based on the story of Judas Priest, a band who replaced their lead singer with a fan, here played by Mark Wahlberg. Once again, Herek fails to utilise his star's best qualities – in Wahlberg's case, that of wide-eyed naiveté in the milieu of sex, drugs and rock 'n' roll. The character development is negligible after the initial set-up and the pay-off kicks in too soon. It compares unfavourably with the similar *Almost Famous* (2000). Timothy Spall, always worth watching, tends to patronise the audience, underlining points they may have missed; at one point he tells the ingenue, 'Your job is to live the fantasy other people only dream of'. Too feelgood, one reviewer called it 'the Muzak version of a Def Leppard hit'.

In *Life or Something Like It* (2002) a rising reporter (a blonde Angelina Jolie) dreams of becoming a household name just as a clairvoyant tells her she has a week to live. Herek again takes a potentially interesting premise and fails to do it justice. Wholeheartedly embracing product placement, the film suggests that a woman's choice of career over romance may be punishable by death; on its release a critic opined, 'When it comes to life or something like it, this film chooses the latter'. Although Herek may not use actors to their full capacity, he has a gift for casting; Jolie is great, as is the woefully underused Stockard Channing, but this is still a movie for multiplex audiences.

Stephen Herek undoubtedly has an ability to make inventive, undemanding and funny movies, which rely heavily on genre conventions but have, on occasion, been reworked to interesting effect. However, the energy and originality of his earlier work seems to have faded and his films have become more conservative, dependent on clichés and crowd-pleasing endings.                                              **FG**

# Marshall HERSKOVITZ

Born in Philadelphia in 1952, Marshall Herskovitz is best known as co-creator of the *Jack the Bear* (1992) television show 'thirtysomething' with Ed Zwick. This was an innovative and influential *Dangerous Beauty* (1998) comedy drama about the compromised ideals of a group of friends in their thirties, which saw cinematic standards of acting, writing and cinematography brought to the small screen.

Herskovitz was a director on a number of episodes of the show. Unlike Zwick, whose features have been epic productions like the Civil War drama *Glory* (1989) and the starry romance *Legends of the Fall* (1994), Herskovitz kept to the intimate family world of his television work with his feature debut, *Jack the Bear* (1992). Written by the talented Steven Zaillian, screenwriter of *Schindler's List* (1995) and writer/director of the superior legal thriller, *A Civil Action* (1999), the story is seen through the eyes of Jack, a twelve-year-old growing up in the early 1970s. His father (Danny DeVito) is a horror movie host on television who has a drink problem and is struggling to bring up Jack and his young brother since their mother died. This fairly traditional rites-of-passage material is mixed in with some darker elements – the schlock monsters of television horror movies are contrasted with the real evil of Jack's sinister neighbour, a sullen Nazi (Gary Sinise). *Jack the Bear* is intriguing but never really comes off. Unlike other films seen through a child's eyes such as *Parents* (1989) and Lynne Ramsay's *Ratcatcher* (1999), there is no discrepancy between Jack's point of view and the objective truth. The creepy Sinise really is a monstrous figure. There is also a sickly tinge to much of the action, although the garish home-movie clips used to evoke the past are well used. Herskovitz and Zaillian do deserve credit, however, for attempting to inject some grimness into the anodyne world of Hollywood children's films.

*Dangerous Beauty* (1998) was released in America as *The Honest Courtesan* and this attempt at a lush period romance is far from the family scenarios of Herskovitz's previous work. Catherine McCormack is Veronica, trained by her mother to be a courtesan in the Venice of the sixteenth century. Despite a vivid evocation of the period, the film resembles a mini-series with hammy performances – from Rufus Sewell and the usually reliable Oliver Platt – and a multitude of anachronisms. Veronica is presented as a kind of proto-feminist and as a result a gloss is put on the ugly reality of female repression during this period. As with the far superior *The English Patient* (1996) and *Gladiator* (2000), it is pleasing to think such seemingly unfashionable, lush period pieces can still be made. But *Dangerous Beauty* is little else.

Despite some interesting touches in both of his films, Marshall Herskovitz has some way to go before his cinematic output can equal his television achievements.        **IC**

# John HERZFELD

Raised in New Jersey, John Herzfeld studied at Memphis State University and the *Two of a Kind* (1983) University of Miami. He made his directorial debut with *Two of a Kind* (1983), from *2 Days in the Valley* (1996) his own script. Zack Melon (John Travolta), in debt to loan sharks, tries to rob a *15 Minutes* (2000) bank, only to have the Australian teller, Debbie Wylder (Olivia Newton-John), take the money herself. Meanwhile, in Heaven, God has once more decided to destroy corrupt humankind, but angels persuade him to relent if two humans, randomly selected, perform a great sacrifice for each other. The rest is obvious. The movie features forgettable songs (including one from Oliver Reed), and unappealing leads reunited for no obvious reason other than their success in *Grease* (1978) – and, presumably, the small fees they could command. Charles Durning, Scatman Crothers and Ernie Hudson are as endearing as ever, and the movie's occasional echoes of such supernatural fantasies as *Here Comes Mr. Jordan* (1941), *A Matter of Life and*

*Death* (1946), *Angel on My Shoulder* (1946), and *The Bishop's Wife* (1947) hint at a genuine affection for a kind of film no longer made. However, the end product was rather unpromising.

Subsequently, Herzfeld worked as an increasingly adept television director, beginning with *Daddy* (1987), from his own script. Starring Dermot Mulroney and Patricia Arquette as high-schoolers ill-prepared for impending parenthood, it is a model of its kind. Of his other television work, Herzfeld has writer or co-writer credit on *The Ryan White Story* (1989), *The Preppie Murder* (1989), *Casualties of Love: The Long Island Lolita Story* (1993), and *Remember* (1993).

He returned to cinematic features with *2 Days in the Valley* (1996), from his own script. It is an entertaining ensemble piece in which a dozen characters are drawn together through chance encounters into a story of murder and redemption. Well-lit and handsomely shot by Oliver Wood, with many stylish compositions, this gentle and unhurried comedy-drama features witty and proleptic associational editing, nicely-judged moments of slapstick, immaculate production design from Catherine Hardwicke (particularly the yuppie art collection), numerous well-staged ironies (such as the near-encounter between cop and killer) and an ambiguous moral. Jeff Daniels wrings considerable pathos from his role as a reactionary cop, and the rest of the cast, especially Danny Aiello, Glenne Headly, Marsha Mason and Paul Mazursky, is very strong. Keith Carradine, Louise Fletcher and, all too briefly, Lawrence Tierney have welcome cameos.

Herzfeld returned to television work with the excellent biopic *Don King: Only in America* (1997), adapted by Kario Salem from Jack Newfield's biography. Ving Rhames is given full reign, and turns in a magnificent performance as the street-criminal-turned-boxing-promoter. Herzfeld's third feature film, *15 Minutes* (2000), is also from his own script. It is that rarity in contemporary cinema, a buddy action movie with a sense of humour *and* at least half a brain. A celebrity homicide detective (Robert De Niro) and a fire marshall (Edward Burns) are thrown together when it becomes clear that the crimes they are investigating are related. Their antagonism is a little too quickly resolved, but this is essential to Herzfeld's reworking of such conventional material into a pointed commentary on a culture obsessed with violence, fame (however fleeting) and the abdication of responsibility. Herzfeld utilises a simple technique to deny his audience sight of the murders, and then makes our complicity apparent by positioning us so that we want to see the heroes behave violently. If *15 Minutes* fails to achieve the satirical savagery of, say, *Network* (1976), it is nonetheless a rewarding exercise in self-reflexive cultural critique, made all the more compelling by the gorgeous, luminous visuals of cinematographer Jean Yves Escoffier.  **MB**

# Peter HEWITT

Born in England in 1965, Peter Hewitt was trained at the London College of Printing and the National Film and Television School. There he made the BAFTA-winning graduation short called *The Candy Show* (1989), about an undertaker's fantasies. Interestingly, the film was partly financed by Harrison Ford, Roman Polanski and producer Tim Bevan, later of Working Title, the company who financed *The Borrowers* for Hewitt in 1997. *The Candy Show* provided a calling card to Hollywood.

As a result he began his professional career directing the sequel to the successful slacker film *Bill & Ted's Excellent Adventure* (1989), *Bill & Ted's Bogus Journey* (1991) – another film in which Death makes an appearance. Well-received for its production design, visual invention and comic detail, all of which were seen as superior to the original, the film was praised for its visual imagination and drew Hewitt even further to Hollywood's attention.

Typically of mainstream Hollywood, Hewitt found himself typecast as a director, being offered *Bill & Ted*-style zany humour and style. For this reason he accepted an offer to direct the first of a six-hour series for American television, about a television executive fascinated with the new technology of virtual reality. *Wild Palms* (1993), which also had episodes directed by Kathryn Bigelow, Keith Gordon and Phil Joanou, allowed Hewitt to initiate a visual style for the show, described as a surreal soap, part science fiction, part noir, and part 'Dynasty'. Using wide lenses and plenty of moving shots Hewitt was able to set a visual tone for the series.

A desire to shift focus towards more family drama led him to Disney and *Tom and Huck* (1995). This darkly heart-warming adventure, set in Alabama in 1845, allowed Hewitt to explore one of his interests – looking at worlds removed from the one in which we live now.

*The Borrowers* would seem a logical move here. Based on Mary Norton's popular books about the tiny Clock family, who live under the floorboards and 'borrow' from the humans who live there, the story requires a keen visual inventiveness. Hewitt's technically sophisticated vision, using enlarged sets, digital mattes, computer generated imagery and stop motion helped create one of the 'other worlds' he is so interested in – resulting in a fantasy/reality hybrid, modern America fused with 1950s Britain. Some bold set-pieces and cartoonish violence (the film's evil lawyer is electrocuted, bug bombed, impaled and scalded) are reminiscent of his previous work.

Hewitt's subsequent film, *Whatever Happened to Harold Smith?* (1999), is another work demanding care with the details of setting up and delivering visual jokes and creating the right pop culture look sometimes at the expense of character and story. It has been reviewed as a quirky and original love story, utilising Hewitt's love of colour in its dream territory production design. It includes his customary mix of romance, eccentricity and nostalgia.

*Thunderpants* (2002), Hewitt's most recent release, is a children's fantasy about a young boy whose farting prowess is utilised in all sorts of technological innovations, finally culminating in space travel.                                    **JD**

# George HICKENLOOPER

Born in 1965 in St. Louis, a graduate of Yale University's BA in Film and History, George Hickenlooper is a true cinephile, as evidenced by his documentaries about film-making such as *Art, Acting, and the Suicide Chair: Dennis Hopper* (1988) and *Monte Hellman: An American Auteur* (1997), and 'Reel Conversations', his collection of interviews with notable critics and directors. It is clearly Hickenlooper's appreciation of cinema that makes his documentaries work so well; not only is he genuinely enthusiastic and knowledgeable, but he makes the actors and directors he interviews appear natural and at ease.

His most well-known and enduring piece of non-fiction work is undoubtedly *Hearts of Darkness: A Filmmakers Apocalypse*, a mesmeric piece of movie lore about the long and troubled filming of *Apocalypse Now* (1979), for which he won an Emmy. Interviews that took place after the release of Coppola's film are inter-cut with Eleanor Coppola's footage of the shoot; full of incident, helicopters are called away into battle at a crucial moment of filming, Martin Sheen has a heart attack, the cast are high on drugs, and Marlon Brando fixates on his weight, further exacerbating an already tense atmosphere. *Picture This: The Times of Peter Bogdanovich in Archer City, Texas* (1991) is also well worth a look. Made during the filming of *Texasville* (1990), the sequel to *The Last Picture Show* (1971), it is packed with interesting facts, movie gossip and character detail, not only about the stars but also the inhabitants of writer Larry McMurty's hometown.

Hickenlooper's fiction film-making tends to involve characters that have reached an existential crisis point in their life; he has commented of his own work, 'All of the characters in all of my films are trying to fill a void inside themselves.' *Some Folks Call It a Sling Blade* (1994), a short starring Billy Bob Thornton as a character who is reluctantly being released after 25 years in an asylum for murdering his mother and her friend, was acclaimed at many festivals and formed the basis for the feature *Sling Blade* (1996). Shot in black and white, featuring Molly Ringwald and a perfectly cast J.T. Walsh, it is packaged on the video with an illuminating 'making of' documentary. Well written, acted and directed, it is the best kind of short film-making: simple, effective and memorable.

Having made *Grey Night* (1993), a horror film set during the Civil War, which has been variously released as *The Killing Box* and *Ghost Brigade*, Hickenlooper released one of his more autobiographical pieces, *The Low Life* (1996). With touches of Doug Liman's *Swingers* (1996), it focuses on a group of Yale graduates who work boring jobs and hang out in bars. Generally self-obsessed, when of them gets a new roommate, a naïve out-of-towner, they mercilessly exploit him, losing sight of life's bigger picture and

*Picture This: The Times of Peter Bogdanovich in Archer City, Texas* (1991)
*Hearts of Darkness: A Filmmakers Apocalypse* (1991)
*Some Folks Call It a Sling Blade* (1994)
*The Low Life* (1996)
*Persons Unknown* (1997)
*Dogtown* (1997)
*The Big Brass Ring* (1999)
*The Man From Elysian Fields* (2002)

any compassion. Sean Astin is particularly good as the relentlessly optimistic Andrew, and Kyra Sedgwick is great as the cheerfully depressive, kooky love interest.

*Persons Unknown* (1997), his next, is a noir thriller that treads similar ground as much of John Dahl's work. Complete with femme fatales and ruthless double-crossers, it stars Joe Mantegna as a troubled ex-cop; having had a one-night stand, he becomes embroiled with two sisters – a pre-*Mulholland Drive* (2001) Naomi Watts and a brittle Kelly Lynch – who have tried to swindle some crooks and are now being pursued. Against his better judgement, he takes them to a 'safe' hide-out and the requisite complications ensue. Although there are a few too many off-kilter shots, the characters are intriguing – particularly their chequered pasts – and it is hard to know which way the narrative will lead, which is certainly refreshing.

Hickenlooper makes good use of location in all his films and particularly so in *Dogtown* (1997), where a small-town milieu is created in all its fascinating detail, complete with wide, open blue skies, empty streets, and the inexorable boredom of nothing to do. When Philip Van Horn (Trevor St. John) returns to his hometown, the inhabitants assume that he has made a great success of his acting career, but LA has not proved to be quite the land of opportunity he thought it would be. Having left to make something of himself, he has returned no better, in a sense, than anyone he left behind, and he still holds a torch for Dorothy (Mary Stuart Masterson), a girl who taunted him at school. Once a beauty queen, she has also failed to realise her dreams. Well-paced and written, paying attention to character and set detail, the result is curiously affecting.

Hickenlooper made *The Big Brass Ring* (1999) for under $7 million; an adaptation of an unproduced Orson Welles script, it was nominated for a Golden Globe. A story of political chicanery, intrigue and ambition, the narrative follows Blake Pellarin (William Hurt), an independent candidate who is running for governor in Missouri. As the ghosts of his past come back to haunt and engulf him, the personal and political collide, and machinations increase. In strong support, Miranda Richardson plays his rich, bored and disillusioned wife, Irene Jacob is a journalist interested in his shady past, and Nigel Hawthorne is the controlling former senator determined to make waves. St. Louis provides a perfect backdrop to the murky goings-on, at once macabre and carnivalesque.

*The Man From Elysian Fields* (2002), Hickenlooper's most recent release, builds well on the promise of *The Big Brass Ring* and an equally intriguing premise. Andy Garcia, who sadly seems to feature less and less in cinema, plays struggling writer Byron Tiller, in need of money. Happily married with a child, when Luther Fox (Mick Jagger), who runs a male escort agency, tries to recruit his services, Tiller thinks of his family and agrees. He begins dating a young woman (Olivia Williams) and discovers that her husband is a famous, ailing Pulitzer Prize-winning author, Tobias Allcott (James Coburn). When Allcott asks for his help in writing his final work, Tiller enthusiastically rises to the challenge; his motives become cloudier and his actions more self-destructive, however, as the action unfolds. For the most part, the dialogue is suitably dry and witty, but on occasion strays towards the clichéd. Like *Sunset Boulevard* (1953), the story is Faustian and cautionary: lured by opportunity and personal gain, the protagonist risks the happiness he has known and his sanity. While the tone may be dark, the off-kilter humour alleviates any gloominess.

Hickenlooper is currently in post-production on a feature documentary, *Mayor of the Sunset Strip*, which chronicles the life of disc jockey and rock impresario Rodney Bingenheimer; and in development with a dark romantic comedy, *The Space Between Bill Buckner's Legs*; a drama starring Susan Sarandon, *A Whale in Montana*; and a farce about police brutality, *2.2*.                                                             **HP**

# Tim HILL

*Muppets From Space* (1999)
*Max Keeble's Big Move* (2001)

No stranger to the family comedy genre, Tim Hill has worked for several years with Nickelodeon, Nick Films, Nick at Nite and Disney Television. One of his highlights while working for Nickelodeon was the stop-motion animated short series 'Action League Now' (1997), which he wrote, directed and produced. Other notable projects he has worked on include the theatrical short *Rock-A-Big-Baby*, which featured the rock group KISS playing a concert for a garage full of action figures.

Hill made his feature film debut with the latest entry in the Muppets film series. With *Muppets From Space* (1999), Hill followed in the footsteps of other great family/comedy film directors, Jim Henson and Frank Oz. He hit all the right marks as he followed Gonzo's quest for family on this and other planets, weaving together humour, music, warmth and touching themes, and showing great ability in keeping every member of the audience interested in the story and its characters.

After the success of *Muppets From Space*, Hill directed the family film *Max Keeble's Big Move* (2001). The story centres on Max Keeble (played by Alex Linz), a boy who finds out that he is moving to another city and tries to exact revenge on all those who bullied him in school. Told lightly and with much 'tongue in cheek' humour, the film was a silly comedy for children and families. While many criticised the film for its juvenile approach, it is a welcome enough, whimsical diversion. Hill is currently working in pre-production on several projects for Disney and Nickelodeon.                    **JM**

# Walter HILL

In his long career, Walter Hill has primarily been associated with the action genres of post-classical American cinema. Veering between mainstream commercialism (*48 Hrs.* (1982), *Brewster's Millions* (1985)) and a more personal art cinema (*The Driver* (1978), *Wild Bill* (1995)), Hill's movies display a recurring thematic concern with masculine identity and male codes of honour, loyalty and betrayal. With few exceptions, women are relegated to the margins of Hill's fictional worlds, while romance, where it exists, usually interrupts the drive toward narrative goals.

Born in Long Beach, California in 1942, Hill studied English literature and history at Michigan University before embarking upon his cinematic career as a screenwriter and assistant director. His directorial debut, *Hard Times* (1975), concerns a bare-knuckle fighter (Charles Bronson) who fights (literally and metaphorically) for survival during the 1930s Depression. Though not a huge commercial success, *Hard Times* does establish thematic and stylistic motifs that dominate Hill's subsequent work. The pace of the film (particularly for an action movie) is slow and meandering. Chaney (Bronson), the first of Hill's tough, taciturn male protagonists, is indifferent to romantic relationships. There is also an ambiguous sense of good and evil and characters are only heroic to the extent that they are able to survive in a violent environment.

Hill's recurring fascination with outsiders and outlaws continued in his second film, *The Driver*. This is a contemporary heist movie that returns to the narrative terrain Hill had previously explored in his script for Sam Peckinpah's 1972 film, *The Getaway* (on which Hill also served as second unit director). *The Driver* is, however, more pared down and existential in tone than Peckinpah's movie. The setting (dismal streets and tawdry neon) is bleak; characters are unnamed and without personal histories, while the performances, particularly of Ryan O'Neal as the driver, are devoid of strong emotions. Indeed, static close-ups of O'Neal's expressionless face repeatedly punctuate the frenzied car-chase sequences. Here, as in most of Hill's work, there is a tendency toward archetypes, rather than psychologically rounded characters.

*The Warriors* (1979) concerns rival teenage street gangs in New York, following the murder of a powerful gang-leader. The film achieved some notoriety upon its initial release, due to press-reports of copycat violence, but here, myth and allegory, rather than social realism, dominate. The film makes overt references to a variety of extra-textual sources (including Greek mythology, Arthurian legend and 1950s teen-movies) and throughout the film, the gangs are without adult constraint or societal context.

Hill's second teen movie, *Streets of Fire* (1984), is a rock-musical set in 'another time, another place'. Styles of pop music and fashion drawn from the history of American youth culture mingle in a postmodern bricolage of teenage subcultures. The cliché-laden plot (concerning the kidnap and subsequent rescue of a female pop singer) along with the formal elements of the film (such as the jagged, page-turn wipes that growl across the screen to mark the transitions between sequences) combine to emphasise its comic book sensibility. It is interesting to note, however, that in this mythic realm, there is an attempt to offer a more progressive representation of women. The tough soldier-female, McCoy (Amy Madigan), is presented as equal (if not superior) to the men.

*The Long Riders* (1980) is the first of Hill's three revisionist westerns, the others being *Geronimo: An American Legend* (1993) and *Wild Bill*. In all three movies,

Hill accentuates generic iconography (panoramic, sunset landscapes and silhouetted horsemen, dusters flapping in the wind) whilst simultaneously challenging Hollywood's traditional representation of Western heroism. *The Long Riders*, for example, offers a sympathetic portrayal of the legendary James brothers and their band of outlaws. Here, family gatherings are bathed in soft, warm colours, while the casting of actual brothers – James and Stacey Keach as the James brothers, David, Keith and Robert Carradine as the Youngers, Randy and Dennis Quaid as the Millers, and Christopher and Nicholas Guest as the Fords – underscores the theme of fraternal loyalty.

The Apache warrior Geronimo is presented as a dignified, softly-spoken statesman rather than the monstrous 'other'. This pro-Native American film shies away from radical revision, however: the extreme white racism is offset by liberal cavalrymen like Lt. Gatewood (Jason Patric). In the sepia toned flashbacks and bright, jarring colours, the legendary gunslinger (Jeff Bridges) is conceived as a scoundrel, drunk, and psychopathic killer. *Wild Bill* undermines the macho posturing traditionally associated with the western hero: in his later years Hickcok is a sad opium addict and almost blind. His code of honour is so bizarre that it becomes ridiculous; a point underscored near the film's opening when Wild Bill shoots a man who had committed the terrible crime of touching Hickok's hat.

*Southern Comfort* (1981) is a Vietnam allegory that uses backwoods Cajuns to represent the Vietcong. The Cajuns use guerrilla tactics to terrorise a group of National Guardsmen on manoeuvres in the Louisiana swamplands. As in John Boorman's *Deliverance* (1978), the wilderness is imbued with beauty and danger. For the Guardsmen (liberal and redneck alike), the everglades form an alien terrain.

Though set in an abandoned factory in St. Louis, Hill's *Trespass* (1992) bears a close resemblance to *Southern Comfort*. In the later film, 'otherness' is personified by a mob of black gangstas (including rap artists Ice T and Ice Cube) who terrorise two off-duty firemen searching the burnt-out building for hidden gold.

The comic buddy movie, *48 Hrs.* (1982), is one of Hill's most popular films and the only one (so far) to have spawned a sequel, *Another 48 Hrs.* (1990). In both films, Reggie Hammond (Eddie Murphy) is released from jail in order to aid a police detective, Jack Cates (Nick Nolte). In his first screen role, Murphy clearly has the more sympathetic (and comedic) character, yet it is Cates – the gruff, cynical loner – who maintains (legal) authority. Hammond is an unpredictable genie freed from the bottle, without whom, Cates is doomed to failure. Notably, both films end with Reggie being confined (back to prison in the first film and to hospital in the second). The popularity of *48 Hrs.* and Hollywood's buddy movies during the 1980s, also led to the modest success of *Red Heat* (1988). Another formulaic partnership of opposites is given a post-Cold War context when Soviet police officer (Arnold Schwarzenegger) is harnessed to world-weary, Chicago cop (James Belushi) to track a group of Russian drug-dealers in America.

During the 1980s, Hill directed a string of mainstream films with varied degrees of success. *Brewster's Millions*, for example, is a feelgood mainstream comedy, bereft of Hill's visual or thematic signature. Hill's film differs from previous versions (1921, 1935, and 1945), by including a black protagonist (Richard Pryor) as the man who will inherit $300 million if he is able to spend $30 million in thirty days. Though the film does offer a liberal perspective in relation to race, as well as class, any political ideology is subsumed within the platitudinous message that 'money can't buy you happiness'. Similarly, the Faustian fable *Crossroads* (1986) descends to banality when teenage guitarist (Ralph Macchio), accompanied by old blues musician (Joe Seneca), engages in a battle of duelling guitars with the devil's (glam-rock) representative. Part buddy movie, part supernatural fantasy, with a plot drawn from the biography of 1920s blues guitarist, Robert Johnson (who claimed to have sold his soul), this film is dominated by the music of long-time Hill collaborator, Ry Cooder.

Though many critics have claimed that Walter Hill's commercial and critical failures following *48 Hrs.* suggest that his career is in decline, *Last Man Standing* (1996) is a quintessential Hill movie. In this remake of Kurosawa's *Yojimbo* (1961), Hill incongruously locates rival groups of gangsters into the rural (Western) wilderness of Texas. Bruce Willis stars as a travelling stranger who drives into town and through a series of gun battles and double-crosses, rescues a kidnapped Mexican woman and thwarts the criminals' plans. As with the best Hill movies, *Last Man Standing* is economic in plot and lavishly shot (with majestic images of the expansive desert landscape). The protagonist is typically stoic and enigmatic (unencumbered by clear motivation or back-story) and his redemption is achieved through violence. For Hill, here as at the outset of his career, heroism is simply being able to survive.

Having withdrawn his name from the credits of the big-budget, science fiction film *Supernova* (2000), Hill recently co-write and directed *Undisputed* (2002), the story of a heavyweight boxing champion who is jailed for rape and subsequently has to fight the prison champion; Wesley Snipe stars. **EC**

# Arthur HILLER

Arthur Hiller, born in Alberta, Canada, in 1923, has sustained a career for nearly fifty years, tackling a variety of genres but having most success with light comedy, reflecting his background in television. He began his career on Canadian radio using knowledge gained from his psychology degree to direct public affairs programmes. The rise of television in the late 1940s and early 1950s gave Hiller the opportunity to diversify and he directed for Canadian television until American broadcaster NBC saw his work and he moved to America in 1955. He directed a vast amount of television, mainly drama series such as 'Alfred Hitchcock Presents', 'Gunsmoke', 'Naked City', and the 'Director's Playhouse' series.

Hiller made an unsure feature debut with a film about a young couple eloping, *The Careless Years* (1957), and followed with *This Rugged Land* (1962), originally made for television but extended for theatrical release, and a Disney film, *The Miracle of the White Stallions* (1962). Already Hiller showed himself to be capable of handling unrelated subjects and completing a competent job.

The brisk, workmanlike *Wheeler Dealers* – a Wall Street comedy – followed in 1963, but it was on his next film that Hiller began his professional relationship with screenwriter Paddy Chayevsky and established himself as a film director. *The Americanization of Emily* (1964) earned him a reputation for flair with sophisticated comedy. He continued this path with his next two films. After *Promise Her Anything* (1965), a briskly paced romantic comedy starring Warren Beatty as a Greenwich Village, dwelling dropout making mail order striptease movies, came the functional comedy thriller *Penelope* (1966), which cast Natalie Wood as a kleptomaniac.

Hiller, who has always directed using 'the same basic technique for all films', changed tack with his next piece of work and took on a special mission war adventure *Tobruk* (1967). In doing so he proved himself able to handle action – particularly in the opening night raid and the gritty finale – although the film is basically just another desert warfare movie. After briefly performing directing duties on J. Lee Thompson's *Eye of the Devil* (1966) Hiller took on *The Tiger Makes Out* (1967), a satire about non-conformity, handled with confidence and imagination.

*The Out of Towners* (1970) marked an obvious return to comedy and the first of two Neil Simon collaborations. The next, *Plaza Suite*, came in 1971. Both incident and dialogue driven, they are crisply directed. Hiller also completed two more films in this period. *Popi* (1969) a semi-serious comedy about a refugee scam, is notable for Alan Arkin's performance and the director's surprising attention to ghetto-life detail. *Love Story* (1970) is probably Hiller's most famous work and certainly his most commercially successful. In a time of hatred and conflict, Hiller felt that audiences were ready for unadulterated love. The film largely ignores social context, aiming instead for mainstream colour-supplement lifestyle and romance evoked in clichéd and sentimental terms.

Hiller's best film followed *Plaza Suite*. With a script by Chayevsky, *The Hospital* (1971) works as a black comedy about disillusionment, with the medical establishment functioning as a metaphor for the chaos of American society. Like Frederick Wiseman's groundbreaking documentary *Hospital* (1970), this film aims to reflect larger social concerns through against a medical backdrop. Wrongful operations, accidental deaths, and murder occur undetected due to the size and complexity of the system under discussion. The film is well served by Hiller's directorial choices. His camera is mobile, roaming the hospital corridors, helping to create a sense of action and movement, reflecting the chaos and confusion in the place.

Hiller later returned to this theme of institutions as a microcosm for society with the inferior *Teachers* (1984). The clichéd story of a teacher who is in touch with 'the kids', and has to fight a lawsuit brought on by fraudulent administration, aims for Chayevskyian satire but misses the mark.

Hiller flopped with the film of a successful play, *The Man of La Mancha* (1972), an ill-judged and unlikely musical set in the seventeenth-century Spanish Inquisition. 1974's gauche and mawkish *The Crazy World of Julius Vrooder* continued the Vietnam theme established in *Confrontation*, but was seen as a distasteful attempt to wring humour from hospitalised veterans. *The Man in the Glass Booth* (1975) lacked the sophistication and intellect of the stage version, famously directed by Harold Pinter. Hiller reduced the cerebral argument of the play to build the movie around Maximillian Schell's showcase performance of a man dealing with questions of identity and Holocaust survival guilt.

Comedy made a predictable return: *Silver Streak* (1976) became the first of two outings for Hiller, Richard Pryor, and Gene Wilder. The second, *See No Evil, Hear No Evil,* was released in 1989. Both rely on visual wit and character for their humour, as does *The In-Laws* (1979), which proved a big success, teaming Hiller collaborators Alan Arkin and Peter Falk in an original comedy about a mild-mannered dentist dragged into an international conspiracy by his daughter's future father-in-law. This has since been re-worked by Jonathan Lynn as *The Whole Nine Yards* (2000).

The biopic *W.C. Fields and Me* (1976) utilised dramatic licence and sentimentality. His 1992 film about Babe Ruth, *The Babe*, bent the truth in similar sentimental style. *Nightwing* (1979), a misfired attempt to cash in on a renewed interest in horror found itself usurped by Ridley Scott's superior *Alien* (1979). His next film, *Making Love* (1982), proved potentially groundbreaking but Hiller refuses the challenge of subversion in this tame tale of a marriage threatened by the husband's attraction to another man. Whilst offering positive gay characters – strong, intelligent and attractive – the film is ultimately coy and judgmental.

Hiller spent the 1980s and much of the 1990s in comedy: *Author! Author!* (1982) about a Broadway playwright; and the appropriately titled duo *Romantic Comedy* (1983) and *The Lonely Guy* (1984). After the comedy blip of *Teachers* came *Outrageous Fortune* (1987) which restored some box-office success to Hiller's career. A female buddy-action comedy with Bette Midler and Shelley Long, it is a predictable but well-played scenario about two women seeking revenge on their mutual boyfriend. There are no pretensions to feminism: the women only become active because they are being betrayed, and they stop in the middle of a dangerous incident to shop for blouses!

After the Pryor/Wilder repeat came *Taking Care of Business* (1991) and *Married to It* (1991). Both comedies directed with typical briskness, the first focused on a conman taking over a businessman's identity, the second on three couples learning about love and marriage. *Carpool* (1996), about the antics following a school run gone wrong, was followed by a sour pause in Hiller's career. Ironically, in a dispute over editing, Hiller removed his name from the credits of his most recent work, the poorly received *An Alan Smithee Film: Burn, Hollywood, Burn* (1997).

Solid and undistinguished, Hiller's work shows a basic flair for comedy and a style more concerned with serving the story than imprinting an authorial signature.     **JD**

# Gregory HOBLIT

*Primal Fear* (1996)
*Fallen* (1998)
*Frequency* (2000)
*Hart's War* (2002)

Forming a consistent body of work in Hollywood is difficult enough for high-profile directors, let alone those lower down the scale. Gregory Hoblit's visual style and recurrent preoccupations with the supernatural, moral and ethical corruption and human relationships make his work unusually distinctive; while sometimes incomplete, his work brims with ideas and the possibilities of cinematic narrative. Hoblit began his career as a director of American television melodramas, including 'Hill Street Blues', 'L.A. Law' and 'NYPD Blue', strong on character, snappily scripted, and well-acted.

His interest in character and the American legal system carried over into Hoblit's feature debut, the courtroom drama *Primal Fear* (1996). The story of an altarboy accused of the murder of a local priest, the film is part psychological thriller, part straight legal-eagle drama, involving twists including sexual abuse and mental manipulation. Hoblit splits the action between the establishing first half and the revelatory second half, using the contrasts between shadowy Freudian interiors and illuminating, illuminated courtrooms for maximum effect. Power shifts and mindgames abound as the film moves towards a final, self-negating twist at the dénouement, a trend Hoblit particularly favours. The film also establishes Hoblit's interest in manipulation and the conflicts of male relationships, but is too melodramatic to satisfy on a deeper level.

*Fallen* (1998) suffers from a similar problem. The high-concept premise, in which a serial killer, actually a dark angel capable of body swapping, escapes his execution and pursues his captor, is simply too much for some to accept seriously. Located somewhere between horror, thriller and action, the film comes across either as farce or gothic genius depending on taste. Hoblit's art direction draws parallels between themes of secrecy, deception, and evil, with brooding buildings, overcast skies, and gloomy settings; secrets of the past again lie at the heart of the film, as does theology and the impact of the supernatural on the everyday. The use of film types and evocative camera angles maximises suspense and contrast between the real and fantastic sequences, and Hoblit again employs a final twist to force reconsideration of the story's events. Though it depends heavily on suspension of disbelief, a problem all of Hoblit's stories share, accepted as a purely fantastic narrative the film is an intriguing variation on the serial killer chase.

*Frequency* (2000) has another unusual premise, in which a man contacts his dead father thirty years earlier by radio and allows him to avoid the fire which killed him, thus changing the present. Hoblit contrasts present day New York with 1960s Queens, again using a consummate range of cinematic tricks including crossfades, flash cuts, film stocks and varying camera styles to explore favoured themes of the supernatural, loss, and male relationships. His handling of the increasingly complex time paradoxes and another use of the twist device are intelligent, as is his sensitive opposition and juxtaposition of the two male leads, but the film is unsatisfying and ends poorly. Far more imaginative and unusual than the norm, Hoblit's films are perhaps too full of ideas.

His thriller, *Hart's War* (2002), taken from John Katzenbach's novel set in a Nazi war camp in World War Two, stars Bruce Willis and has not been as well-received as other such recent genre pieces.                                          **OB**

# Michael HOFFMAN

Born in Honolulu, Hawaii, in 1957, Michael Hoffman has achieved a rather respected position in Hollywood in the past ten years, mainly owing to star-ridden films and lavish productions. Few of them, however, have been particularly successful. His directorial style, at times infused with a sort of bitter irony rarely found in mainstream cinema, is remarkably conservatory and bears the clear mark of Hoffman's stage training.

Hoffman studied Theatre at Boise State University, where he performed at the Idaho Shakespeare Festival's inaugural production of 'A Midsummer Night's Dream', and later pursued his interest for Shakespeare while studying Renaissance Drama as a Rhodes Scholar at Oxford University. It was during this first stay in England that Hoffman directed a number of theatrical productions that led him to the contract for his first feature, *Privileged* (1982). A comedy written by Hoffman and screenwriter Rupert Walters (who later adapted *Restoration* (1995) for him), this undergraduate film featured the debut performances of Hugh Grant, James Wilby, and Imogen Stubbs. The story is a low-profile tale of an Oxford student courting the female lead in his Jacobean college production. Were it not for the interest surrounding the cast, the film itself would be forgettable. Hoffman's later project was a much more charming one. *Restless Natives* (1985) is a gentle off-beat comedy about two young Scottish men robbing tourists from coaches around the Highlands, who eventually become local heroes. In its simplistic idealism, there is something reminiscent of the atmosphere of Bill Forsyth's works.

In 1986 Hoffman returned to his native Idaho, where he rejoined friends from university and became involved in the direction of the Idaho Shakespeare Festival as a founder and member of its Board of Trustees. Alongside this commitment to Shakespearean theatre, however, Hoffman continued pursuing a career in films, writing and shooting two films concerned with small-town adolescence. The first of these is *Promised Land* (1988), an uneven but powerful portrayal of the broken dreams of two former high school acquaintances whose lives tragically meet some years after graduation. The film features more early performances from now affirmed stars (Meg Ryan is particularly powerful) and it was commissioned by the Sundance Film Festival. Compared to this,

*Privileged* (1982)
*Restless Natives* (1985)
*Promised Land* (1988)
*Some Girls* (1989)
*Soapdish* (1991)
*Restoration* (1995)
*One Fine Day* (1996)
*William Shakespeare's A Midsummer Night's Dream* (1999)

*Some Girls* (1989) is a far more light-hearted comedy about the sex education of an American college student who travels to Québec to spend Christmas with his girlfriend, just to discover that she is no longer in love with him. Hoffman writes a dialogue that is both clever and funny, particularly when it comes to the eccentric teachers that the protagonist discovers in his girlfriend's family, and produces a whimsical product, which gained a rather strong cult following.

Departing from the light hand of his early works, in 1991 Hoffman directed *Soapdish* (1991), a farcical comedy about soap opera stars, featuring over-the-top performances from a great ensemble cast. The film, hardly a satire, is more a homage to the nonsensical narratives of daytime television shows, in its succession of unbelievable twists and tongue-in-cheek references. It features Kevin Kline at his best as the alcoholic former soap opera star reduced to play 'Death of a Salesman' in a downtown cabaret bar. However, its fast pace and deliberate referencing of other films diminish its power and make it marginally higher in quality than the material it was inspired by.

After a four-year gap, Hoffman re-teamed with previous leads Robert Downey Jr and Meg Ryan in the adapted costume drama *Restoration*. The film is a rather moving redemption story set in seventeenth-century England about a medical student embracing court life as the Royal Physician and redeeming himself only after being ruined by his lustful weaknesses. However, Hoffman shows here for the first time a flaw that will later pollute his return to Shakespeare. Seemingly preoccupied with the sumptuous representation of the period costumes and settings (particularly the extravagant Court parties), and with an overemphatic expression of moods and feelings, dramatic and farcical alike, the film is ultimately episodic and united only in its foregrounded formality.

In comparison to the previous heritage costume drama, *One Fine Day* (1996) is a much more accomplished piece, and one that provides an interesting and unusually realistic twist. The film is mainly a star vehicle for Michelle Pfeiffer and George Clooney (here at his first feature after the television success in the series 'ER'), yet it manages to enhance their established star personae in pleasant performances that somehow bring depth to the glamorous and glossy confection.

This depth is unfortunately lost in *William Shakespeare's A Midsummer Night's Dream* (1999). The film is built around an exceptionally well cast ensemble of stars, yet it fails to draw together lavish *mise-en-scène* and individual accomplished performances. Hoffman proves beyond any doubt that he is able to exploit his leads' previously-established star personae to produce charming and powerful performances, and shows an in-depth understanding of the Shakespearean text. Yet, despite the original ideas, the acting is lost and scattered among the marvellous and spell-binding settings.

Hoffman has recently finished work on *The Palace Thief*, which is based on a short story by Ethan Canin about a relatioship between a teacher and student over a period of twenty years. **BP**

# Nicole HOLOFCENER

*Walking and Talking* (1996)
*Lovely and Amazing* (2001)

Nicole Holofcener's feature *Walking and Talking* (1996) found critics reaching for comparisons with the New York comedies of Woody Allen. Yet whilst this tale of educated young professionals searching for love in the big city trades in the requisite angst and fatalism, it also falls within the ambit of the contemporary 'chick flick'.

Holofcener was born in 1960 and between graduation from Columbia's film programme in 1988 and *Walking and Talking* she directed a number of shorts. *Your Name in Cellulite* (1995) signals the preoccupation with physical imperfection and body horror which infects her debut feature. Her apprenticeship in shorts is also apparent in the seemingly discrete exchanges of *Walking and Talking*.

Keenly received at the Sundance Film Festival in 1996, *Walking and Talking* underwent a circuitous genesis. Although backed by European television and theatrical distributors, the film taps into entirely American vernacular sensibilities. Citing its 'slightly threadbare look', critic Larry Gross asked why Hollywood hadn't picked up the project, given the vogue for such offerings at the time. Its insistence upon the sanctity of girlhood placed *Walking and Talking* in a tradition inaugurated by Claudia Weill's *Girlfriends* (1978), and plotted in such post-feminist works as *Reality Bites* (1994). The soundtrack is a twangy mix of Billy Bragg, Shrimp Boat, and Greenhouse 27.

Holofcener's preoccupation with friends belonging to friends evokes Woody Allen's assimilationism, yet her multi-stranded narrative suggests the bite-sized flow of television soap opera. Holofcener, in collaboration with Hal Hartley cinematographer Michael Spiller, is already effectively using the frame and narrative space. Adopting a master shot style, with editor Alisa Lepselter cutting to close-ups to catch the inattentions hidden in pauses and hesitations, Holofcener also demonstrates an awareness of the power of metaphor. A beautiful shot of Amelia holding Laura afloat against a sunset backdrop on a lake is not only pictorial but speaks of the support which the film essays. Holofcener managed to cast Anne Heche (Laura) as her star was in ascendance but before mainstream fame. The film also added to Catherine Keener's resumé, contributing to her status as an American art-cinema icon.

Consonant with the post-Tarantino independent sensibility is Holofcener's feeling for the grubbier alleyways of American pop culture – Z movies, porn videos, science fiction moles – locating *Walking and Talking* in a context owing less to traditionalist Woody Allen and more to postmodernists Hal Hartley, Richard Linklater, and Kevin Smith.

This preoccupation assumes confident social resonance in Holofcener's second feature *Lovely and Amazing* (2001), a tender and telling revelation about the vicissitudes of self-image. Gently teasing the 'New You' cultures of cosmetic surgery and self-improvement, Holofcener focuses upon the middle-aged mother Jane's liposuction nightmare and her daughter's various personal misgivings: Michelle (Keener) is approaching middle-age, is unhappily married and can't get her crafts business to work; Elizabeth thinks she is a lousy actress; Annie is an adopted African-American suffering from teenage angst. Handling the undercurrents of these womens' relationships with customary sensitivity, Holofcener, who has also directed episodes of 'Sex and the City', is making this particular contemporary niche her own. **RA**

# Kevin HOOKS

Born in Philadelphia in 1958, Kevin Hooks served his apprenticeship in numerous television movies before turning to feature film directing. He acted throughout the 1970s and 1980s and eventually graduated to directing television movies and movies-of-the-week, including 'V', 'Roots' and 'Fame'. His theatrical debut, *Strictly Business* (1991), featuring early performances from Samuel L. Jackson and Halle Berry, as well as Hooks himself, is a sharp social satire in which the uneven friendship between an ambitious black businessman and his streetwise pal is thrown into confusion when they fall in love with a beautiful waitress. As with several early 1990s black films, Hooks examines the notion that being a black professional renders that person not authentically black. Cleverly, Hooks undercuts the negativity of dozens of black movies, which taught that the only legitimate stance towards white corporate America was to shun it.

*Passenger 57* (1992) starred Wesley Snipes and contains the ultimate kiss-off line – 'Always bet on black'. Lacking the budget and the class of the *Die Hard* trilogy (1988, 1990, 1995), Hooks manages to build up tension but lacks the know-how to sustain the adrenaline and testosterone and throw in the odd bit of relieving humour. Snipes comes across as the black hero of the 1990s, all Shaft and Eddie Murphy rolled into one, while Hooks also allows the predictable English villain (Bruce Payne) enough rope to hang himself. The intensity of the opening scenes may be impressive, but the film's overall lack of clarity leaves the action hamstrung.

*Fled* (1996) plays as a modern-day reworking of *The Defiant Ones* (1958). The pairing of Laurence Fishburne and Stephen Baldwin is hardly Sydney Poitier-Tony Curtis, but the plot (involving a missing floppy disk, the Cuban Mafia and a sinister US marshal) is brisk and fun, provided one does not look too closely at the San Andreas fault-size implausibilities. Hooks directs again with a bracing and breezy knowledge of cinema history; while *Passenger 57* openly referenced *Die Hard* and James Bond, this film allows the leads to ask the question 'Didn't you see...?' and then quote *The Godfather* (1972) or *The Fugitive* (1993).

Hooks' last films have been released straight-to-video in Britain. The most successful, *Black Dog* (1998), stars Patrick Swayze as an ex-con who takes a job as a truck driver. A combination of *Smokey and the Bandit* (1983) and Peckinpah's *Convoy* (1978), Swayze must protect his family when the truck comes under attack and the film treads a fine line between comedy and action that has characterised most of the director's canon, both on television and in the cinema. **BM**

# Tobe HOOPER

Tobe Hooper is a horror film director destined to be associated with one single film for all time. His debut picture is so revered it has in essence eclipsed every other movie he has worked on, and the film-maker has never been able to recreate its zest or spontaneity since.

Born in Austin, Texas, in 1943, Hooper started out making documentaries and industrial films before being appointed assistant director of the film programme at the University of Texas. Using students from this establishment, he embarked upon a semi-professional project which would change the face of modern horror forever. *The Texas Chainsaw Massacre* (1974) is a disquieting inspection of rural insanity, more intricate and less bloodthirsty than the title might connote. Articulating the story of a group of teenagers who come across a house occupied by a deranged, dysfunctional family of unemployed slaughterhouse workers, *Texas Chainsaw* uses documentary techniques – gritty hand-held footage, washed out colours – to efficiently heighten its realism. The true terror, though, comes not from the grisly murders themselves, of which the meat hook incident is the most traumatic, but rather, like the horror films of old, from suggestion: the implied cannibalism and incestuous nature of the family; eerie glimpses of symbolic items inside the house; the hidden visage of cult anti-hero Leatherface (Gunnar Hansen), who shambles around like some gigantic toddler holding a chainsaw instead of a rattle. Like *Psycho* 14 years earlier, *Texas Chainsaw* was inspired by the real life of serial killer Ed Gein, who used the skins of his victims to make furniture. Described by one reviewer as a 'gruelling endurance test', the film has often been emulated – most recently in the outstanding *The Blair Witch Project* (1999) – but has never been surpassed for sheer unremitting, hysterical dread.

Any follow-up was bound to disenchant and *Eaten Alive* (1976) does just that; an obscure and flagrant reworking of *Texas Chainsaw*, but set in and around a sleazy motel not dissimilar to the one Norman Bates owned. Another desecration of the American dream, the movie fails abysmally to recapture the tension of its elder sibling, conspicuously so when it wanders away from its central site. Astonishingly, the composition that does come closest to doing this is *Salem's Lot* (1979), a television mini-series given a theatrical release. Based on the Stephen King book, it cultivates a sense of apprehension gradually, as one by one the inhabitants of an isolated town are transformed into vampires: a threat from both outside and inside. David Soul and distinguished thespian James Mason lend their acting talents and the dramatisation incorporates a tribute to F. W. Murnau's celebrated *Nosferatu* (1922) in the appearance of the vampire Barlow.

In *The Funhouse* (1981), Hooper transplants the action from *Halloween*'s (1978) suburbia and the woods of *Friday the 13th* (1980) to the travelling carnival, but this is by-the-numbers, textbook horror and has little worthwhile affect. *Poltergeist* (1982), his second most popular movie, is an intermittently scary effects-led affair in which Native American shades take their revenge on the average US family for living atop their ancient burial ground. Like *The Thing From Another World* (1951), *Poltergeist* is a film that bears all the stylistic hallmarks of its producer – in this case Steven Spielberg – and it was his name that was used in the promotional trailers. There are several episodes in which Hooper's idiosyncratic signature can be detected, but by and large the horror is curtailed by Spielberg's autocratic, all-pervading presence.

*Lifeforce* (1985), the first of a three-picture deal for Cannon, was the beginning of Hooper's fall from grace: it is a vapid science fiction/horror cross-fertilisation with a deficient premise about space vampires from Halley's Comet. Mathilda May parades naked for voyeuristic value alone and the employment of a mostly British cast, including Shakespearean actor Patrick Stewart, can be construed as a slovenly effort to grant the film respectability.

*Invaders From Mars* (1986) is even more embarrassing. A remake of William Cameron Menzies' 1953 classic, it adheres to the original narrative precisely – right down to the 'surprise' ending – leaving absolutely no room for manoeuvre. The only notable difference between the two is of course the budget, but Hooper's aliens are nowhere near as entertaining as their aged counterparts. Divorced from its 'reds under the bed' context, the film quickly deteriorates into jaded and puerile trash.

In a hasty – and unmitigated – entreaty to fans, in the same year the director devised a sequel to *The Texas Chainsaw Massacre*. However, in order to shock current audiences used to seeing bloodshed on screen, Hooper had to be more direct this time, holding little back in terms of carnage or bestiality (not always to the film's credit) and offsetting this with tongue-in-cheek humour. The scene in which Dennis Hopper engages in a *Star Wars*-style chainsaw duel with Leatherface unequivocally typifies the level he is aiming for.

After this, Hooper's mediocre features would be punctuated by requisite television work, including pilots for shows like 'Freddy's Nightmares', 'Nowhere Man', and 'Dark Skies', as well as television movies like the Anthony Perkins-starrer *I'm Dangerous Tonight* (1990). With *Spontaneous Combustion* (1989) and *Tobe Hooper's Night Terrors* (1993) his reputation plumbed new depths; the first being a *Firestarter* (1984) meets *The Dead Zone* (1983) misfire, while the latter bungles an all-important chance to cogitate on the life and work of infamous sadist the Marquis De Sade, played by Robert Englund, the star of *A Nightmare on Elm Street* (1984).

Englund also appears in *The Mangler* (1995), which is taken from Stephen King's short story about a monstrous Hadley-Watson steam presser that develops a life of its own. The fascinating blending of 1930s aesthetics with contemporary sweatshop practices, plus the anthropomorphising of the machine – a King obsession (*Carrie* (1976), *Maximum Overdrive* (1986)) – works in its favour. However, there are far too many flukish plot devices and one-dimensional characters involved for it to sufficiently appease, leaving viewers yearning for more of Hooper's formative work.

After a prolonged truancy, Hooper returned briefly to cinematic horror in 2000 with *Crocodile* (also known as *Fat Dog*), a truly abysmal monster movie that had the tagline: 'Ever feel like something is watching you?' Even less engaging than *Anaconda* (1997) and lacking the inherent wit of *Lake Placid* (1999), this quite appropriately disappeared without a trace upon release.                                                    **PB**

# Stephen HOPKINS

Stephen Hopkins is a British-born director who has gone from glossy exploitation flicks to starry Hollywood action films. His debut was *A Nightmare on Elm Street 5: The Dream Child* (1989), the fourth sequel to Wes Craven's surreal slasher movie. The *Elm Street* sequels served as something of a training ground for directors eager to make the leap to blockbusters, with *Part 3* directed by Chuck Russell, who went on to *The Mask* (1994) and *Eraser* (1997), and *Part 4* helmed by Renny Harlin, later director of *Die Hard 2* (1990) and *Cliffhanger* (1993). Hopkins' film is a weak addition to the by-then lacklustre franchise. Seemingly keen to play down the sheer nastiness of the paedophile killer of Craven's original, the sequels transformed him into a wise-cracking super-villain and with such a weakened monster, Hopkins relies on special effects to little real effect. There is a notable credit sequence, however, as limbs writhing in close-up are revealed to be lovers conceiving the titular child.

After the efficient Australian television thriller *Dangerous Game* (1990), Hopkins went on to *Predator 2* (1990), the sequel to John McTiernan's silly jungle science fiction/horror hybrid. Hopkins crafts a superior monster movie, shifting the action to the urban US in 1997 and replacing the unkillable Arnold Schwarzenegger with the more human Danny Glover. The numerous action scenes are well-handled with a number of striking murders, chiefly a decapitation and an attack in a speeding subway car.

The director stayed on familiar ground for *Judgement Night* (1993), an urban thriller that can be regarded as a variant on the 'yuppie nightmare' films of the 1980s (such as *After Hours* (1985) and *Something Wild* (1986)). Emilio Estevez, Stephen Dorff and Cuba Gooding Jr. get lost in downtown Chicago en route to a boxing match in a state-of-the-art mobile home and are pursued by heavies. The film is atmospheric and violent, owing much to Walter Hill's *The Warriors* (1979). It can be read as a kind of riposte to 'rural horrors' from *Deliverance* (1971) to *Southern Comfort* (1981), suggesting that deadly terrors lurk in the urban environment.

*Blown Away* is an empty but stylish thriller with a mis-cast Tommy Lee Jones as an ex-IRA terrorist playing cat-and-mouse with bomb squad cop Jeff Bridges. The film offers clichés about 'Oirishness', trivialising the politics of the Troubles in a similar fashion to other Hollywood action fare such as *A Prayer for the Dying* (1987) and *The Devil's Own* (1996). There are, however, a couple of typically exciting set pieces, notably a scary scene where the camera appears to lurk within a series of domestic appliances, any of which could contain a bomb.

Hopkins' next film was *The Ghost and the Darkness* (1993), yet another attempt to re-work *Jaws* (1975), with its story of two man-eating lions eating workers on a railway line in Colonial Africa. The A-list cast (Michael Douglas, Val Kilmer) cannot disguise the essentially B-movie nature of the enterprise. It also feels curiously old-fashioned, a throwback to safari movies like *Mogambo* (1953). Hopkins' stylish 'lions point-of-view' tracking shots cannot energise this. *The Ghost and the Darkness* is particularly disappointing when one considers it is based on a true story and the lions were responsible for the deaths of 130 people!

*Lost in Space* (1997) is Hopkins' biggest project to date. An adaptation of the 1960s television show, itself a science fiction reworking of the Johann Wyss novel 'Swiss Family Robinson', the film was a big summer release. Indeed, the faults of *Lost in Space* are the faults of the modern Hollywood blockbuster, with a promising cast (Heather Graham, William Hurt, and a hammy Gary Oldman) coming second to the special effects. These include a very flashy and impressive credit sequence and an attack by flesh-eating robot spiders. Like other television spin-offs, including *Maverick* (1992) and *Mission: Impossible* (1997), Hopkins' film resembles other event movies rather more than its source material. The thrills, explosions and a time-travel twist cannot disguise the essential emptiness here and the direction is more anonymous than in his earlier low(er)-budget work.

Hopkins' latest is *Under Suspicion* (2000), a thriller with a typically starry cast including Gene Hackman and Morgan Freeman. In many ways, the career of Hopkins resembles a typical career path for American-based directors, from stylish sequels to glossy genre films with A-list stars. As co-director of the popular cult show '24' he has also found success in television.                                                                    IC

# Dennis HOPPER

Dennis Hopper's career as both an actor and a director has, in the course of five decades, swung back and forth between sublime virtuosity and frustrating mediocrity. With a directorial corpus encompassing *Easy Rider* (1969), the film which 'single-handedly created the road movie as a vital post-1960s genre', the audacious experimentalism of *The Last Movie* (1971), the urban nihilism of *Colors* (1988), and the whimsical hack of *The Hot Spot* (1990) and *Chasers* (1994), Hopper has always sat uneasily in Hollywood, where self-conscious stylistic and political militancy represents at best an economic gamble, and at worst, business suicide.

Born in Dodge City, Kansas, in 1936, Hopper was raised on a farm amidst the mythological geography once populated by Wyatt Earp, Billy the Kid, and Wild Bill Hickok. Insofar as Hopper's adolescence informs his cinema, then his relationship with painter Thomas Hart Benton, who urged him to reverse his instincts and 'get tight and paint loose', as well as his photographic studies, are perhaps more instructive to understanding his work than mapping a simple analogue between West and western. For underneath the iconic surfaces of Hopper's best films, one finds aesthetic traces not of a revisionist but a visionary film-maker.

Hopper's directorial debut, *Easy Rider*, is certainly the most famous, perhaps the most important of his films, and the one which best embroiders an aesthetic muse onto ambiguous political cloth. Budgeted for $375,000, the film grossed over $50 million world-wide during its initial release cycle, sling-shotting the film and its creators to the forefront of both the film industry and contemporary counter-cultural politics. That *Easy Rider* variously won or was nominated for a welter of awards in the US and Europe is of less historical significance than its instantaneous canonisation as the reification of the sub-cultural zeitgeist. The critic for the *Washington Post* championed the film as 'lyrical and brilliant, the reflection of its generation', while *Sight and Sound* hailed it as the 'first above-ground movie which treats the culture from the viewpoint of the youth of that culture', producing what Rex Reed described as 'the definitive odyssey of the 1960s'.

However, the reading of *Easy Rider*, and by implication Hopper's auteurism, as a more or less transparent reflection of late 1960s drop-out consciousness is not so straightforward as this historical exegesis implies. The film's canonisation has not only obscured Hopper's subsequent work, but in focusing on its more existential passages the ambiguities of its own political frame and aesthetic economy are lost from sight as well. *Easy Rider* simultaneously articulates geography as an ideogram of American patriotic identity and a *tabula rasa* where revisionist politics can be inscribed. As such, the film is an awkward bedfellow to the revolutionary impulses of 1960s counter-cultural politics. Indeed, inasmuch as there is a discernible genealogy to Hopper's work, it is the positioning of conservative values and rebellious urges in fractious political and aesthetic dialectic that stakes out his particular auteurist credo.

The *mise-en-abîme* logic and impressionist montage of *The Last Movie* (1971) squarely place Hopper with both avant-garde counter cinema and the abstraction of the contemporary plastic arts. The film's violent refusal of verisimilitude and the classical pleasures of identification provoked a litany of upbraiding criticism.

Although the financial deficit which *The Last Movie* left in its wake precluded Hopper from repeating its aesthetic terrorism, it did not, however, foreclose other, more subtle stylistic and political meditations. While the intense punk nihilism of *Out of the Blue* (1980) locates it alongside *Driller Killer* (1979), *Repo Man* (1984), and *Suburbia* (1983) as the apotheosised reflection of disenfranchised 1980s youth culture, it is *Colors* (1988) which not only resonates most powerfully with the political cadence and aesthetic incandescence of *Easy Rider*, but also marks Hopper's descent into mediocrity.

As with *Easy Rider*, the conflicts and negotiations of *Colors'* representational economy take place in geo-territorial terms. However, while the political and aesthetic weave of the former is fashioned against a fecund horizon, the enclosed architectonic of Los Angeles gang-land refuses any sense of optimism. The episodic and deliberately repetitive structure of the film imbue it with a fatalistic nihilism which neither the terror nor wisdom of its protagonists can dent, a logic finally sealed in the death of its only non-violent character.

Hopper's latter-day films have been anodyne in comparison to the aesthetic lasciviousness and political avidity of the early films. One of the more intriguing aspects to the distinctly polite surfaces of *Catchfire* (1989), for which he revoked directorial credit, *The Hot Spot* (1990), and the hackneyed *Chasers* (1994), is the hint that these films are a ruse to ingratiate himself with Hollywood financiers as a prelude to renewed experimentalism.

Ultimately it is a line spoken by George Hanson (Jack Nicholson) in *Easy Rider* that chimes with the complexities and frustrations of Hopper's films: 'Its hard to be free when you're bought and sold in the marketplace.' Hopper's forthcoming project, *The Night Job*, has been described as an updated *Mean Streets* (1973), and will feature himself and Val Kilmer.                                                                                                    **PWa**

# Ron HOWARD

Born in 1954, in Oklahoma, Ron Howard was a child actor before turning professional film-maker, and has since mainly directed comedies, but also produced fantasies and, more recently, thrillers. His style is undoubtedly actor-friendly and his most adept pieces have resulted from work with ensemble casts. He has been quoted as saying that he prefers 'projects that stimulate me so that I don't feel like a manufacturer', which might explain why he has never undertaken a sequel to any of his movies. Incredibly, the director's first taste of show business was at the age of two, when he starred on stage with parents Ranse and Jean Howard in a production of 'The Seven Year Itch'. Working as Ronny Howard, he carved out a career playing innocent boy-next-door roles, but also gained an education at USC. His big break, however, came in 1974 when he secured the pivotal part of Richie Cunningham in the retro television comedy 'Happy Days'. Coincidentally, by the show's conclusion his character had journeyed to Hollywood to become a screenwriter himself – at around the same time his own filmic career was taking off.

Grand Theft Auto (1977), written by Howard and his father, was his incredibly assured directorial debut, making him one of the youngest film-makers in harness at that time. Howard also stars in the film as a smitten youth who elopes with heiress Nancy Morgan and embarks on a madcap matrimonial sprint from LA to Las Vegas – pursued by her father (Barry Cahill), fiancé Paul Linke, and various others along the way. Released the same year as *Smokey and the Bandit*, and paying tribute to *It's a Mad, Mad, Mad, Mad World* (1963), Howard's contribution to the car crash mini-genre is 'tireless' and fetchingly ardent. It's also beholden to Victor Rivers' stunt co-ordination and Joe Dante's judicious editing.

Another five years would pass before he made *Night Shift* (1982), an obscure comedy revolving around morgue attendants and streetwalkers. Starting a trend whereby he would nudge together two impracticably different 'worlds' to observe the results, Howard selects the most tasteless subject matter and forges an amiable cult movie. His old co-star Henry (The Fonze) Winkler plays a mild-mannered night shift worker at the city mortuary who is saddled with boisterous live wire Michael Keaton, a character who listens to rock music whilst prancing up and down the aisles. The pair find common ground, though, running a prostitution racket for Shelley Long's inoffensive hooker.

Howard then took a major step forward with *Splash* (1984) a Disney (Touchstone) movie that does much more than pander to a family audience. The film that made Tom Hanks (from TV's 'Bosom Buddies') a star resurrects the undervalued and underused mermaid theme some thirty years after Glynis Johns' *Miranda* (1948) sequel. Daryl Hannah accepts the mantle graciously, exuding just the right amount of vulnerability and naiveté as 'fish out of water' Madison (taking her name from the avenue). The love story construct is extremely persuasive and Howard sensibly casts the flippers aside for much of the film. However, the perfunctory support from John Candy and a timeworn evil government/scientist sub-plot impair what is otherwise a delightful and fanciful romantic comedy.

*Cocoon* (1985) – from the novel by David Saperstein – has no such handicaps restraining it, and sagaciously feeds off the age-old craving for eternal youth. Aliens Brian Dennehy and Tahnee Welch (daughter of Raquel) return to Earth after 10,000 years to retrieve their kin, left at the bottom of the ocean in large pods. Storing these in a private swimming pool, they inadvertently rejuvenate members of the nearby twilight community who've been sneaking in and utilising the facilities. Howard effectively cranks up the incertitude at the start (are these visitors friendly or not?), before alleviating the tension with humorous episodes and finally ending on a sentimental, almost Spielbergian, note. The entire cast is perfect, but it is the older actors who leave an indelible impression: Wilford Brimley, Don Ameche, and Jessica Tandy in particular.

This makes *Gung Ho*'s (1986) creative and relative box-office shortfall that much harder to comprehend. Perhaps the illogical, contradictory screenplay, which has Keaton returning to try and save an ailing car plant by begging the Japanese for aid, is to blame. Or maybe the fault lies with its stereotypical and racially indefensible portrayal of the oriental industrialists, reinforcing the myth that this is a nation of control freaks, efficient to the point of aberration (so much so that one executive tries to commit suicide after failing to increase production)? Surprisingly, the film can be quite funny when Keaton is in the frame, coming to terms with cultural differences. Yet the dictum appears to be that even though overseas money has saved the US firm, the interlopers should now emulate their way of life. A combination of topics handled with considerably more verve in Ridley Scott's *Black Rain* (1989) and Michael Moore's *Roger and Me* (1989).

*Willow* (1988), his next, denotes a transient frolic in the fantasy genre that bears more of its producer's stamp than Howard's. *Star Wars* meets 'Lord of the Rings' is how one critic phrased it, and this is possibly the most accurate way of describing George Lucas' fable about dwarves, fairies, trolls and the like. A baby princess with a great destiny must be protected from a wicked queen (shades of classical, or even biblical, storytelling) and only the diminutive Warwick Davis, working with renegade swordsman Val Kilmer, can accomplish this. The dialogue ranges from doltish and quasi-mystical, to interminably and intolerably exasperating, but there are some pleasing skirmishes, Indiana Jones-type stunts and Conan-style effects to even this out.

Subtle, yet percipient, self-effacing, yet forthright and candid, Howard's bittersweet *Parenthood* (1989) reads like a *Terms of Endearment* (1983) for those with offspring of all ages. An impassioned project, exquisitely-observed by Howard and his co-scripters, Ganz and Mandel (all parents themselves), it tracks several sets of interrelated families, sometimes delving into the most intimate aspects of their lives. Steve Martin shows that his compelling performance in *Roxanne* (1987) was far from a fluke, here acting as father to an eight-year-old son with emotional problems; Dianne Wiest is a single mother coping with her unpredictable teens; Harley Kozak has a high-flying husband, Rick Moranis, who is pushing their little girl too hard; and Tom Hulce is the prodigal son who returns owing money to some unsavoury types – while patriarch Jason Robards, the head of the family, looks on. A number of the hurdles this middle-class clan have to overcome are particular to the US, but many more are universal and Howard never permits the movie to dwindle into puerile soap bathos.

Family ties are also central to the plot of *Backdraft* (1991), in which William Baldwin follows his brother and late father (both Kurt Russell) into the fire brigade out of a fierce sense of loyalty. Inevitably, the spectacular pyrotechnic displays – painfully authentic and shot in an inspired manner – dominate. Ex-fireman Gregory Widen's script augments the realism, taking viewers behind the scenes at a station house or during an arson investigation. And the presence of legendary names such as Robert De Niro and Donald Sutherland (his finest performance as an eerily placid arsonist) only heighten *Backdraft*'s reputation.

*Far and Away* (1992) sent Howard in another new direction, helming the first big Hollywood period piece in some time and opening the floodgates for a host of imitators. Real-life couple Tom Cruise and Nicole Kidman enjoyed a rare stint filming together to fabricate this account of two Irish immigrants (one a tenant farmer, the other a land-owner's daughter) making their way in America at the close of the nineteenth century. Kidman's contumacious spirit mated with Cruise's raw masculinity (apparent in the bare-knuckle fighting sequences) is a formula for audience success. Alas, the story is sheer unadulterated romanticism, with very little substance or subtext.

*The Paper* (1994) followed, an exposé of life at a busy metropolitan newspaper in the *Broadcast News* (1987) vein; despite a mockumentary flavour, it nevertheless puts its trust in old-fashioned dramatics at times of crisis. Michael Keaton's third film for Howard, it relocates him to the offices of *The New York Sun* where he serves as Metro Editor under Glenn Close and Robert Duvall. The choleric shouting, rushing about and tense humour is fairly representative of the real thing and the main story of two black youths arrested for a double homicide is convincing enough to suspend disbelief. Yet the 'detective' work which constitutes its journalism, and the many coincidences littering David and Stephen Koepp's script, simply do not ring true.

At a time when public support for NASA's expensive space programme was practi-cally non-existent, the appropriately-named *Apollo 13* (1995) whipped up a nostalgic frenzy in the States and made more than $331 million at the box office worldwide. Taking the audience back to that fateful week in 1970 when James A. Lovell Jr uttered those chilling words: 'Houston, we have a problem', Howard spares no expense and cuts no corners in his depiction of what could so easily have been a calamitous incident. Filming was carried out in zero gravity, using a special 'plane diving' technique, Tom Hanks spent time with Lovell to round out his character, and every technical aspect was verified by experts. Howard's greatest feat, though, is in managing to transform a very serious blunder into a righteous advertisement for American bravery and determination without situating the events in any kind of historical or political context.

Visualised by the director as a kind of filmic investigative magazine article, *Ransom* (1996) keeps tabs on an inept kidnap gang holding the son of a wealthy airline mogul for $2 million. Howard refuses to sanitise the boy's ordeal, or that of his father (Mel Gibson) and mother (Rene Russo), but instead uses this situation to his advantage to purvey knife-edge anxiety. Gibson is true to form, and like Jack Nicholson, seems to be able to act in a berserk manner on cue. Yet his character is hardly the exemplar hero-dad (especially near the start), and is doubtful that anyone, even out of desperation, would gamble with their son's life as he does: offering the money as bounty on the kidnappers' heads? At its most basic, *Ransom* holds a magnifying glass up to people under pressure and does so without affectation.

In complete opposition, Howard's next film, *Ed-TV* (1999), introduces us to a man who volunteers for this kind of scrutiny. Matthew McConaughey is Ed the video store worker who puts himself forward to be filmed by a TV crew 24 hours a day. There are plenty of mandatory laughs, with good underpinning from Woody Harrelson as his brother, Liz Hurley as a wanton fame-seeker and Martin Landau as his step-father, plus a satisfying resolution where Ed turns the tables on those executives who are making money out of his 'ordeal'. Still, the movie has some prominent flaws. Ignoring comparisons with the similarly-themed Jim Carrey vehicle *The Truman Show* (1998) (in which the object of attention was voyeuristically filmed), *Ed-TV* is critical of the cult of docusoap personality, pointing the accusatory finger not only at television bosses, but also at the audience itself – surely one of the reasons why it fared so badly in American theatres. Crucial to remember is that Ed is a willing participant in the experiment, which gives his final complaints little credence.

Coincidentally, Howard found himself working next with Jim Carrey on an adaptation of Dr Seuss' Yuletide tale, *How the Grinch Stole Christmas* (2000). Written by Peter Seaman and Jeffrey Price, and with Academy Award-winning Rick Baker in charge of the make-up – which is very close to the book's illustrations – this proved a capable addition to Howard's catalogue. As one might expect, the narrative is thin; but there is still some attempt to explain the origins of the Grinch and why he detests Christmas so fiercely. Still, the overdrawn exposition at the beginning definitely detracts from its subsequently more exciting elements.

Perhaps the pinnacle of Howard's career thus far is his most recent film, *A Beautiful Mind* (2001), winner of Best Picture and Best Director at the 2002 Academy Awards. Russell Crowe stars in the true story of John Forbes Nash Jr, a maths genius who is diagnosed as a paranoid schizophrenic. Rather than exploiting this illness for emotional gain, the director concentrates on the struggle of the person inside – although at times the depiction of Nash's relationship with his wife (another Academy Award winner, Jennifer Connelly) does border on the mawkish. The disease's effects are externalised by allowing the audience to witness Nash's delusions and the final result is an intelligent and powerfully stirring antidote to the glut of more commercial movies on the market at the time of its release.

Howard's next film, due for release in 2003, will be based on the true story of the 1836 siege of Alamo by the Mexican army. **PB**

## George HUANG

George Huang completed the Producing Programme at the University of Southern California before going to Paramount to work as a reader for Howard Koch Jr., then on to Columbia to assist the executive vice-president Barry Josephson. Inspired by the success of independent director Robert Rodriguez, he left his job to write a screenplay drawing on his personal working experiences. Made on a $250,000 budget and with assistance from Josephson, *Swimming With Sharks* (1994) focuses on the acrimonious relationship between a naïve film school graduate and his egotistical studio boss. Sleek and confident in both tone and style, it suffers a little from its claustrophobic setting, some unnecessary repetition, and an overly dramatic ending. That said, it is a worthy addition to the category of cynical Hollywood-on-Hollywood films and a deserved winner of the Critic's Award at the Deauville Film Festival. Kevin Spacey delivers a fine performance as the relentlessly cruel and self-centred executive, as does Frank Whaley as the mistreated assistant who finally manages to turn the tables to his advantage.

Huang's subsequent film, *Trojan War* (1997), a satirical comedy about a man spending the night trying to find a condom, did not receive a wide release. He has since completed several projects for television, including *Live Through This* (2000) and *How to Make a Monster* (2001). **HP**

## Reginald HUDLIN

Born in 1962 in East St. Louis, Illinois, Reginald Hudlin has described his hometown as 'The Blackest City in America'. The birthplace of Miles Davis and Chuck Berry, Hudlin and his brother Warrington lived two doors down from Ike and Tina Turner. He remembers Tina vividly as the Acid Queen in *Tommy* (1975), a scene of early inspiration to him: 'I was a big fan of movies like *American Graffiti*, *Animal House* and *Risky Business*, and I wanted to make that kind of movie about my world'. He and his brother were among the first wave of groundbreaking black talent in Hollywood, making the wildly popular comedy *House Party* (1990). Warrington is also founder of the Black Film-makers Foundation, a distribution and exhibition company established to raise the profile of black film-makers; alumni include Spike Lee who received some financing for

*She's Gotta Have It* (1986). In addition to his features, Hudlin has directed for television – an episode of 'City of Angels' for example – and music videos such as Heavy D and the Boyz's 'Mr. Big Stuff' and George Clinton's 'Paint the White House Black'.

*House Party* was based on a short film of the same name that Hudlin made whilst an undergraduate at Harvard. It is the story of trouble-prone teenager, Kid (Christopher Reid), and his efforts to make it to and from, his best friend Play's party, despite being grounded by his father (Robin Harris). Lean on plot, *House Party* still has incredible momentum, led by infectious rap and dance numbers. Hudlin's energetic camera movements are influenced by the style of comic books and coloured with a fresh hip-hop vernacular. Some critics have argued that he whitewashes the events at the teenage house party; while it lacks critical edge, it is similarly free of moralising. Only an unfortunate homophobic rap near the conclusion mars the fun of the film; it was to be one of the most profitable movies of the 1990s and single-handedly established the genre of hip-hop teen films.

Hudlin's follow-up, the Eddie Murphy vehicle *Boomerang* (1992), has vestiges of *House Party*'s style, but little of its energy, although this did not affect its box-office receipts. The soundtrack, featuring Toni Braxton and Boyz II Men, was particularly popular. *Boomerang* earned $130 million worldwide and again extended a film genre through Hudlin's depiction of the black middle classes. Murphy plays a womaniser who must confront his own behaviour when his new boss (Robin Givens) treats him the way he treats women. Writer-producer Murphy is clearly the driving creative force here and the best moments come with short appearances by the many cast members from *House Party* – including Martin Lawrence, Tisha Campbell, John Witherspoon and Bebe Drake-Massey. The Hudlin brothers also appear as a pair of crooks.

The giddiness of *House Party* returned in *The Great White Hype* (1996), the story of a Don King-like boxing promoter (Samuel L. Jackson) and his plans to bring racial tension back to the world of boxing, finding a white former amateur boxer (Peter Berg) and convincing him to fight the heavyweight champion (Damon Wayans). The film has an energetic pace, weaving between several characters and their schemes and double-crosses. Written by Ron Shelton, who is familiar with sports-themed scripts, the satirical comedy in *The Great White Hype* is dark and sharp, and the racial themes are intelligently considered, despite their cartoonish representation. Hudlin directs Jackson in an appropriately exaggerated performance, and the quick, rap-driven editing is reminiscent of *House Party*. The film's soundtrack was the first release on Hudlin Bros. Record/IEpic Soundtrax and features The Wu Tang Clan and the pairing of Lou Rawls and rapper BIZ Markie.

Hudlin's next film, *The Ladies Man* (2000), was derived from the 'Saturday Night Live' sketch starring Tim Meadows as a libidinous swinger. Leon Phelps and his producer Julie are sacked from his radio show after one too many obscene comments. Unable to find work, he follows up an anonymous letter from a past lover promising him sex and money. Failing to track her down, he begins to settle down with Julie, but then realises that his mystery woman is the wife of the leader of a self-help group who have vowed to castrate Leo. As a sketch this worked quite well but in feature format it lacks consistent character development. 1970s sexual values by way of Austin Powers feel passé rather than retro. The film is most notable for an unusual non-issue-led sex scene involving a black and a white character.

Hudlin's latest offering, *Serving Sara* (2002), is a road movie that he describes as 'a romantic comedy in the *Midnight Run* vein'. It stars Matthew Perry as a New York process server and Liz Hurley as a woman who convinces him to deliver divorce papers to her husband in Texas.  **FG**

# Albert & Allen HUGHES

Whilst Albert Hughes claims that he and his film-making partner and twin Allen, born in Detroit in 1972, would not be making films without Brian De Palma's *Scarface* (1983), their career is more likely the product of the steady practice they received making films from the age of 12, when their mother bought them a camera.

*Menace II Society* (1993)
*Dead Presidents* (1995)
*American Pimp* (1999)
*From Hell* (2001)

Nonetheless De Palma's fast pace and reworking of gangster mythology is evident in the brothers' debut feature *Menace II Society* (1993). The film was in part a reaction to what the Hughes brothers felt was the Hollywood-style sentimentality that had undermined John Singleton's *Boyz N the Hood* (1991), one of the first of the post-Spike Lee black films. Rather than simply relying on an emotive rap soundtrack, the film deals with significant issues in poor black communities, such as 'dead-ending' – the phenomenon of young black men sacrificing themselves, or being sacrificed to, the gangster lifestyle. The film attempts to show the realities of black street life, following the self-destructive cycle of black-on-black violence. Using vérité-style camera work combined with expressionistic lighting, the film's visceral pseudo-documentary style helps to problematise a potentially simple story.

*Dead Presidents* (1995) was more ambitious in its breadth of storyline, covering the lives of a group of friends before, during, and after Vietnam, and the first big-budget film to make the lead veterans all black. The final quarter shows how they utilise their war skills to plan and execute a bank heist and the camera is used to express the emotions and anxieties of the characters, with shaky hand-held mobility and the use of extreme close-ups to heighten tension. Although vaster in scope than *Menace II Society*, *Dead Presidents* also demonstrates that violent actions have their consequences, and here the Hughes brothers show an interest in investigating black ghetto life rather than simply presenting it.

Since then the brothers have transferred their interest in black representation and social context into documentary film-making. *American Pimp* (1999) juxtaposes footage from a range of 1970s blaxploitation films with interviews with the African-American men of the title, to reflect upon the working lives of the pimps and the relationship to black cinematic representations. Free from the enormous technical tasks of *Dead Presidents*, this film uses mainly available light – from tacky neon to table lamps – to attempt a de-glamourisation of the subject.

Their latest work, *From Hell* (2001), moves away from their usual territory to take Jack the Ripper as its subject. Starring Johnny Depp (with a passable Cockney accent) and Heather Graham as prostitute Mary Kelly, the film attempts to add something extra to this oft-told tale, re-figuring the story as a whodunnit by casting Depp's drug-using Inspector Abbeline and his sidekick (Robbie Coltrane) in pursuit of the killer, and proposing an answer to the mystery of the Ripper's identity. The view of Victorian London's Whitechapel that the Hughes brothers provide is a little cliché-ridden in its depiction of cobbled streets, black-toothed pimps and prostitutes straight from Central Casting – something of a waste of the talents of Lesley Sharp and Katrin Cartlidge – but the details and smaller moments are beautifully imagined. The murders, for example, and Abberline's hallucinogenic experiences, are filmed with a visual style that dreamily evokes the darkness and terror of the period. Post-*Se7en* (1995) scratches and light flares are moulded to the directors' own style and the look of these scenes adds to the darkening atmosphere. There are attempts to link the fate of the prostitutes to the sanctioned abuse of women for medical advancements but this is inconsistent and exists more to reinforce the whodunnit plot than offer a social discourse. Furthermore, although the brothers depict Victorian England's class system with some degree of outsider authenticity, there are some classic Hollywood moments – the explosion of a barrel of gunpowder and a coach and horses chase. The love story component is also forced but the visual ambiguity of the resolution of Mary Kelly's story, coupled with Abberline's fate, ultimately rescues the movie from sentimentality.

For some time the Hughes brothers have nursed a pet project – a biopic of Jimi Hendrix – which would restore them to more familiar ground but, typically, it is a subject they will only tackle if they can tell the whole story, not one sanctioned by the Hendrix estate.                                                                                            **JD**

# Bronwen HUGHES

*Harriet the Spy* (1996)
*Forces of Nature* (1999) Bronwen Hughes directed television documentaries including 'Machu Picchu: The Search for Lost Worlds' and 'Elvis: Airborne', as well as segments of the show 'Kids in the Hall' before turning to the cinema. With her debut, *Harriet the Spy* (1996), a film based on Louise Fitzhugh's bestselling book, which won the New York Outstanding Book Award in 1964, Hughes updated the original story to take place in contemporary America. It features a winningly mischievous Michelle Trachtenberg as Harriet, a young girl with ambitions to be a writer who, on the advice of her eccentric nanny, Golly (played with verve by Rosie O'Donnell), practices by making daily observations about the people

around her in her diary. Without being heavy-handed Bronwen uses the story to draw out moral issues involving the nature of friendship and unconsidered action – when her school friends find the diary they turn the tables on her, making her realise how it feels to be the object of unwanted attention. With enough fast-cutting to hold the attention of the MTV generation, it is considerably more interesting than the usual children's fare – mixing just the right blend of humour and realism – and is suitably engaging for adults.

Having opted for a more fittingly colourful and sumptuous visual style in *Harriet the Spy*, with her next film, *Forces of Nature* (1999), Hughes created the visual aspect to act as another character in the piece – Mother Nature. Using slow-motion sequences of hail storms and hurricanes, she mirrors the chaos wreaked on unimaginative blurb-writer Ben (Ben Affleck) when he unexpectedly encounters the free-spirited, rule-breaking Sarah (Sandra Bullock) on the way to his wedding. Forced to travel together from New York to Savannah, they encounter a variety of hurdles and near disasters, all the while becoming more and more attracted to one another. Eschewing the usual romantic-comedy conventions, however, Hughes bravely chooses the non-mainstream ending, having Ben return to his future wife and Sarah find the child she abandoned as a teenager. As an interesting variation of the screwball-comedy and an atmospheric spectacle, the film did undeservedly bad business at the box office, probably because Sandra Bullock did not, as expected, become romantically fulfilled. Nevertheless, with two such competent, varied, and distinctive films behind her, Bronwen Hughes should hopefully be offering more of the same in the not too distant future.          **HP**

# John HUGHES

John Hughes was born in Mississippi in 1950 and briefly attended the University of Arizona then, after trying his hand as an advertising copywriter, novelist, and joke writer, he joined the staff of National Lampoon. Prolific and successful as a writer and producer, he has written all the movies he has directed, and since *The Breakfast Club* (1985), he has produced all the movies he has directed.

*Sixteen Candles* (1984) mismatches teen comedy-drama with the low, broad humour of National Lampoon. Among the movie's strengths are its depiction of the good-hearted chaos of white suburban bourgeois life, and the petty cruelties of sibling rivalry. If its perception of teen anxieties and adolescent male behaviour is clichéd, it is nonetheless sympathetic. Hughes has a good eye for detail, from the set-dressing to the soundtrack: the sparing use of older pop music on a contemporary pop soundtrack plays an important part in establishing the reactionary moral universe of his movies. However rebellious his teen protagonists might seem, they tend to aspire to conformity, and that condition is here normalised through the evocation of an imaginary post-war era of plenty and stability. Romantic fulfilment and a sense of belonging are modulated through nostalgia, and contemporary teen behaviour is perceived as a form of immaturity from which the various couples will emerge into the idealised teen behaviour of the 1950s. *Sixteen Candles* also establishes the ground rules of Hughes' moral universe: children can express consumer desire, but their parents cannot; the self-obsession of others is always a fault, but one's own is always justified; the institutions of romantic love (wedding ceremonies, family relationships) can be mocked, but not romantic love itself; and, of course, non-white people do not really exist. *Sixteen Candles* is unique among Hughes' movies in devoting screen-time to a non-white character, the exchange-student Long Duk Dong (Cedde Watanabe). This portrayal is important in that the extra-diegetic gong accompanying his every appearance, punchline and pratfall establishes that Hughes is not just depicting the racist attitudes of a privileged white world, but exhibiting them himself.

Hughes' two 1985 movies separate the mismatched elements of *Sixteen Candles*. *Weird Science*, in which two geeky misfits make themselves an ideal woman, returns to Hughes' National Lampoon roots. Many critics dismissed it as a puerile, misogynistic comedy about adolescent male desire, but what they overlooked was the fact that the desire in question is not primarily sexual – Hughes is too prudish for that, as are his protagonists. Rather, it is the desire to fit in. The first step in the protagonists' education is a trip to a bar, where they learn to hang out with stereotyped middle-aged African-American men – significantly, Gary (Anthony Michael Hall) achieves this by a poor imitation of how he imagines them to talk and behave. The lesson of this seems to be that if they can fit in with people so very different from themselves, then they can fit in at high school.

In *The Breakfast Club*, Hughes' theme of unlikely friendships comes to the fore and receives its most mature treatment. Five teens – stereotyped as a brain, an athlete, a basket-case, a princess, and a criminal – meet during a Saturday detention, and gradually understanding of each other emerges. Hughes' direction matches this trajectory, with the preponderance of long- and medium-shots early on giving way to more close-ups and two-shots. Unusually for Hughes, differences of social class are allowed to appear (albeit modulated through subcultural markers), but the reasons for difference are attributed to parental distortion of their children. Although the movie suggests that salvation is to be found in freeing the self and each other from this influence, it is significant that the basket-case must be made-over by the princess before the athlete will kiss her, and that the potential relationship between the princess and the criminal is seen as a move in her family's power games. The movie closes as the rich kids are driven home by their parents and the poor kids (both of whom have received a token or trophy) walk home; the lyrics of Simple Minds' 'Don't You Forget About Me' implies that their separation from each other, however regrettable, is final, and that not even romantic love can overcome class difference.

The most benign version of Hughes' universe is found in *Ferris Bueller's Day Off* (1986), the best of his teen comedies. All problems are internal and can be cured: vindictive elders learn better, sibling enmity is overcome, and healing is promised. It is a world without consequences unless you (or your children) decide that your actions should have consequences. The only non-whites to appear are a car thief and a group of African-Americans who spontaneously burst into a choreographed dance routine. The soliloquies and to-camera address occasionally used in earlier movies here become a more significant means of insinuating the viewer into the milieu and viewpoint of the protagonist, winningly played by Matthew Broderick (Hughes has elicited a number of good performances from his young casts, notably Kevin Bacon, Anthony Michael Hall, Elizabeth McGovern, Bill Paxton, Molly Ringwald, Alan Ruck, and Ally Sheedy).

Hughes' inability to understand his characters beyond surface appearances – hence the lack of ideas about what the characters should do between the set-up and dénouement of *Sixteen Candles*, *Weird Science* and *Ferris Bueller's Day Off* – plays a significant part in the failure of *Planes, Trains, & Automobiles*, a blend of *It Happened One Night* (1934) and *The Odd Couple* (1968), starring a lacklustre Steve Martin and a constrained John Candy. *She's Having a Baby* (1988) – a comedy-drama about a young couple becoming parents – seems to recognise this weakness, and attempts to displace this lack of understanding through fantasy sequences and other gimmicks. A more satisfactory solution is achieved in *Uncle Buck* (1989), in which John Candy's persona expands to fill his character – he performs fairly orthodox comic material with a skill rarely sufficiently acknowledged and conveys discomfort with unexpected subtlety. Hughes' most sophisticated movie in visual terms, it – like *Weird Science* – reworks the classic horror movie structure in comic terms so as to celebrate the return of repression.

Of *Curly Sue* (1991), Leonard Maltin sagely observes that 'if there's such a thing as "quintessential James Belushi" this is it'. The film is leaden, formulaic, and pleased nobody, with no sign of the deftness that characterises the director's better work. **MB**

# Bonnie HUNT

*Return to Me* (2000)   Bonnie Hunt, born in Chicago in 1954, a one-time aspiring comic, former cancer ward nurse and character actress better known for her supporting turns in such films as *Jerry Maguire* (1996) and *The Green Mile* (1999), adds writer-director to her list of credentials with *Return to Me* (2000). The film is a comic tear-jerker, guided by the forces of fate and destiny, in which widowed architect Bob (David Duchovny) meets and romances shy waitress Gracie (Minnie Driver), unaware that she received his late wife's heart in a life-saving transplant. While Hunt's movie is unquestionably the work of a first-time director, she nevertheless manages to bring a likeably unvarnished, improvisational feel to her gently contrived script, co-written with Don Lake.

Hunt begins ambitiously, with a unbroken helicopter shot that takes in all of Chicago, then gracefully descends through the clouds to find Bob standing atop a building he has constructed. The shot is echoed later when it floats down to Gracie following her operation, thereby linking the two characters and suggesting a theme of heavenly intervention. Indeed, Catholic imagery abounds in *Return to Me*. Gracie's grandfather prays for her recovery in the hospital chapel, she is later set up on a blind date with an ex-priest, and a trio of nuns serve as a catalyst to bring Bob and Gracie together at the film's end. Elsewhere, *Return to Me*'s style is resolutely old-fashioned, from Hunt's reliance on standards by Frank Sinatra and Dean Martin, to her use of overlapping dialogue and lap dissolves between scenes that quietly evoke the films of the 1930s and 1940s.

Hunt has planned to co-write and direct her next film, Anniversary, a comedy about a separated couple that reunite to attend the anniversary of the man's parent.          **CS**

## Anjelica HUSTON

Award-winning actress Anjelica Huston is probably best known for being the daughter of Irish-American director John Huston, and for her long-lasting and much publicised relationship with Jack Nicholson. Born in Los Angeles in 1952, Huston turned to direction in her late forties, with a debut feature, *Bastard Out of Carolina* (1996). The critically acclaimed film deals with the highly controversial issue of child abuse. Based on the autobiographical best-selling novel by Dorothy Allison, it manages to convey the bleak and traumatic life of Bone, in Greenville County, South Carolina, in the early 1950s. Torn between her mother's blind affection for her brutal husband and his emotional, physical, and sexual abuse, Bone eventually has to find her path in life. This difficult tale of poverty and rape slightly suffers from its televisual concept, which hardly fits the violent topic.

*Bastard Out of Carolina* (1996)
*Agnes Browne* (1999)

Huston's most recent effort, *Agnes Browne* (1999), is a more light-hearted treatment of a family drama about people struggling with poverty, but the importance of the mother-children bond and the villain – Mr Billy, played by a type-cast Ray Winstone – are common elements in both films. Another literary adaptation (from actor Brendan O'Carroll's novel 'The Mammy'), the film is somehow less passionate and convincing than *Bastard Out of Carolina*. In a nostalgic look at stereotypical representations of Ireland, the feature is pervaded with a never-ending humour, which often borders on farce, and an overly emphatic sentimentality. Although the generally light-hearted mood of the film owes a lot to its literary source, playing alongside a long-standing tradition of witty, working-class Dubliners, its style is not particularly impressive.          **BP**

## Peter HYAMS

Peter Hyams is an action and science fiction director whose skills have also extended to those of the cinematographer's trade. Technically and visually outstanding, his films are sometimes criticised for being emotionally barren – possibly because of his earlier career and his renowned impartiality. Born in New York in 1943, educated at Hunter College and Syracuse University, Hyams was a television newsman before he became a director. His first pieces were television movies, written and filmed by himself – a practice he liked to repeat after moving into features proper in the mid-1970s.

*Busting* (1974)
*Our Time* (1974)
*Peeper* (1975)
*Capricorn One* (1978)
*Hanover Street* (1979)
*Outland* (1981)
*The Star Chamber* (1983)
*2010* (1984)
*Running Scared* (1986)
*The Presidio* (1988)
*Narrow Margin* (1990)
*Stay Tuned* (1992)
*Timecop* (1994)
*Sudden Death* (1995)
*The Relic* (1997)
*End of Days* (1999)
*The Musketeer* (2001)

In *Busting* (1974) Hyams used what he had learnt covering crime stories on TV, exhibiting his eye for detail and a streetwise sense of humour. Elliott Gould and Robert Blake, in their last major roles for some time, are scruffy undercover vice squad detectives on the trail of crime lord Allen Garfield. Tough action and furious car chases, including one gallop around a supermarket, play out against an abrasive cityscape of backstreets and littered alleyways (in many ways the inspiration for numerous TV cop shows to come). But the intervening parts of the narrative are equally as entertaining thanks to the rapport of the two male leads.

For *Our Time* (1974), his next film, Hyams foolishly abandoned this grittiness in favour of a nostalgic soap structure, adhering to the screenplay of cinema first-timer Jane C Stanton. Supposedly based on her own student days, this reviews life at a girls school in the 1950s and their relationships with members of the opposite sex. Yet there is no sense of actuality, of authentic recollections; rather this is a hotchpotch of clichés from other teen dramas – national popular memory of the worst kind. Bland, shallow and unsuited to Hyams' style, it marked the first in a two-picture trough for the director. The second low was *Peeper* (1975), originally called 'Fat Chance' and shelved for a year before premiering. Simultaneously mimicking and spoofing private eye films of the 1940s, this starts with a Bogart voice-over and never fully recovers; Michael Caine is an odd choice of gumshoe, who is hired to find Michael Constantine's missing daughter. Conceptually the film is keen, but at a little over 85 minutes it is still too long for comfort.

Luckily, Hyams regained his edge in time to make *Capricorn One* (1978), a science fiction picture with a difference in which the fiction is perpetuated by the US government. Still milking the backlash over Watergate several years later, it proffers a possible faked mission to Mars carrying three astronauts: James Brolin, Sam Waterston and O. J. Simpson. However, the general public is so convincingly deceived by televised reports from the red planet's surface (actually a studio set) that when the dummy shuttle crashes the spacemen must be killed as well. Uncovering the conspiracy is reporter Elliott Gould, whose scenes with Telly Savalas' crop duster near the end are pure gold. An attractive premise handled with considerable aplomb, this is one of the most underrated exercises in shadow state paranoia of the 1970s.

In *Hanover Street* (1979), Hyams applies himself to passionate melodrama but totally miscues. A love story set in the 1940s involving American pilot Harrison Ford and British nurse Lesley-Anne Down only ever reaches its zenith during the war scenes which are designed to be a backdrop for their affair. Indeed, the final few reels where the action elbows its way to the forefront seem jarringly out of place in such a romantic movie.

Hyams is much better helming tight, suspenseful films such as *Outland* (1981), a remake of *High Noon* (1952) which shunts the story into the future and sets it on Jupiter's third moon, Io. The underdeveloped characters are an irritation but the actors endow their parts with individual charisma, especially Sean Connery as the marshal who refuses to turn a blind eye to corruption at the mining colony, and Frances Sternhagen as the doctor who helps him fend off professional hit men. The ingenious ending and restrained effects distance *Outland* from the flurry of laser-blaser pictures which proliferated in the wake of *Star Wars* (1977).

Though *The Star Chamber* (1983) sounds like just such a film, it actually proved to be a timely critique of law courts which are tipped in the criminal's favour. Michael Douglas is an upstanding young judge who finds himself confronted with a vigilante group of his peers, seizing those who've fallen through the cracks in the legal system and treating them to their own particular brand of justice. The thought-provoking script by Hyams and Roderick Taylor locks horns with this issue, and with ample conviction. Yet this is such a weighty and complex socio-political problem it can never fully be explored in under two hours, nor satisfactorily resolved.

The director's next assignment, a sequel to Stanley Kubrick's enigmatic science fiction masterpiece *2001: A Space Odyssey* (1968), was infinitely more daunting. Hyams' first outing as cinematographer and director, *2010* (1984), also comes from a story by Arthur C. Clarke, but this is where the affinity ends. The movie is dragged down by its pessimistic Cold War machinations, evacuating the lyrical and mesmerising flow of *2001* to make way for a recognisable starscape of angular, bulky spacecraft and feuding, territorial governments on the brink of war. In terms of lighting and costume design, certain scenes are even interchangeable with some of those in *Outland*. That said, Roy Scheider is as professional as ever, investigating why the HAL 9000 computer went insane. The sections where Keir Dullea's astronaut, Bowman, comes back from the 'other side' are uncannily eerie, and viewers are at last given a hint as to what those enigmatic alien monoliths really are, thus ending years of speculation and initiating many years more.

Hyams came full circle with *Running Scared* (1986), which is comparable to *Busting* and features comic Billy Crystal and dancer Gregory Hines as cops in pursuit of a Spanish drugs baron, played by future 'NYPD: Blue' star Jimmy Smits. All the obligatory elements are present: shoot-outs, car chases, banter between the two stars and a big finale in the Illinois State Building. Yet there is an unfortunate air of detachment, a lack of humanity and emotion that should ideally be at the hub of a movie such as this.

Hyams toned the action down for *The Presidio* (1988) which contains only three significant sequences that climax in a gunfight at a water bottling plant. This allows Hyams to concentrate more on characterisation and the murder mystery kernel of the narrative. Sean Connery works wonders once more, as an army Marshall whose inquiry into a death on the Presidio base brings him into conflict with the San Francisco police department – represented by Mark Harmon, formerly a disgruntled soldier serving under him. The complication of wilful daughter Meg Ryan falling for Harmon initiates a fiery three-way contention, but the plot inevitability reconciles the two principals.

Hyam's remake of RKO's 1952 money-spinner (which made back a 100 times its budget), *Narrow Margin* (1990), is in some ways superior to its forefather, assisted by incredibly realistic stuntwork which places Gene Hackman's unflappable cop and Anne Archer's murder witness atop a speeding train six whole years before De Palma's *Mission Impossible*. The straightforward story can be preposterous on occasion, but Hyams draws so much inspiration from the Richard Fleischer film he cannot possibly go wrong. It is also refreshing to see a movie where the guardian and charge do not fall hopelessly in love by the end credits.

Reconfiguring the *Tron* (1982) idea, but with television not computers, *Stay Tuned* (1992) strains to be a satirical black comedy told from a non-existent moral high ground. Parents John Ritter and Pam Dawber are plucked from the real world to go on a tour of 'Hellvision' – tumbling into one dire show after the other. The basic objective is reasonable enough and the parodies (trailers for upcoming features include *Three Men and Rosemary's Baby*, *Autopsies of the Rich and Famous* and *Duane's Underworld*), well thought-out. But television actors Ritter and Dawber seem uneasy ridiculing the medium that furnished them both with profitable careers, and it is unclear as to whether writers Tom S. Parker, Jim Jennewein and Richard Siegel want viewers to watch less TV or more. Regardless of this, there is a rare cartoon interlude by Warner Bros. supremo Chuck Jones, which is not to be missed.

*Timecop* (1994) heralded the start of Hyams' brief Jean-Claude Van Damme period, skilfully knitting together a perplexing time-travel episode from a Manga-style comic strip. Working on the assumption that journeying back through time is now possible, the movie also – quite logically – assumes that this technology will be perverted and used for nefarious activities (such as funding unscrupulous senator Ron Silver's campaigns). Van Damme therefore polices the time stream to prevent such acts. The circular script has more discrepancies and paradoxes than is necessary, plus some unwarranted sex which devalues Van Damme's almost spiritual love for his late wife. His decision to tinker with the conventions of action/sci-fi cinema and use the martial art tricks more sparingly certainly pays off, as it does again in *Sudden Death* (1995) because Van Damme's role – a fire marshal at Pittsburgh's enormous Civic Arena – could easily have been filled by any of the major action stars of the day. A *Die Hard* (1988) replica, it is Hyams' direction and Steven Kemper's editing that are the real heroes, taking the audience on the cinematic equivalent of a bobsleigh ride, with Van Damme battling against an ice hockey clock to save his children and defeat a group of less than memorable terrorists.

Fortunately the same cannot be said of Kothoga, Stan Winston's choice monster from *The Relic* (1997). Transporting a minacious and ancient Aztec beast to Chicago's Musuem of Natural History provides the most invigorating creature feature since John Carpenter's *The Thing* (1982) or David Cronenberg's *The Fly* (1986). As superstitious, hard-bitten cop and evolutionary biologist respectively, Tom Sizemore and Penelope Ann Miller are Hyams' most curious pairing yet, reacting in true 'X-Files' fashion to the threat. The more time-honoured shocks are not forgotten, aided by umbrageous lighting and claustrophobic sets. And like the shark in *Jaws* (1975), Hyams keeps the look of Kothoga secret for as long as is realistically possible; though when it does finally appear, it is far from disappointing, an indefatigable mix of VIFX computer animation and animatronics. In essence, *The Relic* is a meritorious adaptation of Douglas Preston and Lincoln Child's bestseller, which even finds a part for veteran monster hunter James Whitmore (of *Them!* (1954) fame).

Hyams persevered with horror for *End of Days* (1999) – Arnold Schwarzenegger's post-heart operation comeback. Re-jigging the *Omen* (1976) formula and interpolating some ferocious action, it posits the notion that the Devil will return just before the millennium to impregnate his chosen bride, thus fulfilling the title's conclusive prediction. Here we see a more fatalistic and downbeat version of the Arnie persona: suicidal, mourning the loss of his family and losing a fight to matronly Miriam Margoyles. But this aside, the film is just as predictable as his other vehicles, with only Gabriel Byrne's seductive Lucifer giving an honourable turn; disparaging twists such as naming the bride

Christine York (Robin Tunney) to symbolise Christ-in-New-York are merely pejorative. In addition the 'faith' ending had to be re-shot when Church leaders complained about Arnold dispatching Satan with man-made weaponry, hence the conflicting message this film advances.

Hyams' most recent project, *The Musketeer* (2001), is a Gene Quintano scripted action drama, starring Justin Chambers as D'Artagnan – the film's central character. Quite possibly the worst ever adaptation of Dumas' legendary story, this seeks to add an inappropriate oriental twist to the swashbuckling, and Hyams' cinematography leaves a great deal to be desired throughout.

He is currently working on *A Sound of Thunder*, which is based on a story by Ray Bradbury and focuses again on the possibilities and perils of time travel.          **PB**

# ICE CUBE

Ice Cube (born O'Shea Jackson) is a true entertainer covering a widening range of media forms. He began as a member of the seminal hip-hop outfit Niggaz With Attitude, leaving to undertake a successful solo career with a spate of huge-selling records before turning his hand to acting, writing and, finally, directing.

Born in Los Angeles in 1969, Ice Cube was educated at the Phoenix Institute of Technology before taking to the music world. He directed music videos for a number of artists including Cypress Hill, Color Me Badd, and Prince, before directing his first full feature, *The Player's Club* (1998). The film is clearly inspired by not only 1970s blaxploitation cinema but also the revived form, which Ice Cube was so much a part of, playing a central acting role in John Singleton's *Boyz N the Hood* (1991). In *The Player's Club* an all-black cast is directed, with the aim of dealing with cultural themes. Ice Cube avoids pointing the finger and instead shows a world with increasingly corrupt power structures at all levels. This first feature takes on several aspects of its predecessors in its styling, yet Ice Cube interestingly chooses to take the perspective of a female lead. The portrayal of the gender divide shows almost all of the male characters in an array of stereotyped, seemingly villainous roles (including Ice Cube himself). The strength of this directorial debut is arguably the taut oral accompaniment to the visuals. With heavy rap blaring through the sequences in the club, Ice Cube succeeds in illustrating a world fuelled and possessed by its own culture.                                    **SS**

# Mark ILLSLEY

Mark Illsley has made a considerable impression with his debut feature, the comedy *Happy Texas* (1999). Born in California in 1957, he attended the USC School of Cinema and Television and worked in different capacities on a number of different projects. The most high-profile of these was as assistant director on *Robin Hood: Prince of Thieves* (1991), the weak, big-budget Kevin Costner vehicle.

*Happy Texas* is an affectionate comedy about two convicts (the bizarrely cast Jeremy Northam and an impressive Steve Zahn) who escape from a chain gang. Hijacking a van belonging to two beauty pageant choreographers, they end up in the titular Texas town and the misunderstandings pile up. Chief amongst these is the way the fugitives, playing the role of gay pageant organisers, have to plan the town festivities while Northam also tries simultaneously to woo the town beauty (Ally Walker), compassionately rejecting the advances of a lonely closeted gay cop (the estimable William H. Macy). This is gentle and amiable stuff set in a Texas where homophobia seems to be non-existent. Illsley, who also co-wrote the screenplay, has a great cast including Ron Perlman, Illeana Douglas and Zahn (fresh from an impressive turn as a stoner in Steven Soderbergh's *Out of Sight* (1998). Fittingly, Zahn won an acting award at the Sundance Festival for *Happy Texas.* Although a little too sweet on occasion, with only Macy's performance hinting at the loneliness and repression that can exist in the rural South, Illsley's film is amusing and absorbing.

His recently completed picture *Bookies*, another comedy, has yet to be distributed. **IC**

# John IRVIN

Born in Newcastle-upon-Tyne, UK, in 1940, John Irvin served as a documentary cameraman in the Vietnam war, and his directorial career began in television in the 1970s, including such prestigious productions as Granada's 1977 adaptation of Dickens' 'Hard Times' and the BBC adaptation of the John Le Carré book 'Tinker, Tailor, Soldier, Spy', in 1980.

Irvin's first four movies were literary adaptations, although from very different sources. *The Dogs of War* (1980), from Frederick Forsyth's bestseller, fails to successfully transform the structure of the novel, resulting in a number of curtailed movements and episodic stretches. The climactic assault offers welcome release after lengthy procedurals which, although not sufficiently detailed to grip, remain interesting. Despite his trademark tics and mannerisms, Christopher Walken is quite effective as the mercenary with a heart of gold. Jack Cardiff's cinematography is an advantage, but the score is not.

*Ghost Story* (1981) follows the plot of Peter Straub's novel but, having excised its detail and resonances, fails to replicate its haunting atmosphere. Key scenes are abandoned, losing the organic logic of the novel. Laboured 'shock' moments and clichéd flashback sequences further detract from its already modest suspense. The cast, which includes Melvyn Douglas, John Houseman, Douglas Fairbanks Jr., and Fred Astaire, struggles against weak dialogue and unimaginative visuals. *Champions* (1983), adapted from jockey Bob Champion's autobiography, recounts his fight against cancer, driven by the desire not only to survive but also to ride Aldaniti in the Grand National. This potentially intriguing study of a man in adversity is reduced to a rather undignified tear-jerker; on that level it succeeds, courtesy of the conviction of John Hurt's central performance and the strong cast that supports him.

*Turtle Diary* (1985), adapted by Harold Pinter from Russell Hoban's novel, again takes little more than the plot from its source but not without good reason. Hoban gives alternating chapters to his protagonists, following the richly patterned and deeply textured free associations of their thoughts and fantasies as they live their quietly desperate lives. Pinter's dialogue – humorous, precise, effective – is in sharp contrast, and his attempts to retain some of the mystery and magic of the tale are undermined by Irvin's unsympathetic and leaden direction. Well-played by another good cast, it is the gentlest of satires on empty middle-class suburban life, and a feeble expression of environmental concerns.

Irvin changed tack again with the crude and humourless *Raw Deal* (1986), arguably the weakest and most reactionary of Schwarzenegger's action movies. Very basic in what it offers, it wastes no time delivering the goods but then bogs down in half-hearted attempts to intersperse narrative complication between fairly unremarkable set-pieces, culminating in a bloody, disorganised, ludicrous climax. A risible coda follows. *Hamburger Hill* (1987), from a screenplay by Vietnam veteran John Carabatsos, follows the 101st Airborne Division as they repeatedly try to take Hill 937 in the Ashau Valley. Intended as a tribute, it makes no mention of the fact that they were ordered to withdraw a few days later, or of the $10,000 bounty US troops put on the head of the Colonel who ordered the attacks, or of the several attempts made on his life. The movie also suffers from heavy-handed ironies, Philip Glass' intrusive score, and a cast of mostly bland young actors who remain fairly indistinguishable. Bizarrely, despite the film's liberal war-is-hell credentials, it nonetheless perpetuates the myth that it was the Vietnamese, not the Americans, who invaded Vietnam.

The revenge-thriller *Next of Kin* (1989) brings Appalachian backwoodsmen into conflict with the Chicago Mafia, lumbering to its predictable climax with unconscionable sloth. Drawn in broad strokes, its attempts to consider the ethics of feuding, revenge and justice are banal and ultimately meaningless. A good cast and score are poorly served by ponderous direction. *Eminent Domain* (1991), a Canadian/Israeli/French co-production shot in Warsaw and Gdansk, is purportedly based on real experiences and events that occurred in Poland before 1979. It tells of Josef Burski, number six in the Politburo hierarchy, who wakes one morning to discover he has been removed from office without any explanation. Opening with an unsubtle depiction of casual corruption and the personal compromises and accommodations made by officials in order to obtain a secure position, it fails to transform into either Kafkaesque parable or a thriller – it lacks the wit and urgency of the former and the suspense of the latter. Shot with a palette as murky as the intrigue it depicts, it recalls something of the seediness and boy's-club-gone-wrong atmosphere of 'Tinker, Tailor, Soldier, Spy', but it is not half as gripping.

*Widow's Peak* (1994) represents another change of direction for Irvin. A period piece set in 1920s Ireland, it veers unevenly from gentle comedy to overblown farce to straight drama. This crisis of confidence, along with the implausible dénouement, leaves the significance of the whole in question. *A Month by the Lake* (1995), based on H. E. Bates' novella, is similarly uncertain as to what it is trying to achieve. Noisy early scenes, in which incident piles on incident, and the frenetic and quirky characterisations, seem at odds with the gentle humour of this tangentially-told period romance. What it lacks in atmosphere and subtlety is compensated for by Pasqualino De Santis' beautiful cinematography.

Irvin returned to action cinema with the post-Tarantino thriller *City of Industry* (1997), a minimalist genre movie that could have been stripped down even further. A stylish black-and-white title sequence gives way to an attractive palette (principally greens and browns), and unfamiliar locations evoke a Los Angeles different from that usually seen in movies. Once again, it suffers from an unnecessary coda and an ill-judged score. With *Shiner* (2001), Irvin returns to Britain with a sleazy mockney thriller about an illegal boxing racket. Replete with echoes of *The Long Good Friday* (1979) and *Carlito's Way* (1993), and full of faces familiar from British television, it is a rather gloomy and unpleasant little film. Fans of Michael Caine might derive some pleasure from his performance, but it is rather weak when compared to those of Martin Landau and Kenneth Cranham. *The Fourth Angel* (2001) is a dull and ludicrous action-thriller in which a magazine editor, played by Jeremy Irons, tracks down the terrorists responsible for the plane hijacking in which his wife and daughters were killed. As Catharine Tunnacliffe observed, 'This is a film that tries to be about the futility of vengeance, but makes better points about the futility of the British trying to make American-style thrillers'.                                                                 **MB**

# Robert ISCOVE

Robert Iscove has been working in television for nearly twenty years, making an array of television films, including *The Little Mermaid* (1984), *Terror on Track 9* (1992) and, more recently, Rodgers and Hammerstein's *Cinderella* (1997). He has also contributed to series such as 'Alfred Hitchcock Presents', 'Miami Vice', and 'Star Trek: The Next Generation'. With his first film produced for cinema he jumped on the late 1990s teen bandwagon to produce *She's All That* (1999), a modern-day variation of George Bernard Shaw's 'Pygmalion'. The narrative is straightforward and predictable: Zach (Freddie Prinze Jr.), the most popular guy in school, takes on a bet to transform dowdy outcast Laney into a woman fit to become the prom queen in just six weeks. She blossoms, he falls in love with her, she discovers the ruse and hates him. They finally end up together. Much of the scenario treads old John Hughes ground – the fact that Laney's from the wrong side of the tracks and her dad's a pool man is reminiscent of a similar situation in *Pretty in Pink* (1986) – and really says nothing new. That said, stylistically, Iscove wisely goes for excess, making good use of high productions values and Fatboy Slim's hip soundtrack. He also exercises a knowing, if faintly nasty, sense of humour, which keeps the audience constantly engaged.

Another romantic comedy, *Boys and Girls* (2000) treads much the same ground and also stars Freddie Prinze Jr, this time alongside Claire Forlani. A case of opposites attract, Prinze's Ryan and Forlani's Jennifer forge an uneasy friendship and begin to rely on one another, particularly during relationship crises. Deftly directed, the end may be inevitable but it's certainly fun to watch the process. **HP**

# James IVORY

James Ivory is the undisputed master of contemporary heritage cinema. Despite his all-American origins and his early interest in India and the cultural clash between the East and British culture, Ivory is best known for his literary adaptations of the 1980s and 1990s, which are now regarded as the canonical examples of British costume drama. Sometimes accused of letting the dazzling visuals of setting and costume prevail over the psychological and emotional interplay of characters, Ivory has in fact managed to draw powerful and award-winning performances from his actors (often stage-trained), only enhanced by the immaculate and detailed backdrop of interiors. Although one is led to wonder if Ivory's films would have been the same without long-lasting partners producer Ismail Merchant and screenwriter Ruth Prawer Jhabvala, there is no doubt about the coherence of his oeuvre.

Throughout his productions, from the very beginning of *The Householder* (1963) to the Cannes-promoted *The Golden Bowl* (2000), Ivory has always been a painter of manners and social conventions, portraying individuals forced to choose between clashing cultures, ideologies or classes. His films often have an episodic quality, sometimes overtly following the tableaux structure (as in *A Room with a View* (1986)) and culminating in party or dance sequences. When the interaction between individuals is restrained by the rules of society the conservatism of Ivory's visual style often clashes with the powerful performances of the protagonists, thus exposing the characters' necessity to compromise with social constraints, a sort of rites-of-passage, and the central conflict in almost all his narratives.

Given these haunting themes of self-inflicted exile, sexual repression, and clashing cultures, it is no wonder that American realist Henry James and British novelist E. M. Forster are the main sources Ivory and Jhabvala have used over the past twenty years. The social and cultural discord at play when American and British citizens travel to Continental Europe and discover the unrestrained and passionate way or life of Mediterranean countries, are the core of both writers' work and also of Ivory's films.

Born in Berkeley in 1928 and raised in Kamath Falls, Oregon, Ivory majored in Architecture and Fine Arts at the University of Oregon. He later enrolled at the University of South California, where he graduated in 1957 with an MA in film-making. His master thesis was *Venice: Themes and Variations* (1957), a half-hour documentary shot in Europe, which already displays the extraordinary formalist quality of his later productions. In 1959 he began showing a keen interest in India, with his second documentary, *The Sword and the Flute*. Conceptually similar to *Venice*, this film is entirely focused on Indian miniature paintings in American collections, yet its driving force is the tension between Ivory's role of intellectual observer and his empathetic response to the paintings' exceptional sensuousness and romantic feeling. The success of this film led to a grant by the Asia Society of New York to make *The Delhi Way* (1964). While in India shooting this documentary, Ivory met local producer Ismail Merchant, with whom, in 1961, he founded the Merchant-Ivory Production Company. Their first feature together was *The Householder* (1963), based on an early novel by Ruth Prawer Jhabvala. Jhabvala also agreed to write the screenplay for the film, thus inaugurating a partnership that still lasts today. A satirical comedy entirely shot on location in Delhi, the film is a coming-of-age tale of a young man facing the conflict between tradition and modern life. In 1964 Ivory completed *The Delhi Way*, whose shooting he had interrupted in order to make *The Householder*. Although much less effective than his earlier work, this documentary displays a concern with the passing of time and its effect on cultures, and acts as an effective bridge to *Shakespeare-Wallah* (1965), in which time and change are main preoccupations.

*Shakespeare-Wallah* was made with money paid by Columbia for *The Householder*, and is based on the experiences of actress Felicity Kendal's theatrical family, and their efforts to keep the spirit of Shakespeare vivid in post-Independence India, while an Indian cinema is emerging. A humorous film of cultural conflict, it showcases in the company's rootless wandering the great dilemma of Ivory's characters, torn between belonging to a culture and living in another. One of Ivory's best works, *Shakespeare-Wallah* was premiered at the Berlin Film Festival and immediately became an international success.

Ivory's third feature, *The Guru* (1969), in a way reverses the theme of the previous film: it portrays a British character travelling to India in search of artistic enlightenment and failing to develop the necessary spiritual qualities. The same structure is present in *Bombay Talkie* (1970), the story of a British artist visiting Bombay hoping for inspiration and discovering the clash between feelings and culture. Shot entirely on location in and around Bombay, the film is at once a psychological drama and a parodic homage to the Indian film scene of the late 1960s and early 1970s. Peculiar in Ivory's career, the feature is really a meta-film – a film about film-making and cinema – in which the viewer is simultaneously involved in what is on-screen and aware of the medium. It also carries forth the classic Ivory themes of cultural misunderstandings that dramatically affect life.

After *Bombay Talkie*, Ivory accepted a commission from BBC Television to shoot a film on Nirad Chaudhuri, a famous Indian polymath. The result was the 1971 television documentary 'Adventures of a Brown Man In Search of Civilisation', where Ivory profiles the 76-year-old scholar while he walks in Oxford and London, professing his love for Western civilisation.

Ivory spent the 1970s going back and forth between America and India. He went to New York to shoot *Savages* (1972), an allegorical tale of people at odds with an unfamiliar environment, inspired by Beechwood, the Colonial Revival mansion, in Scarborough, New York.

He briefly returned to Europe to shoot *Autobiography of a Princess* (1975). Inspired by the research for a documentary on Maharajas, the film tells the story of an Indian princess living in London and the destruction of her nostalgic memories of India, during a tea party to which she has invited her father's former tutor. The film was released after *The Wild Party* (1975), a shrill commercial Hollywood production loosely inspired by a blank-verse narrative poem by Joseph Moncure March about a disastrous Greenwich Village party given by a vaudeville comic. *Roseland* (1977), again based in New York, is chiefly concerned with European exiles dreaming of home in a cavernous and magical New York ballroom. Their three stories, sometimes interconnecting, are centred around the quest to find the perfect dance partner.

In 1977 Ivory was asked by Melvyn Bragg to make a television film for 'The South Bank Show'. The project became almost a detective story, once more about collecting Indian miniatures. *Hullabaloo Over Georgie and Bonnie's Pictures* (1978) was financed by London Weekend Television and proved one of the most difficult collaborations for the Merchant-Ivory-Jhabvala team, with the screenwriter trying to withdraw from the project and shooting beginning before the screenplay was completed. However, upon its release the film received enthusiastic reviews..

The first of Merchant-Ivory's Henry James adaptations, *The Europeans*, was directed by Ivory in 1979. The film depicts the European and American characters reshaping relationships and identities between Puritanism and Continental debauchery, and follows Ivory's own tableaux structure. It displays all the elements that later became hallmarks of Merchant-Ivory costume dramas, the mood-setting use of colours, Ivory's legendary casting instinct (especially as far as actresses are concerned), and the masterful ensemble of interiors and acting.

Ivory's travels between London and America resulted in *Jane Austen in Manhattan* (1980), set in New York and inspired by the sale of a Jane Austen manuscript, the adaptation of which Ivory accepted to direct, only to find out it was just a fragment of a very childish play. However, Jhabvala thought it could be used as the premise for a film in which theatrical groups compete to acquire and produce the Austen play. The film was shot on location with a very tight budget and was closely followed by *Quartet* (1981), an adaptation of the 1928 autobiographical novel by Jean Rhys. The story deals with a love quadrangle between a complicated young West Indian woman, her husband, a manipulative English art patron, and his painter wife. Set in the Golden Age of Paris, with its cafe culture and extravagant night-life, all glitz and intellectualism, the film hints at the sinister core lying underneath the surface, and explores the vast territory between outward refinement and inner darkness. Jhabvala and Ivory's screenplay uses Rhys' novel as a foundation onto which a world is created that is both true to the novel and distinctive in its own right, painting a society that has lost its inhibitions and, inadvertently, its soul.

After completing *Quartet*, Merchant and Ivory returned to India, where they prepared two movies during 1981–82. Ivory directed only the second, *Heat and Dust* (1982), adapted from Jhabvala's Booker Prize-winning novel. The story of two English women living in India more than fifty years apart, *Heat and Dust* cross-cuts between the lives of the women as Anne discovers and repeats the scandal that her independent-minded ancestor caused two generations before.

In 1984 Ivory inaugurated his season of successful literary adaptations with *The Bostonians*, another James novel. The competition of feminist Olive Chancellor (a brilliant Vanessa Redgrave) and a chauvinist lawyer for the affections of a young and passionate speaker is set against the backdrop of Boston's politically active atmosphere – between dinner parties and lectures – and explores the theme already implicit in *The Europeans*. This is the portrait of a nation discovering itself through its arts, ideologies and politics. Two years later, *A Room with a View* (1986) was the first internationally acclaimed Merchant-Ivory production. An outstanding financial success, given its limited budget of $3 million, the film still managed to achieve the lavish and dazzling costumes and sets that won it two of its three Academy Awards (the third went to Jhabvala for her screenplay). The film is a comedy of manners and morals, set in Florence and England, and relies on some career-making performances from Maggie Smith, Daniel Day Lewis and Helena Bonham Carter.

*Maurice* (1987) was the second instalment of the Merchant-Ivory E.M. Forster trilogy. Following the enormous success of *A Room with a View*, the film manages to capture the struggle of the title character as he asserts his identity in the homophobic atmosphere of Edwardian England. This is yet another variation on the long-lasting Ivory theme of internal conflict shaping the life of individuals. After *Maurice*, Ivory returned to the US for two American films. The first of these was *Slaves of New York* (1989), based on the stories of Tama Janowitz, who also wrote the screenplay for the film. The film was well received in Europe but rather neglected by the American audience, possibly due to the remarkably 'un-American' quality of its cinematography and vision.

The nostalgic *Mr and Mrs Bridge* (1990) followed, which was adapted by Jhabvala from the novels by Evan S. Connell. In a long series of brilliant castings, Ivory called real-life couple Paul Newman and Joanne Woodward to play the title characters, a Midwestern couple struggling with the changing reality around them in 1930s America. An excellent supporting cast manages to create the whirlwind of change around the central pair, while helping to expose the drama hidden behind the inability to communicate one's feelings. The film, shot on location in Kansas City and in Paris, was enthusiastically greeted by both public and critics, and was regarded by some as the best film of the year.

Ivory's next project was *Howards End* (1992), which closes the E. M. Forster cycle with an elegant reworking of his 1910 novel. Again, the film's marvellous looks won the team three Academy Awards yet, despite strong and intense performances (especially the award-winning one by Emma Thompson) that make it Merchant-Ivory's greatest financial success, the film lacks much of the conflict and passion present in the book. In comparison, *The Remains of the Day* (1993), reuniting the same central couple of the previous film, is a more quietly intense and dignified period drama. Here the luscious cinematography and the quiet expressiveness of the performances are perfectly balanced in an intelligently and respectfully faithful adaptation of its literary source, Kazuo Ishiguro's Booker Prize-winning novel. *Jefferson in Paris* was Ivory's next project. Released in 1995, the film narrates the events occurring between 1784 and 1789, when Thomas Jefferson travelled with his elder daughter from Virginia to France as American ambassador. Fundamental years in the history of France on the verge of the Revolution, these also shaped Jefferson's public and personal life. Welcomed by French liberals and intellectuals, which he immediately supported after having experienced the corruption Louis XVI's court, Jefferson became the prototype of the American in Paris, exploring all the artistic and scientific riches that the capital had to offer. The film explores this position and the relationship between American Independence and slavery through Jefferson's relationships with painter Maria Cosway and slave Sally Hemings.

*Surviving Picasso* (1996) is loosely based on various published accounts, from Picasso's partners, of what life was like at the side of the great artist. The film is the story of Françoise Gilot's literal survival of her relationship (all other women linked to Picasso either went mad or killed themselves); she was the only woman with enough strength of will to leave Picasso. Interestingly, Picasso's estate banned any reproduction of his art in the film.

In 1998 Ivory shot *A Soldier's Daughter Never Cries*, the adapted story of an American family living in Paris in the mid-1960s, and later moving back to North America, told from the point of view of the daughter, Channe. Against the backdrop of their parents' parties, the children experience their own life-making events, narrated in evocative episodes.

Most recently, Ivory returned to Henry James, with the adaptation of *The Golden Bowl* (2000). Replete with Edwardian artefacts, the film's visual splendour never dwarfs the characters; rather, it acts as a constant reminder of what is at stake in the intricate, nuanced love triangle. *The Golden Bowl* manages a depth rarely achieved in the transposition of literary text to screen, capturing Jamesian double meaning. It was acclaimed at Cannes for its richness and performances. He is currently working on *Le Divorce*, a comedy starring Kate Hudson and Naomi Watts.                    **BP**

# Mick JACKSON

A native of Great Britain where he was born in 1943, Mick Jackson began his film-making career with several television movies produced during the 1980s. Although developing a feature film career that has spanned over ten years, Mick Jackson has not managed to create a distinctive style or personal thematic in his work. In almost every case, Jackson's direction has been superseded by the participation of someone else, whether it be a stellar cast, the screenwriter, or the palette of CGI special effects.

Jackson began promisingly when he burst out of the gate with *Chattahoochee* in 1990, a deliberately different account of a man (played by Gary Oldman) who is wrongfully deemed insane and incarcerated in a Florida mental institution. Aside from the solid cast, which also includes Dennis Hopper, Frances McDormand, Pamela Reed, and M. Emmet Walsh, this adaptation of a true story lacks urgency. Still, the horror show-like mental institution is enough to make the film otherwise notable. Jackson did receive some positive critical marks for his avoidance of mental asylum clichés, but the film was a relative failure overall. Jackson's next assignment was to serve as director for Steve Martin's *L.A. Story* (1991). Similar to Fred Schepisi's participation in *Roxanne* (1987), Martin's performance and screenplay almost makes one forget that he did not direct the film as well. *L.A. Story* is no different: it is Martin's show and Jackson is a competent enough film-maker to know who the true motivating force is. Martin stars as a television weather man who falls in love with an Annie Hall-like character, played by Martin's then-wife, Victoria Tennant. The film is a delight to watch, as Martin's screenplay skewers just about every sacred cow and cultural characteristic of modern Los Angeles. The film is really a love letter to LA and it is for this reason that the film belongs more to Southern California-native Martin than British-born Jackson.

Jackson followed up *L.A. Story* with *The Bodyguard* (1992). While this action love story was a major change of pace from his last two pictures, it still stands as a telling example of Jackson's role as director being usurped by an overriding creator. In this case it is screenwriter and producer Lawrence Kasdan, who originally wrote the film with Steve McQueen in mind and was initially set to direct the picture himself. The film itself is a rather maudlin affair with occasion bursts of energy. Kevin Costner plays the stoic bodyguard who is hired to protect pop superstar Whitney Houston in her film debut as a pop superstar. Jackson confidently directs his two leads in this passionate, if improbable, union. With two large egos to manage on the set, the film could have turned into a disaster. Powered by Houston's rendition of the hit pop ballad 'I Will Always Love You' on the soundtrack, as well as Jackson's confidant blending of action and romance, *The Bodyguard* has turned out to be Jackson's biggest box-office success to date.

*Clean Slate* (1994) heralded a return to comedy but not of the whimsical kind that made *L.A. Story* such a delight. Starring Dana Carvey as a private detective who awakens each morning with no memory whatsoever, the plot has much comic potential, but similarities to the superior *Groundhog Day* (1993), and too many slips into silliness, mire the film in substandard comedic territory. After a turn on cable television with 'Indictment: The McMartin Trial', Jackson directed *Volcano* (1997), a disaster epic that posits a long-dormant volcano erupting in the middle of Los Angeles. Despite a willing cast and benefitting from astounding CGI special effects, *Volcano* is undone by a story that is simply a paint-by-numbers concoction. A full-force marketing campaign and a high-concept story still failed to set the box office on fire.

Jackson's forthcoming feature is based on Po Bronson's novel 'The First $20 Million is Always the Hardest'. **SM**

# Henry JAGLOM

Born in London in 1941, Henry Jaglom started out as an actor, training with Lee Strasberg at the Actors Studio and performing in off-Broadway theatre before moving to Hollywood in the late 1960s. He was contracted to Columbia Pictures as an actor and featured in a number of films including Jack Nicholson's *Drive, He Said* (1971) and Dennis Hopper's *The Last Movie* (1971). Jaglom first became involved with film-making working as an editorial consultant on the cult classic *Easy Rider* (1969).

His first film as writer-director, *A Safe Place* (1971), starred Tuesday Weld, Orson Welles and Jack Nicholson. An exploration of the emotions of a young woman (Weld) going through a crisis, it was not a commercial success but Anais Nin later discovered it and used it in her lecturing as an example of what she called 'the female expression in art'.

Jaglom spent five years putting together $1m to produce his next film, *Tracks* (1976). Starring Dennis Hopper and Dean Stockwell, it tells the story of an army sergeant returned from Vietnam to accompany a comrade's body home for burial; whilst crossing America by train he is haunted by hallucinations. An exploration of the effect of the Vietnam War on America's psyche, Hopper is outstanding as the tormented sergeant. Jaglom's subsequent film, *Sitting Ducks* (1980), was a comedy road movie starring Jaglom regulars Michael Emil and Zack Norman as two small-time thieves in a bid to make their childhood dreams come true.

The reasons for Jaglom's involvement with *National Lampoon Goes to the Movies* (1981), co-directed with Bob Giraldi, are unclear. The film goes against the grain of his other work, it was badly received by the critics and did not gain theatrical release. He followed it up, however, with *Can She Bake a Cherry Pie?* (1983), one of his more successful films, starring Karen Black and Michael Emil. This is an offbeat romantic comedy with Black as Zee, walking up and down Manhattan streets talking to herself and the husband who has just left her. At a café she bumps into Eli (Emil) and an unlikely, funny and touching relationship develops between the two.

Jaglom's next three films all shared the themes of loneliness and the search for love, with Jaglom himself playing the main roles. *Always* (1985) is the story of the break-up of a marriage. *Someone To Love* (1987) focuses on people who are alone and looking for someone to love, and features Orson Welles in his last performance. *New Year's Day* (1989) is a story about starting over again and moving on in life. *Eating* (1990) starred Mary Crosby in a drama about women and eating. The film features three central female characters who throw a joint birthday party and explores the relationship between women and food as the party progresses and not one of the dozens of women there will take a bite of the birthday cake. In *Venice/Venice* (1992) (half filmed in Venice, California and half filmed in Venice, Italy), Jaglom is Dean, a maverick American film director whose most recent film has been chosen as the official US entry at the Venice Film Festival; the film is about the effect of movies on our romantic dreams.

Babyfever (1994) was the first Jaglom film to feature Victoria Foyt (now Jaglom's wife) in a drama about balancing a career and children and the ticking of the biological clock. Foyt was critically acclaimed for her role in this film where, attending a baby shower, she meets a diverse group of women in their thirties and forties who share their mixed feelings about having a baby in today's world. *Last Summer in the Hamptons* (1995) also stars (and is co-written by) Victoria Foyt and Viveca Lindfors. Oona (Foyt) is a successful Hollywood actress who goes to a large country house in the Hamptons, which the owner Helena (Lindfors), a stage actress and ex-movie star, has put up for sale. Helena's extended, talented, theatrical family are all present and have mounted (as is the tradition) a play for a single performance. Oona's unexpected visit wreaks havoc on the group of family and friends. *Déjà Vu* (1997), which Jaglom first wrote as a short story in 1974, is a romantic movie about finding the perfect 'soul mate', starring Victoria Foyt and Stephen Dillane. The two play two very different people from very different backgrounds who against time, location, and previous commitments, find themselves drawn inextricably to one another. More accessible than previous Jaglom films, it marked a move away from the loose structure of previous films to a more straightforward narrative structure.

Festival in Cannes (2001) stars Anouk Aimee, Greta Scacchi and Maximilian Schell. Filmed at the Cannes Film Festival in May 2000, it is Jaglom's second film set and filmed at a major international film festival. Made on a shoestring budget and using natural light throughout, Jaglom uses the festival as a backdrop to the story, which explores the mad world of the international movie business. Scacchi is Alice Palmer, an American actress looking to finance a low-budget script she has written. Aimee is an actress who must choose between a leading role in Palmer's film or a cameo role in a big Tom Hanks film; on the sidelines are a group of up-and-coming actors. *Festival in Cannes* is more accessible than Jaglom's previous films and demonstrates the delicate balance between art and commerce in making films. With actors such as Jeff Goldblum, Holly Hunter and Faye Dunaway playing themselves and distribution by Paramount Classics this film may well reach a wider audience than previous Jaglom films.

*Shopping*, as yet unreleased, stars Rob Morrow and Sam Robards, and is the third in Jaglom's 'women trilogy' of films, which includes *Eating* and *Babyfever*. Many of Jaglom's films tell women's stories from the female viewpoint. He feels strongly that women are not represented on screen because movies are still made largely by and for men; hence films about so-called 'women's issues'.

Jaglom has been criticised for being self-indulgent and narcissistic; however, it could be said that he is the only true maverick of American cinema, producing his films independently, writing the scripts, often editing the films, and acting in them as well as directing. Jaglom can also be described as an auteur whose films reflect personal concerns and individual issues often overlooked by Hollywood.                    **PR**

# Michael Patrick JANN

As one of the founders of New York University's student comedy troupe that went on to create the cult Monty Pythonesque MTV show 'The State', Michael Patrick Jann's humour tends towards the caustic and off-beat. This made him the natural choice to direct *Drop Dead Gorgeous* (1999), a satirical mockumentary based on screenwriter Lona William's experiences of competing in a small-town American beauty pageant. From the same mould as Rob Reiner's seminal *This is Spinal Tap* (1984), and sharing similar thematics to Michael Ritchie's cable film *The Positively True Adventures of the Alleged Texas Cheerleader-Murdering Mom* (1993), *Drop Dead Gorgeous* is a more intermittently derisory, but nevertheless well-realised, piece of satire.

Journeying to Mount Rose in Minnesota to film the local beauty competition, a documentary crew encounter unexpected viciousness lurking behind the apparently charming facades of the town's inhabitants. Spoilt rich kid Becky Leeman (Denise Richards), together with her mother (Kirstie Alley), a former winner herself, will stop at nothing to ensure their success, even if it means murder – in particular that of the naïvely optimistic Amber Atkins (Kirsten Dunst), a girl from the wrong side of the tracks who wants to be like Diane Sawyer. Confident in both style and tone, the film's condemnation of middle America's puritanism rings hollow at times but is, on the whole, wittily realised. The potential flaws are generally offset by the actors' robust and enthusiastic

*Drop Dead Gorgeous* (1999)

performances, which appropriately capture the emotional turmoil experienced by aspirants involved in such proceedings. Well-received upon its release by both critics and audiences, *Drop Dead Gorgeous* won a special mention FIPRESCI Award at the Karlovy Vary International Film Festival.                                                    **HP**

# Jim JARMUSCH

Jim Jarmusch has secured his success with a series of remarkably subtle and humorous films that seem to find a profound richness of detail in even the most seemingly inconsequential situations.

Often compared with directors from Europe and Japan, where Jarmusch has importantly received both finance and great praise, his films offer a fascinating vision of America, replete with geographical and ethnic diversity. However, in this regard the films are also interesting for their tension between the humanistic capacity of his characters to communicate beyond their cultural differences, and a lingering sense of the individual's ultimate existential solitude. It is also noticeable how his more recent films have expanded on his meditations on the role of the self in the world, juxtaposing the outlook of modern Western man to non-Western approaches to life, death, and the human spirit, leading at the same time to a critique of elements of American social history.

Born in Ohio in 1954, Jarmusch graduated in poetry from Columbia University and went on to study film-making at New York University. Here he made his first feature, *Permanent Vacation* (1982), the story of an apathetic teenage loner making a futile trip to visit his estranged mother. In light of the director's subsequent work, *Permanent Vacation* is a deeply disappointing film. Whereas his later films find epiphanic moments in ordinary human interaction (however fleeting this may be), as a film simply composed of meaningless conversations between deeply disturbed individuals, *Permanent Vacation* offers only a banally pessimistic view of otherwise meaningful social relations. Together with the fact that the film's protagonist is so deeply unsympathetic, this makes the film almost painful to watch.

In contrast, *Stranger than Paradise* (1984), the director's second feature, is a far superior work, the success of which depends precisely on the developing camaraderie between its three central characters. Indeed, the film proved so popular as to win the Camera d'Or and secured Jarmusch international recognition. Particularly noticeable is the humour, much of which revolves around the cultural differences between Willie (John Lurie), a Hungarian ex-patriate living in downtown New York, and his less Americanised relatives. The charm of the film lies in the unsentimental way that the somewhat reticent Willie gradually warms to his cousin Eva (Ester Balintz), something that is surprisingly touching given the use of an acting style which only hints at emotion beneath a deadpan exterior. Together with Willie's more openly warm friend Eddie (a comic tour de force from Richard Edson), the threesome later end up travelling to a rather bleak, off-season Florida, where a farcical case of mistaken identity and subsequent miscommunication accidentally forces them into going their separate ways, leaving behind a subtle and pervading sense of melancholy.

Often writing roles for specific actors he already has in mind, Jarmusch is a director who works very closely with his cast, here enabling him to vividly breathe life into his social misfit characters. Yet what makes the film resonate so deeply is its profound sense of rhythm, a testament not only to Jarmusch's staging and skill in using the long take, but also to his understanding of editing. Together with a subtle sense of comic timing this allows Jarmusch and his actors to suggest the richness of the tiniest movement, utterance or gesture.

Continuing the trend of socially marginalised characters, Jarmusch's next work, *Down by Law* (1986), charts the exploits of two New Orleans downbeats, Jack (Lurie) and Zack (Tom Waits – who with Lurie also provides the music), framed by the corrupt local police. The film is carefully structured to draw parallels between the two characters, whose strong similarities actually lead to antagonism rather than friendship. Again stressing the positive role of cultural difference, the madcap humour of a third prisoner, the eccentric Italian tourist Roberto (Roberto Benigni), not only institutes some degree of camaraderie between Zack and Jack but also inspires them to escape to eventual freedom.

Through working with Wim Wenders' regular cameraman Robby Muller, the film is among Jarmusch's most visually impressive, with stunning images of seedy night-time New Orleans and a subsequent shift to beautiful vistas of the surrounding Southern bayou. As such it also adds to the dreamlike texture of the film, with its move from a kind of 'slum naturalism' in the beginning to its sense of fairytale at the end. The film is again deeply endearing without straying into sentimentality, but perhaps because it is structurally so similar to *Stranger Than Paradise*, and with a slightly less interesting dynamic between its characters, there is always the feeling that it does not quite reach the heights of the previous film.

Always demonstrating a loving interest in pop culture, Jarmusch gets to pay homage to rock 'n' roll in his fourth film, *Mystery Train* (1989). Set in Memphis, the whole texture of the film is dependent on its references to music, whether the endless stories told about Elvis or Jarmusch's casting of singer Screamin' Jay Hawkins as a hotel desk clerk. The film has a different narrative structure from his previous works, comprising three stories linked by a gunshot (the source of which gradually becomes clearer) that the characters overhear in their rooms at a dingy hotel. In a welcome change from Jarmusch's other films, *Mystery Train*'s stories actually tackle romantic relationships. Indeed, the depiction of the nascent relationship between a young Japanese couple in the first story is one of his most poignant and acutely observed episodes. The relationship in this story is, however, implicitly compared to the relationship between an older couple who, after a recent break in Memphis, are the world-weary protagonists in the two remaining stories, which slightly lack something of the opening story's skilful characterisation. Yet as well as its interesting use of the omnipresent cultural mythology that surrounds Memphis, the film's structure absorbingly means that the events and locales of one story are subtly intertwined with those in the other stories, again suggesting the significance of ordinary events.

*Night on Earth* (1991) sees Jarmusch structure multiple stories in a different way. With an internationally recognisable cast, the film focuses on a series of conversations between taxi drivers and their passengers, occurring at the same point in time but in different cities throughout the world (Los Angeles, New York, Paris, Rome, and Helsinki). As with Jarmusch's uncompleted series of shorts, *Coffee and Cigarettes*, the stories resemble one-act plays, meticulously structured to highlight the differences and similarities between the featured characters. Humour is again central, although Jarmusch skilfully varies the tone of the comedy from ribald (the episode in Rome starring Benigni) to black (Beatrice Dalle and Isaak de Bankole in Paris) to bittersweet (the episode in Helsinki featuring some of Kaurismaki's regular actors). Whilst never quite finding Jarmusch at his brilliant best, all the vignettes are thoroughly entertaining, and it is also interesting how, in his casting, Jarmusch makes intertextual references to traditions of maverick film-making in European and non-Hollywood cinema.

The director's next film, *Dead Man* (1995), reverts to a single narrative. It marks, however, something of a shift in his work and not simply because it is (loosely) a western. The film focuses on the slow death of William Blake (Johnny Depp), a meek accountant who travels to the barbaric outpost town of Machine only to unwittingly kill a man in a shoot-out. Fatally wounded himself, Blake retreats into the wilderness, where he meets an eccentric mixed-tribe Native American, Nobody (Gary Farmer), who protects him from bounty hunters until his natural death. Although retaining some similarities to its predecessors, the emphasis in *Dead Man* is less on a subtle, rejuvenating vision of the everyday world, and more on the vast differences between the Native American's view of life and death and that of modern, industrialised man. The film not only deals more directly with metaphysical issues, but also addresses political ones, implicitly criticising the barbarism of 'civilised' man towards Native Americans. Like the subsequent *Ghost Dog: The Way of the Samurai* (1999), the film has an incredible density of ideas, also, of course, referencing the mysticism of the poet William Blake. Yet although the film is fascinating to watch in this regard, there does remain something awkward about its tone, juxtaposing often intense feelings of spirituality with a surreal and macabre black humour. Adding to this is a strange ambivalence as to whether Blake, in facing up to death, is ever entirely able to leave behind his modern sensibilities.

After taking time out to make the surprisingly conventional documentary *Year of the Horse* (1997), about American rock group Crazy Horse, Jarmusch returned to fiction film-making with *Ghost Dog: The Way of the Samurai*. Building on the themes of *Dead Man* (and even referencing the film), *Ghost Dog* contrasts the Zen ideals of the eponymous hero with the idea of the self in Western society. The film's meditations on death and human action are, however, tempered by Jarmusch's attention to more concrete issues, namely the emancipation of oppressed black consciousness, for, in an unusual twist, Ghost Dog himself is a corpulent black man (Forest Whitaker).

Working as a hitman for a local mobster who once saved his life, Ghost Dog is inspired by the code of the Japanese samurai but uses a gun rather than a sword. A wrong hit, however, means that he is forced to go to war with the Mob, killing everyone except for his 'master', to whom Ghost Dog's code dictates that he must ultimately surrender his life. Nevertheless, with an emphasis on the cyclical nature of the universe, it is hinted that a young girl whom Ghost Dog has befriended will go on to eventually assume his mantle. Despite the idiosyncrasy of its subject matter and its often outlandish humour, particularly in its hilarious representation of the ageing troupe of mobsters, the intensity of Whitaker's performance helps to ensure that *Ghost Dog* never becomes whimsical. As such, Jarmusch appears to have made a film with enough suspense and action to entertain even a mainstream audience. A better-realised film than *Dead Man* (and with one of the best soundtracks you are ever likely to hear), it is intriguing to anticipate how he aims to improve on this. Alongside directors such as Wim Wenders, he recently contributed a ten-minute short to the project 'Ten Minutes Older'. **CH**

# Vicky JENSON
See **Andrew ADAMSON**

# Norman JEWISON

Norman Jewison is one of Canada's foremost film-makers. Known as an eclectic and unpredictable director, Jewison tackles diverse subject matter, from romantic comedy to epic musical to serious social conscience drama. The unifying thread that runs through these wide-ranging films is a steadfast liberal humanism. Many of his greatest dramas explore questions of racial injustice, focusing on the interaction between whites and blacks in American culture. Recipient of the 1999 Irving Thalberg Academy Award for lifetime achievement, Jewison is a veteran director, well respected by his peers. In the late 1970s he was responsible for creating the Canadian Centre for Advanced Film Studies in Toronto.

Born in Toronto in 1926, Jewison graduated from the University of Toronto, and then wrote scripts and acted for the BBC in London. He moved to the United States in the 1950s, carving out a prosperous career for himself as a director of the popular television music programmes 'Your Hit Parade' and 'Tonight with Harry Belafonte'. Jewison began his film career in the 1960s with the lightweight Tony Curtis comedy *Forty Pounds of Trouble* (1963), a remake of *Little Miss Marker*. His next two comedies, *The Thrill of it All* (1963) and *Send Me No Flowers* (1964), were Doris Day vehicles, interesting for their exploration of the growing impact of commercial culture on suburban sexual politics. *The Art of Love* (1965) is Jewison's least likeable comedy from this period, despite a stellar cast including James Garner, Dick Van Dyke, and Carl Reiner.

*The Cincinnati Kid* (1965) was Jewison's first major hit. Jewison replaced Sam Peckinpah as director of this poker movie made in the tradition of Robert Rossen's 1961 film *The Hustler*. While Jewison's next film, *The Russians are Coming! The Russians are Coming!* (1966), a comedy about a Soviet submarine that lands off the New England coast, was immensely popular, it has not stood the test of time and now does seem dated. Unlike *In the Heat of the Night* (1967), Jewison's most important film. Released during a tumultuous period in American race-relations, the film's portrayal of small-town racism in the deep south struck an immediate chord. Rod Steiger's performance as a redneck sheriff won him a Best Actor Academy Award and Sidney Poitier's portrayal of a northern, black police officer who shows up the dim-witted southern police, is powerful and compelling. The film, which picked up the Best Picture Academy Award, is significant as a historical marker of American racial politics, and it still has pertinence today. Its depiction of the uneasy relationship between Poitier and Steiger is a prototype for contemporary television and cinema's representation of race relations in crime drama.

Although it lacks the thematic import of *In the Heat of the Night*, Jewison's next, *The Thomas Crown Affair* (1968), contains some polished film-making. Featuring Steve McQueen and Faye Dunaway as the charismatic leads, this experimental and sexy crime caper begins with innovative use of multiple screens. He concluded the decade with *Gaily, Gaily* (1969), an unremarkable comedy starring Beau Bridges and Melina Mercouri. Then, disgusted with the conservative political resurgence in the US, Jewison tore up his green card and left his adopted country in 1970, spending the next decade making films in Yugoslavia, Israel and Germany. *Fiddler on the Roof* (1971) is one of the all-time musical classics. Based on the stage musical of the same name, the film is sentimental and hyperbolic, but it is also a deeply entertaining, moving, and ultimately powerful drama about Jewish life in Tsarist Russia. One of the great achievements of the film is that the songs blend naturally into the actions of the characters. The Academy Award-winning Topol superbly plays the central role of Tevye.

*Jesus Christ Superstar* (1973) is arguably a less successful attempt to convert a stage musical for the silver screen. Based on a concept album project written by Andrew Lloyd Webber and Tim Rice, the film follows the final week in the life of Jesus Christ from the point of view of Judas Iscariot, played by Carl Anderson in an excellent performance. The movie was shot on location in Israel and features actors clad in 1970s fashions as modern incarnations of biblical characters.

Jewison ventured into new territory for his next film. *Rollerball* (1975) is a science fiction thriller set in the near future. The dystopian world in which it is set is one where a few huge corporations rule the roost, and rollerball, an ultra-violent game played on roller-skates, is the number one spectator sport. *Rollerball* has aged poorly, but has some interesting ideas about violence and spectatorship. *F.I.S.T.* (1978), an acronym that stands for the Federation of Interstate Truckers, stars Sylvester Stallone in a serious dramatic role as a teamster. Although this epic film is well produced, it is weighed down by an awful script co-written by Joe Eszterhas and Stallone. *...and justice for all* (1979), starring Al Pacino in an over-the-top performance as liberal lawyer Arthur Kirkland, is one of many films in which Jewison explores the workings of a corrupt judicial system. Despite some grating theme music, and a heavy-handed, black and white approach, there is something admirable about the film's moral absolutism. Pauline Kael called it a 'Velveeta comedy ... with banter and gags and an unctuous score'.

*Best Friends* (1982), starring Burt Reynolds and Goldie Hawn, saw Jewison attempting to return to the romantic comedies with which he began his career in Hollywood. Written by Valerie Curtin and Barry Levinson (the screenplay is allegedly based on their experiences as a couple), the film investigates what happens when love becomes institutionalised in marriage. Jewison's next film, *A Soldier's Story* (1984), is far weightier stuff. The second powerful drama in a trilogy confronting racial injustice (*In the Heat of the Night* was the first, *The Hurricane* the last), this little-seen movie starred virtual newcomer Denzel Washington in the title role. Based on Pulitzer Prize-winning playwright Charles Fuller's stage play, the film is an absorbing whodunit. *Agnes of God* (1985), also based on a stage play, tells the story of a young nun who gives birth and then kills the baby. Perhaps Jewison's least successful film of the decade, *Agnes* never bothers to answer any of the difficult questions it raises.

*Moonstruck* (1987) is one of the most successful comedies of the decade and is arguably Jewison's best comedy. Nominated for Best Picture, this playful ensemble piece creates a magical setting against which to explore the workings of love and romance in an Italian family. *Moonstruck* is notable for great acting from Best Actress Cher, Best Supporting Actress Olympia Dukakis, and Best Supporting Actor Vincent Gardenia, along with a wonderful script from John Patrick Shanley. Jewison's final film of the decade, *In Country* (1989), based on Bobbie Ann Mason's novel, is a Vietnam War drama. Although the much-discussed emotional impact of the closing scene at the Vietnam Veteran's Memorial in Washington is undeniable, the film suffers from meandering direction.

Jewison began the 1990s with a return to romantic comedy. *Other People's Money* (1991) features Danny DeVito in the role he plays best: the sleazy opportunist with a twinkle in his eye. *Only You* (1994) is a romance set in a beautifully photographed Italy. Although the film's convoluted plot demands an almighty suspension of disbelief, the good-natured performances of its leads, Marisa Tomei and Robert Downey Jr, along with a beautifully photographed Italy, make for a pleasant, if at times insipid, movie. *Bogus*

(1996), a saccharine yet curiously charming movie, features Gérard Depardieu as a seven-year-old boy's (Haley Joel Osment) imaginary friend.

*The Hurricane* (1999), a film about wrongly convicted boxer Rubin 'Hurricane' Carter, is Jewison's third film to expose the racism of America's legal system. The film, based on Carter's prison memoirs, provides a riveting account of the middleweight fighter's two-decade stay in prison, and the struggle of a group of Canadians to get him released. While a critical and commercial hit, the film was dogged by controversy, accused of misrepresenting the truth in the US. Particularly irksome to Carter's American lawyers was the film's representation of the virtuous Canadians who saved the day. Critics cite the controversy surrounding the film as the reason why it was slighted by the Academy. The film only received one nomination, for Denzel Washington's first-rate performance as the boxer.                                                                    **TH**

# Roland JOFFÉ

Born in London in 1945, Roland Joffé is probably best revealed by the portrait Spalding Gray draws of him in *Swimming to Cambodia* (1987). Gray first met Joffé during casting for *The Killing Fields* (1984) and his vision of him is that of someone possessed: he mesmerised Gray with the story of Cambodia under the Khmer Rouge and of a simple, sustaining friendship between a New York Times reporter and his Cambodian translator. In his portrait of a man obsessed with telling the big, important story, Gray reveals both Joffé's strength and his weakness: he is a director with a great vision and his movies are grand and lush. However, his single-minded decision to make a big point impoverishes his characters and the stories that might have emerged from their interactions.

*The Killing Fields*, Joffé's first feature, displays the director's great skill in building a vast and convincing historical backdrop from meticulous attention to physical detail. New York Times reporter Sydney Schanberg (Sam Waterson) discovers that the US has begun a secret bombing campaign in Cambodia, a fact that Joffé links to the subsequent destabilisation of the Cambodian government and the ascendancy of the Khmer Rouge, who were later to carry out one of the most horrible mass killings in human history.

Against these events, Joffé tells the story of Schanberg and his translator Dith Pran. Schanberg is able to get Pran's family out of the country, but fails to help Pran himself. Considering the rest of the film, its ending is curiously and strangely 'Hollywood'. The message seems to be that love and forgiveness can conquer all; in fact it is more that a good Hollywood ending can efface – or seem to efface – all real complexity.

Joffé's next feature, *The Mission* (1986), continues his theme of the evils of imperialism. Spanish and Portuguese colonists are fighting for possession of a portion of Brazil, waging war against the indigenous tribes, killing and enslaving them in their quest to establish a profitable beachhead in the new world. The tribes can only respond by withdrawing further into the jungle, or suffering under conquerors who treat them as animals. The only defenders of the tribe are a group of Jesuit missionaries who enter the jungle with the aim of converting the natives to Christendom. They succeed beyond the realm of cinematic skepticism, establishing a mission that embodies a Socialist visionary's version of Utopia: a completely rational, environmentally sound, loving community devoted to service and the arts. When the mission is destroyed for economic reasons, natives and Jesuits alike are massacred, and the cause of commerce is brutally sustained. The only resistance is attempted by a colonist-turned-Jesuit (played by Robert De Niro), who answers with force, constituting an ironic counterpoint to Rambo.

*Fat Man and Little Boy* (1989) sustains the theme of imperialism, this time focusing not on the application of force but its invention. The characters of the title are not people, but bombs. Specifically, they refer to the nuclear warheads that the US dropped on Hiroshima and Nagasaki in 1945 to end the war in the Pacific. The film is not about Japan, but about the process of making the bombs themselves; it tells the story of the events in Los Alamos that led to the creation of the Bomb. The film, as it progresses, has the quality of watching a coal lump being transformed to a diamond, with the proviso that the raw materials are pulverised in the process and have little part in the final creation. By portraying the process in slow motion, Joffé illustrates the price to humanity that even the winners must pay to sustain power.

Since *Fat Man and Little Boy*, Joffé's output has continued to address his signature themes but has been even less subtle and less well received. 1992's *City of Joy* saw

Patrick Swayze as an American doctor who travels in India to find himself. (Interestingly, the Indian government fought against its creation.) His past three performances have been equally disappointing: 1995's *The Scarlet Letter*, starring the exhibitionist Demi Moore as Hester Prynne in a loose adaptation of Hawthorne's novel; *Goodbye Lover* (1999), a much-maligned detective thriller with Ellen Degeneres, Patricia Arquette and Don Johnson; and *Vatel* (2000), starring Gérard Depardieu and Uma Thurman. *Vatel* tells the story of a chef-entertainer-opportunist in the court of Louis XIV. Made with French money but recorded in English, *Vatel* was universally booed when it opened Cannes in 2000 and has cast Gaumont, the producing studio, into serious financial trouble.

As regrettable as his many early excesses were, it's difficult not to hope that Joffé will rediscover his early vision and take his rightful place in contemporary cinema: as a thinking person's Oliver Stone. **JA**

# Patrick Read JOHNSON

It takes a brave person to direct children's films these days. With an ever more demanding audience with increasingly inscrutable tastes to satisfy, Patrick Read Johnson can be both endearingly old-fashioned and disappointingly formulaic. Displaying a healthy handle on the often cruel world of childhood, Johnson's films combine originality and timing with an irreverent tone that consistently raises both adult and juvenile laughs. Mixing broad physical gags with moral messages and some often gushingly sentimental moments, the early films display original ideas often let down by hit-and-miss jokes.

*Spaced Invaders* (1990)
*Baby's Day Out* (1994)
*Angus* (1995)
*Life After Donna Dell* (1999)

In *Spaced Invaders* (1990), Johnson's debut, passing Martians intercept a transmission of Orson Welles' *War of the Worlds* and land in a small middle-America town thinking the invasion is underway. Using the amusing reversal of the original human panic to the Wellesian broadcast, Johnson parodies any number of science fiction classics from 1950s B-movies to *Star Wars* (1977), with the genre characters – bumbling sheriff, hokey farmer, gutsy kids – and amusing Martian characters (one is a dead ringer for Jack Nicholson) demonstrating Johnson's irreverent touch and a zany, gag-a-minute style. Johnson's skill lies in his ability to appeal both to childish slapstick and adult in-joke, unapologetic for the downright fun and energy of making a children's film.

*Baby's Day Out* (1994) is much less satisfying, with Johnson sacrificing detailed comedy for a much broader, gaudier comic style more akin to the style of the film's writer, John Hughes. A variation on the *Home Alone* (1990) formula, the eponymous baby is kidnapped by three inept crooks who are then led a merry chase when it escapes. Where the previous film mixed subtlety with outright slapstick, here Johnson moves by numbers from one set-piece to another, including a chase through a taxi, a building site, a bus, a zoo and a department store, employing comic book violence and mishap in favour of subtlety. While the comic timing and pace is there, the film is formulaic and ridiculous, with the script's generic banality and manipulative direction betraying Johnson's usually forthright style.

*Angus* (1995) is much more free and original. Although the story is ostensibly standard fare – a fat but talented kid endures ridicule but constructs a final moment of triumph with the girl of his dreams – the film is again saved from cloying sentimentality by Johnson's ability to make the film work both within genre conventions as a rites-of-passage drama and extend them through its appeal to different levels of sophistication. Preaching the values of diversity and acceptance present in earlier work, Johnson rediscovers his irreverent style, contrasting genuinely funny scenes – Angus learning to dance or trying on a tuxedo – with comic bathos, physical humour and sensitively handled moments of angst. The willingness to show the cruelty of adolescence as well as the hero's flaws result in an unsentimental, honest style and another children's film that manages not to patronise its audience.

As is again displayed in his last feature, *Life After Donna Dell* (1999), Johnson is a director willing to experiment and overcome the straightjackets of the 'kiddie' film, a rare breed in an otherwise unimaginative field. **OB**

# Joe JOHNSTON

With the advent of the standard use of CGI special effects in the 1990s, top-notch film-makers like James Cameron, Robert Zemeckis, Steven Spielberg, and Paul Verhoeven

*Honey, I Shrunk the Kids* (1989)

have created reputations for themselves as expert exploiters of this technology. While these and other A-list film-makers may receive most of the attention, other lesser-known film-makers also make fine use of CGI. One such director is Joe Johnston. Born in 1950 in Texas, and trained as a special effects engineer and artist on *The Empire Strikes Back* (1980) and *Raiders of the Lost Ark* (1981) (for which he and others won an Academy Award for Best Visual Effects), Johnston was an apprentice to such notable film-makers as George Lucas and Ron Howard. He served in a number of positions – as assistant director and production designer – before helming his own feature film *Honey, I Shrunk the Kids* in 1989.

Loud, rambunctious and visually stunning, it is typical live-action Disney fare for kids, only this time the special effects wizardry was so proficient that the film attracted adults as well. Johnston displayed a remarkable talent for handling the demands of a special effects-driven film, whilst also addressing the concerns of narrative such as story and pace. Essentially a modern version of *The Incredible Shrinking Man* (1957), but without the metaphysical thematics, the story is breezy and fun, and instantly forgettable other than for its marvellous effects.

Johnston's next film is one that will hopefully be rediscovered as a pure delight. Based on classic pulp magazines and serial matinee adventures, *The Rocketeer* (1991) played in theatres full of indifferent audiences who had apparently become jaded by the dark, oppressive comic book adaptations of the Batman series. Viewers failed to appreciate many of the inside jokes and witty allusions to figures and places of Golden Age Hollywood, circa the start of World War Two. Graced with astounding special effects, an exciting story, appealing lead characters and exquisite production design, this nostalgic romp through 1930s Hollywood deserved a sequel, unlike many comic book movies since.

After directing an episode of the television series 'The Young Indiana Jones Chronicles' in 1992 for his former boss George Lucas, as well as the live-action scenes for *The Pagemaster* (1994), Johnston embarked on another special effects extravaganza. *Jumanji* was released in 1995, wielding some of the most astounding CGI effects ever put to screen. But unlike *The Rocketeer*, *Jumanji* was not as much fun since the story and characters were obliterated by the barely controlled chaos going on around them. Still, the CGI creatures – a herd of elephants and a band of malicious monkeys – were a strong indication of the direction cinema special effects were headed.

Johnston switched gears for his next film and duly impressed many critics with *October Sky* (1999), a crowd-pleasing sleeper based on a true story of the son of a West Virginia coal miner who becomes a rocket man at NASA. Told with loving attention to detail and a mature resistance towards sentimentality, *October Sky* is a remarkable film from a director like Johnston because of the relative lack of special effects of any kind. Some of the sequences of model rocket launches involved some forms of special effects but, compared to *Jumanji*, this coming-of-age tale is almost unrecognisable as the product of the same director. Johnston also proved his talent with strong, solid actors, particularly Chris Cooper, who plays the stubborn father.

As the second sequel to one of Hollywood's most profitable movie franchises, *Jurassic Park III* (2001) was a tremendous commercial and critical success for Johnston and cemented his reputation as a director adept at mingling thrills and spills with a strong sense of character and a dark streak of humour. Eschewing the ecological techno-babble of the original *Jurassic Park* (1993) and the flabby 'Kong'-esque *The Lost World* (1997), *Jurassic Park III* runs at a brisk 92 minutes, immediately flags its 'tourists-in-peril' credentials and builds upon the CGI work of the original to deliver several scenes of real menace. Co-written by the *Election* (1999) duo, Alexander Payne and Jim Taylor, the film is free of any weightier pretensions and instead cuts straight to the chase. Part of the pleasure is in the acting – world-weary Sam Neill, scream-queen Téa Leoni, flustered billionaire William H. Macy – but also in the new dinosaurs, like the Spinosaurus or the wonderfully sustained pterodactyl sequence, in which Johnston cranks up the tension. Indeed, in such CGI-dominated films, the director is frequently effaced from the process, but Johnston manages to deliver a film that is very different from Spielberg's originals. Lacking the scale or chills of *Jurassic Park*, it nonetheless retains strong elements of wonder, menace and bleak humour.                                                      **SM & BM**

# Spike JONZE

Spike Jonze (born Adam Spiegelin in St Louis in 1969) began his career making skateboarding videos before building his reputation directing music videos for the likes of REM, Bjork and Fatboy Slim. As one of the new wave of pop promo-directors-cum-film-makers (Michel Gondry, Jake Scott, Antoine Fuqua), Jonze maintained his association with independent, innovative material with his first feature, the highly-acclaimed *Being John Malkovich* (1999).

*Being John Malkovich* (1999)
*Adaptation* (2002)

Whilst occasionally falling back on his MTV/advertising background, Jonze demonstrated in this film an admirable understanding of Charlie Kaufman's surreal screenplay. His decision to employ low-key lighting gave the film a distinctly natural feel, ensuring that the weirdness of the material did not detract from the fact that it is a film about human beings. Even at those points when his commercial background became apparent, Jonze refused to let the film evade his grasp: the subconcious chase sequence touching upon the emotional side of childhood; the hallucinatory sequence inside a chimp's memory wonderfully highlighting the anguish of captivity. Similarly Jonze manages to avoid the temptation of adopting a hard-hitting, contemporary soundtrack, instead hitting the perfect note with Carter Burwell's downbeat orchestration. The casting is also immaculate: John Cusack and Cameron Diaz are barely recognisable beneath shaggy hair and trashy clothing; Catherine Keener goes against type to play the delightfully scathing Maxine; and a superb John Malkovich upon whose 'character' the whole piece hangs. If the film can be criticised then one would have to look to the slight decline in momentum as Jonze and Kaufman strive for a point of closure, yet it remains one of the most impressive and highly promising debuts of recent years.

In a typically multi-layered, disorientating fashion, Jonze and Kaufman's subsequent film, *Adaptation* (2002), is based on Susan Orlean's book 'The Orchid Thief' and is also an account of Kaufman's struggles to adapt it.                                                                    **CP**

# Neil JORDAN

Neil Jordan's status as a film-maker might best be summarised as enigmatic. He has worked across independent and mainstream markets in both Europe and America, and it is in the former that he has produced his most successful work. While his œuvre does not display any consistent worldview, his films reveal an affinity with literature and literary sources, and he has returned more than once to issues of Irish social and political history. This is not to suggest, however, that Jordan's films lack any pronounced formal aspect. On the contrary, his work has often demonstrated considerable structural and compositional scope.

*Angel* (1982)
*The Company of Wolves* (1984)
*Mona Lisa* (1986)
*High Spirits* (1988)
*We're No Angels* (1989)
*The Miracle* (1991)
*The Crying Game* (1992)
*Interview with the Vampire* (1994)
*Michael Collins* (1996)
*The Butcher Boy* (1997)
*In Dreams* (1999)
*The End of the Affair* (1999)

Born in County Sligo, Ireland, in 1950, but raised in Dublin, Jordan was educated at University College Dublin where he studied Irish history and English. Following a short and critically successful career as a fiction writer, his crossover into movies came as a 'creative associate' on John Boorman's *Excalibur* (1981); he also made a documentary about the film.

Having scripted Joe Comerford's British thriller *Traveller* (1981), he debuted as a feature director the next year with *Angel* (1982), a bleak and violent revenge thriller set in contemporary Northern Ireland. Witnessing a double sectarian killing, a saxophonist played by Stephen Rea – in his first of many collaborations with Jordan – resolutely pursues the killers across Armagh. At the time, Jordan described himself as a 'literary sophisticate and a cinematic innocent'. While some critics might have anticipated the resourcefulness of his screenplay, and the film's emphasis on naturalistic *mise-en-scène*, through its perceived nods towards Buñuelian surrealism, *Angel* was also acclaimed for its formal schemata, winning the director the London *Evening Standard*'s Most Promising Newcomer award.

By most critical accounts, Jordan consolidated his potential with *The Company of Wolves* (1984), the first of many projects with producer Stephen Woolley. Co-scripted with the original story's author, Angela Carter, and shot on a small budget, *The Company of Wolves* is a surreal, expressionistic revision of the Red Riding Hood myth. The film eschews narrative cohesion in favour of a certain dream logic in which classical realism is displaced and ideas of the fantastic – where wolves morph into human form and vice-versa – abound. Given such iconography, and its propensity towards temporal and spatial blurring, the film has often been read as highly symbolic of suppressed, primordial, feminine sexuality and the duality of danger and seduction in the beast/man.

Co-produced by George Harrison's HandMade Films, Jordan's next film, *Mona Lisa* (1986), garnered both critical and commercial success. Ostensibly a noir love story set in a dehumanising contemporary London, *Mona Lisa* casts Bob Hoskins as an artless, ex-petty hood who, following his release from a lengthy prison term, is hired by former boss Michael Caine to chauffeur chic prostitute Cathy Tyson between jobs. Their relationship gives rise to predictable antagonism before the mismatched couple become mutually dependent: Tyson helps Hoskins to re-adjust to the modern world while he agrees to track down her vulnerable teenage friend who continues to work the streets of Kings Cross. Featuring outstanding performances – Hoskins won the Best Actor award at Cannes for his role – and an unsentimental treatment of its subject matter, *Mona Lisa* made excellent use of London locations.

The success of *Mona Lisa* opened doors for Jordan in Hollywood, where he worked on two comedies. The first of these, *High Spirits* (1988), was a $16 million haunted-house sex farce set in an Irish castle, featuring a star cast including Daryl Hannah, Steve Guttenberg, Peter O'Toole and Beverly D'Angelo. A box-office disaster, the film was universally panned by critics. Jordan, who had no post-production input, has since rued the project, stating that he had envisioned 'a kind of *Whisky Galore* [while] the American producers wanted a raucous teenage comedy'. *We're No Angels* (1989), a David Mamet-scripted remake of Michael Curtiz's 1955 movie, was Jordan's first all-American production. A mistaken-identity caper set during the Depression, in which Robert De Niro and Sean Penn play escaped convicts who are mistaken for priests and take refuge in a Canadian border-town monastery, the film boasted a revered cast. However, it was not the commercial success Paramount had hoped for. Nonetheless, critics generally warmed to De Niro's performance and praised Jordan for his strong sense of period and location.

Disenchanted by his lack of commercial success and the creative constraints placed upon him by the studios, Jordan returned to home territory and to literary themes for his next film, *The Miracle* (1991). Set in the small Irish seaside town of Bray, the film tells the tale of two male adolescent would-be writers who become infatuated with an American actress (Beverly D'Angelo). A romantic rites-of-passage mystery (and Jordan's personal favourite), the film represented something of a critical resurgence for the director, but another commercial disappointment.

The ordeal of transferring *The Crying Game* (1992) from page to screen lasted some ten years. Initially submitted in partial script form as 'The Soldier's Wife' to Channel 4, the project was passed over on the grounds that the subject matter was too sensitive for the time. *The Crying Game* tells the story of a reluctant black British soldier, Jody (Forest Whitaker), who is abducted whilst drunk at an Armagh fairground and held hostage by members of the Provisional IRA. Jody is befriended by Fergus (Stephen Rea), one of his captors, who agrees to look up Jody's girlfriend Dil (Jaye Davidson) should anything happen to him. Fergus fails to carry out an order to execute his prisoner but Jody is killed by a British armoured vehicle while attempting to escape. Having fled to London, Fergus is court-martialled and sentenced to a suicide mission. He befriends Dil and is pursued by his former paramilitary colleagues as the story follows thriller conventions through to their conclusion. *The Crying Game* fundamentally differs from 'The Soldier's Wife' in the film's striking revelation that Dil is a male transvestite.

Since the script juggled the hot potatoes of race, sexual identity and political violence, the film failed to attract American money. It was eventually co-financed by Channel 4 and a syndicate of European and Japanese distribution companies. Moreover, given the film's generic hybridity, *The Crying Game* proved difficult to market and initially flopped in the UK. In the US, however, the film's distributor, Miramax, marketed the film as a straightforward thriller and traded on the film's gender twist – 'the movie that everyone's talking about, but no one is giving away its secrets'. This strategy, coupled with an enthusiastic critical reception, generated huge audiences. By Jane Giles' account, in the period between its release in November 1992 and the Academy Awards in the following March, Miramax increased the film's release prints from six to more than a thousand. The film was nominated for six Academy Awards, including Best Film and Best Director, won for Best Screenplay, and grossed almost $60 million at the US box office alone.

On the back of the *The Crying Game*'s success, Jordan returned to America where he made the first of three films for Geffen/Warner Bros., *Interview with the Vampire* (1994), an adaptation of Anne Rice's cult novel. The episodic events of the film are narrated by a 'reluctant' vampire, Louis de Pointe du Lac (Brad Pitt), who recounts to his interviewer, Malloy (Christian Slater), the details of his two-hundred-year existence. Given its mainstream standing (and a cast including Tom Cruise and Antonio Banderas), the gay sexual overtones of the original novel are predictably reduced to subtext. Considered by some to be narratively laboured, the film is handsomely staged and shot, and did strong business at the US box office.

Jordan chose distinctly Irish themes for his next two films. In the first, *Michael Collins* (1996), he addressed the thorny issue of Irish national history, representing the events surrounding the 1916 Irish rebellion against seven hundred years of British colonial rule. Unsurprisingly, given its politically sensitive subject matter, the film's aesthetic and narrative merits were subsumed by debates over its historical accuracy. Jordan's heroic figuring of Collins (Liam Neeson) – who adopted acts of guerrilla warfare to bring the British to the negotiation table but, in doing so, some have argued, may have created a north/south divide – was particularly criticised. Others took issue with Jordan's unsympathetic representation of the leading figure of the Republican Party, Eamon De Valera (Alan Rickman). Some members of the British press suggested that Michael Collins 'might just as well have been supplied by Sinn Fein's propaganda department' and accused its backers of 'corporate irresponsibility'.

For his next film, *The Butcher Boy* (1997), Jordan turned to an Irish literary source with an adaptation of Patrick McCabe's celebrated novel. Set in a rural Irish community during the early 1960s, the film is an acerbic and breathless coming-of-age picture that depicts events in the life of an orphaned prepubescent, Francie Brady (Eamonn Owens). Rather than dwell upon the often unfettered and romanticised narrative conventions of the genre, the film shows a socially disenfranchised and psychotic boy coming to terms with some terse actualities of adult life – sexual abuse, alcoholism, suicide, and class prejudice. For the majority of critics, the film was a successful amalgam of formal expressionism, narrative realism and comedy. For the wider audience, Jordan's obdurate depiction of an aberrant childhood proved too much of an affront, and the film failed to make any impact on the mainstream market.

With *In Dreams* (1999), Jordan returned to America and turned his attention toward the supernatural/psychological thriller genre. Annette Bening plays Claire Cooper, an illustrator of children's books, who has psychic powers. A psychotic child killer is at large in rural Massachusetts and Claire has premonitions during which she gains clues to the murderer's (Robert Downey Jr's) identity. Predictably, the authorities roundly dismiss Claire's claims and she is forced to hunt down the killer alone. Narratively, *In Dreams* was critically dismissed as formulaic, but was praised for its unsettling, expressionistic dream sequences, in particular, a much celebrated opening scene in which police divers looking for the bodies of the killer's victims swim gracefully through the perfectly preserved homes of a flooded town.

Jordan returned to Europe – and a revered literary source – for his most recent feature, the period drama *The End of the Affair* (1999). Set in London during the Blitz, the film is a loose adaptation of Graham Greene's semi-autobiographical novel that drew on the author's adulterous love affair with Catherine Watson, the American wife of a wealthy farmer. Ralph Fiennes and Julianne Moore play Maurice and Sarah, the adulterous couple, with Stephen Rea taking the role of Sarah's husband, Henry. Quite apart from the narrative's tragic emotional impact, and its deft use of London locations – producer Woolley referred to the city as the film's fourth character – the film's structure is distinguished by its split narration. Jordan has referred to this process as a 'kaleidoscopic exploration of the same pivotal scenes'. Although *The End of the Affair* enjoyed only a modest commercial success, critically it was viewed as something of a return to form for Jordan. It received ten BAFTA nominations, and a Best Actress Academy Award nomination for Moore. Jordan has continued his association with Moore in a 14-minute film, *Not I* (2000), based on Samuel Beckett's play.

He has recently finished making *The Honest Thief*, a remake of Jean-Pierre Melville's *Bob le flambeur* (1955), starring Nick Nolte, which is set for release in late 2002. **TT**

# Mike JUDGE

*Beavis and Butt-head*
*Do America* (1996)
*Office Space* (1999)

Mike Judge is a keen Rockwellian observer of modern society – as filtered through southern United States culture – and has crafted a successful creative career in film and television with his dead-on satiric and often hilarious observations.

Born in Ecuador in 1962, Judge was raised in Albuquerque, New Mexico, and was a shy, unassuming kid who was 'scared to death of talking to girls'. He went on to attend the University of California, San Diego, where he earned a physics degree. Sustaining a life-long interest in animation, he filmed several animated shorts in the early 1990s. His short film *Frog Baseball* (1992) was the genesis of MTV-produced animated series 'Beavis and Butt-head', an irreverent show about two lower-middle-class 14-year-old poseurs obsessed with chicks, heavy metal, and all things cool. Its feature spin-off, *Beavis and Butt-head Do America* (1996), follows the titular characters on a ribald, politically incorrect road trip in search of their most prized property, a television, until they get side-tracked by the possibility of getting laid. Snuggling quite comfortably in the young male-targeted 'idiotic buddy road-trip' sub-genre, the film compares favourably to such standards as *Dumb & Dumber* (1994), *Kingpin* (1996), and other successful dumb duo pictures like *Wayne's World* (1992).

Judge's subsequent live-action film, *Office Space* (1999), demonstrates a hilarious, wickedly dry sense of humour about white collar labour and modern corporate life, when not bogged down by uninteresting romantic tangents and 'whodunit' capers. His forthcoming remake of *The Incredible Mr Limpet* (1964) will combine CGI animation with live action. **THa**

# Gil JUNGER

*10 Things I Hate About You*
(1999)
*Black Knight* (2001)

A decade-long career directing television sitcoms such as 'Ellen' – now infamous for its star's 'coming out' – and the recent 'Daddio', about a stay-at-home dad, seem to have provided Gil Junger with the light touch and attention to comic detail necessary to maintain a feature. Fittingly, when he turned to movies it was Karen McCullah and Kirsten Smith's script dealing with strong females and gender role explorations that caught his eye.

*10 Things I Hate About You* (1999) forms one of the cluster of recent movies again aimed at the established Hollywood demographic – the teenager. Alongside the likes of *American Pie* (1999), rather than the more subversive *Rushmore* (1998), *10 Things* has another bandwagon on which to ride: the trend for modernising classic texts. Like Amy Heckerling's updated 'Emma' in *Clueless* (1995), Baz Luhrmann's *William Shakespeare's Romeo + Juliet* (1996), and a version of 'Les liaisons dangereuses' called *Cruel Intentions* (1999), *10 Things* contemporises 'The Taming of the Shrew' and, like its contemporaries, finds its natural home in the American high school.

The Stratford family parallels the play's central family. Gynaecologist dad, Walter (Larry Miller), knows all the pitfalls of modern teen romance and resolves to refuse lovely Bianca (Larisa Oleynik) a chance to date until her ill-tempered older sister Kat (Julia Stiles) can find someone willing to take her on. The film turns on this dilemma, finding an appealing and feisty heroine in Stiles, and incorporating the teen staples of drunken partying, sexual regret and complicated emotions with a surprising lack of sentiment.

Despite its intentions, the film places its difficult heroine into an ideology espoused by her father, to be 'tamed' by her move into a relationship. Only the guitar given to her by her new love (Heath Ledger as Patrick Verona) suggests that an offbeat creativity and independent sensibility may still be allowed to live on in Kat.

Junger returned to television with the James Belushi show 'According to Jim' and made his second big-screen offering, the Martin Lawrence vehicle *Black Knight* (2001). A comic attempt to discuss race, the film posits Lawrence's Medieval World employee in Hollywood's version of fourteenth-century England after a knock on the head transports him back in time. Here the staple 'fish out of water' plot takes over with Lawrence trying to get to grips with medieval tradition. A farce which involves the opening of a chain of medieval fast-food restaurants, after his accomplished feature debut, it is something of a disappointment. **JD**

# George KACZENDER

Born in 1933, George Kaczender fled his native Hungary, where he had trained at the Budapest Film Academy, and arrived in Canada as a political refugee and joined the National Film Board. The short films that he made under their auspices were sincere, intelligent socio-dramas, dealing with complex educational and family issues. Particularly notable are *World of Three*, a perspective of parenting through a confused three-year-old's eyes, and *Phoebe*, a sensitive piece on teenage pregnancy which won five international awards and remains the second biggest-seller in the Film Board's history.

His features, however, did not rise to expectations. Although his deft direction is apparent – particularly his painterly, graphic style with its occasional surreal touches – his films' sexual politics now leave a peculiarly stale odour. His first feature, *Don't Let The Angels Fall* (1969) portrays his adoptive country, as do many emigrés, in a way that captures the essence of a nation more poignantly than many native inhabitants. This film deals with the fragmentary nature of Canada's social structure in the light of it's colonised past and its cultural identification with the US. The resultant victim/survivor status of Canada is echoed in the microcosm of an urban family cracking apart. The father pursues an affair outside the town, his student son becomes involved simultaneously with protests and a lounge singer, the younger son dreams of running away, and the mother struggles with her increasing inability to nurture her family. The everyday grind of relationships and all-pervading sense of failure whilst still chasing an elusive ideal would became the enduring theme of Kaczender's work. *Don't Let The Angels Fall* won critical praise and is well made but is relentlessly downbeat with no leavening humour or irony.

Kaczender set up his own production company for his second feature, *U-Turn* (1973), which dealt with the changing concept of marriage in a small town. This was selected as the official Canadian entry to the Berlin International Film Festival. The tone attempted to counteract *Angels'* soberness and is a more witty and engaging attack on authority. The ostensible romance and the idealistic search for identity is a compromise between commercial and art movies, but it was generally well received.

*Don't Let The Angels Fall* (1969)
*U-Turn* (1973)
*In Praise of Older Women* (1978)
*Chanel Solitaire* (1981)
*Agency* (1981)
*Your Ticket is No Longer Valid* (1984)
*Prettykill* (1987)
*Maternal Instincts* (1996)

*In Praise of Older Women* (1978) was a very personal one – Stephen Vizinczey, the author of the original book, was the director's best friend. An autobiographical intent was reinforced with the casting of Tom Berenger, Kaczender's exact contemporary, to play the part which he admitted resonated so closely with his own life. The picaresque story follows a Hungarian man who explores a number of relationships with girls and older women and emigrates to Canada where he becomes a philosophy lecturer. Although the film is visually lush, and the music stirring, the sexual encounters are conventional and largely unchallenging. Berenger himself, however, achieves an appropriate stiffness in an uncharacterised role. Karen Black plays the older woman who seduces him, and whilst Susan Strasberg and Alexandra Stewart excel they can do little to raise the film as a whole.

In 1981 he made *Chanel Solitaire*, a French biopic of Coco Chanel played by Marie-France Pisier. The film suggests that she was created largely by the men who surrounded her and largely ignored her work in favour of her love affairs and lesbian experience. In the same year Kazcender directed *Agency*, which was based on a intriguing premise but failed to deliver. Robert Mitchum plays a political leader who takes over an advertising agency with a view to implanting subliminal messages to ensure his political success. Lee Majors is the 'hero' who is dull-witted in the extreme, failing to understand Mitchum's motivation long after the audience. A similar problem of audience underestimation exists in *Prettykill* (1987), an exploitation film which reveals the hooker killer to be the 'split-personality' played by Susan Snyder, by turns incredibly irritating and unintentionally amusing as she plays between her alter-ego Southern daddy and little-girl-lost personas. This movie, tasteless even within this genre, is thus rendered pointless; with no twist to reveal at the dénouement it settles for an unconvincingly happy ending.

Kaczender has since directed many television movies and shows such as 'Falcon Crest' and 'Tour of Duty', and has recently served as a member of the selection committee for foreign films at the Academy of Motion Picture Arts and Sciences.    **FG**

## Jonathan KAHN

*Girl* (1999)  Jonathan Kahn's debut film, *Girl* (1999), is a coming of age tale in which the actors are handled with an adeptness common to solid, well-told, if old-fashioned movies. Starring Dominique Swain, who just two years before seemed marooned in the high-gloss claustrophobia of Adrian Lyne's *Lolita* (1997), *Girl* tells the story of a successful high-school student who explores the grungy world of Portland's rock scene before heading off to the Ivy League.

Stylistically similar to other films of this sub-genre, such as Cameron Crowe's inauspicious but well-loved *Singles* (1992), the film's main virtue is the revelation of Swain. She dominates the movie and Kahn allows her the time and space to do so. Her face is full of interesting, changing expressions as she makes the transition from high school to rock club. Swain's performance aside, the film itself is nothing special. At times distinctly uncinematic, *Girl* is really a television programme that lasts an hour and a half. It is, however, teen television of the quality of 'Dawson's Creek' or 'My So Called Life', rather than the syrupy fare of most 'angst in the afternoon' shows.    **CSo**

## Tom KALIN

*Swoon* (1992)  Tom Kalin worked for several years as a producer for AIDSFILMS, a prevention education
*Plain Pleasures* (1996)  organisation, and with the AIDS activist groups ACT UP and Gran Fury, which he co-founded. He directed a number of short films in the early 1990s, and made his feature debut with *Swoon* (1992), which he also wrote, edited, and co-produced. It is one of the key achievements of the New Queer Cinema. Blending 1920s actuality and fictional footage, tableau, courtroom re-enactments of transcripts, and other non-fictional material with straightforward narrative, *Swoon* is the third cinematic version of the Leopold and Loeb case, but unlike *Rope* (1948) and *Compulsion* (1959) it is able to refer overtly to the homosexuality of its protagonists. Visually and intellectually intriguing, Kalin's well-edited collage represents a determined effort to not produce a positive-image picture, and because it is able to be unambiguous in its discussion of sexuality it succeeds in establishing the cause of their crimes within psychopathology, rather than in some aberrant sexuality which cannot be spoken.

Kalin has continued to direct shorts, the most substantial of which is the 30-minute *Plain Pleasures* (1996), starring Frances McDormand, Will Patton, and Lili Taylor. Various other projects have been mooted, including a biopic of photographer Robert Mapplethorpe, but as yet nothing else of feature length has been forthcoming. Kalin executive produced *Go Fish* (1994), produced *I Shot Andy Warhol* (1996), and contributed dialogue to *Office Killer* (1997), a grim gothic comedy about office downsizing and serial murder.                                             **MB**

# Janusz KAMINSKI

Born in Poland in 1959, Janusz Kaminski graduated from the American Film Institute *Lost Souls* (2000) and quickly became one of the most sought-after cinematographers in American cinema. Principally renowned for his collaborations with Steven Spielberg (he has garnered two Academy Awards, one for the lustrous monochrome of *Schindler's List* (1993), the second for the bleached-out hues of *Saving Private Ryan* (1998)), Kaminski's sole directorial work to date is *Lost Souls* (2000). A hybrid of *Rosemary's Baby* (1968), *The Exorcist* (1973), and *End of Days* (1999), it eerily tapped into the millennial zeitgeist that surrounded all things supernatural. The plot is relatively concise: Winona Ryder is the young woman saved from demonic possession who must then warn writer Ben Chaplin that he may be Satan's next victim. Kaminski conjures up the requisite spooky atmosphere, but *Lost Souls* is ultimately hamstrung by a dysfunctional narrative and a frustratingly unimaginative conclusion. As befits Kaminski's cinematographic roots, the mood is expertly established, all diffuse light and mute colour schemes, while the (necessarily) hammy performances from John Hurt and Philip Baker Hall lends the film a welcome gravitas. Ryder's kohl-eyed ingenue seems out of her depth here (as did Patricia Arquette in the similar *Stigmata* (1999)), but Kaminski's version of apocalyptic horror benefits from an edgy soundtrack and sinewy cinematography. Probably best filed under 'disappointing debut', the film marks a somewhat unimaginative cross-over for Kaminski, but contains ample evidence that his feel for pace and mood may yet warrant further attention.

After *Lost Souls*, Kaminski returned to cinematography with Spielberg's *A.I.* (2001) and *Minority Report* (2002).                                             **BM**

# Charles T. KANGANIS

Charles T. Kanganis began his cinematic career writing the screenplay for 1988's *LA*  *Deadly Breed* (1989)
*Heat*. Working within the sub-genre of police action, made popular in the 1980s after  *A Time to Die* (1991)
such television dramas as 'NYPD Blue' and 'Miami Vice', his first directorial project was  *No Escape, No Return* (1993)
in 1989 with *Deadly Breed*. A violent thriller with white supremacy as its central concern,  *Intent to Kill* (1993)
the film stands at the beginning of a list of similarly hard-core films Kanganis worked on  *Three Ninjas Kick Back*
either as screenwriter, director, or both. As the titles suggest, his portfolio covers a range  (1994)
of glamorous and provocative scenarios: diamond heists (*Chance* (1989)), organised  *Race the Sun* (1996)
crime (*Fist of Honor* (1992)), drug barons (*Intent to Kill* (1992)), prostitution (*A Time*  *Dennis the Menace*
*to Die* (1991)), and police corruption (*No Escape No Return* (1993)).  *Strikes Again* (1998)

This final subject, of police corruption, is a particularly recurrent one, and apparently  *K-911* (1999)
a fascination of Kanganis'. However, where Abel Ferrara, in 1992's similarly-themed *Bad Lieutenant,* boldly opens up his morally-repellent character to us for judgment and also a sympathetic hope for redemption, Kanganis never dares beyond the safe and dependable good-guy, bad-guy opposition. There are no such socially subversive suggestions from him. He brings to the screen such simplified and caricatured characters that no matter how duped the worthy hero is by the suave villain, audience identification could never waver; the enjoyment clearly is meant to be in watching how the heroes outwit (or out-fight) the bad guys.

One problematic issue evident in Kanganis' work is his representation of women. Working in an industry fully informed by the feminist theories which emerged in the 1970s, Kanganis is keen to include a female presence in the very masculine genre he has chosen. Disappointingly, they either play the beautiful victim in a rape storyline or feisty cops who overcome their male assailants with unlikely physical strength. In one scenario from *No Escape No Return*, the antagonism between these oppositional roles produces a highly disturbing system of identificatory pleasure. A policewoman is sent undercover to entice a suspected rapist, but watching from behind a two-way mirror her back-up officers are embittered by her past rejection of their sexual advances. They evidently enjoy watching her overly provocative behaviour with the suspect. By extension the camera's gratuitously slow sweeps of her barely dressed body, and the policemen's voice-over ('yeah, she wants it') invite the audience, too, to take pleasure in watching not only her eroticised body, but its domination by the man. Only after prolonged fetishisation does Kanganis let the scene's narrative agenda resume itself and the back-up policemen enter the room to apprehend the suspect.

More frequently fetishised by Kanganis' camera, however, is the male body, and all its capacity for destruction. By far the most prominent aspect of his films is his penchant for combat. It is usual for his films to start with at least three full-scale fights and a couple of car crashes, the action slowed down for full effect. He seems particularly adept with martial arts but also comfortable with guns and boxing too, and his fight scenes are deftly choreographed and determinedly brutal: muscles flex and blood splashes. Physical prowess and strength are what govern, in terms of the narrative resolution as well as everything Kanganis puts within his frame.

After a gradual increase in emotional sensitivity, and in keeping with the general trends of 1990s Hollywood's action cinema, Kanganis broached the family entertainment arena with *Three Ninjas Kick Back* (1994), a sequel to the successful children's film *Three Ninjas* (1992). This brought him a new audience, more receptive to his simplistic moralising than adults, and the film enjoyed moderate success. Kanganis' action experience endowed the film with an edge not seen in the first of the series, and it tightens up the predictable family drama.

Kanganis has since directed other family-oriented films but with limited success. According to the producers, he was chosen to direct 1996's *Race the Sun* for his ability to work with an ensemble cast and at a low budget. However, the concept of the film – an eclectic group of children race a solar-powered car across Australia – demanded a depth of characterisation Kanganis lacked, and the film failed to meet expectations despite a strong and enthusiastic young cast. Most recently, and with lack of conviction, he has directed *Dennis the Menace Strikes Again* (1998) and the limping *K-9 II* (1999), two sequels for which there was little demand and a sadly insipid reception.     **MS**

# Marek KANIEVSKA

*Another Country* (1984)
*Less Than Zero* (1987)
*Where the Money Is* (2000)

Marek Kanievska has been described as a director of the 'international style', a term which hints at his lack of personal or national stylistic touches. Born in England in 1952, of Polish parentage, he began his career in the theatre. He attempted to gain entry on Television Direction training schemes for both LWT and Granada, but due to the early curtailment of his education and the lack of a degree, he was considered unacceptable. A directorial break in an Australian television drama led to a Penguin Best Adult Drama Award and on his return to England he embarked upon a successful small-screen career ('Coronation Street' and 'Shoestring') and made an Academy Award-winning short, *A Shocking Accident*. His direction of Central Television's 'Muck and Brass' brought him to the attention of producer Alan Marshall who chose Kanievska to direct *Another Country* (1984), the film adaptation of Julian Mitchell's hit play.

Focusing on the education of spy Guy Burgess (Rupert Everett), *Another Country* conjectures upon the circumstances which spawned a defector. It posits, somewhat simplistically, that the traitorous seeds lie in the denial of his entry to the school elite due to an indiscreet homosexual love affair, and are carried on the naïve Marxist invective of his best friend, based on Donald MacLean (Colin Firth). The film won Best Artistic Contribution at its Cannes World Premiere for Peter Biziou's cinematography; lush and elegant but also hard-edged and dark, it elevates the film from soft-focused nostalgia. The scenic beauty of Cambridge serves to underline the oppressive, masochistic hypocrisy of the institution. The direction overcame the verbosity and light tone of the play. However, while it is claustrophobically tight, forcefully directed and maintains an air of tragedy, the substance of Marxism is trivialised; hypocrisy is revealed but privilege *per se* is not questioned. This remains the preserve of the scathing satire achieved in *If...* (1968), a superior film on a similar subject.

Kanievska's next project, *Less Than Zero* (1987), a sanitised and even more superficial version of Bret Easton Ellis's novel, was also concerned with privilege.

Focusing on an affluent bisexual, Julian (Robert Downey Jr), and the attempts of his two best friends to prevent his descent into a self-destructive drug-fuelled binge, the film loses the sexual fluidity of the book's character who becomes forced into 'unnatural acts' to avoid his drug debts. The 1980s may have been a superficial decade but the film's brashness disallows any emotional connection. Although the saturated colour is attractive, the gloss convincing, and the constantly moving camera creates a suitably paranoid atmosphere, the drugs are the only chemistry here. *Less Than Zero* is most notable for Downey's performance, particularly in light of his emergent real-life problems.

A lack of chemistry is also the problem in *Where the Money Is* (2000), which is only saved from complete obscurity by Paul Newman, who plays a criminal who escapes life imprisonment by faking a stroke. Once hospitalised, his suspicious nurse Linda Fiorentino, desperate to escape her drudgery by a bank raid of her own, sets out to convince him to work on one last job. With little tension, suspense, comedy or action, the film relies on its relationship between Newman and Fiorentino, and her outrageous attempts to goad him out of his 'paralysis' by lap dancing, and finally throwing his wheelchair off a dock. Poorly directed, the film never emerges as anything other than a second-rate Newman vehicle.                                                        **FG**

# Deborah KAPLAN
See **Harry ELFONT**

# Jonathan KAPLAN

Jonathan Kaplan is a film-maker whose work treads a provocative and often uneasy line between social exposé and exploitation. Born in 1947 in Paris, Kaplan learned the art of how to make creative, energetic films on a shoestring budget through his experience of working for legendary independent producer Roger Corman (other notables discovered by Corman include Francis Ford Coppola and James Cameron).

*Night Call Nurses* (1972)
*The Student Teachers* (1973)
*The Slams* (1973)
*Truck Turner* (1974)
*White Line Fever* (1975)
*Mr Billion* (1977)
*Over the Edge* (1979)
*Heart Like a Wheel* (1983)
*Project X* (1987)
*The Accused* (1988)
*Immediate Family* (1989)
*Love Field* (1992)
*Unlawful Entry* (1992)
*Bad Girls* (1994)
*Brokedown Palace* (1999)

Kaplan's first two feature films, the sex comedies *Night Call Nurses* (1972) and *The Student Teachers* (1973), are direct products of his collaboration with Corman. Witty and at times subversive of the exploitation genre in which they situate themselves, Kaplan's early films augur the director's later interest in the representation of sexual politics. Kaplan's next three films are violent action pictures. *The Slams* (1973) and *Truck Turner* (1974) are blaxploitation films, featuring pimps and drug dealers as lead characters. *White Line Fever* (1975) is another violent low-budget picture that follows the trials and tribulations of a group of truck drivers. *Mr Billion* (1977) is a bland road action comedy about an auto mechanic who inherits a fortune. Kaplan's final film of the 1970s, *Over the Edge* (1979), stands out as one of his most compelling. In contrast to the pictures that precede it, *Over the Edge* is a film about violence. Scripted by Tim Hunter (who would go on to direct his own chilling tale of nihilistic suburban youth in the 1987 movie *River's Edge*), the film is a disturbing chronicle of alienated youth in a suburban planned community. Possibly the most undervalued teen movie of the last three decades, the film launched the career of Matt Dillon.

The 1980s are Kaplan's most critically and commercially successful period as a director. *Heart Like a Wheel* (1983) tells the story of racing car driver Shirley Muldowney, who struggles against sexism and marital discord to fulfil her dream of becoming a champion on the racetrack. Heralded for its sensitivity to issues of sexual representation, the film boasts a good performance from Bonnie Bedelia. Kaplan's next picture, *Project X* (1987), starring Matthew Broderick, is the story of a young military inductee and his struggle to save a group of chimps from nasty experiments. The film is mainly notable for Kaplan's good direction of the chimps. *The Accused* (1988) is Kaplan's most acclaimed – and most controversial – picture. Based on a real-life case, the film tells the story of Sarah Tobias (played by Jodie Foster in an Academy Award-winning performance), a young woman who is gang-raped in a neighbourhood bar while a group of male spectators stand by and cheer the rapists on. 'The only difference between this and actual rape is that someone is yelling "cut",' Kaplan is reported to have said in regard to his explicit depiction of the rape (shown in flashback at the end of the film). Although some praise the film as a powerful critique of voyeurism, others see the film as submitting to the structures of voyeurism that it professes to subvert. The debate concerning whether the rape scene is 'ethical' or 'exploitative' continues to bear significance: over a decade after its release, the rape in *The Accused* remains one of the most-watched rape scenes in cinematic history.

In the past decade, Kaplan has done extensive work for television, directing several episodes of the hit television series 'ER'. That his career has increasingly shifted in the direction of television is both fitting and ironic given that one of the most frequent criticisms of his feature film work is its resemblance to 'TV movies of the week'. *Immediate Family* (1989) is a film about a yuppie couple and the troubled teenager who decides to give them her baby. It is a competent film with some nice touches but the only thing that really raises it above a standard television melodrama is Mary Stuart Masterson's extraordinary performance as the pregnant teen. *Love Field* (1992), starring Michelle Pfeiffer as the Texan housewife obsessed with Jacqueline Kennedy, is a promising, if generically muddled, film. A road movie that explores racial prejudice in 1960s America, the film tries to be too many things at once. *Unlawful Entry* (1992), an urban paranoia thriller, centres on Kaplan's twin pet themes: violence and the law. While this thriller about a cop-turned-stalker (played to chilling effect by Ray Liotta) is fairly formulaic stuff, Kaplan tries to bring out underlying social issues about everyday citizens and their attempts to protect themselves against violence. *Bad Girls* (1994), his one-time foray into the western genre, is a career low for Kaplan. Despite a powerhouse all-star female cast including Drew Barrymore, Madeleine Stowe and Mary Stuart Masterson, the film suffers from its almost non-existent direction.

Kaplan's most recent film, *Brokedown Palace* (1999), demonstrates his continuing interest in the themes of law and justice. Two girls from Ohio take a trip to Bangkok, fall in with the wrong company, and are eventually sentenced to 33 years in a Thai prison for drug smuggling. Some critics saw xenophobia in the film's bleak portrayal of Thailand.                                                                                                  **TH**

# Jake KASDAN

Son of veteran Hollywood director Lawrence Kasdan, Jake Kasdan, born in 1975, began his career in cinema appearing as a child actor in several of his father's films – *The Big Chill* (1983), *Silverado* (1985), and *The Accidental Tourist* (1988) – and later compiled the companion book to his biopic *Wyatt Earp* (1994). He has also worked in theatre, writing and directing a number of plays, including 'The Behavioural Patterns of Funnyman Tyler Hudson' in 1995 at the Hollywood Playhouse.

Choosing to visit the detective noir genre for his writing/directing debut, *Zero Effect* (1998), he put a fresh spin on the Sherlock Holmes/Dr Watson pairing and created the characters of Daryl Zero (Bill Pullman), a reclusive but brilliantly deductive private eye, and Steve Arlo (Ben Stiller), the frontman who has the unenviable job of meeting clients and feeding information back to his eccentric boss. Faced with a new case involving blackmail and murder, the two relocate to Portland to investigate. Problematically however, having always worked on the premise that observation and objectivity are key to any good detective work, Zero's usually keen perception is dulled when he falls in love with a mysterious paramedic who turns out to be the daughter of the client and a suspect in the case. While adding nothing new to the genre, *Zero Effect* is by no means hackneyed. Tightly scripted, suitably atmospheric (without being wholly derivative), with a compelling soundtrack by Nick Cave and the Greyboy Allstars, the film is intriguingly engaging and humorous. Pullman disarmingly alters his heroic nice-guy President image from *Independence Day* (1996) to become the bad guitar-playing, neurotic genius, and Stiller plays the long-suffering, resentful henchman who simply wants to get married with considerable aplomb.

After making this auspicious debut, Kasdan directed several episodes of television series such as 'Freaks and Geeks', and released his second feature, *Orange County*, in 2002. Starring Colin Hanks (son of Tom Hanks) and Schuyler Fisk (daughter of Sissy Spacek), as boyfriend and girlfriend Shaun and Ashley, it follows his emotional progression from carefree surfer to Stanford applicant; failing to get into the university, he fails also to gain the attention of his family. Injecting the off-kilter humour of *Zero Effect* into the teen genre, the film is considerably deeper than most and benefits from great performances, particularly the presence of Jack Black as Shaun's stoned brother.   **HP**

# Lawrence KASDAN

Lawrence Kasdan has directed some of the most intelligent and compelling films of the 1980s, and also contributed to the screenplays of key films of the period: *The Empire Strikes Back* (1980), *Raiders of the Lost Ark* (1981), and *Return of the Jedi* (1983). He is also a director who enjoys pushing the boundaries of genre and playing with our conceptions of the past. Born in Miami in 1949, and educated at the University of Michigan in English and Education, Kasdan embarked on a graduate film course at the University of California, but did not finish; he spent five years as a copywriter in advertising. In 1980 he collaborated with Irvin Kershner on the screenplay of *The Empire Strikes Back*, a partnership that continued with a further episode, *Return of the Jedi*.

Kasdan made an auspicious feature film debut with *Body Heat* (1981), a stylish updating of the classic film noir *Double Indemnity* (1944). The film is a pastiche of the genre and as such shares some of the genre's common characteristics: a weak man (William Hurt), a dangerous femme fatale (Kathleen Turner, making her feature film debut), tight plotting, and noirish iconography. The director's next feature, *The Big Chill* (1983), is credited as the first film to open the floodgates on the Reagan-era's re-visiting of the 1960s in film. The story centres on a group of former friends who were campus radicals at the University of Michigan in the 1960s, and begins with their reuniting for the funeral of Alex (Kevin Costner). Burying Alex is symbolic of the friends' burial of their idealism and radical ideas, as they come to realise they have become that which they most despised. It is widely regarded as a slicker, more upmarket version of the John Sayles low-budget classic, *Return of the Secaucus Seven* (1980). *The Big Chill* received mixed reviews but was a greater commercial success than the director's debut picture. Kasdan turned his keen eye for genre on the western for his next feature, *Silverado* (1985), with some success. Despite fairly flat characterisations, it is a stylish, knowing, and entertaining re-working of the genre.

Arguably his best film to date, *The Accidental Tourist* (1988) is a poignant and faithful adaptation of Anne Tyler's best-selling novel about a grieving travel writer, Macon Leary (William Hurt). Leary's son has been killed in a random shooting at a burger bar, and he closes off from the world, unable to make sense of the act. He meets Muriel (Geena Davies), who sets about bringing Leary out of his shell. Initially, the fact that *The Accidental Tourist* is a comedy seems to be at odds with Hurt's depressed and downbeat characterisation and the film's initial premise of father grieving for tragically-murdered son. Yet this is the film's genius – the fine counter-balance between pain and laughter. Geena Davies won an Academy Award for Best Supporting Actress, and the film was also nominated for Best Picture, Best Screenplay and Best Music.

Kasdan followed with another comedy, *I Love You to Death* (1990). Based on the true story of a woman who tried to have her husband killed five times, the film stars Kevin Kline and Tracey Ullman as the couple. Kasdan turned to the issues of race, class and violence in his next feature, *Grand Canyon* (1991). The film interweaves several characters' stories from an initial chance meeting between a rich lawyer (Kevin Kline) and a tow-truck driver (Danny Glover). Its message is admirable, if rather overstated at times: that society builds walls between people that need to be broken down. The film was co-written with his wife, Meg Kasdan.

Kasdan returned to the western with his biopic, *Wyatt Earp* (1994); hot on the heels of George P. Cosmatos' *Tombstone* (1993), it is essentially the same story. The film's direction is slacker than Kasdan's previous work and the characterisations curiously empty. He changed genres for his next picture, *French Kiss* (1995), a romantic comedy starring Meg Ryan as a woman dumped by her fiancé (Timothy Hutton) because he has met the love of his life at a conference in Paris. Overcoming her mortal fear of flying, she gets on a plane bound for Paris and meets French jewel thief Luc (Kevin Kline), who stashes stolen gems in her luggage. In an attempt to recover the jewels, Luc pretends to help her win back her fiancé, but en route they fall in love. *French Kiss* is a pleasant – if totally implausible – distraction, particularly in its use of the scenery of Paris and Cannes. It received mixed critical reviews and did modest business at the box office.

Kasdan's subsequent feature is a warm and intriguing comedy, *Mumford* (1999). It focuses on an IRS worker who quits his job, moves to the small town of Mumford, and takes the town's name as his own. Masquerading as a psychologist, he sets about giving the townsfolk radical advice that changes the fabric of life in the town, and Mumford himself (Loren Dean).

*Dreamcatcher*, based on a story by Stephen King, who partially wrote the screenplay, has yet to be released. The tale is classic King realised via the capable direction of Kasdan – four childhood friends from Maine, now in middle age and all dealing with personal crises, meet up for a break in the old cabin they used to frequent as children. Events come to a head after they encounter a mysterious stranger up at the cabin.

Kasdan's contribution to Hollywood cinema in the 1980s cannot be overstated. He has figured in the creation of some of the most popular and best-loved films of the period. In some ways, the director peaked too soon with the highly regarded *Body Heat*, but more recent films such as *Mumford* find him back on top form. **SL**

# Philip KAUFMAN

*The Great Northfield Minnesota Raid* (1972)
*The White Dawn* (1974)
*Invasion of the Body Snatchers* (1978)
*The Wanderers* (1979)
*The Right Stuff* (1983)
*The Unbearable Lightness of Being* (1988)
*Henry & June* (1990)
*Rising Sun* (1993)
*Quills* (2000)

Philip Kaufman's films have been as varied as his colourful career. With stints as an academic, postman, kibbutz worker, and teacher behind him, he found his cinematic calling in the early 1960s, and remains one of the most iconoclastic directors still working in Hollywood. The artistic and ideological liberation of the 1960s resonates through his work. His stories often examine counter-cultural figures at odds with society's norms: the outlaw gunfighters of *The Great Northfield Minnesota Raid* (1972), the fighter jocks of *The Right Stuff* (1983), the street gangs of *The Wanderers* (1979), and the libertarian Marquis de Sade in *Quills* (2000). Strong on mood and atmosphere, his films employ powerful cinematography and a lyrical, poetic style to explore the consequences of colliding worlds and changing eras.

Born in Chicago in 1936, Kaufman grew up in the charged atmosphere of post-war America. Having graduated from the University of Chicago, he had intended to take up a history professorship at Harvard, but was caught up by the counter-cultural tide sweeping America in the early 1960s. He dropped out, became a postman in San Francisco, and befriended a number of influential beat figures, along with the writer Henry Miller, whose relationship with Anaïs Nin later became the subject of *Henry & June* (1990). He lived briefly on a kibbutz in Israel, and became interested in cinema while working as a teacher in Italy, inspired by the guerrilla approach of the Italian New Wave and American independents like John Cassavetes. He returned to the US in 1962 and turned an unfinished novel into his first short film, *Goldstein*, followed by the short crime caper *Fearless Frank*. Contracts for various Hollywood studios followed, and Kaufman quickly fell in with a generation of young directors who, like him, were hell-bent on bringing down the walls of Old Hollywood.

*The Great Northfield Minnesota Raid* was Kaufman's first feature, a 'realistic' western following the last raid of the James-Younger gang, in the mode of recent hits like *Bonnie and Clyde* (1967). Wistful and brutal by turns, Kaufman's film exchanges the mythologising of the traditional western in favour of a gritty examination of outlaw ideology and the passing of the old west, pitting an incendiary Jesse James (played by Robert Duvall) against the measured realism of James Younger (Cliff Robertson). *The White Dawn* (1974) is another violent clash of ideologies, an Arctic western in which a crew of stranded whalers are taken in by a tribe of nomadic Eskimos. The wide-open plains and dusty frontiers of the west become the ice-floes and snow-plains of Arctic Alaska, with the sailors cast as the corrupting white men who disrupt the purity of native existence. The stylistic blend of philosophy and violence, and the fascination with self-destructive figures are characteristic Kaufman.

*The Outlaw Josey Wales* (1976) represents a different standpoint, a comic western in which Kaufman's maverick hero, out to avenge the slaughter of his family, gradually rediscovers the values of tolerance and community. Having scripted the film and finalised the cast, crew and locations, Kaufman was fired days into shooting by the film's star and eventual director Clint Eastwood. Two other projects faltered around this time: a big-screen adaptation of *Star Trek* (Kaufman was told science fiction had no future), and a story developed with George Lucas about a history professor (partly based on himself) who recovers lost relics. Shelved at the time for lack of funds, this later became – with Kaufman's blessing – the first instalment of the Indiana Jones trilogy.

Kaufman's subsequent films moved from a fascination with America's murky past to its complex present. *The Invasion of the Body Snatchers* (1978) exchanges the Cold

War paranoia of the 1955 original for the social revolution of late 1970s America, blending atmospheric horror with a wry satire on new age values. The film's B-movie premise, an invasion myth in which hippy-era San Francisco is slowly consumed by predatory plant-people, becomes a metaphor for a society in flux in which nothing and no one can be trusted. *The Wanderers* (1979) relocates Kaufman's gangland youth in Chicago to the mean streets of the 1960s Bronx, and again shows conflict and violence as perpetual American rites of passage. Rival gangs and their rigid codes of honour clash to a doo-wop and rock 'n' roll soundtrack, while the young bloods rumble their way through various landmarks of the decade, from Kennedy's death to the battlefields of Vietnam. Brimming with tension and charged emotion, this is Kaufman's antidote to the cosy nostalgia of *American Graffiti* (1973) and his wake-up call to a post-hippy America nostalgic for its lost youth.

At some level, Kaufman's films are all concerned with aspects of America, and *The Right Stuff* (1983) is the quintessential example. Adapted from the novel by 'new journalism' guru Tom Wolfe, the film contrasts the new age of the space race and America's first seven astronauts with their forgotten predecessor, ace test pilot Chuck Yeager. For Kaufman, the story becomes a western for a Cold War world, a contrast between the modern era of technology, money and media frenzy, and a purer age of dignity, individualism and Yankee self-reliance. Yeager (memorably played by Sam Shepard) is the laconic cowboy of yore, a warrior of the old world left behind by the new age, the astronauts his ideological sons at the edge of a new frontier. A mix of humour, philosophy and social comment, it is also the best example of Kaufman's lyrical style and fascination with the values of new and old America.

His next two films explored the consequences of sexual and emotional betrayal in a European setting. *The Unbearable Lightness of Being* (1988), from the Milan Kundera novel, explores the ménage à trois of a womanising doctor, his lover and his muse in pre-Communist Prague, an arrangement blown apart by the Russian occupation. *Henry & June* (1990) follows the compulsive love triangle between the writer Henry Miller, his wife June and his literary inspiration Anaïs Nin in 1930s Paris. The notoriously erotic cinematography of both films demonstrated Kaufman's desire to push the boundaries of acceptability (*Henry & June* forced the creation of the new NC-17 certificate) and his interest in exploring difficult and confrontational areas of cinema. *Rising Sun* (1993) is Kaufman's least successful film, a conspiracy thriller based on a Michael Crichton novel in which a prostitute's murder exposes the shady practices of Japanese businessmen in corporate America. Several years of controversy had not helped Kaufman's already delicate relationship with the studios, and he subsequently found himself taking a 'career break' which eventually stretched to eight years.

*Quills* (2000) saw him return in typically confrontational style, exploring the Marquis de Sade's imprisonment in a psychiatric sanatorium. For Kaufman, de Sade becomes a hero of free expression, challenging the covert corruption of church and aristocracy, though the rather more unsavoury aspects of his history (rape, masochism, depravity) are avoided in favour of a contrast between de Sade's imaginative liberation and the repressive values of pre-Revolutionary France.

The parallels between Kaufman's maverick characters and his own artistic struggles in Hollywood seem irresistible. Unlike most of his characters, however – as befits such a director – he seems destined for a happier end.                                    **OB**

# Diane KEATON

Best known as an actress and for her relationship with Woody Allen, Diane Keaton is also a director, producer and photographer. Having left Santa Ana College in California to study acting at New York's Neighbourhood Playhouse, she went on to sing in a band and perform on Broadway in the late 1960s. Popular for her distinct and endearing style of nervous acting, she has turned out a series of notable performances in *The Godfather* (1972), *Looking for Mr Goodbar* (1977), *Shoot the Moon* (1982), and won a Best Actress Academy Award in the title role of *Annie Hall* (1977). In the early 1980s she produced two collections of her photographs – 'Reservations' (1980) and 'Still Life' (1983) – and a short documentary, *What Does Dorrie Want?* (1982), focusing on the life of her sister, a legal secretary. Her next, lengthier documentary, *Heaven* (1987), juxtaposed old film clips and excerpts from religious programmes with a series

*Unstrung Heroes* (1995)
*Hanging Up* (2000)

of interviews in an attempt to explore a range of diverse and challenging concepts of heaven. Subsequent television projects included an after-school special for television, 'Girl with the Crazy Brother' (1990), and episodes of 'Twin Peaks'.

Focusing on her directing work to date some critics have justly labelled her 'precious' and 'overly-sentimental'. At worst she has a tendency to signpost every emotion for the audience, not trusting that they will be drawn into and effected by subtle visual or narrative insinuation. At best she is capable of eliciting unexpected sympathy from the most unyielding viewer. Made for television, her first full-length film, *Wildflower* (1991), is the story of two children who discover an abused and neglected farm girl and seek to educate her. Despite a spirited performance from a young Reese Witherspoon, it is ultimately unfulfilling, its moments of genuine pathos swamped by heavy-handed symbolism and monotonous repetition.

Bolstered by a characteristically offbeat script by Richard LaGravenese, *Unstrung Heroes* (1995) is a far more adept and mature piece of work. Set in Los Angeles in the early 1960s, it is a rites-of-passage tale dealing with the experiences of a twelve-year-old boy and his attempts to come to terms with the fatal illness of his mother (Andie MacDowell). Bewildered and angry, he seeks solace with his charmingly eccentric uncles, one of whom is a conspiracy theorist, the other a rubber-ball collector. Featuring comical and nuanced performances from John Turturro, Maury Chaykin and Michael Richards, its mix of humour and poignancy mark Keaton out as an able and unusual talent.

Her latest directorial offering, *Hanging Up* (2000), is proof that she has yet to realise her full potential. Like *Unstrung Heroes*, the film is focused around a family. But with a bigger budget and well-known stars, it achieves far less intimacy. The unique quirkiness that seemed so natural in her earlier work feels forced here. The manufactured kookiness is intensified by the casting of three neurotically-associated actresses – Meg Ryan, Lisa Kudrow, and Keaton herself – as three sisters trying to deal with the erratic behaviour of their dying father and their strained relationships with one another. Though admirable for its concentration on strong female characters and issues of bereavement, much of the genuine emotion is sanitised by Hollywood sheen.                                    **HP**

# David KELLOGG

*Cool as Ice* (1991)
*Inspector Gadget* (1999)

David Kellogg is best known in the industry for directing high-profile commercials for such corporations as American Express, Apple, Coca-Cola, IBM, Nike and Pepsi, amongst others. After co-producing and directing a segment of a *Playboy* video in 1990, Kellogg directed his first feature *Cool as Ice* (1991). The film is a throwback to Hollywood love stories of the 1950s. A rebellious outsider and motorcycle enthusiast, Johnny, courts a small town's smartest and prettiest young woman while besting her snobbish boyfriend, appeasing her father and rescuing her little brother from her father's would-be killers. Starring Vanilla Ice, rapper and teen sensation of the late 1980s and early 1990s, *Cool as Ice* was marketed by Universal as both a teen drama and modern musical that would capitalise on Ice's star persona. To this end, Kellogg interweaves the film's narrative with frenetically edited song-and-dance numbers that resemble music videos. Universal's high hopes that the film would catapult its star into a successful movie career were dashed when *Cool as Ice* was panned by critics and grossed only $1.2 million, falling far short of its $5.5 million budget.

Kellogg's second film, *Inspector Gadget* (1999), was an unqualified commercial success. Produced by Disney for $75 million, it grossed $22 million in its opening weekend, neared $100 million at the US box office, and was profitably released in dozens of international markets. The live-action film is based on the popular animated television series about a crime-fighter whose body is fitted with gadgets; the film updates this concept with sophisticated special effects, sterling production values and a surplus of spoofs ranging from *The Love Bug* (1969) to *Godzilla* (1998). Though some critics favourably commented on the film's special effects, most felt that matters of plot and narrative cohesion were neglected for physical comedy and visual gimmicks, no doubt to entice children to see the movie more than once. Kellogg's style is indicative of this strategy. *Inspector Gadget* relies on linear editing, action sequences and straightforward dialogue to keep young audiences alert and interested in the story.

Kellogg appears comfortable directing for teen and pre-teen sensibilities. He is currently directing *Flat Stanley*, which is based on the children's book of the same name. Written by Jeff Brown, the book follows the adventures of a boy who is flattened when a bulletin board falls on him. **JPa**

# Rory KELLY

Rory Kelly's film career has been a decidedly west coast affair: both in training and subject matter. Born in New York in 1961, he attended UCLA film school where he received several awards for his student shorts. His two features, *Sleep With Me* (1994) and *Some Girls* (1998), both centre on the tangled web that is the modern relationship for twentysomething Los Angelinos who never seem to work, always have money, and are up for cocktails at any time of day.

*Sleep With Me* (1994)
*Some Girls* (1998)

Kelly has described *Sleep With Me* as 'a movie about a group of friends written by a group of friends,' and this is quite literally the case. *Sleep With Me* is comprised of six vignettes by six different writers and produced by actor Eric Stoltz, who also appears in the film. The fractured, episodic structure of the film is held together by an even tone throughout: a rather arch treatment of love, friendship, and the social gathering. Betrayal, jealousy, and love never have a moment of solitude as another party, wedding, or afternoon tea perpetually loom on the horizon: personal battles must be played out in the public arena. While one critic has noted that 'it is not always clear whether Kelly wants to celebrate or satirise the attitudes and antics of the group', the director embraces the possibility that both can take place. Simultaneously, irony is admired as a defence strategy, and recognised as a limitation.

This dichotomy, a position somewhere between endorsement and condemnation, appears again in Kelly's second feature *Some Girl*. The film, which can best be summed up as a sympathetic portrayal of a female stalker, raises the stakes of *Sleep With Me* by placing an innocent within the swirl of sarcastic banter and careless emotion that is Kelly's LA. However, it is difficult to gauge if the film is supporting, or critiquing, the stance of earnestness; the film remains ambivalent, and is more interesting for doing so. Written as a first screenplay by Marissa Gibisi, starring Gibisi and her brother Giovanni, and produced by their mother, Gay, *Some Girl* gives Kelly a second opportunity to work within a tightly-knit group. Kelly was one of numerous directors to express interest in the screenplay, due to the fact that the film had an A-list star, Juliette Lewis, attached to it from the beginning. The film garnered Kelly a director's award at the 1998 Los Angeles Independent Film Festival.

In 1999 Kelly acted as a visiting assistant professor at UCLA. **LW**

# Lodge KERRIGAN

The 1990s was a decade notable for the alleged renewal of American independent cinema. The problematic use of the word 'independent' not withstanding, there were a handful of promising and radical young film-makers who came onto the scene during this time. Along with Todd Haynes and Hal Hartley, one could easily mention the name Lodge Kerrigan. Although he has only directed two films in the decade – *Clean, Shaven* (1995) and *Claire Dolan* (1998) – Kerrigan has made a name for himself as an independent film-maker whose radical visual style challenges both Hollywood's aesthetic and narratological concerns. Enraptured by protagonists trapped in their own oppressive realities, Kerrigan crafts a film viewing experience that is more interested in provocation than it is in pleasure.

*Clean, Shaven* (1995)
*Claire Dolan* (1998)

Born in 1964, a graduate of New York University, Lodge Kerrigan never entered the business of film-making with the desire to blend in. In one interview he stated, 'When I became an independent film-maker, I thought of being independent as somebody who wanted to attack the status quo'. As both writer and director, he carried this sensibility into the production of his first film, *Clean, Shaven*. The film takes as its protagonist a young schizophrenic named Peter Winter. Peter is desperately trying to wrest his daughter away from an adoptive family but his mental illness too often transforms the world into a disorienting barrage of sounds and images. The content of *Clean, Shaven* liberates Kerrigan to explore certain formal possibilities with the medium that are rarely observed in more mainstream cinema. He has commented that a reliance on dialogue is something that he actively avoids, and situating us in the psyche of a schizophrenic enables him to focus on an overtly mediated reality.

Encouraged by French producers, Lodge Kerrigan directed his second film, *Claire Dolan*. Once again in the role of writer/director, Kerrigan paints a portrait of a female prostitute far removed from the traditionally exotic Hollywood hooker. Claire Dolan is a woman who has attained an incredible degree of control over her male clients. She knows what to say to them to make them happy and she knows how to diffuse their sexual advances. In spite of this ability her own happiness eludes her and she temporarily believes she has found it with a cab driver. Like the male schizophrenic of *Clean, Shaven*, the world we view through the eyes of the female protagonist is one saturated with strange sounds and images. Critic Roger Ebert wrote of the film: 'If a movie like this had a neat ending, the ending would be a lie. We do not want answers, but questions and observations.'                                      **SCh**

# Zalman KING

Born Zalman Lefkovitz in 1941, King has made the transition from cult actor to Hollywood's best-known soft-porn auteur. His 'erotic' films are pitched somewhere between the manic camp of Russ Meyer and the artier hardcore films of the 1970s such as *The Devil in Miss Jones* (1973) and *The Opening of Misty Beethoven* (1976). Although critically reviled (often with good reason), his work has spawned a number of imitators. Indeed, the King-scripted Adrian Lyne hit *9½ Weeks* (1986) created the template for the 'erotic dramas' which are a staple of late-night television.

As an actor, King appeared in some of the best-known TV shows of the 1960s and 1970s, including 'Bonanza', 'Alfred Hitchcock Presents', 'The Munsters', and 'Charlie's Angels'. He also played the lead in two stylish cult movies from the 1970s. *Some Call It Loving* (1973) was a weird hipster re-telling of 'Sleeping Beauty' with Richard Pryor and Tisa (sister of Mia) Farrow and Jeff Lieberman's insane *Blue Sunshine* (1976) was a horror tale with bald LSD casualties going homicidal. King's performances, particularly in the latter film, are very impressive and he makes a peculiar yet charismatic lead.

After writing the story for Alan Rudolph's *Roadie* (1980), he made his name as a screenwriter with the *9½ Weeks*. This risible yet enormously successful would-be thriller, an adaptation of Elizabeth McNeill's novel, detailed an intense sexual relationship between John (Mickey Rourke) and Elizabeth (Kim Basinger). The film is not well-written and suffers greatly from Lyne's flashy direction.

The success of the film, however, led to King's directorial debut, *Two Moon Junction* (1988). This is a Southern bodice-ripper with senator's daughter, April (Sherilyn Fenn), torn between a respectable fiancé and a low-life hunk she meets at a fairground (Richard Tyson). Predictably, her parents are aghast, yet she can't resist the muscle-bound fantasy man. This is pure tosh, with a pre-'Twin Peaks' Fenn (sporting bleached blonde hair) and the 'Chippendale'-esque Tyson giving performances so wooden that the critic Kim Newman wrote 'their nipples are more expressive than their eyes'. There are pleasures to be had here, though – many laughs but not all of them unintentional. An oddball cast delivers wacky performances, including bisexual cowgirl Kristy McNichol, April's creepy mom, Louise Fletcher, and Sheriff Burl Ives. Milla Jovovich, Screamin' Jay Hawkins and Herve Villechaize also make an appearance. King has said that he is trying to appeal mainly to a female audience with his films and here, as in *9½ Weeks*, he offers a slow motion, would-be 'dreamy' brand of softcore far removed from the violent writhings of someone like Paul Verhoeven.

He followed with the over-heated and undistinguished love triangle melodrama, *Wildfire* (1988). A talented cast – Steven Bauer, Linda Fiorentino, Will Patton and Johnny Weissmuller Jr. – are wasted in this run-of-the-mill yarn. *Wildfire* co-writer Matthew Bright (*Freeway* (1996) and *Freeway II: Confessions of a Trick-Baby* (1999)) has done far superior work in a similar vein.

1990 saw King return to soft-core with *Wild Orchid*, a Rio romp, which teamed Mickey Rourke with his wife-to-be Carré Otis. Otis is Emily, a lawyer who falls under the influence of her boss (Jacqueline Bisset) who sets her up with the kinky, impotent Wheeler (a fake-tanned Rourke). This is a re-tread of *9½ Weeks* but Otis is a weaker lead than Kim Basinger and Rourke is laughable; it was this performance that marked the actor's downward turn. The sex is fairly explicit for its time (particularly the end sequence when Emily cures Wheeler's impotence) but the gnomic dialogue ('sometimes you have to lose yourself … in order to find yourself') is rather embarrassing.

Despite the title of King's next theatrical feature, *Wild Orchid 2: Two Shades of Blue* (1992), the film is not a sequel. There are thematic links in this sexy soapy melodrama but instead of 1980s Rio, the setting is the West Coast in the 1950s. The convoluted story tells how Blue (Nina Siemaszko), who lives an itinerant lifestyle with her junkie jazzbo dad (Tom Skerrit), falls into high-class prostitution after he overdoses. Darker than the usual King fare and slightly more lurid, it still has the same writhing and moaning.

*Delta of Venus* (1995), his next film, was more ambitious still, with King adapting the erotic writings of Anaïs Nin and attempting to come over all *Cabaret* (1972) period Bob Fosse, setting his frequent couplings against the backdrop of Nazism in 1940s Paris. This looks more expensive than his previous work but by now, the director's name was as much of a brand-name as Ingmar Bergman's, with its repeated plots (innocence 'defiled'), characters (the virgin who becomes a whore, the more experienced 'corrupter') and visual style (exotic backdrops, high-ish production values, lots of lingerie).

Possibly sensing the limitations of his formulaic soft-core, King made the very untypical *In God's Hands* in 1998, a stylish but pretty empty surf movie. Casting three surfers who hadn't acted before in the lead roles suggests King may have been more interested in the surfing than the (barely developed) plot, but the film is well-shot and pretty to look at. Unlike the only great surfing movie, John Milius' *Big Wednesday* (1978), this would've been much better as a documentary, keeping the surf footage and forgoing the rest.

King was back on familiar ground with the same year's undistinguished *Shame, Shame, Shame*, which features the usual mix of steamy fantasies and R-rated sex scenes and is cast with a mixture of beautiful but blank ingénues (such as Heidi Schanz) and good actors who have fallen on hard times (Valerie Perrine, Olivia Hussey).

His next theatrical feature was the untypical (but typically titled) *Women of the Night* (2000). This is a ponderous but occasionally stylish anthology movie with Sally Kellerman's blind DJ telling the stories of three women, including such stock King characters as the heiress who is fleeing her abusive father and the innocent who is tempted to appear naked in a film. This is faux art-movie material – the Kellerman segment is in black and white and Cassavetes regular Seymour Cassel puts in an appearance – but suprisingly, given King's oeuvre and the film's title, there is very little sex. The marketing, however, with posters of babes in lingerie, exploited the director's reputation for smut.

In addition to directing, King has executive produced a range of 'King-esque' projects, including two by female film-makers: Mary Lambert's weird *Siesta* (1987) and Susan Streitfeld's arty *Female Perversions* (1996), starring Tilda Swinton. Since the early 1990s, he has increasingly worked in television with the popular 'Red Shoe Diaries' series starring a pre-'X-Files' David Duchovny. Indeed, his brand of softcore looks increasingly at home on the small screen, as the tastes of TV viewers become more liberal and sex on screen far more explicit, with hardcore scenes developing in European work such as *The Idiots* (1998), *Romance* (1999), and *Baise Moi* (2000).      **IC**

# Steve KLOVES

Born in 1960, Steve Kloves is one of those Hollywood film-makers who would have been championed by the Americanophilic French film critics that wrote for *Cahiers du cinéma* in the 1950s. He makes pulpy works of narrative, but his eye is clear, his wit is sharp, and his moral sense is keen: he is a true journeyman artist.

*The Fabulous Baker Boys* (1989)

*Flesh and Bone* (1993)

He debuted as a director in 1989 with *The Fabulous Baker Boys*, a Michelle Pfieffer vehicle that also featured Jeff and Beau Bridges as the piano-playing brothers who give the film its title. When bombshell singer Pfieffer comes between the two brothers, the usual sparks fly. Upon its release, however, the film was greeted warmly by critics as being a somewhat formulaic but enjoyably adult romance.

1993 brought a very different film: *Flesh and Bone*. Again, Kloves used big stars (Meg Ryan, Dennis Quaid and James Caan), but he elicited subtle, very unglamorous performances from each of them. Set in a dusty rural wasteland, the film centres around Quaid's character, who travels from town to town maintaining vending machines and is haunted by memories of watching his father (Caan) rob and kill a family when he was a child. In great contrast to *The Fabulous Baker Boys*, Kloves seems to be wrestling here with the formidable legacy of American pastoral, exposing just how soaked in blood that tradition is but also bringing the genre's preoccupation with redemption to centre stage. He frames the violence with a strange kind of uncertainty, but the romantic scenes have a similarly awkward sense about them. This all makes the film feel odd in places, but Kloves is just trying to show us that dad didn't really know how to kill people but did it anyway. When it comes around that his son doesn't really know how to love people but does it anyway, the irony is almost unbearably poignant. It is one of the best, and least seen, Hollywood films of the 1990s.

Kloves has recently concentrated on screenwriting, contributing to Curtis Hanson's 2000 film *Wonder Boys* and the hugely successful Harry Potter series. **JW**

## Chris KOCH

*Snow Day* (2000)   Chris Koch's career began in television in the mid-1990s when he directed the comedy 'Malcolm in the Middle', an animated series called 'Kablam', and spent two years directing 'Remember Wenn' about a Pittsburgh radio station, set in the late 1930s.

This afforded Koch necessary experience in the technicalities of film-making and in directing comedy under pressure, both of which were useful for his feature debut, *Snow Day* (2000). The title of the film refers to the day the children get off school when the extra-heavy snowfall keeps buildings closed, as long as the Snow Plough Man (Chris Elliot) does not get there first to spoil the fun. This sets up the basic premise of the movie – kids trying to outsmart the villainous Elliot – and the film raises some predictable but childishly amusing laughs, including the suspiciously yellow snowball utilised in their anarchy. This runs alongside other main storylines: the television weatherman's attempts to maintain his dignity in a series of ludicrous costumes forced on him by his station controller in a bid to compete for ratings; and his son's public wooing of the high-school beauty to the chagrin of his smart best friend to whom he is more obviously suited.

In spreading the plots across the generations, the film aims squarely at a family audience. Encompassing the working mother guilt factor, the film's good nature is undermined by the mother's admission of failure as she hurries to another meeting, supposedly at the expense of her family. Nonetheless, the action is fast-moving and has a few treats for its adult audience, not least in Iggy Pop's appearance as the ice-rink DJ.

Koch's next film is *A Guy Thing*, a romantic comedy about a man who wakes up next to a strange woman in the morning after his bachelor party and assumes he has cheated on his fiancée. **JD**

## David KOEPP

*The Trigger Effect* (1996)   Born in 1964, David Koepp is the writer directors call on when they need an effects-
*Stir of Echoes* (1999)   driven summer blockbuster. Having written or co-written screenplays for such durable names as Spielberg (*Jurassic Park* (1993) and its sequel *The Lost World* (1997)), De Palma (*Mission: Impossible* (1996) and *Snake Eyes* (1998)), and Zemeckis (*Death Becomes Her* (1992)), it is no surprise that Koepp's two efforts as a writer-director have struck out along similar genre paths. What distinguishes them is his disregard for the audience-pleasing flash that defines him as a scenarist for others, choosing to focus instead on the effect of extraordinary circumstances on simple human interaction.

His first film, *The Trigger Effect* (1996), is a tightly-wound exercise in suburban paranoia that depicts a few sweaty, panic-stricken days in the lives of a young couple, their baby, and a family friend following a mysterious electrical blackout. Koepp is blunt in his suggestion that humanity quickly reverts to savagery in times of strife; his first image is of a pack of wolves, fighting over the bones of a slain deer. He also takes a page from De Palma's book of cinematic tricks, introducing his married protagonists (Kyle MacLachlan and Elizabeth Shue) as part of a long, elaborate tracking shot through a shopping mall. Yet rather than indulge for the sake of style, Koepp uses this opening as a means of illustrating his theme of cause and effect that drives the film, successively following a series of shoppers as each unwittingly enrages the next in a carefully linked chain of mounting aggression. The mall setting is also Koepp's way of commenting on the characters' (and, by extension, the audience's) dependence on the consumer items that are taken for granted daily, from battery-powered phones to computers to gasoline. Once the blackout hits, the director imprisons the cast in a world almost completely devoid of artificial light, submerging his interiors in dappled, underwater-like shadows, and corroding his exteriors until they are bleached and sun-stripped. As vivid as *The Trigger Effect* is, it ultimately lacks the haunting power of other world-gone-wrong pictures (such as Hitchcock's *The Birds* (1961)), or a more contemporary example – like Steve DeJarnatt's *Miracle Mile* (1988)) – due to Koepp's admirable determination to find a hopeful ending to his dystopian vision.

His second feature, the Richard Matheson adaptation *Stir of Echoes* (1999), is equally as effective and problematic as his first. Again, Koepp's focus is on the gradual unravelling of a young family, only this time his framework takes on that of a supernatural thriller, as working-class father Kevin Bacon becomes an open channel for psychic phenomenon after undergoing hypnosis at a party. Setting the picture in a contemporary Chicago of baseball games and backyard barbecues lends the story a sense of blue-collar realism that contrasts nicely with the more otherworldly aspects, a counterpointing of the fantastic with the mundane that recalls the young Spielberg of *Jaws* (1975) and *Close Encounters of the Third Kind* (1977). Koepp delivers a brilliantly understated effects sequence early on, depicting Bacon's hypnosis on a literal level by showing the actor sitting in a darkened theatre, floating slowly towards the screen. He also creates an atmosphere of pervasive dread simply by pointing his camera at a child's face – for scenes in which Bacon's young son, who is also psychic, speaks to unseen spirits, Koepp uses an unsettling subjective close-up of the boy, who appears to stare right through us as he listens and responds to silent voices.

If *Stir of Echoes* runs out of steam by the end, it is partly because the film's air of tension gradually dissipates as it reveals itself to be a more conventional murder-mystery, but mostly because Koepp does little to assuage the fact that an increasing amount of his imagery is closely reminiscent of other, better films (an obsessive Bacon digging up his back garden harkens back to the Richard Dreyfuss of *Close Encounters*, while several other scenes recall Kubrick's *The Shining* (1980)). Perhaps most unfortunately, *Stir of Echoes* was released in the shadow of supernatural blockbuster *The Sixth Sense* (1999), a film with which it shares many coincidental elements.

Koepp was screenwriter on two of 2002's biggest hits, David Fincher's *Panic Room* and Sam Raimi's *Spider-Man*.                                                                      **CS**

# Harmony KORINE

A prodigiously talented director, writer, poet and video artist, Harmony Korine has, in a short space of time, acquired the status of *enfant terrible* of contemporary American cinema. Born Avi Korine in California in 1974, he first came to public attention with his screenplay for the controversial *Kids* (1995). A crudely sensational account of 24 hours in the lives of a gang of teenagers on the streets of New York, the film was criticised for its amoral stance on under-age sex and drug abuse, and its general attitude of malaise towards present-day society. However, it did offer a glimpse of Korine's uncompromising view of the world, fully realised in his first film, *Gummo* (1997).

*Gummo* (1997)
*julien donkey-boy* (1999)

Eschewing a linear narrative in favour of a series of fragmented stories, memories and snapshots of everyday life, *Gummo* is a remarkable attempt to document the lives of the underclass of Middle America – a social group Korine believes the media either chooses to forget, or treats with suspicion and disdain. With sparse narration from one of the younger cast members, the film chronicles life in a town that failed to recover from a devastating tornado which struck two decades earlier. In its frank portrayal of the townspeople's lives, unwilling to pass judgment on their actions, Korine once again courted controversy, drawing fire from a number of critics, moral groups and politicians. However, displaying a wide range of influences, as well as experimenting with the way the images were presented – aided in no small measure by renowned French cinematographer Jean Yves Escoffier – *Gummo* is a disturbingly original film.

*julien donkey-boy* (1999) continues Korine's fascination with documenting life at the heart of America's underbelly, once again offering a challenging, albeit less impressive, piece of film-making. Shot to the strictures of the Dogme 95 manifesto, the film traces the occasionally violent breakdown of a schizophrenic who lives with his eccentric family. Effective in its use of the Dogme mandate, with remarkable performances from Ewan Bremner and Werner Herzog, *julien donkey-boy* remains a minor work when compared with the more expansive and impressive *Gummo*. In many ways a companion piece to its predecessor – often seeming more like an expansion of one of the earlier film's many narrative strands – the film suffers from being confined to one single family, lacking *Gummo*'s insight, poignancy and wry humour. However, *julien donkey-boy* still shows Korine to be a significant talent and a film-maker who is unafraid to challenge both the boundaries of taste and the limitations of film. **IHS**

# Jim KOUF

Jim Kouf's twenty-year career as writer, producer and director has centred on the lucrative blend of action and comedy, combining comic dialogue and mismatched characters with high-octane action sequences to produce films strong on thrill and entertainment value. His more accomplished written work – particularly variations on the modern crime caper – has produced both box-office success and satisfying entertainment, and his own directorial efforts, while initially in the same vein, have more recently shown a willingness to move beyond the confines of screwball action.

Kouf's early career as writer and producer resulted in derivations of popular 1980s genres: his slasher movie parody *Wacko* (1981), the blue-collar comedy *Utilities* (1981), the brat pack movie *Class* (1983), and the romantic comedy *American Dreamer* (1984). All are interesting in the tracing of Kouf's developing sense of comedy, which often borders on farce. *Shaker Run* (1985) added action, blending impressive set-pieces with an ironic script and self-knowing direction, in a breakneck chase/buddy movie combination that was to shape Kouf's career.

After writing the screenplay for *Secret Admirer* (1986), Kouf wrote and produced his first directorial effort, *Miracles* (1986), the story of a divorced couple forced back together in adversity due to their kidnapping by a bank robber. Combining energetic visual thrills with the scattershot dialogue and comic mishaps of Kouf's written work, the film glories in the sheer chaos of uncontrollable events, an adventure farce let down by its unengaging leads. By this point, however, Kouf's style was fixed; comic pairings working together in danger in a combination of spectacle, comedy and sentiment. His next written work, *Stakeout* (1987), shows he was in full control of his material. With Kouf's best comic writing so far, and helped by a like-minded director (John Badham), the film was hugely successful and is the perfect showcase of Kouf's blend of broad laughs and breakneck action.

*Disorganized Crime* (1989), Kouf's second directed feature, was less auspicious. A crime caper involving comically inept robbers planning the perfect robbery, the film bears all the Kouf trademarks, but the usual command of narrative turns and exploitation of dramatic mismatching are lacking. With stereotypical characters and lacklustre direction, and lacking the unapologetic energy of his previous effort, the film feels flat and formulaic. *Gang Related* (1997) is by far Kouf's most developed directorial effort. Following his involvement in *Kalifornia* (1993) and *Con Air* (1997), 1990s updates of Kouf's favoured 'buddy movie' framework, the film is a more thoughtful treatment of his recurrent themes of chance, mishap, and corruption. Where in Kouf's comedies characters are manipulated by events outside their control, here they are entirely responsible for their actions and their consequences with serious rather than comic results. It tells the story of two cops who earn extra-curricular money by killing drug dealers and accidentally kill an undercover agent. The usual narrative twists and character conflict result in the disintegration of the central pairing under the weight of self-aggravated circumstance rather than its eventual triumph – a more downbeat, if more human, conclusion. With intrusive, involving camerawork, deeper characterisation and good use of dramatic tension, it also marks Kouf's move into a more mature style of film-making. As a writer, however, Kouf remains faithful to his action-comedy roots, penning the popular *Rush Hour* (1998) and the comedy *Snow Dogs* (2002). **OB**

# Srinivas KRISHNA

With the release of his startling first feature *Masala* (1991), a project for which the auteur served as director, producer, writer, and star, Srinivas Krishna established himself as one of the most talented and provocative film-makers currently working in North America. Krishna was born in Madras, India, in 1964 and grew up in Toronto, Canada. As a child, he studied South Indian classical singing, and in high school formed an experimental theatre company, Theatre at a Point. After graduating from high school, Krishna attended the University of Toronto where he studied history and painting. While there he became interested in motion pictures; and after earning his Arts degree, enrolled in the film-making programme at Temple University in Philadelphia, Pennsylvania. Krishna made a number of short films at Temple, including *Fingered* (1988) and *The Turned Head* (1989), the latter of which won the Best Short Film Prize at the 1990 Chicago International Film Festival.

He also began work on the script that was to become his first feature, *Masala*, and on completion, returned to Toronto to find a producer for the project. After several failed attempts to secure funding Krishna decided to contact internationally-renowned actor Saeed Jaffrey and ask for his support. Jaffrey was immediately impressed by the project and agreed to star. The film is a testament to its director's extraordinary understanding of the workings of the cinematic medium. Krishna ingeniously makes use of both form and content to tell a story with an approach rarely encountered in a market where decisions are driven by concerns over content. *Masala* blends recognisable elements from different genres and national cinemas to create a compelling portrait of the diverse population of Toronto's South Asian community that simultaneously explores and debunks a variety of established stereotypes. The film garnered rave reviews and was awarded the title of Best Contemporary Drama at the 1991 Birmingham International Film Festival.

After the release of *Masala*, Krishna travelled to London, where, inspired by a classified ad for mail-order brides in *Time Out* magazine, he began work on a project titled 'The Promise of Heaven', which he completed in 1995. The finished film, titled *Lulu*, investigates the myriad ways in which individuals and organisations exploit one another for financial, political and emotional gain. Like *Masala*, Lulu raises pertinent questions about stereotypes and cultural identity. Likewise, both films make stunningly effective use of shifting points of view to illustrate the different ways in which we define the places we live (or once have lived) be it 'a house, a neighbourhood, or a city', as home.

Krishna's most recent projects include the short film, *Forever* (1999), and an audio-visual installment for the permanent collection of the Royal Ontario Museum. His next film is an adaptation of R. K. Narayan's novel 'Waiting for the Mahatma'.          **RC**

# Lisa KRUEGER

Lisa Krueger was a student of semiotician Christian Metz in Paris, and her early work included acting as production manager on music videos and as a script supervisor on indie features including Jim Jarmusch's *Mystery Train* (1989) and *Night on Earth* (1991), and Abel Ferrara's *King of New York* (1989).

*Manny & Lo* (1996)
*Committed* (2000)

Born in 1961 in San Francisco, Krueger's first directorial project was the award-winning short *Best Offer* (1993). This introduced her to the Sundance Festival, where she returned with her first feature script, *Manny & Lo* (1996). Production for *Manny & Lo* was financed independently by producers Dean Silver and Marlen Hecht. The film is an offbeat comedy-drama, which tells the story of two orphaned sisters, 11-year-old Amanda and 16-year-old Laurel, who run away from their foster families and live life on the open road. In the course of the film the two attempt to reconstitute a new family via kidnapping and pregnancy.

Her second feature as writer-director, *Committed* (2000), which Silvers and Hecht again produced, starred Heather Graham in her first role. It tells the story of a young woman who hits the road to search for the no-good husband who left her. Joline (Graham) is a trendy manager of an underground New York night-club whose husband is a frustrated newspaper photographer. She drives two thousand miles on an adventure to track down her wayward husband, who has decided he needs some space, in the hope of renewing their commitments to each other. Joline ends up in El Paso, where she finds her husband but does not make her presence known. Instead she stalks him, protecting him and letting him do his thinking. The film is an introspective and empowering comedy about a woman re-examining her priorities and learning to look to herself for her happiness. Krueger's brother Tom worked as director of photography on both features and won the Excellence in Cinematography award for *Committed* at Sundance 2000.

Krueger is a promising director with a theoretical background who makes films 'about the essence of love or commitment or a bond'. In her first two features she has ensured the integrity of the film-making process by retaining the artistic control possible through working independently and by directing her own material. **PR**

# Stanley KUBRICK

Stanley Kubrick is one of the rare film-makers whose work and reputation appear to have transcended their medium. Conceptually bold, stylistically precise and technically innovative, his films have simultaneously defined and confounded cinematic epochs while dividing critical opinion. Ambitious and perhaps portentous, some see these characteristics as symptoms of a remote control-freakery which manifests itself as a cold, cynical detachment from his subjects. Either way, Kubrick's work stands as a testament to the possibilities and limitations of the total control of the film director. The recurrence of themes and stylistic choices is so pronounced as to lend ammunition to both those who see him as an astute observer of humankind's essential fallibility or a film-maker whose fatalism is perfectly served by the essential ugliness and pessimism of his vision.

Born in New York in 1926, Kubrick's early work as a photographer and documentary film-maker provided apt training for his stubborn independence, and early feature works clearly display an ambition which seeks to rise above their B-movie status. *Fear and Desire* (1953) remains difficult to see, but its philosophical meditation on men at war prefigured the later *Paths of Glory* (1957) and *Full Metal Jacket* (1987). *Killer's Kiss* (1955) is a stark, minimalist interpretation of film noir staples (the fighter, the femme fatale, the mobster) and while characterisation is limited, it is striking for its merging of visual abstraction with realistic location shooting. *The Killing* (1956) reinterprets the conventions of the heist narrative, fracturing its temporal structure in order to dissect the mechanics of an (almost) perfect racetrack robbery. The film benefits from the presence of an accomplished cast, including Sterling Hayden and Elisha Cook Jr. What these films clearly demonstrate is Kubrick's ability to assert his creative personality in a generic framework, a process which would develop over the body of his career.

Kubrick achieved wider industry recognition with *Paths of Glory*, a World War One drama focusing on the bitter class divide and injustice inherent in military structures. While indicting the French military aristocracy (indeed, the film was banned in that country for many years), its themes are universal. Kubrick makes extensive use of architecture in order to offset and emphasise the conflicts of the film's key characters. The smooth tracking shots, depicting the ravaged trenches of the battlefield, would soon become a familiar stylistic trait. Humanitarian in intent, this impulse is hindered slightly by its emotional aloofness and stark fascination with the order and geometry of the military hierarchy.

*Spartacus* (1960) marked the only occasion on which Kubrick served as a director for hire, and the sentimentalisation of the Christian revolt against the Romans seems distinctly uncharacteristic. Yet the precise military formations of the battle sequences display Kubrick's talent for spectacle, and the film is one of the more intelligent widescreen epics of the era. Benefiting particularly from its cast (including Kirk Douglas, Laurence Olivier, Tony Curtis and Peter Ustinov), the film was Kubrick's first major financial success and earned Academy Awards for Ustinov as well as for its costume design, art direction and cinematography.

Kubrick consolidated his new status by adapting Nabokov's scandalous novel of forbidden love, *Lolita* (1962). Overcoming contemporary censorial restrictions by interpreting the story through innuendo, Kubrick transforms Nabokov's prose into a black comedy. This approach was intensified in *Dr Strangelove: or, How I Learned to Stop Worrying and Love the Bomb* (1964). The film again stresses Kubrick's interest in military processes, this time amidst the nightmarish scenario of imminent nuclear destruction. The film's gallery of Cold War grotesques amplifies its satire on the insanity of nuclear annihilation, and Kubrick maintains an icy detachment from his broad caricatures. Nevertheless, the performances of Peter Sellers (in three roles), George C. Scott and Sterling Hayden, transcend the limitations imposed by the striking visual design, sketching the range of paranoid impulses which inevitably collide with devastating results. Less concerned with any political dimension than the inherent human capacity for destructive paranoia, Kubrick presents power structures defined through possession of military technology yet crucially unable to communicate at the most basic human level. Distinguished further by Ken Adam's imposing sets, the film's cynical air is compensated by its often brilliant comedic set-pieces.

*2001: A Space Odyssey* (1968), while concerned with the metaphysical implications of science and the spiritual, relegates its human figures to mere ciphers. Indeed, the progress from ape to human is presented largely as a technological journey (expressed famously in the jump-cut from a bone to a spacecraft) and the film's most expressive figures are its primitive beasts and supercomputer, HAL. Placing humanity in the midst of its spiritual and intellectual superiors, the journey into infinite space is defined ultimately as one of re-birth and possible re-affirmation. Yet Kubrick focuses attention as much on the mechanics and machinations of objects, most extensively in the extended docking sequence choreographed to the 'Blue Danube' waltz. Famously adopted by the Woodstock generation as a trippy 'head' movie, the film's ultimate journey into visual abstraction and obscurantism suggests an unwillingness to fully confront the implications of its initial thesis. Nevertheless, this is cinema as grand, sensory spectacle, and the emphasis on imagery to carry narrative bridged a gap between the experimental and the mainstream.

If *2001* ended on a vaguely optimistic note, *A Clockwork Orange* (1971) presents a world in which moral and ethical boundaries have become cynically eroded. Filtered through the eyes of its young, thuggish protagonist, Alex (Malcolm McDowell), the film's dazzling surfaces serve only to further eradicate the sense of a human centre to Kubrick's universe. The core issue of individuality and free will in the face of institutional oppression is somewhat tempered by the essential ugliness of the figures involved, and the satire often emerges as crude and forced. However, the film is brilliantly designed and constructed, particularly in its early section, in which Kubrick forces the audience to confront or accept the sheer amorality of his scenario.

While received initially as a sumptuous but painfully empty 'coffee table movie', *Barry Lyndon* (1975) now appears to be one of Kubrick's most accomplished and rounded works. Eschewing the melodramatic tendencies of the costume drama, Thackeray's picaresque novel of eighteenth-century social climbing is transformed into a sedate meditation on the ritual and process of societal manners. Kubrick affects the light and compositional effects of period art, placing his protagonist (a fittingly blank and passive Ryan O'Neal) as one more slave to chance in a meticulously recreated past. While suppressing heavily intimate interplay between the characters, the film allows its emotional dimension to simmer painfully below its elegant surface. Making extensive use of visual tableaux, natural lighting (utilising a specially designed lens to capture the effects of low-level lighting), and a slow, elegant zoom, the film often seems to physically reduce its characters to a living death, an appearance apt to Kubrick's ongoing fascination with the mechanics of fate.

*The Shining* (1980) fuses Kubrick's recurring concerns with staple elements of the horror genre. The film blurs the distinctions between the psychological and the supernatural, each impinging on the other as Jack Torrance (Jack Nicholson) slides steadily into homicidal mania. The film can also be read as an analysis of isolation, and the secluded, ghost-ridden mountain hotel becomes an apt metaphor for Torrance's escalating resentments over his frustrated creativity and dissolving family life. The film's array of sub-textual riddles is coupled with an effective implosion of time, and rather than relying on the regular conventions of spooks and dark corners, this is a haunted house whose horrors reveal themselves fleetingly amid well-lit corridors and rooms. Filled with memorable images (a torrent of blood from an elevator door, Nicholson's manic leer through a smashed door frame) and influential, fluid Steadicam work, the film also boasts, in Shelley Duvall, one of Kubrick's most impressive, if thankless (an opinion given weight by Vivian Kubrick's fascinating documentary on the film's production) female roles.

*Full Metal Jacket* presents a cinematic Vietnam unlike any other, shifting the emphasis from jungle to urban warfare. While set against the tumultuous backdrop of the 1968 Tet offensive, the film scales down its action in order to contrast the preparation and enactment of men in combat. An unorthodox structure offsets the extended opening boot camp sequence (in which young men are systematically stripped of their humanity) with the experiences of the recruits in a stark, decimated Vietnam landscape. Narrated by Private Joker (Matthew Modine), the film contrasts the order and precision of the training camp with the chaos of conflict. Intent on producing men fit for war, Drill Sergeant Hartman (Lee Ermey, in an extraordinary role) falls victim to his own creation, a fat, bullied incompetent transformed into a conscienceless killer (Vincent D'Onofrio). Almost in parody of the popular (and revisionist) Reaganite action cycle of the 1980s, the frequent sexualisation of men and military weaponry is strikingly answered in the film's climax in which a platoon is gradually picked off by a lone female sniper.

In light of Kubrick's death during post-production, *Eyes Wide Shut* (1999) seems on reflection an unfinished work. Its take on fidelity, jealousy and dream logic channelled through an array of sub-Freudian motifs appears burdened by its faith to its 1926 source novella, Arthur Schnitzler's 'Dream Story'. The air of sexual melancholy and claustrophobia which permeates the film finds its focal point during an elaborate masked orgy, which may or may not place the film's protagonist (Tom Cruise) in mortal danger. Yet there is an underlying subtlety to the film which takes care to provide all manner of visual and thematic echoes, accommodating the blurring of perceptual distinctions hinted in the film's title. Particularly fascinating is the dismantling of Cruise's established persona, and his often subdued performance is pitched perfectly. Indeed, his central scenes with Nicole Kidman provide an intimacy hitherto absent from Kubrick's work, and their ultimate reconciliation, while somewhat pat in light of the preceding sombre tone, suggests a new, belated optimism in the director's work which alas, we will never see fulfilled.

Ironically perhaps, what audiences did see fulfilled (albeit posthumously) was Kubrick's long-gestating project, *A.I. Artificial Intelligence* (2001). Based on a short story ('Supertoys Last All Summer Long') by science fiction writer Brian Aldiss, Kubrick had prepared detailed pre-production material but never managed to settle on a satisfactory screenplay, despite a range of collaborators. Somewhat startlingly, given his increased lay-off periods, the film reached the screen just two years after his death. The fact that the film was ultimately realised by Steven Spielberg (whose public persona and artistic sensibility are the antithesis of Kubrick's) only added to the anticipation. It has since transpired (in interviews with Kubrick's long time collaborator, Jan Harlan) that Kubrick eventually intended to produce the film for Spielberg, deciding that audiences might have been alienated by his characteristically icy approach to the material. Such a collaboration would, of course, have made for a fascinating marriage (or clash) of creative personalities. However, it is ultimately futile to imagine Kubrick's hypothetical version in relation to Spielberg's final version, despite the intriguing fusion of themes (the fallibility of humanity, the emotional turmoil of childhood, the possibilities of technology) that have frequently fascinated both film-makers. The film's mixed critical reaction and moderate box-office performance seem to suggest that it treads a perilous line between the 'commercial' and the 'difficult'. Nevertheless, it is one of the more interesting summer blockbusters of recent years, not least because it actually takes time to address the themes it raises rather than simply drown them in a suffocating barrage of computer-generated visuals.

As a footnote, it is worth adding that Kubrick had also intended to film a Holocaust drama, 'The Aryan Papers', an idea he dropped only after Spielberg's *Schindler's List* (1993) achieved widespread acclaim and commercial success. It joins 'Napoleon' as Kubrick's great unfilmed project.                                              **NJ**

# Roger **KUMBLE**

Roger Kumble was born in Harrison, New York, in 1966. Before directing his own screenplay for his debut *Cruel Intentions* (1999), Kumble wrote and appeared in *Unveiled* (1994), made uncredited writing contributions to *Dumb & Dumber* (1994), *Mighty Morphin Power Rangers: The Movie* (1995), and *Kingpin* (1996), and wrote *National Lampoon's Senior Trip* (1995), *Provocateur* (1996), as well as the award-winning stageplays 'Pay or Play' in 1993 and 'd-girl' in 1997.

Focusing on the teenage machinations and sexual antics of the spoilt offspring of the East Coast rich, *Cruel Intentions* succeeds in reducing the complexities and ambiguities of Choderlos de Laclos' 'Les liaisons dangereuses', and of previous adaptations, to a dull, confused morality play. Lacking the irony, or even wit, demanded by its premise, *Cruel Intentions* poses its attractive cast attractively in attractive settings. All very pretty, but there is little else to it. The power games it depicts are as transparent as the movie's own cynical, efficient manipulations of its young stars' personas, especially Sarah Michelle Gellar, and its attempts at a cool attitude towards sexual openness are undercut by a deeply-rooted conservatism. Consensual incest, lesbianism, bisexuality and male homosexuality feed a strained kinkiness and all gay sex is depicted as manipulative. Furthermore, despite an early scene's anti-racist hand-waving, its treatment of the only African-American character is appalling. A popular box-office success, it led to creator, executive producer and director credits for Kumble for the prequel television series 'Manchester Prep', which Fox cancelled without airing an episode. The pilot episode, written and directed by Kumble, was released as *Cruel Intentions 2: Manchester Prep* (2000). Its mildly amusing cynicism and calculated would-be shockingness suggests that it would have been moderately successful as a TV show positioned somewhere between 'Buffy the Vampire Slayer', 'Dawson's Creek' and 'Sex and the City'. However, it has a rather confused tone, switching between puerile humour, insincere coyness, intermittent ironies, petty cruelties, and some occasionally pointed comedy about dysfunctional families and institutions, sexual mores, social class and teen sexuality. Kumble's direction is, by and large, unremarkable.

*The Sweetest Thing*, a romantic comedy due for release in 2002, stars Cameron Diaz as a clubber who meets the man of her dreams but is unsure how to approach him. Christina Applegate and Selma Blair also star. Kumble's subsequent project, *The Ugly Truth*, is also a romantic comedy slated for 2003.　　　　　　　　　　**MB**

# Zacharias KUNUK

The director of 19 shorts, Zacharias Kunuk made history at the 2001 Cannes Film Festival, when *Atanarjuat The Fast Runner* (2001) became the first Inuit film to secure an international release, eventually winning the Camera d'Or. A mythic epic set in one of the most inhospitable places on Earth, the film is remarkable both as an ethnographic document of a society living on the boundaries of human existence and as an engrossing drama whose familiarity as a narrative lies in the universality of its themes.

*Atanarjuat The Fast Runner (2001)*

Divided into two distinct sections, the film's first half is more observational, documenting the hardships and sense of community among the small tribe. Kunuk's control over the film's pacing conveys the struggle to survive within the harsh environment, whilst introducing the elements that are central to the main story of two warring families. In addition, Kunuk highlights how the human spirit is harsher and more ruthless than nature. Following the murder of Atanarjuat's brother, and the injuries inflicted on him by the scheming son of the tribe's chief, the film follows the hero's slow journey from recovery to a showdown with his enemy, marking the restoration of peace to the tribe, and the final exorcising of the evil spirit that has cursed it for two generations.

With its lengthy running time, the film allows audiences the space to adjust to the simple, but by no means uncomplicated, lives of the Inuit people. It also enables Kunuk to imbue his film with the generosity of spirit and emotional depth that is missing from so many mainstream films. Bold in its vision, *Atanarjuat The Fast Runner* is evidence that beyond the banality of much contemporary cinema there is still a vibrant, engaging and vital film-making at work.　　　　　　　　　　**IHS**

# Karyn KUSAMA

Making her directorial debut with the 1999 *Girlfight*, Karyn Kusama, born in 1968 in St. Louis, managed to produce a stylish, defiant, and suitably bruising boxing picture that deftly sidestepped many of the common pitfalls and clichés associated with the genre. The disappointing *Blonde Fist* (1991) aside, there are few films that deal with the pugilist's art from a female perspective. In less confident hands this story of a volatile African-American schoolgirl, raised by an uncomprehending father, who takes up the sport as a release from life in the unforgiving New York projects, could have been played purely for novelty value. Yet Kusama, who also penned the perceptive script, conceives spirited visuals, never once allowing the film to become mawkish. Newcomer Michelle Rodriguez is a revelation in the central role, as belligerent, tough, and determined as the film itself. Independently produced by Maggie Renzi, with John Sayles as an executive producer and actor in the film, *Girlfight* garlanded considerable acclaim at the Sundance Film Festival, scooping the Grand Jury prize, hopefully assuring Kusama's future as an intelligent, vivacious and uncompromising artist.　　　　　　　　　　**JWo**

*Girlfight (1999)*

# L

## Bruce LABRUCE

His eclectic mix of hardcore gay porn, semi-porn and camp voyeurism has ensured
Bruce LaBruce a place in the canons of underground film history. Born in Southampton,
Ontario, in 1964, he started off in Toronto as the editor of homo-punk fanzine 'J.D.'
(with G. B. Jones) and then moved swiftly on to producing, directing and starring in
no-budget Super 8 movies such as *I Know What It's Like To Be Dead* (1987), *Boy/Girl*
(1987), *Home Movies* (1988), and *Slam!* (1989).

He came to the attention of the underground, however, with his film *No Skin Off
My Ass* (1991), a gay remake of Robert Altman's *That Cold Day in the Park* (1969),
featuring LaBruce's then-boyfriend Klaus Von Bruckner as the lonely skinhead invited
to live with a camp hairdresser (played by the director himself). He followed this with
possibly his most ambitious film *Super 8½* (1993). This self-referential 'cautionary biopic' stars LaBruce as an ageing former porn star who has broken into the underground
film circuit. As David Macintosh has written, 'he demystifies and defiles the celebrity
industry while mythologising himself within it'.

The film abounds with intertextual references and refuses to be intellectually
deconstructed. In one scene, LaBruce is approached by a film critic who describes
his films as 'early Warhol whilst simultaneously able to achieve those pure moments
of Brechtian middle-Godard'. LaBruce is aware of the intense need to fit him into a
previously constructed and comfortable genre. It is his refusal to be categorised that
makes him interesting as a film-maker. Part *Deep Throat* (1972) part *Valley of the Dolls*
(1967), LaBruce does not fit comfortably in any pre-constructed category.

*Hustler White* (1996) is the closest he has been to the mainstream. Shot with
photographer Rick Castro, the film begins with a homage to *Sunset Boulevard* (1950)
and ends with a twisted reference to *Whatever Happened To Baby Jane* (1962). In
between, his usual mixture of hardcore sex and disjointed narrative makes up a largely
unsatisfying portrait of the Los Angeles hustler scene.

After co-directing two films with Glen Belverio – *The Post Queer Tour* (1992)
and *A Case for the Closet* (1992) – LaBruce came to London to shoot his most
controversial film yet, *Skin Flick* (1999). LaBruce attempts to investigate the inherent

*I Know What It's Like
To Be Dead* (1987)
*Boy/Girl* (1987)
*Home Movies* (1988)
*Slam!* (1989)
*No Skin Off My Ass* (1991)
*The Post Queer Tour* (1992)
*A Case For the Closet* (1992)
*Super 8½* (1993)
*Hustler White* (1996)
*Skin Flick* (1999)

homosexuality within Neo-Nazi Organisations as a critique of contemporary gay society which, he argues, seeks to emulate heterosexual homogeneity instead of standing out in contradistinction to it. However, the film's appropriation of fascistic imagery within gay culture succeeds only on a level of voyeuristic titillation. Nevertheless, the juxtaposition of the gritty and violent world of the skinheads with that of the smug, bourgeois lifestyle of the central gay couple poses an interesting and much needed antidote to mainstream gay culture.                                                                                                                      **BW**

# Neil LABUTE

*In the Company of* If Neil LaBute only made bilious antidotes to a strain of schmaltz in American cinema
*Men* (1997) – mainstream or independent – that would be something; with their lean scripting,
*Your Friends and* disciplined direction and acute casting, his first two comedies of contemporary manners
*Neighbours* (1998) shun accusations of callow nastiness. His strengths are acting and dialogue, rather than
*Nurse Betty* (2000) visual style, and he uses them well, drawing from his theatrical background to thematise
*Possession* (2002) sexual role-playing and the duplicities of language. The results view like Restoration comedies for the soundbite generation; Woody Allen (circa *Manhattan* (1979) without the comforts of philosophy.

Born in Detroit in 1963, LaBute grew in Spokane, Washington, before cutting his theatrical teeth at Brigham Young University, University of Kansas, and New York University. If the titles of plays like 'Filthy Talk for Troubled Times' and 'Lepers' hint at the direction of his later work, his decision to adapt 'Dracula' also suggests the fascination with predatory sexuality that spiked his debut feature, *In the Company of Men* (1997). Part-funded by an insurance windfall following a car accident, the film provoked controversy for mapping the rules of the corporate jungle (much talk of vultures and men with 'the nastiest sacks of venom') onto gender conflicts. The suggestion by white-collared Chad (Aaron Eckhart) to a weasely superior that they date and dump a deaf girl to 'restore a little dignity' to their 'doomed' lives is brutal enough; just as audacious is the way the film's twist turns the tale on anyone seduced by Chad's monstrosity.

LaBute's decision not to punish Chad challenges the audience's position as much as it does Hollywood's glibly cathartic eye-for-an-eye ethos. He shoots the film in static long takes through open doors and in bathrooms while characters whisper conspiratorially. The audience are coerced into becoming uneasy voyeurs, eavesdropping on private worlds. Despite this near-documentary style, we never forget we are watching actors: the 'company' of the title implies it, as does the way the men only act busy while the women actually work. However, the film is not simply an intellectual conceit. Christine, Chad's target, is too complex to be merely a cipher or victim, and actress Stacy Edwards lends her considerable emotional veracity. By contrast, Chad is emotionally dead. He spouts soundbites and asks 'How does it feel?', like someone who only feels vicariously. He listens to himself alone, a theme that is continued in LaBute's second film, *Your Friends and Neighbours* (1998), where emphasis is placed on talking.

*Your Friends* spreads the sexual tension over six characters rather than three. It is even more airless than its predecessor. There are no exterior shots, and its urbane but base characters suit LaBute's pitiless anti-escapism perfectly. They are their own worst enemies: trapped by their egos and in the now (we do not know their histories and can only guess at their futures), trapped by the stylised rituals of mating games, the language they have to articulate emotion and sexuality and, ultimately, betrayed by that language's paucity. In addition to its crisp script and lean plotting, the pleasure of the film comes from the sweet meta-textual revenge LaBute takes on Chad via the actor who played him. Eckhart's new character, Barry, is overweight and masturbatory in *Your Friends and Neighbours*; we never saw Eckhart eat in *In the Company of Men* but this time he shovels it in.

After two such singular films, LaBute's third, *Nurse Betty* (2000), comes as a bit of a disappointment, a diffuse mess of half-baked satire on television soap operas, polite screwball comedy, sweet-toothed schmaltz, rambling road movie and blunt hitman thriller. It is not at all clear what the film's point is, which may be something to do with the director working from someone else's script for the first time. Still, at least Renée Zellweger's performance confirms LaBute's ability to work well with actors; she plays a television soap opera fan who, traumatised after seeing her husband murdered (Eckhart, punished once more), becomes convinced that she is a nurse in her favourite soap.

LaBute's forthcoming film, *Possession* (2002), is an adaptation of A. S. Byatt's book. Eckhart returns to the fold, this time playing an academic whose research into a Victorian love poet, Randolph Henry Ash, brings him into the orbit of a fellow academic, played by Gwyneth Paltrow, who is researching a poet who appears to have been a great love of Ash's. Language, lust and love again, and there will be more of it in LaBute's other new film, *The Shape of Things*, adapted from his own stage play. It is the tale of an English student (Paul Rudd) who becomes the project of an art student (Rachel Weisz). He is infatuated with her and she wants to turn him into something other than what he is – but whether he wants to be turned is open to question. It still proves LaBute to be something of an expert when it comes to skewering the linguistic duplicities of sexual game-playing.                                                                                      **KH**

# Richard LAGRAVENESE

During the 1990s screenwriter Richard LaGravenese, born in New York in 1959, *Living Out Loud* (1998) garnered a considerable reputation with his talent for sketching strong, eccentric female protagonists. In such diverse films as *The Fisher King* (1991), *The Ref* (1994), and *The Mirror Has Two Faces* (1996), LaGravenese displays a rare empathy for his women characters, and a knack for sharp-tongued verbal wit that recalls the best work of Joseph L. Mankiewicz. He writes modern women's pictures with a classic sensibility, his heroines a mix of old school no-nonsense and new age neuroses. *Living Out Loud* (1998), confidently directed by LaGravenese from his own script, manages to stay true to his calling even as his greater autonomy allows him to broaden his palette in looser, spacier directions.

Based on a pair of Chekhov short stories, *Living Out Loud* depicts, in a light-toned vignette style, the gaping hole left in a privileged woman's life in the months following her separation from her husband. Holly Hunter's Judith is a prototypical LaGravenese creation, and the writer-director gives voice to her restlessness with a seamless blend of flashbacks, narration, and fantasy sequences that chart her ever-changing emotional landscape. Her self-exploration culminates in a vibrant, dynamically-staged dance number – in an all-women nightclub – that imagines Hunter reconnecting to her past by dancing with her idealistic younger self (Rachael Leigh Cook). Set in a preternaturally clean vision of New York, Hunter's quixotic journey is contrasted by that of the film's other lead, the lonely, divorced elevator operator played by Danny DeVito, whose own personal trials and yearning for Hunter are captured by LaGravenese in an unaffected 'kitchen sink' style befitting the character's humble origins.                              **CS**

# Mary LAMBERT

In common with several of her female contemporaries (amongst them Penelope Spheeris *Siesta* (1987) and Tamra Davies), Mary Lambert's career began via her involvement in the music *Pet Sematary* (1989) industry. She spent the first half of the 1980s making music videos to accompany *Grand Isle* (1991) the Madonna tracks 'Borderline', 'Like a Virgin', the controversial 'Like a Prayer', and *Pet Sematary II* (1992) the Marilyn Monroe/'Diamonds are a Girl's Best Friend' rip-off, 'Material Girl'. She *Clubland* (1999) established little in the way of visual style with the latter, but demonstrated an energy *The In Crowd* (2000) befitting Madonna's approach to her work.

Lambert made her feature film debut with the weird and wonderful but pretentious *Siesta* (1987), which boasted an array of independently minded American actors (including Jodie Foster and Ellen Barkin) and a bewildering choice of Brits – Julian Sands and 'alternative comedian' Alexei Sayle amongst them. Scripted by Patricia Knop, also responsible for the risible $9\frac{1}{2}$ *Weeks* (1986) screenplay, the film offers a ludicrously abstract and surreal attempt at a thriller, with a bloodsoaked and knickerless Barkin wandering Spanish streets, meeting an array of odd characters, and afflicted by bizarre flashbacks and dream sequences as she tries to make sense of her journey. Overwhelmed with symbolism, the film attempts to be an art-movie thriller but remains inconsistently styled and prey to the kind of narrative gimmicks that become unintentionally hilarious.

Despite this debut, Hollywood came calling and Lambert directed *Pet Sematary* (1989), Stephen King's adaptation of his own bestseller. The novel deals with the way in which the living both fear and long to be reunited with dead loved ones but the movie offers a standard gore-fest of visceral horror and genre clichés. The 'nuclear-family-moves-to-rural-house-and-suffers-mysterious-events-as-a-result-of-the-cemetery-in-their-yard' schtick is predictably represented, yet the movie made enough box-office dollars to ensure that Lambert's Hollywood film career remained stable.

Lambert followed the King adaptation with a return to music video, making a documentary about Bobby Brown, and then a version of 'Tales From the Crypt' for HBO. Before the inevitable *Pet Sematary* sequel in 1992, she directed *Grand Isle* (1991), again based on a novel, this time Kate Chopin's 'The Awakening', about a confused woman's emotional awakening. Produced by and starring Kelly McGillis the movie is another example of Lambert's inconsistent style.

In an attempt to emulate the commercial success of *Pet Sematary*, Lambert was offered the sequel, this time with a relatively starrier cast, including a post-*Terminator 2: Judgment Day* (1991) Edward Furlong, 'ER' star Anthony Edwards, and a gleeful baddy Clancy Brown. Bearing no relation to King's novel, the movie is a shameless sequel exercise, which places a new family in the creepy Maine town. With a predictable degree of gore, reanimated animals and rotting flesh, it marked a descent for Lambert into the world of video games and television movies, all lacking any consistent visual style.

Employing her love of music, she went on to make *Clubland* (1999), starring Alexis Arquette and Terence Trent-D'Arby, the former his usual ludicrous self, and the latter extremely wooden. Although it showcases some of the up-and-coming LA bands of the time, the film cannot rise above the clichéd story of the rock singer whose recording contract requires he dump his loyal band.

Coming hot on the heels of Davis Guggenheim's *Gossip* (2000), *The In Crowd* (2000) – widely panned at the time of release, but begging for late night cult status – deals with ex-psychiatric patient Adrien (Lori Heuring) who works as a waitress in a snobby country club and is befriended by the wealthy college clique who hang out there. Before too long it becomes evident that the clique isn't all it seems, and the teen horror clichés start flying: the appearance of some dark secrets, lesbian betrayals, girl fights and a bloody finale. In a period of original and engaging teen movies, this one was left on the shelf.

At present, Mary Lambert is working in television, fusing her interest in music and horror with a rock 'n' roll version of 'the Twilight Zone'. **JD**

# John LANDIS

The opening credits of 'Dream On', a television series produced and occasionally directed by John Landis in the early 1990s, hint at the formation of the director's worldview: a child is shown growing up in front of a television set in the 1950s, absorbing all of the ensuing ephemera like a pop culture sponge. Like contemporaries Steven Spielberg and John Carpenter, Landis would incessantly rework the themes and motifs of Cold War-era science fiction and horror in his own work. Unlike Spielberg, Landis was unable to ever transcend the gore and gross-out ingredients of such influences and, despite crafting some inspired genre pastiches and a couple of outstanding comedies, looks unlikely to ever produce a *Schindler's List* (1993).

Landis, born in Chicago in 1950 and a sometime stuntman and bit-part actor, broke through on the other side of the camera as a production assistant on *Kelly's Heroes* (1970) before directing his debut, the B-movie homage *Schlock* (1971). His hyperactive and undoubtedly juvenile style was established with *The Kentucky Fried Movie* (1977), a collection of skits based on movies, television, and adverts that unashamedly targeted the lowest common denominator audience that would become his constituency for the next few years. His next film cemented his reputation as a director adept at selling the frat-boy teen audience back their own juvenile antics, becoming a bawdy comedy classic that can retrospectively be credited for the entire career of the Farrelly brothers: *National Lampoon's Animal House* (1978). Treading a fine line between inspired, cultish stupidity and plain old-fashioned banality, the movie was a manic collage of vomit, breasts, and beer barrels, executed with classic slapstick precision and launching the film career of 'Saturday Night Live' comic John Belushi, whose irrepressible Bluto became the public face of Landis' synonymy with all things cinematically sophomoric.

Belushi developed the slob persona of Bluto for Landis' next film, an unlikely and (at least initially) commercially unsuccessful attempt to update the musical genre for a media-savvy generation who had grown up with the soul revues of the 1950s and

1960s: *The Blues Brothers* (1980). Growing out of the concert act developed by Belushi and 'SNL' colleague Dan Aykroyd, the film charts the attempts of renegade soulsters and unreformed jailbirds Jake and Elwood Blues to reform their old band (an all-star combo featuring legendary players like Steve Cropper, Donald Dunn and Matt 'Guitar' Murphy) in a bid to raise funds for the salvation of their cash-strapped childhood orphanage. Landis did a good job of shaping the chaos into a watchable narrative and the movie contains some impressively-mounted dance routines and star musical turns from the likes of Aretha Franklin and Cab Calloway, while simultaneously engaging in some of the most self-indulgently pointless massaging of the egos of cameo performers since *It's a Mad, Mad, Mad, Mad World* (1963). Undisciplined, wild, hopelessly ambitious and touting comedy of the broadest stripe, the film was a notorious $27 million flop on its first release (a large proportion of that budget went on cars that met their end in the spectacularly extravagant demolition derby climax). However, posterity would decide that the film was worthy of cult status, and the images of Jake and Elwood in black suits, white socks and sunglasses became icons adorning a million dormitory walls.

Landis was nothing if not acutely conscious of the popular cultural landscape of 1970s America. Almost all of his successful films would feature the 'Saturday Night Live' stars in one permutation or another, reflecting how high the cultural stock of Belushi, Aykroyd, Chase *et al.* was at the time. Landis used Belushi in *Animal House*; Ackroyd in *Twilight Zone: The Movie* (1983); Chevy Chase and Ackroyd in *Spies Like Us* (1985); Steve Martin and Chase in *Three Amigos!* (1986). Ackroyd and Eddie Murphy teamed up in the life-swap comedy *Trading Places* (1983), a lively and beautifully cast riff on the theme of nature versus nurture imbued with a message concerning the inhumanity of the Reagan era. As a vehicle for Murphy the movie delivered, and the star, one of the biggest of the 1980s, would return to Landis for *Coming to America* (1988), a film principally remembered for Murphy's ludicrous on-set demands and outsize entourage (and for exemplifying creative studio accounting – despite box-office receipts totalling $250 million worldwide, Paramount claimed that the movie was still in the red years later). It is tempting to suggest that Landis' chief directorial skill on this slick but unengaging comedy must have been keeping his preening star's monstrous ego soothed. Landis' third collaboration with the by now passé Murphy was the unwise *Beverly Hills Cop III* (1994), an alleged comedy-adventure whose pitch might well have been 'Die Hard in a Theme Park'. The film, Paramount's big summer hope for 1994, contrived to look hideously cheap while probably costing the earth, and the Landis/Murphy partnership dissolved before Murphy's career renaissance (*The Nutty Professor* (1996), *Doctor Dolittle* (1998), *Bowfinger* (1999)) kicked in.

Before the Murphy days, Landis had experimented with a no-stars approach in *An American Werewolf in London* (1981), a self-explanatory title for a fun, sharp movie that fashioned comedy and genuine thrills simultaneously from a premise straight out of B-movie land. Special effects supremo Rick Baker won an Academy Award for his extraordinary transformation scenes, turning David Naughton into a snarling lycanthrope, while several of scripter Landis' pops at British culture (isolated Yorkshire pubs, sleazy Soho porn cinemas inhabited by zombies) were hilarious.

However, Landis' next feature project would plunge him into professional and personal turmoil. The idea was to resurrect the fondly remembered 1950s science fiction series 'The Twilight Zone' in a postmodern horror portmanteau (all the rage in the 1980s: *Creepshow* (1982), *Cat's Eye* (1984), *Grim Prairie Tales* (1990)). Alongside directors Spielberg, Joe Dante and George Miller, Landis was revisiting the televisual landscape that nurtured his own unnerving instincts for high camp and schlocky thrills. In the event the film was a damp squib, Miller's tale of demonic sabotage on an aircraft standing out, Spielberg's gentle geriatric fantasy by common consensus the weak link. Yet the quality of the film became a side issue as a disaster on the set linked Landis with accusations of gross negligence. Veteran actor Vic Morrow, and two Asian child actors, Renée Chen, six, and My-Ca Lee, seven, were killed when a helicopter was knocked into their path by a huge special effects explosion. Landis and four co-defendants faced charges of accidental manslaughter, but were completely exonerated in 1987. However, the damage had been done to Landis' reputation, as the media homed in on the fact that the children were working after dark illegally, without the appropriate permits or adequate supervision.

As a director, Landis is an unreconstructed genre-blender. The scattershot, channel-surfing approach of *The Kentucky Fried Movie* reflected his postmodern fondness for the mixing of (sometimes inappropriately paired) genres and styles, and his biggest hits would tap into the same television-inflected hyperactivity and condensed attention span in his audience. Sex comedy spliced with coming-of-age flick in *Animal House*; musical-comedy in *The Blues Brothers*; horror-comedy in *American Werewolf* and *Innocent Blood* (1992). Yet such craftsmanship and the ability to turn his hand to different forms has tended to condemn Landis to 'journeyman' status, saddling him with a reputation as a gifted *metteur-en-scène* and crafter of star vehicles. Even his most original works, arguably *Blues Brothers* and *American Werewolf*, are both steeped in the lore of previous genres and texts. Such virtuosity would eventually undermine Landis' position as the hits inevitably dried up and it became too late to try anything else. The treading-water stage of his career began with the mismatched Jeff Goldblum/Michelle Pfeiffer adventure *Into the Night* (1985), entered its middle period with *Oscar* (1991), a woefully unfunny attempt to broaden Sylvester Stallone's appeal, and hit its nadir with the universally reviled sequel *Blues Brothers 2000* (1998), which suffered indescribably without Belushi's mesmerising unpredictability (the late comic was replaced by John Goodman). Landis' and co-writer Dan Aykroyd's desperation was signalled by the incorporation of a ten-year-old, Rayban-sporting orphan into the mix.

Landis seems to have lost the popular touch that he wielded so effortlessly in the late 1970s and early 1980s. He has recently reverted to the 'indie' environment that gave birth to his first feature, *Schlock*, with *Susan's Plan* (1998), although whether this should be viewed as a strategy for artistic rebirth or a loss of major studio favour after a string of costly flops is unclear. Ironically for a director who has generated millions of box-office dollars and created a string of cult hits, what might turn out to be Landis' most enduring achievement is not even a cinema feature. His pioneering 15-minute promo for Michael Jackson's worldwide hit 'Thriller' (1983) married the gore factor of *Werewolf* with a camp, B-movie scenario, Vincent Price cameo, and dance routines that recalled the impressive choreography of *The Blues Brothers*, helping to define Jackson's star persona (unearthly but funky) in the process. Few promos had incorporated dialogue before, and the narrative, as opposed to straight performance, approach would also have an impact in the field. Having benefited from Landis' acumen in inflating the pop promo to cinematic dimensions, Jackson would go on to work with genuine auteurs Francis Coppola and Martin Scorsese, before collaborating once more with Landis on the effects-heavy 'Black or White' promo in 1991, which attracted mild notoriety for some violent content. **MF**

# John LASSETER

Born in Los Angeles in 1957, John Lasseter is a digital storyteller whose pioneering animated features evoke the wonder and the creative spirit of golden age Disney animation. Indeed, it was at a screening of Disney's *The Sword in the Stone* (1963) that the six-year-old Lasseter decided to pursue a career in character animation. Lasseter names the animation of Disney and Warner Bros. animator Chuck Jones as his primary influence. He attended the California Institute of the Arts (BFA 1979, Character Animation) and graduated to a career at Disney Studios, where he became interested in computer animation during the production of *Tron* (1982). He left Disney for LucasFilm's computer animation division in 1983, which was later acquired and christened Pixar by computer magnate Steve Jobs in 1986.

After directing a series of ambitious and critically acclaimed computer-animated short films, Pixar and Lasseter's breakthrough achievement was *Toy Story* (1995), the first ever feature-length computer-animated film. A buddy movie cleverly shifted to the world of animated toys, Lasseter and his storytellers bring a sense of comic sincerity to the love/hate conflict between their main characters, cowpoke doll Woody and space age cosmonaut Buzz Lightyear, as they wrestle for the affection of their whimsical boy owner. Woody and Buzz, brilliantly voiced by Tom Hanks and Tim Allen, are a classic cinematic duo for the ages. Although faithful to its characters and story, *Toy Story* nonetheless contains a dazzling display of high-tech animation that earned Lasseter a Special Achievement Academy Award.

*A Bug's Life* (1998), an Aesop's fable crossed with *Seven Samurai* (1954) and *The Magnificent Seven* (1960), is Lasseter's epic and less successful sophomore effort. On a technical level, *A Bug's Life*'s computer animation is stunning with its gorgeous attention to detail, its graceful shading and lighting, and its elegant organic quality, but the film's humour is too self-indulgent and bogged down in its own cleverness.

*Toy Story 2* (1999) is one of the precious few sequels in cinematic history that tops its predecessor. Moving beyond the small-scale world of *Toy Story*, the sequel adds new dimensions to the already-beloved characters of Woody and Buzz with two cleverly-constructed narrative arcs: a playful but dead-on satire of collector-driven nostalgia when Woody discovers his 1950s television roots, and an ironic battle of wits between Buzz and an industrial-strength version of his former delusional self during a high-stakes mission to rescue Woody.

Lasseter's next film will animate classic cars.                    **THa**

# John L'ECUYER
The history of documentary hangs heavy over Canadian cinema, and the new generation *Curtis's Charm* (1995) of Canadian film-makers have a very strained relationship with that genre. Atom Egoyan's work, for example, is a pretty clear reaction against that tradition, and a lot of Bruce McDonald's output (especially *Hard Core Logo* (1996)) seems to be satirising it. John L'Ecuyer, however, has forged a very different relationship with documentary, making films that are both highly stylised and highly detailed, gritty and stylish at the same time.

His most widely seen work is *Curtis's Charm* (1995), a portrait of a heroin addict living in the slums of Toronto. Produced by Atom Egoyan and Patricia Rozema, the film is a sometimes dreamy, sometimes nightmarish description of his everyday life and a serious attempt to evoke the fragmented way that his mind works. The kind of patronising, liberal concern that often defines films about drug addicts is absent here; it is not that L'Ecuyer is unsympathetic, he is just keenly aware of the brutal reality of life on Canada's streets. L'Ecuyer was, for about seven years, an addict and 'sex-trade worker' in Montreal, and his next film, the documentary *Confessions of a Rabid Dog* (1996) is an attempt to use that personal history to explain the situation of the six other addicts that the film chronicles.                    **JW**

# Mimi LEDER
Born in New York in 1952, Mimi Leder is a television director who has only recently *The Peacemaker* (1997) devoted herself to features. Of the two earliest films she made, both were big-budget *Deep Impact* (1998) projects with an action gist. Yet Leder did not wish to become known for this kind of *Sentimental Journey* (1999) work alone and in the last couple of years she has diversified, making much smaller, *Pay it Forward* (2000) personal pictures which mirror her television origins. But whatever the undertaking, the fact that she received the AFI's Franklin J. Schaffner Alumni Award in 1999 – joining previous distinguished recipients such as David Lynch and John McTiernan – indicates she is a talent worthy of observation.

The daughter of a low-budget independent film-maker, Paul Leder, the director and her brother used to visit his sets often when they were growing up. Leder went on to become the first woman to be accepted on the American Film Institute's cinematography course, before launching her career as script supervisor on the acclaimed 1980s television series 'Hill Street Blues'. She then contributed episodes to 'LA Law', 'China Beach' and 'Crime Story', but found her niche working on TV movies and Michael Crichton's phenomenally successful medical drama 'ER' in the 1990s, directing six of the first season episodes – including the Emmy Award-winning 'Love's Labour Lost'. This brought her to the attention of Steven Spielberg, who contacted her when he was setting up his DreamWorks production company with David Geffen and Jeffrey Katzenberg.

*The Peacemaker* (1997) was the first film out of those hallowed stables and gave Leder the opportunity to direct her 'ER' friend George Clooney on a much grander scale. Though formulaic in every way – from the chase sequences to the explosions – this Clancyesque techno-thriller, in which terrorists hijack Russian nuclear weapons, does level the action out with intelligent plotting. Nicole Kidman is sinfully wasted as the US government nuclear weapons expert tagging along with Clooney's Special Forces hero, but the scenic globetrotting (taking in Vienna and Bosnia) and ticking-clock ending in New York make for appropriate distractions.

Leder's second DreamWorks picture, *Deep Impact* (1998), is vastly superior and possibly the best disaster movie ever made. It was released just as reports of a real-life comet were circulating on the news and in papers. Thankfully that meteorite was never heading directly towards Earth, but if it did happen then events would probably pan out much as they do in this film. There is a certain amount of intrigue and mystery at the beginning, surrounding the discovery of this ELE (Extinction Level Event), and some magnificent special effects, first as the Messiah shuttle tries to destroy the comet, then as parts of it fall to the planet below. However, the real 'impact' comes from the personal traumas of those affected by this rock: the TV reporter who happens upon the greatest story of all time (Téa Leoni's dignified portrayal, tinged with sadness and inner strength); the teenager who accidentally spots the comet (played by Elijah Wood with a maturity beyond his years); the astronauts on the Messiah (including the exceptional Robert Duvall as an ageing space jockey in the John Glenn tradition); the President who must make decisions no one should ever have to contemplate (a steadfast Morgan Freeman); and finally the legion of supporting characters, played by Vanessa Redgrave, Maximilian Schell, and Leder's TV associates. Pre-dating Jerry Bruckheimer's gung-ho Bruce Willis film, *Armageddon* (1998), by about three months, *Deep Impact* delivers human drama of the most inspiring nature, its grave scenario snatching hope from the jaws of adversity. Quite simply a movie free from imperfections and a profoundly poignant emotional experience.

Her next film was the wonderful *Sentimental Journey* (1999), a story very close to her heart: that of her parents' life together. Basing this on a script her father wrote two decades ago, and which her brother, Reuben, has re-written, it tells the tale of an Auschwitz survivor (her mother) and American soldier (her father) who meet and fall in love. Sentiment also informs *Pay it Forward* (2000), which breaks down a humanitarian ideal into its basest components. *The Sixth Sense*'s (1999) Haley Joel Osment plays the schoolboy who comes up with a way to change the world – by suggesting that everyone help three people and those people carry forward the good deeds, therefore creating a domino effect. Liberal in its central premise and execution, the film's sanguinity and unrealistic optimism contribute to its downfall. However, the performances from Academy Award-winners Helen Hunt and Kevin Spacey, who play a major role in the romantic sub-plot, are excellent.                                                                                    **PB**

# Jacques LEDUC

Born in Montreal in 1941, Jacques Leduc studied cinematography at the National Film Office of Canada and worked on the photography of a number of films until his first directorial venture in 1967.

*Chantal en Vrac* is a modest film characterised by beautiful and calming images of the everyday, an approach Leduc took to more extreme ends with his most famous and debated picture, *Tendresse ordinaire* (1973). The film has no recognisable plot: there is a man making his way home after work, and there is his wife waiting for him. While an impatient viewer may find the tardy pace and sparse activity frustrating, what makes it work as a piece of film is Leduc's sensitivity to the pangs of loneliness and longing the couple experience in their separation. The wife waiting at home with impatient eagerness and the weary length of the absent husband's train journey are filmed almost in real time, inviting the viewer to experience the anticipation with them. In this atmosphere, the ordinary human activities, such as cleaning and preparing food, become compelling. The 'tenderness' of the title is the tenderness of coupledom, in all its mundane domesticity, but Leduc also reveals a tenderness for Québec. As much as the film is an evocative glimpse of marriage, it is also a photo-gallery for the majestic scenery of French Canada: the backdrop to the husband's journey is a vast, empty mountain pass, covered in snowy quiescence. It is in this love of the landscape that Leduc reminds us of his cinematographic history.

Staying with an issue close to home, Leduc then experimented with documentary film, a medium he thought was widely considered 'unfashionable'. Described as 'an assessment of delusion' in Leduc's own voiceover, *Charade Cinoise* (1988) explores the militancy of Québec in the 1960s and 1970s, next to the comparable apathy of the

1980s; where the youth had once been a radical force for social change, it was now the most conformist stratum of society. The film, though inherently retrospective, also bears a mission statement: Leduc wants the film to effect an increase in social awareness and action in a generation he finds passive and inert. However, instead of driving the film along, this aim is hindered by the unashamed nostalgia for the previous decades and the film, like those it seeks to challenge, dawdles to an ineffectual closure.

Prominent films that Leduc made in the 1990s include *La Vie fantôme* (1992), which is about marital infidelity. Leduc shows a confidence in dealing with the complex implications of this potent topic, and refuses to rely on easy stereotypes or predictable 'wife' and 'mistress' roles. The result is a defiant picture of a man who cheats, without the burden of reason or morality. *L'Âge de braise* (1998) is a bland film about an old woman coming to terms with the closeness of her own death. It is a subject that could have benefited from a more metaphysical attitude than Leduc wished to take; the film is most enchanting when concerned with the aesthetics, rather than the logistics.

It was in the 1990s that Leduc returned to the art which initially sparked his interest in film, having been involved in the photography for the hugely influential *Jésus de Montréal* (1988). Throughout the 1990s his name appeared on numerous credits for film photography, among them *J'aime, j'aime pas* (1996) which benefits from the acute eye for detail and inspired use of light which is characteristic of Leduc's camera. He seems capable of rendering any location both vivid and gentle, and in this example set in Montreal, even the streets become foregrounded as features of the film. It seems that Leduc has, in revisiting his youthful vocation and his tenderly beheld birthplace, realised his best strength lies in his lens.                    **MS**

# Ang LEE

Ang Lee was born in Taiwan in 1954. He moved to America in 1978, to study Fine Art at the University of Illinois, continuing at New York University, where he graduated with a Masters Degree in Film Production. A director of meticulously crafted dramas, his films analyse the role of the family and personal relationships in terms of generational, cultural and sexual difference. Ranging from Asia to America and spanning two centuries, his work is both intelligent and heartfelt.

*Pushing Hands* (1992)
*The Wedding Banquet* (1993)
*Eat Drink Man Woman* (1994)
*Sense and Sensibility* (1995)
*The Ice Storm* (1997)
*Ride with the Devil* (1999)
*Crouching Tiger, Hidden Dragon* (2000)

Lee's debut, *Pushing Hands* (1992), drew upon his cross-cultural experiences to tell the story of a tai-chi professor who moves to America to live with his son's family, unaware of the distress his presence will provoke. The first of what critics have referred to as Lee's 'father knows best' trilogy, the film balances broad comedy with subtle observations of familial difference across three generations. Central to the film's thematic structure – and much of Lee's work in general – is the close attention paid to the social rituals surrounding eating and the preparation of meals. The father and daughter-in-law's fractured relationship is highlighted within the film's opening scenes through the difference in their eating habits. Only when they accept each other's diet does their relationship show any sign of repair and progression. Similarly, it is the son's destruction of the evening meal, following the disappearance of his father, which symbolises the family in their most extreme state of fissure. Though occasionally sentimental in its representation of the family, the film is well-written and features an excellent performance by Sihung Lung as the elderly patriarch.

One of Lee's most popular films, *The Wedding Banquet* (1993) is an engaging comedy of manners. It centres on an Asian man's attempts to hide his homosexuality from his parents, who have travelled from Taiwan under the assumption that they are attending his wedding. Once again, Lee focuses on the cultural and generational difference between the characters. Homosexuality is treated both as an issue in itself and as a way of exploring the characters' relationships with each other. As with *Pushing Hands*, the film's best moments take place amidst ritual and tradition. In particular, the scenes around the son's dinner table are effective in fleshing out the characters' shifting relationships and the conflict arising out of the predicament they are in. The film won the Golden Bear at the Berlin Film Festival and cemented Lee's reputation as one of contemporary cinema's most adept directors of social comedy.

*Eat Drink Man Woman* (1994) expands Lee's canvas considerably and is the best of his early work. Here, food – or good food – is the nucleus around which the family exists. Sihung Lung plays a retired chef whose inability to taste the food he cooks is symbolic of his lack of connection with his three daughters. Each one is desperate to forge a life of their own, away from their overbearing father. Opening with the preparation of a feast, Lee skilfully plays up the differences between appearance and actuality. The father's meal looks sumptuous, but it tastes dreadful. Similarly, the daughter's lives are never quite what they seem. The eldest appears happy in her role as spinster, but desires freedom. The middle daughter is a successful professional, but unhappy. And the youngest daughter is seen by her family as lacking ambition, but knows exactly what she wants. As their lives intersect with others around them, Lee creates a compassionate portrait of a family not so much falling apart, as transforming with the demands of the modern world. Shot on location in Taiwan, *Eat Drink Man Woman* is one of Lee's most effective studies of the clash between tradition and modernity. His direction is more fluid than in his previous films; his observational style suited to the multiple narratives of his and James Schamus' script. The universality of the film's themes led to the successful transfer of the story to a Latino community in Los Angeles, in director Maria Ripoll's enjoyable *Tortilla Soup* (2001).

Although Lee was brought on to *Sense and Sensibility* (1995) as a gun for hire by producer Lindsay Doran, Jane Austen's novel afforded him the opportunity to explore familiar themes within a very different environment. The clash between tradition and modernity is present, as is the notion of sacrificing happiness for duty and honour. Set in the peaceable English countryside, the film is the bridge between his early, city-orientated films and his more expansive, later work. Eliciting excellent performances from a distinguished cast, Lee's restrained direction is perfectly attuned to the nuances of the British class system, both in the restrictions it places on all echelons of society, and the injustice meted out to those who dare to transcend its boundaries. Building upon Emma Thompson's articulate script, Lee combines pathos and drama, presenting a modern take on an old world, whilst never eschewing the irony of Austen's writing. Certainly one of the best film adaptations of Austen's work, it won Lee his second Golden Bear at the Berlin Film Festival.

*The Ice Storm* (1997) was a dramatic departure from Lee's earlier work and is arguably his best film to date. A bitingly satirical look at family life in 1970s New England, Lee's adaptation of Rick Moody's excoriating novel also marks the director's transformation into a visual stylist of some verve. Unlike his previous films, Lee shot *The Ice Storm* as a series of interconnecting vignettes; photo-realist snapshots of family life at the heart of an America trapped in the mire of political corruption and national discontent. Painting a chilly portrait of New Canaan, Connecticut, Lee documents the tragedy that strikes a community where the family has been relegated by the desire for self-gratification. Aided throughout by Mychael Danna's haunting music, Frederick Elmes' striking photography and sharp editing by Lee regular Tim Squyres, the film draws parallels between the frozen landscape and the emotionless households that inhabit it. The characters move like ghosts through each scene, never quite whole, as a result of insecurity or feelings of hopelessness at their place in the world. Regarded by some critics as a conservative attack on the liberal attitudes that grew out of the 1960s, the film is a more complex attempt to analyse how these values were taken on board by conservatives, for whom tradition was the mainstay of their lives. As such, the film remains Lee's most acute study of the clash between the old and the new, and how rapid change can be as destructive as the refusal to adapt with changing times.

*Ride with the Devil* (1999) is Lee's most ambitious and misunderstood film. A period drama starring Tobey Maguire and Skeet Ulrich as two Southern rebels fighting Unionist soldiers during the American Civil War, it traces the development of their friendship with a black slave, played by Jeffrey Wright. Based on Daniel Woodrell's novel 'Woe To Live On', the film shifts between intimate dialogue scenes and dramatically staged battles. Seen as an unexpected turn by a director previously unfamiliar with physical violence (aside of the hilarious fight in the kitchen of the Chinese restaurant in *Pushing Hands*), the film was criticised for lacking a coherent tone. Thankfully, it has since been reassessed and placed within the context of Lee's previous work. Though certainly more visceral, the themes once again deal with change, this time on a larger scale. The cutting between lengthy discourse and action enable Lee to project the issues facing a small group on to a national stage. And, in contrast to *The Ice Storm*'s depressing ending, the closing moments of *Ride with the Devil* offer hope – although it will still need to be continually fought for.

Once again, Mychael Danna's score, Frederick Elmes' photography, and Tim Squyres' editing complement Lee's vision of the American past. However, it is James Schamus' articulate script that gives such an unconventional film its heart. Perfectly recreating the idiosyncrasies of the nineteenth-century spoken word, as he did for 1970s America in *The Ice Storm* – which won him a Best Script award at the Cannes Film Festival – the film seals Schamus' reputation as one of American cinema's most intelligent screenwriters.

From the favourable reviews following its screening at the 2000 Cannes Film Festival to its Academy Award success, *Crouching Tiger, Hidden Dragon* (2000) cemented Lee's reputation as a world-class film-maker. Based on the novels of Wu Dang Lu, the film is a mythic fable of epic proportions. Set during the last years of the Qin dynasty, it tells the story of two pairs of star-crossed lovers. Seemingly thwarted in their attempts to achieve happiness, the appearance of a criminal mastermind brings the characters together, but threatens to shatter their dreams. Shot on location throughout China, Lee's film is an unashamedly entertaining romp. More than his previous work, it displays his ability to blend action, comedy and moments of intimate drama, creating a wonderful world where characters fly through trees and across rooftops, and suffer the pain of true love. Accompanied by Tan Dun's lush score and Peter Pau's breathtaking photography, as well as martial arts veteran Yuen Woo Ping's choreography, the film dismissed the few remaining critics who still doubted Lee's talents.

Invited by BMW to be one of the five film-makers to direct a six-minute web film to advertise their new range of cars, Lee has also worked outside the cinema. *Chosen* (2001), a mini-thriller starring Clive Owen and Lee's youngest son (his eldest appeared in *Pushing Hands*) boasts the first car chase to be filmed as a tightly choreographed dance number. Though little more than a trifle for the director, its final shot reveals his next project, a blockbuster version of Marvel Comics'™ 'The Hulk'. A significant move into the mainstream, and one that has confounded his critics, Lee shows no sign of being pigeonholed. Having expressed an interest in a biopic of Houdini, a World War Two drama, and a remake of Alain Resnais' Dennis Potter-inspired *On Connait La Chanson* (1997), he remains one of world cinema's most versatile directors. **IHS**

# Malcolm D. LEE

Born in 1970, Malcolm D. Lee has worked in the film industry since he was 17, as *The Best Man* (1999) a production assistant, apprentice editor and assistant director, as well as serving as an assistant to his cousin, director Spike Lee, on the films *Clockers* (1995) and *Girl 6* (1996). A graduate of both NYU film school and a year-long fellowship in screenwriting at Disney, Lee made his debut as a writer-director with *The Best Man* (1999). An effervescent comedic drama with an all-black cast and the broad appeal and charm of an Old Hollywood picture, it puts an African-American gloss on the wedding weekend battle-of-the-sexes classic, *The Philadelphia Story* (1940).

An ensemble piece, *The Best Man* follows several old college friends who gather for a wedding in Manhattan but centres in the main on the groom's best man (Taye Diggs). He is a writer whose barely fictionalised first novel stirs up bad blood and old passions when an advance copy of the book is leaked to the guests. Working from his own classically constructed screenplay, Lee takes great pains to avoid the clichés that restrict the appeal of many films featuring black characters, here creating smart, funny men and women who just happen to be black. Indeed, what's notable about *The Best Man* is its lack of concern with matters of race and Lee wisely allows the very existence of his film to be point enough. What he aims for is a human story on a more universal scale, peopled with recognisable types that any audience can relate to. Gorgeously shot with an eye towards timeless glamour and beautiful faces (both male and female), it establishes Lee as a confident director of actors. He has a talent for sketching interesting, multi-dimensional characters, from a wisecracking, womanising flamenco guitarist to a bachelor party stripper with an intimate knowledge of nineteenth-century poetry. **CS**

# Spike LEE

Born in Atlanta, Georgia, in 1957, Spike Lee continues to be one of the most gifted *Joe's Bed-Stuy Barbershop:* and contentious of contemporary American film-makers. Consistently using the medium *We Cut Heads* (1983) of film to foreground and contest issues of race, class and gender, he also uses it in a painterly way to evolve the very language of cinema itself. These obsessions and persistency in style mark Lee out as an auteur.

Lee studied film at the prestigious New York Film School. One of his first films, *Joe's Bed-Stuy Barbershop: We Cut Heads* (1983) was a product of his studies there and immediately suggested that Lee was a promising young film-maker – one who would write, direct, edit and star in the films he worked on.

Lee's first independently produced film, *She's Gotta Have It* (1986), was shot on a shoestring budget of less than $20,000 and went on to win the Young Cinema Award at the Cannes Film Festival. A contemporary take on the comedy drama, it centres on the sexual relationship that one woman has with the three men in her life. Lee adopts both fictional and documentary realist codes, including direct camera address and the use of grainy black and white footage to cement the authenticity of the *mise-en-scène* and character relationships. This social realist aesthetic has become a recurrent Lee motif. Yet the film is also constructed around what a number of critics have termed his phallocentrism and his use of clichéd black female types.

*School Daze* (1988), his next movie, is set in an imaginary all-black American University where the social divisions that emerge are mostly played for comic laughs. The girls on the campus are split into two distinct groups – lighter skinned black girls and darker skinned black girls – and the confrontation between them offers Lee the chance to articulate their differences through a wonderfully choreographed classical Hollywood-esque musical number. The film acts as a layered rite of passage for adolescent blacks and as social commentary: identity and difference propel the narrative, as it does, Lee would argue, in real life.

*Do the Right Thing* (1989) is not only one of Lee's finest films to date but it is also one of the most important American films produced in the last 15 years. Set in a run-down Bedford Stuyvesant neighbourhood, over a 24-hour period, Lee constructs in microcosm the racial tensions and contestations that undercut the wider American society of the time. The Italian-American Pizzeria owners, the Korean store owners, and the vibrant black underclass who populate the film, represent the hierarchies of power, the diaspora identities, and the dislocated communities that operate in America. For Lee the reality of the black condition is one that calls for moral and political activism, but an activism, at least in terms of the film's resolution, that is ambiguous. The racist murder, by white cops, of Radio Raheem, and the subsequent destruction of Sal's 'Italian-American' Pizzeria by key members of the black community within the film, including Mookie (Spike Lee), who has previously bridged the racial divide, suggest violent action is needed. However, the reconciliatory 'morning after' scene between Sal and Mookie, and the end titles which juxtapose words from both Martin Luther King (advocating peaceful resistance) and Malcolm X (advocating violent resistance), blur this interpretation. What Lee is probably hoping to achieve here is the position where both black and white audiences are forced to see through the fog of their own subject positions.

*Mo' Better Blues* (1990) is a beautifully photographed (by Ernest Dickerson), introspective story of a black jazz musician (played by Denzel Washington) caught between the affections of two women. Through what is a rather clichéd narrative structure, Lee nonetheless manages to construct a powerful, provocative, and often life-determining representation of black culture/history. However, alongside the depictions of what can be seen to be a homoerotic 'musical' masculinity there is also a retrogressive form of macho masculinity and an essentialised notion of feminity. These reductive binary oppositions between black men and women are arguably found across Lee's film work.

*Jungle Fever* (1991), black American slang for unhealthy sexual attraction between races, takes a number of Lee's recurrent political themes and plays them out through the adulterous love affair between a black architect (Wesley Snipes) and a white-Italian secretary (Annabella Sciorra). The film self-consciously articulates their sexual affair through the wider cultural myths that circulate around race. Sciorra is attracted to Snipes because of the promise of his/the black man's sexual prowess, while Snipes is attracted to Sciorra because of the alluring promise of her ideal, white purity, and the status that the possession of her would bring him/the black male. The film attempts to expose and undermine these myths, revealing the race, class, and gender positions of the black and Italian-American communities the films moves in and though.

*Malcolm X* (1992) is the one film that best crystallises Lee's political mission to combine provocative, issues-based cinema – a cinema that gives voice and image to the black American condition – with a 'factional' film aesthetic that represents this condition 'authentically'. *Malcolm X* is 'biographical' in three senses: it re-tells the political story of Malcolm Little; it imagines the 'real' living conditions and social relations of the black community in America at the time; and it reveals Lee's own consciousness as a politically active African-American black male. The film is beautifully shot, is full of Lee's own cinematic touches, including a wonderful tracking, Steadicam opening shot, and mixes fictional cues with hand-held, black and white documentary techniques. The story behind the film is also interesting: running over budget, with Warner Bros. refusing further funds, Lee publicly funded the film through donations from leading black artists (including Bill Cosby and Oprah Winfrey). Racism and black activism in microcosm, no less.

*Crooklyn* (1994) is a semi-autobiographical family-centred drama (scripted with Joie and Cinque Lee) set in the early 1970s, in the Bedford Stuyvesant neighbourhood that Lee first took the audience to in *Do the Right Thing*. The film is full of the sights and sounds of black and white American culture from the time, for example, in one memorable scene the audience see the Carmichael family sing along to 'The Partridge Show' on television. It is rhythms and images such as these which structure the successes, failures and problems of the Carmichael family. *Crooklyn* is one of Lee's most life-determining and optimistic films. The film is also experimental in form, for example in the way Lee uses an anamorphic lens to convey Troy's sense of alienation.

*Lumière et compagnie* (1995) is a documentary (directed by Theo Angelopoulos) in which 40 contemporary directors are asked to make a one-shot film, lasting no more than 52 seconds, using the actual camera first used by the Lumière Brothers at the birth of cinema in 1895. Lee's contribution to this has its roots in his concern and interest in the realist aesthetic: Lee directs a 'home movie' of his baby daughter being prompted to utter her first word, 'Dada'. As the 52 seconds of real time ebb, the daughter manages to utter 'Da' just in the nick of time.

In *Clockers* (1995) Lee uses the vehicle of the investigative, procedural thriller to look at the dehumanising and wasting effect drug-running and guns have on both black and white Americans. The film is predominately pessimistic and brutally violent, capturing superbly the identity crises prevalent in what has come to be known as the postmodern condition. *Girl 6* (1996), by contrast, is probably one of Lee's least successful films. The black girl of the film title is forced into phone sex to make her way. Lee attempts some sort of socio-psychological reading to get at female need, desire, and unequal power relations, but instead produces a reductive, fetishised representation of woman. Nonetheless, *Girl 6* does have some wonderful fantasy moments and does open up a space for Girl 6 to transgress her own gender identity.

*Get on the Bus* (1996) is one of Lee's more inventive, thought-provoking films. Made independently with the financial backing of '15 black men', and shot in both 16mm and video, it follows a group of black men on an organised bus trip to a Nation of Islam protest march. It is a trip that literally takes the men across America and metaphorically takes them (and the audience) on a journey of self-discovery. Each of the characters represents a particular social-male type – on board there is a gay ex-Marine, a member of the Nation of Islam, an estranged father and son, a film student, a light-skinned cop, and a Jewish bus driver. The arguments, discussions and viewpoints raised on this journey provide a bardic function – black American men talking about their black masculinity, about how complex and polymorphous their subject positions are – working out real problems through the fictional narrative drama. The film, however, did extremely poorly on its first run, and went straight to video outside of America.

*4 Little Girls* (1997) was Lee's first full-length feature documentary and, given his desire to capture and represent the real, the documentary form gives him access to the full range of vérité techniques including newsreel footage, interviews, eye witness accounts, real settings, real people and real events. The documentary recounts the racist Alabama church bombing of 15 September 1963, that resulted in the death of four black choir girls. Lee juxtaposes the images and words of the racists against civil rights protesters, home movie shots of the girls, and the lucid memories of relatives and of those there at the bombing to bring the four little girls into textured focus. In short, Lee pitches good against evil, past against present, in what becomes a story that is as much about a contemporary time affected by violence as it is about the loss of the four little girls.

Lee's next film, *He Got Game* (1998), is a wonderful deconstruction of the importance of race and capital to major league basketball. He undercuts the myth of the black American dream through the raw portrayal of all the key manipulators – coaches, girlfriends, club officials – who are all out to snare Jesus (Ray Allen), the nation's top basketball prospect. But this souring of the motives behind basketball is compounded by the role of Jesus' father, Jake (Denzel Washington), a criminalised black who is initially disenfranchised but becomes a source of black empowerment outside, literally and metaphorically, of the rules of the game.

*Summer of Sam* (1999), Lee's first film without a central black cast, takes the serial-killer genre as a vehicle to address social and political issues much in the same way as *Crooklyn*'s generic structure did earlier. The film centres on both the vibrancy and paranoia of a Brooklyn community as the 'Son of Sam' continues to kill women in the area. The sense of an organic community is established but the serial killer persona provides the motor for an 'outsider' mentality to emerge. The central gay character comes to be seen as 'other' and a lynching mentality emerges. The film has a nostalgic feeling to it (pre-Mayor Giuliani and zero tolerance) and foreshadows the breakdown of neighbourhoods during the Reagan and Bush administrations.

*The Original Kings of Comedy* (2000) is Lee's second full-length feature documentary and stars/follows Cedric the Entertainer, Steve Harvey, D. L. Hughley and Bernie Mac – the original stand up Kings of Comedy – as they go on tour. Lee takes the audience behind the scenes and edits together a textured sense of stand-up comedy as a format where racial identity is both constructed and problematised. However, the documentary does have that feel of a vanity project, or at least feels weighed down by Lee's over-indulgence in the subject matter.

*Bamboozled* (2000) is a highly controversial satire on both the mechanisms of television production in the US and the way in which black people are stereotyped on television. It is an exploration of both institutional and cultural racism. Pierre Delacroix (Damon Wayans) is a middle-class black programme executive at a cable TV network who comes up with the idea of a blackface minstrel show that takes place in a watermelon patch on an Alabama plantation. Lee uses this filter as a mirror mechanism to open up the very nature of how black people are imagined within the industry. However, the blackface imagery and the relative sophistication that Lee is demanding of audiences to understand the self-reflexivity, lay the film open to charges that the message is lost in the representation.

Lee's next documentary, *Jim Brown: All American* (2002), is in one sense a warts-and-all biography of one of America's most brilliant athletes. The director constructs a moving account of his life, and typically frames it in terms of the racism and oppression that Brown faces and overcomes. The overall dynamo of the documentary, then, is to show how black men can succeed in an American society that tries to offer them only failure. Lee is currently in production with *The 25th Hour*, the story of the last day of freedom for Monty Brogan before he begins a seven-year jail sentence for drug dealing.                                                                                                 **SRe**

# Jean-Pierre LEFEBVRE

Born in Montreal in 1941, Jean-Pierre Lefebvre is often compared to Jean-Luc Godard – both of them make political films, both favour a semi-Brechtian aesthetics and both came of age in the 1960s. However, Michel Euvrad's assessment of Lefebvre – that he is 'less the cousin of Godard than the nephew of Bresson' – also has validity. Working quietly but steadily in every imaginable cinematic form, Lefebvre is a cinematic poet of tremendous humanistic concern. He began making films, sometimes with the National Film Board of Canada, during the tumultuous 1960s, a period known in Québec as the Quiet Revolution. This saw the opening up of what had been a very closed, repressive culture, and the province's film-makers were at the very head of that cultural movement. Lefebvre was at the vanguard of film-making in Québec.

His early films, such as *Le révolutionnaire* (1965), *Le vieux pays où Rimbaud est mort* (1977), and *Jusqu'au c'oeur* (1968), fitted with the radical politics of Québec. They were also quite artificial – or, in the case of *Jusqu'au coeur*, deeply fragmented

– drawing attention to themselves as productions as all good left-wing narrative films should. More lucid than most of Godard's work, one has the sense throughout Lefebvre's films that he has a genuinely kind, generous, and critical spirit, and that he wants to urge his viewer to consider the world in those contradictory terms. This is especially true of the lovely *Mon amie Pierette* (1968).

In the late 1960s and 1970s he took the work of nurturing the then-nascent Québec cinema very seriously. While working for the NFB he produced a series called 'Premières puvres', devoted to the work of first-time film-makers. In 1969 he and his wife Marguerite Duparc founded the production company Cinak, which produced his own films, in addition to those of such luminaries as Denys Arcand (Cinak produced Arcand's 1973 film *Réjeanne Padiovani*). Some of his later films, such as the pastoral *Les fleurs sauvages* (1982), were more straightforward works of narrative, which, like *Le révolutionnaire*, dealt with the painful dynamics of intimate relationships. *Les fleurs sauvages* won the Critics Prize at the 1982 Cannes Film Festival, and that moment predicted the enormous international acclaim that Québec cinema would find in the 1980s, arguably the province's cinematic golden age.

The 1990s saw Lefebvre turn to video, completing a five-part series he called *L'age des image*. These pieces were deeply personal (and somewhat disillusioned) attempts to come to grips with the cinematic environment around him; some of the episodes were narratives, some diary pieces, and others more experimental meditations.

Unlike more traditional auteurs, Lefebvre's work is wide-ranging and diverse. This is particularly true of his post-1980s films; stylistically there is quite a gap between the gentle, meandering narrative of *Les fleurs sauvages* and the sometimes incoherent, video-art-ness of *L'age des images*. It is hard to believe that they were made by the same film-maker. The key to understanding Lefebvre's ongoing stylistic concerns lies in his early work; the way that narrative and avant-garde strategies are mixed in *Le révolutionnaire* make the film look, in retrospect, like a cross between *Les fleurs sauvage* and *L'age des images*. The 1960s and 1970s are generally considered to be Lefebvre's most exciting and adventurous period, when he was insistent about making his passion for cinematic form and radical politics understood.

In 1998 he made *Aujourd'hui ou jamais*, which completed a trilogy he began with *Il ne faut pas mourir pour ça* (1967) and *Le vieux pays où Rimbaud est mort*. It played in Montreal for barely a week; sadly, Lefebvre's moment, which was itself intimately intertwined with the dream of a sustainable, independence-friendly, and distinct national cinema in Québec, had passed.                                                                **JW**

# Michael LEHMANN

One of the most unconventional directors in Hollywood today, the perennially under-achieving Lehmann very nearly became an academic, having studied philosophy before deciding that he wanted to become a film-maker. Born in San Francisco in 1957, he applied to the University of Southern California to study film, having worked at Francis Ford Coppola's Zoetrope Studios as a Video Project Manager.

His brilliantly original debut feature *Heathers* (1989), a black comedy about suicide, murder and rivalry in a small-town high school was just the kind of project to makes a major studio executive run a mile. Having received a string of rejections it was picked up by the independent New World Pictures and became both a critical and commercial success, and then a cult film. Starring Winona Ryder and Christian Slater in their first starring roles, *Heathers* relies on some extremely bizarre and, to many, sick humour, whilst the shooting style suggested an ability to transcend the conventions of the 'high-school teen comedy' genre.

The satirical swipe at the American way in *Heathers* is also carried over into his next feature *Meet the Applegates* (1990), a film about a family of six-foot Amazonian insects who, having the ability to change into any form, assume that of an appalling middle-American family, in order to blow up a nuclear power station and end the destruction of their natural habitat. Beautifully played by an excellent cast, the film suffers, however, from an over-emphasis on slapstick, whilst the ecological sub-text is never really developed.

Nevertheless, the sheer inventiveness and readiness to take risks with both subject matter and narrative brought Lehmann to the attention of a major studio, producer – Joel

Silver – and co-producer and star – Bruce Willis – who asked him to direct the $40 million dollar extravaganza *Hudson Hawk* (1991). The film is about a former jewel thief (played by Willis) who is forced by a corrupt CIA man, in league with a couple called the Mayflowers, to steal the missing pieces of a Gold Machine, a long-lost invention by Leonardo da Vinci. It has become infamous as an expensive vanity project that went over budget and ultimately flopped. Trapped between a star over-eager to intervene in all aspects of the production, and an aggressive producer, Lehmann was allowed to bring little of the inventiveness or personality evident in his first two features. Willis' smarmy and self-indulgent performance tips the film over into absurd parody though there are occasional glimpses at the kind of wry humour that Lehmann had shown earlier.

It would be three years before Lehmann would direct another film, the more modest *Airheads* (1994), a farce about a rock band who take over a radio station and hold the staff hostage demanding that their demo record be played on the air. The film's narrative scope is the antithesis of *Hudson Hawk*'s and while it lacks real drive, the energy of the performances and a sense of the absurd carry it though. Like *Hudson Hawk* the film was a critical and commercial flop, however Lehmann bounced back with his next feature, *The Truth About Cats and Dogs* (1996), a romantic comedy about mistaken identity and a vet who dispenses advice on the radio. Amidst a welter of romantic comedies, the film stands out as a result of its appealing performances (in particular Janeane Garofalo as the vet) and a perceptive and witty script that seemed to transcend the limits of the genre. *The Truth About Cats and Dogs* echoes *Heathers* in its concentration on the lives of women, and considers friendship and competition as a way of delving into their insecurities and complexities of character.

Having clawed his way back from *Hudson Hawk*, Lehmann threw it all away with the lamentable *My Giant* (1998). The film is a mawkishly sentimental 'comedy' vehicle for Billy Crystal about a showbiz agent who 'discovers' a seven-foot giant in a remote Romanian monastery and takes him back to America to make him a star and reunite him with his childhood sweetheart. With terrible performances (Steven Seagal cannot even play himself), few laughs and a poor script, the film does not befit Lehmann's undoubted talents.   **SH**

# Jennifer Jason LEIGH
See **Alan CUMMING**

# Danny LEINER

The lead guitarist for Brooklyn Garage band The Flying Guacamoles, writer-director Danny Leiner's first short, *Time Expired* (1992), was an unusual tale of a married crook who falls in love with a transvestite whilst in prison. A graduate of the famous State University of New York's Purchase College, his friendship with Bob Gosse and other members of the 'Purchase Mafia' led to his self-scripted low-budget feature, *Layin' Low* (1996). A Brooklyn-set story, it focuses on two underperforming twentysomethings: one, whilst far from intellectual, enjoys reading so much that he would like to try writing, the other is a slacker who dreams of moving to Cleveland between his petty crime and get-rich-quick schemes. Their lives undergo drastic change upon their unfortunate involvement with a local crime baron. Well-paced, the acting is raw and convincing, the dialogue spare and authentic, and the visuals suitably gritty.

*Dude, Where's my Car?* (2000), Leiner's subsequent feature, is one of innumerable *Bill and Ted* rip-offs in which two noodle-heads affably bumble about, in this case in search of their car, meeting aliens, having adventures, and shouting unoriginal catch-phrases 'sweet' and 'dude'. *Dude* co-star, Ashton Kutcher, was the best thing about the film and picked up a Breakthrough Male Performance nomination for the 2001 MTV Movie Awards. Philip Stark's script shows a lack of imagination and *Dude* jogs aimlessly if energetically along to a foregone conclusion. A sequel, also helmed by Leiner, is planned.   **FG**

# Kasi LEMMONS

Born in Missouri in 1961, Kasi Lemmons established herself as a supporting player in films such as *Silence of the Lambs* (1990) and *Hard Target* (1993) before making her remarkably assured writing and directorial debut with *Eve's Bayou* (1997).

Wilfully eschewing the turbulent racial politics of its early 1960s, deep American south setting, the film presents a middle-class black family torn by its internal tensions and secrets. The early confession of patricide (in the adult Eve's opening voiceover) is rendered complex by the ensuing themes of memory, truth and superstition, which all add rich layers to the conventions of family melodrama. While the narrative is female-centred, the shadow of destructive patriarchy informs at all levels. As the doctor and father whose sexual weaknesses initiate the chain of events, Samuel L. Jackson manages to evoke a sense of both pity and disturbance. However, this is a 'women's film' in the best sense of the phrase, buoyed by the impressive performances of its child actors (Jurnee Smollett and Meagan Good) and their adult co-players (Lynn Whitfield, Debbi Morgan, and Diahann Carrol).

Culminating in an ambiguous revelation of incest (indeed, we see two subtly conflicting accounts of the father/daughter taboo), the film balances the significance of old world beliefs (voodoo, spiritualism) with the unreliable and elusive nature of perception and memory. Concluding on a reconciliatory note on the shores of the film's title setting, the film, through reference to figures long gone, carries a sense of the ghosts which continue to impose upon the lives of generations to come. Lemmons shows true potential with this debut feature, a fact reflected in her receipt of both Independent Spirit (Best First Feature) and National Board of Review (Best Debut Director) awards.

Her subsequent film, *The Caveman's Valentine* (2001), is the story of a talented musician, played by Samuel L. Jackson, whose mental instability has led him to live a secluded life in a New York park. The discovery of a corpse nearby draws him out of his cave and back into society.                                                             **NJ**

# Brett LEONARD

Quickly building a reputation as one of Hollywood's new media visionaries and a leading innovator of emerging technologies in the entertainment industry, Brett Leonard's directorial resumé is extremely diverse. It ranges from a schlock horror flick to a pair of virtual-reality features to 3-D productions on dinosaurs and the Las Vegas magician team Siegfried & Roy.

Leonard's directorial debut came in 1989 with *The Dead Pit*, a depressing zombie tale (which he also co-wrote) about an evil doctor who returns from the dead to terrorise hospital staff and mental patients. This fairly inauspicious start to his professional career was more than made up for three years later with *The Lawnmower Man* (1992), a film Leonard based (very loosely) on a Stephen King short story, which eventually grossed more than $150 million around the world. Widely recognised for introducing the concept of virtual reality to pop culture, *The Lawnmower Man* stars Jeff Fahey as a retarded man who undergoes experiments involving intelligence-enhancing drugs and totally immersive virtual-reality technology with disastrous results. Although the movie was criticised for having a weak narrative and wooden dialogue, even its detractors acknowledged the dazzling computer animation sequences (including a sex fantasy/nightmare) and special-effects pyrotechnics at the conclusion. Most impressive of all was the fact that Leonard made the film on a mere $6 million budget.

In 1995 Leonard released two feature films with big-name actors in the lead roles. First came *Hideaway*, starring Jeff Goldblum as a family man who dies in a car crash, only to be resuscitated via an experimental medical procedure. In a twist reminiscent of Wes Craven's *Shocker* (1989) and the more recent supernatural serial killer film, *Fallen* (1998), the hero begins having strange visual sensations, eventually discovering that he is now united with a murderer who somehow entered his mind during death. Continuing to explore the Frankensteinian theme of technology gone awry, *Virtuousity* (1995) places Russell Crowe in the role of a computer-generated entity (code name: SID 6.7) who turns psychopathic and manages to escape his virtual prison. Fortunately, Denzel Washington is there to do battle with SID in reality and finally sends him back to the land of bits and bytes.

Leonard's two most recent films were both made using IMAX 3-D technology. *T-Rex: Back to the Crustaceous* (1998) was a dino-romp which parlayed breathtaking visual effects into a $40 million-plus gross while playing on a very limited number of screens. In contrast, the Anthony Hopkins-narrated documentary, *Siegfried & Roy: The Magic*

*Box* (1999) flopped at the box office, even though it incorporated 20 minutes of special effects into its 45-minute running time (as opposed to five minutes for *T-Rex*).

In addition to his directorial duties, Leonard is founder and co-chairman of the high-tech production company, L-Squared Entertainment, through which he created a highly acclaimed interactive 'Virtual Studio Tour', starring Danny DeVito. Leonard also directed the first music video/motion simulation film, Peter Gabriel's 'Kiss That Frog', which in 1994 won the MTV Music Video award for Best Special Effects.　　　　**SJS**

# Robert LEPAGE

*The Confessional* (1995)
*The Polygraph* (1996)
*Nô* (1998)
*Possible Worlds* (2001)

Born in Montreal in 1957, a graduate of the Conservatoire d'Art Dramatique de Québec, Robert Lepage has achieved success with his innovative theatrical work. Proposing that cinema has done for theatre what photography did for the visual arts – allowing it to become impressionistic, surrealistic and abstract – his application of the conventions of cinema to his own theatre productions created a body of work that presaged his role as a film director. Following various roles in films, including an eccentric Pontius Pilate in Denys Arcand's *Jésus of Montréal* (1989), Lepage moved into film-making. The result is a series of films that play with perceptions of truth and the layers of deceit that mask our daily lives.

*The Confessional* (1995) is a psychological jigsaw puzzle that pays homage to Hitchcock's *I Confess* (1953). Seamlessly shifting between Québec in 1952, when Hitchcock was filming his clerical thriller, and 1989, Lepage's film traces Pierre Lamontagne's (Lothaire Bluteau) attempts to uncover a mystery that has plagued his family for four decades. Delighting in the overt use of Freudian symbolism and cleverly inserting sequences from Hitchcock's film to flesh out his own narrative, Lepage's film is an ambitious debut. Remarkable not only for its overall vision, particularly the use of colour as a metaphor for memory (the red wall inside the Lamontagne house recalls Tipi Hedren's colour/memory association in *Marnie* (1964)), it manages to combine the elements of a whodunit with an articulate and moving account of loss.

*The Polygraph* (1996) continues the central theme – that of the notion of truth amidst lies and deception – with Patrick Goyette's student under suspicion for a murder he cannot remember committing. When a lie-detector test proves inconclusive, he attempts to discover the truth of what actually happened. Based on an early play by Lepage, *The Polygraph* is less impressive than *The Confessional*, both in style and pacing. Weighed down by the claustrophobic nature of its source material – the play's success lay in its taking place in one small space – it lacks both directorial flair and dramatic weight, resulting in an occasionally clever, but ultimately disappointing, film.

Compared with the mood and themes explored in his earlier works, *Nô* (1998), Lepage's most ambitious film to date, initially appears lighter. Adapted from his epic play 'The Seven Streams of the River Ota', it uses the conventions of Feydeauesque farce to look at a volatile period in recent Canadian history and Japan's post-war relations with the international community. Set in 1970, when separatist terrorists were fighting for Québec's independence, and the Osaka World Fair was playing host to a Canadian theatre company, *Nô* contrasts the oppressive atmosphere of a city under martial law with a community celebrating cultural diversity and the freedom of artistic expression, albeit a badly performed French farce. With irreverent humour, Lepage depicts Canada's political troubles as a comedy of errors, portraying both the terrorists and the security forces as bungling fools. However, as the film progresses, it offers a more serious rumination on Québec's political upheavals and the volatile nature of international relations. Shooting the Québec scenes in black and white, a stark contrast to the colourful and more hopeful environment of the Osaka Expo, Lepage returns to the visual daring he displayed in *The Confessional*. More comical than his previous films, *Nô* is further evidence of Lepage's ability to create original and thought-provoking entertainment.

*Possible Worlds* (2001) is a return to the cerebral gameplay of *The Confessional*. A complex psychological thriller, Tom McCamus stars as the victim of a macabre murder whose life is played over and over in a series of different scenarios. Only the ineptly conducted police investigation, which takes place in what could be the present, appears to bear any resemblance to reality. Lepage's most assured film, his interplay between the past and present, the real and the unreal, balances intellectual rigour with emotional depth, offering a moving, if offbeat, musing on the nature of memory and the importance of memories in finding our place in the world. McCamus and Swinton's otherworldly performances match the cool sheen of Jonathan Freeman's photography, which reinforce the ethereal dreamlike world that Lepage and John Mighton's script conjures. Less playful than *Nô*, *Possible Worlds* still remains the work of a trickster. As with all of his work, both in film and theatre, Lepage delights in shifting the boundaries of truth and reality; it is a beautiful, melancholy, and haunting film that once again sees him striving to find his unique voice and vision as a director.                                    **IHS**

# Brian LEVANT

A sworn champion of American pop culture and an avid toy collector, Brian Levant's enthusiasms have been the foundation for a successful career built on purveying popular comedy to audiences around the world. Born in Illinois in 1952, Levant has fashioned a series of films all targeted without apology at the largest possible audience. The director could be said to embody a post-*Home Alone* (1990) aesthetic of family-friendly comedy driven by bright, kinetic gags.

A 1990s Ken Annakin, perhaps, Levant has specialised in brash, bright, multiplex movies that have all been carried by a certain, well-judged level of sincerity amidst the chaos, fantasy and comedy. His films build stories about the forces that threaten family stability. In *Problem Child 2* (1991), Levant's debut feature, he focuses on Junior and his new best friend Trixie as they wreak havoc and strive to make their parents fall in love. In *Beethoven* (1992) – produced by film comedy ace Ivan Reitman – an otherwise happy family feel there is a space that needs filling in their lives. Enter a lumbering St Bernard dog whom they name Beethoven. Slapstick comedy ensues as the family must not only deal with their new 'child' but also the dog's nemesis, a sinister vet.

In *The Flintstones* (1994), the bonds of friendship and family are tested when Fred Flintstone is framed by his cartoonishly evil boss Cliff Vandercave, who plans to embezzle a fortune from the Slate Gravel Company. Fred must find a way to repair the damage, and the film ends with a simple affirmation of friendship. Somehow, amidst the spectacle and combination of practical animatronic creatures and digital creations, Levant elicits appropriately gauged and engaging performances from his leads, notably John Goodman as Fred, Rick Moranis as Barney, Elizabeth Perkins as Wilma, and Rosie O'Donnell as Betty.

Levant directed Arnold Schwarzenegger in the film *Jingle All the Way* (1996), produced by Chris Columbus, director of *Home Alone* and *Home Alone 2: Lost in New York* (1992), telling the very simple tale of a father who must battle another shopper to buy the much-treasured Turbo Man figure for his little boy. *Home Alone* clearly inspired the design of the story and – as with *Problem Child* – the concept feels too familiar and lacks a spin fresh enough to be engaging. *Jingle All the Way*, as a Christmas comedy, lacks any real charm and much of its humour verges on the spiteful.

In the prequel *The Flintstones: Viva Rock Vegas* (2000), Levant recasts the leads with Mark Little as Fred and Stephen Baldwin as Barney. His second outing with the modern Stone Age family is a more confident and charming piece than the first, yet both adaptations faithfully and obsessively recreate the cartoon world in three dimensions – Levant's genuine respect for *The Flintstones* as an icon of pop culture apparent in every frame, his camera moving lovingly across his believably rendered and engaging prehistoric world.

*The Flintstones* and *Beethoven* remain Levant's most creatively successful efforts, both imbued with a giddy populist sensibility which attests to his mission as custodian of good family entertainment. His most recent film, the comedy *Snow Dogs* (2002), is based on the book 'Winterdance', the story of a Miami dentist that inherits a team of sled dogs and decides to train them for the Arctic Challenge race                          **JC**

# Barry LEVINSON

Barry Levinson has been a prolific Hollywood film-maker and writer for over twenty years, working within the mainstream but often on projects with a socio-political message. His films are generally propelled through words, conversations, and character interactions rather than action and spectacle. He therefore seems to be very much a classical Hollywood film-maker in an industry where spectacular excess or high-concept cinema dominates production trends.

Levinson was born in Maryland in 1942 and started work as a comedy writer and performer on local television (winning a local Emmy award) before being asked to write for 'The Carol Burnett Show' in 1967, for which he was to be nominated for two Emmy awards within the space of three years. Levinson's first two screenplays were for Mel Brooks' acclaimed Silent Movie (1976) and High Anxiety (1977). Levinson's third screenplay, co-scripted with partner Valerie Curtin, for the film ...and justice for all (1979), was nominated for an Academy Award.

Levinson's first film, Diner (1982), made with a budget of under $5 million, demonstrates the cinematic power that he could inject into a situational comedy, with a tight, episodic, conversation-cued script (that he also wrote). The first of what have become known as Levinson's 'Baltimore films' is set in an all-night diner in 1959, where a tight-knit group of male teenagers undertake their rites-of-passage into manhood. The superb character performances from the mostly young, first-timer cast (including Steve Guttenberg, Mickey Rourke, Kevin Bacon) propel the film, and with the wonderful, lovingly authentic mise-en-scène, reproduce both a nostalgic yearning for the past, for youth and youth culture, and for an imagined ideal America, or the kind of place that Levinson believes America once was.

Levinson followed this with The Natural (1984), an allegorical baseball movie that again pays nostalgic homage to an American past represented as more authentic, and somehow more magical than the present. Roy Hobbs (played by Robert Redford, returning to the screen after an absence of three years) has an incredible talent for baseball, nurtured by his father, and is destined to play in the major leagues. However, this destiny is only partially fulfilled in the film, and then only made sense of in the final, mesmerising end sequence where, as a man, Hobbs returns to the stadium of his dreams to hit the floodlights out around him, and in effect reclaim his masculine, American identity. The film picked up four Academy Award nominations including one for Caleb Deschanel's 'water-coloured' photography.

Young Sherlock Holmes (aka The Pyramid of Fear, 1985) attempts to combine the roller-coaster aesthetics of a Spielberg movie with the investigative plot dynamic of the thriller. Re-enacting an imaginary first encounter between Holmes and Watson, the film is unfortunately full of some crude stereotypes and never really successfully pulls off its hybrid form.

Levinson's next feature, Tin Men (1987), the second of the Baltimore films, is once again a nostalgic, if caustic, return to late 1950s America. The film concerns itself with the scams of two property salesmen (Richard Dreyfuss and Danny DeVito) who, during the course of the film, become mortal enemies. Their rivalry is played out against a backdrop of changing legislation which threatens their 'fast buck' and macho American way of life. The film is therefore a revisionist frontier movie: Dreyfuss and DeVito, like two dinosaur gun-slingers, are out of place in what is fast becoming a feminised, democratic, more heavily regulated America.

Good Morning, Vietnam (1987) is Levinson's liberal attempt to revise the way Hollywood traditionally has represented the Vietnam war and the Vietnamese people. Through the manic, semi-improvised comedy routines of Robin Williams, playing an army radio DJ, the film constructs an escapist space for audiences to enter into. This opens the way for the film's later utopian moralising in which Williams gets to show the audience how much American suburbanites really are/were like the Vietnamese. When Williams decides to teach the Vietnamese people how to speak English, he does so under a white, privileged imperialist gaze. The film's political rhetoric is nothing more than a gesture; Williams' manic star persona was first cemented here.

Rain Man (1988) is one of Levinson's most celebrated films, winning him Academy Awards for Best Director and Best Picture. Raymond (Dustin Hoffman) is autistic, and has had little contact with his younger and more handsome brother Charlie (Tom Cruise). The film is principally concerned with how the two brothers, who struggle to communicate for different reasons, learn how to communicate with each other – and in part the wider social world – through each other. The film is a typical buddy movie in the sense that initial antagonism between the two protagonists gives way to mutual respect and affection. However, Rain Man sanitises autism for the commercial cinema audiences, and plays out, through what is the metaphor of autism, male identity crises.

Levinson's next film, *Avalon* (1990), is the third of his Baltimore pictures, and also the most reverently nostalgic, drawing on the memories, life patterns, and successes of first-generation immigrants to a welcoming, diasporic America. The film intricately captures the period in question, and enables the myth that the American dream was (and therefore still is) available to all, to re-circulate in contemporary culture. After this came *Bugsy* (1991), a rich, textured story of the mobster Ben Siegel, whose dream it was to build a city of casinos in Las Vegas. The cinematography and production design in the film captures the 1940s setting beautifully, while Warren Beatty's blistering performance as Bugsy portrays the Janus-faced figure fully – sometimes movie wannabe, sometimes ladies' man, but always cold-blooded killer. The film therefore constructs some classic, reductive representations of gender, not least through the enigmatic femme fatale, Virginia Hill (Annette Bening), whose ultimate promise is sex and death.

*Toys* (1992) was both a critical and commercial disaster for Levinson. While lavish in set design, and in its Burton-esque fantasy settings, the film was considered, at the time, to have the most threadbare of storylines. However, more recently, *Toys* has been re-assessed and appropriated by film buffs. The film now has a cult following who marvel at its set pieces (particularly the ending that involves LL Cool J and a host of marvellous action toys), excessive character performances, self-reflexivity, and its over-arching camp aesthetic.

Levinson followed this with *Jimmy Hollywood* (1994), a dark social-realist comedy that tries to offer up a savage critique of Hollywood, and in turn the American dream. The film is a far cry from Levinson's Baltimore films, owing more to *Midnight Cowboy* (1969) and *Taxi Driver* (1976) than to Levinson's own nostalgia pictures. Joe Pesci is by turn manic and pathetic as Jimmy Alto, actor extraordinaire, who cannot find his way into the dream. Levinson captures the feeling of America disintegrating before our eyes through shots such as the camera diving to the bottom of a crystal clear Hockney-inspired pool, only to reveal the cracks and rubbish that lie there.

Academically, much has been written about *Disclosure* (1994), since it seemed to explicitly play out the politics of gender role-reversal that became of cultural concern in the 1980s and 1990s. Meredith Johnson (Demi Moore) is both a literal and metaphorical cross-dresser, taking on the kind of masculine role that is typically conceived as a career-driven individual or lecherous boss. She rapes Tom Sanders (Michael Douglas) and then takes his position within the company. Unfortunately, the film offers a repressive solution to what is or could have been a radical transgression of gender norms. By the end of the film, Meredith Johnson suffers classical Hollywood moral retribution for her sins – those who dare to overthrow patriarchy are themselves overthrown.

In *Sleepers* (1996), Levinson again constructs a narrative that has sexual identity and morality at its core, but here the audience are presented with a homophobically charged rape-revenge movie. Nokes (Kevin Bacon), a sadistic prison guard, sodomises four boys while they are in prison for an 'accidental' murder. When two of the boys later shoot Nokes, the killing is constructed as a morally justified revenge killing, and because they are not found guilty of the crime (because they are given a false alibi by the priest, played by Robert De Niro), the act of homophobic revenge is given religious and state sanction.

*Wag the Dog* (1997) is arguably Levinson's best film to date. A biting, and at times extremely funny, satire of the American political and military machine, the film works best in the context of its fabrications and spin doctoring. The phoney war, soundbites, and spontaneous anthems that circulate around the war are intended to detract from a scandal threatening to engulf the President's (Dustin Hoffman) office. The film's real power lies in the fact that it replays in the immediacy of the scandal that engulfed the Clinton administration. Fact and fiction merge, and the mediated universe the film re-presents is very well handled. *Wag the Dog* won the Silver Bear Award at the Berlin Film Festival.

A disappointing follow-up to this was *Sphere* (1998), a minor science fiction film that fails to reproduce the spectacle of *The Abyss* (1989), from which it borrows, or the tension of the *Alien* films. *Liberty Heights* (1999), the last picture in the Baltimore series, is much more successful, returning the film-maker to the 1950s to play out the film's concern with adolescence and racial segregation. The duality of the narrative, high-school love and other teenage rituals, and the disintegration of a racially-divided America, is generally sensitively handled. However, Levinson's nostalgic refrain indicates that for him it is in the present where something fundamental is lacking – the past has been constructed mythically to allow America a sense of a stabilised identity in a contemporary social context where instability is all around.

An Everlasting Piece (2000), starring Billy Connolly and Barry McEvoy (who also wrote the screenplay), takes place in Belfast in the early 1980s, although the film still has the feel of Levinson's earlier Baltimore pictures. It uses situation comedy – the two main characters, Colm (Barry McEvoy), a Catholic, and George (Brian F. O'Byrne), a Protestant, set up a hairpiece business intending to sell toupees to everyone in the community – to address the political issues of religious sectarianism and the everyday ramifications of living during 'the troubles'. The film has some very funny moments, and some fine performances, and offers a different way into representing Northern Ireland politics.

Levinson's latest film, Bandits (2001), is a major disappointment. Starring Bruce Willis, Cate Blanchett and Billy Bob Thornton, the film, told in flashback, is the story of two bank robbers who both fall in love with Kate (Blanchett), one of their 'unhappily married' hostages, who in turn comes to reciprocate their feelings. Unfortunately, the film produces a confused tone, veering from comedy to pathos to final tragedy. The performances are wooden, and the satire (of the media in particular) feels rather crude and incomplete.                                                                    **SRe**

# Kevin LIMA

Kevin Lima's first piece of direction was on the animated feature A Goofy Movie (1995). Starring the popular Disney character Goofy and his son Max, the story involves them taking a road trip and the supposedly hilarious events that follow. The film is weak, lacking the polish of Disney's big-screen pieces, whilst the music is made up of predictable fare and a number of strange pop-funk tracks intended to enthral a generation weaned on the delights of MTV. The film borrows stylistically from the television cartoon 'Goof Troop' which, due to the obvious constraints, relied much more on the characters than overall polish.

Tarzan (1999) is a much more successful venture. Directed along with Chris Buck, this feature can be seen in a long Disney tradition of family entertainment. For the first time an attempt was made to explain the ability of animals to speak perfect English. When in conversation the animals' and Tarzan's speech is heard as a collection of incomprehensible noises by the human characters; likewise the speech of the human characters remains a mystery to the animals. The audience are thus in the unique position of being able to understand both groups (as, eventually, is Tarzan himself). Along with its tremendous speed of movement, Tarzan heralds an advanced use of computer-aided animation for Disney.

Lima is in line to direct the sequel to Cats and Dogs (2001).                          **SS**

# Doug LIMAN

Of the post-Tarantino crop of young American stylists and pop culture merchants, Doug Liman is one of the most promising in purely cinematic terms. A brace of hip comedies with edge – Swingers (1996) and Go (1999) – have established Liman not only as a film-maker with an ear for the vernacular in the scripts he chooses to work from, but one who is also endowed with a keen cinematic eye and a crisp, energetic storytelling style.

Getting off the mark with campus black comedy Getting In (1994), about the attempts of a desperate student to reduce the waiting list for a place in medical school, Liman found his feet with the indie hit Swingers, recipient of a delirious reception at the Venice Film Festival. Scripted by actor/comedian Jon Favreau, and starring Favreau and Vince Vaughan as slackers with style, the film's nostalgia for the Rat Pack era of Ocean's Eleven (1960) and the Vegas 'Summit' meetings was underplayed just enough to avoid alienating a more enlightened and discerning 1990s audience. In fact, much of the charm of Swingers comes from watching a generation hopelessly cut off from the consequence-free hedonism of the early 1960s trying on the slacks of Frank, Dino and Sammy for size. Favreau's jilted beau is taken on a tour of the Los Angeles club underworld by buddy Vaughan, eventually forging a new relationship with dancing partner Heather Graham. The pairing of Favreau's hangdog, over-sensitive New Man and Vaughan's dapper, unreconstructed playboy is a delight, and proved a star-making turn for Vaughan, who was soon snapped up for Spielberg's *The Lost World* (1997).

Follow-up *Go* forsook the retro styling and show tunes for the rave culture of the late 1990s Ecstasy scene, but retained the close attention to ritualistic detail that characterised *Swingers*. A portmanteau of loosely-linked stories, all hinging on a different sense of the word 'go', the movie unwisely invited comparisons with Tarantino's similarly structured *Pulp Fiction* (1994), but on the whole escaped from the formidable shadow of its forebear, if occasionally coming across like a junior version of the hardboiled hit. Featuring a string of hip new names, mostly culled from teen television stardom (Katie Holmes, Scott Wolf, Jay Mohr, Taye Diggs) alongside the more established indie talents of Sarah Polley and William Fichtner, *Go* demonstrated how Liman had absorbed Tarantino's fondness for a heightened atmosphere of laughs followed by sudden, shocking violence (although in Liman's film the violence is moderate and often comically undercut, as in the scene with J. E. Freeman's Vegas gangster berating his sheepish disappointment of a son for lacking the guts to whack an enemy). Shot (by Liman himself, who also served as his own director of photography on *Swingers*) and edited (by Stephen Mirrione) with exquisite confidence, the film is also notable for being one of the first major American movies to use a rave soundtrack convincingly and to exploit the rhythms of the dance beats for visual effect.

Moving more into the mainstream, Liman has recently directed *The Bourne Identity* (2002), based on Robert Ludlum's book. A thriller starring Matt Damon, it has had a lukwarm reception. **MF**

# Richard LINKLATER

Richard Linklater's films constitute an intelligent reconfiguration of the 'youth movie' for a generation torn between self-conscious cultural savvy and the time-honoured desire to connect. The success of subsequent cheap, chatty and cheerful American independent films such as *Clerks* (1994) and *Go Fish* (1994) suggest the extent to which his debut feature, *Slacker* (1991), crystallised a demographic, but if his films offer an affectionate insider's view on what it's like to be jostled by options between adolescence and adulthood, they certainly don't glibly romanticise youth. Instead, Linklater homes in on a uniformly garrulous generation's fumbling stabs at communication under the weight of solipsism and endless theorising, the loose-looking sprawl of his films belied by their emotional acuity and seemingly effortless narrative economy.

Linklater was born in Houston in 1961 and after working on oil rigs for two years in the Gulf of Mexico, moved to Austin and helped form the Austin Film Society in September 1995. A self-taught film-maker, he started when he was 22 with the help of a Super-8 camera, a projector, editing equipment and a book entitled 'The Technical Aspects of Film-Making'. His first film, *It's Impossible to Learn to Plow by Reading Books* (1988), hinged on themes of travel and restless youth – motifs that recur as *Slacker* opens and a character, played by Linklater, returns from travelling and jumps into a taxi. The significance of Linklater playing *Slacker*'s first slacker suggests his insider's position, and his spiel about alternative realities and the problem of choices maps out the film's thematic and formal concerns.

This self-consciousness about making decisions belongs to generation, director, and character alike. If it begs the question of which story Linklater will tell, the twenty-four hour path his film takes through Austin is one of suitably restless diversions. No sooner do we hear one character's eager rap than the camera fixes on another, resulting in an encyclopaedic day out which views, in retrospect, like a tour of 1990s pop cultural concerns. We hear about conspiracies, JFK, aliens, Armageddon and ecological disasters, and we meet one quasi-Marxist character who talks like a deadpan dead-ringer for a Hal Hartley character. It's a warm, witty and smartly quizzical snapshot of a director, a genre, and a clever but aimless generation in the process of formation, and a prescient one at that.

If *Slacker* foreshadowed the 1990s, *Dazed and Confused* (1993), Linklater's finest film, travels back in time to the break-up of school in summer 1976. Freshmen are brutally initiated by seniors, formative experiences take place everywhere you look, and perennial teenage tensions – peer groups versus teachers, 'visceral experience' versus laying foundations for the future – are lightly, lucidly and warmly articulated over one day's drinking, smoking, making out and hanging out. Linklater just seems to hang out too, his film built like his characters' flares: somewhere between tight at the top and fly-away below. Still, despite the grip it gets on the bell-bottoms and centre-partings of the 1970s, the film is no mere fetishistic, nostalgic period study. Linklater elicits natural performances from his ensemble cast and, between one 'bad ass' senior's commitment to giving freshmen hell and an oppressive games coach, steers clear of marshmallow mythologising. The teenage peer groups are not quite as rigidified as the coach's anti-drugs stance, but, as the presence of one sleazy ex-student-cum-hanger-on suggests, they hint at the possibility of stagnation.

As with *Slacker*, the film closes with a drive to an uncertain future. We don't know where Linklater's characters are going, but *Before Sunrise* (1995) at least offers a brightly romantic holiday snapshot. The film follows Jesse (Ethan Hawke), an American boy, and Celine (Julie Delpy), a French girl, over one shared day in Vienna. Strangers on a train, they hook up on Jesse's argument that it will forestall the moment, twenty years on, when Celine might wonder about that American. Self-consciousness aside, the stage is set for romance, delicately troubled by the possibility that these two – the smart but emotionally capable girl, the dorkish boy with his emotionally impotent theorising – might not last five minutes under other circumstances. Still, as hopeless as Jesse is, and despite Celine's refreshingly no-nonsense jab at any sexual intentions he (and, implicitly, voyeuristic audiences) might harbour, they connect. The knowing avoidance of push-button holiday romance clichés allows this Viennese whirl's spell to take you unawares.

These three films sit so snugly together that it is, perhaps, no surprise that Linklater seemed to go astray in his next two. Maybe it's the result of working from someone else's material, but his knack for character suffered most. Focused on a group of early twentysomethings, and adapted by Eric Bogosian from his own play, *SubUrbia* (1997) is a claustrophobic wake-up call after *Before Sunrise*'s dreamy, ambling night. The seeds of stagnation mildly implicit in *Dazed and Confused* take root here, and for that film's badass seniors, *SubUrbia* offers one near-psychopath. After a slow tour of suburbia over the opening titles, the film's car park setting stalls any travelling motifs, and a tragic conclusion strips garrulous inaction of any romanticism. Still, as bold a revision of Linklater's shtick as all this is, the film struggles with its unconvincing characters and lurching, forced plot twists.

Co-written by Linklater, Claude Stanush and Clark Lee Walker, *The Newton Boys* (1998) is only marginally more successful. Ambitious and liberating after *SubUrbia*, the film ditches the 'hanging out' and 24-hour time spans of Linklater's other films for a western/gangster hybrid set in the 1920s, centred on four likeable brothers who became the most notorious, and possibly sweetest, bank robbers in American history. Still, it remains familiar as a Linklater film because his key theme of how to position yourself in a world that offers more options by the day is only heightened by the period, the burgeoning American city offering a lot more possibilities than the shift from horses to cars alone. Otherwise, Linklater's talents elude him: the trademark sprawl of his plots feels diffuse here, and the characters, though gamely played by the likes of Matthew McConaughey, remain dead on the page. The film peaks with footage of the real Newton boys over the closing credits, and it was pulled from theatrical release in the UK after it bombed in the US.

Thankfully, though, any fears that Linklater had lost the plot have been smartly allayed by his two most recent films. The animated *Waking Life* (2001) sees the director matching his maturing thematic concerns with audacious, low-budget formal experimentation. Ten years on from *Slacker*'s Sundance premiere, the film screened at Sundance 2001 with a plot similar to that of Linklater's breakthrough film: a nameless character (in another nod to Linklater's glory days, it's *Dazed and Confused*'s Wiley Wiggins who provides the voice) dreamily wanders the streets, bumping into numerous individuals who all have a theory about something. But just as *Waking Life* mines Linklater's back catalogue – Ethan Hawke and Julie Delpy appear, albeit animated, and, as in *Slacker*, Linklater voices one of the film's key monologues – it's the innovative use of animation (specifically, a technique called 'rotoscoping') that astonishes, mixing a curiously dreamlike quality with clear-line clarity.

By contrast, *Tape* (2001) depends more on its acute performances than style. Shot on digital video, it is set entirely in one motel room, with Ethan Hawke and Robert Sean

Leonard meeting up and chafing over a horrific, earlier incident involving Uma Thurman's character. Like *Waking Life*, the film shows Linklater at his best: freewheeling and apparently formless on the surface, jostling multiple points of view, but tightly scripted and conceived at the roots, in that, in a sense, it's actually *about* both point of view and a certain tussling for narrative power. After setting an agenda for American independents ten years ago, Linklater's raising the stakes again.                                        **KH**

# Luis LLOSA

Born in Peru, Luis Llosa's credentials mark him as a mainstream action director who falls somewhere short of virtuoso status but can turn in an efficient enough, profitable vehicle – closer to John Badham than John Woo. His first high-profile release was *Sniper* (1993), a tense two-hander centring on Billy Zane's callow government agent learning the rules of combat from Tom Berenger's grizzled, troubled military hard man. Their mission takes them into Panama to unseat an unscrupulous dictator. Most reviews noted the skill with which Llosa executed his action sequences but emphasised the thinness of plot and the risibility of the psychological subtext.

Llosa's next picture was a glossy affair that teamed two huge 1990s stars, Sylvester Stallone and Sharon Stone, just as the profitability and lustre of both passed its peak and started to wane. *The Specialist* (1994) pulls off the familiar action movie trick of casting reputable character actors in subsidiary roles to shoulder the serious acting duties – in this case, James Woods and Rod Steiger. It is a fairly pedestrian thriller, however, the kind that would be rendered obsolete by the post-Tarantino wave of ironic violence. The film looked outmoded even at the time of release, its 'Miami Vice'-era chic serving only to surround its Versace-clad stars with an appropriately shimmering and superficial backdrop. Stone's character is out for revenge; Stallone's bomb-disposal expert discards his lone wolf policy to help her. The stars are clearly meant to generate fireworks in the many contrived erotic scenes but any chance of genuine chemistry is nullified by the clinical procession of lingerie shots and sweaty workouts.

Llosa also maintains a productive career as a producer, both of television programmes in his native Peru, and of mid-budget American sci-fi features such as the Dean Koontz adaptation *Watchers III* (1994) and *New Crime City* (1994). His producer's credit is often found alongside the name of legendary B-movie mogul Roger Corman. Corman's stylistic influence is also stamped all over Llosa's 1997 feature *Anaconda*, a trip into darkest B-movie territory that revisits the predictable generic patterns of 1950s supporting features while also cribbing tricks from the Steven Spielberg of *Jaws* (1975) and *Jurassic Park* (1993). Together with *Deep Blue Sea* (1999), *Lake Placid* (1999) and *Mimic* (1997), it forms part of a new sub-genre, pitting self-deprecating heroes and scenery-chewing baddies against implausible, computer-generated freaks of nature or genetic modification. It is an engaging enough retread of familiar ground with the added 1990s slant of an ironic, cine-literate frame of reference, a welcome development after the emptiness of *The Specialist*.

Jon Voight slums it in the role of Paraguayan snake hunter Paul Sarone, whose malevolent influence leads astray the documentary team led by director Terry (Jennifer Lopez) and anthropologist Cale (Eric Stoltz) in their voyage through the Amazon basin. Hugely derivative of films such as *Alien* (1979), *The Thing* (1982), and *Dead Calm* (1988), the film is a masterclass in reduction and dead-on genre pastiche, every sexual innuendo delivered by the lecherous Sarone backed up with an unsubtle visual image, every set-piece a well-executed rehash of an old favourite. Llosa does attempt to rewrite the generic rules, however, by changing the order in which the victims are usually picked off. White scientist Eric Stoltz is rendered incapable early on and the defence of the boat from the twin onslaught of Sarone and his CGI prey (a forty-foot Anaconda) is eventually left to the resourceful Lopez and her cameraman, played by rapper Ice Cube. All too often the action and horror genres claim marginalised ethnic and gender types as born victims – particularly African-Americans, Latinos and women – but Llosa has a black man and a Latino woman save the day, adding a refreshing twist to the generic formula. This was later emulated in the survivor roles played by black rapper LL Cool J in *Halloween H20* (1998) and *Deep Blue Sea* (1999).                                        **MF**

# Robert LONGO

*Johnny Mnemonic* (1995) Robert Longo was born in Brooklyn in 1953, and graduated from State University College in Buffalo, New York, with a degree in fine arts. In 1974, while still a student, he founded the Hallwalls exhibition/studio space, and during the 1980s he found international success as a major contemporary artist. Having formed Pressure Pictures with partner Victoria Hamburg in 1987, Longo directed a number of music videos for the likes of New Order, REM, Reuben Blades, and Megadeth, as well as several shorts, including *Arena Brains* (1988), and Hamburg's theatrical piece 'Dream Jumbo' in 1989. In 1992 he directed an episode of HBO's 'Tales from the Crypt' called 'This'll Kill Ya', and in 1995 he made his feature debut, *Johnny Mnemonic*, scripted by William Gibson from his 1981 short story of the same name.

Originally conceived as a black and white art film with a budget of $1.5 million, it stalled for a number of years as financial backing repeatedly collapsed and several leading men (Val Kilmer, Christopher Lambert) left. Keanu Reeves joined the project, and the subsequent box-office success of *Speed* (1994) inflated the budget beyond Gibson's skill as a screenwriter and Longo's ability as a director. The McGuffin-led chase narrative sees the high-tech, low-life, near-future world familiar from cyberpunk fiction reduced to the urban-apocalyptic backdrop familiar from countless rock videos; this not only indicates the extent to which cyberpunk was built from conventional genre tropes, but also the speed with which much of what distinguished Gibson's work was recycled and redeployed in popular culture. It is with some justice that the Krokers dubbed *Johnny Mnemonic* 'the day cyberpunk died'.

The movie never recovers from Reeves' dismal opening scene, and although his performance improves, it remains weak. Dinah Meyer is adequate in her underdeveloped sidekick role, and some canny casting – particularly Henry Rollins and Kitano Takeshi, and to a lesser degree Ice-T and Udo Kier – adds much-needed credibility. The strongest elements of the movie are the spectacular cyberspace sequences, in which Longo's visual sense comes into its own. While visually stunning, the city-like architecture and retro design of this virtual space also convey the speed with which technologies become outmoded. **MB**

# Kenneth LONERGAN

*You Can Count On Me* (2000) Born in 1963 in New York, Kenneth Lonergan is a steady and concentrated talent; flavour of the moment, he has penned screenplays for successful films such as *Analyze This* (1999) and *The Adventures of Rocky and Bullwinkle* (2000), three hit plays that have been exceptionally well reviewed – 'This Is Our Youth', 'The Waverly Gallery' and 'Lobby Hero' – and written and directed a debut feature, *You Can Count On Me* (2000), winning the Grand Jury Prize and the Waldo Salt Screenwriting Prize at Sundance.

Watching any of Lonergan's stage plays, it becomes obvious that his interest is in intimate, character-driven narratives – the effects of the past on our handling of the present, and the manner in which we communicate, or more often mis-communicate, with one another. Independently produced, *You Can Count On Me* offers no kooky, cutting-edge surprises. Evenly paced and conventionally shot, it is more traditional in spirit, generically slotting into that category of family drama that too often comprises mawkish tele-movies – thankfully, though, this has all the requisite angst and none of the tawdry melodrama. Rewardingly low-key, the relationships are delicately handled. Laura Linney is superb as a single mother whose capable life gradually becomes more disordered when her younger tearaway brother (Mark Ruffalo) pays one of his infrequent visits and she is assigned a new boss. Having gone from strength to strength since *The Truman Show* (1998), she is given the opportunity to range a plethora of emotions as she attempts to maintain her composure and resist losing the control she so desperately clings to.

More recently, Lonergan has been credited alongside other writers, for the screenplay of Martin Scorsese's forthcoming *Gangs of New York*. **HP**

# George LUCAS

*THX 1138* (1970)
*American Graffiti* (1973) George Lucas was born in Modesto, California, in 1944. An early ambition to be a racing driver was ended by a serious accident in his teens, after which Lucas switched focus

to the more sedate occupation of film directing. A graduate of the USC film school, and award-winner for student short *THX 1138-4EB/Electronic Labyrinth* (1967), Lucas won a Warner Brothers' scholarship to assist on Francis Coppola's ill-fated musical *Finian's Rainbow* (1968). Sharing a utopian vision of a creative film-making environment, Coppola and Lucas formed American Zoetrope, and the reworked feature *THX 1138* (1970) became the debut release of this alliance. A dystopian science-fiction tale, the film is expertly designed in its visual and emotional bleakness. Robert Duvall's eponymous protagonist seeks escape from an underground society where sex and emotions are outlawed. The film's take on the future of humanity is steeped in an Orwellian conception of the diminution of individualism that would creep back, in milder form, in *Star Wars* five years later. *THX 1138* is best seen as part of the pessimistic early 1970s sci-fi cycle that also included L. Q. Jones' *A Boy and His Dog* (1974) and Woody Allen's *Sleeper* (1973). In its refusal to give a human face to an implacably threatening social mechanism, the film anticipates such low-budget, conceptually rich genre entries as Vincenzo Natali's *Cube* (1997).

*Star Wars: Episode IV – A New Hope* (1977)
*Star Wars: Episode I – The Phantom Menace* (1999)
*Star Wars: Episode II – Attack of the Clones* (2002)

Lucas' second feature, *American Graffiti* (1973), could not be more different in feel from *THX 1138*; its social environment (small-town America, 1962) is a wholly benign one. Evoking a sense of popular cultural nostalgia for the first (but hardly the last) time, Lucas depicts a world so familiar and comforting that protagonist Kurt (Richard Dreyfuss) can hardly bring himself to leave it for college. 1973 audiences recognised, with a pang of regret, that just around the corner of Lucas' timeframe lurked Vietnam, an absence in the narrative that nevertheless makes its presence felt in the storyline of young men contemplating uncertain futures and dallying with violent diversions like drag strip racing. The film is cannily based around the totemic locations of the era (the burger bar, liquor store and high school hop) and, significantly, we barely glimpse any parents, removing the traditional teen movie trope of intergenerational conflict but implicitly suggesting that teens define their own social universe. The film's stunning musical selection, framed by the running radio commentary of the mysterious Wolfman Jack, provides another narrative perspective (the audacious 'sound montage' is by the brilliant Walter Murch). Producer Coppola had to fight Universal to get *Graffiti* made, but when the $750,000 movie scored $100 million, no further proof was needed of Lucas' ability to communicate with a mainstream audience.

The financing to make *Star Wars* (1977) was secured by *Graffiti*'s success, but Lucas still endured regular clashes with backers Fox as well as experienced and opinionated crew members. The impact of the film on Hollywood industrial policy is legendary: along with Spielberg's *Jaws* (1975), *Star Wars* inaugurated the second phase of the 'New Hollywood', producing movies designed to reach mass audiences through a combination of recycled popular myths, a tendency towards spectacle over complex narrative, and a host of attendant merchandising and promotional channels that kept revenue streams alive for years after release. Lucas shrewdly negotiated a huge share of profits and personal retention of monies from the unprecedented *Star Wars* merchandising bonanza, a move that guaranteed his role as a major (and largely independent) Hollywood player through his company Lucasfilm. The movie itself is hard to evaluate outside of its enormous success; certainly it is not the greatest achievement of that fertile period in Hollywood history, but it retains the capacity to enthral. Lucas displays utter conviction in his combination of B-grade sci-fi, western and fairytale dynamics, constructing the *Star Wars* universe as meticulously as the detailed narrative worlds of *THX* and *Graffiti*. This fully-realised quality undoubtedly helped the process by which the *Star Wars* myth was widely embraced with utter credence and devotion.

Lucas found the production of *Star Wars* extremely stressful, and vowed never to direct again, abdicating this position on the *Star Wars* sequels to Irvin Kershner and Richard Marquand. Moving himself into a creative producer's role, Lucas developed hits such as the *Indiana Jones* trilogy (in collaboration with Spielberg) and Ron Howard's *Willow* (1988). Known as a commercial over-achiever, Lucas nevertheless presided over one of Hollywood's most notorious flops, *Howard the Duck* (1986); but he also ensured that Lucasfilm maintained a cutting edge, by assisting distribution of the later films of Kurosawa and giving Coppola a home for the underrated *Tucker: The Man and his Dream* (1988). Lucas' ability to return Coppola's early favours (the Zoetrope dream having long since died) reflected the switch in their industrial positions, and underlined the concomitant adjustment in the philosophy of American cinema that made conditions so favourable for the Lucas/Spielberg aesthetic template. Lucas' contribution to the consolidation of the Hollywood system took material form through technological developments like the THX sound system (the importance of sound design is clearly evidenced in all of Lucas' films, especially the early collaborations with Walter Murch). Lucasfilm is even more famous for its effects wing, Industrial Light and Magic, still the industry leader (although pushed hard by facilities like James Cameron's Digital Domain).

The roster of Lucasfilm companies came together to contribute to George Lucas' return to directing, *Star Wars: Episode I – The Phantom Menace* (1999). Sticking to his commitment to produce three films preceding the existing trilogy (although apparently reneging on the originally mooted nine episode cycle), Lucas found the release attended by impossibly high expectations. Although many loyal fans felt disappointed, Lucas supporters pointed out that *Star Wars* had chimed with its original 1977 audience because they were children at the time; now in their late twenties, the fans who felt alienated by the juvenile angle of the new film were missing the point. Indeed, *Episode I* made short work of soaking up another generation of fans and earning $900 million worldwide (although the film's failure to approach the even more awesome commercial achievement of *Titanic* (1997) indicated a narrower appeal).

The narrative of *Episode I* is hardly geared towards children, opening at a snail's pace with the minutiae of galactic trade agreements. Lucas' own dialogue can be excruciating, a weakness masked by the many pithy one-liners in *Star Wars*. More worrying is a murky representational agenda; the scheming overlords of the trade federation speak in accents clearly identified as Japanese, and Jar Jar Binks and Watto are all too easily readable in terms of African-American and Jewish stereotypes. Perhaps sycophantic consensus around Lucas prevented obvious reservations about some of these offensive characterisations being aired. The film crystallises in the solid performance of Liam Neeson as Qui-Gon Jinn, mentor to a young Obi-Wan Kenobi (Ewan McGregor); the climactic battle between the two Jedi and innovative new villain Darth Maul (Ray Park), scored to John Williams' impressive 'Duel of the Fates', is a standout scene in the classic *Star Wars* mould. The almost completely computer-generated 'podrace' sequence, with obvious ancestry in Wyler's *Ben-Hur* (1959), energises a flagging middle section with its impressive speed and perspective effects (typically, cross-promotion encouraged viewers to experience the race for themselves with the LucasArts video game). *Episode I*, thanks to those two key scenes, just about delivered enough to make the promise of the darker *Episode II – Attack of the Clones* (2002) worth waiting for.

With *Star Wars*, Lucas finds himself in the odd position of serving a demanding, difficult-to-please fanbase that will invariably pay to see the film anyway, hardly a scenario that encourages creative risk. More radical is the production basis that the costly *Star Wars* prequels operate on, fully financed by Lucasfilm itself, and only utilising Twentieth Century Fox as a distributor. This arrangement makes Lucas one of the most authentically 'independent' film-makers active in the US, a nice irony that looks back to his cult movie origins. Even more interestingly, *Episode II* is the first blockbuster to be shot entirely on digital video (on high-definition cameras developed by Sony), making Lucas an unlikely bedfellow with digital pioneers such as the Dogme 95 directors. **MF**

# Baz LUHRMANN

*Strictly Ballroom* (1992)
*William Shakespeare's*
*Romeo + Juliet* (1996)
*Moulin Rouge* (2001)

In ten years of directing film, and with only three films to his credit, Baz Luhrmann has established himself as one of the hottest names in international cinema. The offbeat subjects of his films and his distinctive, frenetic style of direction have marked him out as a director of imagination and risk in an industry dominated by convention. Mixing fantasy, melodrama, choreography, music and action with a bravura range of cinematic styles, his full-blown approach to film-making divides audiences down the middle; but love him or loathe him, Baz Luhrmann is a director who is impossible to ignore.

Born in New South Wales in Australia in 1962, Luhrmann started out as an actor, scoring some small parts in television and theatre, and a major role in the Australian drama *Winter of Our Dreams* (1981). He left acting to study at the renowned National Institute of Dramatic Arts in Sydney, where he began to experiment with direction, notably assisting Peter Brook on his 1985 production of 'The Mahabharata'. A half-hour stage version of *Strictly Ballroom*, which later became his debut film, won high-profile accolades at the World Youth Theatre Festival in 1986, including Best Director. Following graduation, Luhrmann founded the Six Years Old Company, where as artistic director he continued to develop his highly visual style of direction, and formed an ensemble of production staff and actors, many of whom would collaborate on his cinematic work. Other notable successes included productions with the Australian Opera of Benjamin Britten's opera 'A Midsummer Night's Dream' in 1984 and a hugely successful version of Puccini's 'La Boheme' in 1990, which updated the setting to the 1950s and laid emphasis on the visual drama of the story rather than the opera itself.

Luhrmann's roots reach directly into his subsequent film career. Following a successful stage revival in the early 1990s, *Strictly Ballroom* (1992) also became his first film. The narrative follows the fortunes of Scott, a maverick young dancer whose unorthodox ideas outrage the conservative establishment. Threatened with disbarment and abandoned by his partner, Scott meets clumsy, short-sighted Fran, a novice who blossoms under his guidance and growing affection and helps him win the national championship against the odds. Hackneyed the plot may be, but the heart of the film is in the telling. Luhrmann's camerawork, choreography and editing give the film a distinctive theatrical style, balancing camp comedy, over-the-top characters and kitsch design with the more down-to-earth drama between the two leads. While never subtle, the film is made with a confidence and imagination that is hard to resist, and became a surprise hit both domestically and abroad. It is a brash, ballsy, and very Australian style of cinema; other examples like *The Adventures of Priscilla, Queen of The Desert* (1994) and *Muriel's Wedding* (1994) also subsequently found success.

Luhrmann's approach to film-making is essentially theatrical, using stylised editing, camerawork, sound and design to create a cinema of spectacle which aims to highlight rather than conceal the conventions of film storytelling. *William Shakespeare's Romeo + Juliet* (1996) applies the same approach in updating Shakespeare's star-crossed tale for a modern audience weaned on MTV and pop culture. Luhrmann packs his version with ideas and theatrical conventions: Verona is made over as Verona Beach, a multi-ethnic melting pot of sprawling industry and cultural tension; the play's prologue is delivered as a television news-flash; the rival families become corporate conglomerates whose sons face off as members of Hispanic and white trash gangs; and the swords and daggers hanging from their belts are revealed as makes of guns. Drawing inspiration from music videos, spaghetti westerns, and high-concept action movies, set to an alt-rock soundtrack, and brave enough (considering its market) to stick to the original text, Luhrmann's film is a bold retelling of a classic tale. Despite being mauled by purists and critics alike, the film was hugely successful, and one of the most interesting aspects of Luhrmann's style seems to be his ability to appeal to a broad range of audiences and ages, from musical-lovers through to the MTV generation.

Though accusations of style over substance have inevitably dogged Luhrmann throughout his career, his most recent film showed little concession to his critics. Undoubtedly his most ambitious (and showiest) film to date, *Moulin Rouge* (2001) is a spectacular modern musical set in a fictionalised version of the infamous Parisian nightclub. The film charts the doomed relationship of a young English writer (Ewan MacGregor) and the consumptive chanteuse Satine (Nicole Kidman) during the creation of the club's sensational new show. Exploring the deliberately overblown idea of (tragic) love as the grandest theatrical theme, it is a story about making stories, which melds fiction, dream and fantasy and plunders the annals of history, film, culture and art for its ideas. Luhrmann's characters are a circus of bizarre archetypes: the doomed femme fatale, the smitten writer, and the Moulin Rouge's grotesque master of ceremonies (Jim Broadbent in a BAFTA award-winning performance) head an assortment of evil dukes, kindly strongmen and weird performers, while the Paris they inhabit is a fairytale city watched over by a singing moon. The film is full of the tricks and arch theatricality which have become Luhrmann's trademark – swooping camerawork, showy editing, opulent production design, fabulous dance sequences, and even musical numbers culled from contemporary song. An extravagant assault on all the senses (taste and subtlety included), *Moulin Rouge* delighted his fans, and confirmed Luhrmann as a unique voice in international cinema, but did little to convince his detractors that there is really something substantial beneath all the glitz and glitter. **OB**

# Sidney LUMET

Born in Philadelphia in 1924, Sidney Lumet is one of America's greatest film-makers and yet his work is rarely discussed outside the confines of academic circles. The arguments for this are many, but perhaps the main reasons are Lumet's eclectic choice of subject matter and his changing directorial style. Another potential factor in Lumet's industry standing is his often disapproving attitude towards the majority of the Hollywood product, a quality which is bound not to endear him to the producers of this material. As Lumet himself notes: 'The essence of any dramatic piece is people, and it is symptomatic that Hollywood finds a way of photographing people directly opposite to the way people are built. CinemaScope makes no sense until people are fatter than they are taller.'

This concern with the character-driven narrative and the anxiety for the individual within any given system is the major theme that Lumet returns to time and time again. Whilst eclectic in many ways, Lumet rarely moves outside of America as a setting for his movies, and it is usually an America in trouble. Television is a concern of his, as *Network* (1976) clearly shows, and Lumet has commented on it in relation to a general concern for the morality of American society and beyond, to an anxiety for people as a whole. For him, television embodies the unseen power that has an ability to affect people in ways that they may not be aware of.

Lumet's career began to reach a wider audience with *12 Angry Men* (1957). At this time he first hit the public and industry awareness, and it is with this film that the individual versus the group is debated in full for the first time. This is a theme developed in a different context with *A Stranger Among Us* (1992), amongst many other examples of his work. Henry Fonda is ideally cast as the unassuming, nameless individual whose concern is for the rights of a defendant. Alongside the role of the individual, Lumet debates the legal system, a theme to be echoed in a number of his works, including *The Hill* (1965), *Serpico* (1973), *Dog Day Afternoon* (1975), and *The Verdict* (1982). Lumet presents his audience with a faceless, corrupt system. However, while *12 Angry Men* ends on a positive note, others are far less optimistic, to the point of brutality.

Whilst the narratives of the majority of his films are involved with conflict, it is the resultant tension that Lumet uses to heighten dramatic effect, and he underpins this with a roaming camera that observes the events from without. This work is often an examination of a hidden and corrupt world, and the resultant debates about good and evil are usually the predominant elements of Lumet's films. *12 Angry Men* epitomises his fascination with debate, whereas *Dog Day Afternoon*, dramatises a real-life incident into a forthright dramatic comment on society at large. *The Hill*, like *Dog Day Afternoon*, debates the notion of justice and, whilst the main protagonists in both films are criminals, they have only been labelled as such by an uncaring society. The debate between right and wrong suddenly becomes much more complicated. It is the essence of the debate that is the enduring memory of these films rather than the clear division in films such as *Serpico* or *Network*. However, in respect of *The Hill*, it is important to note that Lumet is able to stand outside the boundaries of his own immediate cultural experience and to discuss life in a British internment camp. This implies that Lumet's concerns are towards the thematic nature of his storytelling rather than the setting.

In *Dog Day Afternoon* Lumet presents his audience with a range of issues: police versus criminals, individual versus the mass, gay versus straight, and justice versus the law. The majority of the film takes place inside the confines of a bank, a typical physical location metaphorical for a broader issues that Lumet uses throughout his cinema. From *12 Angry Men* to *Dog Day Afternoon*, buildings and rooms throw together people who are dislocated from their normal environment. From *Long Day's Journey Into Night* (1962) to *Night Falls on Manhattan* (1996), Lumet presents his audience with an unforgiving and claustrophobic city. From *The Hill* to *A Stranger Among Us*, a community seeks to exclude and punish those who do not belong. The bleak nature of Lumet's work lies in the inevitable destruction implied by the majority of the settings. The implication is that Lumet makes quality films debating big issues and whilst this may be true in the case of a great deal of his work there are examples which stand outside of this. In many ways his reputation lies in the films he made up to and including *Network*.

In recent years Lumet has tended to settle for at best the mediocre and at worst the truly dreadful. In the latter category comes *The Wiz* (1978) an update of *The Wizard of Oz* (1939) Although *The Wiz* made its costs this was largely due to the all-star cast, including Michael Jackson, Diana Ross and Lena Horne, and the nature of the film as a remake. The film is badly composed, both in terms of a visual dynamic and a narrative progression. This is a flaw that may have been a technique in films such as *Serpico* but now merely look shoddy.

*Night Falls on Manhattan* is one of the prime examples of how Lumet's concerns for the individual versus corruption has become a tired theme. Although Andy Garcia manages to give a convincing performance, Lumet appears to have used the rest of the cast to develop setting. They tend to be stereotyped and one-dimensional. This is a major turn from the early Lumet who seemed to thrive on debate and an absence of clear answers. *Gloria* (1999) did not change the perception of the audience or the critics. It was an odd choice of project – to take a great John Cassavetes film and attempt to re-interpret it for a late-1990s audience, particularly when one of Lumet's talents seemed to be taking a stage play or 'true' story and giving it a very particular cinematic portrayal. Criticism of his latest work aside, Lumet has provided some of the greatest films to have emerged in post-war America. He manages to stay outside of the Hollywood system to produce deeply personal films which, like them or hate them, attempt to deal with interesting and unique themes.

Having made *The Beautiful Mrs. Seidenmann* (yet to be released), a love story set in 1943 about a blonde, blue-eyed Polish woman who attempts to avoid being recognised as a Jew, Lumet has turned to television wityh the drama '100 Centre Street', whcih again concerns the gap between justice and the American system. In eschewing the mannered camerawork and speech patterns of contemporary shows, and choosing high-definition video technology – a more naturalistic medium than that of film – he harks back to an earlier era of realism with, adding the odd stylistically old-fashioned touch.

He has a World War Two picture planned, an adaptation of James Jones' 'Whistle', which is scripted by David Mamet. **REH & FG**

# Rod LURIE

Born in Israel in 1962, Rod Lurie is the former movie critic for KABC radio in Los Angeles and the one-time president of the Broadcast Film Critics Association; he has shown signs of joining a very select band of American scribes, Paul Schrader chief amongst them, in bridging the chasm between writing about films and successfully making them.

The son of internationally syndicated cartoonist Ranan Lurie, he took first tentative steps toward directing with the 1998 short *4 Second Delay*. A political thriller in which a radio station invites one of the original reporters from the Watergate scandal to a call in show with chilling consequences, the theme of political skullduggery was to exert a lasting influence on the writer-director.

A year later, he released *Deterrence*, which is set almost entirely within the confines of a snowbound Colorado diner where the US President (Kevin Pollak), his Chief of Staff (Timothy Hutton) and the National Security Advisor (Sheryl Lee Ralph) are holed up after a freak storm. Tensions simmer between the political bigwigs and the initially mistrustful locals. The film then takes a dramatic change of direction when a television report discloses that Iraq has re-invaded Kuwait. From his snowy bunker the President is forced to deliver a chilling ultimatum: retreat or suffer the full wrath of the US army. A potential global holocaust looms and suddenly the President, without recourse to his enclave of advisors, is forced to turn to the common man for direction. Lurie's thirst for political intrigue promises handsome dividends but ultimately proffers distinctly mixed returns, revealing an Achilles heel for the further shores of plausibility and the wilfully callow belief in the ultimate democracy of the American political system to defeat all evil.

*The Contender* (2000) seemed to offer a significant improvement. A mesmerising Jeff Bridges plays the US president who, aware of the importance of the woman's vote, decides to appoint a female second in command, much to the chagrin of cunning Republican congressman Runyon (an unrecognisable Gary Oldman). Democrat Senator Hanson (Joan Allen), his first choice, is subsequently subjected to a malicious, sexual smear campaign headed by the unscrupulous Runyon whose preferred vice president is the would-be gung-ho hero Governor Hathaway (William Petersen).

The film features brilliant performances from a first-rate cast. Bridges is particularly good; in a neat send-up of presidential power he constantly tries to catch his chief unawares with increasingly outrageous demands for lunch. With sharp writing, which generally engenders the *frisson* of the politically aware American pictures of the 1970s, for the most part it provides intriguing and captivating viewing. Then suddenly, in the final reel, it spectacularly unravels and descends into bombastic, heavy-handed and syrupy sermonising about the wonders of American democracy. Oldman, whose Machiavellian maneuverings are reduced to clear-cut villainy, was so incensed that he threatened to take his name off the production and withdrew his promotional support; he was not the only one to feel somewhat betrayed by Lurie's shallow capitulation.

Unfortunately, *The Last Castle* (2001) was another step in the wrong direction. Court-martialled for disobeying orders, legendary US Army general Eugene R. Irwin (Robert Redford) is sent to 'the castle', a military prison presided over by the ruthless warden, Colonel Winter (James Gandolfini). Gradually, the men in the prison fall under the captivating spell of Irwin and Winter begins to feel his superiority slipping away. As the warden's sadistic thirst for metering out punishment spirals out of control, the men are persuaded by Irwin to undertake a military-style mission to seize control of the prison.

A familiar premise, Lurie's highly reactionary film brings little to the genre. The performances are somnambulant – Redford attempts to coast by on good looks and charm alone and the talents of the excellent Mark Ruffalo are wasted – and both the writing and direction are flabby and conservative. The potentially interesting notion of Irwin as a similarly power-crazed, fallen hero, desperately in search of approbation, is ignored in favour of empty and uncomfortable jingoistic sloganeering about the forces of oppression.

Lurie is currently in production with *Clink Inc*, which is billed as a comedy about a former Wall Street banker who uses the knowledge of the corporate world to make prison life run more smoothly. A writer-director of undoubted talent, one hopes that Lurie will continue to make work of the quality displayed in the first hour of *The Contender*. **JWo**

# David LYNCH

*Eraserhead* (1977)
*The Elephant Man* (1980)
*Dune* (1984)
*Blue Velvet* (1986)
*Wild At Heart* (1990)
*Twin Peaks: Fire Walk With Me* (1992)
*Lost Highway* (1997)
*The Straight Story* (1999)
*Mulholland Drive* (2001)

Drawing from sources as diverse as vintage Americana and surrealism, David Lynch has established himself as American cinema's foremost exponent of the strange. Often wilfully obscure in his intentions (he is always reluctant to expand upon what his films actually 'mean'), critics have nevertheless discovered all manner of significance in his fractured narratives and bizarre visuals. Some have read a disturbing strain of misogyny through Lynch's work. Others have noted an interest in the repressed and hidden secrets of small-town life and a concentration upon an assortment of oddballs and misfits. Of equal note has been his extraordinary sound design, which infuses the films with yet another level of disorientation.

Born in Montana in 1946, Lynch studied painting and film as a student. His early short works *The Alphabet* (1968) and *The Grandmother* (1970) led to his first feature, *Eraserhead* (1977). Shot over five years at the American Film Institute, the film established the director's ability to convey the quality of nightmare and became a regular fixture on the cult movie circuit. The vivid monochrome photography and sparse narrative line allow the bleak industrial ambience to merge freely with vaguely expressed themes and characters. Parenthood, infancy (expressed memorably by a hideous mutant baby), love, sex, death, and fantasy all intermingle with an overwhelming sense of psychological disturbance and claustrophobia. In retrospect, the film serves as a well from which Lynch's later, relatively more conventionally structured, films would draw their themes. Fascinated with the textures and ambience of decay, the film nevertheless allows its central figure, Henry, (played by Lynch regular, Jack Nance) to ultimately escape into a blinding light which seems to represent a life beyond the dread of the physical so forcefully expressed elsewhere.

Impressed with *Eraserhead*, Mel Brooks hired Lynch to direct the story of Victorian England's most famous and fascinating 'freak', John Merrick. *The Elephant Man* (1980) demonstrated that Lynch could sustain a coherent narrative while sacrificing none of the audio-visual qualities which distinguished his earlier work. Indeed, there are many parallels to be drawn between the Victorian industrial age backdrop and that of his previous film, and Lynch frequently runs his camera along the harsh, brutal architecture with relish. Inverting the director's regular theme of a surface beauty, which belies an undercurrent of corruption, the film presents its grotesquely disfigured title figure (John Hurt) as a dignified, loving, human being. This is contrasted with the initial careerism of Frederick Treves (Anthony Hopkins), who comes to love and befriend Merrick, and the brutal exploitation of his side-show 'owner' (Freddie Jones). Highlighting voyeuristic impulses across the Victorian class divide, this is probably the closest Lynch has come to a conscious 'statement' about human nature. Distinguished further by Freddie Francis' photography (again in black and white), the film also demonstrates Lynch's ability to draw rounded performances from his actors. He received an Academy Award nomination for his efforts.

Despite its indisputable visual beauty, *Dune* (1984) is ultimately encumbered by its sprawling, messy narrative, which borders on the incomprehensible. The film again foregrounds Lynch's fascination with design and architecture but demands an epic sweep (present in Frank Herbert's source novel) which is suppressed in favour of often abstract details and events. The frequent references to sensory expansion are familiar from Lynch's other work but their placement here seem like authorial interventions in a form with which he feels uncomfortable. The film marked Lynch's first collaboration with regular screen alter-ego, Kyle MacLachlan.

*Blue Velvet* (1986) is the transitional film of Lynch's career and the one which established his reputation as a twisted commentator on small-town America. Its strangely timeless atmosphere, jarring tonal shifts and appropriation of all manner of cultural signifiers have embroiled the film in debates on postmodernism. Yet, at its most basic level, the film is a murder mystery which, like Hitchcock's best films, explores the thematic possibilities inherent in, but so often neglected by, the form. Upon the discovery of a rotting, severed ear, the seemingly innocent Jeffrey (Kyle MacLachlan) is embroiled in a bizarre narrative involving the seedy underbelly of his picturesque town. This encompasses an array of perverse Freudian thematic motifs. Voyeurism, sadism and masochism play in tandem with a macabre twist on the Oedipal myth in which the film's demented villain, Frank (Dennis Hopper), reverts to infantile cries ('baby wants to fuck!') during his chemically fuelled 'rape' of his captive lover (Isabella Rossellini). This is complemented by Jeffrey's own fascination with the abused woman, and the two men come to reflect each others predilections and peculiarities. It is difficult to discern the film's view of its protagonist's journey, as it frequently veers between fascination for the sensual thrills of violent eroticism and outright disgust. As notions of individual and communal innocence are eroded, the film plays out its thriller narrative in order to restore a now fragile equilibrium, symbolised famously by a patently artificial bird feeding on an insect. In a decade notable for its recuperative Hollywood entertainments, *Blue Velvet* is distinctive in its revelation of the dark heart of the American dream.

*Wild At Heart* (1990) is Lynch's first take on the road movie, featuring a pair of lovers on the run (Nicolas Cage and Laura Dern) and drawing freely from a range of sources encompassing *The Wizard of Oz* (1939) and Elvis Presley. Set in the deep south and making extensive use of its steamy ambience, the film again alternates between black comedy and nightmarish vignette. Particularly disturbing however is the rape-seduction of Lula (Laura Dern) and an extraordinary nocturnal encounter in which a young woman's final moments are rendered through a dreamy soliloquy about her bloodied hair. Even more extreme in its shifting tones than its predecessor, the film demonstrates the common ground between fairytale and nightmare, with its childlike lovers cast adrift in a sometimes oppressive array of monstrous mothers, murderous deviants and surreal landscapes.

Perhaps encumbered by its relationship to the television series, *Twin Peaks: Fire Walk With Me* (1992) was met with both critical and audience apathy. To be fair, a full appreciation of its extensive reference points and allusive imagery demands a knowledge of the series' later developments, and it largely eschews the quirky humour of its television counterpart. Tackling themes of child abuse and corruption, the film charts the last days of Laura Palmer (Sheryl Lee) and is one of the most disturbing interpretations of family horror ever presented. Fusing Laura's fantasy life with her descent into a world of degradation, Lynch presents her imminent demise as a collapse of both her physical and psychological self. While on one level her abusive father is displaced by the monstrous fantasy figure bob through Laura's own projection, on another the film suggests there is a real demonic force capable of possessing and influencing human action. Less concerned with the underbelly of community (an approach enabled by the series format of the television show) than its effect upon one individual, the dénouement recalls the climax of *Eraserhead* as Laura is guided from her debased life by an angelic figure in a fantasy room.

After a five-year hiatus, Lynch returned to features with *Lost Highway* (1997). Probably his most audacious effort since *Eraserhead*, Lynch called it a 'twenty-first-century noir horror film', and the mixing of generic motifs is enhanced by the central premise of a personality which may or may not change, both physically and psychologically. The opening segment, in which Fred (Bill Pullman) becomes racked by suspicion and doubt over his wife's fidelity, is among the most impressively sustained cinema in recent memory. Introducing thematic explorations of the döppelganger, the film is replete with visual and aural rhymes, and the circular narrative is framed by the image of a dark road which opens and closes the film. In addition to Fred's transformation into a young car mechanic (Balthazar Getty), the double motif extends to two femmes fatale (both played by Patricia Arquette) and a pair of mysterious father figures (Robert Loggia and Robert Blake). As personalities converge and perceptual codes collapse, the film eschews any pretence to coherence in favour of a sustained and abstracted exploration of identity. This extends to the film's formal construction itself. Particularly striking is the densely layered sound track, which mixes ambient noise, satanic/death metal and synthesised drones. Largely ignored in the US (the advertising campaign mischievously utilised Gene Siskel and Roger Ebert's 'two thumbs down' judgement as an endorsement), the film demonstrated that after the financial failure of *Fire Walk With Me*, Lynch had lost none of his appetite for sensory assault and confrontation.

It says much for Lynch's oeuvre that the tale of an old man's inter-state road trip on a lawnmower can be considered his most conventional work yet. Indeed, the title pun of *The Straight Story* (1999) suggests a knowing self-consciousness regarding the film's place in Lynch's career. However, where many would have wrung the story for all of its sentimental value, Alvin Straight's (Richard Farnsworth) journey to visit his sick, estranged brother unfolds in a pleasingly understated fashion. Yet for all of its surface Midwestern 'normality', the film's enduring oddness is in its presentation of a world in which everyone is so consistently pleasant and accommodating. There are brief suggestions of an underlying tension – Alvin's war recollections, a woman who regularly knocks down deer in her car – but this is Lynch's warmest work since *The Elephant Man*. Freddie Francis' photography enhances the surrounding landscape and the rural, Iowan space provides Lynch with a welcome respite from the oppressive, interior worlds of his most disturbing works.

For all of its qualities, *Mulholland Drive* (2001) is tinged with the possibilities of what might have been. Made originally as a pilot episode for an intended series for the ABC network, Lynch developed the film into a feature after executives refused to screen it. As it stands, the film is still a considerable achievement, especially as, to all intents and purposes, it is an audacious salvage job. The film provides a feminine spin on the theme of the döppelganger, the almost obsessive interest in doubling and parallel existence established in a pre-credit sequence in which identical jitterbugging young couples move against the backdrop of dancing shadows. While the film's narrative often betrays its origins as a pilot (various characters are introduced only to disappear just as quickly) it is centrally concerned with the relationship developed between Betty (Naomi Watts), an aspiring actress, and Rita (Laura Elena Harring), a mysterious femme fatale. Even here, Rita's sultry exterior masks her inner vulnerability, while Betty's seeming wide-eyed innocence is undercut by the intense sensuality displayed at a film audition. The pair's quest to solve the mystery of Rita's memory loss merely serves as a platform upon which Lynch explores his familiar themes against the sinister underbelly of Hollywood. The film's final sequences become particularly convoluted as each character is transformed into an alternate realm of existence. The film also reveals a striking, reflexive concern with both the business and art of making movies, and by extension, the manufacture of illusion. This is exemplified in the final third when Betty and Rita attend a mysterious nightclub in which both sound and image are exposed as elaborate deceptions. The film's concern with both the blurring of perceptual distinction and the culture of Hollywood is summed up by Betty's description of it as 'this dream place'. Accordingly, the role of Adam (Justin Theroux), a young film director at odds with his paymasters, might be read as a surrogate for Lynch, especially ironic given the fate of the film in its original form. One can only imagine how Lynch's original intentions for the show would have evolved. Nevertheless, he has envisioned a distinct fusion of his recurring obsessions with the business in which he works, a haunting interpretation of faded dreams in the modern Hollywood Babylon.

Lynch has also worked extensively both as a director and producer in television, most notably with the series 'Twin Peaks' and 'Industrial Symphony No. 1' in collaboration with his regular composer, Angelo Badalamenti. Less successful were the series 'On The Air' and 'Hotel Room'.                                                                                      **NJ**

# Jennifer Chambers LYNCH

Although it may be preferable to discuss Jennifer Chambers Lynch without referring to her famous father, David Lynch, having made a sole feature such as *Boxing Helena* (1993), it is difficult to consider her as anything other than the daughter of such a mighty, surrealist visionary of twisted Americana.

Born in Philadelphia in 1968, her career began in her father's 1977 film *Eraserhead* as the little girl. She worked as a production assistant on his *Blue Velvet* (1986) and, more recently, contributed to a television documentary about her father and his work. In between, however, came *Boxing Helena,* a film that she also wrote. Lynch senior's influence is evident in the casting of Sherilyn Fenn in the title role and, more significantly, in the film's premise: a doctor (Julian Sands, developing the oddly seedy persona he had established in his post-Merchant-Ivory films) obsesses about his former girlfriend, cuts off her limbs and keeps her in a box.

Generally poorly received, and carrying the controversy of an infamous lawsuit, which saw Kim Basinger sued for breaking an oral contract to star in the film, Lynch's film has admirable intentions. Its central metaphor suggests the lengths men go to in order to contain women, and Helena's response to her captor – refusing to become dependent on him – offers a moral (of sorts) concerning the way women want to be treated by men. Visually, though, the film borrows too much from the style of David Lynch, which, unfortunately, means that her father's name crops up in association with the movie more than it might otherwise have done.                                              **JD**

# Paul LYNCH

Born in Liverpool, UK, in 1946, Paul Lynch has worked in North America since the early 1970s, dividing his time between directing features and television. His debut, *The Hard Part Begins* (1973), was a forgettable Canadian drama. Having made the legal TV drama, 'Petrocelli', he directed *Blood and Guts* (1978), an awful wrestling movie with biker movie stalwart William Smith. It is hard to believe it took three screenwriters to come up with this material, which doesn't even manage to offer the kind of violent thrills the title suggests. Only the most hardened cult movie freak could be interested in this, drawn by the presence of Smith and writer Joseph McBride (who wrote the fondly remembered *Rock 'n' Roll High School* (1979)).

Lynch followed with probably his best film, the Canadian disco slasher movie, *Prom Night* (1980). Made at the height of the 'stalk and slash' boom that followed the enormous success of *Halloween* (1978), it manages to include all of the required generic conventions and add a dash of *Saturday Night Fever* (1977) for good measure. 'Scream Queen' Jamie Lee Curtis (pre-mainstream stardom) is one of many prom-goers who are stalked by a masked axe killer seeking revenge for the accidental death of a young girl a decade earlier. Although the film is pretty conventional, it has a camp charm: the disco scenes are more frightening than the murders, Leslie Nielsen gives what appears to be a serious performance (disappearing around the half-way mark) and the direction, though derivative, is passable, with Lynch exploiting the dimly-lit school corridors effectively. The identity of the killer is rather obvious, however, and it ultimately pales next to contemporaries such as *My Bloody Valentine* (1981); gore aficionados will be disappointed but the severed head that flies onto the dance floor at the film's climax is worth a look. Trivia buffs should note that the character of Wendy is played by Anne-Marie Martin, the future wife of Michael Crichton and co-writer of *Twister* (1996). *Prom Night* is also clearly the biggest influence on the nouveau slasher film *I Know What You Did Last Summer* (1997).

Lynch subsequently made the terribly titled *Humongous* (1982), in which a hideous, deformed creature dwells on an island, the product of a (sleazily shot) rape years earlier. It picks off a group of annoying teens one by one until (generically) the lone female sets light to it. Not only is the film badly staged and poorly written but it is often played out in almost total darkness – not the noir-ish photography of a film such as Don Siegel's *Escape From Alcatraz* (1979) but actual darkness. Lynch's next film, the erotic thriller *Cross Country* (1983) starring Michael Ironside, was a slight improvement. He also made a great deal of television in the 1980s, directing episodes of shows such as 'Moonlighting', 'Murder, She Wrote', 'Ray Bradbury Theater' and 'Twilight Zone'.

His next theatrical feature was the violent thriller *Bullies* (1986), a Canadian reworking of Sam Peckinpah's bleak and brilliant *Straw Dogs* (1971), about a tyrannical family terrorising a community in British Columbia until they meet violent retribution. The poor thriller anthology *Mania* (1986) followed (with Lynch co-directing). 1986 also saw two other films: the gymnastics movie *Flying* and a poor knock-off of Coppola's *The Conversation* (1974) called *Blindside* with Harvey Keitel (in a mid-80s career slump).

For nearly a decade, Lynch worked exclusively in TV, shooting episodes of 'Hooperman', 'Due South', and 'Star Trek: Deep Space Nine'. In 1994, he returned to features with *No Contest*, a *Die Hard* (1988) rip-off with Shannon Tweed in the Bruce Willis role and Andrew 'Dice' Clay and ex-wrestler Roddy Piper supporting. Even by the standards of the earlier *Blood and Guts*, this is a truly terrible film. Amazingly, the film spawned a sequel in 1997, with Tweed and Lance Henriksen.

Lynch's most recent film, *Frozen With Fear* (2000), failed to secure a theatrical release in the UK.                                                                                    IC

# Adrian LYNE

Born in 1941 and emerging from the group of English directors renowned for their television commercials in the 1970s, Adrian Lyne's most successful films have attempted to tap into the American sexual zeitgeist, often inciting controversy through their crudely provocative narratives.

After the modest teen drama *Foxes* (1980), Lyne achieved a huge popular success with *Flashdance* (1983), a film notable chiefly for its adoption of then relatively new pop video stylistics to convey its female underdog narrative. The film carries the distinct imprint of its production team of Don Simpson and Jerry Bruckheimer, with Lyne's advertising background much in evidence in its slick but empty style.

*9½ Weeks* (1985) continued the concentration on surface effects, this time in the service of a tale of obsessive and supposedly sado-masochistic passion. While the leads (Mickey Rourke and Kim Basinger) strike a series of artful poses, their relationship is stymied by the film's refusal to define the nominally dangerous aspect of their affair beyond tease and allusion. The film's stylistic emptiness reduces its characters to the same level of the decorative objects and lighting effects with which Lyne furnishes the film. Perhaps this is precisely the point, but the film seems to want to say something more profound about the relationship between the sex and death drives (as in *Last Tango In Paris* (1972)), a thematic element reportedly severely damaged during pre-release cutting. Conversely, while the film fails as an adequate marker of mid-1980s sexual attitudes, its series of self-conscious compositions at least serve as a useful reference point for cherished items of the so called 'designer decade'.

*Fatal Attraction* (1987) is a far more accomplished take on the theme of sexual obsession, both through the performances of its leads (Michael Douglas and Glenn Close) and Lyne's more thorough integration of the film's themes with his stylistic choices. However, this is a deeply conservative film which posits the single, hysterical female as a threat to middle-class, patriarchal values. Furthermore, the film has been read widely as a reactionary response to the dangers of promiscuity and infidelity in the AIDS era. Lyne contrasts the warm hues of Douglas' family home with the stark interiors of Close's apartment, and it is left to the latter's skill as an actress to elicit any sympathy for her largely demonised character. The *Grand Guignol* climax (inserted after test audiences objected to Douglas' implication in Close's death) completes the film's take on the independent woman as monster and such is its manipulative hold that we are implored to cheer her punching, strangulation, drowning and shooting, despite her disturbed, pregnant state. Perhaps there is a half-hearted irony in the final shot of a family portrait, seemingly assuring the reconstruction of the family unit in the wake of devastating attack. Yet the dominant impression is that of an apologia for weak, complacent, white male professionals.

*Jacob's Ladder* (1990) has proven to be an anomaly so far in Lyne's career. Part paranoid thriller, part hallucinatory nightmare, the film presents another version of New York as Hell on Earth. This is achieved via a scrambled narrative and fractured chronology which attempts to replicate the disturbed psyche of its Vietnam veteran protagonist (played by Tim Robbins), convinced he is being pursued by sinister, masked figures. The film loses its way in the latter stages as the drug paranoia theme is supplanted by a tale of spiritual redemption while never fully uniting these separate strands. The 'twist' dénouement consequently proves something of a damp squib. At least the film provided Lyne with an opportunity to work beyond the confines of slick sex melodramas, and Robbins' demonic apparitions are often chillingly realised.

Unfortunately, the commercial failure of *Jacob's Ladder* prompted Lyne to return to what he does 'best'. *Indecent Proposal* (1993) is an incredibly stupid film, presenting its central married couple (Woody Harrelson and Demi Moore) as vulnerable in the face of a vaguely Faustian sexual pact with an amoral, billionaire playboy (Robert Redford). After introducing the themes of female objectification, prostitution and sexual manipulation (familiar territory for Lyne), the film is content to resolve its not inconsiderable moral conundrums through simple recourse to standard romantic reconciliation. There is one effective moment of disorientation as Harrelson, desperate and confused amidst a bank of television screens, imagines multiple racehorses transforming into the image of an orgasmic Moore. Ultimately, however, the film's high-concept gloss cannot compensate for its refusal to tackle its themes on anything other than the most superficial level.

This did not bode well for Lyne's adaptation for one of the most scandalous novels of the twentieth century. However, his version of Nabokov's 'Lolita' is a commendable effort, despite the inherent difficulties of transforming the book's dazzling prose and moral ambivalence into a workable narrative of forbidden passion. Filmed previously as a cynical black comedy by Stanley Kubrick, Lyne's *Lolita* (1997) adopts a soft-focus veneer which often unfortunately recalls the 1970s sex films of David Hamilton. But the film is anchored by Jeremy Irons' brave central performance as Humbert and is adventurous in its engagement with his seemingly monstrous acts. Lyne walks a delicate line between a gentle eroticism and blatant softcore romance which sometimes oddly compliments attempts to humanise Humbert, an understanding which achieves some level of discomfort. Therefore, given Lyne's catalogue of abused women, his Lo (Dominique Swain) ironically emerges as his most active, rounded female role. The surreal, bloody climax, in which Humbert confronts his nemesis (Frank Langella), sits uncomfortably in the film as it does not adequately develop their antipathy before this moment. Despite this, the film is the best-realised of Lyne's career to date.

His most recent, *Unfaithful* (2002), is a remake of Claude Chabrol's *La femme infidel* (1969). Starring Richard Gere and Diane Lane, the film examines a couple's relationship after the wife has had an affair. **NJ**

# Jonathan LYNN

Jonathan Lynn is probably best known, in the UK certainly, as the award-winning co-writer of the successful television political satires 'Yes, Minister' and 'Yes, Prime Minister' for the BBC in the 1980s. Born in Bath in 1943, he began his career in the late 1960s, acting in television sit-coms like 'Doctor in the House' (1970) and 'Doctor in Charge' (1972), which he also contributed scripts to. He continued acting and writing throughout the 1970s, completing a film script for James Coburn, *The Internecine Project* (1974). A bad experience curtailed his connection with Hollywood for some years; instead he continued his television career, performing in the Liverpool-set comedy 'The Liver Birds' (1974) and writing for British comedian Harry Worth.

He made two short industrial films in 1983 and 1984. *Mick's People* was about a couple following Barclays Bank scheme to encourage couples to marry and mortgage with the institution, and *The Case of the Short-Sighted Boss* wherein Sherlock Holmes investigates an international company's loss of profits. In 1985 he went to Hollywood to write with director John Landis and made *Clue* (1985), based on the popular board game 'Cluedo'. Starring Tim Curry and Lesley-Anne Warren, the film is intermittently amusing but marred by infantile humour and overripe performances from its usually dependable stars. In America the film was released with three different endings; on the video version the three endings play one after the other. Although not a great success, Lynn got another job from the film – the chance to make *Nuns on the Run* (1990) for Warner Bros. When Lynn and the studio failed to agree about the film (originally set in Boston), producers Jon Peters and Peter Guber obtained the film for Lynn who returned to England to film the newly re-written script with Eric Idle and Robbie Coltrane. Peurile and predictably plotted (borne perhaps out of Lynn's sit-com experiences), *Nuns on the Run* relies on the typical visual gags of any film which places two men, disguised as nuns, in the changing room of a convent gymnasium. A modest success, it led Lynn back to America where his relationship with Peters and Guber had at least left him with some development deals.

After a brief foray into American television with 'Ferris Bueller', a version of the popular film, Lynn made *My Cousin Vinny* (1992), a film about a hopelessly inept and foul-mouthed lawyer defending his cousin on an inaccurate murder charge. Although the film has a verbally dextrous script (by Dale Launer and polished by Lynn) the direction lacks bite and pace, with some scenes outstaying their welcome for want of judicious cutting. He followed this with *The Distinguished Gentleman* (1992), an Eddie Murphy comeback vehicle about a con-man who takes on a dead Congressman's identity and ends up exposing a political scandal. An unsubtle critique of political hypocrisy and corruption, occasionally sharply scripted and directed, the film aims to make the corrupt politicians who abuse their power, rather than the citizens who vote for them, the centre of the comedy. However, it resorts to slush and sentiment, including the staple 'cute child with incurable disease', and once again shows Lynn's intermittent ability with pace and cutting.

*Greedy* (1994), inexplicably influenced by Erich von Stroheim's *Greed* (1924), stars Kirk Douglas as the wealthy manipulative patriarch of a family whose members are waiting for him to die so they can inherit his fortune. Spoilt somewhat by mugging and predictably scatalogical humour, the film saw Lynn consolidate his reputation as a dependable but uninspired director of average comedy. An unpopular film version of the television show, *Sgt Bilko* (1996) came next, updating from the 1950s to the present day, and clumsily re-positioning Fort Baxter as a post-Desert Storm base. In its updating of the setting it uses a few token 'gays in the military' jokes and tries to make comedy out of its gender and racial mix, ultimately to no avail. He film lacks visual wit and, as with Murphy in *The Distinguished Gentleman,* Lynn seems unable to coax an appropriate performance from Steve Martin in a comedy which mixes the sight gag with verbal play, ensemble stupidity and Martin's trademark slapstick to muddled and witless effect.

In 1997's *Trial and Error*, Lynn returns to the courtroom comedy. This time the hapless lawyer is an actor pretending to replace his drunken lawyer friend. Another predictable script, lacking the wit of *My Cousin Vinny,* the film is unaided by Lynn's visual style. Soft filter shots are used every time a man's attraction to a woman needs to be suggested, and slow-motion hair-waving signifying love helps to slow down the film and smother any humour.

*The Whole Nine Yards* (2000) takes its influence from Arthur Hiller's *The In-Laws* (1979). A debt-ridden dentist (played by Matthew Perry) befriends his neighbour, a notorious hitman in a Witness Protection Program (Bruce Willis). Unknown to Perry, his wife is plotting to have him killed and the hitman returned to his former bosses for a tidy financial reward. Another paceless comedy, the film shows that Lynn's career as a director seems to be embroiled in the less distinctive end of the mainstream Hollywood market. He is slated to direct *The Fighting Temptations*, a musical comedy about a hip-hop producer from LA that has to form a gospel choir and make it successful in order to collect his wealthy aunt's inheritance. **JD**

# John MADDEN

John Madden has come to specialise in a brand of heritage drama favoured by cinema-goers as much as executives; stories of forbidden love, set against the obstructing backdrops of repression, restriction and the rules of society. Using period setting and evocative cinematography to conjure the romantic context, together with passionate performances from his male and female leads, he has woven various versions of his love-triangle tragedies, from the weighty New England melodrama *Ethan Frome* (1993) to the moral minefield of racial love in *Golden Gate* (1994). Madden's affinity for period drama with a literary, literate bent is most notably illustrated by the engaging *Mrs Brown* (1997) and the multiple Academy Award-winning *Shakespeare In Love* (1998). There is the inescapable sense of something pre-packaged about Madden's more recent work, however, particularly exemplified by his decision to direct *Captain Corelli's Mandolin* (2001), the sure-fire adaptation of Louis de Bernieres' publishing phenomenon. His reluctance to step beyond the cosy confines of period romance or experiment with more edgy styles and material is in danger of making a misty-eyed old romantic seem something of a bright-eyed cynic.

Born in Portsmouth, UK, in 1949, initially a director of television and theatre, Madden worked in the early 1990s on British and US television series including 'Inspector Morse', 'The Return of Sherlock Homes', and Jim Henson's 'The Storyteller', as well as dramas such as 'Grownups', 'A Wreath of Roses', and the BAFTA-nominated 'The Widowmaker'. Demonstrably a director of considerable dramatic skill, and having additionally directed plays on Broadway, he made his Hollywood debut in 1993 with *Ethan Frome*, an adaptation of an Edith Wharton novel in which New England farmer Frome falls for the cousin of his oppressive, bed-ridden wife. The repressive puritan values of turn-of-the-century New England, mirrored in the film's wintry Vermont landscapes and bleak cinematography, are contrasted with Frome's compulsive love and destructive passion, at once morally illicit and emotionally legitimate.

This is powerful emotional drama of a type much suited to Madden's style, and the various oppositions – love and duty, passion and guilt, emotion and religion – are

*Ethan Frome* (1993)
*Golden Gate* (1994)
*Mrs Brown* (1997)
*Shakespeare in Love* (1998)
*Captain Corelli's Mandolin* (2001)

neatly developed and explored. Less successful is *Golden Gate*, a confused moral drama in which an FBI agent, wracked with guilt over the suicide of a Chinese laundry worker he helped convict, seduces the man's daughter. Set amongst the McCarthy witch-hunts of the 1950s, the film sets out to create a relationship that contravenes the prevailing mores of both societies, but succeeds only in patronising its audience with simplistic characterisations and over-earnest direction. Madden was yet to hit upon the dynamite formula, though these early experiments illustrate the direction in which he was headed: historical romantic-drama with an evocative setting and a tragic streak of unattainability.

*Mrs Brown* was Madden's first large-scale success, and is perhaps his most artistically rewarding film. Initially shot for the BBC, the film snow-balled once Miramax, a company whose entrepreneurial stock-in-trade is the sleeper hit, became involved; following its 1997 presentation at Cannes, Madden was effectively launched into the big-league of British directors. Charting Queen Victoria's prolonged period of mourning following the death of her husband Prince Albert – the time which gave rise to her 'Widow of Windsor' pseudonym – and the constitutional crisis her extended absence caused, the film sets out to explore the private face behind her imposing public figure, particularly the prospect of facing life and the throne as a woman alone. Her relationship with gamekeeper and bodyguard-to-be John Brown is the heart of the story; it is an undeclared but palpable relationship of impossible love and the recuperative force which allows her to face up to responsibility. Madden's skill is in conveying the subtle, covert passionate subtext beneath the surface of decorum and duty – he to his Queen, she to her people – with an understated and engaging touch. This is a different Madden love triangle; the third figure here is two-fold, both the spectre of the dead King whom Victoria would never disgrace, and the country to whom the Queen is inextricably wedded. The complex mix of love and friendship, desire and duty, together with superb performances from Judi Dench and Billy Connolly, makes for intelligent, adult cinema.

*Shakespeare in Love* (1998) is similarly rooted in the contradictory pressures of society and self, but Madden exchanges *Mrs Brown*'s Victorian gravity for an altogether more Elizabethan feel; a bold, sassy, sexy mix of farce, pastiche and romance, a tragicomedy in the true sense of the word. It is an ironic take on a fictionalised relationship in Shakespeare's life in which he falls in love with a woman betrothed to the Earl of Wessex. Shot through with a whole range of post-modern reference points – Shakespeare going to a psychologist, haggling with recalcitrant actors and struggling with writer's block – and directed in an energetic style, the film manages to capture something of the spirit of Shakespeare's wit, wordplay and invention, thanks largely to Tom Stoppard's effortlessly convincing script. Madden delights in any number of in-jokes, pastiches of the plays, cross-dressings and gender-bendings, and the result is an irreverent dose of Shakespeare-lite. The clever-clever style, slightly smug self-referencing tone and pop casting inevitably leave the sense of a film that thinks it is just too smart to pick holes in. Some purists and factual scholars were critical. Whether the film deserved its shower of Academy Awards, and whether it contributes to a wider interest in Shakespeare, is a moot point.

Guaranteed a captive audience, thanks to its origins in a book that reportedly resides in one in twenty British households, *Captain Corelli's Mandolin* shows the same trend as Madden's previous works but none of their charm. It explores the relationship between an Italian captain and a girl on Cephalonia, the Greek island that his army has occupied in World War Two, which flouts not only national allegiances but also her betrothal to simple fisherman Mandras. Comparison with the book is inevitable, particularly given that the film excises large parts of its complex narrative, pares down the subtext love story of Corelli's gay lieutenant for his captain to nothing, and waters down its bleak conclusion to a shamelessly commercial happy ending. Although impressively filmed in Mediterranean hues, and with some exhilarating war sequences, it is badly let down by a simplistic script, some awful accents and the woefully inappropriate casting of Nicolas Cage as the awkward Corelli. Despite having come to the project very late in the day, following original director Roger Michell's heart attack days before the start of shooting, Madden is obviously going through the motions here.                    **OB**

# Guy MADDIN

Guy Maddin is a wonderfully contradictory talent. Cultish and described by Claire Monk as 'no-tech', his films are at once quintessentially Canadian and wholly unique, mock-macho fever dreams of lovesick yearning. Even so, they bulge with references to the likes of Sternberg, Fellini, Sirk, Griffiths and Eisenstein. Some argue that Maddin is creating an imaginary Canadian narrative film history – Canada's film history being documentary-based – distinguished from Hollywood by its lack of heroic individuals. 'Not a "Duke" Wayne among them', Maddin said of Canadian cinema's history of estranged characters. Maybe he is simply indulging a love of cinema. Either way, he has few contemporaries. What other director would publish an opaque statement to that effect, titled 'Salon XXI: A Letter in Severe Terms Suggesting an 8-Point Manifesto for Better Movies'?

Tales from the
Gimli Hospital (1988)
Archangel (1990)
Careful (1992)
Twilight of the
Ice Nymphs (1997)
Dracula: Pages from a Virgin's
Diary (2001)

Many critics find such behaviour unbearable; Marc Horton, for example, was certainly not alone in accusing Maddin of 'pretentious self-indulgence'. But it's a glib dismissal, given the delirious, self-mocking wit and appealingly raw beauty of Maddin's lovingly crafted films – and, indeed, his recent return to striking form.

Born in Winnipeg in 1956, Maddin gained a cult following as early as his semi-autobiographical debut *The Dead Father* (1986) (Maddin's father died when the director was 21), completed after he left a banking career to join the Winnipeg Film Group. It is typical of Maddin's warped humour that, in this tale of father/son conflict, the son's problem is not his father's death – the problem is that death does not make the father less annoying.

Maddin's first feature, a mock-disease movie titled *Tales from the Gimli Hospital* (1988), increased his cult reputation. Having been rejected by 1988's Toronto Festival of Festivals, it was picked up by Ben Barenholtz for midnight screenings at his Greenwich Village Quad cinema. Tapes circulated. Barenholtz did not publicise screenings at the Berlin, San Francisco and Cannes Film Festivals, lending the film an aura of illicit pleasure.

*Tales from the Gimli Hospital* certainly marked Maddin as an individual and acquired taste, putting paid to the David Lynch comparisons which followed *The Dead Father*. Shot for $22,000 on weekends over several months, this pastiche of 1920s silents plays out a bizarre lovers' triangle during a smallpox epidemic in *fin de siècle* Gimli. Although only mildly pustulating for a disease movie, it doesn't stint on necrophilia, AIDS imagery and fatal bouts of butt-pinching. Its cine-literacy is no less rich; Maddin credits D. W. Griffith's *Broken Blossoms* (1919) for the emotionally charged tinting of his print.

Maddin resisted Hollywood's advances to then make *Archangel* (1990), another lovers' triangle movie set in Russia (actually Winnipeg in February) during the Bolshevik revolution. The twist is that the lead characters (notably Lt. Boles, played by Maddin regular Kyle McCulloch) have amnesia and hence do not know who to love. Mixing nods to *Dr Zhivago* (1965) and *Battleship Potemkin* (1925) with absurdism, farce, satire, horror, melodrama, war movie, cannibalism and strangulation by intestine, *Archangel* was an idiosyncratic labour of love and a cut-price triumph. It only cost $400,000, yet the *Village Voice* chose a scene in which rabbits – representing Bolsheviks – fell like snow as 1991's most memorable.

*Careful* (1992) revisits 1920s German mountain films, plays like an early talkie by mimicking Vitaphone and models its vivid look on early two-strip Technicolor. The inspired plot centres on an incestuous family in a mountain village, under constant threat from an avalanche should anyone talk above a whisper. Maddin declared it his 'movie by right of being Canadian, my patriotic take on that commodity of caution'. With its skewed dialogue (from Maddin's long-term collaborator George Toles) and self-consciously wooden acting matched by moments of lyrical beauty, it remains the director's most coherent and irrepressibly cheeky statement. Sadly, Maddin's next film never got made. *The Dykemaster's Daughter* was to be an operetta about a gender-reversed spin on E. T. A. Hoffmann's 'The Sandman', centred on a man and a woman in love with the most beautiful man in the world. Maddin's lack of financial acumen let him down; ironic, given that he trained in economics before making films.

An ambitious project followed. Shot for $1.25 million with Maddin's biggest cast (Shelley Duvall, Pascale Bussieres, Alice Krige, R. H. Thomson, Frank Gorshin and – uncredited – Nigel Whitmey), *Twilight of the Ice Nymphs* (1997) expands the lovers' triangles of his early works into a lovers' hexagon set on the mythical island of Mandragora. The day-glo colour scheme, orchestral score (Maddin: 'And it's in stereo!')

and dense references lend it an air of highbrow melodrama; 'La Ronde' remade by Douglas Sirk in the style of *The Wizard of Oz* (1939) if penned by Norwegian novelist Knut Hamsun. Unfairly savaged by British critics, this overripe delight weeps with unrequited longing, in turn parodied by its hilarious non-sequiturs and mock-phallic chorus of strutting ostriches.

It was closely followed by a one-hour documentary from Noam Gonick, titled *Guy Maddin: Waiting for Twilight* (1997). Narrated by Tom Waits and rich in biographical detail, Gonick's excellent film shows how difficult Maddin found the shoot of *Twilight of the Ice Nymphs*. He talked of not making another, and yet the last couple of years have seen him back on track with a return to silent-movie aesthetics. In 2000, he garnered an astonishing amount of press and praise for a mere six-minute short, commissioned for the Toronto Film Festival. Described by Maddin as 'the world's first subliminal melodrama', *Heart of the World* (2000) is a remarkable piece of work, too theatrical in its imagery but breathtakingly tight in its narrative and thematic condensation.

Maddin again aped silent movie conventions for *Dracula: Pages from a Virgin's Diary* (2001). The Royal Winnipeg Ballet were the stars of this florid take on Bram Stoker's classic, which Maddin takes back to basics with its primitive penetration imagery, expressive performances, stark black and whites (only the odd splash of red), and themes of sex and xenophobia. Again, plaudits all round – even Maddin admits to being proud of the work. What's more, the critical attention looks likely to lead to his biggest film yet: *The Saddest Music in the World*, adapted from an unpublished screenplay by Kazuo Ishiguro. In a time when even a fair few independent and foreign-language films seem intent on imitating Hollywood mores, it's heartening to see one of the world's most idiosyncratic film-makers picking up the thread anew.                                    **KH**

# Maria MAGGENTI

Mario Maggenti began her career as a video activist, making the documentary *Doctors, Liars, and Women* (1988) with videomaker Jean Carlomusto. It focused on ACT UP/New York women's committee challenge to an article in *Cosmopolitan* magazine claiming that women cannot get AIDS from normal heterosexual sex. From 1990 to 1994, she produced several short films, including *Name Day* (1995), which received the Warner Bros. Production award and the Grand Prize at the Hamptons International Film Festival. She claims Billy Wilder, Preston Sturges, Gregory La Cava, Jacques Tati, and Woody Allen as her influences.

When Maggenti wrote and directed her first feature film, *The Incredibly True Adventure of Two Girls in Love* (1995), she was entering into the well-established field of New Queer Cinema. Though new and queer, the film is also a very old-fashioned and heartwarming love story about teenagers who fall in love – a Juliet meets Juliet story. Their different class status matters more than their racial difference and same gender: Evie, elegant and refined, listens to opera and reads poetry; Randy is scruffier, works outside of high school hours pumping gas, and listens to rock music through her headphones. That Randy is raised in a lesbian household – with her aunt, her aunt's lover and her aunt's ex – makes no difference to how embarrassed Randy is by them or how much she rebels against their ways, as any teenager would in any family.

About *The Incredibly True Adventure*, Maggenti has commented, 'I always saw this as a story of first love, because for me being gay is just another authentic American experience'. She prefers to think of her work as independent rather than lesbian and has no illusions about the power of a film to change the world but believes that it 'is part of a cultural landscape that hopefully moves a community forward'.                    **MBP**

# Kelly MAKIN

Canadian directors are often characterised as being the authors of bleak, cold films with little levity, and while the works of artists like Atom Egoyan and David Cronenberg are not overly serious, they are certainly not a light evening's viewing. Kelly Makin makes films in quite the opposite way. A graduate of Ryerson Polytechnic University in Toronto, he began working as an editor and director on the cult-favoured sketch comedy series 'The Kids in the Hall', starring the eponymous Canadian comedy troupe. Makin's closeness to the Kids manifests itself with members popping up in many of his films, from Kevin McDonald's delusional Trekkie in *National Lampoon's Senior Trip* (1995) to Scott Thompson's clumsy FBI agent in *Mickey Blue Eyes* (1999). His work as an editor on the show (as in his later work as a director of commercials and music videos) is apparent in the tightness and economy of his films.

Born in Winnepeg in 1961, Makin's feature debut came with *Tigerclaws* (1992), a low-budget police thriller/martial arts film about a stalker (Bolo Yeung) who is killing martial arts instructors using an ancient technique. The film has inspired two sequels, but did not indicate the cinematic path Makin would take. His second film, *Senior Trip*, follows the Lampoon tradition of endearing losers who manage to defeat the establishment through a series of contrived antics. The film follows the usual group of teens – stoners, nerds, keeners, misfits, and the tramp – who travel from Ohio to Washington to discuss a proposed presidential education bill that is opposed by a corrupt senator (Lawrence Dane). The students are accompanied by a stern principal (Matt Frewer) and spinsterish teacher (Valerie Mahaffey) on a bus driven by drug-addled Tommy Chong (of Cheech and Chong). Although the film is a veritable celebration of low comedy, its efficiency and complete lack of pretension make it a genuinely funny, guilty pleasure. McDonald is brilliant as Travis, the Star Trek-obsessed crossing guard who stalks one of the teens whom he believes is a Klingon leader seeking to form a coalition with the Romulans. Makin directs the film succinctly, with the necessary quick pace. He also shows a surprising restraint in the use bodily function jokes that are usually a standard of such films.

The 'Kids In the Hall' film *Brain Candy* (1996) was a disappointment in many circles, especially to the troupe's legions of Canadian fans, who saw it as a rather diluted, Americanised version of their humour. Their absurdist style, similar to Monty Python, often dealt with ideas of masculinity and how these ideas manifested themselves in society. *Brain Candy*, however, tells the story of a new depression drug being marketed by a greedy pharmaceuticals company and the various people affected by it. The five Kids play most of the parts, often in drag, but the film cannot sustain a consistent level of humour. Although the film is in episodic structure and thus similar to the series, the sketches are uneven in quality. The central idea of the story is simply not strong enough but the film is considered and well paced.

*Mickey Blue Eyes* is the high-concept comedy tale of English art dealer Michael (Hugh Grant), living in Manhattan, who proposes to his girlfriend Gina (Jeanne Tripplehorn), the daughter of a key Mafia figure (James Caan). After her family intercedes in a dispute Michael is having with some delivery truck drivers, he is caught in a web of money laundering and murder between the Mob and the FBI. *Mickey Blue Eyes* is a single joke played out over a hundred-minute running time, with each gag more excruciating than the last. The film displays less of the economical energy of Makin's previous work, perhaps because of scenes added by other directors, but is nonetheless a fun, harmless comedy in the classical screwball vein. Indeed, Grant seems to be making an earnest attempt at playing Cary Grant. **DH**

# Terrence MALICK

Born in Waco, Texas, in 1943, Terrence Malick has been praised by critics and his contemporaries for being one of the most influential directors of the 1970s.

*Badlands* (1973)
*Days of Heaven* (1978)
*The Thin Red Line* (1998)

An enigmatic and assiduously reclusive figure, Malick has been referred to as the J. D. Salinger of the movies. Only recently did he choose to return to directing after a twenty-year self-imposed exile from the film world. A former Harvard and Oxford philosophy graduate specialising in Heidegger, Malick's directorial career began when he enrolled in the American Film Institute in 1969. To date Malick's directing career encompasses a mere 3 films in 27 years. While in no way prolific, Malick exemplifies how narrative cinema has the potential to mesmerise and challenge an audience's perception of reality.

His first film, *Badlands* (1973), offers a metaphysical vision of the world through the eyes of two idealistic teenage lovers, Martin Sheen (Kit) and Sissy Spacek (Holly). The film is based on the true story of 19-year-old Charles Starkweather who, in 1958, murdered the family of his 13-year-old lover. Malick renders the story into a tale of two people numbingly alienated from normality, doomed and adrift in a fantasy of crime. According to critic David Thomson, the film is 'the most assured first film by an American since *Citizen Kane'*. *Badlands* is a curiously passionless road movie told through a seamless blend of lyrical clichés provided by Holly's voiceover. Kit's violent outbursts are deadpan, non-melodramatic and sudden. Accompanied by Holly's detached, indifferent attitude to the violence, a delicately haunting score and the scorched intimacy of the natural landscapes that surround the characters as they flee from the law, Malick presents us with a unique confluence of story, picture and sound.

In 1978 Malick released *Days of Heaven,* a love story set amidst a sea of endless wheat-fields in Texas at the turn of the century. Beautifully shot through with darkly poetic imagery, the film explores the same theme of social outcasts restlessly seeking a niche in a harsh and unforgiving environment. Again Malick uses a female voiceover to cohere and personalise the narrative. Yet the voice-over itself is often fractured and discursive, mumbling so as not to detract from the oppressive imagery of the rural American landscape. Ostensibly the film was a labour of love for Malick and took two years to edit. Quite deservedly it took the Best Director award at the Cannes Film Festival in 1979.

*The Thin Red Line,* Malick's World War Two epic, was released in 1998. Again the same themes of alienation, death and the search for a position in a world ravaged by both natural beauty and violence predominate (often through reference to myth and archetype). The film is a visually stunning piece of work examining the harrowing and often horrific exploits of C for Charlie company during the battle of Guadalcanal. Narrative drive is once again provided in the form of a voice-over. However, rather than a single distanced female character telling the story, in *The Thin Red Line* a series of prophetic male voices provide a series of verbose philosophical clichés about nature, brutality, destruction and sacrifice. This affirms Malick's position as an existential director and screenwriter. Devoted to portraying the insignificance of humanity in the face of nature, Malick's work is exemplary. It is a credit to his skill and vision that his films appeal to both art-house and mainstream audiences.

Malick's three films to date have tapped into the deepest and most resonant strains of the American character. Yet unlike other directors that have attempted to glorify what is the essence of the American dream – the individual against nature – Malick is content to turn the mythology on its head. All three appear to be based on the philosophical question posed at the beginning of *The Thin Red Line*, 'Why does nature contend with itself?' The films are about the very nature of man; man as animal, impelled by the drive to kill, to destroy and to consume his own kind and nature itself (either literally or figuratively). In order to support this philosophy Malick has adopted a film-making technique that is at once alienating and integrative. Firstly, he alienates the audience by distancing them from the characters. He does this through the characters' actions, the insurmountable beauty of the imagery he employs and the often unreliable and precocious nature of the voiceovers. Yet the overall effect of these three strategies when viewed together is to tie the characters and spectators to the very nature of the scene they are viewing. Malick's movies do not simply tell a story, they are inspirational in that they coerce a medium into carrying an overwhelming philosophical message.

Malick is currently working on *The Moviegoer*, an adaptation of a Walter Percy novel, which the director has also scripted.                                                                    **PH**

# William MALONE

Writer-director of two weak and ill-received sci-fi/horror films in the early 1980s (*Scared to Death* (1982), *Creature* (1985)), William Malone has since worked in television directing episodes of 'Tales From the Crypt' and 'Freddy's Nightmares'. He wrote the script of *Supernova* (2000), from which Walter Hill asked his name to be removed. In *The House on Haunted Hill* (1999) Malone's clever use of looks off-screen, cutting, and the sudden placing in the frame of elements designed to frighten (see the sequence where one character, armed with her camera, roams alone around the basement) shows he has learned the right lessons. The film, however, is more of a team effort, and the articulation of script, characterisation, decor and *mise-en-scène* highlights its inscription into a long tradition of film-making. From this standpoint it would be erroneous to reduce the character of Steven Price to actor Vincent. He is also clearly a throwback to William Castle, but his appearance and involvement with an elaborate funfair suggests a parallel with Disney and Anaheim. More to the point, however, is the extraordinary opening where Dr Vannacutt dissects – alive and without anaesthetic – the patients of his asylum while a nurse films the proceedings. It is the spirit of these victims which comes back to haunt the luxury house. Crucial here is the date of the opening, cleverly filmed like a documentary: 1931. As such the film evokes *Frankenstein* (1931), *Island of Lost Souls* (1933), and the horrors of Nazism. Hardly surprising then that production designer David Klassen evokes Albert Speer, although the house clearly shows other influences. A long shot shows an ultra-modern dwelling in an oddly old-fashioned setting. It is patently a model and deliberately artificial, thus contrasting with the film's gruesome realism. On one level this harks back to the castles in *Dracula* (1958) and *White Zombie* (1932), and the homes in *The Old Dark House* (1932) and *The Devil Commands* (a Boris Karloff movie of 1941). At the same time, the marked contrast seems to be a parody of postmodernism, where a play with form tends to eradicate context and history. This shot then stands in for the film itself which represents the return of the repressed of history in the monstrous form of the spirit of the insane, back to exact vengeance from the descendants of the families responsible for their torture. That art is not just a game for wealthy drones is an important theme of this effective, frightening, and decidedly nasty movie.

Malone's forthcoming film, tentatively titled *FearDotCom*, is a thriller about a series of murders that are traced back to a website. **RH**

# David MAMET

In his theoretical book 'On Directing Film', David Mamet states that 'there are some directors who are visual masters – who bring to moviemaking a great visual acuity, a brilliant visual sense. I am not one of them'. Mamet's own self-depreciation alludes to the sense that his films are extensions of his work as one of America's foremost play- and screenwriters. Noted primarily for his forceful male characters and their indulgent macho posturing, Mamet's work as a film director focuses on the nuances of prophetic dialogue over action. This trait of employing often malicious and confrontational verbal scenarios has meant that Mamet creates complex webs of enigma and suspicion within his low-key films that are reminiscent of the dialogue driven narratives of classical Hollywood.

Born in Chicago in 1947, he completed his studies at Goddard College in Vermont and at the Neighbourhood Playhouse School of Theater in New York, and began his career as an actor and theatre writer/director. A playwright of incredible wit and verbosity he would achieve universal critical acclaim for numerous productions, including 'Sexual Perversity in Chicago', 'American Buffalo', and the Pulitzer-nominated 'Glengarry Glen Ross', all of which would later be adapted for the big screen to critical acclaim. Mamet also produced numerous successful screenplays including an adaptation of a James M. Cain novel, *The Postman Always Rings Twice* (1981), Sidney Lumet's *The Verdict* (1982) and the Academy Award-nominated gangland epic *The Untouchables* (1987).

He made his film directorial debut with *House of Games* in 1987, a Hitchcockian drama that follows the descent of an esteemed psychologist, Dr Margaret Ford (Lindsay Crouse) into the shadowy con-artist world of one of her patients, Mike (Joe Mantegna). Buoyed by a strong cast the film is on face value a laconic psychological conundrum of intrigue and deceit yet it works equally well on a variety of levels. The film can also be read as a picaresque drama tracing the emotionally fraught journey of one woman's quest for self-realisation.

Mamet teamed up again with Mantegna in 1988 when he directed his next feature, *Things Change*. Somewhat an anomaly in terms of Mamet's work, the film is a flat whimsical comedy rather than a paranoiac thriller. However, Mamet does still manage to effect some endearing performances from the cast, in particular Don Ameche as the hapless immigrant shoe-polisher framed for a gangland murder. *Homicide* (1991) was Mamet's next release and saw a return to the provocative conspiracy situations of his earlier stage work. The film is an elaborate examination of one man's struggle to understand his personal and national identity. A tough urban cop, Bobby Gould (once again Joe Mantegna), whilst investigating a seemingly routine murder, becomes embroiled in a case of Jewish arms smuggling that leads him to re-evaluate his entire existence. The intrinsic plot, subtle understated subtext and powerful performances all add up to a piece of pure Mamet.

His next feature, *Oleanna* (1994), based on his own play, is a skilfully staged two-character drama that features another Mamet regular, William H. Macy, as a self-important college professor who stands accused of sexual harassment by one of his students, Debra Eisenstadt. The film has been lambasted as racist and misogynist in some quarters yet equally praised in others for being anti-authoritarian and pro-feminist. Ultimately the film received such mixed reception because it dares to challenge the individual whose ideological standpoint is based solely upon established gender tenets. For all its criticism and praise it remains a somewhat staged and stilted film. Yet Mamet's manipulative skill in the use of sharp acerbic dialogue means he still manages to make a relevant, if contentious, point about the hypocrisy and sanctimony of both camps in the so called 'sex wars' of the late 1980s and 1990s.

In 1997 Mamet saw the release of his next project, *The Spanish Prisoner*. Jammed full of nuance and subtlety this film is quintessential Mamet in terms of theme and content. Campbell Scott plays Joe Ross, a scientist who develops a process that is set to earn him and the company he works for a tidy fortune. However, paranoia envelops Joe as he begins to realise that 'you never really know who anyone is'. Trapped in a nightmarish world of double-cross, deceit, treachery and betrayal, Mamet tells an elaborate tale as convoluted and satisfying as any Hitchcock thriller. However, *The Spanish Prisoner* remains very much a theatre director's film because, unlike Hitchcock, Mamet tells his tale without the suggestive camerawork of a purely cinematic storyteller.

*The Winslow Boy* (1999), a faithful adaptation of Terrence Rattigan's 1946 play, sees Mamet breaking with his customary sinister subtexts in favour of a straightforward, elegantly crafted costume drama. Mamet's direction is as restrained and precise as the Edwardian characters in his film. It concerns the plight of Ronnie Winslow (Guy Edwards), who stands accused of a crime he did not commit, and the fight in the courts by his father (Nigel Hawthorne) to restore his son's good name. However, this is neither standard costume drama or courtroom drama fare. Mamet's film is more a closely observed character study concerning the personal sacrifice undergone by a father for the love of his son and for his faith in the judiciary. Although a departure from his earlier themes the film still carries Mamet's signature in the form of dialogue that is often oblique, repetitive and steeped in pathos. *State and Main* (2000) is a comedy focusing on the disruptive presence of a movie crew in a small-town community. This film succeeds in matching the standard that Mamet himself has set as a consummate director who relies on performance style, verbiage and intrinsic plot over the pleasures inherent in the immediacy of special effect and spectacle.

Spectacle should, however, have played a fundamental part in Mamet's latest project, *Heist* (2001), a crime caper featuring Gene Hackman as Joe Moore, an aging criminal forced into 'one last job' involving an aeroplane and a horde of Swiss gold-bullion. The film, being full of Mamet's trademark acidic axioms and plot twists, should, on the level of an atypical Hollywood crime movie, work and run like a well-oiled machine. The problem, however, is that Mamet's contrived dialogue and set-pieces often detract from, rather than add to, any sense of tension that a genre film of this ilk requires. As usual, rather than giving the audience the gratuitous spectacle normally associated with the contemporary thriller, Mamet chooses to focus on intricacies and minutiae. **PH**

# James MANGOLD

*Heavy* (1995)
*Cop Land* (1997)
*Girl, Interrupted* (1999)
*Kate & Leopald* (2001)

Born in 1964, James Mangold is a modern throwback to a classical narrative style of film-making and a firm believer in the idiom of substance over style. Born to artistic parents (his father is minimalist painter Robert Mangold), he was raised in upstate New York around the Hudson Valley area. Mangold attended the California Institute of the Arts where he studied under distinguished British director Alexander Mackendrick and graduated to a high-profile writer-director's contract with Disney Studios. Within a year, creative differences killed his relationship with the studio, and he returned to film school for graduate work at Columbia University from 1989 to 1991 'because it was some kind of shelter from Hollywood'. There, he studied under Academy Award-winning director Milos Forman, who was an influential mentor during the development of Mangold's first feature, *Heavy* (1995).

*Heavy* is an astonishingly elegant and cliché-free film concerning the romantic infatuation of an overweight, small-town pizza cook with a nubile, fresh-faced teenaged waitress newly hired at his restaurant. While North American movie screens around this time were awash with the flamboyant, unrestrained works of New Jack American film-makers like Quentin Tarantino, Robert Rodriguez and Kevin Smith, *Heavy*'s quiet demeanour and gentle emotionalism provided a refreshing alternative to the slick, over-the-top styles of Mangold's contemporaries. Containing strong performances from all involved – especially the leads Pruitt Taylor Vince and Liv Tyler – *Heavy* works tremendously well as a thoughtful treatise on the ambivalence of navigating life's complicated pathways.

A similar thread winds its way through *Cop Land* (1997), Mangold's ambitious attempt at crafting an urban western under the guise of a New York police corruption tale. The film was to be Sylvester Stallone's dramatic film breakout role, but despite his effectively low-key and tender performance as partially-deaf Sheriff Freddy Heflin, *Cop Land* never rises above its conventional plotting and leaves its interesting ideas – like the hero/victim relationship between Stallone and Annabella Sciorra – on the back burner. Mangold continued his exploration of ambivalence, shifting from physically flawed to mentally flawed protagonists, in *Girl, Interrupted* (1999), an adaptation of Susanna Kaysen's intimate memoirs about her late-1960s two-year stay in a mental hospital. Feeling too similar to Forman's *One Flew Over the Cuckoo's Nest* (1975) and structurally too reliant on *The Wizard of Oz* (1939), *Girl, Interrupted* lacks the originality and resonance of Mangold's more personal work.

*Kate & Leopold* (2001), Mangold's most recent film, is an excursion into the romantic comedy genre, and thankfully he brings his practised foot for sincerity along with him. The story of a late-1800s English Duke (Hugh Jackman) who travels through a seam in time to contemporary New York City, it is about restoring honour and integrity to modern courtship. Meg Ryan – who is now a little long-in-the-tooth for this kind of role – comfortably revisits her archetype of the endearing, modern upper-middle-class single girl, but it is Hugh Jackman's wonderful and convincing performance that gives the film its melodramatic fizz. *Kate & Leopold*'s screenplay struggles for plausibility at times, and it would have played stronger had Mangold and his co-writers stripped away its slapstick elements and resisted the lure of cheap laughs, but the film's quality acting and genuine tone lift it above most in its genre.

He is currently working on *I.D.*, a thriller starring John Cusack, in which ten strangers stranded on a desert island are being killed off one by one.              **THa**

# Michael MANN

Few directors in contemporary American cinema are as lionised as Michael Mann. A self-confessed perfectionist, his portraits of obsessional characters caught in transgressive situations are meticulously crafted and serious in intent. His work stands alongside that of Howard Hawks, Sam Peckinpah, Paul Schrader, and Martin Scorsese for its study of masculinity and particular focus on the professional male's uneasy negotiations with society. Formally daring, his films are rarely sentimental or overtly emotional; attempting to mine the consciousness of his characters, he offers complex, but emotionally disengaged, personality studies.

*Thief* (1981)
*The Keep* (1983)
*Manhunter* (1986)
*Last of the Mohicans* (1992)
*Heat* (1995)
*The Insider* (1999)
*Ali* (2001)

Born in Chicago in 1943, Mann studied film-making at London's International Film School, made a series of documentaries and the short film *Jaunpuri*, which won the Jury Prize at the 1970 Cannes Film Festival, and moved back to the US and into television. Having successfully worked as a writer on 'Starsky and Hutch' and 'Police Story', and created the hit series 'Vega$', he earned the respect of television executives, who gave him the go-ahead to make his debut.

*The Jericho Mile* (1979) is the story of Rain Murphy, a convict whose athletic prowess offers him the opportunity to become a member of the US Olympic track team. Obstructed by authorities and the prison's racial barriers, his hopes are dashed but his spirit remains unbroken, resulting in the final, personal victory. Though made for television, the drama excels as a result of Mann's extensive research into the prison system. Set in California's Folsom State Penitentiary, it builds a convincing portrait of prison life, paying particular attention to issues of racial segregation. Murphy has become the prototype of Mann's recurrent central character. Too complex to be either a hero or villain – tropes that the director seems to abhor for their simplicity – his moral compass is dictated by his need to survive in a tough and uncompromising world.

Though much looser in style than his later work, *The Jericho Mile* remains a powerful and intelligent debut.

*Thief* (1981), based on Frank Hohimer's memoir, 'The Home Invaders', remains one of Mann's best films. A studied account of the life of a safe cracker, and Mann's first foray into the territory with which he has become synonymous, it is a tense and atmospheric thriller. Like Neil McCauley in *Heat* (1995), Frank is a professional whose life revolves around his work. A compulsive obsessive, he is thwarted in his attempts to go straight by a local gang boss who coerces him into carrying out a series of jobs. Realising the hopelessness of his situation, Frank destroys every vestige of his life, and his enemies', before driving off into the night alone. *Thief* displays Mann's ability to probe deeply into the psyche of his characters. Bressonian in his attention to the details of Frank's life, particularly in the execution of the robberies, Mann draws out a career-best performance from James Caan, whose edgy acting style perfectly complement's Frank's permanent state of unease. Once again, through his research of the underworld – going so far as to cast both sides of the law in his film – Mann's renders his film more realistic than most crime dramas. Set off by Tangerine Dream's electronic score, *Thief* was critically acclaimed but failed to score with audiences.

The promise Mann showed with his first two films is entirely absent from his only horror film, *The Keep* (1983). Travelling through the Carpathian Alps during World War Two, a Wehrmacht detachment unsuspectingly releases an evil spirit intent on destroying the world. Aided by a Jewish scientist, the spirit is defeated, but only after audiences are put through 96 minutes of gruelling tedium, complete with cheesy effects and crass dialogue. There is little to recommend *The Keep* to anyone but the most ardent Mann completist. The horror is neither horrific nor frightening, and whatever Mann is attempting to say specifically about the treatment of Jews by the Nazis, or the human spirit in general, amounts to little more than glib moralising. Tangerine Dream's score this time hinders the proceedings and a distinguished cast is wasted.

Taking a hiatus from cinema after *The Keep*, Mann concentrated on a number of television projects. Contrary to popular belief, he did not create 'Miami Vice', although he did work on the series which bears the hallmarks of a Michael Mann production; the zeitgeist television programme of the 1980s, its mix of drama, style and music made it an instant success. He subsequently worked on the less popular 'Crime Story', which recreated the Mafia world of the 1960s, and later returned to television in 1989 to produce the Emmy Award-winning 'Drug Wars', based on the true story of DEA Agent Enrique 'Kiki' Camarena.

Revisiting crime on the big screen, Mann directed what arguably remains the best adaptation of Thomas Harris' Hannibal Lecter novels. *Manhunter* (1986), the title changed from 'Red Dragon' because producer Dino De Laurentis did not want the film to be confused with *Year of the Dragon* (1985) or *Red Sonja* (1985), continued his study of obsessives, only this time the attention was focused on a law enforcer. Will Graham is a profiler for the FBI, brought in to search for the Tooth Fairy, a serial killer who murders entire families every full moon. Working against the clock, Graham enters the mindset of the killer in an attempt to pre-empt the next move. As his investigation becomes more involved and time begins to run out, he finds both his family and his sanity threatened. A psychological thriller *par excellence*, Mann's detailed approach to Graham's investigative techniques makes for compulsive viewing. The intelligent script successfully fleshes out his inner conflict – like Frank and Neil McCauley, he is placed in the precarious position of having to choose between the professional and domestic life – but unlike other Mann characters, it is not someone else but himself that becomes his greatest threat. Perhaps because of the threat to his own sanity, Graham is the only one of Mann's contemporary protagonists to actively choose the domestic.

In *Manhunter*, Mann's directorial style matured to a point where his work became instantly recognisable. Adopting certain aspects of his work on 'Miami Vice' – in particular the use of the colour blue – he became adept at drawing suspense from the use of specific locations. In the scene where Graham visits Lecter, who is played with impressive restraint by Brian Cox, Mann creates tension out of the ascetic white space of the cell, shooting back and forth between Graham and Lecter until the bars separating them no longer exist. Inviting the viewer to draw parallels between the two men, the result is chilling.

Mann's subsequent adaptation of James Fenimore Cooper's *Last of the Mohicans* (1992) is his most entertaining film and an enthralling account of adventure and romance on the American frontier. Displaying virtuoso camerawork from the opening sequence – a lengthy tracking shot through a dense forest that begs comparison with Kurosawa – he revels in the freedom of the landscape. Everything on screen is detailed, particularly during the thrilling battle scenes: the manner in which the weapons are used, how they are handled, and the effect a blow or gunshot would have on the body. As a result, the film rattles along with gusto, aided by Daniel Day-Lewis' passionate performance as Hawkeye. As with *The Keep*, the film is problematised by Mann's approach to history: his reworking of James Fenimore Cooper's novel, replacing the native Uncas with his adopted brother Hawkeye as the central character, attracted accusations of racism.

The telemovie *L.A. Takedown* (1989) can be seen as little more than a warm-up for *Heat*, Mann's sprawling crime epic. Based on a script he developed in the 1970s, the low-budget thriller was a rushed effort, doing little justice to the idea he had originally conceived. Comparing the two now is, as Mann commented, similar to 'comparing freeze-dried coffee with Jamaican Blue Mountain'. For some, *Heat* is the finest example of the heist movie. Pitting Robert De Niro and Al Pacino against each other was a guarantee of generating advance press, industry, and public interest in the film. And much of the film delivers on that promise. An epic cat-and-mouse game between Pacino's super-cop, Vincent Hanna, and De Niro's super-con, Neil McCauley, it features a number of audacious set pieces. The opening armoured car robbery and the climactic bank heist are carried out with precise efficiency; Mann's understanding of the tensions of the contemporary urban landscape adds to the scenes' suffocating tension. The film is also successful for the way it elicits audience sympathy. Both Hanna and McCauley are shown to be the best in their profession and as such exist outside the realm of moral judgement, if not above the rule of law; only those who obstruct their spiritual journey are seen to suffer. That said, the film is ultimately marred by Pacino's over-the-top performance. Verging perilously close to a parody of his intense roles of the 1970s, Pacino's externalised style of acting sits uneasily with the studied direction. Exuding an air of confidence, De Niro fits rather better. Another downside, the film highlights Mann's inability to offer more than mere cursory roles to female characters; but such criticisms had little impact on either the film's box-office results or most critics' opinions.

By any standards, his follow up, *The Insider* (1999), is a remarkable achievement. Based on the true story of Jeffrey Wigand, the vice president of a cigarette company who exposed his board of directors as perjurers for the evidence they gave a court hearing, the film documents the campaign of intimidation that Wigand and his family were subjected to. His only ally was Lowell Bergman, the '60 Minutes' producer, who fought to have his story told. Mann and co-writer Eric Roth produced a screenplay from journalist Marie Brenner's article that succeeds in telling a complex tale of boardroom politics in the form of a fast-paced and engrossing conspiracy thriller. If the best films of the 1970s were by the nature of their subject matter political films, then *The Insider* is one of the first contemporary political films. Recent years have seen power move from the courts and halls of government into the boardrooms, where multinationals decide what constitutes law and the information the media can disseminate. *The Insider* exposes the reality of the political power balance in America and Jeffrey Wigand is portrayed as one of the few beacons of hope in a corrupt system. Russell Crowe is remarkable as the persecuted Wigand, a man whose personal demons contribute to his insecurity as much as the pressures of the situation. Unfortunately, both he and the film are let down by Pacino's showy performance as Bergmann – in the second half he descends into the kind of histrionics that marred *Heat*.

Mann's much-anticipated *Ali* (2001) is something of a disappointment. Tracing the tumultuous years between 1964–74, when Cassius Clay became world champion, changed his name to Muhammad Ali, was stripped of his title for refusing to enlist for the Vietnam conflict, and came back to reclaim it in the historic 'Rumble in the Jungle' fight against George Foreman, the film is too superficial in its analysis of one of the icons of the twentieth century. Will Smith delivers an impressive performance as the heavyweight champion, as do Jon Voight as his television sparring partner, Howard Cosell, and Jamie

Foxx as Drew 'Bundini' Brown. Mann effectively asserts Ali's importance during the period covered, particularly in terms of the race movement – his relationship with Malcolm X is well documented, as is his more complex relationship with Elijah Muhammad and the Nation of Islam – but the details of Ali's personal life are disappointingly sketchy. Furthermore, the handling of his relationships, and the movement of women in and out of his life, is schematic and superficial. For the first time since The Keep, Mann's choice of music is questionable. The use of Marvin Gaye places the film within the context of its time, as do the other hits of the period. However, the rousing accompaniment that builds to a crescendo during the boxing scenes is little better than the manipulative score used in the Rocky series; filmed well, the fight scenes hardly need such irritating music to generate suspense. Nevertheless, Ali is an entertaining, if far from insightful, account of a living legend.

Mann is variously rumoured to be working on a film of 'Miami Vice' and an adaptation of Steven Pressfield's novel 'Gates of Fire'. **IHS**

# Joe MANTELLO

*Love! Valour! Compassion!* (1997)
An established theatre practitioner, Joe Mantello has received a Tony nomination for his performance in 'Angels in America' and has directed several plays, including 'Three Hotels', 'Imagining Brad', and 'The Santaland Diaries'. His only cinema release, Love! Valour! Compassion! (1997), is the adaptation of Terrence McNally's Tony Award-winning play which he also directed off-Broadway.

Organised around three seasonal weekend meetings, which take place between eight gay friends in a country retreat, the cast is made up (with the exception of Jason Alexander) of the actors from the original production. The men, all from different professions and backgrounds, spend their time raking over the past, falling out, flirting and ultimately bonding. Shot essentially in a few locations with wordy dialogue and staged action, the film often betrays its theatrical origins. The piece is performance based and Mantello tends to keep the camera conventionally focused rather than attempting anything new or unusual. At times fun, there is nevertheless an underlying seriousness to the camp proceedings with one of the characters dying of AIDS. Considering Mantello's adequate but uninspiring effort one suspects that he may be a theatre director at heart, keen to foray into cinema this once merely because of his familiarity with, and passion for, the material. **HP**

# Stuart MARGOLIN

*Paramedics* (1987)
*Medicine River* (1994)
*Salt Water Moose* (1996)
*The Sweetest Gift* (1998)
Perhaps most familiar as a television actor, in shows including 'Northern Exposure' and 'The Rockford Files', Stuart Margolin has also found a successful niche as a director. Born in Iowa in 1940, much of his directorial experience has come from the small screen, in episodes for shows including 'The Mary Tyler Moore Show', 'Magnum P.I.', 'Bret Maverick', 'Quantum Leap', 'Northern Exposure', and numerous television movies for Canadian and US networks.

Margolin has also directed several feature films. While his early television work, including Glitter Dome (1984), a police drama set in Hollywood, and the comedy-mystery Paramedics (1987), which was given a theatrical release, was generally formulaic and genre-driven, his more recent films have demonstrated a generous humanity and a knack for detail. Medicine River (1993), a rich and humorous exploration of life on a Canadian reserve, was adapted from Thomas King's novel. With Margolin's gentle, insightful touch, Medicine River tells the story of a successful native photographer who returns home to find himself disconnected from his history and culture. If conventional in structure, Medicine River is innovative in content, challenging and overturning the stereotypes of native peoples perpetuated by a century of Hollywood moviemaking.

Margolin has also directed two excellent family films. Salt Water Moose (1996), set along Canada's magnificent north-eastern coast, tells the story of a boy who comes to the rescue of a stranded moose. The Sweetest Gift (1998), made for the Showtime television network, offers a story about two families' struggles to combat and overcome racial prejudice. Both films won awards for family programming, and The Sweetest Gift was featured at the 1998 Berlin Film Festival. **JS**

# Frank MARSHALL

Frank Marshall is perhaps best known as a highly successful producer although he has also acted and directed three feature films. Born in Los Angeles in 1946 and a graduate of UCLA, Marshall learned his trade as an associate producer in the late 1960s and early 1970s under the auspices of Peter Bogdanovich. However, it was in the 1980s that Marshall blossomed, through what was to be a lasting association with Steven Spielberg and his Amblin Entertainments production company. While working in production capacities on such box-office successes as *Raiders of the Lost Ark* (1981), *E.T. The Extra-Terrestrial* (1982), *Back to the Future* (1985), and *Who Framed Roger Rabbit* (1988), Marshall gained experience as second unit director on *Indiana Jones and the Temple of Doom* (1984), *Back to the Future*, *Empire of the Sun* (1987), *Indiana Jones and the Last Crusade* (1989), and *Always* (1989). Following a promising start, however, Marshall's short directorial career has spiralled downward.

*Arachnophobia* (1990)
*Alive* (1993)
*Congo* (1995)

Spielberg's influence is clearly discernible in Marshall's first feature, the horror/thriller *Arachnophobia* (1990). The film depicts a suburban Californian community terrorised by tiny but fatal Venezuelan arachnids whose mother has immigrated via the coffin of a dead resident and who breeds in an old barn. To this slight premise, Marshall brings a series of heart-pounding scenarios that unabashedly and skilfully exploit the phobic fixations of his audience. Allaying the shocks is a splendid comic turn from John Goodman as a self-absorbed gung-ho pest controller. Such fine balancing was to prove enormously popular with audiences, but it was a formula Marshall turned his back on for his next picture, *Alive* (1993). Set in 1972, *Alive* is loosely based on the 'true' testament of an Andes plane crash survivor. In frozen temperatures, the survivors of the crash await the arrival of a rescue plane only to learn (via radio) that they are presumed dead and the rescue mission abandoned. What follows is the realisation that to stay alive the survivors must feed on the bodies of dead victims. Against a relatively forthright representation of acts of cannibalism, the film focuses on the survivors' ethical dilemma over one of simple survival, which, for all its noble intentions, proved unpopular with audiences reared on more shallow disaster fare.

In *Congo* (1995), Marshall's last picture, such lofty themes are abandoned in favour of a nonsensical action/adventure caper. Based on a Michael Crichton novel, *Congo* plunders every conceivable neo-colonial chestnut as Laura Linney and Dylan Walsh head through a Central Africa predictably in the grips of guerrilla insurrection. The former is seeking to discover the fate of her fiancé, who went before her in search of a flawless diamond, while Walsh is returning a cutesy talking gorilla to its natural habitat. To this, Marshall brings a subplot of global communications skullduggery, a laughable Tim Curry as a Romanian racketeer in search of the lost city of 'Zinge', and a bellowing volcano. Unfortunately Marshall leaves his audience with a movie lacking the wit or charm to distract from such gargantuan absurdity. **TT**

# Gary MARSHALL

In the 1970s Gary Marshall was responsible for producing four of the five top-rated sitcoms on network television in America. In the 1980s he would transcribe the romantic familial formula perfected in such shows as 'Happy Days' and 'Mork and Mindy' to the big screen to even greater financial, if not critical, success. Uncompromisingly stalwart in his approach to film-making Marshall is strictly 'old school' in terms of style and subject matter. Working within the mainstream of the industry, Marshall prefers to direct straightforward romantic comedies and melodramas rather than cutting edge independents or effects-laden blockbusters.

*Young Doctors in Love* (1982)
*The Flamingo Kid* (1984)
*Nothing in Common* (1986)
*Overboard* (1987)
*Beaches* (1988)
*The Lottery* (1989)
*Pretty Woman* (1990)
*Frankie and Johnny* (1991)
*Exit to Eden* (1994)
*Dear God* (1996)
*The Other Sister* (1999)
*Runaway Bride* (1999)
*The Princess Diaries* (2001)

His cinematic directorial debut was in 1982 with *Young Doctors in Love*, a somewhat scatological 'spoof' film in the vein of *Airplane!* (1980). The film draws on Marshall's televisual experience and plays somewhat like an extended sitcom even to the point where a plethora of daytime television soap stars appear in cameo roles including Demi Moore and Sean Young. His next feature, *The Flamingo Kid* (1984), is a congenial and tightly constructed coming of age movie. The film stars Matt Dillon as a working-class Brooklyn kid lured by the superficial lifestyle of the patrons at an exclusive beach club. The film's affability is drawn from the moral choice the boy makes between his own dreams of affluence and his familial sense of honour. As with all good American situation comedies, he eventually learns a universal lesson in life and chooses his family as a foundation for his personal development into maturity.

Marshall's next two features, *Nothing in Common* (1986) and *Overboard* (1987), are lightweight, highly inconsistent and callow comedy/dramas. Marshall plays it safe with these films yet does make some poignant jabs at both the immoral politics contained within the corporate world and within relationships between individuals. These piquant remarks are, however, lost within the schmaltzy formulaic construction of both films.

Undeterred by the lukewarm reception both projects received Marshall continued producing romantically sweet comedies, starting with *Beaches* in 1988. A watershed in terms of financial returns for Marshall the film is a veritable soap opera on celluloid. Bette Midler and Barbara Hershey play two people from different sides of the tracks who form a loving and enduring friendship that sees them through relationships, births and tragedy. Not particularly strong on character or motive this is purely emotive, clichéd storytelling at its best. The film's sole intent and purpose is to wring as many tears as possible from the viewer, which it achieves with some aplomb.

After directing a short entitled *The Lottery* in 1989, Marshall capitalised on the success of *Beaches* with the biggest-grossing film of 1990, *Pretty Woman*. The film would eventually make $435 million for the Disney Corporation and launched the career of Julia Roberts as the lovable hooker befriended by a compassionate tycoon, played by Richard Gere. The film, by drawing on the good girl/bad girl dynamic of classical Hollywood, reaffirms another sitcom moralistic standpoint – that deep down all people are good. Denounced in some quarters as being wholly misogynistic in its depiction of the wealthy man literally reshaping the sexual female, the film nonetheless proved enamouring to the female audience.

The success of *Pretty Woman* was followed in 1991 by *Frankie and Johnny*, a film which, considering its respected front-line cast of Michele Pfeiffer and Al Pacino, performed disappointingly at the box office. Based on the play by Terence McNally, the film is a bittersweet if somewhat trite treatise on loneliness in the city. Hampered by the incredulity of the film's two stars playing hapless, world-weary losers and an overlong, overworked script, the film creates a sense of anticipation that can never be fulfilled. Expectations regarding Marshall's next three projects were completely unfulfilled; indeed, many critics were dumfounded when his comedy of sadomasochistic manners, *Exit to Eden* (1994) was released. One critic described the film as 'a strange cinematic catastrophe' the juxtaposition of S&M culture and comedy proving far too disparate for a discerning audience to swallow. *Dear God* (1996) a superficial and deliberately manipulative Capraesque comedy about a postal worker (Greg Kinnear) who replies to letters addressed to God, was equally dismissed by public and critics alike. Similarly *The Other Sister*, a quasi-comedy about the frustrations of an over-protective mother (Dianne Keaton) and her mentally disabled daughter (Juliette Lewis), failed to illicit much response at the box-office.

Marshall returned to box-office form when he reunited with Julia Roberts and Richard Gere in 1999 for the ill-conceived *Runaway Bride*. Second time around the magic between the two stars does not quite gel and Marshall contents himself by rehashing the good girl/bad girl scenario, which pays little in the way of dividends as Roberts' character is so unerringly unsympathetic. He recently directed *The Princess Diaries* (2001), a family comedy about a San Francisco teenager who finds out that her recently deceased father was a European king. He is rumoured to be considering a sequel to *Pretty Woman*.

Marshall remains one of Hollywood's steadfast directors in terms of theme and content. Unswayed by cinematic trends he remains true to his roots as television producer in that his films are, by and large, moralistic familial comedies. By pandering unashamedly to the basest of emotive responses in his pursuit to produce feelgood films that remain endearing and charming, Marshall remains an anomaly amongst his contemporaries. **PH**

# Penny MARSHALL

*Jumpin' Jack Flash* (1986)
*Big* (1988)
*Awakenings* (1990)

Despite being one of the few female film-makers to make it onto the A-list of Hollywood directors, Penny Marshall's films have been spitefully disparaged for dealing in critically unfashionable genres and mawkish themes. Indeed, the set of terms that surface, regular as clockwork, in writing about Marshall's work – sentimentality, nostalgia, warm-heartedness and innocence – revolve around its *in vitro* evocation of the Coca-Cola and blue-jeans view of America before Vietnam and Watergate intervened in the fantasy. As such, Marshall tends to be either praised for making intelligent films in spite of the vapid exigencies of their genre, validated as one of the more accomplished practitioners of the feelgood movie or, more usually, dismissed as one of the more creatively hackneyed members of the Hollywood hoi polloi.

*A League of Their Own* (1992)
*Renaissance Man* (1994)
*The Preacher's Wife* (1996)
*Riding in Cars With Boys* (2001)

Born in the Bronx, New York City, in 1942, Marshall's father was an industrial film-maker and her mother a dance instructor. After briefly studying at the University of New Mexico and improvising variously as a dance teacher, stunt woman, and bit-part actress, her brother, Garry Marshall, executive producer of 'Happy Days', shoe-horned her into the role of Laverne DeFazio, the spit-curled, tough-talking girlfriend of the show's star, 'The Fonze'. The spin-off vehicle, 'Laverne and Shirley', not only elevated Marshall and co-star Cindy Williams to the higher echelons of the celebrity tree, but afforded Marshall the opportunity to direct. As implied by the title of her forthcoming film, *Riding in Cars with Boys*, although her cinema no longer wears the poodle-skirts and cardigan sweaters buttoned up the back, it does, in spite of its grander pretensions, continue to drip with nostalgia for the optimism represented by post-war prosperity.

One critic described *Jumpin' Jack Flash* (1986), Marshall's debut as a feature director, as 'woefully platitudinous' in its sacrifice of plot and generic coherence to Whoopi Goldberg's comedic set-pieces. It is perhaps ironic, therefore, that her next film, *Big* (1988), which trades in similar comic currency, is not only arguably Marshall's most astute work, but also made her the first female to direct a film that grossed $100 million. Indeed, unlike the inanity of Goldberg's character, it is the adroit oscillation between pathos and humour imbued to potentially cloying material by Tom Hanks' virtuoso performance that sets *Big* apart form Marshall's other films, and what prevents it from shrivelling under the weight of hackneyed optimism. Moreover, one can see in *Big* the elements that delineate Marshall's particular auteurist credo: the exultation of solidarity set against the quasi-ideological maxim that 'anyone can make a difference'; the necessity for self-exploration; and psycho-socio issues of identity politics. These are precisely the elements that her subsequent films retune to their respective emotional pitch.

While the sententious moral didacticism of *Awakenings* (1990) haemorrhages schmaltz, especially from a particularly nauseating and pompous Robin Williams, *A League of Their Own* (1992) represents Marshall's most intelligent articulation of identity politics. Set during World War Two, the film's reclamation of the history of the All American Girls Baseball League situates the sisterhood topos as an axiom of popular feminist politics. *A League of Their Own* is at once a female buddy movie and social comedy. In varying degrees of cliché and dexterity, it engages not only with the feminist histories of the masculine depleted culture that emerged in wartime America, but also, perhaps more interestingly, addresses the thorny issue of the difficulty of female solidarity. However, while on the one hand *A League of Their Own* evokes the past in order to construct a community of women, on the other hand, the film's sentimentalised reposit of that history empty it of precisely the socio-political complexities that make it furtive feminist fodder in the first place. In the end, the film does not have the courage of its own convictions and squanders its political grist in between heavy sentimental millstones.

Marshall's latter-day films have failed to capture either the comic vitality of *Big* or the conceptual intelligence beneath the wish-washy patina of *A League of Their Own*. *Renaissance Man* (1994) repeats the sin of its predecessor by levelling down the history of its military milieu to promote its putative catharsis and ultimately drowns in its own mawkish gushing. *The Preacher's Wife* (1996), a weightless remake of Henry Koster's *The Bishop's Wife* (1947), more directly signals Marshall's taste for less frenzied times. Her most recent film, *Riding in Cars With Boys* (2001), stars Drew Barrymore in the story of a young woman who dreams of becoming a writer but has to cope with raising a son.

Although Marshall's work has never been able to swing free from the dead weight of sentiment, to dismiss her films merely as whimsical nostalgia not only misses the genuine sense of pathos which is present in her best work, but also ignores both the considerable popularity of her films as well as her professional status as one of Hollywood's few female mandarins. **PWa**

# Les MAYFIELD

A graduate of the University of Southern California, Les Mayfield has had a lucrative Hollywood career producing television movies with his own company, ZM Productions. Amongst the many to which he has attached his name are *Psycho IV: The Beginning* (1991), *The Shaggy Dog* (1994), and *The Cape* (1996).

Mayfield began directing feature films with *Encino Man* (1992), a comedy about two teens, Dave (Sean Astin) and Stoney (Pauly Shore), who discover a cave man (Brendan Fraser) in the backyard of the former's southern California home. The teens name him 'Link' (as in missing link) and instruct him in the ways of a slacker high-school senior in an effort to become cool. The sheer stupidity of the film's central narrative is matched by that of its characters. Although Fraser gives an exuberant and energetic performance, Astin is too dull an actor to carry the weight of protagonist. The viewer is asked to suspend disbelief infinitely and the improbabilities mount to such an extreme that it becomes thoroughly impossible to maintain interest. Mayfield's direction is sloppy and completely formulaic, down to the customary musical montage.

The director followed *Encino Man* with *Miracle on 34th Street* (1994), a remake of George Seaton's 1947 classic original. It is the story of Kriss Kringle (Richard Attenborough), otherwise known as Santa Claus, who accepts the position of department-store Santa during the Christmas season while trying to convince a sceptical single mother (Elizabeth Perkins) and her daughter (Mara Wilson) of his veracity. If the film never reaches the depths of *Encino Man*, it is largely because of the positivity of the source material. Mayfield's *Miracle on 34th Street* has a lot of charm and is generally good-natured, if somewhat sentimental. However, a central theme – that of the virtue of the traditional suburban, nuclear family – is dated, and can be read as a manifesto for 'family values' conservatives. Attenborough and Wilson are well-cast, but Mayfield's direction is dull and pedestrian, and his sloppiness shows in a silly drawn-out courtroom conclusion.

*Flubber* (1997) is yet another re-make of a family classic, this time of *The Absent Minded Professor* (1961). Produced for Disney, it is the story of Professor Philip Brainard (Robin Williams), a scientist who invents an alternative energy source that takes the form of a cute, animated ball of 'flying rubber'. He is hoping to use the invention to save his financially strapped college. With a total reliance on computer-generated effects, Mayfield is unable to competently tell a story with *Flubber*, and the two dimensional acting is disconcerting. The film is ridiculously stupid, with little humour, and like *Encino Man* is an insult to the collective intelligence of the audience.

*Blue Streak* (1999) is Mayfield's best work to date. Miles Logan (Martin Lawrence) is a jewel thief involved in a botched robbery. Before being arrested, he hides a large diamond in the ventilation system of a building under construction. When he gets out of jail two years later he finds the building is a police station and he must pose as an officer to get in undetected. However, his incidental involvement in a case and knowledge of criminal activities leads to his being perceived as a 'supercop' by the others. *Blue Streak* is a generic action comedy, but its economy and quick pace, as well as a charismatic performance by Lawrence, make it an enjoyable, if lightweight, piece of entertainment. Dispensing with his usual heavy hand, Mayfield handles action scenes well and without the many clichés that usually sink such films. There is also a refreshing lack of sentiment. His most recent feature, *American Outlaws* (2001), focuses on a young Jesse James, whose resistance to a railroad baron intent on acquiring the land of his hometown, gives birth to the outlaw of American legend.

While Mayfield's career is largely unremarkable, he has enjoyed success with 'making-of' films, directing the short *2010: The Odyssey Continues* (1984), producing 'The Secrets of the *Back to the Future* Trilogy' (1990) for television, and the feature documentary *Hearts of Darkness: A Filmmaker's Apocalypse* (1991).          **DH**

# Paul MAZURSKY

Paul Mazursky, the talented actor-writer-producer-director, has been actively working in film for almost fifty years. Much like his creation Larry Lipinsky in *Next Stop, Greenwich Village* (1976), Mazursky was born in Brooklyn (in 1930), discovered acting, and moved to Greenwich Village and then Hollywood, where he found early success playing toughs in such films as Kubrick's *Fear and Desire* (1953) and *Blackboard Jungle*

(1955). *Next Stop, Greenwich Village* is the first in a comic autobiographical series that betrays a set of concerns which constantly resurface, serving to bind together Mazursky's extensive and varying films: the fear of death coupled with thoughts of suicide, the fear of being revealed to be a fraud, the importance of artifice to survival, and the horrifying depths of reality.

Larry presents the young prototype of the Mazursky protagonist. He is charming, neurotic, young and full of life but only dubiously talented. A policeman catches him in an impromptu public performance and mocks him; a rival actor from the famous Studio (played by Jeff Goldblum) questions his commitment; and his own acting teacher implies that his defensive jokiness will prevent him from developing sufficient sensitivity to be truly great. However, if Larry's focus is on playing Shakespeare, his recitals of the bard's words never attempt to assume the appropriate stature. Larry indeed seems incapable of being truly serious; all difficult and real emotions pass quickly across his face only to be transformed and subsumed in a non-stop patter of references and voices, a kaleidoscope of characters that struggle to achieve pride of place in Larry's attention-deprived mind.

Larry's disengagement is a direct product of his need to preserve himself, from his dingy Brooklyn upbringing in general and from his overbearing, guilt-inducing Jewish mother, wonderfully played by Shelley Winters, in particular. In a sense, then, he's not acting at all; he's simply displaying behaviours long learned. As it turns out, those skills are in demand; it's Larry's hamming and get-along personality that land him his first role, implying that the Hollywood that welcomes him is founded on the same sort of escapism that he learned to practice growing up. Hollywood is in some way a projection of the neurotic personality, an illusion generated to hide realities of frailty, fear, and weakness.

A typical situation in Mazursky films is the encounter with the 'other', what one might have become but for the grace of God. Larry's encounter with the over-serious Goldblum is one such moment, as are the awkward encounters with ex-high-school classmates experienced by Alex (Donald Sutherland) in *Alex in Wonderland* (1970) and Harry Stone (Danny Aiello) in *The Pickle* (1993). Run-ins with the homeless also provide moments of truth, as Harry and Dave (Richard Dreyfuss) in *Down and Out in Beverly Hills* (1986) realise. Harry is a highly successful director who is absolutely convinced that his latest film, also called 'The Pickle', will reveal him to be the fraud he knows himself to be. As his limo rolls to a stop at a New York City street corner, a homeless man picking through garbage looks up at Harry and nods politely; Harry rolls up the window and leans back, looking as if his heart would stop.

All these characters feel palpably how precarious their success is; they are convinced that only luck divides them from being pathetic nobody hangers-on or, worse, demented, homeless and lost. Mazursky's performances are distinguished by never losing sight of this fact. He makes comedies, but his comedies all have a dark underside, which always reveals artifice to be fraud and threatens to send character and film-maker alike back to Brooklyn.

Mazursky is able to tease out these subtle yet pervasive fears by maintaining a tight focus on characters and their interactions. His films are talky, and their humour emerges in the interstices between words. Visual counterpoint and clever cutting play their role, but most of the work is done through longer takes that allow actors to develop their parts improvisationally, a vestige perhaps of Mazursky's early work with the Second City improv troupe. These traits are on evidence in Mazursky's first feature, *Bob & Carol & Ted & Alice* (1969), a relationship comedy satirising the fashionable existential misery of two outwardly successful southern California couples. After taking a weekend retreat, Bob and Carol (Robert Culp and Natalie Wood) decide that their lives are too closed and begin fumbling toward more open and honest relationships. They enlist their best friends Ted and Alice (Elliot Gould and Dyan Cannon) in their quest, talking and playing endlessly with openness in all the forms it occurs to them to try, the culmination of which must be (they decide) an orgy in a hotel room – the ultimate expression of love between two couples.

Their yearnings to be freer are undercut, however, by their basic decency and conservatism. They want to be happier and more honest, and conveniently those traits are in fashion. However, it's precisely the lack of artifice that does them in and returns them to themselves. They play at being liberated, never quite acknowledging that it's not working, until they are confronted with the prospect of transgressing something real

– their friendship. In a hotel room wrapped in each other's arms, they realise finally what their newfound openness implies. Their silent faces – practically the first silence in the film – reveal that once all artifice is removed action is impossible. They recoil, and return chastened to their artificial and essentially happy lives.

The play with artifice jumps to the fore in Mazursky's next effort, the Fellini-esque *Alex in Wonderland*, which features Donald Sutherland as a movie director whose first movie has been previewed and is predicted to be a hit. The mere thought of his newfound fame and wealth has made him miserable and begins to tear down the wall between fantasy and reality, between the artifice of chosen roles and the wilds of imagination. On an airplane flight, he looks up at the trapdoor containing oxygen masks, and then dreams that the plane has crashed and hundreds of dead are strewn across the field. He dreams a trip to Italy, complete with beautiful Italian prostitutes and a meeting with a curt, distracted Fellini (played, in cameo, by Fellini himself). He dreams himself part of a fantasia with masked clerics, and dreams that giraffes are wandering through his children's schoolyard. Alex's confusion spills over into the audience; the transitions to his fantasies are often unmarked, and it's impossible to tell at times whether a scene is occurring in Alex's mind or in his reality. But ultimately, the promise of fame engenders its opposite so completely that to make such distinctions would be to miss the point. To watch the film is to be implicated in the whole motion between these characteristic extremes.

*Enemies: A Love Story* (1989) suggests another root for this necessary movement between escapism and difficult actuality. Herman (Ron Silver) is a Holocaust survivor living a double life in and around New York City in 1949. His wife and children were killed by the Nazis, and he marries Yadwiga (Margaret Sophie Stein), a simple, non-Jewish peasant who had hidden and protected him in Poland. She serves him modestly but adamantly, and is anxious to convert to Judaism and for them to have a child. But Herman also has a mistress, the beautiful Jewess Masha (Lena Olin), a cynical and fiery intellectual who is herself a survivor of the camps. Herman is torn between his commitments to Yadwiga and Masha, perpetuating lies to protect both women and to avoid having to take responsibility either for his actions or for his related fear that God has abandoned the Jews.

His lie is soon complicated by the return of his first wife, Tamara (Anjelica Huston), who after all did not die in the camps. Herman carries out a complicated relationship among all three women, until, inevitably, his various lies are exposed. Though it contains many comic moments, *Enemies* doesn't shrug off its burden lightly. Masha kills herself, and it's implied that Herman knows and lets her do it. He leaves New York, choosing to make a life elsewhere while Yadwiga and Tamara jointly raise Herman's and Yadwiga's infant child. *Enemies* emphasises that the materials out of which Mazursky has crafted his comic works dig deeply into the more difficult, even unspeakable, aspects of the psyche. That he has been able to play these tensions out in comedy suggests that powerful psychological motives and needs necessarily underlie the lightest fare.

As Woody Allen, Mazursky's spiritual cousin, has pointed out, one must distinguish between an act of imagination and an active imagination. Mazursky has clearly cultivated a character upon which to project his preoccupations, as when he plays a suicidal, pathetic version of himself in *2 Days in the Valley* (1996). Unlike Allen, Mazursky never plays himself in his own films, which perhaps makes it more difficult to see his work for what it is: a coherent, autobiographical series much like Allen's. One benefit of insisting on surrogates is that Mazursky is able to take up the same themes as he notices them in the fictional Prospero (*Tempest* (1982)) and the biographical Winchell (*Winchell* (1998)). He is a champion of outsiders, and understands well their characteristics. **JA**

# Jim McBRIDE

The career of Jim McBride, born in New York in 1941, has been marked by a mixture of ambitious but failed projects, a few minor hits, and several more critical and commercial flops. However, his first feature film, *David Holzman's Diary* (1968), remains a provocative, engaging film over thirty years after it was first released. It is the story of a young man with a movie camera who films his life as it unfolds over a period of a few days. The film is simultaneously a brilliant distillation of filmic styles and ideas circulating at the time of its production (specifically, the *cinéma vérité* and Direct

Cinema movements) as well as a subtle tweaking of the self-seriousness of those same two movements. A fiction film which uses the documentary format, the movie follows the eponymous protagonist as he intrusively shoots the events of his daily life. In the process he comes to alienate and infuriate those around him who unwillingly end up as subjects in his movie. The film pokes fun at the principals of *vérité* and Direct Cinema, two non-fiction film-making movements which sought to capture reality in its various guises. The movie constantly confronts the viewer with his or her own voyeuristic pleasure in following Holzman deeper into the personal terrain he so desires to depict yet whose depiction only destroys his own 'real' life. Audiences at the San Francisco International Film Festival booed when the end-credits appeared on-screen to indicate that the film was, in fact, fiction. But *David Holzman's Diary*'s brilliance lay in taking those non-fiction movements to their logical conclusion and further blurring the boundaries between the truths to be found in cinematic representation.

Following *David Holzman's Diary*, McBride returned to familiar terrain with another 'mockumentary'. *My Girlfriend's Wedding* (1969) again used the *vérité* style and documentary format to tell the story of the film-maker's relationship to his girlfriend and her decision to marry another man in order to stay in the United States. The film created a tension between the emotional intensity of the relationship between director and subject, as well as the director's own obsession with capturing a certain kind of objective reality. It was another attempt by McBride to address cinema's potential to challenge audiences to think about the film's, as well their own, relationship to the on-screen images.

McBride then moved away from the semi-documentary format and turned to science fiction with *Glen and Randa* (1971). The story of a teenaged couple living in the aftermath of a nuclear holocaust, the film deals with their efforts to survive, reconstruct the semblance of civilisation, and find their way to Metropolis after they discover a 'Superman' comic book not destroyed in the blast. McBride followed with *Hot Times* (1974), a low-budget comedy about a teenager trying to lose his virginity, which failed to gain much attention or broad distribution. McBride spent the next several years doing odd-jobs and pitching projects until directing *Breathless* (1983), a dismal remake of Jean-Luc Godard's revolutionary 1959 film *A bout de souffle*. Whereas Godard's movie sought to re-invigorate cinema by turning the visual codes of classical narrative film-making against themselves, McBride's remake now seems like an attempt to re-inscribe those same codes and to disavow the original's attempt to create a new cinematic style.

McBride next directed *The Big Easy* (1987), the story of a corrupt yet likeable New Orleans detective and a straight-laced district attorney who fall for each other. The two run into trouble with their friends, family, and the Mob when they try to uncover the source of the now-institutionalised kickbacks. A solid and well-received thriller, McBride coaxed a number of strong performances and utilised a mobile camera, economic cutting, and lively score which captured the distinct flavours of New Orleans. The results briefly catapulted the director onto Hollywood's A-list.

With a larger budget and a high-powered cast, McBride next directed *Great Balls of Fire!* (1989), an adaptation of the meteoric rise and fall of rock 'n' roll pioneer Jerry Lee Lewis. The film's dismal reviews and box-office failure made it difficult for McBride to work again on feature films in Hollywood. Instead he turned to overseas production and television work as a way to continue his directorial career. A series of made-for-TV movies and B-grade thrillers from 1991 to the time of writing would follow. Both *Uncovered* (1994) and *The Informant* (1997) combine a newfound concern for historical periods and settings with the thriller's fascination with police procedure. Despite being relocated to the sphere of the less prestigious made-for-TV movie, McBride has nevertheless managed to maintain a thematic and stylistic consistency in which he attempts to probe the historical, moral, and social 'grey areas' by humanising characters who might otherwise be viewed as evil or corrupt. **MR**

# Dan McCORMACK

Dan McCormack is a director who has yet to touch upon the mainstream. While his two features, *The Minotaur* (1994) and *Other Voices* (2000), have been greeted with acclaim, this Brown University graduate has not broken out of the festival circuit to achieve the sort of alternative cinema stardom of, say, Hal Hartley or Robert Rodriguez. So far, directing has punctuated, rather than superseded, McCormack's day job as a television writer in Los Angeles.

*The Minatour*, his debut, is an odd meditation on celebrity; an interview with its eponymous subject, who embodies the substance-addled, faded days of former fame. A comment on the 'stud' power America inflicts upon its male superstars, this bullish man takes the viewer on a modern baroque journey (fifties kitsch welded to seventies disco abandon), settling an ambivalent gaze on the celebrity phenomenon. An examination of living out the expected hedonism in front of a flashbulb, the Minatour – as one critic has noted, a mix between Elvis and John Belushi – is both bent on his own self-destruction and, at the same time, aware of the fact that he has little self to destruct: he is public property. A truly off-beat piece, *The Minatour* played at the 1994 Sundance Film Festival.

McCormack's second feature, *Other Voices*, also in Dramatic Competition at Sundance, where it was nominated for a Grand Jury Prize, depicts a marriage shot through with jealousy and suspicion. Against a background of dark millennial fervour, the film examines the tension of a present plagued by doubt and a future devoid of both faith and trust.                                                **LW**

# Bruce McDONALD

One of the central figures of the recent Canadian resurgence in feature film-making, Bruce McDonald is known for creating movies with a quirky sense of humour, high energy, and endearing oddball characters. Working closely with writer-director-actor Don McKellar, McDonald has directed a number of well-made films.

Born in Kingston, Ontario, in 1959, McDonald first gained international attention with *Roadkill* (1989), a rock-and-roll road movie that won the Best Canadian Feature award at the 1989 Toronto Film Festival. Co-written by McKellar, the film follows the journey of an assistant rock promoter (Valerie Buhagiar) who is sent to track down a missing band, only to find herself transformed by the strange characters she meets. A similar conceit drives McDonald's *Highway 61* (1991), a movie that traces a trip from Canada to New Orleans taken by two strangers and a corpse. Good-natured and briskly paced, the film was also written by McKellar, who stars along with Valerie Buhagiar.

More ambitious is *Dance Me Outside* (1994), adapted from W.P. Kinsella's stories about a fictional Canadian reserve. This ensemble piece explores a number of interlocking stories. In one, a native woman returns home with her husband, hoping to get pregnant. Another strand follows two teens determined to postpone adulthood, and a third involves a murderer who, after killing a native woman, is given a token jail sentence. Touching, ambitious and funny, if at times uneven, *Dance Me Outside* is a more grounded, insightful, and emotionally expansive work than McDonald's road films.

With *Hard Core Logo* (1996), however, McDonald returned to the road. This mock documentary investigates the reunion tour of a washed-up punk band. The members of the band, seeing their youth and rebellion slipping into the past, struggle to retain their idealism. At its best, *Hard Core Logo* taps into a powerful vein of nostalgia and discontent.

The short film *Elimination Dance* (1998), adapted from a story by Michael Ondaatje and created with McKellar, was popular at festivals, winning awards at Brussels International Festival of Fantasy Film, Cinequest, and the Torino and Santa Monica Film Festivals. McDonald has also directed numerous television movies and programmes. **JS**

# Ross McELWEE

Born in North Carolina in 1947, documentary film-maker Ross McElwee invites the viewer to look deeply at both its subject and his own subjectivity. Through McElwee's tireless examination of his family, friends, and the places where he grew up, we experience how inevitably autobiographical film is. An exploration of McElwee's films is an exploration of his life, as he and the life that he lives become both subject and story, woven into all of his documentaries.

Since the popular reception of *Sherman's March* (1986), the documentary form that evolved from *cinéma vérité* and is often called 'personal documentary' resurged

in the late twentieth century with significant popular interest. *Sherman's March* unites
McElwee's own awkward pursuit to meet the woman he desires, while also vaguely
tracing the steps of Civil War General William Tecumseh Sherman's destructive march
through the Southern US in the final months of the war. McElwee weaves the events of
his own life – his loneliness and the comic escapades intended to relieve his suffering
– with both the historic significance of the route of his journey and the anxieties of the
global politics of the early 1980s. The success of *Sherman's March* was preceded by
films of equal complexity, and was followed by films demonstrating the evolution of
McElwee's themes and strategies for exploring them.

While attending MIT's Film Section in the 1970s, and encouraged by instructor
film-maker Richard Leacock, McElwee completed his first feature film. *Charleen* (1978)
brought to the screen his North Carolina friend and poet Charleen Swansea. While we
are privileged to experience the relationship between an artist and her portrait-maker,
through the presentation of Ms. Swansea, we see a hidden landscape of the South as
understood by one of its women. Equally personal, *Backyard* (1984) is a documentary
that characterises many film-makers' struggles with their family's judgment of career
and lifestyle. McElwee's surgeon father, and doctor-to-be brother, personify the rite
of passing the profession of one generation onto the next. While McElwee reverently
presents his family, he stands as the self-deprecated outsider who puzzles his family
with his odd habit of filming them. In both of these films, we see McElwee responding
to the circumstances of his life, and we hear in his narration his thoughts on what these
events might mean. These characteristics persist throughout his films.

In the early 1990s, McElwee married film-maker Marilyn Levine, and was due to
become a father. What began as a celebration of this life transformation became an
exploration of personal tragedy. In the period of a few months McElwee survived his
father's and grandmother's death, and the miscarriage of his first conceived child. *Time
Indefinite* (1993) is a testimony on mortality, and the means to accept its overwhelming
significance. Indeed McElwee did eventually become a parent and went on to make
another film. *Six O'Clock News* (1997) beckons the question of how we might raise
a child in a world defined by the daily disasters presented in the newscasts of local
television. McElwee travelled across the United States to portray the lives of people who
were the subject of sixty-second sensational news stories. What dignity might have been
deprived in the superficial presentations of local network news, McElwee restores with
the relationships we watch him make with each of these survivors.

Perhaps the most renowned practitioner of the personal documentary in the US,
Ross McElwee allows the viewer to experience the inevitable humanity of the person
who looks through the lens. And in so doing, he uses the cinema as a mirror to see and
understand himself.                                                                    **SSc**

# Scott McGEHEE

Scott McGehee and David Siegel burst onto the American independent scene in
1993 with their effortlessly confident and sophisticated debut feature, *Suture*. Executive produced by Steven Soderbergh, the film concerns Vincent (Michael Harris), a
wealthy, unprincipled dilettante and his estranged identical twin brother, Clay (Dennis
Haysbert), a construction worker. Out of the blue, Clay is invited to spend time with
his brother, unaware that Vincent intends to murder him and assume his identity.
Miraculously, Clay survives a lethal car explosion and is physically reconstructed, but
as Vincent. Troubled and confused, Clay attempts to disengage the enigma of his past
with the help of various doctors and psychologists but finds himself at the centre of a
murder enquiry. Meanwhile, the real Vincent is desperately plotting another attempt
on his brother's life.

Shot in sumptuous black and white, *Suture* combines the classic themes of the
hardboiled, film noir genre – murder, amnesia and mistaken identity – and gives them a
knowing post-modern spin, creating a smart and cerebral but hugely enjoyable media-
tion on psychoanalytical (particularly Lacanian) theories of identity and self. Visually, it
is strikingly accomplished for a first film, with keen composition and *mise-en-scène*, and
features wonderful performances from Harris and Haysbert, both of whom have since
been employed to ill effect. There are numerous humorous touches – such as a doctor
named after René Descartes – but the masterstroke is having the identical twins played

by black and white actors. In a film in which nothing and nobody is what they seem, it makes perfect sense.

Fans of *Suture* – of which there were many – had to wait some eight years to see if the first film's combination of taut narrative and intelligence was just a happy coincidence. Fortunately, *The Deep End* (2001) proved that it was not. Tilda Swinton gives a career best in this update of Max Ophuls' *The Reckless Moment* (1949) as Margaret Hall, the Lake Tahoe mother of a young gay man who is involved in the accidental murder of his older lover. Believing that she is protecting him from the legal consequences, Margaret dumps the body in the lake but finds herself held to ransom by an unscrupulous stranger who knows of the connection between the corpse and her son.

Like *Suture*, *The Deep End* (a reference not to the lake itself but to an aquatically themed club) chooses to take an inventive detour around the conventions of the thriller genre – as indeed did Ophuls' original, which is something of a key film for feminist critics – adding issues of sexuality to the simmering treatise on matriarchal instincts and morality. Shot in widescreen, highly coded use of colour signifies emotion and physical and metaphorical locations, demonstrating McGehee and Siegel's fondness for visual motifs. Tremendously assured, it is a highly palatable piece of entertainment that manages to work through highbrow ideas without pretension. **JWo**

# Jim McKAY

In a relatively short time, Jim McKay has become a central figure in New York's thriving independent film scene. Through his production company C-Hundred Film Corp. (formed with Michael Stipe), McKay has supported numerous emerging film-makers, including Chris Smith (*American Movie*, 1999), Hannah Weyer (*La Boda*, 2000), Jem Cohen (*Benjamin Smoke*, 1999), and Tom Gilroy (*Spring Forward*, 1999). McKay is also an advocate for film-makers as a member of the board of directors of the Association of Independent Video and Film-makers.

However, McKay's most important work has been done behind the camera. After directing numerous music videos, McKay turned to feature film-making, and his first two efforts – *Girls Town* (1996) and *Our Song* (2000) – demonstrate a distinctive aesthetic, combining fly-on-the-wall realism with the restraint (and long master shots) of the Japanese transcendentalists. McKay's camera is observant but never obtrusive, and he uses it as a political weapon, revealing a misrepresented and misunderstood subculture: urban teenage girls.

*Girls Town*, a multiple award-winner at the 1996 Sundance Film Festival, forgoes dramatic devices and clichés to provide an honest, sometimes wrenching portrayal of teenage life. The film is immersed in the lives of three high-school seniors – a single mother trying to pass her final classes, a tough, Columbia-bound scholar, and a sensitive African-American poet – who struggle to come to terms with the death of a friend. Over the course of a few weeks the three absorb, and seek to counteract, some of the harsh socio-political realities that many teens encounter as they move into adulthood.

McKay completed his second film, *Our Song*, in late 1999. Created in collaboration with its young cast, *Our Song* visits a housing development in Brooklyn's Crown Heights neighbourhood, focusing on four girls who juggle jobs and social lives, wrestling with issues that may define the course of their lives. More accomplished and ambitious than *Girls Town*, the film seems to move organically from one poetic moment to the next, as in the exquisite closing credits sequence, which isolates two friends as they travel into separate futures.

Taken together, *Girls Town* and *Our Song* represent the work of a committed and engaged activist-artist who recognises the power of the moving image to communicate deeper and socially significant truths. **JS**

# Don McKELLAR

The list of people Don McKellar has worked with reads like a Who's Who of Canadian cinema. He has acted in at least 22 films, among them films from David Cronenberg (*eXistenZ* (1999)), Patricia Rozema (*When Night Is Falling* (1995)), François Girard (*Thirty-Two Short Films About Glenn Gould* (1993), *The Red Violin* (1998)), and Atom Egoyan (*The Adjuster* (1991), *Exotica* (1994)). He co-wrote both the Girard films, was involved in at least five films at the 1998 Toronto International Film Festival, and recently staked his claim as an important writer-director with the release of his debut feature, *Last Night* (1998).

Born in Toronto in 1963, McKellar began his career in theatre and moved to directing film with *Blue* (1991), a short featuring David Cronenberg as a pornography addict working in a carpet factory. McKellar's other shorts include *The Bloody Nose* (1992) and, as co-writer, *Elimination Dance* (1998). If these suggest that McKellar is at his best with low-key, intimate and guardedly upbeat subject matter, *Last Night*, made for the French '2000, Seen By' series (the millennium seen from ten different national perspectives), offers further confirmation. While Hollywood saw the millennium as an opportunity for apocalyptic bluster, McKellar's slight riposte to such multi-million dollar millennial clunkers as *Armageddon* (1998) and *Deep Impact* (1998) hones in on a group of characters filling the six hours until the world's end.

McKellar offers no reason for the apocalypse, and we quickly note an accompanying absence of asteroids, mile-wide UFOs and stern-jawed heroes. Without such crowd-pleasing histrionics, McKellar's sometimes sombre, sometimes witty hymn to human longing freely prioritises people over pyrotechnics, with a concomitant emotional potency capped by the use of Pete Seeger's buoyant 'Guantanamera' over the closing credits (trust the co-writer of the two Girard films mentioned to use music so well). Buoyancy might sound odd in such apocalyptic fare but, despite charges of bourgeois sterility, McKellar's coup lies in blending a wry detachment towards family life, sexual obsession and vocation – Cronenberg plays a gas company executive intent on thanking all his clients from A to Z before the world ends – with warm compassion.

Deservedly, *Last Night* scooped the Prix de la Jeunesse at Cannes, 1998. McKellar may yet become one of Canadian cinema's key figures – if he is not already.     **KH**

# David McNALLY

Born in 1960 in Montreal, David McNally dropped out of college to tour with Canadian rock band The Pinups, going on to make music videos and commercials. His 'lobster' advert for Budweiser attracted Jerry Bruckheimer's attention and McNally became his prodigy; Bruckheimer, infamous for producing high-concept films such as *Con Air* (1997) and *Armageddon* (1998), has his signature all over *Coyote Ugly* (2000), McNally's feature debut.

*Coyote Ugly* (2000)

It is reported that Julia Roberts used to work at a real-life 'Coyote Ugly' and perhaps for this reason alone a poor-man's Julia Roberts, Piper Perabo, plays Violet, the film's central character. A wannabe songwriter for 'Whitney, Mariah, whoever...', she leaves New Jersey and ends up working in the bar. As well as counting her tips in a mini-skirt at four in the morning in a back alley, unmolested, she also meets the nicest guy in New York, an Australian played by Adam Garcia, who helps her tackle her stage fright. The film smacks of *Showgirls* (1995), *Cocktail* (1988), and *Flashdance* (1983); with a harder edge, and any exploration of character, *Coyote* could have been a reasonable film. Although the music moves the movie along at a cracking pace, characterisation is minimal, and the join-the-dots plot is clichéd. The comic dialogue – which includes the line 'I don't care if they pay in lobster, I'm not sticking my hand in that fishy bin' – is risible. Bruckheimer may have perfected his money-making methods by finding music video and commercial directors to direct his action movies but scenes in *Coyote Ugly* that have dramatic potential are sorely neglected.

*Down & Under*, slated to begin shooting in 2003, is the next McNally/Bruckheimer effort in which two friends get caught up with the Mob and are forced to deliver $100,000 to Australia where the money is lost to a wild kangaroo.     **FG**

# John McNAUGHTON

John McNaughton is a director with a powerful personal vision. It is his ability to tap into the darker side of human nature and his legendary black humour that make his films so honest, so frightening and so mesmeric.

*Henry: Portrait of a Serial Killer* (1986)
*The Borrower* (1991)
*Sex, Drugs, Rock & Roll* (1991)
*Mad Dog and Glory* (1993)

Born in Chicago in 1950 to a factory worker and a seamstress, McNaughton graduated from college in 1972 and worked in factories, then in an ad agency and a travelling carnival show. Upon his return to Chicago he teamed up with producer-musician Steve

Jones and, at the behest of video distributor Waleed B. Ali, contrived to make a low-budget horror film.

Influenced by a 20/20 documentary on Texas serial killer Henry Lee Lucas, McNaughton and co-writer Richard Fire aimed to 'take the audience inside the mind of a man who has absolutely no conscience or empathy'. Their achievement is self-evident in *Henry: Portrait of a Serial Killer* (1986), the most chilling psychological profile of a murderer since Hitchcock's groundbreaking archetype. Beginning with a montage of bodies and ending with another victim stuffed inside a suitcase, it accompanies ex-con Michael Rooker as he goes to live with prison acquaintance Tom Towles and coaches him in the techniques of slaying. More suggestive than grotesque (although certain killings take a strong stomach), the detachment and documentary realism are what really make *Henry* so scary. Unlike Anthony Hopkins' suave and enigmatic Lecter from *Silence of the Lambs* (1991), Rooker is no flashy anti-hero; indeed, it is the very monotony of his existence that animates him so, and the motiveless slaughter that repulses. Providing no sympathetic characters, nor any punishment for the crimes committed, *Henry* was given the dreaded X certificate by the MPAA who cited 'moral' grounds. It remained unreleased four years after its completion in 1986, and even then was only granted a limited run before Charles Parello brought it to a wider audience. Ironically, it did receive massive critical acclaim, with nominations for several festival awards and top choice listings.

McNaughton's next film, *The Borrower* (1991), a cheap sci-fi nasty with film school effects, also languished on the shelves for some time: a consequence of Atlantic Films' collapse rather than objections to its content. This unintentionally mirthful tale of a banished alien who must 'borrow' heads from the people of Earth because his own has exploded, is a complete about-face for the director – his one and only experiment with so-called 'splatter' horror.

It was his movie version of Eric Bogosian's one-man off-Broadway show, *Sex, Drugs, Rock & Roll* (1991), that established McNaughton in the major leagues, and so for *Mad Dog and Glory* (1993) the director found himself working with heavyweights Robert De Niro, Bill Murray, and Uma Thurman.

The television disaster 'Girls in Prison' followed in 1994, then two exceptional features. *Normal Life* (1996), the first, tracks the affair of a quixotic cop (Luke Perry) and his unstable girlfriend/wife, Ashley Judd, who encourages him to start robbing banks when he loses his job. Derived from a true story again, this descent into self-delusion and self-destruction is an admirable appetiser for *Wild Things* (1998). From its metaphorical opening, juxtaposing the alligator-infested swamps of Florida with the shiny skyscrapers of Miami, it hints at danger below the superficiality, of recondite desires and Daedalian plot twists worthy of *The Usual Suspects* (1995). Nothing is to be taken for granted in this story of rape, murder and betrayal starring Matt Dillon, Neve Campbell and Denise Richards – with credit due to Stephen Peters, whose Byzantine script is still revealing secrets during the closing credits sequence.

McNaughton's more recent projects have included *Condo Painting*, a documentary about New York-based artist George Condo, made in 1998 but not released until 2000, a TV chronicle of ganster Meyer Lansky's life, told in flashback by Richard Dreyfuss as Lansky senior; and *Speaking of Sex*, a comedy which lambastes prudish attitudes towards sex and relationships through the device of marriage guidance counseling, which is yet to be distributed.                                                      **PB**

# John McTIERNAN

John McTiernan is a director of lovingly-crafted action thrillers who has a reputation for consistently setting the standards others must follow. Headstrong and meticulous, he excels at making the films he would like to see himself. Some call them 'boys' adventures', others simply cinematic spectacle.

McTiernan was born in New York in 1951, educated at Juilliard and, in due course, attended the American Film Institute. He initially wanted to be a theatre director, but was swayed toward film by François Truffaut's *Day for Night* (1973). McTiernan honed his skills making commercials and films for television, before writing and directing *Nomads* (1986). Reminiscent of 'The Fugitive' television series, it boasts the acting talents of Pierce Brosnan as a derelict, and Lesley-Anne Down as the doctor who discovers his mysterious secret. A serviceable start, *Nomads* was followed by his first big-budget studio movie, *Predator* (1987).

(1999)

*The 13th Warrior* (1999)

*Rollerball* (2002)

Riding on the short-lived wave of Vietnam war films, such as the previous year's *Platoon* and Kubrick's *Full Metal Jacket* (1987), this movie takes the familiar iconography of soldiers in the jungle and grafts on a science fiction narrative about an invisible alien hunter. As a decisively flagrant morality tale aimed at blood sports supporters, it is hard to take seriously. However, the innovative use of thermal point-of-view, the almost unbearable suspense, and the prospect of Arnold Schwarzenegger actually facing a far superior foe accounts for some of its appeal.

McTiernan sustained this level of intensity with one of the most influential action pictures of recent years. *Die Hard* (1988) is a film the director likens to 'A Midsummer Night's Dream' (on festival night all the fools become princes and vice versa), and offers Bruce Willis an opportunity to shine away from the relative safety of his TV show 'Moonlighting'. The basic western premise of lone gunman against a gang of outlaws translates into this modern-day thriller – this time the windswept town becomes a tower block. Part disaster movie (in reverence to *The Towering Inferno* (1974)), part heist film, part high-octane 'shoot 'em up', the action only heightens the suspense rather than overwhelming it. One drawback is the narrow-minded script, which seems intent on propagating out-dated myths about feminism wrecking family life and Europeans being untrustworthy. However, *Die Hard* made McTiernan a major player in Hollywood.

*The Hunt for Red October* (1990), adapted from Tom Clancy's international bestseller, endeavours to be a symbiotic political/action film but actually succeeds in being neither. Instead, continual switching from the tense underwater scenes involving a rogue Russian submarine commander (Sean Connery) to the planning of his capture on dry land guarantees that the film veers off course. Excepting Connery's performance, the characters seem trite and unmotivated, which is unfortunate because in every other respect the authenticity is first rate (thanks in no small part to a full-scale submarine set that could roll and tilt for the battle scenes).

Connery also starred in *Medicine Man* (1992), a misinformed attempt to exploit ecological awareness in the early 1990s and a chance for McTiernan to try something different. Unfortunately there is little scope for him here, this being the lacklustre story of a scientist in a remote African jungle, working towards finding the cure for cancer. The only point at which it becomes engaging is when Connery makes his way through the jungle's network of rope riggings (which actually repudiate the conservation message), or as his leading lady Lorraine Bracco dangles on a branch above a gorge, but even these sequences seem forced. A bid to recreate the magic of films like Bogart's *The African Queen* (1951), this only proves that McTiernan should remain within the genre to which he is most suited.

*Last Action Hero* (1993) is McTiernan's second Schwarzenegger vehicle and signals another downturn in his fortunes. A self-referential, postmodern jumble of cinema in-jokes, this awkward parody of the action films that made them both famous completely misses its mark, possibly because the genre has already become a parody of itself. Its fantastical 'plot' (used before to greater effect in Woody Allen's *The Purple Rose of Cairo* (1985)) hinges on one idea alone. Because the juvenile jokes jar uncomfortably with some of the more adult concepts (such as the stealing of a corpse at a funeral and the escape of a malicious axe murderer) a dichotomy is created which the film never adequately resolves.

Thankfully, *Die Hard with a Vengeance* (1995) sees McTiernan back on his old form. His refusal to make a carbon copy of his own original elevates this above the standard of Renny Harlin's first sequel. Using the whole of New York as his exclusive playground, McTiernan this time pits Willis against a mad bomber with a grudge and a hidden agenda (Jeremy Irons). But any sense of *déjà vu* is offset by the inclusion of Samuel L. Jackson as Willis' unwitting – and unwilling – shopkeeper partner, an ingenious departure from the buddy-cop blueprint. An astute, capable action movie which doesn't take itself too seriously, *Die Hard with a Vengeance* is a fitting valediction to the trilogy.

*The Thomas Crown Affair* (1999) is an equable revision of the Steve McQueen film from 1968. Arguably better than its forebear (with Faye Dunaway connecting the two), it is certainly as polished and reunites McTiernan with Pierce Brosnan after a gap of thirteen years. Brosnan oozes sophistication as Crown, the bored billionaire who masterminds an improbable art theft, while Rene Russo is the insurance investigator who apparently falls for his charms. More thought-provoking than McTiernan's usual fare, its major failing lies in the fact that it is difficult to appreciate Crown's ennui.

Quite different in tone, *The 13th Warrior* (1999), which stars Antonio Banderas, is a refreshingly unconventional historical adventure based on a novel by Michael Crichton and set in tenth-century Northern Europe. McTiernan's most recent venture is an updating of Norman Jewison's *Rollerball* (1975), the vehement future-sport movie starring James Caan. Featuring LL Cool J and Chris Klein, it has been universally panned.                                                                                                    **PB**

# Christopher McQUARRIE

*The Way of the Gun* (2000)  Film is a director's medium, and even for a writer of Christopher McQuarrie's calibre, the lure of the director's chair seems irresistible. Best known for his collaborations with director Brian Singer (with whom he attended high school), having written *Public Access* (1993) and the Academy Award-winning *The Usual Suspects* (1995), McQuarrie recently moved into direction with the provocative *The Way of the Gun* (2000).

His stories use convoluted structures, multiple viewpoints, and a host of narrative twists and techniques to experiment with the conventions of the crime caper. *Public Access* (1993) follows a sociopathic anti-hero who sets out to corrupt a small-town through public access television, and explores some provocative ideas about middle American values, but it was the narrative invention and dynamite conclusion of *The Usual Suspects* (1995), in which five criminals try to discover the identity of the master criminal who connects them, that marked McQuarrie out as a major talent. *The Way of the Gun* deliberately strips the crime film of its Hollywood gloss, following two low-grade criminals who hold a pregnant woman to ransom, only to discover that she is carrying the surrogate child of a mob boss. McQuarrie ties up his ensemble of characters in a web of ulterior motives and double-crosses, and shows a flair for non-verbal narrative, using editing and the talents of his cast to great effect. Movie clichés, like the car chases, Mexican stand-offs, and climactic shoot-out are given a realistic twist – bullets look like they hurt, and the good guys, as in real life, just don't exist – but the lack of sympathetic characters, constantly shifting perspectives and amoral stance make for a curiously empty spectacle. McQuarrie is as smart as they come, but cinema should be more than a simply intellectual exercise.                                                                                     **OB**

# Peter MEDAK

*Negatives* (1968)  Peter Medak was born in Budapest in 1937 and emigrated to England in 1956,
*The Ruling Class* (1972)  where he worked as a sound and film editor, second assistant director (Hammer's
*A Day in the Death of Joe Egg*  *Captain Clegg* in 1962), second unit director and associate producer (Jack Smight's
(1972)  *Kaleidoscope* (1966)). His directorial debut, *Negatives* (1968), concerned an odd,
*Ghost in the Noonday Sun*  unmarried couple who pattern themselves on the murderous Dr Crippen (previously the
(1973)  subject of three films, one British) and his wife. The mutability of identity is a theme
*The Odd Job* (1978)  found again in Medak's adaptation of Peter Barnes' black comedy, *The Ruling Class*
*The Changeling* (1980)  (1972). Peter O'Toole stars as the 14th Earl of Gurney, whose legacy is incumbent on
*Zorro, the Gay Blade* (1981)  his family convincing him that he is not, as he believes himself to be, Jesus Christ. The
*The Men's Club* (1986)  family's exhaustive efforts pay off and O'Toole ends the film not only believing himself to
*The Krays* (1990)  be Jack the Ripper, but racking up the body count to support the delusion.
*Let Him Have It* (1991)       Filmed prior to, but released after *The Ruling Class*, was *A Day in the Death of Joe*
*Romeo is Bleeding* (1993)  *Egg* (1972), Medak's adaptation of Peter Nichols' stage play, in which Alan Bates and
*Pontiac Moon* (1994)  Janet Suzman consider the mercy killing of their handicapped child. Medak's lighthearted
*Species II* (1998)  follow-up, the 1973 pirate comedy *Ghost in the Noonday Sun*, was sabotaged from
within by the tantrums of star Peter Sellers, who fired his producers, antagonised co-star Anthony Franciosa, and issued the mid-production dictum that his character's name of 'Jack Scratch' be changed for fear of reprisals from the Devil. Despite the desperation hiring of Sellers' ex-Goon pal Spike Milligan to heighten the comic possibilities of the disastrous production, the film could not be saved and was barely released by Columbia, which wrote the debacle off as a tax loss.

Medak then concentrated on television assignments before teaming up with Monty Python trouper Graham Chapman for 1978's *The Odd Job*, in which a suicidal man hires an assassin to do the deed for which he has no courage; when Chapman changes his mind, the hitman is less easily persuaded with predictably madcap results. More television assignments followed before Medak's next theatrical release, the contemporary ghost story, *The Changeling* (1980). George C. Scott starred as a composer mourning the loss of his wife and daughter but haunted by the ghost of another child, long dead and possibly murdered, when he retires to a rural mansion. A mature and eerie study in loneliness and accountability, the film is still avidly discussed among genre fans as an example of the Victorian ghost story successfully translated to the big screen.

Medak's next theatrical release was an extreme about-face from such grim meditations – 1981's *Zorro, the Gay Blade*, which was an attempt to fashion another lucrative comedy for star George Hamilton in the wake of his unexpected success with the Dracula spoof *Love At First Bite* (1979). Following the cool reception of this problematic lampoon, Medak delved into half a decade of undistinguished television assignments before his return to feature films with the curious *The Men's Club* (1986). Based on the novel by Leonard Michaels (who also scripted), the film – about a cadre of male friends who form their own encounter group, with ruinous complications – was a box-office non-starter despite an exceptional cast that included Harvey Keitel, Richard Jordan, Roy Scheider, Stockard Channing, and Jennifer Jason Leigh.

True to form, Medak again retreated to television, directing episodes of several American series, before his return to cinema with a pair of remarkable dramas based on true events in British crime. *The Krays* (1990) was about the infamous twins who ruled the London underworld during the 1960s (played here by Spandau Ballet's Martin and Jeremy Kemp, with Billie Whitelaw as their frighteningly protective mother). *Let Him Have It* (1991) focused on the 1950s execution of Derek Bentley (Chris Eccleston) for his involvement in the shooting death of a British bobby (the episode also inspired the Elvis Costello song, 'Let Him Dangle'). Tom Courtney and Eileen Atkins provided solid support as Bentley's troubled parents. Perhaps encouraged by the positive critical response of these two films, Medak continued with two offbeat, unconventional projects – the blackly comic neo-noir *Romeo is Bleeding* (1993) and the family drama *Pontiac Moon* (1994). Although capably directed and well cast, neither production was a critical or popular success, and Medak's only other theatrical film to date is *Species II* (1998), a crass sequel to a dumb, violent and poorly-received science fiction film about a murderous mutant running rampant in Los Angeles.          **RHS**

# Deepa MEHTA

Known best for the features she shot in India, *Fire* (1996) and *Earth* (1998), Deepa Mehta's film-making is marked by her trans-nationality. Born in Amritsar, India in 1950, she has lived in Canada since 1973. The daughter of a film exhibitor, her own films combine the accessible style of the Hindi popular cinema of her youth with challenging subject matter.

*Sam & Me* (1991)
*Camilia* (1995)
*Fire* (1996)
*Earth* (1998)

Mehta's film training began on the job when she abandoned philosophy to join a documentary production company in Delhi. Establishing Sunrise Films in Toronto with her husband and brother, she continued to make documentaries but also children's programming and episodic television. *Martha, Ruth & Edie* (1987), produced and co-directed by Mehta for television, initiated her move into drama. The personally-inspired *Sam & Me* (1991), which she co-produced as well as directed, was her first feature. A wry, poignant, but unsentimental story, *Sam & Me* tells of the friendship that develops between Nik, a young Indian immigrant, and Sam, the feisty Jewish octogenarian who is put in his care. Initiating the themes of tolerance for difference and revolt against constraint which run throughout her films, Nik and Sam's friendship develops from their shared outsider status and pleasure in small moments of freedom. Mehta developed the scenario with Ranjit Chowdhry who plays Nik, and also appears in most of her films. Mehta's is a repertory style: she works as often as possible with the same actors and creative team.

*Sam & Me* won the Honorable Mention in the Camera d'Or (first feature category) at Cannes in 1991 and an offer to direct one, and later the final, episode of George Lucas' television series, 'The Young Indiana Jones Chronicles' – 'Benares' (1992) and *Travels With Father*, a movie of the week. Lucas' support and respect encouraged Mehta to trust the director-for-hire role. She was thus pleased to be chosen to direct *Camilla* (1994), starring Bridget Fonda and Jessica Tandy in her last part. The story focuses on Camilla (Tandy), who enlists Freda's (Fonda) help in escaping her well-intentioned but controlling son. They travel to Toronto, ostensibly to relive Camilla's success as a violinist, but also to rendezvous with the man she left behind long ago. Camilla's example gives Freda the courage to realise her own dreams. More sentimental than *Sam & Me*, *Camilla*'s lack of success was blamed on Mehta, who countered that she was not given the final cut; she decided to never again lose control over her films.

Feeling restricted by rules governing Canadian subsidies, Mehta returned to India to finance her films herself. She wrote, produced and directed *Fire* (1996), about a lesbian relationship that develops within a middle-class extended Hindu family. Celebrated actor Shabana Azmi plays Radha, the self-sacrificing wife who is seduced into love by Sita, her younger and equally unhappy sister-in-law, played by Mehta's discovery, Nandita Das. Hindu fundamentalists in India responded to Mehta's message by setting fire to theatres. However, Mehta claims that *Fire* was not a lesbian film but rather a film about choices. Visually more studied than any of her previous films (Mehta chose a colour palette based on the Indian flag), *Fire* is also more textured and sensual. The lovemaking takes place within mosquito netting's diaphanous white cocoon, while the tan glow of the women's skin echoes the saffron of a sari billowing in the wind, the metaphor in an earlier scene of their growing love.

In *Earth* (1998), her subsequent film, Mehta recounts the 1947 Partition of India into Muslim and Hindu states. Basing her script on Pakistani Parsi writer Bapsi Sidhwa's 'Cracking India', Mehta places a cross-ethnic love triangle against the historical canvas of communal violence. Shanta, the Hindu nanny (sensually played by Nandita Das), is loved by two men – Masseur, whom she eventually chooses, and his rival, Ice Candy Man, both Muslims. Mehta adopts the earth tones of India, but the film is also more 'Indian' in its music production values and its acquiescence to Bollywood's star system. Here, however, Aamir Khan as Ice Candy Man is more than a Bollywood heart-throb. Transforming himself from entertainer and seducer to villain, his performance is chilling as he reiterates Mehta's theme of tolerance for difference.

Mehta intended to complete *Fire* and *Earth* with *Water* to make a trilogy, but violent attacks again by Hindu extremists forced her to halt production early in 2001. Currently in Canada, she is completing the comedy *Bollywood Hollywood* and plans to begin production of an adaptation of Alice Walker's novel 'By the Light of My Father's Smile' for Columbia-Tri-Star, again as a director for hire.                                    **JL**

# Eric MENDELSOHN

*Judy Berlin* (1999) Before *Judy Berlin* (1999), his directorial feature debut, Eric Mendelsohn had acted as a costume designer on several Woody Allen films. The influence of Allen's *Manhattan* (1979) is visible in Mendelsohn's film (which he also wrote), not least in the monochrome rendition of a particular aspect of New York life.

Unlike Allen's film, however, it plays not against the romantic vistas of the Big Apple but in a suburban milieu where hope fades in the face of reality. This is epitomised by a would-be actress (Edie Falco) and failed film-maker (Aaron Harnick) whose lives converge during an eerily protracted solar eclipse. The sparse narrative and deliberate, slow pace imbue the film with a reflective quality, which is served further by bittersweet comedy. However, the cosmic significance of the eclipse metaphor is tempered by the sometimes affectionate portrayal of intertwining, middle-class, suburban dreams. The film earned the Best Director award at the 1999 Sundance Film Festival.          **NJ**

# Sam MENDES

*American Beauty* (1999) With his debut feature, *American Beauty*, Sam Mendes became the directing sensation
*The Road to Perdition* (2002) of 1999. Born in Gloucestershire, UK, in 1965, he began his stellar career directing theatre, most notably at The Donmar Warehouse in London, and like many stage directors, was keen to transfer his skills to the cinema. Rather unusually, with just two features to his name, he has already displayed an acute cinematic sensibility.

Based on a screenplay by Alan Ball (writer on the sitcom 'Cybil'), *American Beauty* received almost unanimous critical praise, winning a handful of Academy Awards in March 2000, including Best Screenplay, Director and Picture. Focusing on fortysomething Lester Burnham, the film charts his suburban, disaffected meltdown and the subsequent rekindling of his passion for life and desire to live urgently (albeit with some cynicism). A quintessentially American theme, its sentiments have been travailed many times over in other artistic works such as Sinclair Lewis' novel 'Babbitt'. The film's constant motifs of the red rose (an American Beauty) and the colour red provide a vibrant contrast to the softer, inoffensive pastel tones. Mendes demonstrates real confidence in crafting sequences and juxtaposing them – the heart of the film, which revolves around the poetic footage of a plastic bag caught on the breeze, is pitted against the bitter comedy of the dinner scene immediately afterwards. Mendes' theatrical background also results in universally strong performances. Narratively, dramatically, and in its *mise-en-scène*, the film achieves a sense of wholeness. Initially brittle and cynical, it is ultimately warm and generous. The onscreen action is complemented by one of the strongest music scores of recent years composed by Thomas Newman, which has found a life beyond the movie.

Mendes' cinema career carries a rare promise for a British director working abroad, similar to that of Ridley Scott and Alan Parker in their early days. His second feature, *The Road to Perdition* (2002), is based on Max Allan Collins' graphic novel. Starring Tom Hanks and Jude Law, it is set during the Prohibition era in Chicago.                    **JC**

# James MERENDINO

Born in New Jersey in 1967, James Merendino is a writer-director with a number of low-budget straight-to-video B-movies to his credit. He began his career as director on the fourth film in the Witchcraft series, *Witchcraft IV: The Virgin Heart* (1992), a story of rock musicians who are selling their souls to the Devil for fame and fortune, which was co-written with Michael Paul Girard. He also wrote the screenplay for the fifth film in the Witchcraft series, *Witchcraft V: Dance with the Devil* (1993), directed by Talun Hsu.

*SLC Punk!* (1999)
*Magicians* (2000)
*Amerikana* (2001)

Merendino followed this with another horror movie, *The Upstairs Neighbour* (1994), a tribute to the director Roman Polanski. The film, which plays more as a black comedy than a horror film, was shot on a budget of only $100,000 and is about the paranoia of being stalked by a Satan-worshipper in Los Angeles. *Hard Drive* (1994), a thriller with a typical film noir double crossing, was co-written with Leo Damian, who also appears in the film as Will, a murder suspect and former child star who searches for comfort in computer relationships.

Terrified (1995), Merendino's subsequent film, is a thriller co-written with Megan Heath, which features Heather Graham as Olive, who has been having a rough time. Her husband committed suicide after having killed her lover and she then finds her work colleagues are talking about her, someone is following her, and someone keeps breaking into her apartment, yet the police refuse to take her seriously. *Livers Ain't Cheap* (1997), shot with a bigger budget of $2.5m, is a crime film with James Russo as Rupert, a small-time crook trying to do the right thing; however, when his younger brother gets into trouble and needs a new liver, Rupert brings together his old gang and plans a heist on New Years Eve. *A River Made to Drown In* (1997), was the first film Merendino had directed from someone else's screenplay – Paul Marius, who also appears in the film. The story examines relationships between young male prostitutes and their much older clients and features Richard Chamberlain as an aging lawyer with AIDS who wishes to spend his last days with two young hustlers, the only people he loved. Merendino was not credited as director on this film, the credit instead going to Alan Smithee, a sure sign that he was not happy with the finished product.

Merendino's next film, *SLC Punk!* (1999), is perhaps his best to date and the one for which he has gained most critical acclaim. Starring Matthew Lillard (Stevo) and Michael Goorjian (Heroin Bob), it is about growing up in Salt Lake City, Utah in the mid-1980s and the influence of punk rock on the lives of the two friends. Stevo, the rebellious punk who narrates the film, has just graduated from university, and Heroin Bob is a space cadet who wouldn't dream of taking drugs; the pair are derided as they walk the streets of the town dressed in punk rock garb. The energy and anarchy of the punk rock movement is captured with inventive use of camera and editing and it also works as a satire on the uptight, Mormon, God-fearing community with its outdated curfews and liquor laws. The film blends humour and realism in an examination of the differences between various youth culture movements such as punks, mods, and rockers, as well as the local rednecks. Produced as an independent film for less than $2 million, Sony Pictures Classics bought UK and US rights to the film, which was featured at the Cannes Festival in 1998, and had its US debut at the Sundance Festival in 1999. Music is a large part of the film and the soundtrack features a range of American and British punk from artists such as Blondie and Generation X, as well as earlier influential music from The Stooges, Velvet Underground and Roxy Music.

Merendino's next project, *Magicians* (2000), was a comedy about a con man, Hugo (Fabrizio Bentivoglio), and a struggling professional magician, Max (Til Schweiger). On their way to Las Vegas the two convince a pretty waitress Lydia (Claire Forlani) to join them as Max's assistant; once they reach Las Vegas they meet Milo (Alan Arkin), a longtime professional magician and manager, who thinks Max could be a success as a magician – until he sees him perform. More recently, Merendino has worked on a Dogme film, *Amerikana* (2001), following the set of rules laid out in 1995 by a collective of Danish film directors, including Lars Von Trier. Starring Michael Goorjian and James Duval, it is a road movie about two friends who travel cross-country from South Dakota to their homes in Los Angeles. **PR**

# E. Elias MERHIGE

*Begotten* (1991)
*Shadow of the Vampire* (2000) After crafting three well-received, idiosyncratic shorts – *Implosion* (1983), *Spring Reign* (1984) and *A Taste of Youth* (1985) – E. Elias Merhige (born Edmund Elias Merhige in Brooklyn in 1964) made the move to feature production with the rarely seen festival favourite *Begotten* (1991).

A genuine oddity that features no spoken dialogue, *Begotten*'s plot, such as it is, revolves around a god-like figure that disembowels himself with a razor, setting free from his corpse the spirit of Mother Earth. The spirit wanders into a bleak and unforgiving landscape, finally giving birth to a fully-grown albino child. The child is set-upon and devoured by a pack of vicious cannibals and flowers and insects subsequently grow from the corpse. A symbolically charged, hypnotically powerful work much beloved of Susan Sontag, the film is redolent of the surrealism of Luis Buñuel and early David Lynch – Lynch, in particular, due to the evocation of the body as the source of horror and decay. The washed-out, grainy look, with its empty, desolate landscapes, is comparable with the lingering hopelessness and physical desolation of Aleksandr Sokurov's work, and makes *Begotten* a film worth seeking out.

Merhige's next project, *Shadow of the Vampire* (2000), is an equally imaginative but more conventional affair. Produced by Nicolas Cage, it is a literate, vivid and extremely eccentric account of the shooting of F. W. Murnau's seminal vampire picture *Nosferatu* (1922). The perplexing premise concerns Max Schreck, played with some conviction by a shaven Willem Dafoe, as a real-life vampire prone to the occasional tantrum. He is placated throughout the production by an increasingly demented Murnau (John Malkovich) with the promise that he can feast on the leading lady (Catharine McCormack) once shooting wraps. Knowingly off-the-wall, the film is fun if not taken too seriously. As a director, Merhige shows a fine eye for detail and draws some strong performances from his starry and committed cast. Although a little more restraint could have been exercised, it may well be Merhige's lack of such that makes his work so interesting in the first place.

He is currently working on *Suspect Zero*, a twist on the serial-killer formula, in which the central character realises that the criminal he is tracking is a former agent whose victims are serial killers. **JWo**

# Tim METCALFE

*Killer: A Journal of Murder* (1996) More successful as a writer (*Kalifornia* (1993)), Tim Metcalfe's first and only directorial work is the Oliver Stone-produced *Killer: A Journal of Murder* (1996). Telling the story of sadistic criminal Carl Panzman, the film ultimately sacrifices itself by going soft on Panzman, resulting in a truly awful picture. In trying to establish the all-important bond between Panzman and prison guard Lesser, Metcalfe decides to avoid all questions as to why these two would trust each other, instead offering us the most tedious of eye-contacts. From here on, the film continues on a downward spiral: the use of voice-over narration is clumsy and risible, the camerawork is of the most basic kind, and, perhaps worst of all, is Metcalfe's apparent need to use black and white photography to indicate the use of flashbacks. The switch to colour, presumably to indicate some kind of freedom or redemption, loses all significance in its targeting of the most basic of emotions. The evocation of Panzman's crimes are so absurd it is a struggle not to see them as farcical misadventures.

Metcalfe clearly wishes to put across a meaningful message – about how society creates and then treats such criminals – but this message gets lost in his uninspiring and conventional direction.                                                        **CP**

# Nicholas MEYER

Nicholas Meyer is a novelist and screenwriter-turned-director. Best known for his 'Star Trek' affiliations, he has also tried his hand at comedy and historical dramas over the years.

Born in New York in 1945, Meyer majored in theatre and film at the University of Iowa and subsequently worked as a publicist for Paramount studios. He then defected to Warner Bros. where he became a story editor. His 1974 novel, 'The Seven Per Cent Solution', in which Sherlock Holmes and Sigmund Freud join forces to solve a mystery, was filmed by Herbert Ross two years later and secured Meyer an Academy Award nomination for the script.

*Time After Time* (1979), Meyer's inaugural excursion as director, appropriates much the same abstraction, but exchanges Holmes and Freud for H. G. Wells and Jack the Ripper. Of course, the Time Machine of Wellsian mythology adds another dimension to the story, transporting both men to present-day San Francisco and contrasting the famous author's idealistic vision of the future with the tainted reality. The film is essentially an interesting spin on the antiquated time-travel theme, carried through by the three winsome leads – Malcolm McDowell, Mary Steenburgen, David Warner – and some excellent special effects.

Subsequently Meyer was charged with making a sequel to Robert Wise's emotionally-detached *Star Trek: The Motion Picture* (1979). *Star Trek II: The Wrath of Khan* (1982) is considered by many fans and bystanders alike to be the best in the series, mainly because it recaptures the spirit of the 1960s television show. Superficially the continuance of an episode entitled 'Space Seed', it wrestles with the main characters on a recondite level, using them to raise questions about age, mortality, revenge and family. Add to this dramatic space battles, the startling 'death' of Spock (Leonard Nimoy) – a hook for the second sequel – plus a rousing James Horner score, and the effect is solid science fiction.

In the wake of the furore over his traumatic TV film, *The Day After* (1983), which depicted the cataclysmic aftermath of a nuclear strike, Meyer turned to comedy for light relief. Tom Hanks and John Candy from *Splash* (1984) reunited for *Volunteers* (1985), a tale of tame capers in the Peace Corps, and although both stars are watchable – if out of character – neither can carry such an indifferent jumble. A slightly more serious tone diffuses *The Deceivers* (1988), a historically accurate drama based on John Masters' book. With a cast comprising of many real Indian actors, Meyer goes back in time to tell the true story of the murderous Thuggee cult, worshippers of the goddess Kali. Pierce Brosnan is the quintessential English hero attempting to stop them, however it does stretch the bounds of probability to have him going undercover as a native himself.

Meyer's last two films look at the cessation of the Cold War in very different ways. *Company Business* (1991) follows ex-CIA agent Gene Hackman undertaking a mission to return a former Soviet spy to the Russians. Meyer seems unsure as to whether this should be a grim thriller, a comedy jaunt, or even a spritely travelogue. At least the film addresses what happens to espionage agents when they are no longer needed, and takes a few side-swipes at their respective superiors in the process.

*Star Trek VI: The Undiscovered Country* (1991), on the other hand, comments on the issue less directly – the collapse of the alien Klingon Empire being a metaphor for the disintegration of the USSR. Tensions abound on both sides as Starfleet extends the hand of peace, and the crew of the Enterprise must prevent a conspiracy from undermining their good intentions. Albeit slack in places, there are some fantastically nostalgic moments for long-term followers of Gene Roddenberry's space opera, and Meyer provides a fitting forum for the original cast to sign off – quite literally at the end.

In 1997 the director served as executive producer (along with Francis Ford Coppola) on Andrei Konchalovsky's 'The Odyssey', a lavish television adaptation of Homer's classic story starring Armand Assante as Odysseus and Greta Scacchi as Queen Penelope. Then more recently, in 1999, he helmed a Home Box Office movie *The Vendetta*, the true story of Italian immigrants from the late nineteenth century accused of the murder of a respected New Orleans lawman – headlining Clancy Brown and Luke Ashew.   **PB**

# Nancy MEYERS

*The Parent Trap* (1998)
*What Women Want* (2000)

A former story editor for the film producer Ray Stark, Nancy Meyers is probably best known as the scriptwriter and producer (with director husband Charles Shyer) of films such as *Private Benjamin* (1980), *Irreconcilable Differences* (1984), and *Baby Boom* (1987). What these commercially successful films have in common is Meyers' use of comedy to evoke her views on social and political issues. They all deal with changing female and family roles – women in the armed forces, divorce and its effects on children – and the difficulties facing single women who have to work and raise children simultaneously. Interested in 'meaty parts for women – those with a certain goal who turn their lives upside down', her writing has been influenced by the strong female roles of classic Hollywood. In fact, she has likened Diane Keaton's performance in *Baby Boom* to those of 'Rosalind Russell, Carole Lombard or Katharine Hepburn'.

Her career re-writing existing films into *Father of the Bride* (1991) and *I Love Trouble* (1994), combined with her interest in how modern families live, led to her 1998 directorial debut, the remake of Disney's *The Parent Trap* (1961), which she also scripted. Dealing with separated twins who connive to reunite their divorced parents and enjoy the family they have dreamed of, the film is often warm and humorous but ultimately seems old-fashioned in its faux heartwarming story and style, belonging more comfortably to the period in which the original was made. Her version retained some of the original's knockabout comedy but veered towards the saccharine end of sweet.

Still very much a writer, having not yet established a clear visual style, Meyers' second film, *What Women Want* (2000), is a romantic comedy about a chauvinistic advertising executive who has an accident and develops the power to hear women's thoughts. Starring Mel Gibson and the gutsy duo of Helen Hunt and Marisa Tomei, the story has the potential to provide Meyers with the opportunity to take her socially perceptive interests into more edgily humorous territory. Yet she produces a curiously old-fashioned Hollywood story, pitched somewhere between the partnerships of Hudson and Day or Bogart and Bacall, but sadly lacking the class and style of these classic Hollywood pairings. Despite sold direction, the film soon wanes, concentrating, for instance, on the supposedly funny sight of a man waxing his legs and trying on tights. The more fascinating facts – that Gibson's co-workers loathe his sexism and a rejected employee carries suicidal thoughts – are undermined by aural gags (Gibson hearing a door-woman's thoughts about his 'butt') and a romantic resolution.

Still busy behind the scenes, Meyers has recently executive produced Charles Shyer's *The Affair of the Necklace* (2001), a little-seen film about a young, penniless aristocrat (Hilary Swank) in pre-Revolutionary France trying to reverse her fortunes by stealing a priceless necklace.   **JD**

# Eric MEZA

*House Party 3* (1994)
*The Breaks* (1999)

While Spike Lee continues to deliver hard-hitting polemic essays on the state of black culture, Eric Meza's films have shown a keen eye for the comic potential of aspects of black American life – speech, music, family, society – with an ability to handle both broad physical humour as well as more pointed satire. Meza's first film, *House Party 3* (1994), completes the highly successful series of 'kid and play' movies. The format here is similar to the first two instalments; bright, sassy and energetic, mixing base gags with big characters and lots of hip-hop. Despite the negligible story – mainly an excuse for the leads to goof off – and some crude and misogynistic jokes, Meza's direction is authentic in its direct approach and its awareness of the specific audience it is addressing.

Meza's eye for culture-clash humour is more fully explored in his second feature, *The Breaks* (1999). The film is a neat satire on aspects of the young black American experience. It charts the story of Derrick King, a wannabe-black white kid raised by a black family in LA who gets his wish when he becomes embroiled in a series of mishaps in the Hood, including incarceration by a Confederate flag-wearing LAPD. Serious themes of segregation and prejudice lie behind the skilfully handled laughs and comic situations arising from the endless, *Jerk*-esque possibilities of the central conceit, demonstrating a director unusually capable of satirising as well as addressing cultural issues. He is no less aware than Spike Lee, but an easier pill to swallow.                                    **OB**

# John MILIUS

An obsessive collector of firearms, affectionately known as 'The General' in reference to his bombastic and defiantly right-wing persona, and the inspiration for the demented Vietnam vet in *The Big Lebowski* (1998), John Milius is one of cinema's enduring characters. A member of the 'Brat Generation' of directors which emerged in the late 1960s, Milius worked on many seminal films of the 1970s as screenwriter, a fact which has tended to eclipse his own directorial career. As with many film-makers of his generation, born in the aftermath of World War Two and beginning their careers under the shadow of war in Vietnam, conflict forms a central part of his work. His films explore honour, bravery and individual freedom, often in the context of war, and a fascination with myth-making and male identity.

Dillinger (1973)
The Wind and the Lion (1975)
Big Wednesday (1978)
Conan the Barbarian (1982)
Red Dawn (1984)
Farewell to the King (1989)
Flight of the Intruder (1990)

Born in St. Louis, Missouri, in 1944, Milius had always envisioned a career in the army, but was rejected from national service due to chronic asthma. Consequently, he enrolled in the newly-founded film programme at the University of Southern California, intending to explore a career as a writer while indulging his other great passion – surfing. It proved a fortuitous choice. The new film schools, most notably USC and UCLA, were hotbeds of experimentation and creative collaboration in the late 1960s, producing a generation of innovative young film-makers keen to challenge the rules and conventions of the Hollywood system. Milius quickly caught the creative wave. At USC he wrote and directed two shorts, *The Reversal of Richard Sun* (1966) and *Marcello, I'm So Bored* (1966), a satire of Italian art-house films, and wrote *The Emperor* (1967), a stylish short about an overbearing disc-jockey for one of his class-mates, George Lucas – an idea which undoubtedly contributed to *American Graffiti* (1973).

After graduating, Milius began a prolific period as a screenwriter, beginning with *The Devil's Eight* (1969), a voguish motorcycle movie, and a biopic of stunt maestro *Evel Knievel* (1971). *The Life and Times of Judge Roy Bean* (1972) and *Jeremiah Johnson* (1972), examined men living beyond the law in the old west, while Milius' uncredited writing work on *Dirty Harry* (1971), and his screenplay for the sequel, *Magnum Force* (1973), relocated the frontier to modern-day Los Angeles and turned the quintessential gunslinger, Clint Eastwood, into a loose-cannon detective. Milius' early screenplays set the benchmark for his later work: they all feature archetypal male figures, living outside normal society by a self-defined moral code, thrown into a world in which their values of honour and self-reliance are tested. They also showcase Milius' ear for memorable dialogue (he wrote the immortal *Dirty Harry* line: 'Go ahead, punk. Make my day').

*Dillinger* (1973), Milius' debut directing feature, is a good example of his particular brand of myth-making. Heavily influenced by the Italian westerns of the late 1960s, *Dillinger* portrays its bank-robbing protagonist as a contemporary folk hero, standing up for freedom and individuality against an oppressive government regime in Depression-era America. Stylish, bloody, and snappily written, and peppered with movie references, the film carried strong overtones for a generation at odds with its hippy-hating, commie-bating political machine and demonstrated Milius as a capable director in his own right. *The Wind and the Lion* (1975) is based on an incident in 1904 when an American woman and her children were captured by Arab rebels in Morocco, and focuses on a clash of wills between two authority figures, each a legend in their respective spheres: President Roosevelt and the Arab leader Raisuli. Milius' fascination with conflicting moral codes and impressive desert cinematography make for a vibrant, if rather jingoistic, epic.

Having penned Quint's memorable monologue about the sinking of the USS Indianapolis for Spielberg's *Jaws* (1975), Milius began work on an adaptation of Joseph Conrad's *Heart of Darkness* – a Milius tale if ever there was one – for Coppola's Vietnam epic *Apocalypse Now* (1979). Though much changed in the final version, his influence is still plain to see, particularly in the surfing scenes, the ebullient character of Captain Kilgore, and the conception of Kurtz as a man transmuted into myth. It was

*Big Wednesday* (1978), however, that defined him as a director. A fable of youth, friendship and maturity, structured around the mythology of surfing, the film follows three Californian surfers from youth to middle age: a surfing legend gradually tamed by age, drink and domesticity; a beach-bum who shirks responsibility; and an all-American kid who accepts his duties, fights in Vietnam and returns a changed man. Loosely structured in episodic scenes, with each period linked by the metaphor of shifting ocean swells, the film's philosophy is of its time, but it remains a powerful depiction of the loss of youth and the conflict between freedom and duty. Though it flopped at the box office, it has since become a cult classic, with some of the best surfing footage ever filmed.

Milius' fascination with outlaw heroes and anarchic myth-making continued through the 1980s, but in the reactionary, pro-American fervour of the Reagan years, his films began to lose much of their rebellious appeal. *Conan the Barbarian* (1982), co-written with Oliver Stone, was the most successful. Part spaghetti western, part philosophical fairytale, it is the consummate Milius story, packed with visceral action, grandiose camerawork, a portentous mythology of honour and loss, and a proto-Nietzschean hero out for revenge. It was also the film that unleashed Arnold Schwarzenegger on an unsuspecting public. The later films are less auspicious: *Red Dawn* (1984) examines a group of American teenagers who become guerrilla fighters against a covert Communist invasion; *Farewell to the King* (1989) relocates *Apocalypse Now* to World War Two Borneo, where an Allied resistance party discover an American general in command of a native army; and *Flight of the Intruder* (1990) follows two renegade bombardiers in Vietnam on an unauthorised mission to eliminate a Vietcong missile silo. Milius' flair for action, grand visual set-pieces and great dialogue remains unchecked, and the archetypal figures pushed into violent action are all present and correct, but this is old territory for such a seasoned campaigner.

He has since continued to write for the screen, most recently with *Clear and Present Danger* (1994), and direct the occasional television film, but while his Brat contemporaries continue to push back the boundaries, Milius seems to have lost direction. **OB**

## Rebecca MILLER

*Angela* (1996)
*Personal Velocity: Three Portraits* (2002)

Born in 1962 in the USA, Rebecca Miller, daughter of playwright Arthur Miller, established a steady if unremarkable acting career appearing in a variety of small roles in films such as Alan Rudolph's *Mrs Parker and the Vicious Circle* (1994), Alan J. Pakula's *Consenting Adults* (1992), and Mike Nichols' *Regarding Henry* (1991), before turning more exclusively to writing. Recently, she has published a collection of short stories about women to great acclaim, reinforcing the female-centred themes of her two feature films as director.

Her debut, *Angela* (1996), the story of two young sisters and their mentally ill mother, was a 1995 Sundance Film Festival winner. Concerned with intense and fierce religious fervour, the film follows the sisters as they attempt to rid themselves of the 'evil' they believe to be the cause of their mother's illness; Miller and cinematographer Ellen Kuras capture the girl's visions in a hallucinatory visual style. Slow and lyrical, some have considered this a pretentious debut, yet it promises much both thematically and for its interesting relationship to magic realism.

Her second feature, which is presently on the festival circuit, will more than likely be afforded a wider release. *Personal Velocity: Three Portraits* (2002) concerns three women who seek escape from the men who restrain them and boasts a fine, off-beat cast including Kyra Sedgwick, Parker Posey, Leo Fitzpatrick and Wallace Shawn. Once again, Kuras is responsible for the visual style, her work winning her a Sundance Film Festival award; the film also received the Grand Jury prize. Shot on digital, the personal intensity of the subject suits the format and affords the movie an 'unclean' and 'imperfect' vision. With her personal themes and concerns recurring, and her working relationship with Kuras developing, Miller is forging an interesting film-making career for herself. **JD**

## Daniel MINAHAN

*Series 7: The Contenders* (2001)

With notable credits as co-writer and 2$^{nd}$ unit director on Mary Harron's engrossing *I Shot Andy Warhol* (1996), Daniel Minahan drew upon his experiences working in television on US reality game shows for his self-penned feature debut, *Series 7: The Contenders* (2001).

Cleverly marketed to create the impression that it is a compilation of the install-ments of a popular US television show, the film is a timely critique on the vogue for scheduling programmes that pitch contestants against one another in tests of physical and mental endurance. Minahan takes the conventions of such shows to their logical conclusion – the spoof show, *The Contenders*, boasts that its press-ganged competitors are 'real people in real danger' – and raises relevant questions regarding the dangers of such exploitation. Imbued with a dark, incisive gallows humour it examines the manner in which such shows attract voyeuristic audiences, increasing their thirst for death and destruction. The 'entrants', the all-American girl, the misfit, and the desperate single mom, are all generic types, and Minahan adopts the familiar stylistic formats – hand-held camera, direct to camera confessionals, bombastic voiceovers and ad breaks – to impressive satirical effect.

More *The Truman Show* (1998) than *The Running Man* (1987), *Series 7: The Con-tenders* displays a wily sensibility; it is ultimately uncomfortable, dispiriting viewing, but necessarily so. **JWo**

# Steve MINER

Gore fans will probably be devoted to Steve Miner – his name is synonymous with intermittent reconstructions and recreations of the horror genre, predating Wes Craven's and Kevin Williamson's post-modern irony and tongue-in-cheek humour by over a decade.

Born in 1951 in Connecticut, his two sequels to *Friday the 13th* (1980) – *Friday the 13th Part 2* (1981) and *Friday the 13th Part 3* (1982) – may fail to recapture Sean Cunningham's sickeningly realistic murder situations, but Miner still maintains a high level of suspense and, in the second sequel, displays a certain visual flair by using 3-D shots of popcorn popping and yo-yos going up and down. Yet one of Miner's artistic imprimaturs is his ability to feel at ease in various generic straightjackets. Switching from visceral horror to broad comedy, via romantic melodrama, is a skill that only a few Hollywood journeymen possess, and Miner's canon is full of unexpected twists and turns; he refuses to be shoehorned as a one-genre director.

In between the *Friday the 13th* films and *House* (1986) and *Warlock* (1989) (the former a tale of a writer who moves into a haunted house, the latter a 'stalk 'n' slash' occult thriller that meshes grand guignol, gutsy acting and unsure tone) lies *Soul Man* (1986). The film is an excellent fable addressing the state of racist attitudes in Reaganite Americana. C. Thomas Howell plays the white man who darkens his skin to win a law-school scholarship intended for a black, and both he and Miner excel in their depiction of small-town narrow prejudice, farcical humour and the wider social implications of segregation. The film was an abrupt change of tone for Miner and sits uneasily between his increasingly clichéd horror films that became increasingly moribund during the 1980s.

After directing *Wild Hearts Can't Be Broken* (1991), an absorbing romantic drama about a diving girl, set in the 1930s and starring Gabrielle Anwar, Miner made *Forever Young* (1992). It began a trend of time-travel romance movies that have since become common-place in Hollywood popular culture (*Encino Man* (1992), *Blast From The Past* (1999)). Miner fashions a creditable 'woman's weepie' that was a rousing alternative to the usual summer fare of action movies and animated hi-jinx, and the director shows himself adept at managing to balance the shifts in time and space between 1939 and the present. The production design is remarkable, and the visual quality of the film is one of its high points.

*My Father the Hero* (1994) was a remake of the French classic *Mon Père ce héros* (1991), both of which starred Gérard Depardieu as the leading man. He plays the absentee father who takes his daughter Katherine Heigl on holiday, only to have her impress an older boy by telling him that Gérard is really her lover. The picture at least stands out as an improvement on the usual remakes of European art house far, with both lead actors generating the requisite amount of humour, exasperation and social embarrassment. Miner works the script hard; the material may be formulaic, but in his hands, there are often flashes of gusto and improvisation, especially in the beach landscapes and mistaken-identity scenes.

*Friday the 13th Part 2* (1981)
*Friday the 13th Part 3* (1982)
*House* (1986)
*Soul Man* (1986)
*Warlock* (1989)
*Wild Hearts Can't Be Broken* (1991)
*Forever Young* (1992)
*My Father the Hero* (1994)
*Sherwood's Travels* (1994)
*Big Bully* (1996)
*Halloween H20 – 20 Years Later* (1998)
*Lake Placid* (1999)
*Texas Rangers* (2001)

Miner's most recent features have earmarked him as more than just a hack-for-hire; for the first time, it seems an authorial strain is running through his work that lends greater emphasis to his visual narratives. *Halloween H20* (1998) is undoubtedly the best of the *Halloween* sequels that followed the 1978 original. The innovative camera movements, the eerily simple music and the embattled baby-sitter became staples of the horror genres, and Miner pays tribute to them in this sixth sequel. In the age of Craven 'nudge-nudge' referentiality, Miner places a hockey mask in the film's opening scene (recalling his debut feature) and has Janet Leigh tell daughter Jamie Lee Curtis 'We've all had bad experiences'. The nasty moments in the film remind us that Michael Myers' inexplicability and arbitrariness was the scary thing about the *Halloween* series, and Miner does an expert job of contracting the tension into 87 minutes. There is scarcely a wasted scene in the film; everything counts and all the visual clues and twists are fully integrated into the fluid narrative.

*Lake Placid* (1999) was a hybrid of *Jaws* (1975) and *Anaconda* (1997) – part humour, part prosthetic monster, part deadly seriousness – that proves that spirited B-movie recreations can capture the necessary preposterousness and self-referentiality. Scripted by David E. Kelley (of 'Ally McBeal' fame), he and Miner cram the actors' mouths with sarcasm, wit and scathing humour and this device is played to such an extent that the next one-liner becomes the film's attraction, not the appearance of the giant crocodile devouring inhabitants of northern Maine.

In *Texas Rangers* (2001), Miner's latest film, a group of youngsters band together after the American Civil War to form the Texas Rangers who are charged with the dangerous duty of cleaning up the west. Starring a clutch of Hollywood's hottest young properties (James van der Beek, Rachael Leigh Cook, Usher Raymond), Miner has an enjoyable time riffing on the themes and generics of the western, mixing in familiar faces like Tom Skerritt and Alfred Molina with the requisite guns, explosions and chases. Unlike *Young Guns* (1988), Miner's direction is sure-footed and he is equally adept at romance as suspense. He once again experiments with the genre and fashions an exciting, at times thought-provoking, slant on age-old themes. Horror films and Miner make easy bedfellows, but *Texas Rangers* contains much inventiveness to suggest that he should essay other genres with his trademark wit and clarity.          **BM**

# Rob MINKOFF

*The Lion King* (1994)
*Stuart Little* (1999)
*Stuart Little 2* (2002)

Computers may have expanded the capabilities of animation almost beyond recognition since the golden years of Disney and Hanna-Barbera, but the wit and indefinable magic present in the greatest of their cartoons are qualities often lacking in the age of technological animation. Rob Minkoff has rediscovered something of that old charm; working within the conventions of Disney entertainment, he finds new ways to tell old tales through an astute awareness of the demands of children's narrative and character and the ability to work at the forefront of technology. His films are perfect examples of this synthesis of old and new; traditional Disney stories whose technical innovation may locate them in the present, but whose quality and attention to detailed character are classic in feel.

Initially a traditional animator at Disney in the late 1980s, working on *Basil: The Great Mouse Detective* (1986) and *Oliver and Company* (1988), Minkoff then directed two short cartoons in the influential Roger Rabbit franchise, *Tummy Trouble* (1990) and *Rollercoaster Rabbit* (1990). Much more in the zany vein of Friz Freleng and Tex Avery than Walt Disney, Minkoff invokes their use of breakneck cartoon slapstick, outrageous violence and mishap, and broad characters that appeal as much to an adult audience as a young one. Obviously fluent in cartoon lore and a very capable director, *The Lion King* (1994) further demonstrates Minkoff's technical skill. A rites-of-passage tale in which young cub Simba must reclaim his rightful throne from his father-murdering, usurping uncle Scar, the film is technically fantastic, mixing traditional cel animation with 3D computer manipulation that allows the camera to crane, swoop and move much as in a live-action movie. The film is also lent depth by its 'Hamlet' framework and use of African myth, but it is the sheer energy of execution and characterisation that provide a touch of the old Disney magic.

*Stuart Little* (1999) continues Minkoff's delight in unadulterated children's entertainment, focusing on a family that adopt a mouse as a brother for their only son. Again mixing incredible computer animation of Stuart and his nemesis, house cat Snowbell, with live actors, the story is adapted from E. B. White and is prime Disney fare. Minkoff's command of the genre and animation is faultless and though the film is perhaps overly sweet for some, lacking the self-referential caché of *Toy Story* (1995), his ability to combine old-fashioned entertainment with technical innovation is refreshing in a world where even cartoons have become post-postmodern. He has also directed the sequel, *Stuart Little 2* (2002).                                                    **OB**

# David MIRKIN

Writer, director and executive producer, David Mirkin was born in Philadelphia. Realising that he hated studying electronic engineering, he moved to Los Angeles where he earned a degree in film at Loyola. He began his career in 1982, writing freelance scripts for television and movies, and doing stand-up comedy. He joined 'Newhart' in 1984 as a writer, soon becoming executive producer and taking the opportunity to direct for the first time. His television credits include three Fox series: 'Get A Life!', an invitingly absurd sitcom which was acclaimed by *Entertainment Weekly* as 'one of the ten best shows on television'; 'The Tracey Ullman Show'; and 'The Edge'. He was also a consultant on 'It's Garry Shandling's Show' and 'The Larry Sanders Show', and wrote for 'Three's a Crowd' and 'The Simpsons' – the latter he also began to executive produce.

*Romy and Michele's High School Reunion* (1997)
*Heartbreakers* (2001)

Mirkin is renowned for his sardonic humour, which is apparent in his debut feature, *Romy and Michele's High School Reunion* (1997). Based on the play 'Ladies' Room', *Romy and Michele* is an unusual movie: the set-up is pure buddy movie but with females, and it is a non-conformist mix of irreverent humour and dumb fun. The comedy could easily have centred on the dumb blonde syndrome but instead gives the girls a refreshingly sarcastic edge, flashes of inspiration and plenty of chutzpah. A potential revenge fantasy becomes a hymn to the bonds of friendship, capturing the horrors of high school and the ambivalence of reunions. Dividing critics, it did moderately well at the box office.

His subsequent outing, *Heartbreakers* (2001), failed to build on this promise, largely due to the mediocre script, which Mirkin co-wrote, and also some uneven direction and editing. Despite the fun premise of a Howard Hawks/Preston Sturges-style story of a redeemed con, it pales in comparison. The plot involves a mother-and-daughter team of dupesters. Max (Sigourney Weaver) meets and marries millionaires who are then seduced by the daughter, Page (Jennifer Love Hewitt), caught in the act and subsequently divorced. Things go swimmingly until Max picks chain-smoking tobacco tycoon, William B. Tensy (Gene Hackman), who expires on her before the payoff. In addition, Page decides to go out on her own and falls in love with her first mark (Jason Lee). Either played for laughs like *Dirty Rotten Scoundrels* (1988) or concentrating on the dramatic, mother-child relationship (as in *Grifters* (1990)) would have worked better than this aggregate mix. The film flounders badly, only saved from going under by the energetic performances of the cast.                                                    **FG**

# John Cameron MITCHELL

With only one film to his credit, John Cameron Mitchell, born in El Paso, Texas, in 1963, has already established himself as a rising star amongst the American independent film circle. Adapted from its triumphant success as an off-Broadway cult theatre hit or, as Mitchell labels it, a 'post-punk neo-glam rock musical', *Hedwig and the Angry Inch* (2001) was born from an impromptu friendship with composer/lyricist Stephen Trask. Using a myth from Plato's Symposium, Mitchell created the characters and wrote the dialogue and Trask set the story to music and song. Killer Films, upon seeing the stage version, were instantly convinced of its cinematic value and there was no question as to choice of director. Mitchell was given a budget of $6 million and all the creative freedom one could ask for as a first-time director. Both he and Trask hand-picked the cast and crew (with Mitchell keeping the title role as Hedwig) and refused to sacrifice their artistic integrity, thereby successfully transforming the world of Hedwig from stage to screen. The film is a flamboyant and imaginative tale of a boy named Hansel who leaves his native East Berlin by way of a botched sex-change operation (thus becoming Hedwig) and a marriage to an American sergeant. Having been abandoned in a US trailer park,

*Hedwig and the Angry Inch* (2001)

Hedwig sets off on her quest for true love, stardom and identity. The story wooed critics and audiences alike, and *Hedwig and the Angry Inch* won the 2001 Sundance audience award and director's award. **SK**

# Mike MITCHELL

*Deuce Bigalow: Male Gigolo* (1999)

*Deuce Bigalow: Male Gigolo* (1999), the first feature by Mike Mitchell, is a slight, obscene little film starring 'Saturday Night Live''s Rob Schneider as a fish-tank cleaner who becomes a male prostitute to pay for the broken aquarium of a customer who is a gigolo himself. Deuce's talent comes not with his sexual prowess, but his ability to make his abnormal clients feel good about themselves. He also falls in love with amputee Kate (Arija Bareikis), who is given his services.

The story is merely a conduit for a series of crude jokes on inappropriate topics including blindness, obesity, and Tourette's Syndrome. There is little humour in the film, with the exception of some of the terminology used by Deuce and his pimp T.J. (Eddie Griffin). The film falls in line with the many crude comedies popular in the mid- and late 1990s. *Deuce Bigalow: Male Gigolo* was co-produced by Adam Sandler, perhaps the king of such films and a friend of Schneider, who in turn appears in many of Sandler's films. In this context, it becomes apparent that Mitchell is simply a hired-hand for this high-concept project, intended only as a vehicle for Schneider, and as an easy cash-grab for the producers. The film did well commercially despite its apparent contempt for the audience.

He is currently in production with *Surviving Christmas*, a comedy starring Ben Affleck. **DH**

# Jocelyn MOORHOUSE

*Proof* (1991)
*How-to-Make-an-American-Quilt* (1995)
*A Thousand Acres* (1997)

Jocelyn Moorhouse's oeuvre has so far been both idiosyncratic and anonymous. Creating a buzz with the Australian arthouse hit *Proof* in 1991, subsequent projects have found her sensibility obscured amidst the personalities and conventions of the mainstream. But however disappointing her early American work, her cinematic voice can be perceptive and supremely tempting.

Graduating from the Australian School of Film, Radio and Television in 1984, Moorhouse worked in television as a script editor and writer. It was during this period that she conceived and began developing *Proof*. Opening the Directors' Fortnight and winning the 1991 Camera D'Or at Cannes, *Proof* was an immediate success on the festival circuit. Featuring Hugo Weaving and Russell Crowe, it was seen to herald the second coming of Australian cinema.

Blind from birth, Martin's (Hugo Weaving) only purchase upon the world is through the descriptions he seeks from his friend Andy (Russell Crowe) of the photographs he obsessively takes. Moorhouse finds humour and pathos in this tale of misfits inhabiting a staid Melbourne suburb, their lives straitened by repression yet oddly redeemed by their passion. On one level, the characterful result suggests an antipodean Mike Leigh in the making.

The desire to move beyond the arthouse niche and tell stories to a wider audience clearly informed the move to Hollywood. But whilst *Proof* is ostensibly a man's story, on another level it derives huge poignancy from its tale of Martin's housekeeper Celia and her struggle against loneliness and desire. It is a subtle film which enables such a shift of emphasis, a significant shift given Moorhouse's evolving career. In 1994 she co-wrote and co-produced *Muriel's Wedding*, directed by husband P. J. Hogan. Celebrating a single woman's self-determination and becoming a modest hit in both arthouses and multiplexes, the film was a high-profile episode in the Aussie second wave and presaged women's communities to come.

*How-to-Make-an-American-Quilt* (1995), her first Hollywood feature, was a warmhearted addition to the 1990s 'chick flick' cycle. Finn (Winona Ryder) is spending the summer with her grandmother and great aunt and a sewing circle completing Finn's wedding quilt, while Finn completes her Master's thesis on women's handicrafts. Trading in love found and lost, dreams wished and abandoned, and a series of dewy-eyed turns by such as Ellen Burstyn, Kate Nelligan, Anne Bancroft, and Maya Angelou, the whole awash with Thomas Newman's Coplandesque score, overseer Spielberg's

Amblin Entertainment also lent it, amongst other heritage forebears, more than a little of *The Color Purple*'s (1985) resonance. Whilst sharing with *Proof* a generalised sympathy for the woman whose life remains a fallow expanse of difficult days, the aesthetic overwhelmed the auteur. Indeed, the film begs the question: why are women in Hollywood invariably consigned to 'women's pictures'?

*A Thousand Acres* (1997) is the least successful of Moorhouse's three features. Again, her own voice has been lost in this shrill translation of 'King Lear' to the contemporary Midwest. Co-produced by stars Jessica Lange and Michelle Pfeiffer's production companies, the film is a star vehicle in which Lange and Pfeiffer sought to stretch themselves. Based upon a bestselling novel and mired in the 'herstory' culture of contemporary Hollywood women's cinema, *A Thousand Acres* makes one wish that Moorhouse could break out of this 'woman director' niche.

'When a film really works, it's got the subconscious power of a dream ... to actually by-pass your "safety sieve"', Moorhouse told *Film Comment* in 1992. If she can move beyond the generics of catering to the adult female demographic currently courted by Hollywood, Moorhouse will rediscover whatever it was which by-passed conscious expectations worldwide in 1992. **RA**

# Jonathan MOSTOW

Jonathan Mostow began his career as a film-maker while studying at Harvard, directing a variety of award-winning documentaries and shorts. In 1991 he wrote and directed the television movie *Flight of Black Angel* and received a Cable ACE nomination for Best International Movie. He has also produced David Fincher's *The Game* (1997) and recently joined forces with former Universal Pictures Production President, Hal Lieberman, to form Mostow/Lieberman Productions.

*Breakdown* (1997)
*U-571* (2000)

Judging by Mostow's work so far, it seems that he is carving a niche for himself as a suspense writer/director. Both his feature films – *Breakdown* (1997) and *U-571* (2000) – create dramatic situations which become increasingly more tense thus heightening audience anticipation and emotional involvement. The first, *Breakdown*, which was surprisingly well received on its release, is similar in both narrative and tone to *The Vanishing* (1993). Featuring Kurt Russell and Kathleen Quinlan as a married couple travelling through the American southwest, it focuses on the husband's desperate search through a small desert town following his wife's mysterious disappearance. When all the inhabitants deny any knowledge of her existence, events take a sinister Hitchcockian turn. This is old-fashioned story telling made visually rewarding by arresting cinematography.

The recent *U-571* has had a rather more controversial reception. Set in World War Two, it follows the crew of an American submarine on their mission to capture a top-secret encryption device from a Nazi U-boat. On its release, most British critics were quick to point out its blatant disregard for historical truth and the fact that it was the British who caught the first Enigma machine. Charles Taylor called it 'the shoddiest and most incoherent piece of big-budget action movie-making since *Armageddon*'. Similar in tone to earlier submarine films, this is hardly *Das Boot* (1981), yet it still manages to create a sense of the claustrophobia and panic which the men feel when trapped in a confined space, particularly under the threat of enemy attack. Adhering to conservative values, it upholds the importance of the group over and above the individual and also the notion that good will eventually triumph over evil.

Following *U-571*, Mostow has been entrusted to direct the third Terminator film. **HP**

# Greg MOTTOLA

Greg Mottola was born in Long Island in 1964, and began his career making 16mm films through the arts organisation Pittsburgh Film-makers before attending film school at Columbia University. His short, *Swinging in the Painter's Room* (1989), won a Silver Hugo at the Chicago Film Festival and so impressed film-maker Steven Soderbergh that he offered to support Mottola in his writing of a full-length feature. After several attempts Mottola came up with an idea based on a true incident and Soderbergh agreed to executive produce on a budget of $100,000. Rejected by Sundance, *The Daytrippers* (1996) went on to feature in rival festival Slamdance, winning critical acclaim and the Grand Prize at Deauville.

*The Daytrippers* (1996)

An impressive directorial debut, the film is a road movie of sorts that focuses on a day in the life of a family journeying in their station wagon from Long Island to Manhattan in search of the daughter's errant husband. Effectively utilising the constricted camera movements to create a sense of the mounting tension and claustrophobia felt by each of the characters, it is a fast-paced, bittersweet comedy that knowingly plays around with notions of gender and class. Each actor plays their part to perfection and Liev Schrieber and Parker Posey are particularly good as the ill-suited couple who eventually come to realise their differences.                                                                                        **HP**

# Allan MOYLE

Born in Québec in 1947, Allan Moyle has made the transition from standard arthouse fare to bigger – if not better – films; his best-known deal with teenagers and rock 'n' roll. He initially worked on *Montreal Main* (1974), the downbeat story of a photographer and his relationship with a rebellious teenage boy, as an actor and co-screenwriter, making his directorial debut, *The Rubber Gun*, three years later. Both similar, the latter was co-written with actor/writer/painter Stephen Lack; Moyle even plays the same character in each. *The Rubber Gun* is a grimy trawl through the Montreal drug culture, which is interesting in its own right but also matches the similarly themed *Panic in Needle Park* (1971) and the later films *Drugstore Cowboy* (1989) and *Jesus' Son* (1998). That same year, Moyle appeared in a small role in the David Cronenberg's excellent film *Rabid*.

Moyle's next feature was the cult offering *Times Square* (1980). Probably best known for its soundtrack – featuring Patti Smith, The Ruts, and The Ramones – this is the story of teenage runaways (Trini Alvarado and Robin Johnson) who escape from a mental institution and form The Sleez Girls, a punk rock band. It has a likeable ama-teurish quality and the two leads are great, although its editing is messy and the script frequently lapses into cliché – this is surprising considering that Jacob Brackman, who wrote the dazzling *King of the Marvin Gardens* (1972), is credited as screenwriter. It has strong sociological interest with its scenes of a pre-Guiliani New York of strip clubs and porn cinemas and a strong homoerotic undercurrent between the two leads. Moyle has since suggested that the film was re-edited against his wishes and the lesbian theme was reduced to strong sub-text. Given all of the film's best lines, an unconvincingly accented Tim Curry also puts in an appearance. Independently, *Times Square* is an interesting project but as a New York punk movie, it pales next to a film like Susan Seidelman's *Smithereens* (1982).

Perhaps due to his bad experiences with *Times Square*, Moyle subsequently wrote a novel and left features alone for the next decade. *Pump Up the Volume* (1990) remains his best film to date and continues his fascination with rebellious teenagers and music. Christian Slater is a geek at an Arizona high school who broadcasts a pirate radio show, under the pseudonym Hard Harry, which aims to shake his fellow students out of their lethargy. Like Oliver Stone's *Talk Radio* (1988), where DJ Eric Bogosian uses late-night radio as a weapon, Moyle's script has Harry as a profane voice of truth, blamed for a student suicide and hunted by the school authorities. Although the film's reach exceeds its grasp, it is a noble attempt to make a rabble-rousing teen film, packaging the protagonist as a masturbation-simulating high-school Lenny Bruce 'saying the unsayable' about the powers that be. Slater is fantastic, exploiting his Jack Nicholson mannerisms to pleasing effect as he did in the dark teen picture *Heathers* (1989). Samantha Mathis as a fellow misfit is also impressive. The sequence where she and Slater tease and taunt each other on a suburban lawn at night, which culmi-nates in her taking off her top, is an affecting and erotic seduction scene that makes the overheated likes of *Sliver* (1993) and *Disclosure* (1994) look like Zalman King. Some may regard *Pump Up the Volume* as a smarter and faux-radical John Hughes reworking but Moyle has yet to match it.

His next film was a poor comedy, *The Gun in Betty Lou's Handbag* (1992). With *Empire Records* (1995), Moyle returned to the youth-oriented movies he particularly specialises in but despite an attractive, youthful cast – Liv Tyler, Renee Zellweger, Bren-dan Sexton III – it is a dull story about an anarchic record store. *New Waterford Girl* (1999) is a fairly nondescript comedy and *X-Change* (2000), although a real change of pace for Moyle, is a generic sci-fi thriller. A body-swapping terrorist yarn, it stars Kyle MachLachlan and Stephen Baldwin.

Moyle's most recent film sees him working with another Baldwin brother, Billy, in *Say Nothing* (2001); derivative of *Fatal Attraction* (1985), it sadly wastes the talents of Nastassja Kinski.                                                                                    **IC**

# Geoff MURPHY

With Roger Donaldson, Vincent Ward and Peter Jackson, Geoff Murphy led the new wave of feature film production in New Zealand in the 1980s. After helping to reinvigorate a moribund national film industry, all four have gone on to pursue careers within the American film industry. The varied oppositional or art cinema nature of their output at home has been succeeded by steadily more mainstream productions abroad, but in many ways Murphy's current niche within the cable and television movie industry represents the logical end of his earliest experiments, in adapting an escapist, generic cinematic tradition imported from America to the cultural and commercial demands of the emergent New Zealand cinema.

Murphy's counter-cultural credentials and background represent an important and formative element in his early film-making. After abandoning university education and a teaching career, he joined an eccentric travelling show called BLERTA (the Bruno Lawrence Electric Revelation Travelling Apparition). As well as writing songs and performing in their band, Murphy made short black-and-white films that were shown as part of the group's shows. Later, with Lawrence, Alun Bollinger and Martyn Sanderson, and their respective families, Murphy formed a commune at Waimarama. This group represented one focal point for renewed interest in New Zealand film-making, and from it came one of the most fertile collaborations, with Bruno Lawrence contributing to and acting in four of Murphy's films.

The short film *Wild Man* (1977) grew out of the commune's activities and represented one of the first examples of the emergent film culture. Composed of a series of anarchic sketches linked to a tenuous itinerant narrative, the film established many aspects of the Murphy signature: a celebration of veniality, a robust and black strain of humour often incorporating slapstick, and a penchant for the simultaneous indulgence and ironisation of action and violence. (The director also appeared in a cameo role, as he did in some of his other New Zealand films). These characteristics found a fuller and more successful articulation in the director's next film, *Goodbye Pork Pie* (1980). As one of the most successful New Zealand films to date, *Goodbye Pork Pie* connected with the home audience through its iconic use of local landscapes, its celebration of irresponsibility and iconoclasm, and its nonchalant anti-authoritarianism. The film follows a quixotic odyssey by two determinedly dis-integrated Kiwi males from one end of the country to the other, using an illegally acquired car and engaging in various misdemeanours en route. The film's foregrounding of their indulgence of sex and drugs, and the contemptuous attitude towards establishment efforts to contain them, mobilises these elements as both highly commercial and satiric aspects of Murphy's work. In combining the conventions of the road movie and the buddy movie, and inflecting the counter cultural aspirations of *Easy Rider* (1969) with specific cultural and comedic reference, *Goodbye Pork Pie* became a landmark in New Zealand film and established its director as a significant national voice.

Murphy's subsequent films in New Zealand embodied many of these thematic and stylistic elements, and confirmed his credentials as a self-conscious commercial film-maker. The combination of action, black comedy and the de- (and re-) mythologising of New Zealand history in *Utu* (1983), and of horror, science fiction and the analysis of national identity in *The Quiet Earth* (1985) represent the full fruition of Murphy's writing and direction in his home country. These two films incorporate what is arguably the director's best work, in juxtaposing (to comedic, ironic, challenging and often disturbing effect) the attributes of generic commercial cinema, nationally specific and significant readings of landscape and cultural identity, and pertinent, contemporary issues. In *Utu*, the injustices and ambiguities of the Maori Land War of the late nineteenth century are rendered in the form of the western, both in terms of the classical Fordian cavalry sagas and the 'revisionist' and 'spaghetti' westerns of the 1960s and 1970s. The insoluble racial and ethnic problems of the past are connected with those of the present (and vice versa), through the presence of antagonists and protagonists from the Kiwi, Maori and British groups. Murphy manages to unite these cultural antitheses in a narrative which at once sensationalises, ironises and condemns its spectacles of violence. In *The Quiet Earth*, the initiation of an energy experiment in the Northern Hemisphere affects not only New Zealand but the entire planet, and a frictive group of survivors (again split across ethnic and gender lines) is forced to cooperate to avert disaster. The identification of the threat of the experiment with a reckless and imperious United States suggests that the film allegorises the contemporary ANZUS crisis. New Zealand's defiant, anti-nuclear stand against the military strategy of its American allies in this period can be seen to be mirrored in this science fiction narrative of latter-day political, military and scientific imperialism.

Murphy's last film in New Zealand, *Never Say Die* (1988), is essentially a less-successful recapitulation of the best elements of its predecessors: an odd-couple, road-movie comedy thriller, which parodies Bond films and investigative thrillers irreverently. Subsequently, the director began work on a series of American productions, few of which have been destined for theatrical release. Certain of these projects have cohered very closely with the celebratory and ironic stance towards commercial cinema discernible in the New Zealand films. The updating of western conventions in *Young Guns II* (1990), and the self-conscious execution of action formulae in *Under Siege II* (1995), also reflect and capitalise on Murphy's signature skills (in the staging of chases, stunts and other action sequences). Similarly, his collaboration with Roger Donaldson on special effects for another landmark New Zealand feature (*Sleeping Dogs* (1977)) was repeated on Donaldson's American production of *Dante's Peak* (1997), for which Murphy acted as associate producer and second unit director. Murphy's expertise in this area is also reflected in his second unit direction (alongside Alun Bollinger) for Peter Jackson's *The Lord of the Rings: The Fellowship of the Ring* (2001).

Murphy's tendency to amalgamate, parody and hybridise genres in his New Zealand films has continued in his American films (such as *Blind Side* (1993)). In this respect, the innovations of the 1970s and 1980s have become institutionalised within post-classical and post-modern Hollywood film-making. However, the majority of the director's own most recent films have been minor television or cable productions, with the pilot for the American series of *The Magnificent Seven* (1999) marking a return to the western formula. As such, Murphy's reputation rests on a remarkable body of formally and culturally significant films made in New Zealand, which has been followed by proficient but relatively unremarkable productions in America.          **JR**

# John MUSKER
See **Ron CLEMENTS**

# Daniel MYRICK

*The Blair Witch Project* (1999)  Daniel Myrick (born in Florida) and Eduardo Sanchez (born in Cuba) met while studying for a degree in Film at the University of Central Florida and co-wrote and directed *The Blair Witch Project* in 1999. Sanchez had already written and directed the unreleased student films *Video All* and *Gabriel's Dream* and written a number of screenplays, and Myrick had worked on several commercial and independent films as a director of photography and editor.

Recognising the marketing potential of the internet, during the year preceding the release of the film, they ran a hoax website dedicated to the mysterious deaths and supernatural activity in a remote part of Maryland, supposedly inhabited by the eponymous Blair Witch. Billed as a factual piece, the phenomenon quickly gained a cult following: three young film students who had gone into the haunted woods to make a documentary about the Blair Witch never returned, but their footage was found and pieced together into an 85-minute film.

Myrick and Sanchez were working with a tiny budget that necessitated an original, creative approach to the film-making process and overcame the need for prohibitively expensive film stock by shooting partly on video and partly on 8mm film. They succeeded in convincingly allowing for this anomaly in the plot and structure of the film: the use of the two cameras is a strategy by which the characters attempt to save money, echoing the needs of the directors. The titles that open the films tell the audience that the film-makers never returned from the woods, and that the film is their recently discovered footage. Thus, in this unconventional thriller, much of the horror for the audience is derived from the expectancy of the moments of the characters' death. Furthermore, the directors played on the imagination of the audience, and encouraged audience identification with the characters' fear of the unknown in the dark woods. Such identification also extends to the relationship between Myrick and Sanchez – the 'real' film-makers – and the characters: all film-makers, all young, and, along with the audience, all frightened by the rustles, shrieks and noises in the dark. Indeed, much of the film was shot by the actors themselves, who were sent into the woods and deliberately frightened by the directors. Thus, the distinctions between the real and the imaginary, and between actors and film-makers, are blurred.

*The Blair Witch Project* lacks the visual spectacle of more conventional horror films. As the audience views the action purely through the lenses of the characters' cameras, the audience, like the characters themselves, never actually sees who or what kills them. This lack of the visually spectacular is another strategy by which Sanchez and Myrick militate against their tiny budget, although it heightens the sense of audience identification with the characters and succeeds in instilling fear without the spectacle of a more conventional thriller.

A comprehensive, multimedia approach to marketing, including not only the website but also a hoax television documentary, *The Curse of the Blair Witch* (1999), sustained the belief that the story was factual. The sophisticated marketing campaign and the innovative premise of the film ensured that *The Blair Witch Project* became the most relatively profitable film ever. Both Myrick and Sanchez will be writing and directing *Blair Witch 3* although *Blair Witch 2* was directed by Joe Berlinger, with Myrick and Sanchez acting as co-producers.                                                                 **ES**

# N

## Vincenzo NATALI

Vincenzo Natali, born in 1969, graduated from the Canadian Film Centre in 1996. *Cube* (1997)
Two of his six short films, *Mouth* (1992) and *Playground* (1993), have been broadcast
on CBC; *Elevated* (1997) was completed during a residency at the CFC. During this
period he also directed 'Pentimento', an episode from the 1997/98 series of 'Psi Factor:
Chronicles of the Paranormal' (1996), worked as a storyboard artist on *Boulevard*
(1994), *Blood & Donuts* (1995), and *Johnny Mnemonic* (1995), and on the second
unit of the short *Milkman* (1998).

In 1997 Natali co-wrote and directed *Cube*. Shot on a single set in twenty days for
$300,000, it is rich with echoes of *2001: A Space Odyssey* (1968), *THX 1138* (1971),
*Stalker* (1979), *Hellraiser* (1987), and *I Have No Mouth, And I Must Scream* (1995),
and deserves its growing reputation as a thrilling piece of low-budget science fiction. A
handful of strangers wake up to find themselves caught in a giant cube – quite literally a
plot-engine – consisting of several thousand apparently identical cubes, some of which
are booby-trapped; as they attempt to escape conflicts develop and become deadly.
Inventively shot, with some eerily effective handheld camerawork and intelligent use of
a limited palette, its weaknesses lie in a script and performances which are sometimes
only adequate. Occasionally reduced to a set of loudly-asserted values, characters
struggle to carry the required symbolic weight; this is particularly problematic when the
African-American cop who represents a fascistic will-to-power becomes a stereotype of
black male violence and sexuality. **MB**

## Tim Blake NELSON

The move from Oklahoma to New York is a long one and those artists who have made *Eye of God* (1997)
the journey from the Midwest to the Big Apple have tended to return home in the spirit *'O'* (2001)
of their work. That can certainly be said of Tim Blake Nelson, an artist who has worked *The Grey Zone* (2002)
as director, writer, actor and playwright in the last decade, displaying an interest in the
distinctive charms of small-town life. As an actor he has appeared in a number of films
by directors who have a particular interest in portraying the oddities of small rural places:

The Coen brothers (*O Brother, Where Art Thou?* (2000)), Hal Hartley (*Amateur* (1994)), and Terrence Malick (*The Thin Red Line* (1998)). However, his debut, *Eye of God* (1999), which he also wrote, comes from somewhere else, somewhere more distinctly serious and less ironic. *Eye of God* revolves around a young fast food clerk, well played against type by Martha Plimpton, who falls in love and marries a prisoner. Upon his release the story takes a terrible, biblical turn for the worse. Skilfully controlling the kind of twisting storytelling so prevalent in 1990s films since Tarantino's *Pulp Fiction* (1994), Nelson loads his work with significant metaphors of a literary weight that cinema tends to strain under. The metaphors are religious and concern the glass eye Plimpton wears and its uneasy connection to the title and incident of the film. Nelson further honed his writing skills with *Kansas* (1998), a monologue short for the Seattle Film Festival that was well scripted but visually flawed, despite its rich rural setting.

Despite Nelson's talent as a writer, he acted solely as director on *'O'* (2001), an update of 'Othello'. The least necessary of the spate of teen-versions of classic literature, which should have begun and ended with Amy Heckerling's lovely *Clueless* (1994), the play is concerned with distinctly adult emotions but the film, to its detriment, is not. It takes a similar path to Rob Schmidt's *Crime and Punishment in Suburbia* (2000) by darkening a thus-far fairly bright sub-genre, but the empty horror of Iago and his machinations cries out for Phillip Seymour Hoffman, not some kid fresh from puberty.

Nelson' most recent film, which he wrote and directed, is *The Grey Zone* (2002), a historical drama about a Nazi doctor and a group of Jewish Auschwitz captives that are forced to work against their fellow prisoners. Harvey Keitel and Steve Buscemi star. **CSo**

# Mike NEWELL

Mike Newell's career has been a delicate balancing act. A true survivor of the treacherous waters of British film-making, having consistently worked in television and cinema for the past forty years, Newell has juggled the demands of personal vision and commercial return with varying degrees of success. Employing neither the full-blown, big-budget style of a Ridley or Tony Scott, nor the resolutely, dogmatically home-grown approach of a Mike Leigh or Ken Loach, his best work has a broad crossover appeal. It combines the commerciality of formula with a very British attention to the finer details of character and intimate emotional drama. Moving from modest but well-crafted domestic stories, to the larger canvases allowed by Hollywood budgets, with a concurrent shift of focus from British to American subjects, Newell was a key figure in the revival of fortunes of the British film industry in the mid-1990s. This was due in the main to the phenomenal success of *Four Weddings and a Funeral* (1994), his most widely-known work which inspires vitriol and veneration from its audience in roughly proportionate amounts.

The film's light, shamelessly romantic style is actually unusual for Newell who, elsewhere, is more restrained and often downbeat. The accuracy of tone, however, together with the focus on a strong character-driven script and an emphasis on British issues – relationships, class and codes of behaviour – are indicative of his preoccupations. At his best, Newell is capable of truly brilliant film-making of an old-fashioned, dramatic type, as in *Donnie Brasco* (1997). A worthy addition to the Mob film canon, its fluent exploration of split loyalty and betrayal, and brilliant central performances rank alongside the technical wizardry of *Goodfellas* (1990) or the epic grandiloquence of *The Godfather* (1972).

Born in St. Albans, UK, in 1942, Newell attended Cambridge University, followed by a three-year Granada Television training stint. His initial intention had been to graduate into theatre directing, but he soon found himself directing for television, an occupation which was to largely sustain him for the next twenty years, beginning with *Sharon*, a documentary, in 1964. His basis in television direction, with its focus on domestic issues and settings, and an exclusively British target audience, laid the groundwork for close dramatic work that concentrates on character and situation rather than technical virtuosity. His direction of television plays penned by writers such as David Hare, John Osborne, and Jack Rosenthal was particularly formative.

After his version of *The Man in the Iron Mask* (1976) was deemed good enough to warrant a theatrical release, Newell began to make tentative moves towards the world of feature-film production. His first two efforts were undistinguished schlock pictures produced by a British industry desperately trying to compete with the Hollywood action-horror market. *The Awakening* (1980), a mummy picture in which an obsessive archaeologist believes the spirit of an evil Egyptian queen has possessed his new-born daughter, borrows heavily from seminal horror films *Rosemary's Baby* (1968), *Don't Look Now* (1973), and *The Omen* (1976), but lacks any of their subtlety or verve. *Bad Blood* (1981) is a slightly more convincing thriller, based on the story of Eric Stanley Graham, a farmer who shot several people dead in his isolated community in the 1940s and became the subject of New Zealand's most notorious manhunt. Newell uses the bush setting to heighten the unnerving atmosphere, and handles the climactic chase involving Maori trackers and police well enough, but the film marks his last experiment in the genre.

Also based on a true story, but more compelling, is *Dance with a Stranger* (1985), a film about Ruth Ellis, the last woman to be executed in Britain. Here, Newell finds himself in more familiar dramatic territory. Ellis – a young Miranda Richardson in her debut role – is a social climber, a working-class girl burdened with a ten-year-old son, who becomes embroiled in the seedy world of Soho nightlife in 1950s Britain and an obsessive relationship with high-roller David Blakeley. Austere, grimy London and post-war repression contrast the red-blooded desire of the story, a desire fuelled by lust and the drive to escape the trappings of working-class identity. Filming in a neo-documentary style, Newell is fascinated by Ellis' predicament and by the louche corruption and degeneracy of the world Blakeley represents, playing with visual and dramatic representations of sleaziness and self-destructive behaviour. To indicate her downmarket character, particular emphasis is placed on Ellis' coarseness and lack of social niceties; the true moral degradation is played out around her. London – and Britain – has never felt dirtier.

*The Good Father* (1987) is no less critical of British strictures and structures, but is much funnier in its treatment. It is a battle of the sexes in which Newell explores the emasculating developments of 1960s liberalism and 1980s feminism and their impact on family relationships. In opposition are an emotionally inept father, aided by another ex-husband casualty of female empowerment out for revenge on the sisterhood, and the former's liberated lesbian wife. The film charts their child-custody battle with an unerring comic eye, laying emphasis on the unhealthy motives of all involved. It is especially accurate as a study of male anger and repressed emotion of a peculiarly British type. The intelligent comic tone – half-satire, half-farce – signals Newell's later comic efforts, *Four Weddings and a Funeral* and *Pushing Tin* (1999).

*Soursweet* (1988) examines relationships in Britain from the perspective of an immigrant Chinese family finding their way in a foreign land. It is a clash-of-cultures film in which each generation of the family experience some sort of revelation. British society becomes an agent of change rather than a stagnant and repressive force, and the 'old' way is represented by the Soho Triad gang who pursue an unfulfilled debt, threatening the development of the family's new way of life. Impeccably acted and directed, emotional bite is provided by Ian McEwan's script. *Soursweet* is a strong conclusion to a trilogy of films that demonstrate Newell's fascination with emotional drama, relationships, and the trammels of class, sex and society – sometimes circumstantial, and sometimes self-imposed.

Newell revisits these ideas in *An Awfully Big Adventure* (1994), the story of a love triangle set in a post-war Liverpool theatre, in which a young working-class stage-hand is caught between the intellectual desire for social respectability and the emotional need for love and excitement. Hugh Grant, in an unusual role as the Machiavellian, snobbish theatre owner, represents the former urge, and Alan Rickman's suave, enigmatic lead actor, the latter.

Appropriately enough for a director fascinated by entrapment – an idea explored very differently in *Four Weddings* and *Donnie Brasco* – Newell is also interested in methods of escape. *Amazing Grace and Chuck* (1987), a comic fantasy of wish-fulfilment, examines one form of release, demonstrating cinema's Capraesque potential to transport its audience from the realities of the everyday; and reality doesn't come much more real than mutually assured nuclear destruction. A young American boy strikes from his 'little league' baseball team in protest against a local missile silo, gaining national notoriety and inspiring basketball star Amazing Grace Smith and fellow sports stars to follow in his suit and lobby the President.

Newell revisited the idea of fantasy intruding upon reality in *Into the West* (1992). The contrast in the film becomes intentionally stark, comparing the effect of the grim environs of Irish tower-block life on two children with the fantastic resonance of a white horse brought home by their grandfather. It is Newell's most visually ambitious and striking work, invoking the mythology of both Irish folklore and the Western frontier as metaphors for imaginative liberation and for the rediscovery of family and identity. *Enchanted April* (1992) demonstrates a more realistic form of escape, and revisits Newell's interest in the psychology of repressed and oppressed women. Four 1920s archetypes – a snobbish widow, an aristocrat, a bored housewife, and the unfulfilled wife of a writer – escape from their constraining circumstances to an Italian castle, where their disparate characters, and the contrasting emotional sensibilities of England and Europe, collide. The development of this side of Newell's style – the ability to mix sharp comedy, well-drawn character and drama with sentimentality – was soon to prove financially, as well as artistically, rewarding.

Both of Newell's best films – *Four Weddings and a Funeral* and *Donnie Brasco* — incorporate his talents as a comic entertainer and character director. *Four Weddings and a Funeral* has become something of a pop phenomenon. Instrumental in convincing various movers and shakers of the potential viability and commerciality of home-grown British product, the film is the perfect example of Newell's comic side. It is well-scripted and performed, entertaining and immensely marketable, its characters teetering on the cusp of character and caricature. The central character of a 'serial monogamist' – Hugh Grant in full stumbling schoolboy flow attempting to overcome the binds of English emotional ineptitude in professing his love for a frank American – is a classic Newell protagonist. He is manacled in emotional chains of his own making, as are the sugar-coated issues of repressed love, English reserve, class and character. Newell's skill is in mixing the requisite comic mishaps with emotional punch. The array of neatly packaged British stereotypes – bumbling fop, cheeky Cockney, and hell-raising Scot – overtly panders to an American audience and is too much for some to stomach. Where Newell has the charm and wit to carry it off, later imitators do not. While laying much of the groundwork for the international reception of modern British film-making, *Four Weddings* has also been instrumental in creating some of the straightjackets of subject and character by which those films are bound. It has spawned formulaic romantic comedies and Cockney posturing – outdated stereotypes and one-size-fits-all film-making of the worst kind.

Quite the opposite, *Donnie Brasco* is an understated, unsentimental character study that seeks to break down, rather than perpetuate, well-worn stereotypes, in this case those of the American Mafia. Taking an almost scientific interest in the rules, rituals and routines of low-level Mob life, the film follows Donnie, an undercover cop, and the development of his relationship with Lefty Ruggiero, a long-serving foot soldier who becomes his mentor. Newell's interest is in the dramatic potential of Donnie's split loyalty. He contrasts his home life and the increasingly complex world in which he becomes embroiled, portraying the conflicting demands of profession and friendship that must inevitably come to a head. There is also an affectionate, comic touch at work in the fascination with Mafioso language and Mob etiquette. Sayings like 'fahgedabuoudit', 'fugazi', 'stand-up guy' are explained; the distinction is made between 'a friend of ours' and 'a friend of mine'; nicknames such as Sonny Black, Sonny Red, Lefty Two Guns abound; and at Christmas, both Donnie and Lefty exchange cards with identical wads of cash inside. In their own way, these rules of conduct are as restrictive and defining as the British codes which Newell has explored elsewhere. With its cinematic nods to *Goodfellas* (Scorsese-style montage sequences cut together with a pop soundtrack) and a domestic, low-key approach that deconstructs *Godfather* mythologising, the film is Newell's most compelling drama and his most fluent exploration of the dramatic possibilities of film. It features outstanding turns by Johnny Depp and Al Pacino.

*Pushing Tin* is another glimpse into a parallel, male-dominated world: the testosterone-fuelled profession of air traffic control. It is a high-pressure, competitive environment charged with the type of masculine ego exemplified by top-man Nick Falzone, whose supremacy is threatened by the Zen-like, Indian feather-toting calmness of new man Russell Bell. Another study of male codes of behaviour, the film once again showcases Newell's fluent style and comic timing, as well as his fondness for the slushy ending that *Donnie Brasco* thankfully lacked.

A commercial director in both the positive and negative senses of the word, Newell is a consistently reliable and intelligent film-maker who focuses on cinema's capacity to entertain and emotionally engage rather than provoke or enrage. His next film, *Mona Lisa Smile*, has drawn comparisons to *Dead Poet's Society* (1989) and will star Julia Roberts as a teacher in a women's college in 1953. **OB**

# Andrew NICCOL

A relative newcomer to Hollywood, Andrew Niccol has already developed a name for himself as a distinctive talent, able to examine unusual subject matter in a way which appeals to mainstream audiences. At the age of twenty-one, having left his native New Zealand where he was born in 1964, he spent ten years writing and directing commercials in Britain before having his screenplay for *The Truman Show* (1998) accepted by a major studio. Due to Niccol's lack of experience, veteran Peter Weir was brought in to direct the film with Jim Carrey to star. After a series of production delays, Niccol subsequently wrote and directed *Gattaca* (1997) which were generally well-received by critics upon its release. *The Truman Show* was later nominated for an Academy Award and received a BAFTA for Best Original Screenplay.

*Gattaca* (1997)
*Simone* (2002)

Conceptually, the two films share a great deal in common. Both are set in dystopian near futures and raise issues that are relevant to their contemporaneous societies. *The Truman Show* critiques the powerful gaze of the media and features a protagonist who desires to break free from conformity and establish a sense of his own individuality. *Gattaca* posits a world that is ordered by genetic determinism and a hero with a low social status who is desperate to be accepted. Clearly the work of an advertising director, *Gattaca* has a sleek, honed visual style, complete with modernist designer costumes and stark, minimalist interiors lit through icy, blue filters. While its surface sheen may be necessary to create a suitably clinical atmosphere and heighten the sense of emotional emptiness, the effect at times can be a little distancing for the viewer. Nevertheless, the film is a thought-provoking debut and features a consistently interesting and well-judged trio of performances from Uma Thurman, Ethan Hawke and Jude Law.

Although impressed with Weir's interpretation of *The Truman Show*, Niccol has commented that his personal narrative and stylistic approach would have been far darker. In the future he intends to direct his own screenplays and thereby maintain greater artistic control. Given the success and originality of his efforts so far it is fair to assume that his films will be challenging in both their choice of topic and tone.

Niccol's most recent film is the comedy *Simone* (2002), which stars Al Pacino as a film producer who decides to substitute a computer-generated character for his lead actress when she abandons the shoot. **HP**

# Mike NICHOLS

Born Michael Igor Peschkowsky in Berlin in 1931, Mike Nichols moved to the US in 1939 and began his career as an actor on the New York stage. His 1950s comedy performances with (amongst others) frequent collaborator Elaine May, are widely regarded to have brought improvisational comedy to the US. Nichols carried this sense of innovation over into his work as a film director. Along with Elia Kazan and Arthur Penn, he is a key figure in 1960s Hollywood, making films which were personal and indebted to European cinema while still being accessible; in so doing, he paved the way for the 'Movie Brats' (such as Martin Scorsese, Francis Ford Coppola and Steven Spielberg) who would transform the industry in the 1970s.

*Who's Afraid of Virginia Woolf?* (1966)
*The Graduate* (1967)
*Catch-22* (1970)
*Carnal Knowledge* (1971)
*Day of the Dolphin* (1973)
*The Fortune* (1975)
*Gilda Live* (1980)
*Silkwood* (1983)
*Heartburn* (1986)
*Biloxi Blues* (1988)
*Working Girl* (1988)
*Postcards From The Edge* (1990)
*Regarding Henry* (1991)
*Wolf* (1994)
*The Birdcage* (1996)
*Primary Colors* (1998)

It may well be Nichols' experience as a stage director that led him to adapt Edward Albee's play for his debut feature film, *Who's Afraid of Virginia Woolf?* (1966), an often exhausting tale of marital breakdown and strife among academics on a University campus in New England. The then-tabloid darlings, Elizabeth Taylor and Richard Burton play George and Martha who tear each other to pieces during one boozy night, watched by a naïve colleague and his wife (George Segal and Sandy Dennis). The acting is uniformly excellent, particularly from Taylor who was too often a great star without being a good actor. Nichols uses stark black and white and makes the wise decision not to open out the play too much thus retaining its sense of claustrophobia; he also moves in close with the camera so that we feel uncomfortably close to the characters. Like Kazan's *A*

*Streetcar Named Desire* (1951), this is a stylish and powerful film adaptation of an American classic.

Nichols followed with *The Graduate* (1967). An adaptation of Charles Webb's novel, this is a watershed in Hollywood film-making: the sense of disaffection and frustration on show here mirrors a divided country and a generation that was finding a voice through the protest movement in the second half of the decade. Benjamin Braddock (Dustin Hoffman in a star-making performance) is the eponymous character, alienated from his pushy parents and embarking on an affair with the delectable older woman, Mrs Robinson (Anne Bancroft). Frequent television showings of *The Graduate* may have diluted its power somewhat but this remains a fresh, funny, and pleasingly acidic comedy that shows Nichols' ability to move effortlessly between the witty and the mortifying. Also noteworthy is the use of songs by Simon and Garfunkel, the swimming pool scene (during which a wet-suited Benjamin hides out underwater), and the affecting last shot of Hoffman and Katharine Ross, their smiles fading as they ponder what awaits them. *The Graduate*, like its predecessor, is smart, hip and innovative popular cinema.

Next, Nichols made a Joseph Heller adaptation, *Catch-22* (1970). A difficult project, adapted by *The Graduate* screenwriter, Buck Henry, it is both inspired and turgid in equal measures. Nichols and Henry certainly manage to capture the feel of Heller's anti-war black comedy and the cast is remarkable – Anthony Perkins, Orson Welles, Jon Voight, Charles Grodin, and an impressive Alan Arkin as Yossarian. Yet the tone is wildly uneven and what Heller achieves on the page is harder to capture on film. *Catch-22* is best regarded as a noble, at times brilliant, failure.

Nichols scored again, however, with *Carnal Knowledge* (1971), a coruscating, often painful attempt to expose American masculinity, which follows two characters (Art Garfunkel's weak Sandy and Jack Nicholson's rapacious Jonathan) from the 1950s through to the 1970s. Written by the cartoonist Jules Feiffer, this is one of the best examples of what Hollywood cinema of this decade could do: it is an unashamedly adult movie that isn't afraid to be either unpleasant or technically innovative. Nicholson is incredible and his creepy, misogynistic Jonathan proves that he is an actor who is unafraid to take risks with his image; the scene where he flies into a rage while dressing for dinner is some of the best acting in cinema. More surprising, the singer Art Garfunkel (who had a small role in *Catch-22*) more than holds his own opposite Nicholson. The women in the film are also very good: Candice Bergen, Rita Moreno, Carol Kane and, in particular, Ann Margret as the sexy, screwed-up Bobbie. The direction is exemplary; Nichols makes his actors work hard, giving them lots of straight-to-camera scenes, long takes and close-ups. This is not a date movie and the unpleasantness on show here may be hard for some to take – Feiffer and Nichols are interested in exposing the darkness that lurks within the American male – but as a brilliantly acted, stylish and powerful entertainment, *Carnal Knowledge* takes some beating. The terrifying ending with a bitter and impotent Jonathan being flattered and fellated by Rita Moreno's hooker in a stylised ritual reinforces the fact that *Carnal Knowledge* is arguably Nichols' best film.

After this career peak, Nichols floundered slightly. *Day of the Dolphin* (1973) is a silly romp with George C. Scott and some dolphin assassins. *The Fortune* (1975), a black comedy with Jack Nicholson and Warren Beatty as two con men wooing and trying to kill Stockard Channing's heiress, was hammered by critics. If one doesn't mind the often embarrassing comedy sequences (or can overlook Nicholson's afro-style hair), this is still offbeat, appealing stuff.

The rest of the decade saw Nichols back on Broadway. He didn't make another movie until *Gilda Live* (1980), a Gilda Radner concert movie. After a television film (*The Gin Game* (1981)), he returned to mainstream cinema in 1983 with *Silkwood*, based on the true story of Karen Silkwood, a worker at an Oklahoma nuclear power plant who blew the whistle about safety breaches and then died in suspicious circumstances. This is slick fare, done well and Nichols directs like a less paranoid Alan J. Pakula. As one expects, the acting is strong: Meryl Streep excels in the title role, Kurt Russell is better than usual, and even Cher is pretty good. Although his earlier stylistic flourishes are missing, this is decent mainstream entertainment. *Silkwood* marks Nichols shift from the 'angry' films of the 1960s and 1970s to more polished (and less interesting) star vehicles.

*Heartburn* (1986) is a good example of the latter: written by Nora Ephron (who wrote *Silkwood*), this is an adaptation of her autobiographical novel, detailing her marriage to unfaithful journalist Carl Bernstein (re-named as Rachel and Mark). As expected, heavyweights Streep and Nicholson are good but this is nevertheless pretty insubstantial – although it looks like *Carnal Knowledge* when compared to Ephron's later outings as director, *Sleepless in Seattle* (1993) and *You've Got Mail* (1998). *Biloxi Blues* (1988) is another autobiographical outing, this time written by playwright Neil Simon, and deals with his time spent doing basic training in the army in Biloxi, Mississippi. Frothy but efficient, Matthew Broderick is the lead and Christopher Walken has fun as the CO.

*Working Girl*, released the same year, is an office comedy that proved to be Nichols' biggest hit for a while. A starry cast – Harrison Ford, Sigourney Weaver and a less-annoying-than-usual Melanie Griffith – appear in the story that sees Tess McGill (Griffith) impersonating her boss (Weaver) and predictably proving herself as a skilled high flyer. This is one of those 1980s movies that deals with corporate power and the Manhattan business world, like a less blustering (and funnier) *Wall Street* (1987). Weaver and Ford both seem to have a good time playing away from their trademark action roles and Joan Cusack gets most of the best lines as a whacky secretary – a part for which she received an Academy Award nomination.

*Postcards from the Edge* (1990), Nichols' subsequent film, tackled the druggy autobiographical novel by Carrie Fisher, one-time coke-head star and daughter of Debbie Reynolds. Here Fisher has become Suzanne Vale (Streep again) and Reynolds is Doris Mann (Shirley MacLaine). A mother-daughter-drug-comedy-Hollywood exposé, it collapses under the weight of its ambitions. Streep isn't really a comedienne (and doesn't look out-of-it enough in the first half of the film) but MacLaine is good; there is also effective support from Richard Dreyfuss, Dennis Quaid and Gene Hackman. This is perfectly watchable but Fisher's novel is sleazier and angrier, and the 1990s Nichols is too gentle to really do this material justice – especially when compared to the Altman of *The Player* (1992).

The 1991 Harrison Ford vehicle *Regarding Henry* was a tedious 'yuppie redemption' movie. Like Randa Haines' equally tedious *The Doctor* (1991), it marks the shift from the 'greedy 80s' to the 'caring, sharing 90s' with the tale of a go-getting lawyer (a mis-cast Ford) who, after being shot in the head, learns to appreciate family and the small things in life. This saccharine stuff is far removed from the director's earlier caustic films. Strangely, *Regarding Henry* seems to suggest that a bullet in the head may be just the thing for high-powered men who neglect their families. Annette Bening and Bill Nunn are also wasted, as are the talents of cinematographer Guiseppe Rotunno.

Next came *Wolf* (1994), an unsuccessful blend of horror film and workplace drama with Jack Nicholson playing an executive who is bitten by wolf. Pretty soon, he is howling at the moon in Central Park, urinating over his young office rival (James Spader), and having animal sex with Michelle Pfeiffer. This big-budget monster movie may have worked but Nichols seems much more interested in the business rivalry (revisiting the arena of *Working Girl*) and has little feel for horror. Nicholson is always watchable but his make-up is ridiculous and the talented supporting cast (Spader, Kate Nelligan, Christopher Plummer) has little to do. The screenplay, by Jim Harrison and Wesley Strick, gives occasional glimpses of the film it could have been, with the novel notion of lycanthropy as a blessing rather than a burden, but the Nicolas Cage vehicle *Vampire's Kiss* (1989) is a more successful mix of old-fashioned monsters and the modern workplace.

*The Birdcage* (1996) followed, an ill-advised remake of the popular French farce *La Cage Aux Folles* (1978). Robin Williams and Nathan Lane play two gay Miami club-owners who have to pose as upstanding heterosexuals in order to fool a Jesse Helms-ish Senator (Gene Hackman) whose daughter is engaged to Williams' son. The lightness of touch in the French original is missing here and Williams and (the usually reliable) Lane camp, shriek and flounce their way through this dated comedy of errors. Like other Hollywood remakes of European movies such as *Three Men and a Baby* (1987), *The Assassin* (1993), *The Vanishing* (1993), *Nightwatch* (1998), and *Jakob the Liar* (1999), this is entirely superfluous.

*Primary Colors* (1998) is an adaptation (by Nichols' former comedy partner Elaine May) of the anonymous novel, which was in fact written by Joe Klein, about the Clintons. Like the Barry Levinson satire *Wag the Dog* (1997), the film was overtaken by real events – in this case the Monica Lewinsky affair – but remains slick, polished adult fare, Nichols' best for a decade. John Travolta and Emma Thompson are good as the scandal-hit governor Jack Stanton and his wife and the heavyweight supporting cast includes

Adrian Lester, Kathy Bates, and Billy Bob Thornton. Unlike Rob Reiner's sentimental, superficially similar *The American President* (1995), this is pretty cynical stuff and Travolta in particular seems to be having fun.

*What Planet Are You From?* (2000) is a sex comedy about an alien (Garry Shandling) with a humming, mechanical penis who comes to Earth to mate with Annette Bening. Presumably inspired by the John Gray bestseller 'Men Are From Mars, Women Are From Venus', there are a few laughs here but the film received mixed reviews; the Detroit News comment 'this is *American Pie* for boys-will-be-boys in their mid 50s' was particularly damning. Indeed, Nichols seems unsure as to what kind of comedy this is. Star and co-writer Shandling is best known for his innovative and smart television show 'The Larry Sanders Show' but the sub-Farrelly Brothers humour seems to be attempt to reach the teen crowd. As usual with a Nichols movie, the supporting cast – Greg Kinnear, Linda Fiorentino, Ben Kingsley, John Goodman, and Janeane Garafolo – is excellent.

His latest film is the TV movie, *Wit* (2001), starring Emma Thompson as an English Lit Professor diagnosed with ovarian cancer. Like Nichols' debut, this is an adaptation of a play, in this case by Margaret Edson.

It is hard to say whether Nichols' shift from arty, dark satire to glossy star vehicles is a personal choice or due to the changes in Hollywood over the last three decades. When one looks at the careers of his contemporaries, such as Arthur Penn, William Friedkin, Elia Kazan, and the late Michael Ritchie, it seems to be near impossible for a director to specialise now in the 'difficult', often bitter, mainstream movies which made their name.

Nichols' next film, like *The Birdcage*, will be another remake, this time of the 1949 comedy *Kind Hearts and Coronets*.                                                                    IC

# Christopher NOLAN

*Following* (1998)
*Memento* (2000)
*Insomnia* (2002)

Establishing himself as an original talent with his debut feature, *Following* (1998), Christopher Nolan swiftly capitalised on his critical success with the acclaimed thriller *Memento* (2000) and more recently with the bigger-budget star vehicle *Insomnia* (2002). Favouring small, intense, character-driven stories, his work is heavily influenced by noir narratives and aesthetics. Fashioning protagonists that become the detectives in the mysteries of their own lives, his two first films incorporate flashback narratives.

Born in London in 1970, Nolan experimented with home videos from the age of seven, studied English Literature at University College London, and made three- and four-minute 16mm shorts. *Following*, a hit at Toronto, Slamdance and Rotterdam film festivals, is shot in documentary-style black-and-white, and runs at an economical 70 minutes. Like *Memento*, its plot seems convoluted but is actually simple. An aspiring writer, Bill (Jeremy Theobald), tells the story: having taken to following strangers, his life takes a dramatic turn when one of his subjects, Cobb (Alex Haw), leads him into a life of petty crime. Featuring the customary characters – gangster boss and femme fatale – and the requisite double-crossing, the theatricality of the piece tends towards the melodramatic and at times the acting seems stagey and stilted. However, given that the shoot of 20 days took place over a year, with only one or two takes of each set-up, this is hardly surprising. Variously touching on issues of class, identity, voyeurism and the nature of illusion, the film is well sustained by its intriguing premise.

Nolan's subsequent film, *Memento*, screened in competition at the 2001 Sundance Festival and won the Waldo Salt Screenwriting Award. Based on a short story by Nolan's brother, Jonathan, about a polaroid image which fades rather than reveals itself, in the director's own words it is a 'dis-linear' thriller, 'dealt to us in reverse chronology by a protagonist coping with a trauma-induced condition that prevents him from making new memories'. Guy Pearce plays Lenny, the protagonist in question, perfectly creating a sense of the character's complex past and empty, searching present; with an unreliable memory he tattoos his body in order to remind himself of the important details of his life. Extremely stylish, it cuts between black-and-white and green-tinged colour to delineate time shifts. Like *Following*, it rarely features establishing shots, focusing close in on Lenny's face to heighten the sense of his entrapment and claustrophobia. Joe Pantoliano is suitably ambiguous as Teddy, the contradictory figure who could be friend or enemy, and Carrie-Ann Moss, the spiky, enigmatic love interest, contrasts well with the soft-focus image of Lenny's dead wife.

Nolan's recent *Insomnia* is a remake of a 1997 Norwegian film of the same name directed by Erik Skjoldbjaerg. Al Pacino stars as a troubled cop sent up to Alaska to investigate a nasty murder with his partner (Martin Donovan), and the assistance of a local newcomer to the force (Hilary Swank). A noir set in the constant daylight of 24-hour sun, it benefits from Nolan's ability to fuel psychologically compelling narratives and elicit controlled powerhouse performances.

Like David Fincher or Steven Soderbergh, he fashions stylish, smart and intriguing films that appeal on both an emotional and intelligent level to mainstream and art-house audiences alike.                                                                        **HP**

# Edward NORTON

Since leaving his mark on the Hollywood scene with his cleverly schizoid performance as a murder suspect in the 1996 potboiler *Primal Fear*, Edward Norton has been widely considered one of the finest actors of his generation. Born in Boston in 1970, his understated charisma and broad, 'everyman' appeal has helped lend sympathy to his edgy character work in *Rounders* (1998), *American History X* (1998), and *Fight Club* (1999).

*Keeping the Faith* (2000)

It seems surprising then that Norton chose to make his directorial debut with the relatively light romantic comedy *Keeping the Faith* (2000). However, Norton's second film appearance was in Woody Allen's sunny Manhattan musical *Everyone Says I Love You* (1996), and *Keeping the Faith* shows a deep-soaked Allen influence both in terms of structure and composition. In direct contrast to the visual pyrotechnics favoured by many young directors, Norton's approach is refreshingly unpretentious. As befitting an actor-turned-auteur, scenes are largely staged in medium or master shots, often in single takes, preserving both the integrity of the performances and the film's loose comic energy. Like much of Allen's best work, it is also a love letter to New York City, beginning with a glittering overhead shot of the city at night and extending to his sparkling treatment of such tried-and-true locations as Central Park and the Upper West Side.

A bare bones reading of *Keeping the Faith*'s plot (a priest and a rabbi, friends since childhood, find themselves in love with the same girl) makes it sound like a shaggy dog joke, but Norton – a Catholic himself, who here plays the priest – goes deeper than that, using the script's sitcom contrivance as a springboard for a light-hearted meditation on love and faith, confidently balancing the film's central romantic triangle with a colourful myriad of supporting players. Perhaps fittingly, the bishop who offers guidance to Norton's character is played by another of his real-life mentors, his *The People vs. Larry Flynt* (1996) director, Milos Forman.                                         **CS**

# Phillip NOYCE

Born in Griffith, New South Wales, in 1950, Noyce moved to Sydney at the age of 12. At 17, he made his first short, *Better to Reign in Hell*, about adolescent sexual fantasies. He briefly attended the University of Sydney's law school, later re-enrolling in their fine arts department. *Renegades*, a diary film made over four years, was followed by *Good Afternoon*, which was shot on two linked cameras and had to be projected onto two screens. In 1973, as one of the first students at the Australian Film and Television School, he directed two shorts, *That's Showbiz*, about a vaudeville troupe who hire a stripper to liven up their show, and *Caravan Park*. In the same year, he also made as the award-winning *Castor and Pollux*, a 45-minute documentary about two brothers – a hippy and a biker – and their attitudes towards conventional lifestyles; he would return to the dynamic of this relationship in his first two features.

*Backroads* (1977)
*Newsfront* (1978)
*Heatwave* (1982)
*Echoes of Paradise* (1987)
*Dead Calm* (1989)
*Blind Fury* (1989)
*Patriot Games* (1992)
*Sliver* (1993)
*Clear and Present Danger* (1994)
*The Saint* (1997)
*The Repair Shop* (1998)
*The Bone Collector* (1999)
*Rabbit-Proof Fence* (2002)
*The Quiet American* (2002)

His first professional work was as production manager and assistant director of *The Golden Cage* (1975), as director of *God Knows Why, But It Works* (1975), a docudrama about Dr. Archie Kalokerinos and aboriginal healthcare, as second assistant director on *Let the Balloon Go* (1975), and as director of several Film Australia shorts.

*Backroads* (1977) is a low-budget road movie in which aboriginal Gary (played by activist Gary Foley) and profane bigot Bill drive around with sundry others in various stolen vehicles. After his Uncle Joe murders a wealthy white man whose car they are trying to steal, Gary refuses to surrender to the police and is gunned down. A continuation of Noyce's exploration of the degradation of aboriginal life, it is marred by choppy editing, some inconsistent characterisation, and clumsy stylistic flourishes. Although its attempts at significance largely fail, the dialogue between Gary and Jack remains resonant. *Newsfront* (1978), a detailed and involving period piece, charts the lives of the newsreel cameramen, the Maguire brothers, between 1948 and 1956. Blending actuality footage and reconstructions with a dramatic narrative, it exhibits a significant maturation of Noyce's storytelling skills: the social and political history is never just a backdrop, nor does the narrative become mere illustration. Noyce would return to the conflict between integrity and advancement in *Heatwave* (1982) and the Jack Ryan movies.

After several aborted projects, which included being fired as director of *Attack Force Z* (1982) on the night before shooting was due to start, Noyce directed *Heatwave*, based on the events which also inspired *The Killing of Angel Street* (1981). A routine conspiracy thriller about the destruction of a neighbourhood by property developers, it displays Noyce's growing technical proficiency. Television work followed. In 1983 he directed 'The Dismissal', a mini-series about the sacking of Australia's Labor Prime Minister Gough Whitlam by the Governor General in 1975, and joined the impressive role-call of directors who contributed episodes to the series 'The Hitchhiker'. In 1984, he co-wrote and co-directed 'Cowra Breakout', a mini-series based on the escape of 1,104 Japanese from an Australian prisoner-of-war camp.

Noyce returned to cinema with *Echoes of Paradise* (1987), a film about a woman who must choose between a Balinese Temple Dancer and her philandering husband, and *Dead Calm* (1989), which was rousingly adapted from Charles Williams' thriller. In *Dead Calm*, a haunting opening sequence is followed by a showy and ludicrous flashback, setting the tone for much of what will follow. A dog barks at an empty dawn sea, and a becalmed black schooner is sighted, but the sense of building menace is rapidly discarded in favour of slasher movie plotting; a suspenseful screenplay is marred by shock moments, including one ending too many. Its theme of curing, protecting, and reconstituting the family is reiterated in *Blind Fury* (1989), an updated Americanisation of the Japanese samurai character Zato Ichi. The backstory, in which a US soldier (played by Rutger Hauer) is blinded, taken in by Vietnamese villagers, and trained as a martial arts swordsman, is concluded with alacrity. Before the title sequence is over he has returned to present-day America, where, in order to reunite a child with his father, he must combat the villains. Played with good-humoured relish, this tongue-in-cheek action-comedy is enjoyable if not always successful.

Next, Noyce directed *Patriot Games* (1992), an adaptation of Tom Clancy's novel and a sequel to *The Hunt for Red October* (1990), with Harrison Ford taking over the role of Jack Ryan. It is an effective thriller, despite a typically knuckleheaded portrayal of Ireland and Irish republicanism (which it reduces to a threat to Ryan's family). Of the Ryan movies to date, *Clear and Present Danger* (1994), also directed by Noyce, is the one which most clearly struggles with the narrative form of its source. The solution is to make a straightforward actioneer by beefing up Ryan's role at the expense of those of Clark (Willem Dafoe) and Chavez (Raymond Cruz); unsurprisingly in a screenplay co-written by John Milius, it excises the moral ambiguitites and complexities of Clancy's novel.

Noyce's other American work lacks any sense of development: he remains proficient but is always at the mercy of his scripts. The attractively shot and crisply directed *Sliver* (1993), adapted from Ira Levin's novel, could not overcome Joe Eszterhas' customary sleazy, pretentious and preposterous screenplay. Reshooting was forced upon the production in order to change the identity of the killer, but the central characters are so unsympathetic it is difficult to care. *The Saint* (1997) is a ludicrous action movie bearing little resemblance to Leslie Charteris' gentleman anti-hero, or to previous movie and television adaptations. After a newly-concocted origin story, the cast run around England and Russia in pursuit of one another. Noyce's direction is never less than competent, but his efforts to imbue this witless farrago with some maturity are at odds with a superficial and frequently idiotic screenplay – the near-naked embrace of his leading lady cures The Saint of hypothermia in minutes, and the romance that develops between them *literally* mends her broken heart. The movie does possess a certain goofy appeal, largely due to Kilmer's ill-advised performance, but Noyce, the actors, and, of course, Simon Templar all deserve better than this. *The Bone Collector* (1999) sees a paraplegic and suicidal Denzel Washington enlisted in the pursuit of a serial killer. Adequately reworking material familiar from countless other movies, it is spoiled by platitudes about optimism in the face of adversity.

*Rabbit-Proof Fence* (2002) saw Noyce return to Australia, and to his early theme of the degradation of Aboriginal life, to tell the true story, based on the book by Doris Pilkington Garimara, of three mixed-race girls who were taken from their Aboriginal mothers in 1931 and forced to assimilate into white culture. The title refers to a fence built across the centre of Australia to protect farms from the plague of rabbits. When the girls escape, they follow the fence back home. *The Quiet American* (2002), adapted from Graham Greene's novel, stars Michael Caine and Brendan Fraser. **MB**

# Victor NUÑEZ

A native southerner, born in Deland, Florida, in 1945, Victor Nuñez's films have all explored life in the Deep South, paying rich attention to detail and depth of characterisation. Fiercely independent, his first film, *Charly Benson Returns to the Sea* (1972), established Nuñez's fascination with the linked themes of character, time and place, which were carried over to his second feature *A Circle in the Fire* (1975), based on Flannery O'Connor's short story, and his third, the theatrically released *Gal Young 'Un* (1979). Adapted from a 1932 novel by Marjorie Kinnan Rawlings about a Florida-born rural widow who marries a young bootlegger during the period of prohibition, *Gal Young 'Un* moved beyond the confines of Nuñez's homeland, winning an award at Cannes. The film epitomises a tradition of independent American film that considers the internal actions of characters just as much as the external actions, finding the drama in common, everyday actions.

These techniques, and the experience gained on *Gal Young 'Un*, led to Nuñez's next feature *A Flash of Green* (1984), a television film that gained a small theatrical release. Like his previous films, it was set both in the south (Florida again) and in the recent past, and focused on a conflict between developers and residents over a proposed development on public land. Critical of both formal politics and capital, the film contained Nuñez's main concerns for the everyday lives of the characters.

This concern with the minutiae of characters' lives, and life as a series of anti-climaxes, infuses his first major release, *Ruby in Paradise* (1993). Foregrounding the importance of place, it focuses on Ruby (a remarkable Ashley Judd), an unhappy resident of East Tennessee, who heads for Florida and ends up in the archetypal 'nowheresville', Panama City. Nuñez presents Ruby as an ordinary woman with emotional depth, avoiding any sentimentality in his portrayal of the flip side of the American dream.

Nuñez came full circle with *Ulee's Gold* (1997). Like *Charly Benson Returns to the Sea*, the film features a Vietnam veteran, Ulysses Jackson (nicknamed Ulee), who is played with moving sincerity by Peter Fonda. Like Ruby, Ulee is a solitary figure in the landscape, estranged from his family, introverted and emotionally drawn. In possibly his finest film, Nuñez pulls together all his preoccupations and passions in the character of Ulee, a beekeeper whose son is in jail and whose junkie daughter-in-law is kidnapped by his son's former partners in crime. In the hands of many directors this might have become a predictable tale of revenge, but the tensions in Nuñez's film arise out of the need for the self-contained Ulee to ask for help rather than deal with his predicament alone.

Florida-based *Coastlines* (2002) is Nuñez's first film since *Ulee's Gold*; though the screenplay was written some 15 years earlier, Nuñez could not find a backer. *Coastlines* is a dark revenge thriller about a young drug-runner called Sonny Mann (Timothy Olyphant) who emerges from a three-year prison term determined to claim his share of a lucrative drug trade operated by his former partners in crime, who are reluctant to pay up. As if to complicate matters further he enters into an affair with Ann (Sarah Wynter), the wife of the local Sheriff (Josh Brolin), both of whom are childhood friends. Like many of Nuñez's films, the setting for the film (a region of Florida's Gulf Coast known as the 'Forgotten Coast') and the focus on character are as important and evocative as the story. It was a considerable success at The Sundance Festival and is awaiting release, further confirming Nuñez's reputation as one of North America's most important independent film-makers. **SH**

*Gal Young 'Un* (1979)
*A Flash of Green* (1984)
*Ruby in Paradise* (1993)
*Ulee's Gold* (1997)

# David NUTTER

*Disturbing Behavior* (1998) David Nutter is a veteran television director whose genre experience and workmanlike efforts on such quality programming as 'Millennium' and 'Space: Above and Beyond' earned him a shot at directing feature films in the late 1990s. His career is loosely intertwined with the career of cult television writing/directing duo James Wong and Glen Morgan, a working relationship that started on the Fox television show '21 Jump Street' in 1987. Nutter is probably best known for his work on the popular science fiction anthology 'The X-Files', where he directed several of the series' most highly acclaimed episodes, including 'Ice', 'Beyond the Sea', and 'Claude Bruckman's Final Repose'.

After directing two entries in Full Moon's cult direct-to-video series 'Trancers', Nutter made his feature film debut with *Disturbing Behavior* (1998). An unabashed *Stepford Wives* (1974) clone, oozing with sexy, teen-friendly faces, rock music and pop culture coolness, it is not much better than retrograde bubblegum horror like *I Know What You Did Last Summer* (1997). The film fails on many levels, the most glaring being its compromised narrative, which was apparently gutted from the final cut by MGM/UA against Nutter's wishes. Although *Disturbing Behavior* is technically polished and competently photographed in a style evocative of Nutter's television work, this is not enough to raise the film above its middling aspirations. After his disappointing feature debut, Nutter resumed his genre television career on the teen science fiction series 'Roswell High' and the James Cameron-produced 'Dark Angel'. **THa**

# Alanis OBOMSAWIN

Born in Lebanon, New York, in 1932, Alanis Obomsawin has always seen herself as an activist first and a film-maker second. In the 1960s she was a prominent radical and folk singer, and in 1965 was brought in as a consultant on a film being made by the National Film Board of Canada. She 'got the bug' from this experience, and, more than thirty years later, is one of the NFB's most respected staff directors.

    Her most famous film is *Kanehsatake: 270 Years of Resistance* (1993), which documents the standoff between Mohawk warriors and the Canadian Army, which lasted for several months in 1990. Shot with an unmistakable subjectivity, and clearly intended as a partisan document meant to correct media misrepresentation of the intentions and politics of the Native rebels, it is a fiery, emotionally affecting piece of work. She shot an enormous amount of footage during the crisis, and this lead to two shorter, quieter films about specific people involved in the uprising, *My Name is Kahentiiosta* (1995) and *Spudwrench: Kahnawake Man* (1997), and also to a 'ten years after' film, *Rocks At Whiskey Trench* (2000).

    Indeed, most of her films are moving but restrained works of cinematic activism, many of which are about institutions that help native people. Her short film *Poundmakers Lodge* (1987) is a portrait of an alcoholic recovery centre in Alberta, and *Le Patro, Le Prévost 80 years later* (1991) is about a multicultural day care centre in Montreal. In 1979 and 1980 she did two lyrical pieces for the Canada Vignettes series (1-minute films about life in the sub-arctic), and her first film *Christmas at Moose Factory* (1971) attempted to give cinematic life to drawings by kids from northern Ontario.

    Her film *Incident at Restigouche* (1984) seems like a blueprint for *Kanehsatake*. It documents a dispute over fishing rights on the Québec/New Brunswick border, and an interview in which she loudly argues with Québec's Fisheries Minister about the meaning of sovereignty has become famous. The film feels like a combination of her two sides: a powerful document of a militant uprising, but also a careful, analytical, and lucid consideration of the institutions that led to the confrontation and that gave people the means to cope with it.

*Amisk* (1977)
*Mother of Many Children* (1977)
*Incident at Restigouche* (1984)
*No Address* (1988)
*Le Patro, Le Prévost 80 Years Later* (1991)
*Kanehsatake: 270 Years of Resistance* (1993)
*Spudwrench: Kahnawake Man* (1997)
*Rocks At Whiskey Trench* (2000)

Almost all of her films are centred around long, sometimes rambling, interviews and draw upon voice-over narration (usually done by Obomsawin herself). This is also true of *Incident at Restigouche* and *Kanehsatake*, but in these works Obomsawin favours a pared down form, often portraying the brutality of the Canadian police and army with shaky and jagged images. Overall, she is much more influenced by the National Film Board of Canada's tradition of educational film-making than by *cinéma vérité* but she clearly knows how to powerfully make use of both these formal strategies in order to further the cause of Canada's indigenous people. Her work is, in short, political film-making at its very best.                                                **JW**

# Gavin O'CONNOR

When Gavin O'Connor's breakthrough film *Tumbleweeds* (1999) was released in the US, most film critics immediately compared it to another, very similar film released at the same time, Wayne Wang's *Anywhere But Here* (1999). Both are stories of flamboyant mothers leaving bad husbands and taking their pre-teenage daughters to find happiness in California. The latter film was a big Hollywood affair, with two famous actresses (Susan Sarandon and Natalie Portman) and continent-wide release. O'Connor's film opened in very few major cities and starred two relative unknowns (Janet McTeer and Kimberly Brown), yet it was *Tumbleweeds* that was talked about when awards season came around. While the two films have similar plots, the understated honesty of the performances and direction of *Tumbleweeds* drew almost unanimous acclaim.

O'Connor, a graduate of the University of Pennsylvania, had made only one previous feature, *Comfortably Numb* (1995), although he had also made the short *American Standoff* in 1994, which aired on PBS. *Comfortably Numb*, rated NC-17 in the US and thus disallowed wide distribution, is the story of a young lawyer (Dana Ashbrook) who has a liaison with a prostitute (Angela Shelton). He is further seduced into a hedonistic lifestyle of drugs and parties, and declines from there. Notwithstanding its limited profile, *Comfortably Numb* won the Best New Feature Award at the 1996 Long Island Film Festival.

*Tumbleweeds* is a vastly different film. Adapted from the memoirs of Shelton, O'Connor's then-wife, the script is honest and moving despite being otherwise unoriginal in basic plot. O'Connor uses a roving hand-held camera, successfully achieving a *cinéma vérité* feel, accentuating the honesty of the script by giving the viewer a sense that s/he is watching something authentic unfold. Unlike most contemporary directors who use hand-held camera to achieve a sense of disorientation, O'Connor's camera does quite the opposite, seeking out his subjects and getting into their space. This is where finding actors who can convincingly embody a character becomes so important, and British stage actress McTeer fills the role with force and sensitivity. O'Connor manages to create a dual character study that feels more real than may be comfortable, with characters who have as many flaws as charms.

His forthcoming film, *Pride and Glory*, is the story of a family who have been in the police force for three generations and the drama that ensues when one of them is thought to be corrupt.                                                **DH**

# Pat O'CONNOR

Born in Ardmore, Ireland, in 1943, Pat O'Connor left school at 17 and travelled to England before moving to the United States. He enrolled in a liberal arts programme at UCLA then continued his education in Canada. He returned to Ireland in 1970, when he began work with Radio Telefís Éireann. After a six-year stint in documentary, he moved to drama. He directed several television plays and wrote episodes of the serial 'The Riordans', and in 1982 he directed the acclaimed BBC/RTÉ co-production 'The Ballroom of Romance'. This is a dark, atmospheric tale of repressed sexuality in 1950s rural Ireland written by William Trevor. It won several awards including a BAFTA and a silver award at the New York Festival.

After further television projects co-produced by Channel 4 and the BBC, he came to the attention of David Puttnam, who produced his feature debut, *Cal* (1984). Based on the novel by Bernard MacLaverty, this is the story of the romantic relationship between an IRA getaway driver and the widow of the man his unit have killed. Impressively acted by Helen Mirren and John Lynch, it followed some of the metaphysical threads of 'The Ballroom of Romance', employing similar imagery to evoke a sense of enclosure and oppression. Although some observers criticised the film for retreating from the political context, most responded positively to its passion. It was nominated for the Palme d'Or at the Cannes Film Festival.

O'Connor's next project, *A Month in the Country* (1987), based on the novel by J. R. Carr, is about the tentative friendship which grows between two World War Two veterans who are working on different archeological projects in a Yorkshire village in the 1920s. Like *Cal*, its focus is more on emotions and relationships than issues or politics. Its delicate portrayal of Englishness and the English countryside was admired by both audiences and critics. It won a Silver Rosa Camuna at the Bergamo Film Meeting, and helped to establish the screen careers of Colin Firth and Kenneth Branagh.

O'Connor's promising career began to turn sour with his move to the United States. *Stars and Bars* (1988) features Daniel Day Lewis as an art dealer who encounters eccentric characters while pursuing a Renoir painting. Based on the novel by William Boyd, the film attempts an atmosphere of black comic whimsy that it fails to achieve. It was neither a popular nor a critical success. The situation did not improve with *The January Man* (1989), a mismatch of comedy, thriller and romance with Kevin Kline as a goofy amateur sleuth in search of a serial killer. In both films it appears that O'Connor had no genuine interest in or connection with the material. They share a concern with outsiders and eccentrics but lack any real insight into the characters and their worlds. By comparison with *Cal* and 'The Ballroom of Romance', they are also visually bland. The most notable result of the film was O'Connor's subsequent marriage to its female lead, Mary Elizabeth Mastrantonio.

O'Connor returned to more familiar ground for his next project. *Fools of Fortune* (1990) re-united him with William Trevor in an adaptation of his historical novel about an Anglo-Irish family who attempt to remain outside politics as Ireland fights for independence. Aided by a strong cast and an emphasis on complex relationships between disparate characters, it is a respectful, delicately rendered and handsomely photographed film. It lacks personality, however, falling too easily into the category of 'heritage film'. It was thus eclipsed by the Merchant-Ivory collaborations that were popular at the time of its release.

O'Connor then began a five-year hiatus from feature film-making and worked in television, directing a film on the life of Zelda Fitzgerald for TNT in 1993. He finally returned to the big screen with *Circle of Friends* (1995), a crowd-pleasing adaptation of Maeve Binchy's novel. This US-Irish co-production was supported by a wave of investment in the Irish film industry following changes in the legislation covering tax relief for international financiers. O'Connor's nationality was an asset in getting the project approved and he was also clearly more comfortable with the subject matter. The film introduced Minnie Driver as a small-town girl who attends university in Dublin in the late 1950s. It is a tale of romance, relationships, and coming-of-age of a type familiar to international audiences, and features beautiful images of Ireland and the Irish countryside. Its mixture of warm humour and winning performances proved to be box-office gold. *Inventing the Abbots* (1997) was an eagerly anticipated follow-up that once again featured a young and attractive cast and was set in the late 1950s, this time in America. It follows the story of two working-class brothers who attempt to ingratiate themselves with upper-class girls. Based on a short story by Sue Miller, featuring a cast including Liv Tyler, Joaquin Phoenix, and Jennifer Connelly, it promises much but delivers little. O'Connor is more concerned with romantic universals and family dynamics than with the particulars of class and society. The result is lushly photographed but empty; the film did not generate significant box-office returns.

*Dancing at Lughnasa* (1998), an adaptation of Brian Friel's acclaimed play, provided the director with both an Irish setting and a focus on family. It charts the experiences of five unmarried sisters in rural Donegal in the 1930s following the return of their brother from the missions in Africa. Evoking a rich sense of time and place, it features a talented group of actors including Meryl Streep, Kathy Burke, and Brid Brennan. Yet despite superficial thematic and visual similarities to 'The Ballroom of Romance', it remains stagebound at the cost of potential cinematic dynamism. It was nonetheless nominated for a Golden Lion at the Venice Film Festival and won a Best Supporting Actress award for Brennan at the inaugural Irish Film and Television Academy Awards.

O'Connor's most recent film, *Sweet November* (2001), is an unremarkable remake of the 1968 version. It is a romantic comic drama starring Keanu Reeves and Charlize Theron, the latter as a woman with commitment issues who is pursued by a persistent suitor. **HO**

# Steve OEDEKERK

*Ace Ventura:*
*When Nature Calls* (1995)
*Nothing to Lose* (1997)
*Kung Pow: Enter the Fist* (2002)

Born in 1961 in Los Angeles, Steve Oedekerk is firmly established on the American comedy circuit, and it is his ability to combine free-wheeling improvisation and off-kilter observation that has infiltrated his acting, writing and directing ventures. As a writer on the sketch comedy series 'In Living Color', he worked with Jim Carrey, which led to their collaboration on the 1995 sequel, *Ace Ventura: When Nature Calls*. Originally hired to write the script, Oedekerk took over from directing after Tom DeCerchio left and he was rewarded with a $38 million opening weekend – the highest thus far for a comedy. Unfortunately, the film represents a nadir in Carrey's acting. All spit and vomit gags, this may well be the first film in which a character emerges from the anus of a rhinoceros, and is a simple excuse for the star's brand of lavatorial humour to reach new levels. Scenes of Ace interacting with tribespeople has all the sensitivity of those Warner Bros. cartoons where pygmies cook Bugs Bunny in a pot. Unlike *Dumb and Dumber* (1994) or *Liar Liar* (1997), Oedekerk does not allow Carrey to interact with other talented actors, and so everyone around him becomes a mere cipher.

Writing may be Oedekerk's major forté: he scripted *The Nutty Professor* (1996) and *Patch Adams* (1998), and while both are deeply flawed films, they display an acute grasp of comedy and pace. His directing, however, seems to be constantly atrophied.

In *Nothing To Lose* (1997), Oedekerk teams Tim Robbins and Martin Lawrence in a comedy thriller that wants to be *The Bonfire of the Vanities* (1990) but ends up as a woeful attempt by all concerned to explore and satirise race relations and inject new life into an increasingly moribund genre. Again Oedekerk's writing almost saves the venture; most of the jokes are hit-and-miss, but by subscribing to the *Naked Gun* (1988) philosophy (whereby if you crack enough jokes, at least a few will raise a laugh), the film is never dull, merely anodyne and anonymous.

Oedekerk's most recent feature film, *Kung Pow: Enter the Fist* (2002), is an unfunny attempt to satirise kung-fu films, proof that he mistakenly labours under the belief that ripping off classic scenes from other films constitutes humour and homage. The plot, in which Oedekerk himself avenges the death of his parents at the hands of an evil kung-fu legend, might have been the opportunity for a subtle mélange of black comedy and parody, but instead relies on fart-and-sick gags and unintentionally humorous asides. Any film that spoofs *The Matrix* (1999) by having its hero dodge a cow shooting milk from her teats highlights just how far movie homages have been denigrated; as early as January it was voted the 'Worst Film of 2002'.

Oedekerk has directed two television movies, both moderately successful, which hint at a more comfortable medium for his style of humour. *Thumb Wars: The Phantom Cuticle* (1999) spoofs Lucas' most famous creation, while *steve.oedekerk.com* (1997) combines stand-up comedy and cutting-edge visual effects. He has also written *Jimmy Neutron: Boy Genius* (2001), an engaging enough comedy, which was nominated for Best Animated Film at the 2002 Academy Awards. **BM**

# Peter O'FALLON

*Suicide Kings* (1997)
*A Rumor of Angels* (2000)

Peter O'Fallon graduated from directing commercials to television shows in the late 1980s with episodes of 'thirtysomething'. He directed the premiere episodes of 'Northern Exposure' – gaining an Emmy-nomination for the episode 'Aurora Borealis' – and 'Profiler'; the pilot episodes of 'American Gothic', 'Prey' and 'Odd Jobs'; and episodes of 'Party Of Five' and 'Cupid'.

In 1991 he directed the television movie *Dead Silence* (aka *Crash*), a competently executed variant on the story in which friends conceal a death they accidentally caused. His first cinematic feature – based on Don Stanford's 'The Hostage' – was *Suicide Kings* (1997), one of the recent cycle of movies about spoilt rich kids turning to crime. Following the kidnapping of a young woman, five young men – she is the sister of one and girlfriend of another – kidnap a retired gangster in order to obtain the money to ransom her, but when he discovers that one of them is working with her kidnappers, the situation takes a turn for the worse. A good concept is let down by weak writing. The characters are poorly defined, although Christopher Walken is as engaging as ever and Johnny Galecki works hard to make his teenage Woody Allen likeable. Indecision about how to develop the plot sees it veering from wiseguy comedy to hostage drama to cat-and-mouse games to sting movie and back again, and O'Fallon's frequently mobile camera only adds to the sense of a director looking for his story. Some tension is generated, largely courtesy of Graeme Revell's score.

*A Rumor of Angels* (2000) is adapted from Grace Duffie Boylan's 'lost' Victorian sentimental novel, 'Thy Son Liveth: Messages from a Soldier to his Mother', previously adapted for stage as 'Messages'. Set on the coast of Maine, it tells of the relationship that develops between James (Trevor Morgan), a twelve-year-old boy whose mother died in a car crash two years earlier, and the local crazy lady, Maddy Bennett (Vanessa Redgrave), who still grieves for her son, a signals officer killed in Vietnam. The narrative, such as it is, unfolds at a curious pace, and although the film is handsomely shot (courtesy of cinematographer Roy H. Wagner) not even a cast this good – which also includes Ray Liotta and Catherine McCormack – can rise above such hopelessly sentimental material.                                                                    **MB**

# Frank OZ

Frank Oz is a director who started out working with puppets on children's shows and films, then gradually progressed to making high-profile comedies with star names attached.

Born Frank Oznowicz, in Hereford, England, in 1944, he initially rose to fame with Jim Henson on television's 'Sesame Street' and 'The Muppet Show' in the 1970s, creating, operating and providing the voices for many beloved characters (including Miss Piggy and Fozzie Bear). In the early 1980s he was called upon to bring Yoda the Jedi Master to life for the *Star Wars* trilogy, and made cameo appearances in one or two features – chiefly the John Landis productions *The Blues Brothers* (1980) and *An American Werewolf in London* (1981).

*The Dark Crystal* (1982) was Oz's baptism of fire behind the camera, a task he shared with Henson on this occasion. Though still a puppet film, it is substantially darker than the duo's other work, recounting the efforts of two gelflings in their mission to defeat the wicked flesh-eating Skeksis on a magical fantasy planet. An overtly simplistic and moralistic chronicle of good versus evil, like many a fairytale before it – those of the Brothers Grimm in particular – it functions on various levels (allegorically and metaphorically) and doesn't evade the nightmarish realities of life.

Much brighter was *The Muppets Take Manhattan* (1984), the third film in the sequence and the director's first solo piece. As one would expect, all the old gang are reunited for this fun musical, influenced by Busby Berkeley movies and fuelled by American dreams of success. Kermit and co. are encouraged to take their senior college variety show to Broadway, but find there are many obstacles to overcome – not least of which is prejudice against cute fluffy animals. The Jeff Moss songs (especially the theme tune 'Together Again') are lively, and at times even poignant, the parodies – of *Brief Encounter* (1945) and *Jaws 3D* (1983) for example – are amusing, and the jokes are diverting. If only the story wasn't so slight and the star turns (Liza Minnelli, Joan Rivers, Elliott Gould) so succinct.

Oz's next film was *Little Shop of Horrors* (1986), taken from the stage musical of the same name (basically a spiritless remake of the 1960 Roger Corman quickie), which also contains some state of the art puppetry; a twelve-foot-tall, man-eating plant weighing around 2,000 pounds to be precise. Rick Moranis is the flower shop assistant who unearths this phenomenal foliage, which feeds on human beings and has a rich singing voice. Excess is the key word, but no amount of remarkable effects or catchy melodies can make up for the asinine premise or the exiguous offering from the actors.

For *Dirty Rotten Scoundrels* (1988) Oz again drafted in comedian Steve Martin, with whom he would have a long-term association. Small wonder, as this reworking of the 1964 film *Bedtime Story* is devilishly funny and has a majestic sting in the tail. Both Martin and Michael Caine are brilliant as con men fleecing the wealthy inhabitants of Beaumont-sur-Mer (actually the breathtaking landscape of Nice), but the former truly comes into his own when Oz nurtures his improvisational skills, pretending to be Caine's demented eye-patch-wearing brother. In addition, the sharp script, by the original writers (Stanley Shapiro/Paul Henning) and Dale Launer, has a fabulous time exposing the gullibility of the upper classes.

However, in *What About Bob?* (1991), a tasteless comedy starring Bill Murray and Richard Dreyfuss, the objects of derision are significantly less palatable. Like *The Dream Team* (1989) and *Crazy People* (1990), this depends on the phobias and instability of the mentally ill for laughs – here a patient who follows his psychiatrist to a New Hampshire holiday home. As usual, Murray's antics are humorous in an exorbitantly brazen way, and in the end the egotistical professional, Dreyfuss, is revealed to be more unbalanced than his charge. But this alone cannot justify the insensitive use of such subject matter for entertainment purposes.

*Housesitter* (1992) is a 'romantic comedy about loving, lying and living together' according to the promotional material. In reality it is a vain, slothful waste of time and talent. Steve Martin, as the Boston architect with dreams of the perfect marriage, is never granted the same kind of freedom he enjoys on other sets, having to resort to maladroit horseplay to incite a response. Goldie Hawn reverts to her vertiginous blonde persona of twenty years hence as the prevaricator who takes up residence in Martin's dream house. What could have been a comical, observational piece about relationships and trust in the 1990s is contorted into a calculably lightweight middle-class skit.

*The Indian in the Cupboard* (1995) saw Oz returning to children's films, in collaboration with the writer of *E.T.* (1982), Melissa Mathison. Based on Lynne Reid Banks' book of the same name, the finished product is a spellbinding rites of passage parable. Hal Scardino plays the boy given a magic cupboard for his birthday that can bring toys to life, including a diminutive Indian brave. The picture is mature enough to broach a Native American viewpoint without preaching, and builds the bond between the two main characters tentatively but authentically. Moreover, it is invigorating to see a modern movie that doesn't sacrifice its storytelling for big Hollywood names or overbearing special effects.

Inspired by Tom Hanks' *Philadelphia* (1993) Academy Award acceptance speech, *In and Out* (1997) deals with the tribulations of a small-town teacher (Kevin Kline) 'outed' on global television. Another obscure choice for a comedy, this film does at least have a pronounced message: to accept people for who they are regardless of their sexuality. What grates the most, however, is Kline's reluctance to accept his own preferences, even to himself – which is also the problem with Oz's subsequent film. Ostensibly, *Bowfinger* (1999) is critical of the industry-oriented classical mode of production and its reliance on stars. Yet the movie itself is a product of the very system it berates. The duplicitous stunts of wannabe producer Bobby Bowfinger celebrate the exploitation school of filmmaking popularised by Castle and Corman, but his dire patchwork sci-fier 'Chubby Rain' would find it almost impossible to get a theatrical release in today's climate of hype and hysteria. In all fairness, though, this pairing of Steve Martin (also the screenwriter) and Eddie Murphy is reasonably enjoyable, even if both stars have committed much more expressive work to celluloid in the past.

*The Score* (2001) has recently taken Oz down another path, away from Hollywood introspection. Robert De Niro stars in the film as a thief who is lured out of retirement to do one last job, an altogether too familiar premise. His performance and partnership with the younger criminal, played by Edward Norton, prevents the action from stagnating. In addition, Marlon Brando contributes several key scenes. The director is currently in production with *Ump*, based on James Cohen's 1991 novel. **PB**

# P

## AI PACINO

Alfredo Pacino left college at the age of 17, and took a number of odd jobs while *Looking For Richard* (1996)
simultaneously attending classes at Lee Strasberg's Actor's Studio (continuing what had
been one of the few things he had enjoyed and excelled at during his school days). He
later began his career on the stage in his native New York, where he was born in 1940.
His work as an actor needs little explanation, of course, with his reputation as one of the
most important movie stars of his generation.

Yet Pacino's limited foray behind the camera produced a very interesting result. The
documentary *Looking For Richard* (1996) won the 1997 Directors Guild of America
award for documentary achievement and is, along with *Hearts of Darkness* (1991),
*Hoop Dreams* (1994), and *When We Were Kings* (1996), a film that marked a
renaissance for higher-profile cinema documentaries in the 1990s. In the film, Pacino
builds on his experiences of playing Shakespeare's Richard III on Broadway, and aims to
be an attempt to 'popularise' Shakespeare. Starting from the vantage point of Pacino's
infectious enthusiasm for Shakespeare, *Looking For Richard* sees Pacino assemble a
cast of great names to read through the play, as well as talking to members of the public
to gauge the level of popular understanding of the work. However, during the course
of the film the project becomes more ambitious, as Pacino and his crew attempt more
serious 'cinematic' interpretations of scenes from the play.

Beyond the film's attempts at popularisation, it stands as a much more serious
investigation into Shakespeare (as literature, culture and history) and the understanding
of him (including the controversial question of whether academics or actors are the
'true possessors' of Shakespeare). Ultimately, the film becomes an inquiry into the
nature of film aesthetics (in terms of what can be done with film that cannot be done
with theatre), and a very interesting (and fun) examination of the processes of film-
making itself.

In spite of comments from Pacino that he is 'uncomfortable' with his directorial
abilities, a second outing behind the camera, a filmed version of the Broadway play
'Chinese Coffee' in which he also stars (as he did in the Broadway production), was
reportedly completed in 1998. Other than a few outings on the 2000 festival circuit

(Toronto, Telluride), the movie remains unreleased as yet, and a distribution deal with Fox has thus far failed to bring it to the screen.                                                    **JP**

# John PAIZS

If there were an award for most under-appreciated director, Winnipeg-based John Paizs would most likely be its recipient. Although Paizs, born in 1957, has worked in the industry for over twenty years and has produced several remarkable films, he remains relatively unrecognised outside of Canada.

After graduating from the University of Manitoba's fine arts programme, Paizs produced a series of short films – *The Obsession of Billy Botski* (1980), *Spring-time in Greenland* (1981), *Oak, Ivy, and Other Dead Elms* (1982), and *The International Style* (1983), that introduced his unique brand of humour to viewers across Canada and helped to establish Winnipeg's place in the Canadian entertainment industry.

In an interview with film critic Gemma Files, Paizs summed up his views on film-making: 'a good film is kind of like a Hawaiian pizza – homey stuff next to exotic stuff, like bacon and pineapple'. In his films Paizs transforms seemingly innocent stories with nostalgic settings into works of high camp by inserting unsettlingly incongruous characters and situations. Rituals of middle-class life such as the cocktail party and the family cookout become, in Paizs' films, the settings of nightmares in which dream dates mysteriously drop dead and good guys nearly always finish last. This said, Paizs' films are never cynical or pessimistic. In this respect, they can be seen as the big-screen realisations of the dreams of a generation of Super 8 cineastes raised on 'Creature Feature' and 'Early Show' reruns.

*Crime Wave* (1986), Paizs' first feature, illustrates this point nicely. The film tells the story of Steven Penny (Paizs), a frustrated writer of 'colour crime films' whose attempts to overcome writer's block lead him through a series of fantastic *Wizard of Oz*-inspired adventures. Paizs divides the film between vignettes that depict Steven's hilariously overblown scripts and scenes from his equally quirky life, and ends it with one of the most bizarre tributes to the Hollywood dream factory imaginable. Although *Crime Wave* was a hit with critics and audiences alike, it received poor theatrical distribution in North America; when it finally made it to home video, the companies that released it soon went out of business. Despite these obstacles, *Crime Wave* has amassed a cult of dedicated followers and remains widely discussed in certain film circles and on the internet.

After this rather disappointing episode in his career, Paizs moved to Toronto where he continued to work in the entertainment industry. In the early 1990s he directed episodes of the hit YTV television series 'Maniac Mansion' and segments for the popular 'Kids in the Hall' show. Throughout the 1990s Paizs screened his works at retrospectives and festivals across North America and in Europe, and in 1997, the Manitoba film industry named *Crime Wave* best film ever produced in the province.

The release of *Top of the Food Chain* (1999) marks Paizs' triumphant return to film-making after an almost 14-year silence. His latest work, authored by veteran writers Phil Bedard and Larry Lalonde, is a take-off on 1950s science fiction films and features Campbell Scott, Fiona Loewi, and Tom Everett Scott in lead roles. Although *Top of the Food Chain* had a larger budget than any of Paizs' past projects, its endearingly nostalgic look make it immediately recognisable as a Paizs production.                                        **RC**

# Alan J. PAKULA

Born in New York in 1928, Alan J. Pakula's career spanned five decades. He was perhaps best known for his engrossing political and psychological thrillers, but also applied his unconventional style to romantic comedies, melodramas and a western. Educated at Yale School of Drama, he began his career in the cartoon department of Warner Bros. in 1949. Pakula worked his way through the ranks and left to join Paramount as a producer, where he went on to produce some noteworthy films, including *Fear Strikes Out* (1957), *To Kill a Mockingbird* (1962), and *Inside Daisy Clover* (1965).

He made his directorial debut with the 1969 romantic melodrama, *The Sterile Cuckoo* (1969), which stars Liza Minnelli as a bright young college student who is in love with a fellow student (Wendall Burton). It is a sensitive exploration of young love and well-regarded by critics.

His second feature, *Klute* (1971), established him as a credible director; a classic of 1970s American cinema, it features one of the most interesting and challenging female roles in contemporary cinema. The film is a curious hybrid of tense thriller and melodrama, and at times these elements work against each other. The convoluted plot distracts from the real strength in this film – namely the superb characterisations of Bree Daniels (Jane Fonda) and John Klute (Donald Sutherland). Klute is a suburban policeman working in his own time to find a missing person. He suspects that the missing man is responsible for stalking high-class call girl Daniel; he genuinely feels for the woman's plight and a strange but touching relationship develops. Fonda turns in perhaps the best performance of her career as the prostitute. This is no simple 'tart with a heart' characterisation – she is tough, business-like, intelligent, and, initially, very self-contained. It was rumoured that Fonda spent weeks trailing a real call-girl to help her get into the part, and even spent a night working in a brothel in New York. Sutherland's performance is also one of his finest. As the stoic, gentle cop, he is the perfect dramatic foil for Fonda's intensity.

Pakula followed *Klute* with *Love and Pain (and the Whole Damn Thing)* (1972), a romantic drama about two shy introverts (Timothy Bottoms and Maggie Smith) who fall in love with each other as they tour Spain. After the heavy shades of grey in *Klute*, *Love and Pain* is bright, warm and understated.

Pakula's next two projects reflect the densely paranoid period in American history, post-Watergate. *The Parallax View* (1974) stars Warren Beatty as a journalist investigating the death of a senator and the subsequent deaths of all the witnesses. His work leads him to the shady 'black organisation', the Parallax Corporation. Beatty's character is somewhat one-dimensional, but the plot moves along at such an exciting pace that this is hardly a flaw. Shot on location, the film has a brooding realism, reinforcing the dark, paranoid milieu.

*All the President's Men* (1976) tackles the issue of Watergate head on, as we shadow the two investigative reporters, Bob Woodward (Robert Redford) and Carl Bernstein (Dustin Hoffman), following their story's trail right up to the Oval Office. The film is as much about journalistic practice and processes as it is about the Watergate break-in; centring on dialogue rather than action, it is so efficiently edited that it gathers a genuinely suspenseful momentum. Pakula also makes skilful use of aerial shots, crosscutting and tracking shots to help give the narrative more pace and movement. He shows his immense flair for constructing characters that are compelling agents of narrative, without the distraction of unnecessary personal details. This is the story of a story and both stars and personality traits take a back seat. Widely regarded as one of the best political thrillers of the period, *All the President's Men* won Academy Awards for Best Screenplay, Sound, Art Direction, and Best Supporting Actor (for Jason Robards as the journalists' executive editor, Ben Bradlee).

Pakula followed this with the striking and atmospheric western, *Comes a Horseman* (1978). The story is simple enough – evil cattle baron Ewing wants a hard-working rancher's land. The twist here is that the rancher is a woman, Ella (Jane Fonda), and this is not the pioneer period of the wild west but the final months of World War Two. The film has a dark, foreboding milieu and some critics regard its pictorial style as 'sullen and overblown'; it is mesmerising, however, and entirely appropriate to the context of its wartime setting. James Caan plays Frank, returning to civilian life and eager to find some space and peace. He buys some land from Ella to fulfil his romantic ideals of the simple life of the rancher, but soon falls foul of Ewing. This is a powerful film in a quiet way and certainly merits more critical attention than it has received.

Pakula's next film, *Starting Over* (1979), features a miscast Burt Reynolds as a man falling out of love with his wife (Candice Bergen) and in love with another (Jill Clayburgh). This is a disappointing movie, not least because of the striking parallels with the infinitely superior *The Unmarried Woman* (1978), directed by Paul Mazursky and coincidentally starring Jill Clayburgh.

Pakula's next offering, a contemporary drama about high finance, *Rollover* (1981), reunited him with Jane Fonda. With a ludicrous and rambling plot, this film is not one of his best. However, his next project, *Sophie's Choice* (1982) remains one of the outstanding films of the decade. A faithful adaptation of a William Styron novel, the film exudes humanity and compassion, using dual narration and a series of lengthy flashbacks to tell its story. The principle narrator is Stingo (Peter MacNicol), a young, idealistic, would-be writer from the south, who makes his way to the beguiling north. Sophie (Meryl Streep) narrates from within Stingo's own narration. Streep's performance earned her a well-deserved Academy Award for Best Actress. Kevin Kline also stars as her passionate and idealistic lover, Nathan, and turns in a suitably energetic performance.

Pakula followed this with *Dream Lover* (1986), a thriller in which a young woman (Kristy McNichol) attempts to cure herself of a recurring nightmare through dream therapy. Ultimately, the slow pace of this film prevents the satisfactory realisation of an interesting idea. *Orphans* (1987) is an interesting and well-acted adaptation of a Lyle Kessler play. It centres on gangster Harold (Albert Finney), who is kidnapped by young delinquent Treat (Matthew Modine) and held prisoner. Harold manages to untie himself but does not attempt to escape. Instead he sets about changing Treat and his brother Phillip (Kevin Anderson). Finney played Harold on the stage in London with some success, but the film ultimately fails to translate its complex meanings and character motivations on screen. *Orphans* did little business at the box office and did not impress the critics.

Another romantic drama followed, but in *See You in the Morning* (1989), the romance is a far cry from the subtle intensities of *Klute*, *Comes a Horseman*, and *Sophie's Choice*. An intelligent script and the two central performances from Jeff Bridges and Alice Krige make this film watchable, but it remains disappointing in the context of Pakula's other works.

The director made a return to the genre of the thriller with *Presumed Innocent* (1990), a solid enough rendering of the controversial Scott Turow novel. The film centres around the rape and murder of an attractive and calculating young lawyer, Carolyn Polhemus, played by Greta Scacchi. Harrison Ford's taciturn prosecutor, Rusty Sabich, is assigned to the case but begins to unravel evidence that makes him the number one suspect. The film is adept at weaving its ambiguity, and the cast play with this to great effect. A characteristically laconic and understated performance from Ford works particularly well here, and *Presumed Innocent* was well received by audiences and critics alike.

Next came the disappointing *Consenting Adults* (1992), a suburban thriller starring Kevin Kline and an early Kevin Spacey. Despite an intelligent screenplay, this film made little impact on critics or audiences. Pakula's next feature, *The Pelican Brief* (1993), based on John Grisham's best-selling novel, has been referred to as a 'Nancy Drew for the 1990s'. It centres on a young law student, played by Julia Roberts, who uncovers a plot to assassinate two Supreme Court judges. Despite Pakula's expertise with the political conspiracy theory, *The Pelican Brief* lacks the pace and scope of his earlier work in this genre, such as *The Parallax View* or *All the President's Men*, but it is effectively and economically told.

*The Devil's Own* (1997) is a surprisingly sophisticated tale of the relations between two men: an IRA commander (Brad Pitt), and a New York policeman (Harrison Ford). Despite Pitt's appalling Irish accent, the film is intense and the parallels between the two 'opposites' masterfully drawn. The personal betrayals that occur between Ford and Pitt are at the core, rather than the political differences, and this is the film's major strength.

Pakula was killed in November 1998 in an accident after a metal pipe was thrown from a bridge over the Long Island Expressway; no charges have been brought and the incident remains unsolved. Throughout his career, he was considered to be a master director of thrillers, and the genre was certainly best-suited to his interest in complex plots. However, he has often gone unnoticed for bringing some of the strongest female characterisations to the screen, most notably Bree Daniel (*Klute*), Ella (*Comes a Horseman*), and Sophie (*Sophie's Choice*). His ability to evoke the right mood for the given context made him a director of considerable talent and imagination, and worthy of closer study.                                                                                      **SL**

# Chuck PARELLO

*Henry: Portrait of a Serial Killer Part 2 (Mask of Sanity) (1996)*
*Ed Gein (2000)*

Having worked as a production assistant on Martin Scorsese's 1991 *Cape Fear* re-make and an actor in John McNaughton's underrated *Mad Dog and Glory* (1993), Chuck Parello made an inauspicious entry to feature directing with the unimaginative *Henry: Portrait of a Serial Killer Part 2 (Mask of Sanity)* (1996), which he also wrote. An unnecessary appendage to McNaugton's splendidly dark and uncomfortable original, the film initially favours tone and incremental pacing over gore; replicating the consciously muted delivery of the original, Parello shows a keen eye for disturbing detail. Ultimately, however, as the film reaches its unedifying conclusion, he succumbs to the demands for high blood count and grisly happenings.

He returned to a similarly dark subject with *Ed Gein* (2000), a faithful, somber account of the notorious cannibal who had been the subject of films such as *Psycho* (1960) and *The Texas Chainsaw Massacre* (1974). The film opens impressively with old newsreel footage of the eponymous killer's arrest in his hometown of Plainfield, Wisconsin. It proceeds to offer a deliberately low-key, non-sensationalist look at the factors that shaped the graverobber's unsavoury compulsion to eat flesh and dress in the skin of his victims by moonlight. It is a distinctly unsettling piece of work and Steve Railsback is impressive as Gein. Meticulously detailed production design – lampshades made from human parts – and Parello's methodical, forensic approach to the material pays dividends and suggests that given the opportunity and the right material he can be an original genre director. **JWo**

# Dean PARISOT

A directorial graduate of television shows such as 'ER' and 'Northern Exposure', and an award-winning short film-maker, Dean Parisot made his feature debut in 1998 with *Home Fries*, a satire on the dysfunctional American family unit. Oddball siblings Angus (Jake Busey) and Dorian (Luke Wilson) are manipulated by their demented mother (Catherine O'Hara) into killing their womanising stepfather. When Sally (Drew Barrymore), a cashier in a local burger joint, hears the commotion, she becomes a target for disposal and matters worsen when the mother discovers her identity as the pregnant mistress of her late husband. The scheme falters, however, when Dorian, sent to reconnoitre the burger bar, falls for the downtrodden Sally.

*Home Fries* (1998)
*Galaxy Quest* (1999)

The black comedy and twisted treatment of family values in the film is rendered slightly toothless by a tendency to undervalue the psychotic characters – played with relish and warped Freudian sexual tension by Busey and O'Hara – in favour of the saccharine-sweet romance between Barrymore and Wilson. However, the film, promoted as a vehicle for Barrymore and co-produced by Barry Levinson and Lawrence Kasdan, is engaging, arguably the more so for the enduring sweetness of the central romance in the face of Dorian's screwed-up family. It is also notable for focusing on the sensuality of the pregnant woman – unusual in mainstream Hollywood film – as a lamaze class attended by the shy lovers becomes an unexpected testing-ground for their erotic attraction.

Having convinced studio bosses of his ability to stage both action and comedy (*Home Fries* includes some deftly-handled helicopter chase footage and fight sequences), Parisot was entrusted with a large-scale production for fledgling studio DreamWorks, the sci-fi parody *Galaxy Quest* (1999). In a sense, the film, concerning the exploits of a group of has-been actors from a kitsch science fiction television series who are recruited to fight a real intergalactic battle, develops the concern with family exhibited in *Home Fries*. The stars of the defunct 'Galaxy Quest' show, reduced to earning a living from regurgitating stock catchphrases and improvising answers to inane technical questions at fan conventions, constitute a family too. Their bonding ultimately equips them with the strength to save the childlike alien race that seeks their help.

The obvious target of the parody is Gene Roddenberry's 'Star Trek' and the director deftly plays upon the way in which the programme attracted a fan culture that inflated their own emotional investment in the world of the show to quasi-theological dimensions. Familiar too are the specific characteristics of the crew: the preening, stolidly heroic captain; the curvaceous blonde second officer; the coldly rational alien scientist; and the anonymous, expendable grunt, perpetually worried that his seemingly inevitable unpleasant death is close to hand. While the parody of 'Star Trek' is acutely observed it is never ungenerous and often explicitly affectionate – fans of the show, in spite of the expected digs about their geeky appearance, play a major part in saving the day. The film, despite its central postmodern conceit concerning reality and representation, is never too archly self-conscious for its own good and Parisot proves as comfortable coaxing note-perfect comic turns out of his star players (Alan Rickman, Sigourney Weaver, Tim Allen) as he is co-ordinating computer-generated space battles. The film became a modest hit in the US, ushering Parisot further into the studio mainstream.

His forthcoming film, *Scared Guys*, is a comedy about an agrophobic internet therapist.                                                                                    **MF**

# Alan PARKER

Born in London in 1944, Alan Parker is a vociferous and uncompromising figure in British cinema. Very much the 'working-class boy made good', he entered the film industry via the world of advertising, once describing himself as an 'accidental film-maker'. Starting out as a post boy for an advertising agency, Parker quickly worked his way up to junior copywriter, later to become something of an innovator in the world of television advertisements. He particularly contributed to the development of humour in British commercials, which he thought they lacked, and was responsible for the memorable Leonard Rossiter/Joan Collins Cinzano promotions. Between 1969 and 1978, he made in excess of five hundred television commercials, winning every major industry award. Indeed, Parker's vivid style owes much to his early advertising experience.

In 1973 he wrote and directed a 50-minute film, *No Hard Feelings,* which the BBC bought and aired several years later. His first film produced for the BBC, *Evacuees* (1975), attracted attention from the theatrical marketplace and David Puttnam persuaded him to stand in as a director for a few days on a film he was producing, *That'll Be the Day* (Claude Whatham, 1973). However, Parker's big break into features came with *Bugsy Malone* (1976), a story he wrote with his own children in mind; with 'it being several years before Disney got its act together', there was nothing for them to watch. The film is a delightful musical spoof of gangster movies with a cast made up entirely of children.

Parker's second feature, *Midnight Express* (1978), is based on the true story of an American arrested in Turkey for drug smuggling. It is a powerful and harrowing film; the forbidding locations coupled with dramatic lighting work to create the prison environment in detail. It features superb performances from Brad Davis as Billy Hayes, the hapless amateur drug smuggler, and John Hurt as Max, an eccentric Englishman who acts as a constant reminder to Billy of the ways in which the prison can crush him. *Midnight Express* earned Parker international acclaim, picking up six Academy Award nominations and winning Best Screenplay for an adaptation and Best Original Score. He followed this with a stylish, up-tempo, contemporary musical, *Fame* (1980), a film that spawned the long-running and highly successful television series of the same name.

*Shoot the Moon* (1982), Parker's next feature, is the first film in which he seems to have invested a great deal of himself. It has been described by some critics as autobiographical, and although he has denied this, he does not deny that its uniquely personal feel comes from his own experiences upon the break-up of his first marriage. What possibly added fuel to the autobiography fire was the uncanny likeness of the two leads (Albert Finney and Diane Keaton) to Parker and his wife.

Moving away from the intimate towards the public, Parker's next film, *Pink Floyd: The Wall* (1982), is the masterful expansion of Pink Floyd's concept album. Over the years the film has become both a rock classic and an indication of the size of former Floyd front man Roger Waters' ego. However, this does both the film and Waters a major disservice. Parker himself commented on the ego issue when discussing the experience of making *The Wall*, saying, 'Can you imagine, three megalomaniacs all used to getting their own way'. *The Wall* is a stunning, intelligent piece of film-making, with Parker's direction matching up to the imagination of Pink Floyd's mind-expanding music. Gerald Scarfe's exemplary animation sequences – the giant marching hammers, the school teacher squeezing children into a mincer – would surely figure in any list of the most iconic and enduring images of the early 1980s.

The critically acclaimed *Birdy* (1984), which followed *The Wall*, does not make for easy viewing, with the narrative flow constantly being disrupted by long flashbacks and montage sequences. Nevertheless, it is a moving story directed with sincerity and sensitivity. The film centres on two best friends who have returned from the war in Vietnam: Al (Nicolas Cage), the former high-school romeo, and Birdy (Matthew Modine), a quiet and withdrawn man with an obsession for birds. Both are wounded by their experience of war. While Al's damage is physical, Birdy's is psychological; he withdraws into himself, in his mind becoming a bird; perching, cooped-up and caged. It is a curious film, traumatic, yet hauntingly beautiful. Once again, it is the strong central performances, combined with Parker's use of location and lighting, that renders *Birdy* so powerful and potent.

With his next feature, *Angel Heart* (1987), Parker courted controversy, taking on the MPPA single-handedly for awarding the film an X rating, provoking many Hollywood executives. *Angel Heart* focuses on a private investigator, Harry Angel (Mickey Rourke), who is hired to trace a debtor for Louis Cyphre (Robert De Niro). The superior twist to the film is that Angel realises the person he is seeking is also responsible for a string of grisly murders – a dark, subconscious side of himself. Initially, Parker wanted to shoot *Angel Heart* in black and white, but settled for regular film stock and draining the colour. The stark contrasts between light and dark, and the many shades of grey in between, mirror the film's themes and concerns, signalling Angel's state of mind.

Parker again invited controversy with his next feature, *Mississippi Burning* (1988), a glossy recreation of a famous, civil-rights murder case. The film was praised for its fine performances (most notably, Gene Hackman as a veteran FBI man) but criticised for its flat and inaccurate reworking of history and its perceived anti-Americanism. Parker, however, claimed that *Mississippi Burning* was a polemical film, intended to create debate; to this end, it succeeded. With subject matter that also had the potential to be contentious, *Come See the Paradise* (1990) certainly had an untold story – that of the internment of Japanese immigrants to the United States in camps at the outbreak of World War Two. With a loose script, the film rambled, failing to capture the imaginations of both audiences and critics. It was also heavily criticised for its historical inaccuracies, seen by some as an exercise in historical revisionism.

In his next film, *The Commitments* (1991), the story of the rise and fall of an Irish soul band, based on the first book in Roddy Doyle's Barrytown trilogy, Parker exploited his love for soul music. *The Commitments* is enjoyable but lacks the grit of the novel and other adaptations of Doyle's stories such as Stephen Frears' *The Snapper* (1993) and *The Van* (1996). The soundtrack is exceptional – indulging Parker's obsession for Otis Redding – but this is a feelgood film, amusing for its duration, with little aftertaste.

Following this, Parker both wrote and directed *The Road to Wellville* (1994), adapting it from a novel by T. Coraghessan Boyle. The film centres on Eleanor and Will Lightbody (Bridget Fonda and Matthew Broderick), a couple who journey to Battle Creek, Michigan, at the turn of the century to Dr Kellogg's renowned sanitarium to partake of his cures. A quirky, at times grimly humorous, film, it frustrates more than it satisfies, instituting a number sub-plots then leaving them hanging in mid-air without resolution or explanation.

Parker's next project, *Evita* (1996), was a slick film version of the Andrew Lloyd Webber/Tim Rice musical. Given his lyrical visual style and his adept handling of 'musical films', he was the natural choice to direct. The film did well at the box office but received mixed critical reviews, as projects involving the talents of Madonna invariably do. Whatever the reasons for some critics' dislike of the film, *Evita* is a pleasing and visually alluring piece of cinema. Parker's most recent offering, *Angela's Ashes* (1999), is based on Frank McCourt's bestselling autobiography. It follows the fortunes of Frankie (Robert Carlyle) and his young family, as they struggle to overcome poverty in the slums of 1930s Limerick. The atmosphere of decay reinforces and reflects the spiritual, social and moral decay that Frankie must overcome in his struggles against unemployment, prejudice, and cultural and religious intolerance.

Parker has recently become Chairman of the newly formed Film Council in Britain. His next film, *The Life of David Gale*, will star Kevin Spacey as a Texan professor and anti-death penalty campaigner, who is accused of rape and sentenced to death himself. **SL**

# Trey PARKER

Trey Parker (born Randolph Trey Parker III) is best known as the creator of the very successful, often controversial, television animation series 'South Park'. He was born in Colorado in 1969 and read music theory at college, but eventually his love of cinema took precedence, and he dropped out to pursue practical film studies at the University of Colorado.

*Cannibal: The Musical* (1996)
*Orgazmo* (1997)
*South Park: Bigger, Longer, Uncut* (1999)

His first feature, made while still at film school, is *Cannibal: The Musical* (made in 1993, but released in 1996). Made for next to nothing, the film grew out of a college project, where Parker made a spoof trailer for a non-existent comedy western musical of that title. The 'trailer' was so well-received that Parker was convinced to develop the project into a feature, and he is credited with writing the script and the songs, as well as directing, and taking the lead role. The film is a clear homage to the work of George Romero, with its gory excesses, cartoonish violence, and cut-price aesthetics, but also shows Parker's talent for comedy at an early stage of his career. Whilst comedically patchy, the film contains some very funny jokes and songs.

Following this comes *Orgazmo* (1997), a satire on the pornography industry (and organised religion, as the protagonist, a Mormon Elder, is forced to take work on a porn film to finance his wedding). Again inspired by the work of a low-budget 'excess' director, this time John Waters, Parker clearly has an eye for more financial considerations, as he tones down the excess to secure a wider release. Not wholly successful, the comedy of *Orgazmo* is often described as 'sophomoric'. It is certainly puerile, but occasionally very funny (when it rises above the level of scatological humour) and, through a certain intertextuality, is further indicative of Parker's love of cinema.

Parker's most recent film as a director is his big-screen outing for the phenomenally successful 'South Park' series, *South Park: Bigger, Longer, Uncut* (1999). Following on from *Cannibal*, *South Park* is a remarkably inventive musical. Parker demonstrates a broad knowledge of the generic conventions of the musical, not only in terms of style, but in the animated choreography as well. The songs, whilst parodic of film and theatre musicals (from Disney to 'Les Misérables'), do not mock the form, but celebrate it, and they serve an equally important function in driving the narrative, as generic conventions dictate (again, Parker is co-author of the songs, and was Academy Award-nominated in this respect). Further, *South Park* is one of the most caustic satires of recent years. Analysing its own position, through the use of a film-within-a-film device, Parker justifies his own excesses and sets up a surprisingly intelligent debate on censorship and social responsibility (thereby giving the film a different level from the exceptionally funny comedy narrative on which to work). The film uses the formulae of the cartoon series, and plays with the expectations of the knowledgeable viewer; Kenny's death is expected, whereas his subsequent resurrection and his final self-sacrifice are not. Kenny's sacrifice leads to the film's genuinely moving ending, which is all the more surprising in the light of Parker's record.

With the success of *South Park: Bigger, Longer, Uncut* behind him, Parker went back to televison. 'South Park' continues unabated (though this time they really did kill Kenny, as his weekly deaths were becoming a narrative burden), but his most recent project has proved a costly flop for Comedy Central, who were so instrumental in the development of 'South Park' the series. 'That's My Bush' (which first aired in the summer of 2001) takes the sitcom formula, and throws it with some force at the White House, turning President George W. Bush and family into a typical sitcom family. An interesting conceit, it did not seem to go down well with the conservative audience; the series was cancelled after eight episodes. Undaunted, and with the precedent of the cancellation of 'Police Squad' leading to the phenomenon of the *Naked Gun* movies, Parker is reportedly developing 'That's My Bush' for a cinematic outing.                    **JP**

# Ivan PASSER

*Intimate Lighting* (1966)
*Born to Win* (1971)
*Law and Disorder* (1974)
*Crime and Passion* (1975)
*Silver Bears* (1977)
*Cutter's Way* (1981)
*Creator* (1985)
*Haunted Summer* (1988)
*Stalin* (1992)
*The Wishing Tree* (1999)

Although Ivan Passer arguably directed one of the seminal films of the 1980s, he has not yet achieved his promised potential. He has concentrated on directing comedies, but has maintained a quirky, Czech-influenced humour which has not served him well in the US. He has existed largely in the shadow of lifelong best friend and fellow director, Milos Forman, who Passer admits constantly emerges as the 'best buddy' character in many of his films, which are more often than not about two guys in trouble. Forman seems to have adapted to the US market, whilst Passer's brand of humour, initially instigated to avoid censorship in his home country, shifts between laughter and pain in the Czech manner. He remains a non-conformist director championing the ordinary worker against the corrupt system. His career is opportunistic and haphazard and his projects often chosen for the risk entailed in accepting them.

Born in Prague in 1933, he applied to film school on the spur of the moment merely because he accompanied a friend along to registration; before graduating he was thrown out for lying about passing his high-school diploma on his entrance form. He found himself immediately offered an assistant director position, subsequently discovering that no one else would work with the unstable director. He himself admits, 'every movie I made was a coincidence'.

Passer nevertheless obtained a noted position as a film-maker of the 'second wave' in Europe, working closely with Forman as assistant director and co-author, and with his own directorial debut, the short film *Boring Afternoon* in 1965, and his first feature, *Intimate Lighting* in 1966. *Intimate Lighting* has been described unkindly as the most boring film ever made, but still holds a place in many critics' hearts. A terrible film on paper, Passer nevertheless managed an understated comedy of provincial life in Czechoslovakia, and made Milos Forman's wife Vera Kresadlova a star. An invitation to show *Intimate Lighting* at the New York Film Festival followed, and Passer returned to the festival in 1968 with Forman's *The Fireman's Ball*, which he co-wrote. This Czech comic disaster movie parodied Communist bureaucracy and is reputed to have caused 40,000 firemen to go on strike. Returning from the New York Festival, Passer and Forman found their home country invaded by Russia, and fled back to America to make it their permanent home.

Forman had more immediate success in the US; although Passer garnered some critical praise he achieved little box-office success. His first American feature, *Born to Win* (1971), starring George Segal, is an intelligent comedy which just failed to hit its mark but showed promise. *Law and Disorder* followed in 1974, an uneven but likeable enough lightweight vigilante cop/social comedy. As with many of Passer's films the shift between dramatic tension and humour is not to mainstream tastes.

*Cutter's Way* (1981) was to see the culmination of his talents in setting mood, evoking place and exploring unpredictable states of mind. It is highly likely that this movie would have made Passer's career in the US industry had it not been the victim of one bad review from the notorious Vincent Canby in *The New York Times*, and United Artist's reluctance to promote it in the wake of the *Heaven's Gate* (1980) disaster. Despite almost unanimous subsequent critical acclaim, United Artists broke their contract and pulled the film after its first week on release. *Cutter's Way* is an intelligent, paranoiac, claustrophobic script, handling the disillusionment and psychological damage in post-Vietnam America. This subject held an affinity for Passer, who found parallels with his experiences of the post-war Czech regime. The movie concerns a scarred Vietnam veteran, hell-bent on retribution against a seemingly untouchable tycoon who may be guilty of murder. Not wholly successful, it is an intriguing noir murder-mystery romance, which is richly textured and multi-layered, and has been likened to *Klute* (1971). It is beautifully acted by Jeff Bridges, Lisa Eichorn and particularly John Heard as the mutilated, drunken Vet, and stays in the memory long after other films have faded away. *Cutters and Bone*, as it was then known, won Passer first prize at the Houston Film Festival for Best Director. The film was later released under the new title by Artists Classics.

*Stalin* (1992), which was made for cable and produced in association with Hungarian Television, is particularly memorable for Passer. Apart from its fine acting he has talked about being on location at Stalin's Dacha, surrounded by lookalikes of Stalin (Robert Duvall), Krushchev, and Molotov, when some drunken Russians burst onto the film to announce the end of the Soviet Union. Other of his films are notable as gambles which did not pay off. He took over the bizarre comedy thriller *Crime and Passion* (1975) while film production was in progress without even reading the script (a product of six scriptwriters). He also took a gamble on doing an awful film – *Silver Bears* (1977) which was muddled, with dire performances by Michael Caine and Cybill Shepherd – in a deal which would allow him to make one Czech film of his choice; this was unfortunately cancelled due to *Silver Bears*' dire failure.

Passer has declared that his interest in movies is to do with an intonation and movement which is only possible in film. He has, however, done several projects for the small screen, including the cable production of 'The Nightingale' for The Faerie Tale Theatre, starring Mick Jagger. Whether liked or hated, Passer's work is never unaffecting. He prefers to remain invisible in his direction, disliking showiness and clever camerawork; yet he is always willing to take a risk, whether it be in helming a film no one else will touch (*Cutter's Way*), or casting non-professional actors because they have the right eyes (*Intimate Lighting*). At his best, he is a likeable director capable of producing thought-provoking work. **FG**

# Jonas & Joshua PATE

Identical twins Jonas and Joshua Pate were born in 1970 and grew up in Raeford, North Carolina, a small-town agricultural community where their father was a lawyer. After graduating from university (Joshua from Chapel Hill in 1992 and Jonas from Princeton in 1993) they began their cinematic career in the independent sector of American film.

Their first movie, *The Grave* (co-written by both brothers and directed by Jonas), is a noir-inspired comedy that gained critical acclaim after being launched at the 1996 Sundance Film Festival. Set in Carolina, the film concerns two convicts (Craig Sheffer and Josh Charles) who break out of prison after a condemned inmate tells them about hidden treasure in the grave of an eccentric millionaire. On their quest, the convicts meet a series of grotesque characters, each revealing their own (brutal) histories. The film is notable for its fragmented narrative structure and extreme camera angles. Even in this first, low-budget feature, the Pate brothers self-consciously proclaim their authorship with stylistic excess.

The Pates' second feature film, *Deceiver* (1998), is a taut psychological thriller set in a police interrogation room, where two police detectives (Chris Penn and Michael Booker) question the alcoholic son of a rich Southern family. Wayland (Tim Roth) is suspected of murdering a prostitute (Renée Zellweger) but, when he is subjected to a lie-detector test, provokes the detectives by revealing knowledge of their guilty secrets (one has mob-related gambling debts, the other a series of violent encounters with the murdered prostitute). All three male leads are ultimately presented as contemptible, each inhabiting a web of deceit.

Stylistically, *Deceiver* is even more frenzied than the Pates' earlier film. Once again, the narrative is fractured by a series of flashbacks, whilst the claustrophobia of the interrogation room is emphasised through the use of unusual camera angles and complex tracking shots. As in *The Grave*, *Deceiver* is structured upon a cynical, pessimistic world-view, in which the boundaries between truth and dishonesty, right and wrong are increasingly blurred. Hence, the title of their next project, 'Good versus Evil', can be read as highly ironic.

'Good versus Evil' is a television series created by the Pates (with both brothers writing and directing several episodes). In this supernatural black comedy (influenced by both 'The X-Files' and 'Buffy the Vampire Slayer'), two dead police detectives have returned to earth in order to battle Satan's demons. Here, the stylistic trademarks of the Pates' cinematic authorship are transposed onto an hour-long episodic format. Narrative events are fragmented by a series of flashbacks and flash-forwards, stop-frames and slow motion, featuring elaborate camerawork (including sudden shifts in perspective and sequences in which the camera moves restlessly among the characters).

Like Joel and Ethan Coen (to whom they are, perhaps not surprisingly, most often compared), Joshua and Jonas Pate have quickly established a distinctive authorial signature in their film and television work. **EC**

# Alexander PAYNE

Few commercially successful independent film-makers of the 1990s have cared as much about the incisive political realities of the Midwestern United States as Alexander Payne, who balances the seriousness of the politics in his films with a dark and sardonic humour. Though educated at UCLA's film school, he has fixed the scope of his fiction on Omaha, Nebraska, where he was born in 1961.

His first feature, *Citizen Ruth* (1996), takes aim at the extreme hyperbola of the moral and legal debate over abortion rights, and the rights of the unborn. Ruth Stoops (Laura Dern) has lost one too many children to her drug-addictive habits, and is ordered by a judge to have an abortion. As she contemplates this decision between snorts of aerosol and paint, she befriends a pro-life activist, and later, an abortion-rights activist. Both are looking for another case to exemplify their cause. Despite the extreme dereliction of Stoops, both sides are willing to use her to contradict their adversaries.

Payne is relentless in his satire by showing us the blindness activists will impose upon themselves in the service of their ideals.

*Election* (1999) is no less ruthless in its distillation of US culture and politics. Ambitious and manipulative, Tracy Flick (Reese Witherspoon) will stop at nothing to win a student body election. While making herself appear wholesome, cute and smart, Flick covertly demonstrates unscrupulous contempt for anyone who will stand in her way – namely Carver High's football hero, Paul Metzler (Chris Klein), and Tammy Metzler (Jessica Campbell), Paul's lesbian sister. Each has a stake in winning the election of the student body president but only Flick's instructor Mr McAllister (Matthew Broderick) knows the truth of Flick's character. His chicanery is the ironic and tragic truth that stands as the metaphor for contemporary US politics. We see clearly what motivates the political machines of US society, the choices they imply, and the apathy of the electorate. Yet the temptation to surreptitiously disrupt that system for a higher moral purpose remains the path trodden by fascists.

In both feature films, Payne sustains his metonymic strategy. Omaha, Nebraska is the part that represents the United States. And despite the intensely cynical message, he balances the implied gloom with uproarious humour and memorable performances from his leading female characters.

His most recent work, *About Schmidt* (2002), is an adaptation of Louise Bagley's novel, and stars Jack Nicholson as a newly widowed man who tries to fill the void in his life by controlling that of his daughter.                                                                                    **SSc**

# Kimberly PEIRCE

Kimberly Peirce's stark and stunning first feature, *Boys Don't Cry* (1999), can only be called a labour of love. Originally conceived as a thesis project during her tenure at Columbia Film School, Peirce spent four-and-a-half years researching the true story of Teena Brandon, a sexually-confused teenage girl from Lincoln, Nebraska, who, in the early 1990s, took on the persona of a boy named Brandon Teena and moved to the redneck burg of nearby Falls City, where she was later raped and killed when her deception was discovered.

*Boys Don't Cry* (1999)

While the writer-director cites the novelistic journalism of Norman Mailer's 'The Executioner's Song' as her primary influence, Peirce's film has also rightly and accurately been compared to *In Cold Blood* (1967) and *Badlands* (1973). Like those works, *Boys Don't Cry* combines a gritty, documentary realism and unsentimental tone with a dreamlike expressiveness, while further exhibiting a central romantic yearning all its own. For such a tragic story, Peirce manages to infuse it with many moments of transcendent joy, thanks to a number of expressive cinematic touches and the radiant presence of Hilary Swank in the role of the doomed Brandon, for which she received a Best Actress Academy Award. An early scene set at a roller rink, where Swank (as Brandon) skates with a teenage girl she's picked up, is buoyantly scored to The Cars' 'Just What I Needed' and played almost entirely without dialogue, focusing instead on the looks of pure giddy delight on both their faces.

Peirce gives Teena Brandon a hopeful idealism that borders on the dreamy; through Brandon's eyes, we see stars race across the Nebraska sky and the lights of small-town Falls City smear into a giddy blur of colour, seemingly inspired by a similar effect employed in Godfrey Reggio's *Koyaanisqatsi* (1983). Applying this sense of reverie to the film's central love story – between Brandon and a naive local girl named Lana Tisdell (Chloë Sevigny) – makes a heartbreaking counterpoint to the simmering violence of their backwater surroundings. This finally explodes in the brutality of the last act's barely watchable rape sequence, which Peirce captures with the unflinching eye of the neo-realist.                                                                                    **CS**

# Mark PELLINGTON

Although Mark Pellington's name is not as well-known as many of his contemporaries, his three major films – *Going all the Way* (1997), *Arlington Road* (1999), and *The Mothman Prophecies* (2002) – mark a significant presence in American cinema. His work resembles a low-key Oliver Stone, with its weaving hand-held camera and use of different film stocks, bright lights, and slow motion to punctuate plot points

*Going all the Way* (1997)
*Arlington Road* (1999)
*The Mothman Prophecies* (2002)

and emphasise a sense of disorientation. With this in mind, it is not surprising that Pellington's roots are in music video production and MTV promotions.

Choosing to work within the confines of traditional generic structures, Pellington's style works in the classical auteurist sense, with his personality bleeding through the seams, rather than being put immediately in the forefront. Despite this, and despite differences in the two films that might at once be glaring – the first is a coming-of-age tale set in Indianapolis and adapted from the Dan Wakefield novel; the second, an exciting conspiracy thriller about domestic terrorism and right-wing militias – they share an interesting scepticism about the apparent comforts in the American middle-class existence.

*Going all the Way* begins in 1954, soon after the Korean War, with the return home of two soldiers, Sonny (Jeremy Davies) and Gunner (Ben Affleck), to Indianapolis. Former classmates in high school who had no association with one another, timid photographer Sonny has been serving as a clerk in Kansas City while outgoing jock Gunner has seen battle. While both are seeking ways to change the course of their lives, Sonny has a more difficult time negotiating his rebellious impulses with his religious family and steady girlfriend. *Going all the Way* manages to escape the trap of bittersweetness that so many coming-of-age films fall into, and transcends the genre by introducing a strong homo-erotic undertone in the friendship.

*Arlington Road* is the story of college professor Michael Faraday (Jeff Bridges) who specialises in domestic terrorism. When his new neighbours (Tim Robbins and Joan Cusack) begin to display suspicious characteristics, Faraday decides to investigate their lives, discovering disturbing truths that linger beneath the veil of normalcy. The film questions the security people feel in their lives and the veracity of the information given by the people charged with society's protection. *Arlington Road* also had an excellent sense of immediacy, coming in the light of the terrorist bombing in Oklahoma City and the arrest of the anti-technology Unibomber, and although some critics found the film's story contrived, its ending is astoundingly unconventional with foreshadowing woven excellently into the plot.

A visually stylish and intriguing mystery, *The Mothman Prophecies* stars Richard Gere as a Washington journalist who has lost his wife and child in a suspicious accident. Finding himself drawn to a small town, he begins to investigate reports of supernatural sightings and deaths, becoming more and more embroiled. Based in part on a true story, it falls somewhere between horror and sci-fi – spookily entertaining.

In addition to the three features, Pellington has also directed the video releases 'Single Video Theory' (1998), a documentary on Seattle grunge band Pearl Jam with whom he also made the award-winning video for their song 'Jeremy', and *Destination Anywhere* (1997), a short film to accompany rock singer Jon Bon Jovi's album of the same name. He has also produced several works for PBS.                    **DH**

# Sean PENN

*Indian Runner* (1991)
*The Crossing Guard* (1995)
*The Pledge* (2001)

Born in Santa Monica, California, in 1960, Sean Penn's first success was as an actor, appearing in over thirty movies since 1981. He has also produced five movies, three of which he wrote and directed.

Inspired by Bruce Springsteen's 'Highway Patrolman', and made in the shadow of independent cinema of the period in which it is set, *The Indian Runner* (1991) follows the attempts of Joe (David Morse), a failed farmer-turned-policeman, to come to terms with his younger brother Frankie (Viggo Mortensen), a returning Vietnam veteran and small-time criminal. In an early scene, the transition from a hand-held camera following a bottle as drinks are poured to regulation two-shots indicates the tension at the core of Penn's direction: he is torn between improvisational naturalism and the desire to script and thus control the trajectory taken by individual scenes and the overall narrative. This has severe consequences for the movie, and ultimately the stylistic flourishes reminiscent of John Cassavetes and Hal Ashby (to whom the movie is dedicated) perform the same function as, for example, background television footage of the Chicago police riot at the 1968 Democratic Convention: neither finds resonance with the story being told, and thus they contribute nothing to the movie other than some kind of authenticating period detail. *The Indian Runner* is an elegy to childhood, family, and the potential futures that have been lost, including the cinematic possibilities represented by US independent film-making of the 1960s and 1970s. Yet by becoming a pastiche of such film-making, however sincerely intended, it contributes to its loss. This is evident in the way in which seemingly naturalistic scenes, such as the prison waiting room, are undercut by the knowledge that it is a period piece. It also shows in Mortensen's performance: whereas the unfussy Morse is a solid and convincing presence, and there are good supporting performances and cameos from Valeria Golino, Patricia Arquette, Charles Bronson, Sandy Dennis, Harry Crews, and Eileen Ryan, Mortensen's poor imitation of Sean Penn reduces method improvisation to mere mannerisms.

A sombre attempt to extend his study of masculinity, and the limits of the loyalty and the responsibility it entails, *The Crossing Guard* (1995) reveals a director in greater control of his stylistic tics – ably assisted by director of photography Vilmos Zsigmond – and less in thrall to his models. It is, however, let down by the television movie earnestness of the script and by a closing graveside scene which undermines an otherwise admirable avoidance of sentimentality. Jack Nicholson offers a reasonably restrained performance, but only Anjelica Huston, Priscilla Barnes, and occasionally David Morse, register any convincing feeling. It is unclear what Charles Bukowski, to whom it is dedicated, would have made of it.

*The Pledge* (2001), Penn's most recent film, is an adaptation of Friedrich Dürrenmatt's 1958 Kafka-lite novel, 'Das Versprechen'. It reunites Penn with Jack Nicholson, who plays a retired cop, Jerry Black, sworn to the pursuit of the rapist-killer of an eight-year-old girl. He befriends a waitress – excellently played by Robin Wright Penn – and uses her young daughter as bait for the killer. Fate plays a hand in fine absurdist style, and Jerry is left high and dry, alone and insane. This is Penn's finest film to date, with a less digressive narrative and stronger stylistic control (ably assisted by director of photography Chris Menges), as well as a fuller complement of good performances from Benicio Del Toro, Helen Mirren, Tom Noonan, Mickey Rourke, Sam Shepard, and Harry Dean Stanton. Ironically, in directing his first film from someone else's screenplay, Penn seems to have made the first film that is truly his own, rather than an imitator of illustrious models; he is on the verge of becoming a major director.                  **MB**

# Wolfgang PETERSEN

Born in Emden, Germany, in 1941, Wolfgang Petersen worked for fifteen years as a writer and director in German film and television before the success of *Das Boot* (1981) brought him substantial international recognition. After directing the 1967 short *Der Eine – der Andere*, he co-directed *Ich nicht* (1969) with Jörg-Michael Baldenuis (who worked as his cinematographer five times during the following decade). Like so many of the key figures in the New German Cinema, Petersen was based in Munich during the 1970s, although he has never evidenced the experimentalist bent of many others associated with the movement. He directed three movies during the decade, beginning with *Ich werde dich töten, Wolf* (1971). *Einer von uns beiden* (1973) is a pleasingly grim and complex thriller about an ex-student who attempts to blackmail a professor who obtained his PhD – and subsequent professional and social standing – fraudulently. Their conflict escalates in a morally ambivalent world, and just as it seems the student will triumph the professor commits suicide. The sense of class difference Petersen would later re-articulate as a conflict between men who are just trying to do their jobs and their variously corrupt, conspiring, ineffectual, or ignorant superiors is here at its clearest, manifested through the principals' criminal drive to maintain and advance their positions.

*Die Konsequenz* (1977), which Petersen co-scripted from Alexander Ziegler's autobiographical novel, is a thoughtful drama about a gay romance, attractively shot in black and white. The first half of Petersen's career is, however, dominated by television work, directing several entries in the series of Tatort crime movies: *Tatort – Blechschaden* (1971), *Tatort – Strandgut* (1972), *Tatort – Jagdrevier* (1973), *Tatort – Nachtfrost* (1974), and *Tatort – Reifezeugnis* (1977); as well as *Anna und Toto* (1972), *Van der Valk und die Reichen* (1973), *Smog* (1973), *Aufs Kreuz gelegt* (1974), *Stellenweise Glatteis* (1975), *Die Stadt im Tal* (1975), and *Hans im Glück* (1976), an adaptation of Jacob Grimm's 'Lucky Hans'. Petersen also wrote and directed *Vier gegen die Bank* (1976), *Planübung* (1977), and the bizarre drama *Schwarz und*

*Ich nicht* (1969)
*Ich werde dich töten, Wolf* (1971)
*Einer von uns beiden* (1973)
*Die Konsequenz* (1977)
*Das Boot* (1981)
*Die Unendliche Geschichte* (1984)
*Enemy Mine* (1985)
*Shattered* (1991)
*In the Line of Fire* (1993)
*Outbreak* (1995)
*Air Force One* (1997)
*The Perfect Storm* (2000)

*weiss wie Tage und Nächte* (1978), in which Bruno Ganz plays a computer genius who descends into paranoia after his 'unbeatable' chess program is beaten.

*Das Boot*, a television mini-series and movie adapted by Petersen from Lothar-Guenther Buchheim's autobiographical novel, cast Jurgen Prochnow as the commander of U-96. The settings provide Petersen with ample opportunities to indulge in the rich, warm tones he favours, and his mobile camera is especially effective at generating a sense of claustrophobia. Small details suggest the tedium and discomfort of the submariners' daily routines. The most expensive German movie to that date, it was a popular commercial success, both domestically and internationally. This success has been attributed in part to its refusal to directly address Nazism: Prochnow's commander is a professional soldier whose criticism of the regime extends no further than contempt for the politicians and senior officers who prevent him from doing his job properly; the crew – who share the camaraderie of unruly schoolboys, alternating boredom, excitement, petulance, and fear – join their commander in mocking the only Nazi (an immaculate prig) aboard. Prochnow's line about the need for good men provides a key to much of Petersen's later work and recommends him to US action cinema, itself obsessed with the struggles of such men against both their adversaries and the systems and institutions which are failing to support them.

Petersen next adapted *Die Unendliche Geschichte* (aka *The NeverEnding Story* (1984)) from Michael Ende's novel. With an unprecedented budget of 60 million marks, he was able to utilise the most advanced effects technologies of the day. Although another commercial success, the end result seems at odds with the moral of the story it is trying to tell about the importance of the imagination. Taken together, these movies, with their high production values, full complement of spectacular special effects, and renunciation of the political, announced Petersen as a director amenable to US commercial film-making.

In 1985, $9 million into the budget, and several weeks into shooting in Iceland's inhospitable conditions, Richard Loncraine abandoned his attempted adaptation of Barry B. Longyear's 'Enemy Mine'. Petersen agreed to take over, provided he could begin from scratch, and relocated the production to his familiar Bavaria Studios. Casting Louis Gossett Jr. as the alien sometimes makes this science fictionalisation of *Hell in the Pacific* (1968) seem more like *The Defiant Ones* (1958), but it comes closer than either to actualising the interracial queer romance narrative Fiedler identified as central to American culture. A fantasy mode, matched to seasonal movements, dominates, and an early allusion to *The Creature from the Black Lagoon* (1954) makes it clear that sentimentality will displace the barely-hinted critique of genocidal expansionism and concomitant ecological devastation. The movie is weakened by the variable quality of the effects work, narrative implausibilities, and an alien setting that looks just like a soundstage. However, it gave Petersen entry to American film-making.

*Shattered* (1991), which he adapted from Richard Neely's 'The Plastic Nightmare', produced, and directed, is a solid thriller about business and marital infidelities. Its use of the conventional device of amnesia is effective because the audience only ever knows as much as the protagonist, played by bland Tom Berenger as a character who literally has no character. Subsequently, Petersen has only worked from other people's screenplays, but has retained production credits; he also executive produced *Red Corner* (1997) and *Instinct* (1999), and produced *Bicentennial Man* (1999).

*In the Line of Fire* (1993) represents probably the most successful attempt to develop Clint Eastwood's Dirty Harry persona into an establishment figure. The movie attracted favourable comment for paralleling the protagonist's fate with that of ageing Hollywood action stars, but as in most late-Eastwood vehicles the humour is broad and lazy. Similarly, the positive re-negotiation of gender relations detected by some is platitudinous in the extreme, and as with Petersen's subsequent movie, co-star Rene Russo could just as easily have carried the narrative. *Outbreak* (1995) has a suitably impressive and intriguing opening sequence, shortly followed by a prolonged steadicam shot in which Petersen's ability with a mobile camera is evident. To criticise the performances as one-dimensional is harsh in a movie unashamed of reworking a cheap metaleptic stunt from *The Tingler* (1959): Dustin Hoffman is cannily miscast; Rene Russo is solid in her underdeveloped part; Kevin Spacey relishes his sidekick role; and Donald Sutherland's turn as a barking mad General is more than adequate. *Air Force One* (1997) reworks an airborne *Die Hard* scenario with some skill, but not even the moral dignity Harrison Ford imports from his Jack Ryan movies can overcome the screenplay's cheesy flag-waving. Moreover, if *Das Boot* is to be criticised for its refusal to engage with the politics of its setting, so too must a movie which continues the trend of denouncing nationalist sentiments (unless they are American) and ascribing evil to Asians. Effective as an action-thriller, it is neo-liberal cinema at its most deplorable.

The Perfect Storm (2000), starring George Clooney and Mark Wahlberg, is based on Sebastian Junger's account of the true story of the Andrea Gail, a small fishing vessel which was caught in a massive storm in August 1991. Although the movie makes clear the economic motives which drive the crew into danger, it lacks any real sympathy for their situation, preferring instead to merely propel them into extended jeopardy and spectacular special effects shots.

His forthcoming film, *Endurance*, treads similar ground to *The Perfect Storm*; based on the journey of Sir Ernest Shackleton's Antarctic expedition, it follows the odyssey of the crew's return to civilisation after their ship is trapped in ice.                **MB**

# Daniel PETRIE

Born in Nova Scotia, Canada, in 1920, Daniel Petrie, the father of writer/director Daniel Petrie Jr. and director Donald Petrie, is a routine director who has worked in a variety of genres, returning periodically to films about young people. He began working in television in 1951, making his feature debut with *Bramble Bush* (1960). This was an adaptation of a soapy novel by Charles Mergendahl, starring Richard Burton as a small-town doctor who falls for the wife of a dying friend. Burton looks bored in an unmemorable film.

Petrie's next movie, *A Raisin in the Sun* (1961), was a great improvement, being a sensitive adaptation of the Lorraine Hansberry play. Sidney Poitier stars in the story of a black family in Chicago which has dated considerably but avoids clichés. Petrie travelled to England to make his next four films. *The Main Attraction* (1962) had a miscast Pat Boone alongside veteran British performers like Lionel Blair, John LeMesurier, Warren Mitchell in a dull story of a drifting musician who joins a travelling circus. The following year's *Stolen Hours* (1963) was little better, with Susan Hayward as a dying woman trying to live life to the full. The terrible *The Idol* (1966) was a 'racy' story with a late-period Jennifer Jones as a mother seduced by the same rat who is sleeping with her daughter. *The Spy with a Cold Nose* (1966) was the best film to come out of Petrie's British sojourn, a spoof of the then-fashionable spy genre. Inoffensive and slightly inconsequential, the film benefits from a spirited cast including Laurence Harvey, Denholm Elliott and Colin Blakely.

Returning to the US, Petrie worked in television for some years, making episodes of shows like 'McMillan and Wife' and run-of-the-mill television movies such as *The City* (1971) and *A Howling in the Woods* (1971). Notable from this period is the television movie *Moon of the Wolf* (1972), an effective werewolf yarn set in Louisiana with David Janssen hunting the titular beast. This was followed by *The Neptune Factor* (1973), a wildly different project but no more successful, being a staid submarine 'thriller' with Ben Gazzara. *Cat and Mouse* (aka *Mousey*) (1974) was made for television but got a theatrical release outside America. Kirk Douglas is an effective villain stalking his ex-wife, Jean Seberg. This is a taut, atmospheric thriller and placed alongside *Moon of the Wolf* suggests that perhaps Petrie would be more at ease with slightly darker projects.

The lack of any overt cinematic flourishes in Petrie's work is possibly the reason he could move with such ease from television to features and back again. With *Buster and Billie* (1974), there is once again little in the way of a personal imprint, except for the theme of emergent sexuality amongst the young which tends to crop up often in Petrie's work. The beautiful Jean-Michael Vincent hooks up with ugly duckling Joan Goodfellow in 1940s Georgia but there is a 'seen it all before' quality to the whole thing. Petrie's next, *Lifeguard* (1976) was anything but dark. Sam Elliott is the title character growing old (turning thirty!) disgracefully. This dull, flatly directed beach romp was considered by some critics as having a strong homosexual subtext and it was compared to Visconti's *Death in Venice* (1971), but this makes the film sound much more interesting than it actually is.

The television movie *Sybil* (1976) was a virtual two-hander between Joanne Woodward as a psychiatrist and Sally Field as her patient with 16 personalities. Firmly in TV movie territory, the result was still impressive. The turgid Harold Robbins adaptation

*The Betsy* (1978), with Tommy Lee Jones and Laurence Olivier slumming it, was a tale of power struggles within the auto industry. Petrie followed this turkey with *Resurrection* (1980). This story of a faith-healer, regarded as both saint and sinner, is absorbing if faintly silly. Ellen Burstyn plays the gifted/afflicted protagonist with Sam Shepard as her lover and would-be assassin.

*Fort Apache the Bronx* (1981) is an over-familiar (from countless cop shows and movies) but exciting story of a New York police precinct. The episodic structure increases the similarities to police procedural television material but there are good performances from Paul Newman as a grizzled veteran and Pam Grier as a hooker killing her tricks with a razor blade hidden in her mouth. This was followed by the forgettable *Six Pack* (1982). A would-be heartwarming story of singer Kenny Rogers adopting six delinquent kids, the film is not worthy of note.

This was followed by *The Bay Boy* (1984), which was a Canadian production and stands out amongst the routine projects Petrie specialises in. A self-penned autobiographical rites-of-passage story has Keifer Sutherland coming of age in Nova Scotia in 1937. The personal nature of the story seems to have brought out the best in the director. The photography is striking and good use is made of the unfamiliar setting. Given that this setting is a small mining town, Sutherland's experiences are slightly too exotic: repeated seductions and murder are amongst the things that occur. Yet this stylish and touching film, which won Petrie a Genie, suggests he is capable of being more than a journeyman director.

*The Doll-Maker* (1984), like the earlier (and better) *Cat and Mouse*, was a film for television that got a limited theatrical release. A badly cast Jane Fonda plays a Kentucky housewife and mother who relocates to Detroit in the 1940s. The film offers nothing new. The same could be said for *Half a Lifetime* (1986). Of more interest is the strange *Square Dance* (1987) which resembles a cross between 'Little House on the Prairie' and Tennessee Williams. Winona Ryder is a devout Texas teen whose platonic friendship with the retarded Rory (Rob Lowe) ends in despair for her and genital mutilation for him. Although the film is too slow, good performances make it watchable.

*Cocoon: The Return* (1986) was the awful sequel to Ron Howard's *Cocoon* (1984). Only the veteran cast – which includes Wilford Brimley, Don Ameche, Hume Cronyn, and Gwen Verdon – make this at all bearable. Much more successful was *Rocket Gibraltar* (1988) with Burt Lancaster as an aged patriarch at the centre of a family gathering on Long Island. The script by Amos Poe gives Petrie more to work with than many of his previous outings and the Long Island setting is strikingly rendered, conjuring up memories of *The Bay Boy*.

Amongst more recent television material – like *Mark Twain and Me* (1991) and *Kissinger and Nixon* (1995) – Petrie has directed the fine *My Name is Bill W.* (1989) with an excellent James Woods as the co-founder of Alcoholics Anonymous. Away from the television screen, he directed a routine version of the evergreen *Lassie* (1994) and realised a long-cherished ambition to make *The Assistant* (1997). This adaptation of the Pulitzer Prize-winning novel by Bernard Malamud is a fable of prejudice and tolerance, with fine performances by Amin Mueller-Stahl and Joan Plowright. The film struggled to find its way into theatre but is absorbing, if a little conservative.

Although Petrie is a director capable of making interesting, quality films, he is too often simply a proficient technician.                                                              **IC**

# Daniel PETRIE Jr.

*Toy Soldiers* (1991)
*In the Army Now* (1994)

The son of the prolific director Daniel Petrie, Petrie Jr. started as a literary agent and became a screenwriter capable of excellence before embarking on a less promising directorial career.

Petrie wrote the screenplay for *Beverly Hills Cop* (1984), which was originally intended as a vehicle for Sylvester Stallone. With Eddie Murphy, the film became a box-office smash and made Murphy a star, spawning two sequels (with Petrie involved as a writer on the first one). Jim McBride's *The Big Easy* (1987), an atmospheric and erotic thriller set in New Orleans, was another Petrie script. The considerable sexual charge generated by Dennis Quaid and Ellen Barkin is in no small part due to Petrie's racy dialogue (although it should be acknowledged that director McBride and his colleague Jack Baram do claim to have substantially re-written Petrie's screenplay).

Petrie made his directorial debut with the action movie *Toy Soldiers* (1991). The far-fetched premise has Colombian terrorists occupying a prep school full of alienated rich kids. Like the superior *Red Dawn* (1984) the film is militaristic and jingoistic but the action scenes are disappointing. The young cast are aided considerably by the veteran Lou Gossett Jr. and Denholm Elliott. Although fairly watchable, it is uninspiring and over-familiar.

Petrie's next feature was a Pauly Shore vehicle, *In the Army Now* (1994). The comedian plays one of a pair of idiots who join the army. Shore is clownish and unfunny and yet the film's success is dependent on him. His screen persona makes that of Adam Sandler look like an urban sophisticate. This is a weak comedy of no distinction that bears more resemblance to Petrie's script for the Tom Hanks canine comedy *Turner and Hooch* (1989) than to his more substantial work.

Petrie has considerable talent but the gap between his writing and directing projects is marked and there is a lack of distinction in the two films he has made to date.    **IC**

# Donald PETRIE

Son and brother respectively of directors Daniel and Daniel Jr., Donald Petrie was born in New York and began his career in acting and production. He started directing television series such as 'MacGyver', 'The Equaliser', and 'LA Law', showing that he could economically handle both action and dialogue/character-driven work, and winning awards for 'LA Law'.

He briefly sidestepped into film, making a short for the American Film Institute in 1983. *The Expert* was about the emotional effects on a small-town doctor dealing with the ethical and moral dilemma of preparing the gas chamber at a state prison, and teaching the procedure to a new doctor. He then returned to television, continuing his direction of 'The Equaliser' and new shows such as 'Turner and Hooch The Kid' into the 1990s.

His feature debut, *Mystic Pizza* (1988), was co-written by Amy Jones, who was also scheduled to direct. A studio difference of opinion led to Petrie's involvement in the movie, a female rites-of-passage tale starring a trio of young actresses potentially approaching stardom: Julia Roberts, Lili Taylor, and Annabeth Gish. About three friends working their post-graduation summer in the eponymous parlour while they choose a life path, the film has a sharp script that avoids stereotypes; it also gave Petrie the opportunity to do a different kind of story.

His direction avoids too much sentimentality, and shows visual flair; Petrie shoots Taylor's disastrous wedding from her optical point-of-view, through her wedding veil. He also evokes levels of emotion by using a range of film stocks and making the most of the autumnal setting to imbue the film with a sombre glow unusual for its genre. It was a modest success for Petrie and despite its narrative convention, features funny, perceptive, and emotionally resonant moments.

He moved into comedy with *Opportunity Knocks* (1990), starring Robert Loggia and Dana Carvey, the story of an unsuccessful con man house-sitting for a rich businessman. Although the film demonstrated Petrie's comedic ability, it lacked the visual cohesion of his feature debut and was generally unsuccessful. Paired with professional odd couple Walter Matthau and Jack Lemmon for a version of their successful Neil Simon-based work, Petrie made *Grumpy Old Men* in 1993. A box-office success, this was more to do with the public's desire to re-visit Lemmon and Matthau's earlier, funnier pairings, than a reflection of the movie itself. Unadventurous and predictable, the film rarely gets off the ground, and strong performances by the likes of Burgess Meredith and Ossie Davis are marginalised in favour of the stars. This factor is reinforced by Petrie's decision to include a reel of out-takes and alternative dialogue at the end (a trend becoming increasingly common) as if to capitalise on the most known and loved personae of his stars.

His next film, *The Favor* (1994), languished for three years between completion and release. A marital crisis movie about a woman who asks her best friend to sleep with her ex-high-school hunk boyfriend so she can experience a vicarious affair, it lacks the finesse of Petrie's debut, falling more in line with his more recent clumsy comedy.

Like *Grumpy Old Men*, *Richie Rich* (1994) and *My Favorite Martian* (1999) exploit a general desire for nostalgic entertainment and peddle childish stories for adults. The former refers to Hitchcock in its finale, set against Richie's own Mount Rushmore-style rock faces. Tame and amiable, with pretensions to critique big business, the film fails to reward its ambitions. The same can be said of *My Favorite Martian*, which is based on the popular 1960s television show that timely appeared between 'Red Scares' and space travel. Jeff Daniels is a surprisingly dull hero, Christopher Lloyd a crazy Martian, Elizabeth Hurley the prerequisite love interest, and a talking spacesuit upstages them all. It is a disappointing exercise that struggles to maintain its feature length.

Between these two films, Petrie made *The Associate* (1996), which focused on a female business partnership (between Whoopi Goldberg and Dianne Wiest) that needs a male financial backer to be taken seriously. Described as '*Tootsie* meets *Trading Places* for the politically sensitive 1990s' this promises more than the film delivers, but there are some smart jokes and solid performances. The casting of Goldberg gives the film a political agenda – in the original (Rene Gainville's *L'Associe* (1979)) the central character is a white man – but the film could go further to make some pertinent points about corporate sexism and racism.

A quiet spell followed before Petrie returned to the big screen with the Sandra Bullock vehicle *Miss Congeniality* (2000). The predictable 'ugly duckling turned into a swan' routine combines a recent trend for beauty contest narratives with an action-thriller: it is the story of an FBI agent (Bullock, also the film's producer) who goes undercover at a beauty pageant to prevent a bombing. The premise is promising but the film is comically clichéd: klutzy Bullock trips over her stiletto heels; a camp Michael Caine squeezes as much humour as possible into taming his leading lady's eyebrows; Benjamin Bratt is the oily colleague who, of course, adores the swan that Bullock becomes. Bullock has great fun with her 'before' persona (dribbling food, falling over, wearing baggy t-shirts) and is a game comedy-action heroine, reminding audiences of the blend of deft humour and sweetness she brought to her most likeable roles as she races around the glamorous beauty contest set with her gun. An able supporting cast, which includes Candice Bergen, Ernie Hudson and William Shatner, offer their own comic turns, but of course Bullock takes no risks: everything is resolved satisfactorily, especially for the Miss Congeniality Bullock's FBI agent has become.

Petrie is rumoured to be in production with another romantic comedy, provisionally titled *How To Lose a Guy in 10 Days*. **JD**

# Bill PLYMPTON

Bill Plympton and his self-styled 'Plymptoons' have earned a significant place in the American cartoonal tradition, both for their deadpan auteurist signature style, and their means of production. His short works for MTV established his place as a cult figure, renowned for his surreal address of human obsessions, and the grotesque but playful brutalism in his representation of the body. Describing his own work as 'like an animated David Lynch', Plympton combines the physical excesses of Tex Avery cartoons, the Dali-esque incongruities of form, the sense of absence and presence in the work of Magritte, the 'trip' sensibility of Robert Crumb, and the independent off-centre preoccupations of Jim Jarmusch. His position as a genuine auteur is secure in the sense that he writes, produces, directs, and animates all his own work.

Plympton was born in Portland in 1946 and after leaving Portland State University he joined the National Guard in 1967 to avoid the draft to Vietnam. His five-year stint was followed by a move to New York and a year's study at the School of Visual Arts. Plympton became a graphic designer, illustrator, and cartoonist, creating material for publications as diverse as *Vogue*, *Penthouse*, and the *New York Times*. His move to New York proved particularly important in the sense that the incongruities and brutalities of urban politics, the emergence of the counterculture, and the surrealism seemingly imbued in everyday life, were to be highly influential on his style and outlook. In 1975, he created a political cartoon strip entitled 'Plympton' for *The Soho Weekly News* which was syndicated by Universal to over twenty newspapers nationwide.

Plympton's later, self-taught animation reflects this experience, as he simply removes the logic of the assumptions and consensual habits which are the stabilising elements of contemporary life, and replaces them with an alternative set of perspectives which collapse existence into a chaotic and arbitrary state of mind. The human form is particularly vulnerable in the Plympton universe; the body a site for sadistic and surreal re-definition. Figures inhale each other, are decapitated, crushed, electrocuted, exploded, and imploded – all in the spirit of extending the traditions of artifice in cartoon violence, and foregrounding the vulnerability of the human body as it seeks to transcend its own boundaries. Arguably, there is a great deal of male anxiety about the female form in Plympton's work, but whether configuring breasts as malleable balloon animals or wall-smashing globes serves as a sight to evidence this, or merely serves as the fervent associative invention of an uninhibited comic mind, is open to question.

I Married a Strange Person (1997)
Sex and Violence (1998)
The Exciting Life of a Tree (1998)
More Sex and Violence (1998)
Surprise Cinema (1999)

It is Plympton's prolific draughtsmanship, however, that is even more impressive, creating the significant milestone of *The Tune* (1992), a 90-minute feature animated by one person, in which Del, his leading character, is given 47 minutes to find a hit for his boss, Mr Mega. Partly funded by selling segments of the final film as individual shorts to MTV, partly by commercial work on the 'Trivial Pursuit' and 'Sugar Delight' campaigns, the film was made on a comparatively minimal budget. His technique – loosely drawn animated sequences on paper, transferred to cel and re-coloured and detailed – makes for a spontaneous, active *mise-en-scène*, even when seemingly at its most static and barren. His craving for creative freedom and independence, following in the footsteps of mentor, George Griffin, has also led to him becoming his own distributor, and heightening his profile through putting his material on a website.

Despite a long career in the graphic arts, Plympton did not make his first animation until 1977, with a cut-out film, *Lucas the Ear of Corn*, and did not make a second cartoon until he collaborated on *Boomtown* (1985), a visualisation of a Jules Feiffer song, sung by the Android Sisters, implicitly critiquing American foreign policy and defence spending. *Your Face* (1987), his first 'signature' film, a musical short featuring a slowed-down vocal performance from country singer Maureen McElheron and animation of an ever-contorting face, won an Academy Award nomination. In 1990, Plympton was sought by Disney to animate the fast metamorphoses of the genie in their projected feature, *Aladdin* (1992), but Plympton declined on the basis that he could continue to work independently, having established an international reputation with *One of Those Days* (1988) – a viewer's point-of-view compendium of accidents, *How to Kiss* (1989) – a bizarre guide to kissing, *25 Ways to Quit Smoking* (1989) – an inventive infantry of smoking cures, *Plymptoons* (1989) – animated versions of his most notable print cartoons, *Dig my Do* (1990) – featuring an animated Elvis dog, and *The Wiseman* (1990). *Push Comes to Shove* (1991) plays out a slowhand Laurel-and-Hardyesque escalation of petty yet excessive brutality, while *Nosehair* (1994) engages in the epic struggle between one man and a hair dangling from his nostril, essentially an animated tour de force in what can be achieved with a single line.

Plympton's second feature, *I Married a Strange Person* (1997), includes only one previous short, *How to Make Love to a Woman*, but readily echoes the B-movie, *I Married a Monster From Outer Space* (1958), in its device of a husband, Grant Boyer, being changed by radiation emitted from a satellite dish, which enables him to make his sexual and violent fantasies 'real'. More to the point, this enables Plympton to make these 'realities' yet more excessive and comically implausible. Opening the film by citing Picasso's idea that 'taste is the enemy of creativity', and supporting it, provocatively, with Herman Goering's statement that 'when I hear the word culture, I reach for my pistol', Plympton then proceeds through a catalogue of surreal riffs – bird orgasm, amoeba wrestling, dialogues between tongue and teeth, a comedian who tears himself up and throws himself to the audience, the formation of navel 'fluff', aggressive nipples – it is all here; the body endlessly at war with itself, other people, the media – 'the Smile Corps' – institutionalism, and the environment. The film's set-piece sexual preoccupations are also echoed in *Sex and Violence* (1997) and *More Sex and Violence* (1998).

Plympton has also made two live-action feature films; *J. Lyle* (1994), a comedy about an acquisitive landlord, and *Guns on the Clackamas* (1996), a 'mockumentary' based on the real-life events of the filming of *Saratoga* (1937), when Jean Harlow died and the film had to be completed by using a stand-in, here clothed in typical Plympton excess, as the desperate production financiers of Plympton's mythical western seek to raise funds by selling the dead star's soiled underwear. **PW**

# Jeremy PODESWA

A graduate of the American Film Institute's Centre for Advanced Film Studies, born in Toronto in 1962, Jeremy Podeswa has worked extensively in television and is the

Eclipse (1994)
The Five Senses (1999)

recipient of two Gemini awards. His first film, *Eclipse* (1994), is a contemporary re-working of 'La Ronde'. Tracing the sexual exploits of ten people during the days leading up to a total eclipse, Podeswa draws parallels between the characters' troubled lives and the transitory nature of the solar event. Although unabashed in expressing their sexual desires, each character is traumatised, either by the impermanence of their encounter or the fear of prolonged emotional attachment. Interspersing the episodes are interviews with academics and astrologers, offering their views on the powerful attraction of the natural occurrence. Although Podeswa draws too heavily on the eclipse as a metaphor for the volatile and unpredictable nature of relationships, the episodes are deftly handled, with an intelligent and witty script, and fine performances from the ensemble cast.

*The Five Senses* (1999) is more diverse and accomplished than its predecessor, offering a beguilingly clever study of the foibles of human relationships and the power of attraction. Initially a guessing game about which character represents each of the senses, Podeswa gradually weaves a web of intrigue, as the characters become more deeply embroiled in relationships with the people around them. The senses themselves act as a metaphor for – and the link between – each relationship, emphasising both the senses and characters' inability to function properly on their own. A music lover rapidly losing his hearing learns to find other ways to listen with the help of a prostitute; an aromatherapist is unable to make contact with her daughter; a girl discovers friendship when she loses a child she is babysitting. In one of the film's most comical segments, a professional housekeeper with an unusually high olfactory sense finds himself the object of a young couple's affection, one of whom works for a perfume company. Elegantly written and directed, with more rounded characterisations and emotional depth than *Eclipse*, *The Five Senses* confirms Podeswa's position as one of the most talented film-makers to recently emerge from Canada. **IHS**

# Michael POLISH

Born in 1972, the Polish brothers, Michael and Mark, made their film-making debut with *Twin Falls Idaho* (1999), the story of a pair of conjoined twins, one of whom, Francis (director Michael), is ill. It is the other, Blake (screenwriter Mark), whose stronger heart keeps them alive. The two have checked into a seedy hotel to allow Francis, and thus Blake, to die, but for their birthday Francis has ordered a prostitute (Michele Hicks) for Blake. Although she is initially shocked by the twins, she befriends them, and becomes particularly close with Blake as Francis grows sicker.

A popular success at the Sundance Film Festival, *Twin Falls Idaho* is a quiet, understated film that belies its strange subject matter. Shot in muted tones and made up of sharp precise shots that linger beautifully, it is reminiscent of the work of Stanley Kubrick, down to a deep-focus corridor shot and the theme of dehumanisation. A graduate of the California Institute of the Arts, Michael's consistency of vision is matched by a nuanced screenplay by Mark. Their acting is similarly subtle, with an innate interaction that feels incredibly real; their continual whispering to one another is more like the unspoken thoughts in a person's head. Although Hicks, in her acting debut, is weak, and some of the film's symbolism is obvious, Michael has disguised its extremely low budget well, creating a sublime, if mildly flawed, masterpiece. Their second feature, *Jackpot* (2001), is the story of an ambitious singer who abandons his family to tour the US without a manager.

Michael Polish has also directed the award-winning short film *Bajo del Perro* (1996). Both brothers appeared as a pair of twins in *Hellraiser: Bloodline* (1996). **DH**

# Jeff POLLACK

Having worked in television directing 'The Fresh Prince of Bel Air', like Spike Lee and John Singleton before him, Jeff Pollack entered the cinema attempting to articulate the Afro-American urban experience; exploring the difficulties and dilemmas of the young black male on the margins of American society.

In *Above the Rim* (1994) he visits a familiar subject in this genre – street basketball – and predictably it embodies some characteristic metaphors and messages. It charts the difficulties of a young hopeful on the road to basketball glory and emphasises the importance of staying on the straight and narrow in order to get out of the 'hood'. The narrative centres around Kyle and his moral dilemma in choosing between the influences of a local drug dealer, Birdie (played by Tupac Shakur), and his brother Shep, a gentle school security guard, who has also been a basketball whiz. Typically the plot climaxes in a match between Kyle and Shep and the local gangsters, which they win in the dying seconds, with Kyle ultimately rejecting Birdie and going on to attend college. Pollack touches on themes such as the importance of family, the corrupting desire of material success and hauntings from the past through Kyle's ordeal. The film has been criticised for its clichéd characters and moralising plot.

Like Spike Lee and John Singleton, Pollack's *mise-en-scène* creates a strong sense of the urban context. The location scenes in the dark streets of New York, in the bustling basketball courts of Harlem and Birdie's shady night-club that are accompanied by an upbeat hip-hop score (mostly provided by Shakur) and heavily localised dialogue convincingly create the atmosphere of the ghetto. As in other films from this genre the basketball action is slick, fast-paced and aggressive. However, Pollack's superficial attempt to explore the complex social issues of black urban life lacks the depth of the dramas of Spike Lee.

In *Booty Call* (1997), the story of the sexual adventures of two young black men of contrasting ethics, Pollack reverted to comedy. The slapstick humour travels well from his television days with the plot of mishaps set in just one night. Underlying the laughs is a prevailing message that maintaining moral character is more important than impressing ones friends. It is equally superficial and moral and the varied ethnic characters border on racial stereotypes, leaving Pollack on a plane below directors such as Lee, who have sought to explore and challenge such stereotypes.

In *Lost and Found* (1999), he moves away from the black cinema altogether with a sentimental, stock romantic-comedy, which is set in the cosy white middle-class world of a restaurant owner. In charting the protagonist's efforts to win over his beautiful neighbour Lila (played by Sophie Marceau), Pollack, to his credit, does not succumb to Hollywood's pressure to cast a good-looking, big-name actor for the lead male in romance. **JO**

# Sydney POLLACK

It is unsurprising that Sydney Pollack has been described as an actor's director. Born in Indiana in 1934, this most respected of Hollywood film-makers started his career as a stage actor, so it seems only logical that he has managed to strike up a rapport with some of the biggest stars working in the industry over the past 35 years. Pollack is a straightforwardly commercial director who has happily been a part of the mainstream, unlike such contemporaries as Sidney Lumet and Woody Allen. He has worked in staple genres – western, romance, paranoid conspiracy thriller, gangster, epic historical drama – and has enjoyed much critical and box-office success.

Pollack wanted to act from an early age. He trained at the Neighbourhood Playhouse Theatre School in New York City for a year while in his late teens, under the tutelage of Sanford Meisner (about whom he would later make a documentary). A Broadway debut followed in 1954. After serving in the army for two years (1957–58), Pollack resumed acting, this time in the blossoming medium of television. Simultaneously, he gained a job at the Neighbourhood Playhouse instructing trainee stage actors. Having appeared in a television play directed by his contemporary John Frankenheimer, Pollack struck up a friendship that led to work as a dialogue coach on Frankenheimer's feature film *The Young Savages* (1961). Seeing Frankenheimer at work activated in Pollack a desire to direct. He had a small part in the film *War Hunt* (1962), alongside a young upcoming performer named Robert Redford.

Pollack won several television assignments, directing episodes of such series as 'Ben Casey', 'The Defenders', 'Dr Kildare', and 'The Fugitive'. Such a fast-turnover, low-budget apprenticeship served him well, as he learned expediency and on-set self-discipline that would benefit his major productions later. Supervising the American overdubbing of Visconti's *The Leopard* (1963) was Pollack's breakthrough into feature films. *This Slender Thread* (1965), his full feature debut, was followed by a Tennessee Williams play adaptation, *This Property is Condemned* (1966). The film was most notable for marking the first collaboration between Pollack and Redford as director

*This Slender Thread* (1965)
*This Property is Condemned* (1966)
*The Scalphunters* (1968)
*Castle Keep* (1969)
*They Shoot Horses, Don't They?* (1969)
*Jeremiah Johnson* (1972)
*The Way We Were* (1973)
*The Yakuza* (1975)
*Three Days of the Condor* (1975)
*Bobby Deerfield* (1977)
*The Electric Horseman* (1979)
*Absence of Malice* (1981)
*Tootsie* (1982)
*Out of Africa* (1985)
*Havana* (1990)
*The Firm* (1993)
*Sabrina* (1995)
*Random Hearts* (1999)

and actor respectively, a partnership that would go on to be one of the most enduring in recent Hollywood history.

Pollack flirted with the styles of European art cinema in his work through the late 1960s. He directed one sequence of *The Swimmer* (1968), a successful but somewhat mystifyingly metaphorical effort starring Burt Lancaster as a disillusioned wealthy man who travels across the lavish properties of his friends, swimming in their garden pools along the way. This was followed in the same year by another Lancaster vehicle, the more conventional *The Scalphunters*. A knockabout comedy western, this contained some striking cinematography and winning performances from Lancaster and Ossie Davis as, respectively, a grizzled cowboy and an erudite black slave, who are forcibly teamed to retrieve Lancaster's stolen animal furs from a gang of bounty hunters led by Telly Savalas. Funny and boisterous, *The Scalphunters* marked Pollack as a solid director of easy-going commercial entertainment.

Lancaster appeared a third time for Pollack in the existential war film *Castle Keep* (1969). Apparently intended as a fusion of Hollywood action movie bombast and art cinema metaphor, it was received only as an interesting oddity. *They Shoot Horses, Don't They?* from the same year stands as a key American film of its period. Set during the Depression era, it is a melodrama featuring a motley bunch of misfits, has-beens, and showbusiness wannabes who collectively partake in a gruelling thousand-hour-plus dance marathon contest. Detailing the downbeat private lives of the competitors, the film ends in tragedy for its protagonist, played by an Academy Award-nominated Jane Fonda. Also nominated for Best Director, Pollack conveyed early signs that he could bring together and harness an ensemble cast effectively. The film reaches moments of hypnotic artistry in its cutting, quiet character moments, and energetic dance sequences, while the flashforwards add more art-cinema style internal psychology to the male lead.

Two back-to-back Redford collaborations came in 1972 and 1973. *Jeremiah Johnson*, the first, is an adventure set in the stunning snow-clad mountains of Utah in the 1850s. Redford plays the title part, an ex-soldier who gradually learns how to survive in the wilderness and become one with his habitat. A real sense of what America was like before civilisation encroached is captured in a fascinating sub-western, pseudo-documentary. The second of the consecutive Redford projects is, by contrast, an unashamed attempt to emulate the Hollywood golden age bittersweet romantic tearjerker. Set against a backdrop of political activism (World War Two, the McCarthy witch hunts), *The Way We Were* (1973) utilises Redford and a top-billed Barbra Streisand extremely well. They almost play themselves: he is the WASP college jock and army hero who, on discharge, turns to Hollywood scriptwriting; she is the ugly-beautiful Jewish upstart whose political interests ultimately prove incompatible with Redford's desire merely to live the good life. It pushed all the right buttons with audiences, spawned a hit song for Streisand, and consolidated Redford (in the same year as *The Sting*) as one of the biggest male stars of the era.

Proving his versatility with material, Pollack turned to a gangster project set in Japan, *The Yakuza*, and then shortly after a spy thriller, *Three Days of the Condor* (both 1975). The former was a male-dominated and violent attempt to compare and contrast American and Japanese cultures. The latter remains one of the best films of its director's career. Timed perfectly to ride the crest of the post-Watergate wave, it was a superbly fashioned paranoid conspiracy adventure commanded by an assured star turn by Redford as a naïve CIA operative who suddenly finds himself being pursued by assassins he cannot identify for reasons he does not know. Faye Dunaway provides fine support as the stranger he forces into helping him get out of a desperate situation. Marrying fluid, exciting film-making with a liberal political agenda, *Condor* still holds relevance in today's information age. Also notable is its synthesised funk score by another regular Pollack collaborator, Dave Grusin.

*Bobby Deerfield* (1977) was another European-influenced attempt at an intellectual mainstream offering, this time with a low-key Al Pacino in a darkly tragic love story which was deemed pretentious by critics. More successful was another exploration of liberal politics by the Pollack-Redford partnership in *The Electric Horseman* (1979), a comic romance about a jaded rodeo star who, in an act of frustration with the materialistic nature of his lifestyle, flees to be at one with the wilderness. Jane Fonda appears again for the director as a go-getting reporter who follows – and falls for – Redford. It was a winning combination of accomplished star turns in an undemanding (some might say lazy and pointless) piece of old-fashioned entertainment.

The specific issue of journalistic ethics was dealt with quite successfully in *Absence of Malice* (1981). Sally Field is a crusading reporter who writes a newspaper article, wrongly alleging that Paul Newman's local businessman character has dubious gangland links. Despite top-drawer casting, some critics were by now starting to tire of what they saw as sugar-coated worthiness in Pollack's work. Using likeable stars, it was argued, hampered any serious attempts to tackle important political themes.

*Tootsie* (1982) stands as the box-office peak of Pollack's career. Finishing second only to *E.T.* as the year's top-grossing film, it also did spectacularly well with critics and received ten Academy Award nominations, including Best Picture and Best Director. An incredible Dustin Hoffman, in a tour de force performance, portrays an actor who is so desperate for work that he pretends to be a woman in order to win a part in a daytime soap opera, becoming a celebrity in the process. The jokes are often hilarious, the supporting cast (including Pollack himself as Hoffman's stressed agent) perfection. A beautifully realised crowd-pleaser, *Tootsie* was unusual for Pollack in that he had a torrid experience directing his star actor, the method-obsessed Hoffman. The director later remarked that if he could go back in time he would not have made the film, despite the many millions of dollars it made for him personally.

*Out of Africa* (1985) finally won Pollack the Academy Awards he coveted, for Best Picture and Director. An ultimately downbeat romance, it paired Redford with Meryl Streep. The latter plays Karen Blixen, on whose autobiographical journals the film is based. Long, old-fashioned, well photographed, craftsmanlike, and featuring solid star performances, it is perhaps quintessential Pollack.

Three slick and glossy productions of varying success marked the first half of the 1990s for the by-now veteran director. *Havana* (1990), his seventh and to date most recent teaming with Redford, was another unashamed attempt to revisit grandiose Hollywood entertainment of yesteryear, this time – specifically – *Casablanca* (1942). Centred on the 1958 Cuban revolution with Pollack's favourite leading man in the Humphrey Bogart role and Lena Olin taking Ingrid Bergman's place, it was an expensive and monumentally disastrous commercial and critical failure. It seemed that Pollack's intention to capture a sentimentalised, old-fashioned, and innocent romantic sweep was lost on a sophisticated, cynical late twentieth-century audience. The director bounced back, however, with *The Firm* (1993), based on a best-selling novel by John Grisham. A smash hit in a crowded blockbuster year, it usefully deployed Tom Cruise and Gene Hackman in an unlikely but exciting paranoia thriller about a young lawyer finding himself upsetting the Mafia overlords controlling his new employers. Not unlike *Condor*, there was a sureness of touch in the overall production values that betrayed an experienced directorial hand behind the scenes. *Sabrina* (1995), meanwhile, was another box-office and critical disappointment. Harrison Ford and Greg Kinnear are cast, somewhat uncomfortably, in a frankly pointless remake of Billy Wilder's 1954 comedy romance of the same name, which starred William Holden and Humphrey Bogart.

As well as co-producing many of his own directorial assignments since *The Yakuza*, Pollack has been a prolific producer of other directors' work since the mid-1970s. This reflects his respectable position firmly within the establishment of an industry he is clearly much at ease with. He also revisited his first love in the 1990s, giving by turns dramatic and humorous supporting performances in Woody Allen's *Husbands and Wives*, Robert Zemeckis' *Death Becomes Her*, and Robert Altman's *The Player* (all 1992), and Stanley Kubrick's swansong, the characteristically weird *Eyes Wide Shut* (1999). The latter part was taken at the last minute by Pollack as a favour to a peer he admired immensely when original actor Harvey Keitel quit in exasperation at Kubrick's obsessively meticulous approach to directing. Pollack's most recent own directing effort was the poorly received romance *Random Hearts* (1999), again with Harrison Ford. The future will doubtless see Pollack carry on as before, making one commercial entertainment after another with the biggest stars around. **JMa**

# Léa POOL

Born in Switzerland in 1950, Léa Pool is among the most prominent auteurs in Québecois cinema, sharing the position of leading Canadian female director with Patricia Rozema. Before settling in Montreal in 1978, she only had a brief brush with amateur film-making in her native Switzerland. Her first fiction feature, Strass Cafe (1980), was preceded by a number of television shows, videos and short films, made predominantly for the film studies department at the francophone Université du Québec à Montréal. Scripted and produced by Pool on a shoestring budget, this black and white film brought her four prestigious festival awards. Strass Cafe is a truly experimental art film, created in the tradition of 'dysnarrative' films (like Alan Resnais' Last Year in Marienbad (1961) or Marguerite Duras' India Song (1975)). Like in Duras' films, an insistent music keeps returning as a strange leitmotif, the editing is slow, the shots and the camera immobile, the tone of the narrator monotonous and, finally, the narrative-representative spaces between image and sound are stigmatised in a similar fashion. Pool's characters, like Duras', are portrayed as insubstantial objects, without words or action, held at a distance in space, thus accentuating their dislocation or dissolution. The film seems to relate to a woman in exile who has neither name nor age, and whom 'we call "she" for the sake of convenience'. 'She' and the androgynous man she appears to have met at the Strass Cafe are trapped in a universe of solitude and desire, searching hopelessly for each other.

In 1984 she wrote and directed her second feature, Woman in Transit. Like in Strass Cafe, the boundaries between the artistic and the neurotic personality are blurred. A soft, muted light echoes the muted lives of the three central female characters and the deadliness of the anonymous metropolis in winter becomes an ever-expanding metaphor for the alienation they struggle with. The interrelationship of the film-maker and her actress, and the neurotic woman who resembles her fictitious character, is carefully woven from chance encounters, with the inner and outer realities of the film mirroring and echoing each other. Woman in Transit, Pool's international breakthrough, was recognised by the award of the International Critics' prize at the Montreal International Film Festival; a Geie (Canada's highest film award) for Best Actress, and the prize of the public at Créteil in France.

Anne Trister (1986) is usually interpreted as the conclusive work of this trilogy about displaced identities. It echoes the concerns of other feminist films of the 1980s. Inspired by post-Lacanian psychoanalytic theory, these works are concerned with the acceptance of the mother if a feminist discourse outside the patriarchal (Oedipal) cycle is to be produced. The sketchy plot of this partially autobiographical film follows Anne, a young Jewish woman who, after the death of her father and his funeral in the Israeli desert, breaks with her native country (Switzerland) and moves to Montreal in an attempt to rebuild her inner space. She suffers a breakdown, falls in love with her female therapist (a mother figure), antagonises the therapist's boyfriend (a symbolic break with the father figure), and throws herself into a major environmentalist art project, the visual centre-piece of the film. In the end, unlike the characters from Pool's previous films, Anne breaks free from her emotional dependency. Not always to the film's advantage, however, Pool replaces the audio-visual ambiguity of her other films with sharp, well-lit close-ups, and an over-emphatic and even melodramatic soundtrack.

Straight for the Heart (1988), La Demoiselle sauvage (1991) and Desire in Motion (1994), all scripted by Pool, represent a new phase in her career. While she continues to explore the blurred boundaries between art and reality, between heterosexual, bi-sexual and homosexual love and their vital role in the identity quest, the director becomes increasingly preoccupied with the virtuosity of the camera and the splendour of the images (like those of Montreal and the Swiss mountains). In these films, the sense of brevity of life and love translates into visions, retrospections and dreams that prevent the characters from experiencing the fleeting beauty of the moment. Pool's familiar concern with death acquires a new urgency in her entry 'Rispondetemi' in the 1991 avant-garde six-part travelogue Montreal Sextet. It condenses the life of a young woman, a car accident victim, into only fifteen short scenes flashing before her eyes on the way to the hospital.

Between 1990 and 1997, under the auspices of larger projects, Pool made five documentaries. With Set Me Free (1999) she ventured into stylistic simplicity and narrative clarity for the sake of wider audiences. Set Me Free perfectly fits the description of bildungsroman. Although the coming-of-age tale can assume many different guises, the autobiographical version is a perennial favourite. The director has admitted that the film is her most personal yet, paralleling her own adolescence although moving the venue to Montreal from Switzerland. Hanna is troubled mainly by her mismatched parents: her mother (Québecois star Pascale Bussieres) is a French-Canadian Catholic and her father (Yugoslav actor Miki Manojlovic) is a Jewish immigrant. His image adds new dimensions to constructing ethnicity in Québecois cinema where such a merciless representation of the immigrant experience is yet unknown. Karine Vanasse, in the role of Hanna, gives a strong-willed presence balancing that of Manojlovic, and the film owes most of its charm to this unconventional duo. Vanasse also brings home Léa Pool's Jewish and feminist concerns along with the leitmotif of the sexual identity quest. *Set Me Free* is not only a coming-of-age tale but a coming out tale – another personal motif introduced by the director in an elegant and romantic fashion with tenderness that softens without sentimentalisation. In 1999 France honoured Léa Pool with the prestigious title of Cavalier of Art and Letters in recognition of her artistic achievements.

*Lost and Delirious*, her latest work (premiered in the summer of 2001) is also her first English-language film. Based on Susan Swan's novel 'The Wives of Bath' and scripted by Judith Thompson, it takes one step further the aspirations of *Set Me Free* to reach wider audiences. The director takes her thoughtful explorations of lesbianism and female identity to the territory of teenage melodrama, which explains the emotional and visual excesses of the film and justifies its luxurious romantic setting – an exclusive boarding school for girls. The story, told from the point of view of Mary (or 'Mouse'), a newcomer, balances dangerously on the verge of predictability and mannerism. The plot thickens when she discovers that her roommates, Paulie and Tori, are lovers. In a series of voice-over comments and journal entries, using vocabulary and literary references supposedly characteristic for such a milieu, Mouse (Mischa Barton) is cleverly positioned as mediator between audience and narrative. Thus Pool offers a possibility for identification for those who find the unconventional love story and its steamy developments overwrought or shocking. Piper Perabo as Paulie and Jessica Paré as Tori are also admirable in their earnest attempts to bring to life this intellectual exercise in high-school poetry. Although the film has its fair share of endearing moments, it is far from the elegant confessional lyricism of Pool's previous works, proof that she is not in her element outside of the aesthetics of feminist experimental cinema.

Pool is working on a film starring William Hurt about a dying boy whose last wish is to travel to the Amazon to find a rare butterfly. **CSt**

# Gina PRINCE-BYTHEWOOD

*Love and Basketball* (2000)

Born in California in 1969, Gina Prince-Bythewood is a graduate of UCLA Film School where she received a scholarship for directing for her 16mm thesis film, *Stitches* (1991). She began her career in television as a writer on series such as 'A Different World' and 'South Central', before writing and directing 'What About Your Friends', which won two Emmy nominations for writing and directing, and producing the series 'Felicity'.

*Love and Basketball* (2000), which she wrote and directed, is her feature film debut. The film is produced by Spike Lee's production company, 40 Acres and A Mule, and is a love story which follows Quincy (Omar Epps) and Monica (Sanaa Lathan), who have a passion for the game of basketball and also each other. Prince-Bythewood was keen to write a love story about young African-Americans and, being an athlete herself, about women and basketball. The script was reworked at the Sundance Writer's Lab and Director's Lab and the film was premiered at the 2000 Sundance Festival. Showing the differences between the men's and women's basketball game, as well as the ups and downs in Quincy and Monica's relationship, the film also acts as a reminder of the problems faced by young women wishing to pursue a sport such as basketball. Following the critical success of *Love and Basketball*, Prince-Bythewood made *Disappearing Acts* (2000), a romantic drama starring Wesley Snipes, for television. **PR**

# Pat PROFT

*Wrongfully Accused* (1998)

Born in Minnesota in 1947, Pat Proft worked in theatre and revue, touring as a one-man comedy act during the late 1960s. Regular appearances at the Los Angeles Comedy Store in the early 1970s led to work with the Smothers Brothers and Zucker-Abrahams-

Zucker. His television writing credits include 'The Mary Tyler Moore Comedy Hour', 'The Carol Burnett Show', 'Van Dyke and Company', 'The Smothers Brothers Show', 'Police Squad!', 'The Redd Foxx Show', 'Fernwood Tonite', 'Welcome Back', 'Kotter', and 'The Star Wars Holiday Special'. He also appeared as a series regular on 'The Burns and Schreiber Comedy Hour' and 'Van Dyke and Company'. Screenwriting credits include *Police Academy* (1984), *Bachelor Party* (1984), *Real Genius* (1985), *Moving Violations* (1985), *Naked Gun: From the Files of Police Squad!* (1988), *Lucky Stiff* (1988), *Hot Shots!* (1991), *Hot Shots! Part Deux* (1993), *High School High* (1996), and *Mr. Magoo* (1997).

He made his directorial debut, *Wrongfully Accused* (1998), from his own screenplay. The opening caption reads: 'The following dramatisation is true, based on real events, from other actual movies', and this is a clear indication of what will follow. Leslie Nielsen's mugging and the parodies, incongruities and odd literalisms of Zucker-Abrahams-Zucker movies have become too familiar, although Proft is reasonably successful in maintaining their deadpan style. The end result is brief – some choppy editing suggests numerous gags were excised – and rather dull.          **MB**

# Alex PROYAS

*Spirits of the Air,* Alex Proyas was born in Egypt in 1965, before becoming an award-winning graduate
*Gremlins of the Clouds* (1989) of the Australian Film and Television School. He initially carved out a career as one of
*The Crow* (1994) Australia's most talented music video and commercial directors before achieving success
*Dark City* (1998) on the festival circuit with his first feature, *Spirits of the Air, Gremlins of the Clouds* (1989). A post-apocalyptic western shot on a very low budget, it was an early display of the brand of dystopian science fiction that has since become his trademark.

International success arrived with the release of *The Crow* (1994). An adaptation of James O'Barr's woefully serious graphic novel, Proyas' film revelled in the comic's gothic moodiness, creating a cityscape not too dissimilar to Tim Burton's vision of Gotham, and populated by sociopaths intent on razing the city to its foundations. Toning down much of the novel's extreme violence, preferring instead to emphasise the grief experienced by the eponymous hero, an avenging angel resurrected to wreak havoc on the gang who brutally murdered a musician and his girlfriend, Proyas imbued *The Crow* with a sombre, introspective air. This was further enhanced, albeit unintentionally, by the death of the film's star, Brandon Lee, who was killed in an accident on set.

With the huge success of *The Crow*, Proyas was able to gain funding for a long-cherished project, originally titled *Pedestrian Furniture*. *Dark City* (1998) was a more ambitious film than its predecessor, with influences ranging from *Metropolis* (1926), *Blade Runner* (1982), and *Brazil* (1985), to the writings of Kafka and Calvino. A hybrid of B-movie detective thriller and science fiction extravaganza, the film takes place amidst a bustling urban environment whose architecture and social structure is shaped by the dreams of its inhabitants. Living in a city that has never seen the light of day, the human population are guinea pigs for a nation of aliens intent on controlling their destiny and, ultimately, their bodies. Re-enacting moments from their collective memory, the humans carry on with what they believe to be their real lives, unaware that when the city's clock-tower strikes twelve, the entire population falls into a deep sleep, while the aliens restructure their world. Echoing Fredric Jameson's fears of a postmodern society, *Dark City* is a *mélange* of the fashions, architectures and tastes of American popular culture from the past fifty years. Wearing its influences a little too brazenly, the film remains an intelligent and engaging piece of cinema, confirming Proyas as a talented director who is unwilling to conform to the dictates of the conventional blockbuster.

Pyun is to return to cinema with a musical comedy entitled *Garage Days*, the story of an Australian garage band trying to make it to the top.          **IHS**

# Albert PYUN

*The Sword and the Sorcerer* Hawaiian-born Albert Pyun's debut as a writer and a director came with 1982's *The*
*(1982)* *Sword and the Sorcerer*; costing $3 million, it is one of the better low-budget sword
*Radioactive Dreams* (1985) and sorcery movies of the period. Since then he has directed 35 movies, 14 of which he
*Dangerously Close* (1986) also wrote. Among the theatrical releases, he has directed a number of straight-to-video
*Alien from LA* (1987) movies.

Despite its many flaws, *Cyborg* (1989) was a good early vehicle for Jean-Claude Van Damme, establishing how he would be shot during the following decade (compare the climactic fight sequence with those of *Universal Soldier* (1992) and *Timecop* (1994)), and communicating something of the vulnerability which would be essential to the attempted development of his persona into one more appropriate to mainstream movies. By this point, Pyun's work was already fairly distinctive: slow-motion stylisations, deserted landscapes, casual brutalities, genre-blending (here a science-fiction-samurai revenge-western) and a preference for red and blue tones. Plotting is *non sequitur* and the movie lacks coherence; typically, lots of exciting things happen but there is a lack of tension, and the parts remain greater than their sum.

*Kickboxer 2: The Road Back* (1991) is, in conventional dramatic terms, the best entry in the series. Like all his work, but more so, it benefits from being shot as if its by-the-numbers story might somehow be significant; however, the preponderance of close-ups in the fight sequences detract from it as a martial arts movie. *Captain America* (1991), despite its promising opening sequence, continues the tradition of adapting the Simon/Kirby comic book character to other media very badly, but its epic backstory (the Red Skull has been responsible for all the world's ills during the superhero's fifty-year hibernation) demonstrates Pyun's tendency to establish a massive-scale but off-screen plot to which the particular action of the movie is only vaguely connected. The 1993 Oliver Gruner vehicle *Nemesis* sketches in a global cyberpunk-ish conspiracy as a framework for its action narrative, and in the three sequels, written and directed back-to-back by Pyun as a kind of movie serial, the conspiracy extoliates, but Is narrated rather than shown. This tendency reaches its apotheosis in *Adrenalin – Fear the Rush* (1996) in which minimalist pursuit sequences through empty buildings, streets and tunnels – restlessly shot and edited – completely dominate the epic scale suggested by the opening sequence: there is absolutely no necessary connection between them, or with the title.

*Hong Kong 97* (1994) does a slightly better job of integrating the handover of Hong Kong to China into its narrative. One of Pyun's technically most accomplished movies, it exemplifies the shortcomings of his work even when reasonably well-budgeted: a promising premise and good action sequences are badly let down by a poor script, unsympathetic characters, a wooden leading man and the quirky but counterproductive casting of Pyun regulars.

*Blast* (1996) is a minor *Die Hard* (1988) variant purportedly based on events that could have occurred if the FBI had not discovered an attempted terrorist plot to take the US women's swimming team hostage at the 1996 Atlanta Olympic Games. It exemplifies, in some senses, the opportunistic nature of much straight-to-video action cinema. It is distinguished, however, by a number of factors: Pyun's clever and economical use of his most expensive actor (Rutger Hauer as an Interpol agent with long braids but no legs); the straightfaced ludicrousness of its denouement; its good-hearted cynicism; and the sense of mourning and loss which occasionally overcomes the flat, obvious characterisations of the hero and his ex-wife. *Omega Doom* (1996), a post-holocaust cyborg *Yojimbo* (1961), shares many of these qualities. The comic relief provided by Norbert Weisser, who plays an android head constantly in search of a new body, is overplayed but typifies the fondness with which Pyun can treat even the most hackneyed material. The slow, confused death of one of Rutger Hauer's opponents – surely a riff on his *Blade Runner* (1982) role – lacks pretension and is in danger of seeming dignified.

Within his budgetary constraints, Pyun demonstrates a talent for casting. Familiar faces (Ned Beatty, Kris Kristofferson, Burt Reynolds) appear alongside such regulars as Nicholas Guest, Brion James and Norbert Weisser. He also has an eye to crossover markets. Comedian Andrew Dice Clay appeared in *Brain Smasher ... A Love Story* (1993), and comedian Tim Thomerson has been in nine of Pyun's movies. More recently, Pyun has turned to rappers, making *Mean Guns* (1997), *Crazy Six* (1998), and *Ticker* (2001) with Ice-T, who also produced and appeared in *Corrupt* (1998), *Urban Menace* (1999), and *Wrecking Crew* (1999) (the latter two also feature Snoop Doggy Dogg). This trilogy of short films (they all last for about an hour, and are padded out with ten-minute-long end-credit sequences) is perhaps the most unusual material Pyun has directed. *Urban Menace* and *Wrecking Crew* are fairly straightforward ghetto shootemups, mostly set in a derelict warehouse, which play like really low-budget *Mean*

*Guns* imitators. *Corrupt* is a slightly more complex tale of the impossibility of escaping the ghetto; even those who get out do so by taking the ghetto with them. Shot back-to-back (to judge from their recurring locations, cast and crew), they have the most minimal narratives of any Pyun film and some of the most attractive visuals. They seem to represent vanity projects for Ice-T and his friends, combined with an opportunity for Pyun and Filmwerks to experiment with digital film-making.

Pyun also has the ability to secure actors on their ascent to or descent from bigger, if not better, things (Courtney Cox, Teri Hatcher, Rutger Hauer, Christopher Lambert, Rob Lowe, Charlie Sheen, Van Damme, and Mario Van Peebles) – most recently, it has been the turn of Steven Seagal (along with Dennis Hopper and Tom Sizemore) in *Ticker*.

Kim Newman suggested, a little unfairly, that *Mean Guns* was 'ultimately most interesting as proof that anyone who makes films at the rate Pyun does will eventually turn out something watchable. Now, he should set his sights on making a film that's worth seeing more than once'. Since then Pyun has directed six more movies, but with the possible exception of *Postmortem* (1998), a serial killer thriller set in Scotland and starring Charlie Sheen, he does not seem to have heeded Newman's advice.     **MB**

# Bob RAFELSON

Had Bob Rafelson never made a film again after *Five Easy Pieces* (1970), his name would still be remembered in American film history. That film is a veritable crystallisation of the best of American cinema in the 1970s, and a portrait of disillusionment unparalleled before or since. Although he is best known for that film, Rafelson had been working in television for many years before, most notably as creator, writer, director, producer and actor for the hit series 'The Monkees', which followed the comedic exploits of a Beatles-like group in the late 1960s. Born in New York in 1933, Rafelson's first film was *Head* (1968), The Monkees' feature debut. Co-written by actor Jack Nicholson, with whom Rafelson has made five films, *Head* continues The Monkees' exploits in a series of psychedelic episodes. He went on to form BBS Productions along with Bert Schneider and Steve Blauner, and the company produced the classics *Easy Rider* (1969) and *The Last Picture Show* (1971). As a director, he is best when working with actors in sharp character studies, falling flat with excess plot.

*Head* (1968)

*Five Easy Pieces* (1970)

*The King of Marvin Gardens* (1972)

*Stay Hungry* (1976)

*The Postman Always Rings Twice* (1981)

*Black Widow* (1987)

*Mountains of the Moon* (1990)

*Man Trouble* (1992)

*Blood and Wine* (1997)

Rafelson's breakthrough was with *Five Easy Pieces*. While it is a showcase for the great acting talents of Nicholson, it is Rafelson's beautifully subtle direction and keen eye that make the film a unique visual experience. The story follows Bobby Dupea (Nicholson), a troubled man from a prominent musical family, who has left his home and is working in an oil field. When Bobby's father falls ill, he decides to venture back home, and there must confront the life and cultured values he has rejected. *Five Easy Pieces* is the close reading of one American man trying to discern his environment. He is an angry man who can strike out indiscriminately at almost any time, especially against women. The film's second half, set in the tranquil forests of Washington State, gives no answers for Bobby's mental state. For Rafelson, getting to Bobby's core is the most important story element, and the screenplay by Adrien Joyce (aka Carole Eastman) does just that, accompanied by Rafelson's sombre colour scheme and probing camera.

*The King of Marvin Gardens* (1972) is almost equally moving, and certainly deserves a higher profile amongst the classics of the 1970s. Nicholson plays David Staebler, a radio monologist whose brother Jason (Bruce Dern) is a con man intent on buying a Hawaiian island so the two can open a casino. Rafelson managed to invert Nicholson's already strongly established image by casting him as the quiet, introvert poet against Dern's perfectly flamboyant career criminal. The story achingly shows how David watches his brother's plan, first with knowing apprehension, then cautious enthusiasm, and finally resigned sadness as the plans unravel as he knows they were destined to. The muted tones of the film relay the sadness that is at the heart of these characters, who always hide under a shell of performance – be it a con man's con, a radio announcer's monologues, or sad women in a mock Miss America pageant.

Similar themes run through *Stay Hungry* (1976) as well, and if there is singular proof of Rafelson's ability with actors, it is his direction of strongman Arnold Schwarzenegger in a deeply felt performance as a body-builder looking for meaning in life. The story revolves around Craig Blake (Jeff Bridges), a young southern aristocrat who wants to buy a health-club for a larger real estate scheme, but becomes intrigued by some of the eccentric characters who populate the place. The film is startlingly original – quirky and satisfying – but seems a minor work in comparison to the previous two.

The rest of Rafelson's work is a more straightforward use of generic structures. Yet if *The Postman Always Rings Twice* (1981) was a disappointment to audiences, it was not through lack of trying. For re-adapting the James M. Cain novel (which was originally filmed by Tay Garnett in 1946), Rafelson contracted famed American playwright David Mamet, and cast Nicholson and a young Jessica Lange for the lead roles. Despite beautiful cinematography by Sven Nykvist, the film is a meandering, unpleasant journey with characters whose motivations have little depth beyond the very primal, and does little justice to the film noir tradition from which it is derived.

*Black Widow* (1987) is a well-made – albeit plot-heavy – noir-thriller about a female Justice Department officer (Debra Winger) on the trail of a woman (Theresa Russell) who marries and murders wealthy men. While it is a slickly watchable film, with actors in top form and a refreshingly strong female protagonist, there are few distinguishing points and little suspense. On the other hand, *Mountains of the Moon* (1990) is a superior adventure saga following British topographers Richard Burton (Patrick Bergin) and John Speke (Iain Glenn) as they seek the source of the River Nile in Africa. With beautiful cinematography, intelligent scripting, and outstanding performances by Bergin, Glenn, and Fiona Shaw, the film is as good as any in the genre.

Rafelson's reunification with Nicholson came in the disastrous romantic comedy *Man Trouble* (1992), with Nicholson as a dog trainer and Ellen Barkin as an opera singer who requires his services because of a murderous stalker. Nicholson has only his stock gestures on hand, and the screenplay, by *Five Easy Pieces* collaborator Carole Eastman, falls apart almost immediately. Rafelson's direction in this film has none of the nuance of his earlier work.

*Blood and Wine* (1997), his most recent feature to date, is yet another attempt at film noir, with results similar to *The Postman Always Rings Twice*. Although Rafelson is able to establish a consistent mood, and the acting – especially that of Nicholson and Michael Caine – is of a particularly high standard, the weakness of the characterisations and the flatness of the story mean Rafelson is unable to lift the film above the conventions of the genre, failing to make any point at all.

In addition to the slim nine features in thirty years, Rafelson has directed the television film noir *Poodle Springs* (1998), based on Raymond Chandler's unfinished novel and starring James Caan as detective Philip Marlowe. Short films include *Wet*, Rafelson's contribution to *Tales of Erotica* (1996), and the obscure *Modesty* (1981). **DH**

# Sam RAIMI

Sam Raimi is a director associated with manic, frenetic movies that have a chimerical bent. His films, whether they be within the horror, crime or western genres, are tantamount to live action cartoons; by degrees humorous, infectious, disposable and extremely entertaining.

Born in Detroit in 1959, a cinema enthusiast from a very early age, Raimi began his career making Super 8 shorts at Michigan State University before producing a 30-minute preview 'trailer' with Ivan, his brother, and friend Robert Tapert. *Within the Woods* was used to raise $400,000 from investors, enough to expand upon the original concept and facilitate the shooting of Raimi's debut feature.

The Evil Dead (1982) is a pre-eminent example of inventive low-budget movie making. The shallow plot – whereby five friends accidentally call up Sumerian demons in an isolated log cabin – allows for more experimentation with camerawork, horror clichés and raw special effects, without 'encumbrances' like character development or social comment weighing the piece down. Though justifiably claustrophobic and eerie in places (particularly those scenes filmed in the woods), the overall tone is that of a tongue-in-cheek drive-in movie, embellished by amateurish performances from the cast. It first made its mark at the 1982 Cannes Film Festival, where Stephen King branded it 'the most ferociously original horror film of the year', but it also found notoriety in Britain as one of the original 'video nasty' titles.

Crimewave (1985), known alternatively as The X,Y,Z Murders or Broken Hearts and Noses, came next and represented a serious misstep for the fledgling director. Whilst certainly as energetic and vociferous as The Evil Dead, this comical crime thriller, scripted by the Coen brothers, lacks the vital spark that made his debut so successful. An intriguing premise, involving a falsely accused prisoner (Reed Birney) recounting the events leading up to his incarceration on death row, is marred by assorted idiotic killings and car chases, not to mention tawdry production values.

Much to viewers' relief, Raimi then repaired to the horror genre for Evil Dead 2: Dead By Dawn (1987). More of a polished remake than a sequel, it reduces the previous film's events to an abridged prologue, taking up the legend as incompetent hero Ash (Bruce Campbell) is assailed by mischievous spirits a second time. Hilarious, escapist slapstick blends seamlessly with deliriously paced terror to create a nonpareil cinematic experience; Raimi uses every possible means at his disposal – sound effects, mobile sets, stop-motion animation – to draw the audience into his weird and wonderful world.

Despite being Raimi's first major Hollywood picture, Darkman (1990) loses none of its originator's deranged but edgy Grand Guignol allure. A self-evident homage to classic horror films like Phantom of the Opera (1925) Frankenstein (1931), and The Invisible Man (1933), Darkman also embraces gangster and superhero movie traditions. Remarkable turns by Larry Drake, Frances McDormand, and especially Liam Neeson as the ill-fated scientist working on synthetic skin, complement Raimi's approach perfectly, while Randy Ser's production designs provide a magnificent backdrop. The one letdown is the disorderly script that binds the action scenes together.

Raimi's long-awaited Army of Darkness: The Evil Dead 3 (1993), propelled his signature series even further into the realms of jocose lampoonery, reworking Mark Twain's 'timeless' 1889 novel 'A Yankee at the Court of King Arthur'. However, here it is a chainsaw-wielding Campbell who travels back to medieval times to fight the deadites and woo the maidens. Possibly the most enervated of the three, and the least politically correct, its saving grace is the Jason and the Argonauts-inspired skeletal army itself.

Over the next couple of years Raimi and his production company, Renaissance, launched a number of popular TV shows, the most praiseworthy being 'Hercules: The Legendary Journeys' and its spin-off hit 'Xenia: Warrior Princess'. His 1995 feature The Quick and the Dead proved less enticing, however. Part of a western mini-revival in the mid-1990s, and taking a cue from the previous year's Bad Girls in its choice of Sharon Stone as protagonist, the film attempts to do something fresh with a fairly prosaic recipe. Instead, it simply succeeds in regurgitating set-pieces from Sergio Leone's true landmark 'Dollars trilogy', given a twist by Raimi's disorientating camera angles and obvious showmanship.

More striking is A Simple Plan (1998), probably because it eschews the usual Corybantic flourishes to present a condemnatory study of greed and the damage it can do. Bill Paxton heads a fine cast in this tale of three men who find a fortune in a wrecked plane and decide to keep it, with devastating consequences. His most seasoned film up to now, and his most engaging on a human and intellectual level, A Simple Plan not only confirms that Raimi can operate triumphantly outside of the horror genre, it also verifies that he can make thrillers in the same league as the Coens and De Palmas of this world.

Continuing this trend Raimi made an enlightened film about his second passion, baseball. For the Love of the Game (1999) takes the Crimewave flashback structure and administers it to this story of an ageing pitcher for the Detroit Tigers, Kevin Costner (evoking pleasant memories of Bull Durham (1988) and Field of Dreams (1989)). With the knowledge he could soon be throwing his last ball, his arm failing him, and a turbulent love life taking his mind off the game, he begins to pitch flawlessly as both he and the audience reflect on his career. Raimi's love of America's national pastime shines through, and his poise, especially in the romantic strand, magnifies the director's new-found *savoir faire*.

'The only witness to the crime wasn't even there', states the tagline to Raimi's more subtle horror movie *The Gift* (2000), the complete antithesis of his first film in the genre. No doubt galvanised by the success of *The Sixth Sense* (1999), this tale, scripted by Tom Epperson and Billy Bob Thornton, centres around a young widow with psychic abilities, played to perfection by Cate Blanchett. The town 'fortune teller', she eventually finds herself involved in the search for a missing woman. The immediacy of her visions chill almost as much as Keanu Reeves' underrated performance, here playing against type as a terrifying abusive husband.

However, *Spider-Man* (2002) is a dream project for Raimi, allowing him to expand considerably upon the techniques he used for *Darkman* – a risk mitigated somewhat by the freedom of a much larger budget. More colourful and less grave than both Burton's *Batman* (1989) and Bryan Singer's *X-Men* (2000), this retells the famous Marvel Comics story of a student bitten by a radioactive arachnid. Tobey Maguire brings just the right amount of vulnerability and heroism to the lead, exploring why with great power must come great responsibility while Willem Dafoe lends dramatic credibility as his arch-nemesis, The Green Goblin.                                                                      **PB**

# Harold RAMIS

Harold Ramis is an actor-director-screenwriter who practices his art in the fields of comedy and fantasy entertainment. Though his early efforts tended to be raw and risqué, he has matured into a proficient and appreciable film-maker whose movies always have a tantalising hook.

Born in 1944 in Chicago, and educated at Washington University, Ramis laboured as a mental-ward orderly and joke editor for *Playboy* before writing and performing his own material with the Second City improvisational troupe. A flit to New York brought him into contact with comedians such as John Belushi and Bill Murray, with whom he starred in the National Lampoon's stage show. Towards the end of the 1970s he appeared in SC's TV programme and co-wrote the scripts for *National Lampoon's Animal House* (1978) and *Meatballs* (1979).

Understandably, his first film *Caddyshack* (1980) is of the same ilk, a 'wacky', rampageous, tumultuous farce in the worst conceivable taste – the most 'respectable' gag hinging on a chocolate bar's resemblance to human waste. Contrasting the urbane backdrop of an upper-crust country club with the crass comportment of people like Rodney Dangerfield's nouveau riche member and Bill Murray's lecherous groundskeeper, *Caddyshack* is clearly a well-targeted supplication to the youth market, orchestrated to stimulate quick and easy belly laughs.

His sequel to *Animal House*, *National Lampoon's Vacation* (1983) does much the same, albeit in a slightly less subversive manner. Chevy Chase determines to take his family to the fabled 'Walley World' overland by car, encountering de rigeur catastrophes along the way. An early episodic attempt from John Hughes is adequately played by a cast that includes Beverly D'Angelo as Chase's long-suffering spouse and Randy Quaid as poor backwater cousin, Eddie.

After co-writing and starring in *Ghostbusters* (1984), Ramis strived to breathe life into *Club Paradise* (1986). A last-minute change of leads – Robin Williams replacing Bill Murray – vitiated the production before it could start, as the Brian Doyle-Murray script seems tailor-made for his sibling. Williams vacillates as the incapacitated fireman using his insurance money to buy into a Caribbean club, unable to muster the dry wit needed to deal with his whinging guests.

Described by *Empire* as 'something of a comedy classic', *Groundhog Day* (1993) still remains the pinnacle of Ramis' directorial portfolio. Friend Bill Murray made it on set this time, starring as a cantankerous TV weatherman forced to cover the twee Groundhog Day festival in small-town Punxsutawney PA – over and over again. This déjà vu timeloop, which invariably begins with Sonny and Cher on the radio alarm, graces Murray with plenty of comedic scope, but also shepherds him towards an honourable ending with a well-worn maxim.

'You'll laugh because it's not your family. You'll cry because it is!' expounds the tagline of *Stuart Saves His Family* (1995), in which the latest 'Saturday Night Live' character wends his way to the big screen. Written by and starring Al Franken, the movie satirises the cult of self-help through main character 'Stuart Smalley'. Following this, *Multiplicity* (1996), nourished by developments in genetic engineering during the 1990s, would have the audience believe that the process of cloning humans (not only ethically, but ecumenically frowned upon) has been perfected and tested out on a construction worker with a hectic schedule (Michael Keaton). Ramis takes this premise to extraordinary lengths by duplicating Keaton not once, but three times, investigating the multifaceted sides of his personality (aggressive, tender, infantile). However, in this instance the inspired concept is shackled by the curse of a bloated script and less than impeccable matte work.

Similarly, *Analyze This* (1999), in which Mob boss Robert De Niro seeks help from psychiatrist Billy Crystal because he is losing his nerve, might be a fresh take on an antiquated topic, but it is also morally ambiguous. As Crystal remarks himself, 'What is my goal here? To make you into a happy, well-adjusted gangster?' Hardly the perfect theme for a comedy film. And yet there are some compensatory characteristics – most notably De Niro's re-evaluation of his cinematic image, and the pair's therapy sessions in which they discuss the 'finer' points of psychology.

Ramis' next project was more fantastical. A remake of the 1967 Dudley Moore and Peter Cook movie, *Bedazzled* (2000) gave Liz Hurley her first major role – as a seductive devil determined to corrupt Brendan Fraser. Any serious attempt to contemplate the issues of temptation or desire is quickly forsaken, with preference given to more simplistic comedic set-pieces redolent of Ramis' earlier works.

His latest release reunites De Niro and Crystal for the sequel to *Analyze This*, *Analyze That* (2002). **PB**

# Mort RANSEN

Born in Montreal in 1933, Mort Ransen has worked as a director, writer, and producer of both film and television programmes. Following a short spell acting and directing in the theatre, he joined the National Film Board of Canada in 1961, where he directed 19 films and won several awards. During this time he made his first feature, *Running Time* (1974), telling the story of a friendship between an old lady and a young man which sets off a chain of events that involves a number of people in some bizarre situations.

Ransen quit the NFB to write and direct *Bayo* (1984), for which he co-wrote the screenplay, based on Chipman Hall's novel 'Lightly'. The film features an all-Canadian cast and crew. It is a sensitive and touching account of the relationship between a strong-minded ten-year-old, his crusty grandfather, and his mother. Following this, *Falling Over Backwards* (1990), a romantic comedy written, directed and co-produced by Ransen, is the story of a middle-aged, Jewish school teacher driven crazy by his quarrelsome, divorced father and his complex relationship with his mother. He moves back to his old neighbourhood with his father, and ends up falling in love with his young landlady, who lives upstairs.

Ransen gained commercial success with his fourth feature, *Margaret's Museum* (1995), starring Helena Bonham Carter and Kate Nelligan. He felt that his previous films had not been successful due to the lack of 'household names' and knew that if he were to make another feature, it would need to have a star. *Margaret's Museum*, which took five years to get off the ground, is the story of an independent woman, Margaret (Bonham Carter), and her mother (Nelligan), who struggle to protect family and friends from the ravages of the coal-mining industry in a 1940s Nova Scotia town of Scottish-Irish immigrants. Complications occur when Margaret meets and marries a former miner who washes dishes to survive; he loses his job and is forced back into the mine. This is a touching drama exploring a community that relies heavily on the coal mines, and Ransen uses the romance to tell the political tale. Ransen and Gerald Wexler adapted the screenplay from stories by Sheldon Currie, and Ransen also co-produced the film, which went on to win six Genies in the 1996 Canadian National Film Awards.

The director's next film, *Touched* (1999), was a disappointment after *Margaret's Museum*. He collaborated with Joan Hopper on the screenplay over a five-year period. The film is edited, produced, and directed by Ransen. Starring Lynn Redgrave as Carrie,

*Running Time* (1974)
*Bayo* (1984)
*Falling Over Backwards* (1990)
*Margaret's Museum* (1995)
*Touched* (1999)

*Touched* is a portrayal of healing and love between an older woman and a younger man. Carrie is a hard-drinking woman living on a reserve in British Columbia. Facing eviction from her home and estrangement from her family she meets a handsome young man sleeping in the hayloft of her barn. *Touched* was screened at the Toronto Film Festival in 1999 but was not a critical success.

Not afraid to experiment with new forms, Ransen's films tell stories of intimate relationships between friends and families. He has gained control over his films through taking on the role of producer, as well as that of director. He has said that *Touched* will be his last mainstream film and has decided to close his own production company, Ranfilm, stating, 'it's just too hard to make films'.                **PR**

# Brett RATNER

Born in Florida in 1970, and a graduate of New York University's prestigious Tisch School of the Arts, Brett Ratner is establishing himself as one of today's most promising, directors having already amassed an impressive body of work in music videos and television commercials. Funded by Spielberg's Amblin Entertainment, Ratner's student short *Whatever Happened to Mason Reese?* won various prizes, and in 1997 he formed his own record company, Rat Records, to handle soundtracks for all his future film projects.

In his feature film debut, the comedy *Money Talks* (1997), Chris Tucker (long-time collaborator with Ratner) is turned into an overnight celebrity when he is wrongly accused of planning a prison break. Obviously influenced by Eddie Murphy, Ratner simply cajoles Tucker into a karaoke reprise of Murphy's original fast-paced street talk; Charlie Sheen is forgettable in a role that requires him simply to huff and puff. Ratner resorts to the de rigueur shoot outs and car chases when the narrative begins to sag, and the soundtrack is employed to ominous effect when the director's lexicon runs dry – military drums in the prison, Curtis Mayfield's 'Pusher Man' in a shady nightclub. However, a scene at a posh all-white dinner in which Tucker quotes from Barry White is interesting – America, it seems, is laden with cultural apartheid, and all that his character wants is to cross the divide.

*Rush Hour* (1998) re-teams Tucker with Ratner and also presents Jackie Chan as a bona fide action star. The two play cops brought in to investigate the kidnapping of the Chinese consul's daughter and the rest of the film is simply an excuse to showcase Tucker's motor-mouthed wisecracking routine and Chan's physical elasticity. Much of the dialogue seems improvised, and Ratner eschews any weighty political pretensions about US and British involvement in Hong Kong to put a new spin on the buddy movie. As with Mel Gibson and Danny Glover, there are the inevitable chalk-and-cheese beginnings, but by the close everyone seems to be having such a fun time that Ratner decides to lave the camera rolling and capture the pratfalls and outtakes that have become a necessity in any Chan film. The pool-hall scene in particular is expertly directed, and Ratner shows a visual flair as well as an acute sensibility of the genre.

*Family Man* (2000) stars Nicolas Cage as a Wall Street playboy who stumbles into an alternate universe on Christmas Eve. This romantic comedy, which mixes *Sliding Doors* (1998) with Charles Dickens and Frank Capra, was a moderate commercial and critical success due mainly to Ratner's ability to hone hackneyed narratives into satisfying wholes. As in Capra's *It's A Wonderful Life* (1946), an angelic figure (Don Cheadle) is sent to show Cage the error of his ways, and Ratner has fun playing with the alternate universes – Manhattan glitz and New Jersey claustrophobia. Cage brings his usual earnest gravitas to the role, and although the '1980s greed-is-good' message is hammered home a little too forcefully, the film succeeds largely due to Ratner's ease with the camera, his eclectic soundtrack (Morcheeba, Pavarotti, and Henry Mancini) and strong supporting cast.

His subsequent *Rush Hour 2* (2001) was one of the year's most successful films, benefiting from Ratner's no-nonsense direction and the amiable re-teaming of Tucker and Chan. With the action relocated to Hong Kong (although the show-stopping conclusion is in Vegas), it continues the 'stranger-in-a-strange-land' comic theme that characterised the first film. This time the duo are on the tail of a US consulate bomber and counterfeiter, but the plot is merely incidental; it is the outtakes (which are admittedly funny), Tucker's racial epithets and Chan's remarkable physical elasticity that really matter. Added to the mix is Zhang Ziyi (fresh from the success of *Crouching Tiger, Hidden Dragon* (2000)) and a remarkably brisk running time which in part explains the franchise's success – a move from one action set-piece to another, held together by random plot events and hyperactive acting.

Ratner is currently in production with *Rush Hour 3*, and *Red Dragon* is due for release at the end of 2002. The latter, a remake of Michael Mann's *Manhunter* (1986), charts the early history of Hannibal Lecter and his part in the tracking down of the Tooth Fairy serial killer. Boasting a cast of Anthony Hopkins, Ralph Fiennes, Harvey Keitel, Edward Norton, Emily Watson, and Philip Seymour Hoffman, the project is a radical change of direction for Ratner, and competent handling of the film would go a long way to ensuring his career as a major Hollywood director.                              **BM**

# Robert REDFORD

Critic Robin Wood has commented that Robert Redford's directorial choices mirror his acting choices, defining all his works as 'middle-of-the-road' entertainments, which are 'thoughtful within certain limits, never descending to vulgarity or stupidity but never transcending the bourgeois tenets of "good taste"'. His assertions certainly ring true – Redford has produced a solid and intelligent body of work, respectable but never groundbreaking, either stylistically or in terms of content – but one cannot deny the appeal of his films, specifically the earlier, less sentimental, offerings. Like other actor-directors his style seems to be heavily influenced by his extensive experience in front of the camera and he is able to draw out consistently interesting and moving performances. His films are imbued with a measured, deliberate, and dignified air and his enduring interest in morality and the power of the human spirit gives them both their essence and their substance.

*Ordinary People* (1980)
*The Milagro Beanfield War* (1988)
*A River Runs Through It* (1992)
*Quiz Show* (1994)
*The Horse Whisperer* (1998)
*The Legend of Bagger Vance* (2000)

Born in Santa Monica in 1937, and having attended the University of Colorado and Pratt Institute of Design, Redford went on to study painting in Europe and then acting at the American Academy of Dramatic Arts. His work within the film industry has been diverse and plentiful; his career as a film actor spans from 1962 to the present day and he has received acclaim for performances in films as varied as *Butch Cassidy and the Sundance Kid* (1969), *All the President's Men* (1976), and *Indecent Proposal* (1993). He has also worked as a producer and fundraiser and, in 1981, founded the Sundance Institute, a festival for the exhibition of independent films. Although Sundance has begun to take on a more distinctly commercial edge since its inception, it still crucially provides an invaluable opportunity for first- and second-time directors to showcase their work.

For the direction of his own first film, *Ordinary People* (1980), Redford earned an American Academy Award. A focused study of an upper-middle-class American family, it bravely tackles issues of parenting, guilt, intimacy and suicide against a shifting backdrop of emotional restraint, unspoken recrimination and pent-up anger. All the performances are noteworthy: Timothy Hutton plays the grieving brother with haunting earnestness, Donald Sutherland is the eager father who constantly over-compensates, Judd Hirsch the hard-line but compassionate therapist. Mary Tyler Moore plays against type as the cold-hearted mother, unable to express her feelings; the suggestion that she is not a proper woman or mother because she cannot show her affection is somewhat reactionary but the drama during the moments of verbal conflict are still electrifying. Todd Field's recent family picture *In the Bedroom* (2001), reads rather like *Ordinary People* twenty years on.

The least commercially successful of all his films, *The Milagro Beanfield War* (1988), is one of the most colourful. Working on several different levels, it manages to be both quirky and charming while also raising some serious concerns regarding national identity and the breakdown of community. Dramatising the fight of the little people against corporatism and corruption, it attacks the relentlessness of American hegemony and ultimately celebrates human fortitude.

In many ways *A River Runs Through It* (1992) marked a return for Redford to a study of the family – here living in Montana at the beginning of the 1900s – and an analysis of the ties that bind. Affected by an overbearing, religious father, two sons (Brad Pitt and Craig Sheffer) choose different paths but always maintain their solidarity through their love of fly-fishing. Positioning nature as both a character in the story and an elemental driving force which shapes the behaviour of the central protagonists, it also shares a great deal with his more recent film, *The Horse Whisperer* (1998), but injects a little more humour into the proceedings.

*Quiz Show* (1994), however, is Redford's most enduring and accomplished film to date. Based on the 'Twenty-One' scandals of the 1950s, it uses the past to critique the present, questioning society's deification of television and the malevolent effect of celebrity, commerciality and greed. It cleverly juxtaposes academic elitism with mass entertainment and features an outstanding and complex performance from Ralph Fiennes as the intellectual who, despite his ethical stance, finds it impossible to resist the lure of fame and wealth.

Critical reactions to *The Horse Whisperer* were generally unfavourable. Adapted from Nicholas Evans' bestseller, the story focuses on a young girl (played well by rising star Scarlett Johansson) whose terrible riding accident leaves both she and her horse traumatised. Having heard of a legendary horse healer, her determined mother (Kristin Scott Thomas) decamps to Montana to demand the help of cowboy Tom Booker (Redford). He a mysterious nature-lover, she a street-smart city type, they antagonise one another and romance ensues. However, despite a solid cast – Sam Neill and Dianne Wiest support – it lacks the gentle incisiveness of his earlier work, perhaps because of Redford's decision to play the lead character. It is overly sentimental and self-indulgent in places, emphasising the breathtaking beauty of the rural scenery at the expense of the intensely emotional, people-based drama.

Sadly, *The Legend of Bagger Vance* (2000), his most recent film, starring Matt Damon as a golf-playing World War Two hero and Will Smith as his inspirational caddie, moves in much the same direction. Slow and mawkish, it tries for magic realism – to capture the atmosphere of fable or folklore – and ends up looking great but feeling empty. Although Redford does not set out to deliberately flout convention or take risks with his work, it would be satisfying to see him return to the earlier form of *Quiz Show* and *Ordinary People*, for the attractiveness of his film-making is in its intelligence, subtlety and refinement. He was awarded an Honorary Academy Award at the 2002 ceremony.                                                                            **HP**

# Godfrey REGGIO

*Koyaanisqatsi* (1983)
*Powaqqatsi* (1988)

Godfrey Reggio's background hardly marked him as a future film director. He was born in New Orleans in 1940 and at the age of 14 he took Christian orders, spending the next 14 years in silence and prayer. He followed this through work in education and community work in New Mexico in the late 1960s. In 1972, he founded the Institute Of Regional Education, a non-profit community and arts organisation, through which his work as a film-maker was developed and ultimately released.

His first film as director, *Koyaanisqatsi* (1983, but in production between 1975 and 1982), is a documentary with no explicit narrative, and relies purely on aesthetics to carry the meaning. Using a wide range of visual techniques (slow- and fast-motion, time-lapse photography and so on), Reggio constructs a feature-length montage of images of America, an approach that, upon the film's release, marked Reggio out as a highly interesting figure operating outside of established notions of film-making. Starting from an unblemished landscape, he gradually introduces images of the influence man has had on the environment. From this point, Reggio's project becomes a strong indictment of the manners in which America's mass-production and mass-consumption based culture has taken the soul out of a once vibrant people, and how man's nature is based around destruction (the title of the film is from the language of the native Hopi people, and translates roughly as 'a way of life that calls for another way of living'). The film is not without its problems, however: in an extended central section replayed at high speed, people are equated with factory machinery, which is an interesting comment that is easily made, but due to the extension of the sequence it is one that seems overdone. It almost seems that the faster the film moves, the less it has to say. On the other hand, the film's use of 'portraits' of individuals seems to offer a more emotional connection to the subject matter, and the suggestion of the loss of society's soul. The ultimate irony of the film, however, is that it decries the automation of life, whilst relying on 'mechanical reproduction' to make its point. Nonetheless it remains an impressive piece of purely visual cinema, and it is easy to see it as an impassioned plea from Reggio for a more ascetic or austere way of life.

Five years later, Reggio made a sequel using an almost identical approach, *Powaqqatsi* (1988), the title again a native Hopi word which translates approximately as 'a way of life that consumes the life force of other beings to further its own life'. Here, Reggio offers a very similar project, but with his subject matter transposed to the Third World, the central idea being that geo-political and geo-economic factors induce a mode of drudgery and slavery that stops the emotional development of the people. As social argument, however, the film is much more problematic. The reliance on slow-motion photography throughout the film imbues a National Geographic sensibility that ultimately makes the imagery seem merely pictorial, without the critique that Reggio would like to impose. Further, Reggio's use of sequences dealing with religious and recreational routines seems to suggest that the people of the Third World do not find their situations as difficult as Reggio would have us believe. It is only in the final quarter of the film that it becomes more effective, with the suggestion – through more modern architecture – that the continued poverty of the region is as a result of the power of the West, and his use once again of 'portraits' of individuals in poverty within the context of this modernity makes the point more emphatically.

That either of these films achieves any degree of success is in no small part down to the scores of Philip Glass. With no dialogue, and little diegetic sound, the music is the primary audio signal, and carries the general meaning of the narrative. It underscores the imagery, influences the editing, and generally informs the viewer as to the basic intention of the director. Reggio and Glass are collaborating once again, on a concluding chapter to the 'Qatsi' trilogy, currently in production. Titled *Naqoyqatsi* ('war life'), it aims to present – in the same aesthetic – an examination of the biggest 'displacement' factor of the twentieth century, namely war, and how, beyond the battlefield, technological advancement is actually waging war against the notion of humanity. With his pedagogical bias, and his lack of interest in establishing a film-based career for himself, it seems likely that the conclusion of the 'Qatsi' trilogy will bring to an end Reggio's brief oeuvre, albeit one from a genuinely unique figure in cinema.                    **JP**

# Carl REINER

Born in New York in 1923, Carl Reiner has made a significant contribution to contemporary American comedy, both as a performer and director. Working exclusively in the genre of comedy, his films range from slapstick humour to sophisticated comic parodies of classical Hollywood genres. Carl Reiner is the father of director Rob Reiner.

Reiner made an impressive directorial debut with an adaptation of his autobiographical novel, *Enter Laughing* (1967), centring on a young actor's struggles to make the big time. The director's second feature, *The Comic* (1969), features Dick Van Dyke and Mickey Rooney as silent comedy duo Billy Bright and Cockeye. It is clear from the delightful set pieces that Reiner has both an eye and ear tuned exclusively to the comic frequency.

His next feature, *Where's Poppa?* (1970), is a darkly humorous film centring on two brothers (George Segal and Ron Leibman) and the promise they make to their father, on his death bed, to take care of their mother after he is gone. A witty Oedipal comedy, *Where's Poppa?* received good reviews and did moderate box-office business.

Reiner followed this with *Oh, God!* (1977). The film deals with its controversial subject matter with remarkable integrity. Lacking the 'knock 'em dead' humour of his previous films, *Oh, God!* is a wry and satirical tale which speculates on what might happen if God were to come to Earth to survey mankind. Reiner's next feature, *The One and Only* (1978), is notable for Henry Winkler's fine performance. The film follows the fortunes of a brash young student (Winkler) who becomes a wrestler, and Reiner milks every drop of his star's tragi-comic potential, yet the film only did modest business at the box office.

His next film, *The Jerk* (1979), is a vehicle for comedian Steve Martin and marked the beginning of four collaborations between Martin and Reiner. *The Jerk* is often regarded as the runt of this collaborative litter. Certainly the film is less imaginative, more straight comedy than parody, and its narrative seems little more than a collection of related set-pieces. Yet each set-piece is genuinely funny and Martin steals the film. He plays Navin R. Johnson, the white son of a poor black Southern family, who seeks and loses a fortune. Reiner has a cameo role as a director who causes the deaths of two stunt men by yelling 'cut' too late.

*Dead Men Don't Wear Plaid* (1982) parodies 1940s film noir. The humour stems from the interaction between Martin – as the detective – and clips from a variety of classic noir thrillers. This is a clever, knowing film, but suffers from a wooden script and uneven direction from Reiner. Martin and Reiner then wrote *The Man With Two Brains* (1983), and the film is perhaps the slickest and most successful of their collaborations; a parody of the schlock horror/science fiction films of the classical Hollywood era, featuring Kathleen Turner as a sadistic shrew. Here Reiner's direction is slicker and smarter than in any of his previous work.

In *All of Me* (1984) Reiner tries his hand at romantic comedy to great effect in the last of the 4 Martin/Reiner collaborations. Martin plays the lawyer of wealthy spinster, Edwina, whose spirit jumps into him at her time of death. They promptly fall in love – two spirits in the same body. As ludicrous a premise as this sounds, it works, and this is in some part due to Reiner's ability to capture a certain simpatico between Martin and Tomlin.

The director followed this with a disappointing star vehicle for comedian John Candy, *Summer Rental* (1985). Candy plays the not-so-little man who refuses to let his arrogant employers ruin his family vacation to Florida. Equally disappointing was *Summer School* (1987), which features Mark Harmon as a school teacher forced to spend the holidays with a group of juvenile delinquents. The film failed to ignite critical attention and performed badly at the box office.

Reiner's next film is peculiarly satisfying. *Bert Rigby, You're a Fool* (1989) is a curious generic hybrid of musical and comedy, following the fortunes of a British coal miner who becomes a successful entertainer with a band of travelling artists. The film has a standard 'rise to fame' narrative and a feelgood ending, typical for this kind of 'follow your dream' story. It is widely regarded as being a homage to musicals. It was not a box-office success, and received mixed reviews from critics.

His next feature, *Sibling Rivalry* (1990), is a black comedy featuring the talents of Kirstie Alley and Carrie Fisher. Fisher encourages her sister (Alley) to escape her loveless marriage by having an affair. Her lover dies after their first encounter, triggering dark consequences for the sisters. Well acted by the two leads, but the film suffers from rather heavy handed direction from Reiner.

Reiner's love of spoofs and homages continued with *Fatal Instinct* (1993), a playful spoof of the female killer thrillers of the 1980s and 1990s. It is a stylish piece of film-making, evidencing Reiner's zeal for the project. The humour is silly, the gags predictable, but it is performed and shot with such gusto that it is hard to dislike. It is not playful, irreverent Reiner at his best, but the impeccable timing of the seasoned comedian is still very evident. His last feature film to date, however, is somewhat disappointing. *That Old Feeling* (1997) is a romantic comedy which centres on a young newlywed whose parents reunite for the first time in 14 years at her wedding. The film failed both critically and commercially.

Carl Reiner's contribution to film comedy cannot be over-stated. Unlike many directors, he has stuck with comedy, choosing to bring other genres to his comedy rather than comedy to other genres. His strength also lies in his sympathy for the figure of the comedian, both in terms of depicting comedians on screen and in giving stage and television comedians vital opportunities to break into films.　　　　**SL**

# Rob REINER

Rob Reiner is one of Hollywood's most successful comedy directors of the 1980s. Famed for the broad critical and commercial appeal of his films, Reiner is an old-school director who works hard to please his audience. Greatly inspired by his father, comic actor and writer Carl Reiner, the young Rob Reiner was motivated by a self-confessed desire to carve out his own niche in Hollywood. As Reiner has said: 'You have to fight and find the thing that will identify you and separate you out from your father.'

He was born in New York in 1947 and, after studying drama at UCLA, performed stand-up comedy, founded the improvisational group 'The Session', and wrote for television shows such as 'The Smothers Brothers'. But he first achieved national fame with his Emmy-award-winning role as 'Meathead' (1971–78), the liberal straight man to

the outrageously politically incorrect Archie Bunker on the popular American sitcom 'All *Ghosts of Mississippi* (1996)
in the Family'. Reiner, who also has extensive acting experience in feature film (he has *The Story of Us* (1999)
appeared in numerous pictures including *Sleepless in Seattle* (1993), *The First Wives Club* (1996), and *EDtv* (1999)), is noted for his ability to elicit first-rate performances from his cast. An extremely versatile director, Reiner's body of work moves across several different genres and constitutes an eclectic blend of romance, comedy, fantasy, and drama. Described as a kinder, gentler Woody Allen, Reiner's greatest talent and creative flair lies in his comedic direction, which is arguably at its finest in his earlier work.

In the 1990s, Reiner became politically involved as an advocate for children, playing a crucial role in starting the White House conference on early-childhood development. As part of his campaign for kids, Reiner directed *I Am Your Child* (1997), a celebrity-studded television documentary about child welfare, featuring Bill Clinton, Rosie O'Donnell, and Billy Crystal.

While Reiner's widespread appeal as a director is due to the humanity and warmth of his film-making, his work has an ironic edge. This is certainly the case with *This is Spinal Tap* (1984), his feature film debut, considered by many to be his comic masterpiece. With a clever script written by Reiner and the film's actors Michael McKean, Christopher Guest, and Harry Shearer, this 'rockumentary', in which Reiner plays the film-maker who follows an English rock band on their American concert tour, is a cult favourite that firmly established its director's talent for hilarious satire. The genius of the film, which some mistook for a genuine documentary, lies in its affectionate insight into the foibles of the industry it sends up. *The Sure Thing* (1985), while not approaching the level of comic genius of *Spinal Tap*, is a likeable update of *It Happened One Night* (1934). This sweet, if predictable, road movie contains noteworthy comedic performances from an up-and-coming John Cusack and Daphne Zuniga as the young teenagers who discover that opposites attract, and presages the comedic flair of his later film, *When Harry Met Sally* (1989).

Following this was *Stand By Me* (1986), described by Reiner as his most meaningful movie, a bittersweet coming-of-age story based on 'The Body' by Stephen King. Earning Reiner his first nomination as Best Director from the Directors Guild of America, *Stand By Me* is a signature Reiner film: nostalgic, touching, and above all, entertaining. Distinguished by its moving performances from a talented young cast (including River Phoenix) the film manages, for the most part, to avoid an overly saccharine depiction of boyhood friendship. Reiner's next feature was an adaptation of a William Goldman novel. *The Princess Bride* (1987) is a romantic comedy, action-adventure, swashbuckling spoof that demonstrates Reiner's undeniable talent for engaging humour. As with *Spinal Tap*, the brilliance of Reiner's versatile direction here lies in his ability to parody a genre while simultaneously embodying it.

In 1987 Reiner consolidated his status as a Hollywood establishment figure by co-founding the production company, Castle Rock Entertainment, named after a fictional town in Stephen King's novels. The company, which has produced over fifty feature films, was purchased by the Turner Broadcasting System Inc. in 1993. Reiner concluded the decade on a high note with *When Harry Met Sally*, the first of his films to be produced by Castle Rock. One of the most successful romantic comedies of the 1980s, the film grossed over $100 million dollars at the box office. Cleverly scripted by Nora Ephron, and with good performances from Billy Crystal (Reiner's lifelong friend) and Meg Ryan, the film is a witty exploration of sex, love, and friendship. Reiner uses pseudo-documentary footage of older couples telling the story of how they fell in love to frame the tale of the eleven-year friendship between Harry and Sally. Although the film's narrative of 'happily ever after' is ultimately conventional, Reiner manages to avoid clichés. Authoritatively directed, Reiner's imaginative ability to combine comedy and drama is noteworthy.

In the 1990s Reiner shifted tack as a director, attempting to confront darker, more mature subject matter. The results are dubious at best. It is as if the ugly side of the self-righteous liberalism of 'Meathead' rears its head. *Misery* (1990) is the second of his films to be based on a Stephen King story. Although the film contains an excellent performance from a well-cast Kathy Bates (who won a Best Actress Academy Award for the role), it fails to exploit the full potential of its subject matter. Although the critically and commercially successful *A Few Good Men* (1992) is perhaps the most watchable film of this period of Reiner's career, it is predictable film-making lacking in vision and insight. Nominated for four Academy Awards, including a nomination for Best Picture, the film is shamelessly formulaic, with overblown (if admittedly entertaining) performances from its heavyweight Hollywood leads, including Jack Nicholson (nominated for Best Supporting Actor). Roger Ebert described it as one of the 'worst movies ever made' and Rita Kempley referred to it as '88 of the most painful minutes in movie history'.

The next feature, *North* (1994), was an unqualified embarrassment for Reiner. Featuring Bruce Willis in a bunny suit, the film is in seriously bad taste. A series of vignettes featuring would-be parents is by turns boring and offensive, as a number of regionally and racially stereotyped parents – including the Texans, the Hawaiians, the Eskimos, the Africans, the Amish, the Chinese, and the French – are trotted out and then ridiculed.

*The American President* (1995), a romantic comedy starring Michael Douglas and Annette Bening, can be considered Reiner's most successful film of the 1990s. Given an imbued significance in the wake of the Clinton-Lewinsky debacle, the film's portrayal of the decent left-leaning President and his love affair with an environmental lobbyist reads as a liberal fantasy *par excellence*. As does *Ghosts of Mississippi* (1996), but in a less pleasant way. The film is an account of real-life black activist Medgar Evers, who was gunned down in his driveway in 1963. Smug and self-congratulatory, *Ghosts* plays as white redemption fantasy, giving short shrift to the black characters whose stories it presumes to tell, while foregrounding the heroic deeds of the white man. James Woods' role as the depraved white supremacist earned him an Academy Award nomination.

With *The Story of Us* (1999), Reiner wants to return to the tried and tested formula of wry romantic comedy that worked so well in *When Harry Met Sally*. Derisively referred to by critics as 'When Harry Split From Sally' and 'When Harry Dumped Sally', *The Story of Us*, starring Michelle Pfeiffer and Bruce Willis, was a critical and commercial flop. Self-indulgent, grating and contrived, the film's direction is sketchy and disjointed.

Reiner's next film, which he will also produce, will be an adaptation of Dostoevsky's 'The Gambler'. **TH**

# Ivan REITMAN

Ivan Reitman is a director of comedies and comedy dramas who has also produced virtually all of his own films. He started off making down-market absurdities, but has since carved out a name for himself as one of Hollywood's most dependable investments.

Born in Czechoslovakia in 1946, Reitman was taken to live in Canada at age four by his refugee parents. There he went to McMaster University in Ontario before attending the National Film Board's Summer Institute – his student piece *Orientation* (1968) warranted a theatrical release in Canada. Reitman began producing films a year or so later, but ran into trouble when fined for *Columbus of Sex* (1970).

His first professional directing pursuit was *Foxy Lady* (1971), a relatively short, low-key affair in which 'Good Citizen' Alan Gordon falls for rich girl Sylvia Feigel. Bearing all the hallmarks of a novice assay, especially listless editing and a malnourished script, this nevertheless holds a certain amount of promise.

However, *Cannibal Girls* (1973) shows no signs of improvement. Feeding off the splatter trend in horror films, this has Eugene Levy and Andrea Martin stumbling upon a small-town cannibal haunt. The ravenous girls of the title 'do EXACTLY what you think they do!' says the tagline, and yet this biting comedy horror is neither funny nor horrifying but simply pitiful. American International Pictures apparently added the gimmicky doorbell sound to warn viewers when a gruesome scene approached.

For several years Reitman limited his activities to producing (handling the David Cronenberg pictures *Shivers* (1975) and *Rabid* (1977), plus *National Lampoon's Animal House* (1978)), until he felt sufficiently confident to helm *Meatballs* (1979). Regarded as the apex of zany summer camp buffoonery, it stars Bill Murray as a head counselor training an assemblage of misfits. Base and definitely non-PC comedy predominates, dreamt up by a four-strong writing team (including Harold Ramis) who manage to somehow sidestep many of the usual clichés.

*Stripes* (1981) cleaves to a cognate schema, but in an army camp. The male counterpart to *Private Benjamin* (1980), which is in some respects closer in pitch to the later *Police Academy* (1984), it headlines Bill Murray and Harold Ramis as recruits who accept the glossy military hype and sign up for a tour. Outrageous junketing and practical jokes during the boot camp half keep the entertainment value at a maximum, but the movie exhausts itself towards the end as the cadets see 'real' combat action.

Next came Reitman's most famous film, *Ghostbusters* (1984). Originally planned as a vehicle for Blues Brothers Dan Aykroyd and John Belushi called *Ghostsmashers*, it had to be entirely revamped following Belushi's untimely death in 1982 to include Murray and Ramis from *Stripes* (with Ramis and Aykroyd co-writing the script). A fabulous supernatural comedy in which three disgraced scientists set up a ghost-extermination agency (complete with boiler suit uniforms and traps), cashing in on the fact that a gateway to the afterworld has opened up in Sigourney Weaver's Manhattan apartment block. The film works so spectacularly well thanks not only to the special effects (the crowning glory being the giant marshmallow man), but also because of Murray's spontaneous sarcasm and total disregard for parapsychology.

By way of contrast, *Legal Eagles* (1986) is a stodgy thriller that places too much emphasis on its lead, Robert Reford. But not even his A-List status can redeem this tale of art fraud, theft and murder, particularly when Debra Winger out-performs him as an unflinching lawyer who will do anything to win. The amusing *Twins* (1988) is also less than the sum of its parts. A one-joke movie – Arnold Schwarzenegger and Danny DeVito as 'identical' twin brothers – this does, however, provide its Austrian star with the opportunity to demonstrate his more clement side.

All the original cast returned for *Ghostbusters II* (1989) but as the film itself is forced to admit, the glamour of the first outing had now worn off. Brought out of enforced retirement to battle a pink ooze suppurating beneath New York, the team go through the motions again but to little effect. Only the sequences featuring Sigourney Weaver's baby – actually played by twins – will delight, overshadowing the 'walking' Statue of Liberty.

More children appear in *Kindergarten Cop* (1990), handing Arnold Schwarzenegger his most onerous challenge yet. As an undercover policeman masquerading as a primary school teacher his biggest threat is no longer thugs or drug dealers, but uncontrollable chits. Not only that, he must also 'cope' with the attentions of smitten mothers and fellow teacher Penelope Ann Miller.

*Dave* (1993), however, is a superior political comedy, starring Kevin Kline as a loo-kalike president who takes over when the real leader strokes out. With enough cynical, satirical comment (Dave's small-time accountant friend saves the taxpayers millions over dinner), acting talent (Sigourney Weaver returning as the President's austere wife) and Machiavellian machinations in Gary Ross' script to appease even the most jaded viewer, *Dave* is an absolute joy. The exact opposite of *Junior* (1994), a belated and unavailing reunion for DeVito and Schwarzenegger. The theory about a man carrying a baby to term is probably quite prophetic, but the sight of scientist 'Arnie' locating his feminine side in drag goes one step too far, while Emma Thompson completes the gender reversal by quite literally wearing the trousers as 'father' of the child. More conventional parents abound in *Fathers' Day* (1997), and certainly more contemporary ones. Single mother Nastassja Kinski persuades two old flames, Robin Williams and Billy Crystal, that they are the father(s) of her runaway teenage son. An appalling translation of the French source material, this misuses and miscasts its two main assets – a shame because given a more dynamic vehicle Crystal and Williams would gel perfectly together.

Reitman's subsequent film, *Six Days, Seven Nights* (1998), was an attempt to revitalise the traditional comic romance in which two opposites attract – Harrison Ford's rugged pilot and Anne Heche's sophisticated magazine editor are just too different to bond. Yet the lack of sexual chemistry between the duo, most apparent when they are stranded on a desert island together, is only one of the movie's many mistakes – its tremendous predictability is a major problem. Conversely, *Evolution* (2001) relies wholly on predictability and the audience's acquaintance with science fiction iconography. The story of an alien infiltration, this humorous hybrid of 1950s invasion movies and more up-to-date examples like *Men in Black* (1997) even stars David Duchovny from 'The X-Files'. It is little more than an amusing diversion, often unintentionally. Reitman's next film will be the tenth in the Pink Panther series.                                    **PB**

# Kevin REYNOLDS

Born in Texas in 1952, Kevin Reynolds is an alumnus of both John Milius, for whom *Fandango* (1985)
he wrote *Red Dawn* (1984), and Steven Spielberg, whose company Amblin produced *The Beast* (1988)

his first feature – an expansion of his USC short, *Proof*. The feature, renamed *Fandango* (1985), is a freewheeling, often manic, sometimes muted, road movie about five friends (the Groovers) who graduate from college and are about to do their tours of duty in Vietnam. Led by the reckless, maverick Gardner Barnes (Kevin Costner in an outstanding performance) the Groovers head out across Texas to mark the end of an era and to 'dig up Dom' – a bottle of champagne buried several years before. Barnes' sense of undertaking an epic journey to honour 'the privileges of youth' by defying authority and living for the moment is enhanced by Reynolds' shot compositions – sweeping wide-angle vistas of the barren, endless Texas landscape. The film is carried by a zestful exuberance. Standout sequences, charged with kinetic humour akin to a live action spin on Tex Avery, are the railroad-car towing attempt and the comic-action set piece at the aerodrome built around one character's efforts to prove himself. The film concludes in a more reflective and mature tone as Gardner realises that an era has ended. Reynolds' film made a minimal commercial and critical impact upon its initial release (although it has acquired minor cult status). It marked the first of the Reynolds/Costner collaborations and remains their best effort to date.

The director's second feature, *The Beast* (1988), failed to have a significant commercial impact. An adaptation of the play by William Mastrosimone, *The Beast* told of a Soviet tank lost in the desert during the Soviet invasion of Afghanistan. A character-driven action film, displaying Reynolds' real knack for the genre, *The Beast* is a taut piece in which character frailties and tensions take precedence over action for its own sake.

Reynolds is a significant force in the creation of Costner's on-screen persona, having directing the actor in *Robin Hood: Prince of Thieves* (1991) and *Waterworld* (1995). In both films the maverick, goofy energy of Gardner Barnes is replaced: in *Robin Hood* by something more ponderous and mundane and in *Waterworld* by something appealingly edgy and selfish. Amidst the pyrotechnics and spectacle of *Waterworld*, Costner anchors the chaos with consistent character behaviour. In each collaboration with the star, Reynolds productively employs Costner's graceful physicality – witness *Waterworld*'s energetic and balletic opening 40 minutes in which the Mariner's acrobatics recall, in a more robust way, the endless rushing around of Gardner Barnes.

Across all his work, Reynolds displays a penchant for rugged outdoor terrain and invests his films with a great sense of motion and expanse. The sweeping, energetic compositions and editing patterns tend to be bold and sure, yet the pieces are occasionally marred by his handling of villainous characters. In both *Robin Hood* and *Waterworld* he allows any real sense of danger and threat on the part of the antagonists to dissipate through performances that are too broad and comic. All believable menace is lost.

As in the films of Milius and director John Sturges, all Reynolds' heroes are stoic men of action. In *Rapa Nui* (1994), a historical drama set on Easter Island, the characters are defined through what they do rather than by what they say; here Reynolds savours the opportunity to create a vividly imposing natural landscape.

For *One Eight Seven* (1997), Reynolds shifted from forests, desert and sea settings to contemporary Los Angeles. Samuel L. Jackson portrays teacher Trevor Garfield, who relocates to LA after being stabbed by a student in New York. Sure enough Garfield finds himself confronted by a hostile classroom and is compelled to get tough to survive. Jackson's performance is *One Eight Seven*'s lynchpin and evidence of Reynolds' ability to handle both the performance of his camera and his actors. On occasion, however, the visual strategy is too flamboyant and self-consciously inventive.

Reynolds' most recent offering is the 2002 adventure release, *The Count of Monte Cristo*. More than a dozen adaptations of Dumas' immense novel of revenge have reached the screen and Reynolds makes the effort to infuse the story with a more modern sensibility; rather in the way he intermittently managed with *Robin Hood: Prince of Thieves*. *The Count of Monte Cristo* is anchored by its two leads; Guy Pearce as bad guy Fernand Mondego and Jim Caviezel as Edmund Dantes. Caviezel, in particular, builds upon the promise he showed in *The Thin Red Line* (1998) and *Frequency* (2000). Reynolds' flair for action – specifically men in action – shines through again, and he perfectly balances the necessities of generic expectation with strong character interplay. Shot on location in Ireland and Malta, the work also has a refreshing simplicity about it. Generally well-received, alongside Martin Campbell's terrific *The Mask of Zorro* (1998),

Reynolds' new look at an old favourite stands as one of the best and truest adventure movies of recent years.                                                                                      **JC**

# Jay ROACH

Born in New Mexico and a 1986 graduate of USC's film school, Jay Roach has been a bit of an industry journeyman, finding work as a screenwriter (he penned the story for 1994's bomb squad thriller, *Blown Away*), cinematographer, producer and even camera operator before making his name directing the cult hit, *Austin Powers: International Man of Mystery* (1997), as well as its more successful (but less inspired) sequel, *Austin Powers: The Spy Who Shagged Me* (1999). Both films are fine: generally amusing, only sporadically hilarious comedies buoyed mostly by the charm of co-writer/star Mike Myers and a handful of visually inventive gags. It is Roach's work away from the silly *Powers* series – on 1999's entertaining *Mystery, Alaska* and 2000's slyly funny *Meet the Parents* – that is the better indicator of his artistic potential.

With the first Powers film, Roach found in Myers not only a collaborator, but a kindred spirit infatuated with the same points of pop culture reference: outlandish 1960s spy movies (James Bond, Matt Helm) and the irreverent British comedy of Monty Python, Peter Sellers, and 'The Goon Show'. A fish-out-of-water comedy about a swinging secret agent who is frozen in the 1960s and thawed out in the 1990s (Sellers-like, Myers plays both Powers and his gazoony arch-nemesis, Dr Evil), Roach stylishly captures both eras with bright, comic, panel-coloured widescreen photography. It is a look that is reverent to the glitzy pictures he and Myers are spoofing – a dash of *Danger: Diabolik* (1968), a dollop of *Casino Royale* (1967), and huge chunks of *The Silencers* (1966) – but only enough to suggest a kinship; the images never overpower the film's somewhat uneven blend of witty satire and burlesque farce, and often work in tandem to help enhance the best jokes. Roach has fun inserting quick, 'Laugh In'-inspired musical segues, and even plays with multi-panel editing in one scene (a true 1960's staple if ever there was one). But *International Man of Mystery*'s single greatest gag is a perfectly-timed, winkingly-composed master shot in which everything co-star Elizabeth Hurley touches while she breakfasts in the foreground (a teapot, a magnifying glass, a sausage) serves to conceal Myers/Powers' nudity in the background, at once jokingly alluding to and wryly commenting on the chaste naughtiness of the Bond films.

The second Powers adventure, *The Spy Who Shagged Me*, could be characterised as more of the same, only not as funny. Roach uses his bigger budget to broaden the first film's visual palette, with larger sets and more special effects. (A secret volcano lair in the shape of Dr Evil's head is a nice touch.) It's also a far greater imagined and designed film than the first, if only because this sequel takes place almost entirely in the 1960s, as the intrepid Powers travels back in time in search of his stolen 'mojo'. Unfortunately, *Spy* leans too heavily on both the nauseating physical comedy and indulgent moments of improvisation that sometimes brought the first film to a comic halt, because neither Roach not Myers appear to know when to quit. Most of the picture's biggest laughs are simply recycled versions of ones from its predecessor, such as the opening (and admittedly funny) sequence that turns the hidden private parts routine into a musical dance number that climaxes with a parody of Busby Berkley/Esther Williams swimming pool choreography, while the few original jokes to be found (a montage sequence that elaborates hilariously on euphemisms for the word 'penis', a shadow play that falsely insinuates a cornucopia of items being hauled from Myers' nether regions) linger far too long after hitting their mark.

*Mystery, Alaska* finds Roach adopting an altogether different rhythm, telling the Cinderella story of a scrappy small-town hockey team that takes on the New York Rangers on a much more intimate scale, and showing a sure hand for both light drama and droll character development in the process. *Mystery, Alaska* is shot with the suffused warmth and folksy realism of a Rockwell painting, with Roach this time using his anamorphic frame as more than just a hip joke – it's a perfect proscenium for his beaten-down tundras and white-on-white horizons, further lending a sense of epic, near-Roman grandeur to the roughneck game of ice hockey. (Star Russell Crowe shot this before playing another nobly tarnished arena warrior in *Gladiator* (2000), but the parallels are delicious.) Roach takes equal care with the rich cadre of character players (Burt Reynolds, Colm Meany, Maury Chaykin) at his disposal, drawing on his experience with the improvisational Myers (who cameos here briefly as a former NHL great) to capture their performances in long, sometimes hand-held master shots that allow both them and their story to breathe naturally.

While his first stab at a more realistic brand of humour was met with indifferent box office, Roach's follow-up – the tightly-wound comedy of embarrassment, *Meet the Parents* (2000) – was a bona fide hit. Both broader and more farcical than *Mystery, Parents* centres around one disastrous weekend in the dating life of Jewish male nurse Greg Focker (played to hapless perfection by Ben Stiller), as he tries to fit in with his girlfriend's family, a clan of straight-laced Connecticut WASPs headed by a glowering Robert De Niro. The sharp script stacks the deck against Focker at every turn, making him the victim of a series of misfortunes before revealing De Niro to be a retired CIA profiler who rigorously questions everything from Greg's surname and occupation to his religion, intelligence and honesty; though some critics have compared *Parents* to the domestic capering of 1979's *The In-Laws*, a better precedent might be Woody Allen's harrowing Thanksgiving with Diane Keaton's gentile Midwestern relatives in *Annie Hall* (1977). Roach finds exactly the right tone for this light-hearted nightmare, allowing scenes to play out in enclosed spaces with awkward silences and uncomfortable glances, and deftly executing intricate gag set-ups that pay off through each successive act with the wonky precision of a Rube Goldberg device. He also continues to demonstrate his skill with actors, not only shepherding De Niro through one of his truly great comic performances (far superior, in fact, to his lauded self-parody in 1999's *Analyze This*), but drawing fine, believable work from the likes of Teri Polo, Blythe Danner and Owen Wilson that's never overwhelmed by the film's occasional veerings to raucous slapstick.

Roach's next film, *Austin Powers in Goldmember* (2002), is the third in the Austin Powers series. He is also directing a sequel to *Meet the Parents*, *Meet the Fockers*, as well as a film version of Douglas Adams' 'The Hitchhiker's Guide to the Galaxy'.    **CS**

# Tim ROBBINS

*Bob Roberts* (1992)
*Dead Man Walking* (1995)
*Cradle Will Rock* (1999)

Together with his long-term partner Susan Sarandon, Tim Robbins has often been frowned upon by Hollywood for using his powerful position as an actor to publicise his politically leftist views. While his politics may be less discernible in his choice of acting roles they have certainly affected his artistic decisions both as a writer and director, causing him to produce films which are in opposition to the usual mainstream fare, challenging dominant ideologies and assumptions.

Born in California in 1958, and having acted since the age of twelve with the Theatre for the New City, he studied drama at the State University of New York at Plattsburgh and then transferred to the theatre programme at University of California. In 1981 he co-founded an avant-garde theatre company, The Actor's Gang (of which he later became artistic director), and in 1988 wrote the play 'Carnage' with Adam Simon and established his own independent company, HAVOC. It was in the early 1990s that Robbins really began to earn widespread success and recognition as an actor, starring in the critically acclaimed *The Player* (1992) (winning a Golden Globe and Best Actor at Cannes), *Short Cuts* (1993), *The Hudsucker Proxy* (1994), and *The Shawshank Redemption* (1994).

His feature directing debut, *Bob Roberts* (1992), was inspired by a short film he had made in the mid-1980s for 'Saturday Night Live' and focused on the making of a documentary following the campaign of a far-right American politician/folk singer for a seat as a Pennsylvania senator. Featuring Robbins himself in the title role and viewed by one critic as a 'lament for the fall of the committed American Left', it is full of entertaining satire and refreshingly thought-provoking social awareness, intelligently challenging bourgeois complacency and the cult of celebrity.

His next project, *Dead Man Walking* (1995), was based on the life of the spiritual advisor Sister Helen Prejean and centred on her relationship with a convicted killer (Sean Penn) on Death Row. Penn and Sarandon's multi-faceted on-screen relationship, which encompasses a range of emotions through from compassion to loathing, is truly compelling. Robbins wisely favours a static camera and conventional close-ups. Shot with effecting simplicity, the film manages to convey a humane, liberal message whilst also instilling the horrible reality of his criminal acts. It was nominated for four Academy

Awards, including Best Director, and won Best Actress for Susan Sarandon's compelling and sympathetic portrayal of the nun.

Robbins' third film, *Cradle Will Rock* (1999), is a dramatisation of Orson Welles' attempts to stage Mark Blitzstein's controversial Communist musical about a steel strike. Set in New York during the Great Depression, it features a mix of fictional and historical characters, all played with vivacity by a first-rate cast, including John Cusack, Angus McFayden, Susan Sarandon and Emily Watson. Rich in visual detail and colour, it evokes the volatile atmosphere of the era and a sense of theatricality that never feels stagey.

An actors' director in the truest sense, Robbins has created an ensemble piece shot through with political incisiveness and rumination. It is to be hoped that he will continue to find funding and acceptance in Hollywood for his brand of intelligent and meditative work. **HP**

# Chris ROBERTS

Computer games are moving inexorably towards the expansive plot lines, detailed characters and epic scope of cinema. With big-budget blockbusters using computers to create special effects, superimpose backdrops, and even entire characters, cinema, it may be argued, is going the other way. Chris Roberts has been a pioneer in this process of hybridisation since the earliest days of home computers. His 'Wing Commander' games are part science fiction movie, part space shoot-'em-up, mixing player interactivity, gameplay and cutting-edge graphics with a developed storyline, an enormous cast of characters and a cinematic score. The series works in part thanks to its ability to plunder from cinema, giving players the facility to recreate the dogfights from *Star Wars* and battle *Alien*-style enemies, experiencing design and graphic elements that place them within a sci-fi film as participant rather than spectator. Nowhere is this intention more overtly displayed than in his choice of actor to play the central character Lt. Blair, none other than the crown prince of modern sci-fi – Mark Hamill. Far from concealing his inspirations, Roberts' intention is to ape and invoke classic sci-fi set pieces and narratives, but present them in an entirely novel way.

This is the precise reason why the movie translation *Wing Commander* (1999) fails. The process of reinvention, of translating established science fiction mores into cutting-edge interactive games, obviously disappears in a film version, as does all its related novelty value. Instead the film is simply left with a series of clichés: a hackneyed plot; cut-out characters; and the requisite romantic interest, dramatic sacrifices and character oppositions. Every plot device in the canon is here – the veteran/rookie conflict, the young pilot who proves his worth, the accidental death of a friend and the last-ditch stand against overwhelming opposition. Though Roberts' eye for computer-generated effects is still impressive – even if a little stretched on the big screen – and his fluency in the genre is undeniable, what was innovative as a computer game becomes derivative as a film; homage becomes imitation. Roberts' direction and the actors are all competent, as is the art direction and visual look of the film, but it lacks any mark of the original imagination and approach that Roberts has displayed elsewhere. **OB**

# Phil Alden ROBINSON

Born in 1950 in New York, Phil Alden Robinson's output, in contrast to the bombastic efforts of much of the mainstream, has been marked by sincerity, humanity and occasional stillness. His work as writer and director affirms a sense of community and the power of an idea within the classic Hollywood idiom.

Having worked in radio and making industrial films, in 1979 Robinson wrote two episodes of the series 'Trapper John, MD'. By 1984, he has worked on the original story and script for *Rhinestone* (which was rewritten by Sylvester Stallone) and the Carl Reiner comedy *All of Me*, starring Steve Martin and Lily Tomlin. He made his own directing feature debut with *In the Mood* (1987), a comedy set in 1940s.

Having read W. P. Kinsella's novel *Shoeless Joe* in the early 1980s, in 1989 Robinson adapted the book and directed the story for the screen under the new title *Field of Dreams* – Kinsella's original title for the novel had been 'Dream Field'. A big hit in a vintage year for Hollywood movies, the film focuses on a thirtysomething farmer in Iowa, Ray Kinsella, who hears a voice instructing him to build a baseball field over his cornfield, thereby jeopardising his already dubious financial situation. The film has a quietness about it, which is most evident in John Lindley's dreamy shots of corn, sun-baked highways and vast summer skies. Solitude and space – classic American concerns – underscore the drama. In what may still be the perfect Costner role, Robinson helped forge the actor's screen personal, showcasing his laid-back presence. The film is buoyed further by James Horner's melancholy score and the supporting actors: Burt Lancaster lends a sweet sturdiness to the fantasy; James Earl Jones' bass tones speak on behalf of America's national pastime; and Ray Liotta brings an edginess to the bucolic set-up as Shoeless Joe. Exploring issues of happiness and the bonds and pressures of family, the film also asserts a necessary faith in what cannot be seen.

Robinson followed *Field of Dreams* with *Sneakers* (1992), a comedy drama starring Robert Redford about a goofy team of computer hackers on a mission to steal the ultimate code-breaker. The film is at its best during the interplay between the quirky characters. Efficiently made, it lacks the conviction and durability of his other efforts. Robinson went on to direct a number of documentaries about Somalia and Bosnia for ABC's 'Nightline' programme and the television movie *Freedom Song* (2000), which is set during the 1960s civil rights movement in the US. In 2001 he directed 'Currahee', the opening episode of 'Band of Brothers'; classic Robinson material, it explores the bonds of a 'family' of civilian soldiers.

Robinson's most recent film, *The Sum of All Fears* (2002), is an adaptation of the Tom Clancy novel, and stars Ben Affleck in the role of CIA man Jack Ryan, previously played by Harrison Ford.                                                                              **JC**

# Marc ROCCO

Son of veteran actor Alex Rocco, Marc Rocco has shown a keen awareness of film as the actor's medium. Heartfelt and often powerful, Rocco's films are driven principally by very human concerns – pain, cruelty, love, companionship and betrayal – conveyed through consistently detailed performances and emotive, energetic camerawork. Rocco has not confined himself solely to the realms of realist drama but his predilection for exploring matters of the human heart has found greatest expression in a punchy, uncompromising directorial style, dealing with issues of conflict, survival and injustice.

Rocco's first major film established him as a director capable of producing competent drama. *Scenes from the Goldmine* (1987) is the story of Debi Di Angelo, a talented young musician eager to succeed in the early eighties LA music scene who experiences the cut-throat duplicity that lies behind its glamorous facade. The film is full of 'onstage' and 'backstage' contrast: between over-lighting and under-lighting, noise and silence, and the high-energy gaudiness of the musical set-pieces with the emotional drama played out offstage as Debi discovers her music is being stolen by the lead singer she idolises. Though heartfelt and well-intentioned, the film feels very much an apprentice work let down by a poor script and clichéd morals, and now looks dated thanks to its resolutely 1980s setting. It does, however, showcase Rocco's interest in handling detailed emotional contrast.

*Dream a Little Dream* (1989) is less dramatic but much more entertaining. A body-swap movie in which an elderly man and teenage boy switch minds, it fits into another well-worn genre, but Rocco's imagination for the comic possibilities elevate this film above its many counterparts. His eye for detail – the 'mystical' experiments of the old man, the concurrence of both elderly and teenage love interests, the many well-handled 'generation' jokes – and the pacey direction make for an entertaining, genuine film that again shows Rocco's emotional sensibility.

It was with *Where the Day Takes You* (1992) that Rocco began to show a much more sophisticated, distinctive style. A hard-hitting look at the lives of runaways in Los Angeles, the story is told in a variety of styles – pseudo-documentary, confessional, teen drama and *cinéma vérité*. The intriguing structure, contrasting the testimony of one of the boys to his prison psychologist with his life on the streets, lend the story of his attempts to dissuade his companions from the lures of crime, drugs and violence an inevitable, almost determinist air of tragedy. This innovative treatment, added to Rocco's command of real, emotional film-making and his excellent direction of actors, make for sophisticated cinema with serious themes of isolation, betrayal and companionship in adversity, reminiscent of Coppola's teen dramas *Rumble Fish* (1983) and *The Outsiders* (1983).

The control of directorial style, particularly the ability to move between moments of shocking brutality and delicately handled emotion, becomes a key aspect of Rocco's work in his most successful film, *Murder in the First* (1995). Afforded the gravity of a true story that his previous film carried in spirit if not in reality, the film tells the tale of Henri Young, a harmless petty criminal sent to Alcatraz where he is systematically brutalised by a sadistic associate warden. Rocco creates truly disturbing moments through brilliant performances, evocative art direction and visual restraint; contrasts between the gloom and isolation of solitary cells and the sudden explosions into violence make for fascinating, tense film-making. The later courtroom scenes, too, are expertly handled. Rocco's emotional range and varied style, particularly in his later work, mark him out as a versatile, thoughtful director, capable of attaining an honesty and directness rare in the often formulaic world of modern film-making.

Rocco's forthcoming film, *The Jacket*, is a fantasy thriller about a clairvoyant who is unjustly sentenced and must use his ability to discover who framed him.     **OB**

# Alexandre ROCKWELL

Alexandre Rockwell's career seems to have floundered since the more promising early 1990s when it looked like a whole flock of independent directors might go on to great things. The dream faded, however, and amidst the Richard Linklaters and the Hal Hartleys, only Jim Jarmusch seems to be making films that are far left of the mainstream. Jarmusch is a trenchant comparison for Rockwell, whose own films strike a tonal balance between the Ozu-loving New Yorker's studied aimlessness and the sharp talk brought back into fashion by Quentin Tarantino. Steve Buscemi is Rockwell's characteristic actor, his hangdog face staring out from the grain of the low-budget environs the director tends to favour. Buscemi's ever-growing success, along with Tarantino's and Jarmusch's, stresses how much Rockwell has fallen by the wayside.

*Hero* (1983)
*Sons* (1989)
*In the Soup* (1992)
*Somebody to Love* (1994)
*Louis and Frank* (1998)

His first two films, *Hero* (1983) and *Sons* (1989), are little known. *Sons* is notable for featuring the craggy face of director Sam Fuller, an electric screen presence from Godard's *Pierrot Le Fou* (1965) on, and also re-introducing Jennifer Beals (Rockwell's wife) to a world that had largely forgotten her after *Flashdance* (1983). It was *In the Soup* (1992), however, that was the director's break-out moment. Made in black and white, it features performances from Buscemi and Seymour Cassel that are exercises in scene-stealing but suit the wandering comedy of a pretentious film-maker who earns his production funds through a fast-talking gangster. Already exhibiting a flair for compelling monologues, Rockwell went on to more fully develop his writing skills in his next film, *Somebody to Love* (1994). Betraying Rockwell's prevailing seriousness, the excellent cast includes Harvey Keitel, Rosie Perez, Anthony Quinn, Buscemi again and cameos by Tarantino and Fuller. Each of them play Altmanesque characters who move through the episodic tale in a numb delirium. A genuinely wounded film and hopeless in the best sense of the word, *Somebody to Love* is a genuine achievement.

Hopeless is the word for Rockwell's following two efforts, but only in the critical sense. A contributor to the ill-conceived *Four Rooms* (1995), it was always a danger that Rockwell would struggle for attention next to the flashy talents of Roberto Rodriguez and Tarantino. Better than Allison Anders' opening effort, Rockwell's 'The Wrong Man', concerning a violent sexual relationship which bellboy Tim Roth becomes embroiled in, fades quickly from the mind as soon as Rodriguez's segment begins. Easily overwhelmed by more aggressive stylists, the director has yet to recover.

*Louis and Frank* (1998), resurrects two characters from *In the Soup* but to little purpose. As is often the case with independent directors, it could be that Rockwell would be better suited to more normative dramatic conventions, particularly when oblique postures fail him. His most recent film, *13 Moons*, has yet to be released.     **CSo**

# Mic RODGERS

Sometimes credited as Mic Rogers, Rodgers has collected a number of acting credits since his 1978 appearances in the 'M*A*S*H' episode 'None Like it Hot' and in *Lord of the Rings* (1978). Subsequent roles have tended to be job descriptions, often followed

*Universal Soldier: The Return* (1999)

by numbers (such as Bomb Scene Cop #1 in *Lethal Weapon 3* (1992)), and have often gone uncredited. Perhaps best known as Mel Gibson's stunt double, he has credits for stunts in 34 films since 1982, and as stunt co-ordinator for 21 films since 1984. This has led to work as a second unit director on movies with which he has no stunt connection – *Year of the Comet* (1992), *Fled* (1996), and *Nothing to Lose* (1997) – as well on several for which he worked as stunt co-ordinator – *Braveheart* (1995), *Virtuosity* (1995), *Volcano* (1997), *Lethal Weapon 4* (1998), and *Payback* (1999).

Rodgers' directorial debut, in which he also appears in the typical (for him) role of Big Biker, was *Universal Soldier: The Return* (1999), a belated sequel to *Universal Soldier* (1992), Jean-Claude Van Damme's most financially successful movie. From the outset, action, stunts, fighting, and pyrotechnics are let down not only by the feeble attempt at a screenplay but also by pedestrian camerawork and editing. Although the climactic fight sequence between Van Damme and Michael Jai White is better served by the director, the entire movie looks like second unit work. **MB**

# Robert RODRIGUEZ

Bursting on to the scene in 1992 with *El Mariachi*, the arrival of Robert Rodriguez as a 'Hollywood player' took the industry – and Rodriguez himself – by surprise. Originally intended as a straight-to-video production for the Spanish-speaking market, *El Mariachi* became one of the surprise hits of the 1990s, assuring Rodriguez a place in the mainstream, big-budget business and making him one of the most significant and powerful Latino-American figures in the industry. Born in San Antonio in 1968, his story is a remarkable and enduring one, the American dream made real, which has been a source of inspiration to struggling film-makers everywhere, and has entered Hollywood mythos.

As legend and Rodriguez' book 'Rebel Without a Crew' (subtitled 'Or, How a twenty-three-year-old Film-maker with $7,000 Became a Hollywood Player') has it, in the late 1980s and early 1990s Rodriguez was a low-budget film-maker whose trilogy of home movies, Austin Stories, had taken first prize at a local film festival and shamed the University of Texas-Austin into offering him a film-school place. With some successful shorts behind him, Rodriguez embarked on his first feature, *El Mariachi*, to be made on $7,000 with no crew and starring his friends and family. The budget was notoriously raised through a combination of loans and medical experiment fees and Rodriguez envisioned the film as part of a trilogy that would give him enough experience and cash to put together a decent showreel in order to make a 'real' film. In the event, *El Mariachi* ended up being seen at the ICM talent agency, was acclaimed at Sundance, got international distribution from Columbia and the rest, as they say, is history.

What distinguished *El Mariachi* from countless other low-budget feature debuts was its combination of dynamic plot, inventive editing and evocative visual aesthetic. Pastiche can be the last resort of the unimaginative, but Rodriguez's western-style depiction of gangsters after the wrong guy in a dusty North Mexican town managed to capture the familiar territory of machismo and doomed romance while also invigorating it with some nicely observed humour and ironic touches. The film moves confidently from the expectant stillness of the opening to the frenetic action of the chase sequences and established Rodriguez as a director with a flair for pace, framing and movement, who could turn his hand to everything from camera operation to editing to sound.

*Desperado* (1995) was the next instalment of the planned Mariachi trilogy but proved, disappointingly, that bigger budgets do not in themselves make better films. However, it was significant for a number of reasons, establishing Antonio Banderas as a Hollywood star, further demonstrating Rodriguez' passion for dizzying, choreographed action and violence and, with performances from Steve Buscemi and Quentin Tarantino, establishing the director place among Hollywood's new generation of young mavericks. This was further demonstrated by his contribution to *Four Rooms* (1995), an experiment in collective film-making where Alison Anders, Alexandre Rockwell, Tarantino, and Rodriguez each contributed a segment or 'room'. Although neither a popular nor critical success, Rodriguez' contribution, a 24-minute black comedy entitled 'The Misbehavers', offered some slick, tightly edited, farcical relief from his colleagues' work despite its own grim moments surrounding the discovery of a 'dead whore'.

Rodriguez has become a name that regularly crops up in debates about excessive film violence, his fast and frantic style ensuring that the action is always visceral and flamboyant. Such criticisms neglect the way in which this excess might be seen to lend an element of fantasy to his work. A more disquieting but related issue is the place of women in his films; Rodriguez' work is littered with the bodies of dead and dismembered women, and their deaths are recurrently linked in some way to their sexuality. The infamous Titty Twister nightclub sequence in *From Dusk till Dawn* (1996) is a case in point, a film which also perplexed critics by switching genres from heist-gone-wrong movie to vampire schlock halfway through the proceedings.

Rodriguez' fascination for action continues in his more recent films. With *The Faculty* (1998) he branched out into a pastiche of sci-fi and teen-horror, again demonstrating his self-referential take on genre. In 2001, he expanded his repertoire to take in the family audience, when *Spy Kids'* appealing combination of energetic Bond-style action, over-the-top villains bent on world domination, heroic kids and imaginative, even surreal fantasy sequences, proved a huge hit. *Spy Kids* brought Rodriguez' penchant for frantic pacing and quirky humour to bear in a new context where it translated with massive box-office success and apparent directorial ease, surprisingly perhaps given the restraint it necessitated from the darker moments that characterise his wider oeuvre. In other ways, however, the generic abandon enabled by the children's fantasy picture seems perfectly attuned to Rodriguez' style; this new milieu was evidently more than a solitary departure since the sequel, *Spy Kids 2: The Island of Lost Dreams*, is due for release in 2002. Also up is the final instalment of his *El Mariachi* trilogy, *Once Upon A Time In Mexico*. Starring a number of now familiar Rodriguez regulars, including Banderas, this latest venture promises to be a massive epic, its completion finally fulfilling the early ambitions of the 23-year-old film-maker with $7,000 who became a Hollywood player. **DJ**

# George A. ROMERO

Born in the Bronx in 1940, George A. Romero has never, throughout a thirty-year career, topped his debut *Night of the Living Dead* (1968) for sheer effectiveness. However, this is no cause for shame. Made with a small army of friends and co-workers, Romero's spare, documentary-like feature benefited from all of its limitations to surpass expectations and become not only a cult film but a genre milestone; no comprehensive analysis of the horror film is complete without reference (and deference) to *Night of the Living Dead*. Unfortunately, Romero's Latent Image (a Pittsburgh-based company specialising in television commercials and industrial films) was swindled by its distributor, and neither Romero nor any of his collaborators saw any profit from their labours.

Following the failure of Romero's 1969 romantic drama, *The Affair* (re-released a few years later as *There's Always Vanilla*), the Carnegie-Mellon-educated writer-director returned to the supernatural with *Jack's Wife* (1972), an insightful jab at suburban complacency masquerading as an occult thriller, and as theatrical and dream-informed as *Night of the Living Dead* was numbingly *vérité*. The film did not find favour with audiences, and was hastily re-titled *Season of the Witch* (to capitalise on the Donovan song of the same name) and then again as *Hungry Wives* (in a bid to pass it off as a sex film).

More commercially-minded, but no less impassioned in its politics, *Code Name: Trixie* (1973, later re-titled *The Crazies*) dealt with an Army biotoxin that taints the water supply of a small Pennsylvania township, resulting in an epidemic of madness and destruction. As in *Night of the Living Dead*, Romero's protagonists are another cross-section of humanity who spend as much time fighting one another as they do defending themselves from the raving throng. The use of inhospitable rural locations, mistrust of federal and governmental systems of control, and a downbeat ending result in a deeply cynical but perhaps over-familiar film.

*Martin* (1978) is considered by many of Romero's admirers to be his personal masterpiece. An alienated youth (John Amplas), believing himself to be a vampire, acts out his fantasy in a dying Pennsylvania steel town. Another of Romero's trademark regional casts (including his future wife, Christine Forrest, and make-up artist Tom Savini) helped keep the horror refreshingly local. The grim coda, in which Martin's grandfather (Lincoln Maazel) stakes the boy and buries him in the garden, is all the more poignant because his absence will go unnoticed.

With 1978's *Dawn of the Dead*, Romero fashioned a sequel to *Night of the Living Dead* that in every way opposed the original (colour for monochrome, amusing for grim, optimistic for downbeat) and which comes close to being its horrific equal. A gory satire of acquisitive 'Me Generation' values, Romero's zombies besiege survivors barricaded in a suburban shopping mall. *Dawn of the Dead* proved to be Romero's first runaway hit despite being released unrated – a gambit that paid off with substantial returns.

The success of *Dawn of the Dead* paid for Romero's 1981 noble failure, *Knightriders*. A lengthy character-driven road movie about performers in a travelling Renaissance fair who joust astride motorcycles and re-enact the tragedy of Camelot, *Knightriders* is a lovingly acted and photographed film that nonetheless annoyed Arthurians and horror fans, who expected something less personal. Romero was redeemed in the estimation of the latter with his omnibus *Creepshow* (1982), inspired by the horror comics of William Gaines. Working within the comic book style (comic panels, word balloons and so on), *Creepshow* splashed the screen with primary colours and was Romero's second popular success. The film's naughty *élan* was heightened by game performances from such straight-faced theatre actors as Hal Holbrook, Fritz Weaver and E. G. Marshall. Horror novelist Stephen King provided the script and appeared in one of the blackly comic vignettes.

After bringing the anthology series back to television with his 'Tales From the Darkside', Romero returned to cinema for his third, and to date last, instalment of his 'living dead' trilogy – 1985's *Day of the Dead*. Although a more expensive production had been planned (and scripted), Romero was unable to secure the necessary financing, and so *Day of the Dead* is very much a decoction of his earlier themes. The slapstick velocity of *Dawn of the Dead* is grounded – or rather undergrounded, as the drama plays out in a subterranean bunker – between a small team of scientists and the combative remains of a military unit.

The cool critical and box-office reception to *Day of the Dead* no doubt prompted the more commercial *Monkey Shines* (1988), an adaptation of the novel by Michael Stewart. Shot by cinematographer James A. Contner (*Cruising* (1980), *Jaws 3-D* (1983)) and with an original score by David Shire (*Saturday Night Fever* (1977), *Norma Rae* (1979)), *Monkey Shines* – which attends a quadriplegic bedevilled by his own helper monkey – was the first Romero film to look and sound like Hollywood product, which augured ill for the maverick director's 1990s output.

While technically adroit, Romero's subsequent projects suffered a decided lack of personality. Following his dreadful contribution to the 1990 two-part horror film *Two Evil Eyes* (the other half, an inspired updating of Edgar Allan Poe's 'The Black Cat', was directed by Italian giallo maestro Dario Argento), Romero's next film, *The Dark Half* (1993), an adaptation of the Stephen King novel, sat on the shelf for two years before its theatrical release; a passable thriller that benefits from a charismatic dual performance by Timothy Hutton, the film could have been directed by any number of competent craftsmen and bore few of Romero's trademark touches. As if sensitive to this charge, *Bruiser* (2000) concerned a man who wakes up one morning to find he has no face. Disappointingly, the drama morphs rather quickly into a bloody what-if scenario, with the protagonist exacting revenge on those who have wronged him, squandering a fascinating possibility.

Romero's next projects (a slacker vampire film and another adaptation of a Stephen King novel) have languished in 'development hell', while *Resident Evil*, the theatrical adaptation of the popular video game with which Romero had long been associated, finally passed to another director. Romero's legions of undying fans comfort themselves with the prospect of a fourth 'living dead' film, although definitive plans have yet to be made. **RHS**

# Don ROOS

*The Opposite of Sex* (1998)  
*Bounce* (2000)

Don Roos is arguably the best surprise in recent independent film-making. The ferocious satire of family values and political correctness displayed in his directorial debut *The Opposite of Sex* (1998) proved that a straightforward and original vision can achieve popular success. Roos was born in New York in 1955 and began his career in cinema as a writer. Having studied screenwriting at the University of Notre Dame, and then moving to Hollywood in 1978, he spent eight years there working for television, both writing and producing. In 1992 he wrote the screenplay for *Love Field*, for which Michelle Pfeiffer won an Academy Nomination. The role of the housewife travelling to President Kennedy's funeral was in fact just the first of a string of remarkably complex female characters to which Roos gave life. *Single White Female* (1992), adapted from a novel by John Lutz, the road movie *Boys on the Side* (1995), and even the unsuccessful and disappointing remake of Clouzot's classic, *Diabolique* (1996), all featured great lead performances enhanced by a careful characterisation.

Consistent with his seeming specialisation with female-centred stories, Roos' first feature is told and ruled by the voice of Deedee Truitt, its wicked anti-heroine (wonderfully played by Christina Ricci). Turning from the supposedly audience-pleasing canonical mode of his previous stories, Roos breaks all the rules of traditional screenwriting, and introduces the direct narration (rich in flashbacks and deceiving shots) of an extremely unlikeable character.

Owing to the incredible success of *The Opposite of Sex*, Miramax invested considerably in Roos' next project, the romantic drama *Bounce* (2000). Despite starring Ben Affleck and Gwyneth Paltrow, it was not the expected success. The script for the film, once more written by Roos, displays an interesting shift of attention towards the psychology of a male character, and was possibly a little too contemplative for mainstream multiplex audiences.                                          **BP**

# Bernard ROSE

Born in 1960, a graduate of Britain's National Film and Television School, Bernard Rose was the winner of a BBC young film-makers award when he was a teenager. Having made an early feature, the little-seen *Body Contact* (1987), he directed *Paperhouse* (1988), an unusual and ambitious art-house horror movie; an imaginative spin on Wes Craven's *Nightmare on Elm Street* (1984), it concerns a bored child (the creepy Charlotte Burke) who escapes into a fantasy world that quickly turns nightmarish. The effective use of locations, particularly the windswept coast, and am excellent scare (when a photograph springs into life) make it an unusual British horror movie.

Rose's next film, the disappointing *Chicago Joe and the Showgirl* (1990), features Kiefer Sutherland as a GI stationed in London who graduates from petty crime to murder assisted by Emily Lloyd's prostitute. A variation on *Bonnie and Clyde* (1967), it never really takes off and the leads are pretty poor. The chief point of interest is the artificiality of the visual style: even the exterior scenes were shot on a soundstage to the point where it resembles a Hollywood picture from the 1930s or 40s.

Probably Rose's most well-known film, *Candyman* (1992) was an adaptation of a Clive Barker short story, relocated from Liverpool to Chicago's Cabrini Green. Virginia Madsen plays a student researching urban myths who stumbles across the legend of the Candyman, a hook-handed, bee-covered former slave who emerges from a mirror if you say his name five times. This is stylish and creepy horror, brightly lit and with an evocative Phillip Glass score, although it's hard to shake the feeling that Rose thinks he's making something altogether classier than traditional horror fare – *Candyman* is certainly well done and unusual but it doesn't compare to the nasty, sleazy fun of Barker's own *Hellraiser* (1987). That said, the plot offers up some startling twists and Tony Todd's performance as the title character makes him both scary and sympathetic.

The Beethoven biopic *Immortal Beloved* followed in 1994 with Gary Oldman adding the composer to the list of real-life characters he has played effectively – Sid Vicious, Joe Orton, Lee Harvey Oswald. A classical music romance which owes much to Milos Forman's *Amadeus* (1984), the dramatic nature of the music allows Rose to cut loose and his numerous stylistic flourishes are reminiscent of Ken Russell's films about classical composers (*The Music Lovers* (1970), *Mahler* (1974)). *Anna Karenina* (1997) was a bit of a comedown after *Immortal Beloved*'s bombast and style. Yet another version of the Tolstoy classic, despite a few moments of directorial flourish, it too often resembles a high-quality television adaptation.

His most recent film is another Tolstoy adaptation, but the finished result is of considerably more interest. *Ivans xtc* (2000) relocates 'The Death of Ivan Ilyich' to a contemporary Hollywood setting, with Danny Huston (son of John Huston) playing Ivan, a doomed studio executive. Although this covers familiar ground already traversed Robert Altman's *The Player* (1992) and the neglected Joel Silver-produced television show 'Action', Rose's film is notable for marking his shift (with almost evangelical fervour) to digital video – 'Film is dead. Long live cinema', he has commented about the new medium – and Huston's coruscating performance.                                    **IC**

# Dan ROSEN

*The Curve* (1998) Dan Rosen wrote, co-produced, and appeared (as Deputy Hartford) in *The Last Supper* (1996), a black comedy whose pointed critique of faux-liberalism is not pursued with sufficient vigour. His directorial debut *The Curve* (aka *Dead Man's Curve*) (1998) is shot in his native Maryland, where he was born in 1963, and is far more effective in pursuing its dark vision of the human ability to justify outrageous, even murderous, nastiness. Having learned of their college's policy of giving straight 'A' grades to students whose roommates commit suicide, a couple of students set about murdering a friend so they can get the grades they need to get into Harvard; but all is not as it seems...

Superior to the similarly-premised *Dead Man on Campus* (1998), it became the subject of a bidding war at the 1998 Sundance Festival, but this subsequently led to distribution problems. Although the low budget of $750,000 and tight shooting schedule of just 22 days are occasionally evident in the contrast between several stylishly shot sequences and the efficient, rather less slick, camerawork which dominates, this is compensated for by some sharp dialogue, witty intercutting and associative editing, and some gleefully hammy compositions. A tale of teen cruelty, it is full of mean laughs, spot-on pop references, and Matthew Lillard's trademark mugging. Minor characters are entertainingly fleshed out – particularly the college counsellor who is struggling to quit smoking – and some gentle satirical swipes are essayed at immigration policies, victim culture, big business, and the nature of qualifications and employability.            **MB**

# Rick ROSENTHAL

*Halloween II* (1981)<br>*Bad Boys* (1983)<br>*American Dreamer* (1984)<br>*Russkies* (1987)<br>*Distant Thunder* (1988)<br>*Just a Little Harmless Sex*<br>(1999)<br>*Halloween: Resurrection*<br>(2002) Born in New York in 1949, Rick Rosenthal initially trained as an actor at the Beverly Hills Playhouse so it is no surprise that his directorial work has been character-driven, strong on story and emotional development. Rosenthal has directed with equal success in a variety of styles, ranging from horror to melodrama to romantic comedy, consistently displaying a talent for emotive, if rarely groundbreaking, film-making and a fascination with aspects of modern American life.

After a stint of professional acting, he debuted with *Halloween II* (1981), the follow-up to John Carpenter's landmark horror. Rosenthal uses a neo-Gothic setting in a disused hospital and alternates between suspense and violence with skilful editing and use of music, employing steadicam and point-of-view shots both as subjective projections into the mind of Michael Myers and to implicate the audience in the action. The film showcases Rosenthal's technical ability and sensitive direction of young actors, as does *Bad Boys* (1983), a gritty exploration of teenage gang rivalry and the ineffectuality of 'correctional facilities'. This second movie opposes Brian and Moreno, two tough young hoods whose very American impulse toward destructive, macho posturing results in mutual damage – respectively the murder of a friend and the rape of a girlfriend – and a showdown in borstal. A reaction against the bubblegum brat-pack movie, the film uses disturbing violence and highly-charged camerawork, coupled with powerful performances from its young cast, to create an intelligent tragic melodrama; again demonstrating Rosenthal's ability to juxtapose sophisticated emotion with visceral intensity. It also hints at some recurrent themes, particularly the destructive codes of behaviour and social divisions inherent in American society and the consequences of miscommunication and misunderstanding.

The director's next two films make similar points but in much lighter packages. *American Dreamer* (1984) is a romantic comedy, the story of a woman who escapes a dull marriage by writing romance stories and then, during a bout of amnesia, by believing she is the character of her fictions. Displaying a hitherto unseen comic touch bordering on old-style Hollywood farce, Rosenthal mixes romance and screwball mishap with customary emotional candour. *Russkies* (1987) is another comic farce, here aimed at kids, that refreshingly never pretends to be anything else: a group of boys discover a stranded Russian sailor who embodies Communist peril to their parents but another misunderstood companion to them. By no means groundbreaking, these films nevertheless demonstrate Rosenthal's ability to adapt his style, varying pace and direction according to his intended audience, and an astute awareness of the jingoism and restriction of American values. Both films involve an escape from 'normal' American society, either to Europe and a fantasy world in *American Dreamer*, or to the liberated, unprejudiced world of childhood in *Russkies*.

*Distant Thunder* (1988) examines the flipside of Rosenthal's impulse toward escape and the love/hate relationship with America in its story of a Vietnam vet who, shunned by society on his return, escapes to freedom in the wilderness but also abandons his young son. Both a story of father/son reconciliation and of male bonding in the wilderness, the film condemns the America of small-town narrow-mindedness but asserts long-held values of the American myth. Moving landscape photography and typically sound direction of actors make for more thoughtful if undemanding film-making. Rosenthal's character-driven style ensures that his films avoid the pretentiousness of other issue-based film-makers, while his interest in small-scale, economic drama prompted a long-term move into the television direction which had run alongside his film career.

*Just a Little Harmless Sex* (1999), Rosenthal's first feature in the 1990s, was a return to farcical comedy with a self-analysing twist; a comedy drama of a group of men and women whose lack of communication and mutual misunderstanding display his continuing ability to combine social comment with entertainment. His decision to direct the eighth instalment in the interminable *Halloween* series, *Halloween: Resurrection*, can only be considered a step in the wrong direction.      **OB**

# Gary ROSS

Born in 1956, with only a couple of previously produced screenplays to his credit – *Big* *Pleasantville* (1998) (1988, co-written with Anne Spielberg) and *Dave* (1993) – Gary Ross' sensibility as a storyteller is remarkably clear, utilising elements of fantasy (a boy's wish to be grown up is suddenly granted; the ailing President is replaced by his identical double) to spin illuminating morality tales. In *Pleasantville* (1998), his directorial debut, Ross continues in this vein, transforming a simple high-concept hook (two contemporary teenagers are catapulted into the artificial world of a 1950s sitcom) into a cleverly-mounted, deeply-felt parable about freedom, identity, and enlightenment.

*Pleasantville*'s guiding thematic and aesthetic principles hark back to *The Wizard of Oz* (1939), only reflected in a funhouse mirror. Whereas Dorothy Gale's life is forever changed when she leaves her sepia-toned Kansas for the Technicolor Oz, teens David and Jennifer (Tobey Maguire and Reese Witherspoon) are robbed not only of colour, but of any vestiges of their previous existence when they are deposited in Pleasantville's quaint black and white universe of perpetual re-runs and behavioural loops (the town is as clean and airless as a studio backlot, and intentionally so). In the movie's mythology, 'Pleasantville' is a bland sitcom in the mold of 'Leave it to Beaver', but Ross and cinematographer John Lindley give the black and white photography a tone closer to film noir, favouring baroque set-ups from cockeyed wide-angles that have little resonance with the flat, understandably boxed-in compositions of early television.

Ross shows no interest in slavish stylistic recreation because his film, at its core, is not about television – the story's central conceit is that colour slowly bleeds into Pleasantville only after its naïve citizens are exposed to knowledge (of sex, art, literature) that David and Jennifer bring with them from the outside world. In turn, the teens are only restored to colour when they use their time in Pleasantville as a means to enrich their own lives.

*Pleasantville* marks Ross' entry into a select group of film-makers (including James Cameron and Robert Zemeckis) for whom special effects are merely another tool in the director's pallette, always serving to advance the story, yet at the time of its release *Pleasantville* was said to contain more visual effects than any other film in history. Ross even manages to playfully reference his own theme of forbidden knowledge in one simple grace note, as a teenage girl offers Maguire a newly red apple plucked from a still-grey tree.

He is currently involved in a big-budget romantic comedy, *Dog Years*, about a man whose dead wife comes back to haunt him after he falls in love with a younger woman.      **CS**

# Patricia ROZEMA

Born in Ontario in 1958, Patricia Rozema, like many of her Canadian contemporaries, makes films that chart the tension between a character's private, inner life, and the public world s/he inhabits. Crucially, Rozema recognises that plot is as central to locating her characters as their diegetic space. Her literate, mildly austere, non-realist films are never less than affecting and sensual, but they constantly draw attention to their status as stories told through, and driven by, images. This ranks her with such Canadian directors as Atom Egoyan, who sprang from the same late 1980s boom in Canadian cinema.

The tension between desire and environment may stem from her upbringing in a strict Dutch Calvinist home in Southern Ontario. Having decided that storytelling was her route, she studied philosophy and literature at a religious college before going on to work as an intern on a newspaper, covering arts for a Canadian news show and writing screenplays. Six screenplays were rejected but the seventh was made into a 30-minute, 16mm short called *Passion*. She worked as assistant director to David Cronenberg on *The Fly* (1986) before receiving $350,000 for her debut feature, at a point when, bucking its documentary history, Canada began funding features.

Time has worn *I've Heard the Mermaids Singing* (1987) – the title comes from T. S. Eliot's 'The Love Song of J. Alfred Prufrock' – but it remains an often charming blueprint for Rozema's later work. Her intimate focus on Polly Vandersma, an apparently asexual temp, gauche day-dreamer and part-time photographer, nursing a crush on her boss at an art gallery, reveals a typically Canadian taste for inert outsiders whose fantasy lives sit at odds with the world in which they live, while being more intriguing than surfaces suggest. Polly's 'confessions' are delivered straight to camera; she obsessively watches her employer, Gabrielle, on video. If this implies Rozema's fascination with images, or stories about stories, it also maps onto themes of confession and false idolatry that draw subtle parallels between religion and cinema's claims to educate and enlighten.

*I've Heard the Mermaids Singing* is a film about where and how you place your faith, and what getting to know its object entails. In terms of ideas it works, but it's left to Sheila McCarthy's winning portrayal of Polly to carry the can for characterisation. In retrospect, Rozema's taste for images and ideas over stories is too clear. Still, as she likes to catch the moment when voyeuristic, low-key outsiders have the light turned on them, Rozema's low-key film won her acclaim when Cannes gave it the Prix de la Jeunesse. In a nice metatextual twist, the film's success doubled its plot: something seemingly insignificant making its presence felt on something big.

Rozema's next film, *The White Room* (1990), was a harder piece, free from her debut feature's whimsy. This may explain its relative failure, even though it is a stronger film. Inspired by the work of Emily Dickinson, this determinedly experimental movie swaps its predecessor's female protagonist for Norman, a wimpish male voyeur and fledgling artist; this time, a writer. Despite Norman's often unsettling determination to access female experience, Rozema's mysterious art-house movie maintains empathy for her hero.

If Rozema's Gabrielle towered over the introverted Polly, *When Night is Falling* (1995) puts a lesbian spin on the Cupid and Psyche myth to watch a Polly shack up with a Gabrielle. It's a transformation tale in which Camille, a mythology lecturer at a Christian college, slips free of her emotionally frozen life and faintly smug boyfriend to take the spotlight in the Sirkus of Sorts in tentative pursuit of Petra, a wily lesbian performance artist. Despite superb lead performances – Pascale Bussieres and Rachael Crawford turn clunking dialogue into delicacies – it is Rozema's sensuous direction that carries it. Desire seems to be encoded in the film's form; one elegant cut from Petra blowing out a candle to shooting Cupid's arrow through Camille's bedroom window is exquisite.

If Rozema's debut feature recalled Jane Austen's 'Emma' in its tale of an innocent adrift in a world of sham sophisticates, it was no surprise that she turned to Austen for her next feature. Rozema's sure stylistic hand is evident everywhere in *Mansfield Park* (1999), as is her taste for warmly portrayed, watchful outsider heroines and meta-narratives. Bravely, she risked the ire of Austenites by incorporating excerpts from Austen's letters and journals into her film, acknowledging the writer's own self-conscious narrative voice and making the novel's subtexts – primarily slavery and sex – mildly explicit. English tabloids were briefly afroth at this tampering with their heritage heroine, but the film's acute engagement with the novel's themes simply accepts that literary adaptations are always, first and foremost, interpretations. As such, it brings its literary source to life without paralysing reverence and is certainly the most striking of many 1990s Austen adaptations.

Rozema's only work since has further established her standing as a keen adapter of literary works. Commissioned for a series of adaptations of Samuel Beckett's work, *Happy Days* (2000) sees Rozema, by her own admission, staying out of Beckett's way. It is a work of impressive stylistic restraint, with very little in way of cuts and camera movement. And yet it again shows Rozema's sure hand with her female leads, benefiting immensely from Rosaleen Linehan's superb lead performance as a woman trapped in life's day-to-day rituals and making the best of it. It's another underrated, understated gem – let's hope the subsequent silence from Rozema's camp doesn't last.          **KH**

# Joseph RUBEN

Joseph Ruben was born in New York in 1951, and was educated in Theatre and Film at the University of Michigan, later moving to Branders University, Massachusetts. Ruben made his directorial debut at the age of 24 with a stark psycho-drama, *The Sister-in-Law* (1974), the first of several journeys into the world of the American family. Ruben's next feature, *The Pom-Pom Girls* (1976), marked the first of three forays into the pains and joys of teenage life, being followed by *Our Winning Season* (1978), set in the 1960s, and *Gorp* (1980).

In the middle of this period, Ruben took a detour with *Joyride* (1977), a gripping road movie following two young couples who head out to Alaska looking for adventure but instead find themselves slipping into a life of crime. Ruben then tried his hand at science fiction with considerable style and flair. *Dreamscape* (1984) is part science fiction fantasy and part political thriller, and both aspects work well together. The story centres around psychic Alex Garner (Dennis Quaid), who is enlisted to work on an experiment to enter people's dreams. The political conspiracy gets underway when it emerges that the President of the United States is having nightmares about starting World War Three. Psychic 'bad guy' Christopher Plummer sees a way of manipulating the Presidency and sets about infiltrating and influencing the President's dreams. This is a tightly-scripted, intelligent, and at times visually stunning film, and Quaid turns in an excellent performance as the hero, providing an interesting counterpoint to other science fiction/action heroes of the day.

Ruben returned to issues relating to American family life with the underrated horror-suspense movie, *The Stepfather* (1987). Terry O'Quinn's superb performance, as the psychopath with a yearning for the perfect American family, is at the core of this film's success. O'Quinn's character repeatedly fixates on widows with children in an attempt to obtain the perfect family unit. However, since – as the film shows – families are not meant to be perfect, it is not long before the new man of the house is disappointed. Consequently he murders the 'imperfect family' and moves on to the next. Although considered by some critics to be gratuitous, this is, on balance, an unfair criticism as the film is genuinely disturbing. The terror comes from two areas: the escalating and shocking violence of O'Quinn's character in private, and the fact that the children in the film see him for what he really is, while the mothers are oblivious until it is too late.

Ruben followed this with *True Believer* (1989). James Woods turns in a characteristically wired performance as Eddie Dodd, a fading 1960s icon of counter-cultural America who has carved out a niche defending drug dealers. Redemption comes in the form of a Korean man imprisoned for murder. Dodd takes the case, against his own judgement, encouraged by his idealistic young colleague, Roger Baron (Robert Downey Jr). The film spawned a television series in the United States, 'Eddie Dodd'.

The director's next feature was a star vehicle for Julia Roberts and the director's first major commercial success. *Sleeping with the Enemy* (1991) centres on battered wife Sara (Julia Roberts), who escapes from her millionaire control-freak husband Martin (Patrick Bergen) by faking her own death. Sara becomes Laura and moves to Iowa, but it is not long before her husband tracks her down. The film starts well, but soon degenerates into a straightforward cat and mouse tale, where the evil psychopathic husband torments doe-eyed Roberts.

Ruben's next feature, *The Good Son* (1993) sees Ruben continuing his exploration of family life. Yet this time the aggressor is the child. Cast very much against type, Macaulay Caulkin plays Henry Evans, an evil little monster who drowns his baby brother and attempts to murder both his mother and sister. The problem is in the boy's characterisation – critics complained that the script was too sassy and ironic, and the character too prepossessed to be the nine-year-old boy of the film. Despite Caulkin's box-office profile, the film only did a modest trade upon release.

Ruben's next film, *Money Train* (1995) reunited the stars of *White Men Can't Jump* (1992), Wesley Snipes and Woody Harrelson. The unlikely premise for their pairing in this hybrid action/thriller/buddy movie, is that they are brothers: Harrelson's character (Charlie) having been adopted by Snipes' family when just a boy. The pair work together as transit police, and fall for the same woman (Jennifer Lopez). As with *White Men Can't Jump*, Harrelson's character, Charlie, has a gambling problem. Strapped for cash and in trouble with their boss, the pair become involved in the robbery of a train. There is plenty of high-octane action in this film, and enough witty badinage between Snipes and Harrelson to keep the viewer distracted. However, this is a disappointing entry in Ruben's catalogue. The film did good business at the box office but was not considered a triumph by critics.

Ruben's most recent feature, *Return to Paradise* (1998), tells the story of three friends who travel to Malaysia for a wild holiday of sex and drugs. However, one friend (Joaquin Phoenix) is caught by the Malaysian authorities as he tries to smuggle the friends' stash back to the States and is sentenced to death. Two years later the two friends are tracked down by lawyer Beth Eastern (Anne Heche), who tells them they can save their friend's life if they return to Malaysia and admit their part in the crime. The film is a powerful modern morality tale and works largely because of Ruben's crisp but sensitive direction. Despite some encouraging reviews, *Return to Paradise* was not a major box-office success.

Ruben's work is often unfairly overlooked in considerations of 1980s and 1990s American cinema. The director is at his best when dealing with the darker side of family life and, from this perspective at least, his work deserves wider critical attention.    **SL**

# Saul RUBINEK

*Jerry and Tom* (1998)  German-born Saul Rubinek is a noted character actor with numerous screen credits. Notable performances include his Joel Silver-esque movie mogul in *True Romance* (1993) and Beauchamp, the writer who accompanies Richard Harris' Duke of Death in Clint Eastwood's *Unforgiven* (1992). He also has a major role in the acclaimed US sit-com 'Frasier'.

His directorial debut, and sole feature to date, is the dark hitman comedy, *Jerry and Tom* (1998). Joe Mantegna plays Tom, a veteran hitman, and Sam Rockwell is Jerry, his apprentice whose loyalties are divided between friendship and his murderous job. The film superficially resembles other hitmen thrillers with a similar central duo, such as *The Hit* (1985) and *Cohen and Tate* (1988), yet Rubinek's is a mordant and well-made drama, aided by a magnificent cast. Presumably his status as an often undervalued character actor is what led him to fill his film with other unsung actors of great ability. These include the aforementioned leads and Charles Durning, Maury Chaykin, Peter Reigert, William H. Macy, Ted Danson, and newcomer Sarah Polley. Although it is hard to draw conclusions about a director's promise on the strength of one film, Rubinek demonstrates not only a certain efficiency in his style but also an eye for good casting and the ability to handle a dark subject with a light touch.    **IC**

# Alan RUDOLPH

Born in Los Angeles in 1943, Alan Rudolph, the son of director Oscar Rudolph, grew up in the film industry and learnt about film-making from watching studio people at work. A pioneer of independent film-making, he began as an assistant director on television programmes such as 'The Brady Bunch' and 'Love American Style' before directing two low-budget horror films, *Premonition* (1972) and *Nightmare Circus* (1973, under the pseudonym of Gerald Cormier). Rudolph then entered into a collaboration with Robert Altman that would continue throughout his career. He worked as assistant director on three Altman films – *The Long Goodbye* (1973), *California Split* (1974), and *Nashville* (1975).

In his films Rudolph uses a virtual repertory company of actors and relies on plot lines in which character and motivation are often more important than narrative. These are films about people, their emotions and their relationships. It is because of this emphasis that Rudolph constantly struggles to get his films into production and gain distribution.

*Welcome to L.A.* (1977) was Rudolph's first feature of note, starring Keith Carradine and Geraldine Chaplin. The film is about loneliness and alienation, a satire on the lifestyle of a group of characters who are all inhabitants of LA and all connected in some way with a music-writer (Carradine) and his one-night stands. Rudolph's next film, *Remember My Name* (1978), is a noir-melodrama with Geraldine Chaplin as the vengeful but sympathetic woman who gets out of prison and returns to her ex-husband to wreak havoc on his new marriage. Despite a warm critical reception, neither performed well at the box office.

In order to keep working, Rudolph took on a number of studio projects. *Roadie* (1980) is a film about the rock business starring Meatloaf and featuring cameos from artists such as Roy Orbison, Alice Cooper, and Blondie. *Endangered Species* (1982) is a strange conspiracy sci-fi thriller about a mysterious series of cattle killings and *Return Engagement* (1983) is a documentary following Dr Timothy Leary and G. Gordon Liddy on the college lecture circuit. Producer Sydney Pollack then unexpectedly asked Rudolph, at three days' notice, to take on *Songwriter* (1984), a film set in the world of country and western music, starring Kris Kristofferson and Willie Nelson.

Rudolph's third independent feature, *Choose Me* (1984), is considered by some to be his best to date. With music integral to the story, he was beginning to develop his own unique style of film-making. Again starring Keith Carradine and Genevieve Bujold, the action is set in a Los Angeles bar where Dr Nancy Love (Bujold) hosts a radio love line solving the problems of others although she suffers herself from sexual frustration. The fluid camerawork and seductive, yearning ballads of Teddy Pendergrass work to capture the feelings of the characters. Rudolph creates a similar situation in his next film *Trouble in Mind* (1985). This time the hero is played by Kristofferson, a cop who has served time for a killing and, on his release, visits Wanda's Café which is run by an ex-girlfriend (Bujold again). The film takes place in a mythic 'Rain City' with all the characters in search of some kind of fulfilment and music once again central to the plot as a signifier of meaning. Both films are highly stylised and individual with hints of melodrama and film noir.

*Made in Heaven* (1987) was another studio project on which Rudolph was said to have had difficulties with the three producers (two of whom had written the script). The film stars Timothy Hutton and Kelly McGillis in a story about finding perfect love, losing it and trying to recover it in another life. *The Moderns* (1988) stars Rudolph regulars Keith Carradine, Genevieve Bujold, and Geraldine Chaplin in a romantic evocation of the artistic life of 1920s Paris. The film is about people trying to control the creative process by putting a price tag on art. Another personal project, which has the look and style of Rudolph's previous work, it had a mixed critical reception but did not do as well as expected at the box-office. *Love at Large* (1990) is a noir love-story in which a woman hires a detective to follow her lover. Matters become complicated, however, when he follows the wrong man and uncovers a bigamist. *Mortal Thoughts* (1991) is a more mainstream attempt which injects noir elements into a murder mystery and stars Demi Moore and Bruce Willis.

*Equinox* (1992) is a drama about twin brothers separated at birth whose lives become inter-linked. Matthew Modine plays the role of both twins – one a weakling car mechanic, the other a tough guy – who both live and work in the same city, the fictitious, decaying Empire. The two lead parallel lives and their paths constantly cross as their lives become entwined. Set in 1920s New York, *Mrs Parker and the Vicious Circle* (1994) recreates the life of Dorothy Parker, the writer and member of the Algonquin Round Table. Rudolph's reconstruction of the Algonquin pays detailed attention to costume and décor. The lunch scenes are full of one-liners and filmed with huge swoops of the camera. Shot partly in black and white and partly in colour, Rudolph uses the colour to portray the past and stark monochrome for the present. Jennifer Jason Leigh gives an outstanding performance as Parker, and the atmospheric soundtrack by Mark Isham perfectly evokes the period.

*Afterglow* (1997), seen by many as a return to form, was more of a success at the box office than previous Rudolph films (with the exception of *Choose Me*). This was helped no doubt by the Academy Award nomination of Julie Christie, who plays Phyllis, an ex-actress and wife of Lucky (Nick Nolte), a handyman. The couple's love life has been put on hold since their teenage daughter ran away from home years ago and the film parallels their relationship with that of a younger couple. Jonny Lee Miller and Lara Flynn Boyle have their own problems – she wants to get pregnant, he refuses to have sex. The story is a fable about ups and downs in relationships and how the two couples' lives become intertwined.

Rudolph's next film, *Breakfast of Champions* (1999), was a project he had been trying to get off the ground for a number of years but was only made possible when Bruce Willis bought the rights to the Kurt Vonnegut novel and invested a large amount of his own money. Willis stars in the film as Dwayne Hoover, the area's biggest car dealer and star of his own TV commercials, along with Nick Nolte as Dwayne's sales manager, who has a penchant for dressing in women's underwear. The reviews for this film were mixed, thus limiting its theatrical release. For *Trixie* (2000) Rudolph returns to the familiar noir themes of previous work in a comedy-noir-thriller pastiche. Emily Watson stars as Trixie, a security guard who dreams of becoming a fully-fledged private investigator. Her dream comes true when she gets a job to provide security for a resort casino and becomes involved in a plot to blackmail a lecherous right-wing senator, played by Nick Nolte.

Rudolph's most recent film, *Investigating Sex*, is slated for a 2002 release, a film about a group of bohemian men in the 1920s who decided to discuss at length the nature of sex, with their conversations recorded by two female stenographers. It is being produced by Nick Nolte's production company, and also features the actor in his fourth film in a row for Rudolph.

There is a difference between Rudolph's studio films and his more personal, independent films. It is when working on the projects that he initiates himself that he achieves the best results. His personal style as a film-maker is evident in works such as *Choose Me*, *Trouble in Mind*, *Equinox*, *Afterglow*, and *Trixie* in his use of eccentric but 'realistic' characterisations, places and situations, mirrorings, inversions, and evocative music. Throughout Rudolph's work there is a constant return to the themes of film noir, which are re-imagined according to his own style. Rudolph's most personal work has a dreamlike look about it and utilises elements of different genres, reworking them to produce what could be described as post-modern fairytales. He has planned to adapt Jane Smiley's novella 'The Age of Grief'. **PR**

# Chuck RUSSELL

Having written films such as *Dreamscape* (1984), Chuck Russell directed his first feature, *A Nightmare on Elm Street 3: Dream Warriors*, in 1987; comparing it to Wes Craven's superior original, critics were less than impressed, though it was still regarded as an improvement over the second instalment. In 1988, he directed a re-make of *The Blob* (1958), the film that first introduced Steve McQueen to the world as an actor. A rather ridiculous and excessive horror feature, it nevertheless found more favour with audiences than his debut had. His breakthrough came in 1994 with *The Mask*. A story that started out as a popular comic strip about a 'loveable loser' who finds a mysterious mask and is transformed into a crazy alter ego with a green face and yellow suit, Russell adapted the idea into a screenplay and managed to secure Jim Carrey to play the central character, Stanley Ipkiss. The film is full of amazing special effects, which allow an already unrestrained Carrey to contort his facial expressions even further. Cameron Diaz, in her first main role, is perfectly cast as the love interest. *The Mask* delighted audiences; a box-office hit, it made Carrey one the most sought-after actors of the 1990s.

Russell's next feature, *Eraser* (1996), an action film about a witness protection specialist whose charge is targeted by terrorists, failed to generate the same hype, despite the presence of Arnold Schwarzenegger. Undeterred, Russell released the religious horror *Bless The Child* (2001) starring Kim Basinger – a gritty film in the mould of *Stigmata* (1999), it received equally bad reviews. Working in yet another genre, Russell recently directed *The Scorpion King* (2002), riding the success of *The Mummy*

(1999) and *The Mummy Returns* (2001). Starring The Rock (a WWF wrestler), *The Scorpion King* thunders through fight scene after fight scene but fails to create the same tension as *The Mummy*. Still, it has found a large – mostly teen – audience.      **MRo**

# David O. RUSSELL

*Spanking the Monkey* (1994)
*Flirting with Disaster* (1996)
*Three Kings* (1999)

David O. Russell personifies the more radical, risk-taking side of the American film industry today. Born in New York in 1958, Russell utilises the poetics and politics of film form to say something transgressive about American society, while using the camera like a paintbrush.

Russell's first, independently produced film, *Spanking the Monkey* (1994), which was shot for $200,000, with a relatively unknown cast, heralded his arrival as an important, contentious film-maker – one who had a wickedly dark take on the aspirations and lifestyles of the dysfunctional American middle class. The plot dynamic of the film revolves around identity crises and power, concentrating on the sexually repressed Ray (Jeremy Davies), who, having intended to go to Washington for a highly prized medical internship during his summer vacation, instead has to stay at home to look after his hyper-depressed, and also sexually repressed mother (Alberta Watson). The tensions and dramas of this are played out while his bad-mouthed, white-collar travelling salesman father (Benjamin Hendrickson) desperately struggles to flog videotapes all over the USA, accompanied by his mistress, whom the audience only get to see naked or semi-naked in the film, thus compounding the adulterous angst at its heart). The film's narrative heritage resides, in part, in both *The Graduate* (1967), and Arthur Miller's 'Death of a Salesman'.

*Spanking the Monkey*, like all of Russell's films to date, is hybrid in form, mixing genres and mood. It oscillates between supposed lowbrow, gross-out humour (Ray repeatedly tries to 'spank his monkey' – masturbate – in the toilet during the film, only to be constantly interrupted by his howling dog) and the art cinema taboo of incest (Ray makes love to his compliant, teasing mother in one of the film's most powerful scenes). By the end of the film the audience will have witnessed, and in part laughed at, a storyline that explores incest, adultery, violence, attempted murder, and attempted suicide, as the American dream literally implodes on itself. The film won the Audience Award for the Best Picture at The Sundance Festival in 1994.

Russell's second film, *Flirting with Disaster* (1996), shot for $7 million and produced by Miramax, arguably confirms his status as a film-maker who plays around with both generic form and the sugar candy messages found in much of mainstream Hollywood cinema. The film, deliberately defying easy generic classification, could be called a road movie-cum-rites-of-passage-movie-cum-high farce comedy, with a Pedro Almodovar-inspired cast of tongue-in-cheek dysfunctionals! These include bisexual feds, a leggy ex-dancer councillor, counter-culture drop-outs, neurotic parents, and an angst-ridden thirtysomething (played by indie feature regular, Ben Stiller) who dreams of finding his biological parents. The characterisations, dialogue, and slapstick set-pieces help to flesh out a world that is itself fleshed out of real American psychoses. Russell captures much of the chaos of this world with a jerky, hand-held camera that seems, therefore, to be as dysfunctional as the world that it puts under the microscope.

*Three Kings* (1999), shot for $48 million, is Russell's third film and easily his best. *Three Kings* manages to both re-invent the war film, in part by parody, in part by subversion, and to simultaneously undermine the credo of the American military machine and its global politics (that is, perhaps, until the narrative resolution of the film). In terms of plot, there are clear narrative similarities to *Kelly's Heroes* (1970). However, the film has a radical cut-and-mix style of editing (there are few, if any, establishing shots), and through the disorienting mood jumps (from farce to torture, death, comedy, and back again) the audience is left in the push-and-pull state of not knowing how to respond. The sun-dried tones and third-generation colour stock used to photograph some of the explosive action sequences, the time lapse photography, and the hand-held *vérité*-style cinematography produces a film aesthetic that feels hyperreal. More uniquely, the audience get to sensitively but intrusively meet and understand the racial 'other' in the film, outside of the usual reductive stereotypes found in war pictures. As a consequence, *Three Kings* is a film that subverts the ideology of cohesive American military might, and the binary opposition of simple good versus simple evil – the film suggests to the audience that the Gulf War did happen but not in the way imagined by news teams and journalists at the time. Nonetheless, this is a mainstream, big-budget movie, and in a sense the ending gives us back some of the sugar we would expect of conventional narrative film – disappointingly, a happy conclusion just in the nick of time.

Russell remains an enigmatic figure in Hollywood, with a relative slow turnaround in film projects. In 2002 he produced *The Slaughter Rule* (Alex Smith and Andrew J. Smith), and is set to appear as 'himself' in Spike Jonze's *Adaptation* (2002).          **SRe**

# S

## Michka SAÄL

Born in Tunisia in 1957, Michka Saäl emigrated to Montreal in 1979 and studied cinema at the francophone Université de Montréal. Her first short film, *Far from Where* (1991), is about the anxieties of displacement. Saäl reflects on her roots and cultural formation (she is Jewish, raised in Tunis, and educated in Jerusalem and Paris), juxtaposing the grainy black and white images of her retrospection with images in colour from her life in the new city. The poetic subtlety of this documentary, animated by the director's confessional voice-over, established her professionally and brought her the award of the Québec Film Critics' Association.

One of the lucky few immigrant film-makers in Québec, Saäl developed a small but coherent body of work. Her subsequent short fiction and two documentaries again examine the possibilities for emotional and intellectual survival in that imaginary space between cultures that is opened up by the traumatic exile experience. Her first feature fiction film, *The Snail Position* (1999), is presented like lyrical prose full of jazz music. It depicts Myriam, a young Tunisian-Canadian, trying to find peace within herself, with her love for two men and with her father whom she has not seen in twenty years and who reappears in cosmopolitan Montreal. It is a small and quiet film, well shot and acted. Heavily laden with autobiographical references, in many ways it is a continuation of Saäl's quest as an artist and as a feminist to humanise the abstract discourse on difference and identity.                    **CSt**

*The Snail Position /La position de l'escargot* (1999)

## Louis SAÏA

Louis Saïa's successful career proves that the complex issues of local identity – and rarely are they as dizzyingly distinctive as in Québec – can easily fit into that most turgidly international of genres: the sports movie.

*Les Boys* (1997), Saïa's second feature, followed *Le Sphinx* (1995), a movie that established a partnership with actor Marc Messier that has been the dominant feature of his short career. *Les Boys* is the kind of sophomore success that directors dream of: it broke record after record at the Québec box office, and no native film has ever been

*Le Sphinx* (1995)
*Les Boys* (1997)
*Les Boys II* (1998)
*Les Boys III* (2001)

as successful. Robert Lepage (*Le Confessional* (1995), *Nô* (1998)) may be the most talented Québecois film-maker, but Saïa is the successful son, who in realising that status has strung *Les Boys* into a series of sequels, all of which enjoy success at home but obscurity outside the province.

*Les Boys* and its sequels are about an amateur ice hockey team, who talk politics and sex in the bar, after manfully crunching their way around the rink. They win the final game, of course, and all is neatly resolved. Call that a metaphor for the quest for provincial independence, but only at a stretch – the genre requires the triumphal resolution more urgently than the politicised audience. Ice hockey is an exciting sport, exciting enough that its visual nature (and this could easily apply to other team sports) is sufficiently spectacular without the dynamics of editing – in other words it is naturally suited to the fixed camera positions of television, where its drama forges a kind of natural heroism lost on the big screen. For proof of that try and imagine Wayne Gretsky (ice hockey's greatest ever player) up there, twenty metres high. Diminutive and plain, the heroism of appearance that cinema serves so well is lost on the heroism of action that Gretsky, like George Best, like Joe Montana, embodies.

*Les Boys II* took the amateurs away from Québec to an international tournament in Chamonix in the French Alps – and the mix of authentic French and the bizarre accent found in the province (essentially French with a Canadian accent, which leads to all kinds of strange pronunciations), gave a frisson to a film that was only a minor revision of the original, this time with a slightly increased romantic context. All the actors remained, and a kind of family atmosphere permeated the whole: there is a sense that *Les Boys* could become a Québecois feature film version of 'Cheers', America's long-running, successful comedy that had the same mix of talk, beer and sexual longing, only without the ice. Saïa has already completed *Les Boys III* (2001) and is currently at work on another. **CSo**

# Eduardo SANCHEZ
See **Daniel MYRICK**

# Mike SARGENT

*Personals* (1998) The trend of the indie auteur is nowhere better illustrated than by Mike Sargent. As director and writer of his first feature film, the independently financed and very individual *Personals* (1998), Sargent represents all that is good about low-key American film-making: comic timing, vibrant writing, and sheer enthusiasm for the medium.

The film is the story of a two-timing journalist who, sacked from his job and ditched by both girlfriends, embarks on a series of blind dates prompted by personal ads placed under his real name and his pseudonym. Part romantic comedy, part character satire, the film toys with issues of modern relationships: miscommunication, identity, and gender politics. Sargent throws his womanising central character into an array of comic mismatches – including a Plathesque manic depressive poet and a politicking black woman with a hang-up about Whoopi Goldberg – which will form the basis of his comeback story. Sargent displays admirable imagination in the variety and acuteness of his characterisations – which range from caricature to cliché – while the literate dialogue, deadpan humour and invocation of date movies past and present illustrate his indie credentials. The refusal to succumb to the sanitising influence of political correctness also demonstrates Sargent's individual approach. He revels in the absurdities and self-obsessiveness of people, things normally excised from popcorn romantic comedies, resulting in a truthful, genuinely funny directorial style. With gross-out farces and formulaic rom-coms dominating the current style of Hollywood comedy, an intelligent voice like Sargent's fulfils its 'independent' mantle in more ways than one. **OB**

# John SAYLES

*Return of the Secaucus 7* (1980) Born in Schenectady, New York in 1950, John Sayles, prolific writer, actor and producer, has retained a reputation as a truly inventive and versatile independent Hollywood
*Lianna* (1983) director for the past twenty years. Initially financing his low-budget productions by writing
*Baby It's You* (1983) scripts for Roger Corman exploitation films (*Piranha* (1978), *Alligator* (1980)), Sayles

continues to produce mainly thoughtful political movies funded through independent sources. For the most part his films are allegorical in content, socialist in perspective, and generally focus on communities under threat from the external and internal forces of capitalism, imperialism, and patriarchy. Describing himself as a 'conduit for people's voices', Sayles is often criticised for being overtly sentimental and nostalgic because of his romantic notions concerning the common man. Yet his films, from an industrial and thematic perspective, remain examples of how, with conviction and self-belief, a Hollywood director need not be a slave to a corporate money-making system.

Sayles' directorial debut was *Return of the Secaucus 7* in 1980. It is an unassuming film about the reunion of seven college friends who shared the angst-ridden revolutionary optimism of 1960s campus life but have all chosen different paths since graduation. The film's simplistic façade, however, belies its narrative complexity of vision. Sayles creates – through dialogue alone – a satire on the shallowness of the human spirit, which questions the prevalent mythology of revisionism and radicalism attributed to the 1960s. The film was so inspired that it earned Sayles a 'genius' grant from the MacArthur Foundation that helped to finance future projects.

Sayles' next two films serve to demonstrate his versatility as a genre-hopping director. Both *Lianna* (1983) and *Baby It's You* (1983) are bittersweet romances that analyse the sexual, class, and gender politics inherent in intimate contemporary human relationships. *Lianna* is the more gritty realist drama of the two and is one of the first in a line of 1980s lesbian coming-out movies, while *Baby It's You* is a more whimsical teenage love story, giving Matthew Modine his first big screen break.

Changing generic tack again in 1984, Sayles released the critically well received *The Brother From Another Planet*. The film stars Joe Morton as a black extra-terrestrial slave who escapes his masters only to literally come crashing down to earth in Harlem, New York. Sayles uses the popular generic form of science fiction fantasy to forge a social commentary on the plight of illegal 'aliens' in the US. Unable to understand the language of this strange world the alien, like the immigrant, experiences the innate racial prejudices of a discriminatory and hostile inner-city society. Prejudice and intolerance would again prove to be key themes in his next film, *Matewan* (1987).

A period piece set in a small mining community in the 1920s, *Matewan* is not only a compelling and compassionate drama, but quite simply a remarkably adept piece of storytelling. Focusing on a labour dispute between miners and mine owners, the film draws its power from an impressive symbiosis of the three components that Sayles himself considers essential to successful narrative film-making, creating an adept combination of literary, theatrical, and cinematic elements. Epic in proportion, and beautifully shot by Haskell Wexler, the only real criticism to be levelled at this film is the highly conventional and melodramatic distinctions between the good of the union men and the evil of the corrupt bosses.

Sayles continued to explore the question of labour disputes and corruption in a tight-knit community with his baseball period piece *Eight Men Out* (1988). Based on the infamous 'Black Sox' scandal of 1918, the film contextualises the scandal as a calamitous by-product of a bitter labour dispute between the players and their then all-powerful team owners. The film is wistfully nostalgic and explores the human tragedy of the events that would eventually lead to the banishment of distinguished players, such as 'Shoeless' Joe Jackson, a figure later depicted in *Field of Dreams* (1989).

In his next feature, *City of Hope* (1991), Sayles manages to integrate the thematic threads of his previous films into one narrative. The film is a complex canvas of epic proportions. In parts it is a political commentary on inner city political corruption, while also an Oedipal tragedy, a romance and a sprawling exposition on the tensions of modern urban life. Altmanesque in proportions, the film interweaves parallel narratives with such dexterity that the central theme of change through collective understanding and action is never lost under the weight of diversity.

Sayles abandoned the worthy, sweeping gestures of *City of Hope* for his next project, *Passion Fish* (1992), a microcosmic melodrama focusing on the relationship between a disabled woman (Mary McDonald) and her care assistant (Alfre Woodard). The strength of the film is that it is stripped of the saccharine sweet sentimental charm that Hollywood normally imposes on this particular type of women's picture. The film is an often humorous and moving account of friendship developing across class and cultural divides. Although not hugely successful at the box office the film was to receive two Academy nominations: one for McDonald as Best Actress and one for Sayles for Best Original Screenplay.

In 1994 Sayles turned his hand to children's films with the release of *The Secret of Roan Inish*. Adapted from Rosalie Frye's novella, it is a film made with the oral tradition of storytelling in mind. Using little or no special effects it is Sayles' mythically lyrical answer to the pleasures offered to children by video game culture. Equally, oral tradition proves central to Sayles' next film *Lone Star* (1996). Set near the Mexican border the film examines the romanticisation of the American West through popular mythology. The film, a western/thriller hybrid, uses an elaborate mix of flashbacks, recounted stories and parallel narratives in order to convey its point that history is often corrupt and deceptive and can affect contemporary attitudes for the worse.

*Men With Guns* (1997) continues Sayles' examination of native communities under threat, this time from the dogma of imperialist and late-capitalist principles. A deeply political movie, the film is an allegorical odyssey of self-discovery for its main protagonist Dr Fuentes (Fedrico Luppi), who embarks on a journey into the rural hinterland of Latin America to visit some former students. He discovers a world of corruption and greed where people are literally reduced to commodities and whole communities of impoverished Indians are systematically wiped-out by Men With Guns.

Sayles followed *Men With Guns* with his most surprising film to date, *Limbo* (1999). The film begins in conventional Sayles territory as an exploration of borders – both geographic and emotional – but soon evolves into a thriller and eventually plays out as a tense psychodrama. Set in Alaska, Sayles himself refers to the film as 'a condition of unknowable outcome'. In terms of theme it is a fitting tribute to his exploration of familial tensions in a remote, barren, and often austere community setting.

Sayles continues his journey through both the state and States of America, with *Sunshine State* (2002). Set in Florida, the film stars Angela Bassett and Edie Falco as two women returning to their hometowns, after their dreams of success have deserted them. Battling against family ties and memories of what they once were, as opposed to what they are now, Sayles' film begins modestly, building gradually into an account of small-town life and the often destructive nature of the family unit. With echoes of *Passion Fish* and the more expansive *Lone Star* and *City of Hope*, it is one of the director's warmest and entertaining films.

Sayles' work to date has been both continually inspired and informed by a distinct political agenda. This tendency towards a didactic style of film-making has produced adverse criticism, yet it remains his strength as an independent director. Sayles' films are maybe over-long at times, politically rigorous, and nostalgically Hemingway-esque in their depiction of the tensions inherent in communities, yet they remain intelligent and resourceful homilies to both independent film-making funding and technique.

He has recently completed *Casa de Los Babys*. The story of six women who travel to South America to adopt babies and find they are forced, by law, to live there, the film stars Daryl Hannah, Lili Taylor, Mary Steenburgen, Rita Moreno, Maggie Gyllenhaal and Marcia Gay Harden.                                                                                      **PH & IHS**

# Eric SCHAEFFER

Born in New York in 1962, Eric Schaeffer acts in, writes, and directs New York-based quirky romances, like a bargain basement Woody Allen. Although the quality of their respective output varies wildly, Schaeffer has gone one step further than Allen to exert control over his output by forming his own production company, Five Minutes Before the Miracle.

*My Life's in Turnaround* (1993) was Schaeffer's debut, co-written with Donal Lardner Ward, and starring both as desperate would-be film-makers. They attempt to meet celebrities (including Phoebe Cates), encounter a venal producer (a funny cameo by independent icon John Sayles), and flounder around in the netherworld of low-budget Hollywood. As films about film-making go, *My Life's in Turnaround* hasn't got the bitterness of Robert Aldrich's *The Big Knife* (1955) or the wonder of *Day for Night* (1973), but is rather an amiable, slightly self-indulgent romp in the mould of *The Big Picture* (1989) and *Living in Oblivion* (1995).

The inoffensive charm of this debut is largely absent from his second film, *If Lucy Fell* (1996). A slacker, generation-X take on the romantic comedy, the silly story has two friends (Sarah Jessica Parker and Schaeffer himself) who vow to jump off the Brooklyn bridge if they are still single at thirty. Despite the presence of Ben Stiller (who is not at his best here) and Parker, the result is lightweight and the characters irritating. Schaeffer plays an artist who becomes passionate about supermodel Elle MacPherson, which only serves to reinforce the impression of *If Lucy Fell* as a vanity project.

*Fall* (1997) was a slight improvement. Again, the director plays the lead, a writer-turned-quirky New York City cabbie. He starts an affair with a supermodel (an embarrassing Amanda de Cadenet) while her boyfriend is out of the country. Although considerably more stylish than his previous effort, this is still dull fare. *Fall* seems to be striving for something more profound than a relationship drama but remains undemanding. While actor-writer-directors such as Woody Allen and Albert Brooks rely on humour to deflect any suspicion that they may be producing vanity projects, Schaeffer's films aren't funny enough.

*Wirey Spindell* (1999) was based on the first screenplay the director wrote. More ambitious in scope than its predecessors, it explores the anxieties of the eponymous protagonist as his wedding day approaches. The film revisits different experiences from various stages of his life to illuminate the causes of his (many) problems – this includes the seven-year-old Wirey as an actively bisexual heavy drinker. Although a worthy attempt to step outside of his usual creative sphere, ragged and undisciplined as it is, *Wirey Spindell* ultimately doesn't work.

Schaeffer's most recent film, *Never Again*, was released in the US in 2001. A familiar 'rom-com with a twist' – that the lovelorn protagonists, Christopher and Grace, are middle-aged – it features a great veteran cast, including Jill Clayburgh, Jeffrey Tambor, and Bill Duke, who lend his work film necessary bite. Treading familiar comedy ground, although Schaeffer's ambitions as a director are admirable, his worthy intentions often lead to films that are messy and self-indulgent. **IC**

# Fred SCHEPISI

Born in Australia in 1939, Fred Schepisi symbolises what became known as the Australian New Wave in the 1970s, although he actually started out as a documentary film-maker and producer of television commercials in Australia in the early 1960s. He directed a short called *The Party* (1970) and contributed an episode called 'The Priest' to the film *Libido* (1973). He turned to features in 1976 with *The Devil's Playground*, which, like 'The Priest', was set in a Catholic seminary and focused on sexual repression and moral indoctrination. Along with his second feature, *The Chant of Jimmie Blacksmith* (1978) – about a young Aboriginal man who embarks on a killing spree as a result of racial subjugation at the hands of whites – the film reflected a rather jaundiced view of an isolated and inward-looking Australian culture. Released in the US in 1980, *The Chant of Jimmie Blacksmith* enabled Schepisi to make the transition to Hollywood, where he followed in the footsteps of fellow Australian directors Peter Weir and Bruce Beresford.

His first American feature, a western, was the interesting but commercially unsuccessful *Barbarosa* (1982), which follows the friendship between a Texan outlaw (Willie Nelson) and a farm boy (Gary Busey). Like *Barbarosa* and *The Chant of Jimmie Blacksmith*, Schepisi's next American feature, *Iceman* (1984) – about a scientist on a polar expedition who discovers a living prehistoric man – concentrated on the outsider. The generally kind critical reception of *Iceman* led to him being immediately offered the film adaptation of David Hare's stageplay 'Plenty'. With Academy Award-winning star Meryl Streep taking on the central role of Susan Traherne who the ex-Resistance fighter who finds it difficult to adapt to post-war Britain and what she sees as its stifling conformity, *Plenty* (1985) was Schepisi's first big commercial success.

As with *Barbarosa*, Schepisi collaborated (uncredited) on the screenplay, fashioning a film that capitalised on some excellent supporting performances – in particular John Gielgud's depiction of imperious diplomat Sir Leonard Darwin. In many ways the film's weakness is its coldness, particularly that of Streep's performance, which, despite displaying all of her technical prowess, nevertheless fails to engage the audience. However, the film seemed instrumental in cementing Schepisi's considerable technical ability with its use of widescreen images, in particular the way Schepisi's camera exacerbates Susan's growing detachment from the world and the people around her.

*Plenty* also seemed to echo the themes of Schepisi's previous two American films, exploring the isolated and trapped individual.

His next feature, the romantic comedy *Roxanne* (1987), was in some ways a marked departure in content and form, although once again the film was a star vehicle, this time for Steve Martin, who also penned the script based on 'Cyrano de Bergerac'. Again, the film centres on an outsider, but this time with altogether less depressing results, and the film was a commercial hit. After this dalliance with comedy, Schepisi returned both to a more serious study of outsiders and Australia in *A Cry in the Dark* (aka *Evil Angels* (1988)). The film, co-scripted by Schepisi, was based on the true story of Lindy Chamberlain (played by Meryl Streep), who was accused of murdering her baby but insisted that it had been carried off by a dingo whilst the family were camping near Ayers Rock. *A Cry in the Dark* centred upon the critique of difference and how this clashes with notions of conformity, themes that seem to run throughout much of Schepisi's work. Although not an international commercial success on the scale of *Roxanne*, *A Cry in the Dark* was well received critically. Streep's characterisation of Lindy Chamberlain was far removed from the typical performance of a major Hollywood film star; playing husband Michael, Sam Neill's resemblance is remarkable.

*The Russia House* (1990), based on John le Carré's novel, represents the apotheosis of Schepisi as director of big-budget star vehicles, and in many ways signalled his decline as an interesting and reflexive director. Sean Connery plays a publisher who meets a Russian woman (Michelle Pfeiffer) and becomes drawn into a complex espionage plot to deliver a report on Russia's nuclear capability to British and US intelligence services. Connery's performance notwithstanding, *The Russia House* seems rather devoid of the kind of complex and dynamic characterisation that marked out Schepisi's best work. *The Russia House* also saw Schepisi return to production, which would continue with his next feature, *Mr Baseball* (1992), the story of an ageing baseball player who goes to Japan to play. The film was a vehicle for Tom Selleck, who played the title role. Schepisi's least personal film to date, and his least visually and emotionally arresting, it might be best described as workmanlike.

This engagement with difference was carried through into his next feature, *Six Degrees of Separation* (1993), an adaptation of John Guare's stage play and co-produced by Schepisi. The film is about a well-to-do New York society couple, the Kittredges, who are taken in by Paul, a young man professing to be both a friend of their sons from Harvard and Sidney Poitier's son. As in *Plenty*, Schepisi has to work hard to overcome the film's stage origins, perhaps too hard since so much of the screenplay involved the Kittredges addressing the theatre audience directly, while Schepisi has them address a variety of groups of friends as if they were holding court. On screen it is Schepisi's camera work that compensates, with excellent use of widescreen images of both New York's exteriors and interiors.

He seemed to be treading water with his next film, *I.Q.* (1994), a romantic comedy in which Albert Einstein assists a garage mechanic in wooing his niece, which is a pleasant if totally inconsequential piece. His next outing as director was *Fierce Creatures* (1997), although this was, more accurately, as co-director: he was brought in by writer, star, and producer John Cleese (with whom he was having discussions about playing Don Quixote) to shoot additional scenes, including a new ending. These had been deemed necessary because of poor test screenings, while original director Robert Young was by then unavailable.

*Last Orders* (2001), Schepisi's subsequent film, has seen him return triumphantly to cinemas with his adaptation of Graham Swift's Booker Prize-winning novel, about a group of working-class friends from London, Ray (Bob Hoskins), Vic (Tom Courtenay), and Lenny (David Hemmings), who travel to Margate to scatter the ashes of their dead friend Jack (Michael Caine) along with Vince (Ray Winstone), Jack's son. Eschewing the complex (and un-filmable) structure of the novel, Schepisi's screenplay has the audience join the men on their journey from the capital and, through a series of flashbacks, examines their relationships going right back to World War Two. Alongside, the film focuses in particular on the memories of Ray and Amy (Jack's wife, played brilliantly by Helen Mirren), who had a brief love affair. With such a wonderful ensemble cast, Schepisi's film offers a poignant and utterly authentic meditation on the importance of memory, both individual and collective, whilst detailing a working-class milieu that never panders to soap opera-style clichés.

He is currently in production with *Smack in the Kisser*, a comedy starring Kirk, Michael, and Cameron Douglas, about the attempts of a dysfunctional family at reconciliation. **SH**

# John SCHLESINGER

John Schlesinger's films have brought a dazzling array of dreamers, losers and fighters to the screen; a character of contradictions, he describes himself as 'a romantic cynic'. Born in London, UK, in 1926, he was subsequently educated at Balliol College, Oxford. When World War Two interrupted his studies, he joined the Combined Services Entertainment Unit. During this time he made an amateur film, *Horrors*, and upon resuming his studies, chose to follow an acting career, joining the Oxford University Dramatic Society and becoming president of the Oxford Experimental Theatre Company. An encounter with Roy Boulting during Schlesinger's acting career re-ignited his interest in film-making. This led to a 15-minute documentary, *Sunday in the Park* (1956), that in turn attracted the attention of the BBC.

Schlesinger went on to make a series of documentaries for the BBC – 26 in total – most notably *Terminus* (1961), an acutely observed documentary about visitors to London's Waterloo Station. *Terminus* went on to enjoy commercial distribution and won a Venice Film Festival Golden Lion Award and a British Academy Award.

His first feature, *A Kind of Loving* (1962), is a social realist text based on the novel by Stan Barstow that uses locations in the industrial north of England. The film is the first indication that Schlesinger's oeuvre was concerned with character observation – the politics of the personal rather than the social. The story centres on Vic Brown (Alan Bates), who embarks on a relationship with Ingrid Rothwell (June Ritchie); when it fails the couple go their separate ways, until Ingrid tells Vic she is pregnant. They marry and move in with Ingrid's mother (Thora Hird). The marriage is an unhappy one and Vic takes up the 'angry young man' mantle. Like all angry young men, Vic grows up, and he and Ingrid walk off into the uncertain, smog-filled horizon, hand in hand.

Schlesinger's next feature, *Billy Liar!* (1963) tells the story of Billy Fisher (Tom Courtenay), a young man in a dead-end, routine job. Billy is ambitious but lazy. Without sufficient application in the real world, he lapses into moments of fantasy. The film features fine performances from a solid British cast including Courtney, Julie Christie and Wilfred Pickles. *Darling* (1965) also starred Julie Christie, this time as the hip youngster, Diana Scott. Diana is never satisfied and flits from modelling, through acting and into the arms of an Italian prince via a series of affairs, flings and an orgy. Her voice-over narration should bring us closer to the workings of Diana's mind, but the superficiality of her character prevents the audience from empathising with her. The film is strangely disjointed because of this, but the superb performances that Schlesinger extracts from his cast, the tight editing, and the film's style and settings make this a classic of 1960s British cinema. *Darling* won several Academy Awards – Best Actress (Christie), Story and Screenplay (Frederic Raphael), and Costume Design (Julie Harris).

Schlesinger's next project, *Far From the Madding Crowd* (1967), again starred Julie Christie and Alan Bates in a big-screen adaptation of the novel by Thomas Hardy. The film elicits exceptional performances from its principle cast members, including Christie, Bates, Peter Finch, and Terence Stamp. Lovingly recreated and beautifully shot, the film never achieved the critical acclaim it deserved. *Midnight Cowboy* (1969), however, brought Schlesinger international recognition. With his interest in characters re-ignited, the result is two of the most moving characterisations in contemporary cinema. The film follows the fortunes of Joe Buck (Jon Voight), a young country boy who heads for the bright lights of New York to make it at as a gigolo. He is soon down on his luck and reluctantly pairs up with Enrico 'Ratso' Rizzo (Dustin Hoffman), who teaches him how to survive in the city. New York is filmed as a grimy, seedy, and shallow place. The film was praised for its realism upon release, but has since been criticised for its perceived anti-Americanism. However, the setting could, broadly speaking, be any big city in industrialised society, where poverty and deprivation are neighbours with wealth and opulence. Schlesinger employs many interesting camera techniques in the film. Described in recent years by some critics as 'gimmicky', the experimental work was bold and compelling. *Midnight Cowboy* won several Academy Awards – Best Director, Best Screenplay for Waldo Salt, and Best Picture, the first X-rated film to do so. *Midnight*

*Cowboy* is an influential and powerful film, and its impact can be seen in films such as Jerry Schatzberg's gritty *Panic in Needle Park* (1971), Susan Seidelman's *Smithereens* (1982), and Gus Van Sant's *Drugstore Cowboy* (1989).

Schlesinger returned to the UK for *Sunday Bloody Sunday* (1971) to continue his exploration of characters at crossroads in their lives – only in this film, their roads are intertwined. It centres on an unusual love triangle between divorcee Alex Greville (Glenda Jackson), a gay doctor, Daniel Hirsh (Peter Finch), and their mutual lover, a young sculptor, Bob Elkin (Murray Head). The film received a muted critical response but did respectable business at the box office. He also directed the final segment in *Visions of Eight* (1973), a compendium of eight different directors' views of the 1972 Olympic Games in Munich, including Milos Forman, Arthur Penn, and Mai Zetterling.

Schlesinger followed with *The Day of the Locust* (1975), an adaptation of a Nathaniel West novel, about the underbelly of Hollywood in the 1930s. The film received mixed reviews upon its release and was not a major box-office success. Better known is *Marathon Man* (1976), an adaptation of the popular novel by William Goldman. Schlesinger is reunited with Dustin Hoffman, who plays young Jewish graduate Babe Levy, foiling a gang of Nazi thieves in New York. The film is as fast-paced and furious as thrillers come and features perhaps the most painfully memorable scene of cinematic dentistry in film history. His next feature, *Yanks* (1979), took American GIs stationed in Britain during World War Two as its subject. While it creates a certain rosy nostalgia that some critics saw as pandering to American audience sensibilities, *Yanks* is effective but too long and overly sentimental in places.

If *Midnight Cowboy* was Schlesinger's high point then *Honky Tonk Freeway* (1981) has to be his all-time low. A comic road movie, it has the dubious honour of nearly bankrupting the studio. Schlesinger never attempted another comedy in his film-making career. Licking his wounds from his *Honky Tonk* experience, he then embarked on two projects for British television, *An Englishman Abroad* (1983), and *Separate Tables* (1983), an adaptation of Terence Rattigan's play.

His next big feature, *The Falcon and the Snowman* (1984), was based on the true story of two young Americans who sold America's secrets to the Soviet Union. Plot is secondary to characterisation and there are echoes of *Midnight Cowboy* in the relationship between clean-cut government office boy, Christopher Boyce (Timothy Hutton), and his jumpy, drug-dealing friend and co-spy, Daulton Lee (Sean Penn). *The Falcon and the Snowman* was well-received, particularly in the US.

*The Believers* (1987) marks the director's only foray into the horror genre. It has some slick moments, and Schlesinger shows how adept he is at manipulating audience emotions. However, despite the presence of Martin Sheen, it is a disappointing film. His form rallied again in his gentle and intelligent film, *Madame Sousatzka* (1988). Once again, plot takes a back seat as Schlesinger takes his time to explore the relationship between an eccentric piano teacher of Russian decent, Madame Sousatzka (Shirley MacLaine), and her young student Manek (Navin Chowdhry).

Schlesinger's next project, *Pacific Heights* (1990), might be best described as a 'yuppie nightmare film'. The film centres on a young couple (played by Melanie Griffith and Matthew Modine), who buy a property and rent out a couple of the apartments. Enter Carter Hayes (Michael Keaton), the tenant from hell, who arrives complete with jig-saw, to make their lives a misery. The problem with *Pacific Heights* is the lack of back-story, leaving us to guess as to why Keaton's character is so off-kilter. *A Question of Attribution* (1992), an espionage thriller based on the Burgess-Maclean-Philby spy scandal, starred James Fox. *The Innocent* (1993) was a German/UK co-production. A Cold War spy thriller, it is unusual in its emotional force; the central protagonist is a young British engineer (Campbell Scott), caught between the seductive influence of a German agent, Maria (Isabella Rossellini), and the duplicitous, fast-talking CIA man, Bob (Anthony Hopkins). Despite its respectable status, *The Innocent* did not achieve release in the States until 1996. He followed with *Cold Comfort Farm* (1995), which was made for the BBC.

Schlesinger's next feature was the brutal would-be post-feminist vigilante shocker, *Eye for an Eye* (1996). The film re-works the *Death Wish* (1974) scenario by making the avenging parent the mother (Sally Field), whose daughter is murdered by the irredeemably evil Robert Doob (Kiefer Sutherland). Often described as 'exploitative', the film certainly milks every negative emotion and the attack scenes are rather grisly, but it is redeemed by some interesting and imaginative camera work and lighting, and strong performances from Sutherland and Field. However, as a film it looks like a better-than-average television movie, lacking the grandeur of some of Schlesinger's earlier work.

His most recent feature, *The Next Best Thing* (2000), did good business at the box office, but drew mixed reactions from critics. The title refers to the unconventional family created when Abbie (Madonna), a straight yoga instructor, and Robert (Rupert Everett), a gay horticulturalist, conceive a child after one drunken night of passion. They agree to stay together to raise the child; all goes well until Abbie falls in love with Ben (Benjamin Bratt) and is given a chance to form the 'traditional' family. *The Next Best Thing* is a well-meaning, credible attempt to explore contemporary definitions of 'family', raising difficult questions within a mainstream context. It nudges tentatively at boundaries, not merely in terms of its themes, but also through its use of multi-generic narrative. The film has all the hallmarks of romantic comedy, but soon becomes a mixture of tragedy, courtroom drama and melodrama – a kind of 'Will and Grace'/*Kramer vs Kramer* (1979) hybrid. It is in the handling of these diffuse elements that Schlesinger ultimately fails. The majority of the film's detractors, however, chose to focus on the performance of Madonna, applying the usual adjectives to her acting style – wooden, lightweight and amateurish.

Schlesinger's contribution to cinema has been remarkable and enduring: an innovator in documentary early on in his career, a contributor to the British New Wave, and the director of some of the most influential international contemporary films. Many of his films have been interpreted from various political standpoints by critics and theorists. Yet, surprisingly, Schlesinger professedly has little interest in politics or social messages: 'I agree with Goldwyn – if you want to send a message send it Western Union.'     **SL**

# Rob SCHMIDT

It is rare these days for directors to come to film with some background in the less glamorous parts of the industry, but Rob Schmidt, before his debut in 1999 with *Saturn*, had worked in those two brilliantly named jobs down near the bottom of the ladder: grip and gaffer. That route in is neatly old-fashioned, like a relic from the days when working your way up was the only means to make it in movies. The two films Schmidt has made so far, however, are old-fashioned in a different way – old in the way film trends can seem instantly past their sell-by date.

*Saturn* stars Scott Caan as a young man caring for his Alzheimers-ridden father. He meets an old friend who tempts him into a lurid world of drug dealing, and a wild sexual relationship with the obligatory girl, played here by Mia Kershner. Part Abel Ferrara, part movie-of-the-week, the film did enough business on video to secure Schmidt a higher-profile gig in Hollywood for *Crime and Punishment in Suburbia* (2000).

There have been some odd ideas and some bad ideas in the recent trend for teen-movie updates of literary classics, and *Crime and Punishment in Suburbia* is both of these, transplanting Dostoyevsky's tortured man in search of salvation wholesale into the body of a high-school girl. The original title of the piece was in fact *Crime and Punishment in High School*, and despite the film's laudable attempts to darken a breezily banal genre, the absurdity of that original title, another ten steps down the line from the film's already ridiculous name, shows the sad confusion of its intentions.

Schmidt is currently in production with *Wrong Turn*, a horror film about six teenagers that become trapped in the woods of West Virginia.     **CSo**

*Saturn* (1999)
*Crime and Punishment in Suburbia* (2000)

# Julian SCHNABEL

Born in New York City in 1951, and trained at the University of Texas, the 'neo-expressionist' Julian Schnabel has built a reputation for himself as the 'self-proclaimed lion of the New York art world': a painter, sculptor, and now writer, director and musician, Schnabel found his niche in the avant-garde of New York's 1980s art scene. Using his experiences and choosing a subject he knew well, Schnabel wrote and directed his first feature, *Basquiat* (1996), the biopic of young painter Jean-Michel Basquiat, who was famed for his graffiti-style paintings, adored by the art world crowd, patronised by the wealthy dealers and collectors, and died of an overdose at 27. Schnabel is a passionate but often overwhelming presence – he writes, includes his family in significant roles,

*Basquiat* (1996)
*Before Night Falls* (2000)

composes the score, and casts a well-preserved Gary Oldman as his alter ego. The inclusion of a first-rate cast of American independent film actors (including Michael Wincott, Benicio Del Toro, Willem Dafoe, and Parker Posey) results in some strong performances, but these are sometimes undermined by the occasionally clumsy visual metaphor, including the recurring 'surfer dude' image over the Manhattan skyline, and clichéd dialogue.

After creating the original artwork for Wim Wenders' *The Million Dollar Hotel* (2000), Schnabel directed *Before Night Falls* (2000), about the poet and novelist Reinaldo Arenas, who is played by Javier Bardem in a universally acclaimed performance. Another lavish biopic about a passionate and pained artist, and the relationship between creation and self-destruction, the film covers similar ground to *Basquiat*. It is also bolstered by a collection of cameos, notably from Johnny Depp, and marked once again by Schnabel's energy and zeal. Episodic in structure, it presents its world with a commendable authenticity, but lacks a political dimension that may have better informed Arenas' troubled decision-making. It tends to favour the visual cliché of its predecessor – a floating balloon represents freedom from entrapment – but its dark tones and immediacy mark Schnabel out as a maturing film talent, with already discernible recurring themes. **JD**

# Paul SCHRADER

*Blue Collar* (1978)
*Hardcore* (1979)
*American Gigolo* (1980)
*Cat People* (1982)
*Mishima: A Life in Four Chapters* (1985)
*Light of Day* (1987)
*Patty Hearst* (1988)
*The Comfort of Strangers* (1990)
*Light Sleeper* (1991)
*Witch Hunt* (1994)
*Touch* (1997)
*Affliction* (1997)
*Forever Mine* (1999)
*Auto Focus* (2002)

Paul Schrader's name is often uttered in the same breath as that of Martin Scorsese, and he still remains better known as the screenwriter of four Scorsese films – *Taxi Driver* (1976), *Raging Bull* (1980), *The Last Temptation of Christ* (1988), and *Bringing Out the Dead* (1999) – than as a director in his own right. This, however, has not prevented him from becoming a much mythologised, iconoclastic figure: like Travis Bickle in his *Taxi Driver* script, he seems 'partly truth, partly fiction, a walking contradiction'. He wrote under the influence of alcohol for over 15 years, and Bickle's urban paranoia is largely autobiographical. (Schrader even used to sleep with a loaded gun in his mouth.) Yet he is also an aesthete and an intellectual. He was born in Michigan in 1946 and raised a strict Calvinist, not seeing a film until he was 18. A graduate of theology and film studies, he was taken under the wing of Pauline Kael and began his film career as a theorist and critic – famously being fired by the LA Free Press for a review in which he trashed *Easy Rider* (1969).

David Thomson has argued that Schrader could describe how to make the perfect commercial hit, but that some kind of rugged integrity prevents him from making one himself. This certainly seems correct, but it is also worthwhile to note that Schrader's two most important writings – the essay 'Notes on film noir' and his book 'Transcendental Style in Film', a study of form and theology in the works of Robert Bresson, Carl Theodor Dreyer, and Yasujiro Ozu – together prefigure much of his own film work, which frequently intersects crime narratives with religion. Ironically, these themes and theories come together most clearly in Schrader's biggest hit to date, *American Gigolo* (1980), the most Bressonian of American films and the movie which made Richard Gere a star. A remarkably cold and linear film noir, full of austere camera moves and straight lines, it epitomises Schrader's theories on transcendental style, wherein the paring down and formalising of aesthetics serves to heighten the aura of the transcendent when it is revealed at the film's conclusion – evident in the religious iconography of the final shot of Gere, which points to more than simply a moral or secular redemption of his character.

*American Gigolo* was Schrader's third film, before which he directed *Blue Collar* (1978) and *Hardcore* (1979). One of his finest, though least typical films, *Blue Collar* is a solid drama about three factory workers who perform an ill-fated heist only to discover their union is just as corrupt as the company. Few films are as incisive about how the working classes are exploited by the system, or as poignant – particularly in the tragic consequences of each man being pitted against the other by corporate and governmental forces. Schrader also elicits terrific performances from his three leads: Harvey Keitel, Yaphet Kotto, and especially Richard Pryor, who transfers all the energy and anger of his stand-up routines into a tremendous dramatic performance.

In *Hardcore*, Schrader most explicitly addresses his own religious upbringing, as a stern Dutch Calvinist (George C. Scott) tracks down his runaway daughter, who has disappeared into the Los Angeles pornography scene. As with *Taxi Driver*, the film is a variation on *The Searchers* (1956), this time using the narrative to probe the place of hard-line religious beliefs in contemporary society, with Scott being forced to address (and become) everything that he loathes. Like those two earlier films, *Hardcore* also ends with an ambiguously happy ending, in which it is left open as to whether the girl will be able to re-integrate back into the society from which she fled.

Scott's character in *Hardcore* and Gere's Julian Kay in *American Gigolo* are both, like Travis Bickle, disconnected, obsessive and narcissistic men – a type of character with whom Schrader himself seems obsessed. An ambivalent voyeur, both enthralled and self-loathing, Schrader's camera loves to watch Gere as much as Gere loves to be watched. The strength of *American Gigolo* is the manner in which Schrader uses this camera style to wed the 'transcendental' paradigm to his fascination with male narcissism, so that Gere's spiritual redemption is inextricably linked to the purging of his isolationism and vanity. This is most evident in the way in which Schrader's austere transcendental style becomes fused with the pared-down, depthless surface textures of image-obsessed 1980s California – aided immeasurably by Ferdinando Scarfiotti's visual design and the work of the two Giorgios, Moroder and Armani.

Following *Cat People* (1982), a seductive, animalistic and sexually charged remake of the Val Lewton classic, Schrader returned to the themes of obsession and male narcissism with *Mishima: A Life in Four Chapters* (1985), one of the most striking films of the decade. A biopic of the controversial author and militarist Yukio Mishima, the film is unconventional in every respect, featuring Ozu-like black-and-white flashbacks of Mishima's childhood, boldly stylised adaptations of three of his novels, and docu-drama sequences of the failed attempt to lead the Japanese military into rebellion that ended in his suicide. Schrader uses his subject to delve into the relationships between life and art, with Mishima attempting to merge the two and achieve a 'harmony of pen and sword'. It seems emblematic of Schrader's integrity that he should film an already uncommercial project in Japanese – a language in which he is fluent.

Returning to America, *Light of Day* (1987) was a film by a rock 'n' roll addict, detailing the battles faced by Michael J. Fox and Joan Jett's small-town rock band and featuring a title song written by Bruce Springsteen. However, the film is a small and sober family drama set under the wintry Ohio skies, and it seemed to please neither the rock 'n' roll nor the art-house crowds. Also underrated and overlooked were two films Schrader made with Natasha Richardson: *Patty Hearst* (1988), an account of the heiress' abduction by the Symbionese Liberation Army, and *The Comfort of Strangers* (1990), an adaptation of the Ian McEwan novel, with a script by Harold Pinter.

*Light Sleeper* (1991) saw Schrader return again to the lonely male figure that he previously essayed as Travis Bickle and Julian Kay, with Willem Dafoe playing a drug delivery boy suffering from a mid-life crisis and moral concerns about his job. All three characters are alienated night-workers and men living in the cocoons of themselves, but here much of the earlier insanity has mellowed (with age) into a more gentle resignation. The film was hailed by many as his finest achievement, but that did not prevent Schrader having continued difficulties in acquiring funding.

When his next theatrical release, the odd and quirky *Touch* (1997), finally hit the screens, it was virtually lost in a sea of other Elmore Leonard adaptations. Yet it remains a vital work. Based on Leonard's least typical novel – a satiric parable about faith, exploitation and the media, in which a stigmatic miracle healer becomes a celebrity – the film again sees Schrader fusing pulp fiction with religion. But *Touch* is also light and comic, and we can sense Schrader loosening up and for once allowing himself some fun.

The bleak and wintry *Affliction* (1997), another difficult film, won considerable acclaim for the performances of Nick Nolte as a small-town cop and James Coburn as his abusive father. It is also another film about male violence and obsession, examining how violent behaviour is passed on from one generation of men to the next. At times this theme is perhaps overstated, but watching Nolte's hopeless downward spiral remains an uncompromising, powerful experience.

*Forever Mine* (1999) effectively went straight to video, despite it starring the then-hot Joseph Fiennes. An erotic revenge-thriller, it received perhaps the worst reviews of Schrader's career. *Auto Focus* (2002) stars Greg Kinnear and Willem Dafoe in a biopic of Bob Crane. The film again sees Schrader on familiar turf, probing the seedier side of male obsession: Crane was the star of 'Hogan's Heroes', then descended into the world of strip clubs and amateur pornography, before being bludgeoned to death with a camera tripod in 1978. One suspects Schrader's budgets and his audiences will continue to remain small – a fact he attributes to his being out of sync with teen audiences – but Schrader is a survivor, with much more still left to say.  **AS**

# Barbet SCHROEDER

Like the Dutch director Paul Verhoeven, Barbet Schroeder has crossed over from the European art cinema of the 1970s into the realm of glossy Hollywood productions. However, unlike Verhoeven, who specialises in lurid sex and gore blockbusters, Schroeder makes both schlocky genre films and more personal projects.

Born in Iran in 1941, he studied philosophy at the Sorbonne and wrote criticism for *Cahiers du cinéma*. He formed a production company – Les Films du Losange – with Eric Rohmer, which led to his working with the director in a variety of capacities, from producing to acting and narrating. His company was also involved in bringing films by other European directors to the screen, such as Rainer Werner Fassbinder's *Lola* (1981).

He debuted as a director with *More* (1969), a film about heroin addiction, and followed with *La Vallée* (1972), an exploration of hippies in search of paradise. Taken together, these films demonstrate Schroeder's interest in subcultures and obsessive, often anti-social, activity. This fascination with obsession was also evident in the most acclaimed of his documentaries, *General Idi Amin Dada* (1974). A black and often humorous study of the egocentric Ugandan dictator and self-proclaimed King of Scotland, it is another of the director's examinations of grotesque, extreme characters. They recur again in *Barfly* (1987) and *Reversal of Fortune* (1990).

*Maîtresse* (1976), shot in Paris, is one of Schroeder's greatest achievements. The story of a burglar (Gérard Depardieu) who falls in love with a dominatrix (Schroeder's wife and long-time collaborator Bulle Ogier) is presented in a sober and unsensational style. There is a non-judgmental approach to the human ashtrays, spankings and rubberwear, with the director's use of real S&M devotees helping to present a frank portrait of a subculture rather than a freakshow. The film looks ravishing, Schroeder's lush *mise-en-scène* rendering everything, even the graphic killing of a horse, beautiful. Indeed, Schroeder has called the film 'joyous and life-affirming'. However, scenes of spanking and nipple piercing led to the film being X-rated in the USA and banned outright in Britain. It was eventually released five years later but with heavy cuts.

After the oddity, *Koko le Gorille qui parle* (*Koko, A Talking Gorilla*) (1977), the director examined gambling in the little-seen *Tricheurs* (1984), which can be regarded as another almost-sociological look at an extra-social group. This was Schroeder's last French film before he left for America to make a long-cherished project, *Barfly*, an original autobiographical script by the celebrated American writer, Charles Bukowski. Indeed, so cherished was the project, Schroeder threatened to sever a finger in an executive's office to demonstrate his commitment to the film. Incidents like this encourage one to draw parallels between Schroeder's protagonists and the man himself.

In *Barfly*, Mickey Rourke plays Henry Chinaski, a drunken LA low-life and acclaimed writer who boozes and brawls his way through an episodic series of events, including a bittersweet romance with an unusually dowdy Faye Dunaway. The film is a successful hybrid of European art film and American star power. Like a number of other American movies made by European emigrants, such as John Schlesinger's *Midnight Cowboy* (1969) and Ivan Passer's *Cutter's Way* (1981), *Barfly* is disillusioned with America. 'Why does everyone have to be something?' Chinaski asks. 'Why can't they just be?' The film resists melodrama in favour of a rambling structure, best demonstrated in the way Schroeder begins the action with a long tracking shot into the bar where much of the film is played out and ends it with a reverse track out of the bar.

*Reversal of Fortune* (1990) is also based on a real-life character. The story of the aristocratic Klaus Von Bulow and his trial for the attempted murder of his wife could have been done as a courtroom-bound TV movie. But Schroeder and writer Nicholas Kazan place a bizarrely cast but effective Jeremy Irons (who won an Academy Award for the role) and an equally impressive Ron Silver as Bulow's lawyer within a complex narrative full of strange devices and flashy camera movement. Like *Barfly*, the film has a European feel to it, with stylised moments and an air of ambiguity – Schroeder, for example, refuses to come down on one side or the other on the issue of Bulow's guilt.

*Single White Female* (1992) wasn't quite as successful. Although initially creepy, the film ends up as a psycho-thriller reworking of Bergman's *Persona* (1966). Bridget Fonda has a flat-mate from hell in the form of Jennifer Jason Leigh, who steals her appearance, her boyfriend, and tries to steal her life. The increasing melodrama as the film reaches a climax includes death by high-heeled shoe.

In *Kiss of Death* (1995) Schroeder injects his recurrent themes into a traditional genre piece. Although it is credited as a remake of Henry Hathaway's 1947 film noir, Richard Price's script is a very loose adaptation. David Caruso plays a car thief pressured into informing on Nicholas Cage's Junior, a grotesquely pumped-up gangster with a penchant for white leisure wear. The film has a number of shocking twists, notably the scene where Caruso's wife is killed, and a number of memorably weird characters, such as Stanley Tucci's sinister DA and Samuel Jackson's cop who constantly sheds tears from one eye due to an earlier shooting. This is a far more American film than the freewheeling *Barfly* and the multi-layered *Reversal of Fortune*. The film has an eerily clear look about it, Schroeder abandoning the shadowy neo-noir of someone like John Dahl for a hyper-real *mise-en-scène*. The camera work, too, is showier than before, complete with crane shots and a striking credit sequence. Fittingly for a director so interested in strange characters, Cage's villain, who hates the taste of metal in his mouth and weight-lifts with busty strippers, completely eclipses the rather bland Caruso.

Schroeder's next couple of films were disappointing. The family melodrama *Before and After* (1996), with Liam Neeson and Meryl Streep as a couple torn over the possible involvement of their son (Edward Furlong) in a murder, was well-acted but talky and turgid. This was followed by the oddball *Desperate Measures* (1998), a convoluted and far-fetched story in which Andy Garcia is a cop hunting psycho Michael Keaton, the only person who can donate life-saving bone marrow to his dying son. Although moderately exciting, the ludicrous premise sinks the enterprise.

Although Schroeder has made a successful relocation to America, he seems to find it more difficult to relocate his dominant themes within Hollywood genre vehicles. This may well have been the reason he abandoned Hollywood for his next project. *Our Lady of the Assassins/Virgen de los Sicarios* (2000) is a Spanish language feature, shot in Columbia. A weird, magical realist, violent melodrama with shades of Hitchcock's *Vertigo* (1958), it is the story of Fernando (German Jaramillo), a middle-aged man who swears revenge after his teenage criminal lover (Anderson Ballesteros) is gunned down but instead finds love and falls for a lookalike of the dead man. Somewhat rambling, Schroeder's film is still fairly powerful stuff, drawing most of its power from the unfamiliar, striking backdrop of the Medellin and the film owes a clear debt to Hector Babenco' powerful and grim Brazilian film about street gangs, *Pixote* (1991). Schroeder wrote a production diary for the *Guardian* newspaper and the result was both thrilling and depressing: kidnappings, bombings, and drug-related shootings abound. His most recent film, *Murder by Numbers* (2002), is a crime comedy-thriller starring Sandra Bullock and the impressive Ryan Gosling. Schroeder seems to have grown discontented with the Hollywood schlock of *Desperate Measures* and is rumoured to have a French production in the pipeline.                                                                              **IC**

# Tom SCHULMAN

Working on films such as *Honey, I Shrunk the Kids* (1989), *What About Bob?* (1991), and *Medicine Man* (1992), Tom Schulman is well established as a screenwriter. His industry reputation was secured by his receipt of the Academy Award for his work on *Dead Poets Society* (1989) in 1990. He has also acted as executive producer on *Indecent Proposal* (1993) and *Me, Myself & Irene* (2000).

*8 Heads in a Duffel Bag (1997)*

His sole directorial work on *8 Heads in a Duffel Bag* (1997) is disappointing. As a black comedy, the film is overly reliant on its one joke premise in which a Mob hitman (Joe Pesci) finds that a bag in which he has stored the heads of eight men, ordered killed by his paymaster, has been accidentally switched at an airport with that of a young medical student. Predictably farcical, the film draws heavily from Pesci's self-parodic performance while failing to maximise the potential in the macabre scenario. Particularly poor is the hysterical mugging of George Hamilton and Dyan Cannon, their manic contortions exemplifying the film's substitution of broad caricature for wit. Lacking the energy of the Farrelly brothers' excursions into poor taste, the film is flat and static, despite the exertions of the cast.                                                              **NJ**

# Joel SCHUMACHER

Joel Schumacher is a director who started out making trivial comedies and youth-oriented pictures, but has progressively leaned more towards hard-hitting adult tracts. Often criticised for not delving deep enough or taking a stand in his movies, Schumacher's glossy style is instantly recognisable and has earned him a reputation as one of Hollywood's top money-spinners.

Schumacher's love of fashion paved his way into films. Born in 1939 in New York, he began by working as a display artist for Henri Bendel whilst still at design school, eventually setting up his own boutique. After offering his services as a costume designer for films like *Play It as It Lays* (1972) and *Sleeper* (1973), he started writing screenplays (*Sparkle* (1976), *Car Wash* (1976), *The Wiz* (1978)). His first dallies in film-making appeared on television in the late 1970s but it wasn't long before he made a feature for general release.

Regrettably, *The Incredible Shrinking Woman* (1981) was an unpropitious start, besmirching the good name of Jack Arnold's *The Incredible Shrinking Man* (1957). Instead of radiation provoking the shrinkage, household products cause comedienne Lily Tomlin to contract. And replacing the incontrovertible tension and inescapable dread is a slender, benumbed plot to kidnap Tomlin then reproduce the formula. The result is a leaden, insecure critique of consumerism and big business that employs suitably half-hearted effects. Likewise, *D.C. Cab* (1983) implores its audience not to take it seriously, which is emphasised by the tagline: 'When these guys hit the streets, guess what hits the fan!' Desperate to be a filmic version of 'Taxi' (the television series that completed its run that same year), Washington-based *D.C. Cab* invests in neither the acting nor the writing talent of its 'poorer' cousin. With its token stockpile characters – muscleman Mr T and middle-aged hippy Max Gail – and deficit of one-liners, the film galls at every turn.

This probably accounts for the change in gear with *St Elmo's Fire* (1985), Schumacher's anterior youth movie. Nostalgic, communicative, and resigned to the traumas of early adulthood, this focuses on a band of graduates bracing themselves for the daunting realities of life beyond academia. A wonderful cast on the brink of superstardom, Rob Lowe, Demi Moore, Ally Sheedy, and Emilio Estevez, complement the film. It is flawed only by its motivational deficiency and inability to reach any solid conclusions.

In *The Lost Boys* (1987) Schumacher applies this youth ethic to the vampire sub-genre, suggesting that the missing adolescents of society are really Nosferatu. Obviously feigning 1985's *Fright Night*, the story, by Janice Fischer and James Jeremias, dwells on one such recruit, played by Jason Patric, who is lured by a femme fatale into becoming a Lost Boy. Although the movie does grate when his little brother (Corey Haim) and company pledge to defeat the undead, it still serves as a canny lecture on how cults and biker gangs swell their numbers.

An Americanised and updated remake of Jean-Charles Tacchella's 1975 comedy, *Cousins* (1989) works specifically because of the relationship between Ted Danson and Isabella Rossellini. *Flatliners* (1990) conversely disintegrates because of the total absence of comparative chemistry between the brat pack leads. Only Julia Roberts is plausible as the introverted medical student who is party to her friends' experiments with death. Its fundamental flaw, however, is its inclination to raise not only expectations, but also questions about the afterlife it cannot possibly answer.

Death is the subject of Schumacher's seventh film, as viewed from the perspective of a 28-year-old leukaemia sufferer (Campbell Scott). *Dying Young* (1991) is an example of exploitative cinema, preying on humanity's morbid fascination with such issues. In addition, the director's use of Julia Roberts as a contracted nursemaid and object of Cambell's unconsummated desire seems designed solely to attract male viewers to the film. It is a cloyingly sentimental adaptation of Marti Leimbach's novel that has no hope of a mollifying dénouement.

In *Falling Down* (1993) Schumacher probes another taboo subject, that of mental breakdown: a result of the stressful, accelerated pace of our modern world. The film is also a fascinating study of the reactions of white middle-class America increasingly threatened by multicultural social transformation. For Michael Douglas' white-collar worker all the traffic jams, pollution, fast-food parlours, and sleazy inhabitants of LA have become too much, and accordingly he embarks on a violent – often darkly humorous – trek across the city to reach his 'home' and a life he used to lead. First-rate performances from Douglas, Barbara Hershey (as his ex-wife), and Robert Duvall, playing the 'last day' cop on his trail, combine with sweaty location shooting to create a convincing portraiture of a man on the edge.

The first of two John Grisham adaptations, *The Client* (1994) is a soporific legal drama in which Brad Renfro overhears a Mafia lawyer's suicide secrets – expressly the whereabouts of a murdered senator – and soon finds himself hounded by the police, the media, and intimidating Federal Prosecutor Tommy Lee Jones. Susan Sarandon (recipient of an Academy Award nomination and a BAFTA) is excellent as the inexperienced lawyer he turns to – a typical Grisham hero – but not even her tremendous commitment can bridge the elongated void of suspense.

In 1995 Schumacher acquired the Batman franchise, hoping to improve upon the takings for Tim Burton's underrated but financially disappointing *Batman Returns* (1992). He would achieve his goal ($333 million worldwide) at a cost. *Batman Forever* is a colourful, camp explosion of noise and fury, with handsome – if inanimate – Val Kilmer replacing dangerous Michael Keaton in the title role. Whereas Burton's vision was influenced by Bob Kane's original gothic strip, Schumacher's is more reminiscent of the psychedelic 1960s television show, but with less adept action sequences. Symptomatic of this change in tone is the debut of Chris O'Donnell's carnival Robin and the invaluable casting of Jim Carrey as The Riddler who, like Jack Nicholson before him, monopolises the proceedings. Other performers (Tommy Lee Jones, Nicole Kidman, Drew Barrymore) become unwitting victims of character overflow, as well as inept structuring, and the perplexing story has all the depth of a Warner Bros. cartoon.

*A Time to Kill* (1996) is Schumacher's second Grisham film. More controversial and thought-provoking than *The Client*, it is the story of a vigilante father (Samuel L. Jackson) who kills his daughter's redneck rapists. Matthew McConaughey is the lawyer who defends the man's actions, thus suffering the wrath of the Ku Klux Klan in the process. At least thirty years out of date, its problematic ideology (McConaughey pleads with the jury to imagine it was a white girl who was raped) and judgments (that cold-blooded murder is justifiable if you believe the legal system is corrupt) compete for attention with McConaughey's male model posturing and clean-cut heroics. As one of the few high-profile Hollywood films to even consider racial politics, *A Time to Kill* is seemingly earnest in its intentions. Sadly, as happens all too often, the arguments are broken down into simplistic good versus bad digestible chunks.

Schumacher's continuation of the Dark Knight saga, *Batman & Robin* (1997), duplicates all the mistakes of his initial attempt and makes a thousand more. After Arnold Schwarzenegger's icy quips as Mr Freeze and Alicia Silverstone's cod-feminist ramblings as Batgirl, no amount of lavish sets or expensive effects can cover the cracks. The same is true of his incautious *Se7en*-pretender *8MM* (1999), which no amount of darkened rooms or intense stares from lead Nicolas Cage can salvage. Bleak for the sake of it, this psychological crime thriller, peppered with plot holes and dead ends, is just another example of Schumacher's preference for style over content.

Mercifully, *Flawless* (1999) is a more considered choice, living up to its name in every respect. Robert De Niro plays the uptight security guard who suffers a stroke and has to take singing lessons from drag queen Philip Seymour Hoffman as part of his treatment. *The Odd Couple* (1968) taken to ridiculous lengths, its worthwhile message about the roles we play in society is professionally disseminated through impressive exchanges.

Contributing to the war film resurgence, *Tigerland* (2000), filmed on an unusually low budget with an unknown cast, concentrates on the training of Vietnam recruits in 1971. Raw, tense, and shot with an extremely keen eye – Matthew Libatique's cinematography is visually stunning – this is a worthy addition to both the Vietnam sub-genre and Schumacher's canon. The recent *Bad Company* (2002), an action comedy thriller, stars Chris Rock as the twin of a dead CIA agent alongside heavyweight Anthony Hopkins; *Phone Booth* (2002), a thriller in which a man answers a ringing public phone and finds his life in danger, features Colin Farrell and Forest Whitaker. In addition, Schumacher is reportedly directing a film about the 1996 assassination of journalist Veronica Guerin. **PB**

# Martin SCORSESE

Since emerging from the generation of film-makers which revolutionised American cinema in the 1960s and 1970s, Martin Scorsese has established himself as one of the great directors of contemporary cinema. While Hollywood has steadily retreated into safety and convention, and while his contemporaries have collectively burned out, sold out, or cashed in, Scorsese has continued to produce some of the most challenging and influential cinema that America has to offer. From the experimental short films of the late 1960s, through an astonishing run of films that included *Mean Streets* (1973), *Taxi Driver* (1976), and *Raging Bull* (1980), to the more expansive works of recent years like *GoodFellas* (1990), *Casino* (1995), and *Kundun* (1997), he has remained at the forefront of modern direction for over thirty years.

Hollywood has always enjoyed an uneasy relationship with Scorsese. The controversial subjects, morally complex characters, and confrontational style of his films have often jarred with a studio system driven by money and market research, compounded by the fact that his films have rarely enjoyed great commercial success. He has never received an Academy Award, despite being nominated three times as director and twice as screenwriter, and has usually found greater recognition amongst European audiences; perhaps appropriate given the influence European cinema and its great directors has had on his work.

Fittingly for a film-maker who learned to direct by watching other people's movies, cinema is one of Scorsese's prime subjects. Through experimentation with techniques of camera, editing and production, literate allusions to classic films and great film-makers of the past, and particularly his trademark use of montage and music, his films explore an ongoing fascination with the craft of film-making and his own cinematic heritage. His stories revisit subjects and characters that seem inexorably connected with his own life – the divided heart of an Italian-American, the religious man riven by doubt, the child raised on the city's mean streets. His characters, whether loners or artists, gangsters or saints, small-time hoods or made-guys, undergo the same trials of temptation, suffering, and self-doubt on the journey to redemption or retribution. In a wider sense, however, his films trade on universal themes: loyalty, betrayal, honour, family, and friendship, together with the twin pillars of violence and religion. Through long-standing partnerships with writers (notably Paul Schrader, Mardik Martin and Nicholas Pileggi), actors (particularly Robert De Niro) and editors (Thelma Schoonmaker), Scorsese's films have explored a unique personal vision which also allows rare insight into the relationship between a great director and his work.

Born in 1942 in Long Island, New York, and raised in Little Italy, Scorsese's upbringing was the authentic Italian-American experience. His parents were second-generation Sicilian immigrants; his father Charles worked in a variety of blue-collar jobs, while his ebullient mother Catherine controlled the Scorsese household. Both parents would appear regularly in Scorsese's films, most notably in *Italianamerican* (1974). Family, church, the neighbourhood, and organised crime were the dominant forces in the lives of young Italian-Americans, and Scorsese was no exception, though he increasingly found escape from the reality of everyday street life and the limitations of his asthma through the cinema. During this time, he began to make amateur films, including *Vesuvius VI* (1959), a mini-epic set in Ancient Rome inspired by popular TV shows. Following a brief flirtation with joining the priesthood, Scorsese enrolled in New York University's fledgling film programme, and was caught up in the explosion of European art cinema sweeping American screens, particularly the Italian Neo-Realist movement and the French New Wave of Truffaut, Resnais and Godard.

Scorsese's early films were heavily influenced by the artistry of these film-makers, together with the maverick techniques of the American Underground, especially directors like John Cassavates and Sam Fuller who used film as a means of personal expression. *What's A Nice Girl Like You Doing In A Place Like This?* (1963), a ten-minute short about a young man who becomes obsessed with a picture of a boat on a lake, uses a stylised voiceover to narrate a collection of still photographs and filmed sequences. The film ends on a fashionably surreal note when he disappears into the picture. *It's Not Just You, Murray!* (1964) looks forward to the small-time gangsters of Scorsese's later work, and prefigures many ideas, especially the use of a story told in flashback, voiceovers which cut comically against the action and stylised montage sequences.

Scorsese graduated from NYU in 1964 and began intermittent work on his first feature, *Who's That Knocking at My Door?* (1967), conceived as the second part of a trilogy about his experiences growing up in Little Italy. The film centres on J.R., an Italian-American boy played by Harvey Keitel, both a version of the young Scorsese and an early incarnation of Charlie in *Mean Streets*. J.R. falls for a cultured young woman unlike the neighbourhood girls he has known, but their relationship is destroyed by the revelation that she was raped by a former boyfriend, together with J.R.'s inability to reconcile the conflicting influences on his life: religious guilt, sexual desire and the pressures of street life among his friends. An experimental version of the film, shown in 1965 under the title *Bring on the Dancing Girls*, was poorly received, and a second version, entitled *I Call First* and screened in 1967, similarly failed to make any impact. Frustrated by the lack of progress, Scorsese completed *The Big Shave* later that year, a short film conceived as a surreal allegory of the Vietnam War, which depicts a clean-cut young man who cuts his face while shaving and continues until he is drenched with blood.

In 1968, having been fired from *The Honeymoon Killers* only a week into shooting (apparently for overindulgent direction), Scorsese found occasional work as an editor-for-hire and as a film instructor at NYU. *Who's That Knocking At My Door?* finally secured a cinema release later that year (thanks to an added nude scene) and Scorsese's direction, particularly his use of music and vibrant depiction of urban Italian-American life, began to draw notable attention. In 1970 he became involved in two documentary projects· as post-production director on *Street Scenes*, which followed street demonstrations against American involvement in Indochina; and as an editor on *Woodstock*, the film of the landmark music festival of the previous year, directed by his old NYU compatriot Michael Wadleigh.

In 1971, Scorsese moved to Los Angeles in an attempt to break into the mainstream industry, where he met several other innovative young film-makers, including Spielberg, Lucas, Coppola, and old New York friend Brian de Palma. After editing the rock documentary *Medicine Ball Caravan* (1971), he was hired by Roger Corman to direct the exploitation thriller *Boxcar Bertha* (1972), a film which in many ways became his apprenticeship to fully-fledged direction. Inspired by the vogue of graphic thrillers begun by *Bonnie & Clyde* (1967), the film follows Bertha, a young Arkansas farm girl, as she teams up with a stalwart trade unionist, his black companion, and a slippery New York conman. Together they embark on a crime spree which ends in a violent showdown with the lawmen on their trail. Despite the derivative plot, Scorsese manages to cram the film with energy and numerous film references, and demonstrates a growing fascination with the aesthetics of violence and even a crucifixion scene in which the unionist hero is impaled on a boxcar.

It was *Mean Streets*, however, that finally brought Scorsese to a wider audience. Originally titled *Season of the Witch*, and intended as the third part of his autobiographical trilogy, the film revisits many of the ideas Scorsese had explored in *Who's That Knocking at My Door?* A young Italian-American, Charlie, another version of the young Scorsese played by Harvey Keitel, finds himself torn between irreconcilable forces: his taboo relationship and sexual desire for his cousin Catherine; his sense of Catholic guilt; the wish to impress his uncle, a local crime boss; and his friendship with the dangerously unpredictable Johnny Boy, a young punk from the neighbourhood played by Robert De Niro in his first Scorsese role. Using raw, experimental camerawork, a loose story structure, and largely improvised performances, Scorsese places emphasis on the emotional realism of his characters and the undercurrents of crime and violence that control their lives. Wise-guy dialogue, hand-held camera, and rapid editing inject the film with a sense of restless urgency. Both an authentic snapshot of life on the streets and a technical *tour-de-force*, *Mean Streets* was widely hailed as one of the most vital and innovative American movies of the decade.

Scorsese's next film, *Alice Doesn't Live Here Anymore* (1974) aimed to demonstrate his versatility and address the male-dominated bias of his films. A young widow takes to the road with her son after the death of her husband, determined to revive her singing career; after a series of scrapes, she ends up working as a waitress and falls into a tentative romance with a divorced farmer. After the incendiary impact of *Mean Streets*, the simple, old-fashioned story and Scorsese's low-key treatment is surprising, but the film has a similar emotional honesty and edgy, realistic feel. It also showed his growing facility with actors, with an Academy Award-winning performance from Ellen Burstyn in the title role. *Italianamerican* followed shortly after, a touching and funny documentary in which Scorsese's parents reminisce about their early experiences of life in New York (and which includes Catherine Scorsese's personal recipe for meatballs).

In 1975 Scorsese began to develop a low-budget project by a little-known writer called Paul Schrader. Schrader's script was edgy, controversial and distinctly uncommercial, centring on a lonely, insomniac Vietnam veteran who embarks on a vigilante crusade to wipe the corrupt New York streets clean. With a minimal budget and limited shooting time, Scorsese had little idea that the project was to become both a defining work and one of the most influential films of the 1970s. *Taxi Driver* is both an allegory of urban isolation and a relentlessly realistic study of one man's descent into insanity. Scorsese's visceral camerawork and Bernard Herrmann's menacing score brilliantly reconfigure the landscape of the city into a contemporary hell of neon and shadow, in which the film's anti-hero Travis Bickle, played by De Niro, casts himself as the avenging angel. Sequences of surreal fantasy, dream and realism collide as Travis narrates his mission, which he perceives as a righteous spiritual quest to clean up the collective body and soul of the city, but which leads him into an attempt on a politician's life and a supremely bloody final confrontation with a gang of pimps. Many sequences – especially Travis' celebrated mirror monologue, one of numerous mirror scenes in Scorsese's work – have become classics of modern cinema, and the film continued his fascination with extremes of violence, character and emotion. It was released to critical acclaim, and resonated with a disenfranchised, post-hippy America waking up to the realities of the modern world. *Taxi Driver* won the coveted Palme d'Or at the 1976 Cannes Festival, and has become symbolic of the independent spirit of the new American cinema of that decade.

Scorsese's next films explored his love of music in differing ways. *New York, New York* (1977) is his homage to the Hollywood musical and follows the relationship between a jazz saxophonist, again played by De Niro, and a mainstream big band singer, played by Liza Minnelli. Scorsese recreates the milieu of the musical era with lavish detail and extravagant choreography, contrasting the glittery show-biz surface with the domestic fragmentation behind the scenes, but the film is indulgent, over-long, and went massively over-budget, failing to recoup its costs at the box office. *The Last Waltz* (1978) drew on Scorsese's experience in music documentary, mixing impressive footage of The Band's final concert with revealing backstage interviews. *American Boy: A Profile of Steven Prince* (1978) documents another of Scorsese's acquaintances, recognisable as the gun salesman in *Taxi Driver*. Prince's vivid tales of rock 'n' roll excess touring with Neil Diamond and of a life filled with drugs, guns, and violent events, have been suggested as an inspiration for Scorsese's portrayal of the character of Travis Bickle.

The failure of *New York, New York* after the critical success of his early films left Scorsese depressed and creatively frustrated. His response, appropriately enough, was to come out fighting. *Raging Bull*, based on the life of the middleweight boxing champion Jake La Motta, is one of Scorsese's most fluent explorations of violence and masculine codes of behaviour. Filming in expressive black and white, Scorsese charts the chronological progression of La Motta's career, through his early fights, championship victories, and eventual downfall, juxtaposing in often harrowing detail the brutality of his professional existence with the uncontrollable rage, self-hatred and self-destruction of his personal life. Visually, however, it is Scorsese's stunning interpretations of the fight sequences which are most memorable, particularly his elegant cinematography to create a style of violence which possesses its own visceral rhythms and compelling beauty. Combining elements of biopic, melodrama, newsreel and art film, it is another brilliantly crafted example of Scorsese in complete control of his medium. Thelma Schoonmaker's editing and De Niro's performance as the complex, self-punishing La Motta, another Italian-American wracked with religious and social guilt, both won Academy Awards; Scorsese, nominated for Best Film and Best Director, received nothing.

The previous decade had been exhausting both creatively and emotionally for Scorsese, and his films during the early 1980s were more modest. *The King of Comedy* (1982) is a blackly comic counterpart to *Taxi Driver*, in which Robert Pupkin, an obsessive, no-hoper comedian, takes his television idol hostage in a desperate attempt to break into celebrity and success. De Niro's Pupkin is a bizarre masterpiece of buttoned-up mania and paranoia – Travis Bickle reimagined as a stand-up comedian – and

Scorsese's first foray into comedy turns into an eerie exploration of loneliness and creative frustration. *After Hours* (1985) was his version of screwball comedy, following a hapless computer programmer through a bizarre catalogue of accidents on New York's night-time streets. A strange and often uneasy combination of ultra-black humour and disturbing realism, the film won Scorsese the Best Director award at Cannes. *The Colour of Money* (1986) was his sequel to the pool-hall classic *The Hustler* (1961), and offered him the chance to revisit a classic 1950s movie and make it over in the images of contemporary cinema. Paul Newman reprises his role as 'Fast' Eddie Felson 25 years on, now the mentor of young, talented, and obnoxious pool player Vincent Lauria (Tom Cruise). Where the original was shot through with the hardboiled realism of 1950s film-making, Scorsese's film is a monument to the 1980s: glossy, slick, and showy, driven by ideas of money, ambition, and pride. His depiction of the rituals of pool playing is typically original, and the dynamic of mentor and pupil, in competition both with each other and their own sense of masculinity, gives a new slant to Scorsese's depictions of male relationships.

Scorsese rediscovered controversy in spectacular fashion with *The Last Temptation of Christ* (1988) which fulfilled his longstanding ambition to film the life of Jesus. The project had originally been developed in 1983, but financial problems and nervous studios delayed production for several years. Adapted by Paul Schrader from Nikos Kazantzakis' book, the film aims to provide a domestic portrait and psychological interpretation of Christ, played by Willem Defoe, as a man torn between a sense of his divine duty and his human emotions – love, doubt, fear, anger, pain, and desire. Scorsese's style is deliberately anti-epic, juxtaposing realism and fantasy to explore the drama of the Gospel stories: the everyday reality of Christ living, preaching, struggling, and dying as a man, while simultaneously experiencing the surreal powers and visions of the divine. It is a fascinating but inevitably provocative approach, and the film met with a storm of controversy on its release, especially the final 'temptation' sequences, which depicts Christ being led from the cross by an angel and offered the chance to live as a normal man, that is, as a husband and father. It is also one of Scorsese's most beautiful films, combining striking desert cinematography with the composition of classical painting.

His next project was understandably more low-key. *Life Lessons* is the first segment of *New York Stories* (1989), a three-part film co-directed with Francis Coppola and Woody Allen, and focuses on the disintegrating relationship between a middle-aged painter and his young girlfriend, also an aspiring artist. Located almost entirely in his studio and filmed in an intimate documentary style, the film is both a sharp satire of the 1980s art world and another of Scorsese's convincing studies of a relationship in the throes of breakdown.

Scorsese's films of the 1970s mined his own life and experiences for their subjects. His 1980s films experimented with styles and genres which both courted and confronted mainstream expectations – a boxing film that was more art-house than sports movie, a religious film that was more character study than historical epic, comedies which were more frightening than funny. The 1990s marked both a mature return to his roots and a simultaneous move to broader canvases.

*GoodFellas* revisits the gangster world of his early work. Adapted by Nicholas Pileggi from his book 'Wiseguy', the film follows three mobsters through three decades of Italian-American organised crime: the ambitious young foot soldier and the film's narrator, Henry Hill (Ray Liotta), his Mob mentor Jimmy Conway (De Niro) and violent loose-cannon Tommy DeVito (Joe Pesci). Right from the opening on the bustling streets of 1950s New York, filmed in sweeping camera moves and punctuated by freeze frames to underscore Henry's narration, the film is a virtuoso display of Scorsese's style, full of elaborate camerawork, stylish editing, dazzling montage sequences, brutal violence, and a brilliant period soundtrack which stitches together the complex narrative and time-frame. Like *Casino*, it is a story about the American Dream gone bad, charting the rise and fall of a criminal lifestyle which relies, ironically, on the institutional values of trust, loyalty, and stoicism, but which is ultimately brought down by the vagaries of human emotion – greed, ambition, fear, and the desire for self-preservation. Crucially, Henry Hill is Irish-Italian, not Italian-American, and thus always destined to remain an outsider; when the moment of truth comes, his loyalty is to himself, not the wider 'family'. *GoodFellas* is arguably Scorsese's most accomplished film: more a social canvas than character study, and as seductive as the lifestyle it depicts. Scorsese again received none of the Academy Awards for which the film was nominated, including Best Picture, Director and Screenplay.

*Made in Milan* (1990), his subsequent documentary about Giorgio Armani, continued Scorsese's fascination with Italy, and followed the making of two stylish black-and-white advertisements for the company, filmed in homage to Italian neo-realism. *Cape Fear* (1991) marked Scorsese's first treatment of a traditional Hollywood thriller, remaking the classic 1961 film starring Robert Mitchum. In Scorsese's version, Robert De Niro plays Max Cady, a psychotic criminal and serial rapist who returns to exact revenge on the family of Sam Bowden (Nick Nolte), the defence lawyer who concealed evidence that could have helped him escape conviction. Interestingly, Scorsese adds a religious framework to the original story: each family member reveals sins – Bowden's guilt and adultery, his wife's neuroses, his daughter's sexual desires – for which Cady, covered in biblical tattoos and endlessly quoting scripture, becomes the instrument of redemption. Though undoubtedly his most commercial film, *Cape Fear* is stylishly made, packed with efficient thrills, and evidence of Scorsese's ability, should he so choose, to move effortlessly into different genres. *The Age of Innocence* (1993) provided further proof. Adapted from an Edith Wharton novel, the film is a historical romance set in high-society New York in the 1870s, a world seemingly far removed from the normal environs of a Scorsese film. In fact, the story explores social rituals and hierarchies as rigid as those of his gangster films, and deals with many of the same themes – jealousy, desire, betrayal, and loss. Scorsese's attention to detail and sumptuous cinematography are as impressive as ever, and the film demonstrates his continuing desire to explore new territory.

Late in 1993, Scorsese was approached to contribute to a documentary series celebrating the centenary of cinema, in which he was asked to discuss American films which had influenced him. His contribution eventually ran to over four hours – enough for the entire series – and developed into a project in its own right. *A Century of Cinema* (1995) provides invaluable insight into his inspirations and views on American cinema, cut together with excellent archive footage. Scorsese's sheer enthusiasm for his medium has also been evident in several other extra-curricular projects, including the foundation of his own film archive and an ongoing campaign to address the problems of fading colour film stock.

Scorsese's late 1990s films are the work of a mature director at the height of his powers, and bear interesting comparison with his earlier films. *Casino*, based on another Nicholas Pileggi novel, is perhaps his grandest canvas, and examines the Mob's role in the development of Las Vegas through two central characters: Sam Rothstein (De Niro), a gangster and inveterate gambler, who takes over a major Mob casino, and the volatile Nicky Santoro (Joe Pesci), whose violent antics constantly threaten the status quo. The film is a kind of West Coast companion piece to *GoodFellas*: brash, showy, and extravagant, employing two principal voiceovers, a huge cast of characters, and a typically elaborate style that moves from straight documentary into a glossy, hyper-colourful examination of greed, pride, and corruption.

*Kundun* echoes many of the themes of *The Last Temptation of Christ*, but in an entirely different spiritual framework: Tibetan Buddhism, and the fourteenth reincarnation of the Dalai Lama, or Kundun. The film follows the young Kundun's discovery in a rural community in 1935, his estrangement from his family, and his subsequent monastery education, through to the invasion of Chairman Mao's Communist forces in 1950 and his enforced escape to India in 1959. Though it follows a chronological structure, *Kundun* is one of Scorsese's most experimental works. Using a cast mostly composed of non-actors, no explanatory voiceover and little dialogue, the film relies instead on expressionist editing, symbolic images, beautiful cinematography, and Philip Glass' primal score to reflect the world through the young Kundun's eyes. His conflict is again between his desire for a normal life and his duty to a higher cause; between his fascination for the modern world of science, maps, mechanics, and newspapers, and the spiritual world of ritual, pageantry, and faith which he struggles to understand. It is one of Scorsese's most suggestive films, exploring ideas of pacifism and violence, self and nationhood, reality and dream, and contains some of his most devastating visual direction.

With *Bringing Out the Dead* (1999), Scorsese revisited the mean streets of New York from a very new perspective. The film focuses on Frank Pierce (Nicholas Cage), a lonely, detached paramedic with a heavy-duty drug habit supplied from his own emergency bag and a serious case of compassion fatigue. Scorsese seems to have come full circle: a Paul Schrader script which follows an isolated anti-hero through the city's infernal streets; a series of harrowing encounters with a cast of junkies, madmen, victims, and lowlifes (some of whom are Frank's colleagues); and intense, kinetic direction that reflects Frank's fragile (and frequently wired) state of mind. Where *Taxi Driver* offered apocalypse, however, *Bringing Out the Dead* offers macabre humour, and like Travis Bickle, Frank Pierce finally seems to find a form of peace having served his time in Hell.

Most recently, *Il Mio viaggio in Italia* (1999) documented Scorsese's love of Italian neo-realism in a similar style to *A Century of Cinema*, cutting together personal testimony with illuminating film excerpts. The forthcoming *Gangs of New York*, first mooted as a project in 1987, charts the rise of organised gangs in nineteenth-century New York, and has developed into his most expensive and time-consuming project yet. The film is scheduled for release in late 2002, while his biopic of Dean Martin and the Rat Pack, provisionally entitled *Dino*, is still in development.  **OB**

# Campbell SCOTT

Born in New York in 1961, the son of legendary actor George C. Scott, Campbell Scott *Big Night* (1996) majored in Theatre and the Performing Arts at Lawrence University, Wisconsin, graduating *Final* (2001) in 1983. Having acted in a variety of films, and working as an executive producer on Greg Mottola's *The Daytrippers* (1996), Scott finally stepped behind the camera to co-direct 1996's *Big Night* with fellow actor and high-school friend Stanley Tucci.

Whilst the film sets up the conflict between the old and the new from the outset, it never takes the easy step of falling down on one side or the other, instead distributing equal amounts of sympathy to the main protagonists, Primo and Secondo, the two brothers. The camera is used throughout to highlight the differences between them: remaining fixed in the company of the traditional, sweeping around to meet the demands of the modern. Perhaps most incredible of all is the tension and suspense that is built up around the culinary delights, and in particular 'Il timpano'. Having seen the preparation of the dish in an early scene, the film then stalls in its unveiling, simply reminding us that something magical awaits. And when it comes, Scott enhances our experience by employing a fast-moving, hand-held camera, allowing us to join the characters as they devour the stunningly presented food. To close the film, Scott decides to go with the silent pledge of solidarity between the brothers. One suspects that other directors would have shied away from such a resolution, but it remains an exquisitely touching choice.

His next feature, following a made-for-television adaptation of 'Hamlet', is a science fiction drama about a hospitalised man who believes he was cryogenically frozen for four hundred years as part of a government experiment. *Final* (2001) was the first in the InDigEnt series, a new digital film-making initiative dedicated to exploring new cinema technologies and restoring creative control to the entire crew.  **CP**

# Ridley SCOTT

Born in Durham, UK, in 1937, and trained at the National Film and Television School, *The Duelists* (1977) Ridley Scott has had a successful career in television and advertising, and is one of *Alien* (1979) Britain's most successful mainstream directors. Often derided by critics for his tendency *Blade Runner* (1982) to emphasise style over substance, particularly in the use of inexplicable, though *Legend* (1985) atmospheric, light sources (a quality he shares with his brother Tony), Scott has created *Someone to Watch Over Me* a vision of the past, present and, most dramatically, the future, that has influenced a (1987) whole generation of film-makers. *Black Rain* (1989)

His feature debut, *The Duellists* (1977), loosely based upon a Joseph Conrad story, *Blade Runner – The Director's* is a flamboyant exercise in period style. Harvey Keitel and Keith Carradine play two *Cut* (1991) French officers who embark upon a series of duels with each other across the war-torn *Thelma and Louise* (1991) devastation of Napoleonic Europe. Beautifully composed, with the leads coping as well *1492: Conquest of Paradise* as they can with a perfunctory script, the film is interesting, if only for the attention (1992) lavished upon every aspect of period detail. Though visually impressive, it is a dull drama *White Squall* (1996) that offers little more with repeat screenings. *G.I. Jane* (1997)

Moving away from the ponderous into the fast lane of mainstream Hollywood *Gladiator* (2000) cinema, Scott directed *Alien* (1979). Skilfully blending the stalker genre with the space *Hannibal* (2001) movie, the film is a testament to his ability to transform the most rudimentary material into something more complex and suspenseful. Novelist J. G. Ballard noted the difference between the script's clichéd dialogue and the completed film, identifying its strengths as 'one of the most original horror movies ever made, the throwaway dialogue perfectly set off the terrifying vacuum that expanded around the characters'. Emphasising their solitude in the vastness of deep space, Scott creates a static environment where lives are trapped in a suspended state. The most banal functions of living appear to take hours and each day bleeds uneventfully into the next, creating a monotonous existence. Even the Nostromo spaceship limps listlessly through the vast reaches of deep space. Looking less like a craft capable of travelling to the furthest corners of the universe than some decaying behemoth, the combination of leaking pipes, dank chambers and underlit corridors bear more resemblance to the haunted houses of old B-movies than the result of technological advancement. Camouflaged in such an environment, H. R. Giger's monstrous creation is the embodiment of the fears and desires of the Nostromo's crew, as it violently and mercilessly hunts them down.

Also helping to elevate the film above the realm of the conventional horror/sci-fi movie is Sigourney Weaver's remarkable central performance as Ripley; succeeding in subverting generic conventions, she presents a complex female character as much a predator as she is a victim. Setting the ground for future female action characters, such as Sarah Connor in the *Terminator* series, Weaver's presence ensured that the *Alien* series would continue beyond Scott's involvement.

Scott remained in the future for his next project, *Blade Runner* (1982), an adaptation of Philip K. Dick's story 'Do Androids Dream of Electric Sheep?' and the film that launched a thousand doctoral theses. His best to date, it remains a triumph of vision and intelligence. Once again, Scott plays with generic conventions, positing the murky world of the noirish detective thriller within the confines of dystopian science fiction. The Los Angeles of 2019 is envisioned as a melting pot of past, present and future, with 1940s fashions colliding with Eastern cuisine, and architectural styles ranging from Mayan to Bauhaus. The hectic streets, illuminated by neon lights and littered with wastrels, urchins and black marketeers, are dominated by the over-designed super-structures of a faceless corporate technocracy. Scott successfully created a world immediately recognisable yet simultaneously alien and exotic. The lack of geographical perspective added to the otherworldliness of the environment, unwilling to map out the locations within the sprawl of the future LA. As a result, the audience remain as confused and lost as the film's protagonist, Deckard (Harrison Ford).

Released in 1982, the original *Blade Runner* was different to the version Scott had originally conceived. Responding to test audiences' confusion and dissatisfaction with the narrative and downbeat ending, studios demanded a voice-over to accompany the action, the removal of certain scenes, and a happier ending. Although the voice-over accentuated the noirish feel to the film, it emptied it of its subtlety and ambiguity, whilst the closing moments appeared as inauthentic as the androids themselves. With his director's cut in 1991, Scott removed both the voice-over and the end, inserting the famous unicorn sequence, which raises interesting questions about Deckard's identity as a 'replicant'. More satisfying than the original, it reasserted Scott's film as a masterpiece of science fiction cinema.

After *Alien* and *Blade Runner*, *Legend* (1985), his next film, was something of a disappointment. An attempt to rework the fairytale for a modern audience, it tells the story of a boy whose infatuation with a young forest girl offers the Prince of Darkness the opportunity to plunge the world into permanent night. Too violent for infants, yet too infantile for adults, the film is overlong and a waste of Scott's undoubted talent. Both Tom Cruise and Mia Sara are hardly credible as the leads, while dozens of extras are corralled into a spectacular display of hackneyed Irish accents and impish expressions. Only Tim Curry, stunningly made-up as the film's villain, manages to rise above the mediocrity, breathing life into a one-dimensional role. Limping from one expensive and pointlessly picturesque sequence to the next, no amount of style can help a film that borders on the tedious. It is Scott's weakest and most self-indulgent work.

His next, *Someone to Watch Over Me* (1987), was the first with a contemporary setting and something of a pleasure after *Legend*. Transforming a dull and dreary 1980s Manhattan into a glittering metropolis, Scott combines the elements of a thriller with a domestic drama: a love triangle between Mimi Rogers' wealthy murder witness,

Tom Berenger's cop and Lorraine Bracco's suspecting wife. It is most effective when contrasting the ordinary lives of Berenger and his wife against the fabulous lifestyles of Rogers and her friends. Both the Guggenheim Museum and Rogers' apartment offer Scott opulent backdrops to the drama, emphasising the emptiness of Rogers' life and her vulnerable position both as a witness and the object of a married man's desires. An intelligent and entertaining thriller, Someone to Watch Over Me proved Scott's ability as a director able to work effectively on something other than an effects-driven spectacular.

Scott stayed in the present with Black Rain (1989), although he goes to extraordinary lengths to transform Osaka into a futuristic urban landscape; small compensation for the crude representation of Japanese culture. From the scenes in a steelworks to the film's climactic shootout in a rain-drenched countryside, Scott ensures his locations have an otherworldly feel. Unfortunately, there is little quality in the writing, which posits a maverick, super-hero American cop against a host of racial stereotypes. Michael Douglas plays Nick Conklin, a 1990s Dirty Harry who is ordered to work with the Japanese police force after a high-ranking Yakuza member escapes from his custody. A lazy reworking of the fish-out-of-water theme, Black Rain is a thinly plotted thriller whose intermittent visual elegance fails to hide the tasteless American imperialism lurking beneath.

Deservedly, Scott achieved enormous international success with his next film, Thelma and Louise (1991), one of his best to date. A clever variation on the conventional road movie, it posits Geena Davis and Susan Sarandon's eponymous heroines against the men in their lives, who have cheated, robbed and abused them into becoming fugitives from a repressive patriarchal society. In many ways Scott's most conventional film, his directorial style appears equally at ease in the vast open plains of Midwest America, as it is in the heart of urban life. The expansive landscape, beautifully shot by Adrian Biddle, becomes a metaphor for the women's recently acquired freedom, where they find themselves as free and as powerful as the men who oppress them. A well-paced film, it offers the leads enough room to create a convincing bond of trust and loyalty, and with excellent support from mostly male cast of boyfriends, husbands, lovers and cheats.

In contrast to Thelma and Louise, 1492: Conquest of Paradise (1992) is a visually stunning, but dramatically leaden epic. Released to coincide with the 500th anniversary of Christopher Columbus' arrival on American shores, it stars Gérard Depardieu as the explorer, sent by Sigourney Weaver's Queen Isabela in search of land and wealth to expand Spain's immensely powerful empire and its already burgeoning coffers. An attempt to balance Columbus the myth with the man who brought destruction upon a civilisation, the film is too enamoured with the former, carving out a heroic figure of the explorer. Although efforts are made to account for the genocide that followed in the wake of the Spaniards' arrival, the perceived heroism of Columbus' actions prevents any scathing portrait of one nation's barbarism. However, Scott succeeds in creating a number of impressive set pieces, even if he fails to give the film an even pace.

Scott's next film, White Squall (1996), begins as a traditional rites-of-passage drama, but soon transforms into a terrifying fight for survival, affording him the opportunity to employ his trademark skill as a visually arresting director. Set in 1960, it tells of the disaster that befell the captain and teenage crew of The Albatross when they encountered a hurricane in the usually calm waters of the Caribbean. After a passable first half, in which each member of the crew is introduced and indulges in bonding and kinship, the film steadily gains pace as the storm moves in on The Albatross. A riveting piece of film-making, disorientating and emotionally devastating, Scott pulls out all the dramatic and technical stops to show The Albatross' last, terrifying moments. Ending with a court scene that attempts to investigate the skipper's liability for the boy's deaths, White Squall is a remarkable feat of suspense and drama trapped in an all-too-ordinary film.

Scott's most controversial work, G.I. Jane (1997), bears close resemblance to Tony Scott's work for 'high-concept' producers, Jerry Bruckheimer and Don Simpson. Marketed as a female version of Top Gun (1986), and equalling the earlier film in terms of its lack of intelligence and reliance upon a collection of overused clichés, it is a loud, brash and ultimately depressing film. It follows Demi Moore's transformation from an officer in the US Naval Ops room to a hardened member of the Marine Corps, charting the political minefield she has to traverse to get there. Unable to hold a shot without cutting every few seconds – a signature of the production team of Bruckheimer and the late Simpson

– the film attempts to create a drama out of every scene. Even the sight of Moore shaving her head warrants the use of rousing music and an aggressive, cod-masculine expression from the film's star. Any lucid attempt to analyse the place of women in the modern fighting force is lost through shallow characterisation and a risible script. *G.I. Jane* is a reactionary, unsubtle, and all-too-frequently offensive piece of film-making.

Gladiator (2000), however, is Scott's best film since *Thelma and Louise*. A tour-de-force of special effects and old-fashioned storytelling, it succeeds through the careful blending of the familiar and the new. The awe-inspiring sets that dominated the old epics are made more impressive with the use of CGI effects, as are the monumental battle scenes, including a chariot race that echoes *Ben Hur* (1959). Also present are the scheming siblings, political intrigue and clichéd dialogue. However, these elements are updated, to satiate the appetite of a more knowing, contemporary audience. Scott draws fine performances from a large cast, including Russell Crowe and Joaquin Phoenix, and never allows the battles to dominate the drama.

Following *Gladiator*, hopes were high for Scott's version of Thomas Harris' bestseller 'Hannibal'. Although Jodie Foster refused to reprise her role as Clarice Starling, the FBI agent who forms an intimate, yet dangerous, bond with the renowned serial killer, Hannibal Lecter, Julianne Moore's involvement guaranteed the presence of another strong female character actress. However, *Hannibal* (2001) is a veritable cornucopia of Scott trademarks. From a surprisingly lazy adaptation by David Mamet and Steven Zaillian, Scott drowns the film in atmospheric lighting and morning mists, accompanied by a bombastic Hans Zimmer score. As a result, the film never achieves the sense of menace that haunted both *Manhunter* (1986) and *Silence of the Lambs* (1991). Best are the scenes in Florence, where Anthony Hopkins' operatic performance is matched by the surrounding architecture, whose decadent past suits the flamboyant psychopath. Once the action returns to America, the film becomes a routine cat-and-mouse thriller. Hopkins' campiness looks out of place, while Moore flounders in a role that seems to have lost its sense of purpose. Only the scenes with Gary Oldman, who plays Lecter's surviving victim, and the final, grotesque dinner scene, provide the macabre mood that the rest of the film desperately lacks.

Black Hawk Down (2001), Scott's most recent release, tells of the ill-fated 1993 mission by a group of US Army Rangers in Mogadishu, Somalia. A dawn raid that went disastrously wrong, the film documents the Rangers' attempts to escape the labyrinthine passages of Mogadishu's market area, whilst fighting off the army of a corrupt Somalian warlord. The ensuing battle resulted in the death of 19 Rangers and over 1,000 Somalians. Scott's film presents a blow-by-blow account of how the mission went wrong, from the shooting down of the first Black Hawk helicopter to the wholesale destruction of the centre of Mogadishu and the Rangers' eventual escape. Continuing the hyperreal style adopted by Steven Spielberg for *Saving Private Ryan* (1998), Scott's recreation of one of the most bloody battles in recent military history makes for mostly uncomfortable viewing. With little exposition to explain the complex political situation in Somalia and the merest hint of characterisation, the film is a cacophonic assemblage of fast cuts punctuated by bursts of ear-splitting gunfire, bomb blasts and helicopter drones. The band of trapped Rangers are frequently indistinguishable from each other, whilst the Somalians are portrayed as little more than a faceless aggressor; this is highlighted in the closing credits where each dead Ranger is named and the Somalians are mentioned only in the number of their dead.

Deeply unsettling, *Black Hawk Down*'s attempt at verisimilitude inadvertently raises questions about the function of mainstream cinema. Like many effects-laden blockbusters, the film is technically impressive. However, it is hardly an entertainment. Lacking little more than a skeletal narrative, it may be considered anti-war or a testament to the bravery of the soldiers trapped in the most formidable situation. Either way, it sits uneasily with the contemporary notion of the big-budget, multiplex release. And as such, it may prove to be one of Scott's most fascinating films.                **IHS**

# Tony SCOTT

*The Hunger* (1983)  Tony Scott is probably the ultimate post-MTV film-maker. Born in the UK in 1944
*Top Gun* (1986)  and educated at the Leeds College of Art and Royal College of Art, he formed part of a
*Beverly Hills Cop II* (1987)  wave of British-born Hollywood directors emerging from the field of advertising in the

1970s (including his brother Ridley). Scott's films have been unashamedly commercial and, working mostly within the action/thriller genres, he directed some of the most financially successful features of the 1980s for the production team of Don Simpson and Jerry Bruckheimer. This creative collaboration helped to redefine commercial American cinema, placing emphasis on slick, high-concept narratives while drawing heavily from the diffused, neon-tinged visual style of music videos and commercials, complete with rapid-fire editing and prominent rock soundtracks. Seemingly crass and impersonal, the films have nevertheless been hugely influential, both in their stylistic bombast and their ultimate reduction of the action genres to pure masculinist fantasy. Ridley Scott has defined his brother's aesthetic as 'rock 'n' roll' while the critic John Harkness called him 'the crown prince of the inexplicable light source'.

Scott's first feature is in many ways one of his most interesting. The Hunger (1983) puts a fresh spin on the vampire myth, cushioning its thin narrative of immortal lovers in a series of emptily sumptuous visuals. Its modish surface design outweighs any deeper engagement with the vampire myth but it is a commendable attempt to update the sub-genre. Unusually for Scott, the film centres on two female characters (played by Catherine Deneuve and Susan Sarandon) but the sexual dimension to their relationship is too entrenched in male fantasy to be completely convincing. The film also provides David Bowie with one of his best screen roles.

Scott subsequently embarked on his Simpson and Bruckheimer period, testosterone-fuelled action fantasies in which the signature of the production team was as prominent as that of the director. Top Gun (1986) clumsily appends Reaganite Cold War politics to a male rites-of-passage saga, its homoerotic undertones in constant tension with its hyper-masculine form. Dubbed memorably by one critic 'Phallus in Wonderland', the film is the neo-conservative military fantasy par excellence, shamelessly manipulative but depressingly schematic in its conflict resolutions. However, its impressive aerial action sequences lend the film genuine excitement and it consolidated Tom Cruise's status as a major star. Unfortunately, both Beverly Hills Cop II (1987) and Days of Thunder (1990) are abysmally retrograde films, the former diluting the social force and humour of its predecessor, the latter failing spectacularly in its attempt to transfer the narrative project of Top Gun onto a car-racing scenario. The film also brought the collaborative blockbuster success of Scott, Simpson and Bruckheimer to a temporary halt.

Revenge (1990), a male-centred melodrama starring Kevin Costner, was little seen upon its release. The straightforward action thriller The Last Boy Scout (1991) was a much more confident work, however, benefiting from a flip, profane, Shane Black script and some amusing interplay between the leads, Bruce Willis and Damon Wayans. The film gleefully sends up the dynamics of the buddy/action genre while delivering the requisite brutality in regular doses. The film's philosophy is summed up by the sequence in which Willis reduces a potential assassin to hysterics with a stream of wisecracks before plugging him full of bullets.

Scott carried this new sense of irony and parody over into True Romance (1993), resulting in his best film to date. Working from Quentin Tarantino's script and taking advantage of an eclectic cast, which includes Dennis Hopper, Brad Pitt, Gary Oldman, and Christopher Walken, the film achieves the allusive, pop culture sensibility of its writer's directorial work while retaining Scott's familiar visual design. Drawing from a 'lovers on the run' scenario (played in a strangely touching fashion by Christian Slater and Patricia Arquette), the film veers between extreme violence and comedy, fusing these elements brilliantly in the fatal verbal showdown between Hopper and Walken. Yet there is little in the film of genuine, tangible substance beyond its relationship to the popular culture it regurgitates.

Scott's subsequent work in the 1990s has been patchy and not always confined to the screen. In 1994 he headed a consortium – along with brother Ridley – to buy Shepperton studios, evidence perhaps of a desire to establish a solid production base in his home country. However, he continued to work as a director exclusively in the commercial American industry. Crimson Tide (1995) is a suspenseful military thriller that benefits from a pair of strong lead performances by Gene Hackman and Denzel Washington. Although its Cold War themes seem a little anachronistic, it handles the attendant masculine conflicts in a much more delicate fashion than Top Gun. The Fan (1996) only scrapes the surface of its potentially rich material, the study of sports celebrities and their relationship to fans, giving way to standard psycho-thriller conventions. The film relies on Robert De Niro's title performance, an interesting variation on his gallery of unhinged loners, albeit one that does not match similar material in Martin Scorsese's *The King of Comedy* (1983).

The Will Smith vehicle *Enemy of the State* (1998) is a high-tech thriller in which any genuine paranoid frisson is negated by standard chase scenes and explosions. Gene Hackman's presence, in a role which recalls his character in Francis Ford Coppola's *The Conversation* (1974), only serves to remind the viewer of a time when conspiracy thrillers actually inspired the audience to think. Scott attempted to fashion a more thoughtful spy thriller in *Spy Game* (2001) but the results are decidedly mixed. Told in a series of flashbacks, the film often plays like a checklist of recent covert operations by the US intelligence services. Attempts to give the themes some kind of relevance are drowned in Scott's familiar stylistic bombast. Furthermore, the surrogate father/son dynamic established between the male leads (Robert Redford and Brad Pitt) hints at darker Oedipal undertones but it is resolved in an all-too-familiar rescue climax. Relishing the chance to photograph a variety of international locations, the film seems to yearn for the Cold War era it recreates. Indeed, while attempting to develop complex motivations in its protagonists, Scott ultimately makes sure we know just who the good guys and the bad guys are. **NJ**

# Susan SEIDELMAN

The films of Susan Seidelman are characterised by her strong female protagonists and a concern with the female point of view. Born in Pennsylvania in 1952, Seidelman attended the Drexel Institute of Technology, Philadelphia. From there, she entered the Graduate School of Film and Television at New York University, where she enjoyed success as a film student. Her first short film *And You Act Like One, Too* won a Student Academy Award.

Seidelman's first feature, *Smithereens* (1982), tells the story of Wren, a selfish young punk who wants to make it in the music business. A truly independent film, Seidelman managed to raise a total of $80,000 by forming limited partnerships with friends and family. *Smithereens* enjoyed critical success and entered the main competition at the 1982 Cannes Film Festival.

Wren foreshadows the character of Susan in her next feature, *Desperately Seeking Susan* (1985). The film is a romantic comedy centring on bored housewife Roberta (Rosanna Arquette), who is tired of being a mere accessory for her yuppie husband (Mark Blum) and becomes mixed up in the life of the street-smart and nomadic Susan (Madonna). Much of the film's success has been attributed to the rise of Madonna as a pop artist. Yet it contains some sharply observed moments: its opening sequence provides a neat subversion of the fetishisation and dissection of women's bodies under the traditional male gaze. *Desperately Seeking Susan* received generally favourable reviews and earned back six times its original cost of $5 million.

After the success of *Desperately Seeking Susan*, Seidelman was offered a three-picture deal with Orion, marking the beginning of a difficult period for the director. *Making Mr. Right* (1987) took an interesting idea – a woman falling for an android – and mixed the genres of science fiction and comedy, unsuccessfully. Acting as both director and an executive producer for her next feature, *Cookie* (1989) did little business commercially and generally disappointed critics. Seidelman's final picture in the Orion deal was *She-Devil* (1989), which she produced and directed. Despite the hostile responses of critics – 'an abysmal piece of junk' – the film satisfactory rendered Fay Weldon's tale of a spurned, frumpy housewife (Roseanne Barr) taking revenge on her shallow, cheating husband (Ed Begley Jr) and his mistress (Meryl Streep).

In 1992 she was commissioned by Scottish Television to make a documentary, *Confessions of a Suburban Girl* (1992). It provides great insight into the development of Seidelman's oeuvre as director: her fascination with tough, bad girls; her observations on the material conditions of women's lives; and society's obsession with beauty. She has since directed a short film, *The Dutch Master* (1995), which was nominated in the 1995 Academy Awards competition for Best Live Action Short. From 1996 to 1999, Seidelman worked in television directing episodes of popular television shows including 'Early Edition', 'Now and Again', and 'Sex and the City', and directed a television movie, *Beauty and Power* (2001).

Her most recent feature, *Gaudi Afternoon* (2001), is an engaging and unconventional comic mystery with a noirish flavour that centres on Cassandra (Judy Davis), an American translator working in Barcelona. To supplement her income she agrees to track down the husband of the enigmatic Frankie (Marcia Gay Harden), which leads her to various truths about herself and the peculiar characters she meets. The plot is somewhat convoluted but the performances are strong enough to carry the twists and turns. Well received by critics, *Gaudi Afternoon* is a welcome return to form from one of the foremost female directors working in the contemporary scene. **SL**

# Henry SELICK

Henry Selick is an important and distinctive figure, championing and perpetuating the art of stop-motion animation in feature-length form. Resisting traditional cel animation, and the high-gloss dynamics of computer generated imagery (CGI), Selick's work represents enhancement and continuity in a field stretching back as far as the pioneering 'trick' films of J. Stuart Blackton and Albert E. Smith at the turn of the twentieth century.

*Seepage* (1979)
*Nightmare Before Christmas* (1993)
*James and the Giant Peach* (1995)
*Monkeybone* (2001)

Selick's collaboration with Tim Burton, *Nightmare Before Christmas* (1993), which references Ray Harryhausen's work in featuring Jack Skellington, a skeletal hero, effectively re-established stop-motion animation as a 'low-tech' approach to film-making, promoting the use of the technique to carry the complete narrative of a film, rather than merely using it in effects sequences. The distinctive style and movement added to the sense of surreal beauty and supernatural eccentricity at the heart of the film. Drawing upon influences as diverse as Fred Astaire, Francis Bacon, Dr Seuss, Edward Gorey, Mario Bava, and F. W. Murnau, Selick conjures an elegance and sophistication in the work that has the hallucinatory spirit of dream and the heightened – and sometimes perverse – energy of celebration. Its almost Brechtian operatic quality foregrounds tour de force sequences of black humour that far outweigh any nominal redemption in Disney-esque sentimentality.

Selick was born in New Jersey in 1958 and subsequently became an Art Major at Syracuse University. He also trained at St. Martin's School of Art in London, and was a graduate of the California Institute of the Arts, where he was taught by Jules Engel. Joining Disney, he worked on the title characters for *The Fox and the Hound* (1981), created alien creatures for *Watcher in the Woods* (1981), and made an influential pilot film called *Slow Bob in the Lower Dimensions* (1990), a collage work featuring dancing scissors. Other significant work includes his 'as filmed' storyboards for the 'Claymation' sequences of Walter Murch's *Return to Oz* (1985) and challenging MTV inserts. He also made his own short film, *Seepage* (1979), using life-size stop-motion figures, which is executed in a modernist style, recalling cubism and expressionism.

Selick's most significant achievement to date is *James and the Giant Peach* (1995), which combines stop-motion animation with CGI, hand-painted backgrounds and effects, and live action. Sensitively re-writing Roald Dahl's popular story, Selick sought to use the extended animated sequence in the middle of the film, bookended by live action, to achieve an Oz-like transition into a colourful and exciting fantasy world. Alongside the seamless gleam of the CGI, the director envisaged an approach which echoed the *bunraku* puppetry of Japan, in which the puppet mechanism and the puppeteer are observed. This sense of the 'home-made' in the *mise-en-scène* suits the theatricality of the main insect characters as they perform on the literally limited 'stage' of the peach. Selick's tour de force underwater sequence, featuring a cameo by Jack Skellington, is another direct homage to Harryhausen's skeleton fight, but also to Disney's *Pinocchio* (1940).

Selick's most recent feature, *Monkey Bone* (2001), progresses his work, stretching the boundaries of the psychological, emotional, geographical, and supernatural environments his technique can embrace. The story, based on a graphic novel by Kaja Blackley, concerns a cartoonist (payed by Brendan Fraser) trapped in a coma, who is given twelve hours to find a way out of the labyrinth of his own dreams and nightmares before he eventually dies. Selick's achievement and influence should not be undervalued, as it represents both a continuity in the form, and the maintenance of a predominantly European aesthetic tradition, and consequently, demonstrable 'art', in feature-length Hollywood products. **PW**

# Dominic SENA

Born in 1949 in Ohio, Dominic Sena established a reputation in the 1980s by directing music videos for high-profile artists such as David Bowie, Janet Jackson, Elton John, and Sting. His approach was highly energetic and visually lavish, aspects of style he has brought to his cinematic projects *Kalifornia* (1993), *Gone in 60 Seconds* (2000), and *Swordfish* (2001).

*Kalifornia* is a member of the long-standing road movie genre, but one that also attempts to explore psychopathology, sexual and class politics, and the media's voyeuristic obsession with serial killings. David Duchovny plays Brian, a writer researching serial killers, who shares a trip to California with his sexy photographer girlfriend and a poor redneck couple, one of which emerges as a brutal murderer. The premise is self-reflexive: even as Brian is forced to face the subject of his once-objective fascination, and literally learn what motivates a killer, the audience are implicated as the hungry voyeurs that fuel the media's demand for visceral inside information about such killers. However, the film doesn't appear to know what to do with this potent concept (which pre-dates the much more socially-debated *Natural Born Killers* (1994)), preoccupied as it is with the sensational images of murder. It negates its own agenda by simply supplying the food of voyeurism, rather than analysing or critiquing it: shockingly close-up images of stabbings and shootings are interspersed with stylised scenes of violent weather and dark interiors, which seek to generate excited anticipation of the pending doom. Brad Pitt's idiosyncratic performance as killer Early Grayce won the attention of the media, but the overpowering presence of his inarticulate hillbilly render pale the rest of the film's efforts, and Sena's flash visual style merely adds a veneer to the weak narrative frame.

A long time coming, Sena's second feature *Gone in 60 Seconds*, is a remake of the 1974 film by H. B. Halicki. Nicolas Cage, with his proven on-screen charisma, signed up for the lead role and is supported by Academy Award-winners Robert Duvall and Angelina Jolie as well as imported British stars Christopher Eccleston and Vinnie Jones. Produced by blockbuster veteran Jerry Bruckheimer, it is the story of a retired car-thief who, to save his brother's life, has to do one more theft and steal fifty cars in one night. From its speedy MTV-like credits the film moves with dizzying energy, roaming the various LA locations and jumps headlong into the central dilemma. Although the thumping soundtrack compounds this edgy pace, during the critical car chase moments, it diffuses, rather than heightens, the tension. Critics tended to dislike these scenes and compared the film unfavourably to classics such as *Bullitt* (1968), *The French Connection* (1971), or even *Ronin* (1998); it seems Sena's kinetic camera work, which he relies on to create excitement, is too fast for the cars themselves. A tired and clichéd script furthers the disappointment.

Sena followed up the flash-and-dazzle of *Gone in 60 Seconds* with *Swordfish* (2001), a techno-thriller that is also technically proficient but narratively slack. Hugh Jackman plays a computer hacker roped into a billion dollar heist by a psychotic John Travolta in a plot that is predictably flaccid and overly reliant on *Dog Day Afternoon* (1975) and *Heat* (1995) influences; still, it retains an enjoyable boy's own quality replete with witty one-liners, a cast of indie oddballs (Don Cheadle, Sam Shepard), and the requisite 'money shot' – in this case a huge explosion that Sena lovingly films in sepia slowmotion. The rest of the film seems almost in awe of the opening sequence, which may explain its lack of narrative cohesion and anti-climax. Jackman plays the embittered hacker with brio, but the real star is Travolta, whose charisma and sex-appeal has never been better captured, and whose opening gambit – 'You know what the problem with Hollywood is – they make shit' – is hopefully an ironic counterpoint to Sena's superficial yet dynamic direction. **MS & BM**

# Tom SHADYAC

Born in 1960, Tom Shadyac moved to Hollywood in 1983 and, at age 23, became the youngest staff joke writer ever for comedian Bob Hope. After completing a film degree at UCLA in 1989 (which included the critically acclaimed short *Tom, Dick and Harry*), he worked in movies-of-the-week and stand-up comedy before turning into one of Hollywood's most sought after comedy writer-directors. In the space of four years he has worked with America's three funniest men – Jim Carrey, Eddie Murphy, and

Robin Williams – and although his output has been either woefully crass or criminally overplayed, he has maintained a level of toilet-humour and *Carry On*-esque mock innocence that cleverly taps into audiences' collective consciousness.

His debut feature, *Ace Ventura: Pet Detective* (1994), in which Jim Carrey plays the eponymous 'hero', made over $65 million in the States, despite its self-indulgent japes and reliance on the star's sledgehammer subtlety. Shadyac instantaneously created the Carrey phenomenon (all mugging and rubber-mouthed), handed Sean Young the most demeaning role of her career (women mean little to Shadyac), and proved that woeful parody of other films could effectively efface the role of the director.

He teamed up with Eddie Murphy to film *The Nutty Professor* (1996), a remake of the 1963 Jerry Lewis vehicle. Murphy plays Klump, a 28-stone scientist who discovers a potion that overnight turns him into a slim, suave dandy. As with *Coming to America* (1988), the best bits of the film are when the star plays several different characters sat around a table – the requisite fart jokes and fat gags are all present and correct – and allows Murphy free rein to indulge. This seems to be the leitmotif of Shadyac's work, penning scripts that allow his leading men to run riot with improvisation, mugging and, occasionally, inventiveness.

The same is true of Carrey in *Liar Liar* (1997), a film in which his lawyer is foced to tell the truth for a whole 24 hours by his son after he forgets his birthday. Probably the most mainstream of Shadyac's films, the narrative can at least purport to be a serious/comic look at the US's depiction of lawyers. Carrey's role as a father is also questioned, leading to debates about paternal responsibility and tradition. Beneath this veneer of profundity, however, lies a swamp of overacting and elastic buffoonery from Carrey, who by now was quickly beginning to grate.

He reached a nadir with *Patch Adams* (1998), in which Robin Williams essays his worst ever role. Set in 1969, it is the story of Dr Adams and his decision to shake up the medical profession by cheering up terminally ill patients through the healing power of laughter. Warm and fuzzy, Williams runs the gamut of emotions. Shadyac and company have taken the admittedly radical source autobiography ('Gesundheit: Good Health is a Laughing Matter') but shaved off all the interesting adjuncts (trips around Europe, Adams' status as conscientious objector) to concentrate on his effect in the hospital. Shadyac insists on placing reaction shot after reaction shot of patients bent over double in laughter – by the end, the audience is numbed into believing we have just watched two hours of Williams' shtick rather than the development of a character. Shadyac employs real cancer patients in the hospital scenes which is a gross miscalculation; that they are wheeled in at the end as a kind of syrupy punchline highlights the director's career reliance on his star's egotism to the detriment of socio-politically grounded humour or ironic treatment of American institutions.

In a distinct change of pace, Shadyac's most recent film, *Dragonfly* (2002), stars Kevin Costner as a man whose deceased wife tries to communicate a message to him from beyond the grave. Clearly trawling the same territory as the infinitely superior *The Sixth Sense* (1999), it still manages to thrill and chill in equal measure, and the last-reel twist is refreshingly innovative. Most critics were unimpressed with Costner's somewhat wooden central performance, but he plays his role with the required subtlety and stillness; he is ably supported by Kathy Bates and Linda Hunt. Ultimately, the film is a typical curate's egg – somewhat derivative and slack, it still convinces through solid acting, experimental camera work, and a strong central premise.

His next film, *Bruce Almighty*, will star Jim Carrey once again, this time as a man who constantly complains and is challenged by God to do a better job.          **BM**

# Ron SHELTON

A former baseball player, born in California in 1945, whose film influences range from Buster Keaton to Sam Peckinpah, Ron Shelton is best known for a body of work that uses sport to examine the role of masculinity in American society. Probing the divide between the real lives of sporting heroes and the myths that surround them, Shelton focuses on the outsider and their attempts to achieve success, often at great personal cost.

*Bull Durham* (1988) is a scabrous comedy that charts the fall and rise of a minor league baseball team over one season. By employing the construct of the love triangle, with all three characters playing a pivotal role in the success of the team, Shelton draws hilarious parallels between the ball players' professional and personal lives. Central to the drama is the turbulent relationship between Kevin Costner's seasoned pro and Tim Robbins' talented but hot-headed rookie. Competing as suitors for the attention of Annie (Susan Sarandon), who picks the most promising player as her sexual partner for the season, 'Crash' Davis (Costner) and 'Nuke' Lalouche (Robbins) enter into a jocular battle to assert their dominance amidst the sweaty environment of the locker room. Annie, whose commentary on masculine pride and mens' relationship to women, sex and sport, gently mocks the male ego. An immensely enjoyable debut, *Bull Durham* highlights Shelton's knack at revealing more about the nature of sport off the field rather than on it.

*Blaze* (1989) remains Shelton's most offbeat and unsuccessful film. The story of Earl K. Long's (brother of Huey) affair with stripper Blaze Starr, the film is little more than a vehicle for Paul Newman. As governor of Louisiana during the 1950s, Long was famous for his radical view on politics, which included enfranchising the black vote. However, Shelton's script is too lightweight to show more than scant interest in Long's political career, preferring to focus on his relationship with Blaze. Although Newman is well cast as the charming and eccentric politician, Lolita Davidovich's role is so underwritten, it becomes difficult to understand why Long would risk his career for the stripper. As a result, the film fails to satisfy as either a political satire or light drama.

*White Men Can't Jump* (1992) is Shelton's most commercially successful film to date, returning to the masculinity-in-crisis themes of *Bull Durham*. Woody Harrelson and Wesley Snipes play Billy and Sidney, two competing, small-time basketball hustlers who agree to forget their differences in order to pursue higher stakes, which will resolve Billy's debts with a group of loansharks. A fast-paced, well-written comedy that plays like an invigorating variant of the buddy formula, Shelton draws excellent performances from Snipes and Harrelson, while Rosie Perez offers strong support as Billy's dreamer girlfriend. Most impressive of all is Shelton's ability to transfer the excitement of basketball to the screen. Whizzing around the court, the camera becomes another player in the game, transporting the audience to the centre of the action.

Shelton's second baseball film, *Cobb* (1994), has been referred to as the *Citizen Kane* (1941) of sports movies. An account of journalist Al Stump's collaboration with Ty Cobb, on the baseball legend's biography, it is an articulate attempt to deal with the nature of myth through a man who was a hero to a nation but a liar, bully and killer to those who knew him. Narrated by Stump, whose desire to tell the great, all-American hero story conflicts with his belief in revealing the truth at any cost, Shelton offers an uncompromising biopic of the greatest player in baseball history. It succeeds because of Shelton's unwillingness to shy away from Cobb's violent and bigoted personality, as well as Tommy Lee Jones's remarkable performance. Impressively incorporating fake documentary footage and flashbacks to Cobb's youth, it is Shelton's most impressive piece of film-making to date.

After the commercial failure of *Cobb*, Shelton returned to the romantic comedy of *Bull Durham*. In *Tin Cup* (1996), Kevin Costner plays Roy 'Tin Cup' McAvoy, a golf pro who has hit hard times, spending most of his days knocking balls out into the wastelands of West Texas. When he meets Molly Griswald (Rene Russo), he finds a reason to go back to the professional circuit. Another entertaining comedy of egos, *Tin Cup* offers relaxed performances from Costner and Russo. Again, Shelton toys with representations of masculinity and the character's desire to achieve greatness, but the film differs from *Bull Durham* in documenting how Roy's ambition is transformed into blind obsession. Ultimately, his victory is more pyrrhic than triumphant. *Tin Cup* may not be Shelton's strongest film but it is a fine example of his brand of intelligent, mature entertainment.

*Play it to the Bone* (1999) also toys with representations of myth and heroism. Woody Harrelson and Antonio Banderas play two ageing boxers, whose desire for greatness is contrasted against the reality of their situation. When they are offered the chance to fight each other in the supporting bout of a Mike Tyson match, they hardly consider the ramifications the fight may have on their friendship. Shelton's most visceral film, *Play it to the Bone* incorporates the darker tone of *Cobb* amidst the banter recognisable from most of his work. As a result, it is an unsettling comedy, which never shies away from the brutality of the sporting world. Gone is *Bull Durham*'s rhapsody to the life of the all-American sportsman. In its place is the zealous pursuit of fame and fortune. In a world where money has a stranglehold on the Olympian image of the sporting hero, Ron Shelton's romanticism is gradually transforming into grim fatalism.

His latest film, *Dark Blue* (2002), is a police drama adapted from a story by James Ellroy and based on the 1992 LA riots.                                                    **IHS**

# Sam SHEPARD

Sam Shepard was born in California in 1943 and as a director of just two films, is better known as America's most popular and prolific playwright, but has also featured as an accomplished actor in films such as Terrence Malick's *Days of Heaven* (1978). Many critics have referred to his preoccupation with rural America, its mythologised history, and troubled contemporary masculine identities. Indeed these familiarities of his theatre have prevailed in his transitions to film-making.

*Far North* (1988) is Shepard's first feature film, which many claimed to be a failure. Based around a father's attempt to have the horse that put him in hospital killed, it is fair to say that this film offers little narrative development. However, the domestic realism and mythic imagery hint at Shepard's brilliant theatrical renderings of the decline of the American cowboy. The references to the lack of 'menfolk', Shepard's attention to the squabbling all-female family left on the ranch in the father's absence, and the dream sequence of the hardworking men from the farm sitting down to a hearty meal together connote a nostalgia for strong rural male figures, the Marlboro men, that were recurrent in Shepard's plays. This small-town, domestic comedy, responds to a crisis in masculinity in post-industrial America and predates Alan Taylor's *Palookaville* (1996).

In the character Bertrum, and his symbolic death premonition involving wild native American chanting, *Far North* also touches on, without fully developing, an anxiety about America's buried history. *Silent Tongue* (1993) elaborates on this anxiety. As in much of his theatre Shepard offers a bleak view of the family unit in the McCrees, when Eamon sells both his daughters in exchange for horses. However, this film is better remembered for its supernatural sub-plot of Talbot Roe's (River Phoenix) deceased half-Indian wife who was sold like a slave, returning as a ghost seeking to avenge her misery. The use of haunting native-American music, the subtle symbolism of the savage desert eagle, the Indian paintings and the terrifying, menacing, face-painted Awbonnie who rises from the flames, bring to Shepard's cinema a distinct uneasiness about America's past which is at once identifiable with Jonathan Demme's later adaptation of Toni Morrison's *Beloved* (1998), a story of a sacrificed slave child returning to haunt.                            **JO**

*Far North* (1988)
*Silent Tongue* (1993)

# Cindy SHERMAN

Born in Glen Ridge, New Jersey, in 1954, Cindy Sherman trained in art before turning to photography, perhaps as a result of her relationship with, and interest in, the work of photographer Robert Longo. By the early 1980s, as the New York art scene was thriving, Sherman was exhibiting early small black and white prints. She developed themes concerning the representation of women as seen in paintings, and, more significantly, in movies. Turning to self-portraiture as a means of dealing with her lack of confidence, her series 'Untitled Film Stills' positions her in a variety of traditional, passive female roles. Although some are in colour, lending them a Sirkian tone, many are in black and white, resonant of the earlier classic period of Hollywood movies. Utilising high-contrast lighting, and sharp angles, the photos are both a witty and disturbing attempt to deconstruct femininity and female identity, with Sherman photographing herself in a variety of 'feminine' guises. The dichotomy between the inference of the moving image offered by the film stills, and the frozen photographed image itself, present much of work's power and meaning. Intrigued by the grotesquerie of Hans Bellmer's doll exhibits, Sherman also began to produce darker work, in which a vivid interest in death is evident.

These influences and working styles combined on Sherman's first, and thus far only, venture into feature film-making, *Office Killer* (1997), which was made for $300,000 with the backing of Christine Vachon and Ted Hope's Good Machine production company. The film's debt to the New York independent film scene is also evident in the writing – Tom Kalin co-wrote and Todd Haynes contributed dialogue. The film – in which Sherman does not appear – concerns the reaction of office underdog Dorine Douglas

*Office Killer* (1997)

(Carol Kane) when her job is down-sized to a home job. Before she leaves, an accidental electrocution of a colleague unleashes murderous tendencies; she continues killing her co-workers until her mother's basement is a makeshift office of corpses, whose deaths are a triumph of B-movie gore.

Seen as a form of morality tale, the film suffers from its intellectual approach and lacks the high camp that has made many Hollywood B-movies successful. Like other feminist artists venturing into feature film-making, Sherman imposes a theoretical approach. The 'hysterical glamour' of her visual style involves some typical Sherman-esque images, mainly in the dominant headshot close-ups of Dorine's victims and of perky rival Kim (Molly Ringwald) smoking on the stairs, which convey Sherman's interest in the seductiveness of the superficial. A backstory involving Eric Bogosian as Dorine's abusive father, whom she killed years before, awkwardly justifies her behaviour. Dimly-lit, and partially experimental, the film did not achieve the success of Sherman's still photographs, which, ironically, considering this film's proud B-movie status, sell for Hollywood-style dollars.                                                                              **JD**

# M. Night SHYAMALAN

*Praying With Anger* (1992)
*Wide Awake* (1998)
*The Sixth Sense* (1999)
*Unbreakable* (2000)
*Signs* (2002)

At the very end of the twentieth century, M. Night Shyamalan seemingly appeared out of nowhere to inject some surprising life into the box office with his supernatural hit, *The Sixth Sense* (1999). It was actually the writer-director's third film, but it instantly established him as a fully-bloomed talent, a contemporary master craftsman on the level of a Spielberg or a Cameron. With his imaginative but economical camerawork, light touch with actors (especially children), and an apparently inherent knack for spinning a cracking good campfire yarn, Shyamalan is that rarest of birds: a crowd-pleaser with a brain.

Born Manoj Shyamalan in India in 1970 ('Night' is a stage name the director chose while still in his early teens), the future auteur was raised by doctor parents in the privileged Penn Valley area of Philadelphia. Like his hero Spielberg, Shyamalan's zeal for film-making was incited early on, with the gift of a Super 8 camera at age eight. After graduating from NYU's film program, and with his family's help, he raised the $750,000 necessary to fund his first film, the cultural and spiritual coming-of-age story, *Praying With Anger* (1992). The picture traces the emotional awakening of an Indian-American exchange student (played by Shyamalan himself), who is forever changed after he spends a semester abroad in the homeland of his mother and recently deceased father. Visually, the film belies its modest budget, capturing both the vibrancy and grandeur of India and displaying Shyamalan's eye for elegantly composed *mise-en-scène*. *Praying With Anger* also plants the early seeds for a number of Shyamalan's thematic concerns. His character's quest for spiritual truth (he's introduced first-hand to Hindu faith and beliefs) prefigures the arc of his next film, *Wide Awake* (1998), while several scenes based in and around a seance foreshadow the otherworldy musings of *The Sixth Sense*. Interestingly, the director's first three films feature young protagonists forced to deal with the consequences of death, but only *Praying With Anger* visualises this struggle with a touch of magic realism, in a enchanting moment that has a lone Shyamalan joined by the spectre of his late father, who's seen cast as a shadow on the wall next to his own.

*Wide Awake*, Shyamalan's second film as a writer-director, and his first for a studio, is a markedly less successful effort. Released by Miramax, it was reportedly badly mishandled throughout its production, the delicate story becoming the unravelled victim of ego clashes and differences of opinion. The narrative of a young boy who begins questioning the existence of God after the death of his beloved grandfather, it was shot at the Philadelphia-area Catholic school Shyamalan himself once attended. There's not much here that delivers on the promise of *Praying With Anger*, or that hints at the ambition of his later work, as *Wide Awake* settles instead into the overly cloying, sentimental rhythms of a warm-hued family picture. Only the film's final moments give an indication as to the next step in Shyamalan's evolution as a storyteller, with a final metaphysical plot twist that's almost more moving than it is mawkish.

The metaphysical plot twist of *The Sixth Sense*, on the other hand, is central to its classy, B-movie effectiveness. Handsomely photographed (by Jonathan Demme collaborator Tak Fujimoto), it is a melancholy ghost story that revolves around yet another troubled young boy (Haley Joel Osment) – one who has the unwanted psychic ability to 'see dead people' – and his relationship with the determined therapist (Bruce Willis) who attempts to help him. Shyamalan constructs his deceptively simple narrative with the skill and flair of a magician, playing with audience expectations even as he deftly subverts them, quietly building to the final and unexpected revelation that Willis has himself been dead throughout virtually the entire film. Shyamalan is able to accomplish this feat through the subtle withholding of information, smartly presenting Willis' 'life' as the character himself perceives it: that he and his wife have grown apart because of his uneasy recovery from a gunshot wound inflicted a year earlier, which we learn in the final few moments was, in fact, fatal. Nowhere is this idea better presented than in the film's poignant anniversary dinner scene, captured in a single, insinuating shot as Willis arrives and makes his apologies for being late, only to have his wife turn away and ask for the check. What on the surface appears to be a sharp, pithy observation of a marriage in crisis gains unexpected depth when revisited later; indeed, the film's greatest strength is the airtight logic of Shyamalan's clever visual double meanings in every scene featuring Willis. Here as elsewhere, the director builds suspense and atmosphere with graceful, gliding camera work that lends his film the floating sensation of a lingering dream.

Shyamalan and Willis reunited a year later for *Unbreakable* (2000), a vastly underrated and misunderstood picture that furthered the young writer-director's themes of loss and responsibility even while it covered new ground in its modern, highly adult exploration of the superhero myth. Once again, death – and the inevitability of it – hangs over Shyamalan's characters: David Dunn (Willis), the unharmed sole survivor of a horrible train wreck, and Elijah Price (Samuel L. Jackson), a comic book collector with a debilitating bone condition, who seeks out and befriends Dunn, believing him to be the earthly manifestation of one of his four-colour heroes. Derided by critics and audiences who expected another supernatural thriller in the mold of *The Sixth Sense* (and were, for their trouble, treated to another story-redefining twist ending), *Unbreakable* turns out to be the more daring piece of work; an action movie premise that plays out as deliberately paced psychological drama, as Dunn gradually comes to understand precisely who and what he is. Shyamalan once again shoots with an eye towards minimal coverage, letting many of his scenes play out in elegantly composed masters that recall the bold panel illustrations of a graphic novel. He also uses an upside-down frame as a recurring visual motif, nicely reflecting the dynamic, funhouse mirror opposition of the Willis and Jackson characters. Like *The Sixth Sense, Unbreakable* is most notable for the skilful balance of cool intelligence and genuine emotion Shyamalan brings to an oft-disrespected genre.

Shyamalan has shown no indication of losing interest in otherworldly events; his most recent film, *Signs* (2002), which stars Mel Gibson, involved mysterious crop circles. **CS**

## Alex SICHEL

Alex Sichel first made an impression on the film festival circuit with her short, *Amnesia*, *All Over Me* (1997) but her first feature, *All Over Me* (1997), which she wrote, produced, and directed, premiered and was part of the official selection at the Sundance Film Festival.

The film is a painful and often grim tale of the dissolving relationship between teenage friends Claude (Alison Folland) and Ellen (Tara Subkoff). Set in Hell's Kitchen, its coming-of-age and coming-out narrative takes place against the back-drop of drug abuse, street violence, and homophobia. The film provides an edgy and honest depiction of the two kids' disaffection – from the 'joys of youth' and, increasingly, from each other – and of Claude's first 'proper' lesbian encounter. In its honest, bleak, but *vérité* style the film has more in common with Larry Clark's *Kids* (1995) than with the defiance and charisma of New Queer Cinema. Nevertheless, *All Over Me* offers the rare depiction of a gay context to the brutal realities of teenage sexuality. The performances by the little-known actors were praised, and the film picked up a couple of awards at the Berlin Film Festival. **MA**

## Brad SILBERLING

Born in 1965, Brad Silberling left UCLA and went on to direct several high-profile US *Casper* (1995) television shows, including 'LA Law', 'Brooklyn Bridge' and 'NYPD Blue'. He caught *City of Angels* (1998) the attention of Steven Spielberg and went on to direct his first feature in 1995, the sleeper hit *Casper*. Following in the same vein as *Who Framed Roger Rabbit* (1988), the film combines animation and live action in a tale of Casper the ghost who falls for the daughter of a ghostbuster. Eric Idle pops up as his typical English twit helping a scheming Cathy Moriarty find buried treasure. That his apprenticeship was served in the gritty realms of realism accounts for Silberling's failure to grapple with the grandiose extravaganza of CGI effects and skewed Gaudi-esque haunted-house sets. Similarly, the characters are ciphers; inanimate imprimaturs that are never allowed to detract from the wonder of the high-tech gadgetry. In this respect, Silberling places spectacle over substance as freely as his mentor Spielberg and the picture resembles the very worst of 'event' film-making.

*City of Angels* (1998) is a vast improvement thanks to its stars' winning charm and art-house antecedents. A remake of Wim Wenders' *Wings of Desire* (1987), the action is transported from pre-free Berlin to Los Angeles, the ultimate 21st-century city, all artifice and sprawl. Nicolas Cage plays an angel who falls in love with dowdy nurse Meg Ryan and so 'falls' to earth to live with her. It's a hybrid of *It's A Wonderful Life* (1946), *Superman 2* (1980), and any conventional romantic comedy, but Silberling displays a visual grammar that allows for tricksy camera work and a capturing of the distance modern urban life places between people. The opening shot, a point-of-view pan across the city, is a masterstroke; not only does it symbolise the perpetual omniscience of Cage's angel, but it also shows the full extent of the urban swamp that the 'city of angels' has become. Silberling articulates as well as Wenders the loneliness of the afflicted and the power of simple things (smells, sights) to exert pangs of love and nostalgia. Silberling's back catalogue is no preparation for his treatment of Hollywood's rarely tackled subject: transcendence. Style tries to win out (the angels wear Gucci overcoats) but the mood is perfectly pitched. Freed from the shackles of CGI behemoths, *City of Angels* displays a charm that is naïve, yet never sentimental.

Silberling's next film, *Moonlight Mile*, is a family drama starring Dustin Hoffman. **BM**

# David SIEGEL
See **Scott McGEHEE**

# Scott SILVER

Scott Silver is a director who seems to be drawn to intriguing projects but fails to deliver satisfactorily. His debut feature was *johns* (1996), an independent about street prostitutes in LA. With impressive turns from David Arquette and Lukas Haas, the film suffers from over-familiarity. As well as films like *Midnight Cowboy* (1968) and *My Own Private Idaho* (1991), both of which are extremely stylish and visually innovative, young street hustlers are staple subjects for numerous television documentaries and crime shows. Silver adds little that we have not seen before, offering a rambling and episodic narrative that seems to owe a little to Richard Linklater's work, notably *Slacker* (1991). The weak device whereby everyone John (Arquette) meets is either a 'john' (client) or his namesake typifies the lacklustre quality of the writing and the tragic ending is telegraphed early on. Only Arquette's final scene, with the doomed hustler dancing for the john who will kill him, stays in the memory as a bizarre and moving moment. This moment aside, Silver's debut is disappointing.

His next feature was *The Mod Squad* (1998). This was an update of the weird, camp 1960s television show wherein three 'cool' kids work as undercover cops busting hipster criminals. Rather than an ironic and funny update, such as that given in *The Brady Bunch Movie* (1995), Silver offers something that seems to take the outlandish premise too seriously. A plot which is convoluted to the point of being baffling, involving a cache of cocaine stolen from a police station, combines with a visual style best described as a bargain-basement *Romeo + Juliet* (1996). The talented cast, which includes Dennis Farina, Claire Danes, and Oma Epps, are left floundering in this humourless mess of a movie. The chief reason to watch is the performance of Giovanni Ribisi that seems to be from another film entirely and can be read as a rebellious response to the shortcomings of the script. *The Mod Squad* represents a wasted opportunity and is a far lesser film than other television spin-offs such as *Mission: Impossible* (1996) and *Lost In Space* (1997). **IC**

# Adam SIMON

Currently poised on the brink of mainstream horror film success, even stardom, forty year-old writer-director Adam Simon has already lived multiple and sundry lives in the movie business. Born in 1962, the son of eminent sociologist William Simon (a pioneer in sexology research), he received his early schooling at the Laboratory School of the University of Chicago. Thanks to a 3rd grade teacher who had previously worked editing television documentaries for none other than William Friedkin (in his pre-*Exorcist* days), Simon acquired his first piece of equipment: a small Super 8 editing setup which allowed him to view and recut short films.

Amazed by the ethnographic documentaries of Robert Gardner and determined to obtain a richer education than a traditional film school program could provide, Simon did his undergarduate work in the Visual and Environmental Studies Department at Harvard University. Gardner served as his advisor there, and assisted Simon in designing a programme which enabled him to study broadly in the liberal arts while continuing to make films. In 1982–83, Simon went to Paris, where he attended the seminars of renowned film theorist Christian Metz and worked under such cinema studies luminaries as Jacques Aumont and Marc Vernet. That same year he published his only piece of academic writing – 'Film as Creatura: towards a non-reductive theory of film' – in the journal *Iris*. While in France, Simon also got to meet influential film scholar Tom Gunning, whose assistant he would be for the year 1984–85.

After Harvard, Simon attended the University of Southern California film school, staying there long enough to make a short, *The Blue*, a ghostly World War Two story that brought him to the attention of independent producer and B-movie icon Roger Corman. Always on the lookout for new talent, Corman offered Simon the chance to rewrite and direct an old script by Charles Beaumont (core writer of the original 'Twilight Zone' series as well as three Edgar Allen Poe adaptations for Corman's 1960s A.I.P. cycle). Produced by Corman's wife Julie, the script became *Brain Dead* (1990), Simon's first feature. This unsettling tale of paranoia, madness and open-skull brain surgery (anticipating *Hannibal* (2001) by over a decade) quickly developed a cult following, and still makes the rounds on late-night cable television.

After *Brain Dead*, Simon spent nearly a year working with John Landis on a film which never got made before returning to the Corman fold to direct two other pictures: the erotic thriller *Body Chemistry 2* (1992; ironically, Simon had walked off the original *Body Chemistry*, which Corman had planned to be his next project) and the $800,000 dino movie, *Carnosaur* (1993). Despite sacrificing sophisticated effects technology for hand-puppets and miniatures, *Carnosaur* had more than enough humour, gore, and 1970s retro-horror ambiance to capitalise on its near-simultaneous release with *Jurassic Park* (1993). The film would go on to become the top-grossing Corman production of all time.

In the years immediately following *Carnosaur*, Simon worked mostly as a screenwriter, often with Tim Metcalfe (writer-director of *Killer: A Journal of Murder* (1995)) as partner. Then in 1996, after being invited to direct by Tim Robbins and with financial support from the British Film Institute, Simon switched gears to make a documentary on American indie film legend Samuel Fuller (*Underworld USA* (1961), *Shock Corridor* (1963), *The Big Red One* (1980), etc.). With insightful commentary from such notable Fuller fans as Quentin Tarantino, Jim Jarmusch, and Martin Scorsese, *The Typewriter, the Rifle & the Movie Camera* (1996) won numerous festival awards and marked the beginning of an ongoing relationship with then-head of BFI TV, Colin MacCabe. Since then, the pair have conceived a couple of major series which are in the early stages of development: one is a revisionist history of film, the other a revision of John Berger's classic 'Ways of Seeing' series.

In 2000, Simon directed his second award-winning non-fiction 'film essay' (a term he prefers over 'documentary'), *The American Nightmare*. This close and revealing look at US horror cinema of the late 1960s/early 1970s includes in-depth interviews with most of the genre's biggest names: Wes Craven, Tobe Hooper, David Cronenberg, George Romero, John Carpenter, and Tom Savini. The film succeeds in showing just how much the modern classics of this period, from *Night of the Living Dead* (1968) to *Halloween* (1978), were direct responses to – and distorted reflections of – what their creators saw as real-life nightmares in the world around them (political assassinations, the Vietnam War, sexual promiscuity, new and frightening technologies).

Simon's most recent credit was for co-scripting the Ernest Dickerson horror film *Bones* (2001), starring Snoop Dog as a gangster ghost back from the dead to wreak revenge on his murderers some thirty years after the fact. Currently, Simon is writing (with Metcalfe) a completely new version of the 1980 slasher film *Prom Night*, as well as working on an adaptation of Robert Heinlein's gnostic horror tale 'The Unpleasant Profession of Jonathan Hoag' for Michael Mann's production company. Although horror remains a passion, Simon writes in other areas as well and has expressed interest in making films outside the genre.                                                   **SJS**

# Bryan SINGER

If Bryan Singer's films were systematically rounded up and put in a line-up similar to the one in his film *The Usual Suspects* (1995), the most apparent characteristic would be that nothing is easily apparent. Born in 1966 in New Jersey and a graduate of USC Film School, Singer already has four feature films under his belt. Each of his projects delves deep beneath the surface of his characters to examine the nature of evil, deception and façade. His mastery of gradual revelation has made him one of Hollywood's brightest young stars.

In his first film, a low-budget thriller entitled *Public Access* (1993), Singer brings a handsome stranger into the idyllic town of Brewster to ask the question: 'What's wrong with Brewster?' via a cable-TV show. The stranger, the responses, and the reality of Brewster are slowly revealed to be much darker than they initially appear. Winner of the Sundance Jury Award, this film is most rewarding for its early glimpse into Singer's confident style. The haunting camerawork of this film recurs in his later projects.

*The Usual Suspects*, Singer's breakout follow-up, is a noir puzzle-box of a film, which follows the misdeeds of five career criminals brought together in a police line-up. Winner of two Academy Awards – Best Original Screenplay to Christopher McQuarrie and Best Supporting Actor to Kevin Spacey – this film contains enough twists and turns to leave the audience shaking its head long past the roll of the credits and, according to detractors, to almost nullify itself. Featuring stellar performances from the likes of Gabriel Byrne, Chazz Palminteri, and Kevin Pollak, the premise is a flashback-filled interrogation of Spacey's character Verbal Kint, the lone survivor of a boat explosion/coke deal gone bad. The mastermind behind the heist is Keyser Soze, the embodiment of evil and the riddle inside this conundrum of a movie, although even he is less than straightforward. Singer's *mise-en-scène* is always about peering beneath the surface, epitomised by his use of the slow zoom-in. In a film where deceit and treachery rule, Singer himself turns out to be the biggest manipulator of them all, making this a film that is perhaps best appreciated a second time around, due to its structural complexity and grandly twisted ending.

*Apt Pupil* (1998) is a measured two-person character study into the essence of evil. Brad Renfro plays Todd Bowden, a gifted high-school kid who realises a neighbour (played by Ian McKellen) is actually Kurt Dussander, a Nazi war criminal. Instead of exposing the man, Bowden demands that Dussander tell him everything about the concentration camps. In the process of the telling, however, something evil is unleashed in Bowden and reawakened in Dussander. McKellen gives a densely layered performance in this movie, moving from reluctant old storyteller to gleeful participant as he and Renfro's character engage in a high-stakes power struggle that neither character is able to break free from. Treading the line between conventional horror film and psychological thriller, the film delves into the question of the origin and nature of evil, whether it is innate or learned. Although not a huge box-office success, the film is unmistakably Singer's: the plot is twisted, identity is slowly stripped away, and conventional justice is thwarted.

Based on the popular comic book, the Hollywood blockbuster *X-Men* (2000) looks into the future to a time where genetically mutated people are both feared and persecuted by humanity. When Magneto, a mutant played by Ian McKellen, vows revenge and world domination, it is up to a group of mutants called the X-Men to defend the ungrateful planet. 'We're not what you think,' Patrick Stewart pronounces gravely as Professor Xavier, the X-Men's leader, in the effects-heavy trailer. The same could be said for all of Singer's work. He will also direct the sequel.                                       **DHo**

# Tarsem SINGH

Born in India in 1962, Tarsem Dhandwar Singh (who frequently goes by the single moniker, 'Tarsem') was educated at a Himalayan boarding school before arriving in the US to do a business degree at Harvard University. Deciding that he wanted to pursue a film career instead, he soon left Harvard to attend the highly-regarded Art Center in Pasadena, California.

After graduation Tarsem began directing music videos, and in 1991 his video for REM's 'Losing My Religion' won the MTV Best Video Award. That same year he also received two Cannes advertising tropies, which led to his becoming a highly sought-after director of television commercials around the world.

Renowned for his uniquely expressive and dynamic visual style, it was only a matter of time before Tarsem made the move to Hollywood. When he agreed to direct *The Cell* (2000) – and an opportunity to take a science-fictional journey inside the mind of a serial killer – New Line Cinema fast-tracked the film for production. As producer Julio Caro notes, before *The Cell*, Tarsem had been 'aggressively looking for a project that would capture his sensibility and his aesthetic'. Despite lukewarm reviews and criticism of Jennifer Lopez in the lead role, the astonishing creativity and luxuriousness of the film's *mise-en-scène* ensured modest profits which have since increased following the DVD release.

Tarsem was next scheduled to direct an adaptation of the popular DC-Vertigo comic book, 'Hellblazer'. Starring Nicolas Cage, the Warner Bros.-produced film (retitled 'Constantin') generated a great deal of anticipation. But in January 2002, trade papers reported that Tarsem stepped down because of budgetary constraints. By now used to having near-total control over his projects, Tarsem evidently felt no need to compromise his artistic vision even for a major studio.                                     **SJS**

# John SINGLETON

Born in Los Angeles in 1968, John Singleton directed his first feature, *Boyz N the Hood* (1991), at the age of only 23, emerging as one of a new wave of black film-makers in the early 1990s. His rapid rise to prominence was largely as a result of Columbia's attempt to build on the success of Spike Lee's black-orientated films. Unlike the overtly cinematic Lee, whose films are often dazzling and reflect the influence of film-makers from Billy Wilder to Martin Scorsese, Singleton is, stylistically, much more traditional.

His debut, a rites-of-passage story, focuses on the attempts of Tre (Cuba Gooding Jr) to escape from the cycle of gang violence in LA. Although the film, which was also written by the director, is involving enough and the acting good – particularly from rapper-turned-actor Ice Cube, Laurence Fishburne, and Angela Bassett in an underwritten role – this often seems like a TV movie. Comparisons may be unfair, but it is hard not to place Singleton's film alongside Spike Lee's far angrier, frequently unsettling *Do The Right Thing* (1989) and the The Hughes Brothers' exciting and nihilistic *Menace 2 Society* (1993). The lack of striking visuals and the sentimentality of *Boyz N the Hood* render it less successful and more palatable to the Academy of Motion Picture Arts and Sciences, who rewarded Singleton with a Best Director nomination.

Possibly in an attempt to tackle charges of sexism levelled at his first feature (and the sexual politics of *Boyz N the Hood* are a little unreconstructed), his second film, *Poetic Justice* (1993), centred on females. The film is hampered from the outset, however, by singer Janet Jackson's poor acting. She plays the titular character Justice who writes poetry and the title's corny pun sums up the plot. Alienated and angsty, she agrees to go on a cross-country mail run with a friend and finds a soul mate in Tupac Shakur's postman, Lucky. Shakur, a rapper-turned-actor, who was killed at a young age, is very good here (and even better in his cinematic swan-song, Vondie Curtis Hall's drug comedy, *Gridlock'd* (1997)) but the film is uneasy in tone and doesn't really go anywhere.

Singleton's 1995 film *Higher Learning* met with a hostile critical reception. Although it may be a bit of a mess there is much to recommend this look at college life. A great cast (Omar Epps, Michael Rapaport, Jennifer Connelly join *Boyz N the Hood* stars Cube and Fishburne) appear in a multi-stranded look at the students and their respective cliques at fictional Columbus University. Many of the stereotypes of the high-school movie are here: irascible professor (Fishburne's pipe-smoking West Indian), career student (Ice Cube's black militant), and naïve freshman (Rapaport's hick-cum-fascist). The material is often overwrought – it ends for instance in a very dramatic but highly implausible massacre – and the sexual politics sometimes suspect as Connelly's predatory lesbian homes in on Kirsty Swanson's date-raped student, but Singleton creates a polished soap which is highly watchable, provocative and full of good performances. Epps is a decent actor and Rapaport makes the faintly ludicrous skinhead subplot believable. Like Spike Lee's equally maligned high-school movie, *School Daze* (1988), *Higher Learning* doesn't entirely work but it is still interesting and occasionally gripping.

*Rosewood* (1997), which was made for television, was the first film that Singleton didn't write. Its based on a true story about the African-American community of Rosewood, Florida, that was destroyed in a racist attack in 1923. There are powerful performers here – Ving Rhames, Jon Voight, the underrated Don Cheadle, and Michael Rooker – and the mood is part historical epic, part western with Rhames, in particular, playing a generic outsider, but Singleton's direction is a bit flat and too often, not cinematic enough. As a result the film is upsetting because of what happened at Rosewood, not because of Singleton's skills at storytelling.

The 2000 remake of the Gordon Parks 1971 blaxploitation classic *Shaft* was Singleton's biggest project to date. Samuel L. Jackson is great as the title character and wears the black leather trench coat well but the big ingredient missing here is sex. The protagonist's name is clearly a sexual reference and in the low-budget original Richard Roundtree is barely out of bed for more than a couple of scenes at a time but here Jackson is given little opportunity to reprise the cop-stud-style icon persona. The production was beset by problems – reported tensions between Jackson and the writer Richard Price, and rumours of studio meddling – which may account for it being a non-event. Some stylish action scenes and Jackson (ill-matched by Christian Bale's pasty-faced, weedy villain) are the real attractions here.

Singleton's most recent film, *Baby Boy* (2001), is an ambitious and interesting drama about sexual politics. Model-turned-actor Tyrese plays Jody, a young black man who still lives with his mother, despite having two girlfriends, one the mother of his baby. Singleton explores the phenomenon of 'baby fathers', men who have children with several different women, and he seeks to condemn them while also acknowledging the racism that affords them few other opportunities to prove themselves. Tyrese looks good but doesn't deliver on the acting front and the film is at its most interesting when Ving Rhames is on screen playing the ex-con who is romancing Jody's mother. *Baby Boy* is reflective rather than hysterical (unlike *Higher Learning*) and hints at Singleton's newfound maturity.                                                                                          **IC**

# Gary SINISE

Born in Illinois in 1955, Gary Sinise is better known for his varied acting roles than for his direction. Although he has directed numerous plays for the famous Steppenwolf Theater Company (which he co-founded with John Malkovich in 1974), Sinise is still to make a lasting impression as a film-maker.

After directing episodes of various television dramas ('thirtysomething', 'China Beach', and 'Crime Story'), Sinise debuted on the big screen with *Miles From Home* (1988), starring Richard Gere and telling the story of two brothers' struggle to survive on a farm ravaged by floods. A story of revenge and the exploitation of farmers by Corporate America, the film seems heavily influenced by Terrence Malick (particularly *Badlands* (1974) and *Days Of Heaven* (1978)) and, by Sinise's own admission, Bruce Springsteen's album 'Nebraska'. With an almost Lynchian feel for the dispossessed populations of small-town America, Sinise introduces a strange assortment of characters that serve to further isolate his main protagonists. However, the film is seriously hindered by the casting of Gere as farmer Frank Roberts. Perhaps attempting to reinterpret his role in *Days Of Heaven*, Gere never seems to get to grips with his character, and the results are lifeless and insincere.

Sinise's next film, *Of Mice and Men* (1992), is far more successful. Based on John Steinbeck's novel and adapted by Horton Foote, the film is quiet, intense and emotionally raw. As one would expect from a Steppenwolf collaborative project, the film's strength lies in its performances. Sinise, as George Milton, and Malkovich, as

Lennie Small, dominate the screen. Sinise's love of the text shines through his simple but powerful interpretation of the story.

Both of Sinise's films (and much of his theatre work) rely heavily on relationships that are tested or destroyed by societal deprivation. Like Sam Shepherd before him, Sinise sees the dusty and barren American Midwest as a counterpoint to the American dream and as a symbol of the basic failure of a society entrenched in excess and consumerism. For Sinise, the adage 'I struggle, therefore I am' gives weight to the interpersonal relationships of his characters that are so important in his films. Often in contrast to his high-profile acting roles and to the Hollywood establishment that he vociferously courts, Sinise's films represent a theatrical and literary tradition that eschews spectacle and concentrates on raw emotion and troubled interpersonal relationships.          **BW**

# Kari SKOGLAND

Kari Skogland established herself in the world of commercials and music video as an editor, gradually picking up a range of directorial assignments in television. (She is reputedly the first woman to direct an American beer commercial.) Her feature work has been restricted thus far to films that have received attention on the festival circuit but circulated most widely on home video.

*The Size of Watermelons* (1996)
*Men with Guns* (1997)
*Children of the Corn 666: Isaac's Return* (1999)
*Zebra Lounge* (2001)

Her debut, *The Size of Watermelons* (1996), adopts the Generation X sensibility familiar from *Clerks* (1994) and *Slacker* (1991) but lacks the zeitgeist-defining conviction of those films. Centring on the tribulations of a young film maker (Paul Rudd), it is uneven in tone and the dialogue-heavy sequences often seem laboured and derivative. The low budget deficiencies are compensated by an oft-misplaced irony. *Men with Guns* (1997) is a more assured work. While parodying elements of the crime/action cycle (an approach signalled by its knowing title), Skogland directs the requisite violence with a kinetic energy. Emphasising the frustrations and insecurities of its downtrodden, humiliated protagonists (Donal Logue and Gregory Sporleder), the seedy ambience is balanced by a sense of insight and compassion. Indeed, the film features a moral centre absent from many of the blankly ironic crime films which followed in the wake of Quentin Tarantino's success. As a crime lord, Paul Sorvino recalls his role in *GoodFellas* (1990).

Unfortunately, *Children of the Corn 666: Isaac's Return* (1999) is a step backwards. Displaying many of the desperate contrivances familiar from such horror video franchises, the film resurrects a character absent in the series since the original entry. A few visual flourishes and the presence of Stacy Keach and Nancy Allen cannot make up for sheer predictability. Her next film, the coldly-received thriller *Zebra Lounge* (2001), focuses on a married couple that decide to alleviate their sexual boredom with the help of a couple they meet in a swinger's magazine. She is currently in production with *Liberty Stands Still*, a thriller starring Wesley Snipes and Linda Fiorentino.          **NJ**

# Charles Martin SMITH

An excellent character actor turned director who has delivered a series of impressive acting performances in films as varied as *American Graffiti* (1973), *Pat Garratt and Billy the Kid* (1973), and *Deep Cover* (1994), Charles Martin Smith has directed some enjoyable films from decidedly unpromising material.

*Trick or Treat* (1986)
*Boris and Natasha* (1992)
*Fifty/Fifty* (1993)
*Air Bud* (1997)

Born in California in 1953, he made his feature debut in 1986 with the horror film *Trick or Treat*. Clearly inspired by the bizarre claims of American religious groups that heavy metal albums contain hidden satanic messages, the story concerns itself with a dead rock star whose final album, when played on the radio at the stroke of midnight on Halloween, will destroy the world. Despite this daft premise, Smith crafts a witty and undemanding, often clever romp. Possibly due to the fact that the film lampoons the concerns of censorious pressure groups, real-life rock stars, including Ozzy Osbourne, have cameo appearances.

*Boris and Natasha* (1992) was a lame, live-action up-date of the 'Rocky and Bullwinkle' cartoon series, recently re-made more successfully with Robert De Niro. Although the Cold War romps may have seemed topical when the film was in production, it seemed dated by 1998. There are a few funny moments and cameo's from John Candy, Anthony Newley and John Travolta as himself but Smith can do little to bring his material to life. Although intended for theatrical release, the film premiered on cable.

Equally weak was *Fifty/Fifty* (1993), a would-be action thriller with Peter Weller and Robert Hays as CIA-affiliated mercenaries in Central America, dodging bullets and romancing princesses. Although the film offers the director in a substantial role and some fairly well-staged action scenes, it is still minor fare, fatally weakened by a poor script and a budget substantially lower than the blockbusters it seeks to emulate.

On paper *Air Bud* (1997) seems to be a turkey. This Disney effort about a lonely kid and the basketball playing dog who becomes his friend turns out to be quite enjoyable. Although squarely aimed at a young viewership, the film manages not to patronise its audience – it deals well with the grief of the central protagonist as he mourns the death of his father. Smith's chief asset, however, is the dog itself. A genuine sport-playing dog, Bud became well known as one of the 'pets who do stupid tricks' on the David Letterman chat-show. So impressive are his ball-playing skills, it comes as a shock to the viewer to see the declaration in the end credits that no special effects were used. Michael Jeter is also impressive as the nasty clown who was once Bud's owner.

Although in no immediate danger of eclipsing his acting with his directing, Smith has shown in his relatively short and patchy career that he is capable of crafting some efficient work from concepts with little promise. However, It would be good to see him use his skills for something more substantial than cartoon rehashes and ball-playing canines. **IC**

# Chris SMITH

Fascinated by the backwater America eschewed by mainstream Hollywood, Chris Smith's films are dramas of the little men, the oddballs, also-rans and everyday joes of American society. His films document the hopes, frustrations and imperfections of life in small-town America, exploring the schisms and contradictions of the American character in all its peculiar forms with a wry narrative style and keen documentary eye. Like many other independent directors fascinated by dysfunctional America, his films have been criticised for exploiting their offbeat subjects for the purposes of comedy and entertainment. But Smith is in the long tradition of American artists who employ modest subjects to hint at larger themes: his targets of satire are broader than the foibles, doubts and hopes of his characters, focusing instead on the contrasts between everyday life in contemporary America and the hopes and delusions of the American dream.

Smith's first film, *American Job* (1995), a festival favourite, is a fictionalised documentary that follows its average-white-boy protagonist Randy through a variety of mundane jobs: working at a factory, swabbing a fast-food restaurant, cleaning motel rooms. The film is a pæan to boredom, filmed as low-grade *vérité*, with long sequences donated to the routine of Randy's life, and by implication that of millions of other average Americans.

The story unfolds without the frame of voiceover or explicit narrative, following Randy from job to job through an ever more bizarre roll call of characters and situations, and relying on skilful editing and subtle comedy to make its points. Smith's comic timing and affinity for his characters are obvious, but it is his distinctive ability to make a peculiar kind of art out of everyday material that mark him out as a young film-maker of talent.

While applying the finishing touches to *American Job*, Smith became involved as cinematographer on a documentary about corporate America called *The Big One* (1997), helmed by the investigative comic and fellow champion of the absurd Michael Moore. It was during work on a final cut of *American Job* at Wisconsin University, however, that he unwittingly stumbled across the subject of his own next project – an aspiring young film director called Mark Borchardt, whose struggles towards cinematic greatness are documented in the brilliant, hilarious and touching *American Movie: The Making of Northwestern* (1999). The film follows the making of Borchardt's debut film, a splatter horror short entitled *Coven,* inspired by the guerrilla film-making tactics of directors like Roger Corman and Sam Raimi, and intended to finance the making of a feature-length film about small-town life called *Northwestern* (hence the subtitle). Hindered by a lack of resources, a disbelieving family and a brow-beating girlfriend, Mark remains unswervingly assured of both the project and his talent, despite the mounting complications of recalcitrant actors, unreliable equipment, reluctant financiers (namely his caustic, half-senile grandpa), and the obstacles set in his way by everyday life. Smith's detached narrative style and *vérité* camerawork give the film a fine balance of humour and pathos, and crucially never quite allow us to decide whether Borchardt is a film-maker of actual talent or one doomed to perpetual disaster. Borchardt becomes a kind of flawed American hero, hopelessly seduced by the promises of art, fame and fortune; the film's brilliance lies in showing the flipside, the skewed nobility of Borchardt's pursuit of his dreams in a country increasingly characterised by apathy and disillusionment. Funny, sharp, sad and uplifting, *American Movie* deservedly won the Documentary Award at the 1999 Sundance Festival, and Borchardt has fittingly become something of a cult hero in its wake; but, as yet, *Northwestern* has remained just another American dream.

Smith's most recent portrait of contemporary America, *Home Movie* (2001), brings together an eclectic collection of characters and stories from across the continent, and from a variety of backgrounds, ages and professions. Unveiled to great accolades at the 2001 Sundance Festival, international audiences can only hope the film secures the same kind of distribution deal as *American Movie*. His stories might be made in, about, and for America, but Chris Smith's films carry a universal appeal.  **OB**

# Kevin SMITH

Not only does film-maker Kevin Smith, born in New Jersey, in 1970, epitomise the notion that anyone can make a movie, he lives by it, because – by his own unpretentious estimation – he's anyone. A self-described 'movie brat' weaned on mainstream studio fare and comic books, his writing and directing aspirations were effectively galvanised following a midnight screening of Richard Linklater's *Slacker* (1991) on his twenty-first birthday. Linklater's low-tech approach, as well as those of fellow indie directors Spike Lee, Hal Hartley, and Jim Jarmusch, inspired Smith to make his scrappy first feature, *Clerks* (1994), for a mere $27,000. Produced under Smith's own aptly-named View Askew shingle, his smart, irreverent comedies are not to all tastes. They shamelessly traffic in inside jokes and knowing references to other movies (chiefly by Spielberg and Lucas), and have – until recently – rarely displayed anything above a grudging nod to technical adequacy. Ironically enough, it is also these very qualities that serve to distinguish Smith as a likeable, unique voice among his generation.

The episodic *Clerks* charts a day in the life of hapless counter jockey Dante and his sardonic best friend and fellow wage slave, Randall. Photographed in black-and-white for economic rather than artistic reasons, and shot nights in the very Quick Stop convenience store where Smith was then employed, it is the cinematic equivalent of a brainy, foul-mouthed underground comic strip. The eager-to-impress flash of most American debuts is absent; Smith appears most concerned with just getting his words and performances in the can. Scenes are built around Smith's rapid-fire dialogue, mostly captured in long, static takes against flat backgrounds in the manner of early talkies. The closest he comes to assembling an action scene is the impromptu afternoon hockey game played on the Quick Stop's roof, and his discomfort behind the camera is apparent – it ends up looking rushed and awkward. In the closing credits, Smith generously dedicates his first film to Hartley, Linklater, Lee, and Jarmusch 'for leading the way'.

*Clerks* is notable for forging a rough version of the template upon which the later chapters of Smith's so-called 'Jersey Trilogy' (1995's *Mallrats* and 1997's *Chasing Amy* form the second and third parts) are based. His twentysomething characters are witty, well-spoken orators on a wide range of topics, scatalogical or otherwise; at their best, their musings are as pungent and inspired as a great stand-up comedy routine, and as metronomically precise as a Mamet play. Sharply drawn archetypes, they inhabit a world in which people and situations from Smith's other films are given free reign to cross over and impact the narrative. (*Clerks* also introduced two characters who have appeared in all of Smith's films to date, the comic relief drug dealers Jay and Silent Bob, played by Jason Mewes and Smith himself.) But at heart, the films are buddy movies. Smith's protagonists are young men unlucky in love and unsure of their place in the world. Drifting and insecure, his heartbroken heroes typically find it easier to be intimate and truthful with each other than with a woman, suggesting an underlying (and fairly kidded) homoeroticism that is finally confronted head on in *Chasing Amy*'s climactic threesome proposal.

*Mallrats* was Smith's first film for a major studio, his first multi-million dollar budget, and, coming hot on the heels of *Clerks*' grassroots success, his first failure. Conceived by Universal as a return to the T&A teen films of the early 1980s (in their words, 'a smart *Porky's*'), the picture is an oddball, nearly incongruous hybrid of crass, *National Lampoon*-style gags and Smith's shrewd dialogue. It also has an undeserved reputation as an unmitigated disaster. Like *Clerks*, *Mallrats* follows the rambling story of two best friends, Brodie (Jason Lee) and T.S. (Jeremy London), who retreat to the local mall following a dual break-up with their respective girlfriends. Smith broke with indie ranks to dedicate *Mallrats* to mainstream directors John Landis and John Hughes, and the result is a canvas that's bigger and broader, but not necessarily so far removed from the anarchic spirit of his breakthrough. Affectionately lowbrow, it is also a visual leap past *Clerks*, featuring dolly and crane shots and a greater confidence in his staging of slapstick comedy bits. *Mallrats'* only crime may be that it was released before *There's Something About Mary* (1998) and *American Pie* (1999) marked a more successful return to big-screen vulgarity.

Smith's watershed came with *Chasing Amy*, a daring, emotionally-complicated romantic comedy that returned the director to his independent origins. Re-teaming with actor Lee, he also cast two other *Mallrats* alumni, Joey Lauren Adams and Ben Affleck, in the lead roles of, respectively, a free-spirited lesbian and the lovestruck comic book artist who winds up falling for her. *Chasing Amy* features more of Smith's penchant for movie geek cross-referencing (a hilarious scene of one-upmanship between Lee and Adams, with the two of them comparing scars received during oral sex, is a direct lift from Spielberg's *Jaws* (1975), but balanced with an honesty and truthfulness that's as startling as it is raw. While visually a step back to the cruder-looking *Clerks* (the film was shot on a shoestring in order to preserve the story's integrity), Smith lets the grittier style work to his advantage here, particularly in capturing a wrenching parking lot breakdown by Adams' confused character that comes after she and Affleck have fallen in love. As a bittersweet footnote, the script was inspired in part by Smith's real-life relationship with Adams, adding in no small way to its verisimilitude.

1999 saw the release of Smith's most ambitious film, the controversial Catholic satire *Dogma*. The story of two fallen angels (played by Affleck and Matt Damon) whose plan to re-enter Heaven threatens to bring about the Apocalypse, Smith (a Catholic himself) attempts to cast off the paradigm of his previous films, aiming for a tone of dark fantasy closer to the adult-themed graphic novels of Neil Gaiman ('Sandman') and the loopy science fiction of Douglas Adams ('The Hitch-Hiker's Guide to the Galaxy'). While Smith is often hampered by his own self-confessed limitations as a director, failing to give the picture the epic sweep his script demands (odd, considering his cinematographer here is Robert Yeoman, best known for the hyper-real snap of Wes Anderson's films), *Dogma* works as a pointed, comic, and ultimately moving dissertation on the idea of faith. Also of note is Smith's inspired, risky casting: George Carlin as a press hungry Catholic cardinal; comic Chris Rock as Rufus, the forgotten 13th Apostle; and Jersey Trilogy regulars Jay and Silent Bob as a pair of irreverent prophets.

After an aborted attempt to bring *Clerks* to life as a prime-time animated series (the show was cancelled after a mere two episodes), Smith set his sights on spoofing himself, his films, and pop culture in general with *Jay and Silent Bob Strike Back* (2001). As the title suggests, it is not only the writer-director's most obvious homage to George Lucas, but also an opportunity for his two most recognisable and doggedly persistent characters to finally take centre-stage. *Jay and Silent Bob* is built around the thinnest of premises – our clueless heroes get into *Blues Brothers*-sized trouble as they travel from New Jersey to Hollywood to stop production of the movie that's being made about them – all with the intention of kissing goodbye to Smith's overpopulated 'View Askewniverse'. What's notable about *Jay and Silent Bob* is its willingness to bite the hand that feeds it, and Smith takes self-referential chomps at his own Internet fanbase, famous friends like Affleck and Damon (who appear as themselves on the set of a *Good Will Hunting* (1997) sequel), and even the studio that released the film (Miramax, which also distributed *Clerks* and *Amy*) with a last-meal gusto. Crammed with more cameos than a *Cannonball Run* movie (many actors from Smith's previous films reprise their roles here), it is also Smith's slickest, best-looking production to date, and the director goes out of his way to adorn it with elaborate digital effects and well-planned comic action sequences that play like a defiant middle finger to critics of his competence as a film-maker. It's a true shaggy dog of an in-joke, but at least it's a funny one.

Smith's next film is *Jersey Girl*, a smaller-scaled comic drama about fatherhood, which is scheduled for production in 2002. **CS**

# Steven SODERBERGH

In 1989, at the age of 26, Steven Soderbergh won the Palme d'Or for his debut feature, *sex, lies and videotape*. Overnight he became the darling of the US independent movie scene. However, since this early acclaim, Soderbergh has confounded both critics and public alike with his choice of material. Both idiosyncratic and diverse, Soderbergh's work is disparate and difficult to categorise, although he does tend to return to a recurring theme of a solitary individual seeking truth in a dishonest world of (self) deceit.

sex, lies and videotape is a modern day morality play. The film is a character-driven study portraying a quartet of people, Graham (James Spader), Ann (Andie McDowell), John (Peter Gallagher) and Laura (Laura San Giacomo), who are shaped and constrained by their desires, impulses and sexual drives. Soderbergh explores their motives and inhibitions using a series of strikingly detailed close-ups and subtle camera movements to create a voyeuristic view of marital deception and emotional infidelity. Coupled with an ethereal score and bewitchingly sensitive performances from the lead characters, this is indeed a profoundly moving film.

Soderbergh followed up the success of this film with *Kafka* (1991). Set in post-World War One Prague, the film takes the claustrophobia and fateful inevitability of Franz Kafka's 'The Castle' and mixes it with the politics of a modern-day cinematic conspiracy thriller. The result is a visually eccentric, sometimes terrifying and inspired film. Ultimately, however, it becomes an awkward experiment in zeitgeist as it ambles towards a very un-Kafkaesque and Hollywood-friendly ending.

*King of the Hill* (1993), like *Kafka*, was a box-office flop. Once again the film features a single male protagonist – an impoverished boy, Aaron (Jesse Bradford) – trapped in a world beyond his comprehension. Set against the backdrop of the Great Depression the film is another darkly comic character study surveyed through the haze of Elliot Davis' romantically tinted cinematography. Soderbergh's next film *Underneath* (1995), an icy remake of the noir thriller *Criss Cross* (1949), was also financially unsuccessful. Disenchanted, Soderbergh returned to his independent roots and directed *Gray's Anatomy* (1996), a monodrama featuring Spalding Gray, and *Schizopolis* (1996), a postmodern fable focused on a tragi-comic hero's inability to deal with a failing marriage.

In 1998 Soderbergh confounded his critics with the acclaimed *Out of Sight*, a neo-noir romantic thriller starring George Clooney and Jennifer Lopez. Soderbergh's formalism brings a meticulous air of elegance to this genre piece by using vivid close-ups and fluid camera work to produce an air of emotional expectation in what could easily have been a high-gloss Hollywood star-vehicle. Soderbergh's return to Hollywood mainstream cinema was complete in 1999 with the release of *The Limey* starring Terrence Stamp. Soderbergh's misleading synopsis that the film is '*Get Carter* remade by Resnais', belittles his own stylish direction and unique use of montage, ellipses and linear logic. What he produces is a smart, intensely black comic-thriller that enhances his auteur status by drawing on modernist ideas of alienation in a corrupt and morally bankrupt world.

As if to cement his new found status as 'bankable' Hollywood director, Soderbergh released his most accessible film to date, the Julia Roberts star vehicle *Erin Brockovich* (2000). This is a confident and somewhat predictable movie that follows Soderbergh's latent obsession with truth and lies as he focuses on one woman's struggle against corporate insensitivity and negligence. Yet the film also serves to illustrate Soderbergh's mastery of direction. In lesser directorial hands it is a film that could have easily descended into a winsome, mush-laden drama focusing on courtroom struggles and embittered romances. Instead Soderbergh uses the full range of his skills to produce a naturalistic and subtle film about the ordinariness and idiosyncratic nature of blue-collar middle America.

Soderbergh's films are about character. His distinct talent lies in his ability to use his camera in an unobtrusive fashion that draws our attention to performance over style. Yet this is somewhat of a clever conceit. In foregrounding performance he hides the richness and complexity of his unique approach to film-making. Making films that are hailed critically as stylistically natural is not an easy task and amongst his contemporaries, Soderbergh remains a leading exponent of realist cinema.

With *Traffic* (2000), Soderbergh returned to the more experimental style employed in *The Underneath*. Using a triptych of criss-crossing narratives and a palette of contrasting filters, he charts the attempts made by the American and Mexican drug administrations to prevent the open and ever increasing flow of drugs into the US. Michael Douglas plays the judge appointed by the US President to head up a task force to counter drug trafficking across the Tex-Mex border. Catherine Zeta-Jones plays the wife of a drug barron who, although shocked at first to discover her husband's real profession, takes over his business as he awaits trial for trafficking and possession. And in the film's best strand, Benicio Del Toro appears as an incorruptible Mexican cop whose only desire is to see children in Mexico have a chance of leading a life free from crime and the danger of the drug trade. In a remarkable performance, Del Toro becomes both the film's heart and voice. Although the film is effective in conveying the urgency of America's drug problem, and would appear more overtly political than *Erin Brokovich*, it stops short of suggesting that the proliferation of drugs in the US may have been aided by US foreign policy. Instead, the State is seen, at worst, to be ineffectual in its role as guardian. Nevertheless, for such a strident film to break through to the mainstream and even garner success at the 2000 Academy Awards is quite an achievement.

If *Traffic* saw Soderbergh finally achieve universal industry, critical and audience acceptance, then *Ocean's Eleven* (2001) displayed his passion for cinema as an entertainment medium. A superior remake of the lazy Brat Pack vehicle, the film features an impressive array of stars. George Clooney, Brad Pitt, Matt Damon, and Don Cheadle star as members of a mostly organised outfit of crooks who plan to empty the central vault of three Las Vegas hotels, owned by mobster Terry Benedict. Bankrolled by a victim of Benedict's avarice, the gang's only problem is Danny Ocean's affections for his ex-wife, now involved with Benedict. Aside from Julia Robert's pointless appearance in the role originally played by Angie Dickinson, Andy Garcia's lacklustre performance as Benedict, and the occasional lapse in pacing, the film is an entertaining comedy thriller.

Showing no signs of slowing, Soderbergh recently completed *Full Frontal* (2002), with Blair Underwood, Julia Roberts, David Hyde Pierce, and David Duchovny. A follow-up to *sex, lies and videotape*, and featuring mostly improvised scenes between the actors, the release is seen as a minor project prior to Soderbergh's involvement in his forthcoming *Solaris*. Once again starring George Clooney, and produced by James Cameron, many await what may be one of Soderbergh's toughest challenge; following Andrei Tarkovsky's acclaimed 1972 adaptation of Stanislav Lem's science fiction classic.

Soderbergh has also signed up to direct *The Informant* (scheduled for 2003), a timely account of corporate corruption. **PH & IHS**

# Todd SOLONDZ

Todd Solondz's work as a film-maker to date has sparked much controversy and conflicting critical opinion for its alleged 'perversity' and 'cynicism'. Effectively foregrounding the marginalised experiences of isolated social outcasts, his films are relentlessly honest and rarely gratuitous, although the fine line between satire and misanthropy is becoming increasingly blurred.

Born in New Jersey, the actor-writer-director attended film school at New York University and produced several shorts, one of which caught the eye of both Fox and Columbia and led to two three-picture deals. His first feature, *Fear, Anxiety and Depression* (1989), the story of a man searching for romantic and artistic fulfilment, was recut by the studio against his wishes, causing him to give up film-making for a while to teach English as a second language to Russian immigrants.

Eventually persuaded back into the business, he directed from a script that he had written a few years previously. A mixture of black comedy and serious commentary, *Welcome to the Dollhouse* (1995) is a biting portrayal of an 11-year-old girl's coming of age. Bullied by her schoolmates for being unattractive, ignored by the object of her desire and ill-favourably compared to her insipid younger sister, she is confused but tenacious, and determined to establish a sense of her own identity and become accepted. Combining an excellent performance from Heather Matarozzo with insightful writing, the film deservedly won the Sundance Festival Grand Jury Prize.

Focusing on three suburban Jewish sisters and a series of other lonely, interconnected characters, *Happiness* (1998) has, despite a generally ecstatic critical reception, also found ill favour. Dismissed by Andrew Lewis Conn for being the '*Armageddon* of the indies' and dropped by its original backers because of its dark, dystopian view of life, it actually sustains a cleverly interweaving and over-lapping narrative, tackling difficult and emotive issues with respect and honesty. Featuring some excellent, nuanced performances – particularly from Dylan Baker as the paedophile father – it won the International Critics Prize at the Cannes Film Festival and remains one of the most absorbing independent films of recent years.

His most recent film, *Storytelling* (2001), has prompted further accusations of misanthropy. It is split into two sections – 'fiction' and 'non-fiction'. 'Fiction' is shorter and more arresting. Focusing on a creative writing student (Selma Blair) whose boyfriend has cerebral palsy, it shows their break up and her subsequent one-night stand with a black writing teacher. Looking for thrills, she is alarmed by his sexuality and writes a story based on her 'true' experiences, which is then ridiculed by her classmates for its lack of believability. 'Non-fiction' is a little meandering and more uneven. It opens with a down-on-his-luck, would-be film-maker (Paul Giamatti) who decides to make a documentary about a suburban Jewish American family; completely dysfunctional, with an over-bearing father (John Goodman) and an ineffectual mother, the children are unsympathetic and mistrustful of one another. The result of the film-maker's interfering efforts to chart their lives, referred to as 'glib and facile' by one character, is less than fruitful. Like *Happiness*, *Storytelling* concentrates on sensitive issues – in this case race, disability, and class-consciousness – challenging the viewer to think about the disparity between their genuine reactions and the politically correct reactions that they publicly display.                                                                                             **HP**

# Stephen SOMMERS

As a film-maker trying to reinvent the big-budget B-movie for the twenty-first century, Stephen Sommers' last two films, *The Mummy* (1999) and *The Mummy Returns* (2001), have been relentlessly successful. Both have undoubtedly reinvigorated the flagging comedy-horror genre in American cinema, and kept Industrial Light and Magic technicians in work for several years. Yet his heightened visual and sensorial style – his directing technique of 'more-is-less' – has harmed the lasting potential of all of his films, however rip-roaring, tense or playful they might have been.

Born in Indianapolis in 1962, Sommers attended the USC School of Cinema-Television in Los Angeles, where he wrote and directed the award-winning short *Perfect Alibi*. His debut feature, *Catch Me If You Can* (1989), was filmed on location in his home town of St. Cloud, Minnesota. The story of a group of high-school kids who try to raise money for the school through illegal road races was a somewhat inauspicious beginning for Sommers – the twee, faintly ridiculous script is helped by an eclectic soundtrack of 1950s and 1960s teenybopper hits yet there is a sense that Sommers is more interested in a paean to his home town than expanding his craft. The participation of M. Emmet Walsh and Geoffrey Lewis is welcome but the rest of the cast are largely forgettable – what might have developed as a *Rebel Without A Cause* (1955) for the 1980s frat-pack remains a noisy cocktail of cliché and flimsy dialogue.

Sommers continued his writer-director apprenticeship with *The Adventures of Huck Finn* (1993), a thoroughly modern adaptation of the classic Mark Twain novel. Elijah Wood plays Huck, who flees from his brutal father and goes on the run with Jim (Courtney B. Vance), an escaped slave. He directs efficiently: never resorting to indulgent tricks, he imbues their river adventures with just the right amount of pathos and vigour. In a nod to Lean's *Great Expectations* (1946), the opening few scenes are frighteningly gothic; it is only when the two friends take to the Mississippi that Sommers' tone lightens and the anti-slavery messages filter out. Strong support is supplied by Robbie Coltrane and Jason Robards. This is cute, no-risk film-making that seems too in awe of its source material to try anything too daring or innovative.

The same could not be said of Sommers' next venture, another literary adaptation of a children's novel – *The Jungle Book* (1994). Re-working Rudyard Kipling's novel for Disney, he eschews reverence, adding twists to the original and a sense of pace and fun. Jason Scott Lee plays Mowgli, the Indian boy brought up by jungle animals who falls in love with rich English girl Lena Headey. Added to the mix are stiff upper-lipped Sam Neill, roguish Cary Elwes and eccentric John Cleese, as well as the requisite beautiful scenery – all sun-dappled lakes and verdant forest. Not content to focus on Mowgli's integration into polite society, Sommers creates a sub-plot involving a treasure hunt in the Lost City. This diversion is surprisingly effective, heightening the sense of fun and moving the film into 'Indiana Jones' territory. The pace is relentless – the project often feels like a try-out for *The Mummy* franchise – and the characterisation a little one-dimensional, but the enduring sense of wonder is enough to carry it through to a somewhat mechanical conclusion.

After *The Jungle Book*, Sommers was an executive producer on the 1997 television version of 'Oliver Twist'. His next feature film, *Deep Rising* (1998), was a poor attempt to reinvent and revitalise the sub-aqua shenanigans of *The Abyss* (1989) and *Alien Resurrection* (1997). The film is tiresomely cannibalistic – the set-up recalls the original *Alien* (1979) with its assortment of mismatched characters cramped together in a doomed cruise-liner threatened by giant sea creatures. With shallow dialogue, unconvincing CGI and a stolid earnestness, its execution is risible. Only in the final scene does Sommers develop a sense of humour; until then his run-of-the-mill direction and pedestrian pacing render the film a mish-mash of half-conceived ideas.

He has since made *The Mummy* and *The Mummy Returns* – two of the most profitable movies of the last few years. *The Mummy* is essentially a rehash of the all the old Mummy films: Karl Freund's 1932 original and the 1950s Hammer version are seamlessly merged, allowing Sommers to develop a more tongue-in-cheek approach to the narrative. A long theme-park ride of a film, complete with street chases, marauding zombies, Biblical plagues and man-eating beetles, it is leavened by a healthy dose of irony and some rip-roaring performances. As adventurer Rick O'Connell, Brendan Fraser brings a mixture of brawn and doe-eyed beauty to his role, while Rachel Weisz and John Hannah play the 'English abroad' with typical self-deprecation and pomposity. Sommers maintains the pace throughout, scarcely pausing to add any atmosphere of mystery or wonder to his rollercoaster narrative. In tone and mood, he is clearly indebted to *Raiders of the Lost Ark* (1981), but where Spielberg's pumped-up B-movie was a triumph of wit and plausibility, *The Mummy* is a playful two hours that relies too much on state-of-the-art special effects.

While there is no denying the humour and non-stop action sequences of the sequel, *The Mummy Returns* still suffers from over-indulgence. Sommers foregrounds his showmanship through a skilful blend of action and romance yet the film remains a series of self-contained sequences that never quite fuse into a satisfying whole. Where *The Mummy* bore the traces of a plot, the second film privileges CGI monsters and gruesome set pieces over any depth of character. Everyone from the original is present (WWF star The Rock is the only notable addition), and there is a distinct sense of déjà vu; the man-eating beetles and zombies return, as does Imhotep's ability to be in two places at once.

Sommers has written and produced, though not directed, a second *Mummy* sequel, *The Scorpion King* (2002).                                                                      **BM**

# Barry SONNENFELD

Barry Sonnenfeld is a director who always plumps for ambitious, off-kilter projects, which ably reflect his own personality. To quote one star who worked with him, 'His view of things, his sense of humour ... They're *different*. He has a style all of his own.' And it is this style that has enabled him to bridge the gap from cinematographer to fully-fledged film-maker, working on movies with budgets in excess of $150 million.

Born in New York in 1953, educated at NYU, where he gained a degree in political science, Sonnenfeld enjoyed a brief spell as a photo technician before becoming a film student alongside Joel and Ethan Coen. He went on to serve as director of photography on their films *Blood Simple* (1984), *Raising Arizona* (1987), and *Miller's Crossing* (1990). The natural progression for him was to directing and his first break came after a decade in the business.

*The Addams Family* (1991) bypasses the kitsch 1960s television show and looks to the original Charles Addams *New Yorker* cartoons for inspiration. The gothic setting, costumes, and perspective mimic the source material splendidly, as do the actors involved – Anjelica Huston (Morticia), Christina Ricci (Wednesday), and versatile Christopher Lloyd (Uncle Fester) are each deserving of a special mention. Tragically, the movie never advances beyond its initial concept: that of a warped family of eccentrics rebelling against the conventions of respectable society. The jokes are pithy rather than funny, the residue of a plot is at its best preposterous, and the opportunity to confront these non-conformists with the real world they shun is fatally squandered when the clan are tricked out of their fortune.

An expeditious sequel came next, but *Addam's Family Values* (1993) is a vast improvement on the first attempt. While there is still perilously little substance to the script, *Values* does contain more character development, dealing as it does with the arrival of a new baby Addams (complete with Gomez pencil-moustache) and consequent sibling rivalry, Fester's amorous intentions towards a *Hand that Rocks the Cradle*-style nanny, Joan Cusack, and Wednesday's awakening hormones, which reach fruition at a nauseating summer camp for rich kids.

However, Sonnenfeld's second movie of that year, *For Love or Money* (1993), takes a serious step backwards. Thanks to another inadequate screenplay, the film's outcome is forced to rest almost entirely on the charisma of its star, Michael J. Fox – who falls back on his customary screwball persona. As the concierge of an up-market hotel who can obtain anything the guests desire, his character has promise, particularly when he interacts with the hotel staff or bargains with street traders for goods. But the actual quandary the title suggests – which is more important, love or money? – takes up too much of the storyline for anyone to really care.

*Get Shorty* (1995) is the most significant milestone in the director's career. Based on the novel by Elmore Leonard, this film is a dexterous composite of *The Bad and the Beautiful* (1952) and *Goodfellas* (1990), drawing scathing parallels between the Hollywood system and the criminal underworld. A post-*Pulp Fiction* (1994) John Travolta bolsters his cinematic comeback as the movie-buff debt collector desperate to become a producer – 'Where the real money is!' – but finds that tinseltown is already brimming with mobsters. The meretricious epigrammatic dialogue, intricate and ingenious plotting, resourceful use of camera, and the way Sonnenfeld counterpoises the violence with humour, all combine to make this his most proficient entry.

*Men in Black* (1997) rides a close second, having the extra advantage of a broader audience base. An unexpected hit in a summer of sequels, this was another comic book conversion, but more perceptive and self-reflexive than most. The proposition that aliens live among us, regulated by a clandestine government agency, paves the way for a myriad of puns about Elvis, Spielberg, and New York taxi drivers (consolidated by Industrial Light and Magic's effects). At the centre, Tommy Lee Jones plays straight man to smart-mouth rapper Will Smith, both bedecked in *Reservoir Dogs* attire and hefting unfeasibly large ray guns. Like *The Addams Family*, the embryonic idea and sense of fun has to compensate for a lackadaisical narrative, yet the incredibly fast pace and short running time ensures that tedium never sets in.

Sonnenberg's affection for 1970s television shows came to the fore, evidenced not only by his resurrection of 'Fantasy Island' for a new run starring Malcolm McDowell, but also the adoption of *Wild Wild West* (1999) as his next movie cause. Seen as a 'dream ticket', the director once again consorted with Smith, though the results this time are far less intoxicating. The film professes to be a James Bond spy thriller set in the old west, but is actually more of a genre-bending and bewildering sci-fi western with an action-adventure bias. There is no depth to the production, the characters have infinitesimal motivation, the chemistry between Smith and Kevin Kline (as a mad inventor) is non-existent, and Kenneth Branagh's paraplegic villain is scornful. The only high points – a characteristic it does share with many Bond films – are the gadgets, which range from a jet-powered Penny Farthing to a gargantuan mechanical spider. In spite of this it still took $50 million over its opening weekend in America.

His two most recent films are *Big Trouble* (2002), which is based on Dave Barry's book and follows several diverse Miami residents whose lives intersect, and the sequel *Men in Black 2* (2002), which offers Smith and Jones the chance to work together again for the top secret alien agency. **PB**

# Kevin SPACEY

Kevin Spacey has been one of the finest and most prolific film and stage actors of the 1990s. He was born in New Jersey in 1959 and, having studied drama at the Juilliard School, his popularity and good reputation were particularly shaped by his performances in the most notable noirs of recent years, including *The Usual Suspects* (1995), for which he won an Academy Award, *Se7en* (1995), and *LA Confidential* (1997).

In 1996 Spacey made his debut feature, *Albino Alligator*, a claustrophobic thriller of low-profile criminals trapped by the police in a basement bar. Doomed by a uninteresting and rather badly written screenplay, the film hardly recovers from failure through the performances of its central characters, which are in turn either too exaggerated (in the case of Matt Dillon) or unreasonably underplayed (Gary Sinise). Spacey's direction is overall conservative and unengaging, although he attempts some interesting camera work (especially with some unusual angles), and the noir atmosphere of the film seems to rely only on explicit references to the genre, including the ever-present Bogart poster hanging behind the bar.

However, what is particularly disappointing about Spacey's direction is his handling of actors. Given the situation of the story (a group of characters forced to share the same space for long hours), and Spacey's own experience, the film would have made a great opportunity for character study. Instead, the characterisation is generally weak, even without reproducing traditional good/evil polarities, and the final philosophy – 'None of us are heroes' – is rather cheap and unconvincing.                    **BP**

# Penelope SPHEERIS

Penelope Spheeris emerged from the 1980s as an important figure on the fringes of independent film-making. Her films are noted for their sharp, contemporary observations of popular youth culture. However, in her keynote speech to the Digital Video Conference in 1999, Spheeris lamented the pigeon-hole Hollywood has placed her in and argued that she is not taken seriously enough but is seen as simply a director of bland comedies.

Born in New Orleans in 1945, she attended the University of California in Los Angeles, where she studied film, and later attended the American Film Institute in Los Angeles. Prior to her career as a film-maker, Spheeris worked as a film editor. She set up her own company in the 1970s called Rock 'n' Reel, making films for up-and-coming rock bands – early or 'proto' rock videos.

Spheeris went on to work in television, producing seven comedy shorts for Saturday Night Live, directed by Albert Brooks. Her first foray into features was as a producer for Brooks' *Real Life* (1979). However, it was with her first venture as a director, producer and screenwriter that she made her reputation. *The Decline of Western Civilisation* (1981) is the definitive documentary examining the punk scene in Los Angeles, and achieved widespread critical acclaim, as well as modest commercial success.

Spheeris followed this with *Suburbia/The Wild Side* (1983), which had a cultish appeal due to its post-punk concerns but was not as successful as her previous work, and then *The Boys Next Door* (1986), a tale about youth gone bad. She subsequently turned her hand to comedies for her next two features, *Hollywood Vice Squad* (1986) and *Dudes* (1987). Neither film was well received and they did little business at the box office. Spheeris then took a break from solely making films and returned to working in television, most notably as a story editor on 'Roseanne'.

In 1988 she made *The Decline of Western Civilisation Part II: The Metal Years*. Here Spheeris skilfully crafts a documentary that balances the views of performers such as Kiss and Ozzy Osbourne, against the often deranged fantasies of metal fans. She then contributed to *Prison Stories: Women on the Inside* (1991), a trilogy of dramas centring on the struggles of women in prison; 'New Chicks' follows the character of a pregnant maximum-security prisoner as she fights for better treatment.

*Wayne's World* (1992), based on 'Saturday Night Live' characters created by Michael Myers and Dana Garvey, saw a return to comedy and to her 'Saturday Night Live' roots. The film was an enormous commercial success and achieved critical acclaim as a stylish, knowing, and highly self-referential piece of postmodern popular culture. With its alternative endings and its double-dealing media executives, the film is as much about Hollywood film-making and the media industries as it is about the rise of two small-town dudes and their cable television show.

Spheeris' next two projects saw her attempt to breathe yet more cinematic life into popular television comedy. *The Beverly Hillbillies* (1993) was a failure, both commercially and critically, despite the same kinds of pop culture references and slick self-referentiality used in *Wayne's World*. *The Little Rascals* (1994) fared little better.

Spheeris wrote and directed her next feature, *Black Sheep* (1996). A comedy structured around three former 'Saturday Night Live' comedians, it follows the story of a gubernatorial candidate (Tim Matheson) as he attempts to keep his half-witted brother (Chris Farley) out of the public gaze. He hires a minder (David Spade), and much of the comedy is centred on Spade's sarcasm and Farley's pratfalls. *Black Sheep* was a flop at the box office and achieved little, if any, critical acclaim.

Spheeris began filming a third instalment in the *Decline of Western Civilisation* series in 1996, revisiting the Los Angeles punk scene she first filmed back in 1981. This was released in the US in 1998. Her next feature, *Senseless* (1998), was critically unacclaimed, relatively shallow and disappointing. She followed this with two unremarkable feature films, the comedies *Posers* (2001) and *Closers* (2001). *Closers* is allegedly a comedy centring on a bureau which has as its tagline 'You pick the target and we guarantee you get laid'.

Spheeris has had more success working in the film-making mode with which she has most sympathy – documentary. Her latest offering, *We Sold Our Souls To Rock 'n' Roll* (2001) sees her return to one of her key documentary subjects, heavy metal music, as she follows the massive Ozzfest to thirty cities. The film successfully conveys a sense of the multi-generational appeal of metal from the older Sabbath fans to the new wave of metal freaks like Slipknot. Spheeris claimed that she worked for free on the Ozzfest film, saying, 'I do them for the love of the art, the love of the craft, the art of film-making'. After running into legal trouble, however, concerning music rights, a theatrical release for *We Sold Our Souls To Rock 'n' Roll* seems doubtful.

Spheeris' next film, *Spam On Rye*, is the story of a young man (David Arquette) who steals a car to impress his date and is then chased by a Mob boss, the LAPD, and a shotgun-wielding movie producer. She will also direct an adaptation of John Lydon's autobiography about the Sex Pistols, 'Rotten: No Irish, No Blacks, No Dogs'.          **SL**

# Steven SPIELBERG

Steven Spielberg, along with sometime collaborator George Lucas, is widely credited with rescuing American cinema from the commercial doldrums of the 1960s. However, he is just as frequently accused of reducing of the artform of the Hollywood movie to a merchandise-friendly beacon for dominant values. Spielberg's cinema strongly reflects both of these simplifications, but also contains largely unheralded thematic discourses (especially concerning the fragility of family bonds) as well as an unparalleled capacity to integrate technological innovation with the narrative forms of mainstream cinema.

Born in Ohio in 1946, Spielberg's family circumstances meant that he travelled around a lot as a child, and he was traumatised by the 1966 divorce of his parents (an episode that seems to echo in many of his works). Spielberg got his first chance in television, directing luminaries like Joan Crawford in NBC's 'Night Gallery'. In the late 1960s the ownership of a major film studio was a volatile business, and the most farsighted executives, like Lew Wasserman at MCA-Universal, were leaning heavily on the more reliable sideline of television production. Wasserman pioneered the concept of the 'Made-for-TV movie', and entrusted one such production, *Duel*, to Spielberg in 1971. The narrative of a motorist menaced by a dehumanised and relentless truck driver is slim, but Spielberg's action scenes effortlessly suggest a bigger stage (appropriately, *Duel* earned a cinema release in the UK). As a reward for making a splash with *Duel*, Spielberg was given bigger stars (including Goldie Hawn) and a bigger budget on his first cinema feature, *The Sugarland Express* (1974), a chase caper with mild hints of *Duel*'s vision of a depersonalised society (George Lucas' contemporaneous *THX-1138* (1970) is an instructive point of reference for both *Duel* and *Sugarland*).

Spielberg applied his maturing visual intelligence to *Duel*'s pessimistic theme of unpredictable menace to devastating commercial effect in *Jaws* (1975), an adaptation of Peter Benchley's popular novel and a film regarded as a blueprint for the new corporate era in Hollywood. *Jaws*' extraordinarily effective blend of action and character dynamics, and Spielberg's talent for masking unconvincing special effects with shrewd use of editing and music, is often overlooked due to its place in film history as the benchmark for all the summer 'event' movies to come. Utilising extensive television and press advertising and a 'saturation' release strategy (as opposed to normal practices of progressively widening a movie's number of screen engagements to encourage word-of-mouth), *Jaws* was a massive gamble for Universal that paid remarkable dividends at the box office. The film also established Spielberg's significant motif of the errant father, appearing here in versions both domestic (Roy Scheider's obsessed police chief) and civic (the craven mayor of Amity Island).

Richard Dreyfuss portrays another distracted father in *Close Encounters of the Third Kind* (1977), a film that makes a telling progression from the irrational threat of *Jaws* to a completely benign alien visit that is misinterpreted by hostile authorities. Here, the visit from the unknown is an opportunity for transcendence. Dreyfuss plays one of a series of ordinary people – nevertheless all marked as sensitive, artistic types – who receive a calling from the mysterious visitors, only to run into bureaucratic obstacles barring their goal of physical contact (the 'third kind' of inter-species encounter named in the title). Dreyfuss eventually bypasses human intervention by demonstrating his emotional affinity with the creatures and is last seen in the alien 'mothership', apparently turning his back on his own responsibilities as a father for an exploration of the unknown. Spielberg's film achieves a true sense of wonderment through special effects, and the film makes several references to Walt Disney's *Pinocchio* (1940), establishing a link to the Disney worldview that would remain pertinent throughout Spielberg's career.

Spielberg's first misstep was *1941* (1979), an unwieldy, overcooked, and unfunny Pearl Harbor comedy that represents a surprising anomaly in the context of Spielberg's later track record of representing World War Two. He bounced back from the thoroughly negative experience by collaborating with George Lucas on *Raiders of the Lost Ark* (1981). The film represents the first time that Spielberg zeroes in on the audience demographic that would provide his biggest hits, establishing a Spielbergian sub-genre that film theorist Peter Krämer has identified as the 'family-adventure movie'. The wide appeal of *Raiders*, and its sequels, lies in the alliance of Lucas' proven sense of big-screen nostalgia with Spielberg's ability to keep spectacle and emotion in the right balance. An exhilarating entertainment replete with wartime setting and comic-book Nazi villains, *Raiders* once again foregrounds the blend of old and new Hollywood traditions in Spielberg's cinema. Older viewers recognised the standard plot twists and stock characters of fondly remembered Saturday morning serials, while their accompanying children gained pleasure from Harrison Ford's charismatic (but fallible) hero and the brisk pace of the adventure. In *Indiana Jones and the Temple of Doom* (1984), the all-important younger viewers were given their own surrogate in the character Short Round (Jonathan Ke Quan). The plot – Indy confronts the murderous members of the 'Thuggi' death cult – is purloined from George Stevens' classic *Gunga Din* (1939), but darker themes of moral corruption and the oppression of children, as well as an increased degree of onscreen violence, mark the film as a more threatening proposition than its predecessor. Rounding out the trilogy, and helping the saga to mature a little more, *Indiana Jones and the Last Crusade* (1989) introduces an Oedipal theme that is mostly played for laughs, with Ford and Sean Connery (perfectly cast as Indy's grail expert father) turned against each other by the beautiful Nazi collaborator Elsa Schneider (Alison Doody). Indy's Oedipal narrative is finally resolved when he locates the grail, although yet another ambiguous father figure in a Spielberg text cannot pass unnoticed.

The 'family-adventure' movie inaugurated by *Raiders* reached its zenith with *E.T. The Extra Terrestrial* (1982), a film that even more effectively distils Spielberg's preoccupations into a format tailored to the intergenerational moviegoing experience. The 'Peter Pan' principle seen in *Close Encounters* and *Raiders* is inverted in *E.T.*; whereas those films focus on men who frequently act like impetuous young boys, *E.T.* centres on Elliot (Henry Thomas), a boy from a single-parent family who is forced to grow up when he takes a stranded alien botanist under his wing. The ageless E.T. is both father figure and child to Elliot, who learns the complexities of family life and reconsiders his deserted mother's position in the light of E.T.'s arrival. Elliot instructs the alien in the codes and rituals of suburban life, and the creature blends in perfectly; as in *Close Encounters*, Spielberg hints at the merry weirdness that is released by the impulse of imagination, but also indicates the emotional cost of 'wishing upon a star'. The film is directed with warmth, and includes moments of genuine magic (the airborne bicycle framed against the moon becoming an instant icon of Spielbergian values and perfectly encapsulating the mastery of mundane technology that drives his flights of cinematic fancy). However, when E.T.'s life is drained away as his desire to return home overcomes him, only for a Christ-like resurrection to ensue, one might feel Spielberg's emotional message becoming indigestible. Executives at Universal, Spielberg's second home since *Duel*, were not complaining; the film's huge success redefined the family demographic that would become Hollywood's very own 'holy grail' in the 1980s.

Spielberg's contribution to the ill-fated portmanteau film *Twilight Zone: The Movie* (1983) is of little interest, but his next pair of films after *Indiana Jones and the Temple of Doom* saw the director change tack and attempt to adapt his style to more complex literary sources. Both *The Color Purple* (1985) and *Empire of the Sun* (1987), adapted from works by Alice Walker and J. G. Ballard respectively, found Spielberg apparently making amends for a decade of transparently commercial work by exploring notions of racial intolerance and the shaping of the individual by historical forces. However, the idea that adapting an acclaimed book automatically results in a richer film experience is a facile one, and despite providing star-making turns for Whoopi Goldberg in *The Color Purple* and Christian Bale in *Empire*, the feel of inherited gravitas that settles on both pictures points more towards a creative identity crisis in Spielberg than any true development of style.

A more moderate success, from the same year as the third *Indiana Jones* episode, *Always* (1989) is an awkward love-beyond-the-grave yarn that fails to avoid the twin pitfalls of incredulity and sentimentality. Spielberg's next film, *Hook* (1991), his first direct treatment of the Peter Pan legend, is also below par. Quite apart from a troubled production history which saw an uncertain Spielberg allow the budget to spiral to $75 million, the film is fundamentally flawed. As a chronicler of suburban mores with an eye for the fantastic, Spielberg has always hit the mark when depicting ordinary worlds touched by unearthly or unnatural visitors (*Close Encounters*, *E.T.*, and *Jurassic Park* (1993) exemplify this). However, these terms are unsuccessfully reversed in *Hook*, where an adult Peter Pan (Robin Williams) is forced to revisit a half-forgotten Never Never Land to rescue his own children; this time, a man who considers himself ordinary steps into a fantastical world. The result is Spielberg's creakiest, least engaging 'family-adventure' picture. Despite huge sets and showy all-star casting (Dustin Hoffman, Julia Roberts), the film sacrifices the genuine old-fashioned magic of the Pan legend for a half-heartedly post-modernist update which is only interesting for its treatment of the trademark negligent dad figure (Pan's children are tempted away by Hook because they feel alienated from their workaholic father).

The uncertainty induced by the *Hook* fiasco would soon abate; as is usually the case with Spielberg, there was another era-defining hit around the corner. *Jurassic Park* ushered in a new phase in the use of special effects, trumping the 'morphing' technique displayed in James Cameron's *Terminator 2: Judgment Day* (1991) with an extraordinary blend of photo-realistic CGI and animatronics. All credit went to Spielberg for bringing the film's dinosaurs to life, with nobody commenting on the irony of *Jurassic Park*'s 'bad science' theme in the face of such technological celebration. Notably, the narrative sees a return to the proven Spielberg territory of a realistic world visited by unbelievable creatures, and another canny move sees Spielberg fill the cast out with familiar faces (Sam Neill, Jeff Goldblum, Laura Dern) that, nevertheless, do not detract from the spectacle of the dinosaurs. For all the technical skill on display, Spielberg cleverly realises that the power of scale depends on a strategy of comparison, as is demonstrated in the rippling glasses of water that announce the approach of a rampaging T-Rex. Scenes such as that brought the best out of the brand new DTS digital sound system introduced by MCA with the film, underlining *Jurassic Park*'s role as showcase for state of the art cinema technologies in the early 1990s. Like *Jaws*, *Jurassic Park* served as an unrepentant advertisement for an American cinema of spectacle and technology, and as such, represented a perfectly bred intermedia monster for MCA-Universal. Its sequel, *The Lost World: Jurassic Park* (1997), saw Spielberg in treading water mode, although the action scenes are once again exquisitely co-ordinated.

Spielberg followed *Jurassic Park* with a movie that represented his most concentrated effort yet to attain serious plaudits. Demonstrating Spielberg's uncanny ability to anticipate public responses to his material, *Schindler's List* (1993), a long and frequently distressing account of the plight of Polish Jews in World War Two, actually went on to commercially outperform *Hook* at the worldwide box office. Spielberg signals his serious intent with the film's monochrome palette, shorthand for a sense of newsreel authenticity, but also registering a determination to keep a respectful historical distance – although Spielberg's success in this regard is questionable, and the film's treatment of history caused wide and impassioned debate at the time of release. In contrast to *The Color Purple*, Spielberg gives an impression of total conviction with the difficult material involved in *Schindler's List* (adapted from Thomas Keneally's book *Schindler's Ark*), and does not flinch from depicting Nazi brutality. The compression of the story of thousands of Jewish inhabitants of the Krakow ghetto into the personal dilemma of their potential saviour, German factory-owner Oskar Schindler (Liam Neeson), opens the film to questions of narrative reductionism. However, Spielberg is clearly most comfortable dealing with the effect of the war, and the conflict it raises, within the soul of an individual (a classic Oscar-baiting strategy that rewarded him with the Best Director trophy). The film is undeniably powerful, and relatively under-romanticised, although translations of such emotionally and culturally-charged material for a mass medium like cinema will always raise criticisms, and Spielberg earned his fair share.

The two films that bookended the release of the *Jurassic Park* sequel displayed both sides of Spielberg's newly-established maturity: a burgeoning sense of duty to historical testimony and a tendency to fudge delicate issues with sweeping sentimentality. *Amistad* (1997) undoes some of the good work laid down by Spielberg's restrained approach to *Schindler's List*, turning a critique of America's nineteenth-century enslavement of Africans into an inert courtroom drama. *Saving Private Ryan* (1998) pressed the right buttons for audiences (and the Academy), but forsakes the promise of its brutally effective opening combat scenes for another digression upon the quandary of the symbolic individual life in the context of the common good (familiar from *Schindler's List*). In this case, Matt Damon's Private Ryan, sole survivor of a set of fighting brothers, is rescued from the World War Two frontline by the unit led by Tom Hanks' Captain Miller, and told by the stoical Miller to 'earn' his respite by living a good life. The film attempts to prove that representing the 'Greatest Generation' has not become safe or unproblematic territory for Spielberg, but ultimately *Ryan*'s sense of morality seems one-dimensional.

Although its merits are debatable, *Saving Private Ryan* saw Spielberg continue in the more mature vein of film-making initiated by *Schindler's List*. Returning to science-fiction, perhaps aiming to blend the new, more 'adult' dimension of his approach with a favourite commercial genre, Spielberg embarked upon *A.I. Artificial Intelligence* (2001). Heralded in advance publicity as an epic meeting of *auteur* consciousnesses, Spielberg's development of a screen concept that originated with the late Stanley Kubrick could not help but disappoint on some levels. Yet the movie is surely one of Spielberg's most personal works, filled with visual and thematic references to his other films, and sustains critical interest for its overdetermined, neurotic reworking of *E.T.*'s discourse of family. David (Haley Joel Osment) is a robot child introduced into the lives of Henry and Monica Swinton, a couple whose only son, Martin, is in a coma. Programmed to love unconditionally, David finds himself excluded when Martin returns from his illness and cruelly enlightens David as to his inescapable difference. Osment copes well with the transition from David's early, spooky omnipresence around the house (he becomes another form of domestic appliance, underscoring the relatively harsh view of commodification implied in David's creation) to the development of real emotions and the conflict they produce. The first hour of the film captures something of the hyped meeting of styles, the Spielbergian feel for family dynamics balanced by an observational coldness (enhanced by starkly modern set design) that is very much Kubrick's signature. However, after the stunning scene where Monica abandons David in the woods (signalling narrative affinities with the old *Close Encounters* reference point *Pinocchio* as well as darker tales like Shelley's 'Frankenstein'), Spielberg lets the narrative reins slip somewhat, resulting in an interminable journey through a visually incoherent and uncharacteristically derivative neon cityscape. David's search for the 'Blue Fairy' that can turn him into a 'real' boy takes him across millennia, and an audience duped by several false endings may feel the choice of timeframe is apposite. That said, although the ending is obscure and stretches credibility (even in the appropriate generic context), the final fantasy of reunion with Monica powerfully articulates the overriding themes of the film – maternity, family and the 'authenticity' of feelings. *A.I.* is uneven and poorly structured, and its narrative concern with robotics seems oddly quaint; but its seething Freudian undercurrents make it a fascinating addition to Spielberg's oeuvre.

Spielberg is the 'movie brat' who grew up and acquired his own studio, forming Dreamworks SKG with Jeffrey Katzenberg and David Geffen in 1995; and the consequences for American cinema of his ascendancy cannot easily be overstated. As a director, Spielberg often revisits the same themes, but, significantly, his distinct worldview is also stamped on the productions where he acts as executive producer (running from *Gremlins* (1984) to *Men in Black* (1997) and beyond), and the various television series that have emerged under his aegis ('Band of Brothers', 'Animaniacs', 'Amazing Stories'). The works associated with Spielberg are instantly recognisable in stylistic and narrative terms, and his signature is identifiable across media forms (*A.I.* was notable for one of the most sophisticated internet marketing campaigns yet conducted) and film genres. With *Jaws* Spielberg ushered in the ruthlessly commercial second phase of the 'New Hollywood', however it would be wrong to simply cast him as the pantomime corporate villain of post-classical film. In any true account of popular cinema, he has a claim to be one of Hollywood's pre-eminent auteurs, for rarely has a single film-maker had such a huge influence on the narrative and industrial practices of American movie culture.

His most recent film, *Minority Report* (2002), which stars Tom Cruise, is set in 2080, an age when crimes can be detected before they happen. *Catch Me If You Can*, with Leonardo DiCaprio playing a conman and Tom Hanks as a federal agent, is due for release in 2003.                                                                     **MF**

# Roger SPOTTISWOODE

Born in England in 1943, Roger Spottiswoode began his career as a successful television and documentary editor in Britain, before embarking on a career in America. His early work in Hollywood included editing two of Sam Peckinpah's films (*Straw Dogs* (1971) and *Pat Garrett and Billy the Kid* (1973)), before making his directorial debut with *Terror Train* (1979). Despite a patchy period for the director in the early 1990s, Spottiswoode proved himself to be a safe and capable pair of hands with a big-budget project with the Bond film, *Tomorrow Never Dies* (1997).

*Terror Train* is one of a series of *Halloween* (1978) clones. It also features 'scream queen' Jamie Lee Curtis as one of a band of teens at the mercy of a psychopath, as they party the night away on a moving train. The director's next feature, *The Pursuit of D. B. Cooper* (1981) is a comic chase caper starring Treat Williams as an escaped robber who parachutes from a hijacked plane with thousands of dollars, and is hotly pursued by law enforcers, including Robert Duvall. This is a disjointed film, which suffered a series of problems during its making (several directors and major re-writes of script).

Spottiswoode finally had the opportunity to demonstrate his considerable abilities with *Under Fire* (1983). Set in Nicaragua in 1979, during the last days of Somoza's dictatorship, this is a graceful and spirited tale centring on three American journalists and their reactions to the revolution taking place around them. Fine performances from an exceptionally strong cast (Nick Nolte, Gene Hackman, Joanna Cassidy) make this a gripping and passionate piece of mainstream cinema. Spottiswoode directs this film with exceptional style and flair.

*The Best of Times* (1986) saw Spottiswoode reunited with Ron Shelton, who wrote *Under Fire*. The film is essentially a buddy movie, centring on former high-school football team mates, Jack (Robin Williams) and Reno (Kurt Russell), and Jack's inability to live down a humiliating sporting defeat in his youth. Jack obsesses about re-staging the game, and this obsession draws the two leads closer together while adding enormous strain to their respective marriages. The film successfully avoids the syrupy-sweetness that so often comes with films of this ilk, but did little business at the box office.

Spottiswoode again ventured into the territory of the buddy movie with his next feature, *Shoot to Kill* (1988) consists of the staple 'buddy' formula of two male protagonists with nothing in common brought together for a mission. The film is worth more than a passing glance for several reasons. Firstly, it marked Sidney Poitier's return to acting after ten years behind the camera. Secondly, the performance of Clancy Brown as the villain is chillingly superb and it is easy to see how he has carved a career out of such roles (see *Highlander* (1986), *Shawshank Redemption* (1994)). Spottiswoode's background in editing informs every shot, every sequence, and it is a textbook example of mainstream Hollywood film-making. Despite this, the film did only modestly well at the box office.

Spottiswoode's next feature was popular with audiences but much maligned by critics – and rightly so. *Turner & Hooch* (1989) is an appalling cop flick starring Tom Hanks as an anally retentive detective whose only witness to a murder is a slobbery and clumsy dog named Hooch. Despite the ridiculous premise, audiences flocked to the cinema to see America's box-office favourite act with a dog. Spottiswoode does a fairly standard job in terms of direction, thus ensuring he would at least stay in work in Hollywood for the foreseeable future. And maybe that was the point.

Yet the cinema-going public were not to be fooled by the director's next two offerings: both action comedies, and both huge flops, despite the presence of top stars. *Air America* (1990) features Mel Gibson and Robert Downey Jr as pilots working for the CIA during the Vietnam War. *Stop! Or My Mom Will Shoot* (1992) stars Sylvester Stallone as a cop who has just split up with his lover and boss (JoBeth Williams). His mother, played by Estelle Getty, of television's 'Golden Girls' fame, comes to comfort her son. Spottiswoode's direction is ham-fisted, clichéd, and handicapped further by a script that is at best lightweight.

Spottiswoode's next feature, *Mesmer* (1994), is a biography of the eighteenth-century Austrian physician, Franz Anton Mesmer. Despite a solid performance from Alan Rickman in the lead role, this is a plodding, somewhat episodic film. Spottiswoode did not make another cinematic feature until 1997, though during this time he made two respectable television movies – *And the Band Played On* (1993) and the Canadian/Japanese collaboration, *Hiroshima* (1995). However, the director redeemed himself in the eyes of studios and their accountants with *Tomorrow Never Dies*. The film, as with the majority of the Bond series, was highly successful in terms of its world-wide box-office receipts, and generally highly rated amongst critics. Spottiswoode handles the Bond brand with style and its trademark action sequences are directed with the sharp eye of an editor.

His subsequent feature, *Devil's Pale Moonlit Kiss* (2000), is set during the end of the Cold War and centres around an American porn publisher's attempts to help a young East German ice skater to defect. Spottiswoode's deft hand raises the somewhat flimsy plot to an average piece of film-making but it is disappointing after the high octane thrills and spills of *Tomorrow Never Dies*. Spottiswoode's most work capitalises on current debates in science surrounding the issue of cloning. *The 6th Day* (2000) is set in a near-future America, where scientists have developed cloning technologies. Despire the fact that the world's leaders and scientists have agreed that every form of life can be cloned, with the exception of humans, mad scientists and their pay-masters are happily and covertly cloning people for their own evil needs. Arnold Schwarzenegger plays Adam Gibson, who returns from work to find he has been replaced by a clone of himself, the result of an accident that occured during a terrorist attach. Spottiswoode seems content to put all his faith in the impressive special effects. Robert Duvall turns in a characteristically fine performance as the scientist, which unfortunately throws Schwarzenegger's lack of acting ability into sharp relief. Although it enjoyed a moderate success at the box office, the film was panned by critics for its pump action and somewhat vacuous delivery.

Spottiswoode has proved himself to be a capable director in terms of producing films in the New Hollywood. Despite a low period in the early 1990s, his career as a Hollywood film-maker seems to be on an upward curve. His films are stylish and unpretentious, but he is yet to deliver work of the directorial standard of his earlier *Under Fire* – Spottiswoode at his best.                                                          **SL**

# Salvatore STABILE

*Gravesend* (1997)  Born in New York in 1975, Salvatore Stabile dropped out of New York University Film School and went on to make *Gravesend* (1997). What started as a short film grew into a full-length feature when Stabile was able to finance the film through money left to him after the death of his grandmother.

Although *Gravesend* is an ambitious first project, the film never seems to find an original voice within the constant, deafening roar of its main characters, who scream furiously, and pointlessly, at each other throughout the film. Essentially the story of four young Italian Americans in Coney Island and their desperate attempts to dispose of three bodies, the film suffers from a complete lack of dramatic tension. Instead, it maintains a crescendo of dialogue and action that is superfluous to any plot development. Its attempts to be hard-hitting are undermined by the lack of any credible characterisation and its circuitous plot is interminably frustrating. The characters, like the director, seem to be in a constant state of indecision and appear interchangeable, leading to a complete lack of sympathy for their situation. Visually, however, the film is impressive. Mixing frenetic hand-held camerawork with dimly lit real locations, the film conveys the frantic pace of lives spiralling out of control.

Although all the characters in *Gravesend* seem to be products of a disinterested society and a violent upbringing, Stabile never broadens his scope to encompass this, leaving a confused, testosterone-fuelled portrayal of repressed rage and violence that says little. **BW**

# Darren STEIN

Darren Stein has completed two feature films as writer and director, both branded with an individual style and mordant wit unusual amongst the standard fare produced by Hollywood. These films occupy a strange territory, mixing the box-office appeal of well-worn genres – the road movie, the buddy movie, the teen flick – with the de rigeur cross-referencing and black humour of the self-respecting indie. But denied the caché of true independent film-making, and the low-concept, high-return appeal of the *American Pie*-style teen movie, Stein's films have proved difficult to market, while his visual style, cartoonish and gaudy, often makes his films seem one-dimensional. Stein possesses a genuinely black comic sense, however, with a sharp ear for bathetic, deadpan dialogue that unfortunately is often obscured by over-indulgent direction lacking any real emotional depth.

*Sparkler* (1998), Stein's first film, is the story of Melba May, naïve but well-intentioned trailer trash, who seeks a new life in Las Vegas following the infidelity of her husband. Fascinated by the cinematic potential of sleaze and full of self-consciously quirky characters, the film has comic potential, but Stein's direction lacks any real satirical bite, using over-obvious gags and visual slapstick at the expense of character development or detailed comic interplay. With obvious flair for art direction and some smart editing and use of contemporary songs, Stein's second feature, *Jawbreaker* (1999), is a more focused affair. The story of a fatal prank practised by queen of school Courtney Shane, and the lengths to which she goes to cover up her deeds, the film has more point to its satire. It delineates the crude politics of high school and invokes any number of cinematic counterparts, including *Carrie* (1976), *Heathers* (1989) and *Scream* (1996). Stein again uses his cartoonish visual style, with the full range of snap-cuts, fades, montages, fantasy reveries, and comedy sound effects. Here they seem more appropriate in illustrating the absurd melodrama of high-school life, and the snappy script, coupled with Stein's tangible sense of disgust, make the film a more developed experience, though one still threatened by a sense of caricature.

Stein's films make for curiously uneasy viewing, hinting at a director not entirely in control of his enthusiasm or his material. Obviously brimming with ideas, Stein is undoubtedly a talent for the future, with a passion for the cinema of spectacle and a still-developing sense of real drama. **OB**

*Sparkler* (1998)
*Jawbreaker* (1999)

# Ben STILLER

Born in New York in 1965, Ben Stiller's work on 'The Ben Stiller Show' was rarely less than hilarious, tagging him as a talented, imaginative talent who worked well with others – Janeane Garofalo, an old 'Ben Stiller Show' hand, chief among them. His work as a film director, however, has been more complicated.

His debut, *Reality Bites* (1994), came out at a time when the US was awash in talk of Generation X, slackers, and lazy twentysomethings; it was basically two hours of solid media-spawned cliché. The mainstream press, including many hip urban weeklies, lauded the film, proclaiming Stiller to be uniquely in touch with the malaise gripping America's young people. However, for those with any ability to detect someone pandering to a popular perception rather than exploring it, the disappointment was unmistakable.

Stiller's second film, *The Cable Guy*, has become a kind of shorthand for a 'studio film gone horrifyingly wrong'; starring Jim Carrey and released in the summer of 1996, it

*Reality Bites* (1994)
*The Cable Guy* (1996)
*Zoolander* (2001)

was a huge box-office flop. Despite this reception, *The Cable Guy* was one of that year's best Hollywood films. Carrey is hilariously and exhilaratingly out of control throughout the entire film; Matthew Broderick makes for a near-perfect straight man. The acidic story satirises our obsession with television, and it's hard not to cringe when that obsession is transplanted into every bit of the consciousness of Carrey's cable guy. The narrative is savvy and brutally efficient, and Stiller is often visually ambitious – a scene where he tries to make a basketball game seem operatic, complete with a slow motion shattering of the backboard, is impressively pulled off. It was a film that could have used some critical championing but all could be heard in the American press, however, was the carping of critics who weren't interested in a piece so darkly, sometimes incoherently and excessively, goofball. A honourable exception was the *Village Voice*'s J. Hoberman, who included the film in his top 10 list for 1996.

Stiller's third feature, *Zoolander* (2001), is a minor film but still a worthwhile effort. A satire of the excess of the fashion industry, it features Stiller in the title role of Derek Zoolander, a vapid male supermodel. Will Ferrell, of 'Saturday Night Live' fame, gives his first really solid performance as the evil fashion magnate, Mugatu, and Owen Wilson gives a credibly spacey turn as Zoolander's stoner rival, Hansel. Although Stiller seems to be shooting fish in a barrel here – the fashion industry practically satirises itself –some of the gags that Stiller comes up with are genuinely original, and occasionally quite insane; Zoolander and his airhead model friends, for example, playfully fight with gasoline nozzles. The character Derek Zoolander was originally created as a sketch for the VH-1 Fashion Awards and Stiller has enough sheer comic energy to make the transition workable.

Stiller is planning to make a film of Budd Schulberg's infamous 1941 book, 'What Makes Sammy Run?'                                                                                      **JW**

# Whit STILLMAN

Born in Washington in 1952, the son of a Democrat politician, Whit Stillman graduated from Harvard in 1973 and worked in publishing before entering the film business as a seller of Spanish language films. Whilst working in New York on a Spanish film called *Skyline* (*La Linea del Cielo*) (1984) with director Fernando Colomo, Stillman began to contemplate the possibilities of low-budget film-making. Along with Steven Soderbergh's *sex, lies and videotape*, released in the same year, Stillman's *Metropolitan* (1990) defined the possibilities for US independent cinema at the beginning of the 1990s. Made for $80,000, it is an extremely elegant film that relies on a highly literate screenplay and an excellent cast of unknowns. The world portrayed in the film – preppies living in New York's Upper East Side – is straight out of Stillman's own experience. At first sight this would seem to be a particularly unappealing world full of privileged characters, but Stillman concentrates upon them as young people in transition and endows them with doubts and fears that make identification considerably easier.

Stillman again raided his own background to write and direct his next film, *Barcelona* (1994). Though largely written before *Metropolitan* the film can be seen as further cementing Stillman's approach to storytelling, which is to consider a small and close-knit group in the context of social and cultural change. *Metropolitan* deals with the decline of the old urban social order, whilst *Barcelona* – the story of an uptight American businessman, Ted (Taylor Nichols), and his US Naval officer cousin, Fred (Christopher Eigeman) – takes place in the context of anti-NATO riots and anti-American feeling in Spain. As in all of his films Stillman has to work hard to make the two men sympathetic for audiences. This is a particularly difficult task in the case of Fred, although Stillman manages, in contrast to *Metropolitan*, through the judicious use of melodramatic plot devices. Nevertheless, the film marks a clear development for Stillman, particularly in the way he has sought to naturalise the internal and external worlds of the characters.

In his most recent film, *The Last Days of Disco* (1998), the context for social and economic change is evoked through the decline of disco music and New York's Studio 54. In contrast to the masculine focus of *Barcelona*, *The Last Days of Disco* is effectively told from the point of view of two women, Charlotte (Kate Beckinsale) and Alice (Cloë Sevigny), though the ensemble characters are essentially those from *Metropolitan*. Stillman's real skill, in consistently opting for ensemble pieces, is in establishing the worlds in which the characters move so interestingly whilst refusing to succumb to the temptation (all too prevalent in mainstream Hollywood) to conflate all of the incumbent themes – romance, tragedy, change, betrayal, love – into one or two characters.    **SH**

# Oliver STONE

Born in New York in 1946, Oliver Stone is one of the few major film-makers still prepared to provoke. Displaying radical ambitions, many of his films present an admirable but overwrought attempt to address the role of masculinity and violence amidst the political upheavals of post-1960s America. Tension between Stone's role as 'political' film-maker (embodying a problematic notion of 'truth') and undercurrents of misogyny and hysteria ensure that his work never achieves the clarity and coherence necessary to fulfil its radical potential. Nevertheless, for better or worse, he remains one of the most important directors working in Hollywood today. His work as screenwriter (for example *Midnight Express* (1978), *Conan The Barbarian* (1982), *Scarface* (1983), and *Year of the Dragon* (1985)) merely adds to the rich contradictions.

After dropping out from Yale University in 1965, Stone served in Vietnam from 1967–68, a period which has informed much of his later film work. Subsequently, he attended New York University Film School (where he was taught by Martin Scorsese). His first directorial efforts, *Seizure* (1974) and *The Hand* (1981), use the horror genre to reveal his interest in both a loss of masculine control and the creative fusion of fantasy and reality, ideas which would later emerge fully formed.

Stone established his reputation as a political film-maker with *Salvador* (1986). Set in 1980 as Ronald Reagan achieved Presidential power, the film initially contrasts photojournalist Richard Boyle's (James Woods) personal exploitation of El Salvador with the increase in US military aid to the right-wing government. His redemption is achieved through coverage of the left-wing uprising and the film raises issues of both political and media complicity in foreign affairs. While condemning the upsurge in Reagan's new Cold War, the film also gives voice to a romantic view of American democracy (Boyle stresses how America stands for 'something ... a constitution, human rights for everyone on the planet') which sullies its overall impact. It remains one of Stone's more controlled, measured explorations of American imperialism.

*Platoon* (1986) marked the director's move into widespread prominence after a slew of Academy Awards (including one for his direction). Drawing from his own experiences in Vietnam, Stone presents a grunt's eye view of a tour of duty. Recounted through the letters (in an overstated voiceover) of Chris (Charlie Sheen), his rite-of-passage emerges as a struggle between the good and bad father (Sgt Elias (Willem Dafoe) and Sgt Barnes (Tom Berenger)) for the 'possession of his soul'. This Oedipal slant is complemented by the sacrifice of one father (in an appropriate crucifixion pose) and Chris' elimination of the other. The film also emphasises the class and racial exploitation of the ordinary soldier. A My Lai-type incident on which the film turns presents the only characterisation of the Vietnamese people and the narrative unfolds as an American tragedy ('the enemy was in us', recounts Chris at the conclusion). There is little political dimension to the film, electing instead to convey the senselessness of the whole conflict through the fears and hysteria of its largely disenfranchised grunts. The final call for veterans to teach and rebuild reverberates throughout much of Stone's subsequent work.

*Wall Street* (1987) presents another Oedipal conflict, this time in the contemporary world of corrupt finance. Young broker Bud (Charlie Sheen) is forced to choose between the seductive allure of corporate raider Gordon Gecko (Michael Douglas) and his union member father (Martin Sheen). The film posits wealth as a primary tenet of masculinity and divides its protagonist between his material aspirations and class loyalty. The unwitting betrayal of his literal father leads to redemption and downfall through the rejection of his new mentor. Weighing the business values of old and new America, the film offers a sustained critique of capitalism while fully emphasising the seductive allure of Gecko's 'Greed is Good' credo.

*Talk Radio* (1988) is smaller-scale Stone but one of his most impressive films. Adapted from Eric Bogosian and Tad Savinar's play of the same name and Stephen Singular's book, 'Talked To Death' (about real-life radio host Alan Berg), the film presents a culture of disembodied voices shaped by Barry Champlain's (Bogosian) confrontational radio show. Champlain's contempt for the world around him masks a deep self-loathing and the film contrasts his personal life with the public revelations and humiliations he deals out professionally. Highlighting the class, race, generational, and sexual tensions in contemporary America, the airwave confrontations create a genuinely disturbing ambience. For all the operatic grandstanding of Stone's 'major' works, he demonstrates here an ability to convey the psychological disturbances of his protagonist through a more controlled editing strategy and a visual pattern which repeatedly underscores Champlain's isolation. The face to face conversation with a Generation X stoner and a caller who claims to be a multiple rapist ranks as some of Stone's best work.

*Born on the Fourth of July* (1989) moves on from Platoon by individualising the tragedy of America's involvement in Vietnam before presenting the possibility for political action. Based on Ron Kovic's autobiographical account, Stone presents his journey from 'Yankee Doodle Boy' to Democratic Party conference spokesman as a process of acceptance and re-evaluation. Paralysed in the war, Kovic (Tom Cruise) sees his patriotism become eroded by the surrounding social and political developments. His own resentments are presented as not only a reaction to the war but also a resentful response to his domineering, God-fearing mother. Kovic's symbolic castration is paralleled with his inability to perform sexually and his former role as object of female adoration (his mother, his childhood sweetheart) is cruelly dismantled. Concerned as much with the restoration of male power as the socio-political aspects of the war, Stone again eschews a precise analysis of the relationship between the individual and the conflict in favour of an often hysterical presentation of masculine crisis. However, Stone won his second Best Director Academy Award for the film.

*JFK* (1991) demonstrates Stone's schizophrenic attitude to 'truth' through his dazzling yet highly problematic approach to the various conspiracy theories surrounding the assassination of John F. Kennedy. Concentrating on the attempts of New Orleans District Attorney Jim Garrison (Kevin Costner) to bring a prosecution, the film mixes documentary and reconstruction until they become inseparable. Images of Costner at the White House and his final courtroom speech recall *Mr Smith Goes To Washington* (1939) but Stone's view of democratic ideals veers far from Capra's populist convictions. Indeed, invoking Stone's familiar Oedipal project, the film is torn between concepts of democracy and a yearning for a slain father figure. Seeking truth through narrative speculation, the film manages to implicate everyone from the Mafia to President Lyndon Johnson. The ultimate result is a stylistic hysteria (perfected in *Natural Born Killers* (1994)) which, while persuasive and forceful on the surface, conceals the film's numerous ideological ruptures and tensions. While no one can doubt Stone's convictions, his grasp of history is less sure. Still, the film demonstrates his continual capacity for provocation.

*The Doors* (1991) evinces a different form of hero worship. As much an exploration of sensory expansion as a straightforward rock biopic, the film places Jim Morrison amidst a swirl of chemical excess, social unrest, and Native American mysticism. Bold in its experimentation, the film lacks a proper sense of perspective and is often cringeworthy in its near deification of Morrison. Like its prematurely dead subject, the film runs a steady road to self-destruction.

Based on the memoirs of Phuang Thi Le Ly Hayslip, *Heaven and Earth* (1993) is a rare attempt by Hollywood to tackle the Vietnam conflict from a Southeast Asian perspective. Significantly for Stone, it also contains a female protagonist (played by Hiep Thi Le). Consequently, despite an attempted historical sweep, the film emerges as a Vietnamese melodrama in which America's violation of the country complements its heroine's torture, rape, exploitation but ultimate personal victory. Her American husband (Tommy Lee Jones) is a typically emasculated figure, and much of the film's latter section is devoted to his gradual breakdown. Demonstrating Stone's interest in Eastern philosophy and spiritualism, the final voiceover echoes that of *Platoon*, albeit from an alternate viewpoint.

Stone's next feature, *Natural Born Killers,* is a defining film of our time and all the more disturbing for it. Based on a Quentin Tarantino script (who later distanced himself from the final product, taking only story credit), it feeds its tale of a mass-murdering couple on the run (Woody Harrelson and Juliette Lewis) through a multimedia shredder, resulting in an elaborate postmodern nightmare. Ostensibly a satire on the media and public fascination with violence, the array of film stocks, fast cuts, narrative digressions and formats creates an aesthetic of violence which reduces it to one more surface sign amidst an overwhelming information overload. This may be partially the point for Stone and there is no denying the sensory charge present in some of the film's chaotic set-pieces. Populated by a variety of grotesques and caricatures (played by, among others, Tommy Lee Jones, Robert Downey Jr, and Tom Sizemore), the film revels in chaos and any points which are made concerning the relationship between media images and violence are sucked into incoherence. Referencing the mysticism introduced in *The Doors* as an alternative to the debased society it presents, Stone has inverted the ironies of the Tarantino generation and sensed a sickness at its very heart.

*Nixon* (1995) is a surprisingly sober work considering Stone's established view of America's political Right. Richard Nixon (Anthony Hopkins) emerges as a tragic figure in the classic sense, architect of his own downfall as much as slave to history. The film presents his deep-rooted class resentments as a key factor in his pursuit of power, compounded by gradual conflicts with both his political enemies and ultimately himself. As Nixon's internal demons become inexorably bound with his political ambitions, the film demonstrates the intimate link between the personal and the political on the grandest scale. Like *JFK*, the film is stylistically dense but this time in the service of a more considered approach to the importance of one of history's key recent figures.

Stone's most recent films have continued his inquiry into masculinity. *U Turn* (1997) is a contemporary re-working of film noir motifs. *Any Given Sunday* (1999) transfers the male group ethic to the world of American football. Both films are more consciously commercial than previous efforts but contain key elements familiar from Stone's filmography. Next, he will direct a biograhpical epic of Alexander the Great.　　**NJ**

# Lynne STOPKEWICH

Lynne Stopkewich, born in Montreal in 1964, is a bridge between two very different strands of English-Canadian cinema: the work of David Cronenberg and that of new sensualists like Jeremy Podeswa (*Eclipse* (1994), *The Five Senses* (1999)). Cronenberg's anxiety about the body, fear of violation, and fascination with the abject can be seen in both of her feature films; but so can Podeswa's interest in melancholia, redemption, and sensuality. This is an ambitious straddling act, but Stopkewich pulls it off with confidence and emotional impact, marking her as an important part of Canada's changing cinema.

*Kissed* (1996)
*Suspicious River* (2000)

Her first feature film, *Kissed* (1996), deals with subjects that have occupied Cronenberg, but in a more restrained manner. Given that the film is about a young undertaker who starts having sex with the corpses entrusted to her care, the temptation to resist such restrain must have been great. When a young man falls awkwardly in love with her, he struggles to find some way to connect with her. Although *Kissed* was acclaimed by many critics, it was also castigated by pundits in both Canada and the US. While some viewers may find *Kissed* disgusting, it is also hard not to also find it oddly touching and melancholy.

Her second film, *Suspicious River* (2000), was also controversial for the manner in which it took its characters to extremes. Molly Parker stars again, this time playing a quiet, depressed young woman in an unnamed small town in the Pacific Northwest. She falls in with an apparently charming, but eventually psychotic and sadistic, drifter played by Callum Keith Rennie. His abuse of her forms the dramatic core of the film, and its depiction is graphic; the film's last few reels are breathtaking in their sheer grimness. This bleakness is echoed through Stopkewich's use of setting; this seems to be the fag-end of the badly-dressed mid-1980s, and the use of the soggy, decaying 60s and 70s buildings contributes to the feeling of terminal depression.

In 2001, Stopkewich also directed *Lilith on Top*, a documentary portrait of the third and last year of the travelling women's music festival organised by Sarah MacLachlan.　　**JW**

# Barbra STREISAND

Barbra Streisand was highly acclaimed on the Broadway stage in the early 1960s, and has had a successful career as both film actress and recording artist. Born in Brooklyn in 1942, she has directed only three films: *Yentl* (1983), *The Prince of Tides* (1991), and *The Mirror Has Two Faces* (1996). This limited number indicates not only how selective she is of the projects she works on, but also the criticism which plagues her

*Yentl* (1983)
*The Prince of Tides* (1991)
*The Mirror Has Two Faces* (1996)

directorial work. The beauty and richness that characterises Streisand's singing voice translates onto the screen as the visual splendour and emotional depth of (in particular) *The Prince of Tides*. Yet the sentimentality and self-occupation that commends the torch-song chanteuse frequently damns the director. Such were the charges levelled, especially at *Yentl* and *The Mirror Has Two Faces*. Despite the accomplishment and success of *Yentl* and Streisand's status as the first woman to direct, produce, co-write, and star in a Hollywood film, the Academy has neither acknowledged nor rewarded this achievement.

*Yentl* is an ambitious directorial debut, in which Streisand took the title role of the young Jewish woman who disguises herself as a boy (Anshel) in order to study at *yeshiva*, and who marries a woman in order to stay near the man she loves. This transgressive tale is an amusing, compelling, and sometimes steamy story. Streisand also contravenes the rules of the musical: Yentl sings all the songs. Ultimately *Yentl* is just another love story, but it demonstrates Streisand's talent for re-scripting the conventional, and her uncompromising intervention into the mainstream.

The romanticism of *Yentl* is re-conjured in *The Prince of Tides*. Based on Pat Conroy's best-selling novel, this is Streisand's most accomplished piece; a well-crafted, intricate, and often spellbinding film. The complex material which it deals with – the traumatic recollections of Tom Wingo (Nick Nolte) – is skilfully cultivated through an evocative recreation of the past. *The Prince of Tides*, like *Yentl*, is grounded in the compulsory romance narrative – Tom and Lowenstein become lovers – but, again, all is not sacrificed to it. The film is a tribute to Streisand as director and Nolte's excellent Academy Award-nominated performance (although his agility as an actor grazes against Streisand's more monothematic skills).

Jewishness is a key characteristic of Streisand's films, visible in the New York backdrop to *The Prince of Tides* and *The Mirror Has Two Faces*, and the *shtetl* and *yeshiva* setting for *Yentl*'s romantic comedy. *The Mirror Has Two Faces* sees Streisand's return as quirky Jewish girl, as 'ugly duckling', the role punctuating her acting career. She plays professorial Rose who platonically dates and marries handsome Greg (Jeff Bridges). However, her marriage is only to be fully enjoyed and consummated after her physical transformation into a Lowensteinian New York woman. *The Mirror has Two Faces* is safe Streisand – she is the comical, self-deprecating, Jewish New Yorker. There are many laughs here but this is Streisand's least successful directorial work. The film is not only formulaic, but thin and troubling. **MA**

# Susan STREITFELD

*Female Perversions* (1996)  Susan Streitfeld studied at film school in New York in the late 1970s. Since then she has found it difficult, even in the second wave of American independent film-making in the 1980s, to make films. Before writing and directing *Female Perversions* (1996) she busied herself as an agent to Hollywood actors, including Danny Glover.

Streitfeld took as her starting point Louise J. Kaplan's book 'Female Perversions', a Freudian feminist study of female behaviour and sexuality. Typically for its subject the film addresses female dilemmas of identity and confidence via its complex lawyer heroine Eve (Tilda Swinton), her relationship with her dysfunctional family, and her attempts to overcome her lack of self-confidence to progress in her life and work.

Despite its literary origins, the film strives to be cinematic. It is important to her to bring, as Streitfeld says, 'the visual side and the story side of a film so that they fit together seamlessly and unravel in your psyche'. Thus, the sparse set and cold colours signify Eve's sense of isolation in contrast with the lush golden desert to suggest Eve's internal polarisation. Hard-edged, glossy, and cool, the film presents an antidote to the typical Hollywood take on female empowerment, friendship, and dysfunctional relationships. Here the heroine is cold and aloof, struggling to reconcile strength and independence with acceptable notions of traditional femininity. A result of this is her move into the perversions of the title, here rendered the inevitable outcome of any woman's struggle with her inner self and that which society deems acceptable for her. Sexually explicit, the film threatens to belie executive producer Zalman King's input as it strays into the territory of the erotic thriller, a fate that often overcomes feminist directors (similarly Lizzie Borden's *Love Crimes* (1991)) when they attempt honest depictions of female sexuality. **JD**

# Kevin Rodney SULLIVAN

Born in San Francisco in 1959, Kevin Rodney Sullivan has been working in Hollywood How Stella Got Her Groove in various capacities since the age of 19. Starting as an actor, he appeared in *More* Back (1998) *American Graffiti* (1979), *Night Shift* (1982), and *Star Trek II: The Wrath of Khan* (1982). He then gained a regular role in the later seasons of the popular television series 'Happy Days', whilst also writing screenplays, including an episode of 'Fame'. He later served as an executive producer on the short-lived television series 'Knightwatch'.

Sullivan's feature film directorial debut came with *How Stella Got Her Groove Back* (1998), the story of ambitious forty-year-old American stockbroker Stella (Angela Bassett) who goes to Jamaica on vacation and falls for a twenty-year-old Jamaican named Winston Shakespeare (Taye Diggs). Although both she and others around her question the sense of falling in love with a younger man, they connect on a level that goes beyond the purely carnal.

*How Stella Got Her Groove Back* features an incredible performance by Bassett, but its slow plotting and length ultimately weighs it down. Sullivan and screenwriters Ron Bass and Terry McMillan, who adapted it from the latter's novel, seem too connected to the novel's narrative and allow divergent storylines to detract from the main narrative. The most glaring fault is the attention paid to Stella's close friend Delilah (Whoopi Goldberg) and her illness and subsequent death. Sullivan cannot decide if the film is character-based or plot-based, and ends up with a compromised version of both; too many characters and narrative lines end with little development, giving the narrative as a whole little plausibility. *How Stella Got Her Groove Back* is a positive representation of middle-class black Americans, and marks a forward step for black film-makers such as Sullivan, who shows a strong connection to his characters and an earnest desire to tell a mature story. Ultimately, it is a showcase for Bassett though, and even she cannot sustain a weak narrative.

Sullivan has also directed a segment of the multi-narrative feature *America's Dream* (1996) as well as the HBO movie *Soul of the Game* (1996) about early black players in Major League baseball. Additionally, he co-directed the HBO movie *Cosmic Slop* (1994) with Reginald and Warrington Hudlin.                                                                    **DH**

# John SWANBECK

*The Big Kahuna* (1999), John Swanbeck's only film to date, is an impressively engaging The Big Kahuna (1999) work that manages to discard its theatrical underpinnings and come to life through its magnetic performances and its cinematic assuredness. Shot in a mere 16 days, the film is based on the play by Roger Rueff, who also wrote the screenplay. That it works at all is a tribute to Swanbeck though, who manages to keep the narrative engaging throughout. An experienced theatre director, Swanbeck is clearly confident working in film, as is apparent in his handling of the three actors who drive the narrative: Kevin Spacey, Danny DeVito, and relative newcomer Peter Facinelli. Spacey, who also produced *The Big Kahuna*, sometimes has a tendency to take his characters a little further than necessary. Conversely, DeVito has almost never acted to his potential in film. Swanbeck allows both to shine, by reigning in Spacey and allowing DeVito to blossom.

The film is the story of three industrial lubricants salesmen – braggart Larry (Spacey), dour Phil (DeVito), and young idealist Bob (Facinelli) – who wait in a hospitality suite at a convention in Wichita, Kansas for the Grand Kahuna, the representative of the company whose account they feel will keep their own company afloat. In the meantime discussions on sex, business, life and death, and the existence of God, keep the men occupied. The variety of topics it covers, which in a sense are all variations on a single topic, gives *The Big Kahuna* an excellent momentum. Keeping the film to a strict ninety minutes, Swanbeck proves that he has grasped the innate static limitations of a play-based film.                                                                    **DH**

# T

## Rachel TALALAY

Rachel Talalay's film career began in an unlikely way. A mathematics major from Yale
University, she worked as a computer analyst in her hometown of Baltimore, where she
hooked up with Baltimore's most famous – and freakish – son, film-maker John Waters.
Hearing about an open casting for his *Polyester* (1981), she offered her services on the
production side and ended up working with Waters again, producing *Hairspray* (1988)
and *Cry Baby* (1990).

Freddy's Dead: The Final
Nightmare (1991)
Ghost in the Machine (1993)
Tank Girl (1995)

In between, whilst working as an accountant at New Line (the film company she
became Vice President of in 1987), Talalay became involved with Wes Craven's *A
Nightmare on Elm Street* franchise, and after years on the production side of movies
like *Girls Just Want to Have Fun* (1985) and *Sid and Nancy* (1986), she made her
directorial debut with 1991's *Freddy's Dead: The Final Nightmare*, based on her own
story idea.

Although poorly received, this film introduced the visual style which Talalay would
utilise in her other directorial outings. Full of gimmicks, shock special effects, 3D
sequences and a frantic camera which moves and zooms almost constantly, the film
was criticised for exploiting the topic of child abuse and for providing what was, at the
time, the final nail in the coffin of the original franchise.

Thematically, her next film, *Ghost in the Machine* (1993), is similar to *The Final
Nightmare*, about the soul of a serial killer on the loose, able to travel via electrical
currents to distribute lethal revenge. Again, the film uses special effects but incoherently
and without any real sense of Talalay's visual style.

Her next project, the big-budget MGM-produced *Tank Girl* (1995), tanked. A
well-publicised open casting, the replacement of Emily Lloyd with Lori Petty in the
eponymous role pointed towards the disaster story the film was to become. Based on
Jamie Hewlett's cult comic strip, the film's look was visually true to that of the strip
– Hewlett was heavily involved in production design. Returning to an incoherent visual
variety, Talalay included a song and dance number and animation, but with a hostile
studio demanding cuts (including the infamous sex scene between the heroine and her
half-man, half-kangaroo lover) it was difficult for her vision to remain on-screen. Talalay

remains protective of her project and refers to it somewhat optimistically as 'Ren and Stimpy' meets 'The Brady Bunch' meets 'The Girls of St Trinian's' meets 'Roadrunner' meets 'Beetlejuice'. After this critical panning Talalay moved to television directing for a while, using her British contacts to work on the 'Band of Gold' and 'Touching Evil' series and 'Randall and Hopkirk Deceased'.

*Preacher* – delayed in production and release – is a $20 million movie of the cult comic book of the same name. This violent mythological story of a disillusioned preacher fighting evil in the old west marks a return to Talalay's obvious interest in the dystopian environment of the comic strip. **JD**

# Lee TAMAHORI

*Once Were Warriors* (1994)
*Mulholland Falls* (1996)
*The Edge* (1997)
*A long Came a Spider* (2001)
*Die Another Day* (2002)

Born in Wellington, New Zealand in 1950, Lee Tamahori began his career as a commercial artist and photographer, only joining the New Zealand film industry in the last 1970s as a boom operator, and graduating to assistant director ten years later.

After working as a television director, making diverse dramas such as *Thunderbox* (1989), *Usher II* (1990), and *The Long Rain* (1992) in the late 1980s and early 1990s, Tamahori's first feature film, *Once Were Warriors* (1994), was the powerful and affecting story of a contemporary Maori family in urban New Zealand. Based on Alan Duff's highly controversial and best-selling novel, it went on to become the highest-grossing film in New Zealand's history. Rena Owen gives a strong central performance as the mother trying to keep her dysfunctional family together – her eldest son is a gang member, her gifted daughter her hope for the future. Temuera Morrison is the violent yet charismatic husband. It is a moving melodrama, made all the more meaningful and profound thanks to the electric acting and Tamahori's nuanced style. He carefully balances humour, tenderness and gritty urban violence, and displays an acute sense of time and place. The film garnered several major prizes at film festivals, including Best First Film at Venice and the Jury Prize at Montreal.

Tamahori's first American feature was *Mulholland Falls* (1996), a tentative fusion of *Chinatown* (1974) and *Reservoir Dogs* (1992) that tried hard to play with established Hollywood generic codes. However, the finished article was a far cry from the authenticity and gritty social comment that characterised Tamahori's debut. LAPD detectives Nick Nolte, Chazz Palminteri, Chris Penn, and Michael Madsen – nicknamed 'the hat squad' – are investigating the death of a young prostitute in the early 1950s. The resulting neo-noir is packed with star cameos (John Malkovich, Bruce Dern, Andrew McCarthy) and possesses a stark visual style and high-level production values. Yet the film falls flat. Despite its promising ingredients, Tamahori never manages to blend them into a satisfying whole; there is too little substance, too much narrative complexity, and, after the promising opening, an overwhelming sense of disappointment. Unlike the similarly-themed and designed *LA Confidential* (1997), *Mulholland Falls* never allows the audience to empathise with the characters and situation – Tamahori and Pete Dexter's screenplay is all surface sheen and little emotional depth.

*The Edge* (1997) did provide Tamahori with a strong screenplay and initial premise. Scripted by David Mamet, the film tells the story of a billionaire recluse (Anthony Hopkins) whose plane crashes in the Alaskan wilderness, where he is forced to survive alongside a photographer (Alec Baldwin). Mamet's twist is to suggest that Hopkins' wife, played Elle Macpherson, may or may not have been having an affair with Baldwin. Tamahori's direction is at its most effective when handling the middle section of the film when Hopkins and Baldwin are being stalked by a grizzly bear – these scenes lend a metaphorical, almost mythic nuance to the screenplay. Tamahori also succeeds in sketching out the characters' lives and reining in Hopkins' oft-displayed hamminess. For all of its 'Lord of the Flies' pretensions, the film most clearly resembles a Beckett play – two men placed in an alien landscape are forced to work together to escape. Although the conceit and staccato dialogue is trademark Mamet, Tamahori skilfully crafts a tense 'Boy's Own' drama.

His most recent film, *Along Came a Spider* (2001), is a second instalment of the Alex Cross detective thrillers written by James Patterson. The first, *Kiss the Girls* (1997), was a routine crime thriller elevated above pulp status by Morgan Freeman's central performance, and it is his *basso profundo* gravitas that gives *Along Came a Spider* its real essence. The plot is pure airport fiction – a serial killer's work is plotted by rogue elements within the Security Service – and Tamahori never really allows the film to break out of its generic shackles. He brings a listless efficiency to proceedings, even directing the requisite chases and gun-play with a lethargy and lack of invention. Despite lustrous photography and off-beat performances from stalwarts such as Dylan Baker and Penelope Ann Miller, the film fails to spark enough interest. It is left to Freeman, and his customary displays of wisdom and stillness, to involve the audience and earn their sympathy.

Tamahori's most recent film, is the twentieth instalment of the James Bond series, *Die Another Day* (2002), which stars Halle Berry and Judy Dench alongside Pierce Brosnan.                                                                                     **BM**

# Quentin TARANTINO

Quentin Tarantino emerged in the 1990s as one of Hollywood's most prominent young film-makers, raising interesting questions regarding the relationship between auteurs and the prevalent popular culture. Born in Tennessee in 1963, his personality, as expressed through both the films and his public image, has informed issues as diverse as the ransacking of film history, a celebration of 'junk' Americana and a wilfully amoral take on screen violence. Bound within an allusive, postmodern sensibility, Tarantino's work conflates 'high' and 'low' cine-cultural forms, referencing an array of seemingly incompatible sources such as Jean-Luc Godard, 1970s blaxploitation and Hong Kong action cinema. Consequently, his avowed trash aesthetic runs in constant tension with self-conscious art cinema aspirations, a paradox which has been instrumental in transforming the face of both the crime film and the American independent cinema in general. Dissenting critics have suggested that the films offer an empty pastiche, in which the only tangible points of reference are other films and television shows. Indeed, the Tarantino phenomenon would seem to simultaneously exemplify and deny Roland Barthes' proclamation about the 'death of the author', de-centred through his absorption and dissemination of a multitude of cultural discourses while nevertheless achieving the status of central creative entity.

*Reservoir Dogs* (1992)
*Pulp Fiction* (1994)
*Jackie Brown* (1997)

What has been remarkable about Tarantino's rise is the short time span in which his name has become almost adjectival as a generic reference point. In a two-year period, he directed two films, *Reservoir Dogs* (1992) and *Pulp Fiction* (1994), from self-written screenplays, as well as having two other scripts (*True Romance* (1993) and *Natural Born Killers* (1994)) brought to the screen by Tony Scott and Oliver Stone, film-makers with their own distinct authorial imprint. Tarantino, while praising Scott's film, openly rejected Stone's on the basis of changes made to his original screenplay. After receiving the Palme d'Or at the 1994 Cannes Film Festival, Tarantino was presented with the 1995 Academy Award (along with co-writer Roger Avary) for *Pulp Fiction*'s original screenplay, an indication, along with the film's $100 million American box office gross, that his particular cinephile sensibility had crossed over into mainstream acceptance. Working thus far exclusively within the crime genre, there is already a pronounced sense of a Tarantino 'universe' in which specific generic types, situations, and signifiers are utilised and inverted. The repeated use of actors, a fracturing of narrative chronology, and the interspersing of criminal activity with pop-cultural trivia are all underlined by a play on genre structures and iconography. Comparisons with a previous generation of 'movie brats' have been rife – Paul Schrader called Tarantino 'Scorsese with quote marks around him' while the writer and critic Raymond Durgnat called him 'the bastard son of Martin Scorsese'.

*Reservoir Dogs* belongs ostensibly to the heist movie sub-genre but defies its conventions through a refusal to depict the crime itself. Dissecting the build-up and aftermath of a robbery gone bloodily wrong, it uses its generic canvas to take on a series of diversions. The film introduces Tarantino's strategy of placing the crime genre within the broader context of its cultural production, the intensely homo-social bond of the central characters operating in conjunction with a refined pop cultural sensibility. Madonna, Charles Bronson, John C. Holmes, The Fantastic Four, The Rat Pack, Hong Kong action cinema (the film shamelessly plagiarises Ringo Lam's *City On Fire* (1987)), Lee Marvin, Pam Grier, and 1970s bubblegum pop music are just a few of the multiple verbal or visual references which buttress the film's aesthetic sensibility. The fractured chronology, long takes, and emphasis on spatial composition are redolent of art cinema practices but are utilised here to merge freely with the conscious celebration of both popular and 'trash' cultural forms. The film's casting also solidifies its genre pedigree by using actors familiar from both the contemporary and classic crime film. Harvey Keitel's method intensity, combined with Lawrence Tierney's more conventional yet equally imposing acting style, fuses the golden age of the B-movie gangster with the contemporary screen hoodlum. As a 'pure' genre experience, the film retains the familiar bonding rituals of a highly masculinised world, defining the crime family in terms of its male interrelationships and their potential for violence. Presenting an exclusively white, male criminal sub-class, the film's racial and sexual discourses are appropriately ferocious.

If *Reservoir Dogs* presents a microcosmic version of the white criminal underworld of Los Angeles, *Pulp Fiction* extends into a macrocosmic representation of a multi-cultural criminal community. Consequently, those racial and sexual elements neglected by the former are highly visible and active in the latter. Intimate yet epic in its construction, *Pulp Fiction* supersedes its predecessor's notion of a 'family' of professional criminals bound by a perverse code of ethics with a milieu comprising hitmen, drug dealers, junkies, sodomite rapists, and stick-up artists. The film's anthology format allows Tarantino to extend the temporal digressions of *Reservoir Dogs*, playfully interweaving the separate narrative strands. Moreover, the film heightens its pop cultural allusions through the physical construction of a kitsch 1950s-style diner replete with celebrity lookalikes. Indeed, its 1990s setting is countered by its artificially constructed yesteryear wherein cultural signifiers from different generations interact and assimilate: 1970s icon John Travolta meets lookalike of 1950s icon Buddy Holly before twisting to Chuck Berry under the watchful gaze of an Ed Sullivan clone. The film utilises crime genre narrative staples and transforms their progression through often grotesque means. A male rape, an exploded head, and an accidental overdose provide violent yet perversely comic set pieces which balance the extended verbal exchanges. Inspired in its casting choices (Samuel L. Jackson, Uma Thurman, Bruce Willis, and Travolta all produce some of their best screen work) and bold in its ambition, the film is a key work of the 1990s. Yet it is curiously aloof at its centre and ultimately has nothing of import to say beyond the celebration of its surface dazzle. Travolta's description of the film's retro diner, 'a wax museum with a pulse', may yet serve as its final epitaph.

The less said about the abysmal *Four Rooms* (1995), the better. Intended as a 'document' film from Tarantino, Allison Anders, Robert Rodriguez and Alexandre Rockwell, it is a conceited, turgid work sunk further by Tim Roth's truly bad linking performance as a bumbling bell boy. *Jackie Brown* (1997) is, despite its length, a far more restrained film and displays signs of a move beyond the allusive tendencies of its predecessors. Yet, in many ways it plays like an extended love letter to its female lead and former queen of blaxploitation, Pam Grier. Based on Elmore Leonard's novel 'Rum Punch', it is linear in its chronology (except for one key sequence) and withdraws from the extended pop culture-inflected dialogue of its predecessors. Despite his alterations to the source, Tarantino's take on Leonard provides him with a greater depth of character and he once more demonstrates his skill with actors – Grier, Robert Forster, and Samuel L. Jackson carry the weight of the narrative quite brilliantly, while the LA low-life ambience is effectively coloured by a supporting cast that includes Robert De Niro, Bridget Fonda, and Michael Keaton. It is Tarantino's most mature film to date and its quiet nuances of mood and character proved a brave move in the wake of his previous spectacular success. After a long absence, he will return to the cinema with *Kill Bill*, an action thriller about an assassin (to be played by Uma Thurman) who is gunned down at her wedding, along with everyone present, but survives and sets out for revenge.      **NJ**

# Mark TARLOV

Mark Tarlov is best known as a Hollywood producer with an equally successful eye for comedy – *The Man Who Knew Too Little* (1997) – and thrillers – *Copycat* (1995). With the bravery to produce John Waters' 'mainstream' efforts, including *Serial Mom* (1994), *Pecker* (1998), and *Cecil B. DeMented* (2000), Tarlov always seemed poised for a move to the director's chair.

*Simply Irresistible* (1999), his debut, is a romantic comedy toying with ideas of love, magic and food; the story of a struggling chef who, with the assistance of a magic crab, manages to translate her emotions into her cooking and thereby enchants a dashing young department store owner. Criticised for its similarity to the excellent *Like Water for Chocolate* (1991), to which it bears more than a passing resemblance, the film is nevertheless a casebook Hollywood romantic comedy: a love story peppered by mishap, enlivened by plenty of light comedy, attractive young leads and slick direction. Though its use of a fairy-tale framework – the intrusion of magic powers on a mundane world, the transformation from pauper to princess, the handsome young Prince Charming – is intriguing, the film is nevertheless disappointingly predictable fare. Some smart *mise-en-scène* – the chef imparting sadness to her food and making her entire restaurant weep, for example – demonstrate Tarlov's comic ability and assuredness, but the inevitable conclusion and the inability to escape the staples of its genre make this unstimulating even for aficionados. For a producer capable of marketing the brash high camp of John Waters, this is a surprisingly formulaic choice for a directorial debut. **OB**

# Alan TAYLOR

Alan Taylor has shown the promise of a director capable of taking a British style of black comedy set by Mike Leigh and Peter Cattaneo across the Atlantic, a feat which many of his North American counterparts are attempting, including Steve Buscemi and Vincent Gallo. In addition to his film work he has directed episodes of several television series, such as 'Homicide: Life on the Street', 'Oz', 'Sex and the City', and 'The Sopranos'.

*Palookaville* (1995)
*The Emperor's New Clothes* (2001)

His first feature, *Palookaville* (1995), based on Ítalo Calvino's tragi-comic short stories of misadventure, is a comedy about a group of unemployed men in a dead suburb of New Jersey, on the fringes of the bustling New York scene, who are desperately trying to ascend from their abysmal small-town existences. Underlying the comedy of their escapades are serious themes which denote a crisis in contemporary masculine identity. The main protagonists – Jerry (Gallo), who cannot afford to support his family, Russ (Adam Trese), who lives at home with his mother, and the socially inept Sid (William Forsythe), living alone with his dogs – are reminiscent of the unemployed losers from the decaying industrial town of Sheffield in *The Full Monty* (1997). Thematically, Taylor seems influenced here by Uberto Pasolini, who has a strong interest in portraying marginalised working-class men and with whom he has worked on both of his film projects. The narrative style of interwoven stories and mishaps is reminiscent of Tarantino, but unique in the North American context in its focus on everyday characters and situations that are easy to identify with and also very funny. Taylor has represented the emasculated contemporary man with both subtle humour and seriousness.

Having worked only with contemporary, urban narratives in his previous work, Taylor explored unfamiliar territories with *The Emperor's New Clothes* (2001), which is based on the nineteenth-century parable of Napoleon's secret return to France from St Helena – according to the history books he died whilst in exile. There is a familiar sense of innocent misadventure about this fairytale of conspiracy and faked identity, and Taylor adds a comic human element to his revision of the demise of the famous Frenchman, which is becoming his trademark. **JO**

# Julie TAYMOR

Julie Taymor is part of a new breed of film directors who draw inspiration and imagination from the theatrical stage. Not content with adapting plays for the screen, she adapts theatrical concepts to create a unique film vision. As one of the most imaginative and stylistic theatrical directors and designers today, she has established her place in theatre history. Always one to push mediums and integrate styles, Taymor released the visually stunning and conceptually daring *Titus* in 1999, and seems poised to take command of the film world, as she did with the theatrical stage.

*Titus* (1999)
*Frida* (2002)

Born in Massachusetts in 1952, at a very early age Taymor was introduced to puppetry and theatre while working at The Theater Workshop of Boston. At the age of 15, she studied abroad in Sri Lanka and Paris. After returning to the United States to finish her formal education at Oberlin College, she again embarked on a journey to Japan, Indonesia and Europe.

Back in the US again, she directed and designed numerous theatrical productions, all drawing extensively from her world experience, culminating in her production of 'Juan

Darien' in New York. Most, if not all, were widely heralded for their use of puppetry, mask and movement. Other productions included 'The Magic Flute', 'The Tempest', and 'The Green Bird'.

In 1991, PBS utilised Taymor's services for an American Playhouse adaptation of Edgar Allan Poe's story 'Hopfrog', which was retitled *Fool's Fire*. As a theatre director Taymor had never shied away from style, and this production allowed her to push her vision to the filmed medium. Consisting of both 35mm film and High Definition Video, the film was daringly experimental, consisting entirely of puppetry and showcasing Taymor's unique talent as a director and artist. *Fool's Fire* premiered at the American Film Festival and was aired on PBS in early 1992. Her film directorial debut was a success, winning her a Best Drama award at the Tokyo International Electronic Cinema Festival. PBS provided Taymor with her next film opportunity when they filmed the live stage version of 'Oedipus Rex' in (1992). Although the film was predominantly a filmed stage performance, Taymor did shoot some scenes. The show was another huge success.

Taymor finally burst into the public's consciousness in 1998 when she adapted Disney's *The Lion King* (1994) on Broadway. Again she used masks and puppetry to present a highly stylised version of the popular Disney animated film. The show was a smash, winning Taymor two Tony awards (Direction and Costume Design). She turned her sights to feature film-making and in 1999 released her first full-length feature, *Titus*, starring Anthony Hopkins, Jessica Lange, and Alan Cumming. The film, an adaptation of Shakespeare's 'Titus Andronicus', follows the recent trend of re-imagining Shakespeare for new viewers. However, unlike other recent Shakespeare adaptations, such as Richard Loncraine's *Richard III* (1995) and Baz Luhrmann's *Romeo + Juliet* (1996), Taymor places her film in a unique and flamboyant context. She blends time periods and uses elaborate costumes and set-pieces so that themes can appear fresh to the viewer. Utilising the motifs of revenge, murder, racism, and envy, she allows the words of Shakespeare to combine with the postmodern with dizzying success, seamlessly making the leap from theatre to film, creating a new standard of visual excellence within cinema. The film was a critical success and was nominated for an Academy Award for Best Costume Design.

Taymor's sophomore feature, *Frida* (2002), recalls the flamboyant and painful life of famed Mexican artist Frida Kahlo. Starring Salma Hayek as Frida and Alfred Molina as her abusive husband, Diego Rivera, Ashley Judd, Geoffrey Rush and Antonio Banderas also appear. The film was shot in Mexico during 2001 and promises to be another visual treat, this time utilising the talents of The Brothers Quay to create some unique stop-motion animation sequences depicting Frida's addiction to drugs.          **JM**

# Andy TENNANT

Andy Tennant's films have a picturesque, fairytale quality that provides feelgood entertainment as they engage the viewer to share the characters' struggles for happiness. The films all have a polished, stylish look that emphasises the good looks and charm of the Hollywood casts. Indeed, all of Tennant's films have been star-vehicles that have drawn on the actors' popularity to propel the storylines and present a beautiful, fantasy-filled world for its audiences.

Born in Chicago, Tennant studied theatre at the University of Southern California under John Houseman and began his career as a dancer in the film *Grease* (1978). His first directorial effort was a comedy showcasing the talents and appeal of the twin child actors, Mary-Kate and Ashley Olsen, in *It Takes Two* (1995). Tennant's second film, the romantic comedy *Fools Rush In* (1997) starred two likeable stars – Matthew Perry and Salma Hayek – as complete strangers who decide to wed after a one night stand leads to an unexpected pregnancy. The film, while relying on the formulaic 'opposites attract' subject matter of many contemporary romantic comedies, marked the star power draw of both actors and presented its story in a refreshingly genuine way, mostly due to the amiability of its cast.

*Ever After* (1998) was a bigger box-office success than the first two films and garnered much critical praise. It firmly established Drew Barrymore, in the central role as the orphaned and mistreated Danielle, as an actor capable of single-handedly carrying a film. In its re-telling of the Cinderella fairytale with a more feminist touch, *Ever After* proved that audiences appreciate an old-fashioned love story in which the woman takes an assertive and independent role. The film features delightful touches of whimsy in imagining the actual story behind the fairytale, in particular the role of Leonardo da Vinci in place of the fairy godmother. The winged dress he creates for Danielle to wear to the royal ball truly looks like it was produced by magic. Although the film gets a bit weighed down by the unrepentant and caricatured portrait of the stepmother, played by Angelica Huston, and a somewhat bland Prince Henry, Barrymore manages to keep the whole film afloat by imbuing pluck and a surprising strength in all her scenes. One particularly nice touch is the small appearance of Jeanne Moreau as the narrator, telling the story of her ancestor to the sceptical Brothers Grimm, at the start of the film.

*Anna & the King* (1999), although based on a true story, looks almost like a fairytale. Based on the diaries of Anna Leonowens, the Englishwoman who served as tutor to the children of the King of Siam in the 1860s, and whose story served as the basis of the musical *The King and I* (1956), this non-musical re-telling presents an unrequited love story, historical epic, and costume drama all in one. However, the real strength of the film lies in its gorgeous costumes and set design. While Jodie Foster, as Anna, and Hong Kong action star Chow Yun Fat, as King Mongkut, give admirable performances, the film never really serves up all the adventure and romance that it aspires to produce. *Anna & the King*'s musical predecessor, a cinematic classic that successfully captivated its audiences, may have haunted this dramatic interpretation of the story, drawing attention to its heavy-handed seriousness, in contrast to the musical's zest and playful quality. While the lavish luxury of the royal Siamese court and the palace intrigues, and Bail Ling gives an impressive performance as the doomed newest bride for the King, the film lacks a sense of realistic urgency on one hand and complete flights of imagination on the other. Yet Tennant succeeds in bringing to life a sumptuous past that most people never had the opportunity to witness, and it is a handsome recreation.

Tennant's forthcoming film *Sweet Home Alabama* (2002) is a romantic comedy starring Reese Witherspoon.                                                                   **EK**

# Betty THOMAS

Best known for her portrayal of Lucy Bates on the long-running 1980s cop drama 'Hill Street Blues', Betty Thomas, born in St. Louis, Missouri, in 1947, has since joined the ranks of other actor-turned-auteurs as Penny Marshall, Danny DeVito, and Rob Reiner. Having carved out a niche for herself as a director of mainstream comedies, Thomas appears most attracted to material with darker underpinnings, lacing her best films with clever satire and a subversive sense of wit.

After a stint directing episodic television and movies of the week, not to mention an inauspicious cinematic debut with the Andrew McCarthy/Kelly Preston romantic comedy, *Only You* (1992), Thomas hit her stride with 1995's *The Brady Bunch Movie*. Based on the absurdly sophomoric 1970s television series, *The Brady Bunch Movie* spins off from the notion that life with the upbeat Brady clan has remained unchanged for 25 years, even as the world around them has moved on. While it will never be mistaken for *Citizen Kane* (1941), Thomas manages to bring this premise to zany life, finding precisely the right notes for both the scenes in and around the Brady compound and those on the outside world, painstakingly photographing the former with the same flat, stagey camera and lighting set-ups as the series (even the old, omnipresent, incidental music is layered in, to hilarious effect) and Thomas effectively contrasts this with the brashly exaggerated 'reality' of the latter. (It helps that she has a garishly-dressed, note-perfect cast – led by Shelley Long and a freakishly accurate Gary Cole as the Brady parents – at her disposal.) Part parody, part tongue-in-cheek social commentary, *The Brady Bunch Movie* is the witty antidote to a deluge of leaden boob tube adaptations.

Television was also the inspiration for Thomas' next picture, the slashingly funny made-for-cable movie, *The Late Shift* (1996). Based on Bill Carter's book, which detailed the behind-the-scenes power struggle between late night hosts David Letterman and Jay Leno for the retiring Johnny Carson's 'Tonight Show' throne, her film is a brisk, knowing ride through the cut-throat machinations and back room wheeler-dealing of the entertainment industry. Produced by Ivan Reitman, the subject matter of The Late Shift formed a natural segue to their next collaboration, and Thomas' best film, the Howard Stern biopic *Private Parts* (1997).

Pitched somewhere between a gleefully crude National Lampoon-style farce (and written by Len Blum, who penned the previous Reitman hits *Meatballs* (1979) and *Stripes* (1981)) and a cuddly romantic comedy, *Private Parts* unfolds around the schizoid life of Stern, a popular shock radio DJ whose brutally frank humour and on-air antics with nude women are balanced by the sweet, loving relationship he shares with his wife and daughters. Thomas finesses her wealth of great material into the shape of a hip, lewd mini-epic, shooting Stern's childhood through a gauze of gold-hued nostalgia one minute, interrupting the movie for a hand-held recreation of one of Stern's radio pranks the next. She also elicits warm, natural performances from Stern and the rest of his on-air gang, all first-time actors appearing as themselves. Thomas gets a juicy, anti-establishment kick out of Stern's hilarious clashes with his various superiors, but shows real skill in the trickier scenes involving Stern and his wife Allison (Mary McCormack), finding a relatable emotional centre of true love and faith amidst the comic anarchy.

*Dr Dolittle* (1998) found Thomas relaxing into effects-driven blockbuster mode, updating and retooling the Hugh Lofting stories (not to mention the 1967 Rex Harrison musical version) as a gimmicky summer hit for Eddie Murphy, who stars as the famous physician who can 'talk to the animals'. Thomas scores points for utilising such adult comic talents as Garry Shandling, Ellen DeGeneres, Chris Rock, and Albert Brooks as neurotic animal voices in what is essentially a children's film, but this craftsmanlike effort is ultimately the movie equivalent of fast food: quick, satisfying, and altogether impersonal.

Better, and more in keeping with the left-of-centre sensibility of *Private Parts*, was her jittery rehab comedy, *28 Days* (2000). Thomas smartly enlisted perpetual Girl Next Door Sandra Bullock to play the film's self-centred, alcoholic heroine, whose destructive, drunken breakdown at her sister's wedding gets her shipped off for a month-long recovery at a secluded retreat. The director sands off Bullock's cute edge and helps her deliver a performance of great emotional honesty; likewise, *28 Days* finds Thomas defying convention to shake up what could have been a standard Hollywood morality tale. In an apparent nod to the grainy, hand-held realism of such Dogme 95 films as *Festen* (1998), flashbacks to Bullock's troubled childhood and party girl excesses are captured on digital video, lending the picture an immediacy and pulse that jerks it, however momentarily, out of the mainstream. Thomas also chooses to go hand-held (with film this time) in several funny ensemble therapy scenes set inside the rehab centre, and even breaks into the narrative for mock interview segments with the centre's other 'guests', further establishing the picture's offhand sense of comic *vérité*.

Her next film, *I Spy*, the story of a secret agent and a basketball player who team up to recover a missing jet, will star Eddie Murphy. **CS**

# Billy Bob THORNTON

After labouring for years in relative obscurity as an actor and a writer, Billy Bob Thornton became a major Hollywood figure almost overnight. With the release of his 1996 film *Sling Blade*, he drew comparisons to cinema's greatest multifaceted geniuses, including Orson Welles and Sir Laurence Olivier. Although the hype is clearly premature — his subsequent two films have done nothing to advance his reputation — *Sling Blade* certainly signalled the arrival of an intriguing new American auteur.

Born in 1955, Thornton's career was marked by numerous false starts. Hoping to break into movies, he took an ill-fated trip from his native Arkansas to New York City, a trip that lasted a single day. After retreating to Arkansas, where he spent time as a drummer in a rock band, Thornton moved, with writing partner Tom Epperson, to Los Angeles. He scored a few small roles (in films including *Hunter's Blood* (1987), *Babes Ahoy* (1989), and *Chopper Chicks in Zombietown* (1989)), but continued to struggle in anonymity for several years. According to legend, Thornton – too poor to afford any food other than potatoes – was once hospitalised for malnutrition.

Having worked with George Hickenlooper on the short, *Some Folks Call It a Sling Blade* (1993), Thornton began raising money for the feature *Sling Blade*. Completed for less than $1 million, the film premiered at the 1996 Telluride Film Festival to overwhelming response. Critics and audiences were dazzled by Thornton's performance, the film's offbeat sense of humour and its refreshingly straightforward *mise-en-scène*.

This provocative tale of a man struggling to do the right thing follows the moral evolution of Karl Childers, a semi-retarded man who murdered his mother and her lover at age twelve. Karl is about to be released from the mental institution he has called home for twenty years, left to face his own demons and the unfamiliar demands of the world outside. The character of Karl Childers is in many ways a cipher – neither a clinical representation of a mentally ill patient nor a typical portrait of an underdog. Instead, Karl seems to serve as a kind of experiment in morality. What does it take to push someone to violence? When is an immoral act justified? Thornton's confident, taut handling of his subject matter (and his skill at enacting a character defined largely by a set of mannerisms) mark the film as an important one.

After a four-year gap, Thornton saw his labour-of-love western *All the Pretty Horses* released in 2000. Adapted from Cormac McCarthy's award-winning novel, it was shot in New Mexico and stars Matt Damon as a young Texan cowboy who drifts across the Mexican border in search of deeper truths about his own life. Restrained, intelligent and sophisticated, *All the Pretty Horses* nonetheless did little to advance the sorry state of Hollywood westerns. Perhaps relying too heavily on landscape as metaphor, and sometimes falling into cliché, the film is an admirable but less-than-groundbreaking work for a director faced with enormously high expectations. The film was released in a two-hour version – Thornton's cut reportedly ran four hours.

After many delays, *Daddy and Them* (2002), a black comedy set in Arkansas and starring Thornton, Laura Dern and Jim Varney, has had limited screening. It remains to be seen if it will be released more widely or go straight to video. **JS**

# George TILLMAN Jr

Scenes for the Soul (1995)
Soul Food (1997)
Men of Honor (2000)

When *Soul Food* (1997) – George Tillman Jr's second film – was released, it surprised many in the film industry by out-performing other, more heavily promoted films in its first and subsequent weeks of release. Part of a positive string of films in the mid- and late 1990s telling the personal stories of middle-class black families and friends (e.g. *Waiting to Exhale* (1995), *The Wood* (1999)), the film is a touching examination of a family and the troubles it experiences when its matriarch Mother Joe (Irma P. Hall) falls ill and is no longer available to provide the traditional Sunday dinner.

Tillman had earlier written and directed the little-seen *Scenes for the Soul* (1995), but it was *Soul Food* that showed his promise to the commercial film industry. He subtly directs a large cast into honest performances, and his screenplay is given focus by concentrating the point-of-view onto Ahmad (Brandon Hammond), Mother Joe's oldest grandchild. The film is a celebration of family, and sees connection to family and home as the key element in keeping people centred. The weekly dinner serves as a metaphor for the need to maintain a connection to one's roots in order to understand oneself. Mother Joe is the connection to the past and to the South, where the delectable meals are also rooted. Tillman is also an executive producer of the spin-off television series 'Soul Food'.

His next film, *Men of Honor* (2000), was based on the true story of Carl Brashear, the first black diver in the US Navy. Starring Cuba Gooding Jr as Brashear, it focuses on his relationship with his embittered trainer Leslie Sunday, who is played by Robert De Niro. **DH**

# James TOBACK

Fingers (1978)
Love And Money (1982)
Exposed (1983)
The Pick-Up Artist (1987)
The Big Bang (1989)
Two Girls and a Guy (1997)
Black and White (1999)
Harvard Man (2001)

James Toback graduated a year early from Harvard and returned to New York (where he was born in 1944) to receive a master's degree in English from Columbia University. After teaching work at the City University of New York, Toback turned to full-time writing, eventually providing director Karel Reisz with a screenplay for *The Gambler* (1974), in which James Caan stars as an edgy academic whose addiction to games of chance borders on becoming a deathwish. The closing image of Caan, examining his own razor-slashed face in a mirror, is pure Toback in its reflection on the divided self of the thinking man.

1978 saw the release of Toback's directorial debut, *Fingers*, based on his own script about the son of a numbers man whose aspirations to become a concert pianist conflict with his obligations as a debt collector. Grittier, more violent and less ponderous than

*The Gambler*, *Fingers* benefits from a characteristically intense central performance by Harvey Keitel and the offbeat support casting of Tisa Farrow and former blaxploitation icon Jim Brown (the subject of an earlier book by Toback).

Toback's sophomore effort, *Love and Money* (1982), widened the director's vision from the urban neighbourhood to the world of international intrigue; in its depiction of the affairs (business and extra-marital) of the affluent, *Love and Money* was not well received and is perhaps best remembered for the appearance of legendary Hollywood director King Vidor in a supporting role.

Perhaps striving to find a middle ground between the lavatory sink realism of *Fingers* and a global theatre in which to set his philosophical morality plays, *Exposed* (1983) told the story of a Midwestern farm girl (Nastassja Kinski, who had appeared opposite father Klaus in *Love and Money*) leaving behind an autocratic father to relocate to New York City, where a modelling career brings her into contact with international terrorists (led by *Fingers* star Harvey Keitel). Originally treated by the press as a curio for the offbeat casting of dancer Rudolph Nureyev as the film's nominal, tragic hero (Toback's cameo as an amorous philosophy professor went mostly unnoticed), *Exposed* did poorly and four years passed before Toback attempted another film.

*The Pick-Up Artist* (1987) was a lighter return to familiar themes, with Robert Downey Jr's grad-school lothario romancing the tour guide daughter (Molly Ringwald), unaware of her familial connection to organised crime. Toback saw out the end of the decade with the documentary *The Big Bang* (1989), in which the director posed 'The Big Questions' to a disparate assembly of thinkers, from basketball star Darryl Dawkins to Hollywood producer Don Simpson. Although *The Big Bang* was easily the best received (or least reviled) of all of the director's post-*Fingers* films, it would be nearly a decade before he directed another feature film. In the meantime, Toback would provide Barry Levinson with an Academy Award-nominated screenplay for his acclaimed underworld biopic, *Bugsy* (1991), brokering for himself a cameo appearance as Gus Greenbaum.

Televised footage of actor Robert Downey Jr being led to jail for drug abuse inspired Toback's next work, *Two Girls and a Guy* (1997). Downey stars as a composer whose dual love life is telescoped by the chance meeting of his two girlfriends (Heather Graham and Natasha Gregson Wagner) and the women's resolve not to let his irresponsible man-child off the hook. Theatrical and claustrophobic, the film was cut for an R-rating, which might explain why works best as an exercise that doesn't quite deliver enough genuine emotional intensity.

Toback's *Black and White* (1999), a hip-hop-informed meditation on contemporary urban race relations (the scandal-sheet casting includes Brooke Shields, boxer Mike Tyson, supermodel Claudia Schiffer, and familiar face Downey Jr) begins with a Central Park ménage-à-trois between an aspiring black rapper and two white teenage girls. Shot without a script, the scenes were guided by Toback and improvised by his actors; the film's most discussed moment occurs when Downey's closet case comes on to Tyson, who knocks him to the floor and kicks him – an act that horrified the rest of the cast, for whom the line between acting and reality was instantly smudged.

Although Toback's subject – upper-middle-class 'wiggas' appropriating black culture – is clearly his most timely, *Black and White* faded fairly quickly from memory. The direct-to-video *Love in Paris* (1999) was a markedly gentler rites-of-passage tale about American private school boys on the make in the city of lights; *Harvard Man* (2001) is a return to familiar themes of risk and corruption, and involves a college basket-ball player who, torn between his feelings for a mobster's cheerleader daughter and sexy philosophy professor, fixes the outcomes of games. Although remaining active behind the camera, Toback's reputation remains linked less to his cinematic output than numerous tabloid accounts of his attempts to seduce young women from the streets of New York and Los Angeles with the promise of film work. **RHS**

# Robert TOWNE

Born in Los Angeles in 1934, Robert Towne was part of that lucky generation that reinvented American cinema in the early 1970s. An early student of Roger Corman and friend to Jack Nicholson, Towne wrote and helped write some of the finest screenplays in post-classical Hollywood cinema. His credited work includes *The Last Detail* (1973), *Chinatown* (1974), and *Shampoo* (1975). He also has done uncredited work on *Bonnie and Clyde* (1967), *The Godfather* (1972), *The Parallax View* (1974), and *Reds* (1981), as well as a large body of second-tier work on many movies in the 1980s and 1990s.

Towne's efforts as a director have not earned the same place in the pantheon of American film. Since his 1970s heyday he has written and directed three features: *Personal Best* (1982), a film about a young woman striving to make the 1980 Olympic team, starring Mariel Hemingway; *Tequila Sunrise* (1988), a disappointing cop-and-robber story about old friends on different sides of the law vying for the love of a woman; and a second track and field movie, *Without Limits* (1998), starring Billy Crudup and Donald Sutherland in a biopic about the short but eventful life of early 1970s American track star Steve Prefontaine. *Personal Best* is Towne's directorial masterpiece, a surprisingly complex, atmospheric performance worthy of his best writing. Contrasting it with *Without Limits* suggests the chasm between a film that bears second viewing and a Hollywood product much more easily forgotten.

Despite fine performances from Crudup and Sutherland, *Without Limits* has the feel of a very well done TV movie. The main characters seem little more than stubborn, and the supporting cast – especially Pre's nice blond girlfriend – seem only to fill dramatically expedient roles. Pre (Crudup) is a driven prodigy, a 'front-runner' for whom beating all competition into submission transforms running into art. His coach, Bill Bowerman (Sutherland), sees Pre's conviction, and the demons that drive him, as counterproductive to realising his talent. Each exemplifies and is defined by his belief about the nature of running, but they are both so stubborn that real understanding, or even an evolving relationship, seems impossible. After finishing fourth in his event at the 1972 Olympics, Pre falls into a deep depression, which makes him temporarily susceptible to Bowerman's message about the importance of pacing. Unfortunately, a James Dean-like early death (unfortunate for Pre and film alike) prevents us from knowing whether he would actually change. Sutherland's stirring eulogy suggests that Pre has changed him in some way, although it is never clear precisely how. His triumph, a running joke through the film, is his invention of the Nike running shoe.

If *Without Limits* can to some extent be thought of as a message movie, the much finer *Personal Best* cannot. It presents us with a world so intimate and believable that at times it is embarrassing to be eavesdropping on it. In loving slow-motion, Towne's camera caresses the bodies, often naked, of his female athletes. His attentions are reminiscent of Leni Riefenstahl's in her *Olympia* (1938), but this Fascist worship of perfect bodies is mitigated by the emotional fragility of the women who have been blessed with them. Hemingway's Chris falls in love with Tory (Patrice Donnelly), a fellow athlete who brings Chris into her track club. The two train side-by-side, and as Chris improves the lovers begin to struggle against one another, both on and off the field. The meaning of the title is soon completely lost in the emotional complexity of the characters' lives. 'Personal Best' refers to performances on track and field, but it also refers to human character, a character that is tested repeatedly by the intense pressure of training and competition. With the goading of their sadistic coach, the athletes' bodies and psyches are kept near breaking point. Ultimately, the lovers are driven apart, and the film's final race, which pits them against one another, illustrates exactly the tension between individual achievement, sympathy, love, and team spirit that have been kept in such marvellous suspension throughout the film.

Those expecting from Towne the director something approaching the achievement of Towne the writer should stick with *Personal Best*. Towne continues to be sought after as script doctor and guru, although in interviews he clearly laments the passing of the Golden Age of American cinema that to some extent he helped invent. **JA**

# TRAKTOR

It is debatable whether directors who come from a background in advertising ever stop making adverts. Ridley Scott is the most capable of examples and even with the excellent quartet of *The Duellists* (1977), *Alien* (1979), *Blade Runner* (1982), and *Somebody to Watch Over Me* (1987) behind him, he has not lost the penchant for beautifully lit but pointless shots of objects that may well be for sale. The mysteriously named Traktor, a Swedish collective of six film-makers including Pontus Lowenhelm and Patrick von Kruserstyerna, look set to be another in the list of ex-advertising heads who have moved to features with visual ideas, but little idea of what makes a good film.

*Chain of Fools* (2000)

*Chain of Fools* (2000), having been stalled in its journey from the studio for some time, has the kind of unholy plot still trying to surf the Tarantino bandwagon nearly a decade after the release of *Reservoir Dogs* (1992). The plot is as convoluted and clichéd a mess of misguided ideas as has managed to secure $20 million of Warner Bros. funding for some time. Salma Hayek plays a detective trying to catch a hapless baker who comes into the possession of some stolen treasure. That the treasure is ancient coins with some mystical force and that the two leads fall in love, are only the most reasonable of the unlikely plot twists. As unpromising as it all sounds, it is at least another chance to see Hayek, an actress who has the divine ability to seem like a walking advertisement for her own assets. **CSo**

# Rose TROCHE

*Go Fish* (1994)
*Bedrooms and Hallways* (1998)

Rose Troche, born in Chicago in 1964, completed her degree in film and photography at the University of Illinois. Though wary about making an overtly lesbian debut feature, she decided to target her core audience and work with familiar material. She subsequently co-wrote the romantic-comedy *Go Fish* (1994) with partner Guinevere Turner and began directing scenes in her free time. When they had depleted their funds the pair managed to find support from producers Christine Vachon and Tom Kalin and completion money from John Peirson at Islet Films. Having premiered at Sundance, the film burst on to the independent New Queer Cinema scene and unexpectedly confounded all expectations, arousing the curiosity and admiration of both gay and straight cinema-goers alike. Filmed in black and white, *Go Fish* endearingly and frankly portrays the day-to-day lives of five friends and the romantic searchings of the long-term single Max (Turner). Refreshingly disregarding questions of sexual identity and gender politics, the film encourages the viewer to empathise with the angst-ridden yearning of its characters in an entertaining and touching manner.

Determined for her work to be socially relevant, Troche chose a script by Robert Farrar as her next project. Set in London, *Bedrooms and Hallways* (1998) is a pacey, quirky film that explores the shifting boundaries of sexuality in an attempt to shatter any preconceived notions or prejudice. Focusing on Guy, a gay man who thinks he's desperate to find a settled relationship, it also incorporates a range of other confused characters whose relationships force them to question their assumed sexual choices. Despite some out-dated New Age references and a glossy sheen, it effectively incorporates flashbacks and dream sequences to be, as one critic has pointed out, 'a fun-loving rather than a profound film'.

With two successes behind her, Troche has decided to continue as an independent director, retaining greater artistic control and thereby ensuring the integrity of her work. Her latest project, for which she is writing the screenplay, is an adaptation of a book of short stories by A. M. Holmes entitled *Safety of Objects*. **HP**

# Stanley TUCCI

*Big Night* (1996)
*The Impostors* (1998)
*Joe Gould's Secret* (2000)

Before making his directorial debut with *Big Night* in 1996, Stanley Tucci, born in Katonah, New York, in 1960, was a little-known character actor with a string of acting credits to his name.

Co-written and directed with high-school friend Campbell Scott, *Big Night* is a low-budget production focusing on the trials and tribulations of two Italian restaurateurs, brothers Primo and Secondo (Tucci and Tony Shalhoub), who struggle for gastronomic success in an indifferent 1950s New Jersey setting. As a pae an to Italian food the film works beautifully. Tucci serves up a veritable soft-focus feast of sublime expressions and posturing as the ensemble cast (Ian Holm, Minnie Driver, Isabella Rossellini) devour a banquet prepared by the brothers in a last ditch effort to save their ailing restaurant. Yet the film is more than a nostalgic period piece. It is, at its core, a delicately understated exposition on the tensions between commerce and art, the old world and the new, business and family. Ultimately the film offers no easy resolution to these oppositions. Instead Tucci opts to end with a melancholic five-minute long-take of the brothers making omelette together as they silently make peace with each other and the tensions explored within the film's narrative.

Tucci's second feature, *The Impostors* (1998), met with far less critical and public acclaim than his first. Unlike *Big Night*, with its lingering long-takes and theatrical set pieces, *The Impostors* is an ambitious and valiant effort to recreate the look and feel of a fast-paced classic screwball comedy. Unfortunately the film is somewhat flawed as it becomes over-worked and frenetic in its desperate attempt to extract laughs from its audience. His latest offering, *Joe Gould's Secret* (2000), is an adaptation of Joseph Mitchell's writings, which are themselves based on the true story of Joseph Ferdinand Gould, the bohemian eccentric who spent forty years on the streets if New York.   **PH**

# Jon TURTELTAUB

Jon Turteltaub is the maker of largely inoffensive mainstream Hollywood product. He is the son of Saul Turteltaub, a writer on the US sitcoms 'Sanford and Son' and 'Kate and Allie', and screenwriter of the movie *Roseanna's Grave* (1996).

His debut, made for Disney, was the children's film *Three Ninjas* (1992). A harmless if derivative story of kids using martial arts skills to battle bad guys, the film offers plenty of post-*Home Alone* (1990) pre-teen violence against adults. His next feature was *Cool Runnings* (1993), a broad comedy about a Jamaican bobsleigh team. Based on a true story from the 1988 Winter Olympics, the film combines some broad slapstick with the recurring generic traits of the sports movie post-*Rocky* (1976) – the unlikely under-dogs win through and a washed-up figure (John Candy as the disgraced coach) finds redemption in victory. This mixture is amiable enough, although much of the humour comes at the expense of the 'unsophisticated' Jamaican characters. One could expect a harder edge given that the screenplay is co-written Michael Ritchie, the sharp 1970s auteur responsible for the impressive *Downhill Racer* (1969) and *Smile* (1975), but this is not indicative of his past glories.

*While You Were Sleeping* (1995) was Turteltaub's next feature and it stands as his best film to date. This vehicle for Sandra Bullock, fresh from her impressive turn in *Speed* (1994), is a romantic comedy with an implausible but well-crafted premise. Bullock is a train ticket-seller who nurses a crush on a handsome commuter (Peter Gallagher). When he is injured at the station, Bullock saves his life but is mistaken for his girlfriend by his grateful family. When the injured man's brother (an effectively cast-against-type Bill Pullman) arrives on the scene, he is suspicious, particularly when a romance starts to develop between himself and the hapless Bullock. Turteltaub crafts an amusing and convincing love story out of this contrived situation and there are winning performances from all concerned, particularly Bullock and Pullman. The film also avoids too much sentimentality – the rugged, blue-collar family provide a refreshing alternative to the wealthy suburbanites who normally populate Hollywood romantic comedies.

*Phenomenon* (1996) was a considerable letdown after *While You Were Sleeping.* This is a slice of mawkish New Age sci-fi about a humble garage mechanic (John Travolta) who develops strange powers after being enveloped in a mysterious white light. The film suggests both extra-terrestrial and celestial origins for this miraculous conversion but the screenplay seems to be striving for profundity. John Travolta has always been a fine actor who seems incapable of consistently choosing good projects. As *Saturday Night Fever* (1977) was followed by the woeful *Moment by Moment* (1978), so *Phenomenon* trails some way behind Quentin Tarantino's *Pulp Fiction* (1994). Here, Travolta relies too much on the same irritating man-child mannerisms he displayed in *Michael* (1996).

Turteltaub's next film, the silly thriller *Instinct* (1999), starring Cuba Gooding Jr and Anthony Hopkins, was even worse. Hopkins is a renowned anthropologist who 'goes ape' after studying primates, and kills a couple of hunters, and Gooding is the psychiatrist who has to find out why. Aside from the oft-repeated jokey line that refers to Gooding's Academy Award-winning turn in *Jerry Maguire* (1996), summing up Turteltaub's film as 'Show me the monkey!', there is little of interest. Hopkins is below par in this murky psychological drama that reinforces the fact that, despite the insubstantial likes of *Cool Runnings* and *Phenomenon,* the director has no real feeling for darker material.

Turteltaub's most recent film is the Bruce Willis comedy *The Kid* (2000). After his thriller outing, this mercifully sees the director return to sentimental comedy. A jaded adult (Willis) is visited by his eight-year-old self who has travelled forward in time from the 1970s to deal with his future self's mid-life crisis. The film has opened well at the box office but has been savaged by the critics for being the latest in a recurring cycle of Willis flops and Turteltaub's second under-performer after *Instinct.* Like the director's previous work, it seems *The Kid* is insubstantial and corny but crucially lucrative.

He is currently in production with *Enchanted*, a hybrid animation and live-action film that will star Susan Sarandon and John Travolta. **IC**

# David TWOHY

*The Arrival* (1996)
*Pitch Black* (2000)
*Below* (2002)

Born in 1956, David Twohy may be best known for co-writing one of the most popular action pictures of the 1990s, *The Fugitive* (1993). While also involved with writing other notable high-profile pictures, such as *Terminal Velocity* (1994), *Waterworld* (1995), and *G.I. Jane* (1997), Twohy's directorial body of work rests comfortably within the arena of modestly-budgeted science fiction. True to his writer's roots, Twohy only directs films he has scripted or co-scripted: 'It gives me a foundation that other directors wouldn't have ... I don't really understand, never having directed someone else's script completely, how a director [who is not involved with the writing] gets fully prepared to do a film.'

Clean, simple premises and clever narratives distinguish Twohy's workmanlike genre films. His focus is squarely on the character conflicts driving the logic of his story, not on the often empty special effects-driven 1990s science fiction blockbusters. *The Arrival* (1996) takes the familiar science fiction theme of alien invasion and puts a refreshing, hard-science spin on it with marvellous results. Easily outclassing cheesy big-budget contemporaries like *Independence Day* (1996), *The Arrival* does so with a fraction of the budget and a good measure more tension, excitement, and enthusiasm. The film has a respectable number of set-pieces for its tight budget, and B-grade actor Charlie Sheen is effectively used to relay a high dose of paranoia as geeky, hyperkinetic SETI astronomer Zane Ziminski. *The Arrival* does not aspire to escape genre conventions, but still manages to feel progressive in its execution.

*Pitch Black* (2000) is another rollicking science fiction yarn, a low-rent mesh of *The Lost Patrol* (1999) and *Aliens* (1986), with a slightly bigger budget and visual appeal than Twohy's first effort. The budget is wisely spent on its exotic filming locale (the remote desert town of Coober Pedy, Australia) and visual effects rather than a Big Name cast. The ensemble cast of relative unknowns from the art-house and independent circuit is refreshingly ethnic and multi-gender, giving Twohy the freedom to vary from stock science fiction characterisations. Like earlier Twohy projects, the film benefits from solid storytelling with just enough scares and unpredictability to bring tension and suspense to the proceedings while pressing all the right genre buttons.

Having garnered respect and success in the science fiction genre, Twohy's next film, *Below* (2002), is a horror movie about a a World War Two American submarine that comes across a sunken British ship. **THa**

# Ron UNDERWOOD

Born in San Francisco in 1959, Ron Underwood is a director who has worked in a wide variety of established genres with variable results. Fittingly, he began his career working in various capacities on a number of horror/sci-fi films in the 1970s. On *Futureworld* (1976) and *Capricorn One* (1977) he was production assistant and location manager, respectively, graduating to assistant director on the striking horror, *Tourist Trap* (1979).

After two shorts, including the animated sci-fi *Library Report* (1982), he made his feature directorial debut with *Tremors* (1990), an extremely enjoyable, high-quality monster movie. In this affectionate update of 1950s B-movies, Fred Ward and Kevin Bacon are two Nevada hicks battling huge, carnivorous subterranean worms. Starting out as deceptively comedic, the film becomes scarier and more intense with a small band of survivors under attack as the monsters lay waste to their town. Reminiscent of 'big bug movies' like *Them!* (1954) and *Tarantula* (1955), Underwood's film manages the difficult task of both parodying the genre while exploiting its abilities to thrill. The director seems equally comfortable with the humorous banter between Bacon and Ward (who are a winning double act) and the often deadly worm attacks. There is an extra frisson from the way the horrors are staged in the bright sunshine rather than the more generic night-time setting. *Tremors* seems all the more impressive when set alongside later attempts at reviving B-movies, such as *Independence Day* (1996) and *Mars Attacks!* (1997).

Although *Tremors* was a modest success, Underwood's next film was the box-office smash *City Slickers* (1991). This was a comedy western which, like the sci-fi westerns *Back to the Future 3* (1988) and *Wild, Wild West* (1998), repackages this unfashionable genre for a contemporary audience. Billy Crystal and office pals attempt to head off various mid-life crises and get in touch with their masculinity by joining a two-week cattle drive. Jack Palance won an Academy Award as the genuine western article, with a performance that is basically a slightly more benign version of his villain from *Shane* (1953). There are a lot of jokes arising from the clash of cultures but the writers, Lowell Ganz and Babaloo Mandel, often seem to be striving for profundity, as in their earlier *Parenthood* (1989). This results in the sort of lapses into sentimentality that are a frequent occurrence in Hollywood comedies. Although not a great film, *City Slickers,* even with its saccharine flavour, stands as a good example of a mainstream comedy. *Hearts and Souls* (1993) represents another forage by Underwood into earlier Hollywood forms, this time the 1940s sub-genre of after-life/ghostly comedies (which includes *Heaven Can Wait* (1943) and *A Guy Named Joe* (1943)). This is a deliberately old-fashioned tale of passengers on a crashed bus lurking in the after-life and watching over a baby that grows up to be Robert Downey Jr. Basically silly but well-crafted, the film benefits considerably from great performances from a heavyweight cast including Downey Jr, Charles Grodin, Alfre Woodard, Tom Sizemore. As a sweet supernatural romp, the film is considerably more pleasurable than the earlier, similarly-themed (and far more profitable) *Ghost* (1990).

A great deal less successful is *Speechless* (1994), Underwood's take on the screwball comedy. In a scenario typical of the genre, Michael Keaton and Geena Davis meet in a bookstore and fall in love, unaware that they work as speechwriters for opposing politicians. Unlike the celebrated *Bringing Up Baby* (1938) where an audience withholds its disbelief as the comic misunderstandings pile up and enjoy the ride, *Speechless* is just irritating. This is clearly, to some degree, due to the more cynical times but it is also down to the leaden script and the uncharismatic performances from the two leads. Despite trailers heralding the film's appearance on British screens, it ended up as a direct-to-video release.

*Mighty Joe Young* (1998) was an efficient if uninspired remake of the King Kong imitator from 1949. Like the remake of *The Blob* (1988), the principal motivation for this update seems to be the superior effects technology available today. Bill Paxton and Charlize Theron fall in love and attempt to prevent big-game hunters from getting hold of her giant ape. Undoubtedly fun for kids, this monster romp fails to engage an adult audience in the manner of *Tremors.* His most recent film, *The Adventures of Pluto Nash* (2002), is science fiction comedy starring Eddie Murphy. **IC**

# Kinka USHER

*Mystery Men* (1999)

Kinka Usher has worked as a commercials director since 1992 (including prestigious assignments for Hallmark, HBO, Miller Lite, Mountain Dew, Nike, Nissan, Pepsi, Polaroid, and Taco Bell), and received the 1998 Director's Guild of America Commercial Director of the Year Award. His movie debut was the 1999 adaptation of Bob Burden's *Mystery Men*, a spin-off from the enjoyably strange 'Flaming Carrot' comic. There is a lot to like about this tale of ordinary people who subscribe to masked crimefighter ethics but do not have the necessary superpowers. It is visually impressive, courtesy of director of photography Stephen H. Burum and production designer Kirk M. Petrucelli. Despite running the gamut from fart jokes to thirtysomething observational humour, Neil Cuthbert's script contains more hits than misses. The cast – particularly William H. Macy, Paul Reubens, Wes Studi, and Janeane Garofolo – are spot-on. And where previous adaptations of Dark Horse Comics' characters – *The Mask* (1994), *Barb Wire* (1996) – have stripped them of their distinctive tone in the quest for a mainstream audience, *Mystery Men* compensates for this by sustaining an ironic self-awareness of the conventions not only of superhero comics but also of movie adaptations of superhero comics: everyone finds personal redemption, but in each instance, and as the attempted sincerity of the closing 'teamwork' speech indicates, the movie is massively insincere in its observance of such ritual moments. These elements, however, never quite gel: the cast is criminally underused, and Usher's abilities seem dwarfed by the scale of the project. **MB**

# Jim VAN BEBBER

Jim Van Bebber has managed to attain a cult status without any of his films having a *Deadbeat at Dawn* (1988) wide theatrical release. His epic mockudrama on the infamous 1969 Manson murders, *Charlie's Family* (1997) *Charlie's Family* (1997), was cobbled together between 1988 and 1997 whenever funds were available and has become an underground cause célèbre, though it has only been shown as a work-print at specialist festivals and on pirate tapes. In his refusal to give in to economic realities he has become a beacon for other no-budget film-makers; critics meanwhile have wondered how his work would change if he was given decent production funds.

Born in Dayton, Ohio, in 1961, Van Bebber began making his own shorts at age eleven with a used 8mm camera. Mainly stop-motion fantasies in the style of his then-hero Ray Harryhausen, they are surprisingly sophisticated considering the equipment used and usually star the director himself battling dragons or dinosaurs. In High School he made a 40-minute 'karate-rock' drama inspired by the *Mad Max* films, which was enough to gain him a college scholarship. However, after shooting some mini street-gang epics he decided to drop out in his third year and use his student loan to finance *Deadbeat at Dawn* (1988). This was both a homage to the old American International films as well as a reaction against the rather limited US martial-arts pictures of Chuck Norris, full of fights, gore, drugs, and sleazy people, with the director himself starring as the anti-hero lead. Inspired by the success of Sam Raimi's *The Evil Dead* (1982), Van Bebber had hoped for a theatrical release; as late as 1999, however, he was unhappy with the quality of the US DVD, and Britain's censor had refused the film a video certificate.

Using seed money and enthusiasm, both the result of an initial over-optimistic response to *Deadbeat at Dawn*, the epic *Charlie's Family* was an ambitious project merging the experimental stylistic devices of modern transgressive underground film-makers such as Richard Kern and Lydia Lunch with speed editing and the shock sequences of post-Corman exploitation movies.

During the project's long gestation, governed by availability of cast, crew and cash, Van Bebber also shot smaller items like *My Sweet Satan* (1993), based on a true story about Devil-worshipping rock fans who murder a friend for kicks. Other shorts include

*Roadkill – The Last Day of John Martin* (1994), a grisly nut-with-a-chainsaw gorefest from, as he says, 'the days before serial killers were on cereal boxes'. He has also has dabbled in rock videos – *Spasmolytic* for Skinny Puppy and another for the New Orleans group Necrophagia – and shorts to interest investors.

If they gave Academy Awards for sheer tenacity, Van Bebber would surely win one. At this point, however, it is hard to say whether he will become an important director. Would money help him create a masterpiece or would it do no more than put him at the mercy of 'the system' while alienating his underground fans? On the evidence of *Charlie's Family* – uneven, but still the best thing on Manson – somebody should write a cheque and let us find out.                                                         **SR**

## Mario VAN PEEBLES

Mario Van Peebles can be seen as the offspring of blaxploitation cinema in both directorial style and in his family. As the son of famed actor and movie director Melvin Van Peebles (whose work spearheaded the movement with *Sweet Sweetback's Baadasssss Song* (1971)), the two have frequently worked together as actors and directors a range of collaborations.

Born in Mexico in 1957, Mario was educated at Columbia University where he graduated with an economics degree. From this point he flitted between a financial career and some small-time modelling before setting himself up as an actor. His directorial debut came in the harrowing ode to New York, *New Jack City* (1991). Filled with profanity ably applied by a cast including Ice T, Wesley Snipes, and Chris Rock, this powerful first film shows many of the themes that were to become prevalent throughout his later work. An uncomfortable 'cop buddy' film sees a mixed-race partnership putting their personal differences aside to battle the drug dealers. The finale surrounds the failings of the American legal system and filters through to a written end thought which pushes the point concerning the dangers of drugs in the black community.

Maintaining a political stance, Van Peebles then attempted to tell the 'real' story of the Wild West, showing a western filled with black and Latino frontiersmen. *Posse* (1993) is an impressively competent piece, and although it does little to further the genre, it uses its more popular aspects proficiently. The film is interspersed with dream sequences, which show a preacher being persecuted for his beliefs, and allows a chance for a political message to be aired during the body of the piece. The end thought this time turns on Hollywood cinema, condemning it for ignoring the black experience in the western.

Revisionist history was once again on the agenda for the tale of the militant reformist group, *Panther* (1995), which was unveiled to huge media outcry. In a film version of the novel written by his father Van Peebles attempted to tell the forgotten story of the Black Panther group. Showing a strong use of historical footage the film rattles along as a convincing account of the struggle.

*Gang in Blue* (1996) was a television movie, reuniting father and son in a joint directorial feature. This is a tired piece which treads old ground about the evils of the police, a theme much better explored in his earlier work. In his first film to stray from political debate and views of degrading authorities, *Love Kills* (1998) probably exists as his most engaging and mainstream film to date. *Love Kills* creates a serene and peaceful world that is interrupted by the past and the sense of greed that leaks from every part of the plot. Driven by a Simon Le Bon soundtrack, the movie is not only Van Peebles' best directorial work but also features a particularly dynamic role played by himself.     **SS**

## Gus VAN SANT

Born in Kentucky, USA, in 1952, Gus van Sant has carved an impressive niche for himself within Hollywood, managing to alternate between high-concept crowd-pleasers and deeply personal independent films. Described by one critic as the 'bard of dysfunction', van Sant populates his narratives with hustlers, junkies, sociopathic weathergirls and troubled geniuses; his peculiar, skewed version of middle America is often rendered with a mixture of revulsion and the poetic. Having made autobiographical shorts during his school years, in 1970 he attended the Rhode Island School of Design, where he was introduced to such avant-garde directors as Stan Brakhage and Andy Warhol. In 1976, he moved to Los Angeles and became a production assistant to writer-director Ken

Shapiro; he also began to spend his time hanging around Hollywood Boulevard, mixing with the socially marginalised who would become key figures in his later films.

Van Sant's debut, *Mala Noche* (1985), focused on these fringe elements of Los Angeles. Adapted from Portland writer Walt Curtis' semi-autobiographical novella, the film is a brief study of obsession between a homosexual store worker and a heterosexual Mexican immigrant. It showcases several of van Sant's recurring concerns: unfulfilled love, a dry humour and, most importantly, a refusal to judge homosexuality. Shot in lustrous black and white, for only $25,000 on 16mm, *Mala Noche* was an overnight success on the independent circuit and named Best Independent Film by the *Los Angeles Times*.

On the back of his newly acquired kudos, van Sant relocated to Portland, Oregon, where he made his breakthrough film, *Drugstore Cowboy* (1989), the story of four young drug addicts who rob pharmacies to support their habit. The film features a strong central performance from Matt Dillon; he excels as the junkie who decides to kick the habit, aided by Kelly Lynch, Heather Graham, and James Le Gros. Dispensing with facile moralising, van Sant develops a cool, detached, and often comic look at 1970s drug culture, and overall the piece benefits from his low-key, almost languid film-making style. Apart from the rushing clouds that accompany Dillon's fantasies, his direction is necessarily slow, which makes the scenes of drug excess all the more horrific. The film benefits from William Burroughs' cameo as a junkie ex-priest the group meet on the run, both fragile and firebrand in the same breath.

Portland also provided the backdrop for *My Own Private Idaho* (1991), van Sant's subsequent film about the outer fringes of society. Centring on the events surrounding two male hustlers – narcoleptic River Phoenix and rebellious Keanu Reeves – the story encompasses concepts of unrequited love, the family unit, and the alienation of marginals within American culture. Phoenix is superb as Mike who, along with Scott, sets off to try to trace his long-lost mother. More than just an off-beat road movie, the film has specific Shakespearean overtones, not least in the playful deconstructing of the Prince Hal and Falstaff storyline. As Bob, William Richert is a true Falstaffian figure, and the interplay between all three characters is electrifying. Van Sant's visual style is also highly developed – the urban landscapes are moodily shot and framed – while the haunting score lends a deeper resonance. A key film of the early 1990s, Reeves proved to the world that he could act, and Phoenix gave the best performance of his tragically curtailed life; van Sant won an Independent Spirit Award for his screenplay, assuring his position as the flag-bearer for US independent cinema.

It was a short-lived success, however. His next film, *Even Cowgirls Get the Blues* (1993), overtly eccentric and self-parodic, was a resounding commercial and critical flop. Adapted from Tom Robbins' novel, the $8.5 million budget featured an eclectic cast – Uma Thurman, John Hurt, and Keanu Reeves – but suffered from cuts, re-writes and a delayed release. Thurman stars as the world's greatest hitch-hiker with enormous thumbs, and the film charts her weird and wonderful journeys across America. Once again exploring the conventions of the road movie, van Sant offers his typically skewed vision of a particular time and place, yet the film never fuses into a satisfying whole. There are too many eccentric cameos that hinder the plot, and the end product is neither camp, cult, or even cute.

His reputation was restored in 1995, however, with *To Die For*, arguably his most accomplished film. An adaptation of Joyce Maynard's novel, this black comedy stars Nicole Kidman as the murderously ambitious weather-girl who will stop at nothing to get on television. With Matt Dillon as her husband and Joaquin Phoenix as her lover, the trio of central performances are uniformly excellent – as is the kitsch production design and Danny Elfman's score. Van Sant's first film for a major studio (Columbia), it was a minor success, and undoubtedly works better as a satire on the effects of television culture than a black comedy, highlighting the best of van Sant's eclectic techniques. In the same year, he was an executive producer on Larry Clark's *Kids* (1995) – Clark's photographs of junkies had served as a starting point for him when he was prepping *Drugstore Cowboy*.

Van Sant truly entered the mainstream in 1997 with his Academy Award-winning *Good Will Hunting*. Written by and starring Ben Affleck and Matt Damon, the film charts the story of Will Hunting, a troubled genius trying to fit into Boston society. Robin Williams won an Academy Award for his role as the psychiatrist who tries to get beneath Damon's skin, and Minnie Driver excels as the troubled girlfriend. Again, van Sant attempts to focus on an outsider, this time from within the stuffy intellectualism of MIT. There is an obvious tension, however, between his own visual and narrative preoccupations and the studio's desire to craft a feelgood movie about a blue-collar genius. Devoid of his usual array of marginals, and the strange landscapes they frequently inhabit, his directorial touches become subsumed within a saccharine narrative and pat ending. While the film does not disappoint – there are several standout scenes – van Sant's presence is minimal.

Taking a hallowed text and recontextualising it, van Sant's 1998 shot-for-shot remake of Hitchcock's classic 1960 film, *Psycho*, is a classic post-modern exercise. He was pilloried by critics though, and charged with adding nothing new to the original and instead imbuing his remake with a bland, kitsch self-awareness. This arguably misses the point: as much an academic exercise as it is a piece of multiplex film-making, van Sant and his performers were afforded the opportunity to play with indelible images without ever needing to displace or replace them. Anne Heche is gauche as Marion Crane, and both Julianne Moore (a spiky Lila) and William H. Macy (as Arbogast) seem only vaguely uncomfortable. Vince Vaughan has the impossible task of trying to 'do' Anthony Perkins. His bulkier physique and nervous laugh are poor substitutes for Perkins' birdlike movements and stutter, but he possesses a strong screen presence. Van Sant crucially adds his own directorial touches during the famous shower scenes, while Norman's inner fantasies (speeding clouds and a cow) seem overblown and gratuitous, and lack the spareness of Hitchcock's razor-sharp editing. Van Sant famously described his experiment as a 'cover version'; while it is certainly far removed from conventional remakes such as Martin Scorsese's *Cape Fear* (1991), the film never really answers the question of how a shot-for-shot version can differ from the original. Still, it is curious and never less than watchable.

*Finding Forrester* (2000) strongly resembles *Good Will Hunting*. Van Sant essentially trawls the same material – a young black writer (Rob Brown) finds guidance from a famous, reclusive author, played by Sean Connery, and they end up bonding – but the script lacks the inventiveness that characterised *Hunting*. As a buddy film, the narrative mirrors the friendships in *My Own Private Idaho* and *Mala Noche*, and Sean Connery is impressive as the cranky author who has a chance for redemption. Although van Sant attempts to inject the film with his customary quirkiness and deal objectively with American institutions, ultimately his work feels lightweight and lacks invention. His most recent film, *Gerry* (2002), is a semi-improvised comedy starring Matt Damon and Casey Affleck as characters who find themselves slowly dehydrating after becoming lost in a desert.

Despite his recent forays into the mainstream, van Sant's cinematic contribution is best summed up by the late Ken Kesey: 'When people go to see a movie by, let's say, Gus van Sant, they're doing it not just to be entertained, they're doing it because they want to be better warriors'. He has recently published a novel, 'Pink', which explores his grief over River Phoenix's death. **BM**

# Gore VERBINSKI

With only three features to his name, Gore Verbinski has quickly accumulated enough cachet to become a director of high-concept films. Having graduated from commercials, he made his debut feature, *Mouse Hunt* (1997), a hybrid of 'Tom and Jerry', 'Laurel and Hardy', and *Home Alone* (1990). When brothers, played by Nathan Lane and Lee Evans, inherit their father's mansion, they assume that by renovating it to its former glory they will be able to pay off their string factory's debts. They have not bargained on an obstinate mouse, however, who becomes the catalyst for all manner of mayhem, slapstick humour, and vaudevillian one-liners. Verbinski's direction is all the more assured because the concept is so simple. He expertly directs Lane and Evans, exploiting their contrasting physicality and speech patterns to perfection, includes a wonderfully judged cameo from Christopher Walken, and underscores the entire venture with a sureness of tone, eye for detail, and expert pace.

On the back of the film's critical success, Verbinski went on to make *The Mexican* (2001), which is notable for pairing two stars of the day, Brad Pitt and Julia Roberts. Full of brio and panache, it never delivers on its initial promise, unsure whether it's an off-beat road movie, a gangster comedy, or a romantic western. The story of a man in hock to a local Mafioso who goes to Mexico to locate an antique pistol seems like a curious blend of Guy Ritchie and Robert Rodriguez, and despite the much-heralded union of Pitt and Roberts, their few scenes together are a disappointing anti-climax. Most impressive is James Gandolfini as a gay hitman sent to shadow Pitt. He brings just the right amount of Tony Soprano bulk and menace to the part, but Verbinski unnecessarily saddles him with all the usual 'sensitive gay' stereotypes. The film's lack of understatement is also a problem: every explosion or gunfight is over-extended and over-performed, leaving an uneven, if momentarily enjoyable, aftertaste.

Verbinski's most recent film, *Ring* (2002), is a remake of the chilling 1998 Japanese original, in which a journalist (Naomi Watts) discovers a disturbing videotape with a bizarre history – everyone who watches it dies within seven days.                    **BM**

# Paul VERHOEVEN

Paul Verhoeven is no stranger to the label 'controversial'. His films are often criticised for their violent content, but the director argues he is merely reflecting a violent society. Verhoeven's films pay close, almost scientific, attention to detail, particularly in scenes of a sexually explicit nature. Verhoeven claims there are elements of autobiography in the erotic content of his earlier Dutch films, *Turkish Delight* (1973) and *The Fourth Man* (1983).

Born in the Netherlands in 1938 and subsequently educated at the University of Leiden in maths and physics, he began his career in film as a documentary film-maker for the Dutch Royal Navy and Dutch television. Verhoeven made a transition to fiction with the Dutch television series 'Floris'. 'Floris' gained him much attention and in 1971 Verhoeven made his feature debut, *Business is Business*, about the life of a young prostitute. Verhoeven's second feature, *Turkish Delight*, earned him notoriety. It is a deliciously erotic tale focusing on the marriage between a sculptor (Rutger Hauer) and a middle-class girl (Monique van de Ven). Controversial upon its release, it is a brash and stylish film that shows Verhoeven developing a specific oeuvre. As well as earning its director and stars a certain notoriety, the film was a success in the Netherlands and internationally.

He followed this with *Katie's Room* (1975), a historical drama centring on a working-class woman (Monique van de Ven) and her struggle to rise up the social ladder of nineteenth-century Holland. Verhoeven made a further three Dutch-produced films. The highly acclaimed *Soldier of Orange* (1977), is a drama set during the German occupation of Holland and focuses on the effects of the occupation on the lives of six young university students. *Spetters* (1980) is a gritty portrayal of the lives of wild teens. The film's sexually explicit nature has given it a certain notoriety.

His final Dutch film during this period, *The Fourth Man* is a visually stunning erotic psycho-thriller featuring Renee Soutendijk as a widow who may or may not be responsible for the deaths of three men. An impoverished and manipulative writer, Gerard (Jerome Krabbe), believes he could be next. The film is regarded as a precursor to Verhoeven's later 'killer-chick' flick, *Basic Instinct* (1992). There are similarities certainly, but *The Fourth Man* has more ambiguity, and is more engrossing and visually exciting.

After the success of *The Fourth Man*, Verhoeven directed his first American film, a violent, swashbuckling adventure, *Flesh and Blood* (1985). But Verhoeven made his name in Hollywood with his next feature, the contemporary science fiction classic, *RoboCop* (1987). Slick and engaging in its comic book style, *RoboCop* takes us to a Detroit of the near future. Crime is at epidemic proportions but a big corporation thinks it has the answer: mechanised crime fighters. However, a rethink is required after a demonstration model kills a junior executive in the boardroom, a genuinely disquieting scene and trademark Verhoeven in its black humour. The answer comes in the form of a brutally-murdered cop, Alex Murphy, whose brain is fused with cybernetic technology, turning him into RoboCop. The film is intelligent, provocative, violent, and unremittingly pessimistic about the future.

*RoboCop* paved the way for his next foray into science fiction, the gung-ho science fiction adventure, *Total Recall* (1990), based on a story by Philip K. Dick ('We Can Remember It For You Wholesale'). Arnold Schwarzenneger plays Doug Quaid, a construction worker with a pleasant lifestyle and a beautiful wife (Sharon Stone). Or is he? Disturbed and preoccupied by nightmares of a life on Mars, he goes to the Rekall Company for an implant, to give him the memories of a Mars adventure he never experienced. What follows are constant shifts in the reality of the narrative as the plot twists and turns, punctuated by high-octane action. *Total Recall* has been described as a 'swashbuckling space opera'. The film won an Academy Award for its stunning special effects, which more than make up for the plot defects, anomalies, and the wooden acting of Schwarzenegger.

Verhoeven caused a storm of controversy with his next feature, *Basic Instinct* (1992). The film focuses on the hunt for the killer of a rock star. Investigating the case is San Francisco cop Nick Curran (Michael Douglas), who becomes fascinated by key suspect, writer Catherine Tramell (Sharon Stone). The film contains the essential Verhoeven love-affair-with-ambiguity, as Tramell may or may not be guilty, depending on whether you sympathise with her character or detest her. The film sparked controversy among feminists who largely objected to the (allegedly surreptitious) filming of a pantieless Stone as she crosses and uncrosses her legs during a police interrogation scene. Gay activists were so outraged at the film's portrayal of lesbians that one strategy devised in protest was to reveal the film's ending. A director's cut was released in 1993 featuring 42 seconds of footage censors asked Verhoeven to remove, comprising 8 shots of erotic action between Douglas and Stone.

*Showgirls* (1995) was universally panned by critics, particularly for its weak screenplay and risible dialogue. It focuses on a young woman, Nomi Malone (Elizabeth Berkley) who comes from nowhere to Las Vegas, starts as a lap dancer and becomes a top-rated showgirl. Despite an energetic performance from Berkley and slick production values, the film was not a major box-office success.

Verhoeven followed this with *Starship Troopers* (1997), a camp science fiction/action movie. The film was a major success at the box office, although critical reactions were mixed. Set in the future, the film centres on Johnny Rico (Casper Van Dien), who joins the war against the bug-like aliens of Klendathu out of a desire to be a good citizen. A lot of the action is tongue-in-cheek, and the special effects are excellent. But the weak narrative – a kind of *Top Gun* (1986) in space – and the one-dimensional characters make this a disappointing film in the context of Verhoeven's past work.

*Hollow Man* (2000), Verhoeven's updating of H. G. Wells' 'The Invisible Man', received mixed reviews. Despite impressive special effects, the film suffers from a lack of sustained suspense and gratuitous treatment of sexual representation. Kevin Bacon and Elizabeth Shue do their best to lift the narrative but seem ultimately bound by the director's vision and dubious ethical positioning.

Verhoeven is a skilled craftsman, but it is clear that Hollywood typecasts its directors just as it does its stars. As a consequence, the director's work has become synonymous with action, violence and sex. This does him a major disservice, neglecting as it does his fine attention to detail, his black humour, and rich, slick visual style. His films are violent but the violence is often ironic. Verhoeven ascribes this to his childhood experiences during World War Two, and concludes, 'If it hadn't been for the German occupation and then the American occupation, I would never have been a film-maker.' **SL**

# Denis VILLENEUVE

Denis Villeneuve, born in 1967, is one of the most promising talents to emerge from Québec in recent years. He cut his teeth in rock videos and numerous shorts, the latter including the winning entry of twenty short videos into Radio Canada's 1990/91 Europe-Asia Race. It's too early to find clear themes, but spatial and geographical displacement (he has published an impressionistic travel notebook), wry hints of mock-machismo, subtle philosophical tendencies, a striking visual sensibility, and a passion for the French New Wave seem to be his trademarks to date.

For producer Roger Frappier, he wrote and directed 'The Technician', a segment for the film *Cosmos* (1996). This black and white, French language film wraps six individual short stories by six film-makers around the character of a Greek taxi driver in Montreal. In its sly existentialism and comically bittersweet take on relationships, it's not unlike Villeneuve's debut feature as a writer-director, *August 32nd on Earth* (1998). This enigmatic two-hander combines a study in narrative space with a streak of twentysomething existential disorientation and an almost melodramatic tale of ill-fated love; the line 'I'm not asking for the moon' plays like Villeneuve's mini-homage to *Now, Voyager* (1942).

Still, if the presence of a Jean Seberg poster in the film suggests that this strikingly cine-literate love letter goes to the French New Wave rather than Hollywood, it's borne out by similarities to Godard's *Pierrot le Fou* (1965). Even then, Villeneuve reverses concomitant gender expectations by, thinking of *Breathless* (1959), keeping Jean-Paul Belmondo in mind for Pascale Bussieres, Simone and Seberg in mind for Alexis Martin's Philippe. When Simone decides to rethink her life after a car crash, she asks her friend Philippe to help her have a child. It is when they travel to the Salt Lake City desert to have sex that Villeneuve truly finds his feet, bringing his experiments in the relationship between characters and their environment to life in some breathtaking desert scenes.

If this sounds like a film school experiment, Villeneuve amply compensates by eliciting warmly witty performances from his leads. The result is a suavely stylised take on the quest for a kind of liminal space, with a slick combination of brisk plotting, winning characterisations and a French New Wave-style probe into visual and generic convention.

As twists on the rules of melodrama go, though, the opaque, skittishly stylish *Maelström* (2000) initially looks like a very different kettle of fish. Indeed, it opens with a fish that, about to be disembowelled, assumes the role of narrator – and outside of *Monty Python's The Meaning of Life* (1983) that's something of a rarity. However, from the way it charts the strange routes of romance to its beguilingly eclectic soundtrack, *Maelström* betrays many winningly oddball affinities with *August 32nd*. The main narrative thread is precipitated by a car crash: a woman drunkenly ploughs down a fishmonger (a befuddling riff on *I Know What You Did Last Summer* (1997) perhaps?) and does a runner. When she discovers that she killed him, she finds his son, pretends to be his neighbour and, finally, falls in love with him. It's a conventional narrative in some respects, but Villeneuve's clearly finding new veins for old blood – and it's hard not to warm to a film that features 'voice of fish entity' and 'infernal fishmonger' among its list of characters. **KH**

# Norton VIRGIEN

As director for a number of episodes of the popular cartoon show 'Rugrats', Norton *The Rugrats Movie* (1998) Virgien has used his first attempt at a feature film to extend much of his previous work. 'Rugrats' won awards for its unusual animation style, which takes a childish view of the world, with distorted characters and images from everyday life given a very different spin. *The Rugrats Movie* (1998), which Virgien co-directed with Igor Kovalyov, continues in the same vein but adds a new dimension to the already garish colour scheme of the show, aided by a use of depth, which results in the images seeming much fuller than their small-screen counterparts.

The simple action of the film is improved by the intelligent use of perspective and some well thought out tracking shots, but the decision to include a fully computer-generated sequence is a little mystifying as it seems out of place with the general style of the feature. The difficult job of trying to blend together a child's film with something for the adults to enjoy is attempted, if a little unsuccessfully. However, the homage paid to Indiana Jones is a good touch. **SS**

# Tony VITALE

Tony Vitale has stated that the '[New York] Independent Feature Project was like my *Kiss Me Guido* (1997) film school, and the Independent Feature Film Market was like the finals week'. Born in New York in 1964, and a volunteer at the market for four years in the early 1990s, Vitale worked in various aspects of film production before finding himself in the hub of the 'micro-budget' film boom; a period when young unknowns were encouraged to forego shorts, and trailers, regardless of budget – the mantra at the time: make a feature. Vitale took this advice, and made his first film, *Kiss Me Guido* (1997), under the aegis of Redeemable Features, a New York-based independent production company.

*Kiss Me Guido* charts the clash of sensibilities between an Italian, Bronx-bred, macho young man – the eponymous 'Guido' – and his new roommate, a Manhattanite, gay actor who is confident about both his sexuality and his respective position within the queer community. By placing itself within the arena of off-Broadway hopefuls, the film highlights performance, identity, and the relation between the two. The film trades in stereotypes rather than characters, but this strategy works, focusing attention on how markers of identity circulate the mainstream, and the surprising, ironic points of intersection between gay and straight culture. Championing a liberal line, the film evokes enough acerbic wit to avoid the pedestrian and add some edge to its sweetly humanist leanings.

Revisiting the Italian community (although to very different effect), Vitale's second feature, *Very Mean Men*, has a bartender determined to wrangle a decent tip out of a late-night customer, by telling him the tale of a brutal Mob war between the Minettis and the Mulroneys. Despite the appearance of some decently sized names in the cast, and despite snagging a New Cinema Award at the Seattle International Film Festival, *Very Mean Men* has yet to have a theatrical release in the US.

Curiously perhaps, Vitale's third film, which is currently in production, *Jungle Juice* is a daffy romp set in a Club-Med-like vacation spot. It stars Christopher Walken, Morgan Fairchild, Richard Wagner and Rutger Hauer. **LW**

# Daisy VON SCHERLER MAYER

Born in New York in 1965, and grandaughter to famed screenwriter Edwin Justus Mayer (Ernst Lubitsch's *To Be or Not To Be* (1942)), Daisy von Scherler Mayer is a graduate of the Film Studies programme at Wesleyan University, and her first feature, *Party Girl* (1995), is rife with Wesleyan contributors. No less than 17 school alumni take their place in the production credits, and these same 17 comprise the cast of extras in the film. *Party Girl* is a young woman's coming-of-age story, but this young woman, Mary, happens to be New York's biggest scenester; or at least, she attempts to be. But the scene proves monotonous; and Mary is feeling frazzled and unfinished, until a career in the library sciences beckons.

*Party Girl* played at the 1996 Sundance Film Festival, and left critics divided over its merits. Parker Posey's outstanding lead performance has either been lauded for its chutzpah and bravado or denigrated for its brittle, sarcastic egoism. Von Scherler Mayer has described her central character as 'modelled after a certain sensibility'; and indeed, this sensibility has provided the film with an appreciative female audience. Mary may not be a nice person – she is capable of gross ingratitude – but she's funny, feisty, and massively stylish, and, as Parker plays her, capable of defining her independence in the insouciant manner of a Bette Davis or Barbara Stanwyck. Casting her own mother, Sasha von Scherler, as the senior librarian, the director gives an extra-diegetic resonance to the necessity of supportive female familial bonds to surmount the generation gap and open up a space for common ground.

Von Scherler Mayer's second feature, *Woo* (1998), is fairly standard Hollywood fare that went nowhere commercially and critically, although once again, the film showcases a strong performance by its female lead. Like *Party Girl*, Woo wants to argue that a woman can be smart, sexy, fun, and strong, but while this message registered lucidly in the former, it becomes muddled in the latter, which is unable to effectively challenge its undercurrents of homophobia and chauvinism.

Interestingly, with her third feature, a children's film, *Madeline* (1998) (based on the books of Ludwig Bemelman), von Scherler Mayer recaptures the feminist promise of *Party Girl*. Once again, the female centre, in this case eight-year-old Madeline, is a strong-willed, maverick heroine who takes the world on her own terms. Madeline proves herself more than capable of saving the all-girl school she attends, while the surrounding female community provides both a wellspring of support and the sense of family Madeline so wants to retain. *Madeline* is an intelligent children's film, and its celebration of a young girl's boisterous path to self-reliance is refreshingly free of the moralising ethos that usually accompanies films geared towards family viewing.

If nothing else, *Madeline* demonstrates that von Scherler Mayer is comfortable working with a budget after the no-budget days of *Party Girl* when the production staff were paid with money that flew out the back door of a passing van. Von Scherler Mayer's most recent work, re-titled *The Guru* (2002), is the tale of an Indian man in New York who finds himself mistaken for a Deepak Chopra-like sex guru, a case of mistaken identity that soon has him enmeshed in the porn industry. With a talented high-profile cast, and based on a story idea by Shekhar Kapur (screenwriter for *Elizabeth* (1998)), *The Guru* may well prove to be von Scherler Mayer's crossover work. **LW**

# Larry & Andy WACHOWSKI

Brothers Larry and Andy Wachowski have written and directed only two films to date, *Bound* (1996)
yet both have achieved comprehensive critical and financial success. Born in 1965 and *The Matrix* (1999)
1967 respectively, they both originate from Chicago. Inspired by Frank Miller's stylish
comic-book series 'Sin City' and the work both brothers undertook at Marvel comics
writing dialogue for the 'Hellraiser' series, their work is heavily stylised, seductive, glossy,
and richly laden with mythological and theological conceits.

Their first feature, *Bound* (1996), is a neo-noir thriller concerning an ingenious
heist plot perpetrated by a lesbian plumber (Geena Gershon) and a frustrated gangster's
moll (Jennifer Tilly). Made on a $4 million budget the film subverts the stereotypical
conventions of the noir genre by creating a scenario in which the femme fatale escapes
punishment – indeed, she even gets the girl in the end. Applauded as a slice of lesbian-
noir chic, the film is as erotic as it is violent, yet is tightly structured without pandering
to senseless titillation.

In 1999 the brothers saw the release of their cyber-punk epic *The Matrix*. A veritable
hybrid smorgasbord of kung fu, comic-book posturing, science fiction cool, video game
kinetics, and dystopian mythology, the film is a 'virtual' masterpiece. Drawing on
religious, literary and philosophical allusions, the film casts a bewildered Keanu Reeves
in the role of Thomas 'Neo' Anderson as the reluctant messiah attempting to awaken
humanity from a technological nightmare. For all its flaws, such as the sometimes
inconsistent and confused plot, *The Matrix* is an effects-driven experience that redefines
the aesthetics of the science fiction film. Incorporating such techniques as 'flo-mo', a
process of filming whereby action is seemingly frozen whilst the camera spins dizzyingly
around the protagonists, the Wachowski brothers have produced a film that sets the
benchmark for other cyber-punk films to emulate. They are currently working on a sequel
due for release in 2003. **PH**

# Alan WADE

Alan Wade's films have thus far received scant distribution. His first feature, *Julian* *Julian Po* (1997)
*Po* (1997), based on the novella 'The Death of Mr Golouja' by Serbo-Croatian writer

Branimir Scepanovic, is an understated dark comedy which provides a variation on the theme of a stranger in a small town. Here, the eponymous figure (played by Christian Slater) is a nondescript book keeper who keeps an audio journal and decides to visit the ocean for the first time in his life. After his car breaks down, he finds himself in a closed community that, after initial suspicion and fear, begins to offer bizarre support to Julian's stated plan to kill himself. Julian's off-hand comments and advice are interpreted literally by several townsfolks and have a variety of repercussions. Touching the sexual, spiritual, and social fabric of the town, Julian seemingly finds new hope in the guise of an affair with a vaguely angelic figure (Robin Tunney) who has awaited his arrival for years. Toying only superficially with themes of death and fate, the film strives to make connections between the anonymous banality of both individual and community. However, the reduction of the town dwellers to quirky ciphers exemplifies the film's lack of overall focus. Veering between the sinister and the sincere, the film achieves not ambiguity, but an uncertainty of tone that restricts deeper engagement with the essentially uninteresting characters.

Wade's second feature, *The Pornographer: A Love Story*, awaits release.    **NJ**

# Rupert WAINWRIGHT

*Blank Check* (1994)
*The Sadness of Sex* (1995)
*Stigmata* (1999)

The feature films of English-born music video director Rupert Wainwright are made using many of the tricks of the video form. That all three are tremendously diverse demonstrates the versatility of video techniques, as well as Wainwright's own talent – from the childrens' fantasy *Blank Check* (1994), to the mental wandering of a poet in *The Sadness of Sex* (1995), and finally to the religious apocalypse in *Stigmata* (1999).

A better than average childrens' film with a comparatively complex plot, the Disney-produced *Blank Check* is the story of Preston (Brian Bonsall), a young boy who is given the eponymous document when his bicycle is run over by a convicted thief (Miguel Ferrer) who is in the process of laundering a million dollars cash with a complicit bank manager (Michael Lerner). Preston coincidentally cashes the cheque for a million dollars, causing a mix-up for the bank manager, as he confuses the boy for the intended pick-up man (Tone Loc). Preston then proceeds to live the high life as he is pursued by the three criminals. While it is virtually a paean to consumerism, Wainwright infuses *Blank Check* with some personal style outside the usual sentimental Disney dross. The camera tilts and quick editing, as well as an interesting noirish opening and fetishisation of television monitors and video games, betray Wainwright's video roots. He gives the film efficiency and urgency so that the viewer never loses interest.

*The Sadness of Sex* is an experimental collaboration with spoken word performer Barry Yourgrau, consisting of 15 segments illustrating stories of love and sex the latter delivers while on stage. Influenced by Oliver Stone's *JFK* (1991) and *Natural Born Killers* (1994), Wainwright uses multiple film stocks and other tricks, including some computer and stop-motion animation, to give the film a glossy sheen despite a budget of less than a million dollars.

*Stigmata*, the director's most recent film, is a tailor-made project for his hyperkinetic style. A collage of quick cuts, tilted camera, circular pans, zooms and special effects, it is the story of a young Pittsburgh woman (Patricia Arquette) who becomes stigmatic after receiving the gift of a South American rosary. At the time of its release, the film was attacked by many critics for what they saw as an affront to the Catholic Church. The film does indeed seem to be taking a stand against the Church, but more its institutionalism than its Christian faith. While it has the potential to bring a truly provocative statement forward, *Stigmata's* overbearing and self-conscious style – continuous rain, simulated flames, doves flying in slow motion – detracts from its being a conduit for any kind of higher message. The film is essentially an elongated music video with an inflated narrative. The industrial score by The Smashing Pumpkins' Billy Corgan further enhances this impression.    **DH**

# Randall WALLACE

*The Man in the Iron Mask* (1998)

Once compared to the English novelist Charles Dickens, Randall Wallace has made a stunning leap from novels to the world of film. While still evoking the epic style and lyricism of his novels, he has created a body of film work that has made him one of the most sought after writer-directors in Hollywood today. Choosing to depict personal and complex human drama in the context of horrific and monumental social contexts, Wallace has carved out a unique niche in his career as a screenwriter, historian and humanitarian.

*We Were Soldiers* (2002)

Wallace caught the writing bug while attending Duke University, where he studied religion and Russian literature, and was introduced to the works of Chekhov and Pushkin. Attracted to the style of the Russian classics, he began to write novels and by the time he had completed his fifth, had earned high praise from critics for his rich body of work.

In 1995, Wallace turned to Hollywood and wrote the screenplay for the film *Braveheart* (1995), which told the story of William Wallace (no relation) and Scotland's attempts to free itself from England's tyrannical rule. Wallace's weaving of action, romance, and chivalry was a hit with audiences and critics alike. With this screenplay Wallace became an instant commodity in Hollywood; it was nominated for both an Academy Award and a Golden Globe and won the Writers Guild of America award for Best Screenplay.

Despite numerous writing opportunities, Wallace turned to directing, adapting an Alexendre Dumas' classic *The Man in the Iron Mask* (1998). Starring an international cast such as Gabriel Byrne, Gérard Depardieu, and Jeremy Irons, the film is a swashbuckling action-adventure, heavy on drama and splashed with comedy. Wallace combined all of these elements perfectly to create a fun rollercoaster of a film. Unfortunately the film suffered from a heavy backlash due to the inappropriate casting of Leonardo DiCaprio in the lead role and its success was minimal.

While searching for his next directing project, Wallace returned to writing penning the screenplay for the highly anticipated World War Two action drama *Pearl Harbor* (2001). Choosing to tell the story of two brothers (Josh Hartnett and Ben Affleck) who fall in love with the same woman, Wallace and director Michael Bay tried to repeat the formula of the film *Titanic* (1997), setting up an intricate story of love against the monumental backdrop of war and the bombing of Pearl Harbor. The film was widely heralded for its spectacular visual effects, but suffered from the fact that it took over an hour to get to them. It also suffered from several others flaws, including choice of actors and Wallace's less than stellar screenplay, which was nominated for a Razzie Award for Worst Screenplay of 2001. The film opened big at the box office but quickly fizzled.

Having suffered two setbacks in a row, Wallace turned back to the man who brought him his initial success in Hollywood, Mel Gibson. With *We Were Soldiers* (2002), Wallace pulled double duty, both directing and also writing the screenplay, which he adapted from the book 'We Were Soldiers Once ... and Young: Ia Drang, The Battle That Changed the War in Vietnam' by Harold G. Moore and Joseph Galloway. Based upon real events during the battle of Ia Drang, the film highlights the honour and valour of Lt. Colonel Harold Moore (played by Mel Gibson) and his men as they fight what is considered one of the bloodiest battles during that war. Once again, Wallace chooses an epic setting for an interpersonal look at human relationships. **JM**

# Anthony WALLER

Born of British nationality in Lebanon in 1959, Anthony Waller attended school in Beirut and the UK. In 1978, he was the youngest student ever to have been admitted to Britain's National Film School. In 1981, his short *When the Rain Stops* won the first prize for a work of fiction at the first European Student Film Competition, and he also received the annual Shakespeare Scholarship to study film in Germany. After a year at the Munich Film and TV School, he started work in German television as a vision mixer and editor. He has directed and edited a number of pop videos and movie trailers and, since the mid-1980s, over 100 commercials (for IBM, Camel, Super Nintendo, and others). In 1991 he was awarded the Gold Medal at the New York Advertising Film Festival.

*Mute Witness* (1994)
*An American Werewolf in Paris* (1997)
*The Guilty* (1999)

*Mute Witness* (1994), which he wrote, directed, and produced, is a complex thriller about a mute special effects make-up artist who witnesses a brutal murder and is drawn into the snuff-movie *demi-monde* and criminal underworld of the former Soviet Union. Originally set in Chicago, it was rewritten and relocated to take advantage of the possibility of shooting in Russia (Alec Guinness' scenes were shot in Germany in 1985) and consequently its bilingual cast sometimes struggle with poor dialogue. Occasionally a little too self-conscious, stylistically and in its repeated narrative rug-pulling, it is well-staged and beautifully shot. Playing almost in real-time, it is replete with allusions to Alfred Hitchcock and Dario Argento.

Waller went on to direct *An American Werewolf in Paris* (1997), a belated and sophomoric sequel (sort of) to the quintessential modern horror-comedy movie *An American Werewolf in London* (1981). Frequently unconvincing CGI effects replace the groundbreaking physical effects of the original, and filming in Amsterdam and Luxembourg prevent Paris from being as essential to the movie as London was to Landis' film. A nicely shot opening sequence, again alluding to Hitchcock and Argento, gives way to direction and camerawork that is as pedestrian as the humourless rock soundtrack. The camera is at its best when it is mobile, but too many shots and sequences look as if they have been taken verbatim from adverts.

Subsequently, Waller directed *The Guilty* (1999), a thriller about a young lawyer accused of assaulting his assistant, and executive produced *The Little Vampire* (2000), an adaptation of Angela Sommer-Bodenburg's novel.                                    **MB**

# Wayne WANG

Stylistically Wayne Wang continues to defy categorisation. His directorial style embraces both gritty, offbeat, realist dramas and the visually excessive family melodrama. His films always retain a humanist perspective that focuses on community and the multifaceted, often contradictory, nature of personality in multicultural America. Born in Hong Kong in 1949 and educated in an English-speaking Jesuit school, Wang (named Wayne by his father as a homage to his favourite actor, John Wayne) eventually moved to California in 1967 to study at Foothill College. Given the diverse nature of his upbringing, it is of little wonder that Wang's films often have issues concerning identity crisis at their heart.

His first feature film, *Chan is Missing* (1981), centres on a thinly disguised narrative that sets out to capture the social and political attitudes that constitute masculine Chinese-American identity. Shot for less than $20,000 in 16mm, Wang employs a *vérité* style of film-making reminiscent of early Godard. His use of black and white film stock and non-professional actors makes this more a travelogue through San Francisco's Chinatown than the conventional thriller that it purports to be. The film achieved critical acclaim on the festival circuit, despite not having a general release. Wang subsequently produced a companion piece to this film with his next feature, *Dim Sum: A Little Bit of Heart* (1983). This film focuses on the often confrontational relationship between a second-generation Chinese-American woman and her Chinese mother, exploring and developing themes from a female perspective that were touched on in *Chan*. Again the film was hailed by critics, but failed to make any impression at the box office.

*Slam Dance* (1987) emerged as his first commercial venture. Not only is the film a complete departure from the humanist aesthetics of his first two films, it also reversed his popularity with the critics. Ultimately the film is a confused and over-stylised mess of ideas concerning a hyperactive Tom Hulce running amok in LA. Lambasted for its empty packaging of cheap thrills and lifeless melodrama, *Slam Dance* served only to severely dent Wang's reputation as a director of integrity. Harmed by his critical mauling, Wang defied expectations with his next two projects. *Eat a Bowl of Tea* (1989) is a return to his cultural roots. This sedate comedy of manners about Chinese newlyweds languishing under the censorious gaze of their New York community finds Wang again exploring familiar themes of familial angst. Surprisingly he followed this up with a deliberately frenetic and unorthodox thriller, *Life is Cheap ... But Toilet Paper is Expensive* (1990), a film that tries to evoke the chaotic mood that prevailed in Hong Kong prior to the re-integration with China. Shot on location, the film is as idiosyncratic as it is confrontational, a combination which did little to enhance Wang's standing at the box office.

Desperate for a 'hit' movie, Wang finally found success in 1993 with his adaptation of Amy Tan's novel 'The Joy Luck Club'. Using a predominantly female cast, Wang follows the trials and tribulations of a family of Chinese immigrants as they attempt to adapt to a new life in the US. In many ways the film compromises his earlier *vérité* humanist work, as this is an epic tearjerker that is as emotionally excessive and as glossily stylised as any Douglas Sirk melodrama.

Now recognised as a 'New Hollywood' player, Wang turned his back on the Asian-American experience to focus on a pet project he had been nurturing with novelist Paul Auster since the beginning of the 1990s. Their collaborative work resulted in two of the most whimsical and innovative films of the decade. Both *Smoke* (1995), and its companion piece, *Blue in the Face* (1995), revolve around a cigar shop and its street-corner philosopher owner Augie Wren (Harvey Keitel). The films are set in Brooklyn in 1990, and offer a unique, character-driven insight into the often diverse and complex nature of New York City neighbourhood life. Of the two films, *Smoke* is by far the more lyrical in its treatment of the themes of fate, friendship, and family. It is both melancholic and beautifully crafted in its delicate interweaving of connected narratives concerning loss, redemption, love and companionship, themes that uphold the humanist spirit of Wang's earlier films. *Blue in the Face*, however, is more scatological and anarchic in its attempt to offer an insight into community life. Seemingly lacking any coherent narrative and using vox pops, soundbites and improvised cameos from the likes of Madonna, Jim Jarmusch, and Lou Reed to convey its point, the film is, according to Auster, a veritable 'hymn to the great people's republic of New York'. Off-hand and freshly inventive, the two films mark a departure from traditional Hollywood film-making practices and recovered Wang's reputation with the critics.

However, as if to confound his critics even further, Wang's subsequent work has found him reverting to the lavish bittersweet melodrama. *Chinese Box* (1997) finds him revisiting his native Hong Kong, and the latent themes of loss and cultural identity, as photojournalist John (Jeremy Irons) struggles with the weighty trauma of unrequited love, leukaemia and the impending transfer of Hong Kong to Chinese administration. With only months to live, John, with the aid of a few friends, takes a digital video camera and prowls the streets, seeking to document the 'real' Hong Kong one last time. No less emotionally fraught is *Anywhere But Here* (1999), a straightforward, if somewhat flat, mother-daughter tears-and-laughter coming of age movie that failed to ignite any real burning passion amongst audiences.

His latest film, *The Center of the World* (2001), another collaboration with scriptwriter Paul Auster, is anything but lacking passion. The film, shot on digital video, follows a damaging sexual game between an isolationist dot-com millionaire called Richard Longman (Peter Sarsgaard), and drummer-by-day-stripper-by-night career woman Florence, played with convincing aplomb by Molly Parker. Part *Pretty Woman* (1990), part *Last Tango in Paris* (1973), in some ways the film is a complete departure from the latent humanism of his earlier work. Set amongst the plasticity and kitsch of Las Vegas it is a highly cynical, bleak portrayal of the modern malaise of soulless sex amongst over-worked, under-loved individuals in corporate America.

Wayne Wang remains something of an anomaly. Equally hailed as the voice of a new Chinese-American cinema that failed to materialise, as quirky humanist auteur, and as director of overblown lush familial melodrama, he retains a flair for focusing on the delicate, idiosyncratic nature of relationships and identity in a multi-cultural America.                                                                                                    **PH**

# David S. WARD

Having gained an Academy Award and a Golden Globe nomination for his screenplay *The Sting* in the late 1970s, David S. Ward's move to directing did not earn him the critical success of his screenwriting. Born in 1945, his first production, *Cannery Row* (1982), which he both wrote and directed, was an adaptation of the John Steinbeck novel of the same name, blended with the author's other novel 'Sweet Thursday'. On the whole, this feature slips too easily into the category of populist romance with no real directorial innovation to give it autonomy. Thoughtful performances – from Nick Nolte as the ex-baseball player turned marine biologist and Debra Winger as the love interest – elevate it into the realms of the watchable.

This was followed seven years later by *Major League* (1989), written and directed by Ward and charting the rags-to-riches tracks of the Cleveland Indians, a motley crew of a baseball team at the hands of an new owner and an imminent move to Florida. The film is flawed by its overtly formulaic nature, relying on set-pieces already employed in previous baseball movies, but still occasionally amusing in its parody of baseball mannerisms.

*Cannery Row* (1982)
*Major League* (1989)
*King Ralph* (1991)
*The Program* (1993)
*Major League II* (1994)
*Down Periscope* (1996)

In Ward's next feature, *King Ralph* (1991), a similar theme of accidental affluence permeates the narrative; when the entire English monarchy are wiped out in an unexpected accident, Las Vegas club owner and washout Ralph Jones finds himself next in line for the throne. Concentrating on the Anglo-American culture divide, this film unfortunately shares with *Major League* the predictability of a concept-driven comedy, foreseeable gags and all. Commentators at the time complained that John Goodman – in the starring role – was underused.

Both *The Program* (1993) and *Major League II* (1994) continue the interest in sport. *The Program* pays homage to real American footballer Daniel E. 'Rudy' Ruettiger and his quest in the 1970s to make the Notre Dame team. The film is, at best, unimaginative. Equally disappointing, *Major League II* is an onslaught of clichés that pays little respect to the intelligence of the audience. It is perhaps worth considering that these films hold appeal for younger audiences who may revel in the crass quality of the humour and the enactment of sporting glory.

*Down Periscope* (1996) runs along similar lines to Ward's previous work, in that it regurgitates a formulaic narrative (this time a submarine theme) in a similarly clichéd manner. It stars Kelsey Grammar in his first feature since success in the television series 'Frasier', taking the helm of a dilapidated submarine along with a helpless crew in a contest against more sophisticated nuclear ships. He provides an enjoyable performance, as do the rest of the cast, and although there have been doubts, most critics agreed that this film is amusing. **LB**

# John WATERS

John Waters' oeuvre can be delineated by two signifying date frames: an early period lasting between 1964 and 1977 and, following a one-movie transition period in 1981, a later phase beginning in 1988. While there is undoubtedly a consistency of worldview across both periods, for many observers the latter phase has seen Waters perform something of a Hollywood kow-tow in chase of a wider audience. Conversely, that he was a figure who came to be institutionally embraced at all was for others (Waters amongst them) the very essence of popular American culture.

Born in Baltimore in 1946, and claiming as early influences his middle-class Catholic upbringing and Baltimore's sex cinemas, Waters began to experiment with 8mm shorts. Between 1964 and 1969 he produced four shorts of artistic pretension and modest notoriety: *Hag in a Black Leather Jacket* (1964), *Roman Candles* (1966), *Eat Your Makeup* (1968), and *The Diane Linkletter Story* (1969). It was during this early period that Waters drew together an acting coterie of social nonconformists that included his regular cohorts Mink Stole and the corpulent transvestite, Divine (Harris Glen Milstead), around whom events in the narrative were typically played out.

Waters' first feature, *Mondo Trasho* (1969), which has Divine carrying around the corpse of a woman she has killed with her car, set the tone for a corpus of early work that offered gleeful vulgarity and tastelessness represented through sorrowful production values. *Multiple Maniacs* (1970), allegedly based on the Sharon Tate murders, featured Divine as a mass murderer and boasted a rape-by-giant lobster scene and a pseudo lesbian deflowering in a church, while *Pink Flamingos* (1972), Waters' 'breakthrough' film, took as its premise a competition to find the 'World's Filthiest People' and featured the now legendary closing shots of Divine feasting on freshly passed poodle shit. Although Waters never again plumbed the depths of degeneracy achieved with *Pink Flamingos*, he has remained true to his kitsch vision of a Baltimore populated by devotees of trashy glamour and who perform acts of capricious criminality. In *Female Trouble* (1975), Divine – who in this movie must surely have achieved the distinction of being the only actor to have been cast as both victim and perpetrator of the same rape – plays Dawn Davenport; simultaneously a maternal role model, mugger, glamour model and murderer. *Desperate Living* (1977), the last of Waters' early cycle (and the first not to feature Divine), is a trash fairytale set in a neverland populated by a criminal, lumpen proletariat who are sexual fodder for the sadomasochistic wicked queen. However, Waters conforms to fairytale convention with a happy ending in which the princess is freed from a life of heterosexual misery by a group of lesbian transsexuals.

Given the above, it would seem an idle exercise to offer any solemn criticism of a film-maker who has joyfully gone about the business of lauding the artless aesthetics of trash and who has said that 'someone throwing up at one of his movies would be the equivalent of a standing ovation'. It is for this reason that many of Waters' critics have viewed his move towards a more mainstream audience as signifying something of a betrayal of principles. This shift took its first tentative steps with *Polyester* (1981). Despite certain Waters signifiers including the central casting of Divine and the trashy gimmick of 'Odorama' (which offered the cinema spectator an opportunity to smell the movie by means of screen prompts and a 'scratch 'n' sniff' card) the film eschewed Waters' trademark violence and sexual deviancy in favour of high-camp soap opera. The production values were more agreeable as well and even boasted establishing shots filmed from a tracking helicopter.

Following a six-year sabbatical in which he divided his time between teaching film classes in Baltimore prison, writing film journalism and contributing material for National Lampoon, Waters returned with the bubblegum movie *Hairspray* (1988). For all its concessions to good taste, *Hairspray* is a wonderfully exuberant piece of coy kitsch. Set in a racially segregated 1960s Baltimore, the film recreates the primary-coloured veneer of teenage life set around a local televised dance competition. While the depravity may have gone, the film manages to retain Waters' skewed worldview – most triumphantly through the film's overweight lead (Ricki Lake) winning the dance competition and the love of the local hunk against ghastly hard-bodied opposition. Waters trawled similar teenage territory in his next movie *Cry-Baby* (1990) in which Johnny Depp stars as Wade 'Cry-Baby' Walker the leader of the leather clad 'Drapes' gang. Set in mid-1950s Baltimore, Depp predictably woos the charms of the girl from the right side of the tracks and lures her into a world of 'rampant juvenile delinquency'.

While subtlety will clearly never be Waters' trump card, his next three movies indicate a shift to a more overtly satirical cinema. *Serial Mom* (1994) shows off a full-hearted comic turn from Kathleen Turner as a maternal homemaker who responds to the trifling misdemeanours of her neighbours by killing them. On one hand, the film, which includes one of Turner's victims being clubbed to death with a leg of cooked lamb (for failing to rewind a video tape); another with a phone receiver (for the fashion crime of wearing white shoes after Labor Day), is a typically high-kitsch affair. On the other hand, *Serial Mom* sets out to mock the celebrity status that is given to murders in contemporary America, through such scenarios as a gloriously farcical trial for which the courtroom square is home to a booming *Serial Mom* merchandise stand. *Pecker* (1998), turns its mildly contemptuous lens towards the art establishment through the story of a burger chef-cum-amateur photographer (Edward Furlong), whose naff portfolio of Baltimore's finest disenfranchised becomes the toast of the New York art scene. As with its predecessor, Pecker's conceit is too camp to function as cutting edge satire. Nonetheless the film offers an amusingly tender portrait of blue-collar Baltimore measured against a sweetly virulent swipe at the haughty nocturnes of the New York art world.

Waters' latest film, *Cecil B. DeMented* (2000), stars Melanie Griffith as a Hollywood star who is abducted by a group of activists campaigning against mainstream cinema. Full of industry in-jokes and cheap jibes at the movie-making machine, the film is heavily supplemented by a trademark trash aesthetic and excessive gore. Released to mixed reviews, it may not be his best movie to date but Waters displays a continuing appetite to shock and ridicule.                                                                                              **TT**

# Lance WEILER

When Lance Weiler made *The Last Broadcast* (1998) he was singled out by *Wired* *The Last Broadcast* (1998) magazine as one of the 25 people helping to reinvent entertainment. Co-written, co-directed, and co-produced with Stefan Avalos on a budget of just $900, it was shot on borrowed digital and analogue video cameras, and edited with off-the-shelf Adobe software on a 166MHz PC. Weiler was also the cinematographer, and appears as Locus Wheeler.

Its subject matter is rather appropriate: David Leigh is making a documentary about the mysterious deaths of the hosts of the Public Access show 'Fact or Fiction' who, in order to boost ratings, had put together an expedition into New Jersey's Pine Barrens in search of the mythical Jersey Devil. Despite flawed evidence, Jim Suerd, the sole survivor, is convicted of their murders. When Suerd dies, Leigh receives the mangled remains of the missing last video-tape shot in the Barrens; a magnetic-media restoration specialist promises to reveal the face of the real killer.

The movie raises important epistemological and ontological questions about the implications of data collection and manipulation in the digital age, and the ambiguity surrounding the precise nature of the 'surprise' revelation reinforces Leigh's view of an unknowable world and irrecoverable truth.

After some festival success, Weiler and Avalos formed Wavelength Releasing to facilitate *The Last Broadcast*'s theatrical release. On 23 October 1998, using borrowed equipment, the movie was digitally encoded, beamed via satellite to theatres in Minneapolis, Orlando, Philadelphia, Portland, and Providence, routed through Windows servers, and then digitally projected. Subsequent distribution has been via the Internet and cable modems, as well as more conventional media. **MB**

# Peter WEIR

Peter Weir is one of the few directors working within contemporary Hollywood who makes commercially successful films which are original and unusual in their content. His career is divided into two phases: the Australian and the American. His earlier Australian films are stylistically and narratively inclined towards the abstract and more obviously defined by a European art-house aesthetic. His American films, by contrast, are narratively linear and more commercially biased, yet they often subvert generic conventions and confound expectation. Despite this aesthetic shift, his work is unified by remarkably similar thematic concerns. Each film, to a greater or lesser extent, embodies his interest in cultural myths and dreams, issues of conformity and personal freedom, rites-of-passage, and the idea of alternative realities which exist beneath the apparent surface realities.

Born in Australia in 1944, and having studied arts and law at the University of Sydney, Weir became disillusioned with academia and dropped out to work in his father's real estate business. Inspired by the youth counter-culture of the 1960s, he subsequently travelled around Europe before returning to Sydney to train in television. He directed a number of shorts and documentaries and then progressed to feature films. Primarily a storyteller rather than an effects-driven director, he constantly resists academic labels and maintains that his films should reach the widest possible audience. As a consequence he has sometimes been labelled as middlebrow, criticised for renouncing his Australian roots and selling out to the mainstream.

*The Cars That Ate Paris* (1974) was Weir's first full-length feature film. It charts the experiences of a car crash survivor who realises that the corrupt inhabitants of a small town in New South Wales are deliberately causing accidents in order to strip and steal parts. Combining horror and black comedy, it effectively creates a sense of unease, revealing the dangers that lurk behind an apparently innocuous facade. His next feature, *Picnic at Hanging Rock* (1975), was considered by many to be the film that led the renaissance of the Australian film industry and its reputation as classic still survives today. Set in 1900, it focuses on a party of schoolgirls, some of whom disappear during their visit to a sacred Aboriginal rock. Profoundly affected by the primeval forces of nature, the girls experience the burgeoning of their sexuality and a spiritual freedom which is contrasted to the confining conformity of their academic institution. Although at times a little self-conscious, achieving its soporific, dream-like atmosphere through slow-motion shots, misty photography and pan-piped music, it is nevertheless an intriguingly atmospheric mystery.

More successful outside Australia than within it, *The Last Wave* (1977) afforded Weir more opportunity to explore the dramatic effects of culture clash. Evoking the mythical and spiritual dream-world of the tribal Aborigines to disrupt the order and rationality of contemporary Australian society, the film is replete with symbolic images and unanswered mystery. After *The Plumber* (1979), another film about the disturbance of order, this time made for Australian television, Weir achieved greater international success with *Gallipoli* (1981). Although considered by one critic to be an 'anonymous international picture', it effectively deals with personal issues within the greater context of national concerns. Based on the Anzac landings in the Dardenelles in 1915, where thousands of Australian and New Zealand men were killed during an attempt to provide a diversion for the British, it is a rites-of-passage tale of manhood and lost youth. It is also about the search for a national identity, unencumbered by British imperialism. Described by Weir as his 'graduation' film, it launched the international career of actor Mel Gibson, who went on to star with Sigourney Weaver in the director's first fully-funded American film, *The Year of Living Dangerously* (1982).

Despite being set against a backdrop of Indonesian unrest, *The Year of Living Dangerously* marked a move away from public concerns towards private issues for Weir. The film is more a story of individual love and friendship than one of politics. Like *The Last Wave* it explores a cultural clash, but here the opposition is between the mysticism of the East and the logic of the West. Compared to some of his other work, the ending is unusually upbeat. The journalist figure chooses love and personal fulfilment over social responsibility. Combining eerie music with a noir-inspired voiceover, the film is unusually haunting. Weir's next film, *Witness* (1985), was a success for everyone involved and received eight Academy Award nominations. Harrison Ford altered his Indiana Jones image to play a tough yet sensitive homicide detective. In the process of protecting a young Amish boy who has witnessed a murder he ends up falling in love with his mother. The simplicity of the Amish community is, both visually and spiritually, beautifully contrasted with the shadowy immorality of the encroaching outside world. Incorporating and subverting elements of the western and cop genres, the result is a thought-provoking, atmospheric thriller.

The critical reactions to Weir's next film, *The Mosquito Coast* (1986), were, understandably, not so kind. The protagonist is an inventor who becomes disillusioned with American consumerism and ships his family to the Honduran jungle. Adapted from a Paul Theroux novel, the film is filled with interesting ideas, none of which are adequately explored. When the inventor's plans for a utopian existence fail, he gradually descends into madness, but the lack of tension in the film and its tendency towards self-indulgent melodrama ultimately distance the viewer. Despite its relative failure, Weir's reputation as a commercially viable director was re-established with *Dead Poets Society* (1989). Set in a boys' school in the late 1950s, the film raises the ghost of McCarthyism and, like *Picnic at Hanging Rock*, embodies the central theme of conformity versus freedom. When a new English teacher (played by Robin Williams) arrives at the school, preaching the importance of dreams and individuality, a group of boys are inspired and virtual anarchy ensues. The film ambiguously ends on a note of tragedy and hope as one boy commits suicide and the others bravely swear their allegiance to their teacher and his message of liberation. Although on occasion the film is too emotionally manipulative, it proved Weir's ability to draw out unexpectedly in-depth performances from established comedy stars, a practice he would continue later with Jim Carrey in *The Truman Show* (1998).

His next film, *Green Card* (1990), which he wrote as well as directed, was a modern re-working of the 1930s and 1940s screwball comedies. Continuing the theme of culture clash, its heroine's self-imposed order and constraint are shattered when she enters a marriage of convenience with a sensual, free-spirited Frenchman. *Fearless* (1993), undeservedly, did not do well at the box office. Centring on the after-effects of a plane crash on two survivors, its abstract themes of death and renewal proved too sobering and thought-provoking for most audiences. Despite some unevenness in the second half, the film's allusive symbolism and religious connotation, together with Jeff Bridges' haunting and compelling central performance, make it an absorbing viewing experience.

For its mix of drama and humour, Weir has cited Stanley Kubrick's *Dr Strangelove* (1965) as the inspiration for *The Truman Show*. The film is about a television show that is broadcast live to a global audience, seven days a week, twenty-four hours a day. Its protagonist is unaware of his celebrity status and dreams of adventure and freedom from the constraints imposed by his small-town environment. As much a rites-of-passage story as a media satire, it charts the gradual process by which he comes to realise that there is an alternate reality existing beneath the apparent surface of phenomena. The boldness of the film's concept foregrounds most of Weir's thematic preoccupations: the potential oppression of conformity, the need for individual aspiration and the notion of shifting realities.

The enormous critical and commercial success of *The Truman Show* has consolidated Weir's reputation as an original, innovative director working within the Hollywood mainstream. He is currently in production with *The Far Side of the World*, based on Patrick O'Brian's novel 'Master and Commander', starring Russell Crowe as Captain Jack Aubrey and Paul Bettany as Dr Stephen Maturin.          **HP**

# Chris & Paul WEITZ

In the brief span of their young careers, brothers Chris (born in 1970) and Paul (born in 1966) Weitz are already notable for two things: co-writing the computer-animated bug adventure, *Antz* (1998), and revivifying the long-dormant teen sex comedy genre with *American Pie* (1999). While both directed the lowbrow but good-hearted *Pie*, which details the hi-jinx of four high-school males who make a pact to lose their virginity by graduation, strict Director's Guild of America regulations make it especially difficult for first-time helmers to receive joint credit. As a result, Paul was acknowledged as the sole director of their debut, with Chris rather ungenerously demoted to co-producer.

Built around a series of bawdy sight gags (a *Suspicion*-styled sequence involving an ejaculate-laced beer, a graphic sexual encounter with the title pastry), the film's most obvious structural antecedent is the string of smutty practical jokes in Bob Clark's *Porky's* (1981), an admitted influence. But the brothers, while delivering on the genre's required dosage of nudity and slapstick, mark their picture with a tone of sexual frankness and tarnished innocence, not to mention a refreshing lack of misogyny, that places it closer in spirit to Martha Coolidge's *Valley Girl* (1983) and Amy Heckerling's *Fast Times at Ridgemont High* (1982).

Undistinguished visually, what sets *Pie* in this company is its evenhandedness with regard to its female protagonists. Familiar stock characters all – from the horny exchange student and the slut-in-geek's-clothing, to the lusty older woman and the sexually-cautious 'good girl' – they ultimately (and realistically) call the shots in relation to their various men. Paul and Chris smartly direct their actors with an eye towards naturalism rather than caricature, particularly in the touchingly emotional and raucously comic pay-offs of the film's climactic deflowering sequence.

They stepped out from behind the camera to appear, to humorous effect, in director Miguel Arteta and screenwriter/star Mike White's squirmy indie comedy *Chuck & Buck* (2000). Chris co-stars as Chuck, the former childhood friend that Buck (White) obsesses over and eventually stalks. When Buck later turns his unrequited affections into the thinly-veiled basis for a play, Paul makes an appearance as the dim-witted actor hired to portray Chuck's onstage alter-ego.

Their next production was the long-delayed, reportedly troubled *Down To Earth* (2001), and the first film to credit the brothers as co-directors. A racially-centred remake of both *Here Comes Mr. Jordan* (1941) and *Heaven Can Wait* (1978), *Earth* stars Chris Rock as a black comic who is accidentally killed, sent to heaven, and gets another chance to live when he is returned to earth in the form of a white, middle-aged millionaire. Reported artistic conflicts between the directors and Rock delayed the film's post-production schedule, and while the end result displays some of the same good-hearted humanism that distinguished their first effort, the picture is muddled at best.

After co-producing (but not co-directing) the stale *American Pie 2* (2001), they were unlikely candidates for their next and best picture, an adaptation of British author Nick Hornby's biting comic novel 'About a Boy'. The film stars Hugh Grant as Will, a charmingly caddish bachelor who adopts the notion of inventing an infant son so he can date single mothers, a plan that backfires when he finds himself becoming unlikely friends with twelve-year-old Marcus (Nicholas Hoult). Adapted by the brothers along with Peter Hedges, *About a Boy* (2001) lifts great chunks of Hornby's wry first-person narrative for both the Grant and Hoult characters, delivered in dueling voice-overs that cleverly counterpoint the visuals. Visually, the film is their most accomplished work to date, especially in a recurring motif that depicts the shallow, self-involved Will reflected in a series of mirrors, and events are tugged along by a buoyant pop song underscore by Badly Drawn Boy that invokes both *Breakfast at Tiffany's* (1961) and *The Graduate* (1967). *Boy* can also be linked thematically to *American Pie* in its clear-eyed depiction of lost young men and their relations with no-nonsense women – among others, Toni Collette as Marcus' mother and Rachel Weisz as Will's eventual paramour – as well as the brothers' humanistic approach to its flawed but likeable characters.　　**CS**

# David WELLINGTON

With only a few feature films to his credit, film-maker David Wellington has established himself as one of the most innovative young directors to emerge in the wake of the so-called Canadian New Wave. Like the works of his contemporaries Guy Maddin and

Patricia Rozema, Wellington's films centre on the lives and experiences of outsiders *Long Day's Journey Into Night* (1996) and misfits, but do so in such a way as to make these characters both sympathetic and understandable.

Born in 1963 in Montreal, Wellington is a graduate of the film programme at Concordia University and of the director's programme at the Canadian Film Centre in Toronto. In addition to his feature film work he has directed several commercials and short films, including *Nostalgia*, *Killing Time*, *Three Steps to Heaven*, and *Junk Shop*, and in television, directing episodes of the series 'The Hidden Room'.

Wellington's first feature, *The Carpenter* (1989), defies easy classification. It is the story of a young couple whose dream home is haunted by the spirit of the carpenter who began building it, but died before its completion. Instead of focusing exclusively on the more horrific aspects of the plot, *The Carpenter* also explores the troubled relationship between the young husband and wife, suggesting that doubt and mistrust can be far more destructive than the stuff of our nightmares.

Wellington's second feature, *I Love a Man in Uniform* (1993), tells the story of Henry Adler (Tom McCamus), a mild-mannered bank clerk who moonlights as an actor on a reality-based television series. Henry's inability to cope with the violence and disrespect he sees around him leads him to take on the identity of his television character, Officer Flanagan. He steals his uniform from the costume department and begins to walk a nightly beat. Before long, Henry becomes a swaggering, contemptuous cop who speaks in TV show cliches. Soon he discovers a formerly hidden world of corruption and murder that confronts him with the incontrovertible truth that life isn't like the movies. *I Love a Man in Uniform* has been widely discussed in film studies and Canadian studies circles for its depiction of the identity crises that arise in the wake of the monopolisation of Canada's entertainment and cultural industries by American images and interests.

Wellington's third feature takes a decidedly different direction. An adaptation of Eugene O'Neill's play, *Long Day's Journey Into Night* (1996) transforms the classic story of a dysfunctional family into an exercise in desperation and claustrophobia. Tom McCamus, the star *of I Love A Man In Uniform*, stands out in the role of Edmund. The film received limited distribution and played at several festivals, but reached its largest audience on broadcast television.

Wellington's latest film, which was made for television, *Restless Spirits* (1999), takes the real-life story of two French aviators as a point of departure. In 1927, Lieutenant Charles Nungesser (Lothaire Bluteau) and his navigator François Coli (Michael Monty) leave Paris with the hopes of beating Charles Lindbergh in his race across the Atlantic. After a promising start the two disappear in a fog somewhere off the coast of North America and their plane is never found. Wellington's film turns history into legend by having the two aviators be doomed to endlessly re-attempt their flight each time the fog returns. It is finally only with the help of a young girl (Juliana Wimbles) that the two restless spirits are finally able to succeed in their mission and end their eternal torment. **RC**

# Audrey WELLS

Born in San Francisco in 1961, Audrey Wells earned her reputation in Hollywood as a *Guinevere* (1999) screenwriter. After working as an uncredited writer for *Jumanji* (1995), she wrote *The Truth About Cats and Dogs* (1996), a successful and charming romantic comedy for which she was also the executive producer. Her proven ability to write smart screenplays that appeal to general audiences led her to co-write *George of the Jungle* (1997) and *Runaway Bride* (1999), both grossing more than $100 million at the US box office.

Following those successes, Wells wrote and directed her first feature film for Miramax Studios, *Guinevere* (1999). The movie is a departure for Wells, who had previously written only fantasies and comedies. By contrast, *Guinevere* is a romantic drama that soberly and uncompromisingly explores a love affair between a young Harvard law student and an indigent photographer nearly twice her age. With *Guinevere*, Wells shows that she is not only a promising new director but also a writer of impressive depth and versatility, talents that were noticed at Sundance, where the film earned her the 1999 Waldo Salt Screenwriting Award.

The film's so-called unconventional romance between an older man and younger woman generated some controversy among critics who believed the film perpetuated a discriminatory Hollywood practice of casting attractive young women opposite older leading men, thus excluding female actors over forty from provocative roles. These critics faulted *Guinevere* for sheepishly conforming to the industry's conservative gender codes and compared the casting decision to such mainstream contemporaneous films as *Entrapment* (1999). Though Wells attempted to examine the relationship's complexities in earnest, *Guinevere* was overshadowed by a casting gimmick that led to both absurd and melodramatic situations. Other critics, however, approved of the casting, arguing that it was motivated by neither marketing strategies nor a deeper Hollywood prejudice. Unlike blockbusters that exploit sex appeal, Wells portrays the May-December romance unglamorously, creating an intellectual *Bildungsroman* instead of a degrading sex tale.

Having written *The Kid* (2000) for Walt Disney Pictures, Wells is currently directing *Only Game for Grownups*, a comedy about a group of young people working on a congressional campaign that she co-wrote with Rafal Zielinski. Continuing her active screenwriting career, Wells is also co-writing *Golden Gate Bridge* with Will Richter, to be produced by Imagine Entertainment.　　　　　　　　　　　　　　　　　**JPa**

# Simon WELLS

An American Tail: Fievel Goes West (1991)
We're Back! A Dinosaur's Story (1993)
Balto (1995)
The Prince of Egypt (1998)
Casper 2 (1999)
The Time Machine (2002)

A graduate of De Montfort University in the UK, Simon Wells has made extraordinary progress in the animation industry, now consolidating his place as one of the key figures in the development of animated films at DreamWorks SKG, the studio brainchild of Steven Spielberg, ex-Disney executive Jeffrey Katzenberg, and music industry mogul David Geffen.

Having begun his career working with university colleagues on the first fully computer-generated children's television series, 'Reboot', he quickly found a place with the Amblin division working on *Who Framed Roger Rabbit* (1988), where he took on the role of supervising animator. Having established himself with this project, he then co-directed the first fully animated features released by Spielberg's Ambimation Studio: *An American Tail: Fievel Goes West* (1991), *We're Back* (1993), and *Balto* (1995).

*Balto* is the extraordinary story of a real dog named Balto, who pulled a sled over fifty miles to Nome, Alaska in February 1925, to bring anti-toxins to an ailing community. Wells' impressive use of the emergent Softimage CGI packages brought variety to the designs of snow-covered landscapes, which enhanced the sense of Balto's epic struggle against the elements, Steele (a jealous dog), and his own self-doubt about being a mongrel breed of half-dog, half-wolf.

Wells – and co-directors Brenda Chapman and Steve Hickner – can already count *The Prince of Egypt* (1998) as a masterpiece in the animated feature film. Although controversial in its subject matter, the film is a tour de force which combines technical dexterity and innovation, with a full commitment to the adult-orientation of the material, resisting the pressures to succumb to the modern conventions of feature animation – animal characters, gags and songs of romantic yearning. Wells insisted that the film must not retreat from the pivotal moment when Moses kills the guard who is marshalling the brutalities of Hebrew slavery. Portraying this, in itself, is crucial in setting a tone for the film, which ultimately embraces murder, plague, and exodus. However, this creative decision, along with the contrivance that Moses, voiced by Val Kilmer, and Rameses, voiced by Ralph Fiennes, play out a sibling rivalry that may be read as a tension between Jewish and Egyptian imperatives are at the heart of the criticism levelled at the film.

Jeffrey Katzenberg, the executive producer of the film – in the light of the debates that previously surrounded *Aladdin* (1992) – anticipated potential difficulties, and consulted Rev Jesse Jackson, preacher Billy Graham, Rabbi Marvin Hier, and Michel Shehadeh (of the Anti-American Anti-Discrimination Centre), the latter of whom pronounced the film as 'a human rights film against repression'. Katzenberg also showed the film to 75 cardinals at the Vatican, and gained the approval of the Jewish intellectual magazine 'Tikkun' when Rabbi Michael Lerner pronounced the film 'an outstanding contribution to the task of reintroducing Torah to the world'. All to no avail, alas, as leading Egyptian journalists like Adel Hammouda of *al Ahram*, accused DreamWorks SKG of making a Jewish revisionist history of ancient Egypt by implying Moses ruled Egypt, was the architect of its civilisation, and that the people were punished after the Jewish exodus, in essence, because they were left with no value or worth. Egyptian film director Hani Lashin also called it 'poison-laced chocolate': 'It is very nice and we are hungry, but we must tell the people not to eat it', implying that the film was technically brilliant but sent an inappropriate, and indeed, potentially censorable message. On this basis, Malaysia and the Maldives banned the film as offensive to Muslims.

If nothing else, the fact that an animated feature, previously regarded as merely 'a second cousin' to live-action cinema, or merely children's entertainment, can raise such high levels of debate is a testament to Wells' endeavour in itself. The fact that it also progresses the art of animation must also be fully acknowledged.

Wells' most recent film *The Time Machine* (2002), an adaptation of H. G. Wells' classic science fiction novel, has had a lukewarm reception despite the presence of Guy Pearce and Jeremy Irons. **PW**

# Wim WENDERS

Born in Düsseldorf in 1945, Wim Wenders is a leading member of the diverse and relatively loose co-operative of German film-makers who began their work in the mid to late 1960s, and became known collectively as the *Neues deutsches Kino* or the New German Cinema. Whilst not appearing to share any of this group's ideological agendas, for which he faced sharp criticism from some of his colleagues, Wenders looked to the cinema as an instrument capable of helping to return a sense of identity to Germany, a nation still under shock in the post-war years. Wenders' became a *film*-political and *film*-ideological stance characterised by an almost fanatical love of images and a consistent refusal to allow narrative any more presence than as a rudimentary frame for the presentation of images. Wenders' filmography includes all genres and formats, but he probably remains best known for his road movies, for the atmospheric images and music soundtracks that dominate his films, and for the simplicity of his narratives.

With initial academic courses in medicine and philosophy in 1964–65, Wenders' career could have taken a different direction altogether. However, he broke off his studies to join the first film class at Munich's Film and Television Academy in 1967. Wenders graduated from film school in 1970 with his first feature *Summer in the City (Dedicated to The Kinks)* (1970), which essentially compresses all the elements of the previous shorts into a more coherent but still minimalist, slow-paced, episodic narrative structure. Hans (Hans Zischler), the main protagonist, is on the run from some unknown and unseen criminal associates. His solitary flight from Munich to Berlin and finally to America is emblematic of the road movie elements introduced in the shorts and that typify Wenders' work at least until 1989, combined with Hitchcock-inspired suspense devices and an active suppression of narrative development.

Also peppered with Hitchcockian suspense devices is Wenders' first commercial production, *The Goalkeeper's Fear of the Penalty Kick* (1971). This unspectacular road movie repeats the searching motifs of its predecessor. Originally conceived as a television film, it won its director the Film Critics' Prize at Venice in 1972.

Wenders' second made-for-television movie in 1972, *The Scarlet Letter*, based on Nathaniel Hawthorne's novel of the same title, proved to be a disappointment for Wenders, for whom the historical setting was so far removed from the real world that the capabilities of the filmic medium as a commentator of time risked being compromised. Thematically, Wenders might have been encouraged by the novel's isolation motif, as Esther Prynne, the main protagonist, is cast out by her village for adultery and forced to wear a scarlet letter 'A' for 'adulteress' on her breast.

*Alice in the Cities* (1974) is the film that brought Wenders international attention as an independent director, constituting also a breakthrough from the point of view of Wenders establishing a personal aesthetic. Philip Winter (Rüdiger Vogler), is a journalist who accepts the responsibility of looking after a young girl, Alice (Yella Rottländer) for a few days, and learns a lot about himself as he accompanies her from New York to Amsterdam, then through half of Germany, seeing the world through Alice's eyes. Alice is the first in a string of child characters in Wenders' movies to whom Wenders ascribes a particularly pure visual perception, describing this kind of perception as 'the eyes I would wish for my films'. *Alice* also represents the beginning of a more critical approach to Americana, which had until then been a primary source of inspiration for Wenders.

The following two films, *Wrong Move* (1975) and *Kings of the Road* (1976) are generally considered to form a trilogy with *Alice*, due to the travel motif and the use of the same lead actor, Rüdiger Vogler. *Wrong Move*, based on Peter Handke's adaptation of Goethe's epic novel 'Wilhelm Meister's Apprenticeship', was described by the *Süddeutsche Zeitung* as the most important post-war German film. It follows the voyage of a middle-class hero on the fruitless search for an artistic and personal identity, exposing on its way the depressive and grey reality of life in the provinces and the city suburbs. *Kings of the Road* opens with a dramatic suicide trip into a river and ends on a much more optimistic note at the end of a journey along the East German/West German border from one provincial cinema to the next in a removals truck. The film is a statement on the predicament of provincial cinemas in Germany in the 1970s, which were forced by the mainly US-controlled distributors to show mostly commercial and pornographic material. At the end of the film the camera rises up from street level to see the demoralised Winter tearing up his itinerary, but a ray of hope is suggested in the reflection in the window of his truck's cab of the initials of the director, Wim Wenders, suggesting there is hope for the cinema and that Wenders will be instrumental in securing its future.

Based on Patricia Highsmith's novel 'Ripley's Game', *The American Friend* (1977) is one of Wenders' most consciously genre-driven films in that it allows the plot a much stronger presence than any of the previous films, has internationally known stars (Dennis Hopper and Nicholas Ray), and contains the unmistakable motifs of any typical gangster or noir film. Thematically, however, the film is far from a gangster movie: instead, Wenders attempts to express the potential dangers he perceives to be posed by American cultural domination in Europe. Tom Ripley is a shady art dealer who deals in the paintings of a presumably dead artist (who is in fact alive and well, living in New York). His glamorous jet-set lifestyle attracts Jonathan (Bruno Ganz) and induces him to accept an assassination job for the Mafia, for which he, a family man with a small business in Hamburg, seems wholly unsuited. Yet the fascination holds him and this drives Jonathan to his death.

In 1977, Wenders went to Hollywood to work on a Francis Coppola production, an adaptation of Joe Gores' novel 'Hammett'. Set in the 1930s, *Hammett* (1982) stars Frederic Forrest as the ex-detective turned crime novelist Dashiell Hammett, who is dragged into a new case by an old colleague. This visually stylistic movie is a reflection on writing and experiencing stories, and on the fascination of the classic B-movie. Wenders complained that the American modes of production were detrimental to his artistic identity and to the quality of the end product, but more recently he has admitted to 'quite liking' the film.

More interesting than *Hammett* are perhaps the films Wenders made 'on the side' and partly in reaction to the problems he had working with Coppola. In the striking and hard-hitting *Nick's Film: Lightning Over Water* (1979), Wenders turned to his early idol Nicholas Ray for inspiration from one who had succeeded as an outsider in Hollywood. *The State of Things* ('*Der Stand der Dinge*' (1982)) is a bitter re-telling of the experience with Coppola in which Friedrich Munro (Patrick Bachau), a European director for whom 'stories only exist in stories', makes a movie in black and white using American cash and is murdered by the shady backers who insist on colour and a story for a commercial success. This is perhaps Wenders' darkest movie, expressing the dilemma he felt he was in at the time, but it earned him a Golden Lion at Venice 1982.

Wenders' next film, *Paris, Texas* (1984), was an attempted answer to those who began demanding stronger story in his films. With a cast including Harry Dean Stanton, Nastassja Kinski, and Dean Stockwell, a script by Sam Shepard, an opening sequence in the familiar and classic western setting of Monument Valley in the south-west of the USA, and with an atmospheric soundtrack by blues guitarist Ry Cooder, this film offers a lot that the average American cinema-goer could recognise. Consequently, *Paris, Texas* was one of Wenders' biggest commercial successes. The film follows Travis Henderson (Stanton), yet another solitary hero from the desert to Los Angeles, where he is re-united with his lost son Hunter (Hunter Carson), and then, together with Hunter, to Houston in Texas, where they find Jane (Kinski), Travis' wife and Hunter's mother, working in a peep-show. Travis returns Hunter to Jane at the rather over-emotional end of the movie, and then disappears back into the night. Again, the subtext of the movie – a comment on the power of images to degrade (Travis had an image of Jane as a whore when they still lived together, which she effectively became) – is more important than its banal love story.

The next film, *Wings of Desire* (1987) vies with its predecessor for the status as Wenders' best-known work. The film takes up the theme of Germany's division after World War Two in Berlin, the city where the scars of division remain most visible, to use it as a metaphor for the evils of division in general. Damiel and Cassiel, the two main characters, are angels through whose eyes we see the city. On one of his daily flights of discovery Damiel encounters a circus performer named Marion (Solveig Dommartin) with whom he falls in love. But he is an angel and can neither touch nor speak to her. By some divine will Damiel manages to 'fall' to earth as a human, where he discovers that there are other ex-angels moving around the city (most notably Peter Falk playing himself), and then finds Marion, who makes a poetic declaration of love for him in a long, drawn-out speech at the end of the film. The film makes the suggestion that language provides the key to the healing of divisions – of man and woman, East and West, black and white and colour, modern and postmodern, and so on – and can serve as a model for a cinema able to reach out to people in the media age. *Wings of Desire* won Wenders the Best Director prize at Cannes.

In 1989 Wenders finally got to work on a mammoth project he had been planning since 1977 when Coppola had called him away to America: *Until the End of the World* (1992). Set in 1999–2000, the film warns of the potential dangers of images if they are allowed to invade every aspect of life. The film follows a group of characters in pursuit of Sam Farber (William Hurt), a presumed criminal, around the globe. Farber stole a device invented by his father Henry Farber (Max von Sydow), which was then appropriated by the CIA, that enables the visualisation of brain patterns on monitors. Approximately half-way through the four-hour-long released version, a nuclear communications satellite crashes to earth, knocking out all electromagnetic systems and leaving the main characters stranded in the Australian desert. Somehow they all come together at Henry Farber's laboratory where Sam is eagerly awaited. First experiments in conveying Sam's collected images to his blind mother (Jeanne Moreau) succeed, but when she dies, sad after seeing her family for the first time since her childhood, the equipment is converted to record the dreams of the two main characters, Sam and Claire Tourneur (Solveig Dommartin), to which they become addicted. In the end, older art forms like aboriginal paintings and stories seem to provide the cure for the illness of images.

Along with Peter Greenaway's *Prospero's Books* (1991), *Until the End of the World* is the first film in which HDTV, a digital imaging technology, was used for image manipulation in a film (in the dream sequences). The beautiful musical accompaniment features internationally known artists such as U2, Talking Heads, and Peter Gabriel, and many of those who have seen the full six-hour version consider it a masterpiece.

Wenders' next film, *Faraway, So Close* (1992), is a sequel to *Wings of Desire*, again set in Berlin after the Wall had fallen. Most of the original actors make a second appearance but times had changed, Germany was no longer divided, and the film met with a mostly negative critical response.

This was followed by another small film, commissioned by the Portuguese Government for the Expo '98 in Lisbon, *Lisbon Story* (1994). Originally conceived as a pure documentary, this film became an exploration of the city of Lisbon through the eyes (and ears) of a sound engineer, Philip Winter, who goes to help a friend finish his film in Lisbon. In 1995, Wenders co-directed the disappointing *Beyond the Clouds* with the now frail Michelangelo Antonioni, and directed *A Trick of the Light*, a touching short documentary on the Skladanovsky brothers, co-inventors of cinema.

Wenders' next feature project was *The End of Violence* (1997), set in Los Angeles and starring Bill Pullman and Andie McDowell: a haunting meditation on violence in life and art. Mike Max (Pullman), a successful producer of sex-and-violence movies, realises the error of his ways when he is kidnapped, narrowly escaping execution. The plot device, in which an image accidentally caught on camera is gradually manipulated until it reveals the kidnapping, is strongly reminiscent of the central premise of Michelangelo Antonioni's *Blow-Up* (1966). The film is a visually arresting drama built around seemingly unrelated characters who Wenders gradually links in surprising ways.

In 1999, Wenders directed the most commercially successful documentary in German film history, *Buena Vista Social Club*, following a group of legendary Cuban soneros from the 1930s, 1940s, and 1950s, through the streets of Havana and into their homes. The group then give immensely successful concerts organised by Ry Cooder in Amsterdam and New York's Carnegie Hall. The concerts were the first time this perfectly suited, yet almost coincidentally formed group – average age over eighty – would perform on the same stage.

Wenders' latest film, *The Million Dollar Hotel* (1999) – scripted by Nicholas Klein, Wenders, and U2 singer Bono in their fourth collaboration – is Wenders' third independent American production in a row, and is again set in Los Angeles. In this circularly structured tale, beginning and ending with the suicide of its hero Tom Tom (Jeremy Davies), an almost Shakespearean ensemble of crazies, jokers, whores, alcoholics, and junkies who reside in an actual LA hotel of that name become involved in a separate murder investigation, which turns out to have been the suicide of another of their lot, Izzy (Tim Roth), an artist and billionaire's son. The FBI special agent (Mel Gibson) investigating the case gets nowhere as he tries to play the hotel residents against one another to find the alleged killer. Tom Tom, Izzy's best friend, falls in love with Izzy's girlfriend, the seemingly autistic but captivatingly beautiful Eloise (Milla Jovovich), to whom he confesses to having stood by as Izzy jumped to his death from the roof of the hotel. Yet, as with the other movies, the plot is not as important or as present as its atmosphere, its images and its music. The subtext is a statement about the search for sensation in modern media, and how this can affect artistic production and the appreciation of art in the public eye, especially in reference to cinematic production.

Wenders is currently working on two projects, a pseudo-documentary, *Vill Passiert*, on the German rock band BAP, and another road movie to be shot in the USA.  **AG**

# Simon WEST

<table>
<tr><td>Con Air (1997)</td></tr>
<tr><td>The General's Daughter<br>(1999)</td></tr>
<tr><td>Tomb Raider (2001)</td></tr>
</table>

With a professed love of David Lean and Stanley Kubrick, one a true-blue Brit and one an adopted son, it is a shame that fellow countryman Simon West has eschewed his heroes' flair and depth for a shallow visual style. Born in London in 1961, West directed several well-known television commercials and music videos, before he embarked upon his feature film career.

This is evident in his debut, *Con Air* (1997), for the dialogue, when it can be heard, is sharp and witty. As a graduate of the Jerry Bruckheimer school of cinema (loud and then louder still, as in *Beverly Hills Cop* (1984), *Days of Thunder* (1990), *Crimson Tide* (1995)), the film centres on Nicolas Cage as a tough parolee who joins forces with the police when his plane is hijacked by a group of master criminals led by John Malkovich. With an eclectic cast (including established character actors John Cusack, Steve Buscemi, and Ving Rhames) and thumping visuals, the film may fail on basic levels of cohesion and believability, but provides the audience with a sensory trip that ups the ante on every previous film in this genre. Indeed, Bruckheimer is arguably the auteur here – *Con Air* mixes the dogged earnestness of his earlier 1980s films with a knowing, self-reflexive humour typical of the visceral type of cinema that followed the release of *Pulp Fiction* (1994). The film seems to revel in its own absurdities and does little to deny it, inviting us to buy into such hyperkineticism with lines like 'Somehow they managed to get every creep and freak in the universe on this one plane'.

At least his next feature, *The General's Daughter* (1999), allows women to share some screen time with West's testosterone-charged misogynists. CID officials, played by John Travolta and Madeleine Stowe, investigate the murder of a war hero's daughter. Predictably, the investigation runs up against all manner of obstruction, suspicion, and closed ranks. It is a well-made thriller that at least allows the audience to pause for breath, but the death of Elisabeth Campbell is so gruesomely framed that the film is tinged with an unwarranted sordidness and voyeurism. Admittedly, West's visual flair creates a gloomy Gothic feel, which is similar to film noir in its use of light and shadow, and he again proves adept at choreographing verbal sparring. With a little help from Academy Award-winning writer William Goldman, he films the conversation with Travolta and James Woods as a cross between a sex scene and a title fight.

His most recent release, *Tomb Raider* (2001), stars Angelina Jolie as the eponymous computer game heroine and has proved West's biggest commercial earner to date ($120 million and rising). It is a hybrid of *Indiana Jones* and the classic 'shoot-'em-up' laced with a strong feminist undercurrent. West's affinity with the film is obvious – he rejected the chance to direct *Erin Brockovich* (2000) – and he treats the narrative with a kind of stolid earnestness that avoids tongue-in-cheek humour and pays due reverence to the game's original aesthetic. Full of swooping tracking shots, balletic gunfights and CGI visuals, *Tomb Raider*'s charged narrative almost papers over the generic deficiencies (lack of a 'boo-hiss' villain, woolly backstory, confusing Macguffin) but lacks the kind of characterisation and intricate plot that *Raiders of the Lost Ark* (1981) provided in spades. Still, *Tomb Raider* is a competent addition to West's portfolio, combining a slick action adventure with some astute casting. What the film misses in consistency is tempered somewhat by the joyful laddishness of it all – gadgets, end-of-level baddies, and Jolie, all cleavage and collagen.

West in currently in pre-production on a big-screen adaptation of the 1960s cult television series 'The Prisoner'. **BM**

# Anne WHEELER

Since the mid-1980s Anne Wheeler has made a niche for herself as a director – and sometimes writer and producer – of features with a particular range of feelings and subject matter. All of them are marked to at least some degree by a strong social conscience, appeals for tolerance of difference and co-operation, a kind of practical feminism and a resolutely optimistic standpoint which tries to find something positive in even the most painful situations. She has shown an affinity for period settings (especially the 1940s and 1950s), often gravitating towards family subjects – though these are by no means the basis of all of her work. She has also consistently demonstrated an ability to get the very best out of actors, especially very young or inexperienced ones.

*Loyalties* (1986)
*Cowboys Don't Cry* (1988)
*Bye Bye Blues* (1989)
*Angel Square* (1990)
*Better Than Chocolate* (1999)
*Marine Life* (2000)
*Suddenly Naked* (2001)

Born In Canada in 1946, Wheeler first made her mark as a film-maker in her native Edmonton during the late 1970s making documentaries and short fiction films, often in association with the North West branch of the National Film Board of Canada. The culmination of her activity as a documentarist was *A War Story* (1981), an 82-minute film based on the diaries kept by her late father in a Japanese POW camp, which had voiceover readings by Donald Sutherland, black and white re-enactments, and interviews with camp survivors. It concluded with brief home movies from the postwar era, featuring the subject himself. A restrained but very moving and personal work, *A War Story* shows a creative approach to documentary form and remains one of Wheeler's best films – perhaps still her most powerful one.

After this she moved exclusively towards fiction film, first with a number of short subjects, and finally to features, with *Loyalties* (1986). This Canada/UK co-production, much admired by critic Robin Wood, stages conflicts of gender, race and class in a story of a middle-class English family which resettles in a small town in Alberta and comes into contact with aspects of Native culture. The 'loyalties' of the title are those of sisterhood and human solidarity, which win a hard-fought battle against the cultural conditioning of traditional patriarchal and class values.

*Cowboys Don't Cry* (1988) was based on the well-known 'young adults' novel by Marilyn Halvorson and deals with a rodeo cowboy and his teenaged son, who are trying to cope with the loss of their wife/mother while settling some personal issues and trying to make a new start in life. This very good little family melodrama, like so many of Wheeler's films, features excellent performances from a unstarry cast and a fine eye for the nuances of human relationships. Wheeler's next feature was *Bye Bye Blues* (1989), a period story in which she fictionalised her mother's life as a wartime wife taking up a career as an itinerant musician to support her family while her husband languished as a POW. This engaging film is at its best in capturing the sharply-focused details of time and place in rural Alberta during World War Two, and in its understated observation of many secondary characters and relationships.

*Angel Square* (1990), based on Brian Doyle's novel, is a film in the classic mold for and about pre-adolescent children. Again a period piece, it is set in an unspecified bilingual Canadian city during the late 1940s, and follows the adventures of a boy besotted with World War Two action comics who tries to solve a case of assault on the father of one of his friends. Then came three features for CBC television. *The Diviners* (1993) is a fine adaptation of Margaret Laurence's novel, a canonic pillar of Canadian literature which follows the life of a Manitoba woman from youth to middle age, and features a commanding central performance from Sonja Smits. *The War Between Us* (1995) is a sensitive study of Japanese-Canadians displaced to a small town in the BC interior during World War Two, while *The Sleep Room* (1998) deals with the inmate-victims of a CIA program of experimentation with psychotropic drugs in a Montreal psychiatric institution during the 1950s and the lawsuit it gave rise to decades later.

*Better Than Chocolate* (1999) is a wholesome comedy about lesbian sex, centring on the amorous adventures of a double brace of young practising or aspiring lesbians – an artist, the owner and an employee of a gay/lesbian bookstore, and a transsexual. They meet the challenges of parental and social barriers with energy and optimism, and all grimmer or more conflicted perspectives are happily elided in the prevailing stream of positive thinking and cheerful welcoming of difference. Whether one finds the result funny and heartwarming or rather facile is a matter of personal predisposition, but there is no doubting the film's thematic kinship with Wheeler's whole output, or the skill with which it is fashioned.

She has since made *Marine Life* (2000), which is based on a collection of short stories and traces the affair between a middle-aged singer (Cybill Shepherd) and a younger man and explores the impact on her teenage daughter. *Suddenly Naked* (2001), her most recent feature, is based on a similar premise, the relations between an older successful female writer and a much younger male writer.    **WB**

## Forest WHITAKER

Born in Texas in 1961, Forest Whitaker is probably best known for his work as a character actor, particularly in Neil Jordan's *The Crying Game* (1992). After studying Music at the Pomona College, University of South California, he began his acting career on stage in the US and London, and made his film debut in 1982. However, despite his prolific and varied acting career, little could have prepared the viewer for his directorial debut, *Waiting to Exhale* (1995).

Constructed as a multi-star vehicle shaped around the personae of Whitney Houston, Angela Bassett, Loretta Devine, and Lela Rochon, the film is an embarrassing display of soft-focus and slow motion camera, with a haunting soundtrack provided by Houston. A gallery of ludicrous male characters seem to reverse the politically correct effect of an all-black cast by hinting that all black men are rascals. The film, which begins as a parable about friendship and the bonds between women who share problems and a minority identity, completely abandons any attempt to explore their troubles and ultimately reduces their lives to a glamorous tale of success. Unfortunately, Whitaker's penchant for sentimentality and trouble-free gloss did not abate after his first effort.

In 1998 he teamed up with actress-producer Sandra Bullock for another star vehicle, *Hope Floats*. Again, the qualities of the cast – Gena Rowlands as Bullock's mother and Mae Whitman as her daughter – cannot make up for the old-fashioned style (abundant use of soft-focus and soft colour filters) or the ludicrous storyline. A common fault in Whitaker's film-making seems to be the overly romantic, simplistic handling of potentially dramatic stories, which reduces them to dullness.    **BP**

## Hype WILLIAMS

Hype Williams (born Harold Wilson) exemplifies the late 1990s MTV rap video. He studied film production at Adelphi University in Long Island, New York before moving to advertising and then on to music videos. Often quoted as wishing he had more competition in his own field Williams has produced some two hundred videos, filled with his trademark use of elaborate colours and a 'bug-eyed' lense, allowing the figures to become part of the overblown fantasy landscapes he creates. Widely regarded as the definitive music video artist, Williams' client list ranges from hardcore rap artists to Chanel.

The conversion to cinema allowed Williams to persevere with the motifs and images that had made his work so unique. Employing a host of hip-hop stars to act in the roles of his first movie, *Belly* (1998), made the experience difficult as the collection of stars battled to make their acting convincing. The piece is patchy, with its strength being outstanding attention to visual styling. The effect is a film made up of several set-pieces which each embody Williams' work in the music video field. The down side is that the plot is allowed to stagnate while the indulgent moments blossom. The movie was panned for the reckless views of drug taking and violence that it battles with, drawing uncomfortable comparisons between American ghettos and Jamaican townships.    **SS**

# Kevin WILLIAMSON

Kevin Williamson was born in New Bern, North Carolina in 1965. Beginning with *Scream* in 1996, there is little doubt that his postmodern, intertextual writing contributed greatly to the resurgence of the teen flick that occurred in the late 1990s. Contemplating generic conventions from an ironic position, his body of writing reads as both hit (*Scream*, *The Faculty* (1998)) and miss (*I Know What You Did Last Summer* (1997)), whilst remaining successful. Clearly taking advantage of this fact, Williamson took the opportunity to control the camera with his directorial debut, *Teaching Mrs. Tingle* (1999).

Sadly, the transition has not been a smooth one, with Williamson appearing to be content with simply going through the motions, resulting in a film that seems to have had very little life injected into it. Those familiar with his work on the hugely successful American television series 'Dawson's Creek' will notice an alarming similarity between the characters in both – Holmes' character in particular feels like little more than an extension of her television alter ego, Joey. What is interesting, however, is the noticeable difference between the theatrical trailer and the eventual release. Arriving in the wake of American high-school shootings, not only was the film renamed (originally titled *Killing Mrs. Tingle*), but there have clearly been a number of significant cuts, and without seeing the director's intended version, it is difficult to know whether these are responsible for the film's lack of atmosphere and suspense. Despite all this, the film remains, as with all of Williamson's work, strangely entertaining, enough to suggest that he could succeed in this new career. Hopefully with his next film, the romantic comedy *Her Leading Man*, another attempt to subvert genre convention in a similar manner to *Scream*, Williamson will be able to present his desired version so that we may make a fairer assessment of his talents. **CP**

# Hugh WILSON

Born in Miami in 1943, Hugh Wilson made his writer-director feature debut in 1984 with the seminal screwball comedy *Police Academy*. With a solid background in television (having won awards for writing 'Frank's Place' and producing and directing 'WKRP Cincinnati'), his seven movie features to date have all been situated within the comedy genre.

Combining a fast-paced flow of set-pieces, coincidental incidents and crass gags, *Police Academy* (1984) features an eclectic bunch of officers who are brought in to the Academy as regulations regarding sex, weight, height, and IQ are phased out. Wilson makes the most of the supporting cast and the abundant comic sound effects at his disposal. His work is reminiscent of the *Carry On* films in that the majority of its humour is based upon a politically incorrect and stereotypical premise. However, this silliness proved to be hugely popular with audiences and prompted a further six features to be made, though Wilson himself did not go on to direct any of them.

Less well-known, Wilson's next feature *Rustler's Rhapsody* (1985) was a spoof on matinée westerns, opening in black and white for a shoot-out parody and then moving to colour. Inoffensive, with infrequent passages of humour, this character-based comedy did not harness the audience appeal of Wilson's debut.

In Wilson's 1987 feature *Burglar*, Whoopi Goldberg is cast as a cat burglar who, upon witnessing a murder, turns detective before she is then blamed for the crime herself. Apart from the occasional instance in which Goldberg is allowed to break into a comic skit, the narrative of this feature has little to offer. Cited by many critics as manufactured and hugely conventional, it is clearly a star vehicle for Goldberg. Additionally disappointing is cinematographer William Fraker's attempt at a high-speed motorbike chase through San Francisco.

The unexpected on-screen pairing of Shirely MacLaine and Nicolas Cage as former first lady and reluctant bodyguard forms the basis of reasonable comedy *Guarding Tess* (1994). The plot of this film is familiar and as in *Driving Miss Daisy* (1989), *The Bodyguard* (1992), and *In the Line of Fire* (1993), features incongruent characters in forced proximity who slowly learn to value and understand each other. It plays itself out with low-key comedy until a farfetched kidnap scenario sends the quality quota plummeting; it is saved only by the performances of the main stars. Wilson's next venture was the 1996 feature *The First Wives Club*, starring Goldie Hawn, Bette Midler, and Diane Keaton as three abandoned wives out for revenge. On attending the funeral of a friend who committed suicide upon being replaced by her husband for a younger model, the threesome vow to procure retribution from their philandering spouses. Thus the cartoonesque humour ensues but sadly loses its pace in the film's second half. However, this was the second of Wilson's films to gross over $100 million, after *Police Academy*.

1999 saw the release of two Wilson films, the first of which was *Blast from the Past*. Having retreated into an underground bunker during the Cuban Missile Crisis, a Californian family emerge in the present day and send their son (Brendan Fraser) in search of food and a companion of the female variety. This film does not exceed the expectations which one might have of a romantic comedy and its attempts to moralise on the lost art of courtesy fall short of what Wilson must have intended. It does, however, remain more watchable than some of his past efforts. His second film of that year, *Dudley Do-Right,* was an adaptation of the comic strip Mountie who takes on a battle of wits (although he does not have many) with a melodramatic villain. The film features Brendan Fraser, in his second appearance in a Wilson project, and Sarah Jessica Parker, who is criminally underused in this role. Aimed at a younger audience, the trademark slapstick gags may prove a little overbearing but *Dudley Do-Right* shows some success where other comic-to-screen features have failed.

Wilson's most recent film, *Mickey* (2002), is a baseball-themed family drama, scripted by John Grisham. The two will collaborate again on an adaptation of 'Skipping Christmas'. **LB**

# Theodore WITCHER

*lovejones* (1997) Theodore Witcher is a young director who has attracted considerable interest with his debut feature. *lovejones* (1997) is a relationship drama involving a group of urban middle-class African-American twentysomethings. The plot is familiar enough, being centred on the 'will-they-or-won't-they' romance that develops between Larenz Tate and Nia Long. But *lovejones* is notable for the director's determination to craft a 'black' story without the rap, gangs, guns, and drugs that for many audiences define African-American cinema.

The violent, nihilistic gangstas and secondary female characters of films such as *New Jack City* (1991) and *Menace 2 Society* (1993) differ from their 1970s blaxploitation antecedents because their actions are placed within a wider political context. Yet violence, crime and drugs are still seen as fixtures in the black urban experience. Witcher deliberately rejects what could be deemed the 'ghettosploitation' genre; his sophisticated young characters are interested in poetry, wine, photography, jazz, reggae and dance. Only 27 when *lovejones* was released, Witcher provocatively relegates rap (frequently used as a soundtrack to the new black cinema) to the car stereo of one of his few unsympathetic characters, a loudmouth sexist. A clear influence here is Spike Lee, whose witty debut, *She's Gotta Have It* (1985), contained the credit 'This film contains no drugs and no jeri curls'. The cinematography of *lovejones* also seems to owe something to Lee's impressive jazz story, *Mo' Better Blues* (1992). *lovejones* looks ravishing, if a little too polished. Although the affluent world featured here is a riposte to the 'hood movies', it looks as seductive as a well-done television advert. Intending to attack preconceptions about what a 'black film' should be, Witcher used Ernest Holzman, who photographed 'thirtysomething', to provide the lush cinematography.

Given this impressive debut, the director's only other credit to date comes as a disappointment. The heist thriller *Body Count* (1998), which was written by Witcher and directed by Robert Patton-Spruill, wastes a great cast (including David Caruso, Ving Rhames, Linda Fiorentino, and Forest Whittaker) and wasn't released theatrically. **IC**

# James WONG

*Final Destination* (2000)
*The One* (2001) James Wong met his writing and producing partner, Glen Morgan, at high school in San Diego. They both studied film at Loyola Maymount University (Wong transferred to the film department after initially studying engineering), where they developed early

screenwriting projects, including *Trick or Treat* (1986), the screenplay for *The Boys Next Door* (1986), and scripts for the teen-based television series, '21 Jump Street' (1987). Television production company Stephen Cannell Productions hired Wong and Morgan in 1990, and there they wrote episodes of television series (including 'The Commish' in 1991) before beginning to work as writers-producers on early series of 'The X–Files'. Since then, Wong and Morgan have created two short-lived television series: a science fiction adventure, 'Space: Above and Beyond' in 1995, and a supernatural thriller 'The Others' in 2000.

Wong's cinematic directorial debut (co-written by Wong, Morgan and Jeffrey Reddick) is *Final Destination* (2000), a horror movie in which a party of teenage students and their teacher narrowly escape death by abandoning their scheduled flight to Paris when one student, Alex (Devon Sawa), has an accurate premonition that the plane is about to be destroyed. His subsequent panic causes the group to be removed from the plane minutes before it explodes, but they subsequently begin to die in a series of bizarre accidents. *Final Destination* knowingly reformulates the conventions of the contemporary teenie-kill pic, while also referring to classical cinematic horror. The script (over)emphasises this homage to generic traditions in characters' names (the teacher, appropriately, is called Valerie Lewton, whilst Chaney, Shreck, Murnau, and Hitchcock feature among the characters). As in Val Lewton's 1940s B-movies, there is no unambiguous monster here. Instead, everyday objects within the *mise-en-scène* are imbued with foreboding and menace as all but three of the principal characters meet their deaths. *Final Destination* is an impressive first film for Wong, demonstrating his deft construction of suspense and shock, his ironic use of diegetic music and his fragmentation of *mise-en-scène* to convey a sense of unease.

*The One* (2001), Wong's second feature film as director, is far less distinctive. This generic hybrid of science fiction and Hong Kong martial arts movies features the Hong Kong action star Jet Li, as both the hero (Gabe) and villain (Yulaw, who is travelling between parallel universes to systematically kill his alternate selves in order to become the all-powerful 'one'). Parallels (rather than oppositions) are drawn between Li's characters, implying that there is a tenuous boundary between good and evil. Yet the film does not fully exploit its central theme of duality and the basic premise of the plot remains confused. *The One* is most impressive during the martial arts sequences (choreographed by Corey Yuen) featuring Li's two characters in Kung Fu combat with each other, and gives further confirmation of Wong's primary association with the fantasy genres.

He is currently working on a remake of the 1971 horror film *Willard*.    **EC**

# John WOO

Probably the most prosperous law-abiding graduate of Hong Kong's Kowloon slums, John Woo Yu-sen, born in 1946, in Guangzhou, China, found in Western cinema a temporary escape from a life affected by privation, gang warfare, the death of his father from tuberculosis, and temporary homelessness. The beneficiary of a college education made possible by Christian charity, the young John Woo wrote for a student newspaper, acted in theatrical productions, and shot and edited his own 8mm and 16mm short films. Briefly considering the priesthood (but deemed too undisciplined for seminary school), Woo parlayed his love for film-making into work as a grip, set dresser, and script assistant at Cathay Studios. Learning the hard way that youthful enthusiasm held little currency in Hong Kong's tradition-bound film industry, Woo switched allegiances after two years to the rival Shaw Brothers. At the larger studio, Woo was assigned to assist director Chang Cheh, whose Mandarin language métier was 'the brother film', dealing in issues of fellowship and chivalry – themes that would remain close to the heart of the fledgling director.

Cheh's popular 'chop sockey' programmers – *7 Blows of the Dragon* (1972), *Ten Fingers of Steel* (1973) – proved successful both domestically and in North America, proving that lofty concerns could be wed successfully to escapist fare. In 1973, Woo was finally allowed to direct his first feature film, at the unheard of (for Hong Kong) age of 27.

The extreme violence of Woo's gang warfare drama *The Young Dragons*, made in 1973 but shelved and released in 1975, resulted in its ban in Hong Kong, but Woo's

*The Dragon Tamers* (1974)
*The Young Dragons* (1975)
*Hand of Death* (1975)
*Princess Chang Ping* (1976)
*From Rags to Riches* (1977)
*Money Crazy* (1977)
*Follow the Star* (1978)
*Last Hurrah for Chivalry* (1978)
*Laughing Times* (1981)
*Plain Jane to the Rescue* (1982)
*To Hell With the Devil* (1982)
*The Time You Need a Friend* (1984)
*Run Tiger Run* (1985)
*A Better Tomorrow* (1986)
*Heroes Shed No Tears* (1986)
*A Better Tomorrow II* (1987)
*Just Heroes* (1987)
*The Killer* (1989)

style so impressed Golden Harvest (the renamed Cathay Studios) that they signed him to an exclusive three-year contract. Woo's follow-up films, *The Dragon Tamers* (1974) – about the rivalry between martial arts schools – and *Hand of Death* (1975), were low-budget kung fu features shot in Korea. For the latter, Woo cast himself opposite future superstars Chan and Sammo Hung. He broke from action films to direct *Princess Chang Ping* (1976), based on a Chinese opera about forbidden love and a remake of the 1959 movie, *Tragedy of The Emperor's Daughter*. The success of this lush costumer encouraged Woo to try his hand at comedy. The results were *From Riches To Rags* (1977) – the screwball story of a man who, thinking himself terminally ill, arranges for his own murder only to learn he is in perfect health – and the hugely successful *Money Crazy* (1977), which starred comedian Ricky Hui. Shifting back to action mode, Woo made *Last Hurrah for Chivalry* (1978), the last of his martial arts films, which combined a period setting with the writer-director's pet concerns of honour and loyalty. A revenge thriller worthy of his former mentor Chang Cheh, *Last Hurrah for Chivalry* is perhaps the last great kung fu film of the decade.

Despite his experience helming bloody actioners, Woo had developed a reputation as a 'King of Comedy'. His subsequent efforts were a string of largely unfulfilling gagfests on the order of *Follow the Star* (1978), an episode of the omnibus *Hello, Late Homecomers* (also 1978) and the Chaplinesque farce *Laughing Times* (1981), which Woo made for Cinema City while still under contract to Golden Harvest (necessitating the directorial alias 'Wu Shang-fei'). *Plain Jane to the Rescue* (1982) was a poorly received feature film vehicle for television actress Josephine Siao in the third of her 'Lam Ah-chun' films, about a sweet-natured bumbler who runs afoul of an evil corporation. As if to cleanse his artistic palate, Woo turned out *To Hell With the Devil* (1982), easily his strangest film to date. With its depiction of a tangible Heaven and Hades, the film (which concerns a singer selling his soul to the Devil) makes literal what is often figurative in Woo's anguished meditations of good versus evil.

More comedies followed: the 1984 film *The Time You Need a Friend* – a Taiwanese take on The Sunshine Boys, in which two ageing, estranged comedians are reunited to host a telethon – and *Run Tiger Run* (1985), an updated 'The Prince and the Pauper' embroidered with scatological humour and metaphysical asides. Woo was then invited by American-educated Chinese director-producer Tsui Hark (who had split from Cinema City to found his own independent studio, Film Workshop) to write and direct the film that would turn the tide of his career. *A Better Tomorrow* (1986) is the story of a dedicated police cadet whose brother is a syndicate counterfeiter. Television actor Chow Yun Fat was chosen to play the matchstick-chewing gunman – patterned after Alain Delon's existential hitter in Jean-Pierre Melville's *Le Samouraï* (1967) – whose ultimate sacrifice allows the estranged brothers to be reconciled beneath a shower of shell casings. The kinetic and stylish film, which elevated gunplay to the acrobatic heights of martial epics and instigated the subsequent 'Heroic Bloodshed' subgenre of Hong Kong action films, exceeded all expectations to win the Hong Kong Film Award for Best Picture in 1987. It became the most successful film in the history of Hong Kong cinema.

*A Better Tomorrow II* (1987) shifted the action to New York and brought back Chow Yun Fat as the twin brother of his martyred gunman. More extreme in every way, *A Better Tomorrow II* was another success for Woo and Tsui Hark, who argued bitterly throughout the production, from scripting to editing. When the studio demanded that the film's length be brought down to under two hours, Woo and Tusi split the film and recut their halves separately. While Tsui directed the series' prequel *A Better Tomorrow III* (1989), Woo's name recognition prompted the belated release of *Heroes Shed No Tears* (1986), directed by Woo half a decade earlier but shelved by Golden Harvest for its then unfashionable extreme violence. This Vietnam war story concerned a mercenary hired by the Drug Enforcement Agency to apprehend an opium smuggling Vietnamese general in Thailand's Golden Triangle. Woo's first follow-up to *A Better Tomorrow II* was *Just Heroes* (1987), co-directed with Wu Ma as a benefit for mentor Cheng Cheh. Danny Lee starred in this gangland 'King Lear' variant – a nod to Japanese director Akira Kurosawa's *Ran* (1985). Despite their difficulties, Tsui Hark and Woo were reunited here as producer and director, as they would be for Woo's next film *The Killer* (1989). Danny Lee again stars as a relentless cop out to get Chow Yun Fat's guilt-ridden hitman (this time named 'Jeff', yet another nod to *Le Samouraï*), who has accidentally blinded a beautiful nightclub singer (Sally Yeh). The killer who wishes to retire and the cop not above breaking the law to uphold it make for quintessential Woo. Chow Yun Fat's dedication to restoring sight to the blind songbird prompted critic J. Hoberman to crack that *The Killer* played out like '*Magnificent Obsession* remade by Sam Peckinpah'. In his bloodstained linen suit, Chow Yun Fat even begins to resemble Warren Oates' dissolute piano player in Peckinpah's *Bring Me the Head of Alfredo Garcia* (1974). As violently balletic as *A Better Tomorrow*, *The Killer* also boasts a devastating ironic humour typified by the tense moment where cop and killer train guns on one another over the head of the unseeing chanteuse, who thinks them old friends and blithely sets out tea. Although *The Killer* flopped in China, Woo's international reputation was growing. An American remake was planned, but the perceived homoeroticism of the film's central relationship has forestalled its realisation for well over a decade. *The Killer* was the last collaboration between Tsui Hark and Woo, who are not known to have spoken since.

Woo's script ideas for *A Better Tomorrow III* were eventually filmed by him as *Bullet in the Head* (1990), which remains one of the director's most personal works despite an obvious debt to Michael Cimino's *The Deer Hunter* (1978). Spanning the years 1967–74, the film follows a trio of boyhood friends from an honour killing in their native Hong Kong through their experiences as smugglers and prisoners of war during the Vietnam conflict. Partially inspired by the 1989 Tiananmen Square massacre, the film is less reliant on high-octane action but is as gruelling as Woo's Hong Kong action work. Considerably more light-hearted than either *The Killer* or *Bullet in the Head* (both domestic box-office failures), the 1990 caper film *Once a Thief*, which starred Chow Yun Fat as a dandified art thief, proved Woo could remain stylish even when forfeiting extreme violence and bloodshed. Casting Chow Yun Fat as a dedicated cop avenging the death of his partner, *Hard-Boiled* (1992), Woo's last Chinese language film and his last work as a writer-director, upped the violence ante to near mythic proportions. It features a jaw-dropping opener set in Hong Kong's landmark Wyndam Teahouse, where Chow, his face dusted with cornstarch, blows away the gangster who has killed his partner.

*Hard-Boiled*'s apocalyptic hospital climax, in which innocent victims are mowed down by the dozens with machine gun fire, was executed as both a distillation of all of Woo's great action moments and as his farewell to Hong Kong cinema.

Relocating to America, Woo directed *Hard Target* (1993), a vehicle for Belgian action star Jean-Claude Van Damme. Shorn of twenty minutes by Universal (and reportedly sent back by the censor seven times before being passed), the moderately successful film remains a passable updating of *The Most Dangerous Game* (1932). Van Damme's Vietnam vet takes on a maniacal big game hunter during New Orleans' chaotic Mardi Gras – a fair approximation of Chinese New Year.

Somewhat more ambitious in terms of casting and budget was *Broken Arrow* (1996), the story of two American military men – one dedicated (Christian Slater), the other mercenary (John Travolta) – locked in a battle of wits over a stolen warhead. Again compromised by studio interference, *Broken Arrow* manages to be both bland and preposterous, but urged Woo towards larger and more expensive projects. Between prestige studio projects, Woo turned out *John Woo's Once A Thief* (1996), a made-for-television reworking of his earlier film. Set in Hong Kong and Vancouver, this series pilot suffers from a considerable diminution in energy, but allowed Woo the opportunity to work with a small crew and less administrative interference.

Woo turned down an offer to direct Pierce Brosnan's debut as James Bond in *Goldeneye* (1995) to reunite with actor John Travolta for the 1997 *Face/Off* (originally planned as a science fiction film, but rewritten to suit Woo's gritty milieu). Travolta plays a federal agent who receives a face graft from terrorist Nicolas Cage in order to infiltrate the criminal's inner circle.

When Cage turns the tables by stealing Travolta's dermal mask, the two get to explore how the other half lives. Although a huge box-office success, *Face/Off* is ultimately less Woo than Wooesque, even recycling *The Killer*'s church shoot out, which here has all the resonance of a Madonna video. It would have benefited from a smaller budget, nixing the expense of the tacked-on speedboat chase (surely the most egregious of all action film pursuits) that concludes the film. Following *Blackjack* (1998), an unsold, Canadian-lensed television pilot, starring Dolph Lundgren as a security guard suffering from the fear of the colour white, Woo moved onto the considerably more high profile *Mission: Impossible II* (2000). Hand picked by producer-star Tom Cruise to direct, Woo was clearly a hired gun on this $100 million production, which was ultimately re-edited by another director employed by Paramount to make their investment more marketable. Woo's direction of MGM's big-budget World War Two film, *Windtalkers* (2002), was plagued by pre- and post-production delays. Based on true events, the film concerns a Native American soldier whose Navajo dialect is used as a wartime code. A Marine (Nicolas Cage) is assigned to protect the soldier and ordered to execute his charge rather than let him be captured, an assignment that is complicated by growing respect and friendship between the men.

Bumped from its original release date by the terrorist attacks of 11 September, the film was scheduled to premiere the following summer, which put it behind the release of several Hollywood films with wartime settings, such as Ridley Scott's *Black Hawk Down* (2001) and Randall Wallace's *We Were Soldiers* (2002). Although it is encouraging to see Woo engage the themes of brotherhood during crisis, expectations remain fairly low among his original fans, many of whom have neglected to update their tribute websites since the release of *Face/Off*. Among Woo's upcoming projects are a second *Mission Impossible* sequel and a comedy that will reunite him with former leading man Chow Yun Fat.

Between film projects, Woo has produced films by other directors – Chow Yun Fat's American debut, *The Replacement Killers* (1998), and the poorly received *The Big Hit* (1998) – directed some television commercials, and indulged in his preferred pastime as an amateur chef.

His next film, set in San Francisco in the nineteenth century, will star Chow Yun Fat as a Chinese immigrant who arrives in American to find that he has been sold into slavery. **RHS**

# Y

# Boaz YAKIN

Boaz Yakin made an impact with his first feature, the urban crime story *Fresh* (1994), a far cry from his undistinguished generic scripts for *The Punisher* (1989) and *The Rookie* (1990). Although *Fresh* was dismissed by some as a generic 'hood film' – in the mould of John Singleton's *Boyz N the Hood* (1991) or Ernest Dickerson's *Juice* (1992) – Yakin's film is something quite different. Fresh (Sean Nelson) is a street-smart twelve-year-old who is torn between crime (running drugs for local dealers) and intellectual pursuits (represented here by his excellence at speed chess). This conflict is personified in the twin father figures of Sam (Samuel L. Jackson), Fresh's estranged father and Esteban (an excellent Giancarlo Esposito), the heroin dealer who is the boy's employer. Sam is homeless but in regular chess matches with his son seeks to instil values of discipline and self-reliance.

The film offers a considerable amount of moral ambiguity, with Sam, on the one hand, seemingly unable to live by his own code and Esteban both a gangster drug dealer and a considerate father. Fresh, too, is presented as a complex figure, a child who is both a victim and part of the problem. This complexity is summed up in Nelson's powerful blank-faced performance. What makes the film particularly notable, however, is the tone. Rather than the liberal hand-wringing of *Boyz N the Hood* or the nihilistic rush of *Menace II Society* (1993), *Fresh* has a bleak down-beat tone which is all the more affecting for the lack of platitudes and easy solutions.

Yakin's subsequent film was the less successful *A Price Above Rubies* (1998). Set in the Orthodox Jewish community of New York, the title refers to a biblical quotation, 'a price above rubies, a woman of fortitude'. Renée Zellweger is such a woman, struggling in different ways with the patriarchal world she inhabits. Trying to establish herself as an independent person, she befriends and starts an affair with a Hispanic jeweller. She is blackmailed for sex by her sinister brother-in-law, Sender, visited by the ghost of her dead brother, and ends up cast out by her husband, finally finding the freedom she desired. Although the film contains good performances, it buckles under the weight of its complex plot – there is a lot here, from romance to blackmailing villains and ghosts – and this flaw becomes particularly conspicuous when compared to the streamlined,

*Fresh* (1994)

*A Price Above Rubies* (1998)

*Remember the Titans* (2000)

even sparse narrative of the director's debut. The production was disrupted by frequent protests from Jewish groups.

In 1999 Yakin returned to his roots in genre screenplays, penning *From Dusk 'Til Dawn 2: Texas Blood Money*, a poor sequel to the wildly overrated Quentin Tarantino-scripted Mexican-set noir-vampire outing. His most recent film, the Denzel Washington vehicle, *Remember the Titans* (2000), is a feelgood melding of sports movie (American college football) and anti-racist parable made for Disney. Washington and the perennially underrated Will Patton are football coaches in a Virginia college in 1971 who strive to turn their first interracial team into winners. This is efficiently executed, cornball fare that feels like so many other sports movies such as *Slap Shot* (1977), *The Mighty Ducks* (1992), and *Varsity Blues* (1999). It sidesteps some clichés (the white coach isn't a racist for instance) but the triumphant heroics on show are pretty familiar – all the more surprising considering that the film is based on a true story.

From the innovative *Fresh* to the ambitious, if flawed, *A Price Above Rubies*, to the bland family fare of *Remember the Titans*, Yakin seems to be following the path of many a young American director and becoming more and more anonymous.    **IC**

# Robert M. YOUNG

Born in New York in 1924, Robert M. Young directs socially conscious films of variable quality. He began his career making television documentaries and his interest in themes of poverty and racism manifested itself early, when he was fired from NBC for making his documentary *Cortile Casino* about slums in Sicily. Hard-edged, it was never broadcast, eventually surfacing as a theatrical release in 1993. In 1964 he collaborated on *Nothing But a Man*, an important independent feature directed by Michael Roemer. In the next decade, Young frequently worked as a writer on television shows such as 'Kojak' and also penned the exciting and surprisingly serious Disney film *Escape to Witch Mountain* (1975).

Having debuted with the dull horror *Trauma* (1962), Young returned to the screen 15 years later with a raw and brutal prison movie, *Short Eyes* (1977). Miguel Pinero's screenplay opens up his play to powerful effect and the location shooting at the New York City Men's House of Detention considerably aids this grim story of a child molester (Bruce Davison). Young followed this with *Alambrista!* (1978), the story of Roberto (Domingo Ambriz), a young Mexican seeking work in the United States as an 'illegal' immigrant. The film owes something to the Italian Neo-Realists, using hand-held camera to create a vérité style. Young lived undercover with illegal Mexican workers for nearly a year in order to imbue his film with the necessary authenticity. Regrettably, it feels familiar and any insights that may have come to him as a result of this experience are absent. It did, however, win the Camera d'Or at Cannes in 1978.

*Rich Kids* (1979) is, at first sight, an unlikely Young project, set amongst the New York upper classes. The story of a boy and girl who befriend and support each other through parental divorce, it resembles the work of Woody Allen with its up-market Manhattan locations. Typically, the director eschews overt melodrama and stylistic excess for a low-key look at friendship. Robert Altman was an executive producer.

Young's next film, *One Trick Pony* (1980), starred musician Paul Simon, who also wrote the screenplay. This story of a singer (Simon) trying to keep his marriage together is more than the vanity project it could have been but is still not exceptional. *The Ballad of Gregorio Cortez* (1982) followed, made for and originally screened on the US PBS channel. The true story of the titular Mexican who killed a sheriff in 1901 during an interrogation, the film offers a low-key, if solemn, variant on the western and sees Young continuing his interest in Latino subjects. The director's frequent collaborator Edward James Olmos plays Cortez, who became a folk hero after being pursued by six hundred Texas rangers, captured, tried and imprisoned, only to be pardoned by the Governor. Young seems to resist the opportunity the story offers to create a mythic character along the lines of *Ned Kelly* (1970) and *Dillinger* (1973) but this means the film also eschews many of the thrills such a tale offers. The *mise-en-scène* is constructed through painstaking period detail (such as filming court scenes in the very court was Cortez was tried).

*Saving Grace* (1985) is a silly and dull drama with Pope Leo XIV (Tom Conti) sneaking away from the Vatican and his routine duties to aid earthquake-stricken villagers in a small Italian town. It is turgid and boring rather than heartwarming. *Extremities* (1986), which Young may have considered socially conscious, is pure exploitation. Farrah Fawcett is surprisingly good as a raped woman who turns the tables on her attacker (James Russo), blinding and binding him. The acclaimed play by William Mastrosimone was adapted for the screen by the author but what was claustrophobic and raw on the stage ends up as stage-bound and repetitive, despite Young's attempts to create movement with a revolving camera.

*Dominick and Eugene* (1988), his next attempt, was far more impressive; the story of a medical school intern (Ray Liotta) and his brain-damaged brother (an excellent Tom Hulce) comes across like an earthy, more complex *Rain Man* (1988). Although the film sails close to television movie territory, it is redeemed by sober direction and strong performances. The brutal *Triumph of the Spirit* (1989) seems better suited to Young, with his interest in racism and prejudice. This is the true story of a Greek Jew, Salamo Arouch (Willem Dafoe), who is sent to Auschwitz, and his struggle to survive gladiatorial boxing matches staged by the Nazis. The film adds little to the sub-genre of Holocaust movies, despite being shot on location at Auschwitz-Birkenau. However, the always-excellent Dafoe and a savage Edward James Olmos – playing a brutal gypsy – and some well-staged fights make the film memorable.

Young's most recent films have all been collaborations with Edward James Olmos. In *Roosters* (1993), Olmos is a cock-fighter in a small Mexican town; the drama is unable to shake its stage roots. Similarly underwhelming was the Young/Olmos teaming for the baseball movie *Talent for the Game* (1991), a disappointingly generic sports tale. Young's 1996 film *Caught* was a steamy variation on James M. Cain's 'The Postman Always Rings Twice', again starring Olmos, and can be regarded as something of a return to form. More recently, he has revisited the nature subjects of his early career with *China: The Panda Adventure* (2001). This was a well-received, 1930s-set romp shot in the IMAX format, but as is often the case with IMAX films, the writing and performances come a poor second to the photography. Even the normally reliable Xander Berkley is pretty bad here.

On occasion Young's direction may not be a match for his good intentions yet his commitment to anti-racism and particularly Latino issues render his films important; before American independent cinema embraced movies made by minority groups, Young was a pioneer. **IC**

# Ben YOUNGER

Born in 1973, Ben Younger may be first among a new breed of brash young white *Boiler Room* (2000) American writer-directors, one whose storytelling is as influenced by the jagged rhythms and propulsive attack of hip-hop music as it is by such obvious cinematic forebears as Martin Scorsese, Oliver Stone, and David Mamet. His sole feature credit to date, the attitudinal stock scam expose *Boiler Room* (2000), wears the reputation of *Mean Streets* (1973), *Wall Street* (1987), and the James Foley-mounted adaptation of Mamet's *Glengarry Glen Ross* (1992) on its stylistic sleeve. It is more noteworthy, however, for its portrait of white, suburban – and often, like Younger himself, Jewish – males obsessed with the trappings of black gangsta culture.

Younger sets the tone even before the first frame of his picture rolls, as the familiar New Line Cinema fanfare is 'scratched', club DJ-style. The film energetically documents the rise and fall of an ambitious twenty something, Seth (Giovanni Ribisi). Having run an illegal casino out of his apartment, he begins peddling worthless stocks over the phone in the so-called 'boiler room' of the title – an icily-lit office space crammed with a white-collared army of his avaricious peers. It is overly familiar mano-e-mano territory, infused with rap lingo and a wall-to-wall hip-hop soundtrack. Younger bookends his film's ongoing narration with Seth quoting slain rapper Notorious BIG. He uses rap's insistent beat to inform the jump cuts that plunge us head-first into Seth's corrupt lifestyle, and borrows its snarling braggadocio for his hot-headed, greedy young brokers.

A scene in which they gather around a projection television to openly worship Michael Douglas' *Wall Street* (1987) shark, Gordon Gekko, recalls 'hood' flick progenitor *New Jack City* (1991), where Wesley Snipes' drug lord pays similar tribute to Al Pacino in *Scarface* (1983). Younger's sole female character of any note is a black secretary played by Nia Long, whom Seth romances and finally beds after asking her for 'chocolate love'. It's a sure sign of the ongoing assimilation between black and white culture that these racial details are not belaboured, but rather accepted (much as they are presented) at face value. It will be interesting to see if Younger continues to explore this personal theme in future projects.                                    **CS**

# Z

## Caveh ZAHEDI

Caveh Zahedi is the court jester of the California art-film scene, an actor and auteur who has relentlessly turned the camera on his own insecurities, failings, and unrealised ambitions. Endearing, infuriating, and insightful, Zahedi has been compared to Henry Jaglom, John Cassavetes, and Woody Allen, but he is also clearly inspired by the great European visionaries such as Godard and Bresson. Working with writer-director-producer Greg Watkins, Zahedi has created a small body of work with a substantial cult following.

Zahedi was born of Iranian immigrants in Washington in 1960. His artistic ambitions were largely unfulfilled through the early years of his career, as he failed to complete projects about Arthur Rimbaud and Eadweard Muybridge or to sell experimental videos based on a Talking Heads song and a poem by the French poet Stephane Mallarme.

The director's first success came with *A Little Stiff* (1991), which he wrote, directed, produced, and edited with Watkins. The film uses real-life participants to re-enact his year-long, obsessive, and unrequited romance with a UCLA art student. Charming in its own fashion, and well-crafted, the film premiered at the 1991 Sundance Film Festival to critical acclaim, and also saw a modest theatrical release.

His next project, *I Don't Hate Las Vegas Anymore* (1994) documents a road trip taken by Zahedi, his talkative father, and his sullen brother. In search of reconciliation with his family and proof of the existence of God, Zahedi injects drugs, endless film-making calamities, and his own garbled metaphysical musings into the film. Rougher in construction and more ambitious than *A Little Stiff*, *I Don't Hate Las Vegas Anymore* won the Critics' Award at the Rotterdam Film Festival. It was largely overlooked in the US.

Zahedi has created numerous shorter experimental works, including *I Was Possessed by God*, an autobiographical document of a hallucinogenic drug experience, and a series of video communiqués that he and film-maker Jay Rosenblatt sent one another, edited down by Zahedi. He has also acted in other directors' projects, including Gregg Lachow's *Money Buys Happiness* (1999), Alexander Payne's *Citizen Ruth* (1996), and Scott King's *Treasure Island* (1999).                                                    **JS**

*A Little Stiff* (1991)
*I Don't Hate Las Vegas Anymore* (1994)

# Steven ZAILLIAN

Born in 1951, Steven Zaillian specialises in the big Hollywood 'message' movie. Best known for writing *Schindler's List* (1993), Zaillian makes historical films that begin with the words 'Based on a true story' and conclude with 'where-are-they-now' end titles. His films are tightly told, but suffer from an urge to make big statements about the human heart, a subtlety-draining failing.

Zaillian adapted both of the films he has directed from best-selling books. The first, *Searching for Bobby Fischer* (1993), tells the story of Josh Waitzkin (Max Pomeranc), a seven-year-old chess genius, who must negotiate between his talent and his conscience, and between over-weaning parents and coaches. The most interesting relationship in the film, however, is between Josh and Bobby Fischer, who is revealed to us only in brief news clips accompanied by Josh's voice-over narration. Josh's Fischer is an enigmatic role model, the genius who 'vanished' at the height of his powers. Largely sanitised from the film are Fischer's reappearances, which revealed him to be a monomaniac whose genius had devolved to mere talent. Zaillian uses Josh to cleanse us of Fischer's unpleasantness. Josh is a genius of the same magnitude, but he will settle for a lesser career in order to remain a normal boy who (the end titles tell us) enjoys fishing and other sports. We never see more than cautionary glimpses into the truly troubled and divided nature of genius; Zaillian wants us to remember only the sweet and normal Josh, whose example warms us and confirms us in our own complacency.

*A Civil Action* (1998) from the book by Jonathan Harr, features Jan Schlichtmann (John Travolta), a successful personal injury attorney who agrees to take on the case of a group of small-town parents whose children have all died of cancer. Initially motivated by greed and professional jealousy, Jan is reborn through the film as a crusader for Truth, for which he must sacrifice his career. Zaillian's message is that the American way of conflicting self-interest fails common people; it must be tempered by compassion and love. As with *Searching for Bobby Fischer*, *A Civil Action* tells its story wonderfully well, but the issues and alliances are put forth so bluntly that any real human complexity has no place. Zaillian's characters are mere illustrations, moral types whose interactions seem not archetypal but awkward. **JA**

# Robert ZEMECKIS

Robert Zemeckis has already proved himself to be one of the most commercially successful directors in Hollywood history and still has a long career ahead of him. In March 1995, his success was cemented critically when *Forrest Gump* (1994) won six Academy Awards, including Best Picture. It was particularly fitting that the Best Director award should be handed to him by none other than his mentor, Steven Spielberg.

Born in Chicago in 1952, Zemeckis' career began, like many others of his generation, in film school (at USC, where there is now a building named after him). His debut feature, *I Wanna Hold Your Hand* (1978), made under the aegis of Spielberg, demonstrated his gift for comedy and a fascination with the nostalgic return to recent American history that would mark most of his later work. Co-written by frequent collaborator Bob Gale, the film details the hysteria surrounding The Beatles' first performance in the United States, on the Ed Sullivan Show, as six girls from New Jersey desperately hunt for tickets.

Following screenwriting duties on Spielberg's first major flop, *1941* (1979), Zemeckis and Gale created another crazy comedy of their own, *Used Cars* (1980), starring Kurt Russell and the great Jack Warden (in two roles). Chronicling the rivalry between two neighbouring car dealerships, and their increasingly outlandish schemes to get customers, the film revels in its own bad taste, but with the good nature that characterises all of Zemeckis' work.

His first massive hit was the action comedy *Romancing the Stone* (1984), which started a virtually unbroken string of commercial successes for Zemeckis. Set largely in the jungles of Colombia, the film stars Michael Douglas as an anti-heroic adventurer and Kathleen Turner as a romantic novelist in search of her kidnapped sister. While it admirably captures the roller-coaster spirit of the *Indiana Jones* series, one might also liken the politics of the movie to those of Spielberg's films from the period. Not unlike the Indians in Spielberg's *Indiana Jones and the Temple of Doom* (1984), released the same year, *Romancing the Stone* propagates myths about non-American nations being either villainous thugs or childlike peasants in need of rescue by the White Man. Such representations of foreign nations are common throughout Hollywood history, but are particularly pertinent to Zemeckis' film given the degree of US intervention in Central America during the 1980s.

His next film, the Spielberg-produced *Back to the Future* (1985), proved to be even more successful and spawned two sequels. Again, Zemeckis could be accused of endorsing Reaganite politics, promoting both consumerism and a rose-tinted view of the 1950s in keeping with the neo-conservative rhetoric of the 1980s. Marty McFly (Michael J. Fox) is accidentally sent back in time from a dystopic present to a cheery 1955 and is required to orchestrate his own parents' courtship, after his mother (Lea Thompson) falls for him rather than his nerdish, bullied father (Crispin Glover). His father is eventually taught to stand up for himself and a happy ending is coded through the transformation of Marty's contemporary family into affluent, middle-class folk. The film, however, is perhaps a little more ambiguous than its detractors might admit. Underlying its neo-conservatism, for example, there is also a somewhat perverse Freudian subtext at work, as Marty finds himself being seduced by his own mother; and, in the case of his mother's alcoholism, there is the suggestion that the supposedly idyllic 1950s actually caused many of the problems of the present.

Zemeckis shot the two *Back to the Future* sequels back-to-back. *Part II* (1989) revels in time travel paradoxes as it zips back and forth between 1955, 1985, 2015 and an alternate 1985, even replaying the climax of *Part I* from alternate perspectives, before ending on a cliffhanger. Many people were confused by the narrative and felt cheated by the ending (which merely advertises the next instalment) and *Part II* turned out to be the least celebrated of the trilogy. *Part III* (1990), much less complicated in its plotting, revisits the western genre as Marty and the Doc (Christopher Lloyd) are stranded in 1885. Heralded by many as the best of the series, it again established Zemeckis as one of the most reliable directors at the box office.

*Back to the Future* had marked Zemeckis' first significant use of special effects technologies, an obsession that would spectacularly blossom in *Who Framed Roger Rabbit* (1988), which famously combined live action with cartoon animation and won several Academy Awards. The film's technical virtuosity is so overwhelming that it is easy to overlook that *Roger Rabbit* is also a fascinating film noir, and is, as some have said, the true sequel to *Chinatown* (1974). Set during the heyday of the Hollywood studio system, the film follows private eye Eddie Valiant (Bob Hoskins) as he investigates the murder of Marvin Acme, owner of Toontown, in what turns out to be a thinly-veiled allegory of the actual dismantling of the Los Angeles public transport system by corrupt forces so that the freeways could be built.

In 1992, he made what is arguably his least satisfying film, *Death Becomes Her*, starring Bruce Willis, Goldie Hawn, and Meryl Streep, all cast against type. A black comedy about vanity, immortality and plastic surgery, it demonstrated the ever-present risk in Zemeckis' work of letting the special effects (which are excellent and Academy Award-winning) get ahead of story and characterisation. But more than that, Zemeckis seemed to lose his gift for comedy, presenting instead a display of grotesque slapstick with few laughs.

He bounced back remarkably with *Forrest Gump* (1994), the most critically and commercially successful film of its year. Perhaps the ultimate Baby Boomer movie, the film seems to have crafted the eponymous Gump (Tom Hanks) as the ultimate blank canvas: a vacant vessel which viewers are encouraged to fill with their own memories as they are taken on board for yet another ride on the Zemeckis time machine. Again, however, Zemeckis was accused of making a reactionary film, a revisionist history lesson designed to promote a 'God Bless America' ideology. This argument is debatable, overlooking as it does the dark irony that underpins the narrative. In the tradition of Jean Baudrillard, the film seems to present America as the ultimate simulation: note, for example, the number of fake sunrises and panoramas (created through special effects) or how the story Gump narrates is a deliberately false history of America (just as Toontown never existed, John Lennon and JFK never met a man named Gump). Moreover, just as Baudrillard argued that the presence of the simulacrum masks the absence of anything underneath, *Forrest Gump* seems to suggest that Americans will believe in something purely because of its appearance, even if it is fundamentally lacking meaning – such as when Gump runs and runs for no good reason at all, but acquires a mass of followers nonetheless.

Developing, like his mentor, a taste for more overtly serious subject matter, Zemeckis followed the triumphs of *Forrest Gump* with *Contact* (1997), an adaptation of Carl Sagan's metaphysical science fiction novel. Once again, Zemeckis sought to fuse elaborate visual effects with more weighty themes than the average blockbuster movie, but again teetered on the edge of the slushy sentiment that many accused him of in *Forrest Gump*. For example, Jodie Foster's journey into outer space is represented rather cloyingly as a chance for her to reconcile with her deceased father.

*What Lies Beneath* (2000) saw Zemeckis try his hand at a Hitchcockian suspense-thriller with supernatural undertones, casting Harrison Ford against type as the creepy husband of Michelle Pfeiffer. That the film feels a little bit like a throwaway experiment is not entirely surprising: it was shot during a break in filming while Tom Hanks lost weight for Zemeckis' other film of that year, *Cast Away* (2000). This latter film again featured a typical Zemeckis protagonist struggling to transcend time, with Hanks playing a clockwatching Fed-Ex man stranded on a desert island. In an *oeuvre* of epic, high-tech, effects-driven blockbusters, the surprising minimalism of *Cast Away* strangely makes it his most ambitious film to date: for more than half of its running time there is virtually no dialogue or music, with the director relying entirely on subtle sound design and Hanks' expert physical performance to carry the drama. It proved to be yet another box-office smash, although its trailer, which gives away the ending, rudely deflating the inherent suspense, left many filmgoers disgruntled.

Zemeckis will no doubt continue to make very successful films and innovate in special effects. One hopes that he can maintain the narratives, the politics, and the humour to go with them. **AS**

# Rafal ZIELINSKI

New censorial permissiveness made 1980s comedy a minefield densely populated with bare breasts and rude intentions. Zielinski is one of those directors who could hesitantly be said to have stood at the forefront of the shift to truly trash movies, and although he followed in the wake of *Animal House* (1978) and *Porky's* (1981) his 1980s films are a prolonged assault on the sensibility which hopes that movies might have the brains as well as the balls to offend those two old enemies: taste and decency.

After studying under *cinéma-vérité* documentarian Richard Leacock at Massachusetts Institute of Technology in Boston, Zielinski debuted with *Hey Babe* (1980), in which he showed little more than that he could make films quickly with virtually no budget – a trend he has merrily continued with for two decades now.

*Screwballs* (1983) is the film he will be remembered for, with its own little cult following to rival *Bachelor Party* (1984) as one of those films people hazily remember enjoying from drunken evenings. *Screwballs* is among the basest of that genre, knowing that it is the type of film teenagers watch as an excuse for a regulated dose of nudity. It is crude (at least *Porky's* makes you wait for visual gratification), but it just about works. It also, in name alone, serves as a reminder that the 1980s sex comedy was in some ways a reprise of those great frantic comedies of the 1930s and 1940s which seemed to threaten social order with their cross-societal mismatching: Capra's *It Happened One Night* (1934), *Bringing up Baby* (1938), and Hawks' supreme *His Girl Friday* (1940). Our standards must have diminished terribly for that to happen though: the only threat in any of these 1980s films was transgression, of pushing the joke too far into tastelessness, and being simply unpleasant. Ultimately, *Screwballs* is safe ground – strip bowling in a school called T&A, with a main character called Purity Bush is crass, but it is a threat easily lost in the moral safety the films finally offer. The film's resolution seemed to preclude sequels – all those stereotypes (the nerd, the jock, the cheerleader) could easily become accountants and middle management as the credits roll, yet *Parts II* and *III* followed, with the laws of diminishing returns firmly at play. All with casts of unknowns, they took the premise of *Screwballs* and made it even more direct, but mysteriously less gratuitous. That really left the films with nothing to offer. The unfortunate existence of the risible *Screwball Hotel* is something no-one should be proud of.

Still, the cheerfulness of the enterprise maintains in Zielinski's other films of that decade, with *Recruits* (1986) (a kind of *Police Academy 6: Citizens On Patrol*-lite if that is at all possible) and *Valet Girls* (1987) easily passing an hour and a half. Films of this type are all about the ridiculousness of their story, breasts, and snigger-worthy names.

Sergeant Hardbutt is a good one from *Recruits*, while *Valet Girls* cuts its losses and gives half its characters the same 'zany' name: Sexy Holiday. At least *Valet Girls* has some claim to worth – the idea of a band of women successfully running their own business under the leers and sneers of a bunch of randy men is some kind of gender revenge. It is clearly not worth travelling too far down that road: madness might lie in trying to justify the top that accidentally comes off at a moment's comic notice as feminist critique – this is hokum. Zielinski's other film of the 1980s was for cultish, camp, and cheap British company Empire Films – who are a story all of their own. Not one of their most outrageous concoctions, *Spellcaster* (1988) did have the virtue of featuring Adam Ant as its villainous magician, the sort of part his pop persona, all make-up and dramatic glares, would seem ideal for.

The type of movie the director makes died an oddly immediate death with the changing of decades – it is most likely that the market, all straight-to-video, just did not need more mullets-and-groping masterpieces, or maybe the demented *Flesh Gordon* series was as much as anyone could take. Video shops are still full of the genre, but they are the same films that were there ten years ago. Zielinski had one final fling in 1994 with a National Lampoon movie (*Last Resort* (1994) – and rarely has a film been more aptly named) starring the two Coreys, Feldman and Haim, but the whole enterprise was so self-consciously cheap and tacky that there was no joy to be found anywhere.

Zielinski drifted in the 1990s, and the move into more serious waters has been of little benefit to anyone. From kickboxing (*Night of the Warrior* (1991)), to undercover insurance investigations, to dramas about teenage killers (*Fun* (1994)) and troubled runaways (*Jailbait* (1994)), the films did not amount to much. When a director moves into ultra-traditional territories it generally underlines the lack of radical spirit in their more characteristic films, and all those 1980s comedies now seem as sadly conventional as the teenager-in-trouble and terminal disease films that make up the bulk of TV movie output. One project, *The Elevator* (1996), had unfulfilled promise. Co-directed with debutant Nigel Dick, it was a series of vignettes told by an aspiring screenwriter to a film producer in the vehicle of the title – and no surprises, they were the kind of films that Zielinski himself might make. **CSo**

# Lee David ZLOTOFF

Lee David Zlotoff worked extensively in television, creating the series 'MacGyver', before embarking on his only feature work to date. *The Spitfire Grill* (1996) is essentially a traditional melodrama/weepie with contemporary twists, incorporating post-Vietnam trauma, incest and abuse. A female ex-con, Percy (Alison Elliot), is given employment at a small-town diner by Hannah (Ellen Burstyn, in a role which echoes *Alice Doesn't Live Here Anymore* (1974)). As various bonds are formed amongst the women in the diner, jealousies and secrets from the past unravel with tragic but ultimately redemptive results. While the film lapses into overwrought sentimentality and narrative contrivance, this is tempered by the atmospheric production design and photography which makes effective use of the Maine forest environment. The film's manipulative tendencies were winning enough to earn it the audience award at the 1996 Sundance Film Festival. **NJ**

*The Spitfire Grill* (1996)

# David ZUCKER

David Zucker is a comedy film director responsible for some of the most memorable films of this genre in the last twenty years.

He was born in Milwaukee in 1947, educated, like his brother Jerry, at the University of Wisconsin, and from there went on to form a partnership with his sibling and his friend Jim Abrahams. The trio brought out their first film in 1980 – *Airplane!* – which owed much to the slapstick tradition of Chaplin and The Marx Brothers. But by allying this with more contemporary parodies from Woody Allen and Mel Brooks, the film found a unique voice in the crowded market of comedy entertainment. Spoofing the already clichéd disaster movies of the 1970s (specifically the *Airport* series), *Airplane!* uses a scattershot method, blitzing the audience with joke upon joke. Sight gags (such as the *Jaws* (1975) homage at the very start) co-mingle with infantile wordplays ('Surely you can't be serious.' 'I am serious. And don't call me Shirley!') – all delivered in deadpan

*Airplane!* (1980)
*Top Secret!* (1984)
*Ruthless People* (1986)
*The Naked Gun: From the Files of Police Squad!* (1988)
*The Naked Gun 2½: The Smell of Fear* (1991)
*BASEketball* (1999)
*The Guest* (2002)

fashion by Leslie Nielsen, Peter Graves, Julie Hagerty, and Robert Hays. The plot concerns are secondary, but given the sheer number of laughs guaranteed this really is a minor remonstrance.

After the similarly staged *Top Secret!* (1984) and the mercenary *Ruthless People* (1986) came Zucker's first solo directing job: *The Naked Gun: From the Files of Police Squad!* (1988). As the title ratifies, this is merely a big-screen revision of Zucker, Abraham and Zucker's short-lived, but hilarious, TV cop show. Obviously Leslie Nielsen leads the cast again as the accident-prone Clouseau clone Lt Frank Drebin, dishing out the toilet humour liberally – and *literally* in one unforgettable scene. As per usual the story is completely ludicrous, this time revolving around an attempt to kill visiting dignitary, Queen Elizabeth II. *The Naked Gun 2½: The Smell of Fear* (1991) follows an identical pattern, but strangely enough attempts to work in environmental concerns surrounding our reliance on nuclear and fossil fuels.

After a considerable period spent producing (*Naked Gun 33⅓: The Final Insult* (1994), *High School High* (1996)), Zucker was coaxed back to the director's chair for *BASEketball* (1998). A case of art imitating life, the scenario was inspired by Zucker's own invention of a new game in the 1980s – a cross between baseball and basketball. Addressing issues of commercialism and 'pure' sport in the US, the picture is spiced up considerably by the creators of 'South Park', Trey Parker and Matt Stone, here playing key roles (in front of and behind the cameras).

His most recent film, however, *The Guest* (2002), is less original and appreciably less entertaining. The story focuses on a young publishing junior, played by Ashton Kutcher, from the equally inane *Dude, Where's My Car?* (2000), who house-sits for his loathsome boss. Shot on location in Vancouver, the entire narrative of this movie is based on a progression of increasingly implausible coincidences and stunts – such as a car driving through the wall of the house. Although it does have its own internal logic, this is still just another reworking of fundamental comedy staples that originated in Chaplin's era.                                                                                 **PB**

# Jerry ZUCKER

*Airplane!* (1980)
*Top Secret!* (1984)
*Ruthless People* (1986)
*Ghost* (1990)
*First Knight* (1995)
*Rat Race* (2001)

Jerry Zucker is a director who started out in the comedy genre, but has since turned his attention to more serious fare. Born in Wisconsin in 1950, he is the younger brother of David Zucker. One third of the Zucker-Abrahams-Zucker writing-producing-directing team, and a founder of the Kentucky Fried Theater – used as the basis for John Landis' 1977 film *The Kentucky Fried Movie* – his first effort, *Airplane!* (1980), became one of the most commercially successful comedies of the decade.

*Top Secret!* (1984), co-directed with brother and close friend Jim Abrahams, strives to do for teen rock 'n' roll and spy films, what *Airplane!* did for the disaster sub-genre. Unfortunately, the modus operandi of quick-fire witticisms and pranks works less well in this picture. There are a number of piquant touches, but on the whole more fun can be had from spotting the filmic references (*Jailhouse Rock* (1957), *The Blue Lagoon* (1980), *The Spy Who Came in from the Cold* (1965), and so on) and watching a young Val Kilmer in his feature debut.

After co-directing *Ruthless People* (1986), Zucker branched out on his own with *Ghost* (1990), a sentimental and supernatural cross-genre film (romance/comedy/thriller) starring Demi Moore and Patrick Swayze. Designed for maximum emotional impact, it concentrates on a murdered man's struggle to save his true love from a similar fate. Though hardly original in its depiction of the spirit world (and heaven as a big bright light), the movie scores highly with the character of Whoopi Goldberg's bogus medium, who discovers that she *can* talk to the dead after all – a part which won her an Academy Award.

Zucker remained within the bounds of fantasy for *First Knight* (1995). And yet this jettisons the mystical and magical trappings normally associated with the Arthurian legend (à la John Boorman's *Excalibur* (1981)), focusing instead upon the characters and the themes of trust, loyalty and pride. Scenic Welsh locations, exemplary acting from Sean Connery as Arthur and Julia Ormond as Guinevere, plus electrifying swordplay, advance the realism, while the costume and set designs give the production a more theatrical atmosphere. The only major frustration is the miscasting of Richard Gere as Lancelot, who may look every inch the knight in shining armour but falters when it comes to expressing himself verbally.

Returning to the director's chair and also to the comedy genre in 2001, Zucker delivered the outrageous *Rat Race*. An oddly-timed excuse to revive the fortunes of the road chase screwball farce, made famous by films like *It's a Mad Mad Mad Mad World* (1963) and *The Cannonball Run* (1981), the movie's infantile stance can be summed up by the scene in which a cow inadvertently gets tangled up in a hot-air balloon's ropes. **PB**

# Edward ZWICK

Born in Chicago in 1953, Edward Zwick started his career as a journalist before moving into television to work as a producer in the early 1980s on 'Family' and later on the highly successful and influential 'thirtysomething'. His first feature, *About Last Night...* (1986), was based on David Mamet's play 'Sexual Perversity in Chicago', though the similarities end with the scenario. The story, about an on-off relationship between two young single people, is both hackneyed and listless, and Zwick's film treatment strips away the caustic and cynical aspect of Mamet's play.

There seemed little in this film to suggest that Zwick could do justice to the epic story of the first black regiment to fight in the American Civil War – not least because 'thirtysomething' presented such a whites-only version of suburban Philadelphia. However, the Academy Award-winning *Glory* (1989) is a considerable achievement. It tells an epic story without ever losing sight of its essential humanity. Zwick plays up the old-fashioned values of heroism, comradeship, idealism and dignity, all within a framework that argues for conciliation in terms of racial conflict.

His next film, *Leaving Normal* (1992), appears at first sight to be the antithesis of *Glory*, yet it marks an interesting bridge between that and Zwick's subsequent work. It follows the journey of two women, Norma and Darly (Meg Tilly and Christine Lahti) from Normal, Wyoming to Alaska, using the changing landscape as a metaphor for their shifting lives. In all the ways *About Last Night...* was clichéd, *Leaving Normal* is fresh and original – Tilly and Lahti both play appealing characters. This period, and *Glory* in particular, marks a turning point in Zwick's work since all of his subsequent films are characterised by the telling of intimate stories set against large backdrop. In *Legends of the Fall* (1994) – a recounting of the life of a family of three brothers and their father in turn of the century Wyoming and beyond World War One – Zwick adopts an epic sweep for what is essentially a rather basic tale. Like *Glory*, the film stresses larger-than-life heroism, but opts instead for a more melodramatic structure and a romanticised version of history.

This emphasis on masculinity and heroism is carried over into his next feature, *Courage Under Fire* (1996), Hollywood's first foray into the Gulf War and Operation Desert Storm, and another large backdrop for an intimate study of individual actions. The interesting slant here is that the film focuses on a female helicopter pilot (Meg Ryan), telling and retelling the story of an incident in which she dies in the Iraqi desert whilst trying to rescue US troops. At the heart of the film are a series of difficult (and familiar) moral issues (loyalty, duty, conscience), which Zwick portrays well. However, the blame for her death is eventually placed on the actions and motivations of one individual soldier. As a result, the film barely criticises military culture and its institutional sexism. Opting once again for melodrama, the actors struggle with under-written roles.

The major criticism of *Courage Under Fire* – that it did not critique US policy in the Middle East – was given an additional twist with the release of *The Siege* (1998). The film is a 'what if' drama about the internment of Arab-Americans and the declaration of martial law in New York under the threat of a terrorist bombing campaign. Densely plotted and provocative, it deals with the impotence of modern states in the face of determined terrorists and the potential for these same states to suspend cherished freedoms. To its credit it also purports to show the injustice of actions on all sides – including that of US foreign policy – but ultimately sacrifices its lofty ambitions to the needs of the thriller genre. **SH**

# Terry ZWIGOFF

The spirit of anti-establishment counter-culturalism lives on in Terry Zwigoff, a confessed misanthrope and eclectic film-maker grounded in underground comic culture and

*Ghost World* (2001) esoteric old-time music. Born in 1948 in the sparsely populated farming community of Weyauwega, Wisconsin, Zwigoff spent his formative years in Chicago after moving there when he was five. He returned to Wisconsin in the late 1960s to attend the University of Wisconsin at Madison and eventually moved to San Francisco in 1970, where he befriended underground comic icons like R. Crumb and Art Spiegelman. Zwigoff became interested in late 1920s rural string band music – primarily country, blues and jazz – and began collecting recordings on 78 rpm LPs. His intense interest in this music and an invitation from Crumb to join his string band The Cheap Suit Serenaders motivated Zwigoff to learn the cello and mandolin. Zwigoff and Crumb, sharing similar mindsets and interests in old-time music, record collecting, and comics, began a long-term friendship marked by intermittent professional collaborations that continues to this day.

Zwigoff's first film project was born from an obsession over one of his 78 records, a 1934 recording of 'State Street Rag' by an artist named 'Louie Bluie'. After a long and convoluted search, Zwigoff found the personality behind 'Louie Bluie', a then-76-year-old, still-working black musician named Howard Armstrong. The charismatic Armstrong is the focus of Zwigoff's debut documentary film, *Louie Bluie* (1985), a fascinating artistic portrait highlighted by distinctive musical performances, and spiced up by candid, sexually explicit musings and artwork from Armstrong's bawdy personal journal. Zwigoff parlayed his friendship with Robert Crumb to film *Crumb* (1995), an intimate, disturbing, yet sympathetic documentary about Crumb's life and art as observed over a six-year period. Focusing on Crumb's highly dysfunctional family, bizarre sexual fetishes, and misanthropic tendencies, Zwigoff somehow manages to bring humour and sympathy to Crumb's unconventional lifestyle and beliefs, often relying on the effective technique of meshing narration to slow camera pans of sketches and comic panels to conceptualise Crumb's essence. *Crumb* also presents a fascinating context of the synergism of art and the irony of fame.

Zwigoff's first narrative feature, *Ghost World* (2001), an adaptation of Daniel Clowes' comic of the same name, came about from the encouragement of Zwigoff's wife Missy, who worked at Last Gasp Publishing, and R. Crumb, a 'Ghost World' reader who left copies of the comic behind after visiting Zwigoff while on holiday in France. *Ghost World* observes two deeply alienated teenage girls, Enid and Rebecca, as they take divergent paths into the 'real' world after graduating from high school. The film favors Enid (Thora Birch), the more alienated of the two, and Zwigoff in essence writes himself into the film as the barely-fictionalised, middle-aged sad sack 78 collector Seymour (Steve Buscemi) to serve as a mentor, father figure, and emotional connection for Enid. The film's passively caustic antisocial and anti-corporate themes are subversively cloaked in hilarious bitchy dialogue that makes great fun of skewering mass-market coffee houses, movie multiplexes, video stores, convenience stores, fast food restaurants, and countless other populist mainstays of modern society. The paradox of Zwigoff packaging his prickly anti-corporate message in a commercial MGM/UA Hollywood studio film boggles the mind, and audiences who celebrate the film's eccentricities are probably clueless that Zwigoff's poison Valentine to pop culture is made at their expense.

His next project, *Bad Santa*, will be a comedy starring Billy Bob Thornton as a character who masquerades as Santa Claus and travels across America robbing stores. **THa**

# Filmography

## A

ABBA: The Movie (Lasse Hallström, 1977)
About a Boy (Chris & Paul Weitz, 2002)
About Last Night... (Edward Zwick, 1986)
Above the Law (Andrew Davis, 1988)
Above the Rim (Jeff Pollack, 1994)
Absence of Malice (Sydney Pollack, 1981)
Absolute Power (Clint Eastwood, 1997)
Abyss, The (James Cameron, 1989)
Accidental Hero (Stephen Frears, 1992)
Accidental Tourist, The (Lawrence Kasdan, 1988)
Accused, The (Jonathan Kaplan, 1988)
Ace Ventura: Pet Detective (Tom Shadyac, 1994)
Ace Ventura: When Nature Calls (Steve Oedekerk, 1995)
Addams Family, The (Barry Sonnenfeld, 1991)
Addams Family Values (Barry Sonnenfeld, 1993)
Addicted to Love (Griffin Dunne, 1997)
Addiction, The (Abel Ferrara, 1995)
Adjuster, The (Atom Egoyan, 1991)
Adrenalin – Fear the Rush (Albert Pyun, 1996)
Adventures in Babysitting (Chris Columbus, 1987)
Adventures of Baron von Munchausen, The (Terry Gilliam, 1988)
Adventures of Ford Fairlane, The (Renny Harlin, 1990)
Adventures of Huck Finn (Stephen Sommers, 1993)
Affair, The (George A. Romero, 1969)
Affliction (Paul Schrader, 1997)
After Dark, My Sweet (James Foley, 1990)
After Hours (Martin Scorsese, 1985)
Afterglow (Alan Rudolph, 1997)
Against All Odds (Taylor Hackford, 1984)
Against the Wall (John Frankenheimer, 1994)
Agency (George Kaczender, 1980)
Age of Innocence, The (Martin Scorsese, 1993)
Agnes Browne (Angelica Huston, 1999)
Agnes of God (Norman Jewison, 1985)
A.I. Artificial Intelligence (Steven Spielberg, 2001)
Air America (Roger Spottiswoode, 1990)
Airborne (Rob Bowman, 1993)
Air Bud (Charles Martin Smith, 1997)
Air Force One (Wolfgang Petersen, 1997)
Airheads (Michael Lehmann, 1994)
Air Up There (Paul Michael Glaser, 1996)
Airplane! (Jim Abrahams, David Zucker & Jerry Zucker, 1980)
Aladdin (Ron Clements & John Musker, 1992)
Alambrista! (Robert M. Young, 1978)
Alarmist, The (Evan Dunsky, 1998)
Albino Alligator (Kevin Spacey, 1996)
Alchemist, The (Charles Band, 1984)
Alex in Wonderland (Paul Mazursky, 1970)
Alfred Laliberté sculpteur 1878–1953 (Jean-Pierre Lefebvre, 1987)
Ali (Michael Mann, 2001)

Alice (Woody Allen, 1990)
Alice Doesn't Live Here Anymore (Martin Scorsese, 1974)
Alice in the Cities (Wim Wenders, 1974)
Alien from LA (Albert Pyun, 1987)
Aliens (James Cameron, 1986)
Alien³ (David Fincher, 1992)
Alive (Frank Marshall, 1993)
All Dogs Go to Heaven (Don Bluth, 1990)
Alley Cat, The (Jean Beaudin, 1985)
All Fall Down (John Frankenheimer, 1962)
All of Me (Carl Reiner, 1984)
All Over Me (Alex Sichel, 1997)
All the President's Men (Alan J. Pakula, 1976)
All the Pretty Horses (Billy Bob Thornton, 2000)
Almost Famous (Cameron Crowe, 2000)
Almost Heroes (Christopher Guest, 1998)
Along Came a Spider (Lee Tamahori, 2001)
Always (Henry Jaglom, 1985)
Always (Steven Spielberg, 1989)
Amadeus (Milos Forman, 1984)
Amateur (Hal Hartley, 1994)
Amazing Grace and Chuck (Mike Newell, 1987)
Amazing Stories: Go to the Head of the Class (Robert Zemeckis, 1985)
Ambition (Hal Hartley, 1991)
Ambulance, The (Larry Cohen, 1990)
American Beauty (Sam Mendes, 1999)
American Boy: A Profile of Steven Prince (Martin Scorsese, 1978)
American Buffalo (Michael Corrente, 1996)
American Dreamer (Rick Rosenthal, 1984)
American Flyers (John Badham, 1985)
American Friend, The (Wim Wenders, 1977)
American Gigolo (Paul Schrader, 1980)
American Graffiti (George Lucas, 1973)
American Job (Chris Smith, 1995)
American Movie (Chris Smith, 1999)
American Nightmare, The (Adam Simon, 1990)
American Outlaws (Les Mayfield, 2001)
American Pie (Paul Weitz, 1999)
American Pimp (Albert & Allen Hughes, 1999)
American Pop (Ralph Bakshi, 1981)
American President, The (Rob Reiner, 1995)
American Psycho (Mary Harron, 2000)
American Tail, An (Don Bluth, 1986)
American Werewolf in London, An (John Landis, 1981)
American Werewolf in Paris, An (Anthony Waller, 1997)
Americanization of Emily, The (Arthur Hiller, 1964)
Amisk (Alanis Obomsawin, 1977)
Amistad (Steven Spielberg, 1997)
Amityville 3-D (Richard Fleischer, 1983)

An Alan Smithee Film: Burn, Hollywood, Burn
(Arthur Hiller, 1997)
Analyze That (Harold Ramis, 2002)
Analyze This (Harold Ramis, 1999)
An American Tail: Fievel Goes West (Simon Wells, 1991)
Anaconda (Luis Llosa, 1997)
Anastasia (Don Bluth, 1998)
...and justice for all (Norman Jewison, 1979)
And Now For Something Completely Different
(Terry Gilliam, 1971)
Anderson Tapes, The (Sydney Lumet, 1971)
Andersonville (John Frankenheimer, 1996)
Angel (Neil Jordan, 1982)
Angela (Rebecca Miller, 1996)
Angela's Ashes (Alan Parker, 1999)
Angel Heart (Alan Parker, 1987)
Angel Square (Anne Wheeler, 1990)
Angelo My Love (Robert Duvall, 1983)
Angels and Insects (Phillip Haas, 1995)
Angels in the Outfield (William Dear, 1994)
Angie (Martha Coolidge, 1994)
Angus (Patrick Read Johnson, 1995)
Anna & the King (Andy Tennant, 1999)
Anna Karenina (Bernard Rose, 1997)
Anne Trister (Léa Pool, 1986)
Annie Hall (Woody Allen, 1977)
Anniversary Party, The (Alan Cumming & Jennifer Jason
Leigh, 2001)
Another Country (Marek Kanievska, 1984)
Another Day in Paradise (Larry Clark, 1998)
Another Girl, Another Planet (Michael Almereyda, 1992)
Another 48 Hrs. (Walter Hill, 1990)
Another Stakeout (John Badham, 1993)
Another Woman (Woody Allen, 1988)
Any Given Sunday (Oliver Stone, 1999)
Anywhere But Here (Wayne Wang, 1999)
Apache Woman (Roger Corman, 1955)
Apocalypse Now (Francis Ford Coppola, 1979)
Apollo 13 (Ron Howard, 1995)
Apostle, The (Robert Duvall, 1997)
Appaloosa, The (Sidney J. Furie, 1966)
Appointment, The (Sydney Lumet, 1969)
Apt Pupil (Bryan Singer 1998)
Arachnophobia (Frank Marshall, 1990)
Ararat (Atom Egoyan, 2002)
Archangel (Guy Maddin, 1990)
Arena (Richard Fleischer, 1953)
Arisha, the Bear and the Stone Ring (Wim Wenders,
1992)
Arlington Road (Mark Pellington, 1999)
Armageddon (Michael Bay, 1998)
Armored Car Robbery (Richard Fleischer, 1950)
Army of Darkness: The Evil Dead 3 (Sam Raimi, 1993)
Arrival, The (David Twohy, 1996)
Ashanti (Richard Fleischer, 1979)
Art of Love, The (Norman Jewison, 1965)
Art of War, The (Christian Duguay, 2000)
Article 99 (Howard Deutch, 1992)
As Good As It Gets (James L. Brooks, 1997)
Assassin, The (John Badham, 1993)

Assassins (Richard Donner, 1995)
Assault on Precinct 13 (John Carpenter, 1976)
Assignment, The (Christian Duguay, 1997)
Assistant, The (Daniel Petrie, 1997)
Associate, The (Donald Petrie, 1996)
Atanarjuat The Fast Runner (Zacharias Kunuk, 2001)
At Close Range (James Foley, 1986)
Atlas (Roger Corman, 1960)
At Long Last Love (Peter Bogdanovich, 1975)
At Sundance (Michael Almereyda, 1995)
Attack of the Crab Monsters (Roger Corman, 1957)
August 32nd on Earth (Denis Villeneuve, 1998)
Aujourd'hui ou jamais (Jean-Pierre Lefebvre, 1998)
Au rythme de mon coeur (Jean-Pierre Lefebvre, 1983)
Aus der Familie der Panzerechsen/Die Insel (Wim
Wenders, 1974)
Austin Powers in Goldmember (Jay Roach, 2002)
Austin Powers: International Man of Mystery (Jay
Roach, 1997)
Austin Powers: The Spy Who Shagged Me (Jay Roach,
1999)
Author! Author! (Arthur Hiller, 1982)
Autobiography of a Princess (James Ivory, 1975)
Auto Focus (Paul Schrader, 2002)
Autumn in New York (Joan Chen, 2000)
Avalanche Express (Monte Hellman, 1979)
Avalon (Barry Levinson, 1990)
Avengers, The (Jeremiah Chechik, 1998)
Avoir 16 ans (Jean-Pierre Lefebvre, 1979)
Awakening, The (Mike Newell, 1980)
Awfully Big Adventure, An (Mike Newell, 1994)

# B

Babe, The (Arthur Hiller, 1992)
Baby Boy (John Singleton, 2001)
Baby Geniuses (Bob Clark, 1999)
Baby It's You (John Sayles, 1983)
Baby's Day Out (Patrick Read Johnson, 1994)
Babyfever (Henry Jaglom, 1994)
Babysitter, The (Guy Ferland, 1995)
Back Door to Hell (Monte Hellman, 1964)
Backdraft (Ron Howard, 1991)
Backroads (Phillip Noyce, 1977)
Back to the Future (Robert Zemeckis, 1985)
Back to the Future Part II (Robert Zemeckis, 1989)
Back to the Future Part III (Robert Zemeckis, 1990)
Backyard (Ross McElwee, 1984)
Bad Blood (Mike Newell, 1981)
Bad Boys (Michael Bay, 1995)
Bad Boys (Rick Rosenthal, 1983)
Bad Company (Robert Benton, 1972)
Bad Company (Joel Schumacher, 2002)
Bad Dreams (Andrew Fleming, 1988)
Bad Girls (Jonathan Kaplan, 1994)
Bad Influence (Curtis Hanson, 1990)
Badlands (Terrence Malick, 1973)
Bad Lieutenant (Abel Ferrara, 1992)
Bait (Antoine Fuqua, 2000)

Ballad of Gregomio Cortez, The (Robert M. Young, 1982)
Ballad of Little Jo, The (Maggie Greenwald, 1993)
Balto (Simon Wells, 1995)
Bamboozled (Spike Lee, 2000)
Bananas (Woody Allen, 1971)
Bandido (Richard Fleischer, 1956)
Bandits (Barry Levinson, 2001)
Band of the Hand (Paul Michael Glaser, 1986)
Bang (Ash, 1995)
Banjo (Richard Fleischer, 1947)
Barabbas (Richard Fleischer, 1962)
Barbarosa (Fred Schepisi, 1982)
Barcelona (Whit Stillman, 1994)
Barfly (Barbet Schroeder, 1987)
Barry Lyndon (Stanley Kubrick, 1975)
Bartok the Magnificent (Don Bluth, 1999)
Barton Fink (Joel Coen, 1991)
BASEketball (David Zucker, 1999)
Basic Instinct (Paul Verhoeven, 1992)
Basil, The Great Mouse Detective (Ron Clements & John
    Musker, 1986)
Basquiat (Julian Schnabel, 1996)
Bastard Out of Carolina (Anjelica Huston, 1996)
Batman (Tim Burton, 1989)
Batman & Robin (Joel Schumacher, 1997)
Batman Forever (Joel Schumacher, 1995)
Batman Returns (Tim Burton, 1992)
Battlefield Earth (Roger Christian, 2000)
Bay Boy, The (Daniel Petrie, 1984)
Bayo (Mort Ransen, 1984)
Beaches (Gary Marshall, 1988)
Beast, The (Kevin Reynolds, 1988)
Beast From Haunted Cave, The (Monte Hellman, 1959)
Beauté de pandore, La (Charles Binamé, 2000)
Beautiful Girls (Ted Demme, 1996)
Beautiful Mind, A (Ron Howard, 2001)
Beaver Trilogy (Trent Harris, 2001)
Beavis and Butt-head Do America (Mike Judge, 1996)
Bedazzled (Harold Ramis, 2000)
Bedford Incident, The (James B. Harris, 1965)
Bedrooms and Hallways (Rose Troche, 1998)
Bedroom Window, The (Curtis Hanson, 1987)
Beefcake (Thom Fitzgerald, 1999)
Beethoven (Brian Levant, 1992)
Before and After (Barbet Schroeder, 1996)
Before Night Falls (Julian Schnabel, 2000)
Before Sunrise (Richard Linklater, 1995)
Being at Home with Claude (Jean Beaudin, 1992)
Begotten (E. Elias Merhige, 1991)
Being John Malkovich (Spike Jonze, 1999)
Believer, The (Henry Bean, 2001)
Believers, The (John Schlesinger, 1987)
Belly (Hype Williams, 1998)
Beloved (Jonathan Demme, 1998)
Beloved, The (George P. Cosmatos, 1970)
Beluga Days, The (Michel Brault, 1968)
Benny & Joon (Jeremiah Chechik, 1993)
Bert Rigby, You're a Fool (Carl Reiner, 1989)
Best Friends (Norman Jewison, 1982)
Best in Show (Christopher Guest, 2000)

Best Man, The (Malcolm D. Lee, 1999)
Best Men (Tamra Davis, 1997)
Best of Times, The (Roger Spottiswoode, 1986)
Best Seller (John Flynn, 1987)
Betsy, The (Daniel Petrie, 1978)
Betsy's Wedding (Alan Alda, 1990)
Better Than Chocolate (Anne Wheeler, 1999)
Better Tomorrow, A (John Woo, 1986)
Better Tomorrow II, A (John Woo, 1987)
Between Heaven and Hell (Richard Fleischer, 1956)
Beverly Hillbillies, The (Penelope Spheeris, 1993)
Beverly Hills Cop (Martin Brest, 1984)
Beverly Hills Cop II (Tony Scott, 1987)
Beverly Hills Cop III (John Landis, 1994)
Beverly Hills Ninja (Dennis Dugan, 1997)
Beyond the Clouds (Wim Wenders, 1995)
Beyond Therapy (Robert Altman, 1987)
Bicentennial Man (Chris Columbus, 1999)
Big (Penny Marshall, 1988)
Big Bang, The (James Toback, 1989)
Big Brass Ring, The (George Hickenlooper, 1999)
Big Bully (Steve Miner, 1996)
Big Business (Jim Abrahams, 1988)
Big Chill, The (Lawrence Kasdan, 1983)
Big Daddy (Dennis Dugan, 1999)
Big Easy, The (Jim McBride, 1987)
Big Gamble, The (Richard Fleischer, 1961)
Big Kahuna, The (John Swanbeck, 1999)
Big Lebowski, The (Joel Coen, 1998)
Big Momma's House (Raja Gosnell, 2000)
Big Night (Campbell Scott & Stanley Tucci, 1996)
Big Picture, The (Christopher Guest, 1989)
Big Trouble (Barry Sonnenfeld, 2002)
Big Trouble in Little China (John Carpenter, 1986)
Big Wednesday (John Milius, 1978)
Bill & Ted's Bogus Journey (Peter Hewitt, 1991)
Bill & Ted's Excellent Adventure (Stephen Herek, 1989)
Billy Bathgate (Robert Benton, 1991)
Billy Galvin (John Gray, 1986)
Billy Liar! (John Schlesinger, 1963)
Billy Madison (Tamra Davis, 1995)
Biloxi Blues (Mike Nichols, 1988)
Bingo Long Travelling All-Stars and Motor Kings, The
    (John Badham, 1976)
Bird (Clint Eastwood, 1988)
Birdcage, The (Mike Nichols, 1996)
Bird on a Wire (John Badham, 1990)
Birdman of Alcatraz (John Frankenheimer, 1962)
Birdy (Alan Parker, 1984)
Birthday Party, The (William Friedkin, 1968)
Black and White (James Toback, 1999)
Black Caesar (Larry Cohen, 1973)
Black Christmas (Bob Clark, 1974)
Black Dog (Kevin Honks, 1998)
Black Hawk Down (Ridley Scott, 2001)
Black Knight (Gil Junger, 2001)
Black Marble, The (Harold Becker, 1980)
Blackout (Allan A. Goldstein, 1996)
Black Rain (Ridley Scott, 1989)
Black Sheep (Penelope Spheeris, 1996)

*Black Stallion, The* (Caroll Ballard, 1979)
*Black Sunday* (John Frankenheimer, 1977)
*Blacktop Lingo* (Rick Famuyiwa, 1996)
*Black Widow* (Bob Rafelson, 1987)
*Blade Runner* (Ridley Scott, 1982)
*Blade Runner – The Director's Cut* (Ridley Scott, 1991)
*Blade 2* (Guillermo del Toro, 2002)
*Blair Witch Project, The* (Eduardo Sanchez & Daniel Myrick, 1999)
*Blank Check* (Rupert Wainwright, 1994)
*Blast from the Past* (Hugh Wilson, 1999)
*Blaze* (Ron Shelton, 1989)
*Blazing Saddles* (Mel Brooks, 1974)
*Blerta Revisited* (Geoff Murphy, 2001)
*Blind Alley* (Larry Cohen, 1984)
*Blind Date* (Blake Edwards, 1987)
*Blind Fury* (Phillip Noyce, 1989)
*Blood and Guts* (Paul Lynch, 1978)
*Blood and Wine* (Bob Rafelson, 1997)
*Blooddolls* (Charles Band, 1999)
*Blood, Guts, Bullets and Octane* (Joe Carnahan, 1998)
*Blood In, Blood Out* (Taylor Hackford, 1993)
*Blood Oranges, The* (Phillp Haas, 1997)
*Blood Simple* (Joel Coen, 1984)
*Bloody Mama* (Roger Corman, 1970)
*Blow* (Ted Demme, 2001)
*Blow Out* (Brian De Palma, 1981)
*Blown Away* (Stephen Hopkins, 1994)
*Blue Chips* (William Friedkin, 1994)
*Blue Collar* (Paul Schrader, 1978)
*Blue in the Face* (Wayne Wang, 1995)
*Blue Steel* (Kathryn Bigelow, 1990)
*Blue Streak* (Les Mayfleld, 1999)
*Blue Thunder* (John Badham, 1983)
*Blue Velvet* (David Lynch, 1986)
*Blues Brothers, The* (John Landis, 1980)
*Blues Brothers 2000* (John Landis, 1998)
*Blume in Love* (Paul Mazursky, 1973)
*Bob & Carol & Ted & Alice* (Paul Mazursky, 1969)
*Bob Roberts* (Tim Robbins, 1992)
*Bobby Deerfield* (Sydney Pollack, 1977)
*Body Chemistry 2* (Adam Simon, 1992)
*Body Contact* (Bernard Rose, 1987)
*Body Double* (Brian De Palma, 1984)
*Bodyguard* (Richard Fleischer, 1948)
*Body Heat* (Lawrence Kasdan, 1981)
*Body Shots* (Michael Cristofer, 1999)
*Body Snatchers* (Abel Ferrara, 1993)
*Bodyguard, The* (Mick Jackson, 1992)
*Bogus* (Norman Jewison, 1996)
*Bohemians* (Rafal Zielinski, 2000)
*Boiler Room* (Ben Younger, 2000)
*Boiling Point* (James B. Harris, 1993)
*Boîte à soleil, La* (Jean-Pierre Lefebvre, 1988)
*Bombay Talkie* (James Ivory, 1970)
*Bone* (Larry Cohen, 1972)
*Bone Collector, The* (Phillip Noyce, 1999)
*Boney D* (Bill Plympton, 1996)
*Bonfire of the Vanities, The* (Brian De Palma, 1990)
*Boogie Nights* (Paul Thomas Anderson, 1997)

*Book of Life, The* (Hal Hartley, 1998)
*Boomerang* (Reginald Hudlin, 1992)
*Boomtown* (Bill Plympton, 1985)
*Boost, The (*Harold Becker, 1988)
*Booty Call* (Jeff Pollack, 1997)
*Border Radio* (Allison Anders, 1967)
*Boris and Natasha* (Charles Martin Smith, 1992)
*Born American* (Renny Harlin, 1986)
*Born in Flames* (Lizzie Borden, 1983)
*Born on the Fourth of July* (Oliver Stone, 1989)
*Born to Be Wild* (John Gray, 1995)
*Born to Win* (Ivan Passer, 1971)
*Borrower, The* (John McNaughton, 1991)
*Borrowers, The* (Peter Hewitt, 1997)
*Bostonians, The* (James Ivory, 1984)
*Boston Strangler, The* (Richard Fleischer, 1968)
*Bottle Rocket* (Wes Anderson, 1996)
*Bounce (*Don Roos, 2000)
*Bound* (Larry & Andy Wachowski, 1996)
*Bounty, The* (Roger Donaldson, 1984)
*Bowfinger* (Frank Oz, 1999)
*Boxcar Bertha* (Martin Scorsese, 1972)
*Boxing Helena* (Jennifer Chambers Lynch, 1993)
*Box of Moon Light* (Tom Dicillo, 1996)
*Boy's Club, The* (John Fawcett, 1997)
*Boy/Girl* (Bruce LaBruce, 1987)
*Boy Meets Girl* (Jerry Ciccoritti, 1998)
*Boys* (Stacy Cochran, 1996)
*Boys and Girls* (Robert Iscove, 2000)
*Boys Don't Cry* (Kimberly Peirce, 1999)
*Boys, Les* (Louis Saia, 1997)
*Boys II, Les (*Louis Saia, 1998)
*Boys III, Les* (Louis Saia, 2001)
*Boys, The* (Sidney J. Furie, 1962)
*Boys in Company C, The* (Sidney J. Furie, 1978)
*Boys in the Band, The* (William Friedkin, 1970)
*Boys Next Door, The* (Penelope Spheeris, 1986)
*Boyz N the Hood* (John Singleton, 1991)
*Brady Bunch Movie, The* (Betty Thomas, 1995)
*Brain Candy* (Kelly Makin, 1996)
*Brain Dead* (Adam Simon, 1990)
*Brain Donors* (Dennis Dugan, 1992)
*Brainscan* (John Flynn, 1994)
*Brain Smasher ... A Love Story* (Albert Pyun, 1993)
*Bramble Bush, The* (Daniel Petrie, 1960)
*Bram Stoker's Dracula* (Francis Ford Coppola, 1992)
*Brave, The* (Johnny Depp, 1997)
*Braveheart* (Mel Gibson, 1995)
*Brazil* (Terry Gilliam, 1985)
*Breakdown* (Jonathan Mostow, 1997)
*Breakfast at Tiffany's* (Blake Edwards, 1961)
*Breakfast Club, The* (John Hughes, 1985)
*Breakfast of Champions* (Alan Rudolph, 1999)
*Breaking Point* (Bob Clark, 1976)
*Breaking Up* (Robert Greenwald, 1997)
*Breaks, The* (Eric Meza, 1999)
*Breathe In, Breathe Out* (Beth B, 2000)
*Breathless* (Jim McBride, 1983)
*Breezy* (Clint Eastwood, 1973)
*Brewster McCloud* (Robert Altman, 1970)

Brewster's Millions (Walter Hill, 1985)
Bridges of Madison County, The (Clint Eastwood, 1995)
Bring Your Smile Along (Blake Edwards, 1955)
Bringing out the Dead (Martin Scorsese, 1999)
Brink's Job, The (William Friedkin, 1978)
Broadcast News (James L. Brooks, 1987)
Broadway Danny Rose (Woody Allen, 1984)
Brokedown Palace (Jonathan Kaplan, 1999)
Broken Arrow (John Woo, 1996)
Bronco Billy (Clint Eastwood, 1980)
Brood, The (David Cronenberg, 1979)
Brother From Another Planet, The (John Sayles, 1984)
Brothers McMullen, The (Edward Burns, 1995)
Bruiser (George A. Romero, 1999)
Browning Version, The (Mike Figgis, 1994)
Bucket of Blood, A (Roger Corman, 1958)
Buena Vista Social Club (Wim Wenders, 1999)
Buffalo 66 (Vincent Gallo, 1998)
Buffalo Bill and the Indians, or Sitting Bull's History
    Lesson (Robert Altman, 1976)
Bug's Life, A (John Lasseter, 1998)
Bugsy (Barry Levinson, 1991)
Bugsy Malone (Alan Parker, 1976)
Bull Durham (Ron Shelton, 1988)
Bullet in the Head (John Woo, 1990)
Bullets Over Broadway (Woody Allen, 1994)
Bullies (Paul Lynch, 1986)
Bully (Larry Clark, 2001)
Bulworth (Warren Beatty, 1998)
'Burbs, The (Joe Dante, 1989)
Burglar (Hugh Wilson, 1987)
Burke and Wills (Graeme Clifford, 1985)
Burning Season, The (John Frankenheimer, 1994)
Business is Business (Paul Verhoeven, 1971)
Buster and Billie (Daniel Petrie, 1974)
Busting (Peter Hyams, 1974)
Butcher Boy, The (Neil Jordan, 1997)
Bye Bye Blues (Anne Wheeler, 1989)
Bye Bye Braverman (Sydney Lumet, 1968)

# C

Cable Guy, The (Ben Stiller, 1996)
Caddyshack (Harold Ramis, 1980)
Cadillac Man (Roger Donaldson, 1990)
Caged Heat (Jonathan Demme, 1974)
Cal (Pat O'Connor, 1984)
Calendar (Atom Egoyan, 1993)
California Split (Robert Altman, 1974)
Camilia (Deepa Mehta, 1995)
Can She Bake a Cherry Pie? (Henry Jaglom, 1983)
Candyman (Bernard Rose, 1992)
Candyman II: Farewell to the Flesh (Bill Condon, 1995)
Cannery Row (David S. Ward, 1982)
Cannibal Girls (Ivan Reitman, 1973)
Cannibal: The Musical (Trey Parker, 1996)
Cannonball (Paul Bartel, 1976)
Can't Hardly Wait (Deborah Kaplan, 1998)
Cape Fear (Martin Scorsese, 1991)

Capricorn One (Peter Hyams, 1978)
Captain Corelli's Mandolin (John Madden, 2001)
Careful (Guy Maddin, 1992)
Careless Years, The (Arthur Hiller, 1957)
Carey Treatment, The (Blake Edwards, 1972)
Carlito's Way (Brian De Palma, 1993)
Carnal Knowledge (Mike Nichols, 1971)
Carnival Rock (Roger Corman, 1957)
Carnosaur (Adam Simon, 1993)
Carpenter, The (David Wellington, 1989)
Carpool (Arthur Hiller, 1996)
Carrie (Brian De Palma, 1976)
Cast Away (Robert Zemeckis, 2000)
Cars That Ate Paris, The (Peter Weir, 1974)
Cartographer's Girlfriend, The (Hal Hartley, 1987)
Case For the Closet, A (Bruce LaBruce, 1992)
Casino (Martin Scorsese, 1995)
Casper (Brad Silberling, 1995)
Casper 2 (Simon Wells, 1999)
Cassandra Crossing, The (George P. Cosmatos, 1976)
Castle Freak (Stuart Gordon, 1995)
Castle Keep (Sydney Pollack, 1969)
Cat Chaser (Abel Ferrara, 1989)
Catchfire (Dennis Hopper, as Alan Smithee, 1989)
Catch Me If You Can (Stephen Sommers, 1989)
Catch-22 (Mike Nichols, 1970)
Cat People (Paul Schrader, 1982)
Cats and Dogs (Lawrence Guterman, 2001)
Cat's Meow, The (Peter Bogdanovich, 2002)
Caught (Robert M. Young, 1995)
Caveman's Shadow, The (Kasi Lemmons, 2001)
CB4 (Tamra Davis, 1993)
Cecil B. DeMented (John Waters, 2000)
Celebrity (Woody Allen, 1998)
Cell, The (Tarsem Singh, 2000)
Center of the World, The (Wayne Wang, 2001)
Century of Cinema – A Personal Journey with Martin
    Scorsese through American Movies, A (Martin
    Scorsese, 1995)
C'était le 12 du 12 et Chili avait les blues (Charles
    Binamé, 1994)
Chaindance (Allan A. Goldstein, 1990)
Chain of Fools (Traktor, 2000)
Chain Reaction (Andrew Davis, 1996)
Challenge, The (John Frankenheimer, 1982)
Chamber, The (James Foley, 1996)
Chambre 666 (Wim Wenders, 1982)
Chambre blanche, La (Jean-Pierre Lefebvre, 1969)
Champions (John Irvin, 1983)
Chan is Missing (Wayne Wang, 1982)
Chanel Solitaire (George Kaczender, 1981)
Changeling, The (Peter Medak, 1980)
Chantal en Vrac (Jacques Leduc, 1967)
Chant of Jimmie Blacksmith, The (Fred Schepisi, 1978)
Charleen (Ross McElwee, 1978)
Charlie's Family (Jim Van Bebber, 1997)
Chasers (Dennis Hopper, 1994)
Chasing Amy (Kevin Smith, 1997)
Chattahoochee (Mick Jackson, 1990)
Che! (Richard Fleischer, 1969)

Chicago Joe and the Showgirl (Bernard Rose, 1990)
Child of Divorce (Richard Fleischer, 1946)
Children of a Lesser God (Randa Haines, 1986)
Children of Fate: Life and Death in a Sicilian Family (Robert M. Young, 1993)
Children of Noisy Village, The (Lasse Hallström, 1986)
Children of the Corn 666: Isaac's Return (Kari Skogland, 1999)
Children Shouldn't Play with Dead Things (Bob Clark, 1972)
Child's Play (Sydney Lumet, 1972)
China Girl (Abel Ferrara, 1987)
China Moon (John Bailey, 1994)
China 9, Liberty 37 (Monte Hellman, 1978)
China: The Panda Adventure (Robert M. Young, 2001)
Chinese Box (Wayne Wang, 1997)
Chocolat (Lasse Hallström, 2000)
Chocolate War, The (Keith Gordon, 1988)
Choose Me (Alan Rudolph, 1984)
Christine (John Carpenter, 1983)
Christmas Story, A (Bob Clark, 1983)
Chuck & Buck (Miguel Arteta, 2000)
Chuck Berry, Hail, Hail, Rock'n'Roll (Taylor Hackford, 1987)
Cider House Rules, The (Lasse Hallström, 1999)
Cincinnati Kid, The (Norman Jewison, 1965)
Circle of Friends (Pat O'Connor, 1995)
Citizen Ruth (Alexander Payne, 1996)
Citizens Band (Jonathan Demme, 1977)
City Girl (Martha Coolidge, 1984)
City Hall (Harold Becker, 1996)
City Heat (Richard Benjamin, 1984)
City of Angels (Brad Silberling, 1998)
City of Hope (John Sayles, 1991)
City of Industry (John Irvin, 1997)
City of Joy (Roland Joffé, 1992)
City Slickers (Ron Underwood, 1991)
Civil Action, A (Steven Zaillian, 1998)
Claire Dolan (Lodge Kerrigan, 1998)
Clay Pigeon, The (Richard Fleischer, 1949)
Clean and Sober (Glen Gordon Caron, 1988)
Clean Slate (Mick Jackson, 1994)
Clean, Shaven (Lodge Kerrigan, 1995)
Clear and Present Danger (Phillip Noyce, 1994)
Clerks (Kevin Smith, 1994)
Client, The (Joel Schumacher, 1994)
Cliffhanger (Renny Harlin, 1993)
Clockers (Spike Lee, 1995)
Clockstoppers (Jonathan Frakes, 2002)
Clockwork Orange, A (Stanley Kubrick, 1971)
Close Encounters of the Third Kind (Steven Spielberg, 1977)
Closers (Penelope Spheeris, 2001)
Club Paradise (Harold Ramis, 1986)
Clubland (Mary Lambert, 1999)
Clue (Jonathan Lynn, 1985)
Clueless (Amy Heckerling, 1995)
Cobb (Ron Shelton, 1994)
Cobra (George P. Cosmatos, 1986)
Cockfighter (Monte Hellman, 1974)

Cocoon (Ron Howard, 1985)
Cocoon: The Return (Daniel Petrie, 1988)
Code 99 (Matthew Harrison, 1996)
Code Name: Trixie (George A. Romero, 1973)
Code of Silence (Andrew Davis, 1985)
Coeur au poing, Le (Charles Binamé, 1998)
Coffee and Cigarettes (Jim Jarmusch, 1986)
Coffee and Cigarettes II (Jim Jarmusch, 1986)
Coffee and Cigarettes III (Jim Jarmusch, 1993)
Cold Comfort Farm (John Schlesinger, 1995)
Cold Front (Allan A. Goldstein, 1989)
Collateral Damage (Andrew Davis, 2002)
Collector, The (Jean Beaudin, 2002)
Collectors, The (Sidney J. Furie, 1999)
Color of Money, The (Martin Scorsese, 1986)
Color Purple, The (Steven Spielberg, 1985)
Colors (Dennis Hopper, 1988)
Coma (Michael Crichton, 1978)
Come As You Are (Bruce LaBruce, 2000)
Come Back to the Five and Dime, Jimmy Dean, Jimmy Dean (Robert Altman, 1982)
Comes a Horseman (Alan J. Pakula, 1978)
Come See the Paradise (Alan Parker, 1990)
Comfort of Strangers, The (Paul Schrader, 1990)
Comfortably Numb (Gavin O'Connor, 1995)
Comic, The (Carl Reiner, 1969)
Coming to America (John Landis, 1988)
Committed (Lisa Krueger, 2000)
Commitments, The (Alan Parker, 1991)
Company Business (Nicholas Meyer, 1991)
Company of Wolves, The (Neil Jordan, 1984)
Complex Sessions, The (Jonathan Demme, 1994)
Compulsion (Richard Fleischer, 1959)
Con Air (Simon West, 1997)
Conan the Barbarian (John Milius, 1982)
Conan the Destroyer (Richard Fleischer, 1984)
Condo Painting (John McNaughton, 2000)
Confessional, The (Robert Lepage, 1995)
Confessions of a Suburban Girl (Susan Seidelman, 1992)
Congo (Frank Marshall, 1995)
Consenting Adults (Alan J. Pakula, 1992)
Conspiracy Theory (Richard Donner, 1997)
Contact (Robert Zemeckis, 1997)
Contender, The (Rod Lurie, 2000)
Conversation, The (Francis Ford Coppola, 1974)
Cookie (Susan Seidelman, 1989)
Cookie's Fortune (Robert Altman, 1999)
Cool as Ice (David Kellogg, 1991)
Cool Runnings (Jon Turteltaub, 1993)
Cool Sound From Hell (Sidney J. Furie, 1959)
Cool World (Ralph Bakshi, 1992)
Coonskin (Ralph Bakshi, 1974)
Cop (James B. Harris, 1987)
Cop Land (James Mangold, 1997)
Copycat (Jon Amiel, 1995)
Cord (Sidney J. Furie, 1999)
Cordélia (Jean Beaudin, 1979)
Core, The (Jon Amiel, 2002)
Corruptor, The (James Foley, 1999)
Cosmos (Denis Villeneuve, 1996)

Cotton Club, The (Francis Ford Coppola, 1984)
Countdown (Robert Altman, 1968)
Count of Monte Cristo, The (Kevin Reynolds, 2002)
Courage Under Fire (Edward Zwick, 1996)
Cousin Bobby (Jonathan Demme, 1992)
Cousins (Joel Schumacher, 1989)
Cowboys Don't Cry (Anne Wheeler, 1988)
Coyote (Richard Ciupka, 1992)
Coyote Moon (John G. Avildsen, 1999)
Coyote Ugly (David McNally, 2000)
CQ (Roman Coppola, 2001)
Cradle Will Rock (Tim Robbins, 1999)
Crack in the Mirror (Richard Fleischer, 1960)
Craft, The (Andrew Fleming, 1996)
Crash (David Cronenberg, 1996)
Crash! (Charles Band, 1977)
Crash and Burn (Charles Band, 1990)
Crazy for You (Harold Becker, 1985)
Crazy Mama (Jonathan Demme, 1975)
Crazy World of Julius Vrooder, The (Arthur Hiller, 1974)
Creator (Ivan Passer, 1985)
Creature (William Malone, 1985)
Creature from the Haunted Sea (Roger Corman, 1961)
Creeps, The (Charles Band, 1997)
Creepshow (George A. Romero, 1982)
Cremaster 1 (Matthew Barney, 1995–96)
Cremaster 2 (Matthew Barney, 1999)
Cremaster 3 (Matthew Barney, 2002)
Cremaster 4 (Matthew Barney, 1994)
Cremaster 5 (Matthew Barney, 1997)
Crime and Passion (Ivan Passer, 1975)
Crime and Punishment in Suburbia (Rob Schmidt, 2000)
Crimes and Misdemeanors (Woody Allen, 1989)
Crime Wave (John Paizs, 1986)
Crime Zone (Luis Llosa, 1988)
Crimewave (Sam Raimi, 1985)
Crimson Tide (Tony Scott, 1995)
Critters (Stephen Herek, 1986)
Critters 2: The Main Course (Mick Garris, 1988)
Crocodile (Tobe Hooper, 2000)
Cronos (Guillermo Del Toro, 1993)
Crooklyn (Spike Lee, 1994)
Cross Country (Paul Lynch, 1983)
Crossed Swords (Richard Fleischer, 1978)
Crossing Guard, The (Sean Penn, 1995)
Crossroads (Walter Hill, 1986)
Crossroads (Tamra Davis, 2002)
Crouching Tiger, Hidden Dragon (Ang Lee, 2000)
Crow, The (Alex Proyas, 1994)
Cruel Intentions (Roger Kumble, 1999)
Cruising (William Friedkin, 1980)
Crumb (Terry Zwigoff, 1994)
Cry Baby (John Waters, 1990)
Crying Game, The (Neil Jordan, 1992)
Cry in the Dark, A (Fred Schepisi, 1988)
Cry Uncle! (John G. Avildsen, 1971)
Cube (Vincenzo Natati, 1997)
Curly Sue (John Hughes, 1991)
Curse of the Jade Scorpion, The (Woody Allen, 2001)
Curse of the Pink Panther (Blake Edwards, 1983)

Curtains (Richard Ciupka, 1983)
Curtis's Charm (John L'Ecuyer, 1995)
Curve, The (Dan Rosen, 1998)
CutThroat Island (Renny Harlin, 1995)
Cutting Edge, The (Paul Michael Glaser, 1992)
Cyborg (Albert Pyun, 1989)

# D

Daddy and Them (Billy Bob Thornton, 2002)
Dagon (Stuart Gordon, 2001)
Daisy Miller (Peter Bogdanovich, 1974)
Dance Me Outside (Bruce McDonald, 1994)
Dance with a Stranger (Mike Newell, 1985)
Dance With Me (Randa Haines, 1998)
Dances With Wolves (Kevin Costner, 1990)
Dancing at Lughnasa (Pat O'Connor, 1998)
Dangerous Age, A (Sidney J. Furie, 1958)
Dangerous Beauty (Marshall Herskovitz, 1998)
Dangerous Game (Abel Ferrara, 1993)
Dangerous Liaisons (Stephen Frears, 1988)
Dangerously Close (Albert Pyun, 1986)
Daniel (Sydney Lumet, 1983)
Dante's Peak (Roger Donaldson, 1997)
Dark City (Alex Proyas, 1998)
Dark Crystal, The (Frank Oz, 1982)
Dark Half, The (George A. Romero, 1993)
Dark Star (John Carpenter, 1973)
Darkman (Sam Raimi, 1990)
Darling (John Schlesinger, 1965)
Darling Lili (Blake Edwards, 1970)
Das Boot (Wolfgang Petersen, 1981)
Daughter of Darkness (Stuart Gordon, 1990)
Daughters of the Dust (Julie Dash, 1991)
Dave (Ivan Reitman, 1993)
David Holzman's Diary (Jim McBride, 1968)
David: Off and On (Martha Coolidge, 1972)
Dawn of the Dead (George A. Romero, 1978)
Day in the Death of Joe Egg, A (Peter Medak, 1972)
Day of the Dead (George A. Romero, 1985)
Day of the Dolphin, The (Mike Nichols, 1973)
Day of the Locust, The (John Schlesinger, 1975)
Daylight (Rob Cohen, 1996)
Days of Heaven (Terrence Malick, 1978)
Days of Thunder (Tony Scott, 1990)
Days of Wine and Roses (Blake Edwards, 1962)
Day the World Ended, The (Roger Corman, 1956)
Daytrippers, The (Greg Mottola, 1996)
Dazed and Confused (Richard Linklater, 1993)
D.C. Cab (Joel Schumacher, 1983)
Dead Bang (John Frankenheimer, 1989)
Deadbeat at Dawn (Jim Van Bebber, 1988)
Dead Calm (Phillip Noyce, 1989)
Deadly Affair, The (Sydney Lumet, 1967)
Deadly Blessing (Wes Craven, 1981)
Deadly Breed (Charles T. Kanganis, 1989)
Deadly Friend (Wes Craven, 1986)
Deadly Illusion (Larry Cohen, 1987)
Dead Man (Jim Jarmusch, 1995)

Dead Man Walking (Tim Robbins, 1995)
Dead Men Can't Dance (Steve Anderson, 1997)
Dead Men Don't Wear Plaid (Carl Reiner, 1982)
Dead of Night (Bob Clark, 1972)
Dead Pit, The (Brett Leonard, 1989)
Dead Presidents (Albert & Allen Hughes, 1995)
Dead Ringers (David Cronenberg, 1988)
Dead Zone, The (David Cronenberg, 1983)
Deal of the Century (William Friedkin, 1983)
Dear God (Gary Marshall, 1996)
Death and the Compass (Alex Cox, 1996)
Death Becomes Her (Robert Zemeckis, 1992)
Death Race 2000 (Paul Bartel, 1975)
Death to Smoochy (Danny DeVito, 2002)
Death Wish V: The Face of Death (Allan A. Goldstein, 1994)
Deathtrap (Sydney Lumet, 1982)
Deceiver (Joshua & Jonas Pate, 1998)
Deceivers, The (Nicholas Meyer, 1988)
Decline of the American Empire, The (Denys Arcand, 1986)
Decline of Western Civilisation, The (Penelope Spheeris, 1981)
Decline of Western Civilisation Part II: The Metal Years, The (Penelope Spheeris, 1988)
Decline of Western Civilisation Part III, The (Penelope Spheeris, 1998)
Deconstructing Harry (Woody Allen, 1997)
Deep Blue Sea (Renny Harlin, 1999)
Deep End, The (Scott McGehee, 2001)
Deep End of the Ocean, The (Ulu Grosbard, 1999)
Deep Impact (Mimi Leder, 1998)
Deer Hunter, The (Michael Cimino, 1978)
Deep Rising (Stephen Sommers, 1998)
Defending Your Life (Albert Brooks, 1991)
Defiance (John Flynn, 1980)
Déjà Vu (Henry Jaglom, 1997)
Delinquents, The (Robert Altman, 1957)
Dementia 13 (Francis Ford Coppola, 1963)
Demoiselle sauvage, La (Léa Pool, 1991)
Dennis the Menace Strikes Again (Charles T. Kanganis, 1998)
Dernières fiançailles, Las (Jean-Pierre Lefebvre, 1973)
Demier glacier, Le (Jacques Leduc, 1984)
Dernier Souffle, Le (Richard Ciupka, 1999)
Desire in Motion (Lea Pool, 1994)
Desperado (Robert Rodriguez, 1995)
Desperate Hours, The (Michael Cimino, 1990)
Desperate Living (John Waters, 1977)
Desperate Measures (Barbet Schroeder, 1998)
Desperately Seeking Susan (Susan Seidelman, 1985)
Deterrence (Rod Lurie, 1999)
Deuce Bigalo: Male Gigolo (Mike Mitchell, 1999)
Deux secondes (Manon Briand, 1998)
Devil in a Blue Dress (Carl Franklin, 1995)
Devil's Advocate (Taylor Hackford, 1997)
Devil's Backbone, The (Guillermo del Toro, 2001)
Devil's Own, The (Alan J. Pakula, 1997)
Devil's Pale Moonlit Kiss (Roger Spottiswoode, 2000)
Devil's Playground, The (Fred Schepisi, 1976)

Diabolique (Jeremiah Chechik, 1996)
Dick (Andrew Fleming, 1999)
Dick Tracy (Warren Beatty, 1990)
Die Hard (John McTiernan, 1988)
Die Hard 2: Die Harder (Renny Harlin, 1990)
Die Hard with a Vengeance (John McTiernan, 1995)
Die Konsequenz (Wolfgang Petersen, 1977)
Die Unendliche Geschichte (Wolfgang Petersen, 1984)
Dig My Do (Bill Plympton, 1990)
Dillinger (John Milius, 1973)
Dim Sum: A Little Bit of Heart (Wayne Wang, 1984)
Diner (Barry Levinson, 1982)
Dionysus in '69 (Brian De Palma, 1970)
Directed by John Ford (Peter Bogdanovich, 1971)
Dirty Money (Denys Arcand, 1971)
Dirty Rotten Scoundrels (Frank Oz, 1988)
Disclosure (Barry Levinson, 1994)
Disorganized Crime (Jim Kouf, 1989)
Distant Thunder (Rick Rosenthal, 1988)
Distinguished Gentleman, The (Jonathan Lynn, 1992)
Disturbing Behavior (David Nutter, 1998)
Doctor, The (Randa Haines, 1991)
Doctor Blood's Coffin (Sidney J. Furie, 1961)
Doctor Dolittle (Richard Fleischer, 1967)
Doctor Ducks Secret All Purpose Sauce (William Dear, 1985)
Doctor Mordrid (Charles Band, 1992)
Docu-Drama (Wim Wenders, 1984)
Dog Day Afternoon (Sydney Lumet, 1975)
Dogma (Kevin Smith, 1999)
Dogs (Hal Hartley, 1988)
Dogs of War, The (John Irvin, 1980)
Dogtown (George Hickenlooper, 1997)
Doll-Maker, The (Daniel Petrie, 1984)
Dollman vs. Demonic Toys (Charles Band, 1993)
Dolls (Stuart Gordon, 1986)
Dolores Claiborne (Taylor Hackford, 1995)
Domestic Disturbance (Harold Becker, 2001)
Dominick and Eugene (Robert M. Young, 1988)
Don is Dead, The (Richard Fleischer, 1973)
Donnie Brasco (Mike Newell, 1997)
Don't Drink the Water (Woody Allen, 1994)
Don't Let the Angels Fall (George Kaczender, 1969)
Don't Say a Word (Gary Fleder, 2001)
Don't Tell Mom the Babysitter's Dead (Stephen Herek, 199?)
Doom Generation, The (Gregg Araki, 1995)
Doomsday Man, The (Sam Raimi, 1999)
Doors, The (Oliver Stone, 1991)
Double Whammy (Tom DiCillo, 2001)
Down and Out in Beverly Hills (Paul Mazursky, 1986)
Down By Law (Jim Jarmusch, 1986)
Down Periscope (David S. Ward, 1996)
Down to Earth (Chris & Paul Weitz, 2001)
Downtown (Richard Benjamin, 1990)
Dracula (John Badham, 1979)
Dracula: Dead and Loving It (Mel Brooks, 1995)
Dracula: Pages from a Virgin's Diary (Guy Maddin, 2001)
Dragonfly (Tom Shadyac, 2002)
Dragon Tamers, The (John Woo, 1974)
Dragon: The Bruce Lee Story (Rob Cohen, 1993)

Dragonheart (Rob Cohen, 1996)
Draw (Bill Plympton, 1993)
Drawing Lesson #2 (Bill Plympton, 1988)
Dr Dolittle (Betty Thomas, 1998)
Dream a Little Dream (Marc Rocco, 1989)
Dream Lover (Alan J. Pakula, 1986)
Dreamscape (Joseph Ruben, 1984)
Dressed To Kill (Brian De Palma, 1980)
Driller Killer (Abel Ferrara, 1979)
Driven (Renny Harlin, 2001)
Driver, The (Walter Hill, 1978)
Drop Back Ten (Stacy Cochran, 1999)
Drop Dead Gorgeous (Michael Patrick Jann, 1999)
Drop Zone (John Badham, 1994)
Dr Strangelove: or, How I Learned to Stop Worrying and
    Love the Bomb (Stanley Kubrick, 1964)
Dr. T & the Women (Robert Altman, 2000)
D-Tox (Jim Gillespie, 2002)
Drugstore Cowboy (Gus Van Sant, 1989)
Dudes (Penelope Spheeris, 1987)
Dude, Where's my Car? (Danny Leiner, 2000)
Dudley Do-Right (Hugh Wilson, 1999)
Duel (Steven Spielberg, 1971)
Duelists, The (Ridley Scott, 1977)
Dumb & Dumber (Peter & Bob Farrelly, 1994)
Dune (David Lynch, 1984)
Dungeonmaster, The (Charles Band, 1985)
During One Night (Sidney J. Furie, 1961)
Dying Young (Joel Schumacher, 1991)

# E

Earth (Deepa Mehta, 1998)
Easy Rider (Dennis Hopper, 1969)
Eat a Bowl of Tea (Wayne Wang, 1989)
Eat Drink Man Woman (Ang Lee, 1994)
Eaten Alive (Tobe Hooper, 1976)
Eating (Henry Jaglom, 1990)
Eating Raoul (Paul Bartel, 1982)
Echoes of Paradise (Phillip Noyce, 1987)
Eclipse (Jeremy Podeswa, 1994)
Edge, The (Lee Tamahori, 1997)
Ed Gein (Chuck Parello, 2000)
Ed Wood (Tim Burton, 1994)
EDtv (Ron Howard, 1999)
Edward Scissorhands (Tim Burton, 1990)
Eiger Sanction, The (Clint Eastwood, 1975)
8 Heads in a Duffel Bag (Tom Shulman, 1997)
Eight Hundred Leagues Down the Amazon (Luis Llosa,
    1993)
Eight Men Out (John Sayles, 1988)
8-Mile (Curtis Hanson, 2002)
8MM (Joel Schumacher, 1999)
8 Seconds (John G. Avildsen, 1994)
Einer von uns beiden (Wolfgang Petersen, 1973)
El Mariachi (Robert Rodriguez, 1992)
El Patrullero (Alex Cox, 1992)
Eldorado (Charles Binamé, 1995)
Election (Alexander Payne, 1999)

Electric Horseman, The (Sydney Pollack, 1979)
Elephant Man, The (David Lynch, 1980)
Elevator, The (Rafal Zielinski, 1996)
Elvis (John Carpenter, 1979)
Elvis Gratton – le film (Pierre Falardeau, 1985)
Eminent Domain (John Irvin, 1991)
Empire of the Sun (Steven Spielberg, 1987)
Empire Records (Allan Moyle, 1995)
Emperor's New Clothes, The (Alan Taylor, 2001)
Enchanted April (Mike Newell, 1992)
Encino Man (Les Mayfield, 1992)
End of Days (Peter Hyams, 1999)
End of Violence, The (Wim Wenders, 1997)
Endangered Species (Alan Rudolph, 1982)
End of the Affair, The (Neil Jordan, 1999)
Enemies: A Love Story (Paul Mazursky, 1989)
Enemy Mine (Wolfgang Petersen, 1985)
Enemy of the State (Tony Scott, 1998)
Englishman Abroad, An (John Schlesinger, 1983)
En Kille och en tjej (Lasse Hallström, 1975)
Enter Laughing (Carl Reiner, 1967)
Entity, The (Sidney J. Furie, 1981)
Entrapment (Jon Amiel, 1999)
Entre la mer et l'eau douce (Michel Brault, 1967)
Equinox (Alan Rudolph, 1992)
Equus (Sydney Lumet, 1977)
Eraserhead (David Lynch, 1977)
Erin Brockovich (Steven Soderbergh, 2000)
Erotique (Lizzie Borden, Clara Law, Anna Maria
    Magalhães & Monika Treut, 1994)
Escape from LA (John Carpenter, 1996)
Escape from New York (John Carpenter, 1981)
Escape to Athena (George P. Cosmatos, 1979)
E.T. The Extra-Terrestrial (Steven Spielberg, 1982)
Ethan Frome (John Madden, 1993)
European Vacation (Amy Heckerling, 1985)
Europeans, The (James Ivory, 1979)
Even Cowgirls Get the Blues (Gus Van Sant, 1993)
Event Horizon (Paul Anderson, 1997)
Ever After (Andy Tennant, 1998)
Everlasting Piece, An (Barry Levinson, 2000)
Everybody's All American (Taylor Hackford, 1988)
Everyone Says I Love You (Woody Allen, 1996)
Everything Put Together (Marc Forster, 1999)
Everything You Always Wanted to Know About Sex
    (Woody Allen, 1972)
Eve's Bayou (Kasi Lemmons, 1997)
Evil Dead, The (Sam Raimi, 1982)
Evil Dead 2: Dead By Dawn (Sam Raimi, 1987)
Evita (Alan Parker, 1996)
Evolution (Ivan Reitman, 2001)
Exciting Life of a Tree, The (Bill Plympton, 1998)
Executive Decision (Stuart Baird, 1996)
eXistenZ (David Cronenberg, 1999)
Exit to Eden (Gary Marshall, 1994)
Exorcist, The (William Friedkin, 1973)
Exotica (Atom Egoyan, 1994)
Experiment in Terror (Blake Edwards, 1962)
Explorers (Joe Dante, 1985)
Exposed (James Toback, 1983)

*Extraordinary Seaman, The* (John Frankenheimer, 1969)
*Extreme Prejudice* (Walter Hill, 1987)
*Extremities* (Robert M. Young, 1986)
*Eye for an Eye* (John Schlesinger, 1996)
*Eye of God* (Tim Blake Nelson, 1997)
*Eye of the Eagle 2: Inside the Enemy* (Carl Franklin, 1989)
*Eyes Wide Shut* (Stanley Kubrick, 1999)

# F

*Fabuleux voyage de l'ange, Le* (Jean-Pierre Lefebvre, 1991)
*Fabulous Baker Boys, The* (Steve Kloves, 1989)
*Face/Off* (John Woo, 1997)
*Faculty, The* (Robert Rodriguez, 1998)
*Faded Roads* (Bill Plympton, 1994)
*Fail-Safe* (Sydney Lumet, 1964)
*Faithful* (Paul Mazursky, 1996)
*Falcon and the Snowman, The* (John Schlesinger, 1984)
*Fall* (Eric Schaeffer, 1997)
*Fallen* (Gregory Hoblit, 1998)
*Falling Down* (Joel Schumacher, 1993)
*Falling in Love* (Ulu Grosbard, 1984)
*Falling Over Backwards* (Mort Ransen, 1990)
*Fall of the House of Usher, The* (Roger Corman, 1960)
*Fame* (Alan Parker, 1980)
*Family Business* (Sydney Lumet, 1989)
*Family Man* (Brett Rattner, 2000)
*Family Viewing* (Atom Egoyan, 1987)
*Famous* (Griffin Dunne, 2000)
*Fan, The* (Tony Scott, 1996)
*Fandango* (Kevin Reynolds, 1985)
*Fantasia 2000* (Eric Goldberg, 1999)
*Fantastic Voyage* (Richard Fleischer, 1966)
*Far and Away* (Ron Howard, 1992)
*Farewell to the King* (John Milius, 1989)
*Far From the Madding Crowd* (John Schlesinger, 1967)
*Far North* (Sam Shepard, 1988)
*Faraway, So Close* (Wim Wenders, 1992)
*Fargo* (Joel Coen, 1996)
*Fast and the Furious, The* (Rob Cohen, 2001)
*Fast Times at Ridgemount High* (Amy Heckerling, 1982)
*Fast-Walking* (James B. Harris, 1982)
*Fat Man and Little Boy* (Roland Joffé, 1989)
*Fatal Attraction* (Adrian Lyne, 1987)
*Fatal Instinct* (Carl Reiner, 1993)
*Fathers' Day* (Ivan Reitman, 1997)
*Father to Be* (Lasse Hallström, 1979)
*Favor, The* (Donald Petrie, 1994)
*Fear* (James Foley, 1996)
*Fear and Desire* (Stanley Kubrick, 1953)
*Fear and Loathing in Las Vegas* (Terry Gilliam, 1998)
*Fear City* (Abel Ferrara, 1984)
*Fear, Anxiety and Depression* (Todd Solondz, 1989)
*Fearless* (Peter Weir, 1993)
*Federal Hill* (Michael Corrente, 1995)
*Feeling Minnesota* (Steven Baigelman, 1996)
*Field of Dreams* (Phil Alden Robinson, 1989)
*Felicia's Journey* (Atom Egoyan, 1999)

*Female Perversions* (Susan Streitfeld, 1996)
*Female Trouble* (John Waters, 1975)
*Femme Fatale* (Brian De Palma, 2002)
*Ferris Bueller's Day Off* (John Hughes, 1986)
*Festival in Cannes* (Henry Jaglom, 2001)
*Few Good Men, A* (Rob Reiner, 1992)
*Fiddler on the Roof* (Norman Jewison, 1971)
*Fierce Creatures* (Fred Schepisi, 1997)
*15 février 1839* (Pierre Falardeau, 2000)
*15 Minutes* (John Herzfeld, 2000)
*Fifty/Fifty* (Charles Martin Smith, 1993)
*52 Pick-Up* (John Frankenheimer, 1986)
*Fight Club* (David Fincher, 1999)
*Fighting Mad* (Jonathan Demme, 1976)
*Final* (Campbell Scott, 2001)
*Final Cut, The* (Roger Christian, 1995)
*Final Destination* (James Wong, 2000)
*Final Guardian* (John Flynn, 2002)
*Final Terror, The* (Andrew Davis, 1981)
*Finding Forrester* (Gus Van Sant, 2000)
*Fine Mess, A* (Blake Edwards, 1986)
*Fingers* (James Toback, 1978)
*Finian's Rainbow* (Francis Ford Coppola, 1968)
*Fire* (Deepa Mehta, 1996)
*Fire and Ice* (Ralph Bakshi, 1983)
*Firefox* (Clint Eastwood, 1982)
*Firm, The* (Sydney Pollack, 1993)
*First Great Train Robbery, The* (aka *The Great Train Robbery*) (Michael Crichton, 1979)
*First Knight* (Jerry Zucker, 1995)
*First Wives Club, The* (Hugh Wilson, 1996)
*Fisher King, The* (Terry Gilliam, 1991)
*Fishing Trip, The* (Amnon Buchbinder, 1998)
*FIST* (Norman Jewison, 1978)
*Five Easy Pieces* (Bob Rafelson, 1970)
*Five Guns West* (Roger Corman, 1955)
*Five Senses, The* (Jeremy Podeswa, 1999)
*Fixer, The* (John Frankenheimer, 1968)
*Flamingo Kid, The* (Gary Marshall, 1984)
*Flash of Green, A* (Victor Nuñez, 1984)
*Flashdance* (Adrian Lyne, 1983)
*Flatliners* (Joel Schumacher, 1990)
*Flawless* (Joel Schumacher, 1999)
*Fled* (Kevin Hooks, 1996)
*Flesh and Blood* (Paul Verhoeven, 1985)
*Flesh and Bone* (Steve Kloves, 1993)
*Fleurs sauvages, Les* (Jean-Pierre Lefebvre, 1982)
*Flight of the Intruder* (John Milius, 1990)
*Flight to Fury* (Monte Hellman, 1966)
*Flintstones: Viva Rock Vegas, The* (Brian Levant, 2000)
*Flintstones, The* (Brian Levant, 1994)
*Flirt* (Hal Hartley, 1995)
*Flirting with Disaster* (David O. Russell, 1996)
*Floating Away* (John Badham, 1998)
*Flubber* (Les Mayfield, 1997)
*Fly Away Home* (Carol Ballard, 1996)
*Fly, The* (David Cronenberg, 1986)
*Flying* (Paul Lynch, 1986)
*Fog, The* (John Carpenter, 1980)
*Follow the Star* (John Woo, 1977)

Fool for Love (Robert Altman, 1985)
Fools of Fortune (Pat O'Connor, 1990)
Follow Me Quietly (Richard Fleischer, 1949)
Fools Rush In (Andy Tennant, 1997)
Footlights and Flatfeet (John Gray, 1984)
Forces of Nature (Bronwen Hughes, 1999)
Fore Play (John G. Avildsen, 1975)
Forever Mine (Paul Schrader, 1999)
Forever Young (Steve Miner, 1992)
For Keeps (John G. Avildsen, 1988)
For Love or Money (Barry Sonnenfeld, 1993)
For the Love of the Game (Sam Raimi, 1999)
For Those Who Will Follow (Michel Brault, 1963)
Formula, The (John G. Avildsen, 1980)
Forrest Gump (Robert Zemeckis, 1994)
Fort Apache the Bronx (Daniel Petrie, 1981)
Fortress (Stuart Gordon, 1993)
Fortress 2 (Geoff Murphy, 1999)
Fortune, The (Mike Nichols, 1975)
Forty Pounds of Trouble (Norman Jewison, 1963)
4 Little Girls (Spike Lee, 1997)
Four Rooms (Allison Anders, Alexandre Rockwell, Robert
   Rodriguez & Quentin Tarantino, 1995)
Four Seasons, The (Alan Alda, 1981)
1492: Conquest of Paradise (Ridley Scott, 1992)
Fourth Angel, The (John Irvin, 2001)
Fourth Man, The (Paul Verhoeven, 1983)
Fourth War, The (John Frankenheimer, 1990)
48Hrs. (Walter Hill, 1982)
Four Weddings and a Funeral (Mike Newell, 1994)
Foxes (Adrian Lyne, 1980)
Foxy Lady (Ivan Reitman, 1971)
Frances (Graeme Clifford, 1982)
Frankenstein Unbound (Roger Corman, 1990)
Frankie and Johnny (Gary Marshall, 1991)
Freddy's Dead: The Final Nightmare (Rachel Talalay,
   1991)
Freedom to Move, A (Michel Brault, 1985)
Freefall (John Irvin, 1994)
Freejack (Geoff Murphy, 1992)
Freeway (Matthew Bright, 1996)
Freeway II: Confessions of a Trickbaby (Matthew Bright,
   1999)
French Connection, The (William Friedkin, 1971)
French Connection II (John Frankenheimer, 1975)
French Kiss (Lawrence Kasdan, 1995)
Frequency (Gregory Hoblit, 2000)
Fresh (Boaz Yakin, 1994)
Fresh Horses (David Anspaugh, 1988)
Freshman, The (Andrew Bergman, 1990)
Frida (Julie Taymor, 2002)
Friday (Felix Gray, 1995)
Friday Night Date, A (Sidney J. Furie, 2000)
Friday the 13th Part 2 (Steve Miner, 1981)
Friday the 13th Part 3 (Steve Miner, 1982)
Fried Green Tomatoes at the Whistle Stop Café
   (Jon Avnet, 1991)
Fritz the Cat (Ralph Bakshi, 1972)
From Beyond (Stuart Gordon, 1986)
From Dusk till Dawn (Robert Rodriguez, 1996)

From Hell (Albert & Allen Hughes, 2001)
From Rags to Riches (John Woo, 1977)
From the Hip (Bob Clark, 1987)
Fugitive Kind, The (Sydney Lumet, 1959)
Fugitive, The (Andrew Davis, 1993)
Full Fathom Five (Carl Franklin, 1990)
Full Frontal (Steven Soderbergh, 2002)
Full Metal Jacket (Stanley Kubrick, 1987)
Full Moon High (Larry Cohen, 1981)
Fun (Rafal Zielinski, 1994)
Funeral, The (Abel Ferrara, 1996)
Funhouse, The (Tobe Hooper, 1981)
Funny Bones (Peter Chelsom, 1995)
Fury, The (Brian De Palma, 1978)

# G

Gable and Lombard (Sidney J. Furie, 1976)
Gabrielle Roy, a documentary/Gabrielle Roy, un
   documentaire (Léa Pool, 1997)
Gaily, Gaily (Norman Jewison, 1969)
Gal Young 'Un (Victor Nuñez, 1979)
Galaxy Quest (Dean Parisot, 1999)
Gallipoli (Peter Weir, 1981)
Game, The (David Fincher, 1997)
Game, The (Stefan Avalos, 1994)
Gang in Blue (Mario Van Peebles, 1996)
Gang Related (Jim Kouf, 1997)
Gangs of New York (Martin Scorsese, 2002)
Garbo Talks (Sydney Lumet, 1984)
Gardens of Stone (Francis Ford Coppola, 1987)
Gars des vue, Las (Jean-Pierre Lefebvre, 1976)
Gas, Food, Lodging (Allison Anders, 1992)
Gas-s-s-s, Or It Became Necessary to Destroy the World
   in Order to Save It (Roger Corman, 1970)
Gattaca (Andrew Niccol, 1997)
Gaudi Afternoon (Susan Seidelman, 2001)
Gauntlet, The (Clint Eastwood, 1977)
General Idi Amin Dada (Barbet Schroeder, 1974)
General's Daughter, The (Simon West, 1999)
George Wallace (John Frankenheimer, 1997)
George Washington (David Gordon Green, 2000)
Georgia (Ulu Grosbard, 1995)
Geronimo: an American Legend (Walter Hill, 1993)
Gerry (Gus Van Sant, 2002)
Get on the Bus (Spike Lee, 1996)
Get Shorty (Barry Sonnenfeld, 1995)
Get To Know Your Rabbit (Brian De Palma, 1972)
Getaway, The (Roger Donaldson, 1994)
Getting Even With Dad (Howard Deutch, 1994)
Ghost (Jerry Zucker, 1990)
Ghost and the Darkness, The (Stephen Hopkins, 1996)
Ghost Chase (Roland Emmerich, 1988)
Ghost Dog: The Way of the Samurai (Jim Jarmusch, 1999)
Ghost in the Machine (Rachel Talalay, 1993)
Ghost in the Noonday Sun (Peter Medak, 1973)
Ghost Story (John Irvin, 1981)
Ghostbusters (Ivan Reitman, 1984)
Ghostbusters II (Ivan Reitman, 1989)

Ghosts of Mississippi (Rob Reiner, 1996)
Ghosts of Mars (John Carpenter, 2001)
Ghost World (Terry Zwigoff, 2001)
Gift, The (Sam Raimi, 2000)
G.I. Jane (Ridley Scott, 1997)
Gilda Live (Mike Nichols, 1980)
Gina (Denys Arcand, 1975)
Ginger Ale Afternoon (Rafal Zielinski. 1989)
Gingerbread Man, The (Robert Altman, 1998)
Ginger Snaps (John Fawcett, 2000)
Girl (Jonathan Kahn, 1999)
Girlfight (Karyn Kusama, 1999)
Girl, Interrupted (James Mangold, 1999)
Girl in the Red Velvet Swing, The (Richard Fleischer, 1955)
Girl 6 (Spike Lee, 1996)
Girls Town (Jim McKay, 1995)
Gladiator (Ridley Scott, 2000)
Gleaming the Cube (Graeme Clifford, 1989)
Glen and Randa (Jim McBride, 1971)
Glengarry Glen Ross (James Foley, 1992)
Glimmer Man, The (John Gray, 1996)
Glitter (Vondie Curtis-Hall, 2001)
Gloria (Sydney Lumet, 1999)
Glory (Edward Zwick, 1989)
Goalkeeper's Fear of the Penalty Kick, The (Wim Wenders, 1971)
Go Fish (Rose Troche, 1994)
God Told Me To (Larry Cohen, 1977)
Godfather, The (Francis Ford Coppola, 1972)
Godfather Part II, The (Francis Ford Coppola, 1974)
Godfather Part III, The (Francis Ford Coppola, 1990)
Gods and Monsters (Bill Condon, 1998)
Godzilla (Roland Emmerich, 1998)
Going All the Way (Mark Pellington, 1997)
Going in Style (Martin Brest, 1979)
Golden Bowl, The (James Ivory, 2000)
Golden Gate (John Madden, 1994)
Golden Hour, The (Lasse Hallström, 1996)
Gone in 60 Seconds (Dominic Sena, 2000)
Goodbye Lover (Roland Joffé, 1999)
Goodbye Pork Pie (Geoff Murphy, 1981)
Good Father, The (Mike Newell, 1987)
GoodFellas (Martin Scorsese, 1990)
Good Girl, The (Miguel Arteta, 2002)
Good Morning, Vietnam (Barry Levinson, 1987)
Good Times (William Friedkin, 1967)
Good Will Hunting (Gus Van Sant, 1997)
Goofy Movie, A (Doug Liman, 1995)
Goonies, The (Richard Donner, 1985)
Gorp (Joseph Ruben, 1980)
Gosford Park (Robert Altman, 2001)
Gossip (Davis Guggenheim, 2000)
Grace of My Heart (Alison Anders, 1996)
Graduate, The (Mike Nichols, 1967)
Grand Canyon (Lawrence Kasdan, 1991)
Grand Isle (Mary Lambert, 1991)
Grand Prix (John Frankenheimer, 1966)
Grand Theft Auto (Ron Howard, 1977)
Grave, The (Joshua & Jonas Pate, 1996)

Gravesend (Salvatore Stabile, 1997)
Graveyard Shift (Jerry Ciccoritti, 1987)
Gray's Anatomy (Steven Soderbergh, 1996)
Great Balls of Fire! (Jim McBride, 1989)
Great Northfield Minnesota Raid, The (Philip Kaufman, 1972)
Great Outdoors, The (Howard Deutch, 1988)
Great Race, The (Blake Edwards, 1965)
Great White Hype, The (Reginald Hudlin, 1996)
Greedy (Jonathan Lynn, 1994)
Green Card (Peter Weir, 1990)
Green Mile, The (Frank Darabont, 1999)
Greetings (Brian De Palma, 1968)
Gremlins (Joe Dante, 1984)
Gremlins 2: The New Batch (Joe Dante, 1990)
Gridlock'd (Vondie Curtis-Hall, 1997)
Grifters, The (Stephen Frears, 1990)
Grosse Pointe Blank (George Armitage, 1997)
Groundhog Day (Harold Ramis, 1993)
Group, The (Sydney Lumet, 1966)
Grumpier Old Men (Howard Deutch, 1995)
Grumpy Old Men (Donald Petrie, 1993)
Guardian, The (William Friedkin, 1990)
Guarding Tess (Hugh Wilson, 1994)
Guess What We Learned in School Today? (John G. Avildsen, 1970)
Guest, The (David Zucker, 2002)
Guilty as Sin (Sydney Lumet, 1993)
Guilty, The (Anthony Waller, 1999)
Guinevere (Audrey Wells, 1999)
Gummo (Harmony Korine, 1997)
Guncrazy (Tamra Davis, 1992)
Gung Ho (Ron Howard, 1986)
Gum (Blake Edwards, 1967)
Gumshoe (Stephen Frears, 1972)
Gun in Betty Lou's Handbag, The (Allan Moyle, 1992)
Gunslinger (Roger Corman, 1956)
Guns on the Clackamas (Bill Plympton, 1996)
Guru, The (James Ivory, 1969)
Guru, The (Daisy von Scherler Mayer, 2002)
Gypsy Moths, The (John Frankenheimer, 1969)

# H

Hair (Milos Forman, 1979)
Hairspray (John Waters, 1988)
Half a Lifetime (Daniel Petrie, 1986)
Half Baked (Tamra Davis, 1998)
Halloween (John Carpenter, 1978)
Halloween H20 — 20 Years Later (Steve Miner, 1998)
Halloween: Resurrection (Rick Rosenthal, 2002)
Halloween II (Rick Rosenthal, 1981)
Hamburger Hill (John Irvin, 1987)
Hammett (Wim Wenders, 1982)
Hamlet (Michael Almereyda, 2000)
Hand of Death (John Woo, 1975)
Hand That Rocks the Cradle, The (Curtis Hanson, 1992)
Hand, The (Oliver Stone, 1981)
Hanging Garden, The (Thom Fitzgerald, 1997)

Hanging Up (Diane Keaton, 2000)
Hannah and Her Sisters (Woody Allen, 1986)
Hannibal (Ridley Scott, 2001)
Hanover Street (Peter Hyams, 1979)
Happiness (Todd Solondz, 1998)
Happy Gilmore (Dennis Dugan, 1996)
Happy Here and Now (Michael Almereyda, 2001)
Happy New Year (John G. Avildsen, 1987)
Happy Texas (Mark Illsley, 1999)
Happy Time, The (Richard Fleischer, 1952)
Happy We (Lasse Hallström, 1983)
Hard-Boiled (John Woo, 1992)
Hardcore (Paul Schrader, 1979)
Hard Core Logo (Bruce McDonald, 1996)
Hard Day for Archie, A (Jim McBride, 1973)
Hard Eight (Paul Thomas Anderson, 1996)
Hard Part Begins, The (Paul Lynch, 1973)
Hard Target (John Woo, 1993)
Hard Times (Walter Hill, 1975)
Hard Way, The (John Badham, 1991)
Harriet the Spy (Bronwen Hughes, 1996)
Harry and the Hendersons (William Dear, 1987)
Harry and Tonto (Paul Mazursky, 1974)
Harry Potter and the Chamber of Secrets (Chris Columbus, 2002)
Harry Potter and the Sorcerer's Stone (aka Harry Potter and the Philosopher's Stone) (Chris Columbus, 2001)
Hart's War (Gregory Hoblit, 2002)
Harvard Man (James Toback, 2001)
Haunted Palace, The (Roger Corman, 1963)
Haunted Summer (Ivan Passer, 1988)
Haunting, The (Jan De Bont, 1999)
Havana (Sydney Pollack, 1990)
Head (Bob Rafelson, 1968)
H.E.A.L.T.H. (Robert Altman, 1979)
Hear My Song (Peter Chelsom, 1991)
Hear No Evil (Robert Greenwald, 1993)
Heart and Souls (Ron Underwood, 1993)
Heartbreakers (David Mirkin, 2001)
Heartbreak Hotel (Chris Columbus, 1988)
Heartbreak Ridge (Clint Eastwood, 1986)
Heartburn (Mike Nichols, 1986)
Heart Like a Wheel (Jonathan Kaplan, 1983)
Hearts of Darkness: A Filmmakers Apocalypse (George Hickenlooper, 1991)
Heat (Michael Mann, 1995)
Heat and Dust (James Ivory, 1982)
Heathers (Michael Lehmann, 1989)
Heatwave (Phillip Noyce, 1982)
Heaven and Earth (Oliver Stone, 1993)
Heaven Can Wait (Warren Beatty, 1978)
Heaven's Gate (Michael Cimino, 1980)
Heavy (James Mangold, 1995)
Heavy Traffic (Ralph Bakshi, 1973)
Hedwig and the Angry Inch (John Cameron Mitchell, 2001)
He Got Game (Spike Lee, 1998)
Heist (David Mamet, 2001)
He Laughed Last (Blake Edwards, 1956)
Hellraiser (Clive Barker, 1987)
Hell Up In Harlem (Larry Cohen, 1973)

He Makes Me Feel Like Dancin' (Emile Ardolino, 1983)
Henry & June (Philip Kaufman, 1990)
Henry Fool (Hal Hartley, 1997)
Henry: Portrait of a Serial Killer (John McNaughton, 1990)
Henry: Portrait of a Serial Killer Part 2 (Mask of Sanity) (Chuck Parello, 1996)
Hercules (Ron Clements & John Musker, 1997)
Hero of our Time, A (Michael Almereyda, 1985)
Hey Babe (Rafal Zielinski, 1980)
Hey Good Lookin' (Ralph Bakshi, 1982)
Hideaway (Brett Leonard, 1995)
Hideous! (Charles Band, 1997)
High Fidelity (Stephen Frears, 2000)
High Crimes (Carl Franklin, 2002)
Hi, Mom! (Brian De Palma, 1970)
High Spirits (Neil Jordan, 1988)
High Anxiety (Mel Brooks, 1977)
High Art (Lisa Cholodenko, 1998)
High Plains Drifter (Clint Eastwood, 1972)
High Time (Blake Edwards, 1960)
Higher Learning (John Singleton, 1995)
Highway 61 (Bruce McDonald, 1991)
Hill, The (Sydney Lumet, 1965)
Hills Have Eyes, The (Wes Craven, 1978)
Hills Have Eyes Part II, The (Wes Craven, 1985)
Hi-Lo Country, The (Stephen Frears, 1998)
History of the World: Part I (Mel Brooks, 1981)
Hit! (Sidney J. Furie, 1973)
Hit, The (Stephen Frears, 1984)
Hit Man (George Armitage, 1972)
Hoffa (Danny DeVito, 1992)
Holcroft Covenant, The (John Frankenheimer, 1985)
Hollow Man (Paul Verhoeven, 2000)
Hollow Point (Sidney J. Furie, 1995)
Hollywood Boulevard (Joe Dante, 1976)
Hollywood Ending (Woody Allen, 2002)
Hollywood Vice Squad (Penelope Spheeris, 1986)
Holy Man (Stephen Herek, 1998)
Home Alone (Chris Columbus, 19901
Home Alone 2: Lost in New York (Chris Columbus, 1992)
Home Alone 3 (Raja Gosnell, 1997)
Home for the Holidays (Jodie Foster, 1995)
Home Fries (Dean Parisot, 1998)
Home Movie (Chris Smith, 2001)
Home Movies (Brian De Palma, 1979)
Home Movies (Bruce LaBruce, 1988)
Home Remedy (Maggie Greenwald, 1988)
Home Team (Allan A. Goldstein, 1998)
Homicide (David Mamet, 1991)
Honey, I Shrunk the Kids (Joe Johnston, 1989)
Honeymoon in Vegas (Andrew Bergman, 1992)
Hong Kong 97 (Albert Pyun, 1994)
Honky Tonk Freeway (John Schlesinger, 1981)
Honkytonk Man (Clint Eastwood, 1982)
Hook (Steven Spielberg, 1991)
Hoosiers (David Anspaugh, 1986)
Hope Floats (Forest Whitaker, 1998)
Horse Whisperer, The (Robert Redford, 1998)
Horseman, The (John Frankenheimer, 1971)
Hospital, The (Arthur Hiller, 1971)

Hotel (Mike Figgis, 2001)
Hot Shots! (Jim Abrahams, 1991)
Hot Shots! Part Deux (Jim Abrahams, 1993)
Hot Spot, The (Dennis Hopper, 1990)
Hot Times (Jim McBride, 1974)
Hot Tomorrows (Martin Brest, 1977)
Hotel Chronicles (Léa Pool, 1990)
Hour of the Assassin (Luis Llosa, 1987)
House (Steve Miner, 1986)
House of Games (David Mamet, 1987)
House on Haunted Hill, The (William Malone, 1999)
House Party (Reginald Hudlin, 1990)
House Party 3 (Eric Meza, 1994)
Householder, The (James Ivory, 1963)
Housesitter (Frank Oz, 1992)
How Stella Got Her Groove Back
(Kevin Rodney Sullivan, 1998)
How the Grinch Stole Christmas (Ron Howard, 2000)
How to Kiss (Bill Plympton, 1989)
How to Make Love to a Woman (Bill Plympton, 1995)
Howards End (James Ivory, 1992)
Howling, The (Joe Dante, 1980)
How-to-Make-an-American-Quilt (Jocelyn Moorhouse,
1995)
Hudson Hawk (Michael Lehmann, 1991)
Hudsucker Proxy, The (Joel Coen, 1994)
Hullabaloo Over Georgie and Bonnie's Pictures (James
Ivory, 1978)
Humongous (Paul Lynch, 1982)
Hunger, The (Tony Scott, 1983)
Hunt for Red October, The (John McTiernan, 1990)
Hurlyburly (Anthony Drazan, 1998)
Hurricane, The (Norman Jewison, 1999)
Husbands and Wives (Woody Allen, 1992)
Hustler White (Bruce LaBruce, 1996)

# I

If Lucy Fell (Eric Schaeffer, 1996)
Iceman (Fred Schepisi, 1984)
Iceman Cometh, The (John Frankenheimer, 1973)
Ice Storm, The (Ang Lee, 1997)
Ich nicht (Wolfgang Petersen, 1969)
Ich werde dich töten, Wolf (Wolfgang Petersen, 1971)
Idle Hands (Rodman Flender, 1999)
Idol, The (Daniel Petrie, 1964)
Idolmaker, The (Taylor Hackford, 1980)
I Don't Hate Las Vegas Anymore (Caveh Zahedi, 1994)
Iguana (Monte Hellman, 1988)
I Know What It's Like To Be Dead (Bruce LaBruce, 1987)
I Know What You Did Last Summer (Jim Gillespie, 1997)
Il ne faut pas mourir pour ça (Jean-Pierre Lefebvre, 1967)
I'll Do Anything (James L. Brooks, 1994)
Illegally Yours (Peter Bogdanovich, 1988)
Illusions (Julie Dash, 1982)
I'll Remember April (Bob Clark, 2000)
I Love a Man in Uniform (David Wellington, 1993)
I Love You To Death (Lawrence Kasdan, 1990)
Images (Robert Altman, 1972)

Imaginary Crimes (Anthony Drazan, 1994)
I Married a Strange Person (Bill Plympton, 1997)
Immediate Family (Jonathan Kaplan, 1989)
Immortal Beloved (Bernard Rose, 1994)
I Mobster (Roger Corman, 1958)
Impossible Object (John Frankenheimer, 1973)
Impostor (Gary Fleder, 2002)
Impostors, The (Stanley Tucci, 1998)
In and Out (Frank Oz, 1997)
Incident at Restigouche (Alanis Obomsawin, 1984)
Incognito (John Badham, 1997)
Incredible Shrinking Woman, The (Joel Schumacher, 1981)
Incredibly True Adventure of Two Girls in Love, The (Maria
Maggenti, 1995)
In Country (Norman Jewison, 1989)
Incredible Sarah, The (Richard Fleischer, 1976)
In Crowd, The (Mary Lambert, 2000)
Indecent Proposal (Adrian Lyne, 1993)
Independence Day (Roland Emmerich, 1996)
Indian in the Cupboard, The (Frank Oz, 1995)
Indian Runner (Sean Penn, 1991)
Indiana Jones and the Last Crusade (Steven Spielberg, 1989)
Indiana Jones and the Temple of Doom (Steven
Spielberg, 1984)
In Dreams (Neil Jordan, 1999)
Informant, The (Jim McBride, 1997)
In Her Defense (Sidney J. Furie, 1998)
In-Laws, The (Arthur Hiller, 1979)
Inner Space (Joe Dante, 1987)
Innocent Blood (John Landis, 1992)
Innocent, The (John Schlesinger, 1993)
In Praise of Older Women (George Kaczender, 1978)
Inside Moves: The Guys From Max's Bar (Richard
Donner, 1980)
Inside Out (Lizzie Borden, 1992)
Insider, The (Michael Mann, 1999)
Insomnia (Christopher Nolan, 2002)
Inspector Gadget (David Kellogg, 1999)
Instinct (Jon Turteltaub, 1999)
Internal Affairs (Mike Figgis, 1990)
Intent to Kill (Charles T. Kanganis, 1993)
Interiors (Woody Allen, 1978)
Interview with the Vampire (Neil Jordan, 1994)
In the Army Now (Daniel Petrie Jr, 1994)
In the Bedroom (Todd Field, 2001)
In the Company of Men (Neil LaBute, 1997)
In the Heat of Passion (Rodman Flender, 1991)
In the Heat of the Night (Norman Jewison, 1967)
In the Line of Fire (Wolfgang Petersen, 1993)
In the Mood (Phil Alden Robinson, 1987)
In the Mouth of Madness (John Carpenter, 1995)
In the Soup (Alexandre Rockwell, 1992)
Intimate Lighting (Ivan Passer, 1966)
Into the Night (John Landis, 1985)
Into the West (Mike Newell, 1992)
Introducing Dorothy Dandridge (Martha Coolidge, 1999)
Intruder, The (Roger Corman, 1961)
Invaders From Mars (Tobe Hooper, 1986)
Invasion of the Body Snatchers (Philip Kaufman, 1978)
Inventing the Abbotts (Pat O'Connor, 1997)

*Ipcress File, The* (Sidney J. Furie, 1965)
*I.Q.* (Fred Schepisi, 1994)
*Iron Eagle* (Sidney J. Furie, 1986)
*Iron Eagle II* (Sidney J. Furie, 1988)
*Iron Eagle IV* (Sidney J. Furie, 1995)
*Iron Giant, The* (Brad Bird, 1999)
*I Shot Andy Warhol* (Mary Harron, 1996)
*Island of Dr Moreau, The* (John Frankenheimer, 1996)
*Island of the Alive* (Larry Cohen, 1987)
*Isn't She Great* (Andrew Bergman, 2000)
*I Still Know What You Did Last Summer* (Danny Cannon, 1998)
*It Conquered the World* (Roger Corman, 1956)
*It Could Happen to You* (Andrew Bergman, 1994)
*It Lives Again* (Larry Cohen, 1978)
*It Runs in My Family* (Bob Clark, 1994)
*It Takes Two* (Andy Tennant, 1995)
*Italianamerican* (Martin Scorsese, 1974)
*It's Alive!* (Larry Cohen, 1974)
*It's Impossible to Learn to Plow by Reading Books* (Richard Linklater, 1988)
*Ivans xtc* (Bernard Rose, 2000)
*I've Heard the Mermaids Singing* (Patricia Rozema, 1987)
*I Walk the Line* (John Frankenheimer, 1970)
*I Wanna Hold Your Hand* (Robert Zemeckis, 1978)

# J

*Jabberwocky* (Terry Gilliam, 1977)
*Jack* (Francis Ford Coppola, 1996)
*Jack Bull, The* (John Badham, 1999)
*Jackie Brown* (Quentin Tarantino, 1997)
*Jackpot* (Michael Polish, 2001)
*Jack the Bear* (Marshall Herskovitz, 1992)
*Jack's Wife* (George A. Romero, 1972)
*Jacob's Ladder* (Adrian Lyne, 1990)
*Jade* (William Friedkin, 1995)
*Jailbait* (Rafal Zielinski, 1994)
*James and the Giant Peach* (Henry Selick, 1995)
*Jane Austen in Manhattan* (James Ivory, 1980)
*Jane Austen's Mafia* (Jim Abrahams, 1999)
*J.A. Martin Photographer* (Jean Beaudin, 1976)
*January Man, The* (Pat O'Connor, 1989)
*Jawbreaker* (Darren Stein, 1999)
*Jaws* (Steven Spielberg, 1975)
*Jay and Silent Bob Strike Back* (Kevin Smith, 2001)
*Jazz Singer, The* (Richard Fleischer, 1980)
*Jefferson in Paris* (James Ivory, 1995)
*Jeremiah Johnson* (Sydney Pollack, 1972)
*Jericho Mile, The* (Michael Mann, 1979)
*Jerk, The* (Carl Reiner, 1979)
*Jerry and Tom* (Saul Rubinek, 1998)
*Jerry Maguire* (Cameron Crowe, 1996)
*Jerusalem File, The* (John Flynn, 1972)
*Jesus Christ Superstar* (Norman Jewison, 1973)
*Jésus de Montréal* (Denys Arcand, 1989)
*JFK* (Oliver Stone, 1991)
*Jim Brown: All American* (Spike Lee, 2002)
*Jimmy Hollywood* (Barry Levinson, 1994)

*Jingle All the Way* (Brian Levant, 1996)
*J. Lyle* (Bill Plympton, 1994)
*Joe* (John G. Avildsen, 1970)
*Joe Gould's Secret* (Stanley Tucci, 2000)
*Joey* (Roland Emmerich, 1985)
*Johnny Dangerously* (Amy Heckerling, 1984)
*Johnny Handsome* (Walter Hill, 1989)
*Johnny Mnemonic* (Robert Longo, 1995)
*Johnny Suede* (Tom DiCillo, 1991)
*Johns* (Scott Silver, 1996)
*John Q.* (Nick Cassavetes, 2002)
*Josie and the Pussycats* (Deborah Kaplan & Harry Elfont, 2001)
*Jour S..., Le* (Jean-Pierre Lefebvre, 1984)
*Joy Luck Club, The* (Wayne Wang, 1993)
*Joy of Sex, The* (Martha Coolidge, 1984)
*Joyride* (Jim Gillespie, 1995)
*Joyride* (Joseph Ruben, 1977)
*Joy Ride* (Cameron Crowe, 2001)
*Judge Dredd* (Danny Cannon, 1995)
*Judgement Night* (Stephen Hopkins, 1993)
*Judy Berlin* (Eric Mendelsohn, 1999)
*Julian Po* (Alan Wade, 1997)
*julien donkey-boy* (Harmony Korine, 1999)
*Jumanji* (Joe Johnston, 1995)
*Jumpin' Jack Flash* (Penny Marshall, 1986)
*Jungle Book, The* (Stephen Sommers, 1994)
*Jungle Boy* (Allan A. Goldstein, 1996)
*Jungle Fever* (Spike Lee, 1991)
*Junior* (Ivan Reitman, 1994)
*Jurassic Park* (Steven Spielberg, 1993)
*Jurassic Park III* (Joe Johnston, 2001)
*Jury Duty* (John Fortenberry, 1995)
*Jusqu'au coeur* (Jean-Pierre Lefebvre, 1968)
*Just a Little Harmless Sex* (Rick Rosenthal, 1999)
*Just Cause* (Ame Glimcher, 1995)
*Just Heroes* (John Woo, 1987)
*Just Tell Me What You Want* (Sydney Lumet, 1980)

# K

*Kafka* (Steven Soderbergh, 1991)
*Kalifornia* (Dominic Sena, 1993)
*Kanehsatake: 270 Years of Resistance* (Alanis Obomsawin, 1993)
*Kansas City* (Robert Altman, 1996)
*Karate Kid, The* (John G. Avildsen, 1984)
*Karate Kid II, The* (John G. Avildsen, 1986)
*Karate Kid III, The* (John G. Avildsen, 1989)
*Kate & Leopold* (James Mangold, 2001)
*Katie's Room* (Paul Verhoeven, 1975)
*Kazaam* (Paul Michael Glazer, 1996)
*Keeping the Faith* (Edward Norton, 2000)
*Kentucky Fried Movie, The* (John Landis, 1977)
*Kickboxer 2: The Road Back* (Albert Pyun, 1991)
*Kickboxer 4: The Aggressor* (Albert Pyun, 1994)
*Kicked in the Head* (Matthew Harrison, 1997)
*Kid* (Hal Hartley, 1984)
*Kid, The* (Jon Turteltaub, 2000)

Lion King, The (Roger Allers & Rob Minkoff, 1994)
Lisbon Story (Wim Wenders, 1994)
Little Dragons, The (Curtis Hanson, 1980)
Little Fauss and Big Halsy (Sidney J. Furie, 1970)
Little Man Tate (Jodie Foster, 1991)
Little Mermaid, The (Ron Clements & John Musker, 1989)
Little Nikita (Richard Benjamin, 1988)
Little Odessa (James Gray, 1994)
Little Rascals, The (Penelope Spheeris, 1994)
Little Shop of Horrors, The (Roger Corman, 1960)
Little Shop of Horrors (Frank Oz, 1986)
Little Stiff, A (Caveh Zahedi, 1991)
Live Wire (Christian Duguay, 1992)
Living End, The (Gregg Araki, 1992)
Living in Oblivion (Tom DiCillo, 1995)
Living Out Loud (Richard LaGravenese, 1998)
Lock Up (John Flynn, 1989)
Lolita (Stanley Kubrick, 1962)
Lolita (Adrian Lyne, 1997)
Lone Star (John Sayles, 1996)
Lonely Guy, The (Arthur Hiller, 1984)
Long Day's Journey Into Night (Sydney Lumet, 1962)
Long Day's Journey Into Night (David Wellington, 1996)
Long Goodbye, The (Robert Altman, 1973)
Long Kiss Goodnight, The (Renny Harlin, 1996)
Long Riders, The (Walter Hill, 1980)
Long Weekend (O'Despair) (Gregg Araki, 1989)
Long Winter, The (Michel Brault, 1999)
Longshot, The (Paul Bartel, 1986)
Look Who's Talking (Amy Heckerling, 1989)
Look Who's Talking Too (Amy Heckerling, 1990)
Looker (Michael Crichton, 1981)
Looking For Richard (Al Pacino, 1996)
Loon (Erin Dignam, 1991)
Loose Cannons (Bob Clark, 1990)
Loose Screws (Rafal Zielinski, 1985)
Lorca and the Outlaws (Roger Christian, 1985)
Lord of Illusions (Clive Barker, 1995)
Lord of the Rings, The (Ralph Bakshi, 1978)
Loser (Amy Heckerling, 2000)
Losin' it (Curtis Hanson, 1983)
Loss of Sexual Innocence, The (Mike Figgis, 1999)
Lost and Delirious (Léa Pool, 2001)
Lost and Found (Jeff Pollack, 1999)
Lost Boys, The (Joel Schumacher, 1987)
Lost Highway (David Lynch, 1997)
Lost in America (Albert Brooks, 1985)
Lost in Space (Stephen Hopkins, 1998)
Lost Souls (Janusz Kaminski, 2000)
Lost World: Jurassic Park, The (Steven Spielberg, 1997)
Lottery, The (Gary Marshall, 1989)
Louie Bluie (Terry Zwigoff, 1985)
Louis and Frank (Alexandre Rockwell, 1998)
Love Affair (Glen Gordon Caron, 1994)
Love and Basketball (Gina Prince-Bythewood, 2000)
Love and Death (Woody Allen, 1975)
Love & Human Remains (Denys Arcand, 1993)
Love And Money (James Toback, 1982)
Love and Pain (and the Whole Damn Thing) (Alan J. Pakula, 1972)

Love at Large (Alan Rudolph, 1990)
Love Crimes (Lizzie Borden, 1991)
Loved (Erin Dignam, 1997)
Love Field (Jonathan Kaplan, 1992)
Love in the Fast Lane (Bill Plympton, 1987)
lovejones (Theodore Witcher, 19971
Love Kills (Mario Van Peebles, 1998)
Loveless, The (Kathryn Bigelow, 1983)
Lovely and Amazing (Nicole Holofcener, 2001)
Love Story (Arthur Hiller, 1970)
Love! Valour! Compassion! (Joe Mantello, 1997)
Lovin' Molly (Sydney Lumet, 1974)
Low Life, The (George Hickenlooper, 1996)
Loyalties (Anne Wheeler, 1986)
Lucas the Ear of Corn (Bill Plympton, 1977)
Lucky Numbers (Nora Ephron, 2000)
Lulu (Srinivas Krishna, 1995)
Lust in the Dust (Paul Bartel, 1985)

# M

Mad Dog and Glory (John McNaughton, 1993)
Machine Gun Kelly (Roger Corman, 1958)
Madame Sousatzka (John Schlesinger, 1988)
Made (Jon Favreau, 2001)
Made in America (Richard Benjamin, 1993)
Made in Heaven (Alan Rudolph, 1987)
Made in Milan (Martin Scorsese, 1990)
Madeline (Daisy von Scherler Mayer, 1998)
Maelström (Dennis Villeneuve, 2000)
Magnolia (Paul Thomas Anderson, 1999)
Main Attraction, The (Daniel Petrie, 1962)
Mattresse (Barbet Schroeder, 1976)
Majestic, The (Frank Darabont, 2001)
Major League (David S. Ward, 1989)
Major League II (David S. Ward, 1994)
Make Mine Laughs (Richard Fleischer, 1949)
Making Love (Arthur Hiller, 1982)
Making Mr Right (Susan Seidelman, 1987)
Mala Noche (Gus Van Sant, 1985)
Malcolm X (Spike Lee, 1992)
Malice (Harold Becker, 1993)
Mallrats (Kevin Smith, 1995)
Mambo Kings, The (Arne Glimcher, 1992)
Mandingo (Richard Fleischer, 1975)
Man from Elysian Fields, The (George Hickenlooper, 2002)
Mania (Paul Lynch, 1986)
Man in the Glass Booth, The (Arthur Hiller, 1975)
Man in the Iron Mask, The (Mike Newell, 1976)
Man in the Iron Mask, The (Randall Wallace, 1998)
Man of La Mancha, The (Arthur Hiller, 1972)
Man on the Moon (Milos Forman, 1999)
Man Trouble (Bob Rafelson, 1992)
Man Who Knew Too Little, The (Jon Amiel, 1997)
Man Who Loved Women, The (Blake Edwards, 1983)
Man Who Wasn't There, The (Joel Coen, 2001)
Man With Two Brains, The (Cad Reiner, 1983)
Man Without a Face, The (Mel Gibson, 1993)

Manchurian Candidate, The (John Frankenheimer, 1962)
Mangler, The (Tobe Hooper, 1995)
Manhattan (Woody Allen, 1979)
Manhattan Murder Mystery (Woody Allen, 1993)
Manhunter (Michael Mann, 1986)
Manny & Lo (Lisa Krueger, 1996)
Mansfield Park (Patricia Rozema, 1999)
Marathon Man (John Schlesinger, 1976)
Margaret's Museum (Mort Ransen, 1995)
Marie (Roger Donaldson, 1985)
Marine Life (Anne Wheeler, 2000)
Mario (Jean Beaudin, 1984)
Married to It (Arthur Hiller, 1991)
Married to the Mob (Jonathan Demme, 1988)
Mars Attacks! (Tim Burton, 1996)
Martin (George A. Romero, 1978)
Mary Reilly (Stephen Frears, 1996)
Masala (Srinivas Krishna, 1991)
M*A*S*H (Robert Altman, 1983)
Mask (Peter Bogdanovich, 1985)
Masterminds (Roger Christian, 1997)
Masque of the Red Death, The (Roger Corman, 1964)
Maternal Instincts (George Kaczender, 1996)
Matewan (John Sayles, 1987)
Matilda (Danny DeVito, 1996)
Matinee (Joe Dante, 1993)
Matrix, The (Larry & Andy Wachowski, 1999)
Maudites sauvages, Les (Jean-Pierre Lefebvre, 1971)
Maurice (James Ivory, 1987)
· Maverick (Richard Donner, 1994)
Max Keeble's Big Move (Tim Hill, 2001)
M Butterfly (David Cronenberg, 1993)
McCabe and Mrs Miller (Robert Altman, 1971)
Mean Guns (Albert Pyun, 1997)
Me, Myself & Irene (Peter & Bob Farrelly, 2000)
Mean Guns (Albert Pyun, 1997)
Mean Streets (Martin Scorsese, 1973)
Meatballs (Ivan Reitman, 1979)
Medicine Man (John McTiernan, 1992)
Medicine River (Stuart Margolin, 1994)
Meet the Parents (Jay Roach, 2000)
Meet Joe Black (Martin Brest, 1998)
Meet the Applegates (Michael Lehmann, 1990)
Melvin and Howard (Jonathan Demme, 1980)
Memories Unlocked (Jean Beaudin, 1998)
Memoirs of an Invisible Man (John Carpenter, 1992)
Memory Run (Allan A. Goldstein, 1996)
Men at Work (Emilio Estevez, 1990)
Men in Black (Barry Sonnenfeld, 1997)
Men in Black 2 (Barry Sonnenfeld, 2002)
Men of Honor (George Tillman Jr, 2000)
Men with Guns (John Sayles, 1997)
Men with Guns (Kari Skogland, 1997)
Men's Club, The (Peter Medak, 1986)
Menace II Society (Albert and Allen Hughes, 1993)
Mercury Rising (Harold Becker, 1998)
Meridian (Charles Band, 1990)
Mermaids (Richard Benjamin, 1990)
Mesmer (Roger Spottiswoode, 1994)

Metalstorm: The Destruction of Jared-Syn (Charles Band, 1983)
Metropolitan (Whit Stillman, 1990)
Mexican, The (Gore Verbinski, 2001)
Mi Vida Loca (Allison Anders, 1993)
Miami Blues (George Armitage, 1990)
Michael Collins (Neil Jordan, 1996)
Mickey Blue Eyes (Kelly Makin, 1999)
Micki & Maude (Blake Edwards, 1984)
Midnight Clear, A (Keith Gordon, 1991)
Midnight Cowboy (John Schlesinger, 1969)
Midnight Express (Alan Parker, 1978)
Midnight in the Garden of Good and Evil (Clint Eastwood, 1997)
Midnight Run (Martin Brest, 1988)
Midsummer Night's Sex Comedy, A (Woody Allen, 1982)
Mighty, The (Peter Chelsom, 1998)
Mighty Aphrodite (Woody Allen, 1995)
Mighty Ducks, The (Stephen Herek, 1992)
Mighty Joe Young (Ron Underwood, 1998)
Milagro Beanfield War, The (Robert Redford, 1988)
Miles From Home (Gary Sinise, 1988)
Milk Money (Richard Benjamin, 1994)
Miller's Crossing (Joel Coen, 1990)
Million Dollar Hotel, The (Wim Wenders, 2000)
Million Dollar Mystery (Richard Fleischer, 1987)
Mimic (Guillermo Del Toro, 1997)
Minotaur, The (Dan McCormack, 1994)
Miracle, The (Neil Jordan, 1991)
Miracle à Memphis (Pierre Falardeau, 1999)
Miracle of the White Stallions, The (Arthur Hiller, 1962)
Miracle on 34th Street (Les Mayfield, 1994)
Miracles (Jim Kouf, 1986)
Mirror Has Two Faces, The (Barbara Streisand, 1996)
Misery (Rob Reiner, 1990)
Mishima: A Life in Four Chapters (Paul Schrader, 1985)
Miss Congeniality (Donald Petrie, 2000)
Mission, The (Roland Joffé, 1986)
Mission Impossible (Brian De Palma, 1996)
Mission: Impossible II (John Woo, 2000)
Mississippi Burning (Alan Parker, 1988)
Miss Julie (Mike Figgis, 1999)
Mister Cory (Blake Edwards, 1957)
Mi viaggio in Italia, Il (Martin Scorsese, 1999)
Mixed Nuts (Nora Ephron, 1994)
Mo' Better Blues (Spike Lee, 1990)
Mod Squad, The (Scott Silver, 1999)
Modern Romance (Albert Brooks, 1981)
Moderns, The (Alan Rudolph, 1988)
Mona Lisa (Neil Jordan, 1986)
Mon arnie Max (Michel Brault, 1994)
Mon arnie Pierette (Jean-Pierre Lefebvre, 1968)
Mondo Trasho (John Waters, 1969)
Money Crazy (John Woo, 1977)
Money Man (Phillip Haas, 1992)
Money Pit, The (Richard Benjamin, 1986)
Money Talks (Brett Ratner, 1997)
Money Train (Joseph Ruben, 1995)
Monkeybone (Henry Selick, 2001)
Monkey Shines (George A. Romero, 1988)

Mon oeil (Jean-Pierre Lefebvre, 1970)
Monster's Ball (Marc Forster, 2002)
Month by the Lake, A (John Irvin, 1995)
Month in the Country, A (Pat O'Connor, 1987)
Monty Python and the Holy Grail (Terry Gilliam, 1975)
Monument Ave (Ted Demme, 1998)
Moon 44 (Roland Emmerich, 1990)
Moonlight Mile (Brad Silberling, 2002)
Moon Over Parador (Paul Mazursky, 1988)
Moonlight and Valentino (David Anspaugh, 1995)
Moonstruck (Norman Jewison, 1987)
More (Barbet Schroeder, 1969)
More about the Children of Noisy Village (Lasse
  Hallström, 1987)
More Sex and Violence (Bill Plympton, 1998)
More Than a School (Martha Coolidge, 1974)
Morning After, The (Sydney Lumet, 1986)
Mortal Kombat (Paul Anderson, 1995)
Mortal Thoughts (Alan Rudolph, 1991)
Moscow on the Hudson (Paul Mazursky, 1984)
Mosquito Coast, The (Peter Weir, 1986)
Mother (Albert Brooks, 1997)
Mother Night (Keith Gordon, 1996)
Mother of Many Children (Alanis Obomsawin, 1977)
Mothman Prophecies, The (Mark Pellington, 2002)
Moulin Rouge (Baz Lurhmann, 2001)
Mountains of the Moon (Bob Rafelson, 1990)
Mouse Hunt (Gore Verbinski, 1997)
Movie Orgy, The (Joe Dante, 1967–75)
Mr and Mrs Bridge (James Ivory, 1990)
Mr Baseball (Fred Schepisi, 1992)
Mr Billion (Jonathan Kaplan, 1977)
Mr Holland's Opus (Stephen Herek, 1995)
Mr. Jones (Mike Figgis, 1993)
Mr. Majestyk (Richard Fleischer, 1974)
Mrs Brown (John Madden, 1997)
Mrs Doubtfire (Chris Columbus, 1993)
Mrs Parker and the Vicious Circle (Alan Rudolph, 1994)
Mrs Winterbourne (Richard Benjamln, 1996)
Ms. 45 (Abel Ferrara, 1981)
Mulholland Drive (David Lynch, 2001)
Mulholland Falls (Lee Tamahori, 1996)
Multiple Maniacs (John Waters, 1970)
Multiplicity (Harold Ramis, 1996)
Mumford (Lawrence Kasdan, 1999)
Mummy, The (Stephen Sommers, 1999)
Mummy Returns, The (Stephen Sommers, 2001)
Muppets From Space (Tim Hill, 1999)
Muppets Take Manahttan, The (Frank Oz, 1984)
Murder à la Mod (Brian De Palma, 1968)
Murder by Decree (Bob Clark, 1979)
Murder by Numbers (Barbet Schroeder, 2002)
Murder in the Family (Denys Arcand, 1984)
Murder in the First (Marc Rocco, 1995)
Murder on the Orient Express (Sydney Lumet, 1974)
Muse, The (Albert Brooks, 1999)
Music of Chance, The (Phillip Haas, 1993)
Music of the Heart (Wes Craven, 1999)
Musketeer, The (Peter Hyams, 2001)
Mute Witness (Anthony Waller, 1994)

My Beautiful Laundrette (Stephen Frears, 1985)
My Cousin Vinny (Jonathan Lynn, 1992)
My Father the Hero (Steve Miner, 1994)
My Favorite Martian (Donald Petrie, 1999)
My Favorite Year (Richard Benjamin, 1982)
My 5 Wives (Sidney J. Furie, 2000)
My Giant (Michael Lehmann, 1998)
My Girlfriend's Wedding (Jim McBride, 1969)
My Life as a Dog (Lasse Hallström, 1985)
My Life's in Turnaround (Eric Schaeffer, 1993)
My New Gun (Stacy Cochran, 1992)
My Own Private Idaho (Gus Van Sant, 1991)
My Stepmother Is an Alien (Richard Benjamin, 1988)
Mystérieuse Mademoiselle C, La (Richard Ciupka, 2002)
Mystery, Alaska (Jay Roach, 1999)
Mystery Men (Kinka Usher, 1999)
Mystery Train (Jim Jarmusch, 1989)
Mystic Pizza (Donald Petrie, 1988)
Myth of Fingerprints, The (Bart Freundlich, 1997)

# N

Nadine (Robert Benton, 1987)
Nadja (Michael Almereyda, 1994)
Naked Gun: From the Files of Police Squad, The (David
  Zucker, 1988)
Naked Gun 2½: The Smell of Fear, The (David Zucker,
  1991)
Naked Lunch (David Cronenberg, 1991)
Naked Man, The (Jay Todd Anderson, 1998)
Naked Paradise (Roger Corman, 1957)
Naked Runner, The (Sidney J. Furie, 1967)
Narrow Margin, The (Richard Fleischer, 1952)
Narrow Margin (Peter Hyams, 1990)
Nashville (Robert Altman, 1975)
National Lampoon's Animal House (John Landis, 1978)
National Lampoon's Christmas Vacation (Jeremiah
  Chechik, 1989)
National Lampoon's Senior Trip (Kelly Makin, 1995)
National Lampoon's Vacation (Harold Ramis, 1983)
Natural Born Killers (Oliver Stone, 1994)
Natural, The (Barry Levinson, 1984)
Near Dark (Kathryn Bigelow, 1987)
Negatives (Peter Medak, 1968)
Negotiator, The (Felix Gray, 1998)
Neighbors (John G. Avildsen, 1981)
Neil Simon's Lost in Yonkers (Martha Coolidge, 1993)
Nemesis (Albert Pyun, 1993)
Neptune Factor, The (Daniel Petrie, 1973)
Network (Sydney Lumet, 1976)
Never Again (Eric Schaeffer, 2001)
Never Been Kissed (Raja Gosnell, 1999)
Never Cry Wolf (Caroll Ballard, 1983)
Never Centurions, The (Richard Fleischer, 1972)
Never Say Die (Geoff Murphy, 1988)
New Jack City (Mario Van Peebles, 1991)
New Life, A (Alan Alda, 1988)
New Rose Hotel (Abel Ferrara, 1998)
Newton Boys, The (Richard Linklater, 1998)

New Year's Day (Henry Jaglom, 1989)
New York, New York (Martin Scorsese, 1977)
New York Stories (Martin Scorsese, Francis Coppola &
    Woody Allen, 1989)
New Waterford Girl (Allan Moyle, 1999)
Next Best Thing, The (John Schlesinger, 2000)
Next of Kin (Atom Egoyan, 1984)
Next of Kin (John Irvin, 1989)
Next Stop, Greenwich Village (Paul Mazursky, 1976)
Nickelodeon (Peter Bogdanovich, 1976)
Nick of Time (John Badham, 1995)
Nick's Film – Lightning over Water (Wim Wenders, 1979)
Night at the Golden Eagle (Adam Rifkin, 2002)
Night at the Roxbury, A (John Fortenberry, 1998)
Night Call Nurses (Jonathan Kaplan, 1972)
Night Falls on Manhattan (Sydney Lumet, 1996)
Night in Heaven, A (John G. Avildsen, 1983)
Night of the Living Dead (George A. Romero, 1968)
Night of the Warrior (Ralal Zielinski, 1991)
Night on Earth (Jim Jarmusch, 1991)
Night Shift (Ron Howard, 1982)
Night They Raided Minsky's, The (William Friedkin, 1968)
Nightbreed (Clive Barker, 1990)
Nightmare Before Christmas (Henry Selick, 1993)
Nightmare Circus (Alan Rudolph, 1973)
Nightmare on Elm Street, A (Wes Craven, 1984)
Nightmare on Elm Street 4: The Dream Master, A (Renny
    Harlin, 1988)
Nightmare on Elm Street 5: The Dream Child, A (Stephen
    Hopkins, 1989)
Nightwing (Arthur Hiller, 1979)
9½ Weeks (Adrian Lyne, 1985)
Nine Months (Chris Columbus, 1995)
1941 (Steven Spielberg, 1979)
99 and 44/100% Dead (John Frankenheimer, 1974)
Nixon (Oliver Stone, 1995)
Nô (Robert Lepage, 1998)
No Address (Alanis Obomsawin, 1988)
Noah's Ark Principle, The (Roland Emmerich, 1984)
Nobody's Fool (Robert Benton, 1994)
No Contest (Paul Lynch, 1994)
No Contest 2 (Paul Lynch, 1997)
No Escape, No Return (Charles T. Kanganis, 1993)
Noises Off (Peter Bogdanovich, 1992)
No Looking Back (Edward Burns, 1998)
Nomads (John McTiernan, 1986)
Normal Life (John McNaughton, 1996)
North (Rob Reiner, 1994)
Northville Cemetery Massacre (William Dear, 1976)
Nosehair (Bill Plympton, 1994)
No Skin Off My Ass (Bruce LaBruce, 1991)
Nostradamus (Roger Christian, 1994)
No Such Thing (Hal Hartley, 2001)
Not a Pretty Picture (Martha Coolidge, 1975)
Notebook on Cities and Clothes (Wim Wenders, 1989)
Not for Publication (Paul Bartel, 1984)
Nothing in Common (Gary Marshall, 1986)
Nothing to Lose (Steve Oedekerk, 1997)
Not of this Earth (Roger Corman, 1957)
No Way Out (Roger Donaldson, 1987)

Nowhere (Gregg Araki, 1997)
Nowhere to Run (Carl Franklin, 1989)
Nuns on the Run (Jonathan Lynn, 1990)
Nurse Betty (Neil LaBute, 2000)
Nutcase (Roger Donaldson, 1980)
Nutcracker: The Motion Picture (Caroll Ballard, 1986)
Nutty Professor, The (Tom Shadyac, 1996)

# O

O Brother, Where Art Thou? (Joel Coen, 2000)
Obsession (Brian De Palma, 1976)
O.C. & Stiggs (Robert Altman, 1985)
Ocean's Eleven (Steven Soderbergh, 2001)
October Sky (Joe Johnston, 1999)
Octobre (Pierre Falardeau, 1994)
Odd Couple II, The (Howard Deutch, 1998)
Odd Job, The (Peter Medak, 1978)
Office Killer (Cindy Sherman, 1997)
Of Unknown Origin (George P. Cosmatos, 1983)
Offence, The (Sydney Lumet, 1973)
Office Space (Mike Judge, 1999)
Officer and a Gentleman, An (Taylor Hacklord, 1982)
Of Mice and Men (Gary Sinise, 1992)
Oh, God! (Carl Reiner, 1977)
Okay Bill (John G. Avildsen, 1971)
Old-Fashioned Woman (Martha Coolidge, 1974)
Oklahoma Woman, The (Roger Corman, 1956)
Oleanna (David Mamet, 1994)
Omen, The (Richard Donner, 1976)
On n'engraise pas les cochons à l'eau claire (Jean-Pierre
    Lefebvre, 1973)
Once a Thief (John Woo, 1990)
Once Around (Lasse Hallström, 1991)
Once Upon a Time in Mexico (Robert Rodriguez, 2002)
Once Were Warriors (Lee Tamahori, 1994)
One, The (James Wong, 2001)
One and Only, The (Carl Reiner, 1978)
One Eight Seven (Kevin Reynolds, 1997)
One False Move (Carl Franklin, 1991)
One Fine Day (Michael Hoffman, 1996)
One Flew Over the Cuckoo's Nest (Milos Forman, 1975)
One From the Heart (Francis Ford Coppola, 1982)
101 Dalmations (Stephen Herek, 1996)
One Night Stand (Mike Figgis, 1997)
One of those Days (Bill Plympton, 1988)
One Trick Pony (Robert M. Young, 1980)
One True Thing (Carl Franklin, 1998)
Onion Field, The (Harold Becker, 1979)
Only the Lonely (Chris Columbus, 1991)
Only You (Betty Thomas, 1992)
Only You (Norman Jewison, 1994)
Operation Petticoat (Blake Edwards, 1959)
Opportunity Knocks (Donald Petrie, 1990)
Opposite of Sex, The (Don Roos, 1998)
Orange County (Jake Kasdan, 2002)
Orders (Michel Brault, 1974)
Ordinary People (Robert Redford, 1980)
Orgazmo (Trey Parker, 1997)

Original Gangstas (Larry Cohen, 1996)
Original Kings of Comedy, The (Spike Lee, 2000)
Original Sin (Michael Cristofer, 2001)
Orphans (Alan J. Pakula, 1987)
Oscar (John Landis, 1991)
Osmosis Jones (Peter & Bob Farrelly, 2001)
Other People's Money (Norman Jewison, 1991)
Other Sister, The (Gary Marshall, 1999)
Other Voices (Dan McCormack, 2000)
Our Lady of the Assassins (Barbet Schroeder, 2000)
Our Song (Jim McKay, 2000)
Our Time (Peter Hyams, 1974)
Our Winning Season (Joseph Ruben, 1978)
Outbreak (Wolfgang Petersen, 1995)
Outfit, The (John Flynn, 1974)
Out of Africa (Sydney Pollack, 1985)
Out for Justice (John Flynn, 1991)
Out of Sight (Steven Soderbergh, 1998)
Out of the Blue (Dennis Hopper, 1980)
Out of Towners, The (Arthur Hiller, 1969)
Out to Sea (Martha Coolidge, 1997)
Outland (Peter Hyams, 1981)
Outlaw Josey Wales, The (Clint Eastwood, 1976)
Outside Chance of Maximillian Glick, The (Allan A.
    Goldstein, 1988)
Outside Providence (Michael Corrente, 1999)
Outsiders, The (Francis Ford Coppola, 1983)
Overboard (Gary Marshall, 1987)
Over the Edge (Jonathan Kaplan, 1979)

# P

Pacific Heights (John Schlesinger, 1990)
Package, The (Andrew Davis, 1989)
Pale Rider (Clint Eastwood, 1985)
Palookaville (Alan Taylor, 1995)
Panic Room (David Fincher, 2002)
Panther (Mario Van Peebles, 1995)
Paper, The (Ron Howard, 1994)
Paper Moon (Peter Bogdanovich, 1973)
Paperhouse (Bernard Rose, 1988)
Paper Wedding, The (Michel Brault, 1989)
Parallax View, The (Alan J. Pakula, 1974)
Paramedics (Stuart Margolin, 1987)
Parasite (Charles Band, 1982)
Parent Trap, The (Nancy Meyers, 1998)
Parenthood (Ron Howard, 1989)
Paris, France (Jerry Ciccoritti, 1993)
Paris, Texas (Wim Wenders, 1984)
Party, Le (Pierre Falardeau, 1990)
Party, The (Blake Edwards, 1968)
Party, The (Fred Schepisi, 1970)
Party Girl (Daisy von Scherler Mayer, 1995)
Passengers 57 (Kevin Hooks, 1992)
Passion Fish (John Sayles, 1992)
Patch Adams (Tom Shadyac, 1998)
Paths of Glory (Stanley Kubrick, 1957)
Patricia at Jean-Baptiste (Jean-Pierre Lefebvre, 1968)
Patriot Games (Phillip Noyce, 1992)

Patriot, The (Roland Emmerich, 2000)
Patty Hearst (Paul Schrader, 1988)
Pawnbroker, The (Sydney Lumet, 1965)
Payback (Brian Helgeland, 1999)
Pay it Forward (Mimi Leder, 2000)
Peacemaker, The (Mimi Leder, 1997)
Pearl Harbor (Michael Bay, 2001)
Pebble and the Penguin, The (Don Bluth, 1996)
Pecker (John Waters, 1998)
Peeper (Peter Hyams, 1975)
Pee-wee's Big Adventure (Tim Burton, 1985)
Peggy Sue Got Married (Francis Ford Coppola, 1986)
Pelican Brief, The (Alan J. Pakula, 1993)
Penelope (Arthur Hiller, 1966)
People Under the Stairs, The (Wes Craven, 1992)
People vs. Larry Flynt, The (Milos Forman, 1996)
Perfect Couple, A (Robert Altman, 1979)
Perfect Furlough, The (Blake Edwards, 1958)
Perfect Murder, A (Andrew Davis, 1998)
Perfect Storm, The (Wolfgang Petersen, 2000)
Perfect World, A (Clint Eastwood, 1993)
Permanent Vacation (Jim Jarmusch, 1982)
Personal Best (Robert Towne, 1982)
Personals (Mike Sargent, 1998)
Personal Velocity: Three Portraits (Rebecca Miller, 2002)
Persons Unknown (George Hickenlooper, 1997)
Pet Sematary (Mary Lambert, 1989)
Pet Sematary II (Mary Lambert, 1992)
Phantom of the Paradise (Brian De Palma, 1974)
Phenomenon (Jon Turteltaub, 1996)
Philadelphia (Jonathan Demme, 1993)
Physical Evidence (Michael Crichton, 1989)
Pi (Darren Aronofsky, 1998)
Pickle, The (Paul Mazursky, 1993)
Pick-Up Artist, The (James Toback, 1987)
Picnic at Hanging Rock (Peter Weir, 1975)
Picture Perfect (Glen Gordon Caron, 1997)
Picture This: The Times of Peter Bogdanovich in Archer
    City, Texas (George Hickenlooper, 1991)
Pink Flamingos (John Waters, 1972)
Pink Floyd: The Wall (Alan Parker, 1982)
Pink Panther Strikes Again, The (Blake Edwards, 1976)
Pink Panther, The (Blake Edwards, 1963)
Piranha (Joe Dante, 1978)
Piranha 2: Flying Killers (James Cameron, 1981)
Pit and the Pendulum, The (Roger Corman, 1961)
Pit and the Pendulum, The (Stuart Gordon, 1990)
Pitch Black (David Twohy, 2000)
Places in the Heart (Robert Benton, 1984)
Plain Clothes (Martha Coolidge, 1988)
Plain Jane to the Rescue (John Woo, 1982)
Plain Pleasures (Tom Kahn, 1996)
Planet of the Apes (Tim Burton, 2001)
Plan 10 from Outer Space (Trent Harris, 1994)
Planes, Trains, & Automobiles (John Hughes, 1987)
Platoon (Oliver Stone, 1986)
Play it to the Bone (Ron Shelton, 1999)
Play Misty for Me (Clint Eastwood, 1971)
Player, The (Robert Altman, 1992)
Player's Club, The (Ice Cube, 1998)

Playing by Heart (Willard Carroll, 1998)
Plaza Suite (Arthur Hiller, 1971)
Pleasantville (Gary Ross, 1998)
Pledge, The (Sean Penn, 2001)
Plenty (Fred Schepisi, 1985)
Plumber, The (Peter Weir, 1979)
Plympmania (Bill Plympton, 1996)
Plymptoons (Bill Plympton, 1990)
Pocahontas (Eric Goldberg, 1995)
Poetic Justice (John Singleton, 1993)
Point Break (Kathryn Bigelow, 1991)
Poison (Todd Haynes, 1991)
Police Academy (Hugh Wilson, 1984)
Polish Wedding (Theresa Connelly, 1998)
Pollock (Ed Harris, 2000)
Poltergeist (Tobe Hooper, 1982)
Polyester (John Waters, 1981)
Polygraph, The (Robert Lepage, 1996)
Pom-Pom Girls, The (Joseph Ruben, 1976)
Pontiac Moon (Peter Medak, 1994)
Popeye (Robert Altman, 1980)
Popi (Arthur Hiller, 1969)
Porky's (Bob Clark, 1981)
Porky's II: The Next Day (Bob Clark, 1983)
Posers (Penelope Sheeris, 2001)
Posse (Mario Van Peebles, 1993)
Possession (Neil LaBute, 2002)
Possible Worlds (Robert Lepage, 2000)
Postcards from the Edge (Mike Nichols, 1990)
Post Queer Tour, The (Bruce LaBruce, 1992)
Postman Always Rings Twice, The (Bob Rafelson, 1981)
Postman, The (Kevin Costner, 1997)
Postmortem (Albert Pyun, 1998)
Poverty and Other Delights (Denys Arcand, 1996)
Powaqqatsi (Godfrey Reggio, 1988)
Power (Sydney Lurnet, 1986)
Power of One, The (John G. Avildsen, 1992)
Practical Magic (Griffin Dunne, 1998)
Praying With Anger (M. Night Shyamalan, 1992)
Preacher's Wife, The (Penny Marshall, 1996)
Predator (John McTiernan, 1987)
Predator 2 (Stephen Hopkins, 1990)
Prehysteria (Charles Band, 1993)
Premature Burial, The (Roger Corman, 1962)
Premonition (Alan Rudolph, 1972)
Presumed Innocent (Alan J. Pakula, 1990)
Pret-à-Porter (Robert Altman, 1994)
Pretty in Pink (Howard Deutch, 1986)
Pretty Woman (Gary Marshall, 1990)
Prettykill (George Kaczender, 1987)
Price Above Rubies, A (Boaz Yakin, 1998)
Prick Up Your Ears (Stephen Frears, 1987)
Primal Fear (Gregory Hoblit, 1996)
Primary Colors (Mike Nichols, 1998)
Prince of Darkness (John Carpenter, 1987)
Prince of Egypt, The (Simon Wells, 1998)
Prince of the City (Sydney Lumet, 1981)
Prince of Tides, The (Barbara Streisand, 1991)
Princess Bride, The (Rob Reiner, 1987)
Princess Caraboo (Michael Austin, 1994)

Princess Chang Ping (John Woo, 1976)
Princess Diaries, The (Gary Marshall, 2001)
Prison (Renny Harlin, 1988)
Private Duty Nurses (George Armitage, 1971)
Private Files of J. Edgar Hoover, The (Larry Cohen, 1977)
Private Parts (Paul Bartel, 1972)
Private Parts (Betty Thomas, 1997)
Privileged (Michael Hoffman, 1982)
Problem Child (Dennis Dugan, 1990)
Problem Child 2 (Brian Levant, 1991)
Producers, The (Mel Brooks, 1968)
Program, The (David S. Ward, 1993)
Project X (Jonathan Kaplan, 1987)
Promise Her Anything (Arthur Hiller, 1965)
Promised Land (Michael Hoffman, 1988)
Proof (Jocelyn Moorhouse, 1991)
Proof of Life (Taylor Hackford, 2000)
Prophecy (John Frankenheimer, 1979)
Prom Night (Paul Lynch, 1980)
Psycho (Gus Van Sant, 1998)
Psycho Girls (Jerry Ciccoritti, 1985)
Public Access (Bryan Singer, 1993)
Pulp Fiction (Quentin Tarantino, 1994)
Pump Up the Volume (Allan Moyle, 1990)
Punch-Drunk Love (Paul Thomas Anderson, 2002)
Punk (Carl Franklin, 1986)
Pups (Ash, 1999)
Purple Hearts (Sidney J. Furie, 1984)
Purple Rose of Cairo, The (Woody Allen, 1985)
Pushing Tin (Mike Newell, 1999)
Pursuit (Michael Crichton, 1972)
Pursuit of D.B. Cooper, The (Roger Spottiswoode, 1981)
Push Comes to Shove (Bill Plympton, 1991)

# Q

Q&A (Sydney Lumet, 1990)
Quartet (James Ivory, 1981)
Queen of Hearts (Jon Amiel, 1989)
Question of Attribution, A (John Schlesinger, 1992)
Quick and the Dead, The (Sam Raimi, 1995)
Quiet American, The (Phillip Noyce, 2002)
Quiet Earth, The (Geoff Murphy, 1985)
Quills (Philip Kaufman, 2000)
Quintet (Robert Altman, 1979)
Quiz Show (Robert Redford, 1994)
Q – The Winged Serpent (Larry Cohen, 1982)

# R

Rabbit-Proof Fence (Phillip Noyce, 2002)
Rabid (David Cronenberg, 1977)
Race the Sun (Charles T. Kanganis, 1996)
Racing With The Moon (Richard Benjamin, 1984)
Radio Days (Woody Allen, 1987)
Radioactive Dreams (Albert Pyun, 1986)
Rage, The (Sidney J. Furie, 1997)
Raging Bull (Martin Scorsese, 1980)

Ragman's Daughter, The (Harold Becker, 1972)
Ragtime (Milos Forman, 1981)
Raiders of the Lost Ark (Steven Spielberg, 1981)
Rain Man (Barry Levinson, 1988)
Rain People, The (Francis Ford Coppola, 1969)
Rainmaker, The (Francis Ford Coppola, 1997)
Raising Arizona (Joel Coen, 1987)
Raisin in the Sun, A (Daniel Petrie, 1961)
Raising Cain (Brian De Palma, 1992)
Rambling Rose (Martha Coolidge, 1991)
Rambo: First Blood Part II (George P. Cosmatos, 1985)
Rampage (William Friedkin, 1988)
Random Hearts (Sydney Pollack, 1999)
Ransom (Ron Howard, 1996)
Rape Nui (Kevin Reynolds, 1994)
Rappresaglia (George P. Cosrnatos, 1973)
Rare Birds (Sturla Gunnarson, 2001)
Ratings Game, The (Danny DeVito, 1984)
Rat Race (Jerry Zucker, 2001)
Raven, The (Roger Corman, 1963)
Ravon Hawk (Albert Pyun, 1996)
Raw Deal (John Irvin, 1986)
Real Blonde, The (Tom DiCillo, 1997)
Real Genius (Martha Coolidge, 1985)
Real Life (Albert Brooks, 1979)
Reality Bites (Ben Stiller, 1994)
Re-Animator (Stuart Gordon, 1985)
Reckless (James Foley, 1984)
Recruits (Rafal Zielinski, 1986)
Red Corner (Jon Avnet, 1997)
Red Dawn (John Milius, 1984)
Red Dragon (Brett Ratner, 2002)
Red Heat (Walter Hill, 1988)
Red Rock West (John Dahl, 1992)
Reds (Warren Beatty, 1981)
Red Sonja (Richard Fleischer, 1985)
Red Violin, The (François Girard, 1998)
Reef, The (Robert Allan Ackerman, 1997)
Ref, The (Ted Demme, 1994)
Regarding Henry (Mike Nichols, 1991)
Regroupings (Lizzie Borden, 1976)
Reindeer Games (John Frankenheimer, 2000)
Reign of Fire (Rob Bowman, 2002)
Réjeanne Padovani (Denys Arcand, 1973)
Relic, The (Peter Hyams, 1997)
Remains of the Day, The (James Ivory, 1993)
Remember My Name (Alan Rudolph, 1978)
Remember the Titans (Boaz Yakin, 2000)
Renaissance Man (Penny Marshall, 1994)
Repair Shop, The (Phillip Noyce, 1994)
Replacement Killers, The (Antoine Fuqua, 1998)
Replacements, The (Howard Deutch, 2000)
Repo Man (Alex Cox, 1984)
Requiem for a Dream (Darren Aronofsky, 2000)
Reservoir Dogs (Quentin Tarantino, 1992)
Resident Evil (Paul Anderson, 2002)
Restless Natives (Michael Hoffman, 1985)
Restoration (Michael Hoffman, 1995)
Resurrection (Daniel Petrie, 1980)
Return Engagement (Alan Rudolph, 1983)

Return of the Pink Panther (Blake Edwards, 1974)
Return of the Secaucus 7 (John Sayles, 1980)
Return to Me (Bonnie Hunt, 2000)
Return to Paradise (Joseph Ruben, 1998)
Return to Salem's Lot (Larry Cohen, 1987)
Revenge (Tony Scott, 1990)
Revenge of the Pink Panther (Blake Edwards, 1978)
Revenger's Tragedy (Alex Cox, 2002)
Reversal of Fortune (Barbet Schroeder, 1990)
Reverse Angle: NYC March 1982 (Wim Wenders, 1982)
Revoir Julie (Jeanne Crepeau, 1998)
Révolutionnaire, La (Jean-Pierre Lefebvre, 1965)
Rhinestone (Bob Clark, 1984)
Rhythm Thief (Matthew Harrison, 1994)
Richie Rich (Donald Petrie, 1995)
Ride in the Whirlwind (Monte Hellman, 1965)
Ride with the Devil (Ang Lee, 1999)
Riding in Cars with Boys (Penny Marshall, 2001)
Right Stuff, The (Philip Kaufman, 1983)
Ring (Gore Verbinski, 2002)
Rising Sun (Philip Kaufman, 1993)
River Runs Through It, A (Robert Redford, 1992)
River Wild, The (Curtis Hanson, 1994)
Roadie (Alan Rudolph, 1980)
Roadkill (Bruce McDonald, 1989)
Roadracers/Rebel Highway (Robert Rodriguez, 1994)
Road to Perdition, The (Sam Mendes, 2002)
Road to Wellville, The (Alan Parker, 1994)
Robin Hood: Men in Tights (Mel Brooks, 1993)
Robin Hood: Prince of Thieves (Kevin Reynolds, 1991)
RoboCop (Paul Verhoeven, 1987)
Robot Jox (Stuart Gordon, 1991)
Rock, The (Michael Bay, 1996)
Rock-a-Doodle (Don Bluth, 1992)
Rock All Night (Roger Corman, 1957)
Rocket Gibraltar (Daniel Petrie, 1988)
Rocketeer, The (Joe Johnston, 1991)
Rocking Horse Winner, The (Michael Almereyda, 1997)
Rock Star (Stephen Herek, 2001)
Rocky (John G. Avildsen, 1976)
Rocky V (John G. Avildsen, 1990)
Rollerball (Norman Jewison, 1975)
Rollerball (John McTiernan, 2002)
Rolling Thunder (John Flynn, 1977)
Rollover (Alan J. Pakula, 1981)
Romancing the Stone (Robert Zemeckis, 1984)
Romantic Comedy (Arthur Hiller, 1983)
Romeo is Bleeding (Peter Medak, 1993)
Romy and Michele's High School Reunion (David Mirkin, 1997)
Ronin (John Frankenheimer, 1998)
Rookie, The (Clint Eastwood, 1990)
Room with a View, A (James Ivory, 1986)
Rooster, The (Lasse Hallström, 1981)
Roosters (Robert M. Young, 1993)
Roseland (James Ivory, 1977)
Rosewood (John Singleton, 1997)
Rounders (John Dahl, 1998)
Royal Tenenbaums, The (Wes Anderson, 2001)
Roxanne (Fred Schepisi, 1987)

# S

Se7en (David Fincher, 1995)
Seven Days in May (John Frankenheimer, 1964)
Sex and Violence (Bill Plympton, 1998)
sex, lies and videotape (Steven Soderbergh, 1989)
Sex, Drugs, Rock & Roll (John McNaughton, 1991)
Sgt. Bilko (Jonathan Lynn, 1996)
Shabat Shalom! (Michel Brault, 1992)
Shadow Conspiracy (George P. Cosmatos, 1997)
Shadow of the Vampire (E. Elias Merhige, 2000)
Shadows and Fog (Woody Allen, 1992)
Shaft (John Singleton, 2000)
Shakespeare in Love (John Madden, 1998)
Shakespeare-Wallah (James Ivory, 1965)
Shallow Hal (Peter & Bob Farrelly, 2001)
Shattered (Wolfgang Petersen, 1991)
Shawshank Redemption, The (Frank Darabont, 1994)
She-Devil (Susan Seidelman, 1989)
She Gods of Shark Reef (Roger Corman, 1958)
She's All That (Robert Iscove, 1999)
Sheila Levine is Dead and Living in New York (Sidney J.
    Furie, 1975)
Shelf Life (Paul Bartel, 1993)
Sherman's March – A Meditation on the Possibility of
    Romantic Love in the South During an Era of Nuclear
    Proliferation (Ross McElwee, 1986)
Sherwood's Travels (Steve Miner, 1994)
She's Having a Baby (John Hughes, 1988)
She's So Lovely (John Cassavetes, 1997)
She's the One (Edward Burns, 1996)
Shiner (John Irvin, 2001)
Shining, The (Stanley Kubrick, 1980)
Shipping News, The (Lasse Hallström, 2001)
Shivers (David Cronenberg, 1975)
Shocker (Wes Craven, 1989)
Shoot the Moon (Alan Parker, 1982)
Shoot to Kill (Roger Spottiswoode, 1988)
Shooting, The (Monte Hellman, 1967)
Shopping (Paul Anderson, 1994)
Short Circuit (John Badham, 1986)
Short Cuts (Robert Altman, 1993)
Short Eyes (Robert M. Young, 1977)
Shot at Glory, A (Michael Corrente, 2002)
Shot in the Dark, A (Blake Edwards, 1964)
Showgirls (Paul Verhoeven, 1995)
Shrek (Andrew Adamson & Vicky Jenson, 2001)
Sibling Rivalry (Carl Reiner, 1990)
Sicilian, The (Michael Cimino, 1987)
Sid and Nancy (Alex Cox, 1986)
Sidewalks of New York (Edward Burns, 2001)
Siege, The (Edward Zwick, 1998)
Siegfried & Roy: The Magic Box (Brett Leonard, 1999)
Siesta (Mary Lambert, 1987)
Signs (M. Night Shyamalan, 2002)
Silence of the Lambs, The (Jonathan Demme, 1991)
Silent Night, Deadly Night III — Better Watch Out!
    (Monte Hellman, 1989)
Silent Tongue (Sam Shepard, 1993)
Silkwood (Mike Nichols, 1983)
Sliver Bears (Ivan Passer, 1977)
Silver Streak (Arthur Hiller, 1976)

Silverado (Lawrence Kasdan, 1985)
Simple Men (Hal Hartley, 1992)
Simple Plan, A (Sam Raimi, 1998)
Simply Irresistible (Mark Tarlov, 1999)
Singing Sculpture, The (Phillip Haas, 1992)
Singles (Cameron Crowe, 1992)
Single White Female (Barbet Schroeder, 1992)
Sister, Sister (Bill Condon, 1987)
Sister-In-Law, The (Joseph Ruben, 1974)
Sisters (Brian De Palma, 1973)
Sitting Ducks (Henry Jaglom, 1980)
Six Days, Seven Nights (Ivan Reitman, 1998)
Six Degrees of Separation (Fred Schepisi, 1993)
Six O'Clock News (Ross McElwee, 1997)
Six Pack (Daniel Petrie, 1982)
Sixteen Candles (John Hughes, 1984)
6th Day, The (Roger Spottiswoode, 2000)
Sixth Sense, The (M. Night Shyamalan, 1999)
Size of Watermelons, The (Kari Skogland, 1996)
Ski Troop Attack (Roger Corman, 1960)
Skin Deep (Blake Edwards, 1989)
Skin Flick (Bruce LaBruce, 1999)
Skipped Parts (Tamra Davis, 2001)
Skull: A Night of Terror (Jerry Ciccoritti, 1987)
Skulls, The (Rob Cohen, 2000)
Slacker (Richard Linklater, 1991)
Slam! (Bruce LaBruce, 1989)
Slam Dance (Wayne Wang, 1987)
Slams, The (Jonathan Kaplan, 1973)
Slaves of New York (James Ivory, 1989)
S.L.C. Punk! (James Merendino, 1999)
Sleeper (Woody Allen, 1973)
Sleepers (Barry Levinson, 1996)
Sleeping Dogs (Roger Donaldson, 1977)
Sleeping with the Enemy (Joseph Ruben, 1991)
Sleepless in Seattle (Nora Ephron, 1993)
Sleepwalkers (Mick Garris, 1992)
Sleep With Me (Rory Kelly, 1994)
Sleepy Hollow (Tim Burton, 1999)
Sling Blade (Billy Bob Thornton, 1996)
Sliver (Phillip Noyce, 1993)
Slow Dancing in the Big City (John G. Avildsen, 1978)
Smack in the Kisser (Fred Scepisi, 2002)
Small Circle of Friends, A (Rob Cohen, 1980)
Small One, The (Don Bluth, 1978)
Small Soldiers (Joe Dante, 1998)
Smash Palace (Roger Donaldson, 1981)
Smell the Flowers (Bill Plympton, 1996)
Smithereens (Susan Seidelman, 1982)
Smoke (Wayne Wang, 1995)
Snail Position, The (Michka Saäl, 1999)
Snake Eyes (Brian De Palma, 1998)
Snake Woman, The (Sidney J. Furie, 1961)
Snapper, The (Stephen Frears, 1993)
Sniper (Luis Llosa, 1993)
Snow Day (Chris Koch, 2000)
Snow Dogs (Brian Levant, 2002)
So Fine (Andrew Bergman, 1981)
So This is New York (Richard Fleischer, 1948)
Soapdish (Michael Hoffman, 1991)

S.O.B. (Blake Edwards, 1981)
Soldier (Paul Anderson, 1998)
Soldier of Orange (Paul Verhoeven, 1979)
Soldier's Daughter Never Cries, A (James Ivory, 1998)
Soldiers Story, A (Norman Jewison, 1984)
Some Call It Loving (James B. Harris, 1973)
Some Folks Call It a Sling Blade (George Hickenlooper, 1994)
Some Girl (Rory Kelly, 1998)
Some Girls (Michael Hoffman, 1989)
Some Kind of Wonderful (Howard Deutch, 1987)
Somebody to Love (Alexandre Rockwell, 1994)
Someone Like You (Tony Goldwyn, 2001)
Someone's Watching Me! (John Carpenter, 1978)
Someone to Love (Henry Jaglom, 1987)
Someone to Watch Over Me (Ridley Scott, 1987)
Something to Do with the Wall (Ross McElwee, 1991)
Something to Talk About (Lasse Hallström, 1995)
Something Wild (Jonathan Demme, 1986)
Sommersby (Jon Amiel, 1993)
Songcatcher (Maggie Greenwald, 1999)
Songwriter (Alan Rudolph, 1984)
Son of the Pink Panther (Blake Edwards, 1993)
Sons (Alexandre Rockwell, 1989)
Sophie's Choice (Alan J. Pakula, 1982)
Sorcerer (William Friedkin, 1977)
Sorority Girl (Roger Corman, 1957)
Soursweet (Mike Newell, 1988)
Soul Food (George Tillman Jr, 1997)
Soul Man (Steve Miner, 1986)
South Central (Steve Anderson, 1992)
Southern Comfort (Walter Hill, 1981)
South Park: Bigger, Longer, Uncut (Trey Parker, 1999)
Soylent Green (Richard Fleischer, 1972)
Spaceballs (Mel Brooks, 1987)
Space Coast (Ross McElwee, 1978)
Space Cowboys (Clint Eastwood, 2000)
Space Truckers (Stuart Gordon, 1997)
Spaced Invaders (Patrick Read Johnson, 1990)
Spanish Prisoner, The (David Mamet, 1997)
Spanking the Monkey (David O. Russell, 1994)
Spare Me (Matthew Harrison, 1992)
Sparkler (Darren Stein, 1998)
Spartacus (Stanley Kubrick, 1960)
Speaking Parts (Atom Egoyan, 1989)
Special Effects (Larry Cohen, 1984)
Specialist The (Luis Llosa, 1994)
Species (Roger Donaldson, 1995)
Species II (Peter Medak, 1998)
Speechless (Ron Underwood, 1994)
Speed (Jan De Bont, 1994)
Speed 2: Cruise Control (Jan De Bont, 1997)
Spellcaster (Rafal Zielinski, 1988)
Spetters (Paul Verhoeven, 1980)
Sphere (Barry Levinson, 1998)
Sphinx, Le (Louis Sara, 1995)
Spider (David Cronenberg, 2002)
Spider-Man (Sam Raimi, 2002)
Spies Like Us (John Landis, 1985)
Spikes Gang, The (Richard Fleischer, 1974)

Spill (Allan A. Goldstein, 1996)
Spirits of the Air, Gremlins of the Clouds (Alex Proyas, 1989)
Spitfire Grill, The (Lee David Zlotoff, 1996)
Splash (Ron Howard, 1984)
Splendor (Gregg Araki, 1999)
Spontaneous Combustion (Tobe Hooper, 1989)
Spudwrench: Kahnawake Man (Alanis Obomsawin, 1997)
Spy Kids (Robert Rodriguez, 2001)
Spy Kids 2: The Island of Lost Dreams (Robert Rodriguez)
Spy with a Cold Nose, The (Daniel Petrie, 1966)
Square Dance (Daniel Petrie, 1987)
St Elmo's Fire (Joel Schumacher, 1985)
St. Valentine's Day Massacre, The (Roger Corman, 1967)
Stage Struck (Sydney Lumet, 1958)
Stakeout (John Badham, 1987)
Stalin (Ivan Passer, 1992)
Stand By Me (Rob Reiner, 1986)
Star Chamber, The (Peter Hyams, 1983)
Star Maps (Miguel Arteta, 1997)
Star Trek: First Contact (Jonathan Frakes, 1996)
Star Trek: Insurrection (Jonathan Frakes, 1998)
Star Trek VI: The Undiscovered Country (Nicholas Meyer, 1991)
Star Trek II: The Wrath of Khan (Nicholas Meyer, 1982)
Star Wars: Episode I – The Phantom Menace (George Lucas, 1999)
Star Wars: Episode II – Attack of the Clones (George Lucas, 2002)
Star Wars: Episode IV – A New Hope (George Lucas, 1977)
Stardom (Denys Arcand, 2000)
Stardust Memories (Woody Allen, 1980)
StarGate (Roland Emmerich, 1994)
Starman (John Carpenter, 1984)
Stars and Bars (Pat O'Connor, 1988)
Starship Troopers (Paul Verhoeven, 1997)
Starting Over (Alan J. Pakula, 1979)
State and Main (David Mamet, 2000)
State of Things, The (Wim Wenders, 1982)
State Park (Rafal Zielinski, 1990)
Stay Hungry (Bob Rafelson, 1976)
Stay Tuned (Peter Hyams, 1992)
Steak, Le (Pierre Falardeau, 1992)
Steal Big, Steal Little (Andrew Davis, 1995)
Steal This Movie! (Robert Greenwald, 2000)
Stepfather, The (Joseph Ruben, 1987)
Stepmom (Chris Columbus, 1998)
Sterile Cuckoo, The (Alan J. Pakula, 1969)
Stick (Burt Reynolds, 1985)
Sticky Fingers of Time, The (Hilary Brougher, 1997)
Stigmata (Rupert Wainwright, 1999)
Still of the Night (Robert Benton, 1982)
Stir of Echoes (David Koepp, 1999)
Stolen Hours (Daniel Petrie, 1963)
Stony Island (Andrew Davis, 1978)
Stoolie, The (John G. Avildsen, 1974)
Stop Making Sense (Jonathan Demme, 1984)
Stop! Or My Mom Will Shoot (Roger Spottiswoode, 1992)
Storefront Hitchcock (Jonathan Demme, 1998)
Stormy Monday (Mike Figgis, 1988)
Story of Us, The (Rob Reiner, 1999)

Storytelling (Todd Solondz, 2001)
Straight for the Heart (Léa Pool, 1988)
Straight Story, The (David Lynch, 1999)
Straight Time (Ulu Grosbard, 1978)
Straight to Hell (Alex Cox, 1987)
Strange Days (Kathryn Bigelow, 1995)
Stranger Among Us, A (Sydney Lumet, 1992)
Stranger than Paradise (Jim Jarmusch, 1984)
Strass Cafe (Léa Pool, 1980)
Streamers (Robert Altman, 1983)
Street Scenes 1970 (Martin Scorsese, 1970)
Streets of Fire (Walter Hill, 1984)
Strictly Ballroom (Baz Luhrmann, 1992)
Strictly Business (Kevin Hooks, 1991)
Stripes (Ivan Reitman, 1981)
Stuart Saves His Family (Harold Ramis, 1995)
Student Teachers, The (Jonathan Kaplan, 1973)
Stuff, The (Larry Cohen, 1985)
Stupids, The (John Landis, 1996)
Subject Was Roses, The (Ulu Grosbard, 1968)
SubUrbia (Richard Linklater, 1997)
Suburbia/The Wild Side (Penelope Spheeris, 1983)
Such a Long Journey (Sturla Gunnarson, 1998)
Sudden Death (Peter Hyams, 1995)
Sudden Impact (Clint Eastwood, 1983)
Suddenly Naked (Anne Wheeler, 2001)
Sugarland Express, The (Steven Spielberg, 1974)
Sugar Town (Allison Anders, 1999)
Suicide Kings (Peter O'Fallon, 1997)
Sum of All Fears, The (Phil Alden Robinson, 2002)
Summer in the City (Dedicated to The Kinks) (Wim
    Wenders, 1970)
Summer of Sam (Spike Lee, 1999)
Summer Rental (Carl Reiner, 1985)
Summer School (Carl Reiner, 1987)
Sunchaser, The (Michael Cimino, 1996)
Sunday Bloody Sunday (John Schlesinger, 1971)
Sunset (Blake Edwards, 1988)
Sunshine State (John Sayles, 2002)
Super 8½, (Bruce LaBruce, 1993)
Superman (Richard Donner, 1978)
Superman IV: The Quest for Peace (Sidney J. Furie, 1987)
Sure Thing, The (Rob Reiner, 1985)
Surprise Cinema (Bill Plympton, 1999)
Surviving Desire (Hal Hartley, 1991)
Surviving Picasso (James Ivory, 1996)
Susan's Plan (John Landis, 1998)
Suspicious River (Lynne Stopkewich, 2000)
Suture (Scott McGehee, 1993)
Swamp Thing (Was Craven, 1982)
Swamp Women (Roger Corman, 1955)
Swann (Anna Benson Gyles, 1996)
Sweet and Lowdown (Woody Allen, 1999)
Sweet Hearts Dance (Robert Greenwald, 1988)
Sweet Hereafter, The (Atom Egoyan, 1997)
Sweet Kill (Curtis Hanson, 1972)
Sweet Liberty (Alan Alda, 1986)
Sweet November (Pat O'Connor, 2001)
Sweetest Gift, The (Stuart Margolin, 1998)
Sweetest Thing, The (Roger Kumble, 2002)

Swimming to Cambodia (Jonathan Demme, 1987)
Swimming With Sharks (George Huang, 1994)
Swing Shift (Jonathan Demme, 1984)
Switch (Blake Edwards, 1991)
Swoon (Tom Kahn, 1992)
Sword and the Sorcerer, The (Albert Pyun, 1982)
Swordfish (Dominic Sena, 2001)

# T

Take the Money and Run (Woody Allen, 1969)
Taking Care of Business (aka Filofax) (Arthur Hiller, 1991)
Taking of Beverly Hills, The (Sidney J. Furie, 1991)
Taking Off (Milos Forman, 1971)
Talent for the Game (Robert M. Young, 1994)
Tales from the Gimli Hospital (Guy Maddin, 1988)
Tales of Terror (Roger Corman, 1962)
Talk Radio (Oliver Stone, 1988)
Tall Tale: The Unbelievable Adventures of Pecos Bill
    (Jeremiah Chechik, 1995)
Tamarind Seed, The (Blake Edwards, 1974)
Tango Schmango (Bill Plympton, 1990)
Tank Girl (Rachel Talalay, 1995)
Tao of Steve, The (Jenniphr Goodman, 2000)
Tape (Richard Linklater, 2001)
Taps (Harold Becker, 1981)
Target: Harry (Roger Corman, 1969)
Targets (Peter Bogdanovich, 1968)
Tarzan (Chris Buck & Kevin Lima, 1999)
Taxi Driver (Martin Scorsese, 1976)
Teachers (Arthur Hiller, 1984)
Teaching Mrs. Tingle (Kevin Williamson, 1999)
Teen Agent (William Dear, 1991)
Teenage Cave Man (Roger Corman, 1958)
Teenage Doll (Roger Corman, 1957)
Telling Lies in America (Guy Ferland, 1997)
Tempest (Paul Mazursky, 1982)
10 (Blake Edwards, 1979)
10 Rillington Place (Richard Fleischer, 1971)
Tendresse ordinaire (Jacques Leduc, 1973)
10 Things I Hate About You (Gil Junger, 1999)
Tequila Sunrise (Robert Towne, 1988)
Terminator, The (James Cameron, 1984)
Terminator 2: Judgment Day (James Cameron, 1991)
Terms of Endearment (James L. Brooks, 1983)
Terror Train (Roger Spottiswoode, 1979)
Terror, The (Monte Hellman, 1963)
Terror, The (Roger Corman, 1963)
Texas Chainsaw Massacre, The (Tobe Hooper, 1974)
Texas Chainsaw Massacre Part 2, The (Tobe Hooper, 1986)
Texas Rangers (Steve Miner, 2001)
Texasville (Peter Bogdanovich, 1990)
That Cold Day in the Park (Robert Altman, 1969)
That Old Feeling (Carl Reiner, 1997)
That Tender Age (Michel Brault, 1964)
That Thing You Do! (Tom Hanks, 1996)
That's Life! (Blake Edwards, 1986)
Thelma and Louise (Ridley Scott, 1991)
Theory of Achievement (Hal Hartley, 1991)

*There's Something About Mary* (Peter & Bob Farrelly, 1998)
*These Thousand Hills* (Richard Fleischer, 1959)
*They All Laughed* (Peter Bogdanovich, 1981)
*They Live* (John Carpenter, 1988)
*They Shoot Horses, Don't They?* (Sydney Pollack, 1969)
*Thief* (Michael Mann, 1981)
*Thieves Like Us* (Robert Altman, 1974)
*Thin Red Line, The* (Terrence Malick, 1998)
*Thing Called Love, The* (Peter Bogdanovich, 1993)
*Thing, The* (John Carpenter, 1982)
*Things Change* (David Mamet, 1988)
*Things to Do in Denver When You're Dead* (Gary Fleder, 1995)
*Thirteen Days* (Roger Donaldson, 2000)
*13th Warrior, The* (John McTiernan, 1999)
*Thirty Two Short Films About Glenn Gould* (François Girard, 1993)
*This Happy Feeling* (Blake Edwards, 1958)
*This is My Life* (Nora Ephron, 1992)
*This is Spinal Tap* (Rob Reiner, 1984)
*This Property is Condemned* (Sydney Pollack, 1966)
*This Rugged Land* (Arthur Hiller, 1962)
*This Slender Thread* (Sydney Pollack, 1965)
*Thomas Crown Affair, The* (Norman Jewison, 1968)
*Thomas Crown Affair, The* (John McTiernan, 1999)
*Thousand Acres, A* (Jocelyn Moorhouse, 1997)
*Three Amigos!* (John Landis, 1986)
*Three Bewildered People in the Night* (Gregg Araki, 1987)
*Three Businessmen* (Alex Cox, 1998)
*Three Days of the Condor* (Sydney Pollack, 1975)
*Three Kings* (David O. Russell, 1999)
*Three Musketeers, The* (Stephen Herek, 1993)
*Three Ninjas* (Jon Turteltaub, 1992)
*Three Ninjas Kick Back* (Charles T. Kanganis, 1994)
*Three on a Spree* (Sidney J. Furie, 1961)
*Three Wishes* (Martha Coolidge, 1995)
*Threesome* (Andrew Fleming, 1994)
*3 Women* (Robert Altman, 1977)
*Thrill Of It All, The* (Norman Jewison, 1963)
*Throw Momma from the Train* (Danny DeVito, 1987)
*Thumbelina* (Don Bluth, 1994)
*Thunderbolt And Lightfoot* (Michael Cimino, 1974)
*Thunderpants* (Peter Hewitt, 2002)
*THX 1138* (George Lucas, 1970)
*THX 1138 4EB: Electronic Labyrinth* (George Lucas, 1967)
*Tian yu* (Joan Chen, 1998)
*Ticker* (Albert Pyun, 2001)
*Tiger Claws* (Kelly Makin, 1992)
*Tiger Makes Out, The* (Arthur Hiller, 1967)
*Tigerland* (Joel Schumacher, 2000)
*Time After Time* (Nicholas Meyer, 1979)
*Time Bandits* (Terry Gilliam, 1981)
*Time Indefinite* (Ross McElwee, 1993)
*Time Machine, The* (Simon Wells, 2002)
*Times Square* (Allan Moyle, 1980)
*Time to Die, A* (Charles T. Kanganis, 1991)
*Time To Kill, A* (Joel Schumacher, 1996)
*Time You Need a Friend, The* (John Woo, 1984)
*Timecode* (Mike Figgis, 2000)

*Timecop* (Peter Hyams, 1994)
*Timerider – The Adventure of Lyle Swann* (William Dear, 1982)
*Tin Cup* (Ron Shelton, 1996)
*Tin Men* (Barry Levinson, 1987)
*Titan AE* (Don Bluth, 2000)
*Titanic* (James Cameron, 1997)
*Titus* (Julie Taymor, 1999)
*To Die For* (Gus Van Sant, 1995)
*To Hell With the Devil* (John Woo, 1982)
*To Live And Die In L.A.* (William Friedkin, 1985)
*Tobe Hooper's Night Terrors* (Tobe Hooper, 1993)
*Tobruk* (Arthur Hitler, 1967)
*Tokyo-Ga* (Wim Wenders, 1985)
*Tom and Huck* (Peter Hewitt, 1995)
*Tomb of Ligeia, The* (Roger Corman, 1965)
*Tomb Raider* (Simon West, 2001)
*Tombstone* (George P. Cosmatos, 1993)
*Tom's Midnight Garden* (Willard Carroll, 1999)
*Tomorrow Never Dies* (Roger Spottiswoode, 1997)
*Tonight for Sure* (Francis Ford Coppola, 1961)
*Tootsie* (Sydney Pollack, 1982)
*Top Gun* (Tony Scott, 1986)
*Top of the Food Chain* (John Paizs, 1999)
*Top of the World* (Sidney J. Furie, 1997)
*Top Secret!* (Jim Abrahams, David Zucker & Jerry Zucker, 1984)
*Tora! Tora! Tora!* (Richard Fleischer, 1970)
*Total Recall* (Paul Verhoeven, 1990)
*Totally F***ed Up* (Gregg Araki, 1993)
*Touch* (Paul Schrader, 1997)
*Touched* (Mort Ransen, 1999)
*Tough Enough* (Richard Fleischer, 1983)
*Tower of London* (Roger Corman, 1962)
*Town and Country* (Peter Chelsom, 2001)
*Toy, The* (Richard Donner, 1982)
*Toys* (Barry Levinson, 1992)
*Toy Soldiers* (Daniel Petrie Jr, 1991)
*Toy Story* (John Lasseter, 1995)
*Toy Story 2* (John Lasseter, 1999)
*Tracks* (Henry Jaglom, 1976)
*Trading Places* (John Landis, 1983)
*Traffic* (Steven Soderbergh, 2000)
*Trail of the Pink Panther* (Blake Edwards, 1982)
*Train, The* (John Frankenheimer, 1964)
*Training Day* (Antoine Fuqua, 2001)
*Trance* (Michael Almereyda, 1998)
*Trance* (Rafal Zielinski, 1998)
*Trancers* (Charles Band, 1985)
*Trancers II* (Charles Band, 1991)
*Trapped* (Richard Fleischer, 1949)
*Trauma* (Robert M. Young, 1962)
*Traveling Hopefully* (John G. Avildsen, 1982)
*Trees Lounge* (Steve Buscemi, 1996)
*Tremors* (Ron Underwood, 1990)
*Trespass* (Walter Hill, 1992)
*T-Rex: Back to the Cretaceous* (Brett Leonard, 1998)
*Trial and Error* (Jonathan Lynn, 1997)
*Tribute* (Bob Clark, 1980)
*Tricheurs* (Barbet Schroeder, 1983)

Trick (Jim Fall, 1999)
Trick of the Light, A (Wim Wenders, 1995)
Trick or Treat (Charles Martin Smith, 1986)
Trigger Effect, The (David Koepp, 1996)
Trip, The (Roger Corman, 1967)
Tripwire (Sidney J. Furie, 1999)
Triumph of the Spirit (Robert M. Young, 1989)
Trixie (Alan Rudolph, 2000)
Trois pommes à côté du sommeil (Jacques Leduc, 1989)
Trojan War (George Huang, 1997)
Troll in Central Park, A (Don Bluth, 1994)
Trouble in Mind (Alan Rudolph, 1985)
Truck Turner (Jonathan Kaplan, 1974)
True Believer (Joseph Ruben, 1989)
True Confessions (Ulu Groshard, 1981)
True Crime (Clint Eastwood, 1999)
True Lies (James Cameron, 1994)
True Romance (Tony Scott, 1993)
True West (Allan A. Goldstein, 1983)
Truman Show, The (Peter Weir, 1998)
Trust (Hal Hartley, 1990)
Truth About Cats and Dogs, The (Michael Lehmann, 1996)
Truth About Charlie, The (Jonathan Demme, 2002)
Tucker: The Man and His Dream (Francis Ford Coppola, 1988)
Tumbleweeds (Gavin O'Connor, 1999)
Tune in Tomorrow/Aunt Julia and the Scriptwriter (Jon Amiel, 1990)
Tune, The (Bill Plympton, 1992)
Turkish Delight (Paul Verhoeven, 1973)
Turk 182! (Bob Clark, 1985)
Turner & Hooch (Roger Spottiswoode, 1989)
Turn on to Love (John G. Avildsen, 1969)
Turtle Diary (John Irvin, 1985)
12 Angry Men (Sydney Lumet, 1957)
Twelve Chairs, The (Mel Brooks, 1970)
12 Monkeys (Terry Gilliam, 1995)
20,000 Legues Under the Sea (Richard Fleischer, 1954)
28 Days (Betty Thomas, 2000)
25 Ways to Quit Smoking (Bill Plympton, 1989)
Twilight (Robert Benton, 1998)
Twilight of the Ice Nymphs (Guy Maddin, 1997)
Twin Falls Idaho (Michael Polish, 1999)
Twin Peaks: Fire Walk With Me (David Lynch, 1992)
Twinky (Richard Donner, 1969)
Twins (Ivan Reitman, 1988)
Twister (Jan De Bont, 1996)
Twister (Michael Almereyda, 1988)
Two Bits (James Foley, 1995)
2 Days in the Valley (John Herzfeld, 1996)
Two Evil Eyes (George A. Romero, 1990)
Two Girls and a Guy (James Toback, 1997)
Two-Lane Blacktop (Monte Hellman, 1971)
Two of a Kind (John Herzfeld, 1983)
Two Small Bodies (Beth B, 1993)
2001: A Space Odyssey (Stanley Kubrick, 1968)
2001: A Space Travesty (Allan A. Goldstein, 2000)
2010 (Peter Hyams, 1984)
Typewriter, the Rifle & the Movie Camera, The (Adam Simon, 1996)

# U

U-571 (Jonathan Mostow, 2000)
Ulee's Gold (Victor Nuñez, 1997)
Ultimatum (Jean-Pierre Lefebvre, 1973)
Un autre homme (Charles Binamé, 1990)
Un succèss commercial (Jean-Pierre Lefebvre, 1969)
Unbearable Lightness of Being, The (Philip Kaufman, 1988)
Unbelievable Truth, The (Hal Hartley, 1989)
Unborn, The (Rodman Render, 1991)
Unbreakable (M. Night Shyamalan, 2000)
Uncle Buck (John Hughes, 1989)
Uncovered (Jim McBride, 1994)
Uncut (John Greyson, 1997)
Undead, The (Roger Corman, 1957)
Under Fire (Roger Spottiswoode, 1983)
Under Siege (Andrew Davis, 1992)
Under Siege 2 (Geoff Murphy, 1995)
Under Surveillance (Rafal Zielinski, 1991)
Under Suspicion (Stephen Hopkins, 2000)
Underneath (Steven Soderbergh, 1995)
Understudy: Graveyard Shift II, The (Jerry Ciccoritti, 1988)
Underworld (Roger Christian, 1997)
Unfaithful (Adrian Lyne, 2002)
Unforgettable (John Dahl, 1996)
Unforgiven (Clint Eastwood, 1992)
Unhook the Stars (John Cassavetes, 1996)
Universal Soldier (Roland Emmerich, 1992)
Universal Soldier: The Return (Mic Rogers, 1999)
Unlawful Entry (Jonathan Kaplan, 1992)
Unmarried Woman, An (Paul Mazursky, 1978)
Unstrung Heroes (Diane Keaton, 1995)
Until the End of the World (Wim Wenders, 1991)
Untouchables, The (Brian De Palma, 1987)
Up at the Villa (Phillip Haas, 2000)
Up Close and Personal (Jon Avnet, 1996)
Urban Legend (Jamie Blanks, 1998)
Urinal (John Greyson, 1988)
US Marshals (Stuart Baird, 1998)
Used Cars (Robert Zemeckis, 1980)
Usual Suspects, The (Bryan Singer, 1995)
Utu (Geoff Murphy, 1983)
U-Turn (George Kaczender, 1973)
U Turn (Oliver Stone, 1997)

# V

Valentine (Jamie Blanks, 2001)
Valet Girls (Ratel Zielinski, 1987)
Vallée, La (Bartet Schroeder, 1972)
Valley Girl (Martha Coolidge, 1983)
Valmont (Milos Forman, 1989)
Vampire in Brooklyn (Wes Craven, 1995)
Vampires (John Carpenter, 1998)
Van, The (Stephen Frears, 1996)
Vatel (Roland Joffé, 2000)
Velvet Goldmine (Todd Haynes, 1998)
Venice/Venice (Henry Jaglom, 1992)
Verdict, The (Sydney Lumet, 1982)

*Very Bad Things* (Peter Berg, 1998)
*Via Dolorosa* (John Bailey, 2000)
*Victor/Victoria* (Blake Edwards, 1982)
*Videodrome* (David Cronenberg, 1983)
*Vie fantôme, La* (Jacques Leduc, 1992)
*Vieux pays où Rimbaud est mort, Le* (Jean-Pierre Lefebvre, 1977)
*Vigilante Force* (George Armitage, 1976)
*Vikings, The* (Richard Fleischer, 1958)
*Village of the Damned* (John Carpenter, 1995)
*Vincent and Theo* (Robert Altman, 1990)
*Violent Saturday* (Richard Fleischer, 1955)
*Virgin Suicides, The* (Sofia Coppola, 1999)
*Virtuosity* (Brett Leonard, 1995)
*Visiting Desire* (Beth B, 1996)
*Voices Unheard* (Beth B, 1998)
*Volcano* (Mick Jackson, 1997)
*Volunteers* (Nicholas Meyer, 1985)
*Von Richthofen and Brown* (Roger Corman, 1971)
*Vortex* (Beth B, with Scott B, 1983)

# W

*Waking Life* (Richard Linklater, 2001)
*Wanderers, The* (Philip Kaufman, 1979)
*War of the Satellites* (Roger Corman, 1958)
*Wasp Woman, The* (Roger Corman, 1960)
*Way of the Gun, The* (Christopher McQuarrie, 2000)
*Wag the Dog* (Barry Levinson, 1997)
*Waiting for Guffman* (Christopher Guest, 1996)
*Waiting to Exhale* (Forest Whitaker, 1995)
*Waking the Dead* (Keith Gordon, 1999)
*Walker* (Alex Cox, 1987)
*Walking and Talking* (Nicole Holofcener, 1996)
*Walk on the Moon, A* (Tony Goldwyn, 1999)
*Wall Street* (Oliver Stone, 1987)
*War at Home, The* (Emillo Estevez, 1996)
*War Games* (John Badham, 1983)
*War of the Roses, The* (Danny DeVito, 1989)
*War, The* (Jon Avnet, 1994)
*Warlock* (Steve Miner, 1989)
*Warriors, The* (Walter Hill, 1979)
*Waterboy, The* (Frank Coraci, 1998)
*Waterworld* (Kevin Reynolds, 1995)
*Way We Were, The* (Sydney Pollack, 1973)
*Wayne's World* (Penelope Spheeris, 1992)
*W.C. Fields and Me* (Arthur Hiller, 1976)
*We're Back! A Dinosaur's Story* (Simon Wells, 1993)
*Wedding, A* (Robert Altman, 1978)
*Wedding Banquet, The* (Ang Lee, 1993)
*Wedding Party, The* (Brian De Palma, 1969)
*Wedding Singer, The* (Frank Coraci, 1998)
*Weight of Water, The* (Kathryn Bigelow, 2000)
*Weird Science* (John Hughes, 1985)
*Welcome Home, Roxy Carmichael* (Jim Abrahams, 1990)
*Welcome to L.A.* (Alan Rudolph, 1977)
*Welcome to the Dollhouse* (Todd Solondz, 1995)
*We're No Angels* (Neil Jordan, 1989)
*We're Not the Jet Set* (Robert Duvall, 1975)

*Wes Craven's New Nightmare* (Wes Craven, 1994)
*Westworld* (Michael Crichton, 1973)
*What About Bob?* (Frank Oz, 1991)
*What Did You Do in the War, Daddy?* (Blake Edwards, 1966)
*Whatever Happened to Harold Smith?* (Peter Hewitt, 1999)
*What Lies Beneath* (Robert Zemeckis, 2000)
*What Planet Are You From?* (Mike Nichols, 2000)
*What's Eating Gilbert Grape?* (Lasse Hallström, 1993)
*What's Up, Doc?* (Peter Bogdanovich, 1972)
*What's Up, Tiger Lily?* (Woody Allen, 1966)
*What Women Want* (Nancy Meyers, 2000)
*When Harry Met Sally* (Rob Reiner, 1989)
*When Justice Fails* (Allan A. Goldstein, 1998)
*When Night is Falling* (Patricia Rozema, 1995)
*When We Were Soldiers* (Randall Wallace, 2001)
*Where the Day Takes You* (Marc Rocco, 1992)
*Where the Money Is* (Marek Kanievska, 2000)
*Where's Poppa?* (Carl Reiner, 1970)
*While You Were Sleeping* (Jon Turteltaub, 1995)
*Whipped* (Peter M. Cohen, 2000)
*White Dawn, The* (Philip Kaufman, 1974)
*White Hunter, Black Heart* (Clint Eastwood, 1990)
*White Line Fever* (Jonathan Kaplan, 1975)
*White Men Can't Jump* (Ron Shelton, 1992)
*White Nights* (Taylor Hackford, 1985)
*White River Kid, The* (Arne Glimcher, 1999)
*White Room, The* (Patricia Rozema, 1990)
*White Sands* (Roger Donaldson, 1992)
*White Squall* (Ridley Scott, 1996)
*Who Framed Roger Rabbit* (Robert Zemeckis, 1988)
*Who Is Harry Kellerman And Why Is He Saying Those Terrible Things About Me?* (Ulu Grosbard, 1971)
*Whole Nine Yards, The* (Jonathan Lynn, 2000)
*Who's Afraid of Virginia Woolf?* (Mike Nichols, 1966)
*Who's That Girl?* (James Foley, 1987)
*Who's That Knocking at My Door?* (Martin Scorsese, 1969)
*Who's The Man?* (Ted Demme, 1993)
*Whose Life is it Anyway?* (John Badham, 1981)
*Wicked Stepmother* (Larry Cohen, 1989)
*Wide Awake* (M. Night Shyamalan, 1998)
*Widow's Peak* (John Irvin, 1994)
*Wild America* (William Dear, 1997)
*Wild Angels, The* (Roger Corman, 1966)
*Wild At Heart* (David Lynch, 1990)
*Wild Bill* (Walter Hill, 1995)
*Wild Heart's Can't be Broken* (Steve Miner, 1991)
*Wild Man* (Geoff Murphy, 1977)
*Wild Party, The* (James Ivory, 1975)
*Wild Rovers* (Blake Edwards, 1971)
*Wild Things* (John McNaughton, 1998)
*Wild Wild West* (Barry Sonnenfeld, 1999)
*Wilder Napalm* (Glen Gordon Caron, 1993)
*William Shakespeare's A Midsummer Night's Dream* (Michael Hoffman, 1999)
*William Shakespeare's Romeo + Juliet* (Baz Luhrmann, 1996)
*Willie and Phil* (Paul Mazursky, 1980)

Willow (Ron Howard, 1988)
Winchell (Paul Mazursky, 1998)
Wind (Caroll Ballard, 1992)
Wind and the Lion, The (John Milius, 1975)
Windtalkers (John Woo, 2002)
Wisegirls (David Anspaugh, 2002)
Wing Commander (Chris Roberts, 1999)
Wings of Desire (Wim Wenders, 1987)
Winner, The (Alex Cox, 1996)
Winslow Boy, The (David Mamet, 1999)
Wirey Spindell (Eric Schaefter, 1999)
Wisdom (Emilio Estevez, 1986)
Wise Guys (Brian De Palma, 1986)
Wiseman The (Bill Plympton, 1990)
Wishing Tree, The (Ivan Passer, 1999)
Witch Hunt (Paul Schrader, 1994)
Without Limits (Robert Towne, 1998)
Witness (Peter Weir, 1985)
Wiz, The (Sydney Lumet, 1978)
Wizards (Ralph Bakshi, 1977)
Wolf (Mike Nichols, 1994)
Woman in Transit (Léa Pool, 1984)
Wonder Boys (Curtis Hanson, 2000)
Wonderful Ice Cream Suit, The (Stuart Gordon, 1998)
Wonderful Life (Sidney J. Furie, 1964)
Woo (Daisy von Scherier Mayer, 1998)
Wood, The (Rick Famuyiwa, 1999)
Working Girl (Mike Nichols, 1988)
Working Girls (Lizzie Borden, 1986)
World Traveler (Bart Freundlich, 2002)
Wrestling Ernest Hemingway (Randa Haines, 1993)
Wrong Man, The (Jim McBride, 1993)
Wrong Move (Wim Wenders, 1974)
Wrongfully Accused (Pat Proft, 1998)
WW and the Dixie Dancekings (John G. Avildsen, 1975)
Wyatt Earp (Lawrence Kasdan, 1994)

# X

Xanadu (Robert Greenwaid, 1980)
X Change (Allan Moyle, 2000)
X-15 (Richard Donner, 1961)

X–Files; Fight the Future, The (Rob Bowman, 1998)
X–Men (Bryan Singer, 2000)
X Rated (Emilio Estevez, 2000)
X: The Man with the X-Ray Eyes (Roger Corman, 1963)
XXX (Rob Cohen, 2002)

# Y

Yakuza, The (Sydney Pollack, 1975)
Yanks (John Schlesinger, 1979)
Yards, The (James Gray, 2000)
Year of Living Dangerously, The (Peter Weir, 1982)
Year of the Dragon (Michael Cimino, 1985)
Year of the Gun (John Frankenheimer, 1991)
Year of the Horse (Jim Jarmusch, 1997)
Yentl (Barbara Streisand, 1983)
You Can Count on Me (Kenneth Lonergan, 2000)
You're a Big Boy Now (Francis Ford Coppola, 1966)
You've Got Mail (Nora Ephron, 1998)
Young Americans (Danny Cannon, 1993)
Young Doctors in Love (Gary Marshall, 1982)
Young Dragons, The (John Woo, 1975)
Young Frankenstein (Mel Brooks, 1974)
Young Guns II (Geoff Murphy, 1990)
Young Ones, The (Sidney J. Furie, 1961)
Young Racers, The (Roger Corman, 1963)
Young Savages, The (John Frankenheimer, 1961)
Young Sherlock Holmes (Barry Levinson, 1985)
Your Face (Bill Plympton, 1987)
Your Friends and Neighbours (Neil LaBute, 1998)
Your Ticket is No Longer Valid (George Kaczender, 1984)

# Z

Zebrahead (Anthony Drazan, 1992)
Zebra Lounge (Kari Skogland, 2001)
Zelig (Woody Allen, 1983)
Zero Effect (Jake Kasdan, 1998)
Zero Patience (John Greyson, 1993)
Zoolander (Ben Stiller, 2001)
Zorro, the Gay Blade (Peter Medak, 1981)